PROPERTY TAX IN EUROPE

Property Tax in Europe: A Changing Landscape is a rich mosaic and living laboratory for the design and practice of property taxes in Europe. Edited by three eminent international scholars, this authoritative volume is full of new information, reform strategies, and insights into ongoing challenges. It delivers important lessons for policymakers, practitioners, and scholars working to improve property taxation around the world.

—**JORGE MARTINEZ-VAZQUEZ**, Regents Professor of Economics Emeritus, Georgia State University

Although property taxes have existed in parts of Europe for well over a thousand years, the systems in each country differ in significant ways. At a time when there is pressure for reform, the authors have done a great service—they provide a sound factual analysis of European property tax systems and share ideas on how these fiscal tools might be improved going forward.

—**PAUL SANDERSON**, President, International Property Tax Institute

Property Tax in Europe is an important contribution to our understanding of the specifics of the property tax and the importance of subnational public finance. Policymakers, academics, and administrators will find their time wisely spent if they read this book and keep it on their bookshelves as a reference. The book is about taxes on property, but it could easily be used in a standard public finance class. The policy chapters are simply that good.

—**GARY C. CORNIA**, Emeritus Dean and Marriott Chair, Marriott School of Business, Brigham Young University and former President of the National Tax Association, USA

This book offers a comprehensive and insightful look at property taxation across European countries. Drawing on statistical analysis and in-depth case studies, McCluskey, Bahl, and Franzsen explain why property taxes vary across countries, evaluate the scope for enhancing revenues, and provide thoughtful reform options to improve the equity and efficiency of the tax. *Property Tax in Europe* is essential reading for anyone seeking to understand the theoretical foundations and practical challenges of property taxation in Europe and beyond.

—**ENID SLACK**, Director, Institute on Municipal Finance and Governance, University of Toronto

The unstable economic situation in many European countries has clearly demonstrated the importance of stable property taxes. This book presents a comparative analysis of property tax systems in various European countries, followed by in-depth case studies. It should be read by all researchers and advisors on tax reform, as well as politicians responsible for implementing these reforms properly.

—MICHAL RADVAN, Masaryk University, Czech Republic

Property tax is one of the most complex, fundamental, and misunderstood revenue sources, essential for the provision of public services. *Property Tax in Europe* provides an in-depth and critical examination of the range of taxes affecting real estate in this disparate region. A complement to the Lincoln Institute's volumes on Africa and Asia, this book is a *must* for anyone involved in property tax administration, the provision of public services, and policy planning.

—DR. FRANCES PLIMMER, FIG Chair, Commission 9, 2011–2014

PROPERTY TAX IN EUROPE

A Changing Landscape

Edited by

William McCluskey, Roy Bahl, and Riël Franzsen

LINCOLN INSTITUTE
OF LAND POLICY

Cambridge, Massachusetts

Library of Congress Cataloging-in-Publication Data

Names: McCluskey, William J. editor | Bahl, Roy W. editor | Franzsen, R. C. D. (Riël C. D.) editor
Title: Property tax in Europe : a changing landscape / edited by William McCluskey, Roy Bahl, and Riël Franzsen.
Description: [Cambridge, MA] : Lincoln Institute of Land Policy, [2026] | Series: Comparative property taxation series ; 3 | Includes bibliographical references and index. | Summary: "The first comparative analysis of property tax systems across Europe. Featured countries include Denmark, Estonia, Finland, France, Germany, Greece, Ireland, Latvia, the Netherlands, Poland, the United Kingdom, Russia, Slovenia, and Spain"— Provided by publisher.
Identifiers: LCCN 2025035563 (print) | LCCN 2025035564 (ebook) | ISBN 9781558444638 paperback | ISBN 9781558444645 epub
Subjects: LCSH: Property tax—Europe | Land reform—Europe | Europe–Economic policy | BISAC: BUSINESS & ECONOMICS / International / Taxation | POLITICAL SCIENCE / World / European
Classification: LCC HJ4125.A4 P76 2026 (print) | LCC HJ4125.A4 (ebook) | DDC 336.22094—dc23/eng/20260114
LC record available at https://lccn.loc.gov/2025035563
LC ebook record available at https://lccn.loc.gov/2025035564

Project Editor: Jennifer Sigler
Production Editor: Angela Piliouras, Westchester Publishing Services
Cover Design: Studio Rainwater
Printing: Books International

Printed and bound in the US and the UK on FSC-certified stock.

Distributed by Columbia University Press.

Lincoln Institute of Land Policy
113 Brattle Street
Cambridge, MA 02138-3400
USA

lincolninst.edu

Contents

Illustrations, Tables, and Boxes

Foreword

With this volume—the third in a series that began with *Property Tax in Africa* (2017) and continued with *Property Tax in Asia* (2022)—we turn to the continent that has some of the world's oldest and newest systems of property taxation. In doing so, we also extend a global path of inquiry that has steadily established the Lincoln Institute as the preeminent authority on property taxation around the world.

Some form of property taxation has existed in Europe since at least feudal times. Over the centuries, each nation has developed its own system, reflecting cultural, legal, and administrative traditions as diverse as the continent's languages and cuisines. Even after the formation of the European Union, no uniform approach was adopted. Today, countries from Ireland to Slovenia offer models and lessons that span a wide spectrum of approaches to property taxation. The Lincoln Institute has engaged directly with officials in countries including Latvia and the Netherlands to strengthen administration, improve equity, and share best practices globally.

When I came to the Lincoln Institute in 2014, I, like many, thought of the property tax as a singular policy instrument. I have come to understand it instead as a complex system—one that depends on the smooth functioning of many interlocking parts. These include a legal framework that empowers local governments, a cadastre or land registry that accurately records ownership, reliable and updated valuation systems, disciplined financial management, transparent enforcement mechanisms, and fair procedures for resolving delinquency and transferring ownership when necessary. Where any of these parts is weak, the system suffers.

This volume presents a comparative analysis of property tax systems across Europe, followed by in-depth case studies by experts from more than a dozen countries. Some nations use area-based models, others value-based; some update property values annually, others rely on decades-old valuations. In some systems, central governments retain all revenue; in others, local governments control the funds. But across these variations, a common truth emerges: In an era of globalization and international tax competition, the immovable nature of real property makes the property tax an especially valuable revenue source—for both its economic efficiency and its potential to support equity and accountability at the local level.

The European experience also provides important lessons for other regions. In particular, the evolution of property tax systems in the post-Soviet states offers valuable insights for countries—especially in Africa—that are building new tax systems or restoring those dismantled in previous eras. These examples remind us that progress is possible even in places where institutional memory is fragmented or where components of a tax system must be rebuilt from scratch.

As political and economic pressures grow—ranging from the need for local fiscal autonomy to the necessity of climate resilience and the energy transition—some countries are turning again to the property tax as a tool for reform. In doing so, they face new challenges: how to explain statistical models to courts and citizens, how to manage state oversight of local tax functions, how to evaluate the effects of exemptions and incentives on the tax base, and how to resolve tensions between innovation and transparency in assessment practices.

In 2016, as the Lincoln Institute prepared to release both a Spanish-language book on the property tax in Latin America and *Property Tax in Africa*, the Organisation for Economic Co-operation and Development's *Fiscal Federalism: Making Decentralisation Work* reminded us of a timeless truth: "Ancient civilizations taxed land and property for thousands of years—long before they discovered income, business, or consumption taxes." This insight is no less relevant today. From soaring housing costs to the fiscal impacts of the pandemic to the existential challenge of climate change, property taxation continues to offer a grounded, adaptable, and resilient tool for meeting the needs of communities worldwide.

This volume—like those before it—aims to illuminate the enduring value of the property tax and to help decision-makers across continents learn from each other. Our hope is that the insights offered here will support the development of more effective and equitable systems, wherever they are needed.

George W. McCarthy
President and CEO, 2014–2026
Lincoln Institute of Land Policy

Preface

This book is about whether, and how, the taxation of real property might play a larger role in mobilizing revenues in Europe. This question has been well studied by eminent scholars, and policy reforms for "better" property taxation have been called for by unhappy taxpayers and interest groups, governments, the International Monetary Fund (IMF), the World Bank, courts, and others. But the last 20 years has been a time of property tax turmoil in several European countries. This period has seen a property tax "freeze" in Denmark, Latvia, and Finland; the continued use of long-outdated tax rolls in France, Germany, and Great Britain; area-based property tax systems in Slovenia and Poland; the move to new systems in Germany and Ireland; the maintenance of a fragmented system in Russia; the introduction of a new but possibly revenue-constrained property tax valuation in Estonia; and constitutional court challenges in Slovenia and Germany. If there are common denominators in all of this, they are the failure of the property tax assessment mechanism to generate growth in the tax base, and the stubborn resistance of taxpayers to higher effective tax rates.

We thought that there was room for further research on this subject, research that would focus on three pillars of good property taxation—a tax structure that could capture real property growth in a fair but economically efficient way, a management system that could lay the groundwork for managing real property taxation, and a valuation approach that could track the growth of property values in real time. Our findings suggest that there is interest in, and a pathway to, taxing land and buildings at a higher effective rate. There is some possibility for getting back to a reasonable valuation approach, especially if a way can be found to take greater advantage of new technologies for mass assessment. There is much to build on in many European countries, including the development of comprehensive cadastral systems. The major obstacles to be overcome are the high cost of revaluation and the resistance of taxpayers and interest groups to accepting any property tax reform that might lead to increases in property tax burdens. With respect to the latter, a good case to be made is that a properly reformed (and properly presented) property tax might be less objectionable to voters than either increased income and consumption taxes or reduced public service levels.

There is no "European model" of property taxation. Countries use different bases, rate structures, and preferential treatments, and they administer their systems in different ways. Some European countries raise property tax revenues at the highest levels in the world, and some have the capacity to implement the most modern of tax administration and valuation approaches. Yet the average effective property tax rate in Europe is only about 1 percent of gross domestic product, with about 60 percent of this amount being raised in France, Germany, and the United Kingdom. In this book, we attempt to explain why property tax revenues are so low and why there is so much diversity across European countries. We find that some of it can be explained by low levels of real property wealth, some by faulty administration and management, some by deliberate underassessment of real property, and some by governments' attempts to hold down statutory property tax rates. Underneath some of these explanations is a well-entrenched opposition to increased property taxation that often does not show the best face of property tax reform.

European countries use discretionary policies and administrative actions to support better housing and land use policies, and to relieve burdens on low-income households. Global concerns are also bringing new challenges to property tax design, such as providing incentives to use energy-efficient buildings and to increase the density of land use. The property tax is a key element of support for fiscal decentralization. New technology is bringing new approaches to valuation that can expand the property tax base. It is a good time to be thinking about property tax reform.

We take both comparative and case study approaches in this book. The former takes advantage of the great amount of comparative data provided mostly by the IMF, the European Commission, and the Organisation for Economic Co-operation and Development (OECD). This has allowed us to find some general and interesting trends such as the stagnation of effective property tax rates in European countries over the past two decades. On the other hand, the many countries in Europe are very different in some of their tax laws, the strength of their property tax administration infrastructure, the ways in which they are governed, and their interests in using property tax policy to protect lower-income families from high tax burdens. To identify such patterns, part 2 contains 14 case studies and one technical chapter. These were commissioned from local researchers. In part 1, the comparative analysis, we bring our own research together with the information from the case studies in part 2 in an effort to answer the main questions posed in the first chapter.

In doing this work, we came up against many limitations that we could not overcome. The number of country studies done was not enough to identify the range of country practices. Some very important countries were not covered because of the space constraint. Clearly, more country studies would have led to better comparative analysis. The datasets from the IMF, European Commission, and OECD were rich but did not include some important information, such as the revenue costs of exemptions or the distribution of tax burdens within the country. This research benefited greatly from earlier studies that broke new ground on this subject, but reviewing it all was impossible. Finally, we note that property tax reform was underway in several European countries at the time of this writing, but it is far too early to report results.

The Lincoln Institute of Land Policy funded this project and provided important administrative support. We owe much to Joan Youngman, Semida Munteanu, and other Lincoln Institute staff whose intellectual leadership added value to our work. The Lincoln Institute contributed one of their research staff, Dr. Wenjing Li, to our team, and she played an important substantive role in the work. We benefited significantly from the work of the authors of the country studies in part 2. Their descriptions, analyses, and insights added greatly to the project.

Roy Bahl, William McCluskey, and Riël Franzsen
May 2025

PART 1

Comparative Analysis

1

Introduction and Context

ROY BAHL, WENJING LI, WILLIAM MCCLUSKEY,
AND RIËL FRANZSEN

There is no universal definition of the optimal structure of the property tax, nor is there a golden rule about the amount of revenue it should raise or even about how revenue raised from it should be spent. All of this depends on what the country is trying to achieve with its tax system and on the role assigned to taxes on property in the overall tax system. In Europe, where total tax revenues are equivalent to about 25 percent of gross domestic product (GDP), and where real property investment and consumption are so important (OECD 2022), a share of less than 2 percent of GDP for general property taxes (our term for recurrent property taxes plus other property taxes; see table 1.1, row 1) across Europe seems small. Even for the 27 member states of the European Union, the average was only 2.1 percent in 2022 (European Commission 2025). Explaining the reasons for this low level of property taxation in Europe is the first goal of this book. The second is to describe and analyze reform paths that could increase European countries' revenue take from the property tax, while not adopting practices that lead to inequities, resource misallocations, and revenue displacements.

What Is Property Taxation?

Part 1 of this book is based on a comparative analysis of the taxation of the ownership, use, and transfer of immovable property (that is, land, buildings, and other improvements) in European countries. To ensure that comparisons are accurate, it is important to define some of the basic concepts at the outset.

The definitions for *property tax* used by the International Monetary Fund (IMF), Organisation for Economic Co-operation and Development (OECD), and European Commission (EC) are similar but not exactly the same. The empirical analysis in part 1 of the book is mostly built on IMF data, because of its broader worldwide coverage, but it also draws heavily on OECD and European Union data and analysis because of their greater depth of information about European countries.

The IMF (2014, 93) defines taxes on property as "taxes payable on the use, ownership, or transfer of wealth. The taxes may be levied at regular intervals, one time only, or on a change in ownership."

The OECD (2023, 14) defines property taxes as "recurrent and non-recurrent taxes on the use, ownership or transfer of property. These include taxes on immovable property or net wealth, taxes on the change of ownership of property through inheritance or gift, and taxes on financial and capital transactions. This indicator relates to government as a whole (all government levels)."

The major difference between the OECD and IMF taxonomies is an important one. The OECD lists taxes on capital and financial transactions (which include property transfer taxes) as a property tax, whereas the IMF—since a 2014 reclassification—does not (Grote and Wen 2024; IMF 2014). For European Union statistical purposes, the EC classifies property transfer taxes as part of "other property taxes," implying that the OECD and EC classify property transfer taxes as property taxes. A report by UN-Habitat on property taxes in Europe correctly points out that there are differences between OECD and EC classification (UN-Habitat 2013), but in an EC 2022 discussion paper it is accepted that the OECD and EC definitions are closely aligned and broadly consistent (Leodolter, Princen, and Rutkowski 2022).

It is noteworthy that, for purposes other than statistical reporting, entities such as the IMF, OECD, and EC and scholars sometimes use the term *property tax* in a broad sense that includes property transfer taxes. The term *property-related taxes* (not defined in table 1.1), which includes an even larger group of taxes, is sometimes used (Franzsen and McCluskey 2017). Property-related taxes usually include taxes on capital gains and may even include value-added tax.

To avoid confusion about property tax terminology used in our part 1 analysis, table 1.1 provides a reader's guide to the property tax labels.

The recurrent property tax, the most recognizable form of property taxation, is an annual tax on real property ownership or use. The category

Table 1.1 Property Tax Nomenclature

Classification	Definition	Includes Revenue from Real Property Transfers?
General property taxes[1]	Recurrent property taxes plus other property taxes	No
Recurrent property taxes[2]	Taxes levied regularly on the use or ownership of immovable property, which includes land, buildings, and other structures. Also includes net wealth taxes	No
Other property taxes[3]	Includes estate, inheritance, and gift taxes; capital levies; betterment levies; and taxes on movable property	No (IMF and OECD) Yes (European Union)
Taxes on capital and financial transactions	Taxes on the purchase and sale of nonfinancial or financial assets (including foreign exchange or securities), taxes on checks and other forms of payment, and taxes levied on specific legal transactions, such as the validation of contracts and the sale of immovable property	Yes
Total property tax	Sum of general property taxes and taxes on capital and financial transactions	Yes

Sources: IMF (2014); OECD (2023).

[1] The term *general property tax* is an author intervention defined for use in this study.

[2] Includes three of the five IMF types of taxes on property (IMF 2014, 93): recurrent taxes on immovable property, recurrent taxes on net wealth, and other recurrent taxes on property.

[3] Includes the remaining two of the five IMF guideline types of taxes on property (IMF 2014, 93): estate, inheritance, and gift taxes, and capital levies.

"other property taxes" includes any annual wealth tax that is imposed, as well as inheritance and gift taxes. The total of "recurrent property taxes" plus "other property taxes" we refer to in part 1 as *general property taxes* (table 1.1, row 1). In accordance with our use of primarily IMF data, general property taxes exclude property transfer taxes. Worldwide, recurrent property tax revenues account for about 90 percent of general property tax revenues.

Property transfer taxes constitute a second focus in part 1 (chapters 2 and 6). As is done by the IMF and OECD, these taxes are included as "Taxes on capital and financial transactions" (table 1.1, row 4) and are one-off taxes levied when a property is sold. Most previous research separates analysis of the general property tax from analysis of property transfer taxes, even though both are levied against the value of land and buildings. The considerable revenues raised in some countries, the impact of transfer taxes on property markets and local-government finance, and the possibility that these taxes might be eventually integrated with the recurrent property tax structure are among the reasons why real property transfer taxes are included in our discussion.

Both the IMF, in its Government Finance Statistics (GFS) database, and the OECD, in its Global Revenue Statistics Database (2025), report revenues from property transfer taxes in a larger category, "Revenues from Taxes on Financial and Capital Transactions" (see table 1.1). However, the category "Taxes on Financial and Capital Transactions" also includes taxes on the purchase and sale of nonfinancial or financial assets (including foreign exchange or securities), taxes on checks and other forms of payment, and taxes levied on specific legal transactions, such as the validation of contracts and the sale of immovable property (IMF 2014). Data for property transfer tax revenues are not shown separately in either the IMF or the OECD revenue series. This issue is discussed in more detail in chapters 6 and 7.

Providing precise yearly revenue figures for property transfer taxes alone is challenging owing to the following factors:

- European countries report taxes in different ways, and data is not always broken down specifically for "property transfer," as is the data for other types of property taxes.
- Comprehensive, final figures for every European country for 2021–2024 are not consistently available from a single source.
- What constitutes a "property transfer tax" can vary and may include stamp duties or taxes on financial transactions related to capital, not just the transfer of real estate.

Background

The general property tax is not a major source of government revenues in most countries. Worldwide, it averaged only about 0.67 percent of GDP in 2022 (table 1.2). There are significant disparities in these revenue amounts

Table 1.2 General and Recurrent Property Taxation in Europe and Other Regions

Jurisdictions	Average General Property Tax Revenue (% of GDP)	Average Recurrent Property Tax Revenue (% of GDP)	Average per Capita GDP (current US$)	Total Population (million)[1]	Number of Jurisdictions[2]
All jurisdictions	0.67	0.59	20,737	4,920	129/218
East Asia and Pacific	0.73	0.62	22,389	2,279	19/38
Sub-Saharan Africa	0.22	0.21	2,685	385	21/48
Latin America and Caribbean	0.61	0.56	11,907	598	26/42
Middle East, North Africa, Afghanistan, Pakistan	0.31	0.28	20,125	338	10/23
North America	3.10	2.66	67,059	373	2/3
South Asia	0.30	0.29	3,899	31	3/6
Europe and Central Asia	0.86	0.76	32,015	917	48/58
Europe	0.93	0.81	36,465	746	41/50
Central Asia	0.47	0.46	5,949	170	7/8

Sources: IMF (n.d.); OECD (2025); World Bank (n.d.-a).

Note: This table is based on a cross-sectional sample with latest available data on general and recurrent property tax revenues as a percentage of GDP between 2007 and 2022 for each country. The primary source of data on property taxes is the Government Finance Statistics database from IMF (n.d.), supplemented by data in the Global Revenue Statistics Database from the OECD (2025).

[1] The total population is the sum of populations of countries with available property tax data within each region group.

[2] The leftmost number represents jurisdictions whose general and recurrent property tax as a percentage of GDP are available in the constructed sample for this table. The rightmost number represents total jurisdictions in each region defined by the World Bank (n.d.-b).

both among and within regions. Some countries in Western Europe (and in North America) tax land and property at three times the international average; for example, France and the United Kingdom. General property tax revenues in Europe range from less than 0.2 percent of GDP in the Czech Republic to about 3 percent in the United Kingdom in 2022 (IMF, n.d.). And where these revenues are used directly or indirectly to support goals such as fiscal decentralization, better land use, housing, environmental policy, and possibly even emergency relief, property taxes can have a special importance that stretches well beyond revenues raised.

Shrugging off such differences as being due to lower national income and lesser administrative capacity is tempting, but that ignores the deeper reasons for these differences. Even some higher-income European countries are bedeviled by some of the same problems faced by lower-income countries in other parts of the world. These include obsolete valuation rolls and excessive tax relief. Moreover, some higher-income European countries have chosen not to use advanced technologies to assist in administering their tax systems, and the taxpaying culture is stronger in some countries than in others.

The differences in revenue outcomes also may be due to how taxpayers see the fairness of the property tax relative to other taxes and to what they see to be the benefits from paying higher taxes. And, as many have noted, the salience of the property tax has contributed significantly to holding back its increased use in public budgets (Cabral and Hoxby 2012). Each country has a separate story.

Property and land taxation in Europe has been extensively studied. A large body of quality work has come from the OECD (2022), EC (Leodolter, Princen, and Rutkowski (2022), IMF (Grote and Wen 2024; Norregaard 2013), and numerous scholars (e.g., Blöchliger 2015a; 2015b). This book only scratches the surface of what might be learned from a fuller reading of this rich literature.[1]

But the property tax may be coming into new territory because of some broad worldwide trends and events (de Mello and Ter-Miniassian (2023). The high cost of housing continues to be a major issue and has accelerated in 2021–2025. The growth in the value of physical infrastructure has not been sustained in some countries. Government policies to address climate change call for changes in land policy that can include elements of property taxation. The COVID-19 pandemic may have revealed new ideas on how the property tax can be used during national emergencies. Technological advances in property valuation and data discovery and management have significantly improved determinations of the base for property taxation and possibly lowered the very high cost of property tax administration. Additionally, the expanded use of technology in data management, combined with the development of intelligent processes, has enhanced collection efficiency. Furthermore, the broader adoption of GIS (geographic information systems) contributes to these advancements.

Changes in urbanization patterns, environmental policy, and the role of subnational governments in the public financing system are underway in some countries, and a broader view of taxes on land and property as a fiscal instrument to shape revenue mobilization could gain interest. In countries where the current systems of housing taxation rely heavily on transaction taxes, the increase in recurrent property tax could balance a reduction in the taxation of labor and bring efficiency gains in the European Union member states (European Commission 2018). And more is yet to come. For example, the full consequences on the property tax of working from home are still emerging, as are the shifts toward energy-efficient buildings in cities.

Study Approach

The research in this book combines comparative country analyses and individual country studies. Part 1 describes and analyzes property tax performance in a comparative context. Part 2 contains 14 country studies, commissioned by the editors and prepared by country experts specifically for this book, and a thematic chapter on recent advances in property tax technology in Europe. Part 1 draws heavily on the country studies to review and analyze the performance of the property tax and the options for reform. It also presents evidence from countries other than those in part 2, though in less detail, and carries out comparative statistical analyses of property tax practices in Europe.

The approach taken here agrees with the view that the specifics of the property tax setting and its tax structure and administration in any country greatly influences its performance. The devils that hold back better property tax performance often are hidden in these details. The countries chosen for study here cover a range of economic and demographic situations. The sample includes small and large countries, higher- and lower-income countries, and countries with different historical traditions in land management (table 1.3). Because it is not a random sample, statistical inferences are not drawn.

Chapter 2 raises several questions about property taxation in Europe: whether its place in the taxation of land and buildings is generally understood, why it raises so little revenue, how the disparities among countries

Table 1.3 Countries in Part 2 Analyses, 2022 Data

Country	Population (million)	Per Capita GDP (2022 US$)
Denmark	5.90	68,091
Estonia	1.35	28,451
Finland	5.56	50,441
France	68.07	41,083
Germany	83.80	49,686
Greece	10.44	20,972
Ireland	5.21	105,235
Latvia	1.88	20,227
Netherlands	17.70	59,123
Poland	36.82	18,891
Russian Federation	144.24	15,620
Slovenia	2.11	28,374
Spain	47.79	30,270
United Kingdom	67.60	46,063
Mean	**35.60**	**41,609**

Source: World Bank (n.d.-a).

might be explained, whether it is a sustainable source of revenues, and whether significant untapped revenue potential exists.

Chapter 3 studies the adequacy of the underlying legal and administrative structure for managing the property tax and how this has supported good practice. It also takes up the important issue of the effectiveness of institutions in supporting the property tax practice in Europe. Chapter 4 makes a comparative review of the structure and impacts of general property taxation in the country studies. It draws heavily from the part 2 country studies and from similar research on other European countries. Chapter 5 is devoted to valuation practices in European countries and to technology advances in these practices.

Chapter 6 studies property transfer taxes and their role in a comprehensive property tax regime. Chapter 7 brings this evidence together to answer the two questions posed for this volume: Why are property tax revenues in Europe so low, and what are the best available reform paths?

Scope of Analysis

Success in property tax revenue mobilization is determined not only by rate and base structure but also by how property is identified and valued, how the tax assessments and collections are managed and administered, and how this all is presented to taxpayers. Leave any step out of this chain and the conclusions reached about property tax revenue mobilization in Europe will likely be flawed (Bahl and Linn 1992; Blöchliger 2015b; Kelly, White, and Anand 2020). This study covers all these issues.

An important storyline here is the constraining influence of the political economy in shaping property tax reform. Political considerations have always exerted a strong influence on the practice of taxing land and property, as they should in democracies. Bad practices are often called out by voters, but otherwise good practices also are sometimes blocked because they lead to higher tax burdens, or because powerful lobbies oppose them, or simply because they involve change.[2] This is taken up in some detail in specific country contexts in part 2.

Limitations

The book's case study coverage is broad but probably not broad enough. There is more to learn about property taxation in Europe and about how to improve it. Including more country studies would have revealed more about structural and administrative strengths and weaknesses in property tax practices and made for a richer policy analysis. Our 14-country sample represents countries of different types but cannot be used to infer typical European practices. We had to leave out some countries with different approaches to property taxation at the cost of excluding important information. Italy, for example, takes a different approach to property taxation compared with other high-income European countries.

Another limitation (and in other ways, another strength) of this study is the data. The comparative analysis in part 1 uses IMF, EC, and OECD data. In some cases, these data series are exactly the same, but in others, the three institutions use different classifications of subitems in their tax statistics. They also lack detailed information on revenues collected from real property transfer taxes, perhaps the biggest data problem to be overcome in this book. The country studies in part 2 use statistical reporting as defined by local practices that may differ from that reported in the three international datasets, but that also provides important insights. European annual country reports offer good data on property taxation in the European Union member states.

All this said, this book's research works a rich database of a 20-year time series of high-quality data on property taxation for 38 European countries,[3] and it matches this with detailed country-level data from the 14 case studies. This research does not have all the underlying data that it needs, but it has a lot.

The nonrevenue impacts of the property tax require more attention than we could give here. Property tax–related schemes to promote the increased supply of housing, increased land use density, reduced urban sprawl, investment financing with value capture, and carbon capture deserve more attention. The property tax has taken on some new roles in recent years, including COVID-19 relief and support for decarbonization initiatives. But other interventions in property markets are not adequately covered here. Among these are inheritance and gift taxes, government ownership and trading of real properties, and leasing and public housing arrangements. Neither does this study take up property taxation of natural resources. Finally, the inputs to this analysis limited the time period that could be covered. Most notably, the country studies in part 2 could not report the status of pending property tax reform because the reforms were still emerging.

Notes

1. The work of the OECD on this subject has been pathbreaking. A useful literature review and analysis of recent property taxation issues is in OECD (2022).

2. Examples are the property tax limitation laws in California and Florida in the United States that cap valuation increases.

3. The 41 European jurisdictions in table 1.2, out of 50, are the ones that have data on general and recurrent property taxes as a percentage of GDP. But data availability for all variables, mainly the data on fiscal decentralization, is restricted in the European sample used in regressions in chapter 2.

References

Bahl, R., W. Li, and J. Youngman. 2024. "Revenue Mobilization from Property Taxation." Paper presented at the Riël Franzsen Symposium: Theory and Practice of Taxation in Africa, Pretoria, South Africa (April 29–30).

Bahl, R. W., and J. F. Linn. 1992. *Urban Public Finance in Developing Countries*. New York: Oxford University Press.

Blöchliger, H. 2015a. "The Challenge of Measuring Fiscal Decentralization." In *Handbook of Multilevel Finance*, ed. E. Ahmad and G. Brosio. Cheltenham, UK: Edward Elgar.

———. 2015b. "Reforming the Tax on Immovable Property: Taking Care of the Unloved." OECD Economics Department. Working paper No. 1205.

Cabral, M., and C. Hoxby. 2012. "The Hated Property Tax: Salience, Tax Rates, and Tax Revolts." National Bureau of Economic Research. Working paper No. 18514.

de Mello, L., and T. Ter-Minassian. 2023. "Decarbonisation and Intergovernmental Fiscal Relations: Policy Challenges and Reform Options." Working paper on Fiscal Federalism No. 43. Paris: OECD. https://doi.org/10.1787/c434c385-en.

European Commission. 2018. "Tax Policies in the European Union: 2018 Survey." Directorate General Taxation and Customs Union (December). https://taxation-customs.ec.europa.eu/document/download/56cc0116-1674-4e98-9a82-071d05b718cb_en?filename=2018-tax-survey-report.pdf.

———. 2025. "Data on Taxation Trends." (March). https://taxation-customs.ec.europa.eu/taxation/economic-analysis/data-taxation-trends_en.

Franzsen, R., and W. McCluskey. 2017. "Introduction." In *Property Tax in Africa: Status, Challenges, and Prospects*, ed. R. Franzsen and W. McCluskey, 3–28. Cambridge, MA: Lincoln Institute of Land Policy.

Grote, M., and J.-F. Wen. 2024. "How to Design and Implement Property Tax Reforms." IMF How to Note 2024/006. Washington, DC: International Monetary Fund.

IMF (International Monetary Fund). 2014. *Government Finance Statistics Manual.* Washington, DC: IMF.

———. n.d. "Government Finance Statistics." Accessed September 19, 2025. https://data.imf.org/en.

Kelly, R., R. White, and A. Anand. 2020. *Property Tax Diagnostic Manual.* Washington, DC: World Bank.

Leodolter, A., S. Princen, and A. Rutkowski. 2022. "Immovable Property Taxation for Sustainable and Inclusive Growth." European Commission, Directorate-General for Economic and Financial Affairs, Discussion paper 156.

Norregaard, J. 2013. "Taxing Immovable Property: Revenue Potential and Implementation Challenges." Working paper 13/129. Washington, DC: International Monetary Fund.

OECD (Organisation for Economic Co-operation and Development). 2019. "Tax Morale: What Drives People and Businesses to Pay Tax?" Paris: OECD. https://doi.org/10.1787/f3d8ea10-en.

———. 2021. "Fiscal Federalism 2022: Making Decentralisation Work." Paris: OECD. https://doi.org/10.1787/201c75b6-en.

———. 2022. "Housing Taxation in OECD Countries." OECD Tax Policy Studies, No. 29. https://doi.org/10.1787/03dfe007-en.

———. 2023. Revenue Statistics Interpretative Guide. https://www.oecd.org/content/dam/oecd/en/topics/policy-sub-issues/global-tax-revenues/oecd-classification-taxes-interpretative-guide.pdf.

———. 2025. Global Revenue Statistics Database. Updated July 8, 2025. Accessed September 20, 2025. https://www.oecd.org/en/data/datasets/global-revenue-statistics-database.html.

UN-Habitat. 2013. "Property Tax Regimes in Europe." Nairobi: United Nations Human Settlements Programme.

World Bank. n.d.-a. "World Bank Country and Lending Groups." Accessed October 3, 2025. https://datahelpdesk.worldbank.org/knowledgebase/articles/906519-world-bank-country-and-lending-groups.

———. n.d.-b. "World Development Indicators." Accessed September 23, 2025. https://datatopics.worldbank.org/world-development-indicators/.

2

Revenue Performance

ROY BAHL, WENJING LI, WILLIAM MCCLUSKEY,
AND RIËL FRANZSEN

Perhaps the most remarkable statistic in this study is the very low effective rate of recurrent property taxation in European countries.[1] Recurrent revenues were less than 1 percent of gross domestic product (GDP) and accounted for only about 5 percent of total government tax revenues in 2022. So far as revenue mobilization is concerned, it is a minor source. However, this research concludes that, in fact, it is an important part of the public financing system in Europe—well more than the 1 percent number suggests. We begin this chapter on that note.

Five issues are taken up:

- The level and rate of property tax revenue growth in Europe in the first quarter of the 21st century was not impressive. The effective property tax rate was lower in 2022 than in 2005. Not surprisingly, evidence from this study suggests a significant unused taxable capacity for property taxation.
- Fiscal statistics understate the revenue importance of property taxes because not all taxes raised against the ownership and use of land and buildings are classified as property taxes. A broader view of what constitutes property tax revenues suggests a greater importance than usually supposed. Also important and also discussed (and also less appreciated) is the broad use of property tax instruments (such as

owner occupancy and mortgage financing) in achieving housing and land use policy goals.

- According to earlier studies, the amount that a country raises in property tax revenues depends on its income, wealth, degree of urbanization, and commitment to fiscal decentralization (Bahl et al. 2022; Bahl and Martinez-Vazquez 2008; Norregaard 2013). This chapter studies these factors in an updated econometric analysis of how European countries compare with each other.
- The property tax is a primary source of financing for local government services in Europe, and its long-run revenue-income buoyancy shows its potential to be a sustainable source of revenue. In some countries and in recent years, however, other local taxes and intergovernmental transfers have crowded out its importance in financing government services.
- The use of discretionary policy to limit the increase in property tax burdens is widespread among European countries. Because the property tax has raised so little revenue, and because it is so disliked by voters, governments may have spent too little political capital to reform it and may have been less dogged in developing and pursuing reforms than they should have been. The major problem in this respect is the failure of many countries to revalue real property at market levels.

Revenue Mobilization

General property tax revenues in 38 European countries averaged about 0.94 percent of GDP in 2022 (table 2.1, column 1; and see appendix). Recurrent (annual) property taxes account for nearly all this total (columns 2 and 3).[2] Only four European countries reached general property taxation above 2 percent of GDP, and 20 countries collected 0.7 percent of GDP or less. Including property transfer taxes (taxes on the sale of real properties) in this mapping raises the (estimated) average to about 1.17 percent of GDP, and to nearly 5 percent in France (columns 4 and 5).

When the effective tax rates reported in table 2.1 are converted to total amounts raised, a picture of Europe's property tax geography emerges. Total general property tax revenues collected in the 38-country sample in 2022 were about 1.51 percent of total European GDP (see the appendix for more discussion on the weighted and unweighted property tax rates). The average level of property tax paid per capita is about US$388, but as

Table 2.1 Property Tax Revenues in 38 European Countries, 2022 (% of GDP)

	(1) General Property Taxes	(2) Recurrent Property Taxes	(3) Non-recurrent Property Taxes	(4) Taxes on Financial and Capital Transactions	(5) Total Property Taxes
Albania	0.61 (23)	0.61 (21)	0.00 (25)	0.11 (21)	0.72 (24)
Austria	0.21 (36)	0.20 (36)	0.01 (21)	0.38 (7)	0.59 (27)
Belarus	0.86 (14)	0.86 (12)	n.a.	n.a.	0.86 (19)
Belgium	2.06 (4)	1.35 (7)	0.71 (2)	1.02 (1)	3.08 (3)
Bosnia and Herzegovina	0.34 (32)	0.34 (31)	0.01 (22)	0.01 (28)	0.35 (34)
Bulgaria	0.55 (24)	0.23 (34)	0.32 (5)	n.a.	0.55 (29)
Croatia	0.74 (18)	0.74 (16)	0.00 (24)	0.31 (10)	1.05 (14)
Cyprus	0.39 (28)	0.39 (26)	0.00 (26)	0.01 (27)	0.41 (32)
Czechia	0.18 (37)	0.18 (37)	0.00 (29)	0.01 (26)	0.19 (37)
Denmark	1.93 (6)	1.67 (5)	0.26 (9)	0.00 (29)	1.93 (8)
Estonia	0.16 (38)	0.16 (38)	n.a.	n.a.	0.16 (38)
Finland	1.11 (10)	0.77 (14)	0.34 (4)	0.34 (8)	1.45 (9)
France	3.23 (1)	2.52 (2)	0.71 (1)	0.88 (3)	4.11 (1)
Georgia	0.83 (15)	0.83 (13)	n.a.	n.a.	0.83 (20)
Germany	0.62 (22)	0.39 (28)	0.23 (10)	n.a.	0.62 (25)
Greece	2.27 (3)	2.15 (3)	0.13 (12)	0.27 (13)	2.54 (4)
Hungary	0.39 (29)	0.36 (29)	0.03 (18)	0.33 (9)	0.72 (23)
Iceland	1.96 (5)	1.64 (6)	0.31 (6)	0.16 (18)	2.11 (7)
Ireland	0.53 (25)	0.41 (25)	0.12 (13)	0.29 (12)	0.81 (21)
Italy	1.32 (9)	1.24 (8)	0.08 (14)	0.02 (25)	1.34 (12)
Kosovo	0.39 (30)	0.39 (27)	n.a.	n.a.	0.39 (33)
Latvia	0.65 (20)	0.60 (22)	0.04 (15)	0.12 (20)	0.77 (22)
Lithuania	0.29 (33)	0.28 (32)	0.00 (23)	n.a.	0.29 (35)
Moldova	0.27 (34)	0.27 (33)	0.00 (27)	n.a.	0.27 (36)
Netherlands	0.97 (12)	0.71 (18)	0.26 (8)	0.46 (6)	1.44 (10)
North Macedonia	0.26 (35)	0.23 (35)	0.03 (17)	0.30 (11)	0.56 (28)
Norway	0.75 (17)	0.75 (15)	0.00 (28)	0.21 (17)	0.97 (16)
Poland	1.00 (11)	0.98 (10)	0.02 (20)	0.14 (19)	1.13 (13)
Portugal	0.68 (19)	0.68 (19)	0.00 (30)	0.68 (5)	1.36 (11)
Romania	0.45 (27)	0.45 (24)	n.a.	0.03 (24)	0.48 (30)
Russian Federation	0.87 (13)	0.87 (11)	n.a.	0.00 (30)	0.87 (18)
Serbia	0.76 (16)	0.74 (17)	0.03 (19)	0.26 (16)	1.02 (15)
Slovenia	0.51 (26)	0.48 (23)	0.04 (16)	0.10 (22)	0.61 (26)
Spain	1.60 (8)	1.19 (9)	0.41 (3)	0.92 (2)	2.52 (5)

Table 2.1 Property Tax Revenues in 38 European Countries, 2022 (% of GDP) *(continued)*

	(1) General Property Taxes	(2) Recurrent Property Taxes	(3) Non-recurrent Property Taxes	(4) Taxes on Financial and Capital Transactions	(5) Total Property Taxes
Sweden	0.65 (21)	0.65 (20)	n.a.	0.26 (14)	0.91 (17)
Switzerland	1.89 (7)	1.71 (4)	0.18 (11)	0.26 (15)	2.15 (6)
Ukraine	0.35 (31)	0.35 (30)	n.a.	0.09 (23)	0.44 (31)
United Kingdom	3.00 (2)	2.73 (1)	0.27 (7)	0.86 (4)	3.86 (2)
Mean	0.94	0.82	0.12	0.23	1.17
Standard deviation	0.77	0.65	0.19	0.29	0.98
Coefficient of variation	0.82	0.79	1.56	1.24	0.83

Source: IMF (n.d.-c).

Note: Column headings are as follows: (1) general property tax revenues (excludes property transfer taxes; International Monetary Fund's Government Finance Statistics [GFS] database category 113 [IMF (2014)]); (2) recurrent property tax revenues (excludes property transfer taxes; GFS 1131 + 1132 + 1136); (3) nonrecurrent general property tax revenues (excludes property transfer taxes; GFS 1133 + 1135); (4) taxes on financial and capital transactions (includes property transfer taxes; GFS 11414); and (5) total property tax revenues (includes property transfer taxes; GFS 113 + 11414).

Ranking is shown in parentheses. n.a. = not available.

shown in figure 2.1, the frequency distribution of per capita revenues is heavily skewed toward those countries with lower per capita collections. Nearly 60 percent of total general property tax revenue was collected in three countries (the United Kingdom, France, and Italy), which together account for about 26 percent of European population and 33 percent of European GDP (figure 2.2).

Trends and Patterns of Change

The long-term trend in general property tax revenues has shown little growth in recent years (figure 2.3). It increased between 2005 and 2014 but then fell during the recession and the pandemic back to about 2005 levels. The effective tax rate on property transfers (financial and capital

Figure 2.1 Frequency Distribution for per Capita General Property Tax Revenues Raised for 38 European Countries, 2022

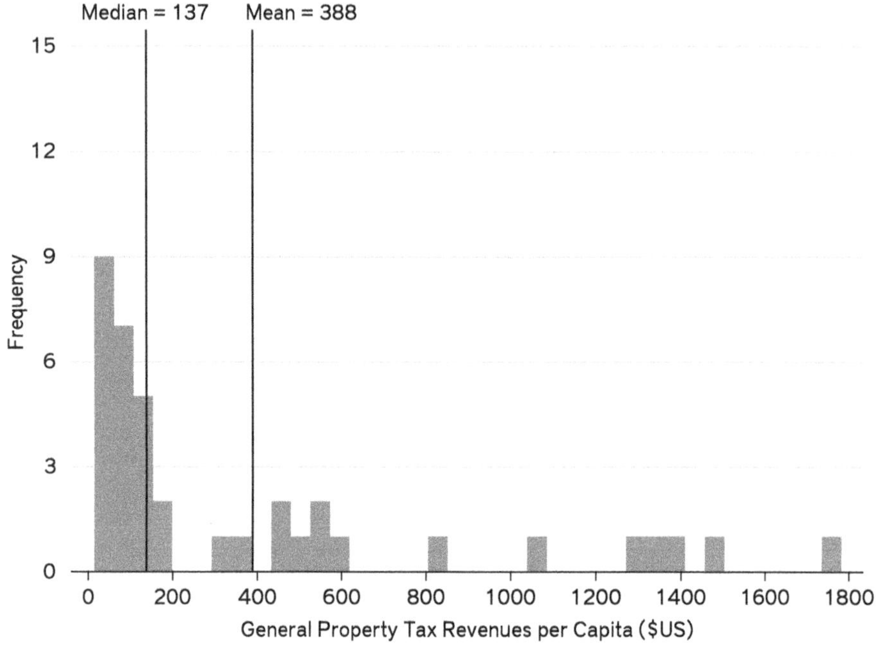

Sources: Data from IMF (n.d.-c); World Bank (n.d.-b).

transaction taxes) also has been declining since 2015, though the patterns of cyclical variation in revenues are not as volatile as some might have expected. What is most important to observe, however, is that the average effective rates for both general property taxes and total property taxes were lower in 2022 than in 2005.

However, outcomes have differed significantly from country to country. As table 2.2 shows, the effective tax rate of 23 of the 38 countries declined between 2010 and 2022, and 7 have been declining since 2005. The average effective rate of property taxation has not increased over the 17-year period of 2005–2022. During this same time span, the average ratio of total tax revenue to GDP also remained constant at about 25 percent.

Broadening the Definition of a Property Tax?

Some levies on the ownership or use of real properties are not reported as property taxes.[3] This leads to an understatement of revenues raised from taxes on land and buildings and contributes to the image of the general

Figure 2.2 General Property Tax Revenue Share for 38 European Countries, 2022

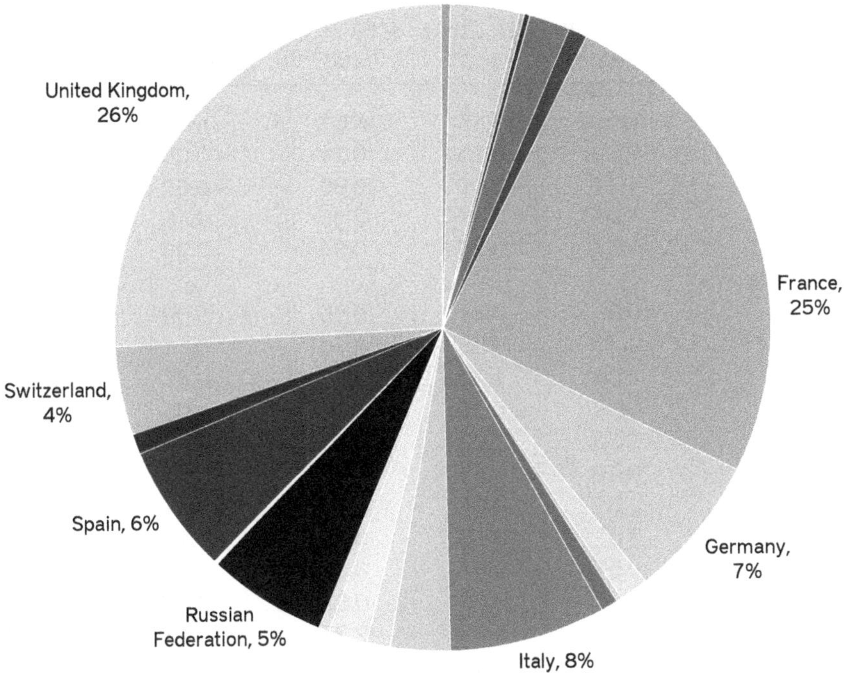

Sources: Data from IMF (n.d.-c); World Bank (n.d.-b).

Figure 2.3 General and Total Property Tax (PT) Revenues for European Countries, 2005–2022 (% of GDP)

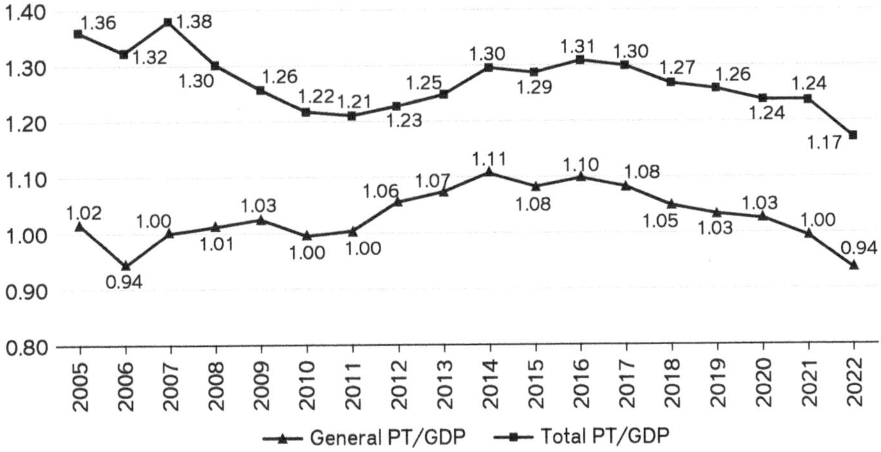

Source: Data from IMF (n.d.-c).

Note: The number of countries reported varies between 34 and 38, depending on data availability.

Table 2.2 Time Series of Effective Property Tax Rate (ETR) in 38 European Countries

	ETR 2005 (%)	ETR 2010 (%)	ETR 2022 (%)	Change 2005–2010	Change 2010–2022
Albania	n.a.	0.15	0.61	n.a.	0.46
Austria	0.29	0.25	0.21	–0.05	–0.04
Belarus	1.71	1.09	0.86	–0.62	–0.23
Belgium	1.91	2.07	2.06	0.16	–0.01
Bosnia and Herzegovina	0.57	0.34	0.34	–0.23	0.00
Bulgaria	0.39	0.48	0.55	0.09	0.07
Croatia	0.71	0.83	0.74	0.11	–0.09
Cyprus	2.06	1.23	0.39	–0.83	–0.83
Czechia	0.18	0.22	0.18	0.05	–0.05
Denmark	1.98	2.23	1.93	0.24	–0.30
Estonia	0.28	0.35	0.16	0.06	–0.19
Finland	0.81	0.83	1.11	0.01	0.28
France	3.87	3.68	3.23	–0.19	–0.45
Georgia	0.51	0.87	0.83	0.36	–0.04
Germany	0.62	0.60	0.62	–0.02	0.02
Greece	0.96	0.89	2.27	–0.07	1.39
Hungary	0.35	0.37	0.39	0.02	0.02
Iceland	1.71	2.11	1.96	0.39	–0.15
Ireland	0.76	0.94	0.53	0.18	–0.41
Italy	0.91	0.81	1.32	–0.09	0.50
Kosovo	n.a.	n.a.	0.39	n.a.	n.a.
Latvia	0.84	0.91	0.65	0.08	–0.27
Lithuania	0.34	0.37	0.29	0.02	–0.08
Moldova	0.62	0.33	0.27	–0.29	–0.05
Netherlands	1.10	0.90	0.97	–0.20	0.07
North Macedonia	n.a.	n.a.	0.26	n.a.	n.a.
Norway	0.75	0.84	0.75	0.10	–0.09
Poland	1.31	1.16	1.00	–0.14	–0.17
Portugal	0.57	0.67	0.68	0.10	0.01
Romania	0.52	0.66	0.45	0.14	–0.21
Russian Federation	1.00	1.11	0.87	0.12	–0.25
Serbia	n.a.	0.40	0.76	n.a.	0.36
Slovenia	0.45	0.52	0.51	0.07	–0.01
Spain	1.30	1.35	1.60	0.05	0.25
Sweden	1.06	0.73	0.65	–0.34	–0.08
Switzerland	1.65	1.60	1.89	–0.05	0.29
Ukraine	0.36	0.80	0.35	0.44	–0.45
United Kingdom	3.07	3.17	3.00	0.10	–0.17

Source: IMF (n.d.-c).

Note: n.a. = not available.

property tax being an inconsequential source of revenues (Bahl, Linn, and Wetzel 2013). These "ghost property taxes" include the following:

- Capital gains taxes on the profits from the sale of real estate that are reported in the government accounts as taxes on individual and company income.
- Taxes on landlord rents that are recorded as individual or company income taxes and impose tax liabilities on the basis of the marginal income tax rate bracket of the individual or the company owner.
- Value-added taxes (VAT) that are usually charged against the (first) sale of newly constructed (and in some countries, refurbished) properties. Future sales of these properties are exempt from VAT but may attract property transfer taxes.
- Tax revenues raised from real property sales (stamp duties or property transaction taxes) that are not included under the heading "property tax" in the International Monetary Fund (IMF) Government Finance Statistics dataset. However, these are counted as property taxes in the Organisation for Economic Co-operation and Development (OECD) dataset (see chapter 1). But neither of these data series separately report revenues raised from the taxes on the transfer of land and buildings. Data reported in the country studies in part 2 suggest that these amounts may be significant when compared with general property tax revenues (see also chapter 6).
- Taxes on real property that are classified otherwise because of historical convention or because of definitions used in the country's tax nomenclature. For example, the "property value tax" is classified as an income tax in Danish official statistics, even though it is levied against the assessed value of real property. In Finland, certain taxes and charges imposed by municipal governments are not classified as property taxes, even though these charges are levied against real property and yield a significant amount of revenues.

The country studies in part 2 examine these ghost property taxes and attempt to determine the amount of revenue raised from them. For some countries, the data could be extracted or at least estimated. For certain taxes and for some countries, the data were readily available. In other cases, no estimate was made.

The results from these country studies, summarized in table 2.3, are too incomplete, and the sample too small and nonrandom, to allow drawing firm conclusions. However, the estimates that could be made in the

Table 2.3 Estimated Revenues from a Broader Definition of Taxes on Land and Buildings

	Landlord Income Tax	Capital Gains Income Tax on Real Property	VAT on New Home Sales	Property Transfer Taxes	Comment
Denmark	n.a.	Most real estate transactions are exempt	New construction and sale of building sites subject to VAT, but calculations are complex	0.31% of GDP in 2020	Property value tax (0.60% of GDP) is classified as an income tax
Estonia	n.a.	n.a.	n.a.	n.a.	
Finland	0.002% of GDP in 2021	n.a.	n.a.	0.396% of GDP in 2021	Revenues from land banking are not reported
France	0.31% of GDP in 2021	0.08% of GDP	0.33% of GDP	0.67% of GDP	
Germany	n.a.	0.14% of GDP	n.a.	0.50% of GDP	
Greece	n.a.	n.a.	n.a.	n.a.	
Ireland	n.a.	0.1200% of GDP in 2021	0.1100% of GDP in 2021	0.1678% of GDP in 2021	
Latvia	n.a.	n.a.	n.a.	0.17% of GDP in 2021	

Netherlands	0.20% of GDP in 2021	0.11% of GDP	n.a.	0.45% of GDP in 2021	
Poland	n.a.	n.a.	n.a.	n.a.	
Russia	n.a.	0.2506% of GDP in 2020 (includes rental incomes)	0.5663% of GDP in 2020	Nominal amounts of stamp duty are levied; 0.0400% of GDP in 2020	
Spain	0.21% of GDP in 2021	n.a.	0.11 percent of GDP in 2020	0.90% of GDP in 2020	
Slovenia	0.1200% of GDP in 2020	0.0260% of GDP in 2020	0.2000% of GDP in 2021	0.1033% of GDP in 2021	
United Kingdom	1.80% of GDP in 2021	0.08% of GDP in 2021;	0.17% of GDP	0.64% of GDP in 2022	Transfer tax as % of GDP is 0.72 (England); 0.47 (Scotland); 0.30 (Wales); 0.20 (Northern Ireland)

Source: Data in part 2 country studies.

Note: n.a. = not available

country studies suggest that the understated amounts of revenue can be large compared with the average effective property tax rate of about 1 percent in Europe. In France, for example, revenue from the general property tax as traditionally defined accounts for an estimated 3.23 percent of GDP in 2022 (see table 2.1). But including property transfer taxes raises this level to 4.11 percent of GDP, and including other taxes on property use and transactions would push it closer to 5 percent. Other examples of the amounts of ghost taxes shown in table 2.3 suggest a significantly greater importance of the property tax.

This discussion omits tax expenditures or tax preferences related to the ownership and use of land and buildings, such as the cost of income tax exemptions for a principal residence from capital gains tax, imputed rents, and mortgage interest.[4] These property tax instruments sometimes make higher income tax rates more palatable.

The bottom line in this discussion is that a lot of revenue collected against the ownership, use, and transfer of land and buildings is not reported (or likely even thought of) as property taxation. The same is true for much income tax relief related to the ownership and use of land and buildings. The argument here is that publication of this information might raise awareness of a larger importance of taxes on real property (and tax relief), thereby nudging governments in the direction of investing more resources and political capital in sustaining the property tax and in improving its structure and administration.

What would it take to further increase awareness about the importance of property taxation? Certainly, there is no reason to call for a new nomenclature of taxation. International agencies and countries deliberate at great length to decide which taxes and surtaxes belong in which category and how to comply with these classification rules. Still, for a fuller picture of how taxes on real property contribute to the revenue base in an economy, adding a statistical crosswalk between general property taxation and other taxes on land and buildings could be an exhibit in international compendia and in country tax department reports. To highlight their special importance, property transfer taxes should occupy a separate line in such an exhibit. Certainly they should be fully reported.

Finally, taxes on land and buildings support policy initiatives broader than taxation. In fact, some property tax functions, such as maintaining a cadastre or registering property transfers, exist primarily for nontax purposes. If done well, however, these taxes can positively affect property tax revenue mobilization (OECD 2022). European countries use property tax instruments to directly support housing and land use program objectives, including taxes on second homes (Austria, Croatia, and Ireland) and vacant properties (Austria, France, Lithuania, and Spain), reduced VAT rates for housing renovations (Belgium and France), and property tax reductions for energy-efficient housing construction (Spain).

Wealth Taxes

A tax on wealth, usually measured as a tax on net worth (assets minus liabilities), is capable of generating significant revenues, with a tax burden that falls disproportionately on wealthy residents. In theory, it could be an important component of the property tax systems in Europe.

A tax on wealth, however, is very different from an annual tax on land and buildings (Zolt 2024). The wealth tax usually covers all assets, whereas the property tax is limited to real estate. Most wealth taxes are calculated on a net worth basis, but property taxes do not allow a deduction for debt. The traditional property tax base usually covers a much larger number of taxpayers than does a wealth tax base.

Twelve European countries in 1990 levied wealth taxes, but by 2018 only four did, and only one limited it to real property wealth. The phasing out of the wealth tax in most of Europe was attributable to base erosion by capital flight and tax avoidance or evasion, revenues falling below expectations, unfavorable equity impacts due to reductions in the after-tax return to savings, and administrative problems (Scheuer and Slemrod 2021).

Wealth taxes have some common features in the four European countries that still levy them (France, Spain, Switzerland, and Norway). The tax base is a measure of the total value of assets held, but depending on the valuation method and the allowed exemption, the effective tax rate can be very low. In none of the four countries does the wealth tax generate more than a minor share of national revenue.

Of the remaining wealth taxes in Europe, the Swiss system produces the most, yielding revenue equivalent to about 1.1 percent of GDP in 2020. It is a highly decentralized tax; individual cantons have rate-setting powers, and municipal governments can add a sur-rate. The widely disparate effective tax rates on wealth result in intercantonal tax competition and migration. Switzerland, however, has neither a federal capital gains tax nor a federal tax on gifts and bequests, which bodes well for the continued use of the wealth tax.

The wealth tax in Norway generates revenues equivalent to about 0.4 percent of GDP. The floor for tax liability is set at about US$160,000 in net worth at a tax rate of 1 percent, rising to 2 percent at a net worth of about US$20 million. However, exemptions, particularly for housing, have significantly narrowed the taxable base. Thoresen et al. (2021) argue that such favorable tax treatment, and the absence of undesirable behavioral and efficiency effects, does not weaken the argument for retaining the tax.

In 2018, France replaced its broader-based wealth tax with a progressive rate tax on the value of real estate wealth. The tax base has a threshold of €1.3 million, including 70 percent of the market value of the main residence, and is net of all related debt. The tax rates range from 0.5 to 1.5 percent. A special feature for French fiscal residents is a wealth tax cap of 75 percent of worldwide income. The real estate wealth tax is self-reported and self-assessed. In 2021, France's wealth tax accounted for 1.86 percent of central-government real estate taxes and 0.09 percent of GDP.

Spain levies its wealth tax on the net value of all forms of personal wealth at a progressive rate. Individuals with a wealth of less than €2 million and family businesses are fully or partially exempt. Income tax and wealth tax together cannot exceed 60 percent of taxable income. When this happens, the wealth tax reduces accordingly. The wealth tax raises little revenue, an average of 0.11–0.13 percent of Spanish GDP. The regional governments retain almost 96 percent of the total tax, and they have some degree of discretion to alter the tax rates. The regions may modify their exemptions at any time.

Intercountry Variations

General property tax revenues in European countries as a proportion of GDP varied from 0.16 percent (Estonia) to 3.23 percent (France) in 2022. Differences in economic development explain some of this variation, but other factors may also contribute, including the concentration of the population in cities, the importance of local governments in providing services, and the level of real property wealth (Bahl et al. 2022). The regression analysis reported in the following specifies the determinants of intercountry differences in the effective property tax rate in European countries and reports their significance.[5]

Specification of the Model

Intercountry variations are studied here using panel data for 34 European nations for 2002–2019.[6] The dependent variable in this regression analysis is total general property tax revenues, standardized by GDP. This study refers to the ratio of general property tax revenues to GDP as the *effective property tax rate*.[7] This convention follows earlier econometric analyses of property tax revenue performance at the national-government level (Bahl et al. 2022; Bahl and Martinez-Vazquez 2008; Norregaard 2013).

The independent variables were selected on the basis of theory, analysis from the part 2 country studies, other research on the determinants of property tax revenue levels in Europe, collinearity among the possible independent variables, and the availability of data. The underlying hypothesis is that the effective rate of general property taxation is determined by the level and composition of the tax base and whether the existing institutional structure captures the revenue-raising capacity. Four independent variables are studied: the urbanization rate, the per capita level of produced wealth, per capita GDP, and the degree of fiscal decentralization.

Urbanization

More-urbanized countries have a greater capacity to raise property taxes. Evidence shows that incomes increase with urbanization (Bahl and Bird 2018, chap. 6; Glaeser 2011). Capturing agglomeration effects has led to productivity increases, which have contributed to higher property values and therefore created a larger property tax revenue potential. Larger and richer cities often have more modern administration practices and provide better-quality public services, thereby holding in check some of the taxpayer resistance to higher property taxes.

National property tax collections tend to be concentrated in larger cities (Bahl and Linn 1992; Bahl, Linn, and Wetzel 2013). By contrast, capacity to pay property tax of those living and doing business in smaller towns and rural areas is lower (on average), and their governments usually rely more heavily on intergovernmental transfers to finance government services. Urban-rural income disparities put more pressure on larger cities to find their own financing and are another stimulus to urban property taxation.

The percentage of national population living in urban areas usually positively impacts the effective property tax rate.[8] However, countries with a higher urbanization rate tend to have a higher per capita GDP and a higher level of produced wealth, making their separate impacts on the effective property tax rate difficult to disentangle in a regression analysis.

Capital Stock

Higher rates of public and private sector investment can lead to higher values of residential housing, commercial and industrial fixed capital, and public sector infrastructure. These investments (and their maintenance) may have increased the value of better-serviced urban land and properties and (indirectly) led to a higher-valued property tax base. The greater a country's wealth base, the more services it can finance without depleting national wealth, and the greater will be its potential to further grow the property tax base. Moreover, the property tax might be directly involved in financing capital maintenance, since a significant share of responsibility for infrastructure finance lies with subnational governments (de Mello and Sutherland 1988). Thus, the wealth of a country would seem a reasonable indicator of its capacity to raise property tax revenues.

The World Bank has worked on the wealth measurement job in its studies on the wealth of nations (2006; 2011; 2021), and Chancel et al. (2022) have contributed analytic work involving the taxation of wealth. The disaggregation of wealth presented in the 2021 World Bank volume includes as a major component of wealth, "produced capital," which includes buildings, structures, machinery, intellectual capital, and residential and nonresidential urban land.[9] This measure includes proxies for some of the underlying factors property taxes are levied against—that is, the wealth in privately owned land and buildings used for residential and business purposes.[10] Produced capital accounted for 31 percent of worldwide total wealth in 2018 and for 40 percent of the total wealth in European countries.

If produced capital is a good indicator of the capacity to tax real property, it suggests that the underlying potential to tax the real property base has increased over the long run. The trends shown in figure 2.4 suggest the real level of produced capital (and total wealth) has grown faster than GDP for most of the last two decades.[11]

To indicate the stock of wealth, this analysis uses the per capita real (in 2018 US$) value of produced capital (with a one-year lag) as estimated by the World Bank (2021). We expect a positive impact on the effective rate of property tax.

Income Effects

Our hypothesis is that families and businesses in countries with higher levels of GDP per capita will demand better services and will have more capacity to pay property taxes.[12] Residential housing values and rents tend to be higher than in lower-income countries, and higher-income countries tend to have a stronger residential and commercial tax base. Assuming that a more efficient tax administration and assessment program will be more affordable for governments in richer countries, and that higher income populations have a greater willingness to pay property taxes, the income effect should drive up property tax revenues.

It is also possible, however, that at the margin, higher levels of GDP can dampen the effective property tax rate. An increase in GDP might lead to larger automatic revenue increases from sales and income taxes than from property taxes, because of the higher built-in revenue-income elasticity of income and consumption tax bases. This in turn could crowd out property taxes in favor of more financing of local governments by intergovernmental transfers and other local-government taxes.[13] The marginal effect of the per capita GDP variable in this regression depends on the strengths of the income and substitution effects.

Figure 2.4 Total Wealth per Capita, Produced Capital per Capita, and GDP per Capita for European Countries, 1995–2018

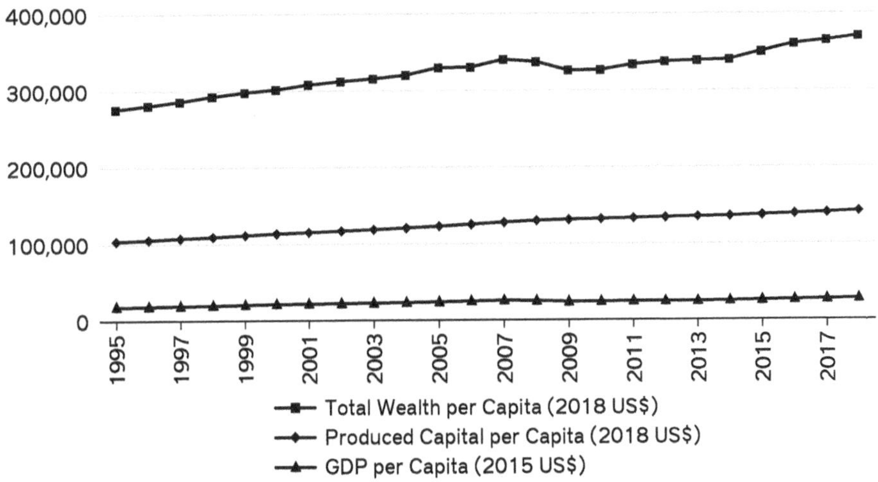

Sources: Data from World Bank (2021; n.d.-a).

Note: Total wealth per capita and produced capital per capita are in 2018 US$, and GDP per capita is in 2015 US$.

Fiscal Decentralization

Central and Eastern European countries adopted fiscal decentralization strategies to achieve economic growth and access to the European Union during their transition to more decentralized governance (Rodríguez-Pose and Kroijer 2009). Countries adopted more fiscally decentralized systems of governance to improve local public service provision. By voting on their budgets (directly or indirectly), local residents can receive public services that more closely fit their preferences than if a higher-level government decided local budgets or set down harder expenditure mandates (Bahl and Linn 1992; Bahl and Martinez-Vazquez 2022; Boadway and Shah 2009; Oates 1981). These desired outcomes, and more accountability, are more likely to be realized if local governments have autonomous taxing powers. This is part of the explanation of why more highly decentralized countries tend to impose higher levels of property taxation. Transitional countries have distinct institutional peculiarities, such as related to landownership, that may affect their relative use of property taxation (Bahl and Martinez-Vazquez 2008). The inclusion of fixed effects in the estimation model controls for such variations across countries.

Using fiscal decentralization as an estimator of the effective rate of property taxation requires addressing the possibility of two-way causation—that is, that higher levels of property taxes may lead to higher levels of fiscal decentralization. If property taxes are a component of the local-government tax base, and if local governments have some discretion in choosing property tax rates, local-government budgets and property tax revenues may be larger. Following Bahl and Martinez-Vazquez (2008; 2022), we treat fiscal decentralization as an endogenous variable measured as the ratio of subnational government expenditures to total government expenditure.[14]

Estimation and Results

This model is estimated with panel data, controlling for country fixed effects.[15] All continuous variables are expressed in logarithms.[16] The model is estimated from an unbalanced panel of 34 European countries from 2002 to 2019. For comparative purpose, we also apply the same estimation to a worldwide sample of 69 countries.

The dependent variable is general property tax revenue as a percentage of GDP (IMF, n.d.-b). The independent variables include fiscal decentralization (IMF, n.d.-a; OECD, n.d.-b), per capita GDP (World Bank, n.d.-a), urbanization rate (World Bank, n.d.-a), and per capita produced capital (World Bank 2021). Data on per capita produced capital was available only up to 2018 when this estimation was carried out. To maximize the sample period, it is lagged by one year in the estimation. The fiscal decentralization variable is measured as the share of expenditures of subnational governments as a proportion of general government spending (Lledó, Gbohoui, and Ncuti 2022).

Following theory and a priori reasoning, a two-stage least squares regression model is estimated with fiscal decentralization treated as an endogenous variable. Instrumental variables used in the first-stage equations are total population (World Bank, n.d.-a) and the Human Development Index.[17] The Durbin-Wu-Hausman test for endogeneity shows that fiscal decentralization is endogenous at the 1 percent significance level for the European sample; however, it is exogenous at the 5 percent significance level for the international sample. To preserve the comparative dimension of this analysis, we apply the same two-stage least squares regression estimation to both samples. The model suffers from a specification error because important information is not available for the independent variable list, such as a control variable for the efficiency of the property tax administration and an index of the pretax distribution of income.

Table 2.4 Determinants of Intercountry Variations in Effective Property Tax Rates, 2002–2019

	Model I	Model II
Variable	**European Sample**	**International Sample**
ln FD	0.7249**	0.7636
	(0.3120)	(0.7219)
ln Y/P	−0.3333***	−0.2863***
	(0.0480)	(0.0624)
ln U	4.9778***	2.2817***
	(0.7078)	(0.4326)
ln L.PK	0.5223***	0.4259***
	(0.1639)	(0.1273)
Constant	−26.4186***	−14.3715***
	(4.3120)	(3.7780)
Observations	581	1,010
Number of countries	34	69
Overall *R*-squared	0.2892	0.4132

Source: Authors.

Note: The dependent variable is ln (general PT/GDP), where general PT/GDP = property tax revenues as a percentage of GDP for both models. The independent variables include FD = fiscal decentralization, L.PK = produced capital per capita in previous year; U = urbanization; Y/P = GDP per capita. All variables are expressed in logarithms. Standard errors are in parentheses.

*** $p < 0.01$, ** $p < 0.05$, * $p < 0.1$

The results for this regression analysis of the determinants of general property tax revenues (table 2.4) for the European sample square with the hypothesized effects. There is a strong and statistically significant impact of the rate of urbanization on the effective property tax rate. The revenue responsiveness to urbanization (the rate at which the effective property tax rate increases with a 1 percent increase in the rate of urbanization) is 4.98 percent of the original property tax rate. For example, if the rate of urbanization increased from its present average level of 71 percent to 75 percent, ceteris paribus, the effective property tax rate would increase from its 2019 average level of 1.08 percent of GDP to an estimated 1.38 percent.[18]

The effective rate of property taxation also responds positively to the value of the physical stock of capital assets. In the European sample, per capita produced capital is estimated to have a significant positive elasticity of 0.52.[19]

The level of per capita GDP shows a significant negative marginal effect on the effective general property tax rate in European countries. For countries *at the same level of urbanization and with the same level of produced capital*, a higher per capita GDP could drive down the effective property tax rate. This would happen because sales and income taxes are more income elastic than are property taxes and, at the margin, they automatically crowd out property taxes. On the basis of these results, for a country with a given level of urbanization and property wealth, a 1 percentage point higher per capita GDP, ceteris paribus, will be associated with a 0.33 percent lower effective property tax rate.[20] By this estimation, the marginal substitution effect (crowding out) dominates the marginal income effect, leading to a lower effective property tax rate.

The results for the international sample are similar, but with two important differences. First, the elasticity coefficients for the urbanization, capital stock, and income effects are larger in the European sample. The effective property tax rate responds more to differences in urbanization and to differences in the level of wealth, and crowding out of the property tax is more pronounced in Europe. Second, fiscal decentralization exerts a statistically significant effect on the effective property tax rate in Europe but not in the larger international sample. These differences might be due to the more developed state of revenue decentralization in higher-income Europe (Bahl and Bird 2018, chap. 6) and to the inclusion of many more lower-income countries in the international sample.

To reexamine the crowding out results for per capita GDP, we drop the property wealth variable from the specification for both models. The results (table 2.5) show that the income variable retains its negative sign in both samples but shows significance only in the European sample. This is consistent with the interpretation of the findings showing a crowding out effect.

Revenue Buoyancy

Understanding how tax revenues respond to economic growth is essential to designing tax policy needs, expenditure limits, and debt planning. The most commonly used measures of the revenue response to economic growth (and decline) are revenue-income elasticity and revenue-income buoyancy. The different meanings of these two coefficients, and their measurement, are important for understanding the sustainability of the property tax (box 2.1).

Table 2.5 Robustness of Estimation of Income Effects

	Model III	Model IV
Variable	**European Sample**	**International Sample**
ln FD	1.3862*	0.5891
	(0.8301)	(1.0475)
ln Y	−0.2174***	−0.1911***
	(0.0482)	(0.0579)
ln U	7.1025***	2.6110***
	(1.7016)	(0.5364)
Constant	−32.7034***	−11.4384**
	(9.8703)	(4.7045)
Observations	581	1,010
Number of countries	34	69
Overall *R*-squared	0.2676	0.3539

Source: Authors.

Note: The dependent variable is ln (general PT/GDP), where general PT/GDP = property tax revenues as a percentage of GDP for both models. The independent variables include FD = fiscal decentralization, U = urbanization; Y = GDP. All variables are expressed in logarithms. Standard errors are in parentheses.
*** $p < 0.01$, ** $p < 0.05$, * $p < 0.1$

Buoyancy

Several arguments support the need for a more buoyant property tax in European countries. Most importantly, it is a primary source of revenues for local governments in their provision of essential local services. Second, a more buoyant property tax supports the development of local government autonomy by forestalling the encroachment of intergovernmental transfers on local government budgets. Third, it relieves the central government of some burden of its financing of local government budgets.

If the property tax is to be strengthened in Europe, it needs to be seen as an important part of the public financing system. The less important a tax is seen in terms of revenue raised to meet budgetary needs, the less effort and political capital will be spent on its reform. And reform of the property tax, no matter how much (or little) revenue it raises, requires great amounts of both. The possible consequences of being perceived as a minor revenue source that does not warrant costly reforms are a shift of tax revenue reliance away from a base celebrated for its immobility, and the loss of a piece

Box 2.1 An Old Question: Buoyancy Versus Elasticity

The revenue-income elasticity coefficient is the automatic percentage change in tax revenues in response to a percentage change in GDP. The elasticity shows the revenue expansion or contraction in response to an income change that might be expected under a "things-as-usual" scenario with no discretionary changes. The problem with the elasticity approach is that the time series of revenue from which the coefficient is estimated must be cleaned of the direct and indirect revenue impacts of discretionary changes (Prest 1962). Discretionary changes might involve rate increases, new exemptions and tax reliefs, changes in the methods of assessment, and most difficult of all, revaluations. Cleaning the revenue statistics of all such changes is nigh impossible.

Estimation of the revenue buoyancy coefficient is based on actual revenue collections, and no cleaning of the data series is required. Some might argue that buoyancy is the more useful measure because keeping property tax revenues in step with budgetary needs in a changing political economy leads to periodic discretionary actions. If the pattern of discretionary changes over the long run has added to revenues more or less consistently, fiscal planners might cautiously assume the pattern will continue–for example, revaluation that is done regularly or tax rate bracket widths that are adjusted periodically. But in most countries, such assumptions are a stretch. Most researchers use the buoyancy measure, largely because the data necessary are more readily available.

of the tax system that (potentially) falls more heavily on higher-income owners of property wealth. Finally, to the extent the property tax is marginalized, local communities in many countries will lose a quasi-benefit tax that contributes to making local-government budgets more efficient.

There is not uniform agreement on an "optimal" long-run buoyancy for the property tax. Countries often begin by proposing a buoyancy-income coefficient of unity, which suggests that the property tax should hold to a constant effective tax rate over time.[21] But certainly there are reasons to challenge this norm. If public service costs rise faster than GDP, even a property tax buoyancy of unity may not generate enough revenue to guarantee sustainability.[22] A country ratcheting up the size of its decentralized public sector with the assumption of more responsibility for providing local public services might seek a higher property tax buoyancy. But other considerations could call for a lower automatic growth of property tax revenues. The revenue buoyancy needed to sustain the place of the property tax in the fiscal structure varies from country to country depending on local and national tax policy and government expenditure preferences.

Measurement

Research on tax buoyancy makes use of a statistical technique (error correction method) that allows separation of the long-run and short-run income buoyancy of a revenue stream. It is important that the revenue growth that is short run (possibly taking the form of an automatic stabilizer and fluctuating annually in response to economic growth and discretionary changes) be studied separately from that which is long run and more accurately reflects the strength and fiscal stability of the economy.

Research on fiscal buoyancy has focused mostly on total tax collections and on the larger sources of revenues, mainly total income and consumption taxes (Dudine and Jalles 2018; Hill, Jinjarak, and Park 2022). A notable exception is the work of Belinga et al. (2014), who use annual property tax revenue data in their study of 34 OECD countries for the 1965–2012 period. Their estimates of short-run buoyancy indicate that property tax revenues in Europe follow a more stable growth path than GDP and adjust more slowly toward long-term buoyancy than do other taxes. Their estimated long-run property tax buoyancy coefficient was not significantly less than unity for these OECD countries, but importantly it was lower than that estimated for other taxes.

New Estimates for Europe

We use an error correction model to reestimate the long- and short-run income-buoyancy coefficients (box 2.2). The panel sample includes data for 37 European countries between 1995 and 2021. The time period varies across countries depending on data availability. Countries with fewer than 10 observations were dropped from the sample. The final sample consists of 917 observations and 37 countries.

Table 2.6 reports the results from this estimation for 1995–2021. The average short-run property tax buoyancy for European countries is 0.375, and the average long-run buoyancy is 1.137. The speed of adjustment is 0.442, suggesting that about 44.2 percent of the discrepancy between the long run and short run is corrected within a year. For the 37 countries in this sample, the null hypothesis of an average long-run buoyancy coefficient of unity cannot be rejected.

These results show a limited response of property tax revenues to GDP growth in the short run. The responses are slowed by assessment lags, continued unpopularity of rate increases, and tax relief measures that usually require administrative lead time. Housing stocks and property valuations are near to fixed in the short run. Discretionary tax policy, however, can lead to short-run countercyclical adjustments in the revenue

Box 2.2 Error Correction Model

1. Specification and estimation

Following Belinga et al. (2014), the error correction model (ECM) is specified as

$$\Delta \ln PT_{i,t} = \lambda_i(\ln PT_{i,t-1} - \theta_i \ln GDP_{i,t-1}) + \varphi_{i,0}\Delta \ln GDP_{i,t} + \mu_i + \varepsilon_{i,t},$$

where $PT_{i,t}$ denotes general property tax revenue in country i in year t, $GDP_{i.t}$ denotes the corresponding level of GDP, μ_i represents country fixed effects, and $\varepsilon_{i,t}$ is the error term. Both the property tax variable and GDP are logarithms. The "Δ" before a variable indicates the first difference of that variable. In this equation, θ_i is the long-run buoyancy coefficient, $\varphi_{i,0}$ is the short-run buoyancy coefficient, and λ_i measures the speed of adjustment.

2. Mean group estimator and pooled mean group estimator

Two techniques estimate the ECM: the mean group (MG) and pooled mean group (PMG) estimators (Blackburne and Frank 2007).

The MG estimator is based on estimating time-series regressions for each group and averaging the coefficients to obtain the panel average coefficients (Blackburne and Frank 2007; Pesaran and Smith 1995). This estimation method allows the intercept, long-run coefficients, short-run coefficients, and speed-of-adjustment coefficients to differ across groups (Belinga et al. 2014).

The PMG estimator combines pooling and averaging of coefficients (Blackburne and Frank 2007; Pesaran, Shin, and Smith 1997; 1999). This approach allows variations in intercepts, short-run coefficients, and speed-of-adjustment coefficients across groups but constrains the long-run buoyancy to be equal across groups. Consequently, the PMG estimator assumes that countries ultimately converge to the same buoyancy but may exhibit divergences in the short run (Belinga et al. 2014).

In this study, we use the MG and PMG estimations for the long-run buoyancy, short-run buoyancy, and speed of adjustment for the panel, and the long-run buoyancy uses the MG estimation for each country.

take. An example is the decision to defer reassessments in some European countries because of the impacts of the COVID-19 pandemic or business cycles on ability to pay (Commission for Economic Policy 2021). Automatic revenue response to GDP changes in the short run will result from new properties coming onto the tax roll, automatic revaluations, and from indexed annual revaluations that might be influenced by GDP (or inflation) changes. On balance, we expect the low short-run buoyancy of 0.375, which is estimated here.

The long-run buoyancy is the more interesting question for this study. The estimate here is a buoyancy coefficient of 1.137. The Wald test of the

Table 2.6 Mean Group and Pooled Mean Group Estimates of Buoyancy, 1995–2021

	Mean Group Estimates	Pooled Mean Group Estimates
Long-run buoyancy	1.137***	1.133***
	(0.102)	(0.019)
Short-run buoyancy	0.375***	0.567***
	(0.077)	(0.064)
Speed of adjustment	–0.442***	–0.326***
	(0.048)	(0.050)

Source: Authors.

Note: Numbers in parentheses denote standard errors.
*** $p < 0.01$, ** $p < 0.05$, * $p < 0.1$ for the significance test of zero coefficient.

long-run buoyancy estimate allows the conclusion that it does not differ significantly from unity at the 10 percent level. This result comes from a combination of economic growth, a strong housing market, and a number of discretionary policies that have enabled some countries to keep their revenues in step with economic growth. But it also reflects country practices to keep the effective tax rate down by postponing revaluations or adding tax base exemptions and preferences. As noted in the country studies, there is ample evidence that these discretionary practices are used.

This result for the mean group estimate is consistent with a conclusion that the property tax has been a buoyant source of revenue in Europe over this study period. Revenues have grown enough to keep pace with GDP. However, note that the time period studied here (1995–2021) included economic downturns, COVID-19, and significant crowding out of property taxation by other revenue sources.

The results for the long-run buoyancy vary significantly by country. Only 7 of the 37 countries in the European sample showed a long-term buoyancy coefficient significantly below unity at a 10 percent significance level (table 2.7), which suggests that in some European countries the property tax was not a sustainable source of revenue during this period.[23] Of these seven countries, only Sweden is among those with an above-average per capita GDP in 2021.

Capturing Fiscal Space

The comparative approach taken in this chapter gives a rough idea about the amount of additional property tax revenues that could be raised in

Table 2.7 Long-Run Buoyancy Estimates, 1995–2021

	Long-Run Buoyancy	Test of Less Than Unity (*p* value)	Test of Greater Than Unity (*p* value)
Albania	3.46	0.023	0.977
Austria	0.67	0.990	0.010
Belarus	0.55	0.850	0.150
Belgium	1.26	0	1.000
Bosnia and Herzegovina	0.76	0.760	0.240
Bulgaria	1.67	0	1.000
Croatia	1.16	0	1.000
Czech Republic	1.01	0.452	0.548
Denmark	0.26	0.592	0.408
Estonia	0.68	0.999	0.001
Finland	1.40	0.084	0.916
France	1.03	0.351	0.649
Georgia	1.14	0.010	0.990
Germany	1.15	0.020	0.980
Greece	2.63	0.205	0.795
Hungary	1.23	0.249	0.751
Iceland	1.03	0.460	0.540
Ireland	0.83	0.665	0.335
Italy	1.26	0.287	0.713
Kosovo	1.50	0.132	0.868
Latvia	0.70	0.992	0.008
Lithuania	0.62	1.000	0
Moldova	0.46	1.000	0
Netherlands	1.06	0.421	0.579
Norway	1.07	0.159	0.841
Poland	0.88	0.879	0.121
Portugal	1.68	0.002	0.998
Romania	1.15	0.304	0.696
Russian Federation	0.89	0.729	0.271
Serbia	2.16	0.398	0.602
Slovak Republic	0.89	0.998	0.002
Slovenia	0.98	0.586	0.414
Spain	1.42	0.037	0.963
Sweden	0.04	1.000	0
Switzerland	1.11	0.330	0.670
Ukraine	1.05	0.465	0.535
United Kingdom	1.21	0.001	0.999

Source: Authors.

Europe based on an average tax effort.[24] Following the traditional tax effort model (Bahl 1971), we used estimates from Model I in Table 2.4 and calculated the tax effort indices for the countries, which allowed us to make cross-country comparisons. The results are shown in Table 2.8. But this level of analysis gives little information about the policy and administrative actions that might be used to erase these revenue shortfalls.

To investigate these shortfalls, one approach is to study the revenue potential of various changes in policy and administration. This usually involves reforming the fiscal instruments that are holding back revenue mobilization: the collection rate, the statutory tax rate, tax reliefs and preferences, and the assessment ratio. The goal would be for countries to use these parameters to develop a policy strategy to capture the excess property taxable capacity. The focus is on the detail of property tax management at the individual country level and on measuring the revenue implications of specific country practices. This is an important component of the design of property tax reform programs.[25]

Estimating revenue potential (capturing fiscal space) can be done with an analytic tool, the property tax identity, that links tax revenue outcomes to specific administrative and policy practices and then estimates the additional revenues that might come from the administrative reforms (Bahl and Linn 1992, 102; Kelly, White, and Anand 2020).

This property tax identity can be stated as:

$$TC/GDP = (TC/TL)\,(TL/TAV)\,(TAV/AV)\,(AV/FMV)\,(FMV/W)\,(W/GDP), \qquad (1)$$

where

TC = property tax revenue collections (excluding arrears)
TL = property tax liability (excluding arrears)
TAV = taxable assessed value of property
AV = total assessed value of property
FMV = full market value of real property
W = produced wealth
GDP = gross domestic product.

Several elements of this identity are familiar: TC/TL is the collection rate, TL/TAV is the average tax rate, TAV/AV takes account of properties excluded from taxation, and AV/FMV is an indicator of the size of the assessment ratio. Government policy and administrative practices can directly influence these first four components in the short run.

An estimate of the potential impact on property tax revenues from increasing the collection rate, moving properties from exempt to taxable, increasing the assessment ratio, or changing the nominal tax rate could be made if the data to populate the equation (1) identity were available for a

Table 2.8 Tax Effort Index for European Countries, 2019

	Actual Effective Rate of Property Tax (%)	Effective Rate of Property Tax at Full Capacity (%)	Gap	Tax Effort Index
Bosnia and Herzegovina	0.36	0.04	0.31	8.37
Moldova	0.28	0.05	0.23	5.30
Georgia	0.96	0.20	0.76	4.73
Serbia	0.82	0.18	0.64	4.59
Greece	2.57	0.67	1.90	3.86
Poland	1.11	0.31	0.80	3.53
Ireland	0.69	0.24	0.45	2.91
Slovak Republic	0.40	0.15	0.25	2.64
Slovenia	0.52	0.20	0.32	2.59
France	3.90	1.66	2.24	2.35
Portugal	0.80	0.39	0.41	2.05
United Kingdom	3.16	1.86	1.30	1.70
North Macedonia	0.23	0.15	0.08	1.55
Italy	1.40	1.03	0.37	1.35
Albania	0.34	0.26	0.08	1.31
Hungary	0.51	0.56	–0.05	0.91
Latvia	0.79	0.88	–0.09	0.90
Belarus	1.19	1.49	–0.30	0.80
Switzerland	1.86	2.39	–0.53	0.78
Spain	1.71	2.60	–0.89	0.66
Russian Federation	1.08	1.73	–0.64	0.63
Lithuania	0.30	0.57	–0.27	0.53
Ukraine	0.47	0.94	–0.47	0.50
Austria	0.21	0.49	–0.28	0.43
Iceland	1.93	4.90	–2.97	0.39
Denmark	2.33	6.18	–3.85	0.38
Finland	1.09	3.68	–2.59	0.30
Estonia	0.21	0.72	–0.50	0.30
Norway	0.88	3.10	–2.21	0.29
Belgium	2.10	7.72	–5.62	0.27
Germany	0.62	2.27	–1.65	0.27
Netherlands	1.05	4.06	–3.01	0.26
Czechia	0.19	1.25	–1.06	0.15
Sweden	0.68	5.19	–4.51	0.13

Source: Authors.

country. In fact, most of the data necessary to simulate revenue potential using this model are available for all countries, either in national compendia or in government department reports. However, the data definitions of different countries may not be the same, or may not be as accurate in some countries than others. So the administrative approach is more suited for individual country analysis than for intercountry comparisons.

The main constraint to populating equation (1) is information about the market value of real property in a country, which is often not available. Some of the country studies in part 2 report or estimate these components of the property tax identity, and these are discussed in chapters 3 and 5. The use of this model for estimating taxable capacity also is demonstrated and discussed in Bahl and Bird (2018, 270–275) and Bahl et al. (2022, 20–22).

Appendix

Weighted and Unweighted Property Tax Rates

The average tax rate of most interest in this study is the mean effective property tax rate across all countries—that is, the unweighted property tax rate. The average Euorpean rates calculated in this study (table A2.1) are driven down by the inclusion of many low-taxing countries. The tax rate can also be calculated as total property tax collected in Europe divided by total GDP in Europe (table A2.2). As discussed in the chapter, a disproportionately large share of property tax collections in Europe is concentrated in a few countries. Finally, tables A2.3 and A2.4 show that OECD data report a larger amount of revenue collections.

Table A2.1 Unweighted Average Effective Rate of General Property Tax, 2020–2023

	2020 (38)	2021 (38)	2022 (38)	2023 (30)
General property tax	1.03	1.00	0.94	1.00
Property transfer tax[1]	0.21	0.24	0.23	0.19
Total property tax	1.24	1.24	1.17	1.19

Source: IMF (n.d.-c).

Note: The number of European countries in each year's sample is in parentheses.

[1] The property transfer tax reports data on "11411 Taxes on financial and capital transactions" as classified in IMF (2014), which is a larger category (see chapter 1).

Table A2.2 Weighted Average Effective Rate of General Property Tax, 2020–2023

	2020 (38)	2021 (38)	2022 (38)	2023 (30)
General property tax	1.66	1.60	1.51	1.32
Property transfer tax[1]	0.33	0.39	0.38	0.25
Total property tax	1.99	1.99	1.88	1.57

Source: IMF (n.d.-c).

Note: The number of European countries in each year's sample is in parentheses.

[1] The property transfer tax reports data on "11411 Taxes on financial and capital transactions" as classified in IMF (2014), which is a larger category (see chapter 1).

Table A2.3 Unweighted Average Effective Rate of General Property Tax, 2020–2023

	2020 (30)	2021 (30)	2022 (30)	2023 (27–28)
General property tax	1.15	1.10	1.04	1.02
Property transfer tax[1]	0.32	0.36	0.34	0.28
Total property tax	1.47	1.46	1.38	1.36

Source: OECD (n.d.-c).

Note: The number of European countries in each year's sample is in parentheses.

[1] The property transfer tax reports data on "4400 Taxes on financial and capital transactions" as classified in OECD (2023), which is a larger category (see chapter 1).

Table A2.4 Weighted Average Effective Rate of General Property Tax, 2020–2023

	2020 (30)	2021 (30)	2022 (30)	2023 (27–28)
General property tax	1.55	1.49	1.40	1.37
Property transfer tax[1]	0.54	0.60	0.57	0.44
Total property tax	2.09	2.09	1.97	1.84

Source: OECD (n.d.-c).

Note: The number of European countries in each year's sample is in parentheses.

[1] The property transfer tax reports data on "4400 Taxes on financial and capital transactions" as classified in OECD (2023), which is a larger category (see chapter 1).

Notes

1. Austria, Estonia, Finland, Latvia, Lithuania, Slovakia, Slovenia, and Spain have low levels of recurrent property taxation (using 2017 figures), ranging from 0.3 to 1.2 percent of GDP (EU 2019).

Revenues from property transfer taxes on land and building sales are reported by the International Monetary Fund's Government Finance Statistics in the category "11414 Taxes on financial and capital transactions" and by the Organisation for Economic Co-operation and Development in the category "4400 Taxes on financial and capital transactions." This total, shown in table 2.1 (Government Finance Statistics data), is about 25 percent of recurrent property tax revenues and pushes the effective property tax rate in some European countries into the range of 3–5 percent of GDP. Chapter 6, part 2 case studies, and table A2.1 provide more detailed data on transfer taxes. Using these data as a proxy for revenue raised from property transfer taxes has important qualifications, as chapters 1 and 6 discuss.

2. The term *effective tax rate* here describes the ratio of property tax revenue to GDP.

3. This has been noted by others, including Blöchliger (2015a, 7) and OECD (2022, chap. 3). But to our knowledge, there are no other attempts to measure the full amount of taxes levied on the real estate sector.

4. OECD (2022) reviews these types of tax expenditures.

5. For comparative purposes, a parallel analysis is carried out for an international sample of 69 countries that includes 34 European countries. The countries were chosen on the basis of availability of data. The non-European countries in the international panel tend to be lower income, have less produced wealth, and be less urbanized, and they also have a lower level of fiscal decentralization. On average, their effective property tax rate is lower.

6. The non-European sample includes all countries for which the required panel data were available. Countries with populations less than 0.1 million were excluded.

7. In analyses at the local government level, the effective tax rate usually refers to property tax payments as a percentage of the value of the property. In our country-level analyses, it refers to property tax payments as a percentage of GDP.

8. Data on the urbanization rate are taken from the World Development Indicators (2022) published by the World Bank.

9. Produced capital stocks are derived from historical investment data using a perpetual investment model that estimates the value of urban land as a percentage of the value of machinery, equipment, and structures (World Bank 2006, 5, 22).

10. Certainly, this is not a perfect measure in that it includes nontaxable properties, and its estimate of the value of urban land is based on a general rule of thumb.

11. The sample size for the yearly averages varies over years. Average total wealth per capita by year is based on 36 countries between 1995 and 2005, and 37 countries between 2006 and 2018; average produced capital per capita by year is based on 38 countries between 1995 and 2018; average GDP per capita by year is based on 38 countries between 1995 and 2007 and on 39 countries between 2008 and 2018.

12. Data on per capita GDP come from the World Development Indicators published by the World Bank (n.d.-a). Average (2019) per capita GDP in the 34 European countries under study here is US$31,574, which is well above the international sample average of US$23,184. This average has considerable variation, ranging from over US$80,000 in Ireland and Switzerland to under US$5,000 in Ukraine.

13. This would happen automatically if the vertical-share entitlements of local governments in the intergovernmental transfer system are a fixed percentage of national collections of the shared tax (Bahl and Bird 2018, chap. 6).

14. Data on fiscal decentralization are taken from the IMF Fiscal Decentralization Dataset (IMF, n.d.-a). Data from the OECD Fiscal Decentralization Database (OECD, n.d.-b) augment the IMF dataset for 12 European countries.

15. The fixed effects model controls for all time-invariant, unobserved factors that affect the effective property tax rate of each country.

16. Because some of the independent variables are expressed in percentages, the interpretation of the elasticities is not straightforward and is discussed in this chapter.

17. "The Human Development Index is a summary measure of average achievement in key dimensions of human development: a long and healthy life, being knowledgeable and having a decent standard of living" (United Nations Development Programme, n.d.).

18. This kind of regression result suggests that most African countries, which are only now urbanizing, will outgrow some of their property tax revenue mobilization constraints. But in Europe, which is more heavily urbanized, countries are less likely to experience such a maturity impact. The calculation of the elasticity is $[(75\% / 71\% - 1) \times 4.98 + 1] \times 1.08 = 1.38$. Note that the expression of GDP in current US dollars and property wealth in 2018 US dollars complicates interpretation of these coefficients.

19. The average annual rate of real increase for the European sample between 2001 and 2018 is 1.17 percent.

20. Supporting evidence for the crowding-out hypothesis is summarized later and discussed in the part 2 country studies.

21. Lagravinese, Liberati, and Sacchi (2020) point out that the value of the tax buoyancy coefficient should converge to 1 in the long run, assuming a long-run relationship between GDP and tax revenue exists.

22. This can happen if more (or different) expenditure responsibilities are assigned to local governments or if the wage bill in the government sector grows faster than that in the private sector (Baumol 1967).

23. The seven countries with a low buoyancy coefficient are Austria, Estonia, Latvia, Lithuania, Moldova, Slovak Republic, and Sweden.

24. Most researchers working in this area argue that tax effort indexes should not be used to give normative advice about the level of taxation. But of course, that is frequently done (or implied) by many if not most advisors.

25. In fact, many countries already use an approach akin to this in revenue estimation.

References

Bahl, R. W. 1971. "A Regression Approach to Tax Effort and Tax Ratio Analysis." *International Monetary Fund Staff Papers* 18, no. 3: 570–612.

Bahl, R., and R. M. Bird. 2018. *Fiscal Decentralization and Local Finance in Developing Countries*. Cheltenham, UK: Edward Elgar.

Bahl, R. W., and J. F. Linn. 1992. *Urban Public Finance in Developing Countries*. New York: Oxford University Press.

Bahl, R., J. Linn, and D. Wetzel, eds. 2013. *Financing Metropolitan Governments in Developing Countries*. Cambridge, MA: Lincoln Institute of Land Policy.

Bahl, R., and J. Martinez-Vazquez. 2008. "The Property Tax in Developing Countries: Current Practice and Prospects." In *Making the Property Tax Work: Experiences in Developing and Transitional Countries*, ed. R. Bahl, J, Martinez-Vazquez, and J. Youngman, 35–57. Cambridge, MA: Lincoln Institute of Land Policy.

———. 2022. "Perspectives in Fiscal Decentralization: Challenges and the Unfinished Agenda." Supplement, *Canadian Tax Journal, Revue Fiscal Canadienne* 70: 69–96.

Bahl, R., W. J. McCluskey, R. Franzsen, and W. Li. 2022. "Context and Comparative Analysis." In *Property Tax in Asia: Policy and Practice*, ed. W. McCluskey, R. Bahl, and R. Franzsen, 3–18. Cambridge, MA: Lincoln Institute of Land Policy.

Baumol, W. J. 1967. "Macroeconomics of Unbalanced Growth: The Anatomy of Urban Crisis." *American Economic Review* 57(3): 415–426.

Belinga, V., D. Benedek, R. A. de Mooij, and J. Norregaard, 2014. "Tax Buoyancy in OECD Countries." IMF Working Papers 14/110. Washington, DC: International Monetary Fund.

Blackburne, E. F., III, and M. W. Frank. 2007. "Estimation of Nonstationary Heterogeneous Panels." *Stata Journal* 7(2): 197–208.

Blöchliger, H. 2015a. "Reforming the Tax on Immovable Property: Taking Care of the Unloved." Working paper No. 1205. Paris: OECD Economics Department.

Boadway, R., and A. Shah. 2009. *Fiscal Federalism: Principles and Practices of Multi-order Governance*. Cambridge: Cambridge University Press.

Chancel, L., T. Piketty, E. Saez, and G. Zucman. 2022. "World Inequality Report 2022." World Inequality Lab. https://wir2022.wid.world.

Commission for Economic Policy. 2021. "Local and Regional Finances in the Aftermath of COVID-19." European Union, European Committee of the Regions. https://data.europa.eu/doi/10.2863/29738.

de Mello, L., and D. Sutherland. 1988. "Financing Infrastructure." In *Decentralization and Infrastructure in the Global Economy*, ed. J. Frank and J. Martinez-Vazquez, 146–170. New York: Routledge.

Dudine, P., and J. T. Jalles. 2018. "How Buoyant Is the Tax System? New Evidence from a Large Heterogeneous Panel." *Journal of International Development* 30(6): 961–991.

EU (European Union). 2019. "2019 European Semester: Country Reports." European Commission. https://commission.europa.eu/publications/2019-european-semester-country-reports_en.

Fatica, S., and D. Prammer. 2017. "Housing and the Tax System: How Large Are the Distortions in the Euro Area?" Working paper No. 2087. Luxembourg: European Central Bank. http://dx.doi.org/10.2866/456421.

Glaeser, E. 2011. *Triumph of the City*. New York: Penguin.

Hill, S., D. Jinjarak, and D. Park. 2022. "Buoyant or Sinking? Tax Revenue Performance and Prospects in Developing Asia." Working paper 656. Manila: Asian Development Bank.

IMF (International Monetary Fund). 2014. *Government Finance Statistics Manual*. Washington, DC: IMF.

———. n.d.-a. "The Fiscal Decentralization Dataset." Accessed December 22, 2023. https://data.imf.org/en/datasets/IMF.STA:FD.

———. n.d.-b. Government Finance Statistics. Accessed December 16, 2023. https://data.imf.org/en.

———. n.d.-c. Government Finance Statistics. Accessed September 19, 2025. https://data.imf.org/en.

Kelly, R., R. White, and A. Anand. 2020. *Property Tax Diagnostic Manual*. Washington, DC: World Bank Group.

Lagravinese, R., P. Liberati, and A. Sacchi. 2020. "Tax Buoyancy in OECD Countries: New Empirical Evidence." *Journal of Macroeconomics* 63 (C). https://doi.org/10.1016/j.jmacro.2020.103189.

Lledó, V., W. Gbohoui, and C. Ncuti. 2022. *Fiscal Decentralization Methodological Note.* Washington, DC: International Monetary Fund.

Millar-Powell, B., B. Brys, P. Reilly, Y. Rehm, and A. Thomas, A. 2022. "Measuring Effective Taxation of Housing: Building the Foundations for Policy Reform." Working paper No. 56. Paris: OECD. https://doi.org/10.1787/0a7e36f2-en.

Norregaard, J. 2013. "Taxing Immovable Property: Revenue Potential and Implementation Challenges." Working paper 13/129. Washington, DC: International Monetary Fund.

Oates, W. 1981. "On Local Finance and the Tiebout Model." *American Economic Review* 71: 93–98.

OECD (Organisation for Economic Co-operation and Development). 2016. "Reforming the Tax on Immovable Property." In *Fiscal Federalism 2016: Making Decentralisation Work*, ed. H. Blöchliger and J. Kim. Paris: OECD. https://dx.doi.org/10.1787/9789264254053-5-en.

———. 2022. "Housing Taxation in OECD Countries." OECD Tax Policy Studies, No. 29. https://doi.org/10.1787/03dfe007-en.

———. 2023. "Revenue Statistics Interpretative Guide." https://www.oecd.org/content/dam/oecd/en/topics/policy-sub-issues/global-tax-revenues/oecd-classification-taxes-interpretative-guide.pdf.

———. n.d.-a. Global Revenue Statistics Database. Accessed January 9, 2024. https://www.oecd.org/en/data/datasets/global-revenue-statistics-database.html.

———. n.d.-b. OECD Fiscal Decentralisation Database. Accessed February 24, 2024. https://www.oecd.org/tax/federalism/fiscal-decentralisation-database/.

———. n.d.-c. Global Revenue Statistics Database. Accessed September 20, 2025. https://www.oecd.org/en/data/datasets/global-revenue-statistics-database.html.

Pesaran, M. H., Y. Shin, and R. P. Smith. 1997. "Estimating Long-Run Relationships in Dynamic Heterogeneous Panels." DAE Working Papers Amalgamated Series 9721.

———. 1999. "Pooled Mean Group Estimation of Dynamic Heterogeneous Panels." *Journal of the American Statistical Association* 94: 621–634.

Pesaran, M. H., and R. P. Smith. 1995. "Estimating Long-Run Relationships from Dynamic Heterogeneous Panels." *Journal of Econometrics* 68: 79–113.

Prest, A. R. 1962. "The Sensitivity of the Yield of Personal Income Tax in the United Kingdom." *Economic Journal* 72(287): 576–596.

Rodríguez-Pose, A., and A. Krøijer. 2009. "Fiscal Decentralization and Economic Growth in Central and Eastern Europe." *Growth and Change* 40(3): 387–417.

Scheuer, F., and J. Slemrod. 2021. "Taxing Our Wealth." *Journal of Economic Perspectives* 35(1): 207–230. https://ssrn.com/abstract=3739647.

Thoresen, T. O., M. A. K. Ring, O. E. Nygård, and J. Epland. 2021. "A Wealth Tax at Work." Discussion Papers 960, Statistics Norway, Research Department.

United Nations Development Programme. n.d. Human Development Index. Accessed March 20, 2023. https://hdr.undp.org/data-center/human-development-index#/indicies/HDI.

World Bank. 2006. "Where Is the Wealth of Nations? Measuring Capital for the 21st Century." Washington, DC: World Bank. http://documents.worldbank.org/curated/en/287171468323724180.

———. 2011. "The Changing Wealth of Nations: Measuring Sustainable Development in the New Millennium." Environment and Development. Washington, DC: World Bank. http://hdl.handle.net/10986/2252.

———. 2021. "The Changing Wealth of Nations 2021: Managing Assets for the Future." Washington, DC: World Bank. https://hdl.handle.net/10986/36400.

———. n.d.-a. "World Development Indicators." Accessed December 22, 2023. https://datatopics.worldbank.org/world-development-indicators/.

———. n.d.-b. "World Development Indicators." Accessed September 23, 2025. https://datatopics.worldbank.org/world-development-indicators/.

Zolt, E. 2024. "Taxation of Wealth." Paper presented at the Riël Franzsen Symposium: Theory and Practice of Taxation in Africa, Pretoria, South Africa (April 29–30).

3

Managing the Property Tax

RIËL FRANZSEN, ROY BAHL, WILLIAM MCCLUSKEY, AND WENJING LI

Institutions Matter

An effective and revenue-productive property tax is more likely to result if the system rests on the foundation of a strong institutional and management infrastructure. While this is not an absolute requirement for levying a property tax (Franzsen and McCluskey 2017), its absence can seriously constrain revenue mobilization.

Greece provides a particularly good example of how a country can improve its revenue yield from the recurrent property tax. At the time of the 2008–2009 financial crisis, it had a failed property tax infrastructure. It has since made significant improvements, mostly as a result of institutional reforms backed by political support.[1] In 2010, recurrent property taxes constituted only 1.0 percent of gross domestic product (GDP). That amount rose to a high of 2.8 percent in 2016 and then decreased to 2.2 percent in 2022—still ranking second in the European Union (EU). As a percentage of total taxes, it was 5.2 percent in 2022, the highest in the EU (European Union 2022).

The administration of the property tax has many moving parts and, often, an array of role players responsible for looking after one or more of these parts. In short, various entities perform different functions collectively integral to the administration of the different property taxes. Coordination, cooperation, and institutional arrangements are essential to avoid overlapping responsibilities. The 14 countries studied here (and most other European countries) have institutional infrastructures for property taxation in place, though each has strengths and shortcomings. Which countries seem to perform better, and why?

This discussion begins with a summary of the main functions necessary to successfully administer property taxes. Some of these functions, such as maintaining a cadastre or registering property transfers, primarily relate to nontax purposes. If done well, and with property-related taxation in mind, they may positively affect the efficacy of these taxes to mobilize revenue and achieve other policy objectives. For example, the national cadastre need capture only data on location, size, and boundaries. But if tasked to also capture data on land use and property values, its database becomes significantly more valuable to revenue authorities and municipalities for tax (as well as nontax) purposes. But none of these good ends could be captured properly without well-developed interministry and interagency cooperation. Legislation in the United Kingdom—the 2017 Digital Economy Act and the 2025 Data (Use and Access) Act—will collectively support a data-sharing environment that may enable tax base verification, tax collection, and enforcement. The UK Treasury Ministry also plays an active role in gathering data on property tax administration.

Well-functioning real estate markets are important for property taxation. These markets generate the tax base as well as a flow of information necessary to make the property tax work. In this regard, both the public sector and the private sector may be involved. The availability of market data supports the imposition of taxes and fees on land and buildings—especially value-based taxes and fees. Fiscal instruments are often used as policy tools to achieve land policy or housing policy goals (OECD 2022). For these reasons, we include in this chapter a discussion of property markets and how property taxes interact with land or housing policy goals.

Need for an Institutional and Management Infrastructure

Countries collect and manage information about real estate for more purposes than property taxation. Four of the most important purposes are land use policy, planning, and management; housing policy; tracking markets related to land and buildings; and the taxation of real estate (land and buildings). This chapter discusses all four, but the focus is the taxation of real estate.

The property tax requires that all buildings and land be valued and then revalued according to a specific calendar.[2] Moreover, property tax rate structures often discriminate against or favor land and buildings according to their value, unused land area, use for business purposes, and more. Finally, valuers typically use other variables to assess the value of property, such as parcel size, number of bedrooms, and the age and quality of construction. All of this suggests that a considerable bank of information is necessary to support an effective property tax (Bahl, McCluskey, and Franzsen 2022, 36).

To tax property, gathering sufficient data on the existence and nature of land parcels and buildings is important. This is usually the task of an entity responsible for capturing and managing cadastral data. Formally registering real rights, especially ownership or leasehold rights, in land and buildings in a register of deeds or titles is critical for tenure security, as is maintaining a record of changes to the property and capturing changes in ownership. A deeds or title office generally performs this function. In some countries—Ireland (box 3.1), the Netherlands, and the United Kingdom—a single entity is responsible for capturing and maintaining all cadastral, spatial, and legal data, which composes the physical and legal cadastre.

Most countries value land and buildings, but reasons vary, one being to impose value-based taxes. A public entity (e.g., a valuation agency, a ministry, or municipalities), or a private sector service provider, or in some instances, property owners themselves may perform the valuation. Valuation for tax (and nontax) purposes may require oversight in the form of objection and appeal processes involving entities such as tribunals and courts and, in some countries, also overall quality control. In Ireland and in Northern Ireland, all public property services (cadastre maintenance, registration, and valuation) are performed by one entity. As discussed later, this may be a model for good practice. Governments at different levels may play a role in determining tax rates and also in determining tax relief. These functions may be the sole prerogative of a central or state government, or of local governments, or may be shared functions. Tax may be collected by a revenue authority (centrally or at the state or regional level) or by local authorities. Notaries may collect, for example, property transfer taxes, as they do in many of the case study countries and in other European countries (e.g., Belgium, Lithuania, Malta, and Romania).

The more entities involved, the more complex the overall institutional infrastructure. Sharing of data among agencies or authorities is therefore critical. In this regard, smaller municipalities in the Netherlands have started to cooperate with other municipalities (as well as polder boards) to establish shared service centers to assess and levy local taxes. This should reduce unit costs as well as intermunicipal competition for sourcing scarce skills and resources.

The private sector and taxpayers may also play a role. Realtors and estate agents may manage price indexes. For example, in Denmark, the Knowledge Centre for Housing Economics, Finance Denmark (a finance industry association), and Boligsiden (a website maintained by a large number of real estate agents) all support various price indexes. In the Netherlands, the real estate listings of brokers and real estate agents are used over and above the sales prices registered in the cadastre, which constitutes the primary source of market data on sales transactions for the mass appraisal and assessment of real estate. In Ireland, property professionals such as estate agents and valuers produce their own databases and rely on sale or rental prices provided by sales agents. Several countries have now established sale price registers to record all transaction prices (chapter 5). In most but not all countries, these data are available to the public.

Accrediting professional entities at a national, regional, or international level may also play a role in valuation. For example, in Ireland, the Society of Chartered Surveyors Ireland and the Institute of Professional Auctioneer and Valuers require prescribed levels of educational, training, and continued professional development. Across the United Kingdom, the majority of valuers involved in property tax–related valuation are members of the Royal Institution of Chartered Surveyors—implying a certain level of professionalism. In Scotland, properties are generally valued by members of the Scottish Assessors Association, who are independent public officials but also must be members of the Royal Institution of Chartered Surveyors. Regionally, the European Group of Valuers' Associations (TEGOVA) determines European valuation standards for plant, machinery, and equipment to assist in valuing industrial plants and some unique nonresidential properties.

Across most European countries, public notaries play an important role in real estate transfers and the overall integrity of tenure security. This is so in Estonia, France, Germany, the Netherlands, Poland, Spain, and Romania. In France and Romania, for example, notaries maintain their own datasets. For a fee, the notaries' PERVAL database in France can be accessed. In France and the Netherlands, a notary office handles formal transfer and registration, organizing the payment to the seller, and paying the property transfer tax on behalf of the buyer.

Taxpayer associations and civil society may also play a role—if only occasionally. The demise of the community charge (the poll tax) that replaced the domestic rating system in Great Britain in 1989 (Scotland) and 1990 (England and Wales) is a glaring example of civil society's influence. The community charge had high administration costs and difficult enforcement, but the mass refusal to pay it and violent poll tax riots brought its end (McCluskey 1991; Youngman and Malme 1994) and led government to hastily replace it with the council tax in April 1993.

Property owners or occupiers and, as taxpayers, individuals and businesses are also important role players. In some systems, self-declaration of property values and declarations of property data (as in Poland) are important, especially for property transfer taxes and capital gains taxes. The Finnish Tax Administration has its own information system on apartment prices, based to a large extent on the self-declared purchase prices of apartment shares.

Detailed recordkeeping for many different taxes is necessary, and numerous actors are involved: owners, occupiers, individuals, businesses, buyers, sellers, estates, notaries, and even governments at various levels. Countries must have some system to keep accurate records on compliance and for purposes of appeals.

Data Capture and Management

Property taxes generally, but recurrent property taxes especially, are data hungry.

In both the Republic of Ireland and Northern Ireland (as part of the United Kingdom), the capture and management of all land and building data by a single government agency has likely led to important efficiency gains—although some jurisdictions have data integration problems. These developments are summarized in box 3.1 and explained in more detail in the relevant country chapters.

The property tax in most European countries is value based (discussed in more detail in chapters 4 and 5). The backbone of valuation practices used in most countries is data taken from real estate sales transactions. A major problem, almost everywhere, is gaining access to accurate and up-to-date property prices. The best source of information on property prices is the sales transactions, and many countries rely on these data for an accurate estimate of current market value. But as discussed in chapters 5 and 6, these declared values are not always reported accurately, especially in countries where third-party data cannot be accessed easily—as in some of the former transitional countries—and why some (Czech Republic, Slovenia, and Poland) at first retained or introduced area-based recurrent taxes in the absence of developed real estate markets.

Some transitional countries lacked well-developed cadastres and registry systems (Šulija 2008). This was not the case in Lithuania and gave impetus to its transition to value-based taxation (Aleksiene and Bagdonavicius 2008). The Czech Republic chose an area-based approach in 1992 because a suitable legal framework for value-based taxation was

Box 3.1 Comprehensive Land Management: Examples from Northern Ireland and the Republic of Ireland

Northern Ireland

Land and Property Services (LPS) demonstrates the powerful synergies from merging government agencies or units within different ministries and previously fragmented service responsibilities. LPS is a data-driven one-stop shop for all land- and property-related services. It carries out the valuation and management of both domestic and nondomestic rates for land and property government services. As an agency of the Department of Finance, the LPS performs mapping, land registration, valuation, and property tax collection for all of Northern Ireland. LPS constitutes a merger of four separate government agencies: Land Registry for Northern Ireland and Ordnance Survey Northern Ireland joined on April 1, 2008, and the Valuation and Lands Agency and Rates Collection Agency merged with it in 2007.

LPS also operates a GIS-based information service (SpatialNI) that provides information on rating valuations and offers publications explaining how values are assessed for rating purposes. LPS is financed by a combination of government funding, fees, and commercial income.

Sources: Greenway (2010); part 2, chapter 21.

Republic of Ireland

On March 1, 2023, the Property Registration Authority and Ordnance Survey Ireland were dissolved and their functions, along with those of the commissioner of valuation and the boundary surveyor, transferred to Tailte Éireann, an independent government agency under the Department of Housing, Local Government and Heritage. This rationalization optimizes the benefits of land information for continuing economic and social development, and it provides citizens, businesses, and policy makers with easy access to and use of property and title information, property valuation data, maps, and aerial imagery. It also ensures the development and maintenance of national spatial information infrastructures, supporting overall better land management.

Tailte Éireann furnishes a range of services, including property registration, valuation, national mapping, and surveying infrastructure for the state. It also provides data on commercial leases and residential sales. Tailte Éireann's valuation division provides stakeholders with accurate, up-to-date valuations of commercial and industrial properties. These valuations are integral to the business rating system in Ireland. Tailte Éireann is financed by government and with commercial and fee income.

Revenue, formerly the Revenue Commissioners, a central-government entity, has charge of the administration (including receiving owners' self-declaration of property value) and, importantly, the collection of the local property tax.

Sources: Tailte Éireann (https://tailte.ie/); part 2, chapter 14.

nonexistent. Despite the development of the real estate market and access to credible data, the area-based system persisted because it is perceived as simple and easy for taxpayers to fulfill their obligations (McCluskey et al. 2024; Rohlíková 1999). Furthermore, the drive to change to an ad valorem system is limited because municipalities (which receive the revenue from the recurrent property tax) are constrained or entirely excluded from having input into the centrally established tax base and tax rate. And because it constitutes municipal revenue, the state has no interest in optimizing its yield (Radvan and Kranecová 2021).

Reported real estate prices may not match up with the legal tax base, such as in countries with separate taxes on land and buildings and in countries that tax the rental values of residential units (France and Germany). The country studies reported in part 2 discuss these issues in some detail.

Property price data come from primarily two sources: the private sector—for example, real estate brokers, listing companies, or research institutes—but mostly, countries extract information from transfer documents, including those that are assisted by notaries (box 3.2).

Especially when third parties (bank and mortgage companies) are involved, these data tend to give accurate estimates of market value, such as in Denmark, France, the Netherlands, and Spain for residential owner-occupied properties. In the Netherlands, for example, 100 percent mortgages are not uncommon—resulting in accurate reporting. In Russia and Poland, data are limited and often do not reflect current conditions.

In most countries, the estimated market values in nationally reported statistics are most accurate for residential owner-occupied properties. In the Netherlands and Slovenia, for example, the national statistics bureau uses sales prices registered in the cadastre to publish a monthly price index for residential real estate across the whole country. This index is publicly available free of charge in the Netherlands. But price indexes for submarkets are not always available. Many countries impose differential rates according to the use of the property—for example, whether commercial or rented. Denmark and the Netherlands report less accurate estimates for commercial property, and Spain and Slovenia report less accurate estimates for rented residential properties. As already noted, obtaining rental data is problematic in most countries.

Countries use these data to varying extents in determining taxable property values, but Finland reports that it does not often use these data for the valuation of apartments, which account for most residential housing. Although more than 50 percent of Germans live in rented accommodation (Housing Europe 2023), current rental data do not factor into property tax.

Managing the Recurrent Property Tax

The key components of property tax systems and infrastructure that must be coordinated are the cadastre, the property registration system, assessment, tax base and tax rate determination, and tax administration.

Cadastre

The cadastre is a methodically arranged public inventory concerning all legal land objects in a country or district. These legal objects are defined on the basis of a survey of their boundaries and systematically designated by, for example, a unique property number. Descriptive data may show for each separate land object the nature, size, value, and legal rights or restrictions associated with the land object. In addition to physical attributes of land objects, a cadastre often contains the official records of rights on the legal land objects (Kaufmann and Steudler 1998). Fiscal cadastres are sometimes developed specifically for land and property tax purposes but in most European countries are now linked with the title and registration system (Denmark, the Netherlands, Slovenia, Spain), in essence representing a comprehensive legal cadastre.

In Spain, the cadastre and the tax administration are well supported through technology and high levels of automation. The cadastre uses information and communications technology (ICT) systems to maintain the data, evaluate accuracy, or discover new properties by checking the territory with GIS as well as information obtained from drones and satellite imagery. The valuation system in the cadastre uses artificial intelligence (AI) to manage and store data and econometric methods to perform the value estimations.

In practice, countries have set up their cadastres, and use them, in different ways. For example, Spain now uses a reference market value, estimated by the cadastral authority, for valuations. Russia taxes some assets at their cadastral value but others at a more outdated book value. In Slovenia, the land cadastre was gradually unified, updated, and digitized at the same time that a register of buildings and parts of buildings was established. This is not unique. In most European countries, the cadastre is integrated with the property register. For example, Slovenia has a land registry that keeps data on all parcels of land, buildings, and parts of buildings. Data for each land parcel include a unique identifier, information on size, and a description of its basic characteristics (such as actual and intended use and, for agricultural and forestland, its productive capacity). For buildings, information includes the year of construction, building type, maintenance, and equipment. The use of GIS has improved the spatial dimension of property data and, through aerial imagery, building feature identification.

Given the nature of the cadastre, its maintenance, verification, and updating are continuous processes. In Poland, the incomplete supply of the central repository with data from the real estate cadastre is a challenge because this repository communicates and exchanges data with all registers (including land and mortgage registers and real estate tax records).

Public access is generally provided to the data in the cadastre (Denmark, Estonia, and the Netherlands), but not in Russia.

Land Titling or Registration

The property management system rests on a title or a deed registration system. This foundation is the legal cadastre—details on ownership and limited real rights pertaining to properties. In a title registration system (the United Kingdom), the government guarantees accuracy of the underlying rights as reflected in the title register, as evidenced by various documents. In a deeds registration system (the Netherlands), documents are paramount in reflecting who the holders of rights are. If operated accurately, a deeds registration system will in practice provide the same tenure security as a titling system. Both systems support good land management, an efficient and orderly property transfer system, and the potential for levying a variety of taxes with land or buildings as taxable objects.

A good property management system identifies all properties by ownership, exact location, and use. Thus, it supports the identification of much of the key data required for a property tax system—that is, details of the taxable object and the ultimate taxable subject (the owner)—as in Denmark. In 2007, the number of local jurisdictions in Denmark decreased from 82 to 24, and land registration was centralized as the Land Registration Court. The Land Registry contains information on all Danish properties, identifying them by their cadastre title numbers. It also provides information about landowners and registered mortgage deeds and other property-related rights (such as rights-of-way and local restrictions), as well as their priority.

The state of registration of properties in Europe varies among countries. In some of the 14 countries discussed in part 2, registration of nearly all properties has been completed and the system is updated regularly, linked to the cadastre, and mostly digitized. These include Denmark, France, the Netherlands, and Spain. In some other countries, such as Poland, Russia (where an active program is still underway), and the United Kingdom, all properties are not yet registered (though unregistered properties when sold must be registered as part of the transfer—a form of sporadic registration).

Ownership

In Finland, where housing companies and shareholders (tenants) own 60 percent of all apartments, tenants' share ownership is not registered. This form of ownership is mainly applied to blocks or flats and terraced housing, but sometimes also detached housing can be structured through a housing company. Apartment ownership in Finland is a form of indirect ownership. The real property unit, including the apartments, is owned by a housing company. There are not yet detailed records of transfers of shareholdings in housing companies. These transfers are taxed at a lower tax rate (2 percent) than the transfer of the actual real estate done by housing companies (4 percent).

Leasehold

An interesting feature across most of the case study countries concerns lease agreements. In Ireland, fee simple, or freehold, is the highest form of landownership. Leasehold is still common, but as in other international markets, leases have become shorter, and leases of 10 to 15 years are now more common.

As short-term rental agreements create only contractual rights rather than real rights, these agreements are not formally registered and rental data are not collected in any formalized manner, as in Estonia and Spain. In Spain, a public institution controlled rental contracts nationally before 1997. This institution has now disappeared, and the rental market has become fully private. Notarizing and registering rental agreements are voluntary, and most contracts are never formally registered. In Slovenia, data on rents received by natural persons are collected once a year from the assessment of tax on rental income.

Lessors in Spain are, however, supposed to declare rental income received as a result of these rental agreements for income tax and possibly value-added tax (VAT) purposes. In Estonia, VAT is charged on rental services but not on apartment rent, which is VAT exempt.

The absence of data on rentals may affect the recurrent property tax in those countries where annual value is the tax base. As argued in chapter 22, the data contained in rental transactions are important and ideally should be considered. In most countries, these data are much less transparent than the data on sales transactions because most countries have no official registration of rental transactions. For that reason, there is also not an organized source of data on these transactions. This could be one of the reasons why valuation rolls in France and Germany became outdated.

Assessment

Area-Based Systems

Traditionally, the transitional countries in Central and Eastern Europe have defined their recurrent property tax base with area-based property tax formulas, albeit with varying degrees of market calibration[3] beyond the size (area) of the property (Bahl and Bird 2018; Brzeski, Románová, and Franzsen 2019; Radvan et al. 2021). Some countries in Europe (Belarus, Bulgaria, Czech Republic, Hungary, Poland, Slovakia, Slovenia, and Ukraine) still use area-based systems (McCluskey et al. 2024; Radvan et al. 2021). In some instances, adjustment coefficients are used to approximate market conditions. The Czech Republic (Radvan and Kranecova 2021), Poland (Miemiec and Zawadzka 2021), and Slovenia (Zibrik and Humar 2021) have attempted moving to a value-based system on one or more occasions (McCluskey et al. 2024). A few countries have moved from an area basis to a value basis, including Albania (Canaj and Lavdari 2021) and Moldova (Buzu 2021).

A major advantage of an area-based system is that it can heavily rely on self-declaration and even self-assessment by the taxpayer. Furthermore, there cannot be objections or appeals about the size unless factually incorrect. In Poland, the taxpayer has the right to formulate objections against the tax decision but also against the tax proceedings preceding its issuance. The objections may concern, for example, incorrect application or misinterpretation of tax law provisions or omission of the evidence requested.

Value-Based Systems

Countries use valuation for reasons including expropriation, compensation, asset management, and taxation. Various institutions undertake property valuations for public purposes. These include public sector and private sector entities. It could even include self-assessment. Chapter 5 describes the different valuation practices in European countries. In most, every taxable property is assigned a taxable value, and this is recorded in the fiscal cadastre.

The underlying infrastructure needed for valuation is a legal system that clearly defines the property tax base and a competent and adequate cohort of trained valuers to carry out the assessments. The legal system that governs valuation practices protects property taxpayers with rules against unfair assessments. Few countries, however, track the quality of these valuations, as discussed in chapter 5. False declarations remain an issue, and therefore monitoring and verification are essential features of value-based systems.

In reforming the Ministry of Taxation in 2018, Denmark created the Property Assessment Agency, which oversees the new valuation system. Data are chiefly taken from the electronic building register (under the auspices of the agency), Land Registry, Danish Geodata Agency cadastre, and Agency of Planning and Rural Districts. Importantly, the new system extensively uses data, implying that more properties may be assessed using an automated statistical model.

Objection and Appeal

In countries using an area-based system, such as Poland, the Czech Republic, Slovakia, and Slovenia, objections and appeals are basically limited to errors in calculating the size of properties. In both Great Britain (council tax) and the Republic of Ireland (local property tax), residential properties are not individually valued but are taxed in value-banding systems.[4] Given the nature of these systems, there are few objections and appeals. But the United Kingdom and Ireland have separate property tax systems for nonresidential properties, in which detailed objections and appeals processes take place.

In Ireland's banding system, owners self-declare residential property values and there are no appeals. This is one of the key administrative advantages of the Irish methodology. The Valuation Tribunal schedules appeal hearings for commercial properties and issues a monthly hearing list (Annual Report 2021). All appeals must go through the call-over system before receiving a hearing date, and all parties involved must appear in person when assigned a slot in the system. Appeals are made to the head of valuation, then the Valuation Tribunal, and finally, on points of law only, the High Court.

UK jurisdictions differ. In England and Wales, for example, an online business-rates-valuation account system applies. In the first stage, largely aimed at discovering factual inaccuracies in the subject property, an objector requests a check from the Valuation Office Agency. The next stage is a formal challenge to the agency, then an appeal to the Independent Valuation Tribunal Service, and then a final appeal on points of fact to the Lands Tribunal. Thereafter, the courts may adjudicate only on points of law. Northern Ireland offers an opportunity for an informal objection, again largely to confirm details. Thereafter, the formal appeal process applies.[5]

Municipalities encourage taxpayers in the Netherlands who object to assessed values to first make an inquiry by telephone or other informal ways before embarking on the formal route. The objection rate (2–3 percent for residential and about 6 percent for nonresidential property) is considered acceptable. When unsatisfied with the outcome of the objection, the taxpayer can appeal to the tax court and eventually the High Court.

Denmark has a sophisticated objection and appeal process. The Ministry of Taxation responds to objections and may agree wholly or partially and settle the case. If the plaintiff is not satisfied or 16 weeks have passed without a decision from the ministry, one of 15 regional assessment appeal boards (consisting of local political appointees and technical experts) settles the objection. If dissatisfied with the appeal board's decision, the plaintiff may appeal to the National Tax Tribunal. About 1.7 percent of property owners objected to the 2010 general valuation of commercial property, and about 0.4 percent objected regarding the 2011 general valuation of owner-occupied dwellings.

In Estonia, tax bills may not increase more than 10 percent annually, thus keeping the effective tax base well below actual market values. As a result, only 15 objections were received regarding the 2022 valuation roll. In Russia, owners may submit comments on the draft valuation report during a public consultation period, primarily to request the correction of errors made by regional valuation agencies. Administrative courts rule on rejections of such requests.

Deciding Tax Rates and Tax Relief

Deciding tax rates and tax relief constitutes important policy—in essence, political—decisions that must be communicated to the public and relief measures explained. The policy decisions on tax rates and tax relief are based, or should be based, on data provided by entities such as the cadastre, the central office of statistics, and the central bank. Intricate tax rate structures presuppose the capacity to administer these policies. European countries, where databases are often comprehensive and well-maintained and systems are generally automated, generally have this capacity.

Tax Administration

Revenue authorities (at the national, state, or local level) are the primary institutions involved in tax administration. Even where a higher level of government collects the property tax, municipalities may still have an important role to play in sharing data about the tax base and taxpayers. Municipal administrative actions, such as granting permission for construction or a change in use, may require another institution to respond with, for example, a supplementary valuation or a reclassification of a taxable property or the owner-/taxpayer.

Billing and Collection

There is no clear indication whether decentralized or centralized collection is preferable. The high collection levels reported in almost all the case study countries suggest that both can function well. The central government or its regional offices collect recurrent property taxes in Estonia, Finland, France, Germany, Greece, Ireland, Russia, and Slovenia. In the United Kingdom, the council tax and the business rates are both collected at the local level. Business rates are also collected locally but pooled nationally and distributed by the central government through a prescribed formula. In Latvia, the 43 municipalities administer the property tax. In the Netherlands and Poland, property tax administration is done locally. The highly digitized system of the Netherlands allows using the base register of assessed values for interrelated administration by the different levels of government. In the Netherlands and Russia, taxpayers can access their tax bills through a government portal. Russian tax authorities calculate the tax amount from records obtained through the interagency exchange from the Federal Service of State Registration, Cadastre, and Cartography (Rosreestr) and from surveying companies that maintain technical records of buildings.

The Estonian Tax and Customs Board calculates land tax via the land tax information system, which directly links to the Land Cadastre, and collects the tax primarily through electronic means. Taxpayers can pay in two installments, unless the amount is less than €64. There is no discount for early payment, and arrears are less than 1 percent.

Denmark municipalities used to collect arrears, but the Ministry of Taxation took over in 2005. Arrears, however, increased in the centralized system, and in 2017, municipalities regained the task of recovering arrears. Under the new property tax system introduced in 2024, the collection of property taxes will again be centralized.

In France, the deconcentrated services of the Ministry of Finance collect the property tax. About 95.5 percent is collected within one year and at least 99.7 percent within three years. France is the only country in this sample that reported in some detail on the cost of collection and percentages attributed to different components of administration. According to the National Audit Office, the management and collection of local taxes in France is rather costly. In 2021, the total collection cost represented about 9 percent of the local tax receipts. The costly administration is attributed to the complexity of dual collection systems that have separate software applications for property taxes on individuals and businesses; the self-declaration and the updating of cadastral values after renovations of residential properties; and the limited use of appropriate software applications (including AI) for property tax administration.

The United Kingdom and Ireland annually publish collection figures, which are subject to external scrutiny.

Enforcement

The primary goal of property tax administration is to collect the full amount of property tax due from each taxpayer while allowing for objections and appeals and minimizing compliance costs. Most of the higher-income countries in Europe have adopted modern methods of property tax payment (online, at banks or other collection points, in installments, etc.). Penalties for failure to comply are clearly stated, and collection rates across European countries tend to be high—for all property-related taxes.

Interestingly, despite easy payment options through bank payments and direct debits to the account of the Finnish Tax Administration, late payments of real estate taxes are reported to be common in Finland.

Enforcement in Spain follows a step-by-step process for all taxes with increasing surcharges (5 percent, 10 percent, then 20 percent) payable with each payment date missed. As a last step, the property can be embargoed. Spanish law declares tax debts extinguished after four years, necessitating speedy action by city councils.

Transparency, Communication, and Compliance

A final piece of the underlying institutional infrastructure for the efficient and fair administration of property taxes is protection of taxpayer rights. In Spain, statistics on property transactions cover almost 100 percent of formal transactions. Relevant data are collected from the notary system, checked against data from the Property Registry, and managed and published by statistical experts in the Spanish Ministry of Transport and Urban Agenda. Data for the whole country are released quarterly.

In recent years, information technology has reduced both administration and compliance costs. Advances in automation and the use of, for example, social media have had a positive impact on voluntary compliance. Electronic service portals that explain systems and how to make payments and allow taxpayers to understand their billings and payment responsibilities have reduced mistrust and reduced compliance costs (OECD 2016).

A further positive influence on taxpayer compliance is the existence of a clear social contract. Not surprisingly, in countries reporting some mistrust in government (Greece and Slovenia), compliance levels are lower. In countries with high levels of trust (Denmark, Finland, the Netherlands, Sweden, and the United Kingdom), tax compliance is high.[6] In the

Netherlands, most communication between inhabitants and different levels of government occurs via the Mijn Overheid (My Government) digital platform. Taxpayers can see the assessed value of their property on this platform, and it also is a gateway to the digital facilities that municipalities offer for questions about the assessment process or the assessed value and how to file an objection. This digital platform facilitates communication with taxpayers before property assessments become available and before tax bills are issued. During the valuation process, taxpayers can verify the characteristics used for their property assessment.

Despite considerable criticism of the council tax in Great Britain and calls for its replacement or reform, it performs exceptionally well as a generator of revenue (McCluskey et al. 2024) and has a high compliance rate. Collection rates are in the high 90 percent range across England, Wales, and Scotland. The collection rate for the local property tax in Ireland is also reported to be more than 90 percent. In Russia, in every year from 2016 to 2021, collection rates were reported to exceed 99 percent of the assessed amounts, and the collection rate of the real estate tax is almost 100 percent in Estonia, where rather curiously, reported payment discipline did not deteriorate during the COVID-19 pandemic.

In a related matter (discussed in chapter 6), most of the case study countries reported that underdeclaration of sales prices or property values for transfer tax purposes is not an issue despite possible substantial property transfer tax rates (France, the Netherlands, and the United Kingdom). Reasons proffered for accurate declarations include adverse capital gains tax implications (especially for the buyer) and the involvement of public notaries in the transfer process.

Slovenia reports underdeclaration in more than 2 percent of cases audited. This may partly be because the existing computer-assisted mass appraisal system is not used for tax purposes and has to some extent been discredited by the adverse 2014 Constitutional Court judgment regarding the value-based property tax.

Table 3.1 lists the most important entities that provide data and administer the recurrent property tax in the 14 countries discussed in part 2. The links between property tax revenue mobilization and the property tax management infrastructure for these countries are summarized in table 3.2. These tables suggest the magnitude of the job of coordinating the actions of the institutions involved in property taxation.

Automation and proper sequencing of notifications of additions or changes to property or taxpayer information are important. Although seemingly obvious, it is easier said than done in practice, especially for property-related databases managed centrally and where local government collects property tax. In the Netherlands, where municipalities are

Table 3.1 Institutional Infrastructure for Property-Related Taxes

	Functions	Responsible Entity
Denmark	Cadastre	Danish Cadastre, situated in the Danish Geodata Agency
	Property registration	Land Registry, in the Land Registration Court
	Property indexes	Statistics Denmark; Finance Denmark; Knowledge Centre for Housing Economics; Boligsiden
	Assessment: Valuation	Danish Property Assessment Agency (previously Ministry of Taxation)
	Rate setting	Municipal councils (within statutory range)
	Tax collection	Ministry of Taxation (previously locally collected)
	Enforcement	Ministry of Taxation
Estonia	Cadastre	Land Cadastre (in the Land Board)
	Property registration	Land Register
	Property indexes	Land Board
	Assessment: Valuation	Land Cadastre
	Rate setting	Local governments
	Tax collection	Tax and Customs Board
	Enforcement	Tax and Customs Board
Finland	Cadastre	Cadastre (in National Land Survey [NLS])
	Property registration	Land Registry (in NLS)
	Property indexes	NLS; Digital and Population Data Services Agency (for buildings)
	Assessment: Valuation	Finnish Tax Administration (land) and Ministry of Finance (buildings)
	Rate setting	Municipalities within a prescribed range
	Tax collection	Finnish Tax Administration
	Enforcement	Finnish Tax Administration

France	Cadastre	Cadastre (Land Registry Service)
	Property registration	Land Registry Service (in the Ministry of Finance)
	Property indexes	Cadastre; Land Registration Service; Cerema; PERVAL (notaries)
	Assessment: Valuation	General Directorate of Finance (i.e., tax authority)
	Rate setting	Municipal (within statutory limits)
	Tax collection	Tax authority
	Enforcement	Tax authority
Germany	Cadastre	Real Estate cadastre (in each federal state)
	Property registration	Real Estate cadastre and Land Register (in each federal state)
	Property indexes	Federal Statistical Office
	Assessment: Valuation	Decentralized regional tax offices
	Rate setting	States and municipal
	Tax collection	Decentralized regional tax offices
	Enforcement	Regional tax offices
Greece	Cadastre	National cadastre
	Property registration	National cadastre
	Property indexes	Bank of Greece (Real Estate Market Analysis Section)
	Assessment: Valuation	Ministry of Finance
	Rate setting	National
	Tax collection	ENFIA: Tax administration; municipality duty: through electricity bills
	Enforcement	ENFIA: Tax administration

(*continued*)

Table 3.1 Institutional Infrastructure for Property-Related Taxes (*continued*)

	Functions	Responsible Entity
Ireland	Cadastre	Tailte Éireann
	Property registration	Tailte Éireann
	Property indexes	Tailte Éireann and Central Statistics Office
	Assessment: Valuation	Tailte Éireann; Revenue (formerly the Revenue Commissioners)
	Rate setting	Central government; local authorities manage local adjustment factor
	Tax collection	Revenue collects the residential property tax; local authorities collect the business rates
	Enforcement	Revenue
Latvia	Cadastre	Cadastre Information System (responsibility of State Land Service–in Ministry of Justice)
	Property registration	Land Registry (maintained by the Court Administration)
	Property indexes	State Land Service
	Assessment: Valuation	State Land Service (overseen by Valuation Board); Cabinet of Ministers
	Rate setting	Central government; limited adjustments by municipalities
	Tax collection	Municipalities
	Enforcement	Municipalities
Netherlands	Cadastre	Cadastre, Land Registry and Mapping Agency
	Property registration	Cadastre, Land Registry and Mapping Agency
	Property indexes	National Statistics Bureau
	Assessment: Valuation	Municipalities
	Rate setting	Municipalities; polder boards
	Tax collection	Municipalities; polder boards
	Enforcement	Municipalities

Poland	Cadastre	Real Estate cadastre
	Property registration	Land and Building Register (at county level)
	Property indexes	Central Statistical Office; Starost
	Assessment: Valuation	–
	Rate setting	Ministry of Finance
	Tax collection	Municipalities
	Enforcement	Municipalities
Russia	Cadastre	Federal Service of State Registration, Cadastre and Cartography (Rosreestr)
	Property registration	Rosreestr manages the Unified State Register of Real Estate
	Property indexes	For improvements (other than buildings)—self-assessment
	Assessment: Valuation	Regional valuation agencies
	Rate setting	Local authorities within federal limits
	Tax collection	Territorial branches of the Federal Tax Services
	Enforcement	Territorial branches of the Federal Tax Services
Slovenia	Cadastre	Surveying and Mapping Authority
	Property registration	Surveying and Mapping Authority
	Property indexes	Financial Administration of Republic of Slovenia (FARS)
	Assessment: Valuation	Surveying and Mapping Authority
	Rate setting	Municipal within centrally determined range
	Tax collection	FARS
	Enforcement	FARS

(*continued*)

Table 3.1 Institutional Infrastructure for Property-Related Taxes (*continued*)

	Functions	Responsible Entity
Spain	Cadastre	Cadastre
	Property registration	Property Registry
	Property indexes	Spanish Institute of Statistics (INE)
	Assessment: Valuation	Cadastre
	Rate setting	Municipalities
	Tax collection	Public administration
	Enforcement	Public administration
United Kingdom	**England:**	
	Cadastre	HM Land Registry
	Property registration	HM Land Registry
	Property indexes	Office for National Statistics (ONS); Morgan Stanley Capital International
	Assessment: Valuation	Valuation Office Agency (VOA)
	Rate setting	Council tax: tax multiplier; business rates: central
	Tax collection	Council tax: local; business rates: local
	Enforcement	Council tax: local; business rates: local
	Northern Ireland:	
	Cadastre	Land and Property Services (LPS)
	Property registration	LPS
	Property indexes	Northern Ireland Statistics and Research Agency
	Assessment: Valuation	LPS
	Rate setting	Domestic rates and business rates: districts and regional
	Tax collection	LPS collects domestic and business rates
	Enforcement	LPS for both domestic rates and business rates

Scotland:	
Cadastre	Registers of Scotland
Property registration	Registers of Scotland
Property indexes	Office for National Statistics (ONS)
Assessment: Valuation	Scottish Assessors' Association; VOA
Rate setting	Council tax: tax multiplier; business rates: Scottish regional
Tax collection	Council tax: local; business rates: local
Enforcement	Council tax: local; business rates: local
Wales:	
Cadastre	HM Land Registry
Property registration	HM Land Registry
Property indexes	ONS
Assessment: Valuation	VOA
Rate setting	Council tax: tax multiplier; business rates: Welsh regional
Tax collection	Council tax: local; business rates: local
Enforcement	Council tax: local; business rates: local

Source: Authors.

Table 3.2 Land Information Systems

	Property Registration System	Data on Property Values	Property Transfers
Denmark	All property is registered, with a cadastre number; information includes property description and ownership details. Registry is administered by the national government and is updated daily. Valuation switched to an automated statistical model in 2016; about 87% digital.	Statistics Denmark publishes regular statistics on price indexes for property sales; various private institutions also publish housing price indexes; data for commercial properties are deemed inadequate.	All transfers must be registered with a purchase agreement and a deed of conveyance; sales values of property tend to be accurately reported.
Estonia	Basic documents are the Land Cadastre and Land Cadastre Map (GIS); Land Board and private valuers are responsible for valuations, which are updated annually.	Database on property transfer values is linked to cadastre; Land Board leads data analysis and does regular updating of values and produces indexes.	Sales data cover about 70% of all transactions. Underdeclarations limited by bank and mortgage requirements. Transaction data collected and submitted by notaries.
Finland	The title and mortgage registry records rights on most properties. The cadastre records information about land use and location. About 60% of apartment ownership is indirect. The housing company (not the individual apartments) is subject to real estate taxes. Reform of property valuation and data collection has been proposed but implementation is on hold.	The real property sales price register collects information on sales prices of property transfers. Reported transfer values do not reflect market values because of municipal government involvement in housing markets. Transaction data are not available for all apartments and commercial properties. Much of the information gathered for property registration is not used for property valuation.	The buyer of a property or the real estate agent submits the transfer tax amount, which is required for registration. Transfers of property may involve value capture based on land use agreements.

France	The land registry (cadastre) covers nearly 100 percent of properties; cadastral value of business properties was updated in 2017.	Transaction values and property characteristics are contained in five databases, including the cadastre. A reliable housing index is available. Data on rental values are too scarce to update the cadastre. The quality of available data is thought to be good.	The process is notary assisted. Underdeclaration of sales values does not appear to be a problem.
Germany	The federal states are responsible for surveying and for managing the cadastre, but implementing regulations have been standardized.	Federal Statistics office provides various indexes of construction and real estate prices; property revaluations have not been done for decades.	Transfers are assisted by a notary public who passes the transfer information to the land register and the relevant tax office. Tax evasion on property transfers is rare.
Greece	National Cadastre documents geographic attributes (location, boundaries, and size) of each property, including building characteristics; registers all transactions that create or alter rights, restrictions, and obligations on properties after verifying legality.	The objective value represents the taxable value of transactions and is derived from the Objective Determination of Real Estate Values System (Ministry of Finance). The objective value is the tax value of the property as assessed by the tax authority and is often lower than market value.	Data for each transfer are collected by the Independent Authority for Public Revenue (AADE), the cadastral offices, or the cooperating notaries. Underdeclaration is common.
Ireland	Registration of freehold and leasehold land is compulsory; 2.8 million parcels are registered by Property Registration Authority; the registry is digitized. The registration of deeds is not compulsory; residential rents are registered.	Private rental sector websites provide information on commercial leases and residential sales but provide little information about the properties. Revenue department data on transactions are not publicly available and in some cases are still in paper form. Detailed indexes on market value of properties are not readily available.	All property sales are registered. The base of the tax is the declared sales price or the market price as determined by a qualified valuer or equivalent.

(continued)

Table 3.2 Land Information Systems (*continued*)

	Property Registration System	Data on Property Values	Property Transfers
Latvia	The property registration system consists of two separate registers: the Land Registry (maintained by the Court Administration) and the National Cadastre Information System, the so-called Cadastre IS (the responsibility of the State Land Service).	Cadastral valuation is the responsibility of the State Land Service (since 1992). The Real Estate Valuation Department (with some 30 valuers, analysts, and GIS specialists) carries out the cadastral valuation for the entire country.	Real estate transfers must be secured in the Land Registry. Securitization of ownership occurs only after the flat state and office fee and outstanding real estate tax have been paid.
Netherlands	All land and apartment rights are registered in the central cadastral registration. Data on property sales are included and made available to the public. The register is fully digitized.	Cadastral registration data are the primary information source for mass appraisals and assessments; a monthly price index (national and main regions) is available to the public. No index is available for commercial and rented property.	Property transactions are notary assisted. There is little underdeclaration of sales prices since most buyers take a 100% mortgage.
Poland	Property transfers are registered, but an adequate land information system is not in place. Data on buildings are incomplete. The cadastre includes data from many sources, including taxpayer declarations, but is badly dated.	A real estate price registry is regularly updated and maintained locally. The quality of the data are not good. Comparative analysis of local data and cadastral records are not regularly carried out.	A notarial deed is required to transfer properties. The deed includes information about the property and about tax and fee payments due. The local tax office reviews the declared sales value for conformity with market value.
Russia	The federal Unified Register consists of 85 databases (one for each region) but does not include all properties. It contains detailed information on each property, including cadastral value, past owners, and property characteristics.	The State Registry includes data on property values. Purchase agreements are in the registry but not available for distribution. Cadastral values are updated on a 2-to 4-year cycle and determined by region valuation agencies. Land leases are set as a % of cadastral values.	Russia has no property transfer taxes. Sales of property are recorded in the property register. Regional governments report significant amounts of missing data.

Spain	All properties are registered in the National Property Registry, which is coordinated with all regions and linked with the national cadastre; the cadastre is the source of property information, and the database used by subnational governments. The property tax base is the cadastral value, which is less than market value. Rental contracts are not registered.	Sales values are compared on all property transactions and released quarterly. Includes price/m^2. Data on rental prices are not included.	A notary system handles property transfers. The notary creates a deed that includes a full property description; declared sales values are reviewed by tax authorities and adjusted if necessary. Transaction costs can reach 13% of total sales value of the property.
Slovenia	The compulsory cadastre registration identifies separate ownership for land and buildings; it includes description of the property and its use. Cadastre and tax-sourced estimates are regularly compared.	The real estate market register includes data from property transfer tax payments and characteristics of the property. Rental prices are estimated from survey data and from transfer tax payments. Rental prices tend to be understated.	The tax base for property transfers is the selling price. This may be corrected by the tax authorities if it is estimated to be less than 80% of the market value. Property values have fluctuated significantly since about 2005.
United Kingdom	Covers, in England and Wales, 88% of properties, and in Scotland, 80%. The system is largely computerized and open to the public. Automation and digitization are ongoing.	Data from market transactions are recorded in the land registry and are made available to the public.	All British governments levy various forms of property transfer taxes. Transactions are usually assisted by a solicitor. Mortgage and bank involvement limit the possibility of underdeclaration of sales prices.

Sources: The country studies in part 2.

responsible for annual valuations, the relevant role players seem to cooperate very well; and data accessibility, verification, and updating are not challenges—as is also evidenced by the shared service centers.

Managing Other Property Taxes

Property transfer taxes are levied in most European countries.[7] Because the transfer tax typically is based on the declared selling price or the market value—whichever is higher—databases are needed to verify the accuracy of these declarations of values. The revenue authorities collecting these taxes may rely on data provided by the cadastre (France, the Netherlands, and Spain), valuation agency (the Netherlands), in-house expertise (Denmark), notaries (France, Germany, the Netherlands, Poland, and Romania), and in some instances, on the honesty of the taxpayer. Moreover, some transfer taxes are structured to help control land prices and owner-occupancy rates, and this requires estimation of their impacts. In general, underdeclaration is not an issue in the high-income countries. In many European countries, notaries play an integral part in the determination and collection of property transfer taxes (box 3.2). The high ethical standards set for and by the notary profession, as well as notaries' general knowledge of the real estate market, may instill some confidence within taxing authorities that the values declared via notaries are indeed market related.

For most of the 14 countries in part 2, property-related taxes nationally levied and collected involve fewer parties. For example, the national revenue authority generally administers capital gains taxes, VAT, and (national) property transfer taxes and largely relies on data and information provided by taxpayers directly or through notaries. Some of these taxes in some of the 14 countries, however, are administered at state or regional level or at local level. For example, Spain levies a type of capital gains tax at municipal level.

Real Estate Market

Another reason why countries regulate real estate relates to tracking land and property markets and developing data to design property-related public policies. The housing and construction sectors are important components of national economies, and tracking their movements is important for property tax policy and administration. Housing prices and mortgage interest rates are regularly reported, which frequently triggers remedial public policies. Business cycles and economic crises matter, greatly. European countries went through a recession and a debt crisis in

Box 3.2 The Role of Public Notaries

France

Registration of any real estate donation or sale in France requires a notary. The notary sends an online copy of the deed to the registry service (in the Ministry of Finance) for recording, collects the property transfer tax, and receives a fixed fee for the notarial service provided. The tax administration provides taxpayers with a tool, Patrim, that searches data collected by notaries and transmitted to the tax administration. Taxpayers use it to compare the purchase price of transactions surrounding their property in recent years and estimate their property's value. For real estate properties, the tax base is the market value of the property as estimated by the notaries on the basis of comparable sales. To estimate the value of the property, notaries have access to their own databases.

Romania

Public notaries in Romania record the transaction price on the sales contract when a property is sold. A chamber of notaries (there are 15) contracts with one or more authorized valuers to prepare annual market reports for each county within the jurisdiction of a specific chamber. These reports provide notaries' indicative prices of real property, garnered from the declared prices, for the property transfer tax. These reports carry some weight and relevance when it comes to the assessment of the tax. Since 2023, valuers preparing market reports have to follow the guidelines set by the National Association of Authorized Romanian Valuers in 2022. The guidelines enumerate sources of information (such as sale contracts, own valuation-related information, and asking prices available in the market) for determining the minimum values in market reports. No central notary database stores this information, and these data have limited accessibility. Romania's National Institute of Statistics offers a residential-properties data capture tool that notaries manage and the statistics institute uses to develop residential property price indexes.

Spain

The notary is a semi–civil servant in Spain. Normally, a notary certifies the aims of two parties in a real estate transaction, their eligibility to act in the transaction procedure, and that the data are true and advises the parties regarding their rights and encumbrances. The document signed by the notary is then sent to the Property Registry, which checks the details and registers it. No assessment of the value is declared for the transaction. The declared price is determined by the contracting parties, and neither the notary nor the Property Registry declares an opinion concerning the value.

Sources: Part 2, chapter 11 (France) and chapter 20 (Spain). For Romania, a restricted-access report from the International Monetary Fund.

the first two decades of this century that called for adjustments in property tax strategy.

In fact, those two decades have been a time of property tax turmoil. Effective property tax rates have fallen in many European countries, and valuation systems have been revamped. Some countries made significant changes in the way they structure their property tax and their administration, such as reintroduction of a recurrent property tax on residential property in Ireland,[8] comprehensive overhaul of the property tax system in Greece, and new property tax systems introduced in Germany in 2025. The changes in Ireland and Greece were effected as part of agreements with the European Commission, the European Central Bank, and the International Monetary Fund.

Data on property rents are more difficult to track but are often required for tax purposes and for monitoring living costs. Except for Slovenia, registries do not capture rents on residential and commercial properties. The private sector adds value in this respect by providing information on real estate asking prices or bank lending practices, and this could be used to help explain the implications and real estate price indexes provided by national government.

Real estate markets in the 14 countries of part 2 are not all the same, and this has affected development of the management infrastructure for property taxation. These countries are at different stages of developing or redeveloping their underlying property tax infrastructure and face different challenges in building it up. This state of affairs almost certainly has affected their rate of revenue mobilization. Take Germany: although it is the largest economy in Europe, it collects relatively little revenue from recurrent property taxation. As a percentage of GDP in 2021, Germany collected only 0.4 percent compared with the European Union average of 1.1 percent. As a percentage of total taxes in 2021, recurrent property taxation was 1.0 percent compared with a European Union average of 2.6 percent (European Union 2022). The following discusses these differences and how they might have affected revenue collections.

Countries in Europe differ in level of development. Of the 14 case study countries, all but Russia are high-income countries.[9] Owner occupancy prevails in almost all Europe. In the European Union, 70 percent of the population live in a household owning their home. Romania has the highest share of ownership (95 percent), followed by Slovakia (92 percent [2020 data]), Hungary (92 percent), and Croatia (91 percent). The remaining 30 percent live in rented housing (European Union 2022). In Germany and Switzerland, renting is more common. In Germany, renting is more common than owning, and just more than 50 percent of the population are tenants. Austria (46 percent) and Denmark (41 percent) also have high levels of tenant occupation (European Union 2022).

The part 2 countries have taken different approaches to property taxation—in particular, the property tax base. Countries that tax the capital values of land and structures have a good database for valuing owner-occupied residential property (the Netherlands), while those that tax rental values (France) often cannot. Northern Ireland provides an excellent example of a jurisdiction that did extensive modeling of all the relevant data on land values, capital values, and rental values to determine the most appropriate base for its recurrent tax on residential property. On the basis of the quantity and quality of data, capital values are used for its system of domestic rates.

Where government plays a more direct role in land markets, cadastral values may not be so accurate. An example is Finland, where municipal governments buy and sell land at prices that do not reflect market levels. In Russia, the credibility of valuation data is also an issue, with inaccurate or missing data on geolocation of properties or land use (see chapter 18).

Property Taxes and Land Policy

Government, the private sector, and the general public all have an interest and involvement in land use management. Apart from increasing the values for property owners, these government decisions may necessitate new infrastructure or the upgrading or extension of existing infrastructure. Land use projects may include zoning and other regulations and, more recently, environmental strictures and conservation initiatives with fiscal consequences, such as providing property tax relief to public and private nature reserves or entitlement to ecological fiscal transfers, such as in France and Portugal (Rodrigues 2016; Santos et al. 2012; Schröter-Schlaack et al. 2014). The development and management of these initiatives require detailed land use mapping, information about land and buildings, and information about the location and quality of public facilities. Government planning agencies regularly gather and use such data. Not infrequently, land use management has implications for the property tax—for example, rezoning agricultural land for urban use or increasing building density.

Given the extensive urban development and redevelopment taking place across Europe as well as a growing need for social housing, governments at the central and subnational levels could benefit from additional resources. One largely untapped resource is land value capture (LVC) instruments. The result could be additional sources of revenue at the central, regional, and city levels. Some LVC instruments are applied as land-based financing tools through which especially local governments expand their revenue base to support their service delivery, infrastructure development, and maintenance responsibilities. Their use has already begun in Europe.

LVC instruments include taxes, fees, and in some instances, regulatory instruments (Ingram and Hong 2011; Smolka 2013; UN-Habitat 2016). They can be determined with reference to value (land value increment taxes, betterment levies) or cost (developer charges, exactions, and impact fees). In an environment where land and property markets are transparent and credible values can in principle be determined, betterment charges (Ireland and the United Kingdom) or even land value increment taxes (Denmark) can raise additional revenue. Land value increment taxes have a revenue focus and betterment charges a goal to recoup value increases attributed to the actual cost of infrastructure needs associated with development. In Ireland, the Planning and Development Act of 2000 paved the way for a new betterment tax that captures up to 20 percent of the value gained from planning for social housing. This law encourages the delivery of private, social, and affordable housing side by side rather than in the traditional segregated approach.

The inefficacy of the recurrent property tax to capture value is strikingly illustrated by the policy and practice in Slovenia, where a 10-year exemption is given to owners of newly constructed or renovated buildings (if building value increases because of renovation by more than 50 percent). The exemption creates an incentive for owners to invest in new buildings or renovations. The value increase is indirectly captured through the issuance of one-off building permits that generate more revenue than the recurrent tax on property. In Latvia, building permits are value based (rather than fixed fees) and levied at rates of up to 2 percent.

In Spain, there is a municipal building and construction tax on developers and other owners of construction projects. The tax base is the effective cost of the construction excluding taxes, professional honorariums, or business benefits. The maximum tax rate, determined locally, is 4 percent. Construction of defined infrastructure (including roads, railways, ports, airports, and sanitation projects) is exempted.

Municipalities in Finland often engage in public land development. According to the Finnish Land Use and Building Act, a landowner who materially benefits from a local detailed plan has the duty to contribute to the costs of the provision of the infrastructure, either as an agreed monetary contribution or, if an agreement is not reached, a statutory fee. Finnish municipalities are also actively involved in land banking and leasing. They can acquire undeveloped land through sale or expropriation, draft plans, and build the necessary local infrastructure. After this, the municipality sells the developed building sites to (private) developers or leases them through long-term land leases, thereby capturing all planning-induced value increases.

In Greece, a social land-for-flats program requires the provision of public land to private investors with a percentage of units to be reserved for the construction of affordable housing (Housing Europe 2023).

The *taxe spéciale d'équipement* in Île-de-France, France, is a variation of the infrastructure levy and was introduced to help fund the Grand Paris Express transit project. It is expected to generate €117 million annually over its existence (OECD 2022).

Property Taxes and Housing Policy

Housing demand has been increasing across Europe for reasons including urbanization, energy efficiency, net immigration, an aging population, and a decline in average household size (Krapp et al. 2020; Segú 2020). Segú (2020, 1) points out that in "a context of low supply elasticity, which characterizes European countries, increases in housing demand tend to capitalize into higher prices. This situation is further exacerbated by a high population density, land scarcity and rigid construction regulation." As a result, interest grows in using fiscal instruments to create incentives for the implementation of certain housing policies.

Residential vacancy plagues Europe. In Greece, for example, 2.25 million out of a total housing stock of 6.37 million houses are vacant (Housing Europe 2023). Various countries in Europe impose taxes or surcharges on vacant housing. France introduced a tax (*taxe sur les logement vacants*) in 1999 levied on the rental value (calculated by the tax administration) of unfurnished properties that have been occupied for less than 30 days in the previous two years. The tax rate increases with each year of vacancy. At first it was introduced in large metropolitan areas (populations exceeding 200,000) where the demand for housing significantly outstrips the supply. It was levied by several French municipalities, and Segú (2020) found that it reduced vacancies by 13 percent on average in the four years following its implementation (OECD 2022). Since April 2013, local authorities in Great Britain can charge vacant units with up to an extra 50 percent of their council tax (Segú 2020). In Ireland, Austria, and Luxembourg, second homes attract additional tax.

Tax relief is also used as an incentive to provide social housing. Some countries grant relief centrally through the personal income tax, corporate tax, or VAT. Belgium, Bulgaria, Czech Republic, Denmark, Estonia, Finland, Greece, Italy, Luxembourg, the Netherlands, Norway, Spain, Sweden, and Switzerland all grant mortgage interest relief. For example, the standard VAT rate is 21 percent in Belgium. However, the rate reduces

Table 3.3 Primary Goal of Property-Related Taxes and Fees Administered in European Countries

Tax, Fee, or Instrument	Revenue Mobilization	Land Value Capture	Housing	Regulating Use and Construction
Recurrent property taxes	Yes			
Property transfer taxes/ stamp duties	Yes			
Value-added tax	Yes		Yes	
Capital gains tax	Yes	Yes		
Inheritance and gift taxes	Yes			
Vacant land tax		Yes		
Vacant house tax	Yes		Yes	
Betterment tax/levy		Yes	Yes	
Developer charge		Yes		Yes
Luxury home tax	Yes			
Special equipment tax		Yes		
Building and construction tax on developers		Yes		
Building permit		Yes		Yes
Land banking		Yes		

Source: Authors.

to 6 percent for renovated private dwellings, private housing for handicapped persons, and demolition to build new housing in a number of cities. For social housing, the rate ranges from 6 to 12 percent (Krapp et al. 2020). In France, new dwellings built in neighborhoods that benefit from the National Urban Regeneration Plan can receive a reduced VAT rate of 5.5 percent when a buyer's income is below a threshold. Furthermore, most social housing programs also benefit from the lower 5.5 percent VAT rate. Similarly, Poland, with a standard VAT rate of 23 percent, taxes the sale of buildings covered by the social housing program at only 8 percent. In Bulgaria, Finland, Greece, Hungary, Malta, the Netherlands, Portugal, and the United Kingdom, property transfer tax or stamp duty relief is given to first-time homeowners. Ireland's 1 percent tax rate on residential property valued below €1 million also provides relief to first-time homeowners (and others).

At the local government level, property tax relief may be an incentive for more environmentally friendly construction or renovation, for example. In Spain, municipalities may grant developers building and construction tax reductions for specific constructions of special interest for the municipality—for example, solar energy systems (95%), private investments in infrastructure (50%), and public housing (50%).

Recurrent property tax payments may also be deferred to address the problem of cash-poor but asset-rich homeowners (Grote, Mansour, and Wen 2024; Grote and Wen 2024), as in Denmark and Ireland (OECD 2022).

Table 3.3 provides an overview of property-related taxes and fees levied in Europe.

Conclusion: Better Management to Mobilize Revenue

The property tax in Europe does not meet its potential as a good tax instrument. Most European countries have put the basic framework in place for good management of the property tax, but few have used these institutions to push property tax revenues to higher levels. Four management-related practices could break the revenue mobilization logjam: the use of technology, better database management, ex post evaluations, and more comprehensive reform strategies.

A comprehensive and up-to-date legal and fiscal cadastre is the basis for a well-functioning recurrent property tax. The results in the United Kingdom show that even with incomplete registration of properties and using a regressive value-banding system, a residential property tax can generate significant revenues. And in France, despite a complex administrative system and a badly outdated tax roll, recurrent property taxes raised more than 2.2 percent of GDP in 2022. Several other European countries, Germany and Finland among them, carry on with old tax rolls but apply rate increases and other patchwork fixes to maintain revenues. In the Netherlands, all the relevant institutions perform well, yet the recurrent property tax still realizes less than 1 percent of GDP, and Spain, where institutions also perform well, realized just above 1 percent of GDP in 2022.

Stopgap measures that bypass institutions are accompanied by significant inequities in the distribution of tax burdens and distortions to land use. Moreover, they cause a loss of confidence in property taxation and set the stage for a significant reform shock when it finally does come. And unfair property taxes are likely not sustainable over a long period. Institutions matter greatly, because they smooth the transitions as property values and the demand for public services grow. Their use is the necessary condition for a good property tax practice.

Germany and Luxembourg are cases in point. Germany's unfair tax system led to major reform beginning in 2025. Luxembourg's recurrent property tax system dates back to the 1930s. In 2024, the government upgraded its computer systems to facilitate electronic tax notifications and technical preparatory work to establish a national register of buildings and housing by the ministry responsible for internal affairs, and the Land Registry and Topography Administration is continuing the work (Grunwald 2024). In 2022 and also July 2025, the government submitted proposed amendments to the property tax law—aiming to address issues with fairness and equity rather than raising more revenue (Afakir and Bentley 2025).

Better management results from implementation of three practices: information technology, linked databases, and evaluation of the accuracy of tax base estimates.

Information technology is critical to a more efficient and equitable administration of property taxes. It contributes in important ways to property identification and base coverage, the quality and regularity of assessments of all properties, modeling of tax burdens, and rate structures and tax relief and is crucial for billing, collection, and enforcement of taxes. Across Europe, countries are digitizing data and automating property registration, the cadastre, and tax administration, or have already done so—significantly reducing administration and compliance costs. Estonia, for example, is a pioneer in its e-government practices for property transactions. The country's paper-free system has reduced the processing time for land transactions from about three months to less than 10 days (Farmer 2021). But despite the progress in digitization and automation, a general revaluation was undertaken only in 2021, 20 years after the previous assessment.

The widespread use of computerized mass appraisal could be a game changer. Conceivably, it could lower the cost of valuation and lessen dependence on having an adequate supply of qualified valuers, thereby softening two of the major constraints to revaluations. At least in theory, it could make valuations more accurate and, even more important, might lead to more regular ex post study of the fairness of valuation outcomes.

Linking databases in the public and private sectors enables more accurate assessments and more regular updates of property details. Not only does this bode well for recurrent property taxes across Europe, but it also opens the door for fiscal measures to change taxpayer behavior toward vacant land parcels (Austria, France, and Luxembourg), second homes (Austria and Ireland), and unoccupied residential property (Luxembourg and Greece). To fully benefit from linking databases, all taxpayers must have easy access. This is being done in countries where all land management functions are performed and managed in one entity (under one roof) (Ireland and Northern Ireland).

In some of the case study countries, revenue authorities use only or primarily in-house property transfer tax databases (Slovenia), but some countries (Denmark and the Netherlands) use third-party databases for verification. And in many countries in Europe, public notaries' role in facilitating property transfers provides opportunities for acquiring important data on ownership and also value. Some countries take the values reported by notaries as a guideline for revenue authorities (the Netherlands, Romania, and Spain). In France, notaries are actively involved in determining values. A generally accepted, ex post evaluation of the accuracy of tax base estimates is needed (see chapter 5). This is not currently done in most countries, but the Waarderingskamer in the Netherlands oversees values determined by municipalities. In some countries, analytic research done on market-related valuations is limited.

Blame for the relatively weak revenue performance of recurrent property taxation in some of the case study countries (especially Germany) falls on not only the underlying administrative infrastructure and management systems but also overall tax policies, tax mix, and political economy (see chapter 4). Property tax reform is overdue in many European countries, and reform that has occurred suffers from three limitations: First, have the reform analyses been comprehensive enough to address the problems—that is, were tax structure and tax administration jointly addressed? Second, were reform proposals adequately publicized to gain buy-in from the people? Third, did external sources (a failing economy, a tax revolt, the courts and judicial system, debt overburden) play a role in curtaining reform initiatives?

With respect to external sources, can the strong revenue performance of the property tax in other countries (Great Britain and more recently in Greece and Ireland) be traced back to well-designed reform strategies and the creation of strong institutional support to strengthen the administration? Interestingly, the reforms in all three of these countries were brought about by pressure exerted on politicians at the political center to effect change—in Great Britain, to find a replacement for the community charge; in Greece, to reform a dilapidated, dysfunctional system; and in Ireland, to reintroduce a tax on residential property (abolished in 1997) to increase domestic revenues in the aftermath of the financial crisis. Ireland, faced with a lack of data on residential properties, looked at the council tax in Great Britain as the answer to the lack of valuation data. But by opting for many more value bands, the regressivity plaguing the council tax especially in Wales was partly addressed. Also, in Germany, politicians had to respond to the Federal Constitutional Court decision condemning the outdated valuations—effectively forcing their hand to (re)act.

In Poland, numbers of valuers to migrate to a modern market value–based property tax are apparently sufficient, but data integration is lacking and so is political will to change the system. Even so, more than 1 percent of GDP is raised with a primarily area-based system, despite disjointed entities and poor data sharing and management. In the Netherlands, in contrast, the data are excellent and up to date, accessible by all, and transparency is paramount, and yet less than 1 percent of GDP is raised from recurrent property taxes. So quality data and well-managed institutions alone cannot explain the revenue performance of property taxes. The role of politics, fiscal decentralization policies, transparency and trust, and proper communication all play a role.

Notes

1. This included creation in 2023–2024 of a valuation unit by the Ministry of Finance.
2. This requirement applies even for countries using area-based systems because the use of land and the usable area of buildings changes frequently.
3. Market calibration typically takes the form of differential tax rates with reference to property type, location in tax (land value) zone, and sometimes city size, in addition to property size (usable area), which, in itself, is a major market calibration factor (Brzeski, Románová, and Franzsen 2019).
4. In the Republic of Ireland owners cannot appeal because they themselves declare the value band. However, the Revenue can challenge the declared band.
5. The Northern Ireland Valuation Tribunal was established April 1, 2007, primarily to hear and determine appeals against new capital values assessed on residential property.
6. The reported compliance largely correlates with Transparency International's corruption perception index (Transparency International 2023).
7. Exceptions are the Czech Republic, Kosovo, Slovakia, and the Republic of Srpska and Brčko District in Bosnia-Herzegovina.
8. Ireland abolished domestic rates in 1978, which resulted in significant dependence of local authorities on subventions from the center (Williams 1999).
9. Across Europe, the vast majority of countries are classified as high income. Albania, Belarus, Bosnia-Herzegovina, Bulgaria, Kosovo, Moldova, Montenegro, North Macedonia, Russia, Serbia, and Turkey are classified as higher-middle-income countries, and Ukraine is the only lower-middle-income country (World Bank, n.d.).

References

Afakir, J., and M. Bentley. 2025. "Amendments to Draft Law on Property Tax and Tax on Land Mobilisation Submitted to Parliament." Atoz Alert. https://www.atoz.lu/media/amendments-draft-law-property-tax-and-tax-land-mobilisation-submitted-parliament.

Aleksiene, A., and A. Bagdonavicius. 2008. "Value-Based Property Taxes in Lithuania." In *Making the Property Tax Work—Experiences in Developing and Transitional Countries*, ed. R. Bahl, J. Martinez-Vazquez, and J. Youngman. Cambridge, MA: Lincoln Institute of Land Policy, 411–435.

Annual Report. 2021. "Valuation Office Annual Report 2020." Dublin. Accessed September 10, 2024. https://www.valoff.ie/en/publications/annual-reports/annual-report-2020.pdf.

Bahl, R., and R. Bird. 2018. *Fiscal Decentralization and Local Finance in Developing Countries*. Cheltenham, UK: Edward Elgar.

Bahl, R., W. McCluskey, and R. Franzsen. 2022. "Current Policies and Practice." In *Property Tax in Asia: Policy and Practice*, ed. W. McCluskey, R. Bahl, and R. Franzsen, 19–88. Cambridge, MA: Lincoln Institute of Land Policy.

Brzeski, J., A. Románová, and R. Franzsen. 2019. "The Evolution of Property Taxes in Post-Socialist Countries in Central and Eastern Europe." African Tax Institute Working paper WP-19-01.

Buzu, O. 2021. "Property Tax Appraisal in Moldova." In Radvan et al., *Real Property Taxes*, 759–798.

Canaj, E., and I. Lavdari. 2021. "Immovable Property Tax System in Republic of Albania." In Radvan et al., *Real Property Taxes*, 585–611.

European Union. 2022. "Housing in Europe: 2022 Interactive Edition." European Union: Eurostat. https://ec.europa.eu/eurostat/cache/digpub/housing/.

Farmer, L. 2021. "Making a Good Tax Better: From Assessment to Collection, Three Places That Built Stronger Property Tax Systems." *Land Lines*, January/April, 43–54.

Franzsen, R., and W. McCluskey. 2017. "Introduction." In *Property Tax in Africa: Status, Challenges, and Prospects*, ed. R. Franzsen and W. McCluskey, 3–28. Cambridge, MA: Lincoln Institute of Land Policy.

Greenway, I. 2010. "Transforming Land and Property Services—Northern Ireland Learns from and Builds on the Australian Experience." Paper presented at the FIG Congress 2010 Facing the Challenges—Building the Capacity, Sydney, Australia (April 11–16).

Grote, M., M. Mansour, and J.-F. Wen. 2024. "How Property Taxes Can Help Low-Income Countries to Develop." IMF Blog, November 11. https://www.imf.org/en/Blogs/Articles/2024/11/11/how-property-taxes-can-help-low-income-countries-to-develop.

Grote, M., and J.-F. Wen. 2024. "How to Design and Implement Property Tax Reforms." IMF How to Note 2024/006. Washington, DC: International Monetary Fund.

Grunwald, A. 2024. "Property Tax Reform Measures Still Several Months Out." Delano, May 4, 2024. https://delano.lu/article/property-tax-reform-measures-s.

Housing Europe. 2023. "The State of Housing in Europe 2023." https://web.archive.org/web/20231110112504/https://www.stateofhousing.eu/The_State_of_Housing_in_Europe_2023.pdf.

Ingram, G. K., and Y.-H. Hong, eds. 2011. *Value Capture and Land Policies*. Cambridge, MA: Lincoln Institute of Land Policy.

Kaufmann, J., and D. Steudler. 1998. "Cadastre 2014. A Vision for a Future Cadastral System." FIG-Commission 7, Brighton, UK. https://www.fig.net/resources/publications/figpub/cadastre2014/translation/c2014-english.pdf.

Krapp, M., M. Vaché, B. Egner, K. Schulze, and S. Thomas. 2020. "Housing Policies in the European Union." (November). https://www.researchgate.net/publication/349767805_Housing_policies_in_the_European_Union.

McCluskey, W. J. 1991. "Rating in England." In *Comparative Property Tax Systems*, ed. W. J. McCluskey, 145–156. Aldershot, UK: Ashgate.

McCluskey, W. J., P. T. Davis, M. McCord, P. Bidanset, J. McIntyre, and L. Hermans. 2024. "Share and Share Alike? Investigating Simplified Approaches to Sharing the Tax Burden for Effective Mobilisation of Property Taxation." Paper presented at the Riël Franzsen Symposium: Theory and Practice of Taxation in Africa, Pretoria, South Africa (April 29–30).

Miemiec, W., and P. Zawadzka. 2021. "Poland." In Radvan et al., *Real Property Taxes*, 117–142.

OECD (Organisation for Economic Co-operation and Development). 2016. *Technologies for Better Tax Administration: A Practical Guide for Revenue Bodies*. Paris: OECD.

———. 2022. "Housing Taxation in OECD Countries." OECD Tax Policy Studies No. 29. https://doi.org/10.1787/03dfe007-en.

Radvan, M., R. Franzsen, W. J. McCluskey, and F. Plimmer, eds. 2021. *Real Property Taxes and Property Markets in CEE Countries and Central Asia*. Maribor, Slovenia: Institute for Local Self-Government Maribor.

Radvan, M., and J. Kranecová. 2021. "Is Ad Valorem Property Taxation a Solution for the Czech Republic." In Radvan et al., *Real Property Taxes*, 47–78.

Rodrigues, L. C. 2016. "Ecological Fiscal Transfer (EFT) in Portugal." Institute for European Environmental Policy. https://ieep.eu/wp-content/uploads/2022/12/PT-Ecological-Fiscal-Transfer-final.pdf.

Rohlíková, A. 1999. "Property Taxation in the Czech Republic." In *Property Tax: An International Comparative Review*, ed. W. McCluskey, 440–454. Aldershot, UK: Ashgate.

Santos, R., I. Ring, P. Antunes, and P. Clemente. 2012. "Fiscal Transfers for Biodiversity Conservation: The Portuguese Local Finances Law." *Land Use Policy* 29(2): 261–273.

Schröter-Schlaack, C., I. Ring, T. Koellner, R. Santos, P. Antunes, P. Clemente, R. Mathevet, M. Borie, and M. Grodzińska-Jurczak. 2014. "Intergovernmental Fiscal Transfers to Support Local Conservation Action in Europe." *Zeitschrift für Wirtschaftsgeographie* [German journal of economics geography] 58(2–3): 98–114.

Segú, M. 2020. "The Impact of Taxing Vacancy on Housing Markets: Evidence from France." *Journal of Public Economics* 185: 104079.

Smolka, M. O. 2013. "Implementing Land Value Capture in Latin America: Policies and Tools for Implementation." Cambridge, MA: Lincoln Institute of Land Policy.

Šulija, V. 2008. "Commentary." In *Making the Property Tax Work: Experiences in Developing and Transitional Countries*, ed. R. Bahl, J. Martinez-Vazquez, and J. Youngman, 436–446. Cambridge, MA: Lincoln Institute of Land Policy.

Transparency International. 2023. "Corruption Perception Index 2023." https://www.transparency.org/en/cpi/2023/.

UN-Habitat. 2016. *Leveraging Land: Land-Based Finance for Local Governments, a Reader*. Nairobi: United Nations Human Settlements Programme. https://unhabitat.org/sites/default/files/download-manager-files/Leveraging%20Land%20%20for%20LBF%20%20Reader.pdf.

Williams, B. 1999. "The Present and Future Role of Property Taxation in Local Government Funding in Ireland." In *Property Tax: An International Comparative Review*, ed. W. McCluskey, 116–129. Aldershot, UK: Ashgate.

World Bank. n.d. "World Development Indicators." Accessed December 22, 2023. https://datatopics.worldbank.org/world-development-indicators/.

Youngman, J. M., and J. H. Malme. 1994. *An International Survey of Taxes on Land and Buildings*. Deventer, Netherlands: Kluwer.

Zibrik, N., and T. Humar. 2021. "Real Property Taxation in the Emerging Economy of the Republic of Slovenia." In Radvan et al., *Real Property Taxes*, 327–373.

4

Tax Structure and Impacts

ROY BAHL, WILLIAM MCCLUSKEY, RIËL FRANZSEN, AND WENJING LI

In 1984, the director of the Fiscal Affairs Department of the International Monetary Fund wrote that "cross-section comparisons of tax structures, like the analysis of taxable capacity and tax effort, have some value in appraising a tax system, but it is doubtful whether they can predict the evolution of systems" (Goode 1984, 100). The more complete story that is called for in this study is an analysis of what is happening at the country level, including the extent to which the legal base is fully taxed, whether properties are adequately valued and revalued for tax purposes, and if the tax administration machinery is doing its cadastre management job adequately. This chapter takes up an analysis of the property tax structures that European countries have put in place. It draws heavily from the country studies in part 2.

The Property Tax Structure in Europe

European countries tax all three of the most frequently used bases (capital value, rental value, and area), and several make use of more than one property tax regime in their system. They give similar exemption and relief packages, but they structure their tax rates and value their properties in very different ways. The similarities and diversities in the tax base are summarized for selected countries in table 4.1.

Recurrent Property Tax Bases

Countries and Legal Jurisdictions (% owner-occupancy rate)	Tax and Tax Base	Number of Different PT Regimes	Vacant Land, Underutilized Property, Second Homes	Intergovernmental Responsibility	Comments
Denmark (48% owner occupied; 20% tenanted)	Land value tax is largest PT; two smaller taxes levied on buildings; land and structures separately assessed	3: LG land tax, LG reimbursement tax on buildings, and CG property value tax on owner-occupied buildings	Developed and undeveloped land is taxed	CG retains tax revenue from property value tax; revenues from the other two PTs go to LG	The 2024 regime includes significant rate and base changes
Estonia (59% of the land is privately owned)	Capital value of land	1: land tax	Developed and undeveloped land is taxed	CG administered; revenues distributed to LG by derivation	Revaluation conducted in 2022
Finland (60% of apartment ownership is in shares of housing companies)	Capital value; land and buildings valued separately	3: land, buildings, and unbuilt building sites	Higher tax rate levied on unbuilt development sites	PT revenue distributed to LG by derivation	Municipal land banking revenues are not treated as budgetary revenues
France (57%; 25% of families own a separate property)	Rental value; residential tax rates applied to 50% of taxable cadastral value; separate business cadastre based on 2017 cadastral value	11 CG PTs equivalent in total to 1.4% of GDP; 14 special-purpose LG and CG PTs	Higher rates charged for second homes and vacant properties; tax base is updated cadastral value	Each CG and LG PT has a designated form of revenue sharing	PT levied on owner

(continued)

Table 4.1 Recurrent Property Tax Bases (*continued*)

Countries and Legal Jurisdictions (% owner-occupancy rate)	Tax and Tax Base	Number of Different PT Regimes	Vacant Land, Underutilized Property, Second Homes	Intergovernmental Responsibility	Comments
Germany (46.5%)	Rental value basis for the real PT, and capital gains basis for the speculation tax; assessment ratio of 35% for nonagricultural property	2: tax on agriculture, forestry, and other real estate, and speculation tax on capital gains from the sale of real property	The second home tax generates little revenue	All real PT revenues belong to municipal governments; speculation tax is a CG levy	After 2024, German states will tax on different value bases, likely moving from rental values to capital values
Greece	Capital market value of land; capital market value of buildings; separate valuation	2 major CG recurrent PTs: ENFIA and supplementary tax. LGs implement their own PT	Undeveloped land is liable for ENFIA	Tax rates for CG PTs are set by Ministry of Finance; revenue is retained by CG	Discussions around allocating PT revenue to LGs
Ireland	Local PT: capital market value of residential property; commercial rates: market rental value	2: LG residential PT; commercial property liable to commercial rates	3% tax on undeveloped land in urban areas; vacant land tax and derelict site levy	Tax rate for local PT set nationally but LG can change this within limits; commercial rates determined by LGs within central limits; CG administration for both taxes	20% of collections distributed as an equalization fund; tax levied on owner for residential property and on occupier for commercial property

Latvia (82%)	Cadastral (capital) value of land and buildings; land and buildings separately assessed	1: recurrent land and building tax	Majority of properties liable to PT	Revenues belong to LGs	Tax levied on owner
Netherlands (60%)	Capital market value	Municipalities and water management (polder) boards each levy PT	No difference between general PT rate and base	PT revenues fully retained by the LGs; equalization grant to municipalities based on assessed valuation covers 70 percent of LG budget	Tax levied on owner; PT regime very transparent
Poland (48% of population lives in urban LGs)	Physical area of land and usable area of buildings; value of business property; cadastral value	3: agriculture, forestry, and built-up sectors	Vacancy tax under consideration	LG revenues	Tax levied on owner
Russia	Asset tax: book value and cadastral value of assets earning rents; natural person's PT: cadastral value of buildings	3: enterprise asset tax, natural person's PT, and land tax	Land tax rate doubled for unused land or unauthorized use	LG revenues	Tax levied on owner
Slovenia (80%)	Area-based PT	2: PT and charge for use of building land	Vacant business property and second homes taxed at a higher rate	PT revenue belongs to LG	Court ruled PT law unconstitutional, mandated return to area-based system in 2013

(*continued*)

Table 4.1 Recurrent Property Tax Bases (*continued*)

Countries and Legal Jurisdictions (% owner-occupancy rate)	Tax and Tax Base	Number of Different PT Regimes	Vacant Land, Underutilized Property, Second Homes	Intergovernmental Responsibility	Comments
Spain (79%)	Cadastral value of property; separate assessment for land and buildings; LG VAT	2: annual PT and LG VAT		Municipal government revenue	Tax levied on owner
United Kingdom: England, Wales, Scotland, and Northern Ireland	Capital value (residential); rental value (business); tax bands set at the regional level	2: residential (council tax) and business (nondomestic rates)	Different treatment in NI and GB	Residential (council) tax is LG revenue source; business (nondomestic) rates are CG taxes distributed among LGs on a formula basis	Council tax levied under a value banding structure except in NI, where it is based on individual property values
England (64%)	Capital value band set by CG and 1991 values; rental values for business tax set by CG	2: residential (council tax) and business property (nondomestic rates)	No rating liability applied to bare development land, derelict property, and agricultural property	Council tax revenues are LG; a formula distributes nondomestic revenues (commercial) among LGs	Tax levied on occupier for business property, normally on owner for residential

Wales	Capital value bands set by regional government based on 2003 values	2: residential (council tax) and business property (non-domestic rates)	No rating liability applied to bare development land, derelict property, and agricultural land	Council tax revenues are LG; a formula distributes non-domestic revenues (commercial) among LGs	Tax levied on occupier for business property, normally on owner for residential
Scotland	Capital value bands, same as England	2: residential (council tax) and business property (non-domestic rates)	No rating liability applied to bare development land, derelict property, and agricultural land	n.a.	Tax levied on occupier for business property, normally on owner for residential
Northern Ireland	Capital values for individual residential properties, based on 2005 values; annual rental value for commercial property	2: domestic and nondomestic rates	Full rating of vacant business properties after three-month exemption; agricultural land is exempt	Property tax revenues are divided among regional and LGs	Tax levied on owner of residential property, on occupier of commercial property

Sources: Part 2 country studies.

Note: CG = central government; LG = local government; n.a. = not available; PT = property tax.

What Is Taxed?

European countries have made different choices about what will be taxed (and, as important, what will not be taxed). Some tax both land and structures, others focus their property tax more on land (Estonia and Denmark), and yet others require separate assessment of land and structures (Finland, Greece, Latvia, Russia, and Spain), as if to set the stage for taxing land at a higher rate than buildings (which theory suggests is a better practice [Vickrey 1999]). In fact, most countries using a split-rate system tax land at a higher rate than buildings, Russia being an exception.[1] Differentiation by sector is also used for taxing businesses versus residences in many countries (including the United Kingdom, Ireland, Denmark, the Netherlands, and Russia), and almost all have a separate regime for imposing lower taxes on agriculture and forestry. "The property tax in Europe" can mean a lot of things.

Value-Based Systems

Most European countries charge the tax rate against the value of property rather than against its physical area. Value-based taxes better reflect the ability of taxpayers to bear the tax burden; are more sensitive to the level of economic development of the local government; can be more effectively used as a tool to reduce the volatility of house prices; are less distortionary and more fair than area-based taxes (Norregaard 2013); and are also used as a base for capital gains taxes, inheritance taxes, and transaction taxes, which leads to economies of scope for tax administration departments.

Some countries make annual assessments of value based on market conditions, and a few countries make heavy use of mass appraisal to regularly update the cadastre (the Netherlands and Denmark are examples of such good practice). Some take a less modern approach that relies on a combination of formulas and expert judgment to determine values at specified intervals, and others do not revalue residential properties at all but simply index, or uplift, the existing taxable property values or levy the tax directly on assessed values from an earlier period (France, Germany, Greece, the United Kingdom, and Finland).

The path of least political resistance seems to be to postpone revaluations and keep the value of tax bases "high enough" with various forms of uplift. While postponing regular revaluations avoids short-run controversy and adjustments, it makes the tax shock greater when it finally does come. It also results in growing assessment inequities in the interim between revaluations. The last general revaluation of residential properties in France was in 1970, and before the reform, in Germany it was 1964 (former West Germany) and 1935 (former East Germany). The uplift approach used by France has, however, led to the highest level of property tax revenue in Europe (see table 2.1). Two jurisdictions in Great Britain have not revalued the residential tax base since 1991. However, the residential property tax generates significant revenue.

Area-Based Systems

Area-based systems directly tax the size of the land plots and the area of structures and do not directly tax property values. In the countries studied in part 2, only Poland and Slovenia use an area-based system.[2] In its purest form, this is a flawed approach to property taxation. It mostly ignores the ability to pay in assessing tax liability and may lead to a regressive structure in the distribution of tax burdens. It does not take account of differential land values in different local-government areas resulting from more productive public investments and different natural endowments. Finally, automatic growth in the tax base is limited, and tax rates (or tax charges) must be changed frequently to raise adequate revenues.

Property tax policy in Poland and Slovenia attempts to address these concerns. Value is indirectly taken into account with annual tax charges (implicit tax rates) that vary by location, land use, and size and condition of the structure. General property tax revenues in Poland have been maintained at a level above the European average, largely by increasing these rates of charge. Taxpayers have rejected moving to a value-based system, mostly because they feel their property tax bills would increase. In Slovenia, the approach to revenue protection has been to weight the area base according to desirability of the neighborhood and the size and amenities of the building. Both of these factors reflect value. Popular opinion and the Constitutional Court have held off the move to a value-based system.

Preferential Treatments and Exemptions

All countries narrow the base of their property tax with exclusions, exemptions, and preferential treatments. The package of exemptions from property tax liability almost always includes properties used for government purposes, places of worship, charities, embassies, and the like. Rarely are these exemptions challenged, or even properly assessed, but they do make a claim on potential property tax revenues. Especially in capital cities, where government buildings and nonprofits can take up prime space (and use government services), these might impose a significant burden.

Other, more targeted relief from taxes on land and buildings is given with exemptions from taxation, reduced tax rates, or assessment preferences.

The summary in table 4.2 describes property tax relief in the 14 countries of part 2 and indicates the practice in Europe. Three categories of preferential property tax relief show up in this review.

The first is property tax relief for families with special needs or with a limited ability to pay, such as low-income families, people with disabilities, the elderly poor, and those living in social housing. This may take the form of outright exemption of properties below a specified (threshold) value, and sometimes (if means testing is possible) low-income families receive preferential low tax rates. France goes a step further by capping total property tax liability at 50 percent of total household income. In some countries (Latvia and Slovenia), discounts on property tax burdens reflect family size. In the United Kingdom, nearly 30 discounts and exemptions are status related—disability, mental health, and occupation by students are some examples. The council tax reduction, which is an income-related benefit amounting to some £5 billion annually, is funded through the tax base. The reduction is effectively a discount given to council taxpayers who live alone in the property.

The second category targets specific activities, either to correct an externality, address an emergency situation, or relieve a certain class of taxpayers. Property tax reductions to reward energy-efficient land use, penalties to encourage development of vacant or dilapidated properties, payment deferrals to address liquidity concerns, lower tax rates for environmentally protected properties, and tax limits to provide general relief are all used in Europe.

Finally, more controversial measures are promoted by special interest groups and often smack of vote seeking. This category includes property tax relief for higher-income families and particularly for residential owner-occupiers. The instruments for this relief include rate ceilings, assessment limits, differentially lower tax rates on certain types of property, and income tax reductions based on property ownership.

Most of the countries surveyed in part 2 do not fully report the revenue cost of their exemption and property tax preference package.[3] Best practice would be the annual publication of property tax expenditure reports. Ideally, countries would regularly review their detailed preferential treatment list to enable public evaluation that might lead to pruning those no longer needed.[4] Otherwise, preferential treatments, once established, can continue for long periods and escape careful reevaluation.

Statutory Tax Rates

The primary role of tax rate setting is to ensure that adequate property tax revenues are raised to support the local-government budget. It also

Country	Special Exemptions	Pro-poor PT Relief	Selected Other Relief	Assessment Biases	Estimated Revenue Costs of Relief
Denmark	Lower rates for retired and for some owner-occupiers; capital gains from owner-occupied housing	n.a.	Since 2003, limits have been placed on the total amount of land taxes paid	Land assessments suspended 2002–2024	n.a.
Estonia	Most residential land; all buildings; growing forests	Pensioners	Reduced tax rate in environment-protected areas	Land tax exemption for most homeowners since 2012	Annual cost of home-owner relief equivalent to about 30% of annual PT revenues
Finland	Churches and non-profits are subject to PT	Adverse personal circumstances; €10 floor for tax payment in 2022	Agricultural land and forestland	Buildings have a lower legal assessment ratio than land	Low floor payment exemption cost €122,000 in 2021, covered only 1.2% of taxpayers
France	n.a.	Social housing; certain elderly and low-income families; PT may not exceed 50% of total household income	New construction exemptions for 2–5 years depending on energy efficiency; offices converted to dwellings can receive exemptions for 5 years	Rebates on cadastral value to develop special economic areas; 30% reduction in tax base for industrial projects to save energy	n.a.

(*continued*)

Table 4.2 Property Tax Relief (*continued*)

Country	Special Exemptions	Pro-poor PT Relief	Selected Other Relief	Assessment Biases	Estimated Revenue Costs of Relief
Germany	n.a.	n.a.	n.a.	Agriculture and forestry assessed at 60%, tax on other real estate at 35%.	n.a.
Greece	Exemptions for religious and charitable properties, cultural and historic buildings, government property	Relief for large families (more than 3 children), disabled persons, low-income households	Agricultural land and buildings	Assessment based on zone value with application of several coefficients	n.a.
Ireland	Exemptions limited mostly to government property	Municipalities can grant up to 90% relief to disabled or poor persons	Agricultural land and buildings; development sites	n.a.	n.a.
Latvia	Property used by government or for religious and charitable uses; historic buildings	Municipalities can grant up to 90% relief to disabled or poor persons	Discounts for families with more than 3 children; Exemptions for certain agricultural and forestry land	Assessment ratio of 50% in Riga	n.a.
Netherlands	Can choose not to levy a PT; can set rates for residential and non-residential property	No low-income exemptions, but special program for relief	Agricultural properties; other relief can be granted upon application	n.a.	Polder boards do not receive transfer from CG

Poland	n.a.	Relief for disabled person, low-income persons	LGs can give discretionary relief for economic development	n.a.	n.a.
Russia	Enterprise assets tax: designated sectoral activities; land parcels	Land tax: deduct 600 m^2 for socially vulnerable people; natural person's PT	Discounts for families with more than 3 children	Land and natural persons' property tax base includes all property owned in the jurisdiction	0.2% of GDP for all 3 PTs
Slovenia	Property tax on residential buildings: 160 m^2; land is exempt; charge for building land: 5-year exemption for new construction	Charge for use of building land: partial or full exemption for low-income families	Lower rates for more than 3 persons in a household; temporary exemption of new or newly renovated properties	Higher tax charges for larger, better quality, newer properties	System awards points for characteristic; municipalities determine the points awarded and the value of a point
Spain	n.a.	Low-valued properties are exempt; less than 1% of private properties are exempt	PT reduced by 50%–90% for construction or refurbishing; other relief for public housing, energy-efficient housing, energy-efficient installations	n.a.	n.a.
United Kingdom	Varies by region within Great Britain	Varies by region within Great Britain	Agricultural land and buildings	n.a.	In 2022: England £10.5 billion, Scotland £1.4 billion, Wales £387 million

(*continued*)

Table 4.2 Property Tax Relief (*continued*)

Country	Special Exemptions	Pro-poor PT Relief	Selected Other Relief	Assessment Biases	Estimated Revenue Costs of Relief
England	25% single-occupancy discount	Charitable and hardship relief; rural properties	Small business, empty buildings	Upward transitional relief from revaluation	n.a.
Wales	25% single-occupancy discount	Charitable and hardship relief	Small business, empty buildings, special relief to other sectors	Upward transitional relief from revaluation	n.a.
Scotland	25% single-occupancy discount	Charitable and hardship relief	Small business, empty buildings, newly occupied buildings	Upward transitional relief from revaluation	n.a.
Northern Ireland	Various industrial property entitled to 75% exemption; historic buildings	Agricultural land and buildings	Commercial property entitled to 3-month exemption if vacant	Value cap of £400,000 for residential property	n.a.

Sources: Part 2 country studies.

Note: Exemptions given in most countries are not listed in this table. CG = central government; LG = local government; n.a. = not available; PT = property tax.

helps implement national and local objectives such as limiting property tax burdens, taxing higher-income household families appropriately, controlling sectoral differences in property tax burdens, reinforcing land use planning, and guarding against a race to the bottom by local governments. Table 4.3 summarizes the considerable variation in European practice.

The best approach in a fiscally decentralized democracy, where hard budget constraints are obeyed by local governments, is to leave rate setting of local property taxes in the hands of local voters and the officials they elect. Tax rates are transparent enough to allow for downward accountability to voters, and the net result of a well-structured decentralization strategy could be a better package of local public services. But setting local-government property tax rates can be an explosive political issue, budget constraints on local governments are not always hard, and voters are not very forgiving about increased property tax rates.

There are two major issues to consider in developing a tax rate policy. One is to set the property tax rate against the value of the property and not to use it as a substitute for proper valuation. Such practices lead to significant and unwanted distortions, as are seen in France, Germany, and the United Kingdom. While tax rates are important for achieving national and local objectives for the tax system, they are not always the best instrument. For example, rather than imposing differential tax rates on residential and commercial property, assessing both at full market value could be a fairer and more economically efficient approach. And while progressive property tax rate structures might improve the vertical equity of the property tax, good revaluations might better accomplish that.

The other major question is whether local governments have adequate discretion to adjust property tax rates within centrally set ceilings. If they do not, imposing fiscal discipline and a hard budget constraint on them may not be possible. Some countries fix their rate ceilings by law. France, for example, imposes a complicated set of rate restrictions, including a parity requirement in rate increases for residential and business properties.[5] The Netherlands comes closest to the full local autonomy model by leaving the determination of rate levels to the local authority. Many central governments in Europe have placed limits on the increases (and floors) that local governments can impose.

Which Is the Best Property Tax Structure?

In theory, any of the three basic choices for a property tax base—capital value, rental value, or area—could produce adequate revenue if backed up

Table 4.3 Statutory Property Tax Rates

Country	Rate Setter	Degree of Rate Discretion for LGs	Differences in Rate Structures Among Sectors	Tax Rate Levels	Preferential Tax Rates
Denmark	Land tax rate and reimbursement duty rate by LG within limits; property value tax rate by CG	Very little; tax rate increases suspended 2002–2024; assessments frozen at 2011 levels	Lower rates for agricultural and forestry land; land value tax levied on commercial but not residential buildings	Average land tax rate in 2021 was 2.6% of taxable value; reimbursement tax rate between 0 and 1% of value of commercial buildings	Retirees, owners of property since 1988 pay a lower rate of land value tax
Estonia	LGs within a national ceiling and floor	Limited	Owner-occupiers have lower effective PT rates.	In 2024 rates will vary from 0.1% to 1%	Revaluation protection measures include maximum tax rate of 0.5% and cap on growth in annual tax of 10%
Finland	LGs within national ceilings	Limited	General rate for most land; rates on buildings depend on use of the property	General rate ranges between 0.93% and 2.00%	Permanent residences, nonprofit organizations
France	LGs within a national ceiling of 56%; rate ceilings limit rate increases and residential/business differences	Rate limitations are complicated	Rate preferences for industrial property	Vary widely depending on the tax	n.a.

Germany	Municipal governments set real estate tax rates; speculation tax rate is national income tax rate	No limits on real estate tax rate	Yet to be determined following the national reforms	910% to 1,050%	Numerous loopholes to avoid speculation tax
Greece	CG	Complete, subject to the law	Limited	Based on the zonal values	Preferential treatment for specific sectors
Ireland	Local PT rates by LGs within central ceiling; commercial rate percentages by local authority	Modest: LG PT rate bands set by CG: local adjustment factor allows 15% annual local rate change; commercial rates set by LGs	Separate rate structures for residential and commercial properties	LG PT has progressive tax rates, 0.1029% to 0.3000%.	None
Latvia	CG	Minimal	No	0.2%–3.0%	None
Netherlands	Municipal and polder boards	Significant discretion for LGs	Residential rates lower than commercial rates	Low rate levels; little difference among municipalities	30% of renter housing is social, with rent-price controls
Poland	LGs within national ceilings	Eight large cities at the maximum rates; smaller municipalities have more fiscal room	Rates may vary according to location land use and technical condition and size of buildings	Ceilings determined annually by Ministry of Finance; 2022 rates were US$5.50 for buildings and US$0.20 for land	De minimis aid for various purposes
Russia	Regional governments and LGs within federal government limits	Not all LGs tax at maximum rate; discretion very limited for land tax	Only nonresidential property pays asset tax; preferential tax treatment of residential land	1.5% for land tax; natural person's PT: 0.1% for residential, 2% for commercial; asset tax rates vary, 2.0%–2.2%	Increases in land tax liability capped at 10%

(continued)

Table 4.3 Statutory Property Tax Rates (*continued*)

Country	Rate Setter	Degree of Rate Discretion for LGs	Differences in Rate Structures Among Sectors	Tax Rate Levels	Preferential Tax Rates
Slovenia	Tax rates (charges) set by LGs	Significant	Businesses pay a higher effective rate than residential properties	Each municipality determines rates and bases	Local authorities have some discretion
Spain	Municipal government within legal limits for PT	Limited discretion	Rates depend on size of municipality and rural-urban classification	Set by municipalities between 0.4% and 1.3% of cadastral value	Minimum rate of 0.1% urban and 0.75% for eligible properties
United Kingdom (Great Britain)	LGs set council rates within limits; business rates set by CG and regional governments	No discretion for business rates; full discretion on council tax for residential property	Rates vary between residential and commercial, and among LGs	Nondomestic rates higher than residential rates	Local authorities have some discretion
Northern Ireland	District rates set by regional government, local rates by LG; nondomestic rates determined similarly	Full discretion on tax rates	Residential property taxed on average at 1% of capital value; commercial property on average at 56% of annual rental value in 2024–2025	Dwellings with a capital value over £400,000 are assumed to have a value of £400,000, and all properties with a capital value below £20,000 are excluded	None

Source: Authors' compilation based on part 2 case studies.

Note: CG = central government; LG = local government; n.a. = not applicable; PT = property tax.

by appropriate policies, good administration, and taxpayer willingness to comply. Revenue mobilization potential depends on how the tax is structured, but it also depends on which tax base can be valued in a reasonably accurate way and, perhaps even more, on taxpayer acceptance.

Capital values are the most-used basis for recurrent taxes on immovable property in European countries. A capital value basis works best when real estate markets are sufficiently well developed, because capital values are commonly estimated using data on recent property transactions (Almy 2014; Slack and Bird 2014).

An area-based property tax structure is probably a better fit for a low-income country without a well-developed property market than for a high-income country. Rental value systems can and do work very well, as in the commercial tax performance in Ireland and Great Britain. However, the availability of accurate and complete data on market rents can constrain good assessment. Moreover, smaller properties tend to have a relatively higher rent-price ratio than large-area properties and to have a regressive bias (Kelly, White, and Anand 2020; Walters 2011).

Once in place, the property tax base tends to have staying power, mostly because of the high costs of transitioning to another base (Radvan et al. 2021). Adopting a new regime puts taxpayers and governments alike on a learning curve, and both sides tend to resist big changes. And, as learned long ago, taxpayers, liking certainty in their taxes, resist new approaches (often because they are new). Poland, for example, has resisted pressure to move away from its area-based system, even though the arguments for change (at least in the eyes of many advisors) seem to be overwhelming.[6] The same was true in Russia, which gave up attempts to consolidate a fragmented system of property taxation in 2014 after many years of trying. Similarly, Slovenia's reform of the existing area-based system has been stalled for many years because of political inertia and by a ruling of the Constitutional Court (Žibrik and Humar 2021). And Estonia proposed in 1991 a land tax with the intention to migrate to a capital value system when the property market matured, but this did not materialize (Youngman and Malme 2008).

Big changes in the property tax base do happen, however. An existing property tax system can get so far out of line with what is acceptable that only a new tax structure will satisfy voters. There are good examples of such a shift in the basis of the property tax in Europe. England, Scotland, and Wales historically assessed annual rental value on each residential property. This was replaced by the community charge in 1989 (Scotland) and 1990 (England and Wales), which in turn was replaced by a capital value basis (the council tax) in 1993 (using value bands). Northern

Ireland, similarly, introduced a discrete capital value basis for residential property in 2007, replacing annual rental value (Gloudemans and Montgomery 2008). A main argument for the shift in Northern Ireland was the absence of sufficient data on open market rents. This, in conjunction with a high rate of owner occupation and ample transaction prices, supported the rationale for adopting discrete capital value assessments. There are other examples. The housing tax in France was phased out. Denmark's property tax was frozen over valuation problems, and Slovenia's migration to a value-based tax was put on the shelf by a constitutional court ruling. And perhaps most notable of all, Germany's property tax is now undergoing a national overhaul ordered by the courts.

Tweaks and nudges also change the property tax structure over the years (Bahl and Bird 2018). Among the many examples of this are mandated revisions of the assessment methods (Denmark and Russia) and automated tax payments. The point here is that today's property tax bases in Europe are as likely to have evolved as to have been fully restructured; and in meeting the new challenges, capital, rental, and area systems have borrowed from each other's approach. Almost all countries use capitalization rates to convert between rental and capital values,[7] and all countries use physical area as part of their formulas for valuing properties.[8] The result of such practices is that the distinctions between a capital value base, a rental value base, and an area base get more and more blurred.[9]

Policy Impacts

The most-watched impacts of property taxation are revenue mobilization, which provides a flow of funds that finances local public services, and the division of tax burdens between higher- and lower-income families and between residential and business taxpayers. Property tax policies also contribute directly to several other public policy issues, such as land use planning, housing supply, and local government service provision. The interventions are not always successful, but for a tax that imposes so little revenue cost, some of the criticisms seem outsized.

The impacts of property taxation are shaped by the economic setting in which it operates, the structure of the tax itself, and the policies countries implement to address these impacts. In the first two decades of the 21st century, European countries have dealt with recession, debt adjustment, and COVID-19. During this period, wealth accumulation has continued to favor those in higher tax brackets. At the same time, the unpopularity of the property tax seems as entrenched as ever, and countries have responded with measures that may have further slowed the natural growth in property tax revenues.

Revenue Mobilization

Three observations summarize property tax revenue mobilization in Europe. First, the general property tax is not a major component of revenues, averaging only about 1 percent of gross domestic product (GDP), with only a few countries raising the equivalent of more than 2 percent of GDP (European Commission 2023). Yet, as discussed in chapter 2, it is an important tax.

Second, individual country performance has varied from country to country since the 1990s. For many, revenue growth has kept pace with GDP, indicating that it can be a productive revenue source. But for several countries, property tax revenues have not kept up, because needed revaluations have not happened and because other revenue sources have crowded out local-government property taxes. In yet others, revenue performance has been maintained (or even increased), but with the use of uplifts and other reform measures that may not be in step with good practice (box 4.1). The findings here suggest that the buoyancy of the property tax is less than that of income and consumption taxes.

Third, the constraints to reaching higher levels of revenues are formidable but not insurmountable. The major hurdles appear to have more to do with the unwillingness to tax real property than with the capacity to do so. Also, flaws in the tax policy and management choices made in some countries have resulted in instruments chosen for property tax reform pushing out others that could have led to higher rates of revenue mobilization. At the top of this list is the failure to revalue property. A path to increased property tax revenue mobilization is open, but it will not be an easy political path in most European countries. Once policies become entrenched—for example, bypassing revaluation, they are not easily dislodged no matter their undesirable impacts.

Equity and Fairness

Fairness is a maxim for good taxation that everyone can agree with. Vertical equity has to do with the way in which property tax burdens are distributed among families at different income levels. The principal concern in most countries is whether the property tax is regressive. Horizontal equity has to do with whether similarly situated properties are treated the same by the property tax. But getting from the agreement about fairness to a set of laws that determine vertical and horizontal equity is no easy trip.

Box 4.1 Indexing and Uplifts to Valuations

Several countries in Europe have postponed revaluations, instead stimulating revenue collections with various types of indexing to increase the property tax base. The countries that use these uplifts structure them differently. These differences have to do with whether they are the same for all local governments, based on a national index such as inflation, and determined by a national body or a local body. In each case, the uplift factor modifies the local-government proposed tax rate. The following table describes some of the indexes used in France, Germany, Great Britain, and Finland.

Country Uplifts to Valuation

Country	Uplift Factor	Comment
Finland	National index, such as inflation	Applied to all local governments
France	Index of national growth; uplifts based on 1980 valuations	The first is voted annually by national Parliament and is an inflation indicator; the second is determined for each department
Germany (formerly)	Multiplier based on size and location of the property	Determined by each municipal government
Great Britain	Tax rate set annually on the basis of the published rate of inflation	Applied only to commercial property and set nationally for each jurisdiction

Vertical Equity

To the extent the property tax is levied on land, it will have a progressive element. But most European countries also tax residential and nonresidential structures. Property tax structures may vary widely, but it is the rare country that escapes the charge that its system is regressive.

In a few countries there is hard evidence that lower-income households pay a higher effective rate—for example, in Denmark. In many countries, the evidence is more based on general observations about features of the property tax structure, such as that assessment is subjective and favors more valuable homes, exemption levels are too low, tax rate structures are not progressive, and businesses do not pay their share. Taxpayers are vocal about their share of the burden and feel that they know the property tax well because they pay it directly. Optics matter.

The public finance research literature is not in full agreement about how the burden of the property tax is shifted to owners or users—that is, whether it is a tax on consumption or a tax on capital (Bahl and Bird 2018, chap. 6). Some even see it as a benefit tax, because households may benefit from local public services in proportion to the amount of property tax that they pay.[10] Much of the reform discussion centers on whether particular elements of the property tax regime place an unduly heavy burden on low-income families or, conversely, too light a burden on high-income families.[11] The bigger question, which often remains unanswered, is whether the burden of the property tax in total is measurably different for higher-income families compared to low-income families.[12]

European countries actively address the distribution of tax burdens. They use tax instruments that are commonly introduced to improve vertical equity, including progressive rate structures, exemptions and surtaxes, low-value thresholds, and targeted tax relief. Table 4.4 summarizes these. Whether their net impact has made much difference in the distribution of tax burdens remains unclear. However, of the 14 country studies in part 2 of this book, four authors concluded that the property tax was regressive, two that it was progressive, and eight saw it as neutral or did not offer a conclusion.

What to do? Every country is different in terms of their problems with property tax equity, and reforms must be country specific. However, on the basis of past research and the experiences of the 14 country studies taken up here, five general reform approaches might be taken to address the vertical equity of property taxes in Europe.

- Tax land at a higher tax rate than buildings (Netzer 1998; Vickrey 1999). Because land is immobile and its ownership is concentrated in higher-income families, this policy could have a progressive effect on the distribution of tax burdens. But local practice can confound such policy reforms. Denmark and Estonia get different results from levying a land tax: Denmark's land tax is progressive, but Estonia's is regressive mostly because higher-income municipalities impose a lower tax rate on land. Another important concern is that higher statutory rates do not sit well with landowners. Other country-specific factors could limit the progressive effect of land taxes—for example, the high concentration of low-income homeowners in Spain, tax exempt land in Estonia, and the difficult business of accurately assessing land values independent of buildings (Franzsen 2009).
- Introduce a progressive property tax rate structure, as Denmark, the United Kingdom, Ireland, and Slovenia have done. The success of

Table 4.4 Property Tax Policies That Affect Tax Burden Distribution

Country	Tax Base Coverage	Tax Rate Structure	Valuation and Assessment Practices	Exemptions and Tax Preferences	Conclusions from Part 2 Studies
Denmark	37% of PT revenue is collected from land tax	Progressive, between 1.4% and 3.6%	Suspended since 2011, leading to undervaluation and inequities in valuation	Ceiling on tax rates including land tax	2019 CG report finds a progressive distribution of PT burdens
Estonia	Tax base is mostly on land, but land under owner-occupied homes is mostly exempt	Low tax rates, 0.1%–1.0%	Only 75% of transaction values covered, including a smaller percentage of commercial than residential properties	Pensioners, most buildings, lower rates on owner-occupiers; tax increase limits	Highly regressive land tax because annual tax bill increase limited to 10%, and wealthy municipalities use lower tax rates
Finland	Broad tax base coverage	Tax rate limits set by CG; minimum tax of €10 in 2021	CG assessment but assessment rates are low	Active municipal land banking program	Regressive because LGs with higher incomes set lower rates
France	Outdated valuations, rental values; taxed base about 20% of rental values	LG determines rates subject to national ceilings; higher rates for second houses and vacant homes	Periodic uplifts based on CG indexing	Social housing; low-income and senior relief; PT cap of 50% of total household income; new construction	Regressive; effective tax rate falls from 1.7% in the 2nd decile to 0.4% in the 9th; computations exclude national wealth tax

Germany	Very outdated valuations; national reforms being rolled out	Less than 1% of municipalities have population greater than 100,000	Complicated valuation method is being revised	Different multipliers uplift different types of properties	Each state can develop a valuation methodology
Greece	Significant issues around the coverage; many properties are outside the value zones	Limited discretion of LGs in setting tax rates	Private sector valuers extensively used to improve valuations	Standard exemptions applied	Considerable work has been done to improve the quality of valuations
Ireland	Tax base coverage is comprehensive for both residential and commercial property	Progressive tax rate on residential property; LGs have some discretion in setting tax rate	Owners self-declare their residential property value; rolling revaluation program for commercial property	Internationally recognized standard exemptions tend to apply	Revaluation of commercial property is progressing but slowly, county by county
Latvia	Good tax base coverage	Limited tax rate discretion for LGs	Centralized valuation	Internationally recognized standard exemptions tend to apply	Quality of some property sector valuations is lower due to lack of data
Netherlands	Broad coverage of base	Tax rates are low and similar across LGs	Equalization grant to municipalities based on assessed valuation	No exemption for low-valued property; high percentage of social housing, rent controls	Progressive at lower end of income distribution, proportional thereafter
Poland	Broad tax base coverage	Area-based tax rates per square meter	Only businesses use an assessment of value	Internationally recognized standard exemptions tend to apply	A value-based PT being discussed

(*continued*)

Table 4.4 Property Tax Policies That Affect Tax Burden Distribution (*continued*)

Country	Tax Base Coverage	Tax Rate Structure	Valuation and Assessment Practices	Exemptions and Tax Preferences	Conclusions from Part 2 Studies
Russia	Considered to have broad tax base coverage	Local discretion of the tax rates	Value-based methodology	Internationally recognized standard exemptions tend to apply	Considerable investment in valuation methodologies
Slovenia	Area of land and buildings; self-reported area with little monitoring	Liberal LG discretion; progressive depending on land use	In a point system, valuations vary by location and amenities	10-year exemption for certain new construction	Not estimated because the 212 underlying municipalities have different practices and different rate/base structures
Spain	Broad tax base using cadastral records	Local discretion	Cadastral value is an estimate of market value, but cadastral values infrequently updated	Standard exemptions apply to religious and charitable uses	Updating of the assessed values is a challenge
United Kingdom	Comprehensive tax base coverage	LGs can set council tax for residential property; national uniform business rate for commercial property	Valuations for both residential and commercial property undertaken by central Valuation Office	Standard exemptions apply to religious and charitable uses; relief for recreational uses; discounts for single occupier of a residential dwelling	Regressive nature of the council tax built into the banding system; lack of revaluations of residential property in Great Britain

Source: Authors.

Note: CG = central government; LG = local government; PT = property tax.

this approach depends a great deal on the tax structure design, such as bracket widths, thresholds, and steepness of the rate graduation. An alternative to a progressive rate structure is a separate tax on real property net wealth, as is done in France and Spain. Yet another approach is to impose a higher tax rate on luxury property ownership, but Slovenia and some French cities have found this not to be very revenue productive.

- Reconsider the differential property tax rate on businesses than on residences. This strategy, followed in many countries in Europe, does not necessarily lead to a more progressive distribution of property tax burdens. The burden of the business property tax on land will fall on owners of businesses that are not mobile and that sell in local markets. The tax on structures might be shifted to consumers, renters, labor, and owners, depending on elasticities of demand and supply. The tax burden for businesses that sell in national markets might be exported. It is probably not clear to most governments who actually pays the property tax.

  In practice, however, most of the 14 countries studied in part 2 tax business property at a higher rate than residential property. In the case of the United Kingdom, it is much higher. This differential tax treatment of businesses is based on impressionistic evidence that businesses are more able to shift the property tax burden than are equally situated residential owners. This is not necessarily the case. A more realistic explanation of the heavier tax on business property is that it is an easy base to identify and that it can keep pressure off the more politically sensitive residential tax base. Moreover, there is a horizontal inequity when the case of online retailers is considered. In short, the vertical equity gains often attributed to taxing business at a higher rate may be overstated.

  What is the right direction for reform? Mirrlees's (2010) proposal to treat real property as an input is likely a nonstarter for local governments. Linking tax payments to benefits received is too complicated and too subjective, though a higher tax rate on business land might be justified.

- Give special exemptions and preferential treatment to lower-income families (or families living in low-valued structures). Almost all countries do this. The most common approaches are establishing property value thresholds below which no tax is levied, giving preferential assessments or tax rates to targeted properties or persons, and providing specific exemptions (see table 4.4). The problem with this policy is that it can be administratively costly, must be periodically reviewed, and carries no guarantee that it will provide relief to poor families.

- Valuation practices can affect the distribution of tax burdens. Dated valuation rolls in countries like France and Germany where property values have grown rapidly in recent years can burden owners whose property values have grown slowest since the last general valuation. If these are lower-income homeowners, the result can be regressive. There is also a concern that valuation may bring a bias against rented versus owner-occupied housing, also leading to a regressive effect (McMillen and Singh 2020).

The thrust of this discussion is that some countries take many policy steps to make their property tax systems less regressive (or perhaps better said, to make their property tax appear less regressive). Precise measurement of their impacts is difficult. Thus, we can pronounce no conclusion and only say that the vertical equity of taxes on land and property probably varies from country to country depending to a great extent on the specifics of how each does property taxation.

Horizontal Equity

The other dimension of fairness in taxation, horizontal inequity, may result from conscious decisions by government to tax property in one sector of the economy or population more heavily than in others. This might be done to discourage certain activities, for income distribution reasons, to simplify administration, to increase revenues, or for political reasons. It also can be the result of property tax policy led by politicians and well-meaning social engineers who champion reforms to favor their special interests (McCluskey, Bahl, and Franzsen 2022).

In one example, several countries in Europe have bypassed general revaluations and increased the property tax base with indexing and rate increases. This led to a significant weakening of the horizontal equity of the property tax in that similarly situated properties are treated differentially without good justification. Another example is that some countries dramatically underassess properties, which leads to pronounced differences in the assessment rate among regions that do not reflect differences in public service levels. In Finland, for example, assessment ratios for housing companies have ranged between 20 and 50 percent, resulting in variations in effective property tax rates from 0.08 to 0.2 percent. Such disparities were observed both within and among municipalities.

Several countries tax business properties at a higher effective rate than residential properties. They do it with higher fractional assessments on business properties, or higher statutory tax rates, or an entirely different tax regime (as is the case of the central-government commercial rates in the United Kingdom and Ireland). To the extent the assumptions that lead to this practice turn out to be incorrect, the result will be a reallocation of resources away from the business sector and away from certain types of business.[13]

Some would argue for a business tax based on benefits received from property taxed public services (roads, utilities, police and fire protection, refuse collection, and the like), but it would be difficult to argue that a uniform tax on business property values matches up with the value of public services received. Moreover, there are variations by types of businesses—for example, local retailers benefit from the location benefits that come from local-government services, but industrial buildings might benefit more from transportation services or water supply.

Arguably, the biggest horizontal equity problem for property taxation comes from the preferential treatment given to owner-occupiers of residential properties. The more important of these tax benefits, depending on the country, are preferential assessments, exemption from capital gains income tax, and the deductibility of mortgage interest.

Finally, the banding approach to valuation in the United Kingdom and Ireland replaces individual assessed values with uniform assessments of all properties within a value band. The practice of taxing all properties in a band at the same level leads to a horizontal inequity for parcels within the band. Banding does not treat similarly situated properties within a band the same, because all properties in a band are not similarly situated. It is largely a question of value: all properties within the same value band have the same tax liability irrespective of property type and location. Properties at the lower end of a band are overtaxed and those at the higher end are undertaxed. Overall, the banding approach is regressive when measured against income, whereas the effective tax rate reduces as the value of property increases.

Fiscal Decentralization

Fiscal decentralization is usually thought of as a policy that has seen most success in higher-income countries (Bahl and Bird 2018). More recently, however, some country-level analyses have seen a tendency toward fiscal centralization in Europe. The following discussion takes up three related issues: the different (and changing) arrangements for fiscal relations between central and local governments in Europe and whether this might compromise property taxation as a good financing fit for local governments; whether there is evidence that the property tax has been crowded out by other sources of local government finance; and whether the concentration of property tax revenue collections in larger European cities could reinforce patterns of fiscal decentralization.

Intergovernmental Fiscal Structure

Even some of the well-developed systems of fiscal decentralization in higher-income countries in Europe have been disrupted by fiscal events in recent years. Finland and the Netherlands are adjusting to cutbacks in their intergovernmental revenues that have put new pressures on their property tax. France and Germany are moving toward property revaluations. France has phased out its main local-government tax on housing. Denmark is ending a long suspension of valuations and rate increases while awaiting the full implementation of a 2024 reform. In 2022, Estonia adopted a new property tax roll after a 20-year hiatus, and Finland continues with indexing a system whose last general valuation was in 1993. Slovenia is still dealing with a court-mandated stoppage on its valuation system. In at least France and Denmark, reforms to address valuation practices have been accompanied by a noticeable trend toward fiscal centralization.

The traditionally centralized United Kingdom has adopted another pattern. It has devolved fiscal and governance powers to Wales, Scotland, Northern Ireland, and more recently, to city regions within England. These devolved governments have fiscal powers, but the fiscal roles and fiscal importance of their local governments vary widely. The German federal system has long provided rate setting autonomy for municipalities, but valuations were done under a uniform national system. Beginning in 2025, however, each of the German federal states has the ability to choose its own valuation approach and property tax structure. How this will affect decentralization remains to be seen.

Despite these changes, the property tax remains a good choice to cover some of the funding gaps in local-government budgets in Europe. It has long been assigned to local governments as a principal revenue source, and central governments have been willing to cede some autonomy in tax structure formulation to local governments.[14] The tax base has been growing in urban areas in response to increasing real estate prices and to new demands for housing and business sites. And it is an attractive tax alternative because it could lead to a more progressive distribution of tax burdens, offer some semblance to a benefit tax, provide for tax increases at the local-government level that can be controlled, and result in tax burdens that fall mostly on those within local-government boundaries (thus limiting intergovernmental conflicts). And it is an alternative to the taxation of labor.

Some European countries are moving toward more local-government autonomy in their revenue systems (OECD 2021). In 2000, local governments in the unitary countries had the ability to set the rates (but not reliefs) for an average of 49 percent of subnational-government tax revenues. By 2018, this share had risen to 68 percent of subnational revenues. Despite this move toward autonomy, however, the effective tax rate of property taxation did not increase in the 2020s by a large percentage (see table 2.2).

The following policy-related factors may have accounted for holding back further increases in property tax revenues in Europe:

- Most national governments in Europe allow local governments to set property tax rates, but usually within a limit, and the limits can be binding. For example, nearly all Norwegian municipalities set their property tax rates at the ceiling level (Borge and Rattsø 2014).
- The property tax is unpopular with voters, and despite its low tax burden and its considerable advantages, political resistance to rate increases and revaluation are strong.
- Equalization grants structured to limit revenue disparities within a country, and those of the Robin Hood type, can dampen local property tax effort (Blöchliger 2015).
- Intergovernmental transfers from higher-level governments and local personal income taxes can crowd out the property tax, and now provide most of the fiscal support for municipal budgets in many European countries.
- Property valuations lag market value growth in many, or maybe most, European countries. Many of the countries covered in part 2 tax on significantly outdated property value rolls, and most do not monitor the accuracy of their assessments.
- National court decisions have not all been friendly to real property valuation regimes (Denmark and Slovenia), and this has contributed to freezes in the value levels. A Constitutional Court decision in Germany, however, led to the phaseout of the long-outdated tax roll.
- Some countries have begun to pull back on fiscal decentralization. For example, starting in the 1990s, Denmark's Parliament reduced local expenditure autonomy and instituted a national tax freeze. After the abolition of the housing tax by Parliament in France in 2017–2018, the financing share of local governments declined dramatically and may not return to previous levels. Estonia has adopted stringent central rules limiting property tax revenue growth during its immediate postrevaluation period.

Crowding Out

Intergovernmental transfers to local governments are often tied to national collection of income or consumption taxes (Bahl and Wallace 2007, 205–250). These have a comparative advantage over property taxes because annual revenues grow faster and more automatically in response to economic growth. This generates an "invisible" increase in taxes, one seemingly more acceptable to voters (Youngman 2016). Local personal income taxes have become a competitor to local property taxes. In the eyes of some voters, intergovernmental transfers and shared personal income tax revenues are a preferred method of financing local-government services because of the illusion that they are "paid by someone else." Local-government personal income taxes have also grown to be an important source of local-government revenues in Finland, Denmark, and the Netherlands.

But reliance on revenue sharing or shared personal income tax bases also has drawbacks for local-government financing (Bahl and Bird 2018). The most important is that the central government may decide to change the structure of the income tax base, which could reduce the revenue flow to the local government or reduce the rate of revenue sharing. Or the central government might decide to reduce the flow of grants to local governments to preserve its own fiscal balance. This appears to have been the case in both Finland and the Netherlands. And most of Europe has a concern about the relatively high tax burden on labor income.

The Property Tax and Large Cities

Macro evidence suggests that property tax revenue mobilization goes hand in hand with urbanization.[15] Large cities and metropolitan areas in some middle- and lower-income countries are responsible for disproportionate shares of total national property taxes raised (Bahl, Linn, and Wetzel 2013; McCluskey and Franzsen 2013). This finding reinforces proposals for giving metro cities more discretion to structure their property tax.

Local governments in large urban areas in Europe are in a good place to move their public financing in the direction of more reliance on property taxes. The quality and value of the capital stock has increased, and a large share of the newly produced capital is likely to have been in urban areas. Moreover, there is heightened interest in Europe in finding alternatives to taxing labor.

The linkages between local-government finance and urban economic development have been studied heavily (Bahl and Linn 1992; Glaeser 2012; Glaeser and Joshi-Ghani 2015). Many larger cities have prospered from adding new roles, including supply chain services and expanding workplaces to support suburban city growth. Agglomeration effects, capturing economies of scale, and the specialization of labor have contributed to productivity increases in the urban areas. Large metropolitan areas also continue to have special appeal to business headquarters and higher-income families. The property tax itself can probably function better in an urban setting. The better level of public services in large cities can make the tax more palatable to voters, sophisticated tax administration and management is more affordable, and urban populations are more able to appreciate the link between property tax payments and the quality of local-government services.

In part 2 of this book, each country study was charged with comparing population and property tax shares in their large cities. The results of this analysis, shown in table 4.5, are mixed.

The proportionate shares of property tax revenues collected in large cities could not be reported for some countries because data were not available in the form needed. In others the computations could be made, and the results are in step with expectations that some urban areas account for a disproportionately large share of the national property tax base or a disproportionately large share of property tax revenues (see table 4.5). Note that Dublin, for example, accounts for 29 percent of Ireland's population but 45 percent of national property tax collections. Tallinn accounts for 34 percent of Estonia's population but 43.7 percent of property tax revenues. The city of Paris is only 3.4 percent of the French population but over 8 percent of the national property tax base. It raises over 4 percent of national property tax revenues even though it has not increased recurrent property tax rates in several years. Moscow and Ljubljana each raise well more than their population shares. These results are due, to varying extents, to a valuable and growing property tax base and to the willingness of urban governments to levy the property tax.

In the other countries, the reported share of property tax raised in large cities was not as impressive. Among the possible explanations for this are a thin property tax base resulting from exemptions and preferential treatments, an intergovernmental system that has crowded out the property tax, a limited assignment of expenditure responsibilities to local governments, and less growth in the value of the tax base. It also may be due to the absence of data to make the correct calculations.

The illustrative calculations for the cities in table 4.5, and interpretations of the results, are limited by the data available. Two issues are of special concern for property tax data for metropolitan areas. First, data on property tax revenue collections are usually available for city governments but not for the amount collected in the city area by overlapping

Table 4.5 Urban Government Finance and Property Taxation, 2021

Country	Cities	% of National Population	% of National GDP	% of National Property Tax Base	% of National General Property Tax Collection
Denmark	Copenhagen (city)	10.8	n.a.	10.2	12.4
	Copenhagen (capital region)	33		41, in 2021	
Estonia	Tallinn	34	51	n.a.	43.7, in 2021
Finland	Helsinki	12.1	35 for the metro area	15.81	12.5
	Next four largest cities	18.14		19.5	18.75
France	Paris (municipality)	3.4	n.a.	8.48	4.39
	Paris (capital city region)	20			
Germany	n.a.	n.a.	n.a.	n.a.	n.a.
Greece	n.a.	n.a.	n.a.	n.a.	n.a.
Ireland	Dublin city	24.7	n.a.	n.a.	35.7
	County Dublin	28.6	47		45.3
Latvia	Riga city	36.5	58	n.a.	31.5
	Riga metropolitan area	63	70		
Netherlands	Amsterdam/Amsterdam Region	5	n.a.	8.6	4.8
Poland	Warsaw	4.8	n.a.	5.2	n.a.
Russia	Moscow	8.7	20	n.a.	16
	St. Petersburg	3.7	7.7		4.0
Slovenia	Ljubljana	14	n.a.	n.a.	25
Spain	n.a.	n.a.	n.a.	n.a.	n.a.
United Kingdom	London	31	n.a.	n.a.	n.a.

Sources: Part 2 country studies.

Note: CG = central government; LG = local government; n.a. = not available; PT = property tax.

regional governments. Moreover, large municipalities may have a different status in some countries than in others. For example, Paris is both a municipal government and a department, so its property tax entitlements may not be comparable to other city governments in France. Second, property tax collections in a central city may not accurately reflect total property tax effort. Some cities often attract a large daytime population of commuter-workers who pay residential property taxes in their home residential communities.

The Property Tax and Markets

The property tax is sometimes used to address market failures, notably housing shortages; deal with subnational land use issues; and make environmental policy corrections. Such interventions may be built directly into the general property tax structure—for example, by charging higher tax rates for land and for underused properties and second homes, and sometimes by adding reliefs or penalties to correct for the results of market failures, such as the failure to address urban sprawl or the construction of energy inefficient buildings. Sometimes these interventions are part of the answer to a broader problem such as a housing shortage. For example, in France, Spain, and Slovenia, property tax reform is used to stimulate housing construction and refurbishment (see table 4.2).

Most countries and local governments do not regularly publish their full inventory of property tax incentive or penalty programs, or the revenue cost of these programs, and more important, some may not regularly review and grade the impacts of these programs. The extent to which these property tax adjustments have succeeded often remains an open question. Casual observation and some research, however, suggests that the use of property taxation for such interventions has expanded in recent years. The brief survey of programs in tables 4.1–4.4 suggests the broad array of property tax measures in place to affect allocation of resources or distribution of income. Some of these—value capture in particular—have significant revenue potential.

Taxing Land

Economists and some social philosophers have famously advocated taxing land, because it is less likely to distort resource allocation than are taxes on income and consumption, and because it seems more fair (George 1879 [1958]; Mill 1848; Ricardo 1817; Vickrey 1999). A land-only approach to property taxation would lead to more intensive and efficient use of land and also add a progressive element to the overall distribution of tax burdens. But in practice, the revenue (and political) attraction of taxing buildings, together with the difficulties of assessing raw land values, has discouraged the separate taxation of land and buildings.

Denmark and Estonia are celebrated for their systems of taxing land (Tiits 2008). However, both countries have also introduced separate taxes on buildings but with a differentially higher tax rate on land. In Denmark, the total tax revenue raised from buildings is equivalent to twice that of land. In Estonia, the property tax base was expanded in 2002 to cover building areas in the two largest cities, but most land under buildings has since been exempted. In Russia, buildings are taxed more heavily than land. In Finland, 77 percent of taxable property value is in buildings.

Of the 14 countries studied in part 2, only 5 require separate assessment of land and buildings. Because of difficulties with assessment, the taxation of land (versus buildings) poses valuation problems. As Franzsen (2009, 46) points out, undeveloped land sales in urban areas are rare, especially in large urban areas. As a result, land is often valued as a residual—that is, as the total property value less the depreciated replacement value of buildings on the property. But this is also problematic if the assessment method used for buildings does not yield an accurate estimate for the present value of the building.[16]

Land Use

Some European countries aggressively use property tax and land use regulation to shape land use patterns. Among the main goals seems to be to increase the density of cities by encouraging the development of vacant properties, penalizing underuse of properties, penalizing the owners of dilapidated properties, and providing incentives for increasing the supply of affordable housing. Property tax policies to support such targeted land use concerns are now on the books in many countries (see table 4.1), and some evidence indicates their success in promoting compact development (OECD 2022).

The *net* impacts of property taxation on land use are not always clear. For example, revaluation would drive up property values and property tax bills, which would in turn encourage the development of cheaper and more distant land, thereby encouraging urban sprawl. The same could be said about a better matching of full market value with liability for property transfer taxes. Such impacts on land use, however, may be less a problem in densely populated European cities.

Finland's municipalities have considerable freedom to control real estate development within their jurisdictions. This includes the acquisition and sale of properties. Municipal land banking and land leasing can capture land value appreciation for the local government or steer the direction of local-area development, but this may come at some cost to property tax revenue mobilization, because municipalities may hold some properties off the market and set their own prices for others. Moreover, land banking revenues are not recorded in local-government accounts.

Decarbonization and the Property Tax

Decarbonization will affect all economic sectors in Europe. Estimates are that Europe's transition to a net zero economy by 2050 will require more than US$30 trillion in new investment (BloombergNEF 2023). The property tax will not directly finance a large share of this investment, but it can play an important supporting role in helping Europe reach net zero.

The implications of national decarbonization policy for subnational government budgets have recently been addressed (Bahl 2025; de Mello and Ter-Minassian 2023; Martinez-Vazquez 2021; Smoke and Cook 2021). Decarbonization will make direct claims on local expenditure budgets, and if the revenue-sharing pool of the central government does not grow, provincial and local-government expenditure budgets will be squeezed.[17] Since property taxation is the mainstay of local-government owned financing, it almost certainly will be called on to fill some of this gap.

The economic displacements that will come from decarbonization will place fiscal pressure on local governments. Oil- and coal-producing regions, and other carbon-intensive production regions, could see significant economic decline. The budgets of subnational governments in such regions will be left with gaps, and local taxes will be called on to fill parts of the revenue shortfall.

The property tax might also be called on to directly support the cost of changing land use patterns and building designs consistent with environmental objectives. The OECD (2021) reports that the residential sector accounts for 17 percent of carbon dioxide emissions. The European Union estimates that 40 percent of European energy consumption and 36 percent of greenhouse gas emissions come from buildings (Leodolter, Princen, and Rutkowski 2022). Reducing this carbon footprint means larger property tax subsidies to support more energy-efficient construction and more environmentally friendly land use patterns and transportation modes. Table 4.2 notes property tax relief for energy-efficient construction for several countries. In addition, new national environmental regulations may lead to an increase in the cost of housing because of, for example, new insulation technologies, solar panels, and heat pumps. To the extent these higher costs are fully capitalized into housing prices, the taxable property tax base will be affected.

Decarbonization will affect the cost of managing local government. Since it touches nearly all areas of the economy, it will result in policy and management reforms, and some of this reform cost will be borne by local governments. A new regulatory system, increased surveillance and monitoring, new subsidy programs, and a new cadre of environmentally skilled local employees will be needed. The property tax will be called on to finance part of this increased cost (Bahl 2025).

The Property Tax and Pandemic Control

The COVID-19 pandemic in 2020 and 2021 interrupted the growth in GDP in most European countries and affected their budgetary performance. The overall tax ratio (total tax revenue/GDP) declined in some OECD countries mostly because of a decline in corporate income taxes, value-added tax, and social security taxes. By 2021, the rebound was underway, and 26 of 37 OECD countries had increased their tax ratio (OECD 2022). Subnational government resilience, intergovernmental transfers, and a housing boom during the crisis was strong enough to avoid much of the shock at the local level (de Mello and Ter-Minassian 2023).

The COVID-19 emergency had the potential for significantly deeper direct and indirect impacts on the budgets of subnational governments. The direct impacts came from increased expenditures on health care and measures to contain the pandemic. Central governments in European countries compensated local governments with increased intergovernmental transfers during this period.

Some European countries, in another direct action, reduced property tax rates or deferred property tax payments by ratepayers to increase the liquidity of local homeowners or businesses. As to indirect effects, growth in the annual property tax base was expected to slow or even decline as economic growth slowed during the 2019–2020 pandemic period. But property tax bases did not change much relative to GDP, in part because the pandemic coincided with an acceleration of housing prices (Frayne et al. 2022). Interestingly, other sources of revenue crowded out the potential property tax reductions.

Good Revenue Outcomes and Bad Practices?

Property tax practices in Europe over the past 25 years suggest that good revenue outcomes do not require good property tax practices. Some European countries (France, Greece, and the United Kingdom) have pushed general property tax revenue mobilization to above 2 percent of GDP by relying on property tax practices that fail the usual tests for good practice. Others have (more or less) followed the rules of good practice without seeing the revenue benefits (Latvia and Lithuania). The discussion that follows is about reconciling (or not) bad practices with good revenue outcomes, focusing on the 14 countries of part 2. The discussion here and the policy analysis in chapters 3 and 5 raise the question of whether good property tax management and good valuation are necessary for good property tax revenue outcomes.

The norms for good property tax practice have been around for a long time. The results of a good property tax are something like this: A good property tax yields adequate revenues with reasonable administrative cost and is transparent (Prammer 2020). Its base is relatively immobile and does not unduly distort the allocation of resources from market-determined levels (see, e.g., Bird 2011). Good practice has been developed over time by academics, practitioners, and international agencies and is a regular part of their consultations with member countries:[18]

- Up-to-date, accurate valuations.
- Testing of whether the valuation roll is reflective of market values. Transparency in reporting the results of this testing.
- A revenue buoyancy high enough to support identified budgetary needs.
- Exemptions and preferential treatments limited to addressing externalities and protecting low-income families.
- Tax burdens distributed in a nonregressive way.

Many European countries have managed to realize good revenue mobilization outcomes, but they were not always the result of good practice. The following are four examples taken from the European experience.

The first is the use of broad uplifts to the existing tax base to stimulate revenues, in order to avoid general revaluation. Such uplifts have been used by France, Germany, and Finland. This approach can impose significant inequities in the distribution of property tax burdens because it raises assessments of all properties at the same rate. In some countries, using such uplifts or indexes to reassess—France, for example—total property tax revenues have increased at a faster rate than GDP in some periods. However, the indexing approach is plagued by fairness problems since present conditions have not been taken into account.

Second, some countries tax different sectors of the economy at different rates to maintain financing targets and public support. The strategy has included differential property taxation on residential and business properties. But differential effective tax rates for different sectors of the economy leads to distortions and possibly significant welfare costs. The taxation of commercial property (business rates) is a particularly contentious issue in the United Kingdom and Ireland, but it has performed well in terms of revenue mobilization and compliance, and it has kept some of the pressure off the residential council tax rates.

The third example concerns the compensation of taxpayers in exchange for accepting a new valuation roll. Bringing in a new and accurate valuation roll is usually a good outcome. But the cost of taxpayer acceptance can be great. It may include rolling back tax rates, phasing in the valuation roll over several years, and offering companion expenditure programs, all meant to soften the immediate hit on taxpayer budgets. In fact, revaluations structured as revenue neutral in their first years are not uncommon. But good policy practice should not include a promise of permanent restrictions on the revenue performance of the property tax under a newly revalued system. Estonia introduced policies that could run a risk of significantly compromising long-run revenue growth, including a pathway to long-term commitments to a lower tax rate, large permanent exemptions to the tax base, and limits on future increases in property tax.

The fourth example demonstrates the opposite problem: sometimes good practice does not lead to good results. The Netherlands seems to obey many of the rules for good practice yet does not generate high levels of revenue. Perhaps the transparency of the system allows voters to focus on a single element—the tax rate—and this explains the quandary.

If the standards of good practice are so widely agreed upon, why are they not always followed? Why do some countries step over the known lines between good practices and questionable practices? There are several answers. Sometimes countries are simply unequipped to carry out the technical tasks required to administer a good property tax, or they cannot afford it. Sometimes voters, and decision-makers on their behalf, are more comfortable with intuition than with informed analysis. Sometimes the political economy (and the voters) reject even proposals straight out of the good practices playbook, and sometimes even the courts object to good reform proposals. The opposition to good property tax reform often involves self-interest, and sometimes is dictated by the necessity of following the path of least political resistance in order to get things done.

Reshaping the Political Economy

The property tax is a favorite of economists, but it has few other champions (McCluskey, Bahl, and Franzsen 2022). Voters see it as a tax that burdens their housing costs but gives them few benefits in return. They regularly reject property tax rate increases and revaluations, and they intimidate politicians enough that increases may not even be proposed.

Politicians do not like the property tax, because their voters do not like it, and truth be known, they are not enthusiastic about the prospects of having to justify property tax rate increases to their constituents. Government bureaucrats at all levels see the need for revaluation but also the monetary cost and realize that most of the increased revenue will go to local governments.[19] Voters often make decisions about property tax reform without fully understanding the impacts. They may even be misinformed. Public voting may be the bedrock of tax democracies, but sometimes special interests take an oversized part in shaping voter views.

The unpopularity of the property tax is a long-standing and well-recognized constraint to increased property taxation (Bahl and Bird 2018; Blöchliger 2015; Cabral and Hoxby 2012; Kelly, White, and Anand 2020; Rosengard 2012). Explanations range from limited tax morality (Torgler 2011) to, in Spain, objection to double taxation of property tax and property transfer tax, to residents paying a tax from which their local governments return few benefits, to the high visibility of the tax. All these considerations have contributed to holding down effective property tax rates. The stories about political economy constraints are well-told in the country studies in part 2.

Can the political economy constraint be loosened? The best route may be major public information campaigns that link property taxation to specific benefits, simplify the tax structure, and better explain how the property tax works. Identifying specific projects paid for with property tax funding could build confidence with voters. So also could structural reforms that remove some of the unfair practices and preferences associated with this tax. And a well-structured progressive property tax can take some of the pressure off the taxation of labor. It is also important for government to better address often-overstated fears, including suggestions that property tax reform will drive people from their homes. A lower cost for administering the property tax, as might come from more use of mass appraisal techniques, could also help.

Information campaigns might succeed. Giaccobasso et al. (2022), working on US education funding in Texas, find evidence that corrections in perceptions about property taxation can increase the willingness to pay taxes. But more work needs to be done in this area. This includes local-government information campaigns that present the dangers of overreliance on transfers from the central government in general and on personal income taxes in particular. Such information campaigns need to be ongoing, not reserved for times of reform.

The property tax is seen as a minor source of revenue mobilization, which is taken by many to mean that it is an unimportant part of the tax system. But when the property tax is combined with other taxes on land

and buildings, its revenue footprint is considerably larger. Its impact can be even greater if central governments rejigger their rules for the distribution of intergovernmental transfers so that property taxes are not so easily crowded out in local budgets.

Finally, the use of modern technology can make for a more effective property tax system. Improved valuation techniques (see chapter 5) might lead to capturing more value for the base, and so would lowering the local government claim on central tax revenues. The same impact might result from a streamlining of the property tax infrastructure (see chapter 3) in some countries. Technology can be very effectively used to ensure that all properties (land and buildings) are captured in the tax base. This is, for example, clearly borne out by the collaboration and coordination among relevant entities in the Netherlands.

Notes

1. Russia uses a separate property tax on enterprise assets to capture the value of rental assets, but the actual coverage of these assets in the tax base varies widely across regions.

2. Area-based property taxation is also used in the Czech Republic and Slovakia (Radvan et al. 2021).

3. In the part 2 country studies, Estonia reported the revenue cost of preferential property tax treatments to be equivalent to 24 percent of property tax revenues raised in 2022. Russia reported 0.02 percent of GDP.

4. While this would be good policy and might lead to better practice, it might force governments to reveal some unflattering decisions that they would prefer to keep less visible.

5. This is a result of a general reassessment of commercial (but not residential) properties in 2017.

6. Despite Poland's and Slovenia's resistance to moving to a value-based approach, they determine tax charges using location coefficients and other value-based indicators.

7. In theory, the annual value and capital value tax bases have an equivalence—that is, the capital value of a property is the present value of the flow of its annual net benefits. The base for the annual value tax is the amount of rent that would be paid in an arm's-length transaction, and for a capital value tax it is the amount for which the property could be sold in an open market. But in practice, this equivalence often gets lost in the way these bases are valued for tax purposes, by government involvement in housing and land markets and by all manner of differential treatments given to certain types of property.

8. In the Netherlands, polder boards (local water management boards) assess non-built-up areas on an area basis, and even in California, an area-based parcel tax is available (Youngman 2016).

9. And always, special cases confuse the issue. For example, apartment ownership in Finland is mostly indirect. Housing companies own the buildings, and individuals own shares of the company.

10. Some governments even structure their property tax to reflect this possibility. For example, the United Kingdom, where the average household size is two, gives a property tax discount for single-family homes.

11. A regressive property tax is usually defined as one in which the effective tax rate is lower for higher-income families.

12. The theories behind determining who pays the property tax have been well studied and well developed (e.g., Mieszkowski 1972; Zodrow 2006).

13. In France, however, the differential taxation of business property is due to a 2017 reassessment of the business tax base. To avoid a differential higher effective tax rate on the business sector, preferential rates have been set.

14. Article 9 of the European Charter of Local Self-Government may be one of the important reasons for this.

15. The tax-urbanization elasticity estimated from regression analysis presented in table 2.4—for the European sample—is 4.98. That is, a 1 percent increase relative to a country's existing urbanization rate (rather than an absolute 1 percentage point rise), ceteris paribus, is associated with a 4.98 percent increase relative to the country's existing effective rate of property taxation.

16. This might happen, for example, if a national average estimate of construction costs is used to estimate building values, as Finland does.

17. For example, Tillu (2021) reports estimates that existing government budgets in China will cover less than 15 percent of the total funding for the low-carbon infrastructure needed to meet carbon neutrality goals.

18. Among these are Bahl and Bird (2018); Kelly (2014); Kelly, White, and Anand (2020); Netzer (1998); and OECD (2022).

19. This point is frequently made but can be misleading. Increased property tax revenues may free up intergovernmental transfers for other purposes and may lead to more efficient local-government spending.

References

Almy, R. 2014. "Valuation and Assessment of Immovable Property." Working paper on Fiscal Federalism No. 19. Paris: OECD.

Bahl, R. 2025. "The Role of Subnational Governments in China's Decarbonization Program." In *Decentralized Governance and Climate Change*, ed. J. Martinez-Vazquez, P. Smoke, and S. Yilmaz. Cheltenham, UK: Edward Elgar.

Bahl, R., and R. M. Bird. 2018. *Fiscal Decentralization and Local Finance in Developing Countries*. Cheltenham, UK: Edward Elgar.

Bahl, R. W., and J. F. Linn. 1992. *Urban Public Finance in Developing Countries*. New York: Oxford University Press.

Bahl, R., J. Linn, and D. Wetzel. 2013. "Governing and Financing Metropolitan Areas in the Developing World." In *Financing Metropolitan Areas in Developing Countries*, ed. R. Bahl, J. Linn, and D. Wetzel. Cambridge, MA: Lincoln Institute of Land Policy.

Bahl, R., and S. Wallace. 2007. "Intergovernmental Transfers: The Vertical Sharing Dimension." In *Fiscal Equalization: Challenges in the Design of Intergovernmental Transfers*, ed. J. Martinez-Vazquez and B. Searle. New York: Springer.

Bird, R. 2011. "Subnational Taxation in Developing Countries: A Review of the Literature." *Journal of International Commerce, Economics and Policy* 2(1): 139–161.

Blöchliger, H. 2015. "The Challenge of Measuring Fiscal Decentralization." In *Handbook of Multilevel Finance*, ed. E. Ahmad and G. Brosio. Cheltenham, UK: Edward Elgar.

BloombergNEF. 2023. "Huge Acceleration Required for Europe to Get on Track for Net Zero." Press Release, May 15. https://about.bnef.com/insights/finance/huge-acceleration-required-for-europe-to-get-on-track-for-net-zero/.

Borge, L. E., and J. Rattsø. 2014. "Capitalization of Property Taxes in Norway." *Public Finance Review* 42(5): 635–661. https://doi.org/10.1177/1091142113489845.

Cabral, M., and C. Hoxby. 2012. "The Hated Property Tax: Salience, Tax Rates, and Tax Revolts." National Bureau of Economic Research Working paper No. 18514. Cambridge, MA: NBER.

de Mello, L., and T. Ter-Minassian. 2023. "Decarbonisation and Intergovernmental Fiscal Relations: Policy Challenges and Reform Options." Working paper on Fiscal Federalism No. 43. Paris: OECD. https://doi.org/10.1787/c434c385-en.

European Commission. 2023. *Annual Report on Taxation 2023.* Directorate-General for Taxation and Customs Union. Luxembourg: European Commission.

Franzsen, R. C. D. 2009. "International Experience." In *Land Value Taxation*, ed. R. Dye and R. England, 27–47. Cambridge, MA: Lincoln Institute of Land Policy.

Frayne, C., A. Szczypińska, B. Vašíček, and S. Zeugner. 2022. *Housing Market Developments in the Euro Area: Focus on Housing Affordability.* Discussion paper 171. Brussels: European Commission.

George, H. 1879 (1958). *Progress and Poverty.* New York: Robert Schalkenbach Foundation.

Giaccobasso, M., B. Nathan, R. Perez-Truglia, and A. Zentner. 2022. "Where Do My Tax Dollars Go? Tax Morale Effects of Perceived Government Spending." NBER Working paper No. w29789. (February). https://ssrn.com/abstract=4045367.

Glaeser, E. 2012. "Triumph of the City: How Our Greatest Invention Makes Us Richer, Smarter, Greener, Healthier, and Happier." *Economic Geography* 88(1): 97–100.

Glaeser, E., and A. Joshi-Ghani, eds. 2015. *The Urban Imperative: Toward Comparative Cities.* New York: Oxford University Press.

Gloudemans, R. J., and E. J. Montgomery. 2008. "Domestic Revaluation in Northern Ireland." *Journal of Property Tax Assessment and Administration* 5(4): 17–31.

Goode, R. 1984. "Government Finance in Developing Countries." Washington, DC: Brookings Institution.

Kelly, R. 2014. "Implementing Sustainable Property Tax Reform in Developing Countries." In *Taxation and Development: The Weakest Link? Essays in Honor of Roy Bahl*, ed. R. M. Bird and J. Martinez-Vazquez, 326–363. Cheltenham, UK: Edward Elgar.

Kelly, R., R. White, and A. Anand. 2020. *Property Tax Diagnostic Manual.* Washington, DC: World Bank.

Leodolter, A., S. Princen, and A. Rutkowski. 2022. *Immovable Property Taxation for Sustainable and Inclusive Growth.* Discussion Paper 156. Paris: OECD.

Martinez-Vazquez, J. 2021. *Adapting Fiscal Decentralization Design to Combat Climate Change (English).* Climate Governance Papers. Washington, DC: World Bank Group. http://documents.worldbank.org/curated/en/099040101252235219/P1725690f4590d06609b0808ead078df321.

McCluskey, W., and R. Franzsen. 2013. "Property Taxes in Metropolitan Cities." In *Financing Metropolitan Areas in Developing Countries*, ed, R. Bahl, J. Linn, and D. Wetzel. Cambridge, MA: Lincoln Institute of Land Policy.

McCluskey, W., R. Bahl, and R. Franzsen. 2022. "Strengthening Property Taxation Within Developing Asia." Background Note for the Asian Development Bank. https://www.adb.org/sites/default/files/institutional-document/782851/ado2022bn-property-taxation-developing-asia.pdf.

McMillen, D., and R. Singh. 2020. "Assessment Regressivity and Property Taxation." *Journal of Real Estate Finance and Economics* 60(1): 155–169.

Mieszkowski, P. 1972. "The Property Tax: An Excise Tax or a Profits Tax." *Journal of Public Economics* 1(1): 73–96.

Mill, J. S. 1848. *Principles of Political Economy*. London.

Mirrlees, J. 2010. *The Mirrlees Review: Dimensions of Tax Design*. Oxford: Oxford University Press.

Netzer, D., ed. 1998. *Land Value Taxation: Can It and Will It Work Today?* Cambridge, MA: Lincoln Institute of Land Policy.

Norregaard, J. 2013. "Taxing Immovable Property: Revenue Potential and Implementation Challenges." Working paper WP/13/129. Washington, DC: International Monetary Fund.

OECD (Organisation for Economic Co-operation and Development). 2021. "Fiscal Federalism 2022: Making Decentralisation Work." Paris: OECD. https://doi.org/10.1787/201c75b6-en.

———. 2022. *Housing Taxation in OECD Countries*. OECD Tax Policy Studies No. 29. https://doi.org/10.1787/03dfe007-en.

Prammer, D. 2020. "Immovable Property: Where, Why and How Should It Be Taxed? A Review of the Literature and Its Implementation in Europe." *Public Sector Economics* 44(4): 483–504.

Radvan, M., R. Franzsen, W. J. McCluskey, and F. Plimmer, eds. 2021. *Real Property Taxes and Property Markets in CEE Countries and Central Asia*. Maribor, Slovenia: Institute for Local Self Government.

Ricardo, D. 1817. *On the Principles of Political Economy and Taxation*. London.

Rosengard, J. K. 2012. "The Tax Everyone Loves to Hate: Principles of Property Tax Reform." Cambridge, MA: Harvard Kennedy School.

Slack, E., and R. Bird. 2014. "The Political Economy of Property Tax Reform." Working paper on Fiscal Federalism No. 18. Paris: OECD. https://dx.doi.org/10.1787/5jz5pzvzv6r7-en.

Smoke, P. J., and M. J. Cook. 2021. *Administrative Decentralization and Climate Change: Concepts, Experience, and Action (English)*. Climate Governance Papers. Washington, DC: World Bank Group. http://documents.worldbank.org/curated/en/099040001252284476/P1725690d761df0fa08f5e0c9bd504c19ae.

Tiits, T. 2008. Land Taxation Reform in Estonia. In *Making the Property Tax Work: Experiences in Developing and Transitional Countries*, ed. R. Bahl, J. Martinez-Vazquez, and J. Youngman. Cambridge, MA: Lincoln Institute of Land Policy.

Tillu, J. 2021. "Financing China's Sustainable Urban Transformation." London: Grantham Research Institute on Climate Change and the Environment (July).

Torgler, B. 2011. "Tax Morale and Compliance: Review of Evidence and Case Studies for Europe." Policy Research Working paper No. WPS 5922. World Bank. http://hdl.handle.net/10986/3690.

Vickrey, W. 1999. "A Modern Theory of Land Value Taxation." In *Land Value Taxation: The Equitable and Efficient Source of Public Finance*, ed. K. C. Wenzer. Abingdon, UK: Routledge.

Walters, L. 2011. *Land and Property Tax: A Policy Guide*. Nairobi: United Nations Human Settlements Program.

Youngman, J. 2016. *A Good Tax: Legal and Policy Issues for the Property Tax in the United States*. Cambridge, MA: Lincoln Institute of Land Policy.

Youngman, J., and J. Malme. 2008. "Developments in Value-Based Property Taxation in Central and Eastern Europe." *Land Lines*, October.

Žibrik, N., and T. Humar. 2021. "Real Property Taxation in the Emerging Economy of the Republic of Slovenia." In *Real Property Taxes and Property Markets in CEE Countries and Central Asia*, ed. M. Radvan, R. Franzsen, W. J. McCluskey, and F. Plimmer, 327–374. Maribor, Slovenia: Institute for Local Self-Government.

Zodrow, G. 2006. "Reflections on the New View and Benefit View of the Property Tax." In *Property Taxation and Local Government Finance*, ed. W. Oates, 79–111. Cambridge, MA: Lincoln Institute of Land Policy.

5

Valuation

Aspects, Issues, and the Future

WILLIAM MCCLUSKEY, ROY BAHL, RIËL FRANZSEN, AND WENJING LI

The law may define the base of property taxation for a country, but more often it is determined by the valuation practice used. Those drafting the law can be cavalier about such concepts as taxation at full market value levels, universal coverage, and exemptions, but valuers are constrained by data availability, limited property registers, tight budgets, and their own skills. And while the timetable for reforming the tax system usually has flexibility, the timetable for sending out the tax assessments does not. The result is that various methods are used to simplify the valuation process, balancing accuracy and efficiency. Few countries are able to maintain assessments at anywhere near full market value levels, and many do not check the accuracy of their assessments (Grote and Wen 2024). Some do not even bother to value property. Most simply try to strike a balance between simplicity and accuracy. And while the property tax laws in many countries may remain unchanged in their basics, valuations may be driven by changes in the real estate markets, such as increasing levels of owner occupancy and by the development of new automated technologies.

Valuers must be consistent in valuations so that all taxpayers are treated equitably. This means all valuers must use the same valuation tax model when deriving the assessments. For example, the Netherlands bases its property tax on the capital value. The capital value of a property could be influenced by the terms of any lease granted by the freeholder.

For instance, a long lease at a low annual rent would depress the capital value of the freehold. The Dutch tax model therefore assumes that the freehold is unencumbered irrespective of the actual condition. Similarly, the nondomestic rating model in the United Kingdom assumes that the property is let from year to year on a full repairing and insuring lease irrespective of the actual lease terms. In addition, the rating assessment is based on current use rather than highest and best use. Hence, understanding the property tax assessment assumptions includes knowing the tax assessment is not necessarily the same as the market value. Other jurisdictions may opt for market value rather than a consistent valuation model.

Valuing the Tax Base

Probably no two countries are exactly alike in how they value real property for tax purposes (Leodolter et al. 2022). But they are similar in recognizing that effective valuation is the key to higher levels of property tax revenue (Grote and Wen 2024). Improving the quality of valuation for recurrent property taxes improves the fairness of the tax and its transparency and thereby increases public confidence in the tax system (Grover et al. 2015). But countries do not all follow the same valuation path to good property taxation (Prammer 2020). This chapter discusses how European countries go about valuing property and with what success.

Value-based assessment uses two broad approaches: capital (or market) value assessment and annual rental value assessment (Blöchliger 2015). *Market value*, *assessed value*, and *cadastral value* are just some of the terms of capital value property tax systems (Franzsen and McCluskey 2013; TEGOVA 2025; UN-Habitat 2013). Where the cadastre is used for valuation purposes, the term *cadastral value* is common, as in Latvia, Spain, and Russia.

Four approaches determine the capital value of land and buildings: capital improved value (i.e., summing the collective value of land and any improvements, generally buildings, on the land), the value of the land and improvements as separate objects (i.e., determining two separate values), unimproved land value or site value (i.e., ignoring any improvements constructed on the land), and the value of buildings only (i.e., ignoring the value of the land on which the building was constructed) (Kitchen 2013).

Capital Improved Value

In jurisdictions where the real estate market is well developed and a property valuer profession functions adequately, capital value can be a viable option. Several Organisation for Economic Co-operation and Development (OECD) countries use it (e.g., the Netherlands and Spain and, for residential property, the United Kingdom and Ireland. In countries where the owner of land also owns improvements on the land, it can prove difficult to determine separate values for the land and the structures on the land. In these countries, land and buildings cannot be alienated, or acquired separately, and therefore there is only one transaction value for a single economic unit of real property. The property is perceived as a whole and therefore taxed with reference to its total value.

Whether properties are valued traditionally, manually case by case, or by an automated mass valuation to determine a discrete market value for every individual property, the system is costly to maintain. It is nonetheless considered a fairer basis for valuation since it spreads the tax burden among property owners according to individually assessed market values. However, the overall fairness of this approach depends on ensuring that the assessed property values reflect the property market.

Given the complexities and administrative burden in valuing every property to a discrete value, two countries—Great Britain (England, Scotland, and Wales) and Ireland—implemented a simplified system based on capital improved values. In 1991, Great Britain replaced its politically unacceptable community charge (otherwise known as the poll tax) with the council tax. The council tax applies only to residential property and is based on the total value of the land and buildings together. This tax combines the assessment and taxation by allocating all dwellings to one of eight value bands, each with its own tax rate.[1] It is a relatively simple way of valuing residential properties but has the advantage that the valuation authority does not have to defend discrete values for every dwelling.

Table 5.1 illustrates the value bands used in England, Scotland, and Wales. Although the methodology simplifies valuation, the value bands need periodic readjustment (their upper and lower limits and their number). Great Britain has failed to do this. The value bands were established on the basis of property values in 1991 and the number and width of the bands have remained unchanged, except in Wales, which revised the number of bands by adding a band in 2005 (McCluskey 2025b).

Research has identified that the council tax needs to be revalued and reformed (Cheshire and Hilber 2021). The values of properties have changed significantly since the council tax was introduced—on average increasing more than twice as much in London as in North East England, for example—yet the distribution of tax burdens has not changed to reflect this (Adam et al. 2020; Leishman et al. 2014; Murphy 2019).

Separate Assessed Values for Land and Buildings

The total market value of a property includes the value of the land and the value of the buildings or structures on the land.[2] Several countries

Table 5.1 Value Bands in England, Scotland, and Wales

Valuation Band	Scotland (£)	England (£)	Wales (£)
A	Up to 27,000	Up to 40,000	Up to 44,000
B	27,001-35,000	40,001–52,000	44,001-65,000
C	35,001-45,000	52,001-68,000	65,001-91,000
D	45,001-58,000	68,001-88,000	91,001-123,000
E	58,001-80,000	88,001-120,000	123,001-162,000
F	80,001-106,000	120,001-160,000	162,001-223,000
G	106,001-212,000	160,001-320,000	223,001-324000
H	Over 212,000	Over 320,000	324,001-424,000
I	n.a.	n.a.	Over 424,001

Source: Compiled by the authors from data at GOV.UK (n.d.).

Note: n.a. = not applicable.

use the capital value–based approach and separately determine the value of land and buildings. Under this methodology, the land can be valued on the basis of market transactions, though these may be few in large urban and highly developed areas. The buildings would then be valued, usually, by new or current construction costs. To reflect the building's age, condition, materials, and so on, would then require adjusting the new costs, typically referred to as the depreciated replacement cost. Several methods can determine either the value of land or the building (New South Wales Government 2019). Finally, as an alternative, the total value of the property could be arbitrarily split between the building and the land.

Given that defendable values must be determined for both the land and the buildings, the valuation cost can be high. Where the property market operates on a total value basis (land and buildings together), splitting and valuing the land and buildings separately becomes artificial. Where sales of vacant land are adequate, the underlying land value can be determined and subtracted from the total sales value to determine the value of the buildings. Splitting the total value into separate land and building values is relatively common and is done in Finland, Latvia, and Slovenia.

The attractiveness of separate values lies in the possibility of applying rate differentiation. In practice, this means that a higher rate can be applied to land, incentivizing development, whereas the building stock—which represents significant capital wealth—is also taxed but at a lower rate.

Land or Site Value

One capital value option reflects only the value of the land or the site, ignoring existing improvements and structures on the land. This does not reflect reality, because all structures on fully developed land, including buildings, parking, fencing, and more, would be disregarded. However, the land value would reflect utilities that service the land and land use zoning regulations.

Generally speaking, a land, or site, value system requires significantly less data, which makes it potentially less costly to administer. Practical issues arise in jurisdictions with a paucity of sales of vacant land parcels for comparison to determine land values for all the properties in the jurisdiction. Taxpayers may find it conceptually difficult to ignore existing improvements in determining a property's assessed value. The exclusion of improvements, which are a highly visible form of capital wealth, may also be politically unacceptable in some countries. Given the narrow tax base (because of excluded improvements), nominal tax rates will need to be high to generate adequate revenues. High nominal rates are generally disliked by politicians and taxpayers, who focus on the tax rate and often have little appreciation for the relationship between tax base and tax rate.

In the 14-country sample, only Estonia takes the value of undeveloped land as the sole basis of the property tax, though Denmark has a separate tax based on the land value. Spain also has a separate tax, administered by municipalities, on the increase in land value over the period of ownership. This is a form of capital gains tax related only to land value.

Assessed Value of Buildings Only

Where land cannot be taxed for political or cultural reasons, buildings provide a viable basis for the property tax. In many cities, the value of buildings as a ratio of total value is considerable. Building values consist of construction costs and depreciation. Compared with determining land values, building values are much more complex and therefore time-consuming and costly. In Finland, building replacement value refers to the estimated costs of a new construction at the date of valuation. The methodology determines individual valuation principles and value estimates for different building types. In other words, residential buildings use a different valuation formula and building cost estimates and depreciation rates than, for example, office buildings. Replacement building costs are generally set by the national government, but those costs can vary by region. The valuation methodology may be set nationally even though the valuations may be done at the subnational level (the Netherlands).

Rental Value Assessment

A common basis of the property tax is the annual market rent the property would command. Market rents are more widely available in the commercial property market than in the residential sector; exceptions are France and Germany. Rents are generally based on the property's current use (for example, the United Kingdom and Ireland). Lease contracts vary regarding lease length, frequency of rent increases, and whether indexation of rents is used. There is a relatively close relationship between rental value and capital, or market, value. The basic formula applies a capitalization rate to the annual rent to estimate the capital value. Hence, the capital value involves two important variables: the estimated rental value and the capitalization rate. Taxpayers can challenge both. Often, just determining the rental value and using that for property tax purposes is appropriate.

France, Germany, Ireland, and the United Kingdom apply a rental value system to nonresidential properties. A rental value system relies on rental evidence obtained from an active rental market with sufficient arm's-length transactions for all relevant property use types. If rent control legislation exists, particularly for residential property, subsidized or controlled rents could skew market rents. Determining a notional market rent for owner-occupied property may also be difficult, especially if its percentage is significant (Ireland, the Netherlands, and the United Kingdom).

Area Basis

As discussed earlier, a relatively common nonvalue approach measures land and the usable area, or net floor space, of buildings (e.g., Poland) (Bird and Slack 2004). The data used in an area-based approach are normally the responsibility of municipalities (Poland and Slovenia). The basic assessment multiplies the (taxable) area of the building and land by a prescribed price per unit. The tax liability is then the product of the area and unit price. To improve equity and fairness, the area basis is often adjusted—for example, to reflect the number of floors in a building or to use the net usable area as opposed to gross area (Connolly and Bell 2009; Lim, McCluskey, and Davis 2008). Many countries modify the calculation further with coefficients to account for property use, age, location, and so on, but these blunt coefficients tend to be selective and to cover fairly large geographic areas. Therefore, granularity is lost, which does not occur for value-based approaches. Although the range and types of adjustment coefficients vary across countries, they all aim to align the tax liability to proxy market value conditions. In Poland, the tax base is the land's usable area, the buildings' usable area, and the assessed value of buildings used for business purposes.

Of the part 2 countries, only Poland and Slovenia use an area-based system.[3] Although revaluation is not a major issue in this system, the annual charge per unit of land or buildings (the tax rate) can be a significant point of contention. Discussions in Poland and Slovenia have led to policies that partially address the problems of area-based taxation. Value is indirectly accounted for with annual tax charges (implicit tax rates) that vary by location, land use, and the size and condition of the structure. Interestingly, Poland has maintained general property tax revenues at above the European average largely by increasing the rates of charge.

Why would a country choose to stay with such a seemingly flawed tax system? Slovenia attempted to replace its area-based system with a market value system but was constrained by a 2013 Constitutional Court ruling and by public opinion (Žibrik and Humar 2021). The Polish government has, on several occasions, rejected moving to a value-based system, and it remains an explosive political issue. Several possible explanations might be given for this state of affairs:

- Taxpayers fear, with good reason, that their property tax bills will be higher under a value-based system. Owners of higher-valued properties, as expected, have raised objections. However, there is also some concern that lower-taxed residences will no longer be affordable to current residents.
- The central government is reluctant to bear the costs of establishing and maintaining an expensive valuation system when it is likely that most of the revenues will accrue to local governments.
- Local politicians might prefer to continue to rely on less transparent sources of finance, such as central-government transfers, over being held accountable by their voters for property tax increases.

Table 5.2 depicts the basis of the recurrent property tax across the part 2 case study countries.

Valuation Practices

Property valuation is among the most difficult and costly activities in property tax administration (OECD 2021). This is largely due to the scale of the valuation exercise, which typically involves hundreds of thousands of properties, all of which require an individual assessed value, usually determined as of the same date.

To conduct fair and correct assessments, accurate and up-to-date information for each property unit is essential (TEGOVA 2025). There are arguments to extend the scope of the Land Administration Domain Model[4] to include valuation information and local and national land and

Table 5.2 Basis of the Recurrent Property Tax

	Capital Value for Land and Buildings						
	Land Value	**Building Value**	**Combined Value**	**Annual Rental Value**	**Land Value Only**	**Area Based**	**Comment**
Denmark			Yes		Yes		Owner-occupied residential property valued to capital improved value; land value is used for commercial land
Estonia					Yes		
Finland	Yes	Yes					Land and buildings are valued separately
France				Yes			Assessed rental values date from 1970, though efforts are underway to revise them
Germany				Yes			Rental values date from 1935 and 1964 in former East and West Germany
Greece			Yes				Zone value per square meter is estimated for a standardized residential apartment
Ireland			Yes	Yes			Capital value applies to residential property; annual rental value for commercial property

Latvia	Yes	Yes					Land and buildings are valued as separate components
Netherlands			Yes				
Poland	Yes	Yes				Yes	Land and buildings generally assessed on usable area; property used for business is assessed on an estimate of market value
Russia	Yes	Yes			Yes		Land tax is based on cadastral value; cadastral value is the preferred basis, though assets can be valued based on book value
Slovenia	Yes	Yes				Yes	The market value of all property is assessed and used for purposes other than the recurrent property tax; land and buildings are assessed separately
Spain	Yes	Yes			Yes		Cadastral value is considered to be below market value; land value increases used as a form of capital gains tax
United Kingdom			Yes	Yes			Capital value applies to residential property; annual rental value for commercial property

Source: Authors' compilation.

property databases (Lemmen, van Oosterom, and Bennett 2015). The extension aims to cover all stages of administrative property valuation—namely, identifying and grouping properties, valuing properties by individual or mass valuation, recording transaction prices, presenting sales statistics, and dealing with appeals (Kara et al. 2018).

Valuation is inherently subjective. Taxable value is determined by an organization, normally a government department, though the private sector can and does have an important role. The Netherlands relies almost exclusively on the private sector for valuation services. The ultimate objective is for the valuation system to ensure a fair, relative allocation of the tax burden across taxpayers (Kelly, White, and Anand 2020).

A property valuation system incorporates standard methods to estimate property value. The three most common are sales (or rent) comparisons, income capitalization, and depreciated cost (Franzsen and McCluskey 2013). The approach selected usually depends on the type of property being valued. The income approach is usually used for expensive income-producing properties, such as office buildings, hotels, and retail malls, for which it is easier to forecast cash flows. Properties with a substantial amount of data on sales, such as small offices, retail spaces, and most residential properties, are commonly valued using sales comparison. Last, properties having almost no sales or no easy way to forecast their income, such as industrial properties, airports, harbors, sports grounds, arenas, and transport infrastructure, are commonly valued using the cost approach. The rule of thumb is that if no sales data are available, a sales comparison makes the most sense, since it directly estimates the capital value (when, as in most cases, the capital value basis is used).

Self-Assessment of Property Value

Given the presumptive nature of the property tax, self-assessment of property value can be useful. It reduces administrative costs but compromises accuracy (OECD 2021). Self-assessments should not be confused with consultation, which usually refers to discussions between the departments that undertake the actual assessments, on the one hand, and taxpayers, on the other. Self-assessments can be useful as a temporary mechanism—for example, when a significant reform to the valuation is planned and resources within government are scarce. But as a permanent solution? Slack and Bird (2015) argue that it results in inaccurate estimates of property values, which tend toward underestimation. Auditing of self-assessments by government then becomes important but could lead to higher administrative costs if large numbers of values are challenged by the government.

There is evidence that self-assessment can work for certain taxes. The United Kingdom uses it for inheritance tax, capital gains tax, and profits tax. It works because of penalties for submitting a false declaration plus interest on the underpaid sum from the date on which the full amount should have been paid. The result is that the taxpayer must hire a private valuer to carry out the assessment to avoid the risk of underpayment. This raises the question of whether self-assessment imposes compliance costs on the taxpayer. Compliance costs are a potential matter of concern since the traditional canons of taxation include that taxation should be convenient for the taxpayer. One of the merits of property taxes can be that compliance costs are minimized if the government carries out assessments. Self-assessment and demands by the government for information from taxpayers increase compliance costs.

Government institutions, in whole or with assistance from private sector valuation firms, primarily estimate assessed value of real properties. Rarely, owners of property submit a declaration of the value of their property; however, some countries do require owners or occupiers to declare their property value (such as Romania, where owners of commercial properties must declare the value). A case in point is the reintroduction of a value-based residential property tax in Ireland, largely based on self-declared values (Turley 2022). A banding system helped in assessments, as owners had only to select the value band that they considered was appropriate for their property. However, the Revenue Commissioners (now Revenue), who administered the residential property tax at the time, provided guidance on average values for typical properties by small geographic areas. Auditing undertaken by the Revenue Commissioners ensured a reasonable degree of accuracy by owners (McCluskey 2025b). Information on sales prices also indicated banding accuracy.

A key objective of Ireland's state valuation service, the Tailte Éireann (previously the Valuation Office of Ireland), has been to accelerate the national revaluation program for commercial properties. To assist the valuation agency in achieving this, legislation specifically provides for elements of self-valuation within the taxation (rating) system, known as occupier-assisted valuation. This amendment allows the valuation agency to explore and test an alternative means of delivering a revaluation. Occupiers of commercial property now have an opportunity to submit their own valuation for property tax purposes. The valuation agency provides supports to occupiers during the valuation submission period. The intention behind the amendment is that this enhanced interaction between the state and taxpayer results in a more transparent process and a better communication and understanding of what the Tailte Éireann is trying to achieve through the revaluation.

Taxpayers in Poland determine the value of buildings used for business purposes. If the taxpayer has not specified its value or provides a value that does not correspond to the market value, the tax authority can appoint a property appraiser to determine the market value.

Revaluations

Most European countries tax the estimated value of property. In implementing their systems, some have taken a path of least resistance and keep the value of their tax bases high enough by inflating them with national indicators, or by legislative fiat, or by raising tax rates on outdated assessments. While this postpones the short-run revaluation controversy and adjustments, it makes the tax shock greater when it finally does come. It also leads to growing assessment inequities in the tax base. Some evidence on the frequency of revaluations is presented in table 5.3.

Regular revaluations are of paramount importance to maintaining the credibility and equity of a market value–based property tax (Leodolter et al. 2022; TEGOVA 2025). Revaluations reflect changes in property value over time and redistribute the property tax burden in a more equitable and fair manner in response to these changes. Without accurate, current values, tax liabilities will be distributed arbitrarily, undermining taxpayer trust in the tax system's legitimacy (Walters 2011). In local submarkets within real estate markets, property values tend to move in unsynchronized ways. Revaluations hence provide the opportunity for the administration to realign assessed values with market prices and in doing so address equity and improve revenue buoyancy (IAAO 2020).

Property values tend to change over time because of factors including supply and demand for specific property types, locational characteristics, cost of debt finance, and physical changes made to the property. To maintain fairness and equity of the property tax, assessed values must be periodically recalibrated with market prices if property values have changed significantly. Legislative, or prescribed, revaluation cycles tend to treat all local governments the same. For some, a five-year revaluation cycle may be too long, particularly where property values are volatile. For rural areas, property values could be static or relative changes in property values are the same, and five-year or longer revaluation cycles could add unnecessary costs, because shorter revaluation periods can be costly. The modus of revaluation and adoption of uniform standards should be managed from the center. Giving discretionary powers to a minister to determine when a revaluation should occur, however (as in the United Kingdom), is inadvisable, since political arguments may postpone a much-needed revaluation.

Table 5.3 Revaluation Calendars

Country	Revaluation Cycle	Date of Last Revaluation	Comment
Denmark	Every 2 years	2022	Initially a 4-year interval; in 1982 an automatic annual adjustment was applied; revaluation planned for 2026
Estonia	Every 4 years	2022	Previous revaluation was in 2001; before 2022, no prescribed cycle. Next revaluation planned for 2026
Finland	None prescribed	1993	Cost prices can be adjusted using indexes
France	None prescribed	Values were set in 1970 for residential property; in 2017 for commercial property	Revaluation planned for 2023 for business property; 2028 or beyond for residential property
Germany	None	Using 1964 values in the former West Germany, 1935 values in East	A new valuation methodology has been developed; the revaluation has yet to be completed
Greece	Every 2 years	2022	No precise revaluation cycle is apparent
Ireland	Every 4 years for residential property tax; every 10 years for commercial property	2021 for residential property. Commercial property revalued under a rolling program over several years by local authority	Residential property values are self-assessed; commercial rates are assessed by the central government

(continued)

Table 5.3 Revaluation Calendars (*continued*)

Country	Revaluation Cycle	Date of Last Revaluation	Comment
Latvia	Every 4 years	n.a.	Before 2016 the revaluation cycle was every 2 years
Netherlands	Every year	n.a.	
Poland	Commercial property values must be declared annually	n.a.	Non-value-based for residential and land Book value for commercial property
Russia	Moscow and St. Petersburg on a 2-year cycle	n.a.	The rest of the country is on a 4-year cycle
Slovenia	Every 2 years	2022	Property values are used not for the recurrent property tax but for other purposes
Spain	Cadastral values updated to ensure alignment with market prices	n.a.	Indexes can be used to update values
United Kingdom	Every 5 years	1991 values used for residential property; 2023 revaluation of commercial property, though values are determined as at 2021	In England and N. Ireland, commercial property is on a 5-year cycle, though a consultation paper has suggested a move to a 3-year cycle

Source: Authors' compilation.

Few countries take revaluations seriously (TEGOVA 2025). However, the Netherlands appears to be an exception because its revaluations are annual. Some take a less modern approach and use increased tax rates and indexes to uplift old assessed values (France and Germany). Several European countries as of 2025 tax on out-of-date assessed property values, including France, Finland, and Northern Ireland (for residential property). Although, in principle, most countries rely on revaluations of property to keep the values current, some properties have not been revalued for decades. For example, Germany is still levying the property tax on values determined in 1964 in the old West Germany and 1935 in the former East Germany (though significant efforts are underway to update assessed values). In England, the value bands for residential property were determined in 1991 and have not been revised. In Estonia, properties were not revalued between 2001 and 2022.

Significant efforts are underway to update assessed values. In accordance with the Valuation Acts 2001–2019, Ireland is rolling out a national program for the revaluation of all commercial and industrial properties across the 31 local authorities. This will be the first nationwide revaluation program since the middle of the 19th century and has been a strategic priority for successive governments. Approximately 150,000 commercial and industrial properties are liable for payment of property rates in Ireland. The revaluation work has taken several years and is due to be completed by 2024–2027 (Department of Housing, Local Government and Heritage 2023). After the initial revaluation, subsequent revaluations are scheduled for every 10 years.

As revenue is a function of tax rates and assessed values, if neither are adjusted relatively frequently, the result is declining revenue-income buoyancy in times when property values are increasing and unfair treatment of some property owners. In many ways, adjusting tax rates in line with inflation or on an ad hoc basis by political leaders is easier. This is the practice in Estonia, Finland, France, Germany, and Greece (Hagemann 2018). But, again, revaluation of all properties in the tax base tends to be costly and is unpopular with taxpayers.

A widely held belief is that revaluations automatically lead to significantly increased tax liabilities. In fact, general revaluations tend to be revenue neutral (Almy 2014), at least in the first years. This then leads to the political economy issue—why spend significant amounts of money on a revaluation if there will be no increase in revenue? Is achieving greater fairness or equity a sufficient reason for a revaluation? The general policy is that total revenue should increase according to the cost-of-living index or the consumer price index only in the year following the revaluation. However, even with this modest increase in total revenue, some properties will face a significant increase in tax liability due to the increased reassessment values, and other taxpayers' property tax liability may fall for the same reason. Hence, revaluation shock needs to be managed. In some cases, relief is given to those whose tax liability has excessively increased. More frequent revaluations better manage the risk of sudden valuation shocks and shifts in tax liabilities (Bird and Slack 2004).

Even though legislation normally specifies the frequency of revaluations, revaluations are commonly delayed, postponed, or canceled (OECD 2021). According to the International Association of Assessing Officers (IAAO 2020), all properties should be revalued at least every four to six years. See table 5.3 for the legislative requirement for timing of revaluations across the countries in part 2.

Revaluation cost depends on many factors, including the type and homogeneity property in the jurisdiction, the number of properties to value, the quality of existing data, the potential of using the private sector, the level of automation and technology, and the ability to use in-house staff. Undertaking valuations for large numbers of properties requires planning and ultimately can be achieved only by using technology, such as automated valuation methods, that many jurisdictions just do not have. Individual discrete (property-by-property) valuations are costly and not always feasible.

An automatic uplifting index, equal for all properties, has potential in updating property values (Ahmad, Brosio, and Jiménez 2019). Automatic updating that uses a recognized standard index such as the consumer price index can be applied. The methodology is not without issues. For example, the index would apply to all properties. This blunt approach may create disparities when the indexed value is out of line with the value of a specific property. Indexation is often thought of as a potentially effective, inexpensive, and quick way to update values. Some European countries have used it as an alternative to individual revaluation.

Residential properties in France have been taxed according to cadastral values (rental values) set in 1970. These values have been under revision since 2020, and new values are scheduled to be applied in 2028. The cadastral rental values for commercial property were revised in 2017 and will evolve to reflect local market dynamics using yearly declarations of landlords. In Finland, the legislation does not prescribe a cycle for revaluation. The land price zones, land values in these zones, and valuation principles were determined in 1993, but some adjustments to land values were made in 2006. Otherwise, adjustments to prices have been based on indexation. Building values are updated using building cost indexes, whereas land values are updated by considering the general land prices in specific areas. But because not all land values are adjusted at the same time, some values in some zones may remain unchanged.

Before 2022, Estonia had no legal valuation cycle. The central government decided when to revalue property. The only requirement for undertaking a revaluation was related to significant changes in the market, but in reality, the central government did not react even when the price increase was significant. According to the amended regulation, the revaluation cycle is now set for every four years; occurring in 2026 and 2030, following the 2022 revaluation.

In Latvia, cadastral values have historically been updated annually, but since 2016 the cadastral values have been frozen. In Slovenia, the revaluation cycle is every two years, though if the market prices indicate that the assessed values have moved outside specific quality ratios, a new revaluation can be effected. In Spain, property values can be updated annually, though the preferred approach is to update values only if the cadastral values and market prices differ. In practice, however, cadastral values across several large Spanish cities remain fixed for several years. A municipality can also request the Center for Cadastral Management and Tax Cooperation to prepare a new set of cadastral values. The center can use estimated revaluation coefficients determined for each municipality and location to reflect the increase in real estate values in the market.

Responsibility for Valuation

Many different organizational designs for managing the valuation administration are feasible, including maps and records identifying taxpayers and taxable properties (Almy 2014; UN-Habitat 2013). When it comes to responsibility for assessing property values for the recurrent property tax (Mikesell 2007), there are several options: the national government; a subnational government such as state, provincial, or local; the private sector; and a combination. The level of government responsible for the valuation and the type of agency that performs it have significant variation among countries. For example, at the central-government level, organizational options include a cadastral authority like Lithuania's State Enterprise Center of Registers and Slovenia's Surveying and Mapping Agency; a specialized valuation department typically falls under the Ministry of Finance, such as the Valuation Office Agency in England and Wales and the Tailte Éireann in Ireland. Practices are summarized in table 5.4.

The valuation of real estate for property tax purposes in Denmark encountered significant impediments. In 2003, valuation responsibility transferred from local municipalities to the Ministry of Taxation. The centralization was partly motivated by the desire for more homogeneous assessments across municipalities and for efficiency savings. Then in 2011, a new central valuation agency (SKAT Ejendomsvurdering) was set

Table 5.4 Responsibility for Valuation Services

Country	National/ Federal/ Provincial	Subnational	Private Sector	Comments
Denmark	Yes		Not used	Municipalities historically were responsible for valuation, though valuation function was centralized for efficiency
Estonia	Yes		Used in the 2022 revaluation	Before 2001, municipalities were responsible; from 2022, the National Land Board has assumed responsibility for valuation
Finland	Yes		Not used	VTT Technical Research Centre determines the valuation methodology; Finnish Tax Administration calculates tax bills and makes collections
France		Yes	Not used	Rental values based on 1970s levels; various initiatives have been suggested to update rental values
Germany	Yes		Not used	Offices of the tax administration perform valuation
Greece	Yes		Determines zone values	Ministry of Finance performs valuation

Ireland	Yes		Self-declared values for commercial property	Revenue is responsible for residential valuation; Tailte Éireann for commercial property
Latvia	Yes		Not used	State Land Service performs valuation
Netherlands		Yes	Used	Central government oversees municipal valuations
Poland		Yes	Not used	For business property, the taxpayer self-declares
Russia	Yes		Not used	Regional valuation authorities perform valuation
Slovenia	Yes		Indirectly used in valuation	Valuation services are embedded with the Surveying and Mapping Authority
Spain	Yes		Not used	The cadastral authority has full responsibility to determine property values
United Kingdom	Yes		Limited use	Valuations done by Valuation Office Agency in Great Britain; Scottish Assessors' Association; Land and Property Services in Northern Ireland

Source: Authors' compilation.

up. An administrative reform of the Ministry of Taxation followed in 2018, wherein a new agency, the Danish Property Assessment Agency (Vurderingsstyrelsen), took responsibility for the new valuation system.

One reason for assigning responsibility for valuation to the central government is that valuations prepared primarily for the recurrent property tax may be used for other purposes, such as social security payments or checking declared transaction prices. In the Netherlands, valuations made for municipal property tax assessments are used for water (polder) board taxes on built property and central-government taxes on imputed income (Bervoets et al. 2024). Spain uses valuations made for the property tax in a net wealth tax. In addition, property tax valuations may be used in a test of the reasonableness of declared values under transfer taxes, gift taxes, and inheritance or estate taxes (Slovenia and Spain). When the assessed value is higher than the declared value, it may be used as the basis for the tax (Spain).

Valuation responsibility is often allocated to state or local government (the Netherlands and Russia). Local knowledge is a critical advantage, but valuation skills may be lacking, hence the potential use of the private sector. Subnational valuation administration has the advantages of familiarity with local conditions, adaptability to them, and facilitating registration of taxpayers who think their concerns are better dealt with by locally based officials. Further, taxpayers can more easily identify the level of government responsible for administering the property tax, and transparency can be lost when a central authority administers the tax levied by a lower level of government. Disadvantages of a subnational administration include the lack of appropriate experienced staff with the requisite valuation skills, the inability to value all specialized property within the local jurisdiction, and an inability to retain staff, resulting in a significant loss of skills and experience. For subnational administration, central government tends to specify in legislation the valuation standards and guidelines for valuation at the local-government level.

The private sector can have an important role in valuations. For instance, commercial properties can involve complex valuations such as for hotels and shopping malls; and unique properties such as sports stadiums, airports, harbors, and railway stations are challenging to value. Valuation and collection services are frequently procured from the private sector, and companies can be contracted to undertake valuations for only part of the tax base. In the Netherlands, municipalities increasingly contract with private companies for valuation services (about half rely on firms and the other half on in-house valuers). Private sector valuers and real estate agents in England and Wales completed about 50 percent of the valuation work involved in assigning residential properties to the council tax bands. Other countries have drawn on companies on a smaller scale. The Estonian National Land Board contracted with private valuers for help during its 2022 revaluation. However, the private sector has not been involved in several countries, including Spain and Russia.

Property tax–related activities, such as property attribute data collection and valuation, should be separate from activities related to land and property title registration. That is, the legal cadastre ideally is distinct from the fiscal cadastre, though valuation functions are undertaken by the cadastral agency in, for example, Poland, Slovenia, and Spain to good effect.

Oversight of Valuation

Quality assurance is an important aspect of every valuation system. Quality assurance procedures ensure compliance with recognized internal, external, and international standards (IAAO 2020). Valuations devolved to regional bodies or municipalities or contracted out to the private sector could lead to inconsistencies among assessment bodies. To counteract this, the Netherlands introduced an oversight body, the Netherlands Council for Real Estate Assessment, with responsibility for quality assurance. The council annually reviews the recurrent property tax valuations for some 100 municipalities. In addition, the council has the power to order a revised assessment if it is not satisfied with the quality and results of the valuation. In Europe, the Netherlands is unique in having an independent body to monitor the quality of valuations. Most other countries rely on internal quality control procedures.

The Potential of Automated Valuation Methodologies

The scale of property tax valuations has led to development of tools to support mass valuation, in addition to the three main methods of valuation (recall they are sales or rent comparisons, income capitalization, and the depreciated cost). These tools improve valuation efficiency by incorporating automated processes driven by technology. One of the most significant recent advances has been the development of computer-assisted mass appraisal (CAMA) valuation (ADB 2023; Raich and Kwak 2023). *Mass appraisal* refers to jointly valuing a group of properties, following standard procedures similar to a single property appraisal; the key difference is CAMA's scale and methods (IAAO 2014). Mass appraisal in essence evolved out of the need to provide uniformity and consistency in valuations (Almy 2013). An equally important aspect was the ever-increasing financial burden of single manual appraisals, particularly during revaluation, when several million taxable units (buildings and parcels) need to be assessed at the same time (IAAO 2017).

Early application of CAMA began in the precomputer era, and advances in computing technology revolutionized valuation (Jason 2021), processing vast amounts of data quickly. The application of multiple regression analysis was seen as a game changer. Multiple regression analysis is a statistical technique used in data analysis to examine the relationship between a dependent variable and two or more independent variables and understand how the independent variables collectively influence the dependent variable. There is significant literature on the use of multiple regression analysis in supporting the estimation of values for property taxation (ADB 2023; Raich and Kwak 2023; Zurada, Levitan, and Guan 2011).

The model specification and application used by CAMA is an automated valuation model (AVM). AVMs are statistical algorithms that estimate the market value of real estate properties quickly and cost effectively (Bidanset 2014). As the name suggests, AVMs automate the valuation process, providing a faster alternative to traditional property appraisals conducted by valuers.

The IAAO defines an AVM as

> a mathematically based computer software program that market analysts use to produce an estimate of market value based on market analysis of location, market conditions and real estate characteristics from information that was previously and separately collected. (IAAO 2018, 4)

The majority of AVMs are built using multiple regression specifications. Their performance is largely driven by the quality and quantity of the transaction data used to calibrate models. IAAO standards deal with regression outputs in terms of accuracy and equity issues. Many countries and jurisdictions have embraced AVMs as being the only realistic solution to the valuation of large numbers of property such as residential, agricultural, and some types of commercial property (Estonia, the Netherlands, Slovenia, and the United Kingdom offer good examples). Benefits of automated valuation include the use of recognized statistical methodologies, the ability to make a large number of valuations within a constrained time period, more-objective assessments of value, and a cost-effective valuation solution. A constraint is the requirement of a significant amount of high-quality property transaction data such as sales prices and rents. For each property that has been sold or rented, it is important to have an accurate measurement of the physical characteristics of the property and locational data (proximity to specific features such as retail malls, medical and educational facilities, and the transport network).

Other constraints are a need for appropriately skilled staff in statistical modeling, the difficulty of explaining models to taxpayers, and providing comparable transactions for estimated values challenged by taxpayers (McCluskey, Cornia, and Walters 2013; McCord et al. 2013).

AVM application is still limited but growing in importance. Table 5.5 depicts European countries embracing this technology. Only four—Estonia, Latvia, the Netherlands, and Slovenia—have seriously invested in the technology, though Denmark, Spain, and Russia have made some limited use of AVMs.

The Impact of Artificial Intelligence

The recurrent property tax relies on large databases with information on the property tax base. Often, data on millions of properties (land and buildings) must be collected, managed, maintained, and stored. The growth in available information, both spatial and nonspatial, combined with much of the data being in digital form creates an environment for the use of artificial intelligence (AI). AI can provide new modalities of working with and analyzing large-scale data. Historically, property assessment organizations made manual valuations on paper using analog methods. Valuation organizations have undergone a quantum shift and now depend on digital data (e.g., spatial data and large databases), data modeling and analysis, computing software and hardware, 3D digital visualization, and data modeling techniques involving AI and machine learning (IAAO 2022).

AI is a broad term that includes technologies such as machine learning, deep learning, data mining, and optimization (McCluskey and Anand 1999). Machine learning, for instance, comprises statistical methods or algorithms that find patterns in massive amounts of data. Advanced neural network applications are well suited to identifying underlying patterns in data that would otherwise remain hidden. Ultimately, the goal is to use these new technologies to estimate or predict property values. But when taxpayers appeal valuations, direct market evidence is the recourse—that is, comparable transactions. The International Property Tax Institute considers AI as the collection of mathematical and statistical methods operationalized in software allowing outputs to be generated absent formal programming from inputted data (IAAO 2022). In addition, machine learning covers a vast array of algorithms that allow software to learn from the data, in the form of textual material, quantitative measures, spatial or locational information, and imagery (such as aerial and satellite).

To integrate AI processes, jurisdictions must develop strategies that involve significant change management. While the use of AI is not yet

Table 5.5 Use of Automated Valuation Models (AVMs) and Computer-Assisted Mass Appraisals (CAMAs)

Country	Application of CAMAs/ AVMs	Comment
Denmark	Yes	Transitioning to statistically based valuation models
Estonia	Yes	The revaluation of 2022 was largely driven by mass valuation
Finland		Some exploratory research into mass valuation for land parcels
France		Proposals have been made to apply mass valuation techniques
Germany		Assessment methodology uses few variables, so automation determines the tax liability
Greece		Automation adjusts the zone value with several coefficients such as age and size
Ireland		Automated valuations were developed only for residential property
Latvia	Yes	Mass valuation models have been developed for the main property types
Netherlands	Yes	Private sector firms have adopted mass valuation techniques
Poland		Academic research is investigating the use of AVMs
Russia	Yes	The provincial valuation authorities are applying mass valuation models
Slovenia	Yes	Mass valuation models have been developed for the main property types
Spain	Yes	Automated methods support annual updates on property values
United Kingdom	Yes	Mass valuation in Northern Ireland is used primarily for residential property; no similar approaches used in Great Britain

Source: Authors' compilation.

widespread, some jurisdictions have begun to adopt it in mass appraisal and mass data collection (IPTI 2021). The reasons for the slow absorption of AI into property tax administration are varied, but among the most important are the lack of competition that has fueled private sector applications, the demand for greater transparency in assessments, and the complexity of AI. AI may eventually produce values that are more accurate than those obtained by traditional equation-based approaches. Additional advantages include objectivity, efficiency, and cost. AI drawbacks include lack of a tangible statistical model, lack of user understanding, and ultimately, lack of industry and taxpayer acceptance. As in other appraisal methods, success depends on data sufficiency and integrity. In addition, a jurisdiction must possess the necessary data analysts and supporting software. In short, AI provides a powerful option for those who have the disposition to use it and the data scientists to test and potentially adopt it (IPTI 2021).

Efficient operating procedures and the need to drive down the administrative cost of valuations is pushing valuation organizations to embrace new technologies and new automated valuation approaches. For many jurisdictions, adopting AI in valuation represents a large leap in business processes and other areas requiring a change management solution.

Quality Control of Valuation

A quality audit gives an objective opinion as to the quality of valuations and comments on the procedures and practices adopted. However, *quality* needs to be defined in terms of what is being measured, how it is being measured, and what the quality standards and benchmarks should be (IAAO 2022; IPTI 2021). Two constituent parts need to be considered: a procedural audit (examining whether legislative requirements have been met, appropriate valuation methods used, and standard guidelines followed); and a ratio study to test for valuation accuracy and uniformity.

A robust system of quality assurance tests the results of large-scale revaluations of predicted property values against quality control standards. The main objective is to have estimated assessed values as close to market prices as possible. In essence, the results of AVMs can be tested through the application of statistically based ratio studies (IAAO 2013). Ratio studies are common in the context of property tax and refer to the analysis of the relationship between assessed property values and their corresponding market prices, ensuring that the tax burden is distributed equitably among property owners (IAAO 2013).

With greater reliance on AVMs there will be a pressing need to undertake quality assurance audits to provide evidence that the estimations of value are in line with recognized international standards (IAAO 2013; 2014; 2017; 2018). Also, such audits provide support when the estimates of value are challenged.

Property Data

Two data components are key to the success of a value-based property tax. The first relates to the coverage of the tax base, or the stock of properties liable to the property tax. The second relates to data supporting the valuation of the tax base, such as sales and other transactions.

First, the property taxation system requires an accurate, comprehensive, up-to-date register of properties. Data quality is of fundamental importance. Ultimately, the quality of the valuations depends on the accuracy of the captured information on all properties. Some countries appear to need to improve data quality. For example, the accuracy of Finland's building data raises significant concerns. Data collection must be a continuous process to reflect daily changes in the property stock. Poor data within the fiscal cadastral and property registration system must be corrected over time using traditional field visits and other manual approaches and technologically advanced techniques such as aerial photography, drone aerial technology, LiDAR (light detection and ranging). Although manual collection is still important, particularly to verify existing data (Poland), countries use multiple modes of data collection (France, the Netherlands, Russia, Slovenia, and the United Kingdom). Mass data collection projects are becoming much rarer primarily because of the cost. The ultimate goal is to have correct, accurate data on all properties; however, given the number of properties involved, this takes time. For example, a jurisdiction with 7.5 million taxable objects (buildings) and land parcels, each having only 10 parameters, results in 75 million bits of information. Any one incorrect parameter of information can cause inaccuracy in the final valuation.

The fiscal cadastre is a comprehensive register of real estate including records of all taxable properties and their characteristics, including taxpayer identification, assessments, and tax obligations (Almy 2014). Essentially, it is a public record of the extent, value, and ownership of land and buildings. Maintaining the fiscal, or property, cadastre is the foundation of a property tax administration system. However, maintaining cadastres and keeping them up to date is difficult, complex, and costly (Almy 2014). It often requires data from several different sources, such as the legal cadastre, building control departments, notaries, and ministries such as land, agriculture, and tourism. Property data for valuation can be stored within the fiscal cadastre typically managed by the valuation authority (as is the case in Ireland and the United Kingdom). In Denmark, the data for property tax assessment are primarily sourced from the digital building register, which from 2018 has been managed by the Property Assessment Agency. Other data draw from entities including the Land Registry, Danish Cadastre, and Agency of Planning and Rural Districts, which supplies planning (zoning) data.

Alternatively, the data can be held and managed by a cadastral authority, which often conducts valuations. For example, Spain's cadastral authority collects property data in three main ways: from the property registry or the notarial system after the transaction is completed, through an owner self-declaring information, and the cadastre's own data collection. There is no requirement to physically inspect the properties because technical and property-related information is contained in official documents, but the cadastre performs inspections if required. In Latvia, the State Land Service maintains the cadastre, in which information concerning land and buildings is registered and updated, including their cadastral values and taxpayers (information drawn from the land register about real property owners, lawful possessors, and taxable users). In addition, it distributes cadastral values and data necessary for the administration of the real property tax to municipalities. Municipalities receive data from the cadastre in a direct (live), daily exchange of relevant information.

The Slovenian land registry holds data on all land parcels, buildings, and parts of buildings and their ownership. Each object has a unique identifier, information on size (usually based on a geodetic survey), and a description of basic characteristics, such as actual and intended use for land; information on productive capacity for agricultural and forest land; and information on year of construction, building type, maintenance, and equipment.

In Russia, state registration in the Unified State Register of Real Estate is generally required for any interest in real estate (including land parcels). Property objects have no tax liability until the ownership is recorded in the Unified State Register. The register contains information on key characteristics of each object of real estate (such as its cadastral number, size, location, and permitted use), legal title (such as current and past owners), and encumbrances (mortgages and easements).

In most countries it is very common for the valuation authority or tax administration to request municipalities to verify data. Municipalities in the Netherlands are required to maintain the inventories of properties within their jurisdictions. These municipal inventories include the details of prescribed primary and secondary object characteristics, or property attributes. Property attributes are manually collected, but updating them is increasingly being achieved through automated detection. This technology, also known as *smart mapping*, establishes, for example, where buildings have changed or vacant properties have been developed. However, physical inspections form a big part of the municipal responsibilities and are mandatory for informing the accuracy of the assessed value of the property.

Self-declaration of property characteristics by taxpayers is commonplace (Finland, Ireland, and Slovenia). The Finnish Tax Administration sends all taxpayers who have been levied real estate taxes a declaration of the property information that defines the tax. The taxpayer has the responsibility to verify the information on such matters as the surface area, building right, planning stage, riparian rights, designated use, and ownership and possession rights, as well as the information used for calculating the replacement value of the buildings. In Slovenia, the Surveying and Mapping Agency manages cadastral data; owners first declare the physical characteristics of their property on prescribed forms. In Greece, each owner (by share of property ownership) declares property characteristics online to the tax administration. This involves some eight million declarations, though no declaration is required if there is no change to the property from the previous year.

Self-assessment of property ownership or occupancy and of physical characteristics of properties is much less demanding than other methods and introduces transparency. The property tax reform in Germany following the Constitutional Court decision has required property owners since July 1, 2022, to submit a property tax declaration as the basis for determining the property tax value. After the federal Ministry of Finance extended the deadline, owners submissions were due January 31, 2023. The scale of the exercise is huge, consisting of some 36 million property tax returns.

A further approach to data management holds valuation-related data in separate registers managed by different government entities. Ideally, these registers are interoperable to allow sharing and exchange of data. For example, municipalities in Finland maintain building registers and are responsible for delivering building information to the Finnish Tax Administration, which performs the valuation. In addition, information about real property units (such as real property identifiers, taxable surface area, ownership data, etc.) is provided by the National Land Survey of Finland, which collects and maintains the information. In Poland, the Integrated Real Estate Information System, a tool that determines the tax assessment by comparing real estate tax records with the real estate cadastre, is not fully operative as of 2025. The main obstacle is the incomplete transfer of data from the Land and Building Register (real estate cadastre), with which all registers communicate (including land and mortgage registers and real estate tax records). The 380 counties in Poland maintain the Land and Building Register.

The Netherlands identifies three main property data sources or base registers for valuation purposes. These are cadastre, register of inhabitants, and register of addresses and buildings. The Netherlands' Cadastre, Land Registry and Mapping Agency collects and registers administrative and spatial data on property and the legal rights. The main property register is the System of Key Registers, which consists of 13 relational databases. The Key Register for Assessed Values (Basisregistratie Waarde Onroerende Zaken, WOZ) is designed in accordance with the Special Act for Real Estate Assessment. The data fields include the WOZ value, valuation date, valuation object (property description), and person liable for payment of the property tax (Bervoets et al. 2024). These property datasets are continually updated and checked by various stakeholders. The market value of property is determined as if all the rights on that property belong to a single party.

Property data held in a country's land and building cadastre is commonly the basis for assessing the recurrent property tax. In Poland, Russia, Slovenia, and Spain, for example, only data contained in the cadastre are taken into account, even if they are incorrect. The data for valuation can be shared with the public; however, openness and transparency must be balanced with respecting the confidentiality of personal data.

Technology and Satellite and Aerial Imagery

Information and communications technology is a transformative tool. It supports valuation authorities and tax administrations in more efficiently administering the property tax (ADB 2023; Raich and Kwak 2023) and has transformed how governments interact with citizens and deliver services (World Bank 2016). Technology is advancing exponentially and becoming increasingly affordable, providing a clear enabler for transformation in public service delivery. For revenue administration, these technologies aid governments in thinking about their business and critically looking at whether their services and business models are aligned to support revenue administration in the 21st century (OECD 2016a). Technology used in valuation is increasingly more affordable, particularly with the availability of open-source systems such as the mapping software QGIS[5] and the statistical software R[6] for data analysis and modeling.

Technologies such as the internet, portal solutions, social media, mobile platforms, cloud computing, aerial imagery, artificial intelligence, machine learning, and big data create opportunities for governments' revenue administration (OECD 2016b). In many countries, information on where properties are located is of primary importance. Satellite imagery is extremely useful in identifying properties, and its cost keeps lowering, to the extent that some online providers have no charge (Ali, Deininger, and Wild 2018). Remote sensing obtains physical properties of a geographic area without actually having to be there. This technology allows an eyes-in-the-sky approach as opposed to feet-on-the-ground, although the latter is still important for verification. It provides a picture at a specific resolution, called *raster data*, captured at a specific point in time. Remote sensing users capture, visualize, and analyze objects and features (such as buildings, parcel boundaries, and transport networks such as roads and railways) on the surface of the earth. Daily, several million images are generated from space by an ever-growing number of satellites. Satellite imagery enables regular remote monitoring of many aspects, such as changes in urban development including newly built-up areas. Earth observation data offer invaluable insights to inform policy decisions and ultimately solve problems.

Satellites, airplanes, unmanned aerial vehicles, and mobile mapping have specialized platforms that carry remote sensing technology. Each type of sensor is suitable for specific conditions. Satellites, for example, capture a large amount of data over a large area quickly, drones are a better solution for flying in small areas and gathering information with high resolution, and airplanes and helicopters take the middle ground (Raich and Kwak 2023). Each type of sensor has its own advantages and disadvantages. Depending on the type of imagery to be captured, several factors must be considered—for example, flight restrictions (unmanned aerial vehicles may have restrictions on flight path altitude and no-fly zones), image resolution, acquisition time, and coverage.

The choice of whether to use satellite, airplane, mobile mapping, or unmanned aerial vehicles largely depends on the scale and objective of the project. Open-source imagery provided by the European Space Agency, National Aeronautics and Space Administration (NASA), the US Geological Survey, and numerous new fleets of small commercial satellites have resulted in an exponential growth in the availability of Earth observation data. Providers of open data allow different levels of free access, from viewing to downloading options for data processing. However, most of the free satellite data available is either dated (from a couple of months or years ago) or low resolution. Free virtual mapping within certain map views and service transactions through satellite imagery are rapidly increasing and available through many sources like Google Earth, Nokia's Here, Microsoft's Bing Maps, Flash Earth, Apple's iOS 3D Maps, and Skyline Globe.

One of the most important ways European countries use aerial technology is to identify changes to properties such as additions, extensions, and swimming pools (Radzali and Tahar 2018). Drones are proving useful for property inspections—for example, where physical access to residential properties (particularly large detached dwellings) is difficult. Given the availability of satellite data, making use of it is a clear course for assessment and valuation organizations.

Transaction Prices

Property transaction prices are an invaluable component of property data, and being able to capture and register transactions as they occur is essential, despite the relatively small number of transactions that occur each year. A notary usually conducts property transfers to ensure registration in the legal cadastre. Transfer documentation normally includes the sale price agreed between the buyer and seller. Declared prices need to be extracted and subjected to a range of quality control checks on the actual price and the property characteristics. Transactions are a multipurpose resource that support market valuations but are also used in developing real estate sectorial indexes such as single-residential properties, apartments, nonagricultural land, and commercial real estate.

Adopting market-based property valuations requires transaction evidence (Franzsen and McCluskey 2013). Underdeclaration of transaction prices occurs in some countries (Greece), but is not a significant issue in the countries in part 2. Several countries have established open and transparent databases of real estate sales prices (e.g., Ireland and Slovenia). A transaction price register primarily verifies declared sales values of the property transfer taxes and the capital gains tax on real properties. A very important second purpose is to support valuations used for the recurrent property tax. Hence, the underdeclaration of transaction prices will lead to a loss of tax revenue and negatively affect the quality of valuations. Understanding why parties might underdeclare the transaction price is important. A generally accepted reason is that the parties want to pay less transfer tax. Another reason is money laundering. Or some transactions may take place informally, and cash is the payment medium, resulting in no tax.

In Slovenia (and many other European countries), if the contract price does not reflect the market value, the tax authority can revise the value to its estimate of market value. Taxpayers unsatisfied with the changed value can provide, at their expense, evidence to justify the declared price. Data on the mass appraised values of the real estate can be used as a guideline, but in the final determination of the tax base, the tax administration relies on comparable market prices.

The position in Spain is that the declared price is agreed upon by both parties of the transaction, and neither the notary nor the Property Registry can change it. The tax authorities, once the transaction is recorded and registered, perform a valuation to estimate the transaction tax. This happens once the buyer has paid the transfer taxes based on the declared value. The tax authorities confirm the property value by comparing it with the location's reference values, adapted to the specific characteristics. Transaction data are collected from the notary system and checked against data from the Property Registry. In 2021, the system to calculate the tax base for verification changed, following the introduction of the reference market value (*valor de referencia del mercado*) as the minimum taxable base for property transfer tax and inheritance tax. The new value is calculated by the cadastre authorities and will be greater than the cadastral value, in some cases up to 90 percent of the market value. These reference values are made public, calculated every year, and on the cadastre's website.

Several features of the French system may contribute to limiting tax evasion. First, the notary fee is proportional to the transaction price. Second, if the declared value is low with respect to the market price, the tax authorities may suspend the transaction. This must occur within two months of the agreement between seller and buyer, and the state or local authority exerts a preemptive right to buy the property at the declared price, in lieu of the private buyer. Third, the tax authorities can fine the buyer and also claim transfer taxes on the true market value. The incentive basis of the whole tax system also plays a role. Buyers who underdeclare pay less stamp duty tax (the sum of the transfer tax and notary and registration fees, 7 to 8 percent of the transaction price) but pay more in capital gains tax in the future.

In Scotland, General Avoidance Rules are applied by Revenue Scotland to protect against tax evasion and avoidance. In particular, the rules can target payment returns made for the land and buildings transaction tax.

In Greece, if the declared sale price is lower than market value (as determined by valuers appointed by banks), the bank making the loan ties it to the declared sale price, and potential borrowers might not receive adequate financing.

Underdeclaration could be a major impediment to a value-based property tax. The following initiatives could discourage it: make mandatory that the proceeds of buying and selling real estate be processed through the banking or financial sectors, prohibit property being purchased or sold unless it is registered in the national legal cadastre, develop a national database of transactions, design an automated system to approve the transaction price or flag suspect prices, reduce or abolish the property transfer tax if it is considered a reason behind underdeclaration, impose stiff penalties on those who willfully and knowingly under- or overdeclare, and electronically share notarized contracts containing the transaction price with the land cadastre and the national database of transactions.

Sales Price Register

Several countries have developed sales price registers and have demonstrated their potential for becoming the definitive source of transaction prices. Essentially a database, the register establishes value parameters for property types and benchmark values for national taxes such as property transfer tax and capital gains tax involving real estate. In France, for example, a research tool, Patrim, allows taxpayers to obtain the purchase price of transactions of neighboring properties and estimate the value of their property. Notaries collect the data and transmit it to the tax administration.

In Slovenia, the Surveying and Mapping Authority manages the Property Market Register, introduced in 2007. The Statistical Office of the Republic of Slovenia, National Bank of Slovenia, Macroeconomic Office of Slovenia, and other sources provide transaction data and rental contracts. The main source for price data is assessment of real estate transfer tax, reported monthly by the tax authority of the Republic of Slovenia. Sellers report prices of real estate transactions for which value-added tax has been paid. The data on rents received by natural persons are collected once a year from the assessment of tax on rental income (Žibrik and Humar 2021). Lessors report information on other rental contracts. Transaction prices are widely used for mass valuation, property indexes, individual valuation, market research for national statistics, and other purposes.

In Ireland, the Property Services Regulatory Authority compiles the Residential Property Price Register using information declared to Revenue for stamp duty purposes. The register provides information on all residential properties purchased since January 1, 2010. The property authority does not edit the data. It simply publishes, in a fully transparent manner, the data from the declarations filed with Revenue. In addition, the property authority produces the Commercial Lease Register pursuant to the Property Services (Regulation) Act 2011. This register includes information on commercial leases entered into since January 1, 2010, such as address of the property, date of the lease, term of lease, and the rent payable.

Since 1998, the State Land Service in Latvia has maintained the Real Estate Market Data Information System, which is integrated into the cadastre. It is comprehensive, containing information for all sales throughout the country. The information about the transaction is received directly from the land register. For mass valuation purposes, the State Land Service reviews all sales and uses only arm's-length transactions. The State Land Service has published raw market data, including basic data analysis (such as price levels, property data, and value maps) on its website since 2021. In part, this strengthens the public's trust and confidence in the cadastral valuation system. Most users obtain transaction data free from the State Unified Computerized Land Register and the State Land Service. The database accumulated some 120,000 transactions during 2010–2025.

The National Land Board in Estonia administers and supervises the Database of Transactions. The system has a direct link to the land cadastre and cadastral map, which enables queries on the basis of location and use of statistical tools. Sales data are used by both the public and the private sectors, although detailed transaction data is limited and not widely available.

Table 5.6 depicts countries that have and have not developed sales price registers. Many registers are stand-alone databases of transaction prices either freely available to the public or subject to a charge. In some cases only registered users can access the register. Recording market transactions is critical in the valuation process and in the verification of declared prices used for capital taxes. Countries that do not have a dedicated sales price register instead capture transaction prices in the land registration system or land cadastre, which impedes retrieval of transaction prices. Often it involves a manual search as opposed to an automated retrieval process.

Assessment Levels

Few countries value properties to 100 percent of actual market value for purposes of the property tax. The relevant property tax or valuation law usually defines the valuation standard, be it market value or assessed value. From a policy and practical point of view, and to increase system fairness, all properties must be valued in a uniform manner. A ratio analysis measures the closeness of estimated market values to their respective sales prices.

Table 5.6 Sales Price Register (SPR)

Country	Established SPR	Responsible Authority	Comment
Denmark	No		Transactions recorded in land registry
Estonia	Yes	National Land Board	Established in 1996; rental contracts not collected; limited public access
Finland	No		
France	Yes	Tax administration	Sales registered in cadastre
Germany	No		
Greece	No		Sales registered in national cadastre
Ireland	Yes	Property Services Regulatory Authority	Full disclosure of details on transaction prices including specific location
Latvia	Yes	State Land Service	Data is open to the public
Netherlands	Yes	National cadastre	Data available to the public
Poland	No		
Russia	No		
Slovenia	Yes	Surveying and Mapping Authority	Public access available; rental contracts collected
Spain	Yes	Tax administration	All transaction flow to the tax administration
United Kingdom	No		Transaction prices are recorded by the Land Registry; the data can be purchased by users

Source: Authors' compilation.

Assessment levels are a different concept and relate more to tax policy. They are set by government and involve applying a fixed percentage to the property's market value to determine its assessed value for tax purposes. On one hand, they are relatively simple and easy to administer, providing a standardized approach to uniformly apply across different properties. On the other, system fairness can decrease, because they assume a constant ratio for all properties regardless of specific characteristics or market fluctuations. The Danish Valuation Authority has adopted a precautionary principle for property assessments, which recognizes that there will always be uncertainty when it comes to a property assessment because the real property value is determined by two independent parties negotiating a mutually acceptable price. The property assessment is reduced by 20 percent, and thus the taxable value is 80 percent of the property's assessed value. For example, if the property assessment of a house is DKK 8 million, 20 percent is subtracted from the property assessment, and the property value tax is calculated on the remaining DKK 6.4 million. The precautionary principle, intended to benefit the individual taxpayer, can complicate taxpayer complaints about a property assessment. Unless evidence proves that the property assessment deviates more than approximately 20 percent from the established property value, the taxpayer's complaint is denied.

Finland deems the taxable value of land as 73.5 percent of the prevailing market price. In Latvia, the degree of accuracy of cadastral value as required by law was 85 percent of market value. Revaluations were conducted on a two-year cycle, and valuations were made one and a half years before the values came into force for taxation purposes. Then legislation in 2017 lowered the mandated accuracy of the cadastral value and increased the valuation cycle to every four years. The real estate market in different territories of Latvia, however, develops differently, and some still value at 85 percent of market value.

Property Tax Reforms

Several tax policies by design deal with relatively small numbers of taxpayers, such as owners of undeveloped land, owners of second homes, and pensioners (deferral programs). However, reform in three major areas could have significant system-wide fiscal impacts: revaluation, the basis of the property tax, and a wholly new property tax. Revaluation is primarily a procedural matter, but the last two are matters of policy.

Revaluations are problematic because they can be canceled, postponed, or deferred for reasons including politics and major calamities (such as COVID-19 and severe climatic events) and because of their cost. Frequent reassessments, often undertaken to maintain revenue neutrality or make a modest increase in line with inflation, increase costs further. As property price movements are asymmetrical by geographic location, a revaluation could have a potentially significant redistributive effect.

Several examples of postponed or deferred revaluations include Estonia, Ireland, and Northern Ireland. Other countries, such as Finland, France, Germany, and Great Britain, have largely ignored revaluing the tax base. Some revaluations were fairly disastrous—for example, Denmark and to some extent Latvia. Using indexing between revaluations is not a perfect solution but arguably better than nothing (though this depends on the type of index used). France and Finland used uplifts, largely to protect revenues. In Great Britain and Northern Ireland, the base values are well out of date but remain fixed, and revenue buoyancy is achieved through annually adjusting the tax rate.

Some good practices are evident where revaluations are conducted more frequently, such as in the Netherlands. In Slovenia, property values are updated regularly but not used for the recurrent property tax. Greece is interesting in that, since the late 2010s and into the early 2020s, the underlying value of properties (referred to as the objective value) has been regularly revised.

Changing the basis of the property tax is quite rare. This means a switch from, say, area-based assessment to one based on property value, or switching between one value basis to another—for example, from land value to capital value. Changing value basis inevitably involves a significant redesign of the property tax in terms of valuation, data, and information and communications technology systems. In addition, new legislation and extensive taxpayer communication will be required. The planning and preparation can take several years, and success depends on full political support from all parties.

Some of the countries in part 2 made a switch, some successful, others less so. A success story is Northern Ireland, where the previous basis of the property tax was the annual rental value (which had been in place since the mid-1800s). The Northern Ireland Assembly decided in 2002, on the basis of a series of diagnostic reports, to adopt capital value as the basis for taxing residential property. The planning took several years, and the reformed residential property tax became operational in 2007 (basing property values on 2005 levels). Disappointingly, no revaluations of the base have yet taken place, though a revaluation may happen in 2030.

The government of Great Britain (England, Scotland, and Wales) replaced the property tax levied on residential property with a non-property-based community charge (commonly referred to as the poll tax) in 1989 (Scotland) and 1990 (England and Wales). A national taxpayer revolt against the community charge resulted in its abandonment and replacement with a capital value–based property tax (the council tax) in 1993 (residential property values were determined as at 1991 levels). In this successful implementation, some 25 million dwellings were valued in less than one year. Wales is the only jurisdiction in Great Britain to revise the value bands and property values (values were revised in 2005 on the basis of 2003 values). The Welsh Assembly is expected to conduct a revaluation in 2028 (Adam et al. 2020). The property values in England and Scotland have not been revised since 1991.

Among the countries in part 2, only the Netherlands abandoned an area-based property tax for one based on market value. In the early 1990s, municipalities could chose to adopt either a value basis or an area basis (McCluskey 1991). Implementing the area basis involved a complex array of adjustment multipliers, and only a few municipalities opted to use the area basis, leading the government to abolish this basis (Youngman and Malme 1993).

Slovenia designed and partially implemented a market value–based system but was unable to replace the area-based property tax with the market value–based one. The assessed market values are, however, used for other purposes such as checking declared transaction prices and as inputs into determining social security payments. No political party has yet taken the initiative to introduce market value as the basis of the property tax.

In Ireland, the residential property tax was abolished in the 1970s, and a local property tax on residential property was reintroduced in 2013. The implementation was a success (undertaken within a relatively short time frame), but since introduction, the planned three-year revaluations have been regularly postponed. However, a revaluation did occur in 2021.

A few countries in part 2 present interesting elements related to valuation reforms.

Estonia

Statistical estimation models assisted in the delivery of the 2022 revaluation of the land tax base. Introduced in 1993, the land tax was based on the market value of the land parcel. Estonia is the only country in Europe to levy the recurrent property tax solely on the basis of the value of land. The object of a valuation is a parcel of land without consideration of buildings, forests, or other crops on the land. Legislation did not prescribe a revaluation cycle but assigned the Minister of the Environment to schedule revaluation, and that became a major issue. The first valuation, in 1993, was followed by revaluations in 1996 and 2001. The next took place in 2022, to become effective in 2024. Amendments to the Land Valuation Act in 2020 now mandate revaluations on a four-year cycle.

The 2022 land valuation increased the taxable value of land significantly, on average by 8.3 times. To avoid future rapid increases in the land tax burden, the maximum tax rates were reduced by up to 20 percent of their previous level for 2024, and the tax was limited to increasing by no more than 10 percent or €5 annually, whichever was smaller. However, these limits have resulted in a situation where some local governments' land tax revenue in 2024 will be lower than in 2023.[7] From 2026, local governments will be able to set their own annual land tax growth limits, ranging from 10 to 100 percent. The amendments to the Land Valuation Act in 2020 eliminate the nationwide area-based exemption for residential land, and from 2026, local governments can set the amount of the exemption for residential land, from €5 to €1,000, meaning that tax must be paid for the portion exceeding the exemption limit.

Denmark

The valuation of land and buildings has been an ongoing problem in Denmark for several years. Attempts to improve the quality of the valuations have resulted in responsibility for valuation shifting among entities. Since 2011, the Danish Property Assessment Agency has had responsibility for valuation. Efforts to improve the quality of the assessed values have largely failed, which has resulted in no revaluations since 2011. A government agency report criticized the Ministry of Taxation for its administration of public property assessments (Office of the Danish Auditor General 2013). The ministry was aware that valuation had been a cause for concern for several years. In an earlier report (no. 2/2011), Rigsrevisionen, the office of the Danish Auditor General, called on the Ministry of Taxation to improve administration of property assessments, criticized for being outdated and inaccurate. As of 2025, the government is comprehensively reviewing the property assessment system. The Danish Property Tax Act, dealing with both the property value tax and the land tax, has been in effect since July 2023. It makes permanent the tax freeze scheme. First implemented in 2001, the scheme freezes the property taxes (property value tax and land tax) at their current level if they increase in the future, until the property is sold. Thus, in reality, this is a loan with a low interest rate.

For several years, the Danish Property Assessment Agency has been developing a new automated valuation system to improve assessment accuracy. In September 2023, the Danish Property Assessment Agency published 1.7 million preliminary assessments for the 2022 tax year. Significant disparities between assessed values and market prices caused major public debate. The office of the Danish Parliamentary Ombudsman announced that it plans to look into the assessment process and the quality of the data used for the preliminary property assessments.

Greece

The taxation of real property in Greece from 2010 to 2015 went through a number of significant reforms. Policy makers saw the property tax as a measure to improve state revenues; however, to property taxpayers it was a severe austerity measure. A recurrent property taxation scheme was introduced in 2011, Special Property Tax for Electrified Surfaces, to be administered through electricity bills. The Greek Public Power Corporation had a property register, but coverage and data were incomplete, though the municipal tax has historically been collected as part of the electricity bill. The recurrent property tax was based on floor-area data, collected by the electricity company. In 2013, Greece's Supreme Court of Civil and Penal Law ruled the special property tax levied through the electricity bills was unconstitutional and in violation of the European Convention on Human Rights. The government in 2014 replaced the electricity bill tax with the Uniform Real Estate Property Tax (ENFIA), a comprehensive tax on real estate. Owners also pay a supplementary tax calculated on the same basis of the property tax.

A significant problem facing the government was the lack of a comprehensive and complete register of taxable land and buildings. The land registration system did not have sufficient coverage or granular enough data on real properties to be useful. To properly administer the new property tax, the state needed data on every property. The Ministry of Finance had the tax administration reengineer the owner self-declaration form, which all owners complete digitally and submit annually.

The main problem with the administration of the property tax was the few revisions of the basis of property value, the objective value, a concept introduced in 1985 to reflect a property's market value. The objective values were updated in 2007 and then more recently in 2020. The objective value is the value of one square meter of a standardized residential property: a new second-floor apartment with frontage on one road. Objective values vary by zone, or an area where properties have similar market values. A property's tax rate is, then, its objective value for the value zone it is in after adjustment coefficients are applied. Commercial properties are valued according to the residential zone value and then adjusted with a coefficient that reflects the trading or commercial quality of the street. This blunt methodology lacks precision in determining discrete property values.

Before 2018, around 10,200 value zones covered only part of Greece's land area; they did not exist outside urban planned areas. The Ministry of Finance expanded the coverage of the property valuation system by defining more value zones, using private sector valuers who followed a prescribed methodology and provided evidence (analysis of comparable sales) they had used to determine the zonal value. A ministerial decision in May 2021 officially adopted, published, and entered into force as of January 2022 ENFIA's new objective value property tax, property transfer tax, and inheritance tax.

Ireland

Ireland needed to broaden its property tax base and implement a pragmatic valuation solution. The recurrent property tax on residential property was abolished in the 1970s, largely due to criticism of the inequities arising from the out-of-date valuation system. It took the 2008–2009 financial crisis to bring focus to reintroducing the tax. The financial support program of the European Commission, International Monetary Fund, and European Central Bank (the so-called Troika) committed Ireland to introduce a residential property tax to widen its tax base.

The Irish government made two bold policy decisions to support the quick introduction of the local property tax (levied only on residential property): use value bands as opposed to discrete value assessments for each property, and have property owners perform self-assessments (Kennedy and Walsh 2016). These policies are not commonly found in property tax systems internationally. According to the OECD (2021), banding and self-assessment could be considered, at least in theory, second-best solutions compared with the more standard forms of valuation and assessment. But the absence of an up-to-date register of residential properties effectively ruled out valuation by the government. Property valuation is not an exact science, and valuation bands ease the valuation challenge (Commission on Taxation 2009). Owner self-assessments seemed appropriate given the time constraints (Turley 2022).

The valuation exercise involved some 1.9 million properties valued by self-assessment as of May 1, 2013 (the same values applied for the following three years). Could the policy choices made by Ireland be considered a success? The new tax was implemented quickly, in months rather than years. A potential successful feature of the tax, and a potential lesson for other jurisdictions reforming property taxes, is the simplicity of the new residential property tax system, relevant for countries wishing to implement a reform but missing information on properties and having scarce property valuation skills (McCluskey 2025a). "The Programme for Government: Our Shared Future" (GoI 2020) outlined the importance of making the local property tax fairer through a revised tax liability methodology linked to an update in property values. A revaluation date of November 1, 2021, was set with the minister for Finance pushing through the necessary legislation that changed the tax charging regime from 2022 onward, including the policy to have revaluations every four years. In 2021, Revenue contacted over 1.4 million property owners of nearly 1.9 million properties that were already included on the Land Registry, setting out the requirements for owners to complete a self-assessed local property tax value estimate for the valuation period 2022–2025.

Germany

The old property tax system has been criticized for years in Germany because of the bizarre, arbitrary, and outdated way it was calculated. Property taxes in the former West German states were based on property values from 1964, whereas taxes in former East German states were based on values from 1935. The authorities had the option of updating these values every six years, but in practice this never happened (Rödding and Uetermeyer 2022). The Constitutional Court's ruling in April 2018 found the former property tax system unconstitutional, mainly due to its values being out of date and, more importantly, levied on different levels of value in different parts of the country. The Constitutional Court also set a deadline for a reform.

The federal government designed the federal tax model for states to use if they chose. Most states adopted the federal model, but five states opted to draft their own legislation and are planning to introduce a different basis of property tax. For example, the state of Baden-Württemberg passed legislation to introduce a state-wide land value tax.

The federal tax model legislation gave tax authorities two years to process an estimated 36 million property tax returns and to issue respective tax assessment notices. But the operation has seen delays since the start. Property owners were required to submit a property tax declaration with information that determines the property tax value. The original deadline for submission was October 31, 2022. The federal Ministry of Finance then extended it to January 31, 2023. Property tax values are determined with the effective date January 1, 2022. Despite a number of issues (box 5.1), the new property tax commenced on January 1, 2025.

Luxembourg

In 2022, a bill (Bill 8082) was introduced in Luxembourg's parliament aimed at reforming property taxes. This bill has several goals: modernize property assessment, encourage owners of vacant land plots to develop the land, and combat vacant housing. To achieve the latter two goals, the bill introduced two new taxes: a land mobilization tax and a vacant housing tax. In July 2025, the original bill was split into two new bills. Bill 8082A deals with property taxes and mobilizing land, while Bill 8082B deals with vacant housing—aiming at accelerating the property tax reforms (DSM 2025).

Great Britain and Northern Ireland

The UK Finance minister (chancellor of the exchequer) is considering making what could be described as significant changes to taxes on real

Box 5.1 Challenges and Issues with Germany's Property Tax Reform

The new recurrent property tax system was supposed to distribute the tax burden fairly and ensure social justice across the entire country. Authorities may have underestimated the complexity associated with self-declaration of data by property owners and the assessment of the almost 36 million properties. The process of revaluing millions of properties and communicating these assessed values to property owners is a huge task. By early 2025, the tax authority had not completed the work of providing all the municipalities with the assessed values, and some municipalities were still issuing payment notices. Hamburg, for example, extended the first payment deadline to April 30, 2025.

The Federal Fiscal Court has expressed its concern about the fairness of the new system. It ruled that property owners must be allowed to challenge their assessments on the basis of overvaluation, especially if the assessed value exceeds the current market value by more than 40 percent. According to the federal model and in Baden-Württemberg, a reduction will be considered only if the assessed value of the property exceeds the market value by €15,000, or in the federal model, the actual value is less than 40 percent of the assessed tax value.

Noncompliance with declaring property data: When property owners do not submit a property tax declaration, the tax authority may estimate the assessed value. Despite the risks involved and a promise of severe penalties, many property owners failed to submit property tax declarations. According to the Federal Ministry of Finance, only about 60 percent of property owners had submitted their property tax data by the deadline of January 31, 2023. The government responded with extensions and grace periods to solicit compliance.

Reassessment and addressing errors: The self-declaration of property data was mostly done on an online platform and resulted in numerous errors, especially regarding building area and living space. Many owners overstated dimensions, due to confusion, for example, about what constitutes living space, resulting in overassessments. Although property owners are allowed to request that errors be corrected, the correct data and concomitant reassessment cannot be applied retrospectively. The tax authority can use the corrected data only from the next year of assessment.

Dealing with objections: The overall complexity of the system, the lack of clarity and transparency, and significant increases in the tax bills of many taxpayers have resulted in large numbers of objections. By April 2025, tax offices across Germany have been swamped by more than 5.2 million objections being filed. This constitutes more than 14 percent of the total number of properties. The highest numbers come from North Rhine–Westphalia (1.5 million) and Bavaria (1.3 million), using the federal model and area-value model, respectively. This large number of objections causes delays and dissatisfaction among all stakeholders.

Revenue neutrality: Keeping the property tax reform revenue neutral, as promised by the federal government, is practically impossible. New values are determined by the tax authority, and tax assessment factors are fixed by law; some federal states opted for different valuation models, and municipalities are able to determine their own tax rate. Some municipalities have been increasing their tax rates and revenues under the old system in 2023 and 2024, so even if they reduce their rates in 2025, on the basis of the 2022 values, many if not most taxpayers will pay more tax. And even if revenue neutrality is achieved at the municipal level, few individual property owners will be paying the same amount in 2025 as in 2024. There will be winners and losers. A nationwide study by a property owners' association of about 2,000 properties indicated that 79 percent of property owners reported an increase in their property taxes.

Transparency: Despite the attempts of some federal states to improve the transparency of the new system, it remains an issue. In Schleswig-Holstein, for example, a transparency register aims to ensure municipalities implement the reform in a revenue-neutral manner, and in Lower Saxony municipalities must publish the revenue-neutral collection rate as well as the actual rate. As property tax can be passed on to tenants, they may also face additional charges.

Sources: Kingston 2024a; 2024b; KPMG, n.d.; Munich Eye 2025; Schlagenhaufer et al. 2025; Tietje 2025.

estate including the capital gains tax, stamp duty land tax, and council tax. Changes are likely to be announced in November 2025 (box 5.2).

Conclusion

"The valuation process is central to the property tax and presents its major administrative challenge" (Youngman 2016, 35). Valuation is largely estimation and as such can be challenged by the taxpayer. Significant efforts are continually made to improve the quality of transaction data in the estimation and in the models used to determine the assessed values. This requires specific skill sets. The entity or institution responsible for determining the assessed values can involve specific valuation departments (as in Denmark, Ireland, Russia, Slovenia, and the United Kingdom). Or the cadastral authority can value properties (as in Estonia, Latvia, and Spain). The private sector tends not to be widely used; the Netherlands is a notable exception.

Box 5.2 Proposed Changes to Real Estate Taxes in Great Britain and Northern Ireland

The capital gains tax (CGT) is a charge on the increase in the value of an asset when it is sold. It applies to the sale of things like paintings, second homes, and stocks and shares, but primary residences are exempt from CGT. The government is considering removing this exemption for expensive dwellings, or those over £1.5 million.

A further change being considered is the abolition of the stamp duty land tax (SDLT), which is a tax on the purchase of residential property in England and Northern Ireland (the equivalent of SDLT in Scotland and Wales is set and collected by their devolved governments). Unlike CGT, this tax does not apply to the change in value of the property but to the actual declared value of the property when bought. The proposal is that SDLT should be replaced with a national proportional property tax, levied on house values above £500,000. This rate would be set by the central government. An annual rate of 0.54 percent, with a 0.278 percent supplement on values over £1 million, would raise the same amount as the SDLT (Leunig 2025). The new tax would be payable on owner-occupied property only after a sale.

Council tax funds part of a local authority's spending. It is devolved in Scotland and Wales, while Northern Ireland uses a different tax system instead of council tax. In England and Scotland, it is based on what the value of the dwelling is in 1991, whereas in Wales, it is based on what the value of the property was in 2003. It is proposed that the council tax should be replaced with a local proportional property tax, levied on house values up to £500,000 with a minimum annual payment of £800 (Leunig 2025). The rate would be set by local authorities. A rate of 0.44 percent would raise the same amount of revenue as council tax. This would be introduced immediately, on all properties, and would be payable by the owner, not the resident.

Therefore, it is proposed that SDLT and council tax should be replaced with two annual and ongoing complementary property taxes related to the value of a dwelling. The receipts from the replacement for SDLT would accrue to national government, while the receipts from the replacement for council tax would go to the local authority as in the current system.

The above are proposals that the current government is considering given the need to raise more revenue from taxes. The proposed changes for CGT and SDLT are considered the easier options from an administrative perspective, whereas changes to the council tax would be rather more complex.

Source: Leunig (2025).

For value-based property taxes, it is hugely important to have processes in place to record transaction prices and rents, needed for assessing the value of taxable properties. Notaries are one of the key groups involved in the administration of transaction prices and rents. The declared price is normally recorded on the contract for sale or purchase, which is then submitted to the land registration or cadastral organization that formally records the change in ownership. The transaction prices need to be accurately recorded. Some countries establish a sales price register that is essentially a database of transactions (Ireland and Slovenia are good examples). The failure to record market transactions in a structured manner is a potential problem for the valuation organization. In the United Kingdom, an abridged document based on the contract and prepared by the notary gives basic information on the property that has been sold—for example, property address, parties, sale price, and date of contract signing. This document is sent directly to the Valuation Office, which stores this data.

Valuation can pose great difficulty in the recurrent property tax administration system. Many of the large-scale reforms across several European countries have involved some aspects of valuation (Denmark, Estonia, Slovenia, and the United Kingdom). Kelly (1993) makes eloquent and ultimately reasonable arguments that the focus of administrative reforms should be on the collection side of the equation as opposed to valuation. This has led to the pragmatic approach of collection-led reform as opposed to valuation-pushed reforms.

Outside Europe, such as in Indonesia (Kelly 1992; 1993; 2004; 2013; Kelly et al. 2020), some focus has been on collection-led strategies. Valuation-pushed or -led reforms have been far more common, such as in the Philippines, Thailand, and Vietnam. The focus in Europe has largely been on valuation, such as in Denmark, Estonia, the Republic of Ireland, and Russia. Greece is to some extent unique in that collection-led strategies were in the fore in the recent reforms. Improvements in tax administration such as developing comprehensive taxpayer databases and significant improvements in property coverage led to increases in revenue collections. These of course were complemented by improvements in the valuation machinery.

Self-declaration of taxable value by property owners is not widely used, though Ireland used this approach with the introduction of a value-based recurrent property tax on residential property. The valuation exercise in Ireland saw some 1.9 million property owners declaring, not the exact value of their property, but the value band it belonged to. To support owners in this exercise, the government provided quite extensive guidance and indicative values at a very local level. Owners underdeclaring the value of their property did not seem to be an issue. According to statistics published by Revenue (Revenue 2021), only 14,900 values were challenged, representing only 0.78 percent of all properties.

Assessment levels (or fractional assessments) are used by only a few countries in Europe (including Denmark, Finland, and Latvia). An assessment level is a policy to determine the taxable value of a property as a percentage of the assessed value. For example, if the assessment level is 50 percent and the assessed value of the property is 100,000 monetary units, then the taxable value is 50,000. If the assessment level is uniform across all properties, in theory there is no impact on effective tax rates. Nonuniform or differential assessment levels would affect effective tax rates. In applying assessment levels, the practice normally is to reduce the number of formal appeals because taxpayers tend to believe their property is assessed below the market value.

Reform of the recurrent property tax can involve policy-related reforms and others more administrative in nature (Grover et al. 2017). Major valuation reforms, however, can lead to taxpayer resistance and political turmoil because the property tax typically affects tens of thousands if not millions of taxpayers (Grote and Wen 2024). The valuation exercise's scale has inevitably resulted in development of automated processes. The introduction of multiple regression techniques that allowed for the valuation of thousands of properties on the basis of statistical formulas was considered a game changer. Developments in the use of AI have been contributing to the use of machine learning algorithms in driving valuation models forward. While these models are not without issues, they will be an important part of supporting valuation activities. Clearly, AI is here to stay and will slowly be integrated into valuation systems. Investment in skilled human resources will be necessary as the valuation techniques become more scientifically based.

Notes

1. The community charge was levied at a flat rate per adult and had itself replaced the long-standing domestic rates, a tax on the gross rental value of each property. The council tax is a compromise between the domestic rates system and the poll tax: the tax liability moved back from a flat charge to one related to property values. The council tax retained a link with the poll tax in its 25 percent discount for single-adult households.

2. Structures can include swimming pools, tennis courts, and so on.

3. Other European countries that use area-based systems are the Czech Republic and Slovakia.

4. The model supports and improves data quality management in real estate administration by focusing on synergy that develops when multiple entities are involved in collecting land-related data. Data standards contribute to the avoidance of inconsistencies and duplication of data maintained by different organizations.

5. Spatial Without Compromise, QGIS, accessed July 24, 2025, https://www.qgis.org/.
6. What Is R?, R Foundation, accessed July 24, 2025, https://www.r-project.org/about.html.
7. Balticnews, "Estonian Govt Approves Bill Seeking to Increase Land Tax," May 11, 2024, https://balticnews.com/estonian-govt-approves-bill-seeking-to-increase-land-tax/.

References

Adam, S., L. Hodge, G. Phillips, and X. Xu. 2020. *Revaluation and Reform: Bringing Council Tax in England into the 21st Century.* London: Institute for Fiscal Studies.

ADB. 2023. *Leveraging Technology for Property Tax Management in Asia and the Pacific: Guidance Note.* Manila, Philippines: Asia Development Bank.

Ahmad, E., G. Brosio, and J. P. Jiménez. 2019. "Options for Retooling Property Taxation in Latin America." Macroeconomics of Development series No. 202 (LC/TS.2019/91). Santiago, Chili: Economic Commission for Latin America and the Caribbean.

Ali, D. A., K. Deininger, and M. Wild. 2018. "Using Satellite Imagery to Revolutionize Creation of Tax Maps and Local Revenue Collection." Policy Working paper No. 8437. Washington, DC: World Bank.

Almy, R. 2013. "A Global Compendium and Meta-Analysis of Property Tax Systems." Working paper. Cambridge, MA: Lincoln Institute of Land Policy.

———. 2014. "Valuation and Assessment of Immovable Property." Working paper on Fiscal Federalism No. 19. Paris: OECD. https://dx.doi.org/10.1787/5jz5pzvr28hk-en.

Bervoets, B. P. P., L. D. Hermans, R. M. Kathmann, and M. Kuijper. 2024. "Lessons from the Netherlands: Real Estate Assessment and Property Tax Systems." Netherlands Council for Real Estate Assessment and the Lincoln Institute of Land Policy. The Hague, Netherlands.

Bidanset, P. 2014. *Moving Automated Valuation Models Out of the Box: A Global Geography of AVMs.* Fair and Equitable. Kansas City, MO: International Association of Assessing Officers.

Bird, R. M., and E. Slack, eds. 2004. *International Handbook of Land and Property Taxation.* Cheltenham, UK: Edward Elgar.

Blöchliger, H. 2015. "Reforming the Tax on Immovable Property: Taking Care of the Unloved. OECD Economics Department. Working paper No. 1205.

Cheshire, P., and C. Hilber. 2021. *Home Truths: Options for Reforming Residential Property Taxes in England.* London: Bright Blue Campaign.

Commission on Taxation report 2009. Government Stationary Office. Dublin, Ireland.

Connolly, K., and M. E. Bell. 2009. "Area-Based Property Tax Systems: Current Practice and Equity Concerns." Working paper. Cambridge, MA: Lincoln Institute of Land Policy.

Department of Housing, Local Government and Heritage. 2023. *Overview of the Rates Revisions in Local Authorities Value for Money.* Dublin: Unit Local Government Audit Service.

DSM. 2025. "Property Tax Reform: A Substantial Overhaul of the Bill." DSM Avocats à la cour (September 4). https://www.dsm.legal/en/property-tax-reform-a-substantial-overhaul-of-the-bill/.

Franzsen, R., and W. McCluskey. 2013. "Value-Based Approaches to Property Taxation." In McCluskey, Cornia, and Walters, *A Primer on Property Tax*. https://doi.org/10.1002/9781118454343.ch2.

GoI. 2020. "The Programme for Government: Our Shared Future." Dublin. https://assets.gov.ie/130911/fe93e24e-dfe0-40ff-9934-def2b44b7b52.pdf.

GOV.UK. n.d. "Check Your Council Tax Band." Accessed March 25, 2026. www.gov.uk/council-tax-bands.

Grote, M., and J.-F. Wen. 2024. "How to Design and Implement Property Tax Reforms." IMF How to Note 2024/006. Washington, DC: International Monetary Fund.

Grover, R., M.-P. Törhönen, P. Munro-Faure, and A. Anand. 2015. "Property Valuation and Taxation for Fiscal Sustainability and Improved Local Governance: Case Studies from the ECA Region." Paper presented at the World Bank Conference on Land and Poverty. Washington, DC (March 23–27).

———. 2017. "Achieving Successful Implementation of Value-Based Property Tax Reforms in Emerging European Economies." *Journal of European Real Estate Research* 10(1): 91–106.

Hagemann, R. 2018. "Tax Policies for Inclusive Growth: Prescription versus Practice." Economic Policy Papers No. 24. Paris: OECD. https://dx.doi.org/10.1787/09ba747a-en.

IAAO (International Association of Assessing Officers). 2013. *Standard on Ratio Studies*. Kansas City, MO: IAAO.

———. 2014. *Guidance on International Mass Appraisal and Related Tax Policy*. Kansas City, MO: IAAO.

———. 2017. *Standard on Mass Appraisal of Real Property: A Criterion for Measuring Fairness, Quality, Equity and Accuracy*. Kansas City, MO: IAAO.

———. 2018. *Standard on Automated Valuation Methods*. Kansas City, MO: IAAO.

———. 2020. *Standard on Property Tax Policy*. Kansas City, MO: IAAO.

———. 2022. "A Review of the Methods, Applications, and Challenges of Adopting Artificial Intelligence in the Property Assessment Office." *Journal of Property Tax Assessment and Administration* 19(1).

IPTI. 2021. "The Potential of Artificial Intelligence in Property Assessment." White Paper. International Property Tax Institute, Toronto, Canada.

Jason, W. 2021. "How the Lincoln Institute Helped Bring Property Taxes into the Computer Age." *Land Lines*, January/April. https://www.lincolninst.edu/publications/articles/2021-01-city-tech-how-lincoln-institute-helped-bring-property-taxes-digital-age/.

Kara, A., P. J. van Oosterom, V. Çağdaş, Ü. Işıkdağ, and C. Lemmen. 2018. "3D Data for Better Property Value Estimation in the Context of LADM Valuation Information Model." Paper presented at the 6th International FIG Workshop on 3D Cadastres, Delft, the Netherlands (October 2–4).

Kelly, R. 1992. *Property Tax Reform in South-East Asia: A Comparative Analysis of Indonesia, the Philippines and Thailand*. Paper presented at Pacific Rim Council on Urban Development Conference, Yokohama, Japan.

———. 1993. "Property Tax Reform in Indonesia: Applying a Collection Led Strategy." *Bulletin of Indonesian Economic Studies* 29(1): 85–104.

———. 2004. Property Taxation in Indonesia. In *International Handbook of Land and Property Taxation*, ed. R. Bird and E. Slack, 117–128. Northampton, MA: Edward Elgar.

———. 2013. *Making the Property Tax Work*. Andrew Young School of Policy Studies, Georgia State University, International Center for Public Policy Working Paper series 13-11. (April). https://hdl.handle.net/20.500.14694/8617.

Kelly, R., R. White, and A. Anand. 2020. *Property Tax Diagnostic Manual*. Washington, DC: World Bank Group.

Kennedy, J., and K. Walsh. 2016. "The Local Property Tax—a Case Study in Designing and Implementing a New Tax. In *Irish Tax Policy in Perspective*, ed. G. Tobin and C. O'Brien. Dublin: Irish Tax Institute.

Kingston, C. 2024a. "Germany's Property Tax Reform Starts Impacting Broader Market." (June 18). https://www.refire-online.com/markets/germany-property-tax-reform-starts-impacting-broader-market/.

———. 2024b. "German Homeowners Brace for Higher Tax Bills from January 2025." (August 18). https://www.refire-online.com/markets/german-homeowners-brace-for-higher-tax-from-january-2025/.

Kitchen, H. 2013. "Property Tax: A Situation Analysis and Overview." In McCluskey, Cornia, and Walters, *A Primer on Property Tax*.

KPMG. n.d. "Impact of Property Tax Reform on Church Property." https://kpmg.com/de/en/industries/church-organisations.html.

Leishman, C., G. Bramley, M. Stephens, D. Watkins, and G. Young. 2014. *After the Council Tax: Impacts of Property Tax Reform on People, Places and House Prices*. York, UK: Joseph Rowntree Foundation.

Lemmen, C., P. van Oosterom, and R. Bennett. 2015. "The Land Administration Domain Model." *Land Use Policy* 49 (December): 535–545. https://doi.org/10.1016/j.landusepol.2015.01.014.

Leodolter, A., S. Princen, and A. Rutkowski. 2022. "Immovable Property Taxation for Sustainable and Inclusive Growth." Discussion Paper 156. Luxembourg: European Commission.

Leunig, T. 2025. "A Fairer Property Tax: A Practical Alternative to Replace Stamp Duty and Council Tax." Onward, UK. https://www.ukonward.com/wp-content/uploads/2024/08/Onward-A-Fairer-Property-Tax.pdf.

Lim, L. C., W. J. McCluskey, and P. Davis. 2008. "Area Based Banding for Property Tax Assessment in Transitional Countries: An Empirical Investigation." *Journal of Real Estate Literature* 16(2): 201–215.

McCluskey, W. J., ed. 1991. *Comparative Property Tax Systems*. Gower, UK: Avebury.

McCluskey, W. J. 2025a. "The Case for Value Banding: The Recurrent Property Tax on Residential Property in Ireland." *Journal of Financial Management of Property and Construction* 22(1): 51–67.

———. 2025b. "Challenging the Conventional Practice: The Use of Value Banding in the Assessment of Residential Properties for a Recurrent Property Tax." *Journal of Property Tax Assessment and Administration* 21(1): 51–67.

McCluskey, W. J., and S. Anand. 1999. "The Application of Intelligent Hybrid Techniques for the Mass Appraisal of Residential Properties." *Journal of Property Investment and Finance* 17(3): 218–238.

McCluskey, W. J., G. C. Cornia, and L. C. Walters, eds. 2013. *A Primer on Property Tax: Administration and Policy*. Chichester, UK: Wiley-Blackwell.

McCord, M., W. J. McCluskey, P. T. Davis, D. McIlhatton, and M. Haran. 2013. "Prediction Accuracy in Mass Appraisal: A Comparison of Modern Approaches." *Journal of Property Research* 30(4): 239–265.

Mikesell, J. L. 2007. "Developing Options for the Administration of Local Taxes: An International Review." *Public Budgeting and Finance* 27(1): 41–68.

Munich Eye. 2025. "New Study Reveals Ground Tax Increases: A Broken Promise," April 23. https://themunicheye.com/new-study-reveals-ground-tax-increases-19092?utm.com.

Murphy, L. 2019. *A Poor Tax: Reforming Council Tax in London*. London: Institute for Public Policy Research.

New South Wales Government. 2019. *Valuer General's Policy: Valuation of Commercial Land*. Sydney, Australia.

Norregaard, J. 2013. "Taxing Immovable Property: Revenue Potential and Implementation Challenges." Working paper WP/13/129. Washington, DC: International Monetary Fund.

OECD (Organisation for Economic Co-operation and Development). 2016a. *Advanced Analytics for Tax Administration: Putting Data to Work*. Paris: OECD.

———. 2016b. *Technologies for Better Tax Administration: A Practical Guide for Revenue Bodies*. Paris: OECD.

———. 2021. *Making Property Tax Reform Happen in China: A Review of Property Tax Design and Reform Experiences in OECD Countries*. Paris: OECD.

Office of the Danish Auditor General. 2013. "Beretning om den offentlige ejendomsvurdering." https://rigsrevisionen.dk/revisionssager-arkiv/2013/aug/beretning-om-den-offentlige-ejendomsvurdering.

Prammer, D. 2020. "Immovable Property: Where, Why and How Should It Be Taxed? A Review of the Literature and Its Implementation in Europe." *Public Sector Economics* 44(4): 483–504.

Radzali, N. M., and K. N. Tahar. 2018. "The Use of Drone in Property Valuation." *International Journal of Engineering and Technology* 7(4): 5–11.

Raich, U., and D.-K. Kwak. 2023. "The Use of Technologies to Enhance Own Source Revenue Mobilization: Applications to the Property Tax." Washington, DC: World Bank.

Revenue. 2021. *Local Property Tax: Preliminary Statistics*. Revenue Commissioners, Dublin, Ireland.

Rödding, A., and S. Uetermeyer. 2022. "Property Tax Reform 2022: A Comparison of Tax Burdens and the Need for Contractual Action in Real Estate Transactions." https://web.archive.org/web/20250324063800/https://www.goerg.de/sites/default/files/fields/content_types/publication/downloads/7220926_Legal%20Update_G%C3%96RG_Grundsteuerreform_eng.pdf.

Schlagenhaufer, S., W. Ranft, J. Schumann, D. Puskepeleitis, H. Meyer, D. Peters, V. Reichardt, D. Dreher, and M. Deutschmann. 2025. "5.2 Million Objections Against New Property Tax." *Bild* (April 28). https://www.bild.de/politik/inland/auch-mieter-betroffen-5-2-millionen-einsprueche-gegen-neue-grundsteuer-67e50315032de159434c205c?utm_source=chatgpt.com.

Slack, E., and R. Bird. 2014. "The Political Economy of Property Tax Reform." Working paper on Fiscal Federalism No. 18. Paris: OECD. https://dx.doi.org/10.1787/5jz5pzvzv6r7-en.

———. 2015. "How to Reform the Property Tax: Lessons from Around the World." IMFG Papers No. 21. Toronto: Institute of Municipal Finance and Governance. https://imfg.org/uploads/325/1689_imfg_no.21_online_final.pdf/.

TEGOVA. 2025. *Valuation and Other Issues for Recurrent Property Taxation*. European Valuation Information Paper (EVIP 4). European Valuation Standards, 10th ed. European Group of Valuers Association.

Tietje, J. 2025. "Tax Tip 14: Property Tax Reform: The Full Extent Is Now Becoming Clear." KPMG Tax Tips, 2025. https://kpmg.com/de/en/insights/corporate-governance-and-compliance/kpmg-tax-tips.html#tabs-d7e0354c89-item-fe1c019c09-tab.

Turley, G. 2022. *The Old and the New: A Tale of Two Local Property Taxes in Ireland*. Paper on Municipal Finance and Governance No. 62. Toronto: Institute on Municipal Finance and Governance, University of Toronto.

UN-Habitat, 2013. *Property Tax Regimes in Europe*. UN-Habitat: Nairobi, Kenya.

Walters, L. 2011. *Land and Property Tax: A Policy Guide*. Nairobi: United Nations Human Settlements Program.

World Bank. 2016. *World Development Report 2016: Digital Dividends*. Washington, DC: World Bank.

Youngman, J. 2016. *A Good Tax: Legal and Policy Issues for the Property Tax in the United States*. Cambridge, MA: Lincoln Institute of Land Policy.

Youngman, J. M., and J. H. Malme. 1993. *An International Survey of Taxes on Land and Buildings*. Boston, MA: Kluwer.

Žibrik, N., and T. Humar. 2021. "Real Property Taxation in the Emerging Economy of the Republic of Slovenia." In *Real Property Taxes and Property Markets in CEE Countries and Central Asia*, ed. M. Radvan, R. Franzsen, W. J. McCluskey, and F. Plimmer, 327–374. Maribor, Slovenia: Institute for Local Self Government.

Zurada, J., A. Levitan, and J. Guan. 2011. "A Comparison of Regression and Artificial Intelligence Methods in a Mass Appraisal Context." *Journal of Real Estate Research* 33(3): 349–388.

6

Taxes on the Transfer of Property

RIËL FRANZSEN, ROY BAHL, WILLIAM MCCLUSKEY, AND WENJING LI

Nearly all European countries tax transfers of real estate, most often as a sales tax on the legal obligation (e.g., contract of sale) and as a stamp duty on a document manifesting a transfer (sales contract or deed of sale).[1] These taxes are fixtures in both industrial and low-income countries but are not often in the forefront of property tax reform discussions (though some commentators believe they should be). This chapter describes property transfer taxation in Europe, tracks its revenue performance, and reviews arguments for reform.

Background

Countries use transfer taxes to affect land and housing markets, provide the baseline information necessary to track property values, and generate revenues. Different countries probably weight these objectives differently. Depending on where one sits, property transfer taxes may be seen as making important contributions to the performance of land and property markets or as harming the allocation of resources and imposing a welfare cost.

Real estate transfer taxes are rarely abolished, but since 2010, more than 60 countries worldwide have lowered tax rates and other fees on property transfers (World Bank 2020). In Europe, some countries have reduced tax rates (Greece and the Netherlands) or even abolished their property transfer taxes (most recently Slovakia and the Czech Republic). Housing prices in Europe have increased by 50 percent in Europe since 2015, which explains some of the recent history and the renewed interest in this tax.

All taxes are objectionable to taxpayers, especially those levied at a high rate, as is sometimes perceived to be the case for property transfer taxes. On one hand, the transfer tax might have been expected to be on the reform agenda long before now. On the other, there are good reasons for the longevity of property transfer taxes. Real property buyers and sellers voluntarily comply because the transfer of rights from seller to buyer is recorded on proof of payment, and compliance costs are low. Governments see it as a progressive tax that contributes revenues. Because it is imposed (mostly) by central governments, local-government voters may not feel empowered to challenge it. In the eyes of most taxpayers, the welfare costs imposed by these taxes (constraints to labor mobility) are theoretical and are not given a heavy weight. Popular opposition to transfer taxes is softened because properties are infrequently transferred. Sometimes the revenues raised from transfer taxes are distributed to or shared with local governments, and in a few cases, property transfer taxes are in the subnational government portfolio. Property transfer taxes seem to check many boxes related to political durability. In fact, property transfer taxes are some of the oldest taxes still used extensively (box 6.1).

This form of taxation has drawbacks, however. Property transfer taxes interfere with market decisions and can impose significant welfare costs, they sometimes are levied at onerous rates that might encourage the underdeclaration of property values, and they may reduce the number of market transactions that would otherwise have taken place (Wallace 2018). In addition, the capitalization of property transfer taxes into land values dampens recurrent property tax collections and biases transactions toward lower-value properties. In doing so, they may encourage urban sprawl.

Property transfer taxes distort economic choices in ways that reduce labor mobility and promote inefficient land use (European Commission 2023). Moreover, the revenue flow from this tax source can fluctuate more widely than for recurrent property taxes. The administrative relationships between property transfer taxes and recurrent property taxes are not always reinforcing, and the policy objectives of the two taxes may conflict. In some corners, and in this book, there is interest in exploring a model that would replace property transfer taxes with an equal-yield increase in recurrent property tax revenues (Blöchliger et al. 2015; Mirrlees et al. 2011; OECD 2022).

Box 6.1 Brief History of Property Transfer Taxes in Europe

Transaction-related fees were already levied across Europe (England, France, and Germany) during feudalism. A tax (in modern guise) on the transfer of assets (including real estate), the *alcabala*, was levied in Spain in the mid-16th century. Various attempts in the Dutch provinces at first failed, but after the Union of Utrecht (1579) the provinces imposed a real estate transfer tax. For example, Holland introduced the 40th penny in 1598. In most continental European countries (e.g., France, the Netherlands), the tax evolved as a levy on the underlying legal obligation to effect transfer of ownership, and the formal registration was a mechanism to enforce payment.

The first stamp act was introduced in Holland in 1624. Stamp tax was collected by embossing a special seal on documents recording legal transactions. It proved to be highly successful, and other countries followed the Dutch example: Spain (1636), France (1673), and Great Britain (1694). The focus of stamp duties is on the instrument or deed, rather than an underlying legal obligation.

Sources: Dowell (1873); Franzsen (1990); Ketelaar (1985); Novotny (1955).

Tax evasion occurs for some countries in southeastern Europe, where the self-declared transaction values are sometimes below the actual selling price and data are not readily available to make corrections (Greece). In particular, not enough data is available to verify declared values with third-party evidence, such as might be provided by banks, insurance companies, or brokers. But in Slovenia, underdeclaration is estimated for only about 3 percent of transactions. Little evidence is available on the revenue cost of this evasion, but it is not believed to be a major problem in the higher-income countries of Europe.

There does not seem to be a groundswell of support for abandoning the current approach to taxing property transfers, despite a housing shortage and population migration issues. A major reason for hesitance in reforming the property transfer tax is that the options for making up the revenue costs with another form of tax on land and buildings are not clearly better. Finally, there is the political economy constraint. Many (if not most) elected local-government officials would probably prefer the transfer of central revenues to their budgets over asking taxpayers for a rate increase in their recurrent property taxes.

Data on property transfer taxes is available but is included with revenues from capital and financial transfers, which greatly constrains comparative research, as described in box 6.2.

Box 6.2 Data Constraints for Comparative Analysis of Property Transfer Tax Revenues

The International Monetary Fund (IMF) and Organisation for Economic Co-operation and Development (OECD) report property (real estate) transfer taxes in a category with "taxes on capital and financial transactions" (CFT). However, this category also includes taxes on foreign exchange, checks, and certain legal transactions (IMF 2014; see also chapter 1), and neither the IMF nor OECD separately report revenues from taxes on real estate transfers.[2]

This is a significant constraint to analytic work in this area.

Effective property transfer tax revenues for 2021, as reported in the 14 country studies in part 2, are compared with those from CFT in the following box table. In two countries, the CFT revenues reported by the IMF were higher than those reported in part 2, but in two others they were lower. In six countries, they were about the same. The largest discrepancies were in France, Ireland, and Spain. In four countries, the differences could not be compared. The remainder of this chapter makes use of this statistical series and of the amounts reported in the country studies in part 2, but the empirical findings from this analysis should be interpreted with caution.

Comparison of 2021 Transfer Tax Revenues from Capital and Financial Transactions (CFT) with Country-Reported Property Transfer Tax Revenues for the 14 Case Study Countries

Country	CFT Revenues (% of GDP) (1)	Property Transfer Tax Revenues (% of GDP) (2)	CFT Property Transfer Tax Revenue (% of general property tax revenue) (3)
Denmark	0	0.31	0.11
Estonia	0	0	0
Finland	0.350	0.396	29.920
France	0.79	0.67	20.07
Germany	0.52	0.50	75.86
Greece	0.19	n.a.	7.21
Ireland	0.28	0.17	61.27
Latvia	0.15	n.a.	18.50
Netherlands	0.45	0.45	37.99
Poland	0.13	0.16	11.36
Russia	0	0	n.a,
Slovenia	0.09	0.10	15.73
United Kingdom	0.63	0.64	21.32

Sources: The data in column 2 are from part 2 country studies. The data in columns 1 and 3 are from IMF (n.d.).

Note: n.a. = not available.

How Do European Countries Tax Property Transfers?

Countries in Europe use different names for property transfer taxes—for example, registration fees in Latvia; state fees in Estonia; asset transfer taxes in Finland; stamp duties in Denmark, Ireland, and the United Kingdom; real estate transfer taxes in Germany and the Netherlands; and local-government capital gains taxes in Spain.[3] Sometimes more than one rate and base regime is used to tax property transfers in a single country, as in Spain and the United Kingdom. Table 6.1 reports property tax revenue structures in the 14 country studies; the part 2 chapters provide a more complete analysis.[4]

Most of the transfer tax bases in the 14 European countries studied here are the estimates of the actual sales price of an (arm's-length) transfer. But they may differ in the degree to which they identify full market value as the legal base. In some countries the base is explicitly stated as the market value of the property, though in Spain the cadastral value (which is set at less than market value) is the base for a transfer tax. Estonia and Russia collect a state fee. In Russia, it is a fixed fee that differentiates between individuals and legal entities. In Estonia, the state fee is a value-based tax on property transfers, as is the registration fee in Latvia.[5]

Most commonly, the value of the transaction is declared by the parties to the sale. This may be overseen to varying degrees by a notary who prepares the documentation for the transfer. The final determination of the base often results from several layers of verification as to whether the declared value is a good estimate of market value. The notary, third parties such as banks, and government all contribute evidence to help make this decision. Even with this checking, there likely are some underdeclarations because the ability (and willingness) to compare with market values is better in some countries than in others.

As noted earlier, significant underreporting is not likely to be a problem in high-income European countries. In the Netherlands, France, and the United Kingdom, for example, arm's-length evidence (mortgage applications and valuations, regularly updated housing sales information, and bank reviews of creditworthiness) is sufficient to verify accuracy of the declared market value. In Spain, the declared values are required to be verified for accuracy by a special monitor before the final tax liability is decided and before a cadastral value is declared. In some countries, however, the degree to which declared sales prices match market prices is more difficult to determine and might include some degree of underdeclaration (Greece, Latvia, and Slovenia).

Property transfer taxes tend to be flat rate levies, but in a few countries (including France, Portugal, and the United Kingdom) progressive rates are used. With respect to nominal rate levels, Belgium, Germany, Malta,

Table 6.1 Overview of Property Transfer Taxes in the 14 Case Study Countries

Country	Tax	Tax Base	Revenues	Nominal Tax Rate or Fee	Determination of Rate and Division of Revenues
Denmark	Stamp duty on registration of transfers and mortgages	Sales and mortgage value; good data on property price levels are available	0.31% of GDP	0.6% on land and 1.45% on mortgages; 0–1% of value of buildings for reimbursement tax	Central government levies the taxes and retains all revenues
Estonia	A state fee is charged, but is value based	Value of the transaction	State fee was 0.03% of GDP	Less than 0.5% of the transaction amount	Central government levy
Finland	Asset transfer tax	Purchase price; limited data on property values	0.396% of GDP	4% of purchase price; 2% for transfer of shares of housing companies	Central government tax
France	Central government stamp duty. Shared stamp duty	Acquisition price; good price evidence available	0.67% of GDP	0.71% on new dwellings. Departments progressive to 4.50%, municipalities 1.20%	Parliament sets national rates, retains revenues. Parliament sets range of rates that are determined by departments; revenues are shared with subnational governments

Germany	Property transfer tax	Total purchase price; verified by cadastral value	0.5% of GDP in 2021	The tax rate varies between 3.5% and 6.5% in the 16 federal states	Federal states retain collections
Greece	Real estate transfer tax	Tax value of the property	0.2% of GDP	3.0%	Central government tax
Ireland	Stamp duty on registration of transfers and leases	Market value on real property transfers; average annual rents on leases	0.1678% of GDP	Separate tax rates on residential and non-residential sectors for real property transfers	Central government determines rates and retains revenues
Latvia	Registration fee	Higher of cadastral value or transaction value	0.16% of GDP in 2021	Varies by type of transfer from 1.5%–2.0%	Central government levies the rate and retains the revenue
Netherlands	Transfer tax	Selling price (declared); good data on property values	0.45% of GDP	2% for residential use, 10% for other use, preferential rate for "starters"	National government tax with no revenue sharing
Poland	Tax on civil law transactions and stamp duty	Market value of the property; weak database on property values	0.162% of GDP	2% of purchase price	Central government sets rate, local government receives revenue on derivation basis

(continued)

Table 6.1 Overview of Property Transfer Taxes in the 14 Case Study Countries (*continued*)

Country	Tax	Tax Base	Revenues	Nominal Tax Rate or Fee	Determination of Rate and Division of Revenues
Russia	No transfer tax is levied, only a fixed fee	Not applicable	Not applicable	Fee differentiation between individuals and legal entities	Not applicable
Spain	Transfer tax; stamp duties	Both are levied on the purchase price of the property; reliable data available	Property transfer tax in 2021 was 0.68% of GDP; stamp duty was 0.20% of GDP. Total is 0.90% of GDP	Varies across autonomous regions	Rates determined by autonomous region governments, and by municipal governments within centrally set limits
Slovenia	Property transaction tax	Selling price based on "corrected" self-declaration	0.1033% of GDP	2%	Rates determined by CG; revenues fully distributed to local governments by derivation
United Kingdom	Stamp duty on sales of real property and leases; levied separately by England, NI, Scotland, and Wales	Sales value of property; net present value of leases	0.64% of GDP: = 0.72% in England; 0.47% in Scotland; 0.30% in Wales; and 0.20% in NI	Rates vary across regions; progressive rate structures; differential rates for residential and business	England, NI, Scotland, and Wales determine their own tax structure; no revenue sharing with local governments

Source: Authors' calculations and definitions based on part 2 chapters.

and Spain are at the high end, having top statutory rates around or above 6.5 percent.[6] Ireland and the Netherlands make provision for a preferential rate for residential properties, and several countries provide special treatment for first-time homeowners, who tend to be heavily burdened by the large one-time payments. This is the case in England, Northern Ireland, and Scotland (but not in Wales), and also elsewhere in Europe (e.g., Hungary and Malta).

Revenues, Revenue Sharing, and Local Autonomy

Taxes on the transfer of land and property can raise significant amounts of revenue. Belgium, France, Spain, and the United Kingdom all raise more than 0.5 percent of gross domestic product (GDP) from this tax.[7] While IMF data are not as complete (or as comparable) for all European countries as might be hoped (see box 6.2 table), the following summaries of the results from the 14 country studies and from the all-Europe sample suggest the revenue importance. On average, property transfer tax revenues are equivalent to about 26 percent of annual general property tax revenues reported in the country study chapters. Total capital and financial transaction tax revenues are equivalent to about 31 percent of annual general property tax revenues for the 32 European countries reported in the IMF's Government Finance Statistics database (see table 2.1).

The 14 country studies show different intergovernmental arrangements for transfer taxes. In most of these countries, the transfer tax is a central-government levy, with rates and base determined nationally and revenues staying in national coffers. But some countries take a more decentralized approach. Spain and Germany retain more control of property transfer taxes at provincial- or state-government levels,[8] and transfer tax rates can vary widely. In Spain, municipal governments are empowered to levy a capital gains tax on property transactions. In France and Slovenia, the national property transfer tax is distributed among local governments on a derivation basis.

Transfer Tax and General Property Tax

Various studies have found statistical evidence that property transfer taxes are capitalized into housing values in European countries. Høj, Jørgensen, and Schou (2018) find that land taxes in Denmark are fully capitalized into market prices. Research in German states finds evidence of overcapitalization (Dolls et al. 2021). The resulting lower home value should in theory be reflected in a lower assessment of the property value. However, changes in assessed values are slow to catch up with changes in market values because, particularly, local governments use discretionary property tax policies to keep short-run revenue-income elasticities low (see chapter 2).

The table in box 6.2 seems to show that property transfer taxes in the 14 case study countries are more heavily used by countries that impose higher effective rates in their recurrent property tax.[9] This might imply that the determinants of higher levels of property transfer tax revenues are some combination of larger property tax bases, more willingness to accept higher property tax burdens, a concentration of property tax wealth in higher income brackets, and limited objections to this central-government tax.

On balance, it would be difficult to identify the direct and indirect effects of eliminating property transfer taxes on taxable property values. Property values would rise with the elimination of the tax, some homeowners would look for residences that better fit their life-cycle stage, and others would make housing choices that reduced their commute to work. Welfare would be increased as consumers got more of what they wanted, but the impact on property values would depend on a number of other factors. However, governments might sweep the windfall into their budgets.

Allocative Effects

Most economists argue that transfer taxes are distortive and do not maximize welfare. Studies on this question have found important lock-in effects of transfer taxes in Europe—for example, the tax dissuades owners from moving when their housing no longer fits their preferences, and a shortage of housing choices may keep many workers from living closer to their workplace (Eyraud 2015; Wallace 2018). As many have noted, the property transfer tax has imposed a significant welfare cost on local populations.

Schmidt (2022, 1), for example, finds that a revenue-neutral abolition of the 2 percent transfer tax in the Netherlands increases the likelihood that homeowners sell their old house and buy a new one by about 40 percent. Eerola et al. (2019) estimate that an increase in the transfer tax rate in Finland led to a 7 percent reduction in household mobility. Sanchez and Andrews (2011) conclude that land use regulations, rent controls, and mortgage regulations had significant effects on residential mobility but that transfer taxes did not. Cho, Li, and Uren (2021) present evidence from Australia that elimination of the stamp duty increases the rate of homeownership, especially among younger owners, and that if it is accompanied by a revenue-neutral increase in annual property taxes, it increases house prices and homeownership rates. Kaas et al. (2020) find

Table 6.2 Correlations Among Wealth, Income, and Property Taxation in 32 European Countries, 2020

	Per Capita Produced Capital (2018)	Per Capita Capital and Financial Transactions (CFT) (2020)	Per Capita GDP (2020)	General Property Tax / GDP (2020)	CFT/ GDP (2020)
Per capita produced capital (2018)	1				
Per capita CFT (2020)	0.6312	1			
Per capita GDP (2020)	0.9234	0.6530	1		
General property tax / GDP (2020)	0.4052	0.4936	0.3347	1	
CFT/GDP (2020)	0.3442	0.8865	0.3148	0.5285	1

Source: Authors.

that higher transfer taxes lead to significantly lower rates of homeownership in Germany.

Intercountry Variations in Property Transfer Tax Revenues

The data in table 6.2 provide an examination of nominal tax rates imposed on transfers of real property (excluding transfer taxes on non–real estate assets) in 2022 in the 27 European Union member states. These comparisons are based on data provided by individual member states (European Commission 2023). According to the European Commission, property transfer tax rates range from around 10 percent in Belgium and Spain to zero in Slovakia and the Czech Republic. Note that several countries use progressive rate structures.

Why do some countries raise a greater share of GDP from property transfer taxes than do others? Some explanations seem obvious, including the level of property wealth. Other obvious indicators are the level of per capita GDP and the rate of urbanization (the latter because property transfer markets tend to be more active in cities). Higher levels of transfer tax revenues are also influenced by the higher transfer tax rates and base coverages that are imposed.

Figure 6.1 Property Transfer Tax Revenue

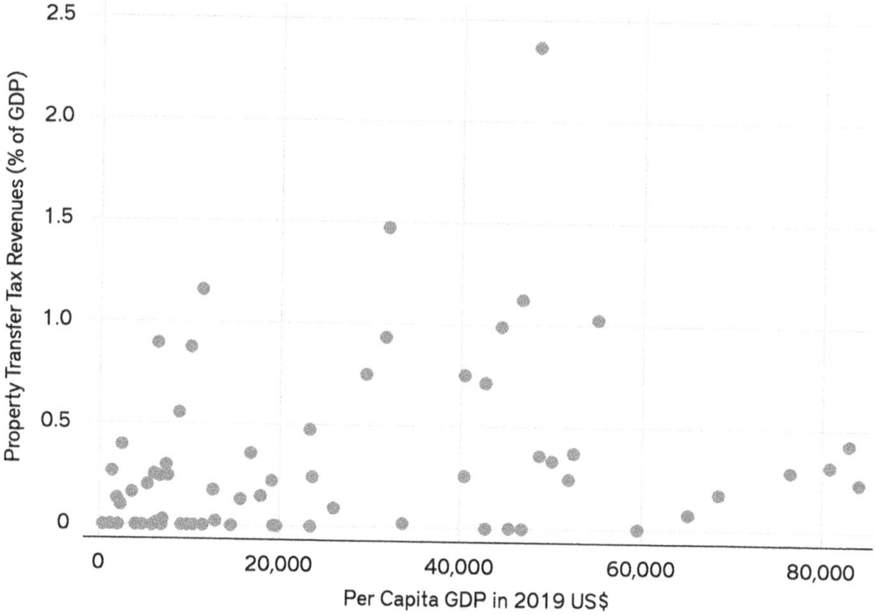

Sources: IMF (2023); World Bank (2023).

Cross-country analysis is limited by data availability. As discussed in chapter 1, taxes on capital and financial transactions include real estate transfers but also a number of other types of transactions, so use of this series could give misleading results (see also box 6.2). In this analysis, we use capital and financial transaction tax revenue (as defined earlier) as a proxy for per capita property transfer tax revenue. To discover patterns among countries in these series, table 6.2 presents a simple correlation matrix. The results show that per capita transaction tax revenues tend to be higher in countries with more wealth and higher incomes. But there is a great deal of variation in these patterns, as shown in figure 6.1.

Discretionary Policies to Modify Property Transfer Taxes

The ability of the government to influence the supply and demand for housing is arguably the primary reason for imposing property transfer taxes. Rate policies can raise prices in an overheated housing market or lower them and are especially important for first-time buyers. Discretionary policies can also account for significant amounts of revenues. And though the tax base is generally thought of as the value of a transaction, it is often modified in ways that have a significant impact on total revenues and on their distribution of property tax burdens. The following European country examples shed light on how property transfer taxes are being restructured to focus more on specific objectives.

The Netherlands

Starting in 2011, the property transfer tax rate for residential property decreased from 6 percent to 2 percent to stimulate the housing market. The rate remained higher for nonresidential purchases and nonprimary residential property. The rate for first-time homeowners was reduced to zero in 2023 to help them overcome liquidity constraints to homeownership (PwC 2023).

Germany

Before the fiscal federalism reform in 2006, a federal property transfer tax rate of 3.5 percent applied. From September 2006, federal states could set the tax rate for the property transfer tax at their discretion (Kholodilin 2025). Bavaria is the only state that still applies a rate of 3.5 percent. Almost all federal states have increased their rates over the years, although Thuringia reduced its rate from 6.5 to 5 percent in January 2024. In 2023 and 2024, some federal states changed their property transfer tax rates, but the tax rate still ranges between a lowest rate of 3.5 percent (in Bavaria) and a highest rate of 6.5 percent (Brandenburg, North Rhine–Westphalia, Saarland, and Schleswig-Holstein), with a simple average in 2024 of 5.53 percent (Mengden 2024). The federal government has been arguing for relief for specific buyer groups since 2021, but according to Kholodilin (2025), by mid-2023 only North Rhine–Westphalia provided such relief from 2022, reimbursing homeowners with 2 percent of the sales value subject to tax up to a maximum of €10,000. In 2023, after 13 years with no change, Hamburg increased its rate from 4.5 to 5.5 percent, which is about the national average rate. The state government undertook to provide relief for young families and social housing, but this had not materialized by mid-2025 (Kholodilin 2025).

Between 2010 and 2020, revenues from property transfer taxes increased across Germany in relative and in absolute terms, with actual revenues quadrupling and its proportion of total revenues doubling over this period. This substantial increase can partly be explained by a 72 percent increase in housing prices between the first quarter of 2010 and the fourth quarter of 2020 but mostly by increases of the tax rate in almost all federal states (Kholodilin 2025). The restrictive monetary policy in 2022 ended the lengthy housing boom, and falling prices and declining sales volume resulted in a decrease in property transfer tax revenue of 7 percent from 2021 to 2022 (Kholodilin 2025).

Ireland

The standard rates of stamp duty for residential property are 1 percent on values up to €1 million and 2 percent on values exceeding €1 million. From May 20, 2021, a higher, 10 percent rate of duty applies to the acquisition of certain residential property (Revenue 2023). These rates were set during the housing crisis of the 2020s and the ongoing, as of 2025, shortage of housing for owner-occupier purchasers in order to discourage purchase of multiple residential units by any one individual or entity. It applies only to people (or an entity) who acquire at least 10 such units during any 12-month period (as of May 20, 2021).

Czech Republic

In September 2020, the 4 percent tax on the acquisition of immovable property was abolished, as was the deduction of interest from loans granted for housing needs. According to the Czech authorities (Explanatory Report 2020), these amendments simplified the tax system and made it more transparent. A further reason given for abolishing the tax was the COVID-19 pandemic and its effects on society. It reduced the tax avoidance scheme that established special purpose vehicles for owning immovable property so that their shares, rather than the immovable property itself, could be transferred without paying tax.[10] Some argued at the time that the tax's abolition would increase investments in real estate. As Radvan and Papavasilevsko (2020) point out, however, little research has been done on the outcomes. The authorities also argue (Explanatory Report 2020) that the taxpayer compliance burden would decrease (as they would no longer be required to submit a tax return or pay for professional assistance when submitting a tax return for acquiring immovable property or conducting tax proceedings).

Hungary

The acquisition tax is 4 percent of the purchase price of the asset up to HUF 1 billion (about US$2.8 million). The tax rate decreases to 2 percent for any portion above that amount, and the maximum amount of tax is capped at HUF 200 million (about US$563,000). The law provides significant relief to buyers of residential property (but comes with seemingly high administration and compliance costs). Some of these provisions are summarized here:

- Buyers of newly built property have no tax obligation up to HUF 15 million (about US$42,150). If the property exceeds HUF 30 million (about US$84,300), a tax of 4 percent is payable on the total sales price.

- If the value of a new home exceeds that of the previous home, the acquisition tax is payable only on the difference in value, providing that the new property purchase occurs within three years after or one year before the sale of the previous house.
- Acquisitions for no consideration between spouses, siblings, or direct relatives (gift or inheritance) are exempt.
- No acquisition tax is payable on real estate purchased with the help of the Family Home Creation Support program, regardless of the purchase price. The exemption does not require use of a support program loan, merely compliance with the program's other criteria.
- Buyers of residential property younger than 35 purchasing their first home are entitled to a 50 percent discount when they purchase a new, residential property with a fair market value of less than HUF 15 million and have not previously owned a property (or at least a 50 percent share in a property). Given the constant increases in house prices, few young people can benefit from this relief measure.

Portugal

Buyers pay the property transfer tax in Portugal on the basis of price. The tax ranges from 0 to 8 percent, depending on property location or whether it is a first or second home in Portugal. Acquisition of more than 75 percent of the shares of a Portuguese real estate company is also subject to the property transfer tax. Rural property is taxed at 5 percent, urban property at 6.5 percent.

For buyers of residential property, different rate structures are applied. Acquisition of a permanent place of residence is taxed on a sliding scale. The first €92,407 is subject to zero tax; above €1 million, the rate is 7.5 percent. The 0 percent rate and the 2 percent rate from €92,407 to €126,403 assist buyers of low-value properties in an environment where transfer tax rates are very high. Second homes and primary residences are taxed on a similar sliding scale, but for primary residences, the first €92,407 is taxed at 1 percent.

Romania

The property transfer tax is more akin to a capital gains tax. Income from the disposal of immovable property by natural persons is subject to a property transfer tax. The state budget equally divides the revenue with the relevant local budget of the property's administrative territorial unit (i.e., local authority). From January 1, 2023, this tax is payable as follows: If the property is sold within three years from acquisition, the tax is

3 percent up to and including RON 200,000 (US$44,000) and RON 6,000 (about US$1,320) and 2 percent on the value exceeding RON 200,000. For taxable property acquired more than three years before the alienation, the tax constitutes 2 percent up to and including RON 200,000 and RON 4,000 (about US$880), and 1 percent on the value exceeding RON 200,000. Donations between spouses and relatives within the third degree are exempt.

These examples make clear that countries can have unique policies for property transfer tax rates and taxpayer relief measures, shaped to encourage certain taxpayer behavior or respond to changes in the real estate market. Table 6.3 provides an overview of tax rates and developments as of 2022.

Policy Issues and Reform Options

Reform of the property transfer tax has not been a front-burner issue in Europe, but many countries have modified its structure and administration. A few countries (Slovakia and the Czech Republic) have abolished it, some have reduced rates or expanded benefits in the last decade (the Netherlands), and the United Kingdom adopted a sliding scale to introduce a higher maximum rate. Transfer taxes can be a prolific revenue raiser, as some countries have shown (see box 6.2 table and Table 2.1). However, it mostly remains a turnover type of sales tax levied separately and not fully coordinated with the recurrent property tax.

We discuss three possible reform directions. The first is continued adjustments to the current system to patch up its shortcomings. The second and third are more far-reaching reforms: One shifts the tax base to capital gains. The other phases out the property transfer tax in favor of a unified property tax.

Improve the Current System

The property transfer tax has significant flaws, but there is no overwhelming consensus on how to change it with comprehensive reform. Two modifications that might be considered for the short run are the following: First, enhance preferential treatment for first-time homeowners. Some European countries have already done this, but further rejiggering their tax structure could make the benefits more accessible to first-timers. Second, transfer all revenues raised from transfer taxes to subnational governments on a derivation basis to compensate them for the negative capitalization impacts on the recurrent property tax base or the management costs of accommodating changes in residential housing values.[11] Other problems with the current system, such as assessment accuracy in

Table 6.3 2022 Nominal Transfer Tax Rates in the 27 European Union Member States and Other Selected European Countries

Country	Tax Rate	Comment
Austria	3.5%	Plus 1.1% registration fee
Belgium	10% to 12.5%	
Bulgaria	0.1% to 3.0%	
Croatia	3%	
Cyprus	3% to 8%	
Czech Republic	No tax	Abolished in September 2020
Denmark	0.6%	Also levies a fixed fee
Estonia	0.27% to 0.4%	
Finland	4%	Acquisition of a first home is exempt if individual (age 18–39) acquires at least 50%; only 2% tax if shares are acquired in a housing company that gives entitlement to ownership of an apartment
France	3.8% to 4.5%	
Germany	3.5% to 6%	Germany is a federal country, and the 16 federal states decide their own rates
Greece	3%	Previously: 8.0% to 10.0% (+ municipal tax of 0.09%, i.e., 3% on the tax payable)
Hungary	4%	
Ireland	1% to 2%	
Italy	2% to 9%	Multiple taxes (registration, cadaster, and mortgage taxes); first-time buyer relief (2% rate)
Latvia	2.5%	
Lithuania	0.2% to 1%	
Luxembourg	7%	Additional surcharge of 3% applies in Luxembourg City
Malta	8%	First-time buyer relief on first €200,000
Netherlands	2%; 10.4%	Reduced in 2011 from 6% to 2% for residential self-occupancy; increased to 10.4% (from 8%) in 2023 for other property acquisitions
Poland	2%	
Portugal	0% to 7.5%	Higher rate for second homes

(continued)

Table 6.3 2022 Nominal Transfer Tax Rates in the 27 European Union Member States and Other Selected European Countries (*continued*)

Country	Tax Rate	Comment
Romania	1% to 3%	Sliding scale with value thresholds
Slovakia	No tax	Abolished with effect from January 1, 2005
Slovenia	2%	
Spain	6% to 10.5%	Both transfer tax and stamp duty are collected
Sweden	1.5%; 4.25%	1.5% rate for individuals and 4.25% rate for corporate buyers
Iceland	0.8%; 1.6%	Lower rate for individuals and higher rate for companies
Kosovo	No tax	
Norway	2.5%	
Russia	Fixed fee	Individuals: RUB 2,000 (about US$30); legal entities: RUB 22,000 (about US$330)
Switzerland	0% to 3.3%	Switzerland is a federal country, and cantons decide on their own rates
United Kingdom	0% to 12%	England and Northern Ireland: stamp duty land tax; first-time buyer relief Scotland: land and buildings transaction tax; first-time buyer relief Wales: land transaction tax; no first-time buyer relief

Sources: Authors' compilation from various sources and part 2 country studies; Grant Thornton UK (2020); PwC (2023).

some countries, will disappear as property markets develop, third-party information on sales gets better, and cadastres improve.

Tax Base Consolidation

The base of property transfer taxes is closely related to that of central-government capital gains income taxes and central-government value-added tax (VAT). Joint administration with one or the other of these taxes might lead to cost economies, could lead to better compliance, and probably would be more fair to taxpayers. Both options have major drawbacks, however, and might move transfer taxes away from their basic mission of influencing property market fluctuations.

Converting the base of property transfer taxes from sales value to capital gains would bring an additional measure of self-checking to the declaration of the sales value. (This is very important because the full transaction price would continue to be reported and would still form the basis of property valuations.) It might make monitoring for underdeclared values easier and less costly.[12] It also would be more fair because it would not double tax the cost of improvements made to the property. For this reason, it could lead to more rehabilitation of properties, depending on how capital gains are calculated. In countries where an effective central-government database of capital gains income tax is in place, some of the development costs of structuring a new property transfer tax would be avoided. The new transfer tax would maintain a separate identity and would include owner-occupied properties. Its revenues could be distributed among subnational governments.

In this reformed arrangement, the transfer tax would be administered alongside the capital gains tax, with a rate and base regime and a collection regime determined by the national government. Revenues from the real estate component would either be retained by the central government or distributed to local governments as an intergovernmental transfer.

Developing this reform would be difficult and require the resolution of several important issues. The definition of taxable capital gains from a real property transfer would need to be revisited, as would the effectiveness of administering the existing capital gains taxes on assets. The regime for taxing capital gains on principal residences would need to be rethought. The subnational governments in a few countries, such as Spain, would lose autonomy in determining their tax base and rate for property transfers. There may also be more difficult legal or even constitutional considerations. None of these are small matters.

Since the capital gains base would be smaller than the sales tax base, a higher nominal tax rate would be needed to preserve revenue neutrality. Another disadvantage to this reform, to some provincial and local governments, is that they would lose control over transfer taxes to any future central-government changes to the definition of the tax base. Finally, the distortive impacts of transfer taxes, such as on housing mobility costs, would not necessarily be reduced by a shift to a capital gains base.

Another option, which we do not consider in depth, would bring all property sales within the ambit of the VAT, which now is levied on sales of new homes in most European countries. Cnossen (1996, 245) argues that property transfer sales values are no more than a poor proxy for the VAT that should be levied on the increase in the value of the immovable property realized in the sale. His proposal does not appear to have been widely taken up because of difficulties about how to tax resales under a VAT (Bahl and Bird 2018).

Phase Out Property Transfer Taxes

Replacing property transfer taxes with a revenue-neutral increase in the recurrent property tax would reduce the economic costs of distortions related to housing choice and increase labor mobility (Mirrlees et al. 2011; OECD 2022). Further, it could remove a bias in favor of lower-value properties, thereby removing an incentive for urban sprawl. Some observers see the current property transfer tax as unjustifiable double taxation. An expert committee on tax reform in Spain in 2012 argued that some taxes, including property transfer taxes, are unfair because they tax property assets that are also taxed by the recurrent property tax and by inheritance taxes.[13]

There would be major drawbacks to such a reform. The recurrent property tax that would replace the revenues from an abolished property transfer tax may be no more efficient. Normal practice in many European countries includes significantly undervalued tax rolls and exemptions and preferences that lead to distorted resource allocation. The property transfer tax is more likely to be a tax on current market values and would automatically update. Moreover, the property transfer tax may be more progressive than the recurrent property tax, and the proposed merger might lead to less progressive total tax burdens. And if there is a universally hated tax, the annual property tax surely wins the prize (Rosengard 2012).

Finally, structuring such a replacement reform involves a significant intergovernmental dimension. First, the absorption of the property transfer tax into the recurrent property tax would be viewed by property owners as a one-time windfall. How would local governments fold this windfall into their current system, with a rate increase for all properties, or with revaluations, or another way? Or would the reform be accompanied by some sort of mandated tax increase by the central government, or would local governments take advantage of the situation with tax rate reductions? Second, the windfall revenue gains would probably concentrate in wealthier urban centers. Would this require adjustment in the formula for distributing other intergovernmental transfers? The replacement of property transfer taxes with the annual property tax would not be an easy policy reform to design.

The drawbacks to this proposal are formidable, and no alternative plan is apparent. Still, a unified tax on land and buildings, with appropriate local-government discretion, has a lot of appeal. It might increase revenue mobilization from the recurrent property tax and direct revenue increases to local government needs. It could allow a more coherent approach in the use of property taxes to support urban planning initiatives. It could make taxes on property more fair and equitable. And it could catalyze governments to reconsider special treatment of owner-occupied properties. Blocking these doors of opportunity is local voters' entrenched and rigid opposition to increasing the property tax.

Notes

1. Countries without property transfer taxes include the Czech Republic, Kosovo, and Slovakia. In 2022, out of 38 European countries surveyed, 30 levied a property transfer tax (OECD 2022).

2. "Comprehensive annual revenue data specifically for property transfer taxes are not readily available, as official sources like the OECD and Eurostat often group them into broader 'taxes on property' categories" (Response to "Property transfer tax revenues in Europe," Google AI, DeepMind, October 5, 2025).

3. Taxes on gifts and inheritances, levied in many countries, are also a form of taxes on the transfer of real property. So too are capital gains income taxes and value-added tax (VAT) on the sales of new homes, though none of the latter group are classified by IMF or OECD as property transfer taxes. We recognize the legal differences between a stamp duty and a tax, but in this study treat both as property transfer taxes (see also Brzeski, Románová, and Franzsen 2019; Radvan and Papavasilevska 2020).

4. A very useful review and comparison of property transfer tax rates is Barrios et al. (2019).

5. The state fee has its origins in Soviet times and is still encountered in a number of former Soviet countries—for example, Armenia, Azerbaijan, Kazakhstan, Kyrgyz Republic, and Uzbekistan (McCluskey, Plimmer, and Franzsen 2021, 7).

6. The Netherlands taxes transfers of nonresidential properties at 10 percent, compared with 2 percent for residential properties. Also noteworthy is that Malta does not have a recurrent property tax.

7. These data are taken from the country case studies in part 2, which use the accounting classifications of the countries. The OECD reckons that, on average, about 27 percent of all property tax revenues in Europe in 2021 were from taxes on CFT (OECD 2022). Data for 2019, the last full fiscal year before the COVID-19 pandemic, show a great variation in CFT revenues as a percentage of GDP, from 0.75 percent of GDP or more in Belgium, Spain, and France to zero in about 10 European countries.

8. Germany is a federal country, so the transfer taxes were retained at the state level, while other taxes were given to the federal government by the states. Although not a federal country, Spain has extensive decentralization.

9. The simple correlation for the 32-country European sample is 0.52, as shown in Table 6.2.

10. Many countries have introduced antiavoidance measures to counter this type of scheme.

11. Several countries already share property transfer taxes with subnational governments, including France and Spain (see table 6.1).

12. Under this regime, stamp duties could be collected against the same base or converted to a cost recovery fee. The VAT on sales of new properties could remain as is.

13. Not all countries in Europe (e.g., Estonia, Latvia, and Russia) levy inheritance and gift taxes (Næss-Schmidt et al. 2011; OECD 2021). Those that do, generally exempt the property transfer tax if inheritance tax is levied—or vice versa (Germany).

References

Bahl, R., and R. M. Bird. 2018. *Fiscal Decentralization and Local Finance in Developing Countries*. Cheltenham, UK: Edward Elgar.

Barrios, S., C. Denis, V. Ivaškaitė-Tamošiūnė, A. Reut, and E. Vázquez Torres. 2019. "Housing Taxation: A New Database for Europe." JRC Working Papers on Taxation and Structural Reforms No. 08/2019. European Commission, Joint Research Centre, Seville.

Blöchliger, H., B. Égert, B. Alvarez, and A. Paciorek. 2015. "The Stabilisation Properties of Immovable Property Taxation: Evidence from OECD Countries." OECD Economics Department Working papers, No. 1237. Paris: OECD. https://doi.org/10.1787/5js0cqq93djg-en.

Brzeski, J., A. Románová, and R. Franzsen. 2019. "The Evolution of Property Taxes in Post-Socialist Countries in Central and Eastern Europe." African Tax Institute Working paper WP-19-01. University of Pretoria.

Cho, Y., S. M. Li, and L. Uren. 2021. "Stamping Out Stamp Duty: Property or Consumption Taxes?" CAMA Working paper No. 1/2021. (January). http://dx.doi.org/10.2139/ssrn.3760893.

Cnossen, S. 1996. "VAT Treatment of Immovable Property." In *Tax Law Design and Drafting*, vol. 1, ed. V. Thuronyi. Washington, DC: International Monetary Fund.

Dolls, M., C. Fuest, C. Krolage, and F. Neumeier. 2021. "Who Bears the Burden of Real Estate Transfer Taxes? Evidence from the German Housing Market." CESifo Working paper No. 8839. Munich.

Dowell, S. 1873. *A History and Explanation of the Stamp Duties*. London: Longmans, Green.

Eerola, E., O. Harjunen, T. Lyytikäinen, and T. Saarimaa. 2019. "Effects of Housing Transfer Taxes on Household Mobility." CESifo Working paper No. 7750. Munich.

European Commission. 2023. *Annual Report on Taxation 2023*. Directorate-General for Taxation and Customs Union. Luxembourg: Publication Office of the European Commission.

Explanatory Report. 2020. Explanatory Report to Act No. 386/2020 Coll., cancellation of the legal measure on the tax on the acquisition of immovable property. LIT283828CZ - latest version of the text.

Eyraud, L. 2015. "The Wealth of Nations: Stylized Facts and Options for Taxation." In *Inequality and Fiscal Policy*, ed. B. Clements, R. de Mooij, S. Gupta, and M. Keen, 121–140. Washington, DC: International Monetary Fund.

Franzsen, R. 1990. "'n Regskritiese ondersoek na hereregte in Suid-Afrika" [A critical legal analysis of transfer duty in South Africa]. PhD diss., Stellenbosch University.

Grant Thornton UK. 2020. "European Transfer Taxes Report 2019/20." https://www.grantthornton.lv/globalassets/1.-member-firms/latvia/pdf/ds1362-european-transfer-tax-report-_v3.pdf.

Høj, A. K., M. D. Jørgensen, and P. Schou. 2018. "Land Tax Changes and Full Capitalization." *Journal of Applied Public Economics* 39(2): 365–380.

IMF (International Monetary Fund). 2014. *Government Finance Statistics Manual*. Washington, DC: IMF.

———. n.d. Government Finance Statistics. Accessed December 16, 2023. https://data.imf.org/en/datasets/IMF.STA:QGFS.

Kaas, L., G. Kocharkov, E. Preugschat, and N. Siassi. 2020. "Low Homeownership in Germany—a Quantitative Exploration." *Journal of the European Economic Association* 19(1): 128–164.

Ketelaar, F. C. J. 1985. "Van pertinent register tot ordentelijk protocol." In *De Levering van Onroerend Goed*. Deventer, Netherlands: Kluwer.

Kholodilin, K. A. 2025. "The Evolution of Real Estate Transfer Tax in Germany." (July 14). https://rpubs.com/Konstantin_Xo/RETT_DEU.

McCluskey, W., F. Plimmer, and R. Franzsen. 2021. "Introduction and Observations." *Real Property Taxes and Property Markets in CCE Countries and Central Asia*, ed. M. Radvan, R. Franzsen, W. J. McCluskey, and F. Plimmer, 1–46. Maribor, Slovenia: Institute for Local Self Government.

Mengden, A. 2024. "Real Estate Transaction Tax Rates in German States." (July). https://taxfoundation.org/data/all/eu/germany-real-estate-transaction-tax-rates.

Mirrlees, J., S. Adam, T. Besley, R. Blundell, S. Bond, R. Chote, M. Gammie, P. Johnson, G. Myles, and J. Poterba. 2011. "The Mirrlees Review: Conclusions and Recommendations for Reform." *Fiscal Studies* 32(3): 331–359.

Næss-Schmidt, H. S., T. T. Pedersen, F. Harhoff, M. Winiarczyk, and C. Jervelund. 2011. *Study on Inheritance Taxes in EU Member States and Possible Mechanisms to Resolve Problems of Double Inheritance Taxation in the EU.* A Copenhagen Economics report for the European Commission Taxation and Customs Union Directorate General. Copenhagen: Denmark.

Novotny, J. M. 1955. "Stamp Duties." *Journal of Economic History* 15(3): 288–290. https://www.jstor.org/stable/2114660.

OECD (Organisation for Economic Co-operation and Development). 2021. "Inheritance Taxation in OECD Countries." OECD Tax Policy Studies, No. 28. Paris: OECD. https://www.oecd.org/tax/tax-policy/inheritance-taxation-in-oecd-countries-e2879a7d-en.htm.

———. 2022. "Housing Taxation in OECD Countries." OECD Tax Policy Studies, No. 29, Paris: OECD. https://doi.org/10.1787/03dfe007-en.

PwC. 2023. "Real Estate Transfer Tax (RETT): An International Overview—17 Countries at a Glance." Amsterdam: PricewaterhouseCoopers. (May).

Radvan, R,. and S. Papavasilevsko. 2020. "Abolition of Tax on Acquisition of Immovable Property: A Tool to Suppress the Negative Consequences of COVID-19 or a Politicum?" *Public Governance, Administration and Finances Law Review* 5(2): 45–57.

Revenue. 2023. "Section 31E: Stamp Duty on Certain Acquisitions of Residential Property." In *Tax and Duty Manual.* Irish Tax and Customs.

Rosengard, J. K. 2012. "The Tax Everyone Loves to Hate: Principles of Property Tax Reform." Cambridge, MA: Harvard Kennedy School.

Sánchez, A. C., and D. Andrews. 2011. "Residential Mobility and Public Policy in OECD Countries." *OECD Journal: Economic Studies* (1): 1–22.

Schmidt, D. J. 2022. "Property Transfer Taxes, Residential Mobility, and Welfare." Tinbergen Institute Discussion Papers 22-042/VI, Tinbergen Institute.

Transparency International. 2023. "Corruption Perception Index 2023." https://www.transparency.org/en/cpi/2023/.

UN-Habitat. 2013. *Property Tax Regimes in Europe*. Nairobi: United Nations Human Settlements Programme.

Wallace, S. 2018. "Property Transfer Taxes." African Tax Institute Working paper WP-18-02, University of Pretoria.

World Bank. 2020. "Registering Property." Subnational Studies—Measuring Business Regulations. https://subnational.doingbusiness.org/en/data/exploretopics/registering-property/good-practices#fees.

———. n.d. "World Development Indicators." Accessed December 22, 2023. https://datatopics.worldbank.org/world-development-indicators/.

7

Conclusions and Reform Options

ROY BAHL, WILLIAM MCCLUSKEY, RIËL FRANZSEN,
AND WENJING LI

Europe is property rich and most of its countries have the capacity to develop and manage a productive property tax system. Yet its recurrent property tax revenues account for only about 1 percent of gross domestic product (GDP), and have not been growing in recent years. The average effective property tax rate in 2022 is less than it was in 2005.[1] The first question we try to answer in this book is why the average country taxes on real property remain so low in Europe. The second is whether there is a viable strategy to increase the effective property tax rate.

The answers we give here are based on statistical analysis of a rich body of data, 14 commissioned European country studies, one thematic study on technology and valuation, and a wealth of existing, high-quality background research on this subject. Of course, there is no one set of answers that fits all countries, and not all European countries have been studied to the same extent in this analysis, but some broad patterns for reform have emerged.

This chapter presents conclusions and reform directions. First, several of the underlying problems that have constrained property tax revenue growth are called out. Second, the reform paths that European countries might pursue are outlined. Finally, this chapter closes with a discussion of some barriers to reform and how they might be softened.

Why Are Property Tax Revenue Levels Low?

The average rate of recurrent property taxes in European countries is low, ranging from 2.73 percent in the United Kingdom to 0.16 percent in Estonia in 2022. The results of a panel data regression analysis in this study show that European countries that are more urban, have a higher level of real property wealth, and govern with a more decentralized fiscal structure tend to levy higher property taxes. But this model explains less than half the variation in the effective property tax rate, suggesting that country-specific policies and practices also play a significant role.

The problem is not a new one. The average effective rate of property tax in Europe did not increase in the first two decades of the 21st century. The tax growth that might have occurred in response to increases in property values has been interrupted by business cycles, the COVID-19 pandemic, and discretionary changes that held off revaluations in some countries and froze tax rates in others. Between 2010 and 2022, the mean effective property tax rate declined for 23 of the 38 European countries studied.

The sustainability of the property tax, its ability to hold its revenue share in a tax system, is an important concern in European countries. The analysis here shows an average long-run revenue buoyancy of 1.1, which is consistent with a conclusion that the property tax has been a sustainable source of revenue in Europe over the two-decade period studied. But this is below the buoyancy level usually found for income and consumption taxes. In recent years, the reliance on property tax financing has been crowded out by intergovernmental transfers and local income taxes, which has reduced its buoyancy.

The Need for Fiscal Importance

The low levels of property taxes are themselves part of the problem. A question often asked is why spend significant effort and political capital to develop a tax that yields so little revenue for public budgets? The question is a good one! So is the response that the revenue importance of property taxation is much greater than that reported in fiscal censuses. The evidence in this book suggests that if all taxes levied on land and buildings—income taxes imposed on capital gains and landlord rents, value-added taxes imposed on sales of new properties, and property transfer taxes—were included in the property tax count, it would be shown to be a much larger tax. If the importance of taxes on land and buildings were to be more fully recognized, the costs of reforming it might seem more justified and local governments might be more interested in reforming it.

Discretionary Actions of Governments

The principal reason for slow property tax revenue growth in Europe is the failure of governments to revalue property at the normally recommended three- to five-year intervals. Valuations are decades out of date in many European countries. Many European countries do not regularly report on the accuracy of their assessments. The major constraints to revaluation are a combination of objectionable (unfair) assessment practices, a lack of resources to do revaluations (both human and monetary resources), and political pushback. Taxpayers and politicians seem to fear that if properties were to be revalued, tax rates may not be adjusted downward to avoid windfall revenue gains. This is confirmed by the reluctance of some German cities to reduce tax rates after the introduction of new assessments (Kingston 2024). Some countries have made a revaluation but failed to implement it because of unfavorable economic conditions (Denmark and Finland) or because of legal or constitutional objections (Slovenia). Other countries (France and—until year-end 2024—Germany) have combined various forms of indexing and rate increases to shore up local budgets.

Reform Path: Constraints

Property tax reform is not an easy path. Two of the most challenging obstacles are the development and upkeep of an infrastructure to manage the property tax and the establishment of a valuation system that can lead to a fair, accurate, and regularly updated property tax base. The first is already in place in much of Europe, but the second still requires a great deal of work.

Management of the Property Tax

The administrative practices for property taxation (i.e., cadastre management, property registration, recordkeeping, identification of taxpayers, assessment, an appeals process, billing and collection, and enforcement) can significantly affect revenue and resource allocation. With only a few exceptions, all or most of these practices are in place and administered properly across Europe. And yet the impact on revenue and resource allocation in some countries remains minimal.

Most European countries have fully digitized cadastres that are integrated with land registries. High-quality data are readily available in many countries, and tax collection rates are near 100 percent in most. The efficiency of the institutions that drive the coordination and collaboration among those responsible for land and property administration and revenue collection are usually satisfactory. Some countries support land use and housing policies through property taxation and also make use of land value capture instruments (e.g., additional taxes, fees, and charges) to finance land development projects at the local level.

The higher-income countries in Europe have a basic infrastructure in place to administer an efficient, comprehensive property tax system. Their registration systems are well designed and cover most if not all properties, What we can therefore conclude is that, for these countries, the root cause of the revenue mobilization problem is not inadequate administrative or management structures. Nor does it seem to be that the institutions in place do not function well or are incapable of collaborating or coordinating. Of course, this is not true for every country in Europe, but it would seem true enough for most. A reasonable explanation might be the failure of politicians (both local and national) to comprehend the damage caused by not properly maintaining a value-based system that is not self-assessed.

Valuation

A good valuation system is central to revenue mobilization. Several European countries have failed the tests of good property valuation. The following are major concerns: First is the failure of most countries to implement computerized mass appraisals on a broad scale. Some countries, such as Latvia, the Netherlands, and Slovenia, rely on automated valuation methodologies, but others less so, including France, Germany, Greece, and Ireland.

Second, a main obstacle to adopting automated valuation approaches is the quality of property value data. This includes the coverage of the tax base, or the inventory of all properties and their characteristics. Collecting and maintaining the inventory is expensive (Greece and Latvia). Generally, the countries in part 2 have processes and systems in place to capture, record, and verify transaction prices (Estonia, Latvia, Ireland, and Slovenia).

Third, the traditional valuation approach that assigns each taxable property a discrete, individually assessed value determined by a government valuation authority is problematic. To get around this, Great Britain (England, Scotland, and Wales) and Ireland use value banding with slightly different numbers and width of bands. In Great Britain, banding was an interim measure when first introduced, to be replaced by the standard practice of a discrete value on each property. Decades after the introduction of banding, there are no immediate plans to replace it. Nor has there been a general revaluation in the 21st century.

The fourth concern is with determining the responsibility for assessing value. European countries have made different choices on this matter, ranging from a government entity (with or without the help of private sector valuers) to owner-driven assessments. Given the possible incentive for owner-occupiers to underdeclare the value of their property, quality assurance by government is needed.

Fifth, most European countries fail to regularly revalue. A tax on a property value that was last estimated decades ago does not build taxpayer confidence. Many countries carry assessment ratios below 50 percent of market value and rely on indexing and rate increases to maintain revenues. The failures to revalue can be attributed to the cost of the required valuation effort, the political will, and problematic external events (such as recessions and COVID-19). Only very recently have some countries in Europe begun to unfreeze their assessments and perform revaluations.

Reform Path: Actions

The second question posed in chapter 1 is whether there are viable reform options for capturing the property tax potential of European countries. This study concludes that there is fiscal space to raise the level of property taxes. Some rich countries (France and the United Kingdom) already tax land and buildings at rates nearing 4 percent of GDP, but others (Germany and Ireland) do not. Many European countries tax at a very low effective rate. Whether increases are viable depends on whether European governments are willing to raise their property taxes even if that effort has significant political and monetary costs.

As the 14 case studies show, countries have not given up on the idea of reform, but they have very different ideas about how to do it and about the costs of delaying it. Sometimes these reforms are based on good property tax practice, but not always. And only rarely is a higher target level for property tax revenues brought up in the early planning stages of a reform, even if it is the main objective. The following discussion considers structural and management reforms that could raise property tax revenues.

Property Tax Structure Reform

Several specific property tax reforms are already on the discussion agenda for certain European countries, and others have been discussed. The following reform directions might be considered.

- The rate ceilings on urban local-government property taxes could be lifted, or eliminated altogether, in countries with decentralized fiscal and governance structures. Property tax policy should be a local government matter, with budget discipline controlled by a hard budget constraint.

- The property tax can be made more revenue productive and more fair by reviewing and reducing preferential treatments for certain taxpayers. Such reviews should be mandated. Special property tax relief such as for housing programs should also be subject to the same program. In general, the central governments should be prohibited from giving unfunded relief from local-government taxes.
- The autonomous property taxing powers of large urban local governments (tax rates) should be strengthened. This could reflect the greater public servicing needs in larger cities and the higher level of services provided. The use of special assessments (value capture) could be encouraged.
- Governments could remove penalties embedded in intergovernmental transfers for local governments that increase property tax revenue mobilization, such as Robin Hood systems of horizontal equalization.
- Intergovernmental arrangements for revenue sharing with local governments could be reformed to lessen the extent of crowding out by other forms of local-government revenues. This could be done with formula adjustments that might favor higher property tax rates.
- Central and local governments should better inform their voters about the negative effects of intergovernmental fiscal policies, especially with respect to potential loss of local autonomy in budget matters.
- Central governments might share directly in covering the cost of revaluation.
- Property transfer tax revenues collected could be allocated to local governments.

Revaluation

Property revaluation is key to pushing up property tax revenue mobilization in Europe. This entails doing a better job with using the underlying property tax infrastructure and with expanding the use of new technology. Both are costly improvements, but both can remove major constraints to property tax revenue mobilization as well as the fairness of the system. Five components of this strategy should be considered:

- Invest in improving the basic data that support valuation. For some countries, this means upgrading the property transfer tax administration and, in others, it means developing mechanisms to discover and efficiently record all transactions, including rental contracts.
- Make more use of automation, including mass valuation, and of self-assessment to control costs. Appropriate use of private sector valuation resources can help.
- Institute quality control mechanisms for tracking assessment quality, which would lead to a more equitable and fair property tax.
- Develop a valuation strategy. Central governments postponing revaluations and then subsidizing the revenue loss leads to a nonsustainable property tax.
- Adopt available technology to administer the property tax.

Resolving the revaluation problem might include cost-sharing arrangements for bringing new valuation rolls on line and a much broader use of automation in mass appraisals. Safer (but possibly less efficient and fair) reforms could include longer periods between revaluations (though there does appear to be a trend to implement revaluations more frequently—Denmark, Estonia, and the United Kingdom for commercial property are good examples) and greater use of general uplifts or indexes. Such reforms might lead to more fairness, but none will likely lead to significantly greater levels of property tax revenue.

Most observers will probably agree that the property tax should be based on up-to-date values of taxable properties (TEGOVA 2025). But doing revaluations is expensive. In a large city it could require determining new values for millions of properties and updating data describing each in some detail. Revaluing the tax roll by traditional property-by-property assessments is a budget-buster for local or central governments. And the political costs of revaluation would continue to hold back revenue increases.

The solution to the valuation problem has two elements. One is to commit to automated mass appraisals of properties. Workable models to predict values are improving and are already in use in some European countries. But model use lags in many other countries. The other is to pay for the revaluation. This might involve limiting the revaluation to larger urban areas, retaining traditional assessments for special properties, and adding a partial cost recovery surcharge on the local property tax and covering the remainder with an intergovernmental transfer. Central governments that reduce intergovernmental transfers to local governments would, in effect, "crowd in" property taxation.

This approach to paying for revaluation has significant constraints, such as whether the valuation authority (often the central government) has the capacity to prepare a new valuation roll. To some extent, using private sector valuers, appropriate self-assessment, and even notaries to assist would overcome this constraint. A second constraint is whether the central government comes to understand the importance of the property tax and makes transfers to cover part of the cost. This strategy could involve an increase in property taxing powers for large urban governments in return for lower intergovernmental transfers from the center. And the most binding constraint of all might be to gain taxpayer approval.

Property Transfer Taxes

Most European countries levy a tax on the sale (transfer) of real estate property, usually a central-government tax whose revenues are sometimes shared with local governments. Its primary goal is to help regulate property markets. It has no formal connection to the recurrent property tax except that it provides information for setting assessed values for the annual property tax.

On one hand, taxes on the transfer of property are easy to levy and have significant revenue potential. In a few European countries (France, Belgium, and the United Kingdom), property transfer taxes have been used to significant revenue advantage. On the other hand, taxes on property sales can harm labor market mobility and have a negative impact on social welfare. Numerous studies have estimated these costs to be significant.

Although a few countries (Czech Republic, Kosovo, and Slovakia) have taken the bold step to abolish transfer taxes, there does not currently seem to be a strong movement in this direction. In fact, most countries have been satisfied to merely modify their structures to encourage more property sales—for example, by lowering rates—especially for first-time homeowners. Planning for major rate or base restructuring has not been given widespread attention, perhaps because of the absence of a good way to recover the revenue loss. One reform option that might attract interest is changing the base of the transfer tax to capital gains to promote fairness and administrative efficiency, but it is not clear that the benefits would outweigh the costs. Another is to create a unified recurrent property tax by abolishing the transfer tax and somehow folding its revenue into the annual property tax. These proposals have not generated much interest.[2] One reason for this apathy could be vertical tax competition—transfer taxes are mostly levied by national governments and recurrent property taxes at the local level.

Governance and Data Issues

Central and local governments need to be reminded of the importance of property taxation in their tax systems. The international agencies could be of great help here by supplementing their annual fiscal censuses with a statistical report quantifying all taxes on land and buildings whether classified as a property tax or not. It should also include an accounting of the total value of tax relief attributable to the ownership or use of real estate, including mortgage interest relief and untaxed capital gains.

Another important data issue has to do with property transfer tax revenues. Property transfer taxes distort housing choices and labor mobility, and by some estimates the welfare costs are large. Someday, perhaps soon, it will be part of the reform agenda, and there will be a significant demand for information about its revenue patterns. Property transfer tax revenues should be—but are not currently—reported separately in either the International Monetary Fund or Organisation for Economic Co-operation and Development data series. They are instead included in the general category "Capital and Other Financial Transactions." The European Commission, however, includes property transfer taxes as "other property taxes" (European Commission 2023) and may therefore have better data on these taxes to assist with property tax reform policy choices.

Socializing the Property Tax

Countries should provide better information to taxpayers and to politicians on the property tax. Keeping valuations current and making the property tax more equitable and fair by reexamining preferential treatments would be a good start. On the advocacy side, governments need to be stronger in identifying and promoting specific projects financed by property taxes and that benefit taxpayers. They should more clearly point out the negatives of centralization, particularly the loss of control over services and the possibility of sudden withdrawal of central support for local budgets. There is ample evidence of both of these problems in Europe. Governments also need to more effectively address the fear tactics of critics (such as "property taxes will cause you to lose your home"). Public information campaigns should be ongoing and long term. The overall thrust should be the public services provided by a property tax and the dangers of leaving local-government finance issues too fully in the hands of the central government. In this context, adherence to Article 9 of the 1985 European Charter of Local Self-Government, dealing with financial resources of local authorities, is critical.[3]

The Way Forward

The next step in developing the discussion of property tax reform is to separate the issue of what is to be taxed from the issue of how much tax will be imposed. A tax on the value of property requires a regularly determined valuation roll of market values. Then, the tax liability that property owners will face can be determined by the tax rate, which will depend on how much voters value the public services provided with these revenues. Once valuations are fixed and maintained to market values, it is up to voters to decide whether they value local services enough to allow tax rates to be higher.

What stops reforms from moving toward such a system? One answer is what Friedman and Friedman (1984) refer to as "the tyranny of the status quo." The champions of keeping things as they are include owners of real property wealth and businesses, who feel they have the most to lose from increased property taxation; rank-and-file taxpayers who resist an increased tax on the most valuable asset they own; and the local-government leadership who covets both these voting blocs. A better socializing of the need for property taxation could help but by itself is not the answer. The game changers could be urbanization that increases demand for improvement to local public services financed by property taxes and the application of new technologies for mass appraisal that could significantly lower the cost of revaluation.

Notes

1. See also chapter 2 appendix.
2. Taxpayers disagree with academics, once again, on this matter. Academics see the general property tax as a good tax whose merits need to be emphasized, and the property transfer tax as a bad one that ought to be abolished. Taxpayers apparently do not see the transfer tax as all that bothersome but are perpetually in revolt over the general property tax.
3. Article 9—Financial resources of local authorities
   1. Local authorities shall be entitled, within national economic policy, to adequate financial resources of their own, of which they may dispose freely within the framework of their powers.
   2. Local authorities' financial resources shall be commensurate with the responsibilities provided for by the constitution and the law.
   3. Part at least of the financial resources of local authorities shall derive from local taxes and charges of which, within the limits of statute, they have the power to determine the rate.
   4. The financial systems on which resources available to local authorities are based shall be of a sufficiently diversified and buoyant nature to enable them to keep pace as far as practically possible with the real evolution of the cost of carrying out their tasks.
   5. The protection of financially weaker local authorities calls for the institution of financial equalization procedures or equivalent measures that are designed to correct the effects of the unequal distribution of potential sources of finance

and of the financial burden they must support. Such procedures or measures shall not diminish the discretion local authorities may exercise within their own sphere of responsibility.

6. Local authorities shall be consulted, in an appropriate manner, on the way in which redistributed resources are to be allocated to them.
7. As far as possible, grants to local authorities shall not be earmarked for the financing of specific projects. The provision of grants shall not remove the basic freedom of local authorities to exercise policy discretion within their own jurisdiction.
8. For the purpose of borrowing for capital investment, local authorities shall have access to the national capital market within the limits of the law.

References

European Commission. 2023. *Annual Report on Taxation 2023.* Directorate-General for Taxation and Customs Union. Luxembourg: Publication Office of the European Commission.

Friedman, M., and R. Friedman. 1984: *Tyranny of the Status Quo.* New York: Harcourt Brace Jovanovich.

Kingston, C. 2024. "Germany's Property Tax Reform Starts Impacting Broader Market." (June 18). https://www.refire-online.com/markets/germany-property-tax-reform-starts-impacting-broader-market/.

TEGOVA. 2025. *Valuation and Other Issues for Recurrent Property Taxation.* European Valuation Information Paper (EVIP 4). European Valuation Standards, 10th ed. European Group of Valuers Association.

Legislation

1985 European Charter of Local Self-Government.

PART 2

Case Studies

8

Property Taxes and Proposed Reforms in Denmark

POUL SCHOU

Denmark has a population of 5.9 million inhabitants covering 43,000 square kilometers (excluding Greenland and the Faroe Islands). This gives a population density of 146 people per square kilometer, somewhat more than the European Union (EU) average of 109 persons per square kilometer (Eurostat 2022a). About 88 percent of the population live in urban areas (World Bank 2022a), for a high degree of urbanization. In the EU, only Malta and the Benelux countries have a higher urbanization percentage (World Bank 2022b).

Denmark is a high-income country. Gross domestic product (GDP) per capita was US$67,800 in 2021, surpassed in the EU only by Luxembourg and the Netherlands (World Bank 2022c). A characteristic of the Danish economy is its high level of public expenditure and a correspondingly high level of taxes. Taxes in Denmark are 47.6 percent of GDP, the highest in the EU, where the average is 41.3 percent (Eurostat 2022b).

Administrative Organization

The system of government in Denmark is unitary. Various reforms of the administrative organization occurred during the last century. The last one became effective from 2007 and divided the country into five regions and 98 municipalities. Both regions and municipalities are led by councils elected locally every four years. The municipalities can levy personal income and property taxes within limits set by Parliament and annual agreements between the government and the association of the municipalities, known as KL–Local Government Denmark. The regions, whose main responsibilities are hospitals, do not have taxing power and are financed solely by financial transfers from the central government.

On average, the 98 municipalities have about 60,000 inhabitants, though there is considerable variation. The least populous municipality, the island of Læsø, has fewer than 2,000 inhabitants, whereas the most populous, the municipality of Copenhagen, has 638,000 inhabitants. The municipalities take responsibility for a large number of areas, among which are primary schools and facilities for childcare and elderly people; social welfare; local environmental and labor market issues; public libraries and museums; and in many municipalities, utilities such as electricity, water, and heating supply. Altogether, 48 percent of government consumption expenditure in 2020 was administered by the municipalities, 25 percent by regions, and 27 percent by the central government (Statistics Denmark 2022a). Municipal expenditures are financed partly by local income and property taxes, partly by transfers from the central government, and partly by revenues from municipal firms such as utilities.

Following a major municipal reform in 1970, fiscal decentralization was quite high, the municipalities having complete discretion in levying personal income taxes. For property taxes, municipal rates were contained within a rather wide band. Also on the expenditure side, many government tasks were decentralized. Starting from the 1990s, however, Parliament gradually issued more central regulations in traditional areas of municipal responsibility—for example, minimum standards for child day care. In 2001, the newly appointed government declared a national tax freeze on increases in centrally mandated tax rates. The tax freeze also stipulated that *average* municipal income and property tax rates could not be raised—an objective to be reached via negotiations with the national associations of municipalities (and the corresponding association for the then-existing counties). During the following years, annual negotiations between the minister of Finance and the local-government associations concerned the local-government budgets. The government introduced economic incentives for the individual municipalities to keep the promises made during the negotiations, though initially with mixed success.

The Budget Law passed in Parliament in 2012 (Law No. 547 of June 18, 2012) introduced budget ceilings for municipalities, regions, and the central government. The budget ceilings are negotiated in annual agreements as before, and municipalities' government transfers are cut, as a fine, if they exceed the budget ceilings. Also, municipal tax rate increases can be made only if agreed on beforehand by the government. In contrast to the agreements of the early years of the 2000s, the budget ceilings have very effectively controlled annual municipal expenditure growth. In tandem, the discretion of the municipalities collectively in changing average tax rates and expenditure levels has practically disappeared.

In 2021, average disposable income in the richest municipality (Gentofte, a traditional high-income area just north of Copenhagen Municipality) was twice the national average of DKK 267,000 (US$39,000),[1] whereas the poorest municipality, the island of Langeland, south of mainland Denmark, had average income 80 percent of the national average. In the municipality of Copenhagen, average income equaled 98 percent of the national level (Statistics Denmark 2023).

Tax Revenues

The relatively high tax revenues needed to maintain the Danish welfare system originate from a detailed tax structure. Personal and to a lesser extent corporate income taxes account for around two-thirds of the total revenue. Duties on goods and services account for another 30 percent of revenue, of which the majority stems from the general value-added tax (VAT). Taxes on wealth, property, and so on, account for around 5 percent. There has been a long-run decline in the relative importance of property taxes, which in 1949 accounted for 11 to 12 percent of the total tax revenue (Statistics Denmark 2022b).

Today there exist three main types of property taxes in Denmark: the land tax (*grundskyld*), the reimbursement duty (*dækningsafgift*), and the property value tax (*ejendomsværdiskat*). The first two form part of municipal budgets, whereas the last one is a tax paid to the central government. In Danish official statistics, only the first two are categorized as property taxes, being indirect taxes, whereas the property value tax is categorized as an income tax, because its purpose is to tax part of the imputed income from owner-occupied dwellings. The same is true for Organisation for Economic Co-operation and Development (OECD) data. However, since its inception in 2000, when it replaced rules for calculation of an imputed rental income from owner-occupied dwellings, which were integrated into the general income assessment rules, the property value tax is levied purely on the assessed value of owner-occupied buildings regardless of the income of the owner (the history of the various property taxes is discussed later). Consequently, in economic analyses it is usually considered an important part of the aggregate system of property taxation in Denmark.

Of the three taxes, the land tax is the most important today in terms of revenue. In 2021, land tax revenues amounted to DKK 27.4 billion (US$3.9 billion), 1.2 percent of GDP and 2.5 percent of total tax revenues in Denmark (table 8.1). The next most important is the property value tax, yielding a revenue of close to DKK 15 billion (US$2.1 billion) and 0.6 percent of GDP (table 8.2). Compared with these two, the reimbursement duty is considerably smaller, bringing in DKK 3.2 billion (US$465 million), or just 0.1 percent of GDP or 0.3 percent of total tax revenue (table 8.3). The three taxes together yield 4 percent of the total Danish tax revenue.

Table 8.1 Land Tax Revenues

	2017	2018	2019	2020	2021
DKK billion	24.7	25.1	25.2	26.4	27.4
% of GDP	1.2	1.2	1.2	1.2	1.2
% of total tax revenue	2.6	2.6	2.5	2.6	2.5

Sources: Statistics Denmark (2022b; 2022c).

Table 8.2 Property Value Tax Revenues

	2017	2018	2019	2020	2021
DKK billion	13.6	13.9	14.2	14.5	14.8
% of GDP	0.7	0.7	0.6	0.6	0.6
% of total tax revenue	1.4	1.4	1.4	1.4	1.3

Sources: Statistics Denmark (2022b; 2022c).

Table 8.3 Reimbursement Duty Revenues

	2017	2018	2019	2020	2021
DKK billion	3.4	3.3	3.2	3.2	3.2
% of GDP	0.2	0.2	0.1	0.1	0.1
% of total tax revenue	0.4	0.3	0.3	0.3	0.3

Sources: Statistics Denmark (2022b; 2022c).

Land and Property

Markets

Danish property law does not generally distinguish between freehold and leasehold. Ownership in land is considered freehold. The registered owner in principle executes unlimited property rights, subject only to certain private and public law limitations, such as zoning and planning regulations. Tenants may be granted certain statutory protections to use the rented property—for example, rules of rent protection and eviction restrictions—(Rosenberg and Tamasauskas 2019).

Some restrictions on property ownership in Denmark apply to foreign nationals. For persons not having had a permanent address in Denmark at some point for at least five years, a special permission from the Ministry of Justice is required to buy real estate. EU citizens are exempt from this requirement owing to the rules of free movement of labor within the EU countries. However, for weekend houses, EU citizens (including Danish citizens) are required to fulfill the requirement of five years of previous permanent address in Denmark.

Of the 2.76 million inhabited dwellings in Denmark, 48 percent are owner occupied; 20 percent are occupied by tenants and owned by private corporations (often pension funds) or individuals, and another 20 percent are nonprofit housing associations. Of all dwellings, 7 percent are housing cooperatives (*andelsboliger*), which are governed by special legislation, and the remaining 4 percent are special kinds of dwellings like official residences and dwellings connected with workplaces.

Of the total area of Denmark, 61 percent was agricultural land in 2016. A further 25 percent was categorized as forests, lakes and streams, and other types of nature, and 7 percent was covered by buildings. About 7 percent of the building area and 9 percent of the total area was owned by national or local government. Of the total area, 80 percent was owned directly by private individuals, another 8 percent by private corporations, and the remaining 3 percent by associations, foundations, and so on (Statistics Denmark 2018).

Registration System

The Danish Cadastre (Matriklen) is the basis for all land registration in Denmark. It consists of a countrywide digital cadastral map, an official register, and a cadastral archive, and it plays a central role in the public management and administration of landownership. It is administered by the Danish Geodata Agency (Geodatastyrelsen), which is part of the

Ministry of Climate, Energy, and Utilities. Any plot of land in Denmark is mapped in the cadastral system and given a title number. The cadastral map displays all registered property boundaries and rights-of-way. The map is updated daily as a part of the registration of cadastral changes. It is based on historical, hand-drawn property maps that have been digitized and georeferenced (Geodatastyrelsen 2022).

Subject to few exceptions, all rights over real estate are centrally recorded in the Land Registry (Tingbogen). The Land Registry, kept centrally by the Land Registration Court (Tinglysningsretten), registers all Danish properties, identifying them by their cadastre title numbers. The Land Registry provides information about the landowner's identity, all registered mortgage deeds and other property-related rights, and rights' priorities. Normally, all other rights and claims such as rights-of-way and local restrictions on construction are also recorded (Rosenberg and Tamasauskas 2019). Information in the Land Registry is publicly available, and the official property assessments rely heavily on the information obtained from this registry.

Until 2007, land registration was handled locally by the courts in each of the 82 jurisdictions. In 2007, together with the reform of the local system of government, the judicial system was reformed. The number of geographic local jurisdictions reduced from 82 to 24, and land registration was centralized in the national Land Registration Court, the 25th jurisdiction, which handled all registration of ownership changes and so on. The Land Registration Court is physically situated in the small provincial town of Hobro. In September 2009, the digital Land Registry was introduced. As of 2025, 87 percent of all registration notifications have been handled automatically and digitally by self-service. The approximately 90 employees in the Land Registration Court in Hobro take care of remaining notifications, typically the more complicated ones.

Transfer of Ownership

All transfers of real estate must be registered with the Land Registry. When purchasing real estate, the parties to the agreement usually electronically sign a purchase agreement and a deed of conveyance. The deed of conveyance is used to register the conveyance with the Land Registry and contains only the material provisions of the transfer agreement, whereas the purchase agreement contains the entire agreement. A buyer must respect any third-party rights registered with the Land Registry but normally not rights that have not been registered and of which the purchaser has no prior knowledge (Rosenberg and Tamasauskas 2019). Registration of ownership transfers or mortgages is subject to a registration fee and stamp duty, discussed later.

Real Estate Indexes

Statistics Denmark regularly publishes price indexes for sales of property, divided into the following exclusive categories:

- Single-family houses
- Residential properties with two or three apartments
- Residential properties with four or more apartments
- Residential and business properties
- Business properties
- Industrial properties and warehouses
- Agricultural properties
- Weekend cottages
- Owner-occupied apartments

In some cases, the indexes are additionally subdivided into each of the five administrative regions and further into ten subregions (constructed for statistical purposes). Data are published monthly, quarterly, or yearly. The current price indexes link back to 1992. There are price indexes for previous years as well, but methodological differences make a direct linkage difficult. Statistics Denmark collects the data weekly from the electronic Land Registry.

Statistics Denmark also administers an EU house price index for purchases of dwellings, and from 2015, a separate index for purchases of existing dwellings—that is, excluding newly built dwellings sold for the first time. The EU house price index includes a subdivision based on urbanization (densely populated areas, intermediate areas, and thinly populated areas) (Statistics Denmark 2023).

In addition, three different private institutions publish price indexes: the finance industry association Finance Denmark; the Knowledge Centre for Housing Economics, financed by RealDania; and the website Boligsiden, maintained by a large number of real estate agents. These indexes differ from those of Statistics Denmark in various ways and may in some cases use more recent data.

Real Estate Taxes

This section provides an overview of the Danish taxes on property ownership and property transfers. The main recurrent Danish property taxes (land tax and property value tax) receive further discussion in the next section.

Central Government–Levied Taxes

Property Value Tax

The property value tax is an annual recurrent tax on the value of owner-occupied dwellings. The statutory rates when the tax was introduced in 2000 was 1 percent of the value of the dwelling until a certain threshold and 3 percent of the value above the threshold. Those who owned the dwelling in question when the law was passed in 1998 would pay only 0.8 percent (rather than the 1 percent) on the value below the threshold as long as they kept living at the address. Retired people with a limited income also would pay only 0.8 percent.

The base for the property value tax was the officially assessed value of the property. In 2002, the tax freeze took effect, ensuring that the property value tax paid on a specific property could not increase in nominal terms (it might decrease if its valuation decreased). More precisely, the tax would be calculated from the lowest value of

- the general assessment value on January 1, 2002;
- the general assessment value on January 1, 2001, plus 5 percent; or
- the latest general assessment value.

As Danish property prices generally rise, on average close to 1 percentage point more than the general annual inflation, the tax freeze implied a continuous decline in the effective tax rate, defined as the ratio of the property tax payment to the market value of the property.

Stamp Duties

Two stamp duties are relevant to real estate: a duty on the registration of transfer of ownership and a duty on the registration of mortgages on real estate. When a transfer of real estate is registered with the Land Registry, a duty of 0.6 percent of the sales price is paid in addition to a fixed fee of DKK 1,750 (US$254). The 0.6 percent payment (but not the fixed fee) is waived if the transfer is the result of a divorce; both elements are waived if the transfer is the result of the death of a spouse and the survivor retains undivided possession of the estate. When a new mortgage on real estate is registered with the Land Registry, a duty of 1.45 percent of the value of the mortgage is paid in addition to a fee of DKK 1,730 (US$254). In 2020, the total revenue of stamp duties from the Land Registration

Court was DKK 7.3 billion (US$1.06 billion),[2] all paid to the central government (Ministry of Taxation 2022).

Estate Tax

Denmark has an estate tax on the total wealth (including housing wealth) of a deceased person above a threshold of DKK 346,000 in 2025 (US$50,260). The tax rate is 15 percent for the part of the bequeathed wealth going to descendants and effectively 36.25 percent for the part going to other heirs. Bequeathals to spouses are exempt from the tax. When computing total wealth of the estate, the actual supposed market value of any real estate should be used, but in practice, the official assessment value plus or minus 15 percent is normally accepted at the discretion of the heirs. The heirs may also choose to have a new independent valuation of the real estate by a professional valuator. Many times, heirs will opt for as low a valuation as possible—the official assessment value minus 15 percent—to minimize the estate tax. Sometimes, heirs want a high valuation—for example, if they plan to sell the property immediately. In that case, they can be taxed by the capital gains from the sale—that is, the difference between the actual sales price and the value of the inherited property according to the estate accounts. As the tax rate on capital gains is higher than the estate tax rate, it may be advantageous to stipulate a high valuation at first.

In 2021, the estate tax revenue was DKK 5.3 billion (US$769 million), all paid to the central government (Ministry of Taxation 2021a).

Value-Added Tax

Real estate transfers are not subject to VAT or other sales taxes apart from the previously mentioned stamp duties. The sales of real estate are thus exempt from the general Danish VAT of 25 percent. However, the sale of building sites and of buildings newly constructed by the seller are not exempt from VAT. The details of exemption or nonexemption from VAT for real estate sales are quite complex (Ministry of Taxation 2010).

Capital Gains Tax

In principle, real estate capital gains are taxed upon realization as ordinary capital income or with a tax rate of 37–42 percent, depending on municipality and income level. Importantly, however, capital gains from the sales of houses, apartments, or weekend houses are exempt if the area of the site is less than 1,400 square meters and the seller lived there at some point. Because of this exemption, the vast majority of real estate capital gains from owner-occupied dwellings are effectively untaxed.

Realized capital gains from real property transactions by corporations are subject to general corporate income taxation of 22 percent insofar as they appear in the taxable profits of the corporations. In 2020, Parliament introduced a tax, to start in 2023, on unrealized (notional) capital gains on rental properties exceeding a value of DKK 100 million (US$14.5 million) and expected to yield an annual revenue of DKK 1.15 billion (US$167 million). After the formation of a new government in December 2022, however, the tax was abandoned.

Local-Government-Levied Taxes

Land Tax

The land tax is an annual recurrent municipal tax on the value of land, levied on agricultural, commercial, and residential land. The tax rate is decided by the elected municipal council within a minimum of 1.6 percent and a maximum of 3.4 percent (traditionally expressed as per mille). In 2021, the average tax rate was 2.62 percent (Statistics Denmark 2022b). Land used for agricultural or forestry purposes has a tax rate 1.48 percent lower than the base tax rate and with a maximum of 0.72 percent, for an effective agricultural land tax rate always between 0.12 and 0.72 percent.

The starting point for the tax base is the officially assessed land value of the property. Since 2003, there have been limits on the annual increase in the tax paid, so that the effective tax rate may be less than the statutory one.

In 2021, 64 percent of the total land tax revenue of DKK 29 billion (US$4.2 billion)was due to owner-occupied dwellings; commercial property (including rental housing and agricultural land) paid the remainder (Statistics Denmark 2021).

Reimbursement Duty

The reimbursement duty was introduced in 1961 as part of the new property tax legislation for counties and municipalities. It is a municipal tax paid on government-owned buildings and commercial property but not agricultural property. The tax rate varies between 0 and 1 percent. For commercial property, the tax base is the so-called difference value (*forskelsværdi*) between the assessed total value of the property and its assessed land value; it is basically a tax on building value. For government-owned buildings, the base is the difference value plus the land value, or the total property value.

In 2021, out of 98 municipalities, 37 levied a reimbursement duty. Most of these municipalities were concentrated in the capital area. The municipality of Copenhagen alone received 42 percent of the total revenue from the duty in 2021 (DI 2021).

Other Taxes

Historically, there have been a number of other direct or indirect property taxes. Until 1903, when the modern income tax was introduced, property taxes were among the most important elements of the tax system, not least the *hartkornsskat*, a tax on the quality of agricultural land. Of the new 1903 taxes, what became the most important one in the long run was the personal income tax, but a new property tax (*ejendomsskyld*) was also introduced as an annual tax of 0.11 percent of the value of both land and buildings of all property. Consequently, a general assessment of all property was carried out in 1904. Whereas the *hartkornsskat* had been on the agricultural quality of a field, assumed constant and thus not requiring revision, after 1903 an explicit tax on the value of properties required repeated valuations, which is why the 1903 tax reform was also the starting point for the regular general assessment system of Denmark. The *ejendomsskyld* was in force until 1985 (Johansen 2007). Also in 1903, a wealth tax was introduced on the overall wealth of citizens above a certain threshold. The wealth tax existed until 1996. Net housing wealth was naturally an important part of the total wealth of many taxpayers.

Additionally, from 1926 to 1966, there was a specific tax on increases in land value (*grundstigningsskyld*).

Finally, the Danish income tax system includes an allowance for interest in the personal income tax. Though the allowance is not limited to interest on mortgages, it is in practice considered a very important element of the tax system, affecting property owners and consequently housing markets. Since 1987, the allowance has been successively curbed, but it still exists today. In 1987, interest could be deducted in incomes paying marginal taxes as high as 73 percent, making the effective tax subsidy 73 percent for interest for people paying the highest marginal income taxes. In 2025, the effective tax subsidy is 25–30 percent, depending on the interest payment.

Recurrent Land and Property Tax

This section treats in more detail the two major recurrent Danish property taxes, the property value tax and the land tax, which constitute both historically and currently the main features of the total taxation of property. Particular attention is given to the assessment on which the taxation rests.

Property Value Tax

The property value tax is an annual tax levied (in principle) on the value of owner-occupied dwellings—that is, all tenanted housing is exempt (but owners pay income tax on the rent income, net of expenses).

The property value tax has existed since 2000. It was part of a major tax reform in 1998, known as the Whitsun Package (Pinsepakken). It replaced the imputed income from owner-occupied dwellings, which had been an integral calculation in the Danish income taxation system since the income tax was introduced in 1903. The imputed income calculation added a percentage of the assessed value of the taxpayer's dwellings to the taxable capital income.

Most economists saw the taxable imputed income of owner-occupied dwellings as an equitable and efficient measure leading to a more symmetric tax treatment of various forms of capital income, even though by the 1990s the rate of imputation (typically 2 percent) was generally considered too low to ensure an effective tax rate comparable to the tax on, for example, interest income. Still, the logic behind the imputation principle was not well understood by taxpayers (Sørensen 2003), making it perhaps the most incomprehensible and unpopular tax for the general public. In the general election in 1998, a major campaign theme for the opposition parties was abolition of the imputed income altogether. The incumbent government and its supporting parties won the election by a narrow margin and that same year removed imputation of income from owner-occupied dwellings from the income tax system. The government announced a new property value tax on the same kind of dwelling but levied as a pure percentage of its value without regard to the income of the owner. The tax rates were designed to ensure roughly the same revenue as the replaced imputation principle (in the short run—in the long run, it was designed to increase revenue slightly). For statistical purposes, however, the property value tax is still treated by the OECD, for example, as an income tax, unlike the land tax and reimbursement duty described later. In economic analyses it is generally considered a tax on the imputed income from owner-occupied dwellings.

As explained earlier in the section "Real Estate Taxes," the tax freeze in effect from 2002 caused the average effective tax rate to decline whenever nominal property prices rose, as they did in normal years. In 2016, the average effective tax rate for the tax paid relative to the officially assessed value was 0.6 percent (Danish Economic Council 2016). In 2021, the Ministry of Taxation reported the average effective property tax rate was less than 0.5 percent (Ministry of Taxation 2021b).

Land Tax

The Danish land tax is an annual tax levied on the value of land, whether used for residential, agricultural, or commercial purposes. It has existed since 1924, and has been collected at various times by national, county, and municipal administrative levels; only municipal collection survives today.

The state land tax grew out of the already existing property tax of 0.11 percent of the value of fixed property, which, as mentioned earlier, was introduced as part of the 1903 tax reform. In the years after the introduction, the property tax was criticized for burdening more heavily smaller landholders in rural areas than had the former *hartkornsskat*, which was levied on the supposed land value exclusively without regard to the buildings on it; buildings make up a larger share of the total value on small holdings than on large holdings (Johansen 2007, 84–85). During the following years, assessing land value independently of buildings on it was discussed. During World War I, the property tax rate was raised to 0.165 percent for 1918 and 0.2 percent for 1919 and the following years, which made the issue more pressing. Also, around 1918, Georgist thoughts on the importance of a pure land value taxation had become influential in some political circles, not least in the social-liberal governing party of Radikale Venstre.

As a result, in 1922 a law change stipulated that the next general assessment in 1924 would make separate land and property assessments. Henceforth, two separate national taxes of 0.15 percent of the land value (the land value tax called *grundskyld*) and 0.11 percent of the building value—the difference between the total value of a property and its land value (called *ejendomsskyld* like the former tax, although now it would be just a building value tax—would be levied. A deduction for expenditures on land improvements could be made for the land tax, and a general deduction of DKK 10,000 (US$1,452) for the property tax was available. Because of the general deduction, many minor properties did not pay any land tax (Johansen 2007).

Both state taxes remained unchanged until the end of the 1950s, except for some modification of the deduction rules. Starting from 1957, tax reforms resulted in a freeze in nominal terms of the revenue from the building value tax and, afterward (from 1966), a phasing out of the national *ejendomsskyld*. The last installments of this tax were paid in 1985. The national *grundskyld* was also paid for the last time in the tax year 1965/1966 and converted to a municipal tax. From that time onward, the municipalities decided the local land tax rate. Gradually, especially from 1971 onward, Parliament restricted the variety of the municipal land tax rates. From 2002, less fiscal decentralization was instituted. Whereas the individual municipalities (and until 2007, counties) in principle could still decide income and land value tax rates, the tax freeze prohibited raising the average municipal and county tax rates, putting significant pressure on the municipalities to maintain revenues via a system of fiscal punishments both individually and collectively. Also in 2002, a ceiling was placed on the annual rise in the nominal land tax payments that remains in force until new tax rules, discussed later, take effect from 2024.

Present Valuation System

Until 1996, the basis for levying the various property taxes was the general valuations normally undertaken every fourth year, the 20th general valuation being carried out in 1996 (Johansen 2007, 265). To avoid large jumps in taxes because of the four-year interval, in 1982 automatic annual adjustments began, based on the prices of sold property (Johansen 2007).

Before each general valuation until the 1970s, all property owners filled out a paper form with size, use, and other property information that became the basis for valuators. In 1977, the electronic building register Bygnings- og Boligregisteret (BBR) was introduced, having been planned since 1972 (Vurderingsstyrelsen 2022). The information in the property owners' forms was transferred in 1977 to the register. From then on, valuators combined the registered information with knowledge of local prices to suggest a valuation, which was sent to the property owner, who agreed with or objected to the valuation (Johansen 2007, 266). This more automated valuation considerably lessened the administrative burden of carrying out general valuations, and they took place annually from 1998.

In 1996, the minister of taxation formed a committee to analyze the assessment process, partly due to criticism of both the accuracy of municipal valuations and their efficiency. The committee reported in 1999. In 2003, assessments transferred from the local municipalities to the Ministry of Taxation, and the process was modified so that valuations of owner-occupied dwellings occurred one year and all other kinds of buildings the next, in a two-year cycle. For each, price adjustments were made in the intermediate years on the basis of changes in the regional price index for properties of the relevant type. The centralization was partly motivated by an ambition to have more homogeneous assessments across municipalities and partly to lower expenses; ministry assessments used half the personnel the municipalities had collectively used. The ministry's organization of the assessment process changed in following years, gradually becoming more centralized. Initially, the 30 regional customs and tax offices performed assessments, to maintain some local knowledge, but in 2009 a new central valuation agency (SKAT Ejendomsvurdering) took over (Office of the Danish Auditor General 2013).

In 2012, the Rigsrevisionen (Office of the Danish Auditor General) investigated the assessment process, publishing in August 2013 a sharp critique of assessment quality that concluded that citizens and enterprises were not ensured a fair and equal treatment in valuations. Even though the ministry had been aware of problems, generally from 2003 and more specifically from 2007, the ministry had not acted to improve quality (Office of the Danish Auditor General 2013). Referring to the report from the Rigsrevisionen, the Parliament-appointed Auditors of Public Accounts (Statsrevisorerne) officially reprimanded but did not prosecute the six ministers of taxation in office in 2003–2013.

Following the report from the Rigsrevisionen, the government in 2013 suspended the whole valuation process and levied taxes (all three kinds) on the basis of the 2011 general assessment for owner-occupied dwellings and the 2012 assessment for commercial property. This remained in effect until 2024, when a new system was introduced (Ministry of Taxation 2021b).

Suspension of the valuation process did not freeze the nominal revenues from the property taxes. On the contrary, the land tax revenues have remained more or less constant as a percentage of GDP from 2009 to 2021. This is mainly due to the limitation on the annual rise in land tax payments combined with a considerable increase in land assessment values from around 2007. Because of the limitation, the effect from the increase in the most recent valuations was delayed for several years. In 2015, only a third of all owners of dwellings had paid the full land tax from the latest (2011) valuation. The remainder had a discount because of the limitation (Ministry of Taxation 2017b).

The valuation law in place until 2024 should result in a prudent valuation, so that the majority of properties are assessed at slightly under the market price. To do this, the analytically suggested values were as a rule reduced by 5 percent to yield the final assessment value.

Various entities report the ratio of assessment values to market values. The Ministry of Taxation each year publishes a so-called distance value (*afstandsprocent*), which measures the rate between the average price of all traded dwellings of a certain type and the average assessment values of the same type in a period. During 2001–2011, the distance value was 13 percent, meaning that market values of owner-occupied properties averaged 13 percent higher than assessment values. During 2012–2016, however, the distance value was between 0 and 2 percent following the large decline in property prices after the 2008 financial crisis. In 2017, the distance value was 10 percent, increasing to 29 percent by 2021 as house prices steadily increased and use of the 2011 assessment values continued. Statistics Denmark started publishing in 2015 its own measure of the two (publishing data from 2004 onward). For owner-occupied dwellings, the market value averaged 12 percent higher than assessed values during 2004–2013. For all real property, it was 85 percent. From 2013, the ratio increased because assessments were not updated and property prices were rising. In 2021, the market value of all owner-occupied dwellings was DKK 3.672 billion (US$533 million), or 146 percent of GDP; 51 percent higher than the corresponding assessment value. The market value of all real property was DKK 4.733 billion (US$687 million), or 189 percent of GDP; 40 percent higher than assessed value (Statistics Denmark 2023).

In the standard procedure for handling property owners' objections to assessments, the Ministry of Taxation reviews the objection and may agree wholly or partially and settle the case. If the plaintiff is not satisfied or 16 weeks have passed without a decision, the ministry must send the objection to one of 15 regional assessment appeal boards (*vurderingsankenævn*), consisting of local political appointees and technical experts. Plaintiffs who do not agree with the board's verdict may appeal to the National Tax Tribunal (Landsskatteretten), a specially appointed court. After a general valuation of commercial property in 2010, there were about 8,000 objections (1.67 percent of all commercial property valuations). In 2011, the general valuation of owner-occupied dwellings resulted in 6,250 objections, or 0.36 percent. The ministry reached an agreement with the plaintiff in 52 percent (2010) and 57 percent (2011) of the cases, respectively; the remaining cases were sent to the regional appeal boards. At the appeal boards, plaintiffs were successful in 47 percent of cases (Office of the Danish Auditor General 2013).

Municipalities used to handle arrears, but the task was centralized and taken over by the Ministry of Taxation in the first decade of the 21st century. In 2005, the ministry initiated an ambitious new administrative system to recover debts to the government in general. The system never functioned properly, however, and turned into an administrative scandal. In 2015, it was canceled, and arrears, including from property taxes, increased considerably. In 2017, the task of recovering property tax arrears returned to municipalities. Once the new property tax system is introduced in 2024, however, as explained later, the central tax authority will collect property taxes and recover arrears.

Development of a Replacement Valuation System

In October 2013, the government instructed an external expert committee (called the Engberg Committee, after its chairman Peter Engberg Jensen, former chief executive at the financial services company Nykredit) to make recommendations for a new assessment system. The Engberg Committee report, published September 2014 (Engberg Committee 2014), called for development of a better statistical model of valuation for owner-occupied dwellings, one based on actual sales prices for comparable nearby dwellings and objective data for the property in question, such as the materials used for its walls and roof. On the basis of the report, the ministry in 2014 founded the Implementeringscenter for Ejendomme (Implementation Center for Properties) to devise assessment principles and practices. Two drawbacks of the old system were that it led to valuations generally too low in large parts of Denmark and that it resulted in land assessments that gave low assessment to apartments compared with one-family houses, especially in large urban areas (Ministry of Taxation 2021b).

In November 2016, a large parliamentary majority agreed to a new property assessment law, and the Implementeringscenter for Ejendomme started developing the new system. In 2018, the new Property Assessment Law (Law No. 654 of June 8, 2017) was implemented, an administrative reform of the Ministry of Taxation took place, and a new agency, the Property Assessment Agency (Vurderingsstyrelsen), was made responsible for the new valuation system.

The new system makes extended use of data, allowing use of an automated statistical model and thus assessment of more properties. Previously, the assessment system used judgments made by the civil servants performing the assessments. The more consistent use of objective data will yield higher transparency, and individual property owners may more easily understand the background for their assessment.

The data chiefly come from the electronic building register BBR (as of 2018 organizationally a part of the Property Assessment Agency), Land Registry, and Cadastre and include planning (zoning) data from the Agency of Planning and Rural Districts (Plan- og Landdistriktsstyrelsen). Most of the sources were available also for the former valuations, but the data collection and organization of the BBR and Cadastre have been revised for the new system. One revision is that from 2018 property owners can themselves—and are obliged to—digitally make relevant changes to the BBR concerning building changes. After municipal approval of building changes, owners enter them directly in the BBR. Data for assessments consist of site size and building size, age, use, material used for roofs and walls, method of heating, and number of bathrooms and toilets. The data also include distance from schools; shopping facilities; infrastructure like railway stations, highways, and other busy roads; and natural amenities like lakes and seaside.

The new assessment model for property values has two steps. First, a market price per square meter is calculated using actual sales data from several nearby reference properties. For one-family houses and row houses, 15 reference properties are used, chosen from properties traded within the last six years. For owner-occupied apartments, 10 reference properties are used, apartments being more homogeneous than one-family houses. The prices of the reference properties are projected to the time of the assessment using a local property price index and are weighted according to their geographic proximity. Second, the square meter price is corrected to take account of the difference between the assessed property and the reference properties in, for example, age, building materials, and distance to major roads, coastline, and so on. The statistical correction models in the second step are based on independent statistical analyses of the influence of various property characteristics on a property's value. Separate statistical models are used for one-family and row houses, owner-occupied apartments, and weekend houses (Skatteforvaltningen 2024). Unlike the previous system, in which valuations were intentionally systematically reduced to slightly underestimate the market value, the new valuation system reflects the market value accurately on average, introducing instead a formal discount of 20 percent in the tax rate to redress inaccuracies. The Ministry of Taxation in 2021 found that assessments in the new system do indeed closely reflect market prices. For one-family houses, assessments differed by less than 20 percent (a high precision) from a newly sold house 70 percent of the time; for owner-occupied apartments, 86 percent (Ministry of Taxation 2021b).

Land Value Assessments

Assessment for the value of land that residential buildings sit on presents particular problems because the assessment is for the land plot as if it were vacant (i.e., with no buildings on it). The new assessment model for land values for one-family houses is consequently based on a statistically estimated correlation between market prices for building sites and for developed (built-up) properties, the so-called land value curve (*grundværdikurve*), which is constructed in the following way:

1. Market prices for land plots are formed by collecting actual sales prices for undeveloped sites, adding data for property sales of built-up sites where the building is immediately afterward demolished (demolition sales), and in some cases, factoring in assessments of real estate agents of the market value of built-up land plots in the hypothetical case that they were undeveloped.
2. For each of these land plots, the (total) property value of a hypothetical property consisting of the land plot in question with a precisely defined standard house is assessed, using the new assessment model for property values described earlier.
3. The land value curve describes the correlation between the land values from step 1 and the property values from step 2. Two national land value curves are constructed, one for permanent one-family houses and one for weekend houses.

In the future when assessing the land value of a specific built-up property, its hypothetical total property value with a standard house on the site will be assessed as in step 2, and the corresponding land value will be then assessed from the land value curve in step 3, and a further adjustment will be made for special circumstances. These could be zoning regulations either allowing or disallowing further development of the property in question.

When determining land values for owner-occupied apartments, data for sales prices of undeveloped sites are even more sparse than for one-family houses. For these, the land value curve for one-family houses is again used to apply a land value assessment that is otherwise similar to the procedure just described.

For business properties (including tenanted housing), the original intentions of renewing the assessment system had to be given up because it was found that data were inadequate. In February 2021, the Danish Parliament consequently agreed to the development of a less complicated system. Assessments of the property values for commercial buildings were simply abandoned so that these properties will in the future receive only a valuation of their land values. For these, a valuation based on the assessment system for corresponding owner-occupied residential buildings was decided on. Consequently, in the future the land value of a specific business property will be assessed as if it was a residential property, after which certain discounts may be employed to reflect differences in the economic value between owner-occupied residential and business properties.

Parliament also changed the future tax base for the reimbursement duty from the building value of the property (that is, the total property value minus the land value) to the land value. Now both recurrent property taxes levied on business properties depend only on the land value, eliminating the need for a recurrent valuation of the total property value for these properties (Ministry of Taxation 2021b).

Property Tax in Large Urban Areas

The metropolitan area of Copenhagen, the capital, has the largest population and contains some of the most valuable properties in Denmark. The Capital Region (Region Hovedstaden), one of five Danish regions, has 1.9 million inhabitants. The region is divided into 29 municipalities, the largest of which is the municipality of Copenhagen (638,000 inhabitants). Regions are often used as a unit for statistical purposes, and sometimes Statistics Denmark defines a metropolitan area of the Capital Region as comprising 13 entire municipalities and parts of 5 others. The metropolitan area in 2022 had 1.345 million inhabitants.

Statistics Denmark publishes extensive statistics for land taxes on a municipal basis, but the same is not true for the property value tax, which is considered an income tax and has no municipal discretion. The metropolitan municipalities have the same possibilities for levying land taxes and reimbursement duties as any municipality. The valuation process also follows the nationally stipulated rules, being administered by the Ministry of Taxation. Consequently, the municipality does not have a valuation department.

Municipalities have a choice regarding the specific tax rates for land taxes and reimbursement duties. The municipality of Copenhagen traditionally levies the highest possible land tax rate, 3.4 percent. The average land tax rate for all the municipalities in the region, however, was 2.675 percent, only slightly higher than the national average of 2.615 percent and lower than in the region of North Jutland. As for the reimbursement duty, Copenhagen levies a duty of 0.98 percent for commercial buildings, or very close to the maximum rate of 1 percent. As commercial property in Copenhagen generally is relatively valuable and most municipalities have a lower or zero tax rate, the municipality of Copenhagen raises 42 percent of the total revenue from the reimbursement duty in Denmark. Also, 25 of the 28 municipalities in the Capital Region levy a reimbursement duty on commercial property, 10 of which levy the maximum rate of 1 percent. Among the 69 municipalities outside the region, only 11 levy such a tax, and none at the maximum rate (Statistics Denmark 2022b).

In Copenhagen, the two property taxes together yielded 12.4 percent of the total revenue for the municipality in 2021. The percentage has been very stable in recent years (table 8.4). The revenue from property taxes constituted 16 percent of the revenue on which the municipality has some direct influence (income and property taxes).

Whereas the nominal growth in land tax revenue was 6.6 percent over the two years from 2019 to 2021, the value of the tax base increased 5.8 percent during the same period (table 8.5). The number of taxable properties increased by 8.6 percent, Copenhagen experiencing a period of high housing demand.

Reform Initiatives and Country-Specific Issues

This section describes in further detail the property tax reforms of 2016–2017 and the later amendments of 2020 and 2021. The reforms are to take effect from January 1, 2024; their full impact is currently not known with certainty.

The reforms consist of a new assessment system to make more accurate assessments of the market value of the taxable properties and a revised set

Table 8.4 Sources of Revenue for Municipality of Copenhagen, 2019–2021 (DKK billion)

	2019	2020	2021	2021 % of total
Municipal income tax	26.122	28.423	27.918	64.5
Land tax	3.851	4.056	4.104	9.5
Reimbursement duty	1.221	1.210	1.244	2.9
Corporate tax	1.752	2.391	1.495	3.5
Certain other taxes	0.286	0.339	0.351	0.8
Intergovernmental transfers	7.138	7.419	7.871	18.2
Interest income, etc.	0.167	0.112	0.234	0.5
Utilities	−0.113	n.a.	0.046	0.1
Total	40.425	43.951	43.263	100.0

Sources: Municipality of Copenhagen (2019; 2020; 2021).

Note: n.a. = not available.

Table 8.5 Taxable Properties and Growth in Value of Tax Base Over Three Years

	2019	2020	2021	2021
Number of Taxable Properties				**% of total**
Municipality	124,265	131,318	134,952	5.6
Region	546,176	557,225	563,997	23.4
Denmark	2,362,704	2,390,168	2,414,091	100
Value of Tax Base (DKK billion)				**% of total**
Municipality	117.720	122.153	124.598	10.2
Region	472.527	488.525	501.719	41.0
Denmark	1,152.701	1,190.276	1,222.371	100

Sources: Statistics Denmark (2020; 2021; 2022b).

of tax rates for all three existing property taxes. A detailed set of transition rules were added to ensure that property owners would not experience increases in their property tax payments because of the reforms.

The need for the reforms was manifold, as explained previously in the section “Recurrent Land and Property Tax”: A reorganization and centralization of the valuation process during the first decade of the 21st century garnered numerous complaints about the accuracy of the assessments. After the Office of the Danish Auditor General issued a sharp critique of the valuation process in 2013, it was suspended altogether, and there was a clear perceived need for an assessment reform.

In addition, there was a considerable political debate on the equity, efficiency, and desirability of the existing property taxation. The main topic during the first decade of the 21st century and early 2010s was the tax freeze for owner-occupied dwellings that entered into force in 2002 and halted increases in the property value tax rate so that the effective rate would henceforth decline concurrently with the rise in nominal house prices. The tax freeze was popular with the general public, especially initially. It was criticized by most independent economists, however, including the Danish Economic Council, an advisory body; several other prominent economic researchers; Danmarks Nationalbank, the central bank; and international organizations like the OECD, the International Monetary Fund, and the European Commission. Initially, the criticism concentrated on the tax freeze locking the existing tax structure, causing an increasing loss of efficiency by eroding the already low value of the property value tax compared with other capital income taxes, thus widening the gap between investment in housing and its tax-induced profitability and business investments. The tax freeze, because it would erode the revenue-to-GDP ratio, was also seen to endanger the long-term fiscal sustainability of the Danish economy.

During and after the 2008 financial crisis, the tax freeze was further criticized for its destabilizing effect on business cycles. Whereas the property value tax originally worked as an automatic stabilizer because it ensured that the tax paid increased and decreased with house prices, the tax freeze would cause effective property tax rates to fall during booms and rise during busts. The Danish Economic Council in 2009 stated that the tax freeze was partly responsible for the bubble in property prices before the financial crisis and its repercussions, which were larger in the Danish property market than in many other countries.

In 2016, the Danish Economic Council in an analysis of the Danish property tax system found another unintended consequence of the tax freeze: it made effective tax rates systematically geographically inequitable. Because house prices had generally risen considerably more since 2001 in the parts of Denmark where they were already high, particularly in and around major cities like Copenhagen and its northern suburbs and Åarhus, effective tax rates were now considerably lower in these municipalities than in the poorer areas of some provincial parts of Denmark. This feature was widely criticized in the press and by main political parties and led to larger political interest in replacing the tax freeze with a more geographically equitable system (Danish Economic Council 2016).

Various proposals to reform the property tax system were raised. Among them either a total abolition of the land tax or a unification of the land tax and property value tax to a single property tax. Some economists and politicians advocated a tax on capital gains from owner-occupied dwellings similar to the Swedish capital gains tax. In 2016, a broad political agreement among the liberal-conservative government, its supporting Danish People's Party, and the main opposition parties (the Social Democratic Party and the Social Liberal Party) was reached concerning principles for a new assessment system, preserving both an assessment of the total value of all properties and an independent assessment of their land values. In May 2017 the same broad coalition of parties reached an agreement on the future property tax system.

The agreement called for a fairer and more accurate assessment system and created the Property Assessment Agency under the Ministry of Taxation, set up new information technology systems, and increased funding to raise the assessment quality. Also, a new structure for assessment objections was agreed on, and all owners who had previously been taxed too highly because of an overvalued assessment were to receive a refund. According to the 2016 agreement, the first general assessment for owner-occupied dwellings under the new system was to take place in 2018, and the first general assessment for commercial buildings, including cooperative and nonprofit housing associations, was due in 2019.

The property tax agreement continued the two main taxes, the land tax and the property value tax, but lowered the statutory tax rates for both. The agreement removed the tax freeze, so that the statutory tax rate would equal the effective tax rate for all new owners from 2021 onward. The new assessments are expected to yield considerably higher valuations than the 2011/2012 ones because of the considerable rises in property prices during the years in question and because land in the major city areas was particularly undervalued on average in the old assessments. To keep the aggregate revenue from the two property taxes in the first year of the reform unchanged, tax rates were lowered accordingly. The agreement expected property tax payments to fall for about 60 percent of all dwelling owners. The remaining percentage of owners would receive a discount ensuring that they would pay no more in 2021 than under the old rules in 2020. In future years, their property taxes would rise with property prices, but the tax increase would be collected only upon the sale of the house. Also, the new agreement stipulated that the tax base for each property would equal 80 percent of the assessment value, to ensure that the uncertainty inherent in the assessment would not lead to too high tax payments.

In 2019, it became clear that the new assessment system would be delayed. The parties behind the original agreement consequently in May 2020 concluded a new agreement that pushed out the new tax system to January 2024. They also created transition rules to compensate owners and furthermore agreed a permanent aggregate tax reduction for dwelling owners of DKK 0.6 billion (US$87 million) compared with the 2017 agreement. The 2020 agreement was later supplemented with provisions for assessment and taxation of commercial property.

The 2024 Rules

From 2024, a new property value tax rate will be effective for the value of all owner-occupied dwellings below the progressive threshold value. The tax rate will be 0.55 percent, but after a deduction of 20 percent of the assessed value of the dwelling, the effective rate will be 0.44 percent of the assessed value. The exact rate will be decided in 2023, depending on developments in property prices and assessments. The progression threshold will be also decided in 2023; the same relative number of owner-occupied dwellings (about 1 percent) will pay the progressive tax in 2024 as in 2023. The progressive tax rate will be 1.4 percent (after deducting 20 percent) of the value above the threshold. The rate increase over the threshold (approximately a doubling) is considerable but still a decrease compared with the former system, which operated with a tripling in the formal tax rate (from 1 to 3 percent).

The land tax rates will also change as of 2024. In 2023, Parliament will set the local tax rates, which will be effective from 2024. The rates will be fixed so that the total revenue in each municipality in 2024 will equal the revenue in 2023. The new land tax and reimbursement duty values cannot be raised (but may be lowered) by the municipalities throughout 2021–2028. From 2029 the municipalities may again decide rates as before the reform, with a maximum of 3 percent. Table 8.6 summarizes the reform.

The development of a new assessment for commercial buildings proved more difficult than foreseen in the original political agreement, and the 2020 amendment consequently postponed a final decision for the reimbursement duty. Starting in 2022, the base for the reimbursement duty was changed from building value (calculated as the difference between the total value of the property and its land value) to the land value of the property. As the new valuation system was still not in place at the time, the duty initially is based on a preliminary valuation by the municipality to be revised later.

Table 8.6 Main Elements of the 2024 Reform

	Base	Assessment	Rate	Preferential Treatment
Property value tax	Owner-occupied dwellings	Revised assessed property value	Expected effective tax rate of 0.44% below threshold and 1.12% above threshold	Reduced rate for retired low-income owners and for people who own their dwelling before January 1, 2024
Land tax	All agricultural, residential, and commercial land	Revised assessed land value	Parliament to decide, to replicate historical revenues; from 2029 to be locally decided with a limit of 3%	Reduced rate for agricultural land; properties listed for reasons of cultural heritage do not pay land tax; government property does not pay land tax, does pay reimbursement duty
Reimbursement duty	Nonagricultural commercial and government land	Revised assessed land value	Parliament to decide; from 2029 to be locally decided with a limit of 1%	

Source: Author.

Administrative Consequences

An administrative consequence of the reform is that the land value tax, which so far has been collected separately by the municipalities, typically twice a year, is now taken over by the Ministry of Taxation and integrated into the general withholding tax of the income tax system (as has always been the case with the collection of the property value tax). The reason for the change is given as administrative simplification, but it is also hypothesized to make the land value tax less conspicuous in the eyes of taxpayers, possibly limiting popular opposition to that particular tax. At the same time, the centralization may lead to less accountability of (local) political leaders to their voters.

Evaluation

The replacement valuation system and related agreements from 2016/2017 came about after a general recognition that the assessment process must be improved, despite the difficulty. The preservation of a separate land tax, the removal of the tax freeze, and a new system securing the same effective tax rates on owner-occupied dwellings across geographic areas were seen as positive features. Though the new rules keep a temporary rate freeze on municipal land taxes, this will not in itself lead to a continuous fall in effective rates. According to the Danish Economic Council, however, property value tax rates will remain low, relative to other Danish capital income taxes, and thus investment in dwellings will be favored over business investment, creating an allocation inefficiency. The Danish Economic Council also deplored the removal of the minimum municipal land tax rate because the very small distortionary effects of the land tax make it an advantageous instrument for raising future taxes.

On one hand, because existing property owners receive a discount that remains in effect for as long as they reside on their property, the reform has a lock-in effect. This leads to decreased mobility in the housing market and may negatively influence labor mobility. On the other, it is a politically necessary feature that creates broad support for the reform. A further consequence of the discount for existing owners is that it will cause house prices to rise through December 2023 and then fall in January 2024, because the 2024 tax bill will be considerably lower when buying a dwelling in December 2023 (or before) than one month later.

Concerning fiscal (de)centralization, the reforms imply a further centralization in the collection of land taxes that is to be transferred from the municipalities to the Ministry of Taxation, integrating it into the general income tax administration, where the property value tax has always resided. Also, the new official land tax and reimbursement rates are initially wholly centrally fixed, and the rate freeze continuation to 2028 additionally limits municipal discretion. Because the 2012 Budget Law and the traditions of the decades since 2000 created an awareness of a very close central management of municipal taxes and expenditures, these are not novelties.

Impacts

Effects of Land Tax

Economists consider the land tax an example of a very efficient—that is, nondistortionary—tax, at least in the pure version in which it is a proportional tax on the value of land (Sørensen and Vastrup 2015). The reasoning is that the tax cannot lead to changes in land supply. Further, the incidence of the land tax has no effect on the owner of the land; later owners will pay the land tax, but are compensated via a correspondingly lower market price of the land. This insight has led to the Danish saying "Old land taxes are good taxes, but new land taxes are bad taxes."

An empirical analysis of data from the local-government reform in 2007 by the Danish Economic Council in 2016 (Høj, Jørgensen, and Schou 2018) examined this hypothesis. The analysis confirmed the proposition that land taxes are fully capitalized into market prices, supporting the nondistortionary property of the tax. In 2007, several smaller municipalities were merged into larger ones, each resulting new municipality having a unitary land tax rate computed as a weighted average of the rates of the constituent smaller municipalities, which had different locally determined land tax rates. Consequently, the reform provided plenty of exogenous variation for examining the effect of a change in land tax rates on house prices. Because of the reform, some landowners experienced a rise and others a fall in their taxation. The reform had a statistically significant effect on the prices of home sales before and after announcement of the reform. Controlling for other potentially important factors, the effect on sales prices was compatible with a 100 percent capitalization of the future land tax changes using a reasonable discount rate (Høj, Jørgensen, and Schou 2018).

Even though the effects of the 2007 local-government reform seem to confirm the traditional economic view that land taxes are generally nondistortionary, two qualifications apply: First, the results hold true only if the tax rate does not vary according to the land's use. This is not strictly true in Denmark, however, as agricultural land is taxed at a considerably lower rate than other land (but see the previous section "Real Estate Taxes"). This might indicate that, though total land in Denmark is inelastic in supply, land used for residential purposes might not be. Individual plot owners, however, do not have the power to determine whether their land is agricultural or nonagricultural (typically, residential); it is instead a decision taken by a political (e.g., municipal) body as part of ongoing physical planning policy. This makes it unclear whether the difference in tax rates has a long-run effect on allocation of land for agricultural or nonagricultural purposes.

Second, for the land tax to be truly nondistortionary, it must tax only the value of the unimproved land plot, and improvements by the owners that increase its value cannot be taxed, in parallel with the irrelevance for the land tax base of the value of buildings on the plot. This feature was recognized and in principle secured by a special allowance for land improvements when developing and parceling out building sites until 2012, when this allowance ended, making the land tax inefficient by reducing incentive to make future land improvements.

Effects of Property Value Tax

As explained earlier, the purpose of the property value tax is to create horizontal equity in the tax system by taxing imputed income from dwellings on a par with other kinds of capital income. If calibrated correctly, so that it reflects average capital income tax rates, the property value tax will not distort decisions to own versus rent dwellings or to invest in residential capital rather than other kinds of business capital. Though there is uncertainty as to how to calculate more precisely the imputed income from owner-occupied dwellings, economists generally judge the actual property value tax rate to be too low to secure tax neutrality between (owner-occupied) housing investment and other investment. The Danish Economic Council in 2016 concluded that a basic property value tax rate of 1.2 percent below the progressivity threshold and 1.8 percent above the threshold constituted a neutral tax rate in this respect. At the time, the effective average property value tax rate at the national level was 0.6 percent. Using macroeconomic models, the council illustrated that raising the property value tax and using the revenue to correspondingly lower the tax on labor income would permanently increase employment and decrease housing capital, which would result in a corresponding increase in nonhousing financial wealth. House prices would fall as soon as the tax took effect, but the models disagree on the permanence of the tax change's effects on house prices (Danish Economic Council 2016).

Effects of Reimbursement Duty and Stamp Duties

Whereas the land tax and the property value tax have generally been viewed as sensible elements of the Danish tax system, economic researchers have criticized stamp duties on the registration of property transfers and mortgage loans. These duties are effectively property transfer taxes, leading to lock-in effects and creating unnecessarily high distortions relative to alternative ways of raising revenue (Danish Economic Council 2016).

The traditional reimbursement duty levied by some municipalities is also considered distortionary, reducing incentives to construct commercial buildings as opposed to residential buildings. In particular, the tax base (commercial building value) of the reimbursement duty until 2022 made construction of commercial buildings less profitable (Danish Economic Council 2021). From 2022, the base of the reimbursement duty is the land value of the property, reducing the distortion. However, it still has the effect of taxing a land plot more highly when used for commercial purposes than when used for residential purposes. Whereas the alternative uses are commonly regulated by physical planning, the planning process itself may be directly or indirectly affected by the differing tax rules.

Distribution Effects

The Danish personal income tax system is generally progressive, because a person's first DKK 48,000 (US$6,900) earned is untaxed by the municipal and central-government proportional income tax and because close to 9 percent of all taxpayers pay a 15 percent surtax on high income. Conversely, indirect taxes are normally considered regressive because the average propensity to consume falls with rising income.

Analyses of equity effects of the main real estate taxes are scant. The Danish Economic Council at various times has analyzed the effect a small rise in the land tax for dwellings and in the property value tax, respectively, has on the Gini coefficient. In 2001, the council found that the property value tax was progressive, so that a small tax rise would decrease the Gini coefficient. For the land tax on dwellings, the movement was the opposite direction (and the effect somewhat smaller in magnitude). The effect of land tax changes is highly sensitive to the assumption of the incidence on inhabitants of rented dwellings. In an unregulated housing market, the owners of tenanted buildings are expected to bear the full burden of a higher land tax. However, in large parts of the Danish housing rent market, price ceilings regulate rent, and tenants pay less than the market rent. Higher land taxes, however, allow a correspondingly higher rent, so that the tenants bear the full burden of the tax change in that case. The council's analyses assume all tenants bear the burden of a land tax rise for tenanted buildings, leading to its conflicting findings on the Gini coefficient (Danish Economic Council 2001).

In a 2008 analysis, the Danish Economic Council confirmed that higher property value tax rates (a proportional increase in the property value taxes for owner-occupied dwellings) would lead to a more even income distribution (Danish Economic Council 2008). The council's major 2016 analysis of the property tax system showed that the amount of land tax paid by property owners generally rose with income. In the highest income decile, owners paid about twice as much as owners in the lowest income decile. For the property tax, the same qualitative result applied, but the progressivity was much clearer. People in the highest income decile paid on average more than six times as much as people in the lowest income decile, and the income share of the tax also rose with each decile, except that the lowest decile paid about the same share of its income in property value taxes as the third-lowest decile and slightly more than the second-lowest decile (Danish Economic Council 2016).

Additionally, the council analyzed consequences for the Gini coefficient of a transition to a purportedly neutral property value tax, abolishing the tax freeze, the special discounts for retired people and for people who had bought their owner-occupied dwellings before 1998, and raising the tax rate below the threshold to 1.2 percent and lowering the tax rate above the threshold to 1.8 percent. It found that abolishing the tax freeze caused a lower Gini coefficient (a more even income distribution), whereas the rise of the general tax rate to 1.2 percent was practically neutral, and a higher Gini coefficient resulted from the other three changes, but chiefly the reduction of the tax rate for the most expensive dwellings (Danish Economic Council 2016).

In 2019, the Danish Economic Council once again examined the equity effects of the property value tax as part of a general analysis of capital income taxation. The results showed once again that the tax was progressive, so that a rise would entail a more even income distribution. This analysis examined independently the two property value tax rates (below and above the progressivity threshold, respectively). Both were progressive in themselves, though the high tax rate naturally considerably more so; indeed, it was the most progressive specific tax of all the 13 tax rates on types of capital and labor income in the analysis (Danish Economic Council 2019). The Ministry of Taxation stated in May 2017 that it expected the property tax reform to be practically neutral on the Gini coefficient in 2021 (the first year the reform was then expected to take effect) (Ministry of Taxation 2017a).

Concerning regional equity, the property tax reform will likely place a relatively larger burden on the metropolitan areas than elsewhere. This is true for two reasons: The future assessment system will raise assessed land values for apartments in residential buildings, most of which are situated in the largest cities. The property value tax will increase for properties that experienced the highest price increases since 2001 (mostly in the metropolitan capital region) and consequently benefited most from the tax freeze and decrease for properties that experienced the lowest price increases (in several rural areas).

Conclusion

The Danish system of property taxation is characterized by two main taxes, each of which has a long tradition and a prominent position in the aggregate tax system: The land tax, applied to land of all types (agricultural, commercial, and residential), and the property value tax (until 2000, a tax on the imputed income from owner-occupied dwellings), designed to make the tax system neutral with respect to gains from household investment in housing and financial investment. The land tax is in effect part of the income tax system. In addition, minor or supplementary taxes affect land and housing markets, such as the reimbursement duty, historically a tax on the value of commercial buildings, and various stamp duties. The allowance for interest expenditures in the personal income tax system, though not limited to mortgage interest, is also an important element of the tax system for property owners and consequently housing markets.

The property tax system has historically been accompanied by a recurrent assessment system, traditionally considered of a relatively high quality by international standards (Almy 2014; OECD 2016) mainly because assessments regularly occur at short intervals. Assessments use standardized methods that access publicly available information on property sales and characteristics of buildings such as age, size, and physical properties.

From an economic efficiency point of view, the two main property taxes are generally considered advantageous elements in reducing the distortions of the relatively high level of taxation in Denmark: the land tax because it is close to an ideal nondistortionary tax, its base having a fixed supply; and the property value tax because it makes the taxation of different kinds of capital income more equal, reducing tax-induced incentives to overinvest in housing. Views of some of the other tax elements have been less favorable, economic researchers pointing out that property transfer taxes in the form of stamp duties on the registration of property transfers and mortgage loans are normally distortionary, though these taxes in Denmark are limited in size compared with many other countries. Also the traditional reimbursement duty is distortionary compared with other ways of financing the same local-government expenditure. Danish economists have differing opinions on the desirability of tax deductions for interest expenses.

Popular and political views of the Danish system of property taxation are less favorable. Both the land tax and the property value tax have been widely attacked in the press. Some people find both taxes illogical and unfair because they do not directly depend on the income of the taxpayer and may seem to overtax some individuals unreasonably. In addition, people have been forced to move because they cannot afford to pay their taxes, perhaps because their property's valuation and consequently its tax payments have increased because of a boom in housing prices. For these reasons, property taxation has been a contentious political issue at times, notably in the 1990s and the next decade, and led to a nominal tax freeze on the property value tax from 2002. The freeze introduced further problems, notably the elimination of the property tax as an automatic stabilizer, which possibly contributed to the house price boom and following bust during the financial crisis, more serious in Denmark than in many comparable countries. When it was established during the 2010s that the tax freeze also had caused a geographically inequitable pattern of taxation—less valuable owner-occupied dwellings in some outskirts of Denmark, typically inhabited by relatively low-income groups, were taxed at a higher effective rate than more valuable dwellings in the major cities and most affluent suburbs—the need for a reform to the property tax system became apparent.

Concurrently, centralization of the assessment process early in the first decade of the 21st century transferred it from the local municipalities to the Ministry of Taxation and, coupled with cuts in the human resources allocated to it, caused a deterioration in the assessment quality. Public awareness of these problems gradually increased, culminating in the 2013 report of the Office of the Auditor General that the assessments were unreliable, after which the standard assessment process was suspended pending a solution.

Changes were necessary, leading to a broad parliamentary majority in 2016 and 2017 to agree to a reform, further amended in 2020 and 2021. The two main property taxes remained, but the reforms made changes in the effective tax rates and other provisions of property taxation. The reform allocated money for a fundamental reorganization of the assessment system, which has proved more difficult than expected, and the new tax rules have been postponed until 2024. Denmark is in a prolonged interim, from the suspension of the former assessment system in 2013 until implementation of the new system of tax rates and rules in 2024. Professional experts and the political majority, including the traditional ruling parties from both sides of Parliament, generally expect that the new system will be an improvement compared with the former.

Postscript 2024

The new system took effect on January 1, 2024. Preliminary assessment values for all owner-occupied dwellings were released in autumn of 2023, and a major media storm followed after examples of hugely incorrect valuations from the new system came to light. But the administrative procedures of the new valuation process were still being tuned and not yet functioning properly, and a final inspection of the automatically produced valuations had not yet occurred. The criticism led to a belated extra check of valuations before tax collection under the new system started in January 2024.

The property value tax rate for 2024 has been finally fixed to 0.51 percent of 80 percent of the assessed value and a higher rate of 1.4 percent for the amount of the value above a threshold of DKK 9.2 million (US$1.3 million). Land tax rates in 2024 were on average lowered to 0.74 percent annually from the 2023 average of 2.7 percent. According to the Ministry of Taxation, 80 percent of all taxpayers will pay a lower amount in property taxes under the new system. For the remaining fifth of property owners, a personal discount ensures they will not pay a higher amount in property taxes in 2024 than they would have under the earlier property tax system.

Notes

1. In February 2023, US$1 = DKK 7.04. US$ amounts are rounded.
2. The total revenue includes stamp duties paid on car loans and so on.

References

Almy, R. 2014. "Valuation and Assessment of Immovable Property." Working papers on Fiscal Federalism No. 19. Paris: OECD.

Danish Economic Council. 2001. *Dansk økonomi, Forår 2001.* Copenhagen.

———. 2008. *Dansk økonomi, efterår 2008.* Copenhagen.

———. 2016. *Dansk økonomi, forår 2016.* Copenhagen.

———. 2019. *Dansk økonomi, forår 2019.* Copenhagen.

———. 2021. *Produktivitet 2021.* Copenhagen.

DI. 2021. "Her er dækningsafgiften i din kommune." https://www.danskindustri.dk/globalassets/dokumenter-analyser-publikationer-mv/analyser/di-analyse/2021/6/provenuet-for-dakningsafgiften-stiger-en-smule/provenuet-for-dakningsafgiften-stiger-en-smule-2.0.pdf/Download.

Engberg Committee. 2014. "Ekspertudvalg om ejendomsvurdering." Copenhagen: Ministry of Taxation. https://skm.dk/aktuelt/publikationer/rapporter/forbedring-af-ejendomsvurderingen-resultater-og-anbefalinger-fra-regeringens-eksterne-ekspertudvalg.

Eurostat. 2022a. "A Growing Population Until 2020." Brussels: Eurostat. https://ec.europa.eu/eurostat/cache/digpub/demography_2022/bloc-1a.html?lang=en.

———. 2022b. "Government Revenue to GDP Ratio Increased in 2021." Brussels: Eurostat. https://ec.europa.eu/eurostat/cache/digpub/european_economy/bloc-4a.html.

Geodatastyrelsen. 2022. The Cadastral Map [database]. Accessed March 4, 2026. https://eng.gst.dk/danish-cadastre-office/cadastral-map.

Høj, A. K., M. R. Jørgensen, and P. Schou. 2018. "Land Tax Changes and Full Capitalisation." *Fiscal Studies* 39(2): 365–380.

Johansen, H. C. 2007. *Indkomstskatter og offentlig vækst 1903–2005.* Vol. 6, *Dansk Skattehistorie.* Copenhagen: Told- og Skattehistorisk Selskab.

Ministry of Taxation. 2010. "Vejledning om moms på fast ejendom er klar." Press Release. October 12. https://www.skm.dk/aktuelt/presse-nyheder/pressemeddelelsesarkiv/vejledning-om-moms-paa-fast-ejendom-er-klar/.

———. 2017a. "SAU, Alm.del—2016–17—Endeligt svar på spørgsmål 381: Spm. om at redegøre for den fordelingsmæssige virkning af aftalen Tryghed om boligbeskatningen af 2. maj 2017 på indkomstdeciler i kroner og øre, i pct. af disponibelindkomst og som andel af den samlede indkomstmasse, til skatteministeren." Answer to Parliamentary Question. https://www.ft.dk/samling/20161/almdel/sau/spm/381/svar/1411317/1764125/index.htm.

———. 2017b. *Skatteøkonomisk redegørelse 2017.* Copenhagen.

———. 2021a. "Skatter—provenuet af person- og selskabsskatter." https://skm.dk/tal-og-metode/statistik/provenu-og-skattestruktur/skatter-provenuet-af-person-og-selskabsskatter.

———. 2021b. *Skatteøkonomisk Redegørelse 2021.* Copenhagen.

———. 2022. "Afgifter—provenuet af afgifter og moms." https://skm.dk/tal-og-metode/statistik/provenu-og-skattestruktur/afgifter-provenuet-af-afgifter-og-moms.

Municipality of Copenhagen. 2019. "Københavns Kommunes årsrapport 2019." https://www.kk.dk/sites/default/files/2021-04/K%C3%B8benhavns%20Kommunes%20%C3%A5rsrapport%202019.pdf.

———. 2020. "Københavns Kommune årsrapport 2020." https://www.kk.dk/sites/default/files/2021-12/K%C3%B8benhavns%20kommunes%20%C3%A5rsrapport%202020.pdf.

———. 2021. "Københavns Kommunes årsrapport 2021." https://www.kk.dk/sites/default/files/2022-05/K%C3%B8benhavns%20Kommunes%20%C3%A5rsrapport%202021.pdf.

OECD (Organisation for Economic Co-operation and Development). 2016. "Economic Surveys—Denmark." Paris: OECD.

Office of the Danish Auditor General. 2013. "Beretning om den offentlige ejendoms vurdering." https://rigsrevisionen.dk/revisionssager-arkiv/2013/aug/beretning-om-den-offentlige-ejendomsvurdering.

Rosenberg, M., and A. Tamasauskas. 2019. "Danish Real Estate Law." https://www.carstedrosenberg.com/danish-real-estate-law.

Skatteforvaltningen. 2024. "Den juridiske vejledning 2024–1." https://info.skat.dk/data.aspx?oid=124.

Sørensen, P. B. 2003. "Statsskatteloven i skatteøkonomisk betydning." *SR-Skat* 3. https://web.econ.ku.dk/pbs/Dokumentfiler/Publications%20(Danish)/Statsskat.pdf.

Sørensen, P. B. and J. Vastrup. 2015. "Boligbeskatningens teorigrundlag." *Nationaløkonomisk Tidsskrift* (Danish Economic Journal) 2015(1): 34.

Statistics Denmark. 2018. "Hvem ejer de bebyggede områder i Danmark?" Copenhagen: Statistics Denmark. https://www.dst.dk/Site/Dst/Udgivelser/nyt/GetAnalyse.aspx?cid=31405.

———. 2020. *Skatter og afgifter. Oversigt 2020.* Copenhagen: Statistics Denmark.

———. 2021. *Skatter og afgifter. Oversigt 2021.* Copenhagen: Statistics Denmark.

———. 2022a. "Kommuner og regioner står for trefjerdedele af det offentlige forbrug." Copenhagen: Statistics Denmark. https://www.dst.dk/da/Statistik/nyheder-analyser-publ/bagtal/2021/2021-18-10-Kom-og-reg-andel-off-forbrug.

———. 2022b. *Skatter og afgifter. Oversigt 2022*. Copenhagen: Statistics Denmark.

———. 2022c. Data Bank of ADAM (Annual Danish Aggregate Model) [database]. Accessed March 4, 2026. https://www.dst.dk/en/TilSalg/ADAM/Databank.

———. 2023. StatBank Denmark [database]. Accessed March 4, 2026. https://statistikbanken.dk/statbank5a/default.asp?w=1920.

Vurderingsstyrelsen. 2022. "Historien bag BBR." Copenhagen: Vurderingsstyrelsen.

World Bank. 2022a. "Urban Population (% of total population)—Denmark." https://data.worldbank.org/indicator/SP.URB.TOTL.IN.ZS?locations=DK.

———. 2022b. "Urban Population (% of total population)—European Union." https://data.worldbank.org/indicator/SP.URB.TOTL.IN.ZS?locations=EU&most_recent_value_desc=true.

———. 2022c. GDP per Capita (current US$)—European Union. https://data.worldbank.org/indicator/NY.GDP.PCAP.CD?locations=EU&most_recent_value_desc=true.

Legislation

Budget Law of 2012, Law No. 547 of June 18, 2012.

Property Assessment Law of 2017, Law No. 654 of June 8, 2017.

9

Estonia

A Revaluation After 21 Years

AIVAR TOMSON, VERONIKA ILSJAN,
AND JOHANNES NÕUPUU

Estonia is situated in the Baltic region of northern Europe, bordered on the north by the Gulf of Finland and beyond that, Finland; to the west by the Baltic Sea and Sweden; to the south by Latvia; and to the east by Lake Peipus and Russia. With a total territorial area of 45,339 square kilometers, Estonia averages 30.6 inhabitants per square kilometer (Statistics Estonia 2021), which is almost a quarter of the average density of the European Union (EU) (World Bank 2020). The capital city, Tallinn, has the highest population density in Estonia, approximately 2,747 inhabitants per square kilometer. Within its municipal borders, Tallinn contains the only areas in Estonia where population density exceeds 10,000 persons per square kilometer (Statistics Estonia 2021).

Estonia is a unitary republic with two levels of government: central and state, and municipal. It is divided into 15 counties, which are state administrative units (not local governments) without separately elected representative bodies or any other significant independent competence (Ministry of Finance 2020). Since the administrative-territorial reform of 2017, there are 79 municipalities; before reform, there were 213. Municipalities are the only level of self-government. The main arguments for merging the municipalities were to increase the administrative capacity of the local authorities, offer better services to local citizens, and efficiently coordinate development and investments in the region (Ministry of Finance 2021).

Figure 9.1 Population Distribution Among Municipalities

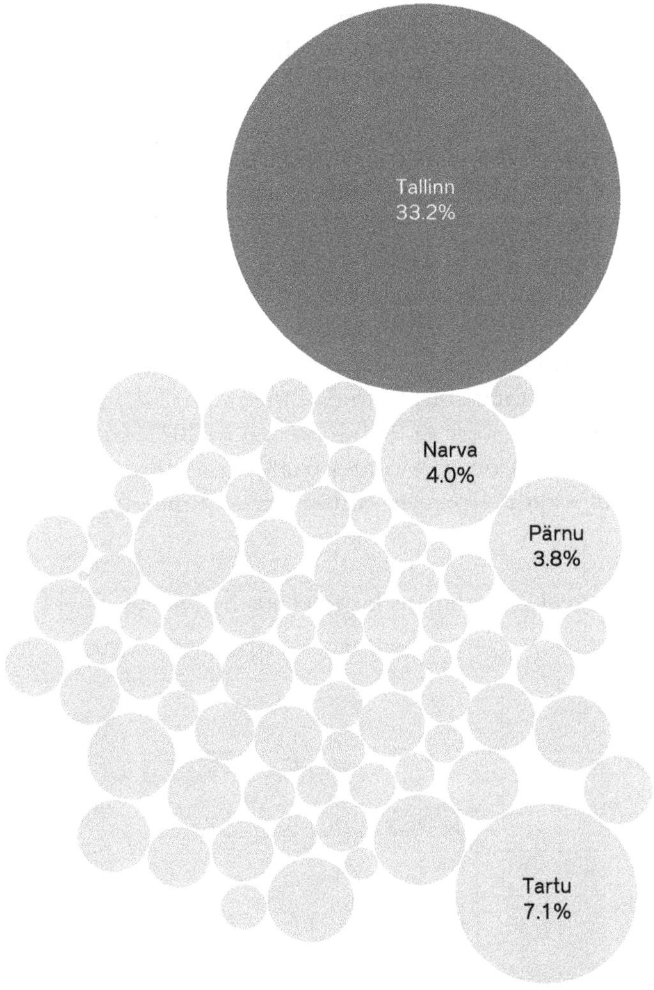

Source: E-Population Register (2023).

At the beginning of 2022, according to Statistics Estonia (2023a), the Estonian population was 1,331,796 people, of whom 69 percent were native Estonians, 24 percent were Russians, and the remaining 7 percent other nationalities.

About one-third of the population live in Tallinn (e-Population Register 2023), which is also the largest city. The 79 local-government units include 15 cities, representing 59.2 percent of the population (figure 9.1). The remaining 64 municipalities are predominantly rural. The average population of municipalities is approximately 16,900, but excluding Tallinn reduces it to 11,500.

In 2022, Estonia's gross domestic product (GDP) was €(2025)36.18 billion, and the Harju and Tartu regions' share in GDP was nearly 75 percent of this total (Statistics Estonia 2023b). Per capita GDP was about €27,167 (Statistics Estonia 2023b), compared with the Organisation for Economic Co-operation and Development (OECD) average of €38,735, as of 2021 (World Bank 2021). In 2022, government debt to GDP was 18.4 percent, one of the lowest in the EU (Eurostat 2023). The COVID-19 pandemic and the Russian invasion of Ukraine increased that percentage to over 20 percent.

In 2022, national tax revenues were €10.31 billion, about 33 percent of GDP, and 44 percent came from social security contributions, 30 percent from value-added tax (VAT), 14 percent from income tax, and 10 percent from excise duty (Statistics Estonia 2023c). In 2017, local-government budget tax revenues were €1.06 billion and in 2022 reached €1.6 billion. The majority of tax revenue comes from personal income tax, and land tax contributes only 4 percent of total tax revenue (figure 9.2). Taking

Figure 9.2 Local-Government Tax Revenue by Category

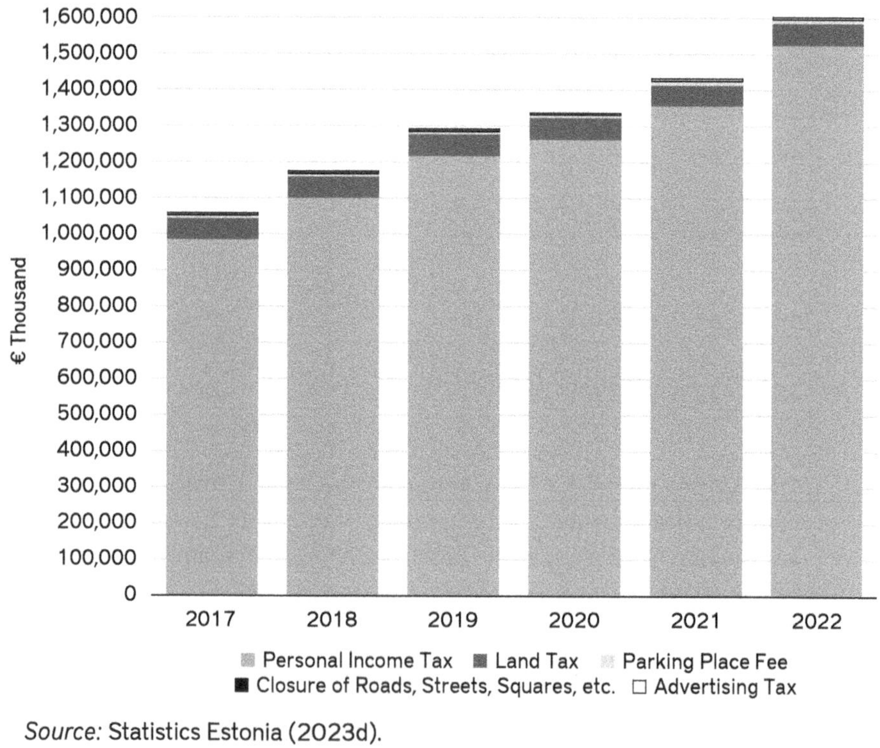

Source: Statistics Estonia (2023d).

Table 9.1 Revenues Raised from Recurrent Property Tax

Year	Total (€ million)	% of GDP
2022	58.98	0.16
2021	58.87	0.19
2020	58.96	0.21
2019	59.08	0.21
2018	57.73	0.22

Source: Statistics Estonia (2023d).

into account that total local-government budgets include other income sources, such as revenue from sale of goods and services and other operating revenues and grants for operating expenses, the receipt of land tax accounts for only 3 percent of the total local municipality revenue (Statistics Estonia 2023d).

The land tax is a state tax, but its revenues accrue in full to the budget of the local government where the land is. The valuation of land and administration of the tax are controlled centrally by the state, but the state does not charge local governments for valuation services (table 9.1).

Municipalities' revenue autonomy (expressed as own revenues relative to total resources available) is low. For example, it was below the EU average (13 percent versus 53 percent) in 2018. The rate of dependency on central-government transfers is higher than the EU average. But dependence on central-government transfers is not the same throughout the country. For example, for Tallinn, it was only 18 percent of operating revenue in 2021, but for Valga, a rural municipality, it amounted to almost half of operating revenue.

Land and Property Markets

Property Registration, Land Tenure

The basis for the current system of land tenure dates back to 1864–1865, when the Russian Empire established the Baltic Private Law Code (Luts 2000, 157). The code included regulation of land rights similar to advanced systems in continental Europe at the time. A radical land reform in rural areas was introduced at the beginning of Estonian independence in the 1920s. Almost all land belonging to large landowners was expropriated, and the land was gifted to veterans of the Estonian War of Independence or sold to small farmers. In 1940, the Soviet Union occupied Estonia and all the land was nationalized. Germany forced out the Soviets from 1941 to 1944, but the Soviets reoccupied the country, and nationalization was followed by the collectivization of agriculture between 1947 and 1949, causing another redistribution of land (Tomson and Eerik 2017, 2).

Changes in land tenure in rural areas started again in the 1980s. After Estonia regained independence in 1991, private landownership was gradually restored. The Land Reform Act, RT 1991, 34, 426, came into force on November 1, 1991, returning to legal owners or their heirs land illegally expropriated after June 16, 1940, restoring private landownership (Tomson and Eerik 2017, 2). Physical restitution was a key component of the Estonian land reform, but owners often opted to accept compensation instead of physical restitution. Restitution was followed by privatization and creation of a property market. The land reform was largely completed by the end of 2022. Owners of only 0.2 percent of the land have not been identified. About 59 percent of the land is privately owned, 39 percent is owned by the state (over 80 percent of Estonia's forests), and 1.4 percent is owned by municipalities.

Legislation for land reform was enacted in the early 1990s. The Land Register defining and protecting private ownership rights and enabling mortgage loans was (re)established in 1993. A few years later, the ease with which a mortgage could be obtained allowed the number of property transfers to increase rapidly. Mortgage loans also contributed significantly to market transparency because commercial banks declared mortgage loans (Tomson and Eerik 2017, 3).

The current land tenure system is similar to that in most of continental Europe. Usually, the landowner owns the buildings on a parcel, and though leasehold is allowed, it is rarely used. Different types of restrictions related to land acquisition and ownership are stipulated. Restrictions on land acquisition were liberalized in Estonia when the country joined the EU in 2004. These restrictions apply to parcels of agricultural and forestland larger than 10 hectares, small islands, and land next to the Estonian-Russian border. There are no restrictions at all on the acquisition of apartments. Another restriction is related to nature conservation, heritage protection, and so on, but it applies to actual use and typically not to acquisition.

Sales Records

The Database of Transactions as a part of the Land Cadastre was introduced by the National Land Board in 1996. It documents property transfers only. Rental data have not been collected. In its early days (1997–2000), the database held only 65–70 percent of sales data, a low number mainly owing to the weaknesses of the legal system (Tomson 2016, 8).

The main attributes of property transfer sales data are type of use, area, existence of buildings, and so on. Data about sellers and buyers is not detailed, but a distinction between legal persons (corporations) and natural persons is made. The National Land Board administers and supervises the sales data to ensure database quality. Transactions data are submitted by notaries. The system has a direct link to the Land Cadastre and cadastral map (a geographic information system, GIS), which enables the use of queries and statistical tools on the basis of location. Both the public and private sectors use the sales data, though access to detailed transaction data is not widely available. Only private valuers, producers of official statistics, research organizations and development institutions, licensed credit institutions, and other persons with legitimate professional interest can use these data (Estonian Land Board 2023a).

The Database of Transactions has direct links to other public databases such as the Building Register, e-Land Register, and cadastral map. However, these linkages are mainly used by the National Land Board; other users lack access to these linkages and must combine data from public databases to meet their own needs. Private users pay a fee based on the number of transactions; there are no discounts for corporate clients (Tomson 2016, 8).

The National Land Board publishes monthly, quarterly, and annual market reviews and annual reviews of certain sectors (residential land, arable land, commercial land, and apartments) market analysis and overviews of sales data; the market overviews are freely accessible on the National Land Board website (https://maaruum.ee/). It provides a freely accessible tool to query price statistics on its website, which returns basic statistics on type of use, location, and so on. The National Land Board does not produce full-scale individual valuation reports, but market data is used for state assets—for example, estimation of initial prices when state land has been sold at auctions.

A rapid reduction of the state fee (transfer tax) on transactions at the beginning of the 1990s began creating a relatively transparent property market. The transfer tax on transactions had previously been up to 5 percent of the sales price. However, real prices were still hidden in most cases. The biggest reduction occurred several years later as a result of the dramatic increase in mortgage lending in the late 1990s. As commercial banks strictly enforced their rights, underdeclared prices mostly vanished. However, not all transactions take place under free market conditions, and in certain cases over- or underdeclared prices remain (Tomson 2016, 8).

Indexes

Some of the real estate indexes were developed and are maintained by private companies. They typically cover residential markets in the larger cities. Information on sales of commercial properties is limited.

Figure 9.3 Price Index of Real Estate

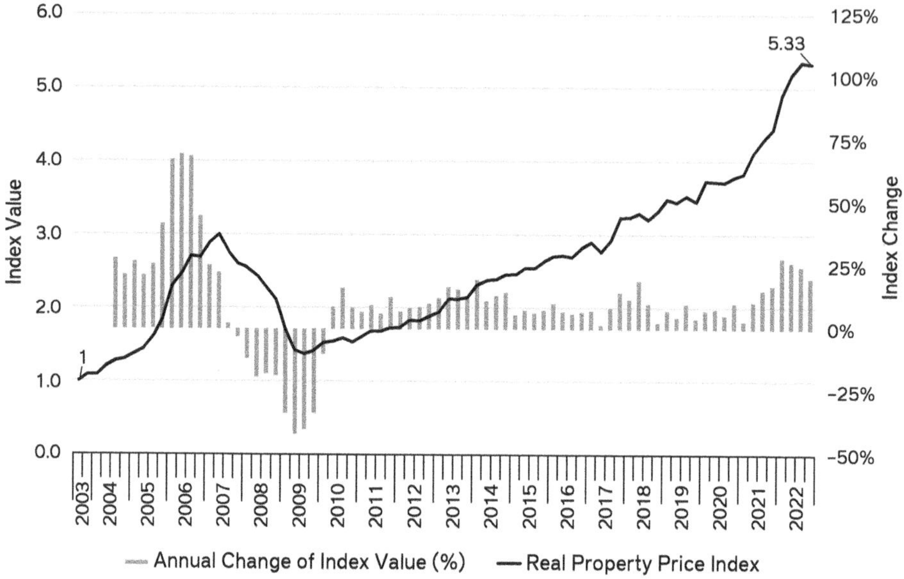

Source: Estonian Land Board (2023a).

The National Land Board indexes draw from the Database of Transactions and provide detailed data of actual transactions made in free market conditions—for example, transactions between relatives are removed, and so are transactions in which the seller is the local government (Estonian Land Board 2023a). The indexes have been calculated quarterly since the third quarter of 2003 (figure 9.3).

The property price index is compiled from the price indexes of three main objects (constituting 85–90 percent of the Estonian property market) and uses the following fixed weights:

- Apartment ownership (includes commercial units)—55 percent.
- Land without buildings—30 percent.
- Residential land with buildings—15 percent.

The price index of apartments is a hedonic regression describing their market price dynamics. It includes apartments from 17 Estonian cities (all county centers and Kohtla-Järve and Narva), which constitute about 75 percent of all sales of apartments in Estonia (Estonian Land Board 2023a).

The price index of land without buildings is a hedonic regression of all transactions of vacant land. The shares of different types of land are set corresponding to the distribution in the market:

- Rural residential land—30 percent.
- Arable land—10 percent.
- Forestland—30 percent.
- Other rural land—30 percent.

The price index of residential land with buildings is a hedonic regression of recurring sales. The index describes price dynamics of residential properties with buildings. Sales not made in free market conditions are removed—for example, sales at a very low price or with a very short time interval and transaction pairs with a large price difference (Estonian Land Board 2023a).

Real Estate Taxes

Tax System

The Estonian tax system is made up of state and local taxes. State taxes are received in the state budget. A part of personal income tax revenues, which in accordance with the Income Tax Act is 11.96 percent of personal income tax (local governments are not able to influence their portion), and land tax revenues in full are allocated to the budgets of local governments. Local taxes are received in the budgets of local governments (State Portal 2023).

State taxes are income tax, social security tax, land tax, gambling tax, VAT, customs duty, excise duties, and heavy-goods vehicle tax. Local taxes are regulated by rural municipalities or city councils in accordance with the Local Taxes Act, RT I 1994, 68, 1169. Local taxes are advertisement tax, road and street closure tax, motor vehicle tax, animal tax, entertainment tax, and parking charge. These are rarely used in practice, and tax revenues are marginal (1 percent of total tax revenue).

Taxes on Transferring Real Property

There is no property transfer tax or capital gains tax on the sale of property, but gains derived from the transfer of immovable property are ordinarily subject to income tax, which is 20 percent of the gain. Certain immovable property transactions are exempt from income tax, and in reality most residential sales are tax exempt because the tax liability is not applied to own-use property of more than two years (Estonian Tax and Customs Board 2023a).

All property sales are subject to low notary fees. For example, for a €100,000 transaction value, the notary fee is €320.80 (0.32 percent); for a €1 million transaction, €2,927.76 (0.29 percent); and for a €10 million transaction, €12,180.63 (0.12 percent) (Notary Fees Act, RT I 1996, 23, 456).

All registrations made in the Land Register are subject to a state fee that depends on the value of transaction and is lower than the notary fee. For example, for a €100,000 transaction, the fee is only €110 (0.11 percent). For all transactions of more than €639,120, the state fee is 0.16 percent but not more than €2,560. Thus, for a €1 million transaction, the state fee is €1,600 (0.16 percent), and for a €10 million transaction, €2,560 (0.03 percent) (State Fees Act 2014).

Real estate sales are generally exempt from VAT, but significant exceptions include transactions of new and significantly renovated buildings. Taxpayers can elect to add VAT to real estate sales prices if certain conditions are met. The rules for rental services do not differ from other types of services; the only exemption relates to apartments, which are always VAT exempt.

According to the Estonian Tax and Customs Board (2023c), the Land Register's total state fees in 2021 was €10.48 million and €11.15 million in 2022.

Inheritance-Related Obligations

Estonia has no inheritance tax, but the Tax and Customs Board still has some inheritance-related obligations (Estonian Tax and Customs Board 2023a). All rights and obligations of the deceased, including obligations to the Tax and Customs Board, are transferred to a successor. Property, such as real estate or money (foreign currency, precious metals, etc.), inherited in Estonia is not subject to taxation upon receipt.

When transferring inherited property (e.g., real estate, precious metals), however, income tax must be paid on the gains, except when an income tax exemption applies to the inherited real estate, such as real estate returned during the ownership reform. This is one of the main exemptions. The values of returned properties were not estimated during the reform, complicating determination of the initial value.

Recurrent Land and Property Tax

Estonia also has no property wealth tax. The only annual (recurrent) property tax is land tax—that is, buildings and the trees of forestlands are not taxed. Land tax is more precisely described later. This section discusses more general aspects and recent changes.

The land tax, from its origin in the early 1990s, applies to market-based value determined by the National Land Board using mass valuation. The valuation results, referred to as cadastral values, are published in the land cadastre. This taxable cadastral value is used as book value in public sector budgets and as a basis for less complicated transactions with state land. Tax assessments are made by the Tax and Customs Board. Tax rates are determined by local governments. The land tax is calculated by multiplying a parcel's taxable value of the land by the land tax rate. Tax exemptions are subtracted.

Land taxation is regulated by the Land Tax Act (RT I 1993, 24, 428), land valuation by the Land Valuation Act (RT I 1994, 13, 231). Three valuations were performed, in 1993, 1996, and 2001. After amendments to the regulations in 2019–2022 and a 21-year break in revaluations, a new valuation was carried out in 2022. These amendments produce a real opportunity to have a positive fiscal effect on local governments.

Before 2022, there was no mandated valuation cycle. The central government decided when to undertake property revaluation. The only precondition related to significant changes in the market, but in reality the central government did not react even when prices significantly increased. The amended regulation requires a four-year revaluation cycle; the next revaluations will be in 2026 and 2030.

As taxation based on the 2022 valuations commenced only on January 1, 2024, its implementation impacts are still unknown. However, it is possible to describe the most important changes and differences before and after 2022.

Major differences in valuation are the following:

- In 2001 and in earlier valuations, the system was more decentralized, and the municipalities were also involved. Sales data were limited, and so valuation relied more on indirect information. The valuation results were displayed as value, or price, zone maps, from which local governments calculated the value of each cadastral unit. Until 2023, the Tax and Customs Board calculated the land tax from the taxable value provided by the local government.
- From 2022, the National Land Board, in cooperation with private valuers, calculates taxable value for each cadastral unit (plot) from transaction data and land value models. The land valuation methodology changed owing to developments in technology and the real estate market and the better availability of transaction and geoinformation data (mass valuation of land in 2022 is discussed later).

Major changes in taxation are the following:

- The National Land Board in 2019 predicted that the taxable value in 2022 could average 7.2 times as much as values in 2001 (see figure 9.3).

The actual increase was 8.3 times (the total value of Estonian land in the 2001 valuation was €3.9 billion, the 2019 estimate was €28.2 billion, and the 2022 valuation was €32.5 billion).

- To mitigate the impact of land revaluation on land tax the maximum tax rates were reduced by about one-fifth—from 2.0–2.5 percent until 2022 to 0.5–1.0 percent until 2024 (up to 2.0 percent in 2025). The tax rate of 0.5 percent for agricultural and forestland remained unchanged.
- A 2024 limit on the annual increase of land tax prevents it from growing by more than 10 percent in any year or by €5, whichever is less. However, the Land Tax Act as amended in 2024 declared a limit of up to 50 percent or €20, whichever is less, from 2025 (Estonian Tax and Customs Board 2025).

Land Tax

Tax Rate

The tax rate interval (between minimum and maximum tax rates) is determined by law. Local governments establish the rates not later than January 31 of the taxation year. In 2024, an exception gave local municipalities until July 1, 2023, to set rates.

The minimum land tax rate is 0.1 percent and has not changed. Before the 2022 revaluation, the maximum land tax rate was 2.5 percent of the taxable value of the land; as of 2024, it is 2 percent. There are some differences in maximum tax rates by land use type:

- Before 2024, the maximum tax rate was 2.5 percent for most land uses and 2 percent for agricultural land.
- From 2024, the maximum tax rate is 1 percent, but for agricultural and forest land it is 0.5 percent.
- From 2025, the maximum tax rate is 1 percent for residential land, 0.5 percent for agricultural land and forestland, and 2 percent for all other land use categories.

Taxable Land

Land tax is the only annual property tax in Estonia. It is applied to the land only, not buildings or trees on forestland. Taxable values are market based, reflecting land's highest and best use. However, land use types are based on cadastral records; and potential changes in land use, and thus value, are not considered—that is, cadastral records must change before land use types change. Land tax is imposed on all land, except that with restricted economic activity:

- Land where economic activities are prohibited by law, except for groundwater-intake sanitary protection zones.
- Nature reserves, special management zones of protected areas, and special management zones for species protection.
- Land adjacent to buildings of diplomatic missions and consular representations of foreign states or parts thereof, land used by a foreign state or international organization by an agreement between it and the Estonian government, and land used for international military headquarters.
- Land belonging to churches and congregations.
- Municipal land under the jurisdiction of a corresponding local authority, except if the tax liability lies on the of user of land.
- Land under public water bodies, water bodies for public use, and public roads; land in state ownership intended for public construction works; and land intended to be public land (Land Tax Act).

Land tax is applied at 50 percent of the land tax rate in the restricted zones specified in the Nature Conservation Act, RT I 2004, 38, 258, where economic activity is partially restricted, and on banks along the water protection zones stipulated in the Water Act, RT I, 22.02.2019, 1.

The tax exemption of municipal land has no impact on the land market because municipal land forms only about 1.4 percent of all cadastral units and because about 89 percent of municipal land is roads, is recreation areas, or fills other social needs and thus not freely transferable in the market.

The revenue from land tax has been relatively stable: €58.87 million in 2021, and €58.98 million in 2022. The tax exemptions described earlier amounted to €14.08 million in 2021, and €14.32 million in 2022 (Estonian Tax and Customs Board 2023b).

Taxpayer

The taxpayer is most often the owner of private land or possessor of public land. In joint ownership, the tax burden is distributed according to the respective shares owned. There are no exceptions for nonresidents or foreigners. For leasehold, the tax burden can transfer to the tenant. Ownership and the other titled rights of all properties are registered in the e-Land Register (https://www.rik.ee/en/international/e-land-register), which allows verification of general data on ownership, restrictions, size, and encumbering mortgages of immovable properties.

Taxpayers can make informal and formal objections and submit appeals to the courts. No appeals have been made for years, because the values and taxes have been stable and low. Now that the taxable values of the 2022 revaluation came into use in 2024, there have been appeals, but so far the few appeals mainly concerned the 10 percent growth limit on the annual increase of land tax.

The Land Tax Act contains several preferential tax treatments—for example, landowners are exempt from the land tax on residential land that is up to 1,500 square meters in cities and other densely populated areas and up to 2 hectares elsewhere. Local authorities may additionally exempt pensioners and repressed persons as defined in the Persons Repressed by Occupying Powers Act (RT I 2003, 88, 589). Homeowner exemptions amounted to €17.03 million in 2021, €17.17 million in 2022. Exemptions made by local authorities totaled €0.118 million in 2021, €0.110 million in 2022 (Estonian Tax and Customs Board 2023b).

Tax Administration

Billing

Once the land value is calculated, the Tax and Customs Board calculates land tax via the land tax information system, which is directly linked to the Land Cadastre. The board sends bills on February 15, and they are distributed electronically or, for some, by post. If the tax is less than €5, the land tax is not imposed.

Collection

The board receives payments primarily electronically. Less than 1 percent of (land tax) taxpayers have tax arrears.

Payment

The tax is paid by the owners of land, or sometimes by the users of land, in two installments, due March 31 and October 1. Amounts of €64 (€100 from 2025) or less are paid in one installment by March 31. Online payment is the most common option chosen by taxpayers. Some direct debit systems are also available. There are no discounts for early payment, but penalties apply for payment delays.

Enforcement

If tax arrears are neither paid on time nor scheduled for payment in installments, the board initiates compulsory execution of tax arrears, such as

- seizure of bank accounts;
- attachment of monetary rights;
- blocking securities or securities accounts;
- adding restraining notes on disposition of property; and
- initiating law enforcement actions if necessary (Estonian Tax and Customs Board 2023c).

These enforcement measures have not been used in practice.

Penalties

Taxpayers in arrears are obliged to calculate and pay interest on unpaid tax by the payment deadline. Interest is calculated beginning the day after the due date of taxes until the date of payment or offset.

Tax Collection

Land tax is a state tax entirely returned to the budget of the local government where the land is. In Estonia, the land tax in 2018 was 0.22 percent of GDP, which is the lowest in OECD countries. It was 0.39 percent in 2000 but declined in following years as GDP increased and land tax collection remained fairly stable (figure 9.4). The Ministry of Finance has suggested gradually restoring the 2000 figure of 0.39 percent of GDP.

Tax collection evolved as follows:

- After the 2001 revaluation, land tax collection gradually increased but at a slower rate than GDP (ratio of land tax to GDP decreased).
- In 2008, the largest municipality, Tallinn, raised tax rates, which increased tax collection, and the ratio of land tax to GDP began to recover.
- After the 2012 implementation in Tallinn, and 2013 in the whole country, of the land tax exemption for homeowners, the land tax collection has remained the same.

The OECD assessed population shrinkage in Estonian rural areas, finding that

Figure 9.4 Land Tax Collection and Percent of GDP

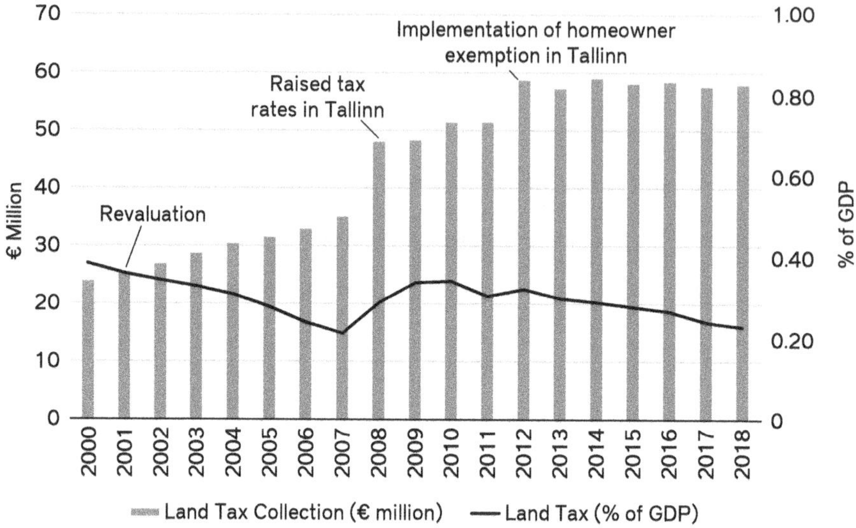

Source: Ministry of Finance (2020).

> municipal finance and taxation systems encourage inefficiency and weaken local decision-making capacity. Eighty percent of central government transfers to municipalities are earmarked. This prevents discretionary decision-making and discourages efficiency gains, as savings cannot be used elsewhere. Greater land tax exemptions exist for residential plots in non-urban areas, adding to distortions harming efficiency. Impact fees, which require developers to bear the cost of development of public infrastructure and services in the vicinity, are not well enforced. (OECD 2022, 11)

The OECD recommended reforming fiscal structures to better prepare for population shrinkage, abandoning or at least considerably reducing the complex earmarked grants system, abolishing land tax exemptions in rural areas, and actively using impact fees.

Property Tax in Large Urban Areas

Despite exemptions and incentives, the amount of land tax revenues collected in Tallinn is remarkable. The country's 2022 overall land tax revenues reached €59.0 million, and Tallinn contributed €25.8 million, or about 43.7 percent of total land tax revenues (Estonian Tax and Customs Board 2023b). Tallinn accounted for 34 percent of the population in 2023 and 51 percent of the GDP in 2021. According to the information received from the Estonian Tax and Customs Board in response to an email inquiry on

December 15, 2022, Tallinn has 15,061 taxable units of nonresidential land and 5,155 exempt units. Of residential land, it has more tax-exempt units (11,505) than taxable units (7,155). This is because of tax relief in the Land Tax Act starting from 2012, which stipulated that most residential land would be tax-free. The tax burden is regressive because this exemption is based on area, and the most expensive land is in Tallinn. The cost of this tax exemption is high in Tallinn but low in many other regions.

Until the 2022 revaluation, the tax base had not changed for more than 20 years, except for some small increases in the land stock. The total value of the tax base, including the values of tax-exempt properties in Tallinn, is around €1.9 billion, which is well below the market value (Estonian Land Board 2023b). The maximum tax rates stipulated in the Land Tax Act were used throughout this relatively long period before the 2022 revaluation.

Looking back to the 2001 revaluation, Tallinn was the only city where the values in the city center were based on building rights—that is, instead of land area, as in the rest of the country, values were based on the gross building area (discussed later). This change in thinking to include the behavior of property markets was a big step forward. The 2022 revaluation made another big step in defining a much bigger area to have building right values, in the central areas of Tallinn and Tartu, the second-largest city. Collection of building right data was challenging.

All properties—exempt and taxed—are valued. In 2001, their valuation was based on the land value in each value zone. In 2022, the valuation was mainly based on geostatistical models that included all the properties. Valuation is still relatively simple because of the limited number of value-based attributes.

Administration on City-Level Total Revenues

The National Land Board carries out all valuations. The Tallinn city government has been involved in mass valuation as a partner of the National Land Board.

Only 15 objections were presented to the National Land Board in 2022. Tallinn probably also received objections. Valuation results were used starting January 1, 2024, and since the annual growth of tax bills was limited to 10 percent, objections remained low. Although taxable values could increase by up to 10 times, the effective tax base was kept well below market values and was mainly influenced by the limit to annual growth. The Land Tax Act was amended once again in 2024, and starting from 2025 the annual growth limit is up to 50 percent. No information is available yet about objections caused by this amendment.

The revenue collected in 2021–2023 remained more or less the same because the tax base had few changes and the tax rate had no changes

Table 9.2 Revenues in Tallinn

	2021	2022	2023
Income tax (€ million)	497.5	585.8	624.7
Land tax (€ million)	26.0	25.6	25.4
Local taxes (€ million)	12.7	14.1	14.2
Central-government grants (€ million)	148.9	162.8	171.7
Foreign grants (€ million)	9.4	23.6	22.1
Sale of good and services (€ million)	82.5	99.9	96.7
Dividends (€ million)	10.0	10.0	6.6
Other income (€ million)	4.2	4.1	5.4
Total (€ million)	791.2	925.9	966.8
Land tax, % of total revenue	3.3	2.8	2.6
Land tax, % of tax revenue	4.8	4.1	3.8

Sources: Association of Estonian Cities and Municipalities (2023); Statistics Estonia (2023d); Tallinn (2023).

(maximum level allowed was 2.5 percent, and this rate has been used in most urban local governments). The land tax revenue in 2020 was €25.8 million; in 2021, €26.0 million; and in 2022, €25.6 million (the last estimation is from the beginning of 2023 and there might be some increase because of delayed payments). Growth in income taxes and central-government grants has been much more robust (table 9.2) (Association of Estonian Cities and Municipalities 2023; Statistics Estonia 2023d; Tallinn 2023).

Mass Valuation in 2022

Valuation Activities by the National Land Board

The National Land Board is a government agency with seven permanent employees in the real estate valuation department. For the 2022 mass valuation (2020–2022), two more people were hired. Others involved were

- a full-time project manager to coordinate information technology projects performed by the private sector;
- full-time GIS experts to support valuers with data analysis;
- professional valuers with extensive experience, three statistical experts from a university to consult on the development of the valuation methodology, and one international auditor involved in the evaluation of valuation models; and

- 15 certified private valuers from different regions to test and evaluate valuation models and aid in valuations.

A mass valuation over 2.5 years after a 21-year break using new technological solutions, new datasets, new methodology developed by a newly formed team, and using an agile framework and approach was a challenge. The real estate valuation department, in addition to mass valuation duties, manages the database of real estate transactions (sales price register), publishes real estate price statistics, conducts market reviews, and makes valuations for transactions of state land.

The results of the 2022 mass valuation are open data and visible to everyone on a web page (https://minu.kataster.ee). When the data describing the land in the land cadastre or in external databases changes, the taxable value of the land is recalculated either immediately or once a year, and the information is automatically forwarded to the Tax Board.

While the mass valuation in 2022 was a one-time project during which new valuation models were developed, valuation models will be continually developed in the future. Valuation is done with automated valuation models that use only machine-readable data from databases. If the source data in the valuation model is incorrect, the landowner (or someone else) can note the correct information in the cadastre. That is sent to the source database for verification and, if necessary, corrected. No physical inspections of property are carried out in the valuation process. However, the manager of the source database may physically verify the data.

Valuation Methodology

There are approximately 760,000 cadastral units, defined in the Land Cadastre Act, RT I 1994, 74, 1324, as an independent parcel of land or public water body, registered in the cadastre. In Estonia, all parcels are valued regardless of how they are taxed. Only land is valued; trees in forests and buildings are excluded. The total value of Estonia's 45,339 square kilometers is €32.5 billion.

The valuation methodology framework consisted of five valuation models and eight location classes. There are four types of land (figure 9.5): forestland, agricultural land (cultivated land and natural grassland), building land (that is, land where residential, commercial, or industrial buildings exist or could exist), and land without an active market (transportation land, wasteland, national defense land, etc.). Each type has its own valuation model that takes into account the factors that affect its value. The exception is building land, which has two different models: a building land model in most locations and a building right model in the most attractive areas.

Figure 9.5 General Land Use Types by Area and Value, 2022

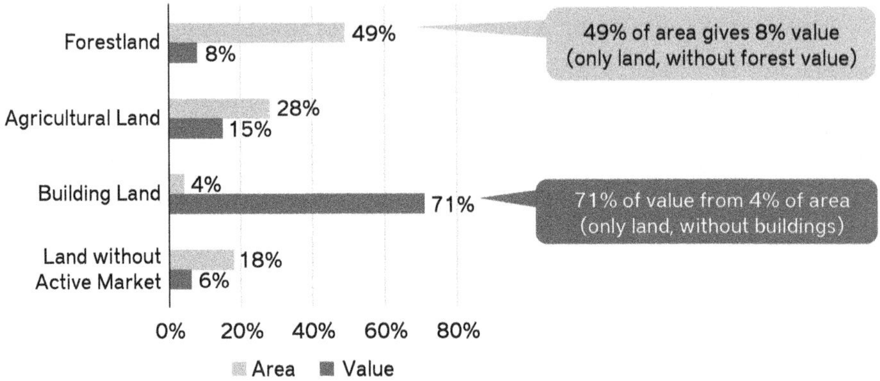

Source: Estonian Land Board (2022).

Figure 9.6 Location Classes Used in 2022 Mass Valuation

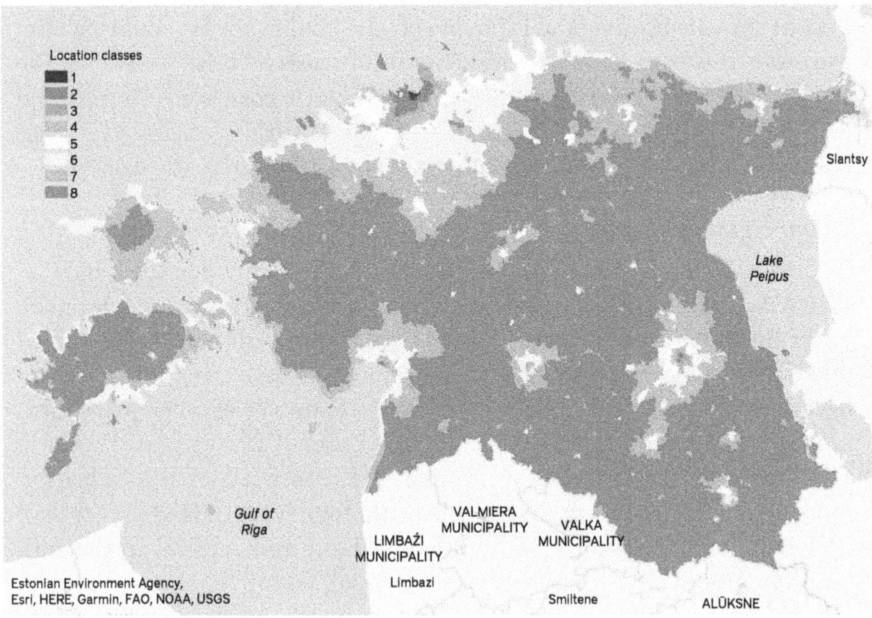

Source: Estonian Land Board (2022).

The division into location classes requires a distinction in the valuation methodology, because the market functions differently in different locations (figure 9.6). The location classes reflect the differences in market price of residential land: the most expensive land is class 1 (over €300 per square meter), and the cheapest is class 8 (below €1 per square meter).

The selection of a valuation model for each cadastral unit is automatic, depending mostly on current land use type. The exception is the building right model, which accounts for building rights according to the land use plan. In some cases, the location class is also important. For example, national defense land in location classes 1–3 is valued as building land (mostly similar to office or industrial land), and in location classes 4–8, as land without an active market.

For the 2022 valuation, the sales data from the transaction database from July 1, 2016, to June 30, 2022, was used. Only sales transactions meeting specific criteria were selected for valuation, and all transactions were indexed to the value date of July 1, 2022. One of the main criteria was that only undeveloped (vacant) land transactions were used.

Before modeling, sales data were combined with spatial and nonspatial attribute data to analyze how different variables affect land value. For calculating different physical and other characteristics of cadastral units, SQL queries were implemented, supported by PostGIS database extender, which is crucial for running different spatial and other location queries.

Five valuation models were implemented:

- Building land model.
- Agricultural land model.
- Forestland model.
- Model for land without an active market.
- Building right model.

Building Land Model

The building land model is a regression-based valuation model whose core is a nonparametric generalized additive model. An unpublished report shared with the authors notes that generalized additive models are well documented throughout academic research as sophisticated predictive algorithms capable of yielding property value estimates more accurate than other common regression-based automated valuation models.[1]

The building land model calculates a base value by analyzing transactions of undeveloped residential land. As coverage of undeveloped residential land transactions is uneven (fewer in dense urban areas) and the market functions differently in different locations, three building land submodels were created: for location classes 1–3, for location classes 4–5, and for location classes 6–8.

Value-affecting variables were selected according to statistical significance and a priori reasoning about what factors determine land value. In the modeling phase, more than 10 variables were considered for the statistical analysis. During the testing phase, it became apparent that considerations of the accuracy of the mass valuation and the volume of data analysis make 2 to 4 factors sufficient to use.

The model intercept, which is the base value for a square meter of building land less than 1,000 square meters and not near a body of water, was left intact. The two other variables used were the land plot area and proximity to a water body. Different adjustments are applied for different location classes and area sizes.

Agricultural Land Model

The agricultural land model functions similarly to the building land model in that it first calculates the base value by analyzing the agricultural land transactions and then adjusts the base value with the value-affecting variables. But to reduce sample bias, the two-step Heckman model was implemented. Variables that showed statistical significance for the agricultural land model were average weighted price for nearest transactions, soil fertility, share of waterlogged soils, share of grassland registered with the Agricultural Registers and Information Board, land plot area, access by road, and selection bias correction (plots not in use are, on average, valued lower).

Because location is not the main driver for agricultural land prices, the price range is small, and location made no difference. The agricultural land model is used for valuation of cultivated (arable) land and also natural grassland. For grassland, a correction coefficient 0.5 is applied.

Forestland Valuation Model

The value of forestland is estimated by multiplying the base value by a quality factor. The base value of forestland is the average price of sales transactions of forestland without trees (in 2022, the value was €1,883 per hectare). The transactions were checked by comparing historical satellite photos with the dates of the transaction to ensure that the set of transactions used in the analysis would consist only of clear-cuts. Then the normalized difference vegetation index was used to determine whether the cadastral unit was covered with dense vegetation, and yearly canopy height values were implemented.

Figure 9.7 Building Right Zone Values in Tallinn

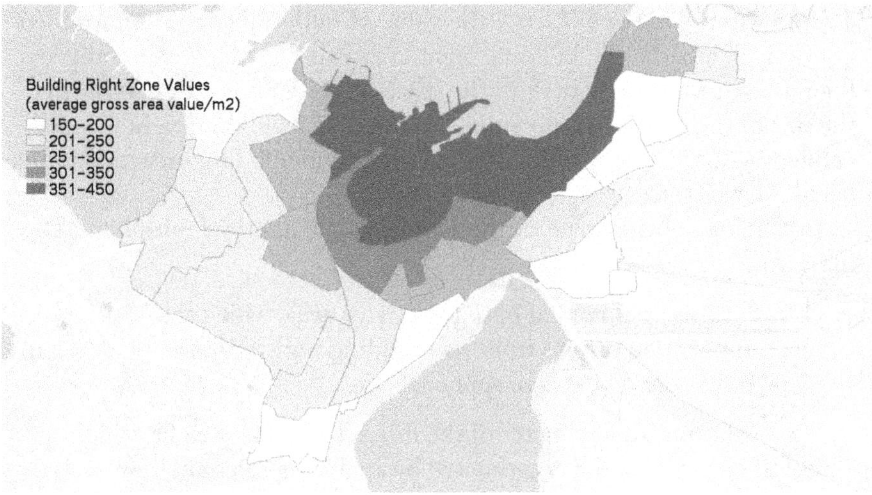

Source: Estonian Land Board (2022).

Quality factors, found in cooperation with forest experts, show the yield of a particular forest stand compared with average forestland, taking into account the site type, soil fertility, and land improvement (draining). Restrictions may decrease the value of forestland:

- The coefficient 0.5 is applied to forestland in nature conservation areas.
- Forestland in nature conservation areas with the strongest restrictions is valued at the lowest rate (€0.04 per square meter).

Model for Land Without an Active Market

Land use types without an active market are, for example, transportation land, waste-storage land, public land, waterbody land—land types that are not in wide circulation on the market and for which there is limited or no sales data.

The value of this type of land is calculated by multiplying the area of the land by the value of its zone. Location classes are used as value zones, and the lowest value of the location class was estimated by analyzing sales data. The lowest values of the location classes (as zone values) were approved by ministerial regulation (the same regulation as the valuation method) to reduce later disputes.

Building Right Model

In active development areas (location classes 1 and 2 in the city centers of Tallinn (figure 9.7) and Tartu), the value of building land is determined not by land area but by building right area—that is, the maximum gross floor area possible to be built in the space. Plot size is less important than the size of the existing or potential building. The building right is mostly defined by the size of the existing building; if no building exists, then the detail plan is used.

In this model the value of the land is calculated by multiplying two indicators:

- The existing or potential building's gross area, which the local government determines from the building register or the plot's detail plan. Area adjustments are applied.
- The value per square meter of the district's building right, which certified private valuers estimated by analyzing sales and rent transactions of land and apartments. A regulation from the minister of Environment validated these values.

Valuation Standards and Quality Control Measures

The valuation methodology complies with the Estonian Property Valuation Standards,[2] and follows good practices of the International Association of Assessing Officers (IAAO 2017). An independent quality control of mass valuation modeling procedures, required by the National Land Board, included review of statistical models for residential land and rural (including agricultural) land.

Testing of the models for building land and agricultural land included basic evaluation metrics, such as adjusted R-squared and Akaike information criterion scores. It also evaluated the distribution of model residuals and checked that they follow a normal distribution. Residuals are the difference between the actual value and the estimated value: negative residuals indicate the model predicts a value too high, positive that the predicted value is lower than the actual value. In a normal distribution, most residuals should remain around zero, and there should be few outliers. Testing also included IAAO (2013) ratio studies and other quality metrics: coefficient of dispersion (CoD), median ratio, the hedonic inequity method, and price-related differential.

Testing revealed that the agricultural land model valuations were quite uniform (CoD 18 percent, median ratio 1.01).

The building land submodels varied in accuracy according to their location classes:

- Valuations for location classes 1–3 were uniform (CoD 18 percent, below the target of 25 percent) and the median ratio (1.02; IAAO [2013] standards are 0.90–1.10) was close to the target median.
- Valuations for location classes 4–5 were less uniform (CoD 39 percent, above the 25 percent target) and the median ratio (1.03) was acceptable.
- Valuations for location classes 6–8 were the least uniform (CoD 57 percent) but the median ratio (1.04) was acceptable. Market experts confirm these location classes have the least active real estate market. It is therefore unreasonable to expect it to have performance metrics comparable with the other models.

Many of these tolerance measures (for example, the CoD) were created by government valuers in the United States who value only one municipality at a time, and the municipalities typically have considerably more resources (staff, budgets, etc.) to appraise significantly fewer properties compared with Estonia. In addition, most US states also have real estate transaction disclosure laws that provide government valuers with ample property and market data in a relatively timely fashion. This allows assessors to capture property characteristics (e.g., size, age, condition), transaction prices, rents, and financing terms of transactions. Considering these advantages, the National Land Board could not hold to the same accuracy and uniformity expectations as municipalities do in the United States and Canada.[3]

In the last testing of the model, the holdout sample (data used for testing the calibrated model) was not included, and therefore not all IAAO quality-control metrics were used. That is because the very small size of the holdout sample meant that testing the model against that sample did not make sense. Even with a split ratio of 80 percent for model specification and training and 20 percent for model testing, the model performance had different results on each run and results seemed strongly dependent on what transactions were used.

Impact

Because the 2022 valuation increased taxable value by a factor of 8.3 and 2024 property tax revenues were likely to be large, strong mitigation measures were applied.

The land tax is a limited revenue source, as shown by its small share of GDP and the marginal amount of local-municipality revenue from it (3 percent of total revenue). After the revaluation in 2001, land tax collection began to increase, but since at least 2012 it has remained constant,

€58 million to €59 million per year. All other tax revenues have increased greatly within the same period.

The same can be argued about land tax impacts on land use. The tax base remained the same for 21 years, and since 2012, revenue collected from the land tax has not changed. The tax base will increase in coming years, bringing opportunities to benefit from the land tax because it encourages taxpayers to use land in more efficient ways. Although abolition of the central land tax restrictions is planned, what kind of changes will be introduced and how municipalities will use these opportunities is unclear.

The land tax is highly regressive. Although its annual growth limit has been set at 50 percent, municipalities have used this limit sparingly because of upcoming local elections in 2025. This is likely to continue into the future because wealthy municipalities have lower tax rates. If the land tax bills remain low in relatively attractive regions, this regressivity will continue.

Land under residential buildings is exempt from land tax (in urban areas the limit is 1,500 square meters; in rural areas, 2 hectares). Some politicians proclaim this as a benefit to taxpayers, but it shrinks the tax base. Removing this exemption would be very complicated, which intensifies the equity issue, particularly because the tax exemption is area-based and does not depend on the value of the land.

Conclusion

In light of international trends and growing competition for land, a limited resource, more questions about land use policy will arise in the coming years. Many observers are looking forward to the challenge of the next stage of Estonia's tax system. The government elected in March 2023 and taking office in April has adopted OECD recommendations and prioritized the fiscal autonomy of municipalities, including their regulation of land tax exemptions. More pragmatic solutions related to fiscal autonomy of municipalities can arise after 2025 elections.

Notes

1. Paul Bidanset, "Final Report for an Independent Assessment of Estonian Land Board Mass Valuation Modeling Procedures," unpublished manuscript, 2022.
2. The Estonian Property Valuation Standards EVS (European Valuation Standards) 875 are prepared by the Estonian Association of Appraisers, https://ekhy.ee/tegevus/standardid/riiklikud-eesti-varahindamise-standardid/.
3. Bidanset, "Final Report."

References

Association of Estonian Cities and Municipalities. 2023. “Omavalitsuste kontaktid ja statistika.” https://www.elvl.ee/omavalitsuste-kontaktid-ja-statistika.

E-Population Register. 2023. “Population in Municipalities.” [In Estonian.] https://www.elvl.ee/elanike-arv.

Estonian Land Board. 2022. “Mass Valuation in 2022.” [In Estonian.] https://maaruum.ee/maakataster-ja-maa-hindamine/maa-hindamine/maa-korraline-hindamine.

———. 2023a. “Statistics on Real Property Transactions.” https://maaamet.ee/en/land-transactions-land-cadastre/land-valuation-and-transactions/statistics-real-property.

———. 2023b. “Tableau Workbook for Aggregate Mass Valuation Results and Changes.” [In Estonian.] https://tableau.envir.ee/views/mkh_koondtulemused/mkh?%3Adisplay_count=n&%3Aembed=y&%3Aiid=2&%3AisGuestRedirectFromVizportal=y&%3Aorigin=viz_share_link&%3AshowAppBanner=false&%3AshowVizHome=n#2.

Estonian Tax and Customs Board. 2023a. “Estate Taxes.” https://www.emta.ee/en/private-client/taxes-and-payment/other-taxes/estate.

———. 2023b. “Open Data of the Estonian Tax and Customs Board.” [In Estonian.] https://www.emta.ee/eraklient/amet-uudised-ja-kontakt/uudised-pressiinfo-statistika/statistika-ja-avaandmed#kov-tulumaks-maamaks-failid.

———. 2023c. “Land Tax.” https://www.emta.ee/en/private-client/taxes-and-payment/other-taxes/land-tax.

———. 2025. “Land Tax Subject to Several Changes This Year.” https://www.emta.ee/en/news/land-tax-subject-several-changes-year.

Eurostat. 2023. “Government Debt Down to 93.0% of GDP in Euro Area.” https://ec.europa.eu/eurostat/documents/2995521/15725185/2-23012023-AP-EN.pdf/02f734a3-f3fe-df4d-db84-f1671933a5c6.

IAAO (International Association of Assessing Officers). 2013. *Standard on Ratio Studies: A Criterion for Measuring Fairness, Quality, Equity and Accuracy.* Kansas City, MO: IAAO.

———. 2017. *Standard on Mass Appraisal of Real Property: A Criterion for Measuring Fairness, Quality, Equity and Accuracy.* Kansas City, MO: IAAO.

Luts, M. 2000. “Private Law of the Baltic Provinces as a Patriotic Act.” *Juridica International,* 157–167.

Ministry of Finance. 2020. “Local Governments in Estonia.” https://www.agri.ee/sites/default/files/documents/2023-07/v%C3%A4ljaanne-2019-estonia-local-governments.pdf.

———. 2021. “Administrative-Territorial Reform.” Updated February 27. https://www.fin.ee/en/administrative-territorial-reform.

OECD (Organisation for Economic Co-operation and Development). 2022. *Shrinking Smartly in Estonia: Preparing Regions for Demographic Change.* OECD Rural Studies. Paris: OECD. https://doi.org/10.1787/77cfe25e-en.

State Portal. 2023. “Taxes and Tax Systems.” https://www.eesti.ee/en/money-and-property/taxation-and-currency/taxes-and-tax-system.

Statistics Estonia. 2021. "Population and Housing Census 2021." https://storymaps.arcgis.com/stories/4badeabbc1474d67877973ad62cdaa4c.

———. 2023a. "Population Figure." https://www.stat.ee/en/find-statistics/statistics-theme/population/population-figure.

———. 2023b. "RAA0050: Gross Domestic Product by Year, County and Indicator." https://andmed.stat.ee/en/stat/majandus__rahvamajanduse-arvepidamine__sisemajanduse-koguprodukt-(skp)__regionaalne-sisemajanduse-koguprodukt/RAA0050.

———. 2023c. "RR01: State Budget Tax Revenues." https://andmed.stat.ee/en/stat/majandus__rahandus__valitsemissektori-rahandus__maksud/RR01.

———. 2023d. "RR02: Local Budgets Tax Revenues." https://andmed.stat.ee/en/stat/majandus__rahandus__valitsemissektori-rahandus__maksud/RR02.

Tallinn. 2023. "Annual Financial Reports of the City of Tallinn." [In Estonian.] https://www.tallinn.ee/et/tallinna-linna-majandusaasta-aruanded.

Tomson, A. 2016. "Property Sales Register as a Tool to Improve the Quality of Valuation and Market Research: Lessons Learned from Selected Countries." Paper presented at the World Bank Conference on Land and Poverty. Washington, DC (March 14–18).

Tomson, A., and Ü. Eerik. 2017. "First Steps and Further Steps: Creation of Property Market. Estonia Case Study." Paper presented at FIG Working Week, Helsinki, Finland.

World Bank. 2020. Population Density (people per sq. km of land area)—European Union. https://data.worldbank.org/indicator/EN.POP.DNST?locations=EE-EU.

———. 2021. "GDP per Capita." https://data.worldbank.org/indicator/NY.GDP.PCAP.CD?locations=OE-EE&name_desc=false.

Legislation

Income Tax Act. *Riigi Teataja* RT I, 30.06.2023, 81.

Land Cadastre Act. *Riigi Teataja* RT I 1994, 74, 1324.

Land Reform Act. *Riigi Teataja* RT 1991, 34, 426.

Land Tax Act. *Riigi Teataja* RT I 1993, 24, 428.

Land Valuation Act. *Riigi Teataja* RT I 1994, 13, 231.

Local Taxes Act. *Riigi Teataja* RT I 1994, 68, 1169.

Nature Conservation Act. *Riigi Teataja* RT I 2004, 38, 258.

Notary Fees Act. *Riigi Teataja* RT I 1996, 23, 456.

Persons Repressed by Occupying Powers Act. *Riigi Teataja* RT I 2003, 88, 589.

State Fees Act. *Riigi Teataja* RT I, 30.12. 2014, 1.

Water Act. *Riigi Teataja* RT I, 22.02.2019, 1.

10

Land and Property Taxation in Finland

HEIDI FALKENBACH AND PAULIINA KRIGSHOLM

Finland is a parliamentary republic, characterized by the Nordic social and economic model of a comprehensive welfare state and large public sector (49 percent of gross domestic product in public spending and 41.9 percent of GDP in taxes). According to the World Bank database, GDP per capita in Finland was US$53,983 in 2021 (World Bank, n.d.). Finland has the lowest population density in the European Union, 18.2 people per square kilometer (Eurostat 2019). Since over 70 percent of Finland's total population of approximately 5.5 million people lives in urban areas (Statistics Finland 2021), most of the country's land area is categorized as rural (Suomen ympäristökeskus, n.d.). The main administrative levels are the state and the local government (municipalities). Both the state and the municipalities have the power to levy certain taxes.[1]

Municipalities are legally autonomous and governed by an elected municipal council. They provide and control many public services, including education (up to upper secondary level and vocational education), water and energy supply, waste management, and land use planning and environmental protection. About 40 percent of total government expenditures are municipal expenditures (European Committee of the Regions 2023). In 2023, there were 309 municipalities in Finland. Between the state and municipalities is an administrative level of regions. Finland is divided into 19 regions, whose main task is to facilitate collaboration between municipalities in the region in the areas of regional planning, economic development, and education. Regions are governed by councils composed of delegates from the municipalities, except for the autonomous region of Åland, which has a permanent democratically elected regional council. In addition, the indigenous Sami people in Finland have a semiautonomous region in Lapland for issues concerning language and culture. Regions are funded by the state.

The Finnish governance structure is undergoing substantial changes regarding the provision of public health care, social welfare, and rescue services. As of 2023, these responsibilities have been transferred from municipalities to a new administrative level referred to as well-being services counties. A total of 21 well-being services counties have been established. The well-being services counties are funded by the state, because the counties have no taxing powers. Municipal budgets, in particular, have been affected by this reform, since part of the income transfers from the state to the municipalities and an estimated 12.4 percent of municipal income taxes are now directed to these counties. From a municipal perspective, the administrative reform has reduced their flexibility in balancing municipal budgets and increased the relative weight of the real estate tax as an income source.

The decentralized governance system translates into a high level of fiscal decentralization: In 2021, municipal tax revenue represented 24 percent of total general government tax revenue, and municipal taxes accounted for about half of the municipal total revenues (OECD n.d., table 9). The municipalities receive the municipal income tax, a flat tax rate decided by the municipal council, and the recurrent land and property taxes (called real estate tax in Finland). In addition, the state transfers income to municipalities to balance the differences between municipal revenue base and costs of providing municipal services. In 2018, for example, such transfers accounted for 29 percent of municipal revenues (European Committee of the Regions 2023).

The main taxes received by the state are progressive income taxes, capital income taxes, and value-added taxes (VAT). A corporation tax is shared by the state and municipalities, with the state's share being about two-thirds of the revenue. In addition, the state receives several specific taxes, such as asset transfer tax, capital gains tax, and inheritance tax. Such taxes, if they relate to real estate, are discussed further in the next section.

Figure 10.1 illustrates the relative shares of the different tax categories in Finland in 2021. The individual income tax includes all types of income tax paid by individuals, such as progressive income taxes, capital income taxes, and pensions and social benefits subject to taxation. Real estate taxes formed less than 3 percent of the total collected taxes.

Figure 10.1 Contributions of the Main Taxes to Total Collected Taxes, 2021

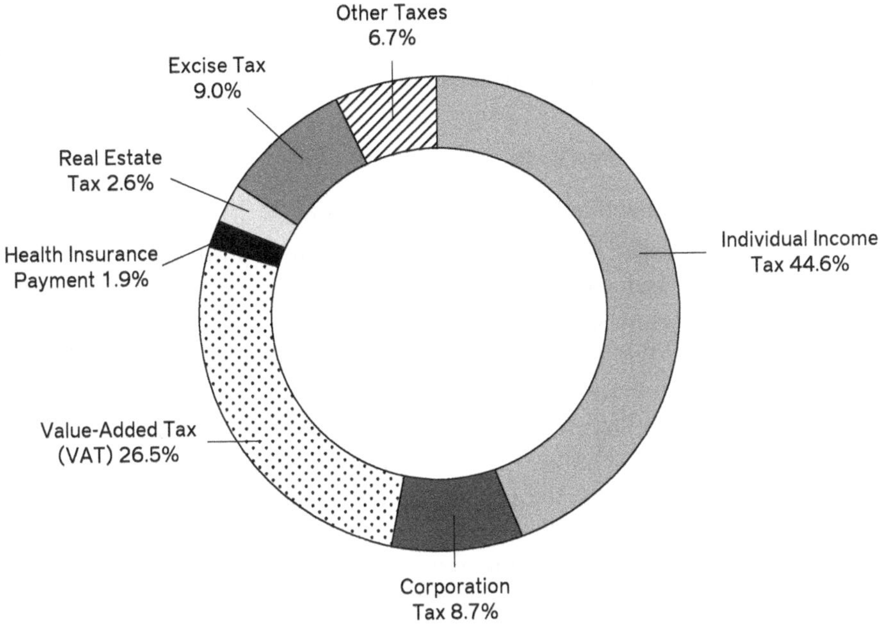

Source: FTA (2021a).

The legal and regulatory landscape of taxation is constantly altering. Recently, for example, the real estate tax categories and the permitted range of real estate tax rates were changed in the Real Estate Tax Act (RETA 654/1992, as amended). This chapter follows legislation in force as of January 1, 2024.

Taxation in Finland is administered by the Finnish Tax Administration (FTA),[2] regardless of whether the tax is received by the state, a municipality, or a church (Tax Assessment Procedure Act 1558/1995). The FTA bills, collects, and enforces taxes and delivers the tax receipts to the tax recipient in all tax categories. In Finland, tax recipients are responsible for returning their taxes. The FTA monitors tax declarations, evaluates their credibility, and if necessary, asks for corrections or further explanations from the taxpayer. In 2022, the monitoring activities identified over €500 million in unpaid taxes (FTA 2023a). The FTA has been very active in testing and using new technologies, such as software robotics, to support analytics and software development, for example. Recently, a single off-the-shelf software product was launched that replaced some 70 end-of-life tax systems (OECD 2019). This change allowed the shift to an electronic service portal called MyTax (https://www.vero.fi/en/e-file

/mytax/). The FTA serves taxpayers through the MyTax portal and a network of local tax offices. Taxpayers can return their forms and documents related to taxation either by mail or electronically through MyTax. All material is digitized and kept in electronic form; the income taxation of natural persons in particular is already largely automatized.

Land and Property Markets

Characteristics of Land and Property Ownership

A real property is the basic unit of landownership in Finland. It consists of the physical land area but also shares of joint property units, easements, and shares of joint special interests and private special interests (see Niukkanen 2014). Property law holds that a real property includes, in addition to the land and water areas, buildings that belong to the landowner (Hyvönen 1982). In Finland, ownership of real property is the most complete and exclusive right to an object. The ownership right covers both the right to use the property and the right of absolute control over the property (Niukkanen 2014).

Apartment ownership in Finland is a form of indirect ownership. The real property unit, including the apartments, is owned by a housing company. Shareholders of the company gain possession of a specified apartment or some other part of the building or site through defined shares (Falkenbach and Nuuja 2007; Puustinen and Viitanen 2015). This form of ownership is mainly applied to blocks or flats and terraced housing, but sometimes also detached housing can be structured through a housing company. Indirect ownership through housing companies is very common in Finland—approximately 60 percent of all dwellings are indirectly owned through shares. The figure is higher in cities—for example, in Helsinki it is more than 90 percent (Statistics Finland 2022a).

Any natural person or legal person (e.g., company or municipality) can acquire ownership rights to a real property through, for example, transaction, exchange, gift, or inheritance. However, real property purchases by natural or legal persons from outside the European Union (EU) or European Economic Area (EEA) must first receive permission. Such real property purchases are monitored by the Ministry of Defense. Persons with a dual citizenship in Finland or any other EU or EEA country are exempt from this rule. In addition, permission is not needed if the real property is purchased jointly with a partner who has citizenship of an EU or EEA country. Monitoring is limited to real property purchases. The monitoring of real property purchases covers the purchases of both built and unbuilt sites (i.e., land or plots). There is no monitoring of, for example, purchases of housing company shares or land leases (Riekkinen et al. 2022).

Land and Property Registration and Market Information

Information on real properties and on the related rights, restrictions, and responsibilities are recorded in the registers of the cadastral system. The Finnish cadastral system consists of three connected elements: the cadastre, the land registry, and the cadastral map. As explained by Niukkanen (2014, 53), "Ownership of land is seen in the Nordic legal system as protected title-based owner-possession." Thus, the land registry part of the system enjoys full positive and negative faith and credit[3] (see, e.g., Krigsholm et al. 2017). The land registry records all rights on real properties (such as information about real property ownership and pledges) but not some types of use rights that are registered in the cadastre. All changes in ownership must be registered. Application for the registration of title needs to be submitted within six months of signing the deed of sale or agreement. The registration process starts automatically if an electronic transaction service is used. In other cases, an application needs to be submitted to the National Land Survey (NLS).[4]

The cadastre records information about the location of real property units and the use of land. The Finnish cadastre does not enjoy the same level of faith and credit as the land registry because of shortcomings resulting from differences registering rights of use, easements, and restrictions (Vitikainen 2013). The cadastre and the land registry complement each other and create a unified entity. A registered real property has the same unique identification number across both parts. Both registers are maintained by the NLS. The cadastral information is accessed via the Finnish Land Information System.

The NLS collects information on transfer prices for real property in the real property sales price register, which is not part of the cadastral system. However, it is a centralized national register that provides information on real property sales (not on apartment sales), particularly for real property valuation for professional purposes, such as in cadastral procedures, land use planning, and credit granting. The real property sales price register information is collected from official notices from the public purchase witnesses and includes information on transfer objects (real properties) and their basic characteristics, use of transfer object, transfer or sales prices, buildings, and the parties to the transfer. Property-level information on real property sales is available through the Finnish Land Information System for certain user groups (e.g., municipalities, civil servants) for free, and for a fee for other users. Statistics on real property sales prices are freely available on the NLS website (https://www.maanmittauslaitos.fi/). The statistics are compiled on municipal, regional, and national levels.

Even though transfers on land are recorded in a public register, transactions on developable land are often affected by land policy measures and cannot be used as evidence of free market transactions. Land with the potential to be used for development anytime in the future is typically purchased by municipalities. As the municipalities have extensive rights for expropriation, even transactions that appear to happen in voluntary markets may have the threat of expropriation affecting both the decision to sell and the transaction price. Similarly, because municipalities engage actively in the land market (e.g., Valtonen, Falkenbach, and Viitanen 2018), most transfers of building sites are by municipalities, and selling prices are determined through administrative means. The public intervention in the land market is explained in more detail in the next section.

Information on buildings and residences is not maintained by the cadastral authority. This information, collected and maintained in close cooperation with municipalities, is stored in the Population Information System of the Digital and Population Data Services Agency. In the Finnish public data infrastructure, certain information is kept in one register only and transferred between different systems via interfaces. The real estate information in the Population Information System, for example, originates from the registers of the cadastral system.

The real properties owned by housing companies and the rights concerning them are registered in the registers of the cadastral system. However, since apartments are not real properties in the Finnish system, the ownership of shares in the housing company (i.e., the de facto right to a specific apartment) is not registered in the land registry. Recently, a new national information system that records apartment ownership has been established. The system, called the Residential and Commercial Property Information System, collects comprehensive information on ownership, pledges, and restrictions of housing company shares. Housing companies established after 2019 are automatically entered in the system. Transferring information on companies established before 2019 is ongoing. In the future, the system will include full-coverage registers of apartment ownership. Although this system is maintained by NLS, it is not part of the cadastral system.

A sales price register for apartments based on the transfers registered in the Residential and Commercial Property Information System does not exist but is being discussed. The FTA has its own information system on apartment prices, based on transfer tax declarations. These data include the self-declared purchase price of the apartment shares.

Commercial properties can be held as property or as shares in mutual real estate companies or real estate companies (Limited Liability Housing Companies Act 1599/2009, § 28, para. 2). Hence, registration of ownership and transactions in these company forms follows that for housing companies. Commercial properties registered as real properties are typically held and transacted through holding companies. Changes of ownership and prices of commercial properties therefore do not systematically enter official registers, and publicly registered data on, for example, pricing is limited. Typically, valuations of commercial properties are done by private valuers that have their own proprietary databases.

Rental transactions are not formally recorded in Finland. Asking rents are, however, widely available through online trading platforms.[5]

The centralized practices on recording information on real estate and apartment transactions and prices are evolving. The institutional characteristics of Finnish land markets (see next section), and particularly the dominant role of municipalities on land markets, hinders the existence and availability of market price data for land. In this setting, obtaining actual land price developments across locations is difficult.

Taxes on Real Estate

Both the state and the municipality levy taxes on real estate. The state levies the asset transfer tax, capital income and capital gains tax, and inheritance and gift taxes.[6] This section describes these tax categories in more detail.

The recurrent land and property tax (real estate tax) is a municipal tax. The real estate tax system, assessment of real estate taxation values, and administration of the real estate tax are described in the next section. Municipalities in Finland also lease public land and impose fees related to development that have tax-like characteristics. Public land leasing and development-related fees are discussed at the end of this section.

The tax types and their main principles have been relatively stable, with no major reforms in recent decades. Tax rates, in contrast, change more frequently. When the state levies a tax, its rate is set in law. For taxes levied by the municipality, the legislation sets the permitted range of tax rates, and the municipalities decide what rate to levy.

National Level

Asset Transfer Tax

Transfers of real estate and securities are subject to the asset transfer tax (Act on Transfer Tax 931/1996, as amended). In 2021, the asset transfer taxes totaled €993 million, increasing by almost 20 percent from the year before. Most of the revenue came from the transfers of real estate and shares of housing companies (FTA 2021a).

The state collects the tax, which is paid by the natural or legal person who acquires the asset. The transfer tax on real property is 3 percent of the self-declared purchase price or the value of other contribution or 1.5 percent of the purchase price for transfer of shares of housing companies and other real estate companies. If the transfer of shares includes a share-specific portion of debt in the company's balance sheet, the tax is paid not on the purchase price but on the so-called unencumbered sales price, equaling the sales price plus the portion of debt. If there is more than one buyer, the tax is paid pro rata—each buyer's percentage share in the property. Assets received as gifts or inheritance are also exempt. If the purchase price is less than 75 percent of the market value of the assets, the difference is regarded as a gift and subject to gift tax.

The buyer is obligated to file the transfer tax return and pay the tax within two months of signing the asset transfer contract. If a real estate agent or broker is involved, the agent submits the transfer tax return, and the tax is paid at the signing of the transfer contract. The payment of the asset transfer tax is a prerequisite for entering change of ownership of real property in the land registry.[7]

The penalty for tax returns late up to 60 days is €50 for individuals and estates and €100 for other taxpayers. For returns more than 60 days late, a penalty is imposed, usually 10 percent of the tax due but can be lower (2 or 5 percent) or higher (15–50 percent), depending on the type of negligence. The penalty is always at least €75 for individuals and estates and €150 for other taxpayers. In addition, late payments of the transfer tax are subject to interest payments. The interest rate is determined by the state, and in 2025 it was 11.5 percent. If the right being transferred (ownership right in a property) is subject to mandatory registration, failing to apply for the registration on time increases the transfer tax by 20 percent for each consecutive six-month period of nonregistration, until a maximum penalty of 100 percent is reached.

Capital Income Tax and Taxation of Capital Gains

Earned income and capital income are taxed separately in Finland (Income Tax Law 1535/1992, as amended). Revenue from the tax on earned income is divided among the state, municipalities, and Finland's two national churches. The capital income tax is received by the state. Capital income tax includes all sources of capital income, such as dividends, entrepreneurial income, rental income, and capital gains. The taxation is progressive: in 2025, the capital tax rate was 30 percent, but for the portion of capital income that exceeds €30,000, the tax rate is 34 percent. The taxable capital income is gross income minus potential deductions. Potential deductions include all expenses related to the acquisition and maintenance of such income and losses on a source of income. In 2020, the total capital income tax was €3.080 million, approximately 9.5 percent of the total individual income tax (FTA 2020). In 2021, the total rental income reported in capital gains taxation amounted to €2 billion and total rental losses amounted to €161 million (FTA 2023b). For a tax rate of 30 percent, the tax revenue from rental revenues is about €551 million. No comparative reporting exists on the capital gains from real estate transfers.

If a seller makes a profit when selling an asset, this profit is subject to capital gains tax. The profit is calculated by taking the asset's sales price and deducting its purchase price (including the transfer tax), along with any expenses incurred in making the profit (e.g., brokerage fees). If the asset was a gift or inheritance, the value used in taxation at the time of receipt is used. The taxpayer can opt to use a deemed acquisition cost instead of the real one. If the asset has been owned for less than 10 years, the deemed acquisition cost is 20 percent of the sales price, otherwise 40 percent. If the asset is a home owned for at least two years and the owner has continuously and permanently lived in the dwelling for this period, the owner can be exempted from the capital gains tax of a dwelling.

Finland used to be among the most generous countries in the EU in allowing deduction of mortgage interest payments in taxation (European Commission 2015). This deduction has been phased out, and interest related to mortgages of an owner-occupied dwelling can no longer be deducted from taxes. If there is a deficit (net negative capital income), 30 percent of the deficit (32 percent for first-time home buyers) can be deducted in earned income taxation. For dwellings rented to third parties, the interest deduction is, with certain limitations, 100 percent.

Inheritance and Gift Taxes

Inheritances and gifts are subject to tax collected by the state (Inheritance and Gift Act 378/1940, as amended). An inheritance worth €20,000 or more is taxed at a rate depending on the monetary value of the inheritance (progressive scale) and the family relationship between the deceased and the recipient. There are two groups of recipients: Group 1 includes the deceased's children, parents, spouse, and spouse's children. In some cases, the unregistered partner of the deceased is included in group 1. Group 2 includes all other parties.

The value of the estate is defined as at the date of death. The estate is liable for making an inventory of the estate's assets, along with a declaration of their value, within three months of the death. The estate inventory can be done by someone informed of the deceased person's wealth (e.g., spouse or child), but services by banks or law offices, for instance, can also be used. The assets are to be valued at their fair value (likely sales price), but there are no requirements for using, for example, external valuers. After the FTA receives the deed of estate inventory, it decides whether to accept the values in the deed as the basis of inheritance tax assessment. The FTA determines inheritance tax and sends the tax decision along with payment details to members of the estate separately on the basis of their share of the estate. The recipients in group 1 and group 2 have different tax rates. For taxable inheritance of €60,000, for example, the tax is €3,500 for group 1 recipients and €8,900 for group 2 recipients. In addition, the spouse receives a €90,000 deduction, and minor children a €60,000 deduction. Inheritance tax is not levied if the taxation value of the inheritance is less than €20,000.

A gift tax is applied to all gifts worth €5,000 or more. The threshold amount applies to all gifts received from the same donor within three years. The recipient of the gift is responsible for filing a tax return on the gift within three months and for paying the tax. The value of the gift is determined by its value at the date of the donation. The gift tax on a €25,000 gift, for example, is €1,700 for recipients in group 1 and €3,900 for recipients in group 2.

Late filing of a tax return on an inheritance or gift incurs filing penalties and increased tax rates. For returns up to 60 days late, the penalty is €50 for individuals and estates and €100 for other taxpayers. For returns more than 60 days late or if the deed of estate inventory or declaration of the gift is incomplete, a punitive tax increase is imposed. The punitive tax relates to the increased tax burden (e.g., if some assets have not been declared or their values have been underreported). The starting punitive tax is 10 percent of the increased tax calculated at group 1 recipient tax rates. An increased punitive tax rate between 15 and 50 percent of the increased tax is imposed for repeated negligence or apparent disregard toward tax filing responsibilities. A decreased punitive tax rate of 5 percent can be applied if the case is ambiguous or there are circumstances that make the application of the base rate unreasonable. A further decreased punitive tax rate of 2 percent is applied if the tax subject corrects a mistake in tax filing that will lead to an increased tax burden (e.g., declares assets omitted from previous filings). If the deed of estate inventory has not been filed or the values declared cannot be used in taxation, the tax authority conducts the tax assessment. In such cases, a punitive tax rate of 25 percent of the increased tax is applied. The punitive taxes are a minimum €75 for individuals and €150 for other taxpayers.

The total tax revenue of inheritance and gift taxes in 2021 was €826 million (Statistics Finland 2022b). No statistics exist on the role of real estate in inheritance or gift tax.

Municipality Level

At the municipal level, the only real estate–related tax is the recurrent land and property tax (real estate tax), discussed in detail in the next section. However, in addition to taxes, municipalities may impose other tax-like payments through their land policy.

These payments, regarded as municipal land policy implementation, not taxation, are not collected by the FTA, and no detailed requirements on reporting or public disclosure exist. The municipalities set, negotiate, and collect these payments. Furthermore, these revenue items are not defined as separate accounting items, and hence their role and magnitude in municipal finances cannot be properly evaluated (see, e.g., Falkenbach et al. [2021] on the lack of transparency of land policy implementation related fees and payments).

Value Capture and Other Levies and Payments Related to Land and Real Estate Development

Finnish municipalities have a pronounced role in land and real estate development within their jurisdictions. They have the independent right to initiate, prepare, and approve detailed plans, and in practice, no significant development can be executed in the absence or in breach of a local detailed plan.[8] Alongside the right to control development, municipalities have the responsibility to provide and maintain related municipal infrastructure.

Most municipalities in Finland prefer drafting local detailed plans on municipality-owned land (Falkenbach et al. 2021). This means that Finnish municipalities, like their counterparts in the Netherlands and Sweden, for example, widely engage in public land development (see Krigsholm, Puustinen, and Falkenbach 2022; Valtonen, Falkenbach, and Van der Krabben 2017). In public land development, the municipality acquires undeveloped land, drafts the local detailed plans, and builds the necessary local infrastructure. The municipality then sells the developed building sites to private developers or leases them through long-term land leases, thereby capturing all planning-induced value increases.

But new development increasingly occurs on privately owned land because of, for example, infill development and regeneration of already developed areas. According to the Finnish Land Use and Building Act (LUBA 132/1999, as amended), a landowner who significantly benefits from a local detailed plan has the duty to contribute to the cost of providing infrastructure. The contribution paid by the landowner is agreed on through voluntary negotiations, but statutory fees can be applied if an agreement is not reached. The contract signed between municipality and landowner that determines the landowner's contribution to the land development fee and other terms and conditions of development is the land use agreement. Although the LUBA (132/1999) defines land use agreements as a cost recovery tool, in practice the contract is commonly based on the value appreciation caused by the plan. Thus, in essence, the agreements are value-capture tools and the fees are tax-like measures. A report found that most municipalities aim to capture between 30 and 60 percent of the value appreciation through these agreements (Falkenbach et al. 2021). The payment schedule is negotiated with the landowner and often tied to the infrastructure construction timeline. Payments are sometimes not monetary, but land transfers or transfers of part of the permitted building volume to the municipality.

Leasing of Municipality-Owned Land

Finnish municipalities are significant landowners. Some of this land originated from historical land donations from the Swedish crown, but municipalities also actively acquire land by voluntary means and sometimes through preemption rights and expropriation. The legislation and planning system supports municipal land banking: The planning monopoly makes the public land development model easy to implement, and a municipality can easily acquire undeveloped land within its jurisdiction. Municipalities also have a right to expropriate real properties if they can justify acquisition as needed for the coordinated development of the municipality.

After developing the land (drafting a plan and servicing the plots), a municipality can sell or lease the plots to developers or to individuals. The Finnish legislation on land leases (Land Tenancy Act 258/1966) is relatively liberal. The law provides for the land lease agreements for building sites to be made for periods of 30 to 99 years. Rent amounts are not regulated nor is the discount rate that the municipality may use in setting the rent. The rent levels tend to be on the moderate side. The annual rent payments can be indexed, to account for the changes in land values during the contract period. Most municipalities apply annual indexation of land rents based on the cost-of-living index of Statistics Finland (https://stat.fi/en/statistics/khi), but some municipalities base the indexation on some house price index. Land values have risen faster than average living costs in recent decades, particularly in growing urban areas, and rent appreciation tends to lag the appreciation of land values in many locations.

Municipal land banking and land leasing is a way for municipalities to capture land value appreciation. A municipality owning undeveloped land can maintain it in forestry or agricultural use and receive income or rent revenues from it. At the same time, any hope value[9] related to development potential will be captured by the municipality. Similarly, when leasing building sites, the municipality captures all land value appreciation.

Recurrent Land and Property Tax

Real Estate Tax System

The real estate tax was introduced in 1993, when several charges and taxes were replaced by one tax (Government Bill 50/1992 for the RETA). The goal was to simplify the legally and economically fragmented system of payments related to ownership of property. The tax is received by the municipality of the property.

The Finnish real estate tax system is a three-tier tax system defined in the RETA (654/1992, as amended).[10] The real estate tax is the sum of taxes related to separately valued components. The two initial components in the tax system were land and buildings, which have separate tax rates. The tax rates for buildings depend on their primary use.

In 1999, the RETA was amended to allow for a higher tax rate on unbuilt building sites. The change was made to create an incentive for developing unbuilt building sites in local detailed plan areas, and thereby increase housing supply and curb increases in house prices (Government Bill 100/1999 for the amendment of the RETA). In 2006, the law was amended, and the increased tax rate was made mandatory for 14 municipalities in the Greater Helsinki area.

In 2023, the RETA rates were amended. Until 2023, the act had recognized a general real estate tax rate that applied to all land and buildings unless otherwise specified. The amendment replaced this general tax rate with two general tax rates: for land and for buildings. The change was made to provide municipalities with improved tools for incentivizing plan implementation and for adapting the tax burden according to local conditions (Government Bill 39/2023 for the amendment of the RETA).

In Finland, real estate is defined as a real property unit (see the previous section, "Land and Property Markets," for the full definition), which is registered in the cadastre. The provisions of the real estate tax are, however, also applied to buildings, where the real property unit is owned by one party and the buildings might be owned by another; unseparated parcels part of a property unit; and building areas part of a joint property or a jointly owned forest. Buildings, in general, are regarded as part of the real estate to the extent they are owned by the same owner as the land area. Apartments owned by housing companies, or other forms of property ownership through the Finnish share system, are not regarded as real estate in the Finnish real estate tax system. Hence, the whole building entity of the housing company (i.e., the whole condominium scheme) together with the land area owned by the company is the subject of real estate taxation.

Coverage of Tax Base

The real estate tax applies to all real properties except agricultural and forest land; abandoned churches, castles, fortresses, and cloisters; buildings used for territorial surveillance and properties used for the needs of defense forces (as fortresses; as military, aviation, or naval bases; as research or test sites; or as storage facilities or depots); areas protected by the Nature Conservation Act (9/2023) but not the buildings and building sites in such areas; and water areas. The tax is also not paid on real estate used as a marketplace, public square, street, public road, railroad, or public airport runway or for real estate used as a graveyard (RETA para. 3). The real estate tax is a general duty—that is, all landowners, including the state, municipalities, the two national churches, and nonprofit organizations, are subject to the tax. Municipalities do not, however, pay real estate tax on the real estate they own within their own jurisdiction (RETA para. 3). The real estate tax is not collected if the tax would be less than €10. In 2021, the total amount of real estate tax was below this limit for 1.2 percent of potential real estate taxpayers. The revenue lost to this exemption was around €122,000 (FTA 2021b).

Taxpayer

The tax is paid by the owner of real property. Holders of permanent tenure on a property and holders of gratuitous tenure because of inheritance or a testament are deemed equal to owners (RETA para. 5). If land area and buildings are owned by different parties, the landowner pays the tax on land; the owner of the building, on the building. The owner of an unseparated parcel is responsible for the tax on the parcel. If a joint property unit includes building land, the unit is responsible for paying the tax. If a real estate has multiple owners, their share of the tax is calculated pro rata to their ownership share. If the responsibility for the tax is divided among many different right holders, the owner pays tax only on the share of the property in the owner's possession (RETA paras. 6–9). In the Finnish real estate tax system, the housing company owns the land and buildings and is therefore responsible for the real estate tax. If a property is purchased for a corporation or yet-to-be-registered entity, as is often the case for new housing companies, the entity that made the purchase is responsible for the tax until the ownership right is transferred to the new legal entity (RETA para. 10). According to implementation measures published by FTA (2022a), the party liable for the tax is the party that owns the property at the beginning of the calendar year. If the property transfers to a new owner during that calendar year, and the previous owner has not paid the real estate tax, the new owner can be held liable for the tax (RETA para. 36).

Owners living outside Finland are subject to the same taxation as local owners, unless levying taxes would be against an international treaty; then, the owner is exempt (RETA para. 4). As international tax treaties do not generally include provisions on real estate taxation, the exemption applies mostly to real estate owned by foreign missions and consulates.

Tax Rates

The RETA defines the range of tax rates. Municipal councils determine the real estate tax rates for their jurisdictions annually in advance, at the same time they decide the municipal income tax rate. The real estate tax rates are set to two decimal places and defined in percentages (e.g., 4.00 percent) (RETA para. 11). The tax is calculated by multiplying the value of the property (or component) by the relevant tax rate. Table 10.1 summarizes the real estate tax rates applied by Finnish municipalities in 2025.

The general real estate tax rate on land applies to most land. This rate must be between 1.30 and 2.00 percent. The municipal council can choose to set a specific tax rate for unbuilt building sites. This rate must be between 2.00 and 6.00 percent. The 14 municipalities in the Greater Helsinki region are obliged to set a specific tax rate for unbuilt building sites, at least 3.00 percent higher than the general real estate tax rate on land but not exceeding 6.00 percent.

An unbuilt building site can be subject to the increased tax rates if the local detail plan for the area has been legally binding for at least a year before the beginning of the calendar year, more than half the planned building right is designated for housing purposes, no building is used for residential purposes and construction for such has not started, the building site has road access or such can be arranged, the property can be connected to a water main and wastewater sewer as defined in the Water Services Act (119/2001 § 10), the building site is not subject to a prohibition according to the Land Use and Building Act (132/1999 paras. 38, 53, or 58 subparagraph 5), and the building site is owned by one owner. A building site is owned by one owner if spouses own the building site jointly or the building site is otherwise owned through specified shares of joint ownership. The increased tax rate can be imposed on plots and other building sites that conform with the local detailed plan and are registered in the cadastre, building sites that are formed according to the binding or indicative plot division as defined in the local detailed plan, and areas designated as building blocks in the local detailed plan without a binding or indicative plot division. The increased tax rate cannot be applied to building sites designated for holiday homes (RETA para. 12a).

Buildings are taxed at the general real estate tax rate for buildings unless a specific tax rate applies to the building type. The general tax rate

Table 10.1 Real Estate Tax Rates in Municipalities, 2025

Tax Rate	Permitted Range	Median%	Minimum%	Maximum%
General real estate tax rate for land	1.30%–2.00%	1.30	1.30	2.00
Tax rate for unbuilt building sites (land)[1]	2.00%–6.00%	3.00	2.00	6.00
Tax rate for unbuilt building sites in specified municipalities (land)	At least 3.00% above the general real estate tax rate for land. Max. 6.00%	4.42	4.30	6.00
General real estate tax rate for buildings	0.93%–2.00%	1.10	0.93	1.90
Tax rate for permanent residential buildings	0.41%–1.00%	0.55	0.41	1.00
Tax rate for other residential buildings	0.93%–2.00%	1.2	0.93	2.00
Tax rate for buildings and land that are owned by nonprofit organizations, and used for public or common-good purposes[2]	Can be set lower than the general tax rate, no minimum threshold	0.00	0.00	1.43
Tax rate for buildings used as power plants[3]		3.10	0.93	3.10

Note: Municipalities of the autonomous region of Åland are excluded from the sample.

[1] Values calculated from data of municipalities that have voluntarily set a rate for unbuilt building sites. Of 292 municipalities, 164 have set a tax rate.

[2] Values calculated from data of the 250 municipalities that have set a rate.

[3] Values calculated from data of the 254 municipalities that have set a rate.

for buildings must be set between 0.93 and 2 percent (RETA para. 11). Buildings used as permanent residences have a lower tax range, between 0.41 and 1 percent. A building is a permanent residence if at least 50 percent of the area of the dwelling is used as permanent residence. A dwelling is assumed to be a permanent residence if that is its recorded use in the Population Information System. Buildings under development and planned for permanent residence are included in this category. Outbuildings and garages associated with permanent residences are taxed at the rate of a permanent residence (RETA para. 12).

For other residential buildings, the tax rate is between 0.93 and 2 percent. This tax rate is applied to a residential building designated for use other than permanent residence (e.g., holiday homes) or under development for such use. Again, associated outbuildings and garages are taxed at the same rate as the main building. This tax rate does not apply to buildings used for lodging services (RETA para. 13).

The municipal council can deviate from the general tax rate for land and buildings owned by nonprofit organizations if the building is primarily used for a public or common-good purpose. For such buildings, the tax rate can be set below the thresholds defined for the general real estate tax rate and can be as low as zero (RETA para. 13a).

The municipal council also has the right to set a specific tax rate for power plants and buildings and constructions used as final storage sites for nuclear power waste. For such buildings, the tax rate can be a maximum 3.10 percent. The application of this tax rate is limited to power plants producing a minimum nominal power of 10 megavolt-amperes. If a group of power plants is connected to a high-voltage distribution network or the main grid through one interface, the nominal power is calculated as the sum of their nominal power capacities. The plant owner is responsible for presenting a statement on the nominal capacity of the plant.

Tax Relief Measures

Generally, tax relief is defined in the Act on Tax Collection (para. 47). The FTA can grant tax relief only in exceptional circumstances, such as the taxpayer's decreased ability to pay taxes due to sickness, unemployment, obligation to pay child support or maintenance, or other special reasons. Having a low income or being heavily indebted are not grounds for tax relief.

The FTA grants relief on taxes paid to the state (e.g., income tax, inheritance and gift taxes). For taxes paid to the municipalities, including real estate tax, each municipality can decide on the tax relief independently and allow FTA to handle them (Act on Tax Collection para. 48). For real estate tax, a taxpayer can be granted relief on the increased tax on an unbuilt building site if the construction has been delayed for reasons other than the actions of the landowner. The tax relief applies to the tax but also to interest and late payment penalties (Act on Tax Collection para. 47).

Valuation for Real Estate Tax Purposes

As of 2025, Peltola (2014) provides the most recent description of valuation for real estate tax purposes in Finland. The valuations of real estate for real estate taxation are done in accordance with the Act on the Valuation of Assets in Taxation (1142/2005). The taxable value is defined as the value of land and buildings in the previous calendar year (RETA para. 15). The FTA defines tax values as of the value on December 31 of the previous calendar year (FTA 2022a).

Basis of the Land and Property Tax

The three-tier tax system used in Finland requires that land and structures (buildings) be valued separately (Act on the Valuation of Assets in Taxation 1142/2005, para. 8). The legislation (para. 29.4) specifies that the following factors be considered in valuing land for taxation purposes: purpose of use of a real property, allocated building rights, location, transport connections, suitability for construction, infrastructure readiness, and reasonable price level, in accordance with sales of comparable units (in both quality and location). Buildings are valued by first calculating a hypothetical replacement value and then subtracting age-based discounts. The estimates used for building costs and depreciation rates are set in the Decree of the Ministry of Finance on the Determination of Replacement Value of Buildings 681/2024, as amended, and apply throughout the country.

Valuation Methodology and Responsibility for Valuations

The valuation methodology is based on current use values. The method for land valuation was developed by VTT Technical Research Centre and the FTA in the early 1990s, before the introduction of real estate tax in Finland. Back then, VTT Technical Research Centre determined moderate current values of buildable land for the whole country. On the basis of these values, municipality-specific valuation guidelines were created. The FTA applies these guidelines in determining land values. These guidelines include plot price maps, which show current land values of different land uses within a municipality (area prices). Hence, area prices are different for plots for residential, commercial, industry, and other uses. Real properties with the same area price form one price zone. Price zones are meant to reflect local market segments and are not tied to a predetermined geographic division such as postal code area. The land values presented in plot price maps and municipality-specific valuation guidelines are average current prices, which are calculated mainly from sales of unbuilt plots. The FTA's target is that taxable value of land be 73.5 percent of prevailing market prices. This target sets the upper bound for taxable land values.

As noted earlier, the Ministry of Finance decree on replacement value of buildings (681/2024, as amended) annually sets the likely cost of new construction at the time of valuation. The decree determines individual valuation principles and value estimates for different building types. For example, residential buildings are valued by a formula, building cost estimates, and depreciation rates different from office buildings'. The somewhat complex calculation principles were drafted back in the 1970s using the building standards at the time. In short, the replacement value is determined on the basis of the building size, quality, and equipment. The decree lists average values per square meter or cubic meter, and these values are used in replacement value calculations. The decree defines the replacement value as 70 percent of average building costs. All buildings are valued using the decree's calculation guidelines. An alternative value can be used only if the real property owner liable for the tax can prove that the building differs substantially from the assumption of average quality of construction. This value can deviate by a maximum of 30 percent from the value determined according to the decree. The taxable value of the building is defined as the replacement value minus annual depreciation (based on the annual depreciation rate determined in the decree). Table 10.2 gives examples of fiscal year 2024 replacement values, and table 10.3 presents the depreciation rates.

Valuation Cycle

Current legislation does not prescribe a revaluation interval. The land price zones, land values for these zones, and valuation principles were determined in 1993. Some adjustments to land values were made in 2006. Otherwise, adjustments to prices have been based on indexation. Building values are updated using building cost indexes, whereas land values are updated by considering the general land price development of areas (in other words, land values can be raised for one area or price zone while they stay the same for another area or price zone at a certain time). Despite the adjustments, building values are estimated to substantially lag their replacement value on average, and land values also fail to meet the target of 73.5 percent of current land prices in many parts of the country (Peltola 2014). Concerns have been raised particularly regarding the

Table 10.2 Replacement Values, 2024

Building Type	Replacement Value
Detached houses, semidetached houses, and row houses	€769.04/m^2
Cellars used as storage space	€263.85/m^2
Blocks of flats	€769.04/m^2
Nonpermanent residences (e.g., summer cottages)	€613.52/m^2
Garages and outbuildings (insulated)	€501.18/m^2
Garages and outbuildings (lightly structured)	€260.97/m^2
Offices	€1,065.71/m^2
Retail buildings	€328.36/m^3
Industrial buildings	€128.14/m^3

Source: Decree of the Ministry of Finance on the Determination of Replacement Value of Buildings (681/2024).

Note: The replacement values can be increased or decreased according to the size, quality, and equipment of the building.

Table 10.3 Depreciation Rates for Building Types, 2024

Building Type	Annual Depreciation Rates (%)
Residential, office, and other comparable-use buildings, made of (1) wood or (2) made of stone, brick, concrete, or similar material	(1) 1.25 or (2) 1
Shop, warehouse, factory, workshop, utility building, and other comparable-use buildings, as well as power stations (not hydroelectric plants) made of (1) wood or (2) made of stone, brick, concrete, or similar material	(1) 5 or (2) 4
Warehouses and other structures	10
A building, dam, pool, or other structure belonging to a hydropower plant	1
A building or structure directly serving nuclear power plant operations	2.5
A building or structure belonging to a wind power plant	2.5

Source: Act on the Valuation of Assets in Taxation (1142/2005, as amended).

intramunicipal variation in relative fiscal values (Peltola 2014), and a need for reform of valuation principles has been recognized (see the later section "Reform Initiatives and Country-Specific Issues" for further details).

Valuation Quality Control Measures

Valuation practices have not been updated for several years. Building valuations are based on average values and the assumption of an average construction level, whereas land valuations rely on moderate current values and price zones that were determined some decades ago. It is widely acknowledged that the valuation quality is far from optimal, and particularly in growing urban areas the taxable values have not developed in accordance with land price and building cost development (Peltola 2014). For instance, according to market information, age decreases building value at different rates in different parts of country, yet the same formula is used in building valuations throughout the country. Moreover, the price zones used in land valuation are often geographically quite large areas, hence differences in micro-locations are not reflected in land valuations (Peltola 2014). No national or international quality standard is applied.

Property Valuation Data

As explained previously, plot price maps developed in the 1990s are the backbone of land value determination in Finland. The NLS delivers information about real property units (real property identifiers, taxable surface area, ownership data, etc.) to the FTA. Building information is provided by municipalities who maintain building registers within their jurisdictions. The building registers, however, are not part of the national data infrastructure, and the quality and validity of building information varies; some buildings are completely missing from the list of taxable of buildings, for example (Peltola 2014). Municipalities also deliver lists of building sites and other relevant information for the administration of the real estate tax for unbuilt building sites.

Administration of the Real Estate Tax

The FTA administers the real estate tax. Taxpayers declare to the FTA their taxable income, deductions in taxation, the information of assets and liabilities, and any other information that could affect their taxation. The FTA annually sends private persons and estates of deceased persons a precompleted tax return based on the information the FTA has received. The precompleted tax return is delivered in the electronic service portal MyTax and by post. The taxpayer confirms the information in the precompleted tax return and corrects errors and reports missing information. If the taxpayer makes no corrections or additions, the FTA considers the precompleted tax return as accepted (RETA para. 16). Corporations and other taxpayers must return their tax information independently (Tax Assessment Procedure Act para. 7).

The FTA sends to all taxpayers a declaration of the property information used in defining the tax: the surface area, building right, planning stage, riparian rights, designated use, and ownership and possession rights, for example, as well as the information used to calculate building replacement value. The taxpayer is given reasonable time to inform the FTA of errors, missing properties and buildings, and any improvements and significant renovations, demolitions, or removals from use (RETA para. 16). The taxpayer does not need to verify the values, only the basis of the information.

Third parties and other authorities, municipalities, and the state may also inform the FTA of information relevant for administering real estate taxes (RETA para. 18; Tax Assessment Procedure Act § 3, para. 18). Conversely, the FTA may submit information on properties and owners to the NLS and the building's municipality for verification, which the authority in question has the duty to fulfill.

Objection and Appeal

The FTA sends the tax decision and instructions for appeal to the taxpayer. The tax decision includes the name or other designation of the taxpayer and identifies the authority that administered the decision along with contact details. The decision must also include a list of all properties subject to real estate tax, the values of these properties, and the tax to be paid. If a building has been taxed with other than the general real estate tax rate, the tax decision also informs the taxpayer about this (RETA para. 24).

The taxpayer, the FTA, and the municipality of the taxed property have the right to appeal a tax decision. Demands for rectification and appeals are regulated by paragraphs 61–71g of the Tax Assessment Procedure Act (1558/1995, as amended). Demands for rectification must be made within three years after the end of the taxation year or within 60 days of being informed about the tax decision. The FTA and the municipality must submit their rectification requests within four months of the end date of the tax assessment.

Appeals of a rectification decision must be made within 60 days in the administrative court of the municipality of the taxpayer's residence. All parties have a right to reply, and the body submitting the appeal can respond to the reply. If the change in tax responsibility is €6,000 or less and the matter is not ambiguous or unclear, however, the administrative court can rule on the case without hearing the FTA.

Administrative court decisions can be appealed to the Supreme Administrative Court within 60 days of notification of the decision. The taxpayer, municipality, or FTA may appeal the decision directly to the Supreme Administrative Court, if it grants leave to appeal, but such leave to appeal requires the consent of both parties. In 2021, altogether 63 appeals regarding real estate tax were made to administrative courts and 11 to the Supreme Administrative Court (FTA 2021c).

Billing

The Act on Tax Collection (11/2018, as amended) defines procedures for billing, payment, and collection of taxes. Each taxpayer receives forms for the payment of real estate tax along with the real estate tax decision. All properties are billed at the same time. If the total of the real estate taxes is less than €170, the tax is billed in one payment. For larger tax payments, there are two bills. The due dates on tax payments vary depending on the end date of the tax assessment. The first payment is due in the second month after the end date of the tax assessment, and the second payment is due in the fourth month after the end date of the tax assessment.

Payment

Taxes are paid through the banking system or deposits to the accounts of the FTA (Act on Tax Collection para. 8).[11] There are no discounts for prompt payments, and late payments are subject to late-payment interest as set in the Act on Surtax and Penalty Interest in Arrears (1556/1995, as amended). The late-payment interest is the previous six-month reference rate (Interest Act 633/1982 para. 12) increased by 7 percentage points or €3, whichever is greater. The interest is paid from the day after the due date up to the day of payment.

Enforcement

Tax receivables are subject to payment enforcement similar to any other receivable. Before starting enforcement activities, the FTA sends a payment reminder to the taxpayer (Act on Tax Collection para. 42). In practice, the FTA sends one to three payment reminders, depending on whether the taxpayer has other unpaid taxes, before notifying the enforcement authorities (FTA 2022b) and informing the taxpayer of this in the payment reminder (Act on Tax Collection para. 42).

Delayed payments of real estate taxes are common. In 2022, more than 20 percent of real estate tax payments for fiscal year 2021 were not paid by their due date. Interest from late payments totaled about €1 million in

2021 (FTA 2022c). In April 2023, unpaid real estate taxes totaled €36 million (FTA 2023c).[12]

If in temporary financial difficulty, a taxpayer can request a payment arrangement. While the payment arrangement is in force, the FTA will not notify enforcement authorities. For corporations, the payment arrangement prevents businesses from being removed from the prepayment register and having their tax debts published on the tax debt register or on the protest list (FTA 2022b). In general, taxes under payment arrangement are subject to interest, as described earlier. If extremely strong reasons indicate the interest is unreasonable, however, interest will not be collected (Act on Tax Collection para 43). The FTA can cease demands of tax receivables when it deems that enforcement will not succeed or that the result will be minor. The FTA also has the right to give detailed prescriptions on its process on tax enforcement and actions made in terms of enforcement (Act on Tax Collection paras. 45, 46).

Taxpayers can have a negligence penalty of up to €2,000 imposed if they fail to submit or correct minor information or submit the information late or in a noncompliant form. If the negligence is substantial and corrected only after a request for correction, a negligence penalty of up to €5,000 can be imposed. If the negligence was intentional or gross misconduct, the penalty can be up to €15,000. Such negligence payments are not imposed on natural persons or estates of the deceased (Tax Assessment Procedure Act para. 22a).

The FTA can impose late-filing penalties and punitive tax increases for real estate taxes (Tax Assessment Procedure Act para. 32). If a taxpayer sends new information on the real estate after the deadline but before the tax assessment has been completed and the information leads to an increase in real estate tax, a late-filing penalty can be imposed. The penalty is €50 for individual taxpayers and estates of deceased persons and €100 for others. Taxpayers who do not file corrections concerning missing units or buildings or have not remedied other errors can have a punitive tax increase imposed. The amount of punitive tax depends on the omission and can be between 2 and 50 percent of the increased tax. The punitive tax increase is approximately 10 percent of the amount of the added tax, but the minimum is €75 for individual taxpayers and estates of deceased persons and at least €150 for other taxpayers. These penalties cannot be imposed if the taxpayer cannot reasonably be assumed to have known of the error in the tax filing. The revenues raised from penalties are given to the municipalities (RETA para. 25).

Taxpayers who have not filed a tax return or have submitted an incomplete, erroneous, or faulty tax return that increases real estate tax, must, in addition to the punitive increase in tax rate, pay late-payment interest on the increased tax (Tax Assessment Procedure Act para. 57). This interest is paid from the original due date of the real estate tax to the due date of the increased tax (Act on Surtax and Penalty Interest in Arrears para. 5b).

Tax fraud is a criminal offense (Criminal Code 39/1889, chap. 29, §§ 1–3, as amended), and taxpayers can be fined or imprisoned for up to four years, depending on the severity of the fraud. If the crime is minor, taking into account the amount of tax and other circumstances, the FTA may abstain from prosecution. In addition, negligence to provide information can lead to fines (Tax Assessment Procedure Act para. 87), but charges and punishment may be waived if a punitive tax increase is deemed a sufficient penalty. Furthermore, no charges can be brought if a punitive tax has already been imposed on the same person in the same case, unless new evidence arises and the previously imposed punitive tax has been annulled (Criminal Code § 11).

Key Figures of Real Estate Tax

Table 10.4 presents an overall picture of the real estate tax in Finland and in its largest cities in 2021. Taxable values are concentrated in the largest cities, where land values are highest and the building stock is concentrated. Note that the taxable values in the first column include the values

Table 10.4 Real Estate Tax, National and Largest Cities, 2021

	Taxable Value as % of GDP	Real Estate Tax Collected as % of Taxable Value	Real Estate Tax Collected as % of GDP
Total	96.18	0.83	0.80
Land	19.00	n.a.	n.a.
Buildings	77.18	n.a.	n.a.
Helsinki	15.21	0.74	0.11
Espoo	6.92	0.78	0.05
Tampere	4.13	0.90	0.04
Vantaa	4.56	0.90	0.04
Oulu	3.16	0.76	0.02

Source: FTA (2021b).

Note: Taxable value as a percentage of GDP includes the taxable values of all properties. When calculating property tax collected as a percentage of taxable value, the taxable value is the denominator. The main difference between the two taxable value bases is that properties owned by the municipality of the property are valued for tax purposes but tax is not levied. n.a. = not available.

Figure 10.2 Growth in Levied Real Estate Tax, GDP, and Apartment Prices, 2014–2021 (2014=100)

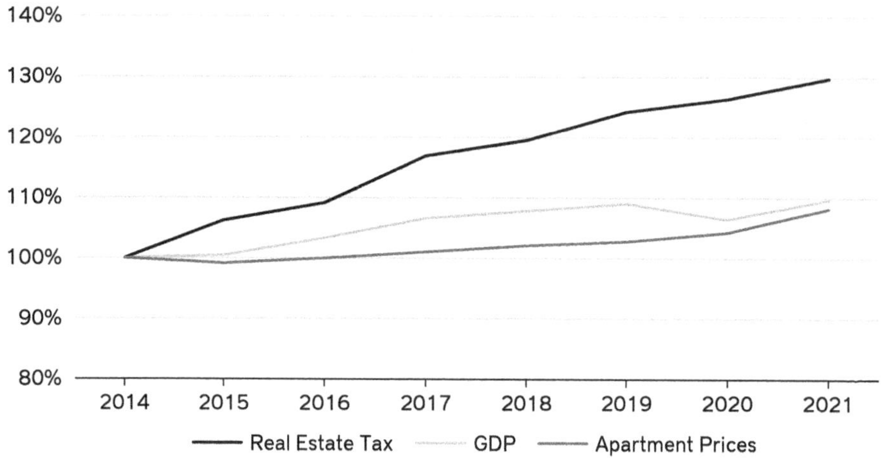

Sources: FTA (2021b); Statistics Finland (2023a; 2023b).

of municipality-owned real estate on municipality-owned land, which are not taxable. Effective tax rates vary among the largest cities because they can choose their property tax rates within a given range and because some cities, such as Helsinki, are a significant landowner. About one-third of the real estate tax is collected in the five largest cities. Nationally, real estate taxes formed approximately 7.6 percent of municipal tax revenue in 2019 (World Observatory on Subnational Government Finance and Investment 2019).

Figure 10.2 presents the growth of the real estate tax, GDP, and apartment prices from 2014 to 2021. Over these seven years, the real estate tax levied grew by some 30 percent, while the total GDP growth was only 10 percent. The apartment price index of the whole country grew 8 percent. The growth in the real estate tax levied was mainly a result of several municipalities increasing their real estate tax rates.

Reform Initiatives and Country-Specific Issues

Between 2013 and 2015, the Ministry of Finance commissioned a series of reports on land and property valuation for taxation purposes (see Haahtela 2013; Peltola 2014; 2015). The report authors concluded that the valuation principles and the current land and building values used in taxation needed reform. Consequently, the ministry launched a reform to renew the valuation system and produce values of land and buildings more accurately reflecting the current land price and building cost levels and the local pricing differences. The existing system of separately valuing and taxing the values of the buildings and land was to be preserved. The reform was expected to increase the equity and neutrality of real estate taxation in Finland.

In 2016, the ministry began a project to revalue the land for taxation throughout the country. The NLS executed the project. The whole country was to be divided into price zones. For each property type (residential, commercial, industrial, etc.), a separate price zone map was to be produced. Additionally, the aim was to create a system with a frequent valuation cycle so that taxable land values better reflected local changes in land value.

A project to revalue buildings in Finland was also introduced by the Ministry of Finance. It started in 2017 and was implemented by Statistics Finland. The aim was to create a building-classification and -valuation system that annually produces an average building cost unit value for different building types that would be used to define the taxable building value. The valuation system accounts for the geographic location of the building, building type, age of building, and size.

Both projects were carried out as planned, but the reform itself was delayed. In September 2022, the government announced the reform was postponed and that it would not propose to Parliament legislative changes during that election cycle. As justification for the postponement, the government pointed to rapid changes in housing-related expenses (e.g., the rapid increase in energy prices in 2022) and the need to prevent other housing-related expenses (e.g., real estate taxes) from simultaneously increasing and causing economic distress for households. The draft of the new legislation on valuation of tax values is scheduled for parliamentary discussion in 2025.

Impact

There is relatively little evidence on how the real estate tax and other property-related taxes have affected land and property markets in Finland. Reasons include limited data, particularly on land markets, which in part is due to municipalities being active landowner-developers and main suppliers of building land. Also, as only a few changes and amendments of policy have taken place, establishing research settings that would allow causal inference has been difficult. Alongside research publications, several reports initiated mainly by the Ministry of Finance address some of the main deficiencies in the current real estate tax system (see Haahtela

2013; Peltola 2014; 2015). This section discusses the research on the effects of taxes and then the allocative and equity impacts of real estate taxation the commissioned reports addressed.

Lyytikäinen (2008; 2009) examines the effect of the increased tax rate for unbuilt building sites on housing construction. Municipalities that set an increased tax rate for unbuilt building sites were the treatment group, and the municipalities that remained within the two-tier taxation regime were the control group. Lyytikäinen finds that in municipalities that adopted the three-rate property tax system construction starts for single-family housing increased roughly 12 percent, but there was no effect on housing density, which Lyytikäinen interprets to be the result of binding planning regulations that limit housing density below its optimal density. Lyytikäinen (2009) notes that the municipalities' application of three-tier taxation was their decision. Hence, the findings may be endogenous to the municipalities' choice and to development decisions. In a robustness analysis, Lyytikäinen (2009) examines and rules out expansive planning policy as such a factor. Additional robustness checks confirm that the general property tax (two-tier taxation) does not affect development.

Saarimaa (2011) examines the effects of imputed rental income and its tax treatment on income distribution in Finland. He finds that imputed rental income has a major effect on homeowners' budgets, constituting almost 10 percent of their disposable income. The tax subsidy resulting from not taxing imputed rents is skewed toward high-income households. When imputed rental income is included in a household's disposable income, the overall inequality measured by the Gini index decreases. These findings suggest the nontaxation has distributive effects. However, Saarimaa observes that the net inequality effects of taxation would depend on how the increased tax revenue would be returned to households.

The effects of housing transfer taxes on household mobility in Finland are studied in a quasi-experimental setting by Eerola et al. (2021). They focus on a tax reform starting in 2013, in which the transfer tax rate of apartments was increased from 1.6 percent to 2 percent, but the transfer tax rate of real properties remained unchanged. This reform allowed a difference-in-difference approach in the analysis. As the treatment group (apartment owners) and control group (single-family homeowners) consisted of different segments in the housing markets, there may have been spillovers across segments. Eerola et al. take this into account by complementing the model with a theoretical model. Combining the two analyses, they find a 7 percent reduction in household mobility due to the tax increase.

Peltola (2014) investigates the relationship between fiscal values and market values (relative fiscal value) and the relationship between real estate taxes and their market values (effective tax rates). The results show that the fiscal values are substantially lower than market values in all Finnish municipalities. The relative fiscal values for real property varied between 20 and 50 percent; for properties held through housing companies, between 20 and 40 percent; and for properties designated for other than housing purposes, between 30 and 70 percent. Correspondingly, the effective tax rates were 0.1–0.3 percent for single-family homes, 0.08–0.2 percent for housing companies, 0.1–0.4 percent for plots designated for housing purposes, and 0.1–0.5 percent for other plots. An alarming observation regarding the horizontal equity was that the relative fiscal values and effective tax rates varied notably both between and within municipalities.

The detailed analyses by Peltola (2014) also show that the relative fiscal values and effective tax rates were notably lower in municipalities where real estate prices are higher than in municipalities with lower real estate prices. Within municipalities, the variations in relative fiscal values and effective tax rates were highest in municipalities with the highest real estate value variations. In general, the largest inaccuracies were observed in relative fiscal values and effective tax rates of housing companies. Peltola (2014) also observes that the fiscal value of land is calculated based on permitted building rights in the plan. If the building rights have been exceeded, the land values do not adjust.

Peltola's observations indicate the Finnish real estate tax system has severe challenges related to achieving horizontal equity. The system is planned to be vertically neutral, to have no progressive or regressive features. But because of the problems in real estate tax valuation, the taxation appears to have regressive features.

The need to improve the real estate tax has also been pointed out by international organizations such as the Organisation for Economic Co-operation and Development (OECD). In its 2018 economic survey for Finland (OECD 2018), the OECD recommended that Finland increase real estate taxation, because real estate tax revenue was below the OECD average. The report also suggested making the tax more progressive: the real estate tax in Finland is regressive because municipalities with higher incomes tend to set lower real estate tax rates.

The tax-like payments applied in municipal land policy, such as the land use fee, have been addressed in recent reports. Häkkänen (2020) provided a legal analysis of the land use fees, concluding that the cost recovery applied by municipalities is not open and transparent and that the fees are often based on land value increases. Land use fees do not align with the mechanism the Parliament intended to create. In particular, Häkkänen (2020) pointed out that land use fees tend to have tax-like characteristics even if they are not regulated as taxes and that their appropriateness should be evaluated also from the constitutional perspective. Falkenbach et al. (2021) broadly evaluated Finnish land policy with respect to instruments, their impacts, transparency, and fairness. Their key conclusions are that availability and accessibility of data related to land policy is poor, especially on the land use fee. The authors contended that lack of data on fees related to development of land impedes evaluations of the policy efficiency and the potential negative subsidiary effects of policies. Policy fairness evaluations are also hindered by lack of data on fees related to land development.

Conclusion

Owning, transferring, and developing real properties are subject to several taxes and charges in Finland. The state imposes the asset transfer tax, capital income and capital gains tax, and the inheritance and gift taxes, while the municipalities impose the real estate taxes. The municipalities collect fees and payments related to land and real estate development that can be considered tax-like payments. Taxes related to real estate make up only a small share of the total collected taxes in Finland, and recurrent land and property tax (real estate tax), especially, is below the OECD average.

Finland employs a three-tier real estate tax system, in which land and buildings are valued and taxed separately. The real estate tax was introduced as a two-tier system in 1993 and was amended later by introducing a third tier, a separate tax category for unbuilt building sites. The valuation system, however, has remained unchanged and most properties are assessed at well below market value levels. This results in revenue loss and in significant inequities. Criticism has focused on the real estate tax valuation principles and on the outdated valuations used in real estate taxation. The disparities in horizontal equity led to development projects to improve the valuation of land and buildings. The outcomes of these projects are yet to be applied in real estate taxation.

Maintaining a fair and neutral system in which land and structures are taxed with separate rates is by no means supported by the Finnish institutional setting, however. Municipalities supply most of the developable land, making market-based observations on land prices scarce. Therefore, providing accurate and reliable valuations of land is difficult, or even nearly impossible in some locations.

Many tax-like payments are also related to real estate. These fees are imposed by municipalities as part of their land policy. The transparency of and reporting related to these fees is not subject to regulation as taxes are, and hence there is practically no data to evaluate the incidence of these fees or their potential effects on horizontal or vertical equity.

Notes

1. In addition to the state and municipalities, the Evangelical Lutheran Church of Finland, the Orthodox Church of Finland, and the Social Insurance Institution of Finland are tax recipients. Their tax receipts do not relate to real estate and are, hence, not discussed further in this chapter.

2. Finnish Customs levies certain taxes, and the Finnish Transport Safety Agency collects the vehicle tax.

3. Full negative and positive faith and credit means that a third party can trust that the rights specified in the register exist (positive) and that there are no rights besides those specified in the land register (negative).

4. For details of different ways to apply for a title registration, see NLS (2022).

5. In addition to market data recorded and registered by authorities, commercial entities provide data on, for example, rents, prices, and cap rates. These data are typically not relied on in real estate taxation and are, hence, not in the scope of the chapter.

6. The property wealth tax was abolished in 2005. Transfers of real estate are not subject to VAT (Act on Value Added Tax para. 27, subsection 1), whereas leasing of real estate may be subject to VAT.

7. Transfer tax is deductible for all taxpayers when capital gains tax is calculated. Transfer tax is hence treated in (individual and business) taxation almost as a component of the purchase price. When firms declare depreciation on buildings in tax filings, the transfer tax affects the depreciation. For example, if you buy a building of 100 units, tax is on 4 units, and your depreciation is calculated as if the purchase price were 104 units.

8. Finland has a statutory planning system that follows a hierarchical structure in which national land use guidelines and regional land use plans steer development of legally binding local plans. Municipalities draft and approve two types of local plans, master and detailed. Typically, local detailed plans allocate building rights.

9. *Hope value* refers to the expectation of getting planning permission for land development and the resultant increase in its market value.

10. Real estate taxation in the autonomous region of Åland is defined and regulated in the Real Estate Tax Act of the Region of Åland (ÅFS 15/1993), whose principles are similar to the RETA. There are small differences in tax rates and their permitted ranges and in tax exemptions.

11. Tax refunds are paid similarly by the FTA, which later charges the municipalities.

12. Finland's public accounting standards use an accrual basis and largely conform with International Public Sector Accounting Standards. Tax revenues are recorded on cash basis in the month the revenue was transferred by FTA to the municipality.

References

Eerola, E., O. Harjunen, T. Lyytikäinen, and T. Saarimaa. 2021. "Revisiting the Effects of Housing Transfer Taxes." *Journal of Urban Economics* 124, 103367. https://doi.org/10.1016/j.jue.2021.103367.

European Commission. 2015. "Tax Reforms in EU Member States 2015: Tax Policy Challenges for Economic Growth and Fiscal Sustainability." Directorate-General for Economic and Financial Affairs. Institutional Papers 8. Brussels. (September). https://www.doi.org/10.2765/274179.

European Committee of the Regions. 2023. "Finland—Fiscal Powers." https://portal.cor.europa.eu/divisionpowers/Pages/Finland-Fiscal-Powers.aspx.

Eurostat. 2019. "Population Density by NUTS 3 Region." https://ec.europa.eu/eurostat/databrowser/view/DEMO_R_D3DENS__custom_672158/bookmark/table?lang=en&bookmarkId=48e7b1e4-7d8d-45db-8717-b7bfd36182a0.

Falkenbach, H., P. Krigsholm, T. Lönnroth, T. Puustinen, A. Ekroos, M. Häkkänen, J. Kortelainen, and M. Toivanen. 2021. "Maapolitiikan nykytila ja tulevaisuus—keinot, vaikuttavuus ja hyväksyttävyys." Valtioneuvoston selvitys- ja tutkimustoiminnan julkaisusarja. http://urn.fi/URN:ISBN:978-952-383-322-7.

Falkenbach, H., and K. Nuuja. 2007. "Flat Ownership and Registration in Europe, an Overview." Paper presented at the XXX FIG General Assembly and Working Week 2007, Hong Kong SAR China (May 13–17, 2007).

FTA (Finnish Tax Administration). 2020. "Taxes and Charges by Groups of Beneficiaries in Statistics on Income Taxation." https://vero2.stat.fi/PXWeb/pxweb/en/Vero/Vero__Henkiloasiakkaiden_tuloverot__lopulliset__verot_maksut/verot_maksut_101.px/.

———. 2021a. "Verotulojen kehitys vuonna 2021." https://www.vero.fi/tietoa-verohallinnosta/tilastot/verotulojen-kehitys/Verotulojen_kehitys_aiempina_vuosina/vuosi-2021/.

———. 2021b. "Statistics on Real Estate Taxation 2021." https://www.vero.fi/tietoa-verohallinnosta/tilastot/kiinteistoverotilastoj/kiinteistoverotus-verovuonna-2021/.

———. 2021c. "Toimintakertomus 2021—Veronsaajien oikeudenvalvontayksikkö." https://www.stat.fi/til/vermak/2021/vermak_2021_2022-03-15_fi.pdf.

———. 2022a. "Implementation Measures on Real Estate Tax Act, dated 7.3.2022." Diary number VH/849/00.01.00/2022. https://www.vero.fi/syventavat-vero-ohjeet/ohje-hakusivu/48453/kiinteist%C3%B6verolain-soveltamisohje4/.

———. 2022b. "Guidance on Requesting a Payment Arrangement." https://www.vero.fi/en/individuals/payments/financial-difficulties/payment-arrangement/.

———. 2022c. "Myöhässä maksetuista veroista kertyi viime vuonna 7 miljoonaa euroa korkoja—Verohallinto suosittelee e-laskun tilaamista." News Release. https://www.vero.fi/tietoa-verohallinnosta/uutishuone/lehdist%C3%B6tiedotteet/2022/myohassa-maksetuista-veroista-kertyi-viime-vuonna-7-miljoonaa-euroa-korkoja/.

———. 2023a. "Verohallinto löysi viime vuonna ilmoittamattomia veroja 534 miljoonaa euroa." News Release. https://www.vero.fi/tietoa-verohallinnosta/uutishuone/lehdist%C3%B6tiedotteet/2023/verohallinto-l%C3%B6ysi-viime-vuonna-ilmoittamattomia-veroja-534-miljoonaa-euroa/.

———. 2023b. "Suomalaiset saivat kaksi miljardia euroa vuokratuloa vuonna 2021—tietojen ilmoittaminen veroilmoituksella vuodelta 2022 on ajankohtaista nyt." News Release. https://www.vero.fi/tietoa-verohallinnosta/uutishuone/lehdist%C3%B6tiedotteet/2023/suomalaiset-saivat-kaksi-miljardia-euroa-vuokratuloa-vuonna-2021--tietojen-ilmoittaminen-veroilmoituksella-vuodelta-2022-on-ajankohtaista-nyt/.

———. 2023c. "Päivittyvä tilastokatsaus veroveloista ja maksuvaikeuksista." https://vero.fi/tietoa-verohallinnosta/tilastot/verovelat-ja-maksuvaikeudet/paivittyva-tilastokatsaus/.

———. 2023d. "Kiinteistöveroja ja mätkyjä rästissä yli 147 miljoonalla eurolla—oikeat maksutiedot löytyvät OmaVerosta." News Release. https://www.vero.fi/tietoa-verohallinnosta/uutishuone/lehdist%C3%B6tiedotteet/2022/kiinteistoveroja-ja-matkyja-rastissa-yli-147-miljoonalla-eurolla--oikeat-maksutiedot-loytyvat-omaverosta/.

Haahtela, Y. 2013. "Kiinteistöjen käyvän hinnan määrittäminen kiinteistöverotusta varten." Haahtela-kehitys Oy. https://tinyurl.com/yrvz97ad.

Häkkänen, M. 2020. "Maankäyttömaksut ja kehittämiskorvaukset: Oikeudellinen selvitys maankäyttösopimuksia koskevista käytänteistä." Ympäristöministeriön julkaisuja. http://urn.fi/URN:ISBN:978-952-361-044-6.

Hyvönen, V. O. 1982. *Kiinteistöjärjestelmä ja kiinteistönmuodostamisoikeus*. Espoo, Finland: Ky Veikko O. Hyvönen.

Krigsholm, P., T. Puustinen, and H. Falkenbach. 2022. "Understanding Variation in Municipal Land Policy Strategies: An Empirical Typology." *Cities* 126: 103710.

Krigsholm, P., S. Zavialova, K. Riekkinen, P. Ståhle, K. Viitanen. 2017. "Understanding the Future of the Finnish Cadastral System: A Delphi Study." *Land Use Policy* 68: 133–140. https://doi.org/10.1016/j.landusepol.2017.07.032.

Lyytikäinen, T. 2008. "Studies on the Effects of Property Taxation, Rent Control and Housing Allowances." VATT research report 140. https://helda.helsinki.fi/server/api/core/bitstreams/ee185634-b4fd-4f07-af05-d0c99920c76e/content.

———. 2009. "Three-Rate Property Taxation and Housing Construction." *Journal of Urban Economics* 65(3): 305–313.

Niukkanen, K. 2014. "On the Property Rights in Finland—the Point of View of Legal Cadastral Domain Model." PhD. diss., Aalto University, Department of Real Estate, Planning and Geoinformatics. Doctoral Dissertations 163/2014.

NLS (National Land Survey). 2022. "Register Your Ownership of a Property by Applying for a Title Registration." https://www.maanmittauslaitos.fi/en/real-property/property-owners/register-your-ownership-property.

OECD (Organisation for Economic Co-operation and Development). 2018. "OECD Economic Surveys: Finland 2018." Paris: OECD. https://doi.org/10.1787/eco_surveys-fin-2018-en.

———. 2019. "Introducing a Commercial Off-the-Shelf Software Solution." Paris: OECD. https://www.oecd.org/en/publications/introducing-a-commercial-off-the-shelf-software-solution_c330fe12-en.html.

———. n.d. "OECD Fiscal Decentralisation Database." Accessed May 19, 2023. https://www.oecd.org/tax/federalism/fiscal-decentralisation-database/.

Peltola, R. 2014. "Kiinteistöjen arvostamisperusteiden kehittämistarve kiinteistöverotuksessa." Valtiovarainministeriö, helmikuu 2014. https://vm.fi/documents/10623/4524211/Kiinteist%C3%B6jen+arvostamisperusteiden+kehitt%C3%A4mistarve+kiinteist%C3%B6verotuksessa.PDF/.

———. 2015. "Maapohjien aluehintojen arviointimenetelmän kehittäminen kiinteistöverotuksessa. Valtioneuvoston selvitys- ja tutkimustoiminnan julkaisusarja 18/2015." http://urn.fi/URN:ISBN:978-952-287-201-2.

Puustinen, T. L. M., and K. J. Viitanen. 2015. "Infill Development on Collectively Owned Residential Properties: Understanding the Decision-Making Process—Case Studies in Helsinki." *Housing, Theory and Society* 32(4): 472–498.

Riekkinen, K., O. Penkkilä, P. Krigsholm, A. Ekroos, and M. Häkkänen. 2022. "Huoltovarmuuden turvaaminen osana kiinteistöomaisuuden valvontaa." Valtioneuvoston selvitys- ja tutkimustoiminnan julkaisusarja 2021:49. https://tietokayttoon.fi/julkaisut/raportti?pubid=URN:ISBN:978-952-383-134-6.

Saarimaa, T. 2011. "Imputed Rental Income, Taxation and Income Distribution in Finland." *Urban Studies* 48(8): 1695–1714.

Statistics Finland. 2021. "Population According to Urban-Rural Classification by Age and Sex, 2000–2021." https://pxdata.stat.fi/PxWeb/pxweb/fi/StatFin/StatFin__vaerak/statfin_vaerak_pxt_11s3.px/.

———. 2022a. "Stat.fi: Statistics on Dwellings and Housing Conditions." https://stat.fi/en/statistics/asas.

———. 2022b. "Verot ja veronluonteiset maksut 2021." https://www.stat.fi/til/vermak/2021/vermak_2021_2022-03-15_fi.pdf.

———. 2023a. "Finland in Figures—National Economy." https://www.tilastokeskus.fi/tup/suoluk/suoluk_kansantalous.html#bruttokansantuotteen-volyymin-vuosimuutos.

———. 2023b. "Prices of Dwellings in Housing Companies." Helsinki: Statistics Finland. https://stat.fi/en/statistics/ashi.

Suomen ympäristökeskus. n.d. "The Finnish Urban-Rural Classification." Accessed October 20, 2022. https://ckan.ymparisto.fi/dataset/kaupunki-maaseutu-luokitus-ykr.

Valtonen, E., H. Falkenbach, and E. Van der Krabben. 2017. "Risk Management in Public Land Development Projects: Comparative Case Study in Finland, and the Netherlands." *Land Use Policy* 62: 246–257.

Valtonen, E., H. Falkenbach, and K. Viitanen. 2018. "Securing Public Objectives in Large-Scale Urban Development: Comparison of Public and Private Land Development." *Land Use Policy* 78: 481–492.

Vitikainen, A. 2013. *Kiinteistöjärjestelmä ja perusrekisterit*. Helsinki: Aalto University.

World Bank. n.d. "World Bank Open Data: GDP per Capita (current US$)." Accessed January 20, 2025. https://data.worldbank.org/indicator/NY.GDP.PCAP.CD?view=chart.

World Observatory on Subnational Government Finance and Investment. 2019. "Country and Territory Profiles: Finland." https://www.sng-wofi.org/country_profiles/finland.html.

Legislation

Act on Surtax and Penalty Interest in Arrears (Laki veronlisäyksestä ja viivekorosta 1556/1995).

Act on Tax Collection (Veronkantolaki 11/2018).

Act on the Valuation of Assets in Taxation (Laki varojen arvostamisesta verotuksessa 1142/2005).

Act on Transfer Tax (Varainsiirtoverolaki 931/1996).

Act on Value Added Tax (Arvonlisäverolaki 1501/1993).

Criminal Code (Rikoslaki 39/1889).

Decree of the Ministry of Finance on the Determination of Replacement Value of Buildings (Valtiovarainministeriön asetus rakennusten jälleenhankinta-arvon perusteista, 29.12.2024/681).

Government Bill 100/1999 for the Amendment of Real Estate Tax Act (Hallituksen esitys kiinteistöverolaiksi, HE 100/1999 vp).

Government Bill 39/2023 for the Amendment of Real Estate Tax Act (Hallituksen esitys kiinteistöverolaiksi, HE 39/2023 vp).

Government Bill 50/1992 on Real Estate Tax Act (Hallituksen esitys Eduskunnalle kiinteistöverolaiksi sekä siihen liittyväksi lainsäädännöksi, HE 50/1993 vp).

Income Tax Law (Tuloverolaki 1535/1992).

Inheritance and Gift Act (Perintö- ja lahjaverolaki 378/1940).

Interest Act (Korkolaki 633/1982).

Land Tenancy Act (Maanvuokralaki 258/1966).

Land Use and Building Act (Maankäyttö- ja rakennuslaki 132/1999).

Limited Liability Housing Companies Act (Asunto-osakeyhtiölaki 1599/2009).

Nature Conservation Act (Luonnonsuojelulaki 9/2023).

Real Estate Tax Act (Kiinteistöverolaki 654/1992).

Real Estate Tax Act of the Region of Åland (ÅFS 15/1993)

Tax Assessment Procedure Act (Verotusmenettelylaki 1558/1995).

Water Services Act (Vesihuoltolaki 119/2001).

11

Property-Related Taxes: The French Case

GUILLAUME CHAPELLE, GUY GILBERT, ALAIN TRANNOY, AND ETIENNE WASMER

France is the second-largest European economy (17 percent of European Union gross domestic product, GDP), after Germany (25 percent), in continental Europe. The GDP per capita in 2024 was €42,600, and France ranks 22nd in the world. France is not as densely populated (120 people per square kilometer) as other European countries, mainly due to having the largest area (543,000 square kilometers). Its 68.6 million people are fairly evenly distributed across the country, but Paris, the most populous metropolitan area in continental Europe (13 million), holds one-fifth of the population. Population also concentrates on the Mediterranean coast and in a few large cities, such as Lyon, Marseille, Lille, Toulouse, and Bordeaux.

France's ranking regarding household wealth is favorable: it placed 16th in the world for wealth per capita at US$312,000 in 2022 (UBS 2023) and 6th in the European Union. Among the explanatory factors are a high savings rate (15 percent) and a preference for investment in real estate, which accounts for 70 percent of household wealth. The portfolio share invested in financial assets is 15 points lower in France than in the United Kingdom (Crédit Suisse 2022), and comparison with other European countries points in the same direction (Trannoy and Wasmer 2022). National net worth is the sum of physical assets and financial assets. However, the net position of the country in terms of financial assets is marginal; foreign financial assets held by domestic agents approximatively equal French financial assets held by foreign agents, so that most wealth comes from physical assets. Among those, the total land value in 2023 amounted to €8 trillion, three times the GDP and almost half the French net worth. Urban land accounts for 84 percent of total land value; roughly speaking, the price of developed land is 17 times that of undeveloped land. Structures and infrastructure come in second, accounting for 40 percent of French net worth. Other physical assets such as machinery and patents represent only a marginal share, about 1/10th. At the same time, the figures for tax burden and public spending are also among the highest in the world, challenging Denmark's crown for these features. All taxes and mandatory contributions are around 45 percent of GDP, and the corresponding figure for public expenditures is about 50 percent. The budget has not been balanced since the 1980s, adding to a public debt that amounts to 114 percent of GDP.

In France, 57 percent of households are owners of real property, and this ratio has not changed since the beginning of the millennium. A study of real estate assets (André and Meslin 2021) shows that a quarter of French households own several dwellings and that two-thirds of the housing stock is held by individuals. However, the degree of concentration of the housing stock varies according to the use of the units. Ownership of rental units is much more concentrated than ownership of primary and secondary homes, and the concentration of ownership is greatest in the central areas of major cities.

Property taxation is fragmented in France. The power to tax property—inherited from the Physiocratic school and taken over by the Revolution—is granted to local authorities. For 150 years there were only two layers of local government, but in the last 40 years or so, two more layers have been added. Therefore, it is necessary to take a detour to present this institutional stacking to understand the fragmentation from which property taxation in France suffers.

France has a four-tier system of local governments (figure 11.1). The base is composed of 35,000 municipalities (communes) that evolved from the medieval parishes. The large number relates to France's physical area. Moreover, France was, for a long time, the most populated country in Europe because the soil of France was and still is fertile (wheat and vineyards). Given that 25,000 municipalities each have less than 1,000 inhabitants, the central government encouraged mergers over the years but with limited success: the number of communes today is only 10 percent less than the number of communes in the 1960s.

A second local-government level with responsibility for coordination and service delivery is the intermunicipal cooperation body (*intercommunalités*). It was created as a response to the large number of smaller municipalities. Today, each municipality belongs to an intermunicipal

Figure 11.1 Subnational Government in France, 2020

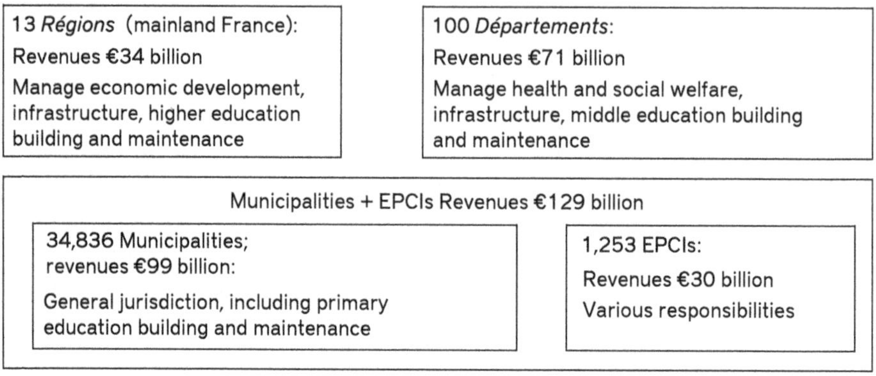

Note: There are no hierarchical relations between the layers of government.

cooperation public body (*établissement public de coopération intercommunale*, EPCI). The map of the 1,253 EPCIs was stabilized with the NOTRe Act (2015).[1] EPCIs can raise rates and their members are now directly elected by the citizens in each municipality in the EPCI area. The need for and scope of cooperation can differ depending on whether the various municipalities belong to a rural or metropolitan area. There are four different kinds of EPCIs to cope with this heterogeneity of situations. The more integrated form of EPCI, the metropole, is tailored to correspond to France's 22 biggest cities. At the top of the pyramid, the metropoles of Grand Paris, Lyon, and Marseille have been granted a special status; in them, cooperation is very high in Lyon, low in Paris, and dysfunctional in Marseille. The picture will be incomplete if we do not mention that there is another, older form of intercommunal cooperation, the intermunicipality union (*syndicat intercommunal*), that has existed since the end of the 19th century to manage public services or activities that go beyond the territorial limits of the communes (water, sanitation, electricity, transport, etc.). These unions cannot levy taxes, and the EPCIs have progressively replaced them.

The municipality may intervene in any area not assigned by law to another level of government. That said, in an intermunicipal setting, public transportation, networks, household waste collection, and economic action are compulsory responsibilities of the intermunicipalities, while the municipal council handles pre-elementary and elementary school maintenance and management, school canteens, housing and building permits, and environmental matters. Urban planning is shared between the two municipal and intermunicipal layers.

The municipal bloc (*bloc communal*), referring to the group formed by the commune and the EPCI, is markedly different from the other two forms of local governments, departments and regions, which are tailored more to public needs from a regional perspective.

The third layer in the administrative structure, created during the French Revolution, is the department (*département*). In each of the 100 departments, deconcentrated units of line ministries coexist within a prefecture with an elected local-government council, which makes the department a unique blend of deconcentration and decentralization. The territorial sizes of the departments are similar, but they are heterogeneous regarding population and wealth. Their responsibilities are mainly in social benefits distribution (children, disabled and dependent people, basic income management), infrastructure (ports, airfields, departmental roads), construction maintenance, and management of junior high schools.

The fourth layer of local government, the region, is the most recent in the landscape of French fiscal federalism. Regions became locally elected authorities with the Decentralization Act of 1982. Five regions are overseas. Each of the 13 regions in mainland France includes an average of 10 departments around a metropole. The goal was that they would become equivalent to German länder (federal states) in size and economic power. At this stage, that goal remains wishful thinking, even though their economic and political power has been growing over time. While departments are mainly local authorities dedicated to managing the welfare state within its boundaries, the regions act primarily on economic matters. They are mainly responsible for economic development, regional planning, intercity transport, construction, maintenance, and management of high schools.

The EPCI and the regional layers of local government are financed by local taxes plus subsidies and shares of national taxes. Altogether, the four layers of local government represent 70 percent of the total public investment in France. But because of their limited financing capacity, they have frequently benefited from national and sometimes European assistance (see Gilbert and Thoenig 1999). This complex system guarantees that the spillover effects of local public goods are correctly internalized. The price to pay is the fixed cost of each structure and the time cost needed to find agreement among them. Lengthy negotiations and more administrative red tape are the downsides of a fair and efficient procedure to allocate the cost of local public goods.

Regarding the tax side, the total tax revenues in 2019 benefiting all local governments add up to €145 billion, 6 percent of the GDP or 13 percent of the total compulsory levies, putting France in a median position in the Organisation for Economic Co-operation and Development (OECD) countries, according to Carbonnier (2019). The two oldest levels of local

Table 11.1 Taxes, Transfers, and Other Revenues of Local Governments (€ billion)

	2018	2019	2020	2021
Taxes	140.90	145.43	143.52	149.18
Local taxes	116.17	117.37	112.57	98.26
Shared taxes	24.73	28.06	30.96	50.92
Transfer from central government	51.07	52.96	53.54	56.39
Other revenues	33.45	34.14	31.51	34.20
Total revenues (except borrowing)	225.42	232.53	228.58	239.77

Source: DGCL (2022).

government, municipalities and departments, receive larger pieces of the tax cake, about 30 percent each. The EPCIs account for about 25 percent and the regions for about 16 percent.

The share of local taxes in local-government revenues declined since 2018 (a drop of 10 points, from 51 percent to 41 percent) in favor of shared taxes and transfers from the central government. The abolition of the housing tax by the parliament in 2017–2018 mostly explains this. The taxing power of local governments has decreased, and it is unlikely that they will regain it in the near future.

Part of the taxes is a share of national taxes, or more precisely, a share of the proceeds of national taxes, because local governments do not set the tax rate, and essentially the same is true at the regional level. These taxes represent about €50 billion of receipts (Table 11.1), and their share is growing over time because two local taxes are gradually being removed, the housing tax (*taxe d'habitation*) and a local value-added tax (VAT) raised on firms (*cotisation à la valeur ajoutée par l'entreprise*), and replaced by shares of the national VAT for local governments.

Taxes decided at a local level finance the other three local-government levels. Table 11.2 (pp. 326–327) breaks down local tax revenues in two categories. The first is taxes calculated by area in square meters, rent value, or property value. We refer to these as property taxes and assimilated taxes. The second category is local taxes imposed on bases other than real property. Table 11.2 shows the current dynamics of revenues from these two groups of taxes. We put the now-abolished housing tax, except for second homes, in the second group because tenants used to pay it. The property tax group is clearly on the rise, mainly because property transfer tax revenues have doubled since 2014, fueled by both the housing price increase (30 percent more) and the rise in housing transactions, which increased by half. Whereas the local tax resources of the departments largely

Figure 11.2 Local-Government Share of Total Government Expenditures, 1978–2020

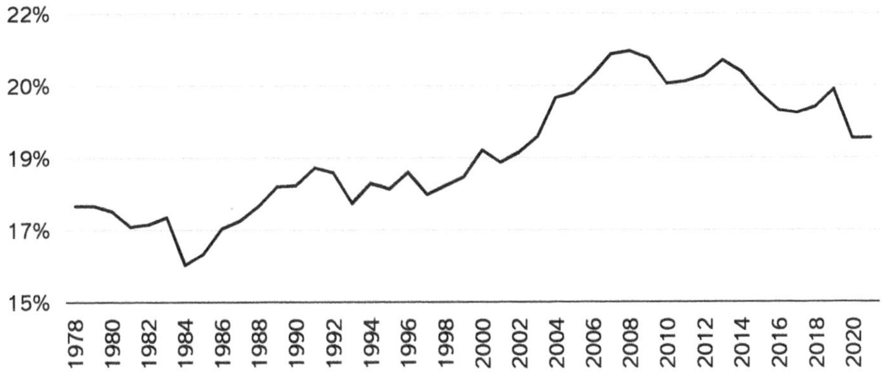

Source: DGCL (2022).

come from the transfer tax, the municipal bloc (the commune and EPCI) benefits from the other, less dynamic tax bases, which are, in a way, a degraded form of a property tax. The principle of tax specialization (each tax benefits one and only one level) across various tiers of local government is increasingly respected in France. Comparing the total property and transfer tax liabilities with private real estate wealth yields an implicit tax rate of about 0.6 percent (€75 billion versus €13 trillion). This figure barely changes when taking into account property taxes to the benefit of the central government—the real estate wealth tax and the capital gains tax, which is a component of the income tax. The amount of tax revenues is comparatively small, about €4 billion.

In total, the expenditure share of local governments represents about one-fifth of government public expenditures. That share was on the rise up until the 2008–2009 financial crisis and then began trending down. Interestingly, this trend remains regardless of the political color of the party in power in Paris (figure 11.2).

Land and Property Markets

Full ownership, tenancy, and sharecropping are the three forms of agricultural land tenure. Tenancy and ownership are the two possible types of land rights in urban areas. The separate ownership of land and structures is not allowed except when buying an apartment from a social housing unit. This is still at an experimental phase through solidarity land offices (*offices fonciers solidaires*). The full ownership of a property may be

Table 11.2 Local Tax Revenues, 2014–2021

	2014 (€ million)	2015 (€ million)	2016 (€ million)	2017 (€ million)	2018 (€ million)	2019 (€ million)	2020 (€ million)	2021 (€ million)	% Change
Property Taxes and Assimilated Taxes									
Property tax	29,312	30,429	31,940	32,723	33,628	34,526	35,264	34,298	117
Property tax on undeveloped land	1,014	1,040	1,046	1,054	1,067	1,092	1,106	1,116	110
Housing tax on second or vacant homes[1]	59	60	69	64	71	75	84	2,841	
Refuse collection tax	6,356	6,553	6,688	6,792	6,924	7,012	7,137	7,432	117
Rent tax on business real-estate	6,974	7,234	7,426	7,663	7,954	8,006	8,265	6,853	98
Stamp duty tax	9,856	11,223	12,167	14,145	14,861	16,363	16,047	19,975	203
Tax on retail space	712	737	753	942	774	791	799	794	112
Development tax	633	1,145	1,287	1,492	1,716	1,784	1,693	857	135
Additional property tax	0	81	87	105	234	270	284	352	
Tax on office space	183	183	183	213	213	213	213	213	116
Total	55,099	58,685	61,645	65,192	67,442	70,132	70,891	74,731	136

Other Local Taxes									
Other local taxes except housing tax	28,505	29,644	30,444	31,754	32,142	33,555	31,626	22,198	78
Housing tax	17,256	17,894	18,164	18,640	16,590	13,682	10,048	1,334	
Total	45,760	47,539	48,608	50,394	48,732	47,237	41,675	23,533	51
Total local taxes (property and assimilated taxes + other local taxes)	100,859	106,224	110,253	115,586	116,174	117,369	112,566	98,263	97

Sources: DGCL (2022, table 5.1); authors' computations.

[1] For 2014–2020, the amounts are for vacant homes only. For 2021, the amount includes an estimate for second homes only, but it is likely high.

divided into two distinct parts: the bare ownership and the usufruct, or the right of use.

Foreigners have no restrictions when buying properties except for agricultural land. Indeed, stringent limits have been introduced for a nonfarmer buying agricultural land. Two mechanisms limit market forces and transactions. French farmers receive priority, and the SAFERs (Sociétés d'aménagement foncier et d'établissement rural) regulate farming land transactions. A limit to ownership right in cities is that the owner of a property in an urban development zone must give the municipality the first chance to make an offer, or the preemptive right (*droit de preemption*) of the public authority. Some big cities have extended this right in land purchases to cap developed land price increases.

Notary services are compulsory for registering donation or sale of real estate (apartment, house, land) but not for a rental transaction. The land registry service (*service de la publicité foncière*), part of the Ministry of Finance, advertises property sales or transfers. The notary for the transaction sends an online copy of the deed to the land registry service for recording, required for any transfer, donation, inheritance, or subdivision of property (between bare property and usufruct). The notary collects the property transfer tax and receives a fixed fee between €1,200 and €1,400 plus 0.8 percent of the transaction price (beyond a transaction of €60,000). Anyone may request information on a property and obtain the identity of the successive owners, the prices of the different sales, and a copy of the real estate sale documents.

The land register (cadastre) covers the whole of France.[2] Digitization started early in the 21st century, so that by 2022 some 34,700 municipalities out of the 35,000 shared an online cadastre. There are 52 million properties registered in the cadastre: 20 million houses, 17 million apartments, 12 million outbuildings, and 3 million industrial and commercial premises. Public entities own a little more than a quarter and individuals own the remainder. About 6 million properties belong to the public sector (social housing plus public bodies).

The entire market (transactions, prices, and property characteristics) is contained in five databases. The first is the cadastre. For the second, a branch of administration, Services de la Publicité Foncière (Directory of Land Advertising Services), receives a copy of each transaction. The third is the Demande de Valeurs Foncières (DVF, Requests for Land Values) of the tax authority (Direction Générale des Finances Publiques), which lists all the property transfers registered by the Services de la Publicité Foncière. The database is free but difficult to use. Fourth, Cerema (an applied research center under the Ministry of Housing) has combined the DVF data with additional land data for more detailed analyses. Fifth, notaries have their own dataset, PERVAL, which can be accessed after paying a significant fee.

Most economists and experts agree the quality of the data on transaction prices is good and underdeclaration of transaction prices is limited, but there is a lack of research studies or fiscal authorities' reports. Evasion of the transaction tax is low. Several features of the French system may contribute to limiting tax evasion. First, the notary fee is proportional to the transaction price. Second, if the declared value is perceived to be too low with respect to the market price, the tax authorities may interrupt the transaction process within two months of the agreement between the seller and the buyer and exert a preemptive right. The state or local authority can then buy the property at the declared transaction price, in lieu of the private buyer. Third, the tax authorities can also claim from the buyer the payment of transfer taxes on the true market value and a fine. The incentive device of the whole tax system also plays a role. Buyers who underdeclare pay less stamp duty tax (sum of transfer tax and notary and registration fees, 7–8 percent of the transaction price) but pay more capital gains tax in the future.

A collaboration of the French statistical institute (INSEE) and the organization Notaires de France (French Notaries) developed a reliable housing price index (indice Notaire-INSEE). INSEE developed a methodology based on hedonic regression techniques for residential property, and Notaires de France gathered transaction data. Unfortunately, the equivalent does not exist for commercial property, but a network of academics, consultants, and firms in this market are making progress in this regard. The SAFER group lists on its website (https://www.safer.fr/) the average price of agricultural land in small homogeneous distinctive zones.

Table 11.3 depicts the tax revenues per region generated by the transfer tax. It shows a contrast between, on one hand, the Paris and Provence regions with their high tax revenues per inhabitant (in Provence, the result of high market prices combined with many second homes) and, on the other, the regions surrounding the Paris region (Île-de-France) with their low tax receipts. Brittany, the Atlantic coast, and the Toulouse and Lyon regions are in-between.

Real Estate Taxes

Property and real estate taxes represent a relatively modest share of national taxes. According to our estimates, the total amount of real estate and property taxes represented 4.66 percent of the French GDP in 2019, of which a significant share is borne by housing (see tables 11.1 and 11.2).

This section provides summary statistics on real estate and property taxes at the national and subnational levels in France and details real estate taxes—that is, taxes on transactions and real estate consumption.

Table 11.3 Transfer Tax Revenues by Region, 2021

Region	Transfer Tax Revenues (€ million)	Population in 2020 (million)	Transfer Tax per Capita (€)	Share in Total (%)
North of France	1,175.0	5.998	195.9	5.8
Île-de-France (Paris region)	5,220.6	12.272	425.4	25.7
Normandy	792.3	3.326	238.3	3.9
East of France	1,031.0	5.563	185.3	5.1
Burgundy	546.9	2.802	195.2	2.7
Centre	561.6	2.575	218.1	2.8
Brittany	973.5	3.374	288.5	4.8
Loire	1,110.5	3.832	289.8	5.5
Aquitaine	1,959.7	6.034	324.8	9.6
Languedoc	1,720.6	5.974	288.0	8.5
Rhone-Alpes (Lyon region)	2,421.1	8.079	299.7	11.9
Provence–Côte D'Azur	2,496.8	5.099	489.7	1.3
Corsica	122.8	344	357.4	0.6
Overseas	204.8	2.203	93.0	1.0
Total for France	20,337.3	67.472	301.4	

Sources: DGFiP (2022); authors' computation.

The next section goes deeper into recurrent land and property taxes. We begin with the national level before turning to subnational taxes.

National Taxes

Real estate taxes that benefit only the national government are a relatively small share of total real estate and property taxes. The taxes shared between the subnational and national levels are detailed later, because the majority of tax receipts go to subnational governments.

Rental income is taxed in two ways: by income tax and through social security contributions.

Rental Income Taxed According to the Income Tax

Principles, Rates, and Tax Base

Physical landlords of real estate properties are subject to a tax on rental income taxed according to the income tax (*imposition des revenus fonciers à l'impôt sur le revenu*). The income tax is progressive; the lowest marginal tax rate is 0 percent and the highest is 45 percent. For 2019, we estimate that about 2.27 percent of the tax base of the income tax is the net rent (real estate deficit subtracted from real estate income). This does not include the rent of furnished dwellings, which represent an increasing share of rental properties. Taxpayers are required to declare the total yearly amount of rent received. The tax base declared can vary because taxpayers may choose between two different regimes. In the most common tax regime (*régime micro-foncier*), the tax base is 70 percent of the gross rental income. Taxpayers who opt out of this tax regime can itemize extra expenditures such as interest payments, local property taxes, insurance, or refurbishments. The tax base is then the net rental income after removing these expenditures. When these itemized expenditures are more than rents, this real estate deficit can be reported from one year to the next.

Special exemptions

Fiscal devices and tax rebates exist for some specific rental investments.

- Furnished rental dwellings: Furnished rentals can benefit from a different taxation regime. The rental income is declared not as real estate income but as industrial and commercial benefits. The tax base is 50 percent of the rental income and is not subject to social security contributions (see later discussion).
- Tax credits for rental investments: Households subject to the income tax can benefit from the Pinel-Denormandie tax rebate when investing in recently built or significantly refurbished rental properties. To receive the tax credit landlords commit to rent dwellings under an income ceiling that remains relatively high and under a rent cap per square meter for at least six years.
- Student rentals and retirement homes: Investments in student rentals or retirement homes can benefit from a tax rebate similar to the Pinel-Denormandie rebate but having no specific restriction on the location of the dwelling and the rent levels. Otherwise, they benefit from the same tax regime as furnished rental dwellings.

Incidence

No specific study on the impact of the income tax on real estate markets has been done, and it is difficult to estimate whether it affects rents or housing prices. Literature is growing, however, on the impact of tax rebates to promote rental investments in new dwellings. These studies consider a previous but very similar scheme and find that these rebates increased land (Bono and Trannoy 2019) and housing prices without stimulating new construction (Chapelle, Vignolles, and Wolf

2018). Moreover, they find that the tax credit increased the share of rental properties in new dwellings at the expense of homeownership, while the social composition of tenants did not change, because income ceilings were not binding. Overall, these studies suggest that the supply of developable land remains relatively inelastic, resulting in a large capitalization of tax credits into land and housing prices.

Suggested reforms

A report from the Council of Economic Advisors to the French prime minister (Artus, Bozio, and García-Peñalosa 2013) suggests reestablishing taxation of imputed rents, or the rent saved by homeowners. This reform, however, seems to generate a strong political opposition and remains unlikely. Chapelle, Fabre, and Lallemand (2020) suggest replacing the tax credits with a lower VAT to reduce their capitalization in land value.

Social Security Contributions

Principles, rates, and tax base

As for income tax, physical landlords are also subject to social security contributions (*imposition des revenus fonciers aux prélèvements sociaux*) composed of three components resulting in a tax rate of 17.2 percent. The tax base is the same as for the income tax: either 70 percent of the rent paid by the tenant or the net rent after deduction of all extra expenditures.

Special exemptions

All rental incomes are subject to social security contributions. If rental income exceeds €23,000 and represents the most important source of income of physical taxpayers, it can be subject to the regime of social security contributions of firms, resulting in different rates.

Capital Gains Tax

Capital gains are also taxed (*imposition des plus-values foncières*) in two ways: by the mean of income tax and by social security contributions. Social security contributions represent 17.2 percent of the final tax base.

Principles, rates, and tax base for the income tax

Capital gains are subject to the income tax and social security contributions. The tax base is the difference between the current transaction price and the last one (or the estimated value at the moment of the transaction). Some expenditures can be deducted from these capital gains, such as the amount of transfer taxes paid (either 7.5 percent of the initial price or the exact amount if higher). Refurbishments of a

Table 11.4 Rebates for Capital Gains Taxation

Years Held	Additional Yearly Tax Rebate as % of Capital Gain–Income Tax	Additional Yearly Tax Rebate as % of Capital Gain–Social Contributions
6–21 years	6	1.65
22nd year	4	1.6
>22 years	0	9
>30 years	0	0

Source: République Française (2025a).

property owned for more than five years automatically reduce the tax base representing 15 percent of the initial price, and the tax base is reduced by a yearly tax rebate (table 11.4). For example, if the real estate asset has been owned for 15 years, the tax base is only 46 percent[3] of the net capital gains for income taxation and 85.15 percent for social security contributions. After 30 years of ownership, capital gains are thus exempt from income tax and social security contributions.

The rate of income taxation is 19 percent. When the capital gain is above €50,000, an additional capital gains tax ranging from 2 to 6 percent can be applied to the capital gain (table 11.5), as described later.

Special exemptions

The main residence of taxpayers is exempted from capital gains taxation. Moreover, if taxpayers use the money from the sale to buy a main residence within two years or if they have not owned a main residence for more than four years, capital gains are also tax exempt. Transactions below €15,000 or dwellings sold to social housing organizations are exempt, as are sellers who are not French fiscal residents. Sellers with an income below €11,276 and who receive a pension, reside in a retirement home, or have certain physical disabilities may be exempt.

Annual Contribution on Rental Income

Principles, rates, and tax base

Firms and not-for-profit organizations that are owners of residential or commercial units and receive a rental income are subject to the annual contribution on rental income (*contribution annuelle sur les revenus fonciers*) if these incomes are above €1,830, but not if they are subject to the VAT and not if the units are older than 15 years. Their tax rate is 2.5 percent.

Table 11.5 Additional Capital Gains Tax

Capital Gain (CG) Range (€)	Additional Tax
50,00–60,000	2% CG – (60,000 – CG) × 5%
60,00–100,000	2% CG
100,001–110,000	3% CG – (110,000 – CG) × 10%
110,001–150,000	3% CG
150,001–160,000	4% CG – (160,000 – CG) × 15%
160,001–200,000	4% CG
200,001–210,000	5% CG – (210,000 – CG) × 20%
210,001–250,000	5% CG
250,001–260,000	6% CG – (260,000 – CG) × 25%
>260,000	6% CG

Source: République Française (2025a).

Exemptions

In practice, relatively few units are subject to this tax because many sectors—social housing, vacant land, retirement homes, or public buildings—benefit from tax exemptions.

Real Estate Wealth Tax

Principles, rates, and tax base

In 2018, the wealth tax (*impôt sur la fortune*) was replaced by a real estate wealth tax (*impôt sur la fortune immobilière*). This is a progressive tax on the value of real estate wealth when the tax base exceeds €1.3 million. The tax base is the total net real estate wealth, which includes 70 percent of the estimated market value of the main residence and the market value of all other real estate assets including the share of companies owning real estate. The tax base is net of outstanding debts contracted for the purchase or maintenance of these assets. The market value is estimated by the taxpayer and declared annually to the fiscal administration. The taxpayer fills out a form reporting all assets with certain characteristics (shares in real estate companies, location of the property, area, number of rooms, purchase price, and estimated value). To aid tax payers in estimating the value of their property, the tax administration provides the research tool Patrim, which allows taxpayers to obtain recent purchase prices of transactions near their property. This data is collected by notaries and transmitted to the tax administration.

According to a Cour des Comptes (the national audit office) report (2022a), the national tax administration exerts little control on the

Table 11.6 Real Estate Property Wealth Tax

Net Real Estate Wealth (€)	Marginal Tax Rates (%)
0–800,000	0
800,001–1,300,000	0.50
1,300,001–2,570,000	0.70
2,570,001–5,000,000	1.00
5,000,001–10,000,000	1.25
>10,000,000	1.50

Source: Adapted from République Française (2025b).

self-declared values (real estate wealth and inheritance taxes) except in special cases (for example, a large gap between self-declared property values and self-declared income). Explanations for this lack of oversight are the complexity of inspection, which is said to be time consuming; the scarcity of human and information technology resources of the national tax services; and the low priority set on regulating these taxes because of the expected tax revenue impact. Garbinti et al. (2023) question the accuracy of the information transmitted by the taxpayer to the tax authorities. They provide causal empirical evidence that a 2011 reform allowing households with less than €2.5 billion to report only a gross estimate of their wealth without many details led taxpayers to underreport their wealth. The data did not allow the study authors to find specific results regarding the reporting of taxpayers' property value.

The tax rate ranges from 0.5 to 1.5 percent (table 11.6). A notch at the €1.3 million tax threshold implies that taxpayers pay nothing if they declare €1.299 million and €1,250 if they declare €1.3 million. This violates a principle of horizontal equity. In 2021, 150,000 households paid real estate wealth tax (DGFiP 2022).

Special exemptions and tax shelter

Commercial real estate assets and real estate used by firms in the production process are excluded from the tax base. Moreover, French fiscal residents can benefit from a tax shelter because the amount of real estate wealth tax cannot exceed 75 percent of their total worldwide revenues. Finally, 75 percent of charitable donations can be deducted from the tax owed, which has a ceiling of €50,000 per year.

Incidence

Studies evaluated the impact of the reform on household disposable income (Jelloul et al. 2019) and the structure of firm governance (Bach et al. 2021). But no academic work to our knowledge assesses its impact on real estate market dynamics.

Gift and Inheritance Tax

Principles, rates, and tax base

Donations and inheritances are subject to a specific tax (*droits de mutations à titre gratuit*). It is a progressive tax on transfers whose rates and tax base depend on the relationship between the donor (or the deceased) and the recipients. Each recipient pays a net tax that corresponds to the estimated value of the total transmission (all assets) minus a rebate that depends on the relationship between the two parties. Table 11.7 summarizes the relationships and taxes. For real estate, the tax base is the market value of the property as estimated by a notary who compares similar real estate transactions. To estimate the value of the property, notaries have access to their own databases (BIEN for Paris and surroundings, and PERVAL for the rest of France). The research tool Patrim and its underlying data can also be used.

Special exemptions

Inheritance between husbands and wives or legal partners is exempt from taxation. Children with disabilities receive additional rebates. An interesting case for real estate taxation is donations of bare dominion. When parents transmit the ownership of property without usufruct (i.e., bare dominion), the tax base is discounted. The tax is applied to a percentage of the estimated value that depends on the age of the person transferring usufruct.

Value-Added Tax

Principles, rates, and tax base

Real estate activities subject to the 20 percent standard VAT (*taxe sur la valeur ajoutée*) rate are mostly sale of developed land parcels, sale of dwellings, redevelopment that increases the floor area of dwellings by more than 10 percent, or addition of a new building to a dwelling within the last two years. Redevelopment of commercial and professional real estate is also relevant. A significant number of activities can benefit from a reduced rate of 10 percent when they contribute to the maintenance of residential dwellings more than two years old. For example, this reduced rate can apply to the labor cost to install kitchen, bathroom, and heating devices. Finally, equipment or interventions that significantly improve the energy efficiency of a dwelling can benefit from a reduced VAT rate of 5.5 percent.

Table 11.7 Donation and Inheritance Tax

		Net Tax Base Computation	
Net Tax Base Brackets (€)	**Rate**	**Donations (one rebate per person every 15 years)**	**Inheritance**
Between Husbands and Wives or Civil Partners			
<8,072	5%	Estimated value – €80,724	No tax
8,072–15,932	10%		
15,933–31,865	15%		
31,866–552,324	20%		
552,325–902,838	30%		
902,839–1,805,667	40%		
>1,805,667	45%		
To Children			
Same as above	Same as above	Estimated value – €100,000 (or €159,325 for children with disabilities)	Estimated value – €100,000 (or €159,325 for children with disabilities)
Between Grandparents and Grandchildren			
Same as above	Same as above	Estimated value – €31,865 (or €5,310 for great-grandparents)	Estimated value – €31,865 (or €5,310 for great-grandparents)
Between Brothers and Sisters			
<24,430	35%	Estimated value – €15,932	Estimated value – €15,932
>24,430	45%		
Between Uncles, Aunts, Nephews, and Nieces			
	55%	Estimated value – €7,967	Estimated value – €7,967
Others			
	60%	Estimated value	Estimated value

Source: Adapted from République Française (2016).

Special exemptions

New dwellings in neighborhoods in the domain of the National Urban Regeneration Plan (Plan National de Rénovation Urbaine) can benefit from a reduced VAT of 5.5 percent when a buyer's income is below a threshold. Most social housing programs also benefit from a reduced VAT rate of 5.5 percent.

Incidence

Carbonnier (2007) analyzed the reduced VAT rate for maintenance work and found that the provision of these services appears relatively elastic and that the reduced VAT rate decreased prices. No impact on quantity was documented.

Corporate Income Tax

Principles, rates, and tax base

Income from rental properties owned by a real estate company is taxed through the corporate income tax (*impôt sur les sociétés*). The tax base is the profit of the firm. The distributed gains are also taxed through the income tax after a rebate of 40 percent. The tax rate ranges from 15 to 25 percent and varies with the turnover of the firm; €38,120 is the exemption threshold.

Exemptions

The social housing sector is exempt from corporate tax.

Stamp Duties and Transfer Taxes

Principles, rates, and tax base

Most stamp duties and transfer taxes are shared between the national level and local authorities, as detailed later. The transfer tax is entirely controlled at the national level and is the contribution that gives legal ownership. The tax on the transaction price is applied at a rate of 0.1 percent. In addition, the central government receives stamp duty tax revenues corresponding to 2.37 percent of the tax revenue of departments and 0.71 percent of stamp duties on new dwellings.

Table 11.8 lists the real estate taxes paid to the central government.

Revenues collected by the central government for social security and national public goods and services funding through the various taxes on real estate totaled €29 billion in 2019, or 1.2 percent of GDP.

Table 11.8 National Real Estate Taxes, 2019

Tax Name	French Name	Tax Revenues (€ million)	Tax Revenues (% of GDP)	Tax Revenues (% of tax on real estate)	Rates	Main Base
Real Estate Taxes, Central Government Only						
Income tax	*Impôt sur le revenu* (IR)	7,575	0.31	6.70	0%–45%	70% of the rent
Social contribution	*Prélèvements sociaux*				CSG: 9.2% CRDS: 0.5% PS: 7.5% Total: 17.2%	70% of the rent
Corporate tax, rentals	*Impôt sur les sociétés* (IS), *loyers*				15%–25%	Corporate benefits
Contribution on rental income	*Contribution annuelle sur les revenus locatifs* (CRL)				2.5%	Commercial and housing rent above €1,830
Capital gains tax	*Impôt sur les plus-values immobilières* (IR)	1,914	0.08	1.69	IR: 19% CSG: 9.2% CRDS: 0.5% PS: 7.5% Total: 36.2%	Capital gains on rental/ secondary homes
Property wealth tax	*Impôt sur la fortune immobilière* (IFI)	2,105	0.09	1.86	0.5%–1.5%	Property value
Inheritance tax	*Droits de succession*	7,656[1]	0.32	6.77	5%–60%	Estimated property value less rebate

(continued)

Table 11.8 National Real Estate Taxes, 2019 (*continued*)

Tax Name	French Name	Tax Revenues (€ million)	Tax Revenues (% of GDP)	Tax Revenues (% of tax on real estate)	Rates	Main Base
VAT, land	*Taxe sur la valeur ajoutée (terrains)*	785	0.03	0.69	5.5%–20%	Value added
VAT, new dwellings	*Taxe sur la valeur ajoutée (logements neufs)*	7,231	0.30	6.4	5.5%–20%	Value added
Contribution for real estate security	*Contribution sur la sécurité immobilière*	790	0.03	0.69	0.1%	Property value
Real Estate Taxes Shared with Local Authorities						
Stamp duty tax	*Mutation à titre onéreux d'immeubles et droits immobiliers (part etat)*	17	0	0.02	n.a.	Property value
Stamp duty	*Taxe de publicité foncière*	542	0.02	0.48	n.a.	Property value
Rent tax on business real estate	*Cotisation foncière des entreprises* (CFE)	3	0	0.00	n.a.	Cadastral rental value
Tax on retail space	*Taxe sur les surfaces commerciales*	196	0.01	0.17	€5.75/m^2 to €35.70/m^2	Weighted commercial surface area

Sources: Service des Données et des études statistiques (2021a; 2021b).

Note: n.a. = not available.

[1] We estimate this by applying the share of real estate in national wealth (50%) to the total tax receipts from the inheritance tax from DGFiP.

Subnational Government Taxes

Housing Tax

Principles, rates, and tax base

The housing tax (*taxe d'habitation*) is one of the main local taxes based on housing consumption. This tax is paid by any household living in a municipality—that is, tenants and owner-occupiers. The base of this tax is the 1970 updated rental cadastral values, which reflect the rental value of a dwelling in 1970 updated with a standard growth rate (described later in box 11.1). Tax rates are determined annually by municipalities and have a ceiling of 2.5 times the national or the departmental average. Many households receive a rebate or exemption based on their financial situation, such as level of income. In 2018, the government enacted a plan for gradually phasing out housing tax on the main residence. It was completed in 2023. Second homes will continue to be liable for the housing tax.

Tax on Vacant and Second Homes

Principles, rates, and tax base

Second homes are taxed at a rate set by municipalities (*taxe sur les logements vacants et résidences secondaires*), usually the same as the housing tax rate. Some municipalities, such as Paris, charge an additional rate for a second residence ranging from 5 to 60 percent of the housing tax. In a tight housing market, dwellings vacant for more than one year are subject to a vacancy tax. The tax base is the updated rental cadastral value of 1970, and the tax rate is 12.5 percent if vacant for two years, 25 percent if three or more years. The owner or usufructuary, if different, pays the tax. In municipalities governed by ordinary law, a local vacancy tax can apply to dwellings vacant for more than two years, in which case the tax rate is the same as the housing tax.

Exemptions

Dwellings that have been occupied for three consecutive months in the last year, and dwellings requiring significant refurbishment (i.e., costs above 25 percent of the dwelling value) are exempt from taxation.

Incidence

Segu (2022) documented that the vacancy tax reduced vacancy by 13 percent between 1997 and 2001, mostly concentrated in long-term vacancy. Results also suggest that most of the vacant units were turned into a primary residence where the owner lives.

Rent Tax on Business Real Estate

Principles, rates, and tax base

Firms and individuals acting as independent workers in a municipality are subject to the rent tax on business real estate (*contribution foncière des entreprises*). The tax base is the rental cadastral value.

The cadastral value of business properties was updated in January 2017. The new cadastral values result from a methodology that introduces 38 broad categories of professional buildings (e.g., storage buildings, offices, shops, garages) and that defines homogeneous areas, clusters of similar buildings within a department having similar average rent per square meter. Each cluster corresponding to a category in a sector is associated with the average observed rent per square meter of this category. The average rent, representing the value of buildings and their underlying parcels, is adjusted to follow market dynamics by departmental commissions on the basis of data gathered from the yearly fiscal declarations of landlords. The final gross cadastral value is computed by multiplying the weighted surface area with the reference rent of its category in its corresponding sector. On the basis of the cadastre, we estimate that the old tax base for the rent tax on business real estate represents about 1/10 of the new tax base.

To achieve revenue neutrality a coefficient (the sum of revised cadastral values divided by the sum of cadastral values from 1970) ensures that the total tax base of a given local authority remains the same as at the transition. Additional coefficients smooth the transition between the former and the new tax base. The tax rate is set by local authorities under a national ceiling of 56 percent. Further updates of rental values to account for market dynamics should be completed December 31, 2022.

Exemptions and rebates

Rebates on the cadastral value apply to several specific activities, and local authorities can grant additional rebates to promote other activities, special economic areas, or neighborhoods. Nationwide, the tax base of industrial facilities is reduced by 30 percent, facilities to reduce pollution or save energy benefit from a rebate of 50 percent, and airports and ports benefit from a rebate of 33.3 percent and 100 percent, respectively. Small craftsman corporations also receive rebates ranging from 25 to 50 percent.

Incidence

A study on correlations between variations of the rent tax on business real estate and firms' behavioral responses found few significant correlations overall. The manufacturing sector appears to adjust its consumption of land when its rent tax rate increases (Urvoy 2019).

Tax on Retail Space

Principles, Rates, and Tax Base

Firms operating facilities with a retail area larger than 400 square meters, with annual sales above €460,000, and that opened after 1960 are subject to the tax on commercial area (*taxe sur les surfaces commerciales*). The tax base is the area open to the public and covered, and where customers buy goods, the firm advertises the goods, and employees circulate to sell goods to customers. The tax per square meter depends on the turnover per square meter and the type of use (for example, retail use versus a facility that sells petrol; table 11.9).

Increases, Rebates, and Exemptions

The commercial area tax can be increased by 50 percent if the area is greater than 2,500 square meters and by 30 percent if the facility is larger than 5,000 square meters and the turnover per square meter is above €3,000. Tax rebates of 30 percent are granted when the main activity is the sale of furniture, cars, construction materials, or agricultural machinery.

Stamp Duties and Transfer Taxes

Principles, Rates, and Tax Base

Transfer taxes (*droits de mutation à titre onéreux*) are mostly local-government taxes and are collected by notaries at the time of the transaction. The value reported is the transaction price net of the estimated values of movable properties (large furniture and home appliances left with the dwelling).

Table 11.9 Tax on Retail Space

Turnover/m^2 (€)	Retail Tax/m^2 (€)	Gas Station Tax/m^2 (€)
<2,999	5.74	8.32
3,000–12,000	[(Turnover/m^2 – 3,000) ×0.00315]+5.74	[(Turnover/m^2 – 3,000) ×0.00315]+8.32
>12,001	34.12	35.70

Source: République Française (2025c).

- Department stamp duties. Departments may set a tax rate on the purchase of real estate (*taxe départementale de publicité foncière*) between 3.8 percent and 4.5 percent. The rate is applied on the declared value of the transaction—validated by notaries (net of compensation for general expenditures and the estimated value of free-moving chattels, e.g., a refrigerator or a wardrobe). In practice, all departments except three apply the highest rate of 4.5 percent. It is paid by the buyer.
- Municipal stamp duties. Municipalities levy an additional rate of 1.2 percent on the same tax base.

Exemptions

Newly constructed buildings sold by firms are subject to the VAT and are thus subject to the reduced rate of stamp duties of 0.71 percent. However, new properties bought from individuals are subject to the standard stamp duties and transfer taxes. Departments can reduce their global rates (in 2022, four departments had a 3.8 percent rate) and offer additional rebates. Dwellings sold by the social housing sector are exempt from stamp duties.

Incidence

In 2014, departments were allowed to increase their tax rates. This tax hike was investigated to find the potential impact of the reform on the number of transactions and prices. One study finds a significant loss of transactions subsequent to the reform but no long-term impact (Bérard and Trannoy 2018). Another study finds a negative impact on the volume of transactions in the long run in eased market condition but no impact on prices, suggesting that the tax burden is mostly borne by the buyer (Bachelet and Poulhès 2017).

Development Tax

Principles, rates, and tax base

The development tax (*taxe d'aménagement*) applies to all projects requiring authorization such as a building permit. Its tax base is the newly built closed and covered area, if greater than 5 square meters and more than 1.8 meters high, multiplied by €820 (€929 in Île-de-France, the Paris region). Solar panels and swimming pools are also taxed. Their tax base is obtained by multiplying their area by €200 (swimming pools) or €10 (solar panels). Municipal rates can bet set between 0 and 5 percent, and departments can set rates of up to 2.5 percent.

Exemptions and rebates

The first 100 square meters of main residences, industrial and artisanal facilities, and social housing projects receive 50 percent rebates. Reconstruction also receives an exemption.

Suggested reform

The development tax is counterproductive. It taxes an investment to develop a property. Moreover, this tax increased by 7 percent in 2022. This tax hinders the renovation of existing housing. Research suggests it should be removed (Cavailhès 2022).

Table 11.10 lists the real estate taxes local-government budgets receive.

Recurrent Land and Property Taxes

Property Tax

Principles, rates, and tax base

All property owners (firms or physical taxpayers) or usufructuaries are subject to the property tax (*taxe sur les propriétés bâties*) on their dwellings and professional or commercial facilities. The tax base is the cadastral rental value of a land parcel and the building on it.

The cadastral rental values for office buildings and commercial facilities were revised in 2017 and reflect local market dynamics by using yearly declarations of landlords (see the previous discussion on the rent tax on business real estate). Departmental commissions upgraded tax rolls in 2022 using current rental data.

Cadastral values for residential properties have been under revision since 2020 and new values are scheduled to be applied from 2028, replacing cadastral values computed in 1970. (A proposed revision of the valuation process is outlined in box 11.1.) The tax rates are set by local authorities (municipalities, their EPCIs, and departments) under a national ceiling and are applied to 50 percent of the cadastral value.

In a large urban area like Paris, cadastral values are an estimated 4 percent of the market rent. The tax base is the cadastral value adjusted by a 1980 departmental coefficient (see box 11.1) plus the yearly growth rates (close to the national inflation rate since the initial tax base assessment the year it was built) voted by the French parliament. This final tax base represents an estimated 20 percent of the current market rent. For new dwellings, rental value is assessed on the basis of the updated location coefficients of the 1970s and accounting for new dwellings being perceived as higher quality.

Table 11.10 Main Subnational Real Estate Taxes, 2019

Tax Name	French Name	Tax Revenue (€ million)	Tax Revenue (% of GDP)	Tax Revenue (% of taxes on real estate)	Rates	Main Base
Real Estate Taxes Paid by the Buyer						
Housing tax	*Taxe d'habitation*	13,756	0.57	12.17	Set locally 0%–58%	Cadastral rental values
Tax on vacant and second homes	*Taxe sur les logements et les residences secondaires*				Set locally 0%–58%	Cadastral rental values
Rent tax on business real estate	*Cotisation foncière des entreprises* (CFE)	8,006	0.33	7.08	Set locally 0.46%–47.34%	Cadastral rental values
Tax on retail space	*Taxe sur les surfaces commerciales* (TASCOM)	791	0.03	0.7	€5.75/m^2–€35.70/m^2	Weighted commercial area
Development tax	*Taxe d'aménagement*	1,784	0.07	1.58	Local rates, (1% up to 5%) +(0% up to 2.5%)	Paris: built area €929/m^2; rest of France: €820/m^2
Stamp duty	*Droits de mutation à titre onéreux* (DMTO)	16,363	0.67	14.48	Set by *départements*, 5% up to 5.7%	Property value
Tax for flood prevention	*Taxe gestion des milieux aquatiques et prévention des inondations* (GEMAPI)	190	0.01	0.17	Budget split among taxpayers after their contribution to the housing, property, and business real estate assets taxes	

Recurrent Property and Land Tax Paid by the Owner						
Property tax	*Taxe fonciere sur la propriété bâtie* (TFPB)	34,526	1.42	30.55	Set locally, 0.02%–63%	Cadastral rental values
Undeveloped property tax	*Taxe fonciere sur la propriété non bâtie* (TFNB)	1,092	0.05	0.97	Set locally, 0.02%–63%	Cadastral rental values
Additional property tax	*Taxe fonciere additionelle*	270	0.01	0.24		Cadastral rental values
Refuse collection tax	*Taxe d'enlèvement des ordures ménagères* (TEOM)	7,012	0.29	6.20	Set locally, 1%–33%	Cadastral rental values
Special additional yearly tax	*Taxe additionnelle spéciale annuelle* (TASA)	80	0	0.07	Total budget of €80 million split among all taxpayers of property tax and rent tax on business real estate in Paris region. The tax is proportional to their respective contribution to these taxes	
Office space tax	*Taxe sur les bureaux* (TSB)	213	0.01	0.19	€0.75/m^2–€23/m^2	Office, retail, and parking area
Sweeping tax	*Taxe de balayage*	110	0	0.10	Tax/m^2 locally set	Ceiling of taxable surface (6 m × parcel street frontage)

Sources: DGCL (2022); DGFiP (2021); Service des Données et des études statistiques (2021a).

Mass appraisal has been proposed but not adopted, and the valuation process used for the revised values is not very technical. The new methodology proposed for the revision is a simple two-entry table containing the property's area and location that is built from observed transactions. While real estate transaction prices are captured in many reliable sources, data on rental values remains relatively scarce, increasing the difficulty of updating the cadastral rental value. This led to several initiatives to gather rental values, either from online advertisements (Chapelle and Eyméoud 2022) or by surveys in large urban areas. To update the cadastral value, the government requires all landlords to declare their dwellings and their associated rental income online. This dataset will be used for future updates; no assessment of its reliability can be made yet.

It is a responsibility of the central government to collect the dataset and manage the database of cadastral values. Department and municipal committees composed of local authorities and taxpayers propose adjustments to the data provided by the state following precise guidelines. If these committees cannot find agreement, the representative of the central government (*préfet*) sets the final values.

Exemptions

Several exemptions provide temporary relief from the property tax. New construction can receive an exemption for two years. Residential construction with high levels of energy efficiency can have its exemption extended to five years. Existing dwellings with significant improvements in energy efficiency can also benefit from an exemption for three years, while offices transformed into dwellings can benefit from an exemption of up to five years. There are other exemptions for being low income, handicapped, or a senior (over 75), or when market conditions do not allow rental of a dwelling. The property tax liability cannot exceed 50 percent of a household's income for a taxable income lower than a certain value.

Social housing receives a long-term property tax exemption (between 15 and 25 years). From 2022, the central government compensates municipalities for the full lost tax revenues for the new social housing stock built after this date (not for the stock).

Government-owned properties (whether national, local, or social housing) are exempt from the property tax. The amount of municipalities' loss of tax revenues is not evaluated and not compensated.

Incidence and reforms

We are not aware of any study that estimates the incidence of the property tax in France. The cadastral rental values for residential dwellings appear outdated and are under revision (box 11.1).

Property Tax on Undeveloped Land

Principles, rates, and tax base

All property owners (firms and physical taxpayers) or usufructuaries are subject to the property tax on undeveloped land (*taxe foncière sur la propriété non bâtie*). The tax base is the cadastral rental value. The tax bases for vacant land date from 1961 and were slightly updated in 1980. Departmental commissions assessed these values according to market values for land with similar crops in the municipality (Cour des Comptes 2023).

No national revaluation has taken place besides homogeneous yearly national increases. To our knowledge, no experimentation was initiated for this purpose. The rates are set by local authorities (municipalities, their EPCIs) under a national ceiling and are applied on up to 80 percent of the cadastral value for agricultural land used for farming. Total tax receipts are modest.

Increase, rebates, and exemptions

Some municipalities in tight housing markets have the right to increase the cadastral value of developable land up to three euros per square meter to limit land retention and stimulate the production of dwellings. Other activities, people, and types of land can benefit from rebates or exemptions: public land, forests, young farmers, some plantations, and protected areas.

Incidence

Some evidence suggests that the additional property tax for developable land increased the use of empty parcels in some municipalities (Guelton 2015; Guelton and Leroux 2016).

Additional Undeveloped Property Tax

Principles, rates, and tax base

The rates for an additional tax for undeveloped properties (*taxe additionnelle sur les propriétés non bâties*) such as stone pits, developable land, private streets, other gardens, railroads, and yards are set by regions, departments, municipalities, and their EPCIs. The tax base is the same as the undeveloped property tax.

Box 11.1 Cadastral Rental Values of 1970 for Residential Dwellings and Their Revision

The 1970 cadastral value, still in use in 2025 for residential property taxes, reflects the rental value of a dwelling (the building and its parcel) in 1970, accounting for location and eight categories ranging from low-quality to luxury dwellings. These categories are based on the architecture of the building, the quality of the construction, and the facilities it contains (toilets, elevator, central heating, etc.). Each *quality category* is associated with a *rent per square meter* reflecting the relative values of these categories in the neighborhoods as defined in 1970. To compute the cadastral value for each dwelling, the rent per square meter of the dwelling's category is multiplied by a *weighted surface area*. The weighted surface area reflects, first, the decline in rent per square meter as the area of the dwelling increases (e.g., for a high-quality dwelling of 400 square meters, the first 20 square meters are multiplied by 3 and the remaining 380 square meters by 0.9); second, how much the building has degraded over time (with a coefficient ranging from 1.2 to 0.8); and third, a dwelling's location and facilities (e.g., the presence of a toilet is associated with an additional 3 square meters, and a shower is associated with an additional 4 square meters). Dwellings built after 1970 are assigned to one of these categories; if a dwelling's characteristics change sufficiently, it is reassigned to another category and its weighted surface area is adjusted. Other than a departmental revision in 1980, these values are only uniformly updated annually. A revision in 1990 was aborted. A study compared the cadastral value with the estimated market rental value of dwellings (Chapelle, Fabre, and Lallemand 2020): the cadastral value in the largest French municipalities and their periphery appears disconnected from the market rental value, estimated through hedonic regression analysis. The study concludes that the cadastral value of new dwellings is underestimated and so is that of dwellings in peripherical municipalities when compared with their central municipalities.

Experimental revision: In 2015, a method for revising cadastral values was tested in five departments following a new methodology for valuation proposed by the national tax authority (DGFiP 2016). It creates four broad categories of dwellings (apartments, single-family dwellings, exceptional dwellings, and isolated dependencies) and subdivides them into subcategories corresponding to size (18 subcategories for apartments, 16 for single-family dwellings, 2 for exceptional dwellings, and 8 for isolated dependencies). Homogeneous areas within a department are grouped into territories according to their average rent per square meter. The tax authority proposes further subdivision of departmental territories into six or seven sectors that group municipalities and cadastral sections (i.e., housing blocks). In practice, the report finds that only the largest municipalities have heterogeneous housing blocks belonging to different price categories. In the end, the proposed valuation methodology accounts for only a few parameters: the type of dwelling and its location and size. Modern mass appraisal tools are not an option because the law constrains the valuation process to simple methods. Chapelle, Fabre, and Lallemand (2020) suggest that a least hedonic regression model could be used to regularly update cadastral values. The national fiscal administration makes only limited use of new technologies. Some artificial intelligence algorithms are being developed that detect swimming pools from satellite imagery (Cour des Comptes 2023).

Data on rental values: While real estate transaction prices are captured in many sources, data on rental values remains relatively scarce, increasing the difficulty of updating the cadastral rental value. This led to several initiatives to gather rental values, either from online advertisements (Chapelle and Eyméoud 2022) or by surveys in large urban areas.

Refuse Collection Tax

Principles, Rates, and Tax Base

All owners or usufructuaries of dwellings are subject to a tax on garbage collection (*taxe sur les ordures ménagères*). The owners of rental dwellings can recover the amount of the tax from the tenant. The tax base is the same as the property tax, 50 percent of the cadastral rental value. The rate is set locally by municipalities or their EPCIs. Local authorities can adjust the tax to account for the volume of garbage produced by households.

Exemptions

Low-income owners exempted from property tax can ask to be also exempted from the refuse collection tax. Owners can ask for rebates when the dwelling is vacant. Instead of a garbage collection tax, local authorities can set refuse collection fees proportional to the real cost of the service.

Tax on Office Space

Principles, Rates, and Tax Base

Owners or usufructuaries of office space in four categories (office space larger than 100 square meters, retail space larger than 2,500 square meters, retail space larger than 5,000 square meters, and parking space larger than 500 square meters) are subject to the tax on office space (*taxe sur les locaux à usage de bureaux*) if in the Paris region (Île-de-France). A tax per square meter is applied to the total area. The rate decreases with the area and depends on the location (table 11.11).

Table 11.11 Tax on Office Space (€/m²)

	Sector 1	Sector 2	Sector 3	Sector 4
Office (corporations)	23.67	19.93	10.90	5.26
Office (associations, public sector)	11.76	9.90	6.55	4.75
Retail space	9.01	8.01	4.21	2.14
Storage space	4.22	4.22	2.14	1.10
Parking space	2.67	2.67	1.44	0.75

Source: République Française (2025d).

Note:

- Sector 1: the 1st, 2nd, 7th, 8th, 9th, 10th, 15th, 16th, and 17th arrondissements of City of Paris and some high-income municipalities of the west and northwest suburbs (Boulogne-Billancourt, Courbevoie, Issy-les-Moulineaux, Levallois-Perret, Neuilly-sur-Seine, and Puteaux).
- Sector 2: the arrondissements of Paris and the municipalities of the Hauts-de-Seine *département* not included in the 1st sector.
- Sector 3: the municipalities included in the urban zone of Paris out of the City of Paris and the municipalities of the Hauts-de-Seine *département.*
- Sector 4: the other municipalities of the Région Ile-de-France and some low-income municipalities of Zone 3 eligible for specific grants in aid.

Sweeping Tax

Principles, rates, and tax base

Owners or usufructuaries of parcels can be taxed by municipalities or their EPCIs to fund street cleaning services. The tax per square meter is locally set and can vary by the type of street. The tax base is the length of the street frontage of the parcel multiplied by half the width of the street up to six meters. Only five municipalities, including Paris, have the legal right to levy this tax.

Cap on Local Tax Rates

The ceilings on local-government rate setting are complex and manifold. They also change quite often, because of changes in the administrative context of tax rate setting (for example, the rise and the diversity of intermunicipal bodies) and changes in economic conditions. The first and simplest ceiling is the uniform ceiling set by legislation for a given tax—for example, stamp duty. A second ceiling governs the increase of rates: a local government may not increase its tax rates by more than twice the average rate of increase of the same tax computed for all local governments of the same layer. The same applies to the local business property tax. A third ceiling restricts the comparative rate of increase in the local taxes on households and that of local taxes on businesses. A local government may not increase the rate on business property tax faster than it raises the rate on property tax on developed land. Similarly, the rate of increase of the tax on undeveloped land may not increase faster than that on developed land. The final tax ceiling relates to businesses liable for local taxes: the sum of local business property tax and local VAT cannot exceed 3.5 percent of a business's annual value added. Symmetrically, individual taxpayers get a rebate in their property tax if their personal income is less than the ceiling set annually by the finance law.

Except for stamp duties, whose rates the *départements* (all but three choose the ceiling rate) and municipalities rarely lower below the highest rate set by the law, no evidence indicates that local governments' property tax rates cluster at the ceiling level. This is especially the case for the local business property tax. Two reasons could explain this apparent oddity. First, as mentioned earlier, the rate itself of the rent tax on business real estate is not capped, but a cap applies to its rate of increase over time with respect to the average rate of increase in all municipalities. Introduced in 2022, this cap's clustering effects on the rates of the rent tax on business real estate are as yet unknown. Second, those rates have an indirect cap: the sum of the rent tax on business real estate and the local VAT as a percentage of the taxpayer value added. As a result, only municipalities where this ratio is high would be fiscally harmed and thus encouraged to limit the growth of the rate of the rent tax on business real estate.

Figure 11.3 illustrates that the local level is the main beneficiary of real estate taxation and that property tax accounts for almost a third of the total revenues.

Administration

A department of the Ministry of Finance, the Direction Générale des Finances Publiques (DGFiP), collects national and local taxes. Households declare income for the income tax and social security contributions online or on paper. The DGFiP then computes the amount of taxes due and prepares tax rolls. Most local taxes, such as the property and housing taxes, are also computed by the DGFiP by combining the tax base and the tax rates voted by local authorities. Tax rolls can be transmitted electronically or on paper. The deconcentrated services of the Ministry of Finance collect the payments. The collection rate is about 95.5 percent after one year, 98.5 percent after two years, and at least 99.7 percent after three years. Households make tax payments via automatic monthly or yearly transfers from their bank account, in cash, or by check. As many as 70 percent of

Figure 11.3 Real Estate Tax Revenues by Level of Government, 2019

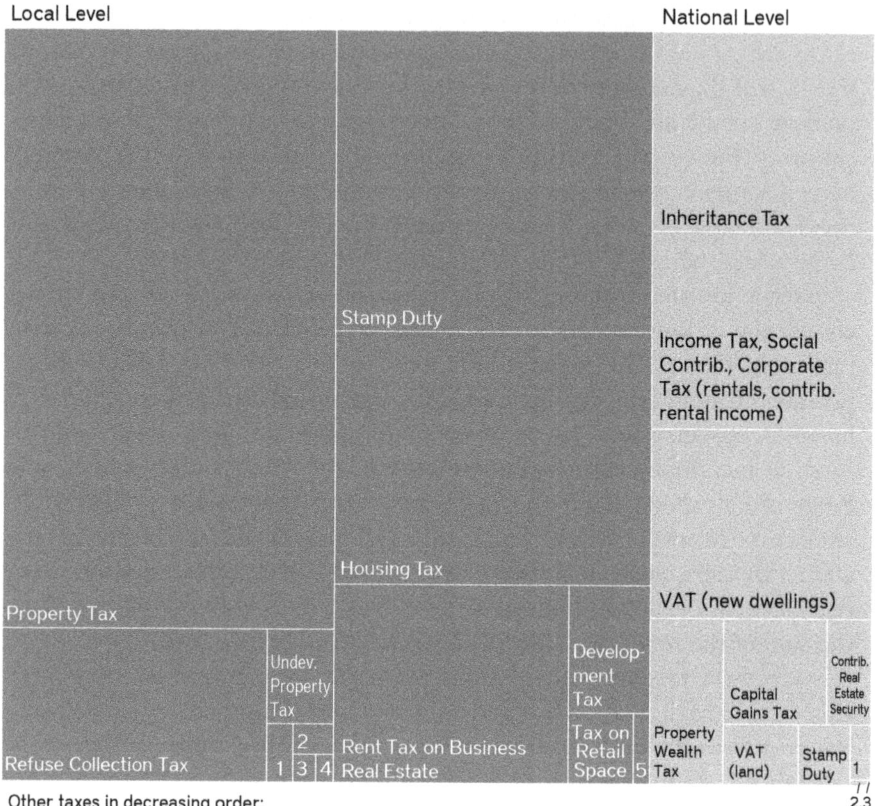

Other taxes in decreasing order:

1. Additional property tax
2. Office space tax
3. Sweeping tax
4. Special additional yearly tax
5. Tax for flood prevention

Other taxes in decreasing order:

1. Tax on retail space
2. Stamp duty tax
3. Rent tax on business real estate

Note: Box sizes correspond to revenue magnitude of each tax. The darker shading on the left indicates local taxes; the lighter shading, national taxes.

taxpayers use automatic bank transfers or online payments. Since the elimination of the local VAT, DGFiP is almost the sole tax collector for firms, which must make an electronic declaration for national taxes such as corporate taxes and VAT. Firms pay corporate tax quarterly, VAT every six months. Management of firms' local taxes is mostly the same as for households.

According to the French national audit office (Cour des Comptes 2022a), the management and collection of local taxes is "particularly costly." The total collection cost[4] of local taxes was €4 billion in 2021, or

9.1 percent of local tax receipts collected in 2021 by the Ministry of Finance. The administrative costs (human resources) represent 40 percent of the total, the tax rebates granted after appeal 45 percent, and unrecovered taxes 15 percent. That 9.1 percent is three times as much as the 3 percent the French Tax Code declared when it gave the central government the right to charge local governments for collection of tax receipts. In other words, according to this estimate, two-thirds of the collection costs of local taxes are borne by the national taxpayer. The percentage breakdown of the total (40, 45, and 15 percent) includes all local taxes. The percentage of collection costs related only to property taxes is unknown.

A 2023 national audit office report (Cour des Comptes 2023) provides additional details on the property tax on developed and undeveloped land. It estimates the contribution of components to the total collection costs relative to property taxes alone: 45 percent corresponds to the definition and uprate of the tax base, 29 percent is tax collection, 21 percent is tax litigation, and 1 percent is tax control. In addition, the report carefully itemizes factors that create complexities in setting local property taxes and thus likely increase collection costs. The first is the split inside the Ministry of Finance between property taxes on individuals and property taxes on businesses, which multiplies software applications and adds delays. Second is the incomplete administrative treatment of self-declarations and updates to cadastral values after dwelling improvements. Third is the limited use of numerical tools for property tax control (including artificial intelligence). Only a few experiments in this area are reported. Among other recommendations, the report argues for an efficient updating of cadastral values and for a broader use of electronic declarations (Cour des Comptes 2022a).

However, as the audit office reports themselves mention, these estimates of factors in property tax collection must be carefully scrutinized. Property taxation, whether local or national, raises the ratio of collection cost to tax receipts. The real estate wealth tax entails administrative (human resources) costs even higher than the local property taxes. In addition, the estimated collection costs include the loss in tax receipts because of tax rebates, which are not collection costs as much as the result of decisions made by the central tax services.

Property Tax in Large Urban Areas

More than 77 percent of the French population, and thus economic activity and income, is concentrated in urban areas. Paris holds 2.2 million residents intra muros (3.4 percent of the general population) and the capital city region, the metropolitan area, 12 million, or one French resident out of five. Paris is unique compared with London and New York in that it no longer contains a major share of the population in its metropolitan area (18 percent) but still accounts for a third of jobs. The area of Paris (only 100 square kilometers) is small compared with other capital cities. The gross national product per capita in Paris is three times as much as the French average, and the median disposable income per unit of consumption is 30 percent higher in Paris than the French average. The concentration of resident population and of economic activity in the capital city area and in some other metropolitan areas (Lyon, Marseille, Lille, Toulouse, Bordeaux) exacerbates the wedge between the residential land values in the center of metropolitan areas, the land values in the suburbs, and those in the other nonurban residential locations (Chapelle et al. 2021). For this reason, the property tax geography in France and, more precisely, the capital city, is of particular importance.

Paris and Multilayer Local Authorities

Characterizing property taxes in Paris raises two sets of difficulties. The first is that some of the property taxes considered in this chapter are levied at a national level, on a uniform tax scheme. Therefore, the related tax revenues are registered where the taxpayer is fiscally resident, irrespective of where the taxed properties are located. Other property taxes that are local taxes are related to properties in the jurisdiction of that local government and levied according to tax rules and tax rates set by it. Those property taxes are locally registered. As a result, the territorial merging of property taxes is so complex that any attempt to study combined local and national property tax revenues collected in large urban cities will be unsatisfactory. This section limits itself to property taxes levied only by the City of Paris (Ville-de-Paris) local government. It treats separately the revenues of other specific or additional property taxes levied by local governments or independent administrative bodies overlapping the Parisian region such as the Métropole du Grand Paris. Nor do we consider the tax revenues related to national property taxes (except real estate wealth tax revenues) levied on Paris-located taxpayers. Given this, our appraisal of the concentration of property taxes in the capital city, a large urban area, is only partial. It takes the viewpoint of the local government taxing property and not the taxpayer facing local or national property taxes on the same tax bases.

The second set of difficulties arises from the City of Paris being since 2017 a specific local government. The elected Council of Paris (Conseil de Paris) has the responsibilities of both an ordinary municipality and a *département* (the third layer of local government in France). Accordingly, the City of Paris merges the previously separate tax resources of these two tiers of local governments. Lyon merges municipal responsibilities with the *département* only partially, and Marseille not at all. Further, local governments in the Paris territory overlap in specific and complex ways. Five layers of local governments exist within the Paris territory: a municipality, an intermunicipal cooperation public body (EPCI), a metropolis (Métropole du Grand Paris), a *département* consolidated with the municipality in the Ville-de-Paris, and a region (Région Île-de-France). Since 2016, the City of Paris has been one of the 12 members of the Métropole du Grand Paris, which covers 800 square kilometers and has a population of just over seven million. Consequently, City of Paris tax resources (including property tax revenues) are split among the City of Paris itself, the Métropole du Grand Paris, and special administrative bodies (Société du Grand Paris, Etablissement Public Foncier d'Île-de-France), and the Île-de-France Region. All these layers of government or public bodies are entitled to levy taxes additional to the municipal property taxes or to receive part of the corresponding tax revenues.

The City of Paris is the largest local government in France. In 2019, it employed 38,000 civil servants, spent €10 billion, or approximately 11 percent of the 2019 total outlay of the almost 36,000 French municipalities and 6 percent of the total outlay of the municipalities and *départements*.

Property Taxes Levied by the City of Paris

In its hybrid status, the City of Paris is entitled to levy the property tax, the property tax on undeveloped land (partly as a municipality, partly as a *département*), the rent tax on business real estate, the refuse collection tax levied on the same base as the property tax, and the stamp duty and transfer tax (partly as a municipality, partly as a *département*). We add to this list the housing tax levied on owners of a second home (*résidences secondaires*) and the housing tax on vacant properties, because we consider them true property taxes.

Other recurrent property taxes, specific to the Paris area, are levied. These include

- a sweeping tax (*taxe de balayage*), which is imposed on the same base as the property tax;
- a specific development tax (*taxe spéciale d'équipement*);
- an additional tax (*taxe spéciale additionnelle perçue au profit de la Région Île-de-France*), which is a property tax on undeveloped land, a rent tax on business real estate, and a housing tax, and whose revenues are assigned to special administrative bodies (Établissement Public Foncier d'Île-de-France and Société du Grand Paris); and

- the same tax bases are subject to another additional development tax whose revenues go to the Métropole du Grand Paris.

Property Tax Bases in Paris

The City of Paris tax bases on improved or unimproved land or on business real estate are estimated in exactly the same way as in other French municipalities—taxpayer declarations. The City of Paris has no central administrative unit (similar to the European Union's Tax Observatory) dedicated to the systematic control of data collection, despite having more than two million taxable properties. We have been told that, in contrast to other large cities (such as Marseille), City of Paris tax services do not consider implementation of a tax observatory a priority. Piecemeal exchanges of information regarding tax bases between City of Paris tax services and the tax services of the central government are reportedly concentrated on the property tax base that affects important urban renewal programs. These exchanges of information are said to be efficient and raise no specific problems. Even in the special cases mentioned earlier, where City of Paris services pay special attention to the fiscal impacts of urban renewal programs, all the administrative activity related to local taxes is by the central-government tax services.

As was done for all tax bases in France, the property tax bases in Paris were set decades ago (1970) following the general revision of rental values. A partial updating took place in 1980. An attempt at general revision took place in 1990 but failed, due to the political opposition of the Parliament. A reestimate of business property and business real estate tax bases began in 2017. The committees in charge of the process use accounting balance sheet methods for the industrial sector and administrative rental value techniques for the other sectors of economic activity. The reestimate is delayed and will likely not finish until 2024–2025. A reestimate of rental values for individuals is not on the current political agenda even if preliminary (unofficial) studies are in progress. As usual, the preliminary results focus on who is affected by the revision and by how much.

Trannoy and Wasmer (2022) report that, in 2003, 47 percent of the Paris cadastre area (covering 62 percent of the total Paris area) was owned by the state (29 percent) and the City (18 percent). Condominiums (multiowner properties) represented 38 percent of the cadastre area, and single-property individual owners only 5 percent. The remaining properties were owned by private companies and miscellaneous profit or nonprofit organizations. No recent overall analysis of the property tax base in Paris is available. Except for large urban renewal programs, the 20 arrondissements' administrative services (arrondissements are subdivisions of the

Paris municipality as boroughs are for London) handle the detailed day-to-day management of these property tax bases.

The leeway left to the Paris municipality on setting the tax base is the same as for all other French municipalities. It consists mostly of setting the minimum tax basis and rate for the rent tax on business real estate. The City of Paris strategy is to maintain stability while granting Paris taxpayers the benefits of low and predictable tax rates. Rebates on the property tax and on the tax on business real estate granted by the City of Paris are negligible; in 2020, it amounted to less than 0.004 percent of the business real estate tax revenue of 2020 and less than 0.0007 percent for the property tax in 2020.

In 2020, the property tax bases (*valeurs locatives municipales nettes*) in the City of Paris represented 8.48 percent of the total of net tax bases of all French municipalities, only 0.03 percent of the tax bases on unimproved land, and 6.7 percent of the business real estate tax base. The per capita property tax base in Paris was €3,690, which is two times as much as the national average (€1,431) for all French municipalities. The per capita tax base for undeveloped land was €3 in Paris compared with €2.50 on average for France. The per capita property tax on business real estate was €920 in Paris, which was twice the average of €467 for France.

Property Tax Rates

The statutory rates of the property taxes on developed and undeveloped land, rent tax on business real estate, refuse collection tax, and stamp duties are set by the elected Council of Paris exactly the same way they are in other French municipalities. They are subject to the same fiscal rules.[5] The tax rates of minor additional property taxes (development taxes, additional development taxes) are not set by the Council of Paris.

The strategy of the City of Paris relative to property taxes rates differs sharply from that of other local governments in France, including other large urban areas. First, since 2011, the tax rates for the property tax, the property tax on undeveloped land, and the tax on business real estate voted by the elected Council of Paris have remained unchanged. Consequently, 100 percent of the change in City of Paris property tax revenues is the result of a change of the tax bases or an increase in the tax rates set by the national law (for stamp duty revenues, for example). The City of Paris statutory tax rates in 2022 were set at 13.50 percent (8.37 percent municipality plus 5.13 percent *département*) for the property tax, 16.67 percent for the property tax on undeveloped land, 16.52 percent for the tax on business real estate, and 6.21 percent for the refuse collection tax. Property tax rates, however, have increased in all other municipalities outside Paris,

Table 11.12 Local Property Tax Rates (2018) and Rate of Change, 2018–2020, City of Paris Versus Other Municipalities

Tax	All Municipalities (Paris excluded) + All *Départements*	City of Paris	Rate of Increase 2018/2017 All Municipalities (Paris excl.) + *Départements*		
	Average tax rates 2018 (%)	Tax rates 2018–2020 (%)	Tax revenue (%)	Tax base component (%)	Tax rate component (%)
Property tax	19.39	**13.50**	+2.8	+2.2	+0.6
Property tax on undeveloped land	49.67	**16.67**	+1.3	+1.0	+0.3
Rent tax on business real estate	17.84	**16.52**	+3.8	+3.3	+0.5
Refuse collection tax	6.92	**6.21**	+1.9	+3.5	–0.6

Sources: DGCL (2021); Laignel and Guené (2022).

Note: The rate of increase of the tax revenue results from the increase of the tax base (tax base component) and an increase (decrease) in the tax rate (tax rate component). For example, the increase from 2017 to 2018 of 2.8% in the property tax revenues is the result of an increase in the tax base of 2.7% and an increase in the tax rate of 0.1%.

mostly before 2018 (table 11.12), and have contributed significantly to the increase of property tax revenues (see table 11.14).

Second, the local property tax rates in Paris are significantly lower than in the other French municipalities (see table 11.12). They are also significantly lower than those in Lyon and Marseille (table 11.13). Despite its low tax rates, the City of Paris significantly increased its property tax revenues since 2015, thanks mainly to the increase in the number and the nominal amount of transactions of properties, which boosts stamp duty revenues (table 11.14). Property taxes amount to half of the City of Paris operating revenues and a third of the total revenues, including investment operations. Two main factors explain this situation. First, in a metropolitan context, other local taxes based on economic activity (a part of the value added registered by businesses in Paris, the local VAT) have been transferred from the municipality to the metropolitan layer of responsibility,

Rate of Increase 2019/2018 All Municipalities (Paris excl.) + *Départements*			Rate of Increase 2020/2019 All Municipalities (Paris excl.) + *Départements*		
Tax revenue (%)	Tax base component (%)	Tax rate component (%)	Tax revenue (%)	Tax base component (%)	Tax rate component (%)
+2.7	+2.8	−0.1	+2.1	+2.2	−0.1
+2.3	+2.2	+0.1	+1.3	+1.2	+0.1
+0.7	+0.5	+0.1	+3.2	+3.3	−0.1
+2.7	+2.8	+0.1	+1.8	+1.8	0

making the tax base of the municipality more dependent on property.[6] Second, the concentration of property values in Paris increases the property tax proceeds. The dependency of City of Paris budgets on property taxes, however, has its dark side. The number of transactions and the market values on immovable goods are cyclical. Consequently, the revenues of the property taxes directly linked to these transactions (stamp duties) are also highly cyclical, as they have been since 2015. In contrast, the disconnection between the administrative rental values and the market values combined with the City's choice to not change the tax rates make the revenues of the true property taxes less cyclical.

City of Paris property tax revenues are not earmarked to any specific purpose. Even revenues of the refuse collection tax, which seems to be a refuse collection user fee, are not earmarked for financing refuse collection but contribute to the current operations budget.

Table 11.13 Property Tax Rates City of Paris, Lyon, and Marseille, 2020

	City of Paris	Lyon	Marseille
Property tax (TFPB)	13.50% (8.37% municipality + 5.13% *département*)	29.81% (18.23% municipality + *département*)	41.66% (municipality only)
Property tax on undeveloped land (TFPNB)	16.67%	21.88%	53.86%
Rent tax on business real estate (CFE)	16.52%	28.62%	26.45%
Refuse collection tax (TEOM)	6.21%	TEOM transferred to the Métropole of Lyon	9.02%

Sources: Cour des Comptes (2021, table 6; 2022b).

The property tax revenues contribute extensively to making the tax capacity of the City of Paris significantly higher than the average tax capacity per capita of other French municipalities. The spread between the two is approximated by the index of the financial potential (*potentiel financier*) per capita used to calculate the contribution of the City to the layers of fiscal redistribution between local governments.[7]

The high per capita tax capacity of the City of Paris entails three major consequences. First, it makes Paris the most important net contributor to the fiscal equalization systems between local governments. Second, it might help increase the rating of the City of Paris on financial markets. Third, the property tax paid by households in Paris represents on average less than 1.5 percent of their disposable income. This share is higher than 2.5 percent in two departments of the suburbs surrounding the City (3 percent in Seine-Saint-Denis and 2.7 percent in Val-de-Marne) and higher than 3.5 percent in some municipalities (André and Meslin 2021). This fact is particularly telling since property ownership in Paris is the highest in France. Households owning five or more units own 40 percent of the capital's housing stock. And in some areas of central Paris, the proportions are more extreme. For example, between 60 and 70 percent of privately owned rental units near Place de la Concorde and the Champs-Élysées are owned by households with five or more units.

Table 11.14 Property Tax Revenues, City of Paris and Other Government/Public Bodies, 2018–2020

Government/Public Body	Property Taxes	2018	2019	2020
City of Paris (municipality + *département*)	*Property tax*			
	Tax revenue municipality + *département* (€ million)	1,048	1,063	1,064
	Tax revenue municipality only (€ million)	640	649	658
	Number of tax articles	1,009,333	1,014,653	1,018,932
	Tax rate (%)	13.50	13.50	13.50
	Property tax on undeveloped land			
	Tax revenue (€ million)	0.01	0.01	0.009
	Number of tax articles	588	591	556
	Tax rate (%)	16.67	16.67	16.67
	Rent tax on business real estate			
	Tax revenue (€ million)	n.a.	336	n.a.
	Tax rate (%)	16.52	16.52	16.52
	Refuse collection tax			
	Tax revenue (€ million)	479	486	493
	Number of tax articles	1,023,237	1,028,819	1,033,178
	Tax rate (%)	6.21	6.21	6.21

(*continued*)

Table 11.14 Property Tax Revenues, City of Paris and Other Government/Public Bodies, 2018–2020 (*continued*)

Government/Public Body	Property Taxes	2018	2019	2020
	Stamp duty			
	Total tax revenue (€ million)	1.524	1.480	1.733
	Tax revenue municipality (€ million)	348	324	382
	Tax revenue *Département* (€ million)	1.176	1.156	1.351
	Tax rate (%)	4.50	4.50	4.50
	Housing tax revenue (only second home part and housing tax on vacant properties)[1]	0.098	0.099	0.1
	Development tax (€ million)	0.012	0.06	0.011
	Sweeping tax	n.a.	n.a.	n.a.
Métropole du Grand Paris and related public bodies (Office foncier du Grand Paris, Société du Grand Paris)	*Additional taxes to the property tax*, to the property tax on undeveloped land, to the housing tax, to the rent tax on business real estate	n.a.	n.a.	n.a.
	Tax on retail space	n.a.	n.a.	n.a.
	Development tax	n.a.	n.a.	n.a.
Région Île de France	*Specific regional tax additional to property tax* and rent tax on business real estate	n.a.	n.a.	n.a.

Central state	*Property wealth tax*[2]			
	Property wealth tax revenues (€ million)	0.388	0.455	0.493
	Number of property wealth taxpayers	34,850	36,715	39,911
	Personal income tax[3]			
	Personal income tax revenues (€ million)	9.953	10.689	10.657
	Number of tax units[4]	850,852	919,903	917,957
	Total property tax revenues City of Paris (€ million)	n.a.	3,695	n.a.
	Property tax revenues City of Paris / City of Paris revenues[5]	n.a.	53.7%	n.a.
	City of Paris property tax revenues / City of Paris total revenues[6]	n.a.	37.6%	n.a.

Sources: DGFiP (n.d.); authors' calculations.

Note: n.a. = not available.

[1] Estimate, based on the ratio of second home properties in Paris (9.5%) and on the assumption that the tax base of second homes and vacant houses is the same as the average rental value of other housing and according to the housing tax rate in City of Paris (13.38%).

[2] Number of property wealth taxpayers registered in City of Paris

[3] Number of taxpayers registered in City of Paris who pay the personal income tax (*impôt sur le revenu*) and its related tax revenues.

[4] Tax unit = a single individual, a couple, a family, etc.

[5] Revenues = revenues registered in the operating budget.

[6] Total revenues = revenues of operating budget + revenues of investment budget.

Parisian owners benefit from the regressivity of the property tax, discussed in the following.

Reform Initiatives and Country-Specific Issues (2015–2022)

Several reforms have taken place since 2015 regarding taxes related to land and property. We start with the reforms regarding local property taxes.

A major change was the abolition of the housing tax on primary residences, which will be fully completed by 2023. The tax cut is about €17 billion for households. Even if the housing tax is not a property tax (see the earlier section "Real Estate Taxes"), the remaining housing tax, which includes second homes and, optionally, vacant dwellings, can be viewed as an additional property tax on these properties. Some municipalities may apply a surcharge. These are the municipalities in areas with tight housing markets and where private sector rents are the highest. These communes are also where the tax on vacant dwellings may apply.

A parallel change is a 50 percent fall in the rent tax on business real estate from 2021. This fall related to industrial activities. Martin and Trannoy (2019) argued in favor of removing some tax surcharges on production costs. Their argument is that these taxes raise the breakeven point of the company. Basing their reasoning on the Diamond-Mirrlees production lemma (1971), they contend that the rent tax on business real estate and the property tax on commercial properties were not the worst and could be kept. The government did not accept this argument and, under pressure from the industrial sector, decided to decrease by 50 percent the property tax on industrial real estate from 2021 onward. The rationale was that deindustrialization in France is due in part to high production costs. This tax rate decrease may improve France's attractiveness to investors but at the detriment of a loss of neutrality of land and property taxation.

Another change was the critical revision of the tax base for the property tax and the rent tax on business real estate. Two measures have been implemented to smooth the transition from the old valuation approach to the revised one. First, a transition period of 10 years, up to 2026, is in place. The company will not pay its full property tax corresponding to the revised value until that date. The annual pace of variation is 1/10th of the tax liability change. A second measure to protect the business sector from the revaluation was introduced, because the revaluation for the residential sector is still pending. If not corrected, the share of the property tax paid by firms would have surged because business property and housing are jointly taxed. The same property tax rate is applied to the two sectors.

The Martin and Trannoy (2019) previous argument suggests, however, that the reform's effects may be limited, and further revision of the property tax base for the residential sector is needed. The 2020 Finance Act provides for a further revision of residential property rental values in 2026 on the basis of the rents recorded in 2023 by category of dwelling and geographic area. The 2023 Finance Act, however, postponed the introduction of the new tax bases to 2028. How to compensate municipalities that lose out after the reform has always been the main cause of the failure of rental value revision. Indeed, a sound revision of rental values would necessarily benefit urban municipalities (and even more, suburban ones), whose tax capacities would increase. On the opposite side, the tax capacities of rural municipalities would diminish. In the meantime, thanks to the successive reforms of local taxation that took place during the past decade, the local power to tax has been considerably reduced and is now concentrated on setting property tax rates. Consequently, the mechanical effect of any revision of rental values should fuel local tax competition, because it is likely to push urban local governments to reduce property tax rates, and the opposite may occur in rural municipalities. The political economy of any revision of property tax bases is thus quite complex in the French context of a highly fragmented municipal mapping (35,000 municipalities). This is exactly what happened in the early 1990s when the reform of rental values introduced by the government faced the successful opposition of the Parliament (Gilbert and Guengant 1998). The political economy of the reform of rental values is thus facing a dilemma between, on one hand, local tax autonomy, which is fundamental to fiscal decentralization, and on the other, a complete centralization of the property tax rate (or an equalization device), which should mitigate the property tax competition between thousands of municipalities (Gilbert 2019).

Properties used for social housing are exempt from the property tax. In the long run, municipalities lose tax revenues when new social housing developments are completed. At the instigation of the Rebsamen Commission, the central government will compensate municipalities for the full revenue loss from 2022 for the new social housing construction flow (not for the already built social housing park).

Finally, the transfer of the departmental share of the property tax to the municipalities (as of the 2021 budget) is worth mentioning. The department property tax is now a municipal tax.

Turning to the national level, the transformation of the wealth tax to a real estate wealth tax occurred in 2018, following a campaign pledge of presidential candidate Emmanuel Macron in 2017. The rationale for this reform was that rich taxpayers fled France to avoid paying the wealth tax. Indeed, a net emigration of rich taxpayers to Switzerland, Luxembourg, Belgium, and the United Kingdom has been documented. The free movement of people and capital is one of the founding principles of the European Union. The absence of wealth taxes in France's neighboring countries[8] made the net emigration of rich French citizens almost impossible to counteract. The restriction of the wealth basis to immobile elements such as housing and land was an individual response from France to stop this net emigration. Another approach would have been to persuade other countries to adopt a similar wealth tax, a much more complex solution to trigger and sustain.

Gilbert and Guengant (1998) studied replacing the property tax with a land tax based on market values, which they called a capitalization tax in reference to the capitalization of property and real estate values (negative capitalization of the property taxes and positive capitalization of local public services). They noted the differences between market values and rental values in certain situations. For instance, slums in city centers have high market value and low rental value, but it is the opposite for some rural premises in attractive tourist areas and likely to become second homes. They discussed the question of the fairness of the land value tax from the point of view of both the fiscal approach of equivalence (benefit principle) and taxpayers' ability to pay. The benefit principle was satisfied because the contribution is intended to capture the unjustified accumulation of wealth enjoyed by owners, who see the value of their property increased by the capitalized value of local public services. The wealth increase is also likely to augment the taxpayer's ability to pay.

The Gilbert and Guengant (1998) proposal was inspired more by the Henry George theorem (Arnott and Stiglitz 1979) than by George's initial proposal (1879). The reverse is true for the proposal made by Trannoy and Wasmer (2022). That proposal starts from the observation that the land values in macroeconomic terms are exceptional in France both in dynamics and in international comparison. Even if landownership in France is not well known, it appears to be unequally distributed. André and Meslin (2021) deliver stark empirical evidence of housing wealth concentration. Half of all households own 3.5 percent of the rental properties. Both efficiency and fairness push toward replacing all property taxes and use of property taxes with a single tax on land value. A simple calculation shows that a 1 percent land value tax enables recovering the tax receipts of all existing taxes. It is a resumption of a Georgist argument in the French economic context of the 21st century. The argument is not known by the French public, which historically has not been widely exposed to Henry George's ideas. We must be aware that in France, in addition to the political economy problems concerning taxpayers, there are also political economy problems with regard to local authorities. These problems are challenging. First, the stacking of the four levels of local authorities makes the compensation of losers quite complex, within a level but also between levels. In addition, municipalities will not easily give up the tax rate freedom on the property tax they currently enjoy because it is the only one they have retained. As a result, the status quo is the equilibrium point in the noncooperative tax game concerning reform of the property tax base.

Related to country-specific issues, there are two concerns.

- The rise of statutory property tax rates in 2022 and 2023 worries taxpayers in some cities after the COVID-19 crisis and with the 2022–2023 energy crisis. On average, built and unbuilt property tax rates will increase by 1.9 percent in 2022. In fact, more than a quarter of the large cities and their ECPIs have increased their taxes this year. In some cities, this local tax has simply soared over the past year, as in Marseille (up 13.1 percent), Strasbourg (up 8.9 percent), and Nantes (up 7.8 percent). Indeed, the abolition of the housing tax leaves few degrees of freedom for municipalities under financial strain. The property and refuse collection taxes are the only options left to balance the budget.
- For departments, the story is different. The poverty rate during the COVID-19 pandemic did not rise, contrary to expectations. The central government paid whatever it cost. So departmental expenditures were contained, and they hugely benefited from the surge of the transaction market in terms of both prices and volumes. The transfer tax receipts have exploded since the pandemic (see table 11.1). The unknown is what will happen next because it is less than plausible that the rally in the housing market will continue as interest rates rise.

Impact

Trannoy and Wasmer (2013a; 2013b) pointed to four major malfunctions in the French housing market: a high vacancy rate in the private housing stock (8 percent), a low price elasticity of the housing supply (0.5, found by Cavalleri, Cournède, and Özsöğüt [2019]) or a high short-term housing price elasticity to credit (0.7, found by Labonne and Welter-Nicol [2016]), insufficient spatial mobility of owners and tenants between employment areas, and a social housing stock whose occupation is not optimized. Overall, it is not clear that taxation is the leading cause of these malfunctions, but inappropriate regulations are undoubtedly one of the major reasons. Because tax bases of the property tax are only loosely correlated to market values, the salience of the tax may not be very high. At the same time, one might think that another taxation system, based only on the land value, could solve most of the first three problems while maintaining the existing regulations. First, a land tax as a substitute for the transaction and capital gains taxes will stop the land retention phenomenon. A more fluid land market will partially solve the land supply problem in urban and peri-urban areas. Furthermore, the housing supply will thrive without any tax on construction, renovation, or building ownership. The housing market frictions will ease because owners will think twice before leaving properties vacant while paying 1 percent of their value each year. In addition, mobility among cities or regions will no longer be slowed with the abolition of the stamp duty tax. Beyond that, it is unclear whether it is easier in political terms to change the tax system or easier to work on each ill-thought regulation to make them more efficient.

From a macroscopic view, the increasing multiple layers of local governments cannot be viewed in itself as a problem, because it naturally aims at solving specific institutional issues arising from small municipality size, which remains a basic feature in France. However, this institutional piling up entails the piling up of responsibilities and raises special difficulties in defining precisely the responsibilities allocated to each layer, where decisive progress is required. Moreover, the piling up of nationally managed policies and local policies leads to complexities, duplications, and lack of internalization of local externalities (see, e.g., Wasmer 2016). On the revenue side, tax specialization (meaning that each layer of local government benefits from an exclusive set of taxes) is almost complete in 2023. In the meantime, successive reforms of local taxation tended to transfer the tax burden from businesses to individual taxpayers. As a consequence, local governments and local individual taxpayers bear more of the political responsibility of raising the local tax rate than in the past. In this context, it is strange that the taxation of capital gains on properties accrues to the national level and not to local governments, whose provision of local public goods is at least partly at the origin of such an increment in property values.

Beyond this global judgment, there are specific deficiencies from an efficiency viewpoint.

- Looking at the balance between the property tax and the property tax on undeveloped land (agriculture), the tax rate seems higher on urban property than on agricultural land in aggregate terms. Looking at the tax revenues in table 11.1 and comparing them with the wealth figures in national accounts for urban wealth and farming land wealth for 2021, the tax rate for urban wealth is double that for farming land wealth. Of course, this global comparison hides heterogeneous situations, but a lack of neutrality should be justified only on the basis of externalities.

- Tenants of residential real estate no longer pay the housing tax. Tenants of business properties, however, continue to pay the equivalent of the housing tax and the rent tax on business real estate. Departing from the principle of tax neutrality regarding land or building use should be motivated by appealing to external effects. That argumentation is missing. Urvoy (2019) shows a significant negative statistical association between the rate of the rent tax on business real estate and that on land and building assets for firms in the manufacturing sector.
- Pending revisions of the cadastral values for residential buildings create significant unfairness between taxpayers but are also a source of large inefficiencies. Two taxpayers who own dwellings with the same rental value will pay different property taxes even if the municipal tax rates are the same. Revision has not occurred since 1970. As a result, in relative terms the actual tax bases overestimate the rental market value of the newest dwellings and undervalue the large homes with many rooms (Chapelle, Fabre, and Lallemand 2020).
- The high transfer tax (7–8 percent plus notary fees) discourages residential mobility. Bérard and Trannoy (2018) showed that the rise of the departmental rate of 0.5 percent in 2014 deterred 40,000 transactions. They did not find a price effect, meaning that prices are quite rigid in the French housing market. Importantly, first-time home buyers bear this transfer tax to a higher degree. Transfer tax first hurts the most mobile and the young. Removing these transfer taxes and increasing property taxes will meet with hostility from the departments, for which this represents the main tax source. As long as expectations about housing prices are rising, first-time buyers can always hope that the future rise will allow them to erase tax losses. Indeed, some advocates of the tax argue that property turnover was as high as 4 percent in 2021. However, in a property market in equilibrium or a downturn, the reasoning does not hold.
- The system of taxes on capital gains on vacant land made available for development has disincentive effects. It leads to land retention. The longer the owner keeps the land, the lower the tax rate. More generally, the same criticism applies to capital gains on housing wealth. Empirical evidence on the impact of the tax schedule of capital gains on the housing market is still missing.

Regarding the progressivity of property and assimilated taxes, we must admit that we do not have a complete picture. We have only empirical information about the progressivity of the local property tax itself and the soon-to-be former housing tax, thanks to Carbonnier (2019), but this study covers only primary homes, not second homes and vacant or rental housing. The corresponding wealth represents 44 percent of the 10th decile's housing wealth and still 23 percent of the 9th decile, which biases the study results against progressivity.

That the housing tax was clearly regressive was put forward as a reason for its abolition. This regressivity was reduced by a cap of 2.4 percent on the ratio of the housing tax to disposable income, transformed into an additional flat tax for payers of the capped tax. Choosing the amount of disposable income as a reference doomed the housing tax. A regressive tax on income is untenable. Only a measure of the value of local public services provided is a valid point.

The progressivity of the property tax is more complex. First, the whole population or the population of landlords could be the scope of the study. Second, among the three determinants of progressivity—the tax base, the schedule of exemptions and deductions that mainly benefit taxpayers below an income threshold, and the spatial differences among local taxes—it is unclear whether spatial differences should be taken into account. According to Tiebout (1956), differences in local tax rates may correspond to different private or public good-bundle choices. Accounting for the disparity in tax rates without accounting for the gap in public good quantity would bias the comparison. More specifically, rich people buy public goods in greater quantity because of an income effect. This yields a positive gradient of local tax rate with local mean income and indicates progressivity in tax rates, which will hide progressivity in local public good services. That said, when including the three determinants the profile of the property tax is regressive among homeowners. The average effort ratio, defined as the ratio of the tax liability to the standard of living (equivalized income taking equivalence scales between households of different sizes and compositions into account), including the imputed rent, goes from 1.7 percent in the second decile to 0.4 percent in the ninth decile. Poor, old, and handicapped homeowners may benefit from exemptions of deductions of property taxes, but it does not seem to have a big impact. It should not be forgotten that one-third of the poorest living-standard decile are homeowners.

A study by André and Meslin (2021) has the advantage of being based on a quasi-exhaustive administrative database. It remedies a drawback of Carbonnier's (2019) work by including all housing properties, and in particular, rentals and second homes. The property tax regressivity is confirmed but only on the bottom part of the distribution (the two first deciles). The share of tax liability in disposable income is almost constant at about 2.5 percent on all the remaining range up to the last centile, where it drops to 1.5 percent.

A caveat is in order. The property taxes at the national level, particularly the real estate wealth tax, are not included in the two studies of the preceding paragraph. By definition, the former is very progressive. So the global picture may be less gloomy than that conveyed by these two studies. Its marginal tax rate of about 0.5 percent will bite the last centile and mitigate or maybe offset the lack of progressivity at the very top of the distribution.

This regressivity of the property tax can only make its current version quite unpopular. Several factors contribute to this, but one driver is the choice of the market rent as the tax base. It is well established that small-area properties have a relatively higher rent-price ratio than large-area properties. In other words, adopting the market price as the tax base would help reduce the regressivity phenomenon. According to Chapelle, Fabre, and Lallemand (2020), the revision of rental values would probably mitigate the regressivity since the richest would see their tax pressure increase by about 10 percent, and the bottom of the income scale would see a reduced magnitude in the opposite direction.

Conclusion

France can be remembered as the country where economists first made a case for land taxation with the Physiocratic school. The tax system initiated during the Revolution followed this recipe to some extent. What was valid in the 18th century is even more true in the 21st, when land value represents almost half the net worth and three times the French national income. Moreover, the very fact that France has the second-highest tax burden in OECD countries makes it even more compelling to find tax bases that are the least distortive (OECD, 2025).

Property tax reforms are hampered by the complexity of the French institutional organization. As soon as the tax bases are modified, both horizontal and vertical losers will appear, and it is therefore necessary to invent equalization and smoothing mechanisms to prevent excessive burdens. This often renders the reforms too complex to be understood. The Gordian knot has never been cut, which has so far prevented any major reform.

France is a land-rich and housing-rich country, and an exception in that dimension in the Western world apart from the United Kingdom. As a matter of fact, both countries have centralized institutions and a large capital agglomeration and secular institutions. Given the capitalization of national wealth into land and housing, it is not surprising that the size and diversity of the housing tax system is so complex and inefficient to a large extent. Many reforms need to be made, and economic reasoning can bring more to the table than it currently does.

Notes

1. A number of municipalities had to be forced to join an EPCI. Tricaud (2022) explains why they might be right to fear joining.

2. Exceptions are the city of Strasbourg and some neighboring communes, for historical reasons related to the occupation of Alsace-Moselle by Germany between 1871 and 1918.

3. $\{100 - [(15 - 6) \times 6]\}$.

4. Total collection cost is the ratio of the cost of central-government tax services to the net tax receipts sent to local governments.

5. The rates of the additional property taxes mentioned above are set by the Finance Act. They could vary from one year to another. For example, from 2019 to 2020, the tax rate of TSE-Office foncier moved from 0.953 percent to 0.223 percent; the TSE-Société du Grand Paris, from 0.243 percent to 0.195 percent; the TSARIF rate, from 0.311 to 0.207 percent; and GEMAPI rate, from 0.124 to 0.0912 percent.

6. In 2021, the increase in the revenues of rent tax on business real estate was transferred from the City of Paris to the Métropole du Grand Paris.

7. The measure is an approximation because the *potentiel financier* index encompasses all local tax capacities, not just the property tax capacity. In addition, the index takes into account a lump-sum subsidy transferred by the central government.

8. This is not true for Switzerland, but rich taxpayers can negotiate rebates of wealth tax.

References

André, M., and O. Meslin. 2021. "Housing Wealth Concentration and Redistributive Impact of Property Tax: Evidence from a Database on French Households' Housing Wealth." Working paper 2021–004. INSEE.

Arnott, R., and J. Stiglitz. 1979. "Aggregate Land Rents, Expenditure on Public Goods, and Optimal City Size." *Quarterly Journal of Economics* 93(4): 471–500.

Artus, P., A. Bozio, and C. García-Peñalosa. 2013. "Fiscalité des Revenus du Capital." *Notes Du Conseil d'analyse Economique*, no. 9: 1–12.

Bach, L., A. Bozio, A. Guillouzouic, and C. Malgouyres. 2021. "Évaluer les Effets de l'Impôt Sur La Fortune et de sa Suppression sur le Tissu Productif." Report Institut des politiques publiques, No. 36.

Bachelet, M., and M. Poulhès. 2017. "Hausse des Droits de Mutation: Quel Impact sur Le Marché Immobilier?" THEMA Commissariat Général. https://www.ecologie.gouv.fr/sites/default/files/publications/Théma%20-%20Hausse%20des%20droits%20de%20mutation.pdf.

Bérard, G., and A. Trannoy. 2018. "The Impact of a Rise in the Real Estate Transfer Tax on the French Housing Market." *Economics and Statistics*, nos. 500–502: 187–209.

Bono, P.-H., and A. Trannoy. 2019. "The Impact of the 'Scellier' Income Tax Relief on Building Land Prices in France." *Economics and Statistics* 507(1): 91–114.

Carbonnier, C. 2007. "Who Pays Sales Taxes? Evidence from French VAT Reforms, 1987–1999." *Journal of Public Economics* 91(5–6): 1219–1229.

———. 2019. "The Distributional Impact of Local Taxation on Households in France." *Economics and Statistics* 507–508: 31–52.

Cavailhès, J. 2022. "Interview d'Alain Trannoy: Habitat individuel et sobriété foncière." Fonciers en debate, January 15. https://fonciers-en-debat.com/interview-d-alain-trannoy-habitat-individuel-et-sobriete-fonciere/.

Cavalleri, M. C., B. Cournède, and E. Özsöğüt. 2019. "How Responsive Are Housing Markets in the OECD? National Level Estimates." OECD Working paper No. 1589.

Chapelle, G., A. Trannoy, and E. Wasmer. 2021. "L'explosion de la des terrains en France est-elle uniforme? Une analyse en Ile-de-France." LIEPP Policy Brief. https://sciencespo.hal.science/hal-03507967v1/document.

Chapelle, G., and J. B. Eyméoud. 2022. "Can Big Data Increase Our Knowledge of Local Rental Markets? A Dataset on the Rental Sector in France." *PloS One* 17(1): e0260405. https://doi.org/10.1371/journal.pone.0260405.

Chapelle, G., B. Fabre, and C. Lallemand. 2020. "Révision des Valeurs Locatives sur les Locaux d'Habitation: une Evaluation sur Grandes Agglomérations." *Rapport Institut des Politiques Publiques* 29. https://www.ipp.eu/publication/decembre-2020-revision-valeurs-locatives-locaux-d-habitation-une-evaluation-sur-grandes-agglomerations/.

Chapelle, G., B. Vignolles, and C. Wolf. 2018. "Impact of a Housing Tax Credit on Local Housing Markets: Evidence from France." *Annals of Economics and Statistics/ Annales d'Économie et de Statistique* 130: 101–131.

Cour des Comptes. 2010. "La fiscalité locale." https://www.ccomptes.fr/sites/default/files/EzPublish/Rapport-fiscalite-locale-conseil-des-prelevements-obligatoires_2.pdf.

———. 2021. *Mission avances aux collectivités territoriales: Note d'analyse de l'exécution budgétaire 2021. NEB Avances aux collectivités territoriales 2021.* Paris: Cour des comptes.

———. 2022a. "La Gestion de la Fiscalité locale par la DGFIP." https://www.ccomptes.fr/sites/default/files/EzPublish/20170201-rapport-gestion-fiscalite-directe-locale-dgfip.pdf.

———. 2022b. "Situation Financière de la Ville de Paris." https://www.ccomptes.fr/sites/default/files/2023-10/IDR2022-04_0.pdf.

———. 2023. "Les Taxes Foncières." https://www.ccomptes.fr/sites/files/20230227-S2023-0028-Taxes-foncieres.pdf.

Crédit Suisse. 2022. "Global Wealth Report 2022." https://bibbase.org/f/nKAPSyp34A9azBzJd/Shorrocksetal2022a.pdf.

DGCL (Direction Générale des Collectivités Locales). 2021. *Guide statistique des finances locales and Rapport de l'Observatoire des finances et de la gestion publique locales.* Ministère de l'Intérieur.

———. 2022. "Les collectivités locales en chiffres." Ministère de l'Intérieur. https://www.collectivites-locales.gouv.fr/.

DGFiP (Direction Générale des Finances Publiques). 2016. "Rapport relatif à l'expérimentation de la révision des valeurs locatives des locaux d'habitation menée en 2015." https://www.senat.fr/fileadmin/Fichiers/Images/commission/finances/evenements/finances_locales/Revision_des_valeurs_locatives_1e_partie.pdf; https://www.senat.fr/fileadmin/Fichiers/Images/commission/finances/evenements/finances_locales/Revision_valeurs_locatives_2e_partie.pdf.

———. 2021. "Annuaire statistique de la Direction Générale des Finances Publiques." (December 6). https://www.data.gouv.fr/fr/datasets/annuaire-statistique-de-la-direction-generale-des-finances-publiques-dgfip/.

———. 2022. "L'impôt sur la Fortune Immobilière en 2021." *Etudes et statistiques*, no. 8.

———. n.d. "Comptes administratifs de la collectivité parisienne." https://www.paris.fr/pages/comptes-administratifs-de-la-ville-retrouvez-toutes-les-infos-27793#comptes-administratifs-de-la-collectivite-parisienne.

Diamond, P., and J. Mirrlees. 1971. "Optimal Taxation and Public Production." *American Economic Review* 61(1): 8–27.

Garbinti, B., J. Goupille-Lebret, M. Munoz, S. Stantcheva, and G. Zucman. 2023. "Tax Design, Information, and Elasticities: Evidence from the French Wealth Tax." Working paper No. 31333. Cambridge, MA: National Bureau of Economic Research (June).

George, H. 1879. *Progress and Poverty: An Inquiry into the Cause of Industrial Depressions, and of Increase of Want with Increase of Wealth. The Remedy.* D. Appleton.

Gilbert, G. 2019. "Les Réformes Empilées de la Fiscalité Locale en France depuis le Milieu du XX ième Siècle." In *L'Echelle des Régulations Politiques XX*[e] *–XXI*[e] *Siècles*, ed. V. Albe, J. Commaille, and F. Le Bot, 59–72. Paris: Septentrion.

Gilbert, G., and A. Guengant. 1998. *La Fiscalité Locale en Question*. 2nd ed. Paris: Montchrestien.

Gilbert, G., and J.-C. Thoenig. 1999. "Les Cofinancements publics—Des Pratiques aux Rationalités." *Revue d'Economie Financière* 1: 7–40.

Guelton S. 2015. "Taxer les Terrains Constructibles Non-bâtis." *Revue fonci ère* 3: 16–18.

Guelton, S., and B. Leroux. 2016. "La Sur-taxation des Terrains Constructibles Non-bâtis." *Revue fonci ère* 9: 35–40.

Jelloul, M. B., A. Bozio, T. Douenne, B. Fabre, and C. Leroy. 2019. "The 2019 French Budget: Impacts on Households." Notes Institut des Politiques Publiques, No. 37. https://www.ipp.eu/en/publication/the-2019-french-budget-impacts-on-households/.

Labonne, C., and C. Welter-Nicol. 2016. "Cheap Credit, Affordable Housing? Evidence from the French Interest-Free Loan Policy." Banque de France. https://acpr.banque-france.fr/en/publications-and-statistics/publications/ndeg-20-cheap-credit-unaffordable-houses.

Laignel, A., and C. Guené. 2022. "Rapport de l'Observatoire des finances et de la gestion publique locales—2022." *Vie Public.* July 15. https://www.vie-publique.fr/rapport/285733-observatoire-des-finances-et-de-la-gestion-publique-locales-2022.

Martin, P., and A. Trannoy. 2019. "Les Impôts pour ou contre la Production." Note No. 52. Conseil d'Analyse Economique.

McKinsey Global Institute. 2021. "The Rise and Rise of the Global Balance Sheet." https://tinyurl.com/547kvpap.

OECD. 2025. "Tax Revenues." https://www.oecd.org/en/data/indicators/tax-revenue.html.

République Française. 2016. "Comment dois-je calculer les droits de succession?" https://www.impots.gouv.fr/particulier/questions/comment-dois-je-calculer-les-droits-de-succession.

———. 2025a. "Impôt sur le revenu—Plus-value immobilière." Last updated June 10. https://www.service-public.fr/particuliers/vosdroits/F10864.

———. 2025b. "Impôt sur la fortune immobilière (IFI)." Last updated February 20. https://www.service-public.fr/particuliers/vosdroits/N20074.

———. 2025c. "Taxe sur les surfaces commerciales (Tascom)." Last updated January 1. https://entreprendre.service-public.fr/vosdroits/F22790.

———. 2025d. "Taxe annuelle sur les bureaux en Île-de-France." Last updated January 1, 2025. Accessed August 1, 2025. https://entreprendre.service-public.fr/vosdroits/F20668.

Segu, M. 2020. "The Impact of Taxing Vacancy on Housing Markets: Evidence from France." *Journal of Public Economics* 185: 104079.

Service des Données et des études statistiques. 2021a. *Comptes satellites du logement 2019:* DGFiP, *Recettes fiscales brutes (2019).* Paris: Ministère de la Transition écologique.

———. 2021b. "Rapport du compte du logement 2019." September 29. https://www.statistiques.developpement-durable.gouv.fr/rapport-du-compte-du-logement-2019-0.

Tiebout, C. 1956. "A Pure Theory of Local Expenditures." *Journal of Political Economy* 64(5): 416–424.

Trannoy, A., and E. Wasmer. 2013a. "Comment Modérer les Prix de l'Immobilier?" Note No. 2. Conseil d'Analyse Economique.

———. 2013b. "La Politique du Logement Locatif." Note No. 10. Conseil d'Analyse Economique.

———. 2022. *Le Grand Retour de la Terre dans les Patrimoines et Pourquoi c'est une Bonne Nouvelle.* Paris: Odile Jacob.

Tricaud, C. 2025. "Better Alone? Evidence on the Costs of Intermunicipal Cooperation." *American Economic Journal: Applied Economics* 17(1): 160–207.

UBS. 2023. *World Global Wealth Databook.* Zurich: UBS. www.ubs.com.

Urvoy, C. 2019. "Impôts sur la Production: Quel Impact sur la Compétitivité? Analyse de Trois Taxes sur Données d'Entreprises." Focus No. 35. Conseil d'Analyse Economique.

Wasmer, E. 2016. "Des Politiques Urbaines Nationales, un Oxymore?" *Revue Economique* 67(3): 667–678.

Legislation

Act on the New Territorial Organization of the Republic (NOTRe Act), Law No. 2015-991 of August 7, 2015 [Loi n° 2015-991 du 7 août 2015 portant nouvelle organisation territoriale de la République (NOTRe)].

Decentralization Act of 1982, Law No. 82-213 of 2 March 1982 on the rights and freedoms of municipalities, departments, and regions [Loi n° 82-213 du 2 mars 1982 relative aux droits et libertés des communes, des départements et des regions].

Finance Act of 2020, Law No. 2019-1479 of December 28, 2019 [Loi n° 2019-1479 du 28 décembre 2019 de finances pour 2020].

Finance Act of 2023, Law No. 2022-1726 of December 30, 2022 [Loi n° 2022-1726 du 30 décembre 2022 de finances pour 2023].

12

Updating to a New Property Tax Structure in Germany

JAN WERNER

Germany has a population of 83.7 million people and a gross domestic product (GDP) of €3.6 trillion as of July 1, 2022. This makes Germany the 19th most populous country in the world, and only the United States, China, and Japan are ahead of Germany in terms of nominal GDP worldwide.

GDP per capita in Germany is over €43,000, a rank of 18th in the world. Like many other industrialized countries, Germany is facing the challenges of an aging population. At the end of 2021, there were 8.3 million people in Germany between the ages of 15 and 24, or 10 percent of the total population. This number is lower both in absolute terms and proportionally than it has been since 1950.

Knowing German history is important to understanding the German public finance system.[1] During the Middle Ages and early modern period, Germany comprised a huge number of small, independent, and self-governed states. Three hundred German states existed during the Holy Roman Empire of the German Nation in the 17th century. For this reason, Germany has a long tradition of federalism and is not a centralized state like France or the United Kingdom, for example. Under the occupation by Napoleon's army, this sectionalism was reduced by creating bigger kingdoms and duchies, but the Germans did not accept this imported territorial reorganization by Napoleon. The second German Empire, which existed from 1871 until 1918, excluded the German-speaking Austria and thus represented the so-called Lesser German solution, still consisting of 26 states, with four kingdoms, six grand duchies, five duchies, seven principalities, three free Hanseatic cities, and the imperial territory of Alsace-Lorraine. However, the kingdom of Prussia contained about two-thirds of Germany's population and territory, and its dominance was also established constitutionally. After World War I, the Weimar constitution aspired to establish the accountability of government to an elected parliament, but it failed to render the latter politically viable and was a highly fragmented party system at a time of major social and political upheavals. The national parliament eventually fell prey to the ploys and threats of the Nazis, which ended the short-lived democracy between the two world wars. Hitler's ascendance to power had proceeded via Berlin and through Prussian institutions, with the other states of the federation being impotent or unwilling to counterbalance his usurpation of power. This is why the Allies abolished the state of Prussia immediately after World War II, thereby eliminating one important asymmetry and source of political instability.

The newly created zones, later *länder*, or federal states, did not necessarily respect historic boundaries, and after the Nazi experience, regional balance and symmetry became guiding principles for the reconstruction of postwar Germany, at least in the former West Germany. However, a concession to German history was the creation of the city-states Hamburg and Bremen, and after unification, Berlin, which introduced a minor asymmetric element into intergovernmental fiscal relations that has more recently attracted the attention of Germany's Constitutional Court. But as a general rule, because the devastation of World War II had left all regions equally poor and deprived of economic resources, balanced regional development and uniform living conditions became attractive features for policy making and institution building. These principles were not only incorporated in the new federal constitution; they became so entrenched in people's minds and penetrated all domains of collective decision-making that they would survive even the quandary of unification in 1990. Indeed, German unification, in which the formerly socialist East Germany represents roughly 20 percent of the population but less than 6 percent of total value added, was, and still is, a major challenge for the political system and the economy.

This history explains why modern German states exert their sovereignty only conjointly at the national level, through the Bundesrat, the upper house, which consists of representatives of state governments, not elected officials as in the US Senate. No individual state is accorded privileges in the Bundesrat other than its vote, which is exerted en bloc and weighted roughly by population. The result of the majority vote is binding for all, and the policy outcome is uniform across the nation, even for tax law and state and municipal taxes (though municipalities are accorded some discretion in setting rates for municipal taxes), and the states are denied any form of own taxation. Tax revenue is typically shared and apportioned among layers of government according to the constitution for income taxes or the law for the value-added tax (VAT), and revenue is disbursed horizontally among regional entities according to formulas with strong equalization components.

A host of intergovernmental transfers aimed at fostering national homogeneity and uniformity of living conditions, combined with the states' inability to use their own tax instruments, exacerbate the almost complete lack of policy discretion at lower tiers of government and the weaknesses of the revenue agenda of state parliaments. This interregional solidarity is pushed to the point that the average command of public resources per capita is now higher in the needier states than in some of the richest states in the western part of the country.

Germany is a federal state with a three-level administrative structure. In addition to the federal government, whose ministries are based both in Germany's capital, Berlin, and in the former capital, Bonn, there are 16 federal states (*Bundesländer*)[2] and 10,796 municipalities as of July 1, 2022. Table 12.1 shows their populations.

Within the local administrative bodies in Germany, a further distinction is made among the regional planning associations,[3] the 294 rural districts (*Landkreise*), the 106 incorporated cities (*kreisfreie Städte*), and the municipalities, which form part of the rural districts and with towns are

Table 12.1 Municipality Populations, 2000 and 2021

Number of Inhabitants	Number of Municipalities, 2000	Number of Municipalities, 2021
<100	226	201
100–499	3,454	1,893
500–999	2,521	1,731
1,000–4,999	4,809	4,016
5,000–9,999	1,288	1,355
10,000–49,999	1,348	1,407
50,000–99,999	109	113
100,000–199,999	43	40
200,000–499,999	27	26
≥500,000	12	14
Total	13,837	10,796

Sources: Various publications of the *Statistisches Bundesamt*.

the smallest local units. After numerous territorial reforms in the respective federal states between 1970 and 1977, the number of small towns decreased.[4]

Tax revenues are distributed among the individual regional administrative bodies both according to own assigned revenues and revenue sharing. This means, for example, that the tax receipts from the real property tax are available to the municipalities in full, while they also receive a fixed percentage of the tax receipts from the VAT and the personal income tax, but not the corporate income tax. Table 12.2 shows the distribution of the most important tax revenues.

Figure 12.1 presents the distribution of all taxes and customs among the central government, the 16 federal states, the local units, and the European Union.

The political accountability for expenditure outcomes is not always clear in Germany. For example, the level and criteria for spending by the social welfare programs are fixed by the central government, but disbursement of grants and examination of the respective social neediness is the responsibility of the local authorities. Moreover, the central government delegates a huge number of administrative duties—mainly for social security—to the federal states and local authorities and bears their

Table 12.2 Tax Revenue Distribution Among Central Government, Federal States, and Municipalities, 2021

Tax	Central Government (%)	Federal States (%)	Local Units (%)	Revenues (€ billion)
Consumption taxes	100			87
Surtax on the personal income tax and corporate income tax	100			11
Inheritance and gift tax		100		10
Property transfer tax		100		18
Lottery tax		100		2
Real property tax			100	14
personal income tax	42.5	42.5	15	318
VAT	51.0	46.4	2.6	250
Corporate income tax	50	50		42
Interest rebate	44	44	12	10
Trade tax	3.7	12.7	83.6	61

Source: Author.

Figure 12.1 Taxes and Customs Distribution of Central Government, Federal States, Local Units, and the European Union, 2011–2021

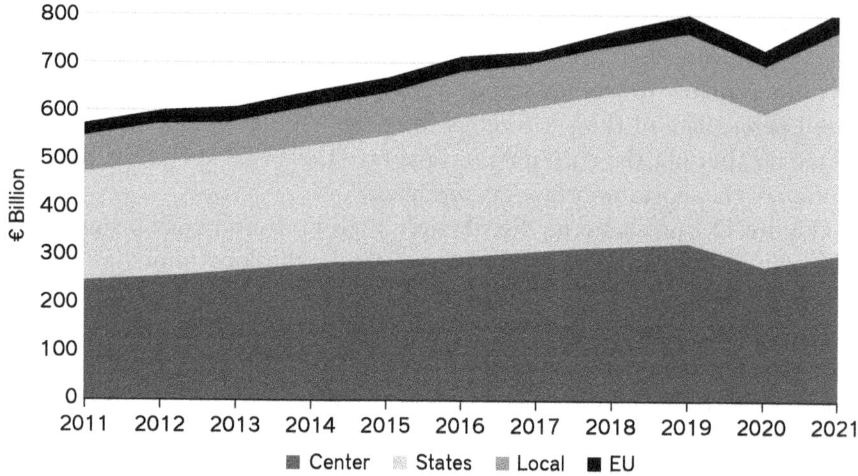

Source: Werner (2018a).

expense. Table 12.3 shows the distribution of the accountability for some areas of expenditure among government tiers.[5]

Land and Property Markets in Germany

In 2020, 50.6 percent of Germany's 357,581 square kilometers was used for agriculture. Forests covered 31.0 percent of the total area. This proportion is slowly decreasing, while the proportion of land devoted to settlements and transport steadily increases. Settlement and transport was the third-largest land use at 14.5 percent in 2020.[6] In addition to housing, public purposes, or trade, settlement and transport use includes recreational areas, cemeteries, and traffic infrastructure. Lakes, rivers, canals, and near-coastal waters take up 2.3 percent of the land area. The remaining 2 percent include quarried land such as gravel or lignite pits; unland (vegetation-free areas) such as rocky areas, former military terrain, or former spoil heaps; and unused vegetation areas such as heathland, moors, swamps, woody areas, and areas adjacent to water bodies.

At the end of 2021, there were 43.1 million apartments in Germany, the majority in buildings comprising three or more apartments.[7] The average apartment size is around 92 square meters, 4.4 rooms plus kitchen and bathroom. Owner-occupied apartments are 120 square meters on average—two-thirds larger than rented apartments, which have an average 72 square

Table 12.3 Distribution of Expenditure Accountability

	Central Government	Federal States	Rural Districts	Municipalities
Foreign policy	Yes	No	No	No
Currency policy	Yes	No	No	No
Defense policy	Yes	No	No	No
Social welfare	Yes	No	No	No
Roads, railways, and inland water transportation	Yes	Yes	Yes	Yes
Education	No	Yes	No	No
Police	No	Yes	No	No
Construction supervision (including building and occupation permits)	No	No	Yes	No
Construction and maintenance of school facilities	No	No	Yes	No
Public transportation	No	No	Yes	No
Construction and maintenance of public hospitals	No	No	Yes	No
Kindergartens	No	No	No	Yes
Fire departments	No	No	No	Yes
Theaters and museums	No	No	No	Yes
Parks and sports facilities	No	No	No	Yes
Waste management[1]	No	No	No	Yes
Electricity supply[1]	No	No	No	Yes
Water supply[1]	No	No	No	Yes

Sources: Adapted by the author based on Werner (2003).

[1] Most municipalities own and politically control special purpose associations for this task. A few have sold their special purpose associations to private companies after making long-term arrangements with them.

meters of floor space. About 47 percent of all apartments in 2018 were owner-occupied.

There are significant regional differences in the ownership structure in Germany. The ownership rates in almost all the former West German non-city-states are traditionally—and still—higher than in most former East German states, although some catching up has taken place in the twenty-first century. This is particularly so in the state of Brandenburg, where the ownership rate has risen by 12 percentage points (table 12.4).

Table 12.4 Residential Ownership in Federal States, 1998, 2010, and 2018 (%)

	1998	2010	2018
Germany	**40.9**	**45.7**	**46.5**
Saxony-Anhalt	36.5	42.7	45.1
Mecklenburg-Western Pomerania	32.3	37.0	41.1
Thuringia	39.2	45.5	45.3
Saxony	28.7	33.7	34.6
Brandenburg	35.5	46.2	47.8
Saarland	58.1	63.7	64.7
Lower Saxony	48.5	54.5	54.2
Rhineland-Palatinate	55.0	58.0	58.0
Schleswig-Holstein	46.8	49.7	53.3
North Rhine–Westphalia	37.4	43.0	43.7
Baden-Wuerttemberg	48.3	52.8	52.6
Bavaria	47.6	51.0	51.4
Hesse	43.3	47.3	47.5
Berlin	11.0	14.6	17.4
(Hanseatic city) Hamburg	20.3	22.6	23.9
(Hanseatic city) Bremen	37.5	37.2	37.8

Source: Statistisches Bundesamt (2020).

The nation's highest ownership rate is still in Saarland, where almost two out of three apartments (65 percent) are owner-occupied.

Differences are also evident between cities and rural areas. Living in the city mostly means renting. The ownership rate in urban areas of Germany in 2018 was just 27 percent. In the largest metropolises (Berlin, Hamburg, Munich, Cologne, Frankfurt am Main, Stuttgart, and Düsseldorf), the ownership rate was as low as 22 percent. In communities adjacent to the metropolises, in the commuter belt or greenbelt areas, the ownership rate nationwide is over 44 percent. In rural districts, more than one in two apartments are owner-occupied. The farther an apartment is from a large city, the more likely it is to be owner-occupied. Whether an apartment is owner-occupied or rented correlates closely with building size. In 2018, four out of five owner-occupied apartments were in a building with a maximum of two apartments. Exactly the opposite was true in apartments occupied by tenants. Here the proportion of apartments in buildings with three or more units was 81 percent. The proportion of rented apartments in buildings with 10 or more units has increased significantly nationwide, from 31 percent for residential buildings built before 2011 to 42 percent for those built between 2011 and 2018. The proportion of owner-occupied apartments in the buildings erected between 2011 and 2018 increased slightly, to 8 percent.

Renting is very common, especially in the city-states. The financial burden of rents are significantly higher in cities than in rural areas.

Construction and real estate prices have risen sharply since 2010. This price development is influenced by many demographic and economic factors. A growing population—immigration—a scarce supply of real estate, and low interest rates have all led to rising prices. Indexes from the Federal Statistical Office document the price rise. The construction price index for residential buildings shows prices for individually planned single-family and multifamily homes. However, only the building is included in this index. The index shows that house prices increased by 29 percent between 2010 and 2020. The inflation rate increased by only 14 percent in the same period. The price index for building land shows prices for undeveloped, designated building plots of 100 square meters or more. Prices for building land increased by 102 percent between 2010 and 2020. The house price index measures the average price of all typical market transactions for residential real estate (condominiums as well as detached and semidetached houses) sold as a complete package of land and buildings. This includes both newly built and existing residential properties. Nationwide, the prices for one- and two-family houses and condominiums rose by around 65 percent between 2010 and 2020.

Munich has been Germany's most expensive city for years. The average price for condominiums in 2021 was €9,732 per square meter. The second-most-expensive city is Frankfurt am Main, where the average is €6,586 per square meter. In the ranking of the Big Seven, the seven largest German metropolises, Hamburg ranks third at €6,489 per square meter, ahead of Berlin at €5,528. Cologne is, comparatively speaking, the cheapest metropolitan city. Here, too, prices rose significantly in 2021. Nevertheless, a square meter in Cologne costs only half as much as in Munich (Postbank 2022, 1–14).

Land and building prices have skyrocketed in Germany since the 2008 financial crisis. Nevertheless, it has so far been comparatively affordable for many owner-occupiers to buy a house or apartment, because no matter how much the prices rose, prospective owners always benefited from the low interest rate policy of the European Central Bank, which led to historically low costs for construction loans.

Then came the trend reversal: since the beginning of 2022, mortgage interest rates have risen by an average of 2.5 percent. Depending on the line of credit and the equity contributed, they effectively averaged 3.2 to 3.5 percent in 2023.

Regardless of whether people are renting or owning, many households feel burdened by their housing costs or live in overcrowded apartments—according to the European definition.[8] The overcrowding rate was particularly high in cities in 2020, when about one in seven people (15.0 percent) were living in an overcrowded apartment. In small towns and suburbs, only about half as many people were affected, with 7.9 percent living in such housing. In rural areas, more living space was usually available, with only 5.8 percent living in overcrowded apartments. Housing allowances are granted to enable low-income households to find appropriate housing.[9]

Real Estate Cadastre

The real estate cadastre is the official register of parcels of land in accordance with Section 2 (2) of the Land Register Ordinance. Federal states have their own regulations for management of the cadastre, in terms of surveying laws, ordinances, and decrees. With regard to the data, the implementing regulations have largely been standardized among the federal states in order to be able to guarantee nationwide data delivery. In most federal states, either the Ministry of the Interior, the Ministry of Finance, or the Ministry of Economic Affairs is responsible for managing the cadastre.

Cadastre offices are structured differently and have different names in the respective federal states, but the tasks are similar:

- Management of the real estate cadastre (cadastral maps are real estate or field maps).
- Management of cadastral books and real estate books.
- Archiving of all historical (paper) documents.
- Digitization of the data.
- Provision of data to, for example, property buyers and sellers, notaries, and courts.
- Cadastral surveying to, for example, determine boundaries on parcels of land.
- Technical processing, such as land consolidation, or reallocation according to the building code, such as converting agricultural land to building land for residential properties.
- Mapping of all properties on the basis of descriptions of plots (area size, numbers, and type and class of use).

For the transfer of ownership of a property, but also for mortgage valuations, the owner or purchaser needs an excerpt from the cadastral book. In a real estate purchase, the buyer also needs a current extract from the cadastre office. The buyer can use this to check whether there are mortgages, heritable building rights, building encumbrances, or other usufructs.

If the property is mortgaged, the seller cannot proceed without the consent of the creditor. A third party who has a heritable building right is not the owner but may construct a building on a specified area of the property. Construction encumbrances are obligations toward an authority. These include actions that a property owner must refrain from or carry out on the property. Usufructs are easements that entitle third parties to use the property in a certain way (right of residence, right-of-way). Anyone with a legitimate interest can inspect the cadastre office digital registry. Inspections take place via the broker, the seller, or as part of the financing application via the financing bank.

If the financing is in place, the legally binding purchase contract can be concluded with the seller. A public notary draws up the purchase contract. The notary fees are laid down in the Court and Notary Costs Act and amount to 1.5 percent of the agreed purchase price. As a rule, the buyer selects the notary, who takes a neutral position between the parties and sends the buyer and the seller a draft contract for review. If there is nothing that needs to be changed, the buyer can meet the seller and notary for certification. After this appointment, the notary has a notice of conveyance entered in the land register. The property can no longer be sold to a third party.

The buyer pays the purchase price to a notary escrow account—this gives more security for both parties. The buyer also receives a notice, sent by post, from the tax office, of the property transfer tax owed. Only after this tax, the land registry fees, and the notary costs have been paid by the buyer is ownership of the property transferred. If a broker was involved in the sale of the property, the broker's commission is now due—as of December 2020, this is generally split equally between buyer and seller. Finally, the buyer receives confirmation of the entry in the land register from the district court. This completes the property purchase, and the buyer is the legal owner.

Because of the involvement of a notary in the recording of the property sale, it is very rare for any of the purchase price to be untaxed. The bank provides credit based on the official contract, and for this reason there are no huge incentives for under-declaration.

Any foreigner can buy real estate in Germany without restriction. Foreigners can make their declarations of intent before a notary through a sworn interpreter. It is even possible to make this declaration of intent

Table 12.5 Revenues from Real Estate Taxes, 2021

Real Estate Tax	German Name	Tax Revenues (€ billion)	Tax Revenues (% of GDP)
Property transfer tax	Grunderwerbssteuer	18	0.50
Inheritance and gift tax	Erbschaftssteuer	9	0.25
Real property tax	Grundsteuer	14	0.38
Capital gains tax within the personal income tax[1]	Spekulationssteuer im Rahmen der Einkommenssteuer	5	0.14

Source: Author.

[1] The personal income tax is divided into seven types of income. The capital gains tax for real estate is a subitem of one type, called other income. All subgroups of other income generate around 6% of the total tax revenue, according to 2018 statistics. The €5 billion is thus only estimated and assumes that roughly two-thirds of other income is generated by the capital gains tax.

abroad, before a German consular officer (Wissenschaftlicher Dienst of Bundestag 2022).

Real Estate Taxes in Germany

The main real estate taxes and their revenues are summarized in table 12.5.

Property Transfer Tax

Real estate sales must be notarized. By law (the Real Estate Transfer Tax Act of 1982), the previous owner and the purchaser are jointly liable for the tax, but either can pay. Generally, the purchase contract specifies that the buyer pays. After certification of the contract, the notary sends it to the responsible tax office, which then sends the property transfer tax assessment to the party to be charged. The tax is due one month after the notification of the tax assessment. Once the buyer pays, the tax office issues a clearance certificate, which is the prerequisite for the transfer of ownership in the land register.

The tax rate varies among the 16 states between 3.5 and 6.5 percent. Table 12.6 summarizes the 2021 tax rates, the tax burden for a purchase price of €500,000, and the total revenues per state.

Table 12.6 Property Transfer Tax Rates and Revenues, 2024

	Tax Rate (%)	Valid Since	Tax Burden for a Purchase Price of €500,000 (€)	Total Tax Revenues (€ billion)
Saxony-Anhalt	5	2012	25,000	0.2
Mecklenburg-Western Pomerania	6	2019	30,000	0.3
Thuringia[1]	6.5	2017	32,500	0.2
Saxony[1]	3.5	1997	17,500	0.4
Brandenburg	6.5	2015	32,500	0.5
Saarland	6.5	2015	32,5000	0.1
Lower Saxony	5	2014	25,000	1.3
Rhineland-Palatinate	5	2012	25,000	0.7
Schleswig-Holstein	6.5	2014	32,500	0.9
North Rhine–Westphalia	6.5	2015	32,500	4.1
Baden-Wuerttemberg	5	2011	25,000	2.5
Bavaria	3.5	1997	17,500	2.5
Hesse	6	2014	30,000	1.9
Berlin	6	2014	30,000	1.3
(Hanseatic city) Hamburg[1]	4.5	2009	22,500	0.6
(Hanseatic city) Bremen	5	2014	25,000	0.2

Source: Author.

[1] Since 2021, some states have changed their transfer tax rates. Hamburg increased its rate from 4.5 percent to 5 percent, and Saxony from 3.5 percent to 5 percent in January 2023; Thuringia reduced its rate from 6.5 percent to 5 percent in January 2024 (Mengden 2024).

Real estate sales are exempt from the German VAT, avoiding double taxation by the property transfer tax of 3.5 to 6.5 percent and a VAT rate of 19 percent. Voluntary payment of the VAT on real estate sales is possible under certain conditions, in which case, the real estate transfer tax is based on the gross amount.

No property transfer tax is levied on transfers subject to inheritance and gift taxes, to avoid double taxation. Real estate acquisitions as a result of a death or through gifts of real estate made by living persons are therefore exempt from property transfer tax.

Furthermore, not all real estate transfer transactions are subject to the property transfer tax. The main exemptions are the following:

- If the value of the land purchase does not exceed €2,500, the purchase is not subject to property transfer tax. This is not an exempt amount, but an exclusion. This means that an acquisition of €2,500 is tax-free, but an acquisition of €2,501 is subject to property transfer tax on the entire amount.
- Donations of real estate subject to usufruct (right of residence) in favor of the donor are completely exempt from property transfer tax.
- The group clause in German property transfer tax law exempts real estate transfers as part of internal restructuring of a group of companies. A group subject to property transfer tax requires a controlling company and at least one subsidiary company. The purpose of the regulation is to make it easier to carry out restructuring that makes economic sense. The European Court of Justice decided in 2018 that the property transfer tax group clause does not constitute state aid and does not violate European law. However, a minimum investment period of five years in the subsidiary company is required before and after the transfer, and the holding company must own 95 percent of the subsidiary company.

Inheritance and Gift Taxes

An inheritance tax is levied on an acquisition mortis causa, and a gift tax is levied on donations inter vivos. Inheritance and gift taxes were introduced in the whole of the German Reich in 1906, having previously applied in only some federal states. In 2021, the taxed assets amounted to €118 billion (Statistisches Bundesamt 2022). The assessed inheritance tax amounted to €9 billion and the gift tax to €2.1 billion in 2021. The actual value of inheritance is around €400 billion per year (Tiefensee and Grabka 2017). The majority of inheritances and gifts are therefore not taxed. The reasons are that the majority of transfers are lower than the personal allowance, and not all transfers are reported to the tax office.

Both inheritance tax and gift tax take capital assets and real estate assets into account. Business assets, or the transfer of an entire company, are also considered. Business assets are a particularly important factor for medium-sized companies, because an entire company could be endangered by a tax burden in the event of inheritance.

The tax burden for both taxes depends on the value of assets and the degree of relationship. Spouses and registered civil partners benefit from the highest tax-free allowance: they can inherit up to €500,000 tax-free. For others, the more closely related they are to the deceased, the higher the allowances. There is an allowance of €400,000 for each child of the deceased, and also for grandchildren if the children of the deceased have already died. If the children are still alive, there is a tax-free allowance of €200,000 for the grandchildren. The allowance for great-grandchildren or parents who inherit from their children is €100,000, and for all other heirs, even if they are not related, it is €20,000.

Tax must be paid on inherited assets in excess of the respective allowance. There are three tax classes, with tax rates between 7 and 50 percent: the most favorable tax rate is tax class I. It applies to spouses or registered life partners, children and stepchildren, and other close relatives. More distant relatives receive the second-lowest tax rates, in tax class II. These include siblings, stepparents and parents-in-law, children-in-law, and divorced spouses. The highest tax rates, tax class III, apply to all other heirs who are not related to the deceased.

Heirs in tax class I do not pay tax on living space they use themselves under certain conditions. This applies if the deceased used the residential property until his or her death and the heir then lives in the inherited property for at least 10 years.

The main reason why the revenue yield from these two taxes is so low—despite the huge number of assets transferred in Germany—is because of the allowance for the acquisition of business assets and the allowance for the gift tax. These allowances can be reclaimed every 10 years. The effect on revenue yield becomes obvious with a simple example: Each parent can transfer up to €400,000 tax-free to a child every 10 years. If the grandparents are still alive, they can each give another €200,000 to their grandchild every 10 years. A child up to the age of 10 can thus receive up to €1.6 million tax-free. If the allowances are used again in the following decade, the child will have received €3.2 million of tax-free assets by the age of 21.

Real Property Tax

Under the German real property tax system, the value of the property—irrespective of the economic profit it generates—is taxed. Properties used for agriculture or forestry are subject to real property tax A, and all other properties are subject to real property tax B. Publicly owned real property is not taxed, and all revenues from property tax A and property tax B belong to the municipalities. Under the real property tax system, the value of the property is multiplied nationwide by a tax assessment figure determined centrally—0.6 percent for real property tax A and 0.35 percent for real property tax B. The resulting amount is then multiplied by the municipal tax rate.

Figure 12.2 Property Tax Burden in Federal States, 2021 (€ per capita)

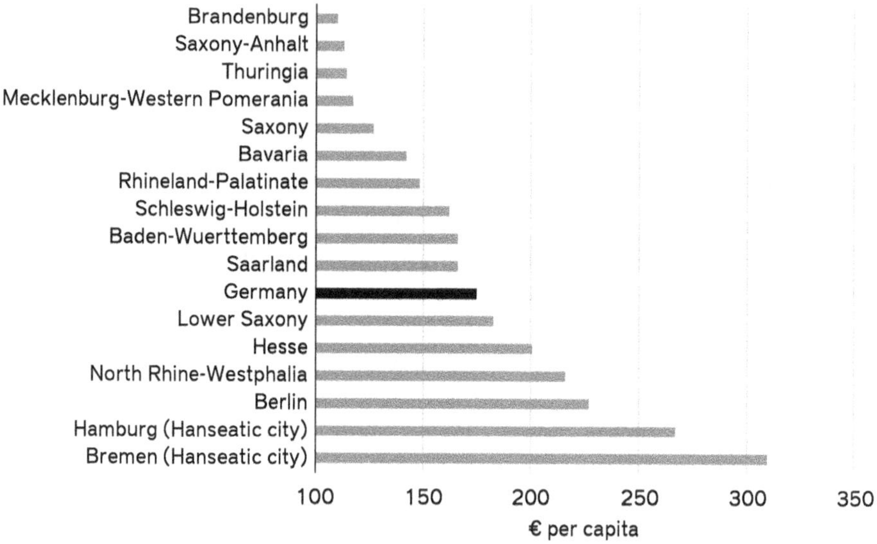

Source: Ernst & Young (2022).

Although the tax assessment figure of real property tax B is lower than that of real property tax A, the tax revenues from real property tax B are significantly higher, in part because municipalities set a higher local tax rate for real property tax B. In 2021, the total tax amount of the real property tax was around €14 billion. The revenue from property tax A (on the assets of agricultural and forestry operations) totaled €0.4 billion in 2021. This was an increase of 0.4 percent compared with the previous year. From property tax B (properties), the municipalities received a total of €14.6 billion in 2021—2.2 percent more than in 2020.

The real estate tax burden in Germany, compared with the rest of the world, has been low for decades.[10] The average per capita tax paid in 2021 was only €175. Figure 12.2 shows the per capita tax burden in all 16 federal states in 2021. In the southern and eastern regions of Germany, the tax burden is lower; and it is higher in the three city-states, as well as North Rhine–Westphalia, and Hesse.

Because of some local fiscal autonomy in the system, the municipalities have complete discretion to fix their tax rate. In 15 municipalities, with the tax rate at 0 percent, inhabitants did not pay any property taxes in 2021. Tables 12.7 and 12.8 present the highest per capita levels of property tax in 2021 and the tax spread, respectively, among the federal states in 2021.

Table 12.7 Highest Local Property Tax Rates, 2021

City	Federal State	Local Tax Rate (%)
Lautertal (Odenwald)	Hesse	1,050
Lorch, town	Hesse	1,050
Nauheim	Hesse	960
Ringgau	Hesse	960
Bergneustadt	North Rhine-Westphalia	959
Bad Karlshafen, town	Hessen	951
Hürtgenwald	North Rhine-Westphalia	950
Bad Emstal	Hessen	950
Bönen	North Rhine-Westphalia	940
Altena	North Rhine-Westphalia	910
Nörvenich	North Rhine-Westphalia	910
Witten	North Rhine-Westphalia	910

Source: Ernst & Young (2022).

Table 12.8 Highest and Lowest Property Tax Rates in Federal States, 2021

Federal State	Municipalities with Lowest Tax Rates	Tax Rate (%)	Municipalities with Highest Tax Rates	Tax Rate (%)
Baden-Wuerttemberg	Büsingen am Hochrhein	0	Tübingen	660
Bavaria	Gundremmingen	150	Gnotzheim	650
Brandenburg	Breydin	300	Potsdam	545
Hessen	Eschborn	140	Lautertal	1,050
Mecklenburg-Western Pomerania	Altenhof	300	Wackerow	700
Lower Saxony	Gorleben	250	Ritterhude	640
North Rhine-Westphalia	Verl	190	Bergneustadt	959
Rhineland-Palatinate	Bergenhausen	0	Lissendorf	700
Saarland	Perl	350	Gersheim	680
Saxony	Weißenborn	300	Leipzig	650
Saxony-Anhalt	Apenburg-Winterfeld	300	Niedere Börde	750
Schleswig-Holstein	Friedrichsgabekoog	0	Glücksburg	700
Thuringia	Kirchgandern	200	Gera	600

Source: Ernst & Young (2022).

Figure 12.3 Average Tax Rates in Federal States, 2021

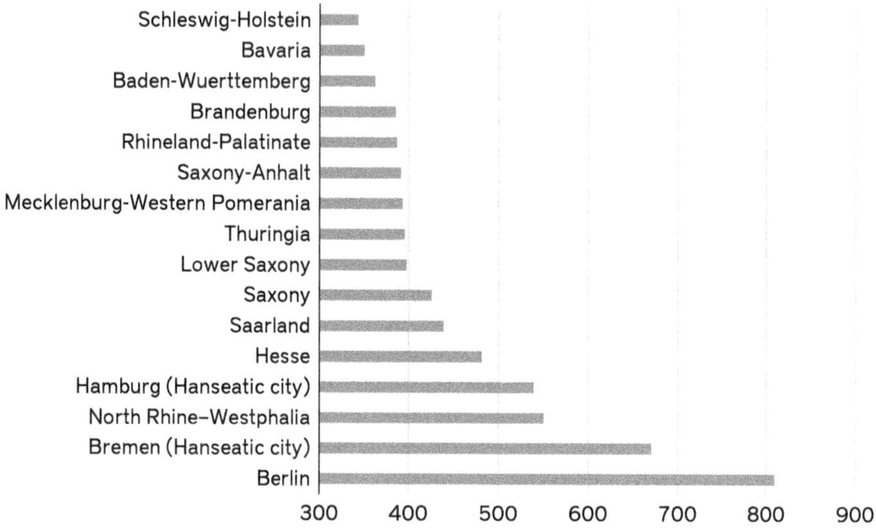

Source: Ernst & Young (2022).

Figure 12.3 presents the average tax rate in each of the 16 federal states in 2021.

The property valuation process for the property tax is detailed later.

Capital Gains Tax

A capital gains tax—called a speculation tax in Germany—on real property transfers is levied under the income tax. This tax must be paid by anyone who does not use a property and sells it within 10 years of purchase. The amount of the tax depends on two factors: the individual's personal income tax rate and the increase in value of the property. The tax base is the profit from selling the property, not the entire sales price. Ancillary costs for buying and selling, such as brokerage fees and property transfer tax, are deducted from the profit margin. Deductions do not include interest payments or repayments for a building loan. If the owner takes a loss in the sale, the tax does not apply at all. In rural areas with a declining population, a loss in value can occasionally occur, but this loss cannot be claimed against personal income tax.

The 10-year period that homeowners must wait before they can avail themselves of the tax-free status begins on the date the purchase agreement is signed. If the buyer buys a plot of land and builds a house on it years later, the date of purchase of the plot of land still counts as the key date, not the year the house was built. If the land sells before the end of the 10 years, the seller must pay the capital gains tax in the year of the sale.

Owners who give away or inherit their property are not exempt from the speculation period—the clock simply keeps ticking. Conversely, for an apartment bought, for example, three years ago by someone who rented it out, inheritors must wait seven years to sell it to avoid the tax.

The capital gains speculation tax is also completely eliminated in the event of a sale before 10 years from the date of purchase if the apartment was used exclusively by the owner (or owner's children) between purchase and sale. For example, an owner who lets a student child move into a one-room condominium and then sells it at short notice does not have to pay capital gains tax, provided that the property owner still has a maintenance obligation for the child—that is, still receives the child tax benefit.

However, even an owner who rents out an apartment for some period within the 10 years has the opportunity to sell it tax-free, thanks to an exception. An owner who first rents out an apartment but then lives in it for three calendar years before the sale does not pay the capital gains tax.

A rarely used option to avoid paying capital gains tax is the hire-purchase agreement. The future buyer of the property first moves into the property as a tenant and, after an agreed period of time, contractually undertakes to buy it. Part or all of the rent paid is deducted from the purchase price.

It is not uncommon for married couples getting divorced to have to pay capital gains tax if they own or rent an apartment together for less than 10 years. For example, if the wife pays her ex-husband for his share of an apartment that he does not live in at the time, he has to pay capital gains tax on the profit from the sale. If no purchase price is paid, the tax office uses the current market value of the property as a basis.

Anyone who concurrently owns several properties or, for example, rents apartments, land, or garages will face another special feature: the three-property limit. Owners who sell more than three properties within five years can establish a business. If they sell a property they have owned for less than 10 years, they pay no capital gains tax but are liable for trade tax, in addition to income tax.

Property Valuation for Real Property Tax

The tax administration is an extremely tangled web. Article 108 of the German constitution stipulates that financial administration is shared between the federal and state governments. Unlike some other European countries, Germany uses a decentralized and multilevel financial administration. The central government possesses a number of special agencies with very detailed areas of responsibility and is alone responsible for

Figure 12.4 Structure of the Central-Government Tax Administration

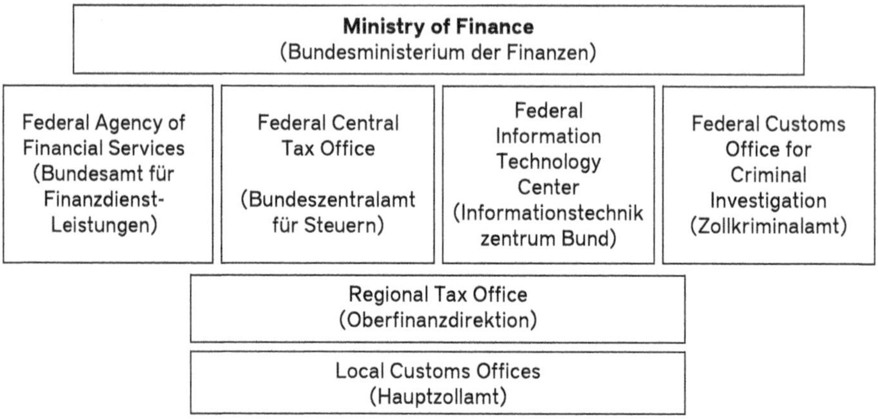

Source: Author.

customs duties, the consumption taxes, the taxes levied within the framework of the European Union, and criminal investigation. The 16 federal states mainly administer personal income tax, VAT, and all other taxes.

The central government bears the expenses for the delegation of tax administration and allocates to the federal states an amount to cover these. The local authorities administer only the petty taxes, like the alcohol tax, the entertainment tax, dog licenses, pub licenses, hunting and fishing licenses, and the second-home tax. The second-home tax generates little revenue: the tax base is the annual net rent of the home multiplied by a local tax rate. The local authorities also send the local trade tax assessment notice and the notice of real property tax to their local taxpayers, although the complete tax base calculations are carried out by the regional tax office.

Figures 12.4 and 12.5 describe the structure of the tax administration of the central government and in the federal states.

Valuation of Real Estate

The 530 local tax offices are responsible for real estate valuations in Germany. But because increased tax yield from a revaluation would go to the municipalities and because the federal states and the central government have to cover the costs for revaluations, they wish to avoid a revaluation of private and commercial property.

In 2018, however, the Federal Constitutional Court declared the existing system of property tax assessments unconstitutional because it treats

Figure 12.5 Structure of the Tax Administration in Federal States

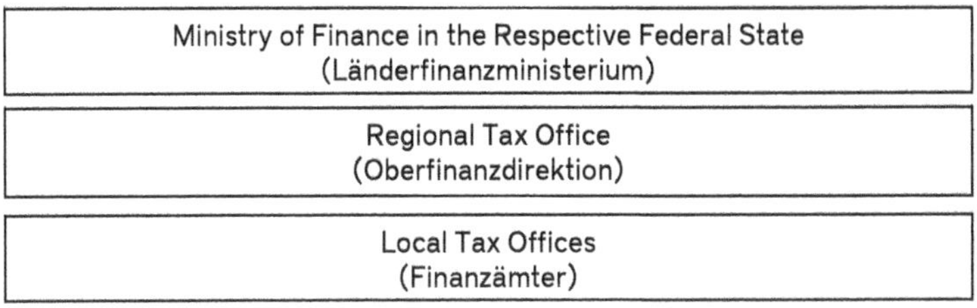

Source: Werner (2006).

similar properties differently and thus violates the principle of equal treatment enshrined in the German constitution. The court ruled that a new law had to be in place by December 31, 2019. Property tax can continue to be levied under the old system on a transitional basis until December 31, 2024. From January 1, 2025, property tax will be levied on the basis of the new law, leading to a patchwork quilt of valuation systems because each federal state will be able to choose its own manner of calculating the tax.

Previous System

Before the reform, calculation of property tax was based on property values that were decades old (the so-called standard values). In the former West Germany, properties were assessed on the basis of their value in 1964. In the former East German states, the underlying values were even older, based on values from 1935.[11] Periodic reassessments were meant to take place every six years but never happened.

Since the values of land and buildings have developed very differently in both east and west since 1935 and 1964, there are currently inequalities in the levying of the tax that, according to the Federal Constitutional Court, are no longer compatible with the Basic Law for the Federal Republic of Germany of 1949 (i.e., Germany's constitution). Because the current valuation system treats similar properties differently for no objective reason, the valuation violates the principle of equal treatment enshrined in the Basic Law. As a result, the standard valuation has been decoupled from the actual values of the property. In other words, significantly different real estate tax payments can currently be due for comparable properties in neighboring locations, as Figure 12.6 shows.

Until 2025, the property tax for developed and undeveloped land continued to be determined using the standard value system, a formal process for determining and establishing taxable values for property. The assessed

Figure 12.6 Different Tax Burdens for Similar Properties in Different Cities

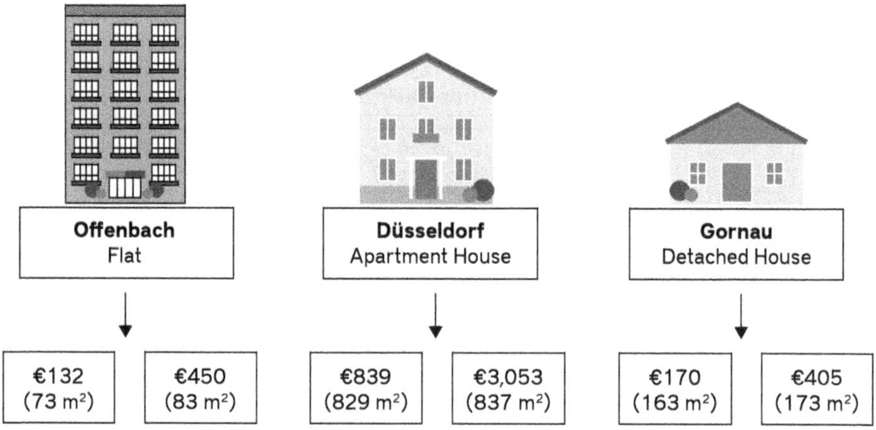

Source: Author.

value is the basis for calculation of several taxes in the literal sense of the word. Since the abolition of the wealth tax on December 31, 1996, and the introduction of the needs assessment for the property transfer tax and for inheritance and gift taxes, standard values (applicable until December 31, 2024) have been required only for property tax purposes.

The local tax offices determine the property tax value for each property, guided by the value ratios that existed at the time of the last and only main assessment done in 1964 and 1935 (as stated), resulting in assessed values that are significantly lower than current market values. In practice, this means that the local tax offices use the gross annual rent that a tenant would have had to pay on January 1, 1964, in the west or on January 1, 1935, in the east.[12] A multiplier is applied and the result can be adjusted with surcharges (value-increasing circumstances) or discounts (value-reducing circumstances).[13] The process is called the earnings method and is used for all developed mixed-use properties, family houses, rental properties, condominiums, commercial properties, and almost all single-family homes. For vacant lots, the area in square meters is multiplied by the 1964 or 1935 land rental value.

If a property has an assessed value of €34,512 and is a single-family house in an old federal state, say, the old western part of Berlin, where the property tax assessment factor is 2.6 per mille and the property tax rate is 810 percent, the formula for determining the annual property tax is $€34{,}512 \times 0.0026 \times 8.10 = €727$.

The index value and the property tax rate are set by the municipality.

Postreform System

On April 10, 2018, the Federal Constitutional Court ordered the federal Parliament to adopt a new statutory regulation concerning the property tax by the end of 2019 and to implement it with effect from January 1, 2025, at the latest. In November 2019, the federal and state governments agreed on a new law, and the Property Tax Reform Act (GrStRefG) was adopted. This law created a federal model, but also gave federal states the opportunity to deviate from the federal model in terms of the definition of a tax base and how the properties were to be valued for property tax purposes.

The Property Tax and Valuation Law contains new valuation rules for the federal property tax. It stipulates that all properties in Germany had to be revalued as of January 1, 2022, with the conditions existing on January 1, 2022. There are an estimated 36 million properties in Germany. For the revaluation, property owners had to submit electronically a declaration to the tax office so that the property tax value can be determined. This involves declaring property-related data, which differs depending on the type of use of the property.

The Property Tax Reform Act (GrStRefG) of 2019 gives the municipalities the right, from 2025, to set a higher rate of assessment for undeveloped, ready-for-building plots of land for urban planning reasons. This law must be read with the Building Land Mobilization Act of 2021. Germany has a significant housing shortage, particularly in metropolitan areas, and land ready for construction is increasingly being held for speculative purposes. In some cases, land is bought only to wait for an increase in value and then sell it for a profit. This speculation prevents the creation of urgently needed housing. In the future, municipalities will be able to set a higher assessment rate for plots of land that are ready for construction but undeveloped. This so-called property tax C makes speculation more expensive and creates financial incentives to actually construct housing units on plots that are ready for construction.

Articles 72, 105, and 125b of the Basic Law were amended to allow for the new property tax dispensation. The Basic Law thus retains the federal government's legislative powers regarding property tax regulation, but, at the same time, the states have been granted the right to introduce their own land tax regulations that deviate from federal law. Five states have made use of this option (Baden-Württemberg, Bavaria, Hamburg, Hesse, and Lower Saxony). In principle, Saarland and Saxony are using the federal model, but they have introduced tax indicators that deviate from the federal law. Figure 12.7 summarizes the different reform models that give rise to Germany's patchwork quilt.

Figure 12.7 Property Tax Reform Models in the 16 Federal States

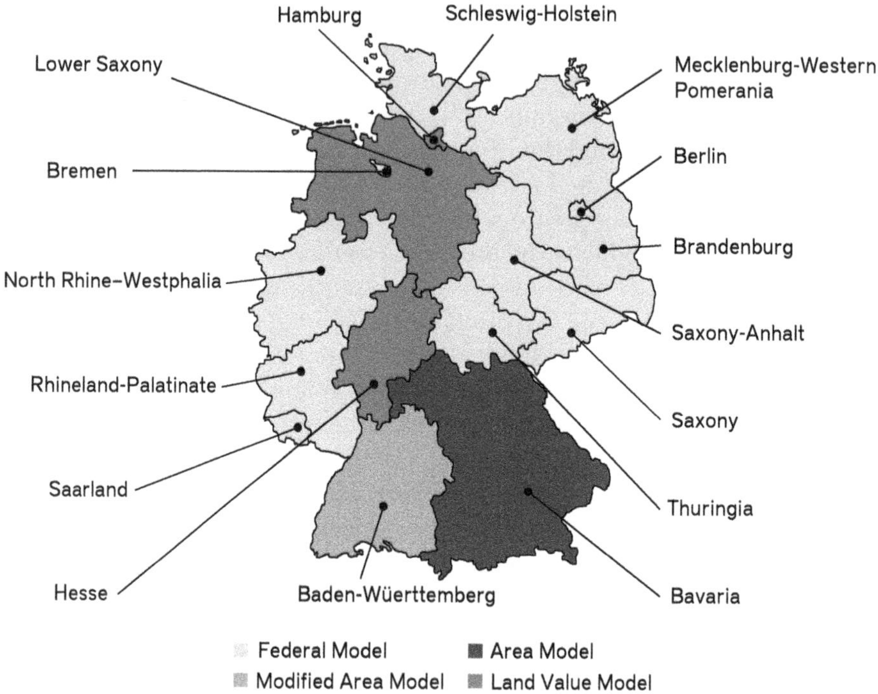

Source: Author.

Property tax will continue to be calculated in three steps in the future: Property value × tax assessment factor × tax rate.

The property value is determined by the tax office on the basis of an assessment declaration provided by property owners. To determine the value of the property, the following elements are considered: the respective value of the land and the average net basic rent in the local community. Other factors include the area of the property, the type of property, and the age of the building. The standard land values can be viewed by citizens in the standard land value information systems on the federal states' websites. The federal Ministry of Finance using data from the federal Statistical Office determined the net basic rent for each municipality.

The new tax assessment factor, as second element, is determined by law and compensates for increases in value, compared with the current values and those that have not been updated since 1935 or 1964. So that the increase in value is not too great, the new tax assessment factor is about 1/10 the previous value. The basic federal rate or tax measurement number thus drops from 0.35 to 0.031 percent for residential properties (single- and two-family houses, rental properties and residential property) and to 0.034 percent for nonresidential properties (commercial properties, mixed-use properties, part ownership, other developed properties). Housing is tax deductible through property tax, because companies offering affordable housing and apartments with social housing subsidies receive an additional deduction of 25 percent from the tax assessment factor. This may be desirable from a sociopolitical point of view, but it clearly contradicts the goal of property tax reform, which is to reduce the various exemptions and to increase tax revenue overall.

The tax rate, as third element, will continue to be determined by the municipalities without restriction. This strengthens their revenue autonomy. If the revaluation results in significant increases in the property tax revenue in individual communities, the tax rates can be adjusted. The municipalities have officially announced that they will also do this—because an increase in property tax on the occasion of the constitutionally required new regulation would not be politically acceptable. Against the background of revenue neutrality, I wonder why this "reform of the century" was started at all.

Five federal states have developed individual models for calculation of the property tax (BMF 2021, 1–8).

Baden-Württemberg passed a state law in November 2020, according to which the property tax is determined using a modified land value model. The valuation multiplies the plot area by the standard land value. The product is the land value for tax purposes. The building is not relevant for the assessment. If the property is used primarily for residential purposes, 30 percent is deducted from the tax assessment factor. The net basic rent is therefore not directly accounted for in Baden-Württemberg.

Bavaria uses a surface-area model based on land and building areas and value-independent equivalence figures (fixed values per area unit of land and per area unit of buildings). These equivalences are multiplied by the respective area and the property tax assessment factor. For living space, a discount of 30 percent is deducted from the property tax assessment factor. The advantage of the Bavarian model is that the basis of assessment was determined once on January 1, 2022, and has to be adjusted only if the size of the area or the use of the building changes.

Hamburg passed a state law in August 2021 mandating an equivalence-based model that takes residential location into account (residential location model). The properties are valued exclusively on the basis of the property size, living space, and usable area. The respective areas are multiplied by an equivalence number and thus represented in an equivalent amount, which forms the starting value for determining the tax measurement amount. The different equivalence numbers reflect potential uses of municipal infrastructure that are not covered by fees and contributions. In addition to preferential treatment for housing, monuments, listed buildings (e.g., privately owned property in an area declared as a UNESCO world heritage site), and social housing, there is also a preferential treatment from the point of view of urban development. A distinction is made between "normal" and "good" residential locations, based on the residential location index of Hamburg's rent index.

Hesse's area factor model, like the land area models of Bavaria, Hamburg, and Lower Saxony, accounts for the areas of land, living space, and usable commercial space and is also based on the equivalence principle. An additional factor takes location into account, since this determines the extent to which benefit can be derived from the municipal infrastructure. This factor increases or decreases the result, depending on how the property's location compares to the average location in that city or county. The standard land value of the property to be valued is used to calculate the location factor of a plot of land in relation to the average land value of the city or municipality, and an exponent of 0.3 is applied to this ratio.

In July 2021, Lower Saxony opted for an area-location model. It is based on the Bavarian model, extended by a location component. Property tax is calculated according to the use of the property. The benefit is not measured solely on the basis of property area. Depending on where the property is located within the city or municipality, a location factor is derived from the ratio of the standard land value to the average standard land value of the city or municipality. This is then multiplied by the equivalent amounts of the land area and the building area.

Conclusion

The taxation of property in Germany is very low, as seen in figure 12.8 showing the percentage of all property taxes in relation to gross domestic product for 2019. Only Sweden, Mexico (Werner 2021), and Austria had a lower value than Germany, and Germany performed worse than the average for 37 Organisation for Economic Co-operation and Development (OECD) countries. This comparatively low level of property taxation, together with a greatly outdated tax base, suggests that the German property taxation system has not reached its potential.

The wealth tax has not been collected since 1997, and the revenues from inheritance and gift taxes on real property are low because of numerous creative possibilities and loopholes for large inheritances and gifts. Profits from the sale of property are commonly tax privileged or completely tax-free after 10 years, while acquisition costs and maintenance costs for rental properties can be deducted from personal income

Figure 12.8 Property Tax Revenues in Selected Countries and Average of OECD Countries, 2019 (% of GDP)

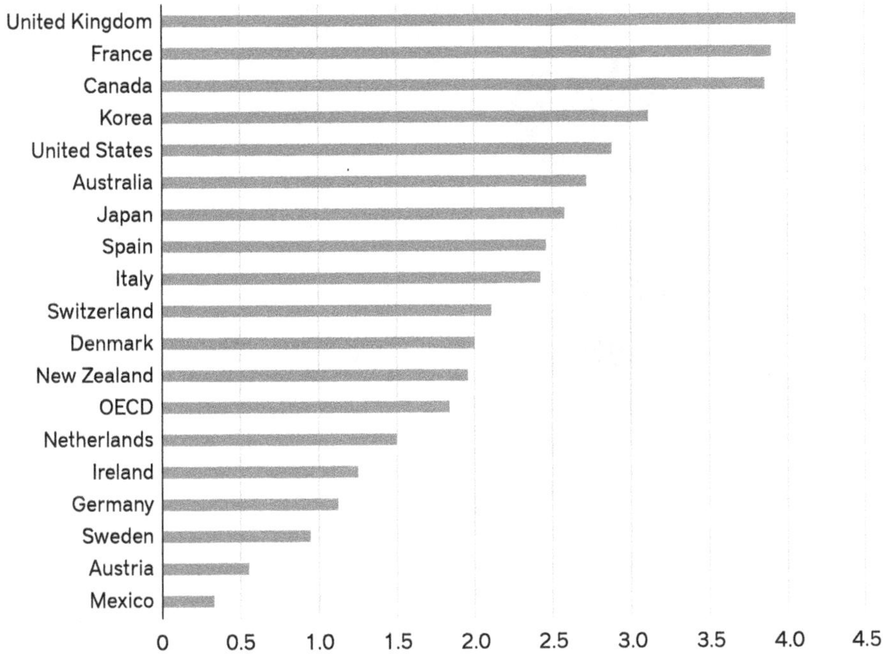

Source: OECD (2021).

tax. These structural facts have held back additional property tax revenue mobilization in Germany.

However, taxes on real property in Germany could play an important role, as they do in other countries. The Anglo-Saxon countries such as Canada, the United States, and the United Kingdom provide their local authorities with an extensive system of property taxation. One advantage of local property tax is that a direct link between the benefits and costs of public goods can be established. This direct link between citizens' preferences in terms of local public goods and the policy makers who have to provide them cannot be created by grants or transfers. Besides levying a local property tax, several other European countries—namely, Switzerland, Belgium, Croatia, and the Scandinavian countries (Werner 2008)—give significant tax autonomy to their local authorities, and therefore a local surcharge on the personal income tax is common. A third means of financing local authorities has been chosen by Austria, Bolivia (Werner 2018b), Germany, Luxembourg, Pakistan (Werner 2019a; 2019b), and Poland, who have developed local tax systems with their own revenues as

Figure 12.9 Revenue Structure of German Municipalities, 2021

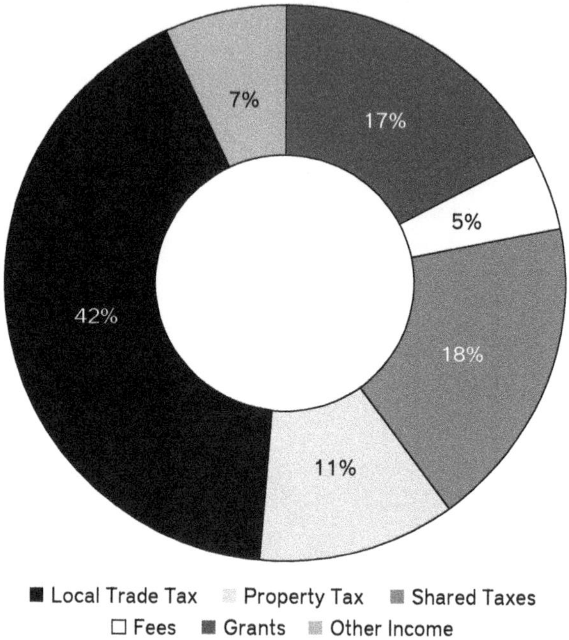

Source: Author.

well as tax-sharing systems. The pros of a tax-sharing system are stable revenues, because the taxes are not as strongly affected by economic fluctuations, and a common tax for all tiers of government, which strengthens the solidarity among government tiers. ("We are all sitting in the same boat.") The cons of tax sharing are the lack of revenue autonomy and the related lower level of local accountability and less transparency than in the Anglo-Saxon model with an intensive property tax or in the Scandinavian model with a local piggyback tax on the national personal income tax. Vertical grants are nevertheless also needed in the Anglo-Saxon, Scandinavian, and German models.[14]

In 2021, the German local units—without the three city-states—had a budget volume of €289 billion. Figure 12.9 presents the main sources of revenue for the municipalities. In addition to the local trade tax, the property tax is the only way for the municipalities to increase their income independently, so we can safely say that the German municipalities have a very low level of fiscal autonomy. The reform of the property tax from 2025 is to be welcomed despite its conceptual weaknesses, because it has brought about the first uniform valuation of real estate for decades.

The future will show whether this also creates the constitutional basis for a reintroduction of the general wealth tax.

Notes

1. The following historical overview relies heavily on Werner (2008; 2014; 2018).

2. Three of the 16 federal states are city-states (Berlin, Bremen, and Hamburg). These three federal states do not separate their municipal budgets from their respective federal budgets and thus have only a federal budget. Similar budget structures are in Austria, for the municipality of Vienna and the federal state of Vienna, and in the United States, for its capital, Washington, DC.

3. The metropolitan regions of Stuttgart, Hanover, and Frankfurt are regional planning associations. A quite similar administration unit also exists in Aachen and Saarbrucken, which consists of a former incorporated city and some surrounding municipalities that were combined in a rural district.

4. Yet Germany is far from creating a realigned municipal structure, which Denmark did when it reformed its territories in 1970 and in 2007 (Werner 2008).

5. Cities combine the accountabilities of a rural district and a municipality in one administration unit.

6. Human settlements occupy 9.3 percent and transport services cover 5.1 percent of Germany's surface area.

7. A building is a residential building if at least 50 percent is used for residential purposes. The totality of all apartments consists of apartments in residential buildings, apartments in nonresidential buildings, and dormitories.

8. According to the Office of the European Union, overcrowding occurs when the living room also doubles as a bedroom, three or more children have to share a bedroom, or a brother and sister, both in their teens, share a room.

9. These percentages are from various publications of the European Union Statistics on Income and Living Conditions and press announcement no. 67 of the German statistical office, November 17, 2022.

10. In 1992, the tax burden per capita was €64, and in 2021 the property tax generated a tax burden of €102 per capita (Werner 2006).

11. Traditionally, property tax has never contributed much to the budgets of German municipalities. For example, in 1894, property taxes in the 17 largest Prussian cities accounted for only 11 percent of total local tax revenue. The municipal surcharges on the personal income tax contributed over 70 percent of the municipal tax revenue for the same year. Property taxes were not a significant source of income for communities during Wilhelm II's imperial era in the 19th century, in the Weimar Republic of the 1920s, and under the Nazi regime. During the democratic period of the Weimar Republic, the federal state of Prussia decided to use the property and building tax again—as it had before 1893—as a source of income for the state of Prussia and gave its communities the option of adding a surcharge to this new state tax. In 1937, 1 percent of the total tax revenue in Germany was generated by the real estate transfer tax and 8 percent by the real estate tax. For a detailed overview of the German local tax system from 1810 until 2005, see Werner (2006, 73–135).

12. If the property is owner-occupied and does not incur rental payments, the comparative local rent for similar properties is used, but it is the comparative local rent from 1935 or 1964. Since the tax office determines the assessed value for each property, property owners do not have to rummage through the archives to find the comparative local rent from 1964. The disadvantage is that the tax office calculations are not transparent.

13. The multiplier depends on the construction materials, year of construction, and the number of inhabitants of the municipality on the respective key dates, and can be

viewed in Annexes 3 to 8 of the German Valuation Act. For example, the multiplier is 13.0 for a house built with stone and steel and in a tiny village with not quite 2,000 inhabitants. The same house in a metropolitan city with a population of more than 500,000 is taxed by a multiplier of 11.9. Houses constructed in wood are divided into wooden houses with brick linings and those with clay infill. Generally speaking, wooden houses have a lower multiplier than stone or steel houses. Further, different multipliers apply to undeveloped and developed land (§ 15 of GrStRefG). The majority of taxpayers are unaware of these multipliers.

14. For an overview of the German equalization system among the federal states, see Spahn and Werner (2007) and Werner (2003; 2014; 2018a).

References

BMF (Bundesministerium der Finanzen). 2021. "Monatsbericht November 2021—Analysen und Berichte, Überblick zur Grundsteuerreform—Wie die Länder das neue Grundsteuerrecht umsetzen." Berlin.

Ernst & Young. 2022. "Wirtschaftsprüfungsgesellschaft: Grundsteuerhebesätze in Deutschland 2005 bis 2021." (August). https://www.bfw-newsroom.de/wp-content/uploads/2022/08/ey-analyse-grundsteuer-entwicklung-deutschland.pdf.

Mengden, A. 2024. "Real Estate Transaction Tax Rates in German States." (July). https://taxfoundation.org/data/all/eu/germany-real-estate-transaction-tax-rates/.

OECD (Organisation for Economic Co-operation and Development). 2021. "Revenue Statistics 2021: The Initial Impact of COVID-19 on OECD Tax Revenues." (December). https://www.oecd.org/en/publications/revenue-statistics-2021_6e87f932-en.html.

Postbank. 2022. "Wohnatlas 2022: Immobilienpreise in Deutschland—Rasanter Preisanstieg—was kostet Wohnen heute?" Bonn.

Spahn, P., and J. Werner. 2007. "Germany at the Junction Between Solidarity and Subsidiarity." *Fiscal Fragmentation in Decentralized Countries: Subsidiarity, Solidarity and Asymmetry*, ed. R. Bird and R. Ebel, 89–113. Cheltenham, UK: Edward Elgar.

Statistisches Bundesamt. 2020. "Eigentümerquote nach Bundesländern im Zeitvergleich basierend Ergebnisse der Mikrozensus-Zusatzerhebung 2018." Wiesbaden.

———. 2022. "Erbschafts- und Schenkungssteuerstatistik 2021." Wiesbaden.

Tiefensee, A., and M. Grabka. 2017. Das Erbvolumen in Deutschland dürfte um gut ein Viertel größer sein als bisher angenommen." *DIW Wochenbericht* 27: 565–570.

Werner, J. 2003. El federalismo Alemán: En Estado de Fluctuación, *Zergak Gaceta Tributaria del Pais Vasco* 25(3): 81–114.

———. 2006. "Local Government Organization and Finance: Germany." In *Local Governance in Industrial Countries*, ed. A. Shah, 43–79. Washington, DC: World Bank.

———. 2008. *Das deutsche Gemeindefinanzsystem: Reformvorschläge im Kontext der unterschiedlichen Einnahmenautonomie der lokalen Gebietskörperschaften in Europa.* Frankfurt am Main: Peter Lang.

———. 2014. "The Financing of Policies in Germany." In *Le financement des politiques publiques*, ed. M. Leroy and G. Orsoni, 347–369. Brussels: Bruylant.

———. 2018a. "Equalisation Among the States in Germany: The Junction Between Solidarity and Subsidiarity." *Revista Presupuesto y Gasto Público* 92: 155–176.

———. 2018b. "The 'Pacto Fiscal' in Bolivia: A Sound Intergovernmental Forum or Just Another Toothless Paper Tiger? In *Mobility in a Globalised World 2020*, ed. E. Sucky, N. Biethahn, and J. Werner, 184–191. Bamberg, Germany: University of Bamberg Press.

———. 2019a. "Options to Support Urban Infrastructure Delivery in Pakistan: A Survey for the Province of Punjab. In *Mobility in a Globalised World 2020*, ed. E. Sucky, N. Biethahn, and J. Werner, 245–257. Bamberg, Germany: University of Bamberg Press.

———. 2019b. "Fiscal Equalisation and Fiscal Conflicts: Junction Between Solidarity and Subsidiarity for Pakistan and especially Khyber Pakhtunkhwa, Pakistan—Lessons from the German Experience." In *Corridors of Knowledge for Peace and Development*, ed. S. S. Aneel, U. T. Haroon, and I. Niazi, 96–123. Lahore, Pakistan: Sustainable Development Policy Institute and Sang-e-Meel.

———. 2021. "Local Public Finance in Oaxaca: Indigenous Traditions and Mexican Reform Efforts." In *Mobility in Globalised World 2020*, ed. E. Sucky, N. Biethahn, and J. Werner, 257–276. Bamberg, Germany: University of Bamberg Press.

Wissenschaftlicher Dienst of Bundestag. 2022. "Rechtsfragen des ausländischen Immobilienerwerbs in Deutschland." Berlin.

Legislation

Basic Law for the Federal Republic of Germany of 1949 (as last amended by the Act of March 22, 2025) [Grundgesetz für die Bundesrepublik Deutschland].

Building Land Mobilization Act of 2021 [Gesetz zur Mobilisierung von Bauland].

Court and Notary Costs Act of 2013 (GNotKG).

Property Tax Reform Act of 2019 [Grundsteuer-Reformgesetz (GrStRefG)].

Real Estate Transfer Tax Act of 1982 [Grunderwerbsteuergesetz (GrEStG)].

Valuation Act of 1934 (as amended by Article 39 of the Law of December 12, 2019, Federal Law Gazette I p. 2451, 2486) [Bewertungsgesetz (BewG)].

13

Property Taxation in Greece: Gordian Knot or Not?

THOMAS DIMOPOULOS

The Hellenic Republic, commonly referred to as Greece, is located at the southernmost point of the Balkan Peninsula in southeastern Europe. It holds a unique geographical position at the convergence of the European, Asian, and African continents. Its land borders are limited to the northern and northeastern regions, where it shares borders with Albania, the Republic of North Macedonia, Bulgaria, and Turkey.

Greece is composed of nine distinct geographical regions and has an estimated population of 10.4 million. The capital and most populous city is Athens, followed by Thessaloniki and Patras. The nation operates as a unitary parliamentary republic and is classified as a developed country. It boasts an advanced high-income economy and a high quality of life, ranking 33rd on the Human Development Index (Wisevoter, n.d.). The political structure is led by a prime minister, who wields significant political power, while the president, as the head of state, assumes primarily ceremonial responsibilities. The executive power is vested in the government.

Throughout the post–World War II era, Greece's economy witnessed rapid expansion and performed commendably for much of the 20th century, characterized by robust growth rates and low public debt. However, it has persistently remained among the least developed economies within the European Union (EU). The 2007 bankruptcy of Lehman Brothers incited a global banking crisis and credit crunch that extended until 2009, necessitating government bailouts of banks in the United States and

Europe. Confronted with escalating borrowing costs and dwindling finances, Greece found itself unable to service its mounting debt (Vinci et al. 2022).

In addition to the international challenges, Greece grappled with its own issues, predominantly due to excessive government borrowing and deceptive accounting practices that obscured the magnitude of the outstanding debt. The elevated ratio of public debt to gross domestic product (GDP) was paralleled by a high budget deficit, which, after multiple adjustments and revisions, was determined to have been relatively constant at just over 100 percent until 2007 (Papanikos 2015). Following corrections, the ratio was disclosed to have reached 10.2 percent and 15.1 percent of GDP in 2008 and 2009, respectively. Consequently, the nation's ratio of public debt to GDP, which had already hit 127 percent of GDP in 2009, seemed to spiral out of control (Skartsis 2018). Moreover, Greece's Eurozone membership significantly limited its independent monetary policy discretion.

In March and April 2010, the EU and the International Monetary Fund (IMF), apprehensive about the euro currency zone's collapse and the potential erosion of confidence in Greece's repayment capacity, intervened by providing two substantial aid packages accompanied by austerity measure requirements. However, these stringent austerity measures failed to rescue the Greek economy and government. Ultimately, Greece, other Eurozone members, and the IMF agreed upon a bailout plan, initially providing €45 billion in loans, followed by an additional €110 billion (IMF 2010). To secure the funding, Greece was obligated to implement strict austerity measures aimed at reducing its deficit.

In 2012, a second bailout amounting to €130 billion (US$173 billion) was approved, contingent upon further austerity measures and financial reforms, and it included debt reduction. After six years of decline, Greece's economy resumed growth in the second quarter of 2014, and by the third quarter, it exhibited the fastest growth in the Eurozone. In July 2015, a third bailout was authorized (Schmitt-Grohé and Uribe 2013). Between 2009 and 2017, government debt in Greece rose from US$300 billion to US$318 billion, an increase of approximately 6 percent (partly due to the 2012 debt restructuring); however, during this period, the crucial debt-to-GDP ratio surged from 127 to 179 percent, primarily as a result of the dramatic GDP contraction amid crisis management (Eurostat 2015). Greece's GDP experienced a 25 percent decline as a consequence of the bailout programs, which profoundly affected the economy. This contraction alone led to an increase in the debt-to-GDP ratio from 127 percent in 2009 to approximately 170 percent. In a 2013 report, the IMF acknowledged that it had underestimated the repercussions of substantial tax hikes and expenditure cuts on the country's GDP, extending an informal apology. The organization admitted to initially underestimating the fiscal multipliers and thus the effect of fiscal consolidation on GDP (IMF 2013).

On August 20, 2018, Greece's bailouts were officially declared successful, and the heightened surveillance regime that had been in place following its three consecutive bailouts from 2010 to 2018 was terminated (Stamouli 2022).

The 2008–2009 financial crisis had a profound impact on Greece's economic and fiscal policies, leading to a series of bailout programs imposed by the Troika—the IMF, the European Commission, and the European Central Bank. A crucial condition of these bailout agreements was the reform of Greece's property taxation system, aimed at increasing state revenues and reducing the country's fiscal deficit. As a result, the Uniform Real Estate Property Tax (ENFIA) was introduced, shifting the tax burden significantly onto property owners. Before the crisis, property taxation in Greece was fragmented and inefficient, with loopholes that allowed widespread tax avoidance. Under Troika supervision, property taxes became a key pillar of fiscal consolidation, generating a stable source of revenue at a time when other tax bases—such as income and corporate taxes—were shrinking due to economic contraction. While this reform increased tax revenues, it also placed a heavy financial burden on property owners, many of whom struggled with liquidity issues due to the broader economic downturn. The introduction of the ENFIA as a permanent tax measure, rather than a temporary crisis response, demonstrates how external pressure played a decisive role in shaping Greece's modern property tax framework. The long-term effects of these reforms continue to influence property ownership and investment in Greece today.

A study from Kapa Research presented at a conference held by POMIDA (the Hellenic Property Federation) on January 25, 2025, found that property taxation remains the primary challenge for property owners, exacerbating the housing shortage (POMIDA 2025a; 2025b).

Land and Property Markets

The Planning System

In addition to its national government, Greece has two subordinate tiers of government: 13 regional entities and 325 municipal divisions. Moreover, there are seven decentralized administrative units that operate as deconcentrated extensions of the national government.

The national government plays a pivotal role in Greece's intricate spatial planning system, bearing the primary responsibilities. These include overseeing the establishment of framework laws relating to regional and urban planning, environmental conservation, and regional development.

Furthermore, it is responsible for the enactment of all related legislation and regulatory bylaws governing the planning process.

Regions possess limited responsibilities concerning land use, predominantly serving advisory roles in formulating certain spatial plans. The decentralized administrative units are tasked with approving detailed land use plans and co-approving four other types of plans alongside the national government. Municipalities provide advisory services during the endorsement of some local land use plans. They were formerly accountable for approving a local land use plan, which was legally abolished in 2014. However, plans of this type that were in progress at the time of their legal abolition are still slated for completion and eventual approval by the respective municipality (OECD [Organisation for Economic Co-operation and Development] 2016).

The year 2025 started with big issues as the Council of State declared several provisions of the New Building Regulation (NOK) unconstitutional in December 2024. These provisions had allowed for increased building heights and densities in exchange for incorporating environmentally friendly features, such as green spaces or energy-efficient designs. The court ruled that such general incentives violated Article 24 of the Greek Constitution, which mandates area-specific urban planning based on scientific studies. Specifically, the court invalidated provisions that

- permitted increased building height and density as incentives for eco-friendly construction; and
- excluded certain structures, such as lofts up to 35 square meters and swimming pools considered as planted areas, from building calculations.

However, the court upheld the provision that bay windows could be excluded when calculating the building factor.

The ruling emphasized that urban planning cannot rely on generalized incentives but must be tailored to the unique characteristics of each area, supported by scientific research. This decision underscores the importance of adhering to constitutional principles in urban development and may lead to more stringent regulations to ensure sustainable and balanced growth.

It is important to note that this ruling does not apply retroactively. Building permits already issued under the annulled provisions remain valid, provided that construction has commenced, but several developers already sold units in projects that were not started, and the planning permit was issued.

The NOK has created significant instability in Greece's real estate sector, particularly following the recent ruling by the Council of State that declared several of its provisions unconstitutional. The annulment of key incentives, which were initially introduced to modernize urban development, encourage sustainable construction, and increase buildable space, has now led to widespread uncertainty among developers, investors, and property owners. Many projects that were designed under the now-invalidated provisions—such as increased building heights, additional density allowances, and green infrastructure exemptions—are now facing legal ambiguities, creating delays in construction and raising concerns over the validity of permits already issued. This regulatory inconsistency has also affected real estate valuations, as properties that were expected to benefit from the expanded allowances may now see reduced market value. Furthermore, the court's ruling has halted investor confidence, as developers remain cautious about future changes in urban planning policy. The government's response—to incorporate some incentives into localized urban planning projects—has done little to reassure the market, as the process remains highly bureaucratic and lacks clear timelines. The lack of a stable regulatory framework is discouraging investment, particularly from international buyers who rely on predictable zoning laws. In effect, the NOK, rather than facilitating growth, has deepened uncertainty, delayed development, and created a legal quagmire that is disrupting Greece's already fragile real estate market.

Land Registration

The National Cadastre of Greece was established in 1995 (by Law 2308/1995 on the Organization and Operation of the Hellenic Cadastre and Other Provisions) and serves as a unified, continuously updated system recording legal, technical, and additional data regarding real estate and associated rights, all under the state's jurisdiction and assurance. Greece faces significant challenges with unregistered and illegal constructions, affecting property taxation. Many properties escape taxation due to discrepancies in the National Cadastre and informal ownership. The government has introduced various amnesty programs to regularize illegal constructions, yet enforcement remains a challenge. Recent efforts to complete the National Cadastre have focused on integrating informal properties into the taxation system. The government has proposed stricter enforcement and penalties for nonregistered properties while also offering incentives for voluntary registration. This initiative aims to enhance tax equity and increase revenue from previously untaxed properties, as described at the presentation of the New Cadastre Bill to the Greek Parliament (*Greek Herald* 2024).

The objective of the bill's formation is to institute a modern, fully automated real estate registration system that guarantees the utmost transparency and transactional security.

The responsibilities of the National Cadastre are

- to document the geographical attributes (location, form, boundaries, and size) of each property, as well as build characteristics;
- to register all transactions that create or alter rights, restrictions, and obligations on properties following legality verification;
- to disclose and systematically document state-owned land; and
- to register rights established through *usucapio*, a common method of ownership acquisition in rural and mountainous regions due to informal transfers.

Greece's property taxation system is significantly undermined by the large number of unregistered properties and illegal or informal constructions, creating discrepancies between the National Cadastre records and actual properties on the ground. Many rural properties and inherited assets remain unregistered due to outdated ownership records, while unauthorized modifications in urban areas often go undeclared, leading to widespread tax evasion. As property tax assessments are based on official cadastral data, unregistered properties often escape taxation, resulting in significant revenue losses and shifting the fiscal burden onto compliant property owners. The lack of legal documentation also complicates tax collection and enforcement efforts. In response, the government has introduced property registration amnesty programs to incentivize owners to declare unregistered buildings with reduced penalties, while the establishment of the new National Cadastre, expected in 2025, will incorporate all properties into the formal tax system. Additionally, stricter penalties have been introduced to deter noncompliance and enhance tax equity. Despite these measures, the persistence of unregistered properties continues to pose a major challenge to the effectiveness of Greece's property tax framework. The establishment of the National Cadastre is a critical infrastructural initiative for Greece, promising substantial benefits to citizens, state governance, the national economy, and environmental protection by

- registering and securing the location and dimensions of every parcel and building;
- boosting transparency and security in property transfers;

- reducing bureaucratic hurdles and accelerating real estate transfer procedures;
- enhancing the property market and attracting significant investments;
- formally demarcating and securing state and municipal land;
- more effectively protecting the environment by defining the boundaries of forests and coastal zones, thereby preventing their encroachment; and
- serving as a crucial tool for the country's rational organization and development.

The new Hellenic Cadastre, which replaced the previous National Cadastre, is a legal entity governed by public law. It was instituted by Law 4512/2018 and is overseen by the Ministry of Digital Governance (Presidential Decree 3/6.1.2021).

Recent efforts to complete the National Cadastre have focused on integrating unregistered properties into the taxation system. The government has proposed stricter enforcement and penalties for nonregistered properties while also offering incentives for voluntary registration. This initiative aims to enhance tax equity and increase revenue from previously untaxed properties. The mission of the Hellenic Cadastre is to ensure the reliability, transparency, and accessibility of spatial and legal data related to real estate and to guarantee public trust and transactional security. This is accomplished through the development, maintenance, and operation of the National Cadastre, which ensures that public legal (registrable rights and encumbrances) and technical (locations and boundaries) information from all registered real property transactions is kept up to date. It also undertakes the geodetic and cartographic coverage of the country through the creation and maintenance of digital geospatial data (Greek Land Registry, n.d.). It is accountable for

- overseeing the establishment, preservation, and function of the National Cadastre;
- sustaining and managing the Registrations and Mortgages system;
- creating, preserving, and modifying fundamental and added-value topographic maps and schematics;
- conceptualizing, establishing, arranging, implementing, and managing the systems necessary for the formation and control of the nation's geodetic infrastructure;

- coordinating, implementing, and supervising photogrammetric and cartographic ventures, from the acquisition of aerial snapshots and satellite imagery to the creation of foundational maps, catering to the needs of the agency, the Greek state, local-government organizations, and public legal entities; and
- administering and maintaining digital geospatial databases.

Real Estate Indexes

As far as property indexes are concerned, the main indexes that come from an official authority are the residential and commercial property price indexes and other short-term indexes that are produced by the Bank of Greece (Bank of Greece, n.d.-b). The Bank of Greece places particular emphasis on developing a central system for gathering and analyzing data related to real estate market activity, with special attention to property values, rental levels, and quality features. The objective is to systematically monitor the sector and provide evidence-based assessments of current conditions and future trends. For this purpose, the bank's real estate market analysis section has established both residential and commercial property price indexes, which are derived from detailed information submitted by domestic credit institutions and real estate investment companies.

These indexes possess several notable advantages:

- They are compiled by an official authority applying contemporary methodologies.
- They are issued consistently, with results announced on predetermined dates.
- They are available at quarterly (residential) and semiannual (commercial) intervals.
- They offer extensive breakdowns—for instance, by geographic location, property type, or building age.

Other statistical series also contribute to a more complete understanding of supply and demand dynamics in the Greek property market, such as indexes on housing rents, construction costs, building activity, construction investment, and sectoral expectations. On the demand side, indicators such as interest rate movements and the evolution of housing loan balances are particularly valuable.

All these datasets are stored in the dedicated database of the Bank of Greece real estate market analysis section and are available on its website (Bank of Greece, n.d.-a), enhancing both transparency and dissemination of information about the sector's current state and outlook. Note that the indexes are compiled not from actual sales transactions but from valuation data—primarily linked to mortgage lending.

Tax System

The tax system of Greece is complicated, although taxes are about as high as (in many cases higher than) in other EU countries. The personal income tax rate is 9–45 percent, while corporate tax is flat at 22 percent. Additional taxes on "luxury items" are imposed on wealthy individuals and companies with large turnovers (Immigrant Invest 2024).

Real estate tax policies are subject to continuous modification. Fiscal policy consistently considers numerous economic and social factors that exhibit heightened volatility, especially in recent years. In Greece, real estate taxes include acquisition and annual property taxes, as well as taxes on rental income generated from property leasing. The prevailing taxes, charges, and fees relevant to privately owned immovable property are outlined in subsequent sections (Residence-Greece, n.d.).

The Greek legislature has established several objective techniques for determining income and property values in order to prevent tax evasion. Individual income taxation and real property taxation are the two most significant applications of this strategy (possession and transfer). The legislation specifies a variety of costs and assets that demonstrate "deemed income" of the taxpayer when it comes to the taxation of individual income. Therefore, if someone were to claim an annual salary of €10,000, they would not be able to justify owning a large home with a swimming pool.

If taxpayers disclose less income than the deemed income, they will be taxed on the considered income based on their personal assets and spending. A chart is used for calculating the income associated with specific assets and expenditures, which are summed together. Similar to this, the legislature established an "objective system" of real property assessment with the passage of legislation 1249/1982 in an effort to prevent tax fraud related to property transactions. This approach establishes a minimum value for real estate based on factors including location, size, nearby public amenities, and age of a structure. It was put in place for the tax authorities to have a minimum value to use as a guide for assessing taxes. This mechanism is often termed "presumptive" or "deemed" taxation, and it is used in many jurisdictions to counteract tax evasion or underreporting of income. By setting minimum taxable values based on easily observable metrics (such as ownership of property or certain expenditures), tax authorities can reduce the chances of people hiding their actual income.

The following is a breakdown of the two systems mentioned.

Income estimation based on assets and expenditures

This method can be seen as a check against income understatement. If someone, for instance, reports an income that is disproportionately low compared with their luxurious lifestyle or the acquisition of high-value assets, this system would allow the tax authority to estimate what the person's income "should" be based on those expenditures and assets. This would then be the basis for taxation.

Advantages:

- It makes it difficult for taxpayers to evade taxes based on underreporting.
- It simplifies the taxation process for some individuals who might not keep detailed records.

Disadvantages:

- The estimation might not always reflect actual income, especially for those who have occasional large expenditures.
- It can be seen as intrusive or arbitrary.

Objective system for real property assessment (legislation 1249/1982)

This system sets a floor value for real estate properties, ensuring that any property transactions that report values below this minimum can be taxed at the presumed value.

Advantages

- The system prevents the undervaluing of property during transactions to evade property transfer taxes or capital gains.
- It provides consistency in the assessment of properties for tax purposes.

Disadvantages

- The assessment might not always reflect the market value, especially in cases where the actual value is lower due to factors not covered by the objective metrics.
- It can sometimes lead to overtaxation in depressed real estate markets.

Both methods are aimed at ensuring that the tax base is protected and that taxpayers pay what they owe. They are especially useful in economies where tax evasion is rampant or where the formal financial recordkeeping is not robust. However, like all systems, they need to be applied judiciously and with regular reviews to ensure fairness and to adjust for changing economic realities.

Objective Value

The "objective value" attributed to real estate assets essentially represents the taxable value of transactions within the Greek real estate market. It is derived from the Objective Determination of Real Estate Values System managed by the Ministry of Finance. The objective value is the tax value of the property as assessed by the Greek tax authorities, and it is often lower than the market value.

The property's location, size, type, age, and other characteristics are used to determine the objective value. This system is based on zone prices (zonal values), which are set per square meter for each zone or area in Greece. Each zone has its own value, which is meant to reflect the market value of properties in that area. Generally, central urban areas have higher zone values than suburban or rural areas. Zone prices play a role in various taxes and fees, including property taxes, transfer taxes when a property is sold, and inheritance taxes (Labropoulos 2019).

The objective system using zone prices was instituted to combat tax evasion and underdeclaring the value of property transactions. Having a government-determined value reduced the potential for parties to misreport the sale price of a property. The basic calculation for determining the objective value of a property involves multiplying the property's size (in square meters) by the zone price for the area where the property is located. Adjustments are then made based on the type of property, its age, its number of floors, and other attributes. The calculation of the objective value is carried out by multiplying a variety of coefficients and factors related to the dwelling in question. The Ministry of Finance provides the data for calculating the value of a house or apartment and a plot of land. The data typically contain detailed information, including zone prices, coefficients, and other factors necessary to determine the value of a property for taxation purposes. Some coefficients necessary for the calculation of objective values are not easy to find. Combined with the fact that the tools can be difficult to understand, this makes the calculation process particularly demanding. These tools, especially when introduced by government bodies, can be complex due to the many factors they attempt to incorporate and regulate and the many instruments, methods, and systems used to assist in determining these values.

The objective value is based on a variety of rates that are multiplied in order to calculate the base value on which the property is taxed. The calculation of the objective value depends on the following factors:

- Zone price (provided by valuers).
- Number of facades of the property.
- Floor on which property is located.
- Commerciality of the street.
- Surface area of the property.
- Width of the external walls.
- Year of construction.
- Construction materials.
- Special conditions, such as damage from natural disasters.
- Completion stage.
- Area of the land being utilized.
- Total buildable area of the plot.
- Central heating and elevators.
- Co-ownership.

These features are categorized into special coefficients. The rates correspond to specific values that are multiplied to calculate the taxable value.

The objective value or the value stipulated in the contract, whichever is higher, is used to determine the necessary transfer taxes. The objective values are often far lower than the market prices, although recently the government has been uplifting the zone value. The government is conducting an ongoing effort to align its standardized property valuation system (objective values) more closely with the real-world property market dynamics (market prices). This balancing act is crucial to ensure both fairness in taxation and appropriate revenue collection for public services. Since not all places in Greece have been appraised, the tax authorities in certain (mostly rural) regions make estimates based on comparable transactions or other information that is readily available.

It is not uncommon for the objective value of a property to be less than its actual market value. To reconcile the discrepancy between the objective value and the property's market value, the former is regularly reassessed, especially when there is a tax revenue shortfall in Greek governments. In many instances, the objective value inaccurately reflects prevailing market conditions and lacks substantiation from comparable evidence. The Greek government sets the objective values for different real estate assets from an external standpoint; and their estimates are, in theory, based on the prevailing market conditions, factoring in demand and supply (Chatzitsolis and Vlamis 2014).

Until 1985, the determination of the taxable value of real estate was made using comparative data from purchases and sales of similar properties. These prices, as well as the basic characteristics of the properties, were recorded in the "Book of Prices of Transferred Real Estate" of the Directorate of Capital Taxation, where the initial search was done on the basis of the name of the street where the property was located. This system was correct in principle, and it also allowed for the creation of a register of market prices, which does not exist today. However, in addition to its limited function in cases where the comparative method was applied, it also allowed a relative subjectivity in its interpretation. This weakness spurred the design and implementation of a more objective system for calculating taxable values (Malliou, Kilatou, and Soultis 2022).

Gradually, from 1985 onward, the Objective Determination of Real Estate Values System came into force, based on Law 1249/03.04.1982 (Government Gazette 43A/05.04.1982), as amended by Law 1473/07.09.1984 (Government Gazette 127A/07.09.1984). Article 41 describes how it was originally applied: "For the purpose of determining the taxable value of immovable property transferred in a sale or because of death, gift or dowry, account shall be taken of the starting prices, fixed in advance, by zones or building blocks and by type of property such as urban property, detached house, apartment, shop, farm and other." Today, it has been supplemented, amended, and updated with a plethora of laws and decisions that have been applied to almost the entire country (Franzsen 2014).

Coverage of Tax Base

The Objective Determination of Real Estate Values System consists of four subsystems, which cover all types of real estate for which the determination of their taxable value is needed:

- **The Subsystem of Objective Values of Real Estate**, which began to be applied in 1985, based on Law 1249/03.04.1982 and Law 1473/07.09.1984 and concerns five basic categories of properties located within development zones, determining the total value of the building and its associated land. The five types of property are

- houses or apartments;
- business premises;
- land plots;
- warehouses; and
- parking spaces for cars.

- **The Subsystem of Objective Values of Buildings**, which began to be implemented in 1996, based on Article 10 of Law 2386/06.03.1996 (Government Gazette 43A/07.03.1996), and concerns
  - special buildings located within development zones; and
  - all buildings that are outside the development zones, but specifies the value of only those buildings, not the land.

  The nine types of properties are
  - houses (excluding detached houses);
  - detached houses;
  - office and shop buildings (business premises);
  - car stations and industrial and craft buildings;
  - agricultural and livestock buildings or warehouses;
  - hotels and tourist facilities, hospitals, and charitable institutions.
  - schools;
  - sports facilities; and
  - buildings not falling under the previous categories.
- **The Subsystem of Objective Land Values**, which began to be implemented in 2000, based on decisions 1144814/26361 &1144816 /26362 (Government Gazette 1328B/31.12.1998) and 1121210/6271/ DTY27.12.1999 (Government Gazette 2260B/31.12.1999), and concerns the land outside development zones and determines only the value of the land.
- **The Subsystem of Comparative Data**, which concerns the areas within development zones (usually within settlements) where the Subsystem of Objective Values of Buildings has not yet been applied, as well as in areas outside development zones where special building conditions apply and where *only the value of the land is determined*. It is carried out by the responsible government official

based on comparative sales data within the administrative boundaries of the property under valuation.

Valuation Cycle

The boundaries of the system zones, the zone values, and the coefficients of the system result from an outturn study of the real estate market of zone area, following a political decision. The initial provision for a review of the system was every two years, which in practice was not implemented, due to the particular difficulties arising from the very nature of the envisaged revision. Every two to three years, the Ministry of Finance adjusts the zone prices, and consequently the objective values of properties change. However, the objective values have been adjusted two years in a row, in 2021 and 2022. It would therefore be reasonable to expect the objective system to be updated on an annual basis, given recent developments. Objective prices are calculated on the basis of zone rates and methods of calculation of the state for imposing taxation (Labropoulos 2019).

Dates of adjustments to the objective value made by the
objective determination of real estate values system:

January 1, 1985
March 15, 1986
January 5, 1987
August 16, 1988
January 2, 1991
January 21, 1993
October 2, 1995
January 1, 1998
March 5, 2001
January 1, 2006
March 1, 2007
May 21, 2015

Another revaluation (change of the objective value) was made in 2019, and the last one was carried out in 2020–2021 and implemented in 2022 (Labropoulos 2019).

Valuation Methodology

The determination of the objective value is carried out according to the type and location of each property, by selecting in combination the appropriate forms, tables, and maps, usually in the following order:

- Locating the property and then selecting a suitable subsystem (from items 1–4 in the foregoing list).
- Determining the property category or type, followed by the selection of appropriate forms applicable to the property type.
- Conducting data extraction from
  - maps (within or outside development zones); and
  - relevant tables relating to zone price, land development coefficient, commerciality coefficient, land area, ground floor exploitation, initial basic value, special basic value, and so on.
- Completing forms (proportional or electronic) and determining the total objective value.

Multiplying the zone price by the area of the property and predetermined incremental or reducing coefficients for each of the factors that differentiate the property under consideration from the reference property finally gives the objective value of the property. In addition to the zone price and the aforementioned coefficients of the factors that affect the value of the properties, the Objective Determination of Real Estate Values System consists of a number of other coefficients, obvious or invisible, which are summarized as follows:

- Land development coefficient: The coefficient that expresses the possibility of building exploitation of the plot. It usually coincides with the building factor of the plot, unless otherwise specified in the relevant tables.
- Commerciality coefficient: The coefficient (greater than or equal to the unit) that expresses the commerciality of a road or a section of road of a particular zone. Its values are given in the relevant tables in detail per street. On roads not mentioned, the following applies: commerciality coefficient = 1.
- Land coefficient: The coefficient that determines the value of the land. It is determined by zone in the relevant tables and is less than or equal to or greater than the unit.
- Ground floor exploitation factor: The coefficient that determines the exploitation size of the ground floor of a property. It is a function of the land utilization coefficient and the commerciality coefficient of the plot.
- Land price: The per square meter value of a plot that has frontage on a single road, with commerciality coefficient = 1. It is a function of the zone price and the land utilization coefficient.

- Land participation rate: The percentage of participation of the plot in the value of the final product, whose inclusion in the tables of the system is not necessary but remains as a tool for analysis, monitoring, and development of the system.

Property Valuation Data

In a transfer, the property is taxed on the higher of the objective value or the value stated in the contract. In the first case, there is a loss of tax revenue for the state, while in the second case there is an overtaxation of the real estate without any real return. The price stated in the contract is not necessarily equal to the sale price of the property and therefore to its market value, since its declaration is free, not subject to restrictions or controls, and the sale price is not known except to the two (or more) parties and brokers who may have intervened. This, combined with the previously high transfer tax (8–10 percent), created a culture characterized by the declaration of low contract prices, in most cases equal to the resulting lower objective value.

Another problem that arises concerns bank lending and especially mortgages, since the financial institution cannot conclude a loan agreement for the purchase of a property in an amount that exceeds the declared sale price or contract price (loan to value), even if the commercial value estimate made by the valuers indicates that the requested loan amount is reasonable and corresponds to the market value of the property. If the declared sale price is lower than the actual market value (as determined by valuers), and a bank's lending is tied to the declared sale price (as in the loan-to-value rule mentioned), then potential borrowers may face challenges in obtaining adequate financing.

The objective value is a standardized method for calculating the value of real estate according to the Greek government. Its purpose is to provide the following:

- Taxation consistency: By setting standard values for different properties based on their attributes and location, the government ensures that similar properties are taxed similarly. This helps maintain a level of fairness and consistency in property taxation.
- Transparency: The objective value system also allows property owners to know how their tax is being calculated and what factors are taken into consideration.
- Prevention of tax evasion: In markets where underreporting of transaction values is common to avoid taxes, an objective value

system can help ensure that the government receives its due tax revenue. It prevents underdeclaration of property values and thus helps in curbing tax evasion.

- Ease of administration: The objective value system simplifies the process of property valuation for tax purposes, making it easier for both the government and the taxpayers.

However, it is worth noting that the objective value in Greece has often been criticized for being out of sync with actual market values and very difficult to calculate (table 13.1).

Table 13.1 20 Taxes, Duties, and Other Factors That Are Determined by the Objective Values of Immovable Property

1. Minimum notional/presumed income from property rental/free use of a property	3% on objective value
2. Presumed/notional income from an owner-occupied commercial property	3% on objective value
3. Objective expenditure ("presumed") of living in an owner-occupied or rented home	Depends on area and price zone
4. Uniform Real Estate Property Tax (ENFIA) per property	Buildings: €2–€16.20/m^2 Plots: €0.0037–€9.25/m^2
5. Supplementary tax on all property–tax-free amount of €250,000	Natural persons: 1.5‰–1.15‰ Legal entities: 2.5‰–5.50‰
6. Municipal real estate tax (buildings and land)	0.25‰–0.35‰
7. Real estate tax for offshore companies	15%
8. VAT on the purchase of newly built buildings and for contractual consideration (Land-for-Apartment Exchange System) (on the value of the buildings)	24%
9. Real estate transfer fees/inheritance tax	3%
10. On property transfer fees/tax:	
a. Municipal tax	3% on property transfer tax
b. Tax in favor of the Prefectural Road Funds (Law 4110/13)	7% on property transfer tax
11. Exchange tax (land consolidation)	1.5%
12. Property distribution tax	0.75%

(continued)

Table 13.1 20 Taxes, Duties, and Other Factors That Are Determined by the Objective Values of Immovable Property (*continued*)

13. Municipal property transfer tax	3%
14. Proportional tax on the transfer of contracts	4.75% on mortgaged registrations 5% + 1% at the new land registry offices
15. Inheritance or parental provision of immovable property tax	See table 13.5
16. Gift/donation of immovable property tax	See table 13.5
17. Proportional transfer fees/tax on donations/gifts and parental provisions	7.75% on mortgaged registrations 8% + 1% at the new land registry offices
18. Proportional land registry tax of the Hellenic Land Registry	1% on objective property value over €20,000 with a limit of €900
19. Town planning fines for the construction or maintenance of arbitrary buildings	See Law 4759/2020
20. Contributions to land and money for inclusion in city plans (Law 1337/83, Law 2508/97, as amended by Article 1(7) of Law 4315/2014, Government Gazette A 269/24.12.2014, etc.)	On land: 10%–50% On money: Up to 25%

Types of Taxes

Taxes, Fees, and Deductions on Income from Immovable Property

When leasing a property in Greece, one is required to pay taxes on the income generated from the rental. The tax rates applied are progressive, varying based on the amount of profit earned from the rent.

For corporations, rental income constitutes a portion of their taxable income. The corporate tax rate is currently 29 percent, accompanied by a 15 percent dividend withholding tax. If foreign investors own Greek companies through an EU-based corporation, they may be eligible for the Parent-Subsidiary Directive exemption, which eliminates the dividend withholding tax in such cases.

The rental income is also subject to a solidarity contribution, which is determined based on a progressive tax scale of up to 10 percent. This contribution is calculated using an individual's total income. It is crucial to report one's complete income, as the Greek government closely monitors landlords with rental properties. Homeowners may face penalties if

Table 13.2 Taxes on Income from Immovable Property

1. Rental Income Tax (breakdown)		15%/35%/45%
Breakdown of Scale of Taxation Based on Income Obtained Exclusively from Real Estate Rental[1]		
Income	**Tax Rate**	
€0–€12,000	15%	
€12,001–€35,000	35%	
€35,001 and above	45%	
2. Stamp Duty + Agricultural Insurance Organisation (excluding income from residential leases)		3.6%
3. Special Solidarity Tax on Natural Persons[2]		2.2%–10%
Breakdown of Tax Scale for Special Solidarity Contribution for Natural Persons		
Income	**Tax Rate**	
€0–€12,000	0%	
€12,001–€20,000	2.2%	
€20,001–€30,000	5%	
€30,001–€40,000	6.5%	
€40,001–€65,000	7.5%	
€65,001–€220,000	9%	
€220,001 and above	10%	

[1] Rental income (excluding income from residential leases) is subject to an additional stamp duty of 3.6%.

[2] Temporarily suspended.

they neglect to declare their rental earnings (Global Citizen Solutions 2023).

A 3.6 percent stamp duty is charged on nonresidential rentals (except for shopping centers and logistics centers subject to value-added tax [VAT]). In general, there may be a 2.4 percent stamp duty on loans and interest. There are a few exclusions, with the main ones pertaining to bank loans and bond issuance. Additionally, it has been made clear that interest-bearing loans made by a person subject to VAT (enterprises), even on a sporadic basis, are free from stamp duty in accordance with current Greek legal precedent. In a few rare instances, additional stamp taxes may be necessary (Hellenic Property Federation 2023) (table 13.2).

Annual Taxes on the Possession of Immovable Property

The most typical methods of gaining property under Greek law are as follows:

- Acquisition through a written contract signed before a notary public and documented between the seller and the buyer (or registered).
- Acquisition by succession, whether through a will or another method.
- Acquisition by a gift or parental grant; acquisition of property at an auction or through a compulsory enforcement action taken against the debtor's property, when the highest bidder ultimately succeeds in acquiring possession of the property.
- Acquisition by a person who has been lawfully occupying a property for ten years (normal or usual usucapion) or acquisition by a person who has been legally occupying a property for twenty years (extraordinary usucapion) (Xythali 2019).

ENFIA

There are a number of annual property taxes associated with the ownership of real estate. The majority of these taxes are related to the Uniform Real Estate Property Tax (ENFIA), levied in terms of Law 4223/2013 on the Uniform Real Estate Property Tax (table 13.3). In 2014 the ENFIA replaced the previous special tax implemented in October 2011, commonly referred to as *haratsi*. In contrast to the *haratsi* tax, the new tax is not incorporated into electricity bills. Instead, an individual invoice is issued by the tax administration, which can be settled either in a single payment or through equal installments over a five-month period (Ministry of Digital Governance of the Hellenic Republic 2022).

The annual tax is applicable to all categories of real estate and is imposed on all property owners, both individual and legal entities. The tax is calculated according to an objective value that is set by the tax authority every year on January 1. The calculation of this part is complex—it takes into account various factors such as property type, size, location, usage, building age, and estimated value.

It consists of two parts:

- The principal tax that is levied on buildings: The floor area, price zone, surfaces, building age, facade, proportion of ownership, and other specific elements are some of the criteria that determine the tax. The principal tax is measured by multiplying the property's area by a coefficient ranging from €2 to €16.2 per square meter.

Table 13.3 Greek Real Estate Property Taxation Overview

1. Main Tax, ENFIA, per Lien on Immovable Property Belonging to a Natural Person or a Legal Entity Based on Rates per Square Meter of Surface Area of Property (applied per property as of January 1 each year)	Buildings: €2.0–€16.2/m^2 Plots: €0.0037–€9.25/m^2

Breakdown of Scale of Basic Tax Rate for Building (built 25 years ago or before):

Price Range	**Tax Rate (per m^2)**
€0–€750	€2.00
€751–€1,500	€2.80
€1,501–€2,500	€3.70
€2,501–€3,000	€4.50
€3,000–€3,500	€7.60
€3,501–€4,000	€9.20
€4,001–€4,500	€11.10
€4,501–€5,000	€13.40
€5,001 and above	€16.20

(*continued*)

Table 13.3 Greek Real Estate Property Taxation Overview (*continued*)

2. Main Tax, ENFIA, per Lien on Urban/Commercial Property Belonging to Natural Persons (provided that the total value of the property exceeds €400,000 and the total value of all property owned by the taxpayer exceeds €300,000)	Range: 0.20%–1.0%

Breakdown of Tax Scale of Additional Tax (formerly property tax) on Individuals as of January 1

Scale (€)	Tax Bracket (%)	Tax Scale (€)	Total Immovable Property Value (€)	Tax (€)
0.01–400,000.00	0.0	0	400,000	0
400,000.01–500,000.00	0.2	200	500,000	200
500,000.01–600,000.00	0.3	300	600,000	500
600,000.01–700,000.00	0.4	400	700,000	900
700,000.01–800,000.00	0.5	500	800,000	1,400
800,000.01–900,000.00	0.6	600	900,000	2,000
900,000.01–1,000,000.00	0.7	700	1,000,000	2,700
1,000,000.01–2,000,000.00	0.9	9,000	2,000,000	11,700
2,000,000.01 and above	1.0			

3. Additional ENFIA on the Total Value of Property Rights on Immovable Property Belonging to Legal Entities	Range: 0.10%/0.35%/0.55%
4. Annual Property Tax (buildings + land)	0.25‰–0.35‰ (potentially up to 10 times is given to local-government organizations
5. Special Real Estate Tax for Companies	15%
6. Readjustment of Property Owned by Businesses Tax (periodic)	Land: 5% Buildings: 8%

- The principal tax that is levied on land: it is calculated by multiplying the area of the land (square meters) by a coefficient ranging from €0.0037 to €9.25 per square meter.

The supplementary tax is applied only to legal persons and is calculated at a rate of five and a half per thousand (5.5‰) on the value of the aforementioned rights, while for real estate that is used by the owner for the production or performance of any type of business activity, regardless of field of activity, the supplementary tax is calculated at a rate of one per thousand (1‰). This distinction emphasizes the Greek government's approach to encourage the active use of properties for business purposes, likely to spur economic activity and employment. By offering a reduced tax rate for properties used in business activities, the taxation system incentivizes entities to utilize properties for productive purposes rather than merely holding them as passive investments. The supplementary tax is decreased to 1 percent for businesses that utilize the property for the purposes of commercial operation of their own. The supplementary tax for individuals is levied at a progressive rate ranging from 0.1 percent to 1.15 percent and allows for a tax-free allowance of €200,000 of the entire value of property rights covered by the ENFIA, excluding the value of agricultural parcels outside urban planning for the year 2018.

Municipality Duty

According to the relevant law provisions, real estate ownership (i.e., ongoing taxation—taxes imposed on the possession of Greek real estate property) is subject to a municipality duty. This duty is levied and collected annually through the electricity bill in favor of municipalities and communities at a currently calculated rate ranging between 0.25 and 0.35 percent on the assessed real estate's value, determined by multiplying the real estate's total building area in square meters by the specific value per square meter, depending on the location of the property (the specific value is determined by the Ministry of Finance), and further multiplied by the rate deriving from the building's age (Kallideris 2023; PwC 2018).

Special Real Estate Tax

The special real estate tax is set at 15 percent of the property's cadastral value and applies specifically to corporations possessing real estate assets. There are multiple strategies to legally avoid paying this tax. For instance, companies that show an income from active trade activities that surpasses their passive income activities are exempt from this tax. This tax is levied on all Greek corporations that own real estate. The government's aim with this tax is to discourage corporations from concealing their real estate assets (Global Citizen Solutions 2023). The tax requires a 15 percent annual payment on the cadastral value of the property unless the corporation falls under certain exemptions, which are as follows:

- Companies with registered shares to individuals are exempted, provided that the companies are resident in Greece or any other European country (with the exception of certain noncooperative states). It is also mandatory for individual shareholders to keep their Greek tax identification number up to date.
- Companies owned by banks and major investors are exempt from revealing ownership details to individuals, as long as these individuals are not based in noncooperative states and are regulated by an approved supervisory authority of a state.
- Organizations having their shares listed on a recognized exchange are exempt.
- Maritime or ship-owning companies with Greek offices that utilize their real estate solely as offices or storage spaces, or lease these properties to other maritime companies, are exempt.
- Nonprofit entities focusing on philanthropic, educational, cultural, and religious activities are exempt for the buildings supporting these activities, including abandoned buildings or other properties they manage. The condition is that all profits must be redirected to the aforementioned objectives.
- Companies engaged in commerce, industry, or manufacturing in Greece are exempt, provided their gross income from these activities surpasses the gross income from the owned real estate in the relevant fiscal year. Regardless of their country of incorporation, such legal entities constructing a space for exclusive use in their commercial, industrial, or manufacturing activities are eligible for a seven-year special real estate tax exemption from the date of submission of all necessary paperwork for the building permit.
- Companies where registered shares or portions are owned by a domestic or foreign institution aiming for philanthropic objectives in Greece are exempt.
- Social security organizations, insurance funds, real estate mutual investment companies, and regulated funds supervised by the competent authority at their place of registration are exempt, excluding those based in noncooperative states (RSM Greece Certified Auditors and Management Consultants 2025).

Taxes: Fees on the Transfer of Immovable Property

The provision and leasing of immovable property are generally not subject to VAT. However, starting from January 1, 2025, a 24 percent VAT will apply to the sale of new buildings before their first occupation. For properties with construction licenses issued after January 1, 2006, the sale of newly constructed homes is normally subject to this VAT. For VAT purposes, "new property" refers to any structure that has not been previously occupied before sale. Exemptions from VAT may apply on a case-by-case basis, subject to request and compliance with specific conditions.

In principle, transfer tax is replaced by VAT, with the tax burden falling on the buyer. However, under Law 4646/2019, the application of VAT to real estate with permits issued on or after January 1, 2006—still under construction or unsold—was suspended until December 31, 2022. This suspension was subsequently extended until December 31, 2025, during which time a reduced 3 percent transfer tax applies, calculated on the property's objective value (or the transaction price, if higher). This measure forms part of broader policy initiatives designed to stimulate construction activity and attract foreign investment by lowering up-front acquisition costs.

Capital gains realized by individuals are generally taxed at a rate of 15 percent. An exception applies, however, to capital gains from the sale of real estate, which remained exempt until December 31, 2024. This exemption, first introduced in 2013, has been consistently extended and is expected to remain in place until a comprehensive reform of real estate taxation is implemented.

Finally, transfer tax, borne by the buyer, applies when there is a change in the legal or economic ownership of Greek real estate. The rate is 3 percent of the property's tax value. However, in cases where VAT is levied on the sale of a new building, the 3 percent transfer tax is waived (RSM Greece Certified Auditors and Management Consultants 2025) (table 13.4).

Inheritance Tax, Parental Provision, and Gift or Donation of Immovable Property

The Greek Civil Code states that the national legislation governing inheritance, possible heirs, and their shares of the bequest are determined by the deceased's citizenship. If the deceased held several citizenships, Greek nationality is given priority. If the deceased did not have Greek nationality, the laws of the nation with which they had closer ties would take precedence. If the dead had no nationality, the laws of their place of

Table 13.4 Property Transaction and Transfer Taxes

VAT on the purchase of newly built buildings and for contractual consideration (Land-for-Apartment Exchange System) (suspended until December 31, 2024)	24%
Capital gains tax on property sales annual property tax (buildings + land) (currently suspended)	15%
Transfer tax/utilization of property tax	3%
Exchange tax (land consolidation)	1.5%
Property distribution tax	0.75%
On property transfer fees/tax: a. Municipal tax b. New tax in favor of the Prefectural Road Funds (Law 4110/13)	 a. 3% on property transfer tax b. 7% on property transfer tax
Proportional tax on the transfer of contracts	4.75% on mortgaged registrations 5% + 1% at the new land registry offices

habitual residence first, then of their place of residency, are applicable (Amoiridis Law Services 2020).

The deceased individual's obligations, as well as real estate and transportable property, are included in the inheritance (private debts, taxes due to the public state, social security debts, loans, etc.) (table 13.5).

Reform Initiatives and Country-Specific Issues

Governments worldwide are employing various strategies to identify affluent individuals for taxation purposes. For instance, Portugal has recently introduced a 10 percent tax on foreign pension income, thus terminating the tax-free status for foreigners initiated during the financial downturn. On the other hand, Greece contemplates tax reduction as a means to draw foreign investors. To transfer their tax domicile to Greece, overseas investors need to make a minimum real estate investment of €500,000. Greek decision-makers are considering the prospect of lowering the unified property tax by increasing the exemption limit from €250,000 to between €300,000 and €350,000 to entice wealthy individuals. In 2018, property taxes constituted a significant portion of Greece's total tax revenue, at 7.9 percent, compared with a mere 4.6 percent for European OECD nations.

Table 13.5 Inheritance Taxes

1. Inheritance or Parental Provision of Immovable Property Tax

Tax Scale for Inheritances–Parental Provisions
CATEGORY A
Inheritance (to spouse, children, grandchildren, or parents)

Scale (€)	Tax Bracket (%)	Tax Scale (€)	Total Immovable Property Value (€)	Proportional Tax (€)
150,000	0	0	150,000	0
150,000	1	1,500	300,000	1,500
300,000	5	15,000	600,000	16,500
Above	10			

Note: There is a special inheritance tax exemption of €400,000 for a surviving spouse (after five years of marriage) and their children who are minors.

Parental Provision to Children (from October 1, 2021)

Scale (€)	Tax Bracket (%)	Tax Scale (€)	Total Immovable Property Value (€)	Proportional Tax (€)
800,000	0	0	800,000	0
Above	10			

Note: The fees for parental provisions are now the notary's fee and the transfer/registration fees as of October 1, 2021.

(continued)

Table 13.5 Inheritance Taxes (*continued*)

CATEGORY B (other descendants and ascendants, siblings, and uncles)
Inheritance

Scale (€)	Tax Bracket (%)	Tax Scale (€)	Total Immovable Property Value (€)	Proportional Tax (€)
30,000	0	0	30,000	0
70,000	5	3,500	100,000	3,500
200,000	10	20,000	300,000	23,500
Above	20			

CATEGORY C (other relatives and nonrelatives)
Inheritance

Scale (€)	Tax Bracket (%)	Tax Scale (€)	Total Immovable Property Value (€)	Proportional Tax (€)
6,000	0	0	6,000	0
66,000	20	13,200	72,000	13,200
195,000	30	58,500	267,000	71,700
Above	40			

2. Gift/Donation of Immovable Property Tax

Tax Scale for Donations

CATEGORY A

To Spouse, Grandchildren, and Parents

Scale (€)	**Tax Bracket (%)**	**Tax Scale (€)**	**Total Immovable Property Value (€)**	**Proportional Tax (€)**
150,000	0	0	150,000	0
150,000	1	1,500	300,000	1,500
300,000	5	15,000	600,000	16,500
Above	10			

Gift/Donation to Grandchildren (from October 1, 2021)

Scale (€)	**Tax Bracket (%)**	**Tax Scale (€)**	**Total Immovable Property Value (€)**	**Proportional Tax (€)**
800,000	0	0	800,000	0
Above	10			

(continued)

Table 13.5 Inheritance Taxes (*continued*)

CATEGORY B (other descendants and ascendants, siblings, and uncles)
Donation

Scale (€)	Tax Bracket (%)	Tax Scale (€)	Total Immovable Property Value (€)	Proportional Tax (€)
30,000	0	0	30,000	0
70,000	5	3,500	100,000	3,500
200,000	10	20,000	300,000	23,500
Above	20			

CATEGORY C (other relatives and nonrelatives)
Donation

Scale (€)	Tax Bracket (%)	Tax Scale (€)	Total Immovable Property Value (€)	Proportional Tax (€)
6,000	0	0	6,000	0
66,000	20	13,200	72,000	13,200
195,000	30	58,500	267,000	71,700
Above	40			

3. Proportional Transfer Fees/Tax on Donations/Gifts and Parental Provisions	7.75% on mortgaged registrations 8% + 1% at the new land registry offices

However, Greece's real property tax system is convoluted and imposes a substantial capital burden, rendering the country less competitive than its OECD counterparts. Greece is positioned 33rd out of 36 nations in terms of real property taxes, according to the "International Tax Competitiveness Index 2019" (Bunn and Asen 2019). To lure foreign investors, Greece has proposed a flat 7 percent tax on foreign pensioners' income and sanctioned a tax exemption for property relocated to Greece during foreign nationals' resettlement.

While these initiatives may prove beneficial, the Greek government needs to meticulously balance the costs of tax incentives with the potential for broader tax reforms. A property tax reform in Greece aimed at simplifying the system, amplifying deductibility against corporate taxable income, and focusing the tax exclusively on land value could serve as a more effective goal than merely targeting incentives for foreigners to shift their tax domicile. Such a reform could stimulate investment and economic activity while potentially enhancing the tax's revenue-generating capacity (OECD 2024).

Law 4549/14.06.2018 (Government Gazette 105A/14.06.2018) established the Independent Department of Real Estate Valuations and Determination, which, among other things, aims to collect and analyze data related to real estate values, create tables of real estate values, revise the Objective Determination of Real Estate Values System, organize procedures, and revise the legal framework of property taxation in the country. In this context, it has already launched a series of projects and formed contacts with all relevant public and private sector bodies, which, in combination with the results of technical assistance that the EU has been providing for the effort in recent years, are expected to soon give results for the upgrade of the Objective Determination of Real Estate Values System, as well as for its transformation into a System of Mass Real Estate Valuations (a computer-assisted mass appraisal [CAMA] system).

Compared with the current system, which is based on objective value and value zones, the upgrade transformation toward a CAMA system can benefit the Greek government in various aspects:

- Accuracy and efficiency: CAMA systems assess property attributes and sales data using statistical modeling, which can produce more accurate and consistent property valuations than human techniques. More equal taxes may result from this enhanced accuracy, which may increase public confidence in the tax system.

- Savings in time and money: By automating the appraisal process, time and resources required for conducting property assessments can be greatly reduced.

- Data management and integration: To manage and analyze a variety of property data, CAMA systems can integrate with geographic information systems and other databases. This data integration can increase tax administration's effectiveness and offer important insights for determining policy.
- Transparency and accountability: CAMA systems can give thorough records of the methods used to calculate property values, which can improve the process's transparency and accountability.
- Data updating: Property valuations can be updated regularly to reflect changes in the real estate market with the aid of CAMA systems. This can ensure that market values are reflected in objective values used for taxation, which has been a major problem in Greece.
- Revenue collection: A CAMA system may boost tax collections by increasing the accuracy of property appraisals. The government may not be making as much money as it could be if properties are undervalued. However, if properties are overvalued, it could result in appeals and conflicts that can be expensive and time consuming.

However, the current situation indicates that there is a long away to go until such a CAMA system is implemented, as one of the projects launched in 2020 by the Ministry of Interior was to synchronize all involved authorities to share available geographic data.

Impact

Greece's property tax system is probably one of the most complicated systems among EU countries. The existing system creates a high tax burden on capital, increases the cost of capital, and potentially drives businesses and individuals to invest in more business-friendly jurisdictions. A complex property tax system can also hinder real estate investment and improvement, which in turn affects economic growth and productivity. The complexity of the system can also lead to confusion, uncertainty, and inefficiencies in the land market, potentially hindering investment and the efficient allocation of resources. Additionally, if the property tax system is not transparent and predictable, it can undermine investor confidence and discourage investment in the land market. Since the postcrisis period (2011–2012), Greece's property tax system has relatively stabilized, with EU monitoring ensuring compliance with fiscal reforms. Efforts have been made to improve tax collection efficiency and reduce tax evasion related to real estate transactions (table 13.6). However, challenges remain in

Table 13.6 Billing and Collection

Fees, Taxes, and Contributions in Favor of Local-Government Organizations and Third Parties	
Municipal cleaning and lighting tax	Determined by each local-government organization
Municipal tax on areas that are electrified	Determined by each local-government organization
Potential municipal fees (with various justifications)	Determined by each local-government organization
Special tax for renewable energy sources	kWh × unit charge (€/kWh)
Tax in favor of Hellenic Broadcasting Corporation	€3 per month
Property sewerage charges (connection and use)	Determined by public enterprises and organizations and each local-government organization
Contributions to land and money for inclusion in city plans (Law 1337/83, Law 2508/97, as amended by Article 1(7) of Law 4315/2014, Government Gazette A 269/24.12.2014, etc.)	On land: 10%–50% On money: Up to 25%
Taxes on Cadastral Registration, Copies, and so on, Paid to the Hellenic Land Registry	
One-off land registration fee	€35 per registration
Proportional tax of 1‰ on property value over €20,000 with a limit of €900, the collection of which is pending	
Proportional tax/fee for the registration of mortgages	8‰
Fixed tax/fee for the registration of each legal transaction	€20
Fee for issuing a copy from the Land Registry's archive	€9.50
Fee for issuing a certificate from the Land Registry's books	€9.50
Fee for issuing an extract from the cadastral map	€15
Fee for issuing a cadastral map	€33
Additional transfer fee on the value of each property	1‰

(*continued*)

Table 13.6 Billing and Collection (*continued*)

Taxes, Fees, and Contributions for Building Permits, Construction of Buildings, Arbitrary Buildings, and so on	
Fee for issuing a building permit within the development zone on property outside the development zone in favor of the Green Fund (Law 4759/2020)	1% of project budget 5% on cost of permit
Construction work tax	Vote KH'/1947
Withheld in favor of the municipality, the Technical Chamber of Greece, and the Public Works, Contractors, and Engineering Fund	On budget
Employer contributions to the Unified Social Security Fund	+90% on the imputed daily wage
VAT on building materials and works	24%
Municipal taxes for pavements	Determined by each local-government organization
Property electricity supply fee (in favor of the Public Power Corporation and the municipality)	Law 4483/65 (Article 8)
Town planning fines for arbitrary buildings, etc.	Defined by Law 4759/2020

assessing the real market value of properties, and there are also constitutional and legal challenges such as the New Building Regulation.

Major issues that arise stem from the fact that neither property transactions nor rentals are recorded in a centralized database, which causes a series of problems, including the following:

- Lack of transparency: Unrecorded property transactions can create barriers to tracking ownership changes and assessing the value of properties, which can result in a lack of transparency in the real estate market.
- Incomplete market information: If transactions are not recorded, it can be difficult to obtain accurate information about property prices and market trends, which can lead to an incomplete understanding of the market.
- Lack of accuracy in property valuations: A lack of information about property transactions can pose challenges for accurately valuing properties, leading to incorrect assessments of property taxes, insurance rates, and other real estate–related charges.

- Difficulty in enforcing property rights: If transactions are not recorded, enforcing property rights and resolving disputes over ownership and possession becomes more difficult.
- Inadequate revenue collection: Accurately collecting taxes and other charges on real estate becomes challenging without records on property transactions, which can reduce the revenue collected by government and other entities.

Conclusion

It is hard to say whether the property tax in Greece has reached its potential, as this depends on a number of factors. However, the property tax in Greece is an important source of revenue for the government and has been used to help fund public services and infrastructure.

The property tax has been used as a tool to help the Greek government raise revenue, particularly during the country's economic crisis. In recent years, the government has made efforts to improve the property tax system, such as by increasing enforcement and cracking down on tax evasion (Petrakis 2020).

Tax reforms generally occur in Greece every 3.5–4 years, when there is a change in government. It can be expected that two to five property tax reforms will take place with the induction of a new government. This is done in order to combat tax avoidance and evasion, problems that have created large gaps in the government's income. Greece holds the unfortunate distinction of having the second-highest incidence of VAT evasion within the European Union, resulting in annual revenue losses equivalent to two years' collections of the ENFIA. The European Commission is urging member states to intensify their endeavors to curb VAT evasion, a problem costing the EU more than €134 billion annually. Specifically, in Greece, the state forgoes approximately €5.35 billion in potential VAT revenue each year, representing about 25.8 percent of the theoretical VAT receipts (Hatzinikolaou 2022).

A significant portion of Greece's GDP is derived from tourism income. Tourism contributes to 18 percent of Greece's GDP and provides employment for over 900,000 individuals, equating to one-fifth of the workforce (Hellenic Republic of Greece in the USA, n.d.). This revenue stream, however, is particularly susceptible to tax evasion due to the ease with which it can be concealed. Notably, in 2019, one in every three businesses in Greece was reported to have breached tax regulations, according to the Independent Authority for Public Revenue (AADE), with businesses associated with tourism and taxi services being primary offenders. To ensure compliance with tax laws, especially in relation to the issuance or accuracy of receipts, special fraud units are expected to carry out daily audits that are considered crucial to addressing the considerable discrepancies observed in the country's revenue (Greek Travel Pages 2022). To address the deficits in the nation's revenue, property tax reforms are implemented as a means to supplement the shortfall. Given that property represents a tangible, physical asset that cannot be concealed, it is challenging to evade revenue generated from property or avoid paying taxes on owned assets. Thus, when there is a substantial need for revenue supplementation, property tax reforms are often carried out.

While the taxation system in Greece appears to be quite structured, there have been criticisms that the country's property tax is still not reaching its full potential. Some experts argue that the system is not as efficient as it could be, and that there is room for improvement in terms of increasing revenue and reducing evasion. This could be achieved through better administration, increased efforts to identify and tax undeclared properties, and the implementation of new technologies to improve the collection of property taxes. The process of collecting money and distributing the tax revenue lacks transparency.

It is worth noting that the property tax is a part of the overall tax system, and its potential is affected by the complexity of the tax laws and regulations, the ability to enforce the laws, the economic conditions, and the level of cooperation of the taxpayers (Labropoulos 2012).

The existing system is complicated, unfriendly, unfair, and obsolete compared with one that might be assisted by a CAMA system.

Additional problems due to the structure and operation of the existing system include the following:

- The lack of a scientific modification of the zone prices rather than modification through the proper handling of tax rates.
- The arbitrary definition of the coefficients of fluctuation of each factor that affects the value of real estate, horizontally for the whole country and all types of real estate, without the use of statistical procedures and analyses.
- The connection of tax practices (e.g., increase of tax of larger properties or maximum age of real estate at 26 years) with procedures for determining the value of real estate.
- The disregard for the spatial dimension of real estate, within each zone, in the differentiation of its value.

- The infrequent review of the system, which leads to strong market distortions, just before and shortly after the date of readjustment, maximizing and minimizing, respectively, the demand and the related operations.

Additional problems particular to Greece include the following:

- There are no official and organized sales prices, while the main source of comparative data for the approximation of real estate value is the "requested prices" from ads, as well as information from brokers. The only approach to commercial values is to use estimates from local property companies, to the degree that they are reliable and to the extent that they are organized, available, and searchable.
- The National Cadastre, which could form the basis of the real estate tax system as the one in Cyprus does, is in a phase of development with a significant time to completion. The rest of the "registers" of real estate—the E9 property register, the Inventory of ELSTAT (Hellenic Statistics Authoity) Buildings, HEDNO (Hellenic Electricity Distribution Network Operator S.A.) meter data, valuation data from the Bank of Greece—either are not available for reasons of personal data protection or cannot be interconnected with the other registers and their data.
- Procedures for urban planning are complicated and building legislation is complex.
- In total, as mentioned, the roughly 45 taxes and fees on real estate place a significant burden on the ownership of real estate.
- The number of debtors who default on their loans has increased significantly, as has the number of properties that have been or are expected to be auctioned.

Although any mass appraisal of the value of real estate cannot determine exactly the market value of each property, the aim is to achieve it to such an extent that it corresponds as much as possible to reality and makes taxation fair. Therefore, the need arises to revise the system so that it is based on modern scientific technologies, methods, and techniques and internationally recognized real estate market data, automated with the least possible human intervention and subject to statistical processing and verification.

The main problem created by the lack of knowledge and disclosure of the sale prices of real estate is that a reliable register of real estate transfer values cannot be created, based on the observations of which the real estate market would be "regulated" and fairer taxable values could be imposed on them. Nevertheless, Law 4484/2017 (Government Gazette 110A/01.08.2017), Adaptation of Greek Legislation to the Provisions of Directive (EU) 2016/881 and Other Provisions, stipulates that the General Secretariat of Public Property of the Ministry of Finance maintains in electronic form a Register of Real Estate Transfer Values, which is technically supported by the General Secretariat for Information Systems and Administrative Support of the ministry for the sole purpose of drawing statistical conclusions and monitoring the real estate market. The data of each transfer are collected by the AADE, the cadastral offices, or the cooperating notaries, according to the AADE circular regarding Law 1040/2018, "Determination of the Sources and Type of Data Collected, the Category of Data Published, as Well as the Time of Keeping the Data in the Register of Real Estate Transfer Values." The register has been in force since March 2017, and when it gathers a sufficient number of comments, its reliability and the extent of its effect can be judged.

References

Amoiridis Law Services. 2020. "Greek Legislation on Inheritance Proceedings." May. https://www.law-services.gr/greek-legislation-on-inheritance-proceedings/.

Bank of Greece. n.d.-a. "Real Estate Market." Accessed March 2025. https://www.bankofgreece.gr/en/statistics/real-estate-market.

———. n.d.-b. "Residential and Commercial Property Price Indices and Other Short-Term Indices." Accessed March 2025. https://www.bankofgreece.gr/en/statistics/real-estate-market/residential-and-commercial-property-price-indices-and-other-short-term-indices.

Bunn, D., and E. Asen. 2019. "International Tax Competitiveness Index 2019." October 2. Tax Foundation. https://taxfoundation.org/research/all/global/2019-international-index/.

Chatzitsolis, N., and P. Vlamis. 2014. "The Boom and Bust of the Greek Housing Market." *Real Estate Issues* 39(1): 9–17.

Eurostat. 2015. "Euro Indicators." News Release. January.

Franzsen, R. 2014. "Legal Framework for an Effective Value-Based Property Tax System." Presented in "Market Value-Based Taxation of Real Property: Lessons from International Experience," Lincoln Institute of Land Policy and Centre of Excellence in Finance course, Ljubljana, Slovenia.

Global Citizen Solutions. 2023. "Your Guide to Property Taxes in Greece." https://www.globalcitizensolutions.com/property-taxes-in-greece-the-ultimate-guide-by-experts/.

Greek Herald. 2024. "Greece to Establish Land Registry by 2025—PM Kyriakos Mitsotakis' Announcement." October 4. https://greekherald.com.au/news/greece-to-establish-land-registry-by-2025/.

Greek Land Registry. n.d. "The Cadastral Project in Greece." Accessed November 25, 2025. https://www.ktimatologio.gr/.

Greek Travel Pages. 2022. "Greece Gets Tough on Tax Evasion in Tourism." May 6. https://news.gtp.gr/2022/05/06/greece-gets-tough-on-tax-evasion-in-tourism/.

Hatzinikolaou, Prokopis. 2022. "VAT Evasion at 5.35 Bln Euros." Ekathimerini, April 27. https://www.ekathimerini.com/economy/1183012/vat-evasion-at-5-35-bln-euros/.

Hellenic Property Federation. 2023. "Real Estate Tax Observatory." https://www.pomida.gr/paratiritirio_foron.php.

Hellenic Republic of Greece in the USA. n.d. "For a Sustainable Tourism Industry." Hellenic Republic—Greece in Brussels. Accessed March 2025. www.mfa.gr/brussels/en/about-greece/tourism/for-sustainable-tourism-industry.html.

IMF (International Monetary Fund). 2010. "Europe and IMF Agree €110 Billion Financing Plan with Greece." May 2. www.imf.org/external/pubs/ft/survey/so/2010/car050210a.htm.

———. 2013. "Greece: Ex-Post Evaluation of Exceptional Access Under the 2010 Stand-By Arrangement." Washington, DC: IMF. https://www.imf.org/en/Publications/CR/Issues/2016/12/31/Greece-Ex-Post-Evaluation-of-Exceptional-Access-Under-the-2010-Stand-By-Arrangement-40639.

Immigrant Invest. 2024. "Property Taxes in Greece for 2024: VAT, Transfer Tax, ENFIA." May 24. Accessed March 25, 2025. https://immigrantinvest.com/blog/greece-property-taxes/en (blog post no longer available).

Kallideris, C. 2023. "Greece—Individual—Other Taxes." PwC. https://taxsummaries.pwc.com/greece/individual/other-taxes.

Labropoulos, A. 2012. International Workshop on Mass Appraisals, Pafos, FIG Commision 9, Neapolis University.

———. 2019. "Seminar for the Objective Value." Association of Greek Valuers. https://avag.gr/video/η-έκδοση-των-ελληνικών-εκτιμητικών-ο/.

Malliou, A., M. Kilatou, and D. Soultis. 2022. "Greece." In *The Private Wealth and Private Client Review*, ed. John Riches, 11th ed. https://www.osullivanlaw.com/wp-content/uploads/2022/10/Margaret-OSullivan-Marly-Peikes-Private-Wealth-and-Private-Client-Review-2022-Canada-Chapter-The-Law-Reviews.pdf.

Ministry of Digital Governance of the Hellenic Republic. 2022. "Uniform Real Estate Property Tax (ENFIA)." https://www.gov.gr/en/sdg/residence/purchasing-and-selling-of-immovable-property/taxation-for-possession-of-real-estate-property/uniform-real-estate-property-tax-enfia.

OECD (Organisation for Economic Co-operation and Development). 2016. "Country Fact Sheet Greece." In *The Governance of Land Use*, 49–87. https://www.oecd.org/regional/regional-policy/land-use-Greece.pdf.

———. 2024. "Greece Economic Snapshot." https://www.oecd.org/en/topics/sub-issues/economic-surveys/greece-economic-snapshot.html.

Papanikos, G. T. 2015. "The Real Exchange Rate of Euro and Greek Economic Growth." *Journal of Economic Asymmetries* 12(2): 100–109. https://doi.org/10.1016/j.jeca.2015.04.002.

Petrakis, P. E. 2020. *The New Political Economy of Greece up to 2030*. Cham: Palgrave Macmillan.

POMIDA (Hellenic Property Federation). 2025a. "42nd POMIDA Conference: Property Taxation and Housing Crisis." January 25. https://www.pomida.gr.

———. 2025b. "KAPA Research Study on Property Taxation." January 25. https://www.pomida.gr.

PwC. 2018. *Greek Real Estate Taxation: A Brief Summary*. https://www.pwc.com/gr/en/publications/greek-thought-leadership/greek-real-estate-taxation-summary.html.

RSM Greece Certified Auditors and Management Consultants. 2025. "Selling and Transferring Greek Real Estate." February 28. https://www.rsm.global/greece/insights/real-estate-insights/selling-and-transferring-greek-real-estate.

Residence-Greece. n.d. "Property Taxes in Greece: What Should an Investor Expect?" Accessed March 2025. https://residence-greece.com/property-taxes-in-greece/.

Schmitt-Grohé, S., and M. Uribe. 2013. "Downward Nominal Wage Rigidity and the Case for Temporary Inflation in the Eurozone." *Journal of Economic Perspectives* 27(3): 193–212. https://doi.org/10.1257/jep.27.3.193.

Skartsis, L. 2018. "2010–2018 Greek Debt Crisis and Greece's Past: Myths, Popular Notions and Implications." https://www.academia.edu/37583185/2010_2018_Greek_Debt_Crisis_and_Greeces_Past_Myths_Popular_Notions_and_Implications.

Stamouli, N. 2022. "Greece Exits Bailout Monitoring, but Austerity Pain Lingers." *Politico*, August 16. https://www.politico.eu/article/greece-exit-bailout-monitor-austerity-economy/.

Vinci, S., F. Bartolacci, R. Salvia, and L. Salvati. 2022. "Housing Markets, the Great Crisis, and Metropolitan Gradients: Insights from Greece, 2000–2014." *Socio-Economic Planning Sciences* 80(101171). https://doi.org/10.1016/j.seps.2021.101171.

Wisevoter. n.d. "HDI by Country." Accessed March 2025. https://wisevoter.com/country-rankings/best-countries-to-live-in/#countries-by-hdi/.

Xythali, T. 2019. "Real Estate Rights and Registration in Greece." Lexology, April 12. https://www.lexology.com/library/detail.aspx?g=8505a359-f2e5-4552-ab9a-05bd386a40e2.

Legislation

Law 1040/2018 on Determination of the Sources and Type of Data Collected, the Category of Data Published, as Well as the Time of Keeping the Data in the Register of Real Estate Transfer Values.

Law 1249/1982 on Real Property Tax and Other Provisions.

Law 1473/1984 on Public Administration.

Law 2308/1995 on the Organization and Operation of the Hellenic Cadastre and Other Provisions.

Law 2386/1996 on Taxation of Income, Tax Audits, Value Added Tax, Capital Taxes, Excise Duties and Other Provisions.

Law 4223/2013 on the Uniform Real Estate Property Tax (ENFIA).

Law 4484/2017 on the Adaptation of Greek Legislation to the Provisions of Directive (EU) 2016/881 and Other Provisions.

Law 4512/2018 on Arrangements for the Implementation of the Structural Reforms of the Economic Adjustment Programmes and Other Provisions.

Law 4549/2018 on Provisions for the Completion of the Agreement on Budgetary Targets and Structural Reforms—Medium-Term Financial Strategy Framework 2019–2022 and Other Provisions.

Law 4646/2019 on Tax Reform and Other Provisions.

Presidential Decree 3/2021 on the Transfer of Responsibilities of the Hellenic Cadastre to the Ministry of Digital Governance.

14

Property Taxes in Ireland

FRANK HARRINGTON, NIALL DEEGAN,
AND ANTHONY KENNEALLY

The Republic of Ireland is an independent state in northwestern Europe with a Celtic heritage. After a period of British rule, it regained its independence in 1922 following the signing of the Anglo-Irish Treaty, which established the Irish Free State. The republic was officially declared through the Republic of Ireland Act in 1949.

Since 1922, the island of Ireland has been divided into the Republic of Ireland and Northern Ireland. The Republic of Ireland is a member of the European Union (EU), while Northern Ireland is part of the United Kingdom and, since Brexit, no longer part of the EU. This chapter focuses exclusively on the Republic of Ireland.

The country covers an area of approximately 70,283 square kilometers, divided into 62 percent agricultural land, 10.9 percent forestry, and 27.1 percent urban land.

Preliminary results from the 2022 Irish Census suggest a population of 5,100,000, representing the first time the Irish population has exceeded 5,000,000 since 1851, with net inward migration of more than 190,000 (CSO [Central Statistics Office] 2022) being a significant factor in this increase. Figure 14.1 shows that the population is concentrated in Dublin, the capital city.

Dublin, as the country's main economic engine, experienced the largest inward migration of 46,559 people in 2022 (CSO 2022). The metropolitan area of Dublin accounts for approximately 53 percent of Ireland's

Figure 14.1 Population by Electoral Division, Republic of Ireland, 2022

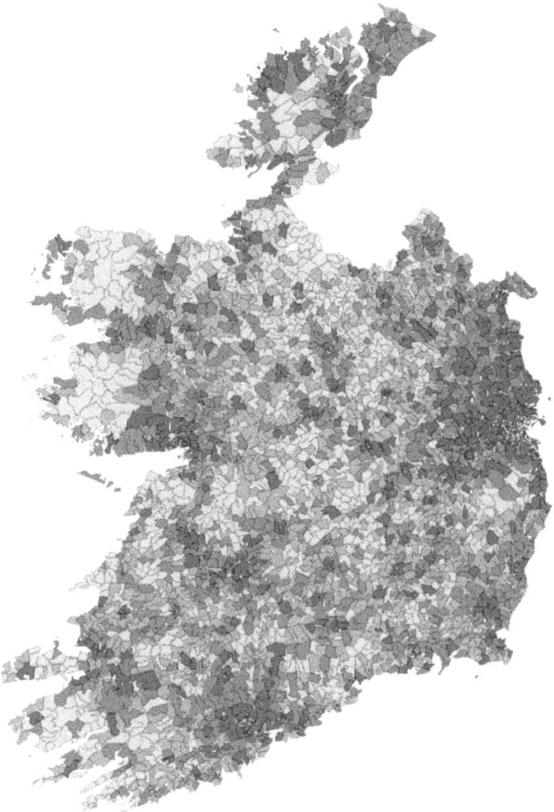

Source: CSO (2022).

gross domestic product (GDP), with the greater Dublin area also representing a significant proportion of economic activity (OECD [Organisation for Economic Co-operation and Development] 2018). The development of the tech sector in Dublin has been a significant factor attracting inward migration, alongside foreign direct investment, which have both been crucial drivers of the Irish economy. In 2022, the estimated per capita GDP was US$128,343, compared with an OECD average of US$49,043 (OECD, n.d.-a).

Based on this measure, Ireland can be considered a relatively wealthy economy. It is worth noting that the cyclical nature of the Irish economy since the beginning of the millennium should be accounted for when considering taxation. Figure 14.2 illustrates Ireland's annual GDP growth and drops in Ireland compared with other OECD members since 1971.

Figure 14.2 GDP per Capita, 2022 (US$)

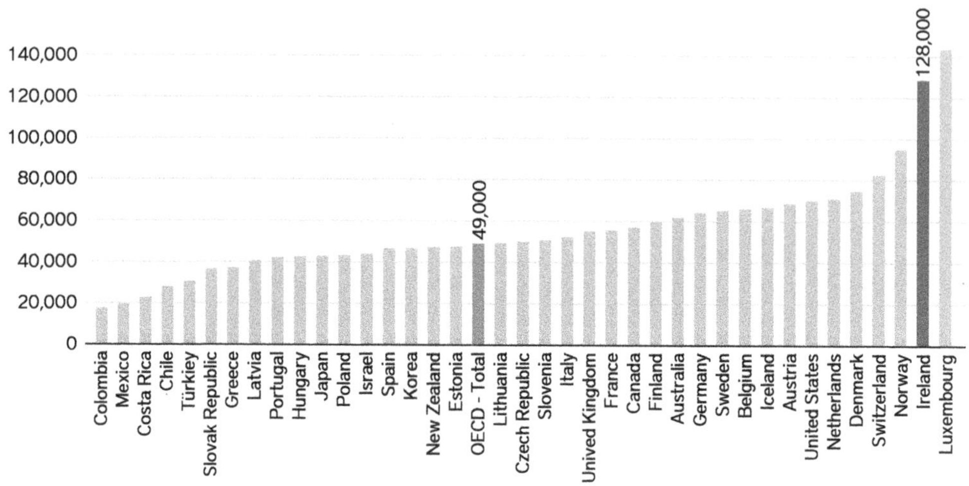

Source: OECD (2023).

In 2021, Ireland's tax revenue to GDP ratio was 21.1 percent compared with the OECD average of 34.1 percent, which ranks it 36th out of 38 OECD countries (Revenue 2022a). While it may be argued that a significant component of GDP in Ireland does not stay in the economy, it broadly suggests that Ireland is a relatively low-tax economy. Despite this, the country's position on tax policy has been influenced by its distinct geographical location and political relationship. Ireland is separated from Great Britain by the Irish Sea, the North Channel, and St. George's Channel to the east and from the Americas by the Atlantic Ocean to the west. As a result, policy makers have had to consider the tax policies of neighboring and other countries due to the importance of external trade and foreign direct investment to the economy. This has led to a debate on whether to follow the "Boston or Berlin" approach to policy decisions (Fischer 2014).

Writing in 1993 in the book *Taxation: Ireland and the New Europe*, Taoiseach[1] Albert Reynolds noted that "there has always been an important international dimension in Irish tax affairs. Given the importance of external trade and foreign investment to our economy, Irish tax policymakers have had to take account of the position of certain neighboring and other countries" (Reynolds 1993, 1). Although this quote is over 30 years old, it remains relevant, particularly as the impact of Brexit continues to be felt. Ireland remains a committed member of the EU while now sharing a land border with Northern Ireland in the United Kingdom. Despite its small size, Ireland is an open economy that has complex relationships with many nations worldwide, and it remains aware of these relationships in its tax policy.

Systems of Government and Responsibilities

The Republic of Ireland is a parliamentary representative democracy, where legislative power rests with the Oireachtas, composed of the president of Ireland and the two houses, Dáil Éireann and Seanad Éireann. The executive power is held by the cabinet, led by the Taoiseach, in Dáil Éireann (Oireachtas, n.d.).

In addition, Ireland has 31 local authorities[2] responsible for a range of local services including

- housing;
- planning;
- roads;
- environment protection;
- libraries; and
- the register of electors.

Article 28A of the Constitution of Ireland recognizes local authorities and guarantees local elections at least every five years. Irish voters currently elect 949 councilors to represent them locally and make decisions at council meetings (Citizen Information 2022). Local authorities are funded by local taxation and central-government funding and are responsible for about 9 percent of total government spending (European Committee of the Regions 2018).

Local authorities in Ireland derive income from a range of sources, including government grants and subsidies, charges for goods and services, commercial rates, and the local property tax. As shown in figure 14.3, government grants and subsidies accounted for the largest share of local authority revenue in 2022, followed by commercial rates, goods and services, and the local property tax.

Ireland's membership in the European monetary union is also worth noting, specifically the transfer of authority over central bank lending rates to the European Central Bank. Interest rates continue to play a crucial role in controlling inflation and consequently controlling housing affordability (Yiu 2023). Since the Irish national government does not have full control over European Central Bank interest rates, there is potential for it to prioritize measures within its control, such as property tax.

Figure 14.3 Local Authority Revenue, Income Breakdown, 2022

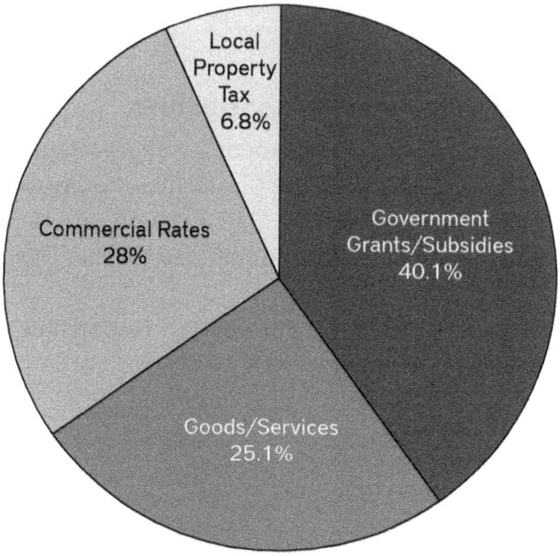

Source: Department of Housing, Local Government and Heritage.

Whether it has done so is something we will return to in the context of property tax and economic rent later in the chapter.

Chapter Overview

This chapter provides a high-level context and overview of property tax in Ireland. The Republic of Ireland is a developed nation with a complex taxation system, many elements of which relate to property. Aspects that are not directly related to property taxes, such as corporation tax and taxation of income from property investments, while they may concern property, will not be covered in this chapter.

This chapter also examines property tax and, in particular, land taxation measures in order to provide a perspective on the following questions:

- Has property tax reached its potential?
- What has held back additional property tax revenue mobilization?
- What reform options (policy, administrative, and management) might increase Ireland's revenue contributions and address societal objectives?

While broad recommendations are made within the scope of this chapter, the authors recognize the complexity of taxation and its impact on a range of societal issues. One of the key issues this chapter raises is the lack of transparent and appropriate property data. Policy makers, working with appropriate stakeholders, should address this problem for the benefit of society as a whole.

In addition to providing an overview, this chapter seeks to provide a framework for future studies and address some of these issues. At the same time, this review of initiatives and recommendations will hopefully add to the debate in this area, which may prove helpful to policy makers in Ireland and internationally to learn from experiences.

Land and Property Markets in Ireland: Legal Framework and Context

This section highlights the primary forms of land tenure and rights, ownership of land and buildings, and any restrictions on ownership that may apply.

Tenure Title

In Ireland, fee simple, or freehold, is the highest form of landownership. Historically, freehold landowners would lease their land to occupiers for several hundred years at what would be considered modest but steady rents today. These long leaseholders often subdivided their lands, creating inferior leases. Such long leaseholders may have granted building leases with permission to construct properties on-site, and such building lessors granted occupational leases. This situation is prevalent in many central urban areas in large cities such as Dublin, Cork, and Limerick.

Occupational leases for retail, office, and industrial units were typically 25 or 35 years, with rent reviews every 5 or 7 years. Lease lengths were driven by institutional investors seeking a long-term secure return and reviewed regularly to keep in line or beat inflation. However, as in other international markets, leases have become shorter since the start of the century, and leases of 10 to 15 years are now more common. If they are longer, they may have a break option, and rent reviews are still typically held every five years. Depending on the state of the market, there may be inducements such as rent-free periods, contributions to fit out, or stepped rents, particularly in the first five years. These may vary depending on whether it is a landlord or tenant's market based on supply and demand.

Commercial and Residential Leases

Commercial leases are agreed upon by estate agents and drafted by solicitors. The leases set out the parties involved—the landlord and tenant—and include the lease start date, its length, agreed-upon rent and inducements, and the property's address. The leases are either full repairing and insuring (FRI) or internal repairing or insuring (IRI). In FRI leases, the tenant assumes all responsibility for repairing and insuring the property. IRI leases, which are less common, are ones in which the tenant is responsible for the property's internal upkeep. Residential leases usually run for a minimum of one year, and all residential tenancy agreements must be registered with the Residential Tenancy Board (RTB) as set out in the Residential Tenancy Act of 2004. The longer the tenant is in situ, the more notice the landlord must give to obtain vacant possession. Vacant possession is possible when the landlord wishes to occupy or sell the property or for nonpayment of rent.

Most residential landlords have between one and two investment properties, while professional landlords with purpose-built, build-to-rent units make up approximately 6 percent of the market (Amárach Research 2021). The RTB settles any residential disputes, although it cannot enforce an award. A court must enforce RTB decisions.

The main sectors in the property market in Ireland are retail, office, industrial, and the private rented sector. Other specialized markets also generate a lot of interest—for example, nursing homes, student accommodation, and hospitality, including hotels, pubs, and license agreements. The office market in Dublin is significant, and occupiers include global tech firms such as Google, Meta, Amazon, and TikTok. Ireland's climate is also well suited for data centers, and there has been an increase in the number of developments in recent years. In addition, it appears that sustainable energy developments, including wind farms, will become even more common in the years to come.

The commercial center of the country is Dublin and the Greater Dublin Area, and most commercial transactions occur in Dublin. The office market has performed well in recent years, with strong demand for modern office space in central Dublin, the Docklands, and the central business district. There is also demand for office space in the suburbs, particularly Sandyford and Cherrywood, which are south of the city and close to the M50 (Dublin's orbital motorway). The tech sector primarily drives office demand, and a significant portion of the net inward migration seeks high-skilled tech employment. An increasing number of institutional investors are emphasizing sustainability and environmental issues when buying an office investment.

Land Registration

The Property Registration Authority (PRA), now part of Tailte Éireann, is responsible for registering all property and land transactions in

Ireland. The PRA is also responsible for the Ground Rents Purchase Scheme under the various landlord and tenant acts. It was set up on November 4, 2006, under the Registration of Deeds and Title Act of 2006 and oversees the Land Registry and the Registry of Deeds (ROD), which are separate entities.

The progress made in information technology has facilitated the extensive documentation of records, the most significant ones being the Integrated Title Registration Information System between 1999 and 2002, the Digital Mapping Project between 2005 and 2010, and the conversion of the entire register and associated indexes to digital form between 2006 and 2009.

The Land Registry was established in 1892 to provide a method of land registration. When properties are registered, the deeds are filed, and all particulars are registered on folios along with maps and plans. Currently, these are recorded electronically. Once recorded, this folio is guaranteed by the Irish state. It is compulsory for every county to register all titles, and to date, 2.14 million titles have been registered, which equates to 2.8 million parcels of land. Registration in the Land Registry is compulsory in the following scenarios:

- Land bought under the land price acts.
- Land acquired after January 1, 1967, by a statutory authority.
- Certain transactions (in the case of freehold land, conveyance on land; in the case of leasehold land, grant or assignment on sale) concerning property in the counties and cities listed in table 14.1.

The ROD, established in 1707, provides a voluntary system for recording deeds and conveyances relating to land. The principal purpose of registration is to establish priority between instruments, although there is no statutory requirement to register. In practice, priority is determined by the order of lodgment, with registered instruments generally taking precedence (Tailte Éireann, n.d.-a; n.d.-b).

The registry operates under Part 3 of the Registration of Deeds and Title Act of 2006 and the Registration of Deeds Rules of 2008. Applications must be accompanied by an ROD application form, which replaced the earlier memorial system. This form records key details such as the date of execution, the parties, and a description of the property. Once lodged, the form is allocated a serial number reflecting the date and time of submission. The registry does not retain the deed itself or verify its legal effect; it merely records its existence (Tailte Éireann, n.d.-g).

As the register is public, searches can be carried out for a fee to determine whether deeds affecting a property have been lodged. However, the effect of

Table 14.1 Counties and Cities with Compulsory Registration

Compulsory Registration Counties Affected	Effective Date
Carlow, Meath, Laois	January 1, 1970
Longford, Westmeath, Roscommon	April 1, 2006
Clare, Kilkenny, Louth, Sligo, Wexford, Wicklow	October 1, 2008
Cavan, Donegal, Galway, Kerry, Kildare, Leitrim, Limerick, Mayo, Monaghan, North Tipperary, Offaly, South Tipperary, Waterford	January 1, 2010
Cork, Dublin	June 1, 2011
Cities Affected	
Galway, Limerick, and Waterford[1]	January 1, 2010
Cork and Dublin	June 1, 2011

Source: Authors' compilation (based on data from the Property Registration Authority and Tailte Éireann).

[1] As defined by Section 10 of the Local Government Act of 2001.

such deeds can be determined only by consulting the original documents, which remain with the lodging party. The application form itself is retained in the registry as the official record (Tailte Éireann, n.d.-c; n.d.-d).

Ground Rents

The PRA manages a program that allows leasehold property owners to purchase their ground rent and upgrade their interest to freehold. Leasehold interest is time limited and subject to rent, whereas freehold interest can last indefinitely. Before implementation of the Landlord and Tenant (Ground Rents) (No. 2) Act of 1978, the purchase of ground rents on dwelling houses was arranged solely by the parties involved, as per the Landlord and Tenant (Ground Rents) Act of 1967. If any difficulties or disputes arose, the county registrar was called upon to make a decision that could be challenged in the circuit court. The buyer was responsible for the landlord's expenses incurred during the transaction.

The Landlord and Tenant (Ground Rents) (No. 2) Act changed this approach by allowing the PRA to undertake the legal work of completion of the purchase of the fee simple for a specified fee. The PRA is entrusted with administering the new scheme instead of the county registrar.

The PRA, now Tailte Éireann, has publicly available websites that provide data on commercial leases and residential sales. While these websites give helpful information, they are not comprehensive in describing properties, providing floor areas, or listing any lease incentives or inducements.

It is important to mention that the Property Price Register and Commercial Lease Register are the only databases available for sale or commercial letting transactions. The Property Price Register records the sale price of residential properties but does not provide any further information on its website, such as the type of house, its size, the number of bedrooms, or its condition. Similarly, the Commercial Lease Register records the terms of commercial lettings, but it may not include additional details such as inducements.

Even though certain government departments, such as Revenue, gather information about sale transactions, including the identities of the buyer and seller, these data are not harvested or provided to the public. In the most favorable scenario, only other government departments can access this information. Also, despite the data usually being stored electronically, additional information may be kept in files or on paper.

As the available data sources do not provide complete transparency, other bodies often resort to advertisements to obtain data. Some local authorities even accept property website advertisements as market evidence. However, reliance on such nonmarket transactions is not considered best practice.

To establish comparable land and property transactions, property professionals, including estate agents and valuers, rely on contacting other sales agents for sale or letting prices. They often produce their own databases and research, which, while sometimes detailed, are not always in the public domain. These unofficial databases have limited use in improving transparency in property taxation. Detailed official indexes for various sectors are limited in availability. The CSO has been working on developing indexes for the residential and agricultural sectors, but both are in their early stages and lack sufficient detail for broad application in local markets. Some major criticisms of these indexes are that they lack detailed characteristics of the sold assets, there is a time lag in their recording of information, and there are exclusions from the data set. Nonetheless, it is significant that they have been developed and that the government is beginning to acknowledge the importance of having accurate property data.

To illustrate the importance of improved property market data, the Finance Act of 2021 demands that local authorities record a list of undeveloped residentially zoned sites exceeding one acre that are capable of development. Landowners on this list must pay an annual land tax of 3 percent of the land's value from 2021 onward. The current absence of development land datasets is a significant impediment to the practical application of introducing and applying property taxes such as these.

This section has highlighted the evident lack of data and transparency in the property market in Ireland. When compared with other asset classes, such as the equity markets, the contrast is stark. There is a need for more comprehensive, transparent, and official datasets for the benefit of all stakeholders.

While the data available are limited, the valuation profession in Ireland is well established. However, there is a strong case for statutory recognition of the profession, as it is currently self-regulated by the Society of Chartered Surveyors Ireland (SCSI) and the Institute of Professional Auctioneers and Valuers, each with different educational, training, and continued professional development requirements. Valuation requires a broad range of skills and an understanding of legal and market frameworks. It also is improved by transparent and comprehensive data. Aligning standards and providing comprehensive data would support the property tax system.

Property Taxes

This section provides an overview of the various tax heads that can be levied on the purchase or transfer of property in Ireland. These include stamp duty, capital gains tax (CGT), capital acquisitions tax (CAT), and value-added tax (VAT). Other taxes related to real estate activities are detailed, including relevant contracts tax (RCT), residential zoned land tax, Irish real estate fund (IREF) withholding tax, IREF income tax, corporation tax, and income tax.

Stamp Duty on Transfers of Property

Stamp duty is a tax chargeable on instruments (written documents) that transfer land and buildings. It is levied at differing rates depending on the transaction type. Stamp duty is a tax that applies to the purchase or transfer of residential and nonresidential properties. For residential property valued at €1 million or less (excluding VAT), a 1 percent duty is applied. If the value exceeds €1 million (excluding VAT), a 2 percent duty applies to the excess amount. For nonresidential property, a stamp duty of 7.5 percent applies. Stamp duty is always payable on the ex-VAT consideration. A 10 percent duty is levied for the bulk purchase of "relevant residential units," an intervention that will be further discussed later in this chapter. This also applies where shares, units, or partnership interests are acquired, which derive value from relevant residential units. Relevant residential units are those purchased in bulk of 10 or more or if the buyer has bought 9 or more residential units in the previous 12 months. Apartments in apartment blocks are not included in this definition.

A stamp duty rebate is available in certain circumstances, such as leasing a residential unit to a local authority or an approved housing body for social housing purposes. A stamp duty rebate is also available for a designated "cost rental dwelling" (Stamp Duties Consolidation Act of 1999, Schedule 1).

The 10 percent stamp duty rate was implemented on May 20, 2021, with the aim of targeting the bulk buying of specific residential units (Stamp Duties Consolidation Act of 2021, Section 31E).

Stamp Duty on Leases

Stamp duty can also apply to the average annual rent and any premium payable under a lease. It is a single tax on a rent contract. The rate depends on the lease term, with a rate of 1 percent of the average annual rent for an indefinite period or term not exceeding 35 years, a rate of 6 percent for a term between 35 and 100 years, and a rate of 12 percent for a term exceeding 100 years.

No stamp duty is payable for a residential lease term of an indefinite period or not exceeding 35 years with an annual rent exceeding €40,000. When a premium is payable in respect of a lease, the applicable duty rate is the same as that for the transfer of property.

Stamp duty is collected through the Revenue Online Service (ROS), a facility that enables taxpayers to file tax returns and make payments online to the Revenue Commissioners. A person needs to make a stamp duty filing within 44 days of the date of execution of an instrument. A charge applies for late filing, and interest applies on late payment.

Usually, in the case of a transaction, the taxable value will be the VAT-exclusive consideration paid for the transfer. This differs in the case of gifts or transfers of property at undervalue, where the property's market value (assessed by a registered valuer or equivalent) at the time of the transfer is used to ascertain the stamp duty rate. The "accountable person" is the person who must pay stamp duty (table 14.2).

In 2021, the tax receipts from stamp duty on property amounted to €728 million (Revenue 2022e) (table 14.3).

CGT

CGT is paid when an Irish property is sold, regardless of the vendor's tax residency status in Ireland. It is levied at a rate of 33 percent on chargeable gains. A CGT clearance certificate (CG50A certificate) must be

Table 14.2 Categories of an Accountable Person

Document	Accountable Person
Conveyance on sale	Buyer/transferee
Lease	Tenant
Any other document	Any party to the document

Source: Stamp Duties Consolidation Act of 1999.

Table 14.3 Stamp Duty Receipts (€ million)

Year	Residential	Nonresidential	Land and Property Total
2017	165.99	214.85	380.84
2018	173.04	486.71	659.75
2019	181.56	535.30	716.86
2020	160.26	405.93	566.19
2021	216.18	512.17	728.35

Source: Authors' compilation (based on data from the Office of the Revenue Commissioners).

obtained from the Revenue Commissioners when an asset is sold for more than €500,000 or when a residential property is sold for more than €1 million. Where a CG50A certificate is not obtained, the purchaser must withhold 15 percent of the purchase price from the seller, which can be reclaimed from the Revenue Commissioners at a later date.

For disposals made between January 1 and November 30, CGT is due to be paid by December 15. For disposals between December 1 and December 31, CGT must be paid by January 31 of the following year. Payments must be made through ROS. Disposals must be disclosed in income tax or corporation tax returns, or a CGT return (Form CG1) must be filed by October 31 of the year after the disposal.

Under the principal private residence relief, certain conditions must be met to qualify for an exemption from CGT on the sale of personal property. Full relief from CGT is available for gains arising from the sale of properties purchased between December 7, 2011, and December 31, 2014, when the property has been held for four to seven years and sold after January 1, 2018. The transfer of a one-acre site from a parent to a child for the purpose of building a house may also be exempt from CGT, provided

Table 14.4 Total Tax Receipts from CGT Relating to Property from CGT Returns and Self-Assessments (€ million)

CGT Liability	2016	2017	2018	2019	2020
Agricultural land/buildings	26	31	30	34	40
Development land	15	26	35	26	26
Commercial premises	80	42	50	44	36
Residential premises	71	105	121	109	122
Total CGT liability relating to property	192	204	236	213	224

Source: Authors' compilation (based on data from the Office of the Revenue Commissioners).

Table 14.5 Total Tax Receipts from CGT Relating to Property from Companies (€ million)

Year	2017	2018	2019	2020	2021
CGT receipts relating to real estate activities	215.38	249.67	288.51	285.48	482.75

Source: Authors' compilation (based on data from the Office of the Revenue Commissioners).

the site is valued at less than €500,000 and conditions specified in the Taxes Consolidation Act of 1997 are met.

Expenditure attributable to the base cost of an asset includes the purchase price and any costs of acquisition, enhancement, or disposal. These are allowable expenses in the calculation of any chargeable gains. Indexation relief (or inflation relief) is available in calculating the chargeable gains for assets sold before 2003. Indexation relief works by increasing any costs paid before 2003 related to the asset, including the purchase price and costs of acquisition, enhancement, or disposal. A personal exemption from CGT is available to individuals for the first €1,270 of capital gains realized for each tax year (tables 14.4 and 14.5).

CAT: Gifts and Inheritances

CAT is levied at a rate of 33 percent on taxable gifts or inheritances (table 14.6). CAT applies to amounts over certain tax-free thresholds dependent on the relationship between the beneficiary and the disponer or transferor. There are several exemptions from CAT on real property, including business relief, agricultural relief, and the dwelling house exemption.

Table 14.6 Total Tax Receipts from CAT, 2017–2021 (€ million)

Tax	2017	2018	2019	2020	2021
Inheritance tax	425.50	466.45	455.35	430.58	480.93
Gift tax	32.47	52.61	59.14	71.00	94.88
Discretionary trust tax	1.96	3.27	6.89	3.51	5.77
Probate tax	0.11	0.17	0.20	0.15	0.18
Total CAT	460	523	522	505	582

Source: Revenue (2022a).

CAT is collected by filing Form IT38 through ROS. The deadline for paying and filing CAT depends on the valuation date. For example, if the valuation date is between January 1 and August 31, the deadline is October 31. If the valuation date is between September 1 and December 31, the deadline is October 31 the following year (Taxes Consolidation Act 1997).

VAT

The VAT treatment of property transactions in Ireland was significantly revised in July 2008. Under the current rules, the first transfer of a nonresidential property within five years of its completion is typically liable for VAT. Subsequent transfers within that five-year period can also fall within the charge, unless the property has been continuously occupied for at least 24 months. In such cases, VAT is generally applied at the reduced rate of 13.5 percent, on the basis of the property's market value.

Certain sales are outside the scope of VAT, including the disposal of undeveloped land, properties developed more than five years earlier, or properties where any development work undertaken in the previous five years is regarded as minor. A further exemption applies to later sales where the property has been occupied for a total of two years or more.

The legislation also allows vendors and purchasers to opt for joint taxation on otherwise exempt transactions. This mechanism, often used to protect VAT recovery under the capital goods scheme (CGS), involves the purchaser accounting for VAT on a reverse charge basis.

For residential property, the first sale by a developer, or a connected person, is always subject to VAT at the reduced rate of 13.5 percent (adapted from PwC 2023; 2025; see also Revenue 2024).

The sale of property in connection with the transfer of business is not subject to VAT, and property that is let will generally qualify for transfer

Table 14.7 Net VAT Receipts by Sector

Tax Year	2017	2018	2019	2020	2021
VAT receipts from real estate activities (€ million)	717.11	721.87	736.30	479.04	380.3
Proportion of total VAT receipts (%)	6.21%	5.85%	5.58%	4.49%	2.78

Source: Authors' compilation (based on data from the Office of the Revenue Commissioners).

of business relief. However, there may be VAT implications for the purchaser. For example, if the purchaser was not entitled to deduct VAT in the absence of transfer-of-business relief, they may face a VAT self-supply charge, depending on several factors.

VAT on Lettings

All lettings are exempt from VAT by default, irrespective of duration. However, where a letting is exempt from VAT, the landlord is not entitled to deduct VAT on costs incurred in respect of the exempt letting. In addition, if the landlord has previously deducted VAT for the letting, the landlord may suffer a VAT clawback under the CGS based on the VAT previously deducted on the acquisition and development of the property. Accordingly, a landlord may tax the letting to preserve its VAT recovery position. The landlord may opt to tax by notifying the tenant in writing or by including a clause opting to tax the letting in the letting agreement.

The option to tax is specific to each letting. When the option is exercised, VAT at the higher rate (currently 23 percent) is levied on rents as they fall due.

While VAT applies across a wide range of goods and services in Ireland, receipts from real estate activities represent only a small proportion of overall VAT revenues. This proportion has fluctuated in recent years, reflecting changes in market activity and transaction volumes. Table 14.7 outlines net VAT receipts from real estate activities between 2017 and 2021, both in absolute terms and as a share of total VAT receipts.

CGS

The capital goods scheme (CGS) is intended to ensure that the VAT deducted on property acquisitions or developments accurately reflects the way the property is used over time. For VAT purposes, a "capital good" generally means a newly constructed property or substantial works carried out on an existing property, such as a refurbishment.

Each capital good is given a defined VAT life, divided into review periods of 10 years for refurbished properties and 20 years for newly developed properties. During these intervals, the original VAT claimed is reviewed and may be adjusted on a time-apportioned basis.

At the end of each review period, the business must reassess its entitlement to recover VAT on that property. If entitlement has increased, additional VAT may be reclaimed (provided it was nondeductible at the time of purchase). If entitlement has decreased, part of the VAT already recovered must be repaid. Where there is a significant change in how the property is used, the CGS can also require accelerated adjustments.

The CGS applies to disposals of freehold and freehold-equivalent interests. If a sale is exempt from VAT, the scheme may trigger a clawback of previously recovered VAT. In contrast, a taxable sale (such as one under a joint option for taxation) may give rise to an additional VAT credit for the vendor. The scheme also applies when an option to tax a letting is exercised and subsequently canceled. Transitional provisions apply to certain properties under construction on July 1, 2008, as well as to occupational leases granted before that date, as set out in the Value-Added Tax Consolidation Act of 2010. Property taxation remains a complex area, and legislative updates are frequent (adapted from PwC 2023; 2025; see also Revenue 2024).

Holding Vehicles

Irish real estate is generally held through a property company or an Irish Collective Asset Management Vehicle (ICAV), a vehicle exempt from Irish tax on income and gains regardless of where its investors reside (ICAV Act 2015).

A property company is subject to corporation tax at a rate of 25 percent regarding net rental income. Expenses that are directly related to running the rental business and are considered revenue in nature (and not recharged to the tenants) are usually eligible for tax deductions against the yearly rental income.

In the calculation of profits liable to corporation tax, depreciation of capital assets is not deductible. However, capital allowances (which are similar to tax depreciation) may be claimed on a straight-line basis over eight years at a rate of 12.5 percent for plant and equipment items (Taxes Consolidation Act 1997).

If individuals are landlords, they are subject to income tax on their rental income. The marginal income tax rate of 52 percent applies to incomes above €32,800, comprising 41 percent income tax, 4 percent social insurance contributions, and a universal social charge of 7 percent (Taxes Consolidation Act 1997).

IREF

An IREF, which is an Irish-regulated fund that derives over 25 percent of its value from Irish land or buildings, is subject to a new taxation regime under the Finance Act of 2016. The regime came into effect on January 1, 2017. If a fund is classified as an IREF, it must operate a 20 percent withholding tax on taxable events such as income distributions and gains on redemptions, unless the distributions are payable to "exempt investors" such as Irish pensions schemes, life insurance companies, regulated funds, and their European Economic Area–based equivalents.

The Finance Act of 2019 introduced changes to the existing IREF regime, including the introduction of an income tax charge at a rate of 20 percent for deemed income in the hands of the IREF where specific interest and debt restrictions are met.

Recurrent Land and Property Tax

While the previous section discussed property taxes that are typically one-off charges, this section discusses recurring taxes. Ireland's primary recurring property tax systems differ based on whether a property is commercial or residential. If a property is residential, the homeowner will be subject to local property tax (LPT), whereas if a property is commercial, the owner or occupiers will be subject to commercial rates. Other recurring taxes include the vacant site levy and the derelict sites list.

LPT

In 2013, LPT came into effect, replacing the annual household charge introduced by the Local Government (Household Charge) Act of 2011, which was payable by residential property owners to local authorities. Before this, there were other forms of property taxation, including a charge on nonprincipal private residences, which applied from 2009 to 2013, and the residential property tax, which was abolished in the Finance Act of 1997.

LPT was implemented to broaden the tax base and provide stable annual funding for local authorities. The tax is applicable to all residential properties in Ireland; the term *residential property* encompasses any building or structure (or part of a building) that can be used as a dwelling, including grounds of up to one acre. LPT does not apply to development sites, farmland, vessels, vehicles, or structures that are not permanently attached to the ground (Finance [Local Property Tax] Act of 2012). LPT is a self-assessment tax collected by the Revenue Commissioners and is calculated based on chargeable value, often referred to as market value bands.

Turley (2022) provides a detailed account of the context surrounding the introduction of LPT, including references to the Commission on Taxation Report of 2009, the Inter-Departmental Group formed in 2012 to establish LPT, and computer-assisted mass appraisal methodologies. It is beyond the scope of this chapter to explore this context in more detail, but interested readers may consult these resources for further information.

What is the basis of value in legislation?

The Finance (Local Property Tax) Act of 2012, as amended, uses the term *chargeable value* to refer to the basis of value. The act states that the chargeable value, "in relation to a relevant residential property, means the price which the unencumbered fee simple of the property might reasonably be expected to fetch on a sale in the open market were that property to be sold on the valuation date in such manner and subject to such conditions as might reasonably be calculated to obtain for the vendor the best price for the property and with the benefit of any easement necessary as would have existed prior to that sale."

While this is broadly in line with the International Valuation Standards common basis, market value, the definition was prescriptive rather than providing a recognized conceptual framework. It appears the government recognized this, prompting it to produce a 2022 circular that notes the chargeable value is essentially its market value. While it provides a conceptual framework, some aspects of the circular add confusion rather than clarity to even experienced valuers. An example is where it states, "It may be necessary to assume the existence of a market where one does not exist" (Revenue 2022b, 7), which could be construed to provide a valuer the flexibility to assume a strong market in poor market conditions. While the authors appreciate the need to differentiate this from the basis of valuation for certain legislative purposes, adopting the definitions and conceptual framework used by the International Valuation Standards Council (IVSC) where appropriate is recommended in the future.

The self-assessment system is led by individual taxpayers, who determine their property values and submit the LPT returns in accordance with Irish tax legislation and Revenue guidance. The first band covers properties worth up to €200,000, and bands increase to a maximum of €1.75 million. If a property is valued at €1.75 million or lower, the tax is set at the basic rate for the band that the value fits in. Properties valued over €1.75 million are assessed on the actual value of the property at 0.1029 percent on the first €1.05 million, 0.25 percent on the portion between €1.05 million and €1.75 million, and 0.3 percent of the portion above €1.75 million.

Table 14.8 LPT Property Bands, 2013–2021

LPT 2013 Valuation Band (€)	LPT Charge Basic Rate in 2013 (half-year charge) in €	LPT Charge Basic Rate for 2014–2021 (full year) in €	Percentage of Properties as of May 1, 2013
0–100,000	45	90	27.2
100,001-150,000	112	225	27.4
150,001-200,000	157	315	20.9
200,001-250,000	202	405	10.1
250,001-300,000	247	495	4.9
300,001-350,000	292	585	2.9
350,001-400,000	337	675	1.9
400,001-450,000	382	765	1.3
450,001-500,000	427	855	0.9
500,001-550,000	472	945	0.6
550,001-600,000	517	1,035	0.4
600,001-650,000	562	1,125	0.3
650,001-700,000	607	1,215	0.2
700,001-750,000	652	1,305	0.2
750,001-800,000	697	1,395	0.1
800,001-850,000	742	1,485	0.1
850,001-900,000	787	1,575	0.1
900,001-950,000	832	1,655	0.1
950,001-1,000,000	877	1,755	0.1
Properties worth more than €1 million are assessed on the actual value at 0.18% on the first €1 million of declared market value of the property as of May 1, 2013, and 0.25% on the portion of the declared market value above €1 million as of May 1, 2013.			0.2

Source: Revenue (2022d).

See table 14.8 for valuation bands and corresponding charges for the years 2013–2021.

In 2019, a review was undertaken that sought to reform the tax in light of increased property prices in the market since its introduction. In 2022, the valuation bands were widened, and the annual charge applicable to the upper bands was increased. See table 14.9 for valuation bands and corresponding charges for 2021–2024.

Self-assessed property valuations apply for four years and determine the amount of LPT to be paid each year, as set out in the Finance (Local Property Tax) (Amendment) Act of 2021. The Revenue Commissioners offer an interactive valuation tool to estimate the average valuation band for properties in an area (Revenue 2021a).

Table 14.9 LPT Property Bands, 2021–2024

LPT 2021 Valuation Band (€)	Annual Charge (€)
0–200,000	90
200,001-262,500	225
262,501-350,000	315
350,001-437,500	405
437,501-525,000	495
525,001-612,500	585
612,501-700,000	675
700,001-787,500	765
787,501-875,000	855
875,001-962,500	945
962,501-1,050,000	1,035
1,050,001-1,137,500	1,189
1,137,501-1,225,000	1,408
1,225,001-1,312,500	1,627
1,312,501-1,400,000	1,846
1,400,001-1,487,500	2,064
1,487,501-1,575,000	2,283
1,575,001-1,662,500	2,502
1,662,501-1,750,000	2,721

Properties worth more than €1.75 million are assessed on the actual value at 0.1029% on the first €1.05 million, 0.25% on the portion between €1.05 million and €1.75 million, and 0.3% of the balance above €1.75 million.

Source: Revenue (2021a).

From 2015 onward, local authorities have had the power to vary the basic LPT rate on residential properties in their administrative area. The "local adjustment factor" allows increases or decreases of the basic rate by up to 15 percent, resulting in different amounts of LPT payable for residential properties of similar value in different local authority areas.

If a local authority passes a resolution to vary the basic LPT rate, it must notify Revenue and publish a notice of the variation of LPT on its website and in at least one local newspaper. Revenue adjusts the LPT liability for residential properties within the local authority's administrative area accordingly.

The Revenue Commissioners administer LPT, and LPT returns must be filed and paid through the LPT online service. LPT exemptions and deferrals are available in certain circumstances. Failure to

Table 14.10 LPT Statistics from End-of-Year Reports, 2017–2021

Year	LPT (€ million)	Total Properties Returned
2017	459	1,920
2018	455	1,920
2019	443	1,920
2020	453	1,868
2021	463	1,861

Source: Office of the Revenue Commissioners (2022a).

meet LPT obligations or the late payment of tax may result in the imposition of interest on the liability at an annual rate of 8 percent. Where LPT and interest remain unpaid, it becomes a charge on the property itself. Any liability must be settled before the property can be sold or transferred (Revenue 2022a).

LPT provides significant funding for local authorities, which will be discussed later in the chapter in the context of other property taxes.

On January 1, 2018, LPT receipts were transferred from Revenue to the Local Government Fund managed and administered by the Department of Housing, Planning and Local Government. Table 14.10 summarizes LPT receipts and the number of properties returned between 2017 and 2021, based on end-of-year reports from the Revenue Commissioners.

The Finance (Local Property Tax) (Amendment) Act of 2021 ensures that all local authorities retain 100 percent of LPT. Before this, well-financed local authorities were obliged to redistribute 20 percent of LPT to less well-funded local authorities.

How is accuracy checked?

Irish property owners are responsible for self-assessing their property's value to calculate their LPT liability. However, the checks in place to ensure that property owners provide accurate information appear limited. This is partly due to the lack of data and the shortage of qualified valuers in the Revenue Commissioners who administer LPT. The Revenue Commissioners do have checks in place, such as

- carrying out random audits of property owners to verify the accuracy of the market values declared;

- conducting targeted audits of property owners who have provided values that are significantly different from the average for similar properties in their area;
- comparing the market values declared by property owners with other data sources, such as planning permissions, building energy ratings, and property sales records; and
- using statistical analysis to identify anomalies and inconsistencies in the market values declared.

In December 2021, Revenue conducted a preliminary analysis of the self-assessed valuations submitted by property owners as of November 1, 2021, comparing the average LPT valuations submitted by property owners to average sales prices from the CSO. Revenue found that these valuations very closely track prevailing average sales. Revenue records show that a total of 22,020 valuations have been increased since 2013, arising from a combination of self-correction and Revenue challenges (audits) (Revenue 2022e).

These checks are welcome, but the limited data and lack of registered valuers within Revenue make it challenging to determine how accurate the LPT is, particularly given the heterogeneity of property. It is an area worthy of more detailed study, but there is a strong hypothesis that statistical measures combined with registered valuers would likely be more accurate.

There are also positives to Revenue administering the LPT—for example, its enforcement powers. If Revenue identifies that a property owner has provided inaccurate or misleading information, it may take enforcement action, including imposing penalties, interest charges, and, in serious cases, prosecution. It is important to note that property owners have a legal obligation to provide accurate and complete information in relation to their LPT liability. Failure to do so may result in penalties and other consequences.

Another advantage of the Revenue Department administering LPT is the fact that Revenue has more experience and authority to collect. A backstop is that if inaccurate figures are provided when a person sells or transfers a property, there are measures to collect unpaid taxes retrospectively. Revenue recently announced a 90 percent compliance rate and that it was stepping up enforcement on those who have yet to pay (Stedman 2023).

However, there appears to be a lack of expert valuers on both the declared valuation side (self-declared) and the Revenue (check) side. Strengthening the valuation profession through regulation and resourcing and further improving links with Tailte Éireann may help to improve the accuracy and reliability of LPT valuations.

Commercial Property Rates

Commercial rates are a tax that local authorities impose on the owners or occupiers of land and buildings used for business or industrial purposes (Local Government Rates and Other Matters Act 2019). The elected representatives of the respective local authorities determine the rates that the local authority requires annually based on the budget to deliver local services. The valuations determine the equity of distribution among the ratepayers. Rates on residential property were abolished in 1967, and LPT is now used in their place.

The rates levied on a property are calculated by multiplying the Annual Rate on Valuation (ARV), also known as the multiplier, by the property's valuation determined by the Valuation Division of Tailte Éireann. The ARV is set each year by the local authority. The commissioner of valuation determines the valuation, and the basis of valuation is the net asset value (NAV).

The determination of the property rates payable is based on valuations provided by the Valuation Office (VO) to the relevant local authority. The ARV is fixed each year based on the budgetary requirements of the local authority for facilities in their jurisdiction. The local authorities publish the valuation roll, which lists the valuations of all properties subject to rates within their jurisdiction. They calculate the final rates liability and collect them according to the Valuation (Amendment) Act of 2015. Rolling revaluations are used to maintain relativity between property types in different locations. Rolling revaluations of a local authority happen every 5–10 years after an order is signed off by the head of valuation of Tailte Éireann and the government minister. Up-to-date market rents are analyzed to help update schemes and come up with the new net annual values placed on commercial properties.

Commercial enterprises are also charged for water usage, typically metered for larger companies, and charged per 1,000 liters used. Commercial rates represent about one-third of total local-government funding. They are a primary source of revenue for local authorities, the remainder coming from central government (Department of Housing, Planning and Local Government 2020). The funds are used to provide essential services such as housing, water supply, waste disposal, maintenance of public areas, and lighting.

In general, liability for commercial rates falls on the occupier of a rateable property at the date the charge arises. There are, however, some exceptions. If a property is vacant, liability rests with the owner at the relevant date. In addition, if a former occupier leaves unpaid arrears, a new occupier can be held responsible for up to two years of those outstanding rates.

Rateable valuations are determined by reference to the rental value of the property at the valuation date. In making this assessment, certain categories of fixed plant and machinery are included. These items are valued using a standard approach based on their construction or replacement cost, together with an agreed formula for allocating value to the site (Tailte Éireann, n.d.-e).

For certain property types, such as licensed or leisure premises, the ratable value can be assessed based on levels of trade. Detailed advice may be required depending on the property type, and the SCSI maintains a list of active rating consultants with expertise in commercial rates (SCSI 2022). A ratable value can be challenged, and appeals can be made to the commissioner of valuation and the Valuation Tribunal. Failure to pay rates by the specified period may result in the issuing of legal proceedings.

Commercial rates amounting to approximately €1.5 billion were waived from March 2020 to the first quarter of 2022 to help businesses affected by restrictions imposed during the COVID-19 pandemic (Government of Ireland 2022). Commercial rates income for 2020 totaled €1.659 billion (23 percent of total revenue income in local authorities), and commercial rates income for 2021 was €1.675 billion. Budgeted income from rates in 2022 was €1.71 billion.

RCT

RCT is a withholding tax that requires a "principal contractor" to retain tax from amounts payable to subcontractors carrying out relevant operations in Ireland. If a landlord engages in developing an asset or engages a development company to act as a subcontractor to develop an asset, the company may be considered a principal contractor and must operate RCT. RCT has three rates: 35 percent, 20 percent, and 0 percent. A "build-to-rent exclusion" is available under certain conditions specified in the Taxes Consolidation Act of 1997.

Residential Zoned Land Tax

The residential zoned land tax is a self-assessed annual tax introduced by the Finance Act of 2021 to replace the vacant site levy as a measure to activate land and encourage the development of vacant sites. It is administered by the Revenue Commissioners and calculated at 3 percent of the market value of land that is serviced and zoned as suitable for residential development, with certain exclusions. Local authorities are required to prepare and publish a map identifying land within the scope of the tax, which is updated annually for changes in zoning and servicing status.

The tax liability for an owner of land zoned for residential development and serviced on January 1, 2022, and on which development has not commenced before February 1, 2024, is payable on or before May 23, 2024. If the land is zoned as suitable for residential development or serviced after January 1, 2022, the tax will be due in the third year after it comes within scope, and it will continue to be payable each year unless a deferral applies or the land ceases to be liable to the tax. Noncompliance with the legislation, including undervaluation of the land and late filings of returns, may result in interest, penalties, and surcharges of up to 30 percent (Revenue 2025).

Vacant Site Levy

This levy was introduced to promote the development of vacant sites and reduce land hoarding under the Urban Regeneration and Housing Act of 2015. It applies to residential land of more than 0.05 hectares where there is a need for housing in the area and where the site is suitable and has not been in use for an extended period; and regeneration land (other than residential land) where the majority of the site has not been in use for an extended period or has a negative impact on existing amenities or the character of the area. Each local authority maintains a register of lands suitable for housing that have not been put forward for development. If a site has been vacant for 12 months or more, the local authority can add that site to the Vacant Sites Register, notifying the owner of its intention, and the owner can then appeal within 28 days. The register must contain the location and map of each site, the name and address of the owner, and the current market value. The levy is paid to the local authority each year until the site is removed from the register at a rate of 7 percent of the market value of the land.

Derelict Sites

The Derelict Sites Act of 1990 defines a derelict site as any land that "detracts, or is likely to detract, to a material degree from the amenity, character or appearance of land in the neighborhood of the land in question because of"

- the existence on the land of structures in a ruinous, derelict, or dangerous condition;
- the neglected, unsightly, or objectionable condition of the land or any structures on it; or
- the presence, deposit, or collection of any litter, rubbish, debris, or waste.

Each local authority maintains a register of all derelict sites in its area, which includes the location, the owner's name and address, any action taken by the local authority, and the current market value of each site carried out by the local authority.

If the property is owned or occupied by the local authority, the register must state the property's current use and the local authority's intended plans. If the owner of urban land is entered into the register, they must pay an annual levy to the local authority. If this levy is not paid within two months of receiving notice, interest will be charged on the full amount at 1.25 percent a month or part of a month. Failure to pay this charge may result in the issuing of legal proceedings. The Minister for Housing, Planning, Community and Local Government can classify any area as urban, so long as it is not part of a county or other borough.

Property Tax Data

This section examines recurrent property taxes, who pays them, and trends in net receipts in more detail. Property tax in Ireland is primarily an urban commercial tax, with the LPT, still in its early stage of development, representing a relatively low proportion of recurrent tax take in 2020 (table 14.11).

As commercial rates continue to be the main recurrent property tax (76 percent), we will examine these in greater detail, including a breakdown of the different local authorities within different sectors.

There are approximately 146,000 commercial and industrial properties paying commercial rates in Ireland. Every local authority has a valuation list that is available to the public. Dublin City Council has the largest number of properties on its valuation list at 19,700, while Leitrim local authority has the lowest at 1,100. Approximately €1.47 billion was collected via the commercial rating process in 2020.

The Central Valuation List / Global Valuations includes 12 public utilities valued at €949,540,000. These utilities include entities such as ESB

Table 14.11 Recurrent Property Taxes Net Receipts, 2020

Commercial Rates (€ million)	LPT (€ million)	Vacant Site Levy (€ million)	Recurrent Property Tax Data (€ million)	LPT as a Percentage of Recurrent Property Tax
1,470	453	11.3	1,934.3	23.42

Source: Authors' compilation (based on data from Tailte Éireann and Central Statistics Office).

Table 14.12 Breakdown of Ratable Properties, 2022

Property Type	Number of Units
Industrial	40,518
Office	34,114
Retail shop	47,960
Retail warehouse	1,962
Service station/fuel depot	2,108
Health facilities	2,049
Hospitality	9,168
Leisure	3,177
Minerals	565
Miscellaneous	4,091
Utility	515
Total	146,227

Source: Authors' compilation (based on data from the Valuation Office website).

Networks, Irish Water, and Gas Networks Ireland. The 31 valuation lists consist of 146,227 ratable properties, of which 40,518 are industrial, 34,114 are office, 47,960 are retail, and 1,962 are retail warehouses, 2,108 service stations, and so on (table 14.12). Table 14.13 compares the valuation of Dublin with other major urban areas.

The elected representatives of the local authority are responsible for determining and collecting the total amount of rates to be collected each year. The Valuation Division of Tailte Éireann, formerly known as the VO, is responsible for calculating the breakdown of commercial property rates to ensure fairness among ratepayers. It is responsible for maintaining the 31 valuation lists and, as of August 31, 2022, employed approximately 140 staff.

Tailte Éireann is an independent government agency under the Department of Housing, Local Government and Heritage, and the Valuation Division provides up-to-date valuations of commercial and industrial properties to ratepayers and local authorities (Tailte Éireann, n.d.-f). These valuations are an essential component of the commercial rating system in Ireland and generate a significant portion of local-government revenue each year. Additionally, the Valuation Division conducts market valuations for state assets and properties.

Some local authorities, such as Dublin City Council, have valuation offices serving various local functions. For example, the Dublin City

Table 14.13 Comparison of Valuation Between Dublin and Other Urban Centers

Local Authority	Number of Entries on the Valuation List	Valuation Base (total value on the valuation list) (€)	Valuation Date/Base Year	Total Amount of Rates Liable for Collection (€)	Annual Rate on Valuation (formerly known as the rate/£)
Dublin City Council	19,743	1,369,102,140	2011	366,919,374	0.268
Limerick City and County Council	6,455	221,439,711	2012	59,279,416	0.2677
Galway City Council	3,979	564,454	1988	38,044,205	67.4
Cork City Council	9,835	1,298,942	1988	97,095,600	74.75

Source: Authors' compilation (based on data from the Valuation Division of Tailte Éireann).

valuation office often operates on behalf of other local authorities regarding valuation matters.

The principal legislation governing property valuation for rating purposes in Ireland is the Valuation Act of 2001, which has been amended several times since it first came into effect. A "working consolidation" of the Valuation Act of 2001 and subsequent amendments (up to August 12, 2020) assists customers and other stakeholders of the Valuation Division of Tailte Éireann.

The value of the property is fixed by a valuer, and the Valuation Division of Tailte Éireann may have to defend its valuation. These values are then put onto a list where the public can inspect them. Vacant properties are not liable for the entire rates liability, and a rebate for some or all of the amount is possible, depending on the local authority.

In terms of valuing the property, Sections 48–55 of the Valuation Act of 2001 set a valuation basis. The primary basis is set by determining the NAV of the property. The NAV is the VO assessment of market rent for a particular asset class in a specific location in an urban area. The NAV is generally lower than the market rent applicable to a subject property. The NAV has a legal definition set out in Section 48 of the Valuation Act as "the rent for which, one year with another, the property might, in its actual state, be reasonably expected to let from year to year, on the assumption that the probable average annual cost of repairs, insurance and other expenses (if any) that would be necessary to maintain the property in that state, and all rates and other taxes payable in respect of the property, are borne by the tenant."

This assumes that the tenant bears all charges for repairs, insurance, and other expenses. The property must be valued in its actual state and existing use. Those who are entitled to appeal are the occupier, an occupier of relevant property in respect of any other property in the same rating area, the rating authority itself, and a person who has an interest in the property.

The rate charge is calculated by multiplying the ratable valuation by the ARV. The commissioner of valuation, now the head of valuation under Tailte Éireann, determines the ratable valuation of a property, and each local authority sets the ARV annually at their budget meetings. The ARV adopted by the council varies annually. To illustrate this, consider a property with a ratable value of €50. If the local authority's ARV is, for instance, 70, the resulting rates bill will amount to €3,500.

Appeals can be made to

- the head of valuation, stating why the value is incorrect and what it should be, referencing the valuation list;

- the Valuation Tribunal, outlining why the head of valuation is incorrect and what the value should have been; or
- the High Court; however, this avenue only examines a point of law rather than the valuation.

The basis of an appeal is a "material change of circumstances" since the last valuation—that is, a change of use from commercial to residential or charitable purposes, amalgamation or subdivision of property, alterations (usually structural), or demolition.

The rating process comprises revision and revaluation. Revision relates to a material change in a property—for example, a subdivision of units, an extension, or the completion of a new property. If an occupier is dissatisfied with a proposed valuation, they have 40 days to make representations upon receipt of the proposed valuation certificate. Revaluation happens when all ratable properties in a local authority are valued at the same time with the same valuation date. Certain counties are selected for reevaluation every few years until the entire country has been revalued. In the most recent revaluation project, there were six local authorities undergoing their initial revaluation: Clare, Galway City, Galway County, Kerry, Mayo, and Donegal. The final valuation certificates for these areas were issued in September 2023, with effectiveness on the list from 2024 onward. The revaluation of Cork City and Cork County, the last two local authority areas, will commence once the current project has finished. Some internal work has already begun to help improve efficiencies for the Cork revaluation. Additionally, there is an ongoing revaluation occurring in Dún Laoghaire Rathdown; however, this is the second time this particular local authority has undergone revision. The COVID-19 pandemic was the reason for the scheduling conflict in this case. As stated earlier, revaluations are carried out on each local authority every 5–10 years to help ensure up-to-date valuations. Again, the final valuation certificates for this local authority were issued in September 2023. In the coming years, the period between revaluations is likely to be reduced due to greater efficiencies and the adoption of more advanced technology within the Valuation Division of Tailte Éireann. An appeal can be made to the Valuation Tribunal within 28 days of issuing the final valuation certificate.

The Valuation Tribunal deals with revision, revaluation, globals (public utilities), and derelict and vacant sites. It was established under the Valuation Act of 1988, followed by the valuation acts of 2001–2015, to deal with the decisions made by the head of valuation. The Valuation Tribunal is independent of the Valuation Division of Tailte Éireann and head of valuation. The decision of the tribunal is final, although an appeal can be made to the High Court. The Valuation Tribunal comprises 1 chairperson, 9 deputy chairpersons, and 24 members.

Due to the overwhelming volume of valuation appeals received, the callover system was implemented. Before being assigned a hearing date, all appeals must go through the callover system, and all parties involved must appear in person when assigned a slot on the callover system. If appellants cannot appear in person, they must communicate this in writing to the tribunal. Repeated nonattendance will result in the appeal being dismissed.

The new software (internally named Axia) is delivered by BearingPoint Ireland. It is based on the Ontario Municipal Property Assessment Corporation system and uses ArcGIS. Using this mapping system to log comparable properties should improve data accessibility; however, the initiative is at an early stage.

The tax works well in that it is established and accepted by ratepayers. The system is fair and transparent, and rate occupiers are allowed to appeal their valuation certificates. With greater efficiencies, revaluation periods will be reduced over the next few years. It could be argued that the system can become congested during busy periods and that more investment is required. However, greater digitization will help improve this.

Exempt Properties

Certain properties and property types exempt from commercial rates are listed in table 14.14. There is no register of exempt properties or data on the number of exempt properties. In addition, exempt properties are not valued and there is no published list or register of them.

Commercial rates continue to be the primary revenue-generating property taxes in the state, representing approximately one-third of local-government funding (Department of Housing, Planning and Local Government 2020) (table 14.15). While new taxes have been introduced in the past decade, this is likely to continue to be the case in the medium to longer term.

Table 14.14 Properties Exempt from Commercial Rates

Exempt Properties and Categories
Agricultural land, farm buildings, public galleries/museums, government-occupied property, domestic premises, community sport buildings, community halls, public schools, public hospitals, public universities, buildings used for charitable purposes, and buildings used for public religious worship.

Source: Authors' compilation from legislation and Tailte Éireann sources.

Table 14.15 Local Authorities with Multiplier, 2021–2023

	Local Authority	Multiplier 2021	Multiplier 2022	Multiplier 2023
1	Carlow County Council	0.2571	0.2571	0.2700
2	Cavan County Council	0.2010	0.2011	0.2211
3	Clare County Council	72.99	75.76	75.76
4	Cork City Council	n.a.	74.75	77.59
5	Cork County Council	74.75	76.99	79.68
6	Donegal County Council	71.81	71.81	71.81
7	Dublin City Council	0.268	0.268	0.273
8	Dun Laoghaire/Rathdown County Council	0.1732	0.1732	0.1801
9	Fingal County Council	0.1796	0.1796	0.1796
10	Galway City Council	67.40	67.4	67.4
11	Galway County Council	66.59	70.59	70.59
12	Kerry County Council	79.25	79.25	79.25
13	Kildare County Council	0.2246	0.2246	0.2268
14	Kilkenny County Council	0.200	0.200	0.206
15	Laois County Council	0.2217	0.2217	0.2217
16	Leitrim County Council	0.2208	0.2274	0.2354
17	Limerick City and County Council	0.2677	0.2677	0.2797
18	Longford County Council	0.2400	0.2400	0.2521
19a	Louth County Council	0.2100	0.2100	0.2191
19b	Louth County Council	n.a.	n.a.	0.2223
20	Mayo County Council	78.42	78.42	78.42
21	Meath County Council	0.1938	0.1938	0.1938
22	Monaghan County Council	0.2260	0.2260	0.2374
23	Offaly County Council	0.2198	0.2198	0.2198
24	Roscommon County Council	0.2250	0.225	0.225
25	Sligo County Council	0.2300	0.2300	0.2415
26	South Dublin County Council	0.276	0.276	0.276
27	Tipperary County Council	0.1919	0.1919	0.2015
28	Waterford City and County Council	0.2648	0.2780	0.2863
29	Westmeath County Council	0.194	0.194	0.194
30	Wexford County Council	0.2460	0.2460	0.2530
31	Wicklow County Council	0.217	0.217	0.217

Source: Authors' compilation from local authority websites.

Note: n.a. = not available.

Figure 14.4 Property Tax Revenue Performance in Ireland, 2005–2020

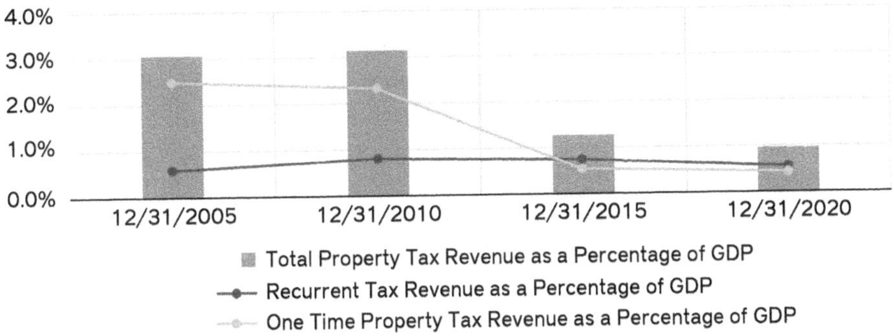

Source: Author compilation from Revenue, CSO, and Tailte Éireann.

As figure 14.4 illustrates, the proportion of property tax to GDP has fallen since 2005, but the drop is almost entirely driven by a falloff in one-off taxes such as stamp duty and capital gains. During this time, recurrent property taxes have remained relatively steady with periods of growth. As previously highlighted, property tax has a significant role in funding local government and local services. There is a strong argument to increase recurring property taxes at the expense of one-time property tax revenue.

Irish Reform Initiatives, Impact, and Conclusions

This section provides a short overview of the merger of the VO, Ordinance Survey Ireland (OSI), and the PRA into the new body, Tailte Éireann, representing one of the most significant administrative changes to the Irish system in decades. It also examines the role of property tax in Ireland as a means of funding local government and supporting societal objectives, such as housing and sustainable taxation. Comments are also made on other relevant administrative issues and consider the property tax's potential impacts and conclusions. It is beyond the scope of this chapter to provide a comprehensive analysis of all property taxes or the delivery of all local-government services. The authors have therefore focused on some key issues and highlighted areas worthy of further research.

Tailte Éireann

Tailte Éireann is a newly established independent government agency under the Department of Housing, Local Government and Heritage. It provides a range of services, including property registration, valuation, national mapping, and surveying infrastructure for the state. Tailte

Éireann was created through the merger of three organizations: the PRA, the VO, and OSI.

Tailte Éireann was established on March 1, 2023; however, the merging organizations have operated under the aegis of the Department of Housing, Local Government and Heritage since January 1, 2018 (Tailte Éireann, n.d.-f). Several such mergers have already taken place as part of the Agency Rationalization Program under the government's Public Sector Reform Plan (Oireachtas Library and Research Service 2015).

A report by O'Keeffe (2012) proposed that the merged organization should focus on customer service, innovative delivery channels, cost reduction, new ways of working, and implementation and delivery. The report also suggested that the merger of the VO, OSI, and the PRA provides an opportunity for more efficient and cost-effective delivery of land, spatial data, and property administration services. As the three organizations hold the most comprehensive set of property and spatial data in Ireland, with full national coverage, there may be a significant benefit in combining these datasets.

The Tailte Éireann Act of 2022 dissolved the PRA and OSI and transferred their functions, along with those of the commissioner of valuation and the boundary surveyor, to Tailte Éireann, effective March 1, 2023. The core business of the organization is to provide a system of ownership registration for land in Ireland, accurate valuations of commercial and industrial properties, and maintenance of the definitive mapping records and physical infrastructure of the state.

Table 14.16 shows a comparison of Tailte Éireann with common features of agencies in other common law countries and states.

It is too early to assess the effectiveness of Tailte Éireann since it was established on March 1, 2023, but the experience of other countries suggests that merging these agencies could be a significant progressive step.

Local-Government Funding and Responsibilities

This chapter has provided an overview of property taxes in Ireland and how they can play a significant role in delivering societal objectives. It has also noted the Irish system of government, which is responsible for providing local services and relies on property tax as a funding source. It is worth noting that local authorities are responsible for providing a multitude of societal services, including planning, housing, roads, economic and community development, environment protection, recreation, amenities, fire services, and the registrar of electors.

While national government and semistate organizations have a role in delivering many of these services, they are listed as local authority

Figure 14.5 Local Government Expenditure as a Percentage of General Government Expenditure

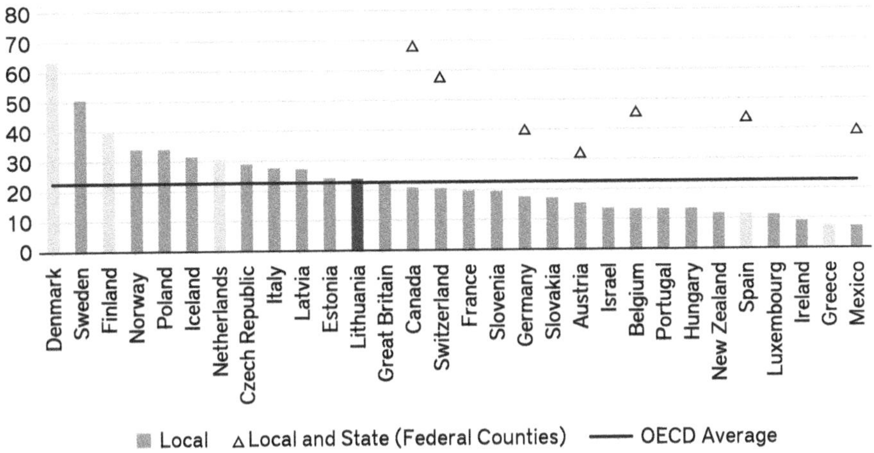

Source: OECD (2019) as cited in Vammalle and Bambalaite (2021).

responsibilities. This raises important research questions: Are local authorities sufficiently resourced to deliver effective local services and societal objectives like housing? Does not having sufficient self-funding inhibit appropriate planning from being undertaken to deliver and monitor effective services? While it is beyond the scope of this chapter to explore these questions in detail, some recent administrative improvements are highlighted. Furthermore, this chapter does not offer a comprehensive analysis of local-government funding, and the authors would direct readers to Vammalle and Bambalaite (2021) for more information. However, that source notes the deficit in funding for local government when considered against its assigned service responsibilities (figure 14.5). It seems clear that, relative to other countries, Ireland does not raise a significant amount of its total revenue at the local level.

Considering this in the context of its other funding arrangements and the political structure is essential. For example, Vammalle and Bambalaite (2021) report the strong integration of financial and regional development plans into the local authority funding model.

Nonetheless, the stark deficit in funding to provide the services and the reliance on central-government funding to supplement the provision of these services may contribute to or lead to a time lag in delivering services. Local authorities typically have first access to both anecdotal and factual data on issues arising with the services (in the housing sector,

Table 14.16 Comparison of Tailte Éireann with Agencies in Other Common Law Countries and States

Country/ State–Agency	Property Registration	Valuation	Mapping/ Surveying	Responsible for National/State Geospatial Data Infrastructure	Organizational Status
Northern Ireland–Land and Property Services	Yes	Yes	Yes	Yes	Executive agency of government department
State of Western Australia–Landgate	Yes	Yes	Yes	Yes	State agency
State of New South Wales (Australia)–Land Property Information	Yes	Yes	Yes	No	Division of government department
State of Victoria–Land Victoria	Yes	Yes	Yes Regulation of valuation only	No	Division of government department
New Zealand–Land Information New Zealand	Yes	Yes	Yes	Yes	Government department
State of British Columbia (Canada)–Land Title and Survey Authority	Yes	No	Yes	No	State agency
Tailte Éireann	Yes	Yes	Yes	Yes	State agency

Source: Extract from Oireachtas Library and Research Service (2015) internal research note on merging property, mapping. and valuation state agencies.

Establishment Rationale	Relationship to Government/ Department	Status of Employees	Statutory Officers	Funding
To streamline delivery of services	Part of government department	Civil servants	Commissioner of valuation; registrar of titles	Government funding and commercial/ fee income
Coordination/ merging of functions	Accountable to government minister	Public servants	Commissioner of titles; registrar of titles; valuer-general	Government funding and commercial/ fee income
Coordination/ merging of functions	Part of government department	Public servants	Registrar-general; surveyor-general; valuer-general	Government funding and commercial/ fee income
Coordination/ merging of functions	Part of government department	Public servants	Registrar of titles; registrar-general; valuer-general; surveyor-general	Government funding and commercial/ fee income
To streamline delivery of services	Part of government department	Public servants	Registrar general of land; surveyor-general; valuer-general; commissioner of crown lands	Government funding and commercial/ fee income
Coordination/ merging of functions	Operating agreement with government department	Nonpublic servants, direct employees of agency	Director of land titles; surveyor-general	Fully self-financing
Coordination/ merging of functions	Accountable to government minister	Civil servants	Registrar of deeds and title; chief state surveyor; commissioner of valuation	Government funding and commercial/ fee income

the demand and supply of local housing, for example). Having sufficient local-government funding to address issues at an early stage may help in limiting or preventing issues with the provision of these services before they become significant or emergencies.

There have been improvements in this regard since the introduction of the LPT. As has been previously noted, transferring the LPT returns from the Revenue Commissioners to the Local Government Fund in 2019 is a progressive step in aligning revenue raised to support local services.

While this provides a simple high-level overview, it would be negligent of the authors not to highlight this funding issue in a chapter on property taxes in Ireland. Adjusting property taxes, having considered the relevant context, provides the opportunity to make targeted equitable interventions to address this gap and provide sustainable and prudent measures for the benefit of all stakeholders.

Property Taxation and Housing

Housing is a key challenge for Irish society. At the launch of the Irish government's most recent plan to address the housing crisis, the Taoiseach stated that housing was "the single most urgent and important social issue facing our country at this moment in time" (Department of the Taoiseach 2021). This section discusses how property taxes may be employed to help address the Irish housing issue. It focuses on one aspect of the property tax, betterment tax, that affects housing supply. This is worthy of particular study due to its role in taxation of betterment and housing strategy. Theories of land value taxation and economic rent are well established by seminal authors such as Adam Smith and David Ricardo. However, recent studies highlight how land taxation affects land prices and housing affordability (Lichfield and Connellan 1997; Ryan-Collins, Lloyd, and Macfarlane 2017).

What Is Part V?

Part V of the Planning and Development Act of 2000 (as amended) is the legislation that captures betterment (referring to land values) in Ireland. Like many developed nations, Ireland has faced challenges supplying its citizens with affordable housing. One of the earliest reports where property taxes and housing affordability were linked was the Kenny report. The minister for local government commissioned the report in 1972 in response to concern about rising land prices affecting housing affordability during the 1960s and 1970s. It considered including betterment taxes to control the price of land required for housing and measures to ensure that increases in land values directly attributable to the actions of public authorities would be used to benefit the common good.

The Irish government rejected these long-term strategic property tax proposals at the time, and Ireland continued to face land price inflation and housing affordability challenges throughout the following decades. The Planning and Development Act of 2000 introduced a reform initiative to create a new betterment tax capturing up to 20 percent[3] of the value gained from planning for housing for the common good. The betterment component formed part of the broader requirement for local authorities to set their own housing strategy, including how much social, affordable, and market housing they required. As part of this plan, local authorities could specify what percentage of social and affordable housing was needed in all new housing developments.

An important and innovative aspect of the act encouraged the delivery of private, social, and affordable housing side by side rather than in the traditional segregated approach. Much evidence suggests that grouping social housing causes many social problems, including antisocial behavior, which can consequently lead to increased expenditure in policing, social welfare, and other areas.

Part V works by estimating a housing development's existing use and development values to determine the betterment occurring due to the grant of planning permission and provision of services by the state. The betterment tax is a percentage of this uplift, and the net value calculated is referred to as a net equivalent monetary value. It requires property developers to meet their legislative requirements by providing a discount on housing units within their development for social and affordable purposes. Local authorities typically purchase these units at a discount on market values equivalent to the net monetary value. Integrating[4] social and affordable housing with private market housing promotes sustainable mixed-tenure communities. The initiative to deliver these units as part of a long-term housing strategy, which was aided by Part V, has been viewed as a positive step in tackling the cyclical nature of economic and housing cycles (Housing Agency 2014).

Academic studies have also found Part V to be an effective method of delivering integrated social and affordable housing despite the original purpose being watered down through some of the amendment acts (Harrington 2011).

Sustainable Property Taxation

The role of property tax in achieving sustainability goals is widely acknowledged. Plimmer and McCluskey (2011) propose that sustainability in property taxation should be considered from three perspectives: the sustainability of the tax object (land and buildings), the sustainability of the tax system itself, and the sustainability of the uses to which the yield from property taxation is put. This section examines sustainability in property tax in Ireland through the lens of previous examples of property tax, incentives, and housing.

The housing measures outlined in the previous section have the potential to contribute to various United Nations Sustainable Development Goals (SDGs), including SDG 1 (reducing poverty), SDG 8 (decent work and economic growth), SDG 9 (industry, innovation, and infrastructure), SDG 10 (reduced inequalities), SDG 11 (sustainable cities and communities), and SDG 13 (climate action) (United Nations, n.d.). This section highlights that property taxation and incentives can significantly contribute to many of the SDGs, and these areas are worthy of independent studies.

The sustainability of the tax object (land and buildings)

There are clear areas where property tax can contribute to the tax object. One proposal is to review the LPT, which is currently self-assessed without direct links to the State Building Energy Rating system. This has the potential to further incentivize the sustainability of the tax object.

The sustainability of the tax system itself

This chapter does not analyze the sustainability of the tax system itself. Nevertheless, the fact that Ireland has been overreliant on transaction measures, such as stamp duty, has been well documented, especially since there was no recurring property tax such as the LPT in place at that time (2000–2007).

Figure 14.6 might help readers understand the issue better. It is important to keep in mind that Ireland has an open economy and is prone to economic cycles, which affect its housing market.

As house prices and transactions fell from 2007 to 2012, so did transaction-based taxes. While some argue transaction-based taxes should be disregarded entirely, we would advocate for refinements. Refining stamp duty and Part V, which would likely include empowering local authorities to accept net equivalent monetary value in certain circumstances, could generate more funds to support countercyclical measures aimed at meeting society's housing needs.

The sustainability of the uses to which the yield from property taxation is put

Figure 14.7 highlights the cyclical nature of Ireland's house prices and transactions. During this period, a limited amount of new housing was constructed due to the economic recession. This came at a time when housing was most needed.

Figure 14.6 Ireland's Cyclical Housing Market

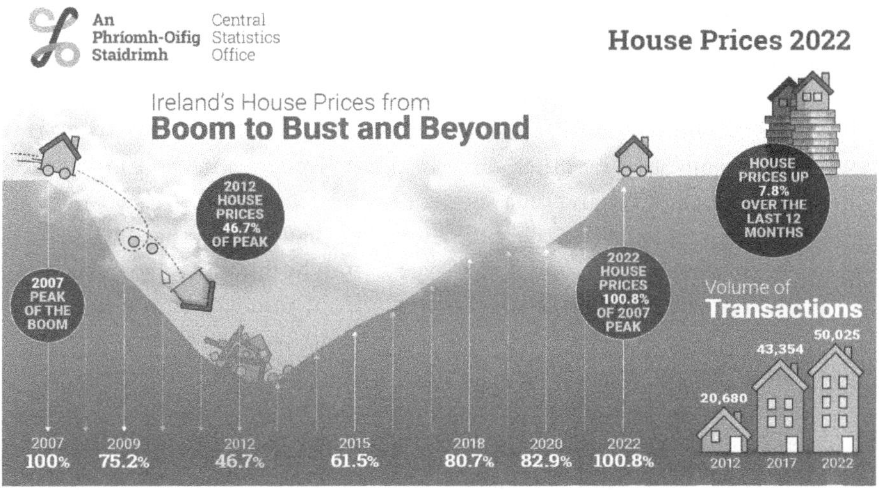

Source: CSO (2022).

Figure 14.7 Housing Supply Graph

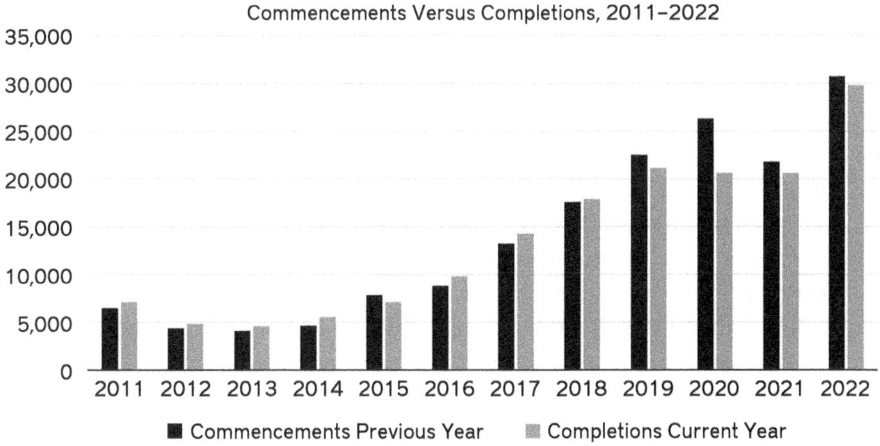

Source: Data compiled from CSO and Department of Housing, Local Government and Heritage (2020).

Expanding the tax base could facilitate interventions in the market through construction and purchase, thereby enhancing the housing supply, supporting economic activity, and adding to the state's housing assets. Additionally, refining Part V to enable local authorities to accept the net equivalent monetary value at the right time would also be countercyclical, provided funds were ring-fenced for housing. These recommendations would empower local governments to make independent decisions that support the delivery of the housing strategy rather than relying on a single, universal approach.

While some may see these measures as urbancentric, there are many ways property taxes and incentives could be employed to support achieving the SDGs in a rural setting. Continuing with the housing example, rural Ireland faces the widespread issue of vacant housing in small towns and villages, despite a significant proportion of new housing being granted planning permission in rural locations outside these rural towns and villages. In Ireland, this phenomenon is known as "one-off houses," and its prevalence is not attributable to the global trend of urbanization alone. There may be opportunities for property taxes and other incentives to play a role in addressing the issue, and ongoing independent monitoring of all potential impacts would seem to be called for.

The Irish government has recently moved to address the issue of vacant housing by introducing a new vacant homes tax in Budget 2023. Dwellings occupied for fewer than 30 days within a 12-month period will be subjected to a self-assessed vacant homes tax at three times the LPT rate in an attempt to return these properties to the housing market. Sherry FitzGerald, a leading Irish residential estate agent, notes that this measure alone will unlikely return a substantial amount of stock to the market (Sherry FitzGerald 2023).

There may be more opportunities to introduce sustainable property tax reforms and incentives to stimulate rural communities and achieve the SDGs. Various incentives, such as those introduced in former urban regeneration projects, should be considered to encourage people back to town and village centers, reduce pressure on providing services; and create vibrant, sustainable communities.

Administrative Issues

We highlight many Irish-specific administrative issues that could improve transparency and confidence in the valuation and property tax systems. These include enhancing the quality of datasets by making them more comprehensive, recognizing and leveraging the expertise of those working in this field, and implementing legislative reforms to increase transparency and instill trust among all parties involved.

An Irish-specific administrative reform worthy of further consideration is the practice of taking derelict redevelopment sites off the commercial rates list. When they are struck off the list, no commercial rates are payable on these properties until they are developed into a new use. While there is a rationale for this, it would seem counter to the purpose of the recently introduced vacant site levy. Adopting a new practice similar to the vacant site levy would bring advantages to most stakeholders, such as generating revenue for the local authority, decreasing the workload of appeals to Tailte Éireann, and promoting development.

Another reform worthy of further research is investigating the feasibility of a centralized service for collecting commercial rates. In Ireland, the collection of rates is the local authority's responsibility, and as has been highlighted, the various local authorities have differing resources. Centralizing these rates would remove the burden from the local authorities and potentially be a more efficient collection method.

Finally, we recommend standardizing some of the terminology used in the field. While some terms have valid and specific reasons for use, others have broadly similar definitions and conceptual frameworks, such as *market value*, *chargeable value*, and *open market value*. Ultimately, differing terminology can reduce transparency and confidence in valuations. Therefore, the IVSC terminology, definitions, and conceptual frameworks are recommended as the basis for future legislation, where possible.

Interventions and Critical Analysis of Successes

Numerous property tax interventions have been implemented in Ireland in recent years, with the establishment of the LPT and Tailte Éireann being among the most significant. Despite facing significant opposition to other proposed taxes, such as water charges, the government's successful establishment of the LPT is commendable. The contribution of the Revenue Commissioners to this achievement cannot be overlooked, particularly in light of the challenges encountered during its implementation.

Although the Revenue Commissioners were central to its establishment, the lack of data and valuation expertise in the declaration or checking process have been highlighted as a limitation in this chapter.

With respect to Tailte Éireann, while it is too early to critically analyze its impact, its successful establishment may be considered an achievement. It has significant potential, as it combines state valuation, legal support, and data centers. Given these attributes, it may be an appropriate time to migrate the administration of LPT to Tailte Éireann.

Figure 14.8 Share of Property Investment in Ireland by International Investors, 2007–2021

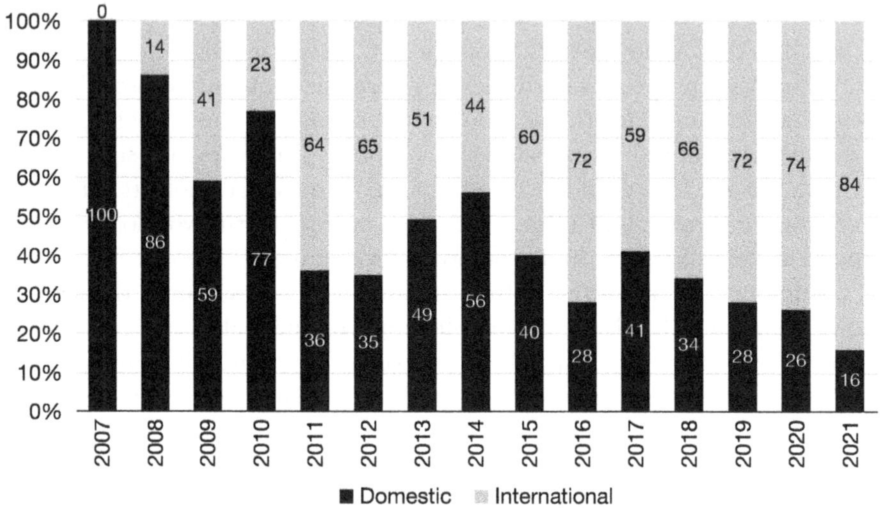

Source: Irish Institutional Property (2023); CBRE.

There have also been various microlevel successes. For example, the introduction of property tax holding vehicles has encouraged investment funds into the Irish real estate market. These measures (ICAVs and real estate investment trusts) were introduced to address a gap in funding, particularly after the previously referenced banking crisis in 2008, when traditional lenders largely exited the market, and the supply of housing and other critical assets was significantly limited.

Figure 14.8 highlights the significant change in funding for Irish real estate since 2007.

Although there are ongoing debates about the focus of funding—for example, build-to-rent (BTR) versus build-to-sell (BTS)—it is important to differentiate between the micro issues that can be resolved through planning regulations, and funding issues. While the interventions may have been successful anecdotally, it is not recommended to rely solely on private sector funding for public services like housing. Rather, such funding should be used alongside state involvement in meeting societal needs. However, long-term independent research and data are lacking, and given the societal importance of this topic, it underscores the need for independent critical analysis.

Another intervention worthy of note is the previously referenced 10 percent stamp duty rate, introduced in 2021 to target the bulk buying of specific residential units. This issue became prominent when a traditional BTS development was removed from the market after the agent announced they had sold all units in bulk to an investor for rental purposes. In this case, investors bought completed units intended for the BTS market and proposed moving them to the rental market. This is distinct from BTR, where it may be argued that there are advantages to investors funding and improving the viability and delivery of development schemes that may otherwise not occur.

When the targeted stamp duty intervention was introduced in 2021, the BTR market was outperforming the BTS market. As a result, the supply of BTS units was limited, and the suggestion to sell a BTS scheme for rental purposes received significant media attention and, ultimately, political intervention. The stamp duty intervention successfully prevented other investors from engaging in this practice (Arthur Cox 2021; Department of Finance 2021; Horgan-Jones, Leahy, and O'Halloran 2021), but it did not address the root cause of why the BTR market was outperforming the BTS market. According to research by TU Dublin, it was a viability issue that could have been better addressed through other property tax measures and interventions. This underscores the need for long-term strategic analysis of property tax interventions, as reactive measures may only be successful in the short term.

Recommendations and Conclusions

Has property tax reached its potential in Ireland? The property tax encompasses several categories, and each can have a substantial impact on revenue generation and society. The purpose of this chapter is not to draw conclusions but to offer talking points and propose suggestions for future research.

In Ireland, it is challenging to determine whether property tax has reached its full potential due to the lack of detailed property data on the long-term effects of such taxes. Therefore, it is recommended that reliable, detailed, and transparent data be made more readily available to inform policy decisions. Additionally, there should be a commitment to independent research to assess the effectiveness of property tax and incentives. Emergency measures are being introduced without a comprehensive understanding of the property market and economic theory. Independent research combined with long-term data could help policy makers address these issues and focus on medium- and long-term objectives.

Despite the limited data and independent research available, this chapter has highlighted some successes achieved through using property tax and opportunities for influential reforms to achieve societal objectives, such as addressing SDGs.

In Ireland, housing is one particular societal issue where property taxes have significant potential to be more influential. While some specific initiatives have been innovative and achieved their objectives, overall, housing policy in Ireland has been unsuccessful. In September 2022, the Irish Parliamentary Budget Office stated that "housing demand still far outstrips supply, with a shortage of properties available to rent and affordability an issue for many" (Parliamentary Budget Office 2022), highlighting the need for a critique of all measures so that lessons may be learned. This chapter has highlighted some areas that warrant further independent study.

Property taxes can be utilized to moderate land prices, which, in turn, can help address issues of housing affordability and inflation while encouraging the supply of private, affordable, and social units through Part V and other measures. Property taxes and incentives can also be used to achieve more sustainable spatial patterns and encourage the development of Irish rural towns, villages, and urban regeneration areas. However, careful consideration must be given to their introduction or modification, having regard for potential impacts on the market.

While this chapter does not offer a conclusive answer on whether property tax in Ireland has reached its potential, it has made clear that property tax can contribute to achieving Irish societal goals.

What Has Held Back Additional Property Tax Revenue Mobilization?

Property tax may have a negative connotation in Irish society and across political parties. For example, while targeted urban regeneration initiatives during the 1980s were successful, follow-on measures that were politically motivated led in part to the creation of ghost estates and received national media coverage. These measures point to a lack of data, of independent research on these projects, and of political motivation to change policy when needed. Recent attempts to introduce water charges during a period of austerity were rejected, reducing the political will to tackle property taxes, even if merited. Despite this, the Irish bailout and current housing crisis have renewed the focus on property tax as a revenue tool.

A caution is that too many unclear measures may add uncertainty and fail to raise revenue or address the societal objectives they have been introduced to address. Instead, refining existing measures should be carefully considered before introducing new ones. Furthermore, improving datasets and aligning definitions to IVSC standards will provide transparency and help to achieve societal objectives.

What Reform Options (Policy, Administrative, and Management) Might Increase Ireland's Revenue Contributions and Achieve Societal Objectives?

Changing the narrative around property tax is a crucial starting point. Increasing transparency and ensuring that funds raised from property taxes are ring-fenced for societal projects like housing, sustainable initiatives, and local services can help to do this. Combining this with the publication of objective research on the successes and failures of interventions would further foster confidence. The current housing crisis has created an opportunity to discuss how evidence-based strategic approaches and property tax amendments can help tackle difficult situations. This discussion could provide a framework to begin to change the narrative.

At a policy level, incentives and disincentives can help Ireland achieve its SDGs and develop critical infrastructure such as housing. It is critical to prioritize measures that address the cyclical nature of the Irish property market in order to deliver a sustained supply of private, affordable, and social housing units. Ongoing analysis of measures is necessary to increase revenue contributions where appropriate and help achieve these objectives.

Housing remains a key priority for the Irish government, and the supply of housing is a crucial component of its housing plan. High land costs and inflationary pressures on construction have made housing schemes, particularly BTS, less viable, putting pressure on the housing supply. Furthermore, as the government has limited control of European Central Bank interest rates, any increase in interest rates will put more pressure on housing scheme viability. However, where the government has control is property tax and incentives, and therefore direct and simple measures are key to improving the housing supply.

In this context, it is clear that property taxes and incentives have a role in solving the current housing crises and maintaining adequate supply through countercyclical measures. Incentives, disincentives, VAT, and stamp duty should be regularly reviewed to support housing viability while also ensuring sufficient resources are available to deliver other societal services.

The Taoiseach, at the time of writing, believes Ireland's housing crisis is "on the cusp of changing" and that government policies are affecting the housing supply (Meskill 2023). While this chapter has highlighted some successes, it is evident more needs to be done in this area in particular. Targeted countercyclical measures are needed to temper the cyclical nature of the Irish economy and the housing market. Ongoing monitoring and analysis are necessary to deliver these measures, and more resources and staff with real estate expertise are required in relevant government departments and Tailte Éireann. Increasing research and engagement with the academic community are also imperative. All these measures should help change the narrative and provide a framework for more sustainable property tax bases and policies to meet societal needs.

Appendix

Property Tax Revenue Performance in Ireland

Table A14.1 Overall Property Tax Revenue Performance in Ireland

Year	Total Property Tax Revenues (€)	Total Property Tax Revenues as % of GDP	Recurrent Tax Revenues as % of GDP	One-Time Property Tax Revenue as % of GDP
2020 (most recent year available)	3,514,970,000	0.94	0.52	0.42
2015 (or similar recent year)	3,322,000,000	1.26	0.73	0.53

Source: PwC (2023).

Table A14.2 Property Tax Revenues from One-Time Sources, 2020

Tax	Amount of Revenue (€)	% of GDP
Stamp duty	566,190,000	0.15
CGT	509,480,000	0.14
CAT	505,000,000	0.14

Source: PwC (2023).

Table A14.3 Property Tax Revenue from Recurrent Sources

Tax	Amount of Revenue (€)	% of GDP	Taxable Value (€)
Commercial rates	1,470,000,000	0.39	7,015,707,694
Residential property tax	453,000,000	0.12	45,300,000,000
Vacant site levy	11,300,000	0.003	n.a.

Sources: PwC (2023).

Note: n.a. = not available.

Table A14.4 Breakdown of Local-Government Revenues in Ireland per Local Authority Budgets, 2022 (€)

Local Authority	Per Capita Local Revenues	Per Capita Property Tax Revenues (LPT and commercial rates)	Per Capita Grants
Carlow	250	345	406
Cavan	205	350	440
Clare	289	406	388
Cork City[1]	308	426	305
Cork County[1]			
Donegal	311	382	277
Dublin City[1]	293	548	399
Dun Laoghaire Rathdown[1]			
Fingal[1]			
Galway City[1]	209	319	332
Galway County[1]			
Kerry	297	399	404
Kildare	156	323	233
Kilkenny	243	314	343
Laois	207	258	446
Leitrim	276	452	522
Limerick	1,094	378	3,057
Longford	334	389	582
Louth	281	321	397
Mayo	276	417	491
Meath	176	279	263
Monaghan	202	399	525
Offaly	197	304	356
Roscommon	237	335	376
Sligo	264	358	381
South Dublin[1]	See collated Dublin County		
Tipperary	287	373	486
Waterford	288	433	480
Westmeath	252	302	385
Wexford	228	346	244
Wicklow	238	289	280

Source: Adapted by authors from Department of Housing, Local Government and Heritage data.

[1] There are 26 county councils, 3 city councils (Dublin, Galway, and Cork), and 2 councils that oversee a city and county (Limerick and Waterford).

Table A14.5 Commercial Property Rates Report, 2023

Local Authority	Number of Properties	Commercial Rates Taxable Value (€)	Ratable Value and NAV (€)	ARV (€)	Total Annual Rates Collectible (€)
Carlow County Council	1,956	58,110,156	58,110,156	0.2700	15,689,742
Cavan County Council	2,501	81,872,655	81,872,655	0.2211	18,102,044
Clare County Council	5,245	125,982,308	629,911	75.76	47,722,098
Cork City Council	10,983	305,080,036	1,525,400	77.59	118,355,799
Cork County Council	18,760	349,468,046	1,747,340	79.68	139,228,069
Donegal County Council	8,104	123,727,124	616,165	71.81	44,246,853
Dublin City Council	19,956	1,412,984,970	1,412,984,970	0.2730	385,744,896
Dun Laoghaire Rathdown County Council	5,228	546,642,174	546,642,174	0.1801	98,450,255
Fingal County Council	6,450	869,544,535	869,544,535	0.1796	156,170,198
Galway City Council	4,363	125,727,132	628,635	67.4	42,370,043
Galway County Council	6,617	103,485,590	517,427	70.59	36,525,238
Kerry County Council	7,243	133,758,014	668,790	79.2500	53,001,613
Kildare County Council	4,974	277,438,574	277,438,574	0.2268	62,923,068
Kilkenny County Council	2,823	103,700,249	103,700,249	0.2060	21,362,251
Laois County Council	1,978	65,928,651	65,928,651	0.2217	14,616,381
Leitrim County Council	1,140	28,964,335	28,964,335	0.2354	6,818,204

Limerick City and County Council	6,623	238,159,771	238,159,771	0.2797	66,613,288
Longford County Council	1,473	36,728,441	36,728,441	0.2521	9,259,240
Louth County Council	4,436	157,494,665	157,494,665	0.2191	34,507,081
Mayo County Council	6,584	108,955,692	544,778	78.4200	42,721,526
Meath County Council	4,875	264,239,558	264,239,558	0.1938	51,209,626
Monaghan County Council	2,440	62,048,643	62,048,643	0.2374	14,730,347
Offaly County Council	2,586	82,427,325	82,427,325	0.2198	18,117,526
Roscommon County Council	2,115	56,351,700	56,351,700	0.2250	12,679,132
Sligo County Council	2,264	60,995,161	60,995,161	0.2415	14,730,331
South Dublin County Council	6,901	526,949,501	526,949,501	0.2760	145,438,062
Tipperary County Council	5,399	182,765,371	182,765,371	0.2015	36,827,222
Waterford City and County Council	3,849	126,267,935	126,267,935	0.2863	36,150,509
Westmeath County Council	3,155	92,269,111	92,269,111	0.1940	17,900,207
Wexford County Council	4,618	163,795,257	163,795,257	0.2530	41,440,200
Wicklow County Council	3,692	144,339,012	144,339,012	0.2170	31,321,565
Total	**169,331**	**7,015,707,694**			**1,834,972,628**

Source: Author compilation.

Notes

We extend our deepest gratitude to the numerous professionals and academics whose valuable insights and expertise enriched this chapter. Special appreciation goes to PwC, and in particular Ilona McElroy, Ailbhe MacGreevy, Macdara Kelly, Aimee Kelly, and Rosaleen Carey, whose contributions were pivotal, notably in shaping the one-off and recurring property taxes sections. We are also indebted to the Valuation Division of Tailte Éireann for their generous provision of time and data; Declan Lavelle and Maurice O'Neill's contributions were invaluable, as were those of Peter Stafford and John McCartney. We acknowledge with heartfelt thanks the indispensable support of all contributors, without whom this publication would not have been possible. Your contributions are deeply appreciated.

1. Executive power in Ireland is exercised by the government, which is led by the Taoiseach (prime minister).
2. There are 26 county councils, 3 city councils (Dublin, Galway, and Cork), and 2 councils that oversee a city and county (Limerick and Waterford).
3. Authority was given to local authorities to set the exact amount with reference to their housing needs in their housing strategy.
4. This was the initial purpose of the legislation, but there were loopholes where social and affordable housing units were not fully integrated alongside private developments.

References

Amárach Research. 2021. *Small Landlords Report 2021.* Clonakilty, County Cork: Residential Tenancies Board. https://rtb.ie/wp-content/uploads/2025/05/RTB-Small-Landlord-Survey-2020-Report-Final.pdf.

Arthur Cox. 2021. "Government Announces Stamp Duty and Planning Measures to Prevent the Bulk Acquisition of Houses and Duplexes." May 19. https://www.arthurcox.com/knowledge/government-announces-stamp-duty-and-planning-measures-to-prevent-the-bulk-acquisition-of-houses-and-duplexes/.

Citizen Information. 2022. "Local Government." https://www.citizensinformation.ie/en/government_in_ireland/national_government/local_and_regional_government/functions_of_local_authorities.html.

CSO (Central Statistics Office). 2022. "Census of Population 2022—Preliminary Results." Press Release. June 23. https://www.cso.ie/en/csolatestnews/pressreleases/2022pressreleases/pressstatementcensusofpopulation2022-preliminaryresults/.

Department of Finance. 2021. "Minister Donohoe Announces Stamp Duty Measure for Bulk Purchasers for Homes." Press Release. May 18. https://www.gov.ie/en/press-release/0b75f-minister-donohoe-announces-stamp-duty-measure-for-bulk-purchasers-for-homes/.

Department of Housing, Local Government and Heritage. 2020. *Value for Money Unit Local Government Audit Service: An Overview of Commercial Rates in Local Authorities December 2018.* https://assets.gov.ie/static/documents/an-overview-of-commercial-rates-in-local-authorities-december-2018-02d79b5b-646e-434f-.pdf.

Department of the Taoiseach. 2021. "Speech by the Taoiseach Micheál Martin at the Launch of Housing for All." September 2. https://www.gov.ie/en/speech/105d4-speech-by-the-taoiseach-micheal-martin-at-the-launch-of-housing-for-all/.

European Committee of the Regions. 2018. "Ireland Fiscal Powers." https://portal.cor.europa.eu/divisionpowers/Pages/Ireland-Fiscal-Powers.aspx.

Fischer, J. 2014. "Boston or Berlin? Reflections on a Topical Controversy, the Celtic Tiger and the World of Irish Studies." *Irish Review* 48: 81–95.

Government of Ireland. 2022. "Government Announces €62.3m Targeted Commercial Rates Waiver for Quarter One 2022." Press Release. December 3. https://www.gov.ie/en/press-release/f4ee1-government-announces-623m-targeted-commercial-rates-waiver-for-quarter-one-2022/.

Harrington, F. 2011. "A Critical Analysis of Whether Part V of the Planning and Development Act 2000 Has Been an Affective and/or Reliable Mechanism of Delivering Social and Affordable Housing in the Mid-East Region Between 2000 and 2010." Dublin: DIT.

Horgan-Jones, J., P. Leahy, and M. O'Halloran. 2021. "Housing Crisis: Hike in Stamp Duty Considered to Deter Bulk-Buying of Homes." *Irish Times*, May 12. https://www.irishtimes.com/news/ireland/irish-news/housing-crisis-hike-in-stamp-duty-considered-to-deter-bulk-buying-of-homes-1.4562439.

Housing Agency. 2014. "Part V Review: Report and Recommendations by Housing Agency." Dublin: Housing Agency.

IIP/CBRE. n.d. "Key Facts About the Role of Institutional Capital." Accessed March 2022. https://www.iip.ie/key-facts.

Irish Institutional Property. (2023). *Residential Development Finance in Ireland—An Overview*. December. https://irp.cdn-website.com/4065c16c/files/uploaded/13_IIP%20Development%20Finance%20Presentation_Digital-b3a14a75.pdf.

Lichfield, N., and O. Connellan. 1997. "Land Value Taxation in Britain for the Benefit of the Community." Working paper. Cambridge, MA: Lincoln Institute of Land Policy.

Meskill, T. 2023. "Housing Crisis on 'Cusp of Changing,' Says Taoiseach." RTÉ News, April 9. https://www.rte.ie/news/politics/2023/0409/1376067-politics-ireland/.

OECD (Organisation for Economic Co-operation and Development). 2018. "OECD Regions and Cities at a Glance 2018—Country Notes: Ireland." https://www.oecd.org/en/publications/oecd-regions-and-cities-at-a-glance-2018-country-notes_11d019fb-en/ireland_d4655699-en.html.

———. n.d.-a. "GDP." Accessed March 2022. https://data.oecd.org/gdp/gross-domestic-product-gdp.htm.

———. n.d.-b. "OECD Fiscal Decentralisation Database." Accessed March 2022. https://www.oecd.org/ctp/federalism/fiscal-decentralisation-database.htm.

Office of the Revenue Commissioners. n.d. "Local Property Tax (LPT)." Accessed March 2022. https://www.revenue.ie/en/property/local-property-tax/index.aspx.

Oireachtas. n.d. "Factsheet." Accessed March 2022. https://www.oireachtas.ie/en/press-centre/factsheet/.

Oireachtas Library and Research Service. 2015. "L&RS Note: Merging Property, Mapping and Valuation State Agencies—Tailte Éireann." Dublin: Houses of the Oireachtas.

O'Keeffe, D. 2012. "Working Group Undertaking the Critical Review of the Proposal to Merge the Valuation Office, Ordnance Survey Ireland and the Property Registration Authority." Dublin: Department of Justice and Equality.

Parliamentary Budget Office. 2022. "The Parliamentary Budget Office (PBO) Has Published Its Pre-Budget 2023 Commentary." Press Release. September 19.

https://www.oireachtas.ie/en/press-centre/press-releases/20220919-parliamentary-budget-office-pbo-publishes-its-pre-budget-2023-commentary/.

Plimmer, F., and W. J. McCluskey. 2011. "Sustainability and Property Taxation." International Federation of Surveyors Article of the Month, August. https://www.fig.net/resources/monthly_articles/2011/august_2011/august_2011_plimmer_mccluskey.pdf.

PwC. 2023. "Tax Facts 2023—VAT & Property." PwC Ireland. https://www.pwc.ie/publications/2023/tax-facts-2023.pdf.

———. 2025. "Tax Facts 2025—VAT & Property." PwC Ireland. https://www.pwc.ie/publications/2025/tax-facts-2025.pdf.

Revenue. 2021a. "Local Property Tax, Property Valuation Guide." https://lpt.revenue.ie/lpt-web/views/login.html?execution=e1s1.

———. 2021b. "Notes for Guidance—Taxes Consolidation Act 1997, Finance Act 2021 Edition, Part 22A, Residential Zoned Land Tax." https://www.revenue.ie/en/tax-professionals/documents/notes-for-guidance/tca/part22a.pdf.

———. 2022a. "Annual Report 2021." https://www.revenue.ie/en/corporate/press-office/annual-report/2021/ar-2021.pdf.

———. 2022b. "Interest Charges." https://www.revenue.ie/en/property/local-property-tax/what-happens-if-you-do-not-comply/interest-charges.aspx.

———. 2022c. "Irish Real Estate Fund (IREF) Guidance Note." Part 27-01b-02. https://www.revenue.ie/en/tax-professionals/tdm/income-tax-capital-gains-tax-corporation-tax/part-27/27-01b-02.pdf.

———. 2022d. "The Valuation of a Residential Property." In *Tax and Duty Manual*, Part 04-01. https://www.revenue.ie/en/tax-professionals/tdm/local-property-tax/part-04/04-01.pdf.

———. 2022e. "Local Property Tax (LPT) for 2021: Statistics Update." https://www.revenue.ie/en/corporate/documents/statistics/lpt/local-property-tax-2021.pdf.

———. 2024. "Supply of Property (Tax and Duty Manual, Part 11—Immovable Goods)." Office of the Revenue Commissioners. https://www.revenue.ie/en/tax-professionals/tdm/value-added-tax/part11-immovable-goods/supply-of-property/supply-of-property.pdf.

———. 2025. "What Happens If You Do Not Comply?" July 25. https://www.revenue.ie/en/property/rzlt/not-comply/index.aspx?utm_source.

Reynolds, A. 1993. Introduction to *Taxation: Ireland and the New Europe*, ed. K. Murphy and M. Mulreany. Dublin: Institute of Public Administration.

Ryan-Collins, J., T. Lloyd, and L. Macfarlane. 2017. *Rethinking the Economics of Land and Housing*. London: Zed Books.

SCSI (Society of Chartered Surveyors Ireland). 2022. "Commercial Rates & Revaluation." https://scsi.ie/business/value/commercial-rates/.

Sherry FitzGerald. 2023. "Reaction to Budget 2023." https://www.sherryfitz.ie/news/reaction-to-budget-2023-.

Stedman, G. 2023. "150,000 Letters Sent About Unpaid Local Property Tax." RTÉ News, April 6. https://www.rte.ie/news/business/2023/0406/1375601-150-000-letters-sent-about-unpaid-local-property-tax/.

Tailte Éireann. 2025. "Land Registry: Compulsory Registration." Accessed August 11, 2025. https://tailte.ie/land-registry-compulsory-registration/.

———. n.d.-a. Registry of Deeds—Practice Directions and Procedures. Accessed March 2022. https://tailte.ie/practice-directions-registry-of-deeds-proccedures/.

———. n.d.-b. "Registry of Deeds FAQs." Accessed March 2022. https://tailte.ie/registry-of-deeds-faqs/.

———. n.d.-c. "What Is the Difference Between the Land Registry and the Registry of Deeds? Accessed November 28, 2025. https://tailte.ie/what-is-the-difference-between-land-registry-title-and-that-noted-in-registry-of-deeds/.

———. n.d.-d. "Search and Copy Services: Official Search—ROD Form 11." Accessed November 28, 2025. https://tailte.ie/our-archieves/search-and-copy-services/.

———. n.d.-e. "Valuation for Rating Purposes." Accessed September 11, 2025. https://tailte.ie/services/valuation/.

———. n.d.-f. "About Tailte Éireann." Accessed August 11, 2025. https//Tailte.ie/about/.

———. n.d.-g. "Requisition for Copy Memorial/Application Form." Registry of Deeds. Accessed March 2022. https://tailte.ie/rod-form-memorial-copy-application-fee-e20/.

Turley, G. 2022. "A Review of Ireland's Local Property Tax." *Administration* 70(4): 1–25.

United Nations. n.d. "The 17 Goals." Department of Economic and Social Affairs Sustainable Development. Accessed March 2022. https://sdgs.un.org/goals.

Vammalle, C., and I. Bambalaite. 2021. "Funding and Financing of Local Government Public Investment: A Framework and Application to Five OECD Countries." OECD Working Papers on Fiscal Federalism 34. Paris: OECD Publishing.

Yiu, C. Y. 2023. "Are Central Banks' Monetary Policies the Future of Housing Affordability Solutions." *Urban Science* 7(1): 18. https://www.mdpi.com/2413-8851/7/1/18.

Legislation

Derelict Sites Act 1990.

Finance Act 1997.

Finance Act 2016.

Finance Act 2019.

Finance Act 2021.

Finance (Local Property Tax) Act 2012.

Finance (Local Property Tax) (Amendment) Act 2021.

Irish Collective Asset-Management Vehicles (ICAV) Act 2015.

Landlord and Tenant (Ground Rents) Act 1967.

Landlord and Tenant (Ground Rents) (No. 2) Act 1978.

Local Government Act 2001.

Local Government (Household Charge) Act 2011.

Local Government Rates and Other Matters Act 2019.

Planning and Development Act 2000.

Registration of Deeds and Title Act 2006.

Republic of Ireland Act 1949.

Residential Tenancy Act 2004.

Stamp Duties Consolidation Act 1999.

Stamp Duties Consolidation Act 2021.

Tailte Éireann Act 2022.

Taxes Consolidation Act 1997.

Urban Regeneration and Housing Act 2015.

Valuation Act 1988.

Valuation Act 2001.

Valuation Act 2011.

Valuation (Amendment) Act 2015.

Value-Added Consolidation Act 2010.

15

Reforming the Taxation of Real Estate in Latvia

SARMITE BARVIKA

Latvia is one of the three Baltic states that renewed their independence in 1991 after the collapse of the Soviet Union. It is situated in northeastern Europe by the Baltic Sea and has borders with Estonia, Lithuania, Belarus, and the Russia Federation. Latvia's border is also the outer eastern border of the European Union (EU). The country has four historical regions (Vidzeme, Latgale, Kurzeme, and Zemgale), 81 towns, and three international ports. The territory covers almost 64,589 square kilometers. The dominant land uses are forests (52 percent) and agricultural land (37 percent), while urban areas form less than 2 percent.

The regions of Latvia are sparsely populated, on average only 28 people per square kilometer. The Riga region, however, is more densely populated, with about 2,021 people per square kilometer. Since 1990, Latvia's population has declined by more than 30 percent. At the beginning of 2022, Latvia ranked third among countries with a population of less than 5 million in terms of population decline (World Population Review, n.d.). In 2021, compared with 2010, the decrease in natural growth was 17,000 people (Central Statistical Bureau, n.d.-a).

In 2021, 98.6 percent of the population lived in 824,800 private households (2.26 people per household), while 1.4 percent lived in 11,200 units of social or institutional housing. In Latvia, 82 percent of dwellings are privately owned, although only 6 percent of the urban population live in detached or terraced houses. Forty percent of the population falls into the group of "unsupported middle class"—that is, they do not qualify for state or municipal financial aid, institutional housing, or loans but cannot afford well-furnished dwellings (OECD [Organisation for Economic Co-operation and Development] 2020).

Economic Indicators

Latvia has been a member of the EU since 2004, and it joined the OECD in 2016. Latvia's per capita gross domestic product (GDP) is €17,890, which ranks it below the OECD average of €38,697. Between 2017 and 2021, the country's GDP has grown by 30 percent, compared with the OECD's corresponding increase of 13 percent. In 2021, the composition of gross value-added sectors as a percentage of GDP was services (57 percent), manufacturing (13 percent), agriculture (3.2 percent), information and communication technology and construction (5 percent), and real estate activities (12 percent).

The COVID-19 pandemic, Ukrainian war, and fuel deficit crisis have had a significant impact on domestic consumption, fuel and heat prices, export capability, and government debt. The most affected industries were hospitality (decline of 20 percent) and energy-intensive industries (construction, wood processing, and agricultural production). In 2019, the income of the richest 20 percent of the population exceeded the income of the poorest population by 6.2 times (in 2014, 6.5 times), and the Gini index was one of the highest in the EU. In 2021, Latvia was the third-poorest country in the EU. In 2021, the Shadow Economy Index grew by 1.1 percent, reaching 26.6 percent of the GDP. The total tax losses from the shadow economy (including "envelope" wages, 46 percent of the total volume, mostly in the construction and real estate sectors) exceed €3.2 billion (Sauka and Putnins 2022).

The Consolidated Budget of the Government

Latvia is a unitary constitutional multiparty republic. The Saeima (Parliament) has legislative power and voting responsibility for the consolidated budget of the government. The government budget deficit declined from 9.6 percent of GDP in 2009 to 1.4 percent of GDP in 2019 (CEIC 2022). Since 2011, when Latvia resumed economic growth, the government fiscal position has improved. From 2017 to 2019, the budget deficit was less than 1 percent of GDP. In 2020, because of the COVID-19 pandemic, it increased to 4.8 percent of GDP. In 2022, Latvia recorded a government budget deficit equal to 7.3 percent of the country's GDP.

Administrative Territorial Structure and Reforms

Since 1990, Latvia has undergone three major administrative territorial structure reforms, in 1990, 2009, and 2021. The last two took place only 12 years apart and led to a reduction in the number of municipalities from 552 to 43.

Since the municipal elections of 2021 and the adoption of the Law on Administrative Territories and Populated Areas, Latvia has been divided into

- 5 planning regions (Kurzeme, Latgale, Riga, Vidzeme, and Zemgale);
- 6 statistical regions (Kurzeme, Latgale, Pieriga, Riga, Vidzeme, and Zemgale); and
- 43 one-tiered municipalities—36 counties (rural municipalities) and 7 municipalities of national cities (Saeima 2020).

Planning regions serve as planning and statistical units. Municipalities have the status of administrative territory as well as planning and statistical unit. The number of towns has increased from 77 to 81. Three national cities (Jekabpils, Ogre, and Valmiera) were integrated into the administrative territories of their respective municipalities. Several municipalities (Saulkrasti, Ikskile, Babite, etc.) appealed the amalgamation decision to the Constitutional Court, but to no avail. In 2022, the law set the requirement to establish residents' councils to support the observance of the interests of smaller communities.

The Spatial Planning System

The Spatial Development Planning Law of 2011 sets an obligation to maintain an up-to-date, coherently coordinated, three-tiered (national, regional, and local) spatial planning system (current, prospective, and historical cartography; descriptive documents and images; etc.). The Land Management Act of 2015 defines the principles of land use planning and development.

A number of national-scale geographic information system (GIS) projects were implemented to improve spatial data infrastructure within the framework of the Infrastructure for Spatial Information in the European Community directive (EU 2007):

- Territory Development Planning Information System (data and document storage and exchange for the spatial planning and Regional Development Indicator Module)—in operation since 2015 (Vides aizsardzības un reģionālās attīstības ministrija 2023).

- Building Information System (data and document storage and exchange for the construction planning process)—in operation since 2017 (State Construction Control Bureau 2023).
- State Land Service's Geospatial Data Geospatial Information System (cadastral information on the cadastral portal)—in operation since 2014 (Barvika and Treija 2014).

Metadata and spatial and descriptive open data (cadastre, large-scale cartography, Regional Development Indicator Module, Official Statistics Portal statistics, etc.) and relevant e-services (Cadastre Information System [Cadastre IS], Land Registry, building permits, land use and construction planning, etc.) are accessible on government portals (e.g., Latvija.lv).

The Budget of Local Governments

The tax revenue share of the current budget of municipalities is 63 percent and draws from three tax sources:

- Personal income tax (PIT) (an 80 percent share of national PIT from 2018 to 2021; 75 percent since 2021).
- Real estate tax (RET) (100 percent).
- Local fees (e.g., building permits) and taxes (at about 1 percent of all tax revenue).

PIT is paid into the state budget. Municipalities receive 75 percent of PIT (as of 2021). This revenue is made up of the share of annual PIT contributions of the registered (declared) residents of the given municipality. The State Revenue Service administers the PIT at the central level. The State Treasury further collects and distributes PIT to the municipal or state budget.

From 2018 to 2021, the municipalities received a special grant from the general government consolidated budget income of 19.6 percent (excluding PIT).

In 2021, municipal tax revenues of €9.66 billion accounted for 18.6 percent, with PIT at 15.5 percent and the RET at 2.5 percent of total local tax revenues. Until 2019, municipal tax revenues tended to increase; however, due to the impact of COVID-19 and the energy crisis, a decrease for PIT was forecast for 2023–2024 (Ministry of Finance 2021) (figure 15.1).

The municipal tax revenue dynamics for 2017–2021 are shown in figure 15.2.

Over the course of five years, there has been a slight decrease in the average share of RET in the total tax structure, and a further decrease was forecast for 2023–2024 (Ministry of Finance 2021).

Figure 15.1 Changes in the Volume Dynamics of the Share of RET and PIT in the Total Municipal Tax Revenue (2017–2023, %)

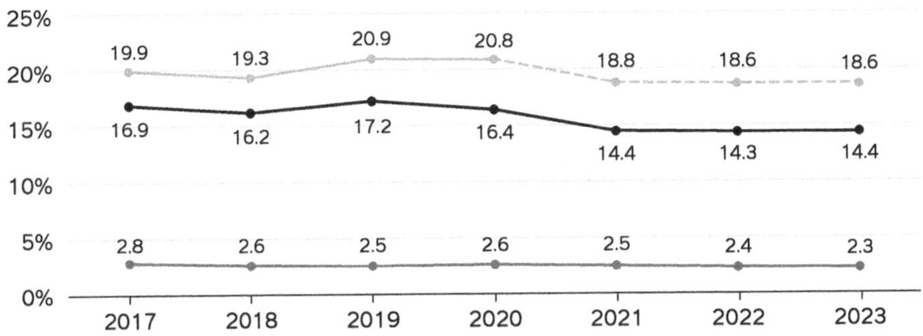

Source: Ministry of Finance (2021).

In 2022, the total estimated tax income of municipalities was €17.56 billion. The bulk of all tax revenue is generated by PIT payments (at about 82 percent). In 2021, the highest RET and PIT revenue per capita (more than €1,050) was in the Riga metropolitan area, and the lowest revenue (less than €450) was in the municipalities in the Latgale region near the state border with Belarus (Central Statistical Bureau, n.d.-a).

In 2022, 8 out of 43 municipalities paid almost €160 million to the Municipal Financial Equalization Fund (MFEF). Wealthier municipalities contribute a part of their income to this fund to support the poorer municipalities. After the administrative territorial reform of 2021, the Cabinet of Ministers, the Latvian Association of Local and Regional Governments (representing all Latvian municipalities), and the 43 amalgamated municipalities reached an agreement to continue with the MFEF payments. In 2023, the annual government budget payment to municipalities was estimated at €81.69 million; the MFEF was €81.08 million, including a special grant of €45.21 million (Ministry of Finance 2021).

System of Registration of Property Rights

The property registration system of Latvia consists of two separate registers, the Land Registry (maintained by the Court Administration) and the National Cadastre Information System, the so-called Cadastre IS (the responsibility of the State Land Service). The Court Administration and State Land Service operate under the auspices of the Ministry of Justice.

Figure 15.2 Tax Income Dynamics of Latvia's Local Governments (2017–2021, € million)

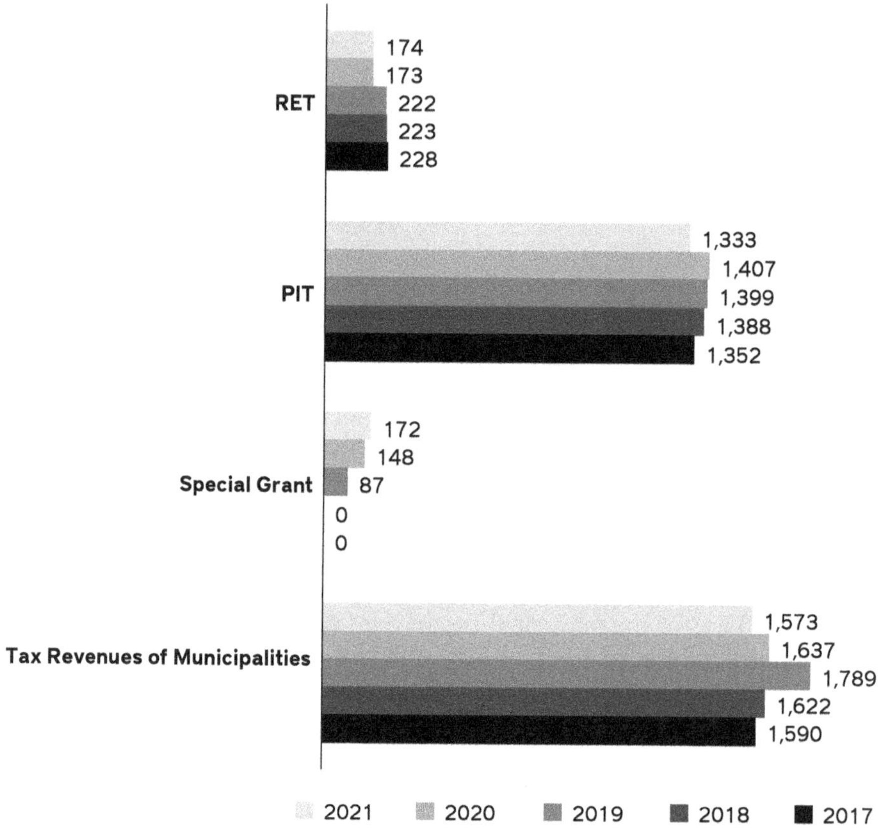

Sources: Central Statistical Bureau (n.d.-a); State Regional Development Agency of the Republic of Latvia (n.d.).

Land Registry System

The securing of property rights is mandatory as laid out in the Land Registry Act and the Law on Immovable Property Tax. The real estate must be secured in the Land Registry district (city) court in whose jurisdiction it is located. Ownership can be granted to residents and nonresidents (individuals as well as legal entities) if there is a legitimate basis (purchase, a lease, a gift, inheritance); there is no conflict with the civil law, the Land Registry Act, or financial liabilities; and a property is acquired by restoring property rights, redeemed or privatized during the land reform process.

Securitization of ownership occurs only after the flat state and office fee and the RET have been paid. Every real estate holding (e.g., land, building, land with buildings, share of building or apartment) shall be secured in a separate section of the Land Registry. The Land Registry portfolios are divided into four parts: the real estate in question, easements and encumbrances, the owner, and the basis of the property rights, pledges, and mortgages.

The Land Registry supports e-services (document submission, legal extracts, and information updates). In the user's account ("My data" in the Land Registry), information about owned properties is available upon registration (Tiesu administrācija 2021). The Land Registry is the only state register that has a legal trust for real estate. Only electronic data of the Land Registry are legally binding.

Digital Land Registry (statistics, transaction prices, and publications) is publicly accessible; and searches in the Land Registry are possible according to the cadastral number, the Land Registry number, the name of the property, or the address.

For 2022, the electronic archive of the Land Registry contains more than 2.5 million document units; almost 1.31 million estates (more than 87 percent were secured); and approximately 3 million lands, land with buildings, buildings, and new construction portfolios (an average of 145,000 portfolios per year were entered).

On January 1, 2022, the ownership breakdown was as follows:

- 59.2 percent natural persons.
- 3.0 percent legal persons.
- 5.9 percent municipalities.
- 30.1 percent state and state enterprises.
- 1 percent free undivided land.

Individuals owned about 71 percent of total territory of Latvia:

- 43 percent was acquired in a transaction.
- 33 percent was acquired by restoration of ownership.
- 21 percent was privatized.
- 1 percent was freehold land.
- Loan or mortgage finance was required for 30 percent of real estate acquisitions.

Cadastral Registration System

The Cadastre IS is the national unified system of real estate registration that provides, maintains, and uses official real estate textual and spatial data. Real estate and its objects are land, land and buildings (structures), buildings (structures), and apartment property. All real estate objects (as defined in the National Real Estate Cadastre Law) must be entered in the Cadastre IS: land, parts of land units, residential and nonresidential buildings, residential and nonresidential groups of premises, and engineering structures.

Cadastral information consists of the following:

- Textual data: Cadastral identification number, address, land area, building or premise area, current or forecasted cadastral value of land, buildings and groups of premises, leased land parts, land use type or purpose, building type, building depreciation, construction year, building amenities, encumbrances and restrictions associated with the cadastral object, and the owner, possessors, or users (except personal identification numbers).
- Spatial data: Land cartographic data, administrative borders, encumbrances, land unit and building borders, topography, land use or type distribution, zonings, cadastral descriptions, and so on.

On January 1, 2022, there were 5.8 million objects in the Cadastre IS:

Real estate:

- land estate (land with buildings): 0.85 million;
- building estate (land for rent): 0.45 million; and
- apartments: 0.64 million.

Objects of the real estate:

- land units: 1.082 million;
- buildings: 1.41 million; and
- engineering structures: 0.35 million (only 13 percent of all engineering structures).

Since 2004, the automated cadastral valuation module has been an integral part of the Cadastre IS. Since 2014, cadastral information has been managed in a digital format that has multiple layers and can be used specifically for cadastral valuation and RET administration purposes. Cadastral information has an informative status only. Cadastral data is used for

- securing property rights;
- establishing real estate transactions;
- land use and building planning;
- cadastral valuation;
- RET administration;
- regional and municipal economic development, environmental, and territorial planning;
- national statistical information; and
- GIS maintenance (which occurs in the portal kadastrs.lv).

Land Reform

The Land Reform (1990–2012) ensured privatization and the restoration of property rights to former owners and their heirs. The denationalization method was used to restore landownership rights in cities and to restore property boundaries as they were determined on June 17, 1940.

Since 1996, land privatization was intensified

- in the countryside (through the acquisition against payment or redemption against privatization certificates); and
- in cities (through privatization of apartments of the modernism period against privatization certificates).

The Land Reform has resulted in shared ownership rights (different owners for buildings and associated land); a forced lease (6 percent of cadastral value) relationship between proprietors (30 percent of all 11,000 multiapartment buildings; and the fragmentation of built-up land through the subdivision of large properties into small parcels. As a result, by 2014, the average size of a rural estate was eight hectares.

The Land Reform officially ended in 2011 in the cities and in 2012 in rural areas. The State Land Service ensured land assessment for redemption and registration of privatized apartments in the Register of Redemption.

Real Estate Market

In 2003, Latvia imposed restrictions on the acquisition of rural land and land in border areas for EU citizens and foreigners for a period of 11 years (until 2014) in terms of an amendment to the Law on Land Privatization in Rural Areas. Restrictions were not binding on EU citizens who have been engaged in agricultural production for three years or have permanently lived in Latvia. By 2014, foreigners already owned about 25 percent of the land of Latvia.[1] In 2022, 50 percent of the largest owners of agrarian land (more than 1,000 hectares) were Latvian citizens. Scandinavian legal entities own a large number of rural properties (in some Kurzeme municipalities, up to 50 percent of forestland).

In 2011, amendments to the Immigration Law of 2002 permitted foreigners to purchase housing but with a price restriction (initially €100,000 in Riga and €50,000 in the countryside, later €250,000 throughout the country) against the issuance of a residence permit—at first for five years but with the option to extend. In 2019, these amendments were suspended until July 2023, because of their negative impact on middle-class residential property supply and housing prices.

Most transactions have occurred with apartments:

- 17,000 transactions in 2012 and 21,000 in 2021; and
- 20,000 transactions in the Riga region and 5,000–7,000 in other regions yearly.

From 2017 to 2022, 5,882 new housing units were sold in Latvia (Cenu Banka, n.d.). In 2020–2021 (during the COVID-19 pandemic), residential property prices increased between 5 percent and 10 percent in response to an increased desire for more space, privacy, and general well-being. In 2021, the prices of apartments of the modernism period increased by 6 percent, highlighting the problem of a shortage of affordable new housing given that about 82 percent of the population live in apartments of the modernism period. In 2022, the average asking price of new apartments was €2,300 per square meter in Riga and Pieriga, although the increase in energy prices and Euribor rates temporarily reduced demand for new housing. The prices of energy-inefficient apartments of the modernism period in Riga dropped by 3 percent. There was a trend to sell larger or redundant homes to avoid high utility bills in coming winter (Latio 2022).

Information on residential rental prices is inconclusive. Census data show that a significant number of citizens (up to 43 percent in the center of Riga and 14–28 percent in the large-scale neighborhoods) live in rented housing units. Just as there are no tenements available, mostly private owners with excess housing units participate in the market (Central Statistical Bureau 2021).

Central-Government Taxes on Real Estate

By comparison with the OECD's average tax levels in 2020, Latvia's tax structure shows a heavier reliance on social security taxes (31 percent for

Latvia versus the OECD average of 26 percent), value-added tax (28 percent versus 20 percent), and other taxes on goods and services (17 percent versus 13 percent). Taxes below the OECD's average are those on personal income and profits or gains (21 percent for Latvia versus the OECD average of 23 percent), taxes on corporate income and gains (1 percent versus 10 percent), and RET (3 percent versus 6 percent). Embedded within each of these are revenues raised from taxes levied on the ownership, use, and sales of real assets.

Property Transfer Taxes

The property transfer tax (in the form of a stamp duty) is a central-government tax paid by new owners before securing property or mortgage rights in the Land Registry. The Cabinet of Ministers' regulations "On the State Fee for the Consolidation of Property Rights and Mortgage Rights in the Land Registry" set the state fee amounts. In 2021, the fee rate for a natural person and legal person to secure ownership rights was reduced from 2 percent to 1.5 percent of the value (but cannot exceed a total of €50,000 for gifts and compulsory auctions).

Rates for certain types of transactions, certain types of properties, and certain types of individuals vary:

- 0.5 percent of the value for people up to the third degree of kinship.
- 3 percent (maximum €50,000) for the disposal of real estate on the basis of a donation.
- 0.5 percent (maximum €500) if the real estate value does not exceed €100,000 and 1.5 percent (maximum of €50,000) if the real estate value exceeds €100,000.

In 2021, the fee for the registration of apartment property for legal entities was reduced from 6 percent to 2 percent of the real estate value. The mortgage registration fee is 0.1 percent of the loan amount.

The amount of transfer tax imposed is based on the highest registered value of the real estate—either the cadastral value or the transaction value. Transaction values are usually applied to calculate the state fee for securing properties sold in the primary market (new constructions), as the cadastral value of newly built properties still lags transaction values owing to flaws in the valuation methodology. In 2021, €55.3 million was collected from real estate registration, including payments by individuals of €25 million (Berzīte and Grumolte-Lerhe 2022).

The securing of property rights is a mandatory requirement under the Land Registry Law and the Law of Immovable Property Tax. Some

Table 15.1 Calculating Capital Gains Tax for Transactions with Real Estate

Real Estate Transaction Type	**Capital Gains Tax Calculation / Taxable Amount**
Sale	Difference between the selling and purchase price, including investments (repair, maintenance, improvement, etc.) made to the real estate
Exchange	Value difference between the purchase values of the acquired and exchanged property
Buildings under construction and existing buildings	The consumer price index is applicable for taxable income calculation
Donations	The sum (less than the cadastral value specified in the agreement)
	The cadastral value in the year of gift, if the agreement does not specify the value: • for properties acquired after December 31, 2000; • dividing cadastral value by the consumer price index for the last 10 years for properties acquired before December 31, 2000

Source: State Revenue Service (2024).

owners (both consciously and unconsciously) do not fulfill this obligation, because the legislation does not specify the conditions for securing property rights. However, failure to secure property rights does not exempt owners from the obligation to pay the recurrent RET. All revenues collected from stamp duty accrue to the central government.

Capital Gains: Income Tax

Latvian residents are liable for PIT and capital gains tax on their worldwide income.[2] Nonresidents are liable for PIT on their Latvian-source income.[3] The obligation to pay capital gains tax on dividends and other income from the capital (e.g., gains on stocks, shares, and property sales) is stipulated by the law on PIT. Capital gains due to real estate sales or exchange and gifts attract a fixed PIT rate of 20 percent (table 15.1).[4]

Capital gains tax is not levied on a sale or exchange of real property owned for 60 months that serves as the person's declared residence for

24 months, or in the case of the purchase of new real estate. It is an individual's duty to declare quarterly income from the capital gains to the State Revenue Service on its electronic declaration system. The capital gains tax must be credited into the state budget immediately for amounts of less than €1,000 and quarterly for amounts that exceed €1,000.

Individuals are liable to pay a PIT of 10 percent on rental income.

Other Central-Government Taxes and Fees on Real Property

In Latvia, there is either a separate inheritance tax or a wealth tax applied on real estate acquisitions. A value-added tax of 21 percent is levied on the sale of unused real estate (new construction) and improved (construction) land.[5] Corporate income tax is levied on a company's real estate rental revenue profit (20 percent, as a company income tax) and differences in value when selling shares of the company as real estate (15 percent). A building permit fee may be set at a rate of up to 2 percent of the estimate of value and may vary across municipalities. It is applied for electronically in the Building Information System and is valid for eight years.

Local service fees are applicable for the maintenance of buildings and their associated territory and infrastructure (seasonal cleaning, landscaping, utilities, etc.). The national service price regulator must approve utility (heating, water, and sewerage) tariffs before they come into effect.

Municipal Finances and Taxes on Real Estate

The RET, state and office fees for transactions with real estate, and inheritance, gift, and capital gains tax are equivalent in amount to 1.02 percent of GDP (RET represents 0.75 percent and other charges represent 0.27 percent). Municipal fees, other than RET and utilities charges, make up less than 1 percent of municipal tax revenues.

The government envisages the implementation of medium-term tax system reform in 2025, increasing total collections by an estimated 30 percent. The tax burden will be shifted from labor to capital gains and consumption taxes (excise tax, RET, etc.). Municipalities will be required to search for new sources of income because the share of PIT in municipal budgets already has been reduced by 5 percent and the decline in the working-age population can be seen throughout the country, except in the Riga region, which dominates income tax collections (figure 15.3).

There is a proposal under consideration to redistribute the corporate income tax between the national and municipal budgets to motivate municipalities to attract more companies. Municipalities have begun to audit

Figure 15.3 PIT Taxpayers by Employees' Declared Place of Residence in Planning Regions (thousands of people)

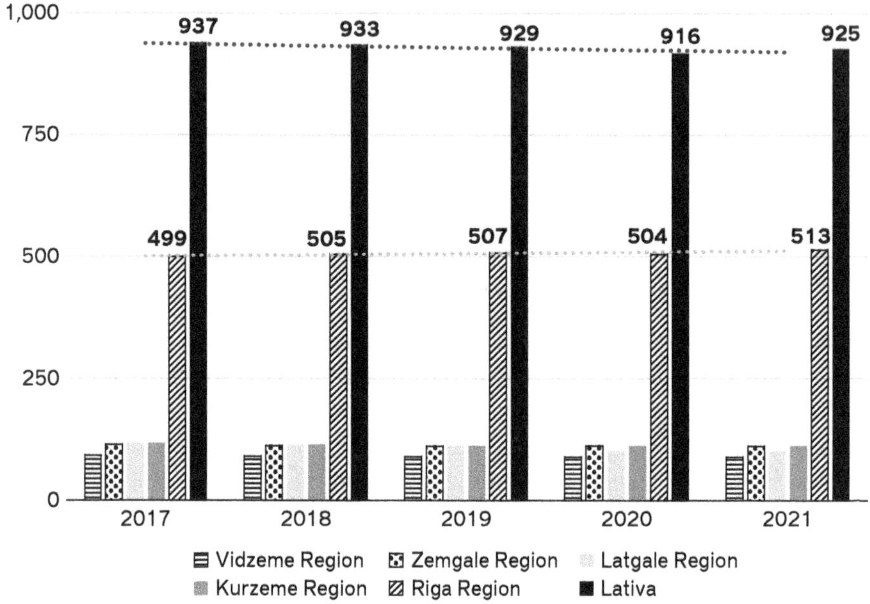

Sources: State Regional Development Agency of the Republic of Latvia. 2023; State Revenue Service.

their housing stock to prioritize offers of well-equipped institutional housing to attract education and medical workers, which could bring in new taxpayers.

The Ministry of Finance plans to introduce taxpayer single tax accounts in order to achieve more integrated tax administration and to allow better assessment of tax burdens on individuals and households. This kind of enhancement to the tax administration might improve taxpayer morale. Since the COVID-19 pandemic and the energy crisis, however, all tax reforms have been stalled.

The legal basis of RET is the Law on Immovable Property Tax, which was passed in 1997. The law initially provided direction on both RET (the taxable objects and subjects, rates, payment schedules, tax relief, and responsible authority) and cadastral valuation (basis, method, information to be used, and responsible authority). In 2006, with the adoption of the National Real Estate Cadastre Law, all cadastral valuation issues were separated from the general RET legislation. The tax basis for RET is the assessed (cadastral) value.

Table 15.2 Institutional Partners Involved in the Implementation of the RET

Authority	Role	Duties
Cabinet of Ministers	The highest executive authority of the country	Approval of: • RET and cadastral valuation regulation • cadastral value base
Ministry of Finance	Tax policy Budgeting	Legislation initiative General principles of taxation and budgeting
Ministry of Justice	Real estate policy Real estate registers Development of cadastral valuation	Legislative and advisory initiatives: • real estate policy • property data registration (Cadastre IS and Land Registry) • cadastral valuation Submission the cadastral value base to the Cabinet of Ministers
State Land Service	Executive body Cadastre IS Address Register	Maintenance of the Cadastre IS Building cadastral surveying Cadastral valuation (cadastral value basis, methodology, and assessment)
Municipalities	Local executive body RET revenues	Local land use planning RET administration Land use purpose determination Registration of illegal or decommissioned buildings

Sources: Barvika (2020); Saeima (2005).

RET Implementation and Administration

Five main authorities are involved in the implementation of the RET: the Cabinet of Ministers, Ministry of Finance, Ministry of Justice, State Land Service, and municipalities, as is evident from table 15.2.

RET Base

The RET is imposed on "tangible things" that are entered into the Cadastre IS. These include land, buildings, noncommissioned buildings, and engineering structures.

The RET is not applied to

- real property of municipalities;
- real property of foreign governments that is used for diplomatic or consular offices;
- graveyards or properties of religious organizations that are not used for economic activities;
- natural preservation areas, where economic activity is forbidden by law;
- state-protected cultural monuments;
- land under public waters, roads, streets, and railroads tracks;
- land under young forest stands;
- state and municipal engineering structures;
- engineering structures that are not used for economic activity;
- national sports facilities;
- buildings or engineering structures used for agricultural production;
- prisons or facilities of national armed forces, police, border guards, or fire and rescue services;
- national security institutions;
- state-financed buildings used for education or health, social care facilities, museums, libraries, and so on; or
- buildings used for environmental protection purposes.

RET Taxpayers and Tax Rates

RET taxpayers are natural and legal entities, including nonresidents. This includes owners or persons with possession rights,[6] and possessors or users of the state or municipal real property. Tax rates vary from 0.2 percent to 3 percent of cadastral value (land, buildings, groups of premises, and engineering structures) as assessed by the State Land Service. Since 2012, the Law on Immovable Property Tax has given municipalities a limited power in their jurisdiction for setting the tax rate for specific taxable objects (uncultivated land, subsidiary buildings of residential estates). Municipalities may also grant relief (up to 90 percent for disabled persons [since 1998] and families with three or more children under the age of 24 [since 2011]).

Municipal governments are empowered to register and tax noncommissioned buildings (since 2016) and tax noncommissioned buildings with expired building permits at a rate of 3 percent (since 2023). The evolution of the RET base and rates is tracked in table 15.3. Until the global financial crisis of 2009, RET policy was focused on increasing the role of municipalities in setting local tax policy.

From 2008, the increase of current land tax could not exceed 25 percent compared with the previous tax year. This rule was abolished in 2010 due to the recession in the real estate market. In 2009, the International Monetary Fund recommended expansion of the RET base (to include new taxable objects), setting tax minimums for the poor and introducing improvements to the cadastral system. Therefore, in 2010, the Ministry of Finance, Ministry of Economics, and Ministry of Justice developed a new midterm taxation strategy that included a reform of the base and rate structure. It also introduced strategies for cadastral assessment and for capturing additional data on construction activities.

In 2010, tax rate reforms were introduced:

- The RET rate increased to 1.5 percent for land.
- A rate of 3 percent was applied for uncultivated EU-subsidized rural land.
- A rate of 1.5 percent was applied to engineering, commercial, and industrial structures.

In 2011, owners for first time paid “housing tax” with rates of 0.1 percent to 0.3 percent depending on the cadastral value. In 2012, effective housing tax rates were doubled.

In 2013, a rate of 1.5 percent of the land’s cadastral value was applied to unoccupied multistory residential buildings of legal entities. Since 2014, municipalities, based on analysis of the social, economic, and spatial developmental problems, began imposing maximum tax rates on empty dwellings and taxing auxiliary buildings.

The RET reforms were adopted first by coastal municipalities with many horticultural communities. The media and society criticized municipalities for tax enforcement on residents (mostly low-income pensioners) with dilapidated building stocks. Since 2020, all municipalities have implemented “residence reliefs” (at the municipality’s discretion) alongside other statutory reliefs—for example, for large families, disabled people, and the poor. Income level and social status are no longer considered when setting the rate on a person’s other occupied or vacant residential properties.

In 2018, municipalities were granted the right to register in the Cadastre IS without the owner’s consent and then tax noncommissioned

Table 15.3 The Dynamics of RET Rates Since 1998

Year	Rate	Taxable Objects	Tax Base	Notes
Until 2007	1.5%	Commercial buildings/ premises	Book value Inventory value	This was the first building taxation object with the application of balance sheets for book value calculation
From 2007	1.5%	Nonresidential buildings/ premises, except agricultural production buildings	Current cadastral value	Increase of building taxation base
Until 2008	1.5%	Land	Current cadastral value	
2008	1%	Land	Current cadastral value	Land tax rate was reduced by 0.5%
From 2010	1.5%	Land	Current cadastral value	Land tax rate was increased to 1.5%
From 2011	1.5%	Engineering structures	Current cadastral value	Increased the tax base

2012	0.1%–0.3%	Residential buildings/premises and associated auxiliary buildings/spaces (garages, parking, cellars, terraces, storages, etc.)	Current cadastral value Rates: • 0.1% up to €56,915 • 0.2% for amounts between €56,915 and €106,715 • 0.3% for amounts above €106,715	Increased the tax base Auxiliary buildings became taxable at the discretion of the municipalities
From 2012	0.2%–0.6%	Residential buildings/premises, auxiliary buildings/premises (garages, parking, cellars, terraces, storages, etc.)	Current cadastral value Rates: • 0.2% up to €56,915 • 0.4% for amounts between €56,915 and €106,715 • 0.6% for amounts above €106,715	Building tax rates were doubled
From 2014	3%	Uncultivated EU-subsidized rural land, slums	Current land cadastral value	Applied on improperly maintained land and buildings
From 2023	3%	Noncommissioned buildings with expiring building permit	Current land cadastral value	Applied at the discretion of the municipality

Sources: Barvika 2020; State Revenue Service 2024.

and illegally occupied buildings based on external survey. Long-term noncommissioned buildings were to be taxable by the Construction Law at the discretion of municipalities beginning in 2023. But this norm was abolished in 2022 due to the State Land Service's lack of capacity to complete the massive number of building cadastral survey requests within the stipulated time. In 2014, the Construction Law set a deadline of October 1, 2022, for putting in operation long-term noncommissioned buildings (with expired building permits). There are about 20,000 noncommissioned buildings with expired building permits, of which 6,000 are situated in Riga.

According to their bylaws, municipalities must declare the effective RET rates and list of taxable objects for the next taxation year by November 1 of the pretaxation year.

RET Management

Property tax administration (tax calculation, notices, database, appeals, and collection and debts) is a responsibility of the 43 municipalities. Each municipality maintains a local taxpayer register and requires all owners to register. RET must be calculated separately for land and buildings, applying current statutory tax rates and local tax rates, as well as statutory and municipal tax reliefs applicable to a person's status.

The RET amounts are calculated based on the current cadastral value of the RET objects (land, building, group of premises, or engineering structures). In order to calculate RET, municipalities must identify in various information systems

- address of the RET payer;
- address of the taxable object or real estate;
- taxable object or real estate registry;
- cadastral value of the taxable object or real estate; and
- applicable reliefs.

Municipalities use the Land Registry to identify property rights and the owners, Cadastre IS to identify the physical parameters and current cadastral value of the property, the Population Register to identify persons and addresses, and the Rural Support Service for information on uncultivated agricultural land. The granting of RET reliefs to low-income taxpayers is done by applying the criteria in the Cabinet of Ministers' regulations, including the person's age and social status category, monthly income, other properties owned, and other assets.

RET Notifications

The taxation period of real estate is a calendar year, commencing on January 1. By February 15 of the relevant year, the local tax authority must notify the taxpayer (by mail or electronically) of the amount of RET for the current taxation year by sending a payment notice. The tax notice contains the following information:

- Name, surname, personal identification number, and contact information.
- RET amounts (land and buildings separately).
- Payment schedule.
- Notification of delayed payments (if any).
- Account number.
- Contact information of tax authority or official.
- Claims regarding cadastral value.

In 2021, there were 740,000 RET payers in the 43 municipalities; about 590,000 (80 percent) were taxpayers who owned one real estate parcel (mostly privatized apartments of the modernism period in urban areas).

RET Payments

The RET becomes payable in the next calendar month after the acquisition of ownership, possession, or right of use of real property, or leasehold for state or municipal property. The RET must be paid into the municipal budget either quarterly (in four equal installments) or annually as an advance payment. In the last few years, municipalities have allowed monthly RET payment upon agreement with the taxpayer. The minimum RET, payable in one installment, is €7. It is payable even in cases where taxpayers are eligible for tax relief.

From the COVID-19 pandemic until 2023, municipalities withheld from charging fines (0.01 percent for each day of delay) for late RET payments, except in the case of enforced debts. RET payment e-service is available by authorization with internet banking (Smart ID application) or e-signature on the national e-service portal Latvija.lv or the websites of municipalities. The State Treasury's municipal RET account information is included in most banks' list of automatic payments, providing also a link to the RET notice.

RET Appeals

The amount specified in the RET payment notice can be contested only to the relevant local tax authority. The contested error can be a calculation (mathematical) error in the land and building tax, an error in the ownership data, or outdated cadastral data applied for cadastral value calculation. The municipality must correct mathematical and RET payers' (owners') data errors. However, if the issue is an assessment or cadastral value error, or the result of outdated land and building data, the request must be addressed to the State Land Service. All requests to update land use must be addressed to the relevant municipality and can only be submitted in the Cadastre IS after the municipality makes its decision.

RET recalculation is carried out only after the cadastral data has been updated and the cadastral value recalculated. Taxpayers very often appeal the RET to the State Land Service, expecting to reduce the cadastral value or base values used for the calculation of cadastral values. The number of appeals in the State Land Service is small, but the consideration of these appeals is a labor-intensive task for its cadastral specialists. Neither the cadastral value base, nor the RET rate, nor the obligation to pay RET can be appealed.[7]

Collection

The collection rate of the RET is almost 100 percent. RET payment discipline did not deteriorate during the COVID-19 pandemic. RET debtors are not listed separately but are included in the total debt recovery statistics.

RET Burden

Some taxpayers (typically the owners of expensive residential properties) argue that the RET should be abolished due to its insignificant impact on municipal finances. In 2019, before the Administrative Territorial Reform of 2021, in about 50 percent of 119 municipalities, the RET collections contributed more than 7 percent of their overall budgets. The range was from 2 percent in Daugavpils to 18 percent in Carnikava (State Regional Development Agency of the Republic of Latvia n.d.).[8]

Comparing the spatial distribution of the RET burden over a 10-year period, it can be seen that the RET income has gradually increased in all 119 municipalities, constantly maintaining the highest values in the territory of the Riga metropolitan area (Barvika 2020).

Figure 15.4 Proportions of RET Total Revenues (land, buildings, and engineering structures) and Household RET Revenues (2017–2021)

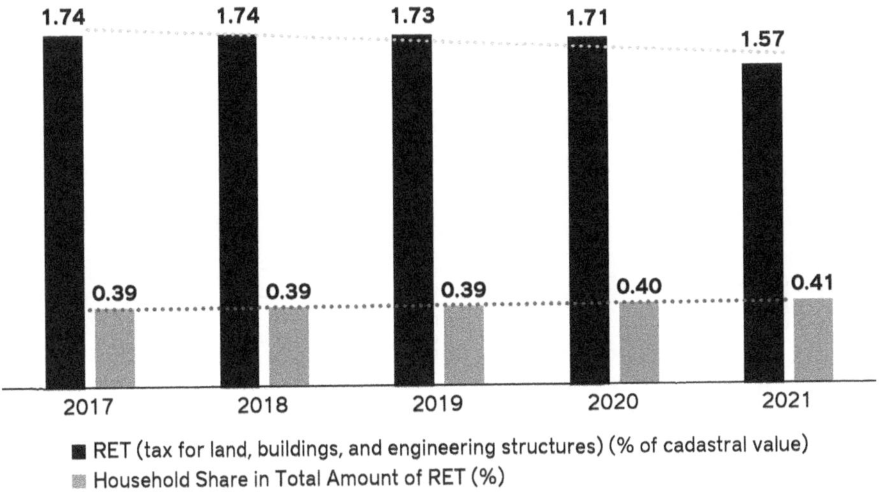

The RET is less than 2 percent of total taxes collected, with a decreasing trend. The household contribution is 0.41 percent, with a slight tendency to increase, whereas the payments of other RET payers are reducing (figure 15.4).

RET Payments and Debt Recovery

RET payments must be made to the budget of the municipality. This may be done electronically, via internet bank installments, or in the Riga Neighborhood Residents Center, at the Latvia Post, or in Maxima supermarket.

The forced RET collection mechanism under the Law on Immovable Property Tax regulations starts from €15 and consists of three steps: reminder, warning (twice a year), and thereafter bailiff enforcement. The maximum term for debt recovery is seven years, unless other circumstances occur (insolvency, liquidation processes, changes in the register of heirs). After seven years, debts in amounts less than €15 are paid off as a priority. RET debt fines were not applicable in 2021 and 2022 to limit the financial impact of COVID-19 (table 15.4).

The collected RET and the respective cadastral value totals are shown in figure 15.5.

The largest RET revenue growth (€17.1 million) has come from the taxation of land and the rate increase from 1.5 percent to 3 percent.

Table 15.4 RET Statistics by Subject of Tax and Impact on GDP (%), 2017–2021

Parameter	2017	2018	2019	2020	2021
Land tax (€ billion)	122.00	118.00	119.00	117.00	118.00
Land tax (% of GDP)	0.48	0.41	0.39	0.40	0.36
Building tax, including engineering structures (€ billion)	106.00	105.00	107.00	105.00	108.00
RET (land, buildings, engineering structures) (€ billion)	228.00	223.00	226.00	222.00	226.00
RET (land, buildings, engineering structures) (% of GDP)	0.90	0.77	0.74	0.76	0.69
Land cadastral value (€ billion)	10,070.00	9,823.00	9,792.00	9,798.00	9,803.00
Building and engineering structure cadastral value (€ billion)	20,300.00	20,457.00	20,716.00	22,639.00	22,836.00
Cadastral value (land, buildings, engineering structures) (€ billion)	30,370.00	30,280.00	30,508.00	32,437.00	32,639.00
Land tax (% of land cadastral value)	1.22	1.20	1.22	1.19	1.10
Building tax, including engineering structures (% of building and engineering structures cadastral value)	0.52	0.54	0.52	0.52	0.47
RET (land, buildings, engineering structures) (% of cadastral value)	1.74	1.74	1.73	1.71	1.57
Households' share in total amount of RET (%)	0.39	0.39	0.39	0.40	0.41

Source: Ministry of Finance (2021).

Figure 15.5 Proportions of RET Revenues and Assessed Cadastral Value Totals (land, buildings, and engineering structures) (2017–2021, € million)

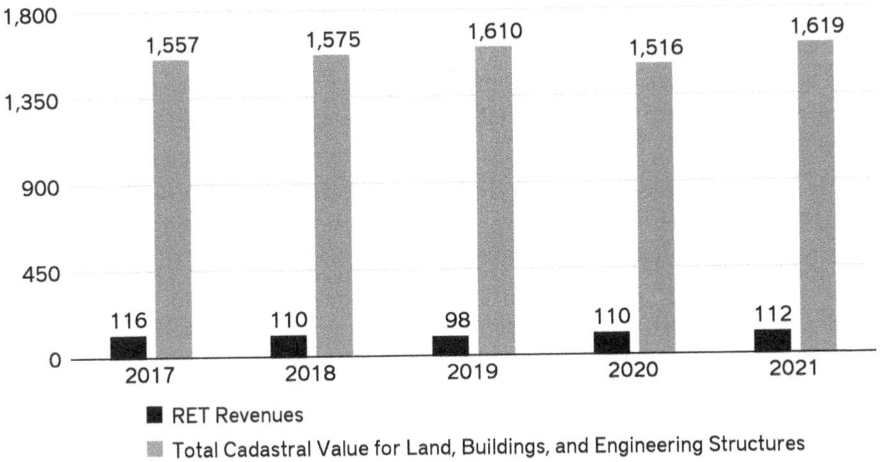

Sources: Berzīte and Grumolte-Lerhe (2022); State Land Service (n.d.).

Cadastral Valuation

The purpose of cadastral valuation[9] is to determine the value of cadastral objects (i.e., land and buildings) in a manner that is consistent with the relevant laws and regulations.

Cadastral valuation is the responsibility of the public sector—that is, under the State Land Service. Commercial properties and industrial properties are valued in the same manner (methodology, models, legislation, and cadastral data) as all other properties within their groups. The cadastral value is determined separately for land and buildings, applying the mass assessment approach—the respective base values and valuation models for land and buildings.

In the determination of the base values of engineering structures, the State Land Service uses the statistical average construction costs of industrial objects, multiplying them by a factor of 0.3 (set in regulation). Commercial and industrial properties are taxed within rates ranging from 0.02 percent to 3 percent.

The assessed cadastral value forms the base for RET (with rates ranging from 0.02 percent to 3 percent), state duties (from 0.5 percent to 2 percent), urban land rent (6 percent), municipal and agricultural land rent (0.5 percent to 4.5 percent), and capital gains tax (20 percent).

The cadastral valuation is prepared in accordance with the National Real Estate Cadastre Law (from 2006), which covers cadastral data updates, cadastral valuation, and the obligation of real estate owners to provide data reflecting changes to property; and the Cabinet of Ministers' "Regulations Regarding Mass Appraisal" (Cabinet of Ministers 2020), which provides the cadastral valuation and land and building valuation models.

The cadastral value should be based on property market value estimated by using the mass valuation approach. Since 2012, the national property valuation standard of Latvia has been consistent with the International Valuation Standards of the International Valuation Standards Council (LVS 2013). In the development of the cadastral valuation methodology, alongside the national and international property valuation standards, the recommendations of international organizations for the mass valuation of real estate must be followed (Saeima 2005). The valuation sequencing, quality control, and accuracy of the assessment thus must comply with the requirements of the International Association of Assessing Officers (IAAO) Technical Standards and IAAO Standard on Mass Appraisal of Real Property (2017).

Responsible Authority

Cadastral valuation is the responsibility of the State Land Service (since 1992). The Real Estate Valuation Department (with some 30 valuers, analysts, and GIS specialists) carry out the cadastral valuation for the entire country. The main responsibilities of this department are

- the development of a cadastral value base;
- Real Estate Market Data Base maintenance;
- market data analysis;
- uniform cadastral valuation methodology; and
- uniform methodical supervision of regional zoning development specialists.

Staff within the Real Estate Valuation Department hold various academic qualifications, including higher education in real estate valuation, engineering, statistics, environmental science, and GIS. There is no requirement for staff to have a market appraiser's certification. Many of the Real Estate Valuation Department specialists obtained their qualifications from partner institutions in Scandinavia, Lithuania, Estonia, and the United States. The cadastral valuation process in Latvia is managed by several specialists who have been working on the cadastral valuation system since the beginning in 1997.

Cadastral valuation activities and results are regularly discussed by the Valuation Board, whose members are from the State Land Service, the Ministry of Justice, Latvia's Association of Property Appraisers, Latvia's Real Estate Transaction Association, the Ministry of Finance, and the Ministry of Economics.

Classification of Taxable Objects

Specific classifications are used for the grouping of the objects by their use types and for classifying land uses and building types (under the Cabinet of Ministers' "Classification of Real Estate Use Types" [2006] and the Cabinet of Ministers' "Classification of Types of Construction" [2018]).

Valuation objects are classified as residential, industrial, commercial, public, and rural properties. Other aspects are considered during the classification process, including

- physical and economic factors;
- the data to be collected; and
- the valuation approach used in the assessment.

Land use determination is a responsibility of municipalities, whereas the determination of building type is a responsibility of the State Land Service.

The minimum number of transactions in a group for analysis is 20 transactions no older than two years. About 1,200 different datasets (at least 20 data points in each data set) were analyzed for the projected value base of 2020. Uniformity of values is homogeneity (objectivity) of value levels in assessments of all property groups and within each data group (type of use, territory, etc.). The average value ratio in the country with the projected cadastral value base in 2020 is 0.97 (corresponds to the situation in the real estate market). These indicators were published with the cadastral value base in 2020. The main problem concerning cadastral and market values is the mismatch between cadastral and transaction data, criteria, and information on the relevant property. Therefore, the calculated cadastral value may not coincide with the sales value of the property. This problem is solved by analyzing the level of values and the uniformity (correspondence) of values within and between data groups.

Objects of Valuation

Land for construction purposes comprises the following groups: land for single residential houses, land for multistory residential buildings, land for construction of commercial buildings, and land for industrial buildings.

There are three groups of rural (agricultural) land: agricultural (arable) land, forestland, and land under water.

There are 67 types of buildings within nine groups.

Value Basis

The process of cadastral valuation consists of the development of separate cadastral value bases for land and buildings and the calculation of cadastral values. The value basis consists of

- value zonings—homogeneous zone maps for each real estate group;
- base values, coefficients of standard area, and correction coefficients for construction (development) land;
- base values of rural land—seven agricultural and four forestland quality groups;
- base values, standard sizes, and coefficients of corrections for buildings; and
- base values for engineering structures.

The development process of the cadastral value base relies on information collection, analysis, proposal, review, and approval, which takes approximately one year. The Cabinet of Ministers must approve the valuation base, which will be in force until June 15 of the pretaxation year. The approved cadastral value base is used for RET forecasting for the next tax year[10] and becomes effective on January 1 of the next year. The cadastral value calculation automatically is added to the Cadastre IS within 48 hours before the effective date.

Market Data Collection

Since 1998, the State Land Service has been maintaining the Real Estate Market Data Base, which has information on some 600,000 properties for the entire country. Some 70 percent to 80 percent of data are automatically stored, while the remainder are manually processed. Automatic data downloads from the Land Registry take place on a daily basis. The Real Estate Market Data Base has built-in statistical analysis software, including online analytical processing, IBM SPSS Statistics, and the statistical software R. The data are an integral part of the Cadastre IS (figure 15.6).

Agricultural land leases are used for the verification of rural land values.

The State Land Service classifies about 40 percent of all the Land Registry raw market data as invalid for assessment purposes. The main data problem is the reliability of transaction prices. Collusion between

Figure 15.6 Real Estate Market Data Integration Between Cadastre IS and Land Registry

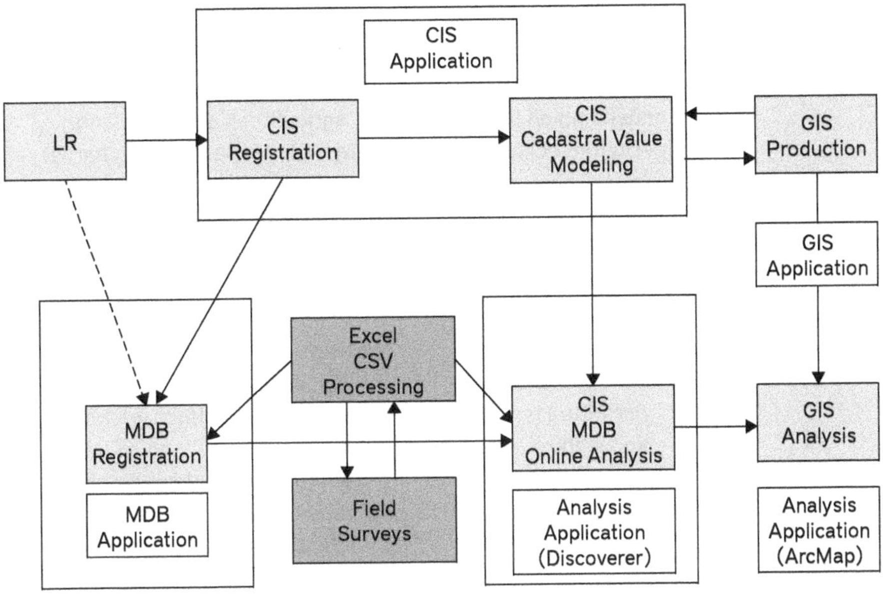

Source: Elkins (2016).

Note: CIS = Cadastre IS; CSV = comma separated values (text file); LR = Land Registry; MDB = Real Estate Market Data Base.

the parties would seem to indicate a reduced price in contracts with undeclared cash payments.

Since 2021, the State Land Service has published raw market data and data analysis (including price levels, accurate data, and value maps) on Kadastrs.lv in order to strengthen the public's trust and confidence in the cadastral valuation system. Most users obtain transaction data free from the Land Registry and the State Land Service (only selective market data analysis), as well as from the portal of the Cenu Banka (which includes asking prices, listing information, and transaction data of all property types integrated with additional features such as textual data, images, cartographic layers, and other analytical tools).

Valuation Models

The valuation models are established separately for land and buildings.[11] Value zones, indexes of cadastral value bases, and base values are accessible on the State Land Service website. In addition, valuation reports are accessible on the website of the State Land Service.

Table 15.5 Main Factors Influencing the Value of Built-Up and Rural Land

Factor	Built-Up Land Model	Rural Land Model
Land use/type	Purpose of land use, depending on the permitted building type	Land use types: • agricultural land (plowland, meadows, pastures, orchards) • forestland • land under buildings/yards • land under fishponds • other land (bushes, marshes, land under waters and roads)
Area	Plot size: • standard plot for permitted building type • above the standard area	Areas of land use types: • agricultural land (plowland, meadows, pastures, orchards) • forestland • land under buildings/yards • land under fishponds • other land (bushes, marshes, land under waters and roads)
Encumbrances	Types and occupied areas	Types and occupied areas
Land quality		Quality (point) groups: • seven for agricultural land • four for forestland
Building impact		Influencing factor of residential building (standard of 1,000 m^2 of residential land, if applicable)

Source: Cabinet of Ministers (2020).

Land Valuation Models

Land valuation principles have been set since 1998. Calculation formulas (pricing models) are defined for buildings and rural (agricultural and forest) land.[12] The main value-influencing factors used in the calculation of land cadastral value are shown in table 15.5.

Standard land areas are set for

- built-up land based on market data analysis to precisely evaluate plots of different sizes of the same use; and
- rural land, depending on the agricultural and forestland quality groups.

The land base values, the standard areas, and the correction coefficients of standard areas must be approved in the valuation regulations. The principles of land value reduction regarding the impact of encumbrances are also set in general valuation rules.

Building Valuation Models

Building cadastral assessment was implemented in 2002. Up until 2012, the calculated values were applied only to tax commercial buildings. Initially a simplified model was introduced. In 2012, the cadastral valuation of buildings was divided into three groups: residential buildings, multifunctional buildings, and other nonresidential buildings. The main value-influencing parameters used for the calculation of cadastral values of buildings and engineering structures are shown in table 15.6.

The base value of detached houses reflects that of a well-equipped building. Cadastral value indicators of residential buildings (building type base values, standard capacity, and adjustment correction coefficients) must be approved in the regulation. Capacity-related criteria can be applied to overcapacity of nonresidential buildings based on analysis of location and current and normative service length. The common correction coefficients applied to the cadastral values are shown in table 15.7.

Cadastral value adjustments are not applicable to buildings that have not been surveyed by the cadastre—the registration was carried out based on mass inventory or a municipal tax collection campaign for noncommissioned buildings.

All correction factors (areas, status, binary data, construction year, registration year, encumbrances, etc.) must be entered in the Cadastre IS before assessment. Factors influencing the value (base land values, standard area, standard area correction factors) must be approved in the valuation regulations.

Implementation Overview

From 1992 to 1998, normative values were used in the cadastral assessment to support the implementation of the Land Reform. The uniform cadastral valuation procedures were implemented with adoption of the Law on Immovable Property Tax (1997).

The implementation of the mass assessment approach began with the assessment of urban land (from 1998 to 2001), then the mass assessment of buildings (in 2002), the assessment of the capital Riga (from 2001 to 2003), the assessment of rural land (from 2000 to 2003), and the assessment of engineering structures (from 2010).

Table 15.6 Main Factors Influencing the Value of Buildings and Engineering Structures

Building Model	Value Correction Factors	Correction Adjustment Factors/Reduction of Cadastral Value
One/two apartment houses	• Location/value zone • Type (stone, wood, summer houses) • Indoor/outdoor space, storage, basement, garage area • Amenities (electricity, sewerage) • Physical condition (foundations, walls, floors, roof)	For areas: • outdoor–0.3 • basement–0.3 • storage–0.3 • garage/storage inside building–0.6 Amenities: • no electricity–0.6 • has electricity, no sewer–0.8
Multifunctional buildings (apartment/office/commercial buildings with residential space)	• Location/value zone • Outdoor/indoor space • Residential and commercial area (office, retail and wholesale, hotel) premises • Residential storage, garages or other premises in the basement floor • Location of residential premises (ground, basement, other level) • Amenities of residential premises (sewerage, sanitary network) • Exterior material (wood, masonry) • Physical condition (foundations, walls, floors, roof)	For areas: • outdoor–0.3 • utility space group–0.3 • space of wooden apartment building–0.8 Amenities of living space: • No sewer, has sanitary network–0.8 • No sewer or sanitary network–0.6 Location of living space: • ground floor–0.9 • basement–0.6
Other nonresidential buildings	• Location/value zone • Building type • Total building capacity • Indoor/outdoor space • Physical condition (walls, foundation, facade, roof)	Outdoor area of building–0.3
Engineering structures (model for nonresidential building)	The capacity of physical condition	Applicable in scale from 1.0 to 0.3 A limit of physical condition–70%

Source: Cabinet of Ministers (2020).

Table 15.7 Common Correction Coefficients for Land and Building Cadastral Values

Adjustment Type	Adjustment Volume
Building physical condition (foundations, walls, floors, roof)	Applicable in scale from 1.0 to 0.1 to: • new construction–1.0 • building with depreciation greater than 80%–0.0
Cultural heritage building	Until 2007: • 45% of cadastral value for national cultural monuments • 35% of cadastral value for local cultural monuments In 2017–canceled From 2018: • 30% of cadastral value applies to all cultural heritage buildings
National cultural monument territory Baltic Sea protection zone (land)	20% of cadastral value
Protected zones Engineering communication land (%)	Maximum cadastral value adjustments: • 45% for encumbered urban plot area • 30% for completely encumbered rural land

Source: Cabinet of Ministers (2020).

The development of the land value base began with the technical assistance of the National Land Board of Finland and the Estonian Land Board. All projects (77 urban and 552 rural) were publicly discussed with municipalities. In 2007, base values of building types were determined by applying value zones. Zones were developed throughout the country cyclically every four years to ensure uniform assessment levels. The base values were updated every second year for rural (separately for agricultural and forestland), residential, industrial, commercial, and public building groups. From 2010, base value updates have taken place yearly in response to rapid property market fluctuations.

This challenge led the responsible authorities to revise the RET and cadastral valuation systems (a new strategy for cadastral valuation and building data collection) to introduce a sustainable fiscal capacity base (generating more revenues) for municipalities. In 2012, the most significant improvements in the model were implemented for the acquisition of value-influencing data for new buildings, including the construction year and amenities (electricity, sewerage, basements, garages, sheds, patios, balconies, terraces, parking lots, depreciation, building floor, etc.). The industrial object zoning was applied for the assessment of engineering structures.

In 2013, the annual zoning and updating of base values came into force.[13] In 2016, due to the effect of the housing tax capture policy across the country and increases in the cadastral value base, the cadastral assessment process received public criticism and was the subject of political discussion. Some 60,500 votes were collected on the public participation portal Mana Balss calling for the "immediate cancellation of a recurrent tax on owners' sole residential property" and citing it "as unconstitutional and a violation of human rights."[14] The cadastral value base was frozen from 2016 to 2020, giving time for the responsible authorities to redevelop the tax regime for residential property.

New Cadastral Assessment Methodology

In 2020, the State Land Service formulated a new cadastral value base methodology to be applied in 2021 (State Land Service 2020) (table 15.8).

The new cadastral value base project had been developed according to the situation in the real estate market as of July 1, 2019. The projected cadastral value increase, compared with 2016, was 79 percent for land and 112 percent for buildings (table 15.9).

Comparing the projected value base with the value base of 2016,

- projected cadastral values correspond to the situation in the real estate market as of July 1, 2019 (median ratio in range of 0.03–0.08); and
- compliance has been significantly improved (ratio in the range of 0.3–0.63) (figure 15.7).

The Real Estate Market Data Base has accumulated some 50,000 transactions during the period 2017–2019. Land values have increased the most in rural areas (126 percent), while building values have increased mainly in the cities (118 percent) (figure 15.8).

Cadastral value totals for the major real estate groups are shown in figure 15.9.

Projected maximum and minimum base values for the main property groups are shown in table 15.10.

The most important increases are shown in table 15.11.

The multiapartment building group comprises some 41,400 buildings (11,000 with wooden exterior walls, 27,900 low-rise, and 2,500 high-rise).

Table 15.8 Methodological Improvements in the Cadastral Assessment Base (2020)

Implemented Change	Methodical Description of the Implemented Change
Compliance with the real estate market value	Statistical assessment of cadastral value and transaction price ratio: • cadastral value and the real estate market situation compliance in 85 percent for all property groups, except 100 percent for agriculture and industrial land • the time period of market data to be used (2016–2019)
Zoning/value zones	All zones: • two-year valuation cycle • single zoning for residential, commercial, and industrial properties Agricultural zoning: • several zones for a municipality
Value base	Cyclical update Agricultural land: • application of timber, development, and reforestation price statistics Buildings: • grouping and subgrouping based on similar value-influencing factors
Encumbrances	Land cadastral value reduction: • 45% for encumbered rural plot area • applied to encumbrances affecting the value of a built-up plot Building cadastral value reduction for local and national monuments: • by 35% if depreciation is less than 35%
Land valuation	Multiapartment land: • application of building rights for setting standard areas Urban forestland: • criterion "logging ban" for land uses "forestry" and "ecological base area" • value corrections in case of reduction of ball-hectares
Building valuation	All buildings/premises: • age/depreciation groups • indoor/outdoor areas (except covered stages) Detached, multifunctional, and nonresidential buildings: • criterion "heating" Multifunctional buildings: • "underground floor" for nonresidential premises • residential premise model for unclassified premises

Source: Cabinet of Ministers (2020).

Table 15.9 Projected Cadastral Value Changes in National Cities, Municipalities in 2020

Territory	Land: Effective 2016 (€ million)	Land: Projected 2020 (€ million)	Land: Changes (%)	Buildings: Effective 2016 (€ million)	Buildings: Projected 2020 (€ million)	Buildings: Changes (%)
National cities	5,206	7,147	38	14,173	30,923	118
Municipalities	4,583	10,360	126	5,532	10,927	97
Latvia	**9,789**	**17,508**	**79**	**19,705**	**41,850**	**112**

Source: State Land Service.

Figure 15.7 Average Compliance of Forecasted Cadastral Values for Major Real Estate Groups as of July 1, 2019 (average cadastral value and median cadastral value, €, 2020)

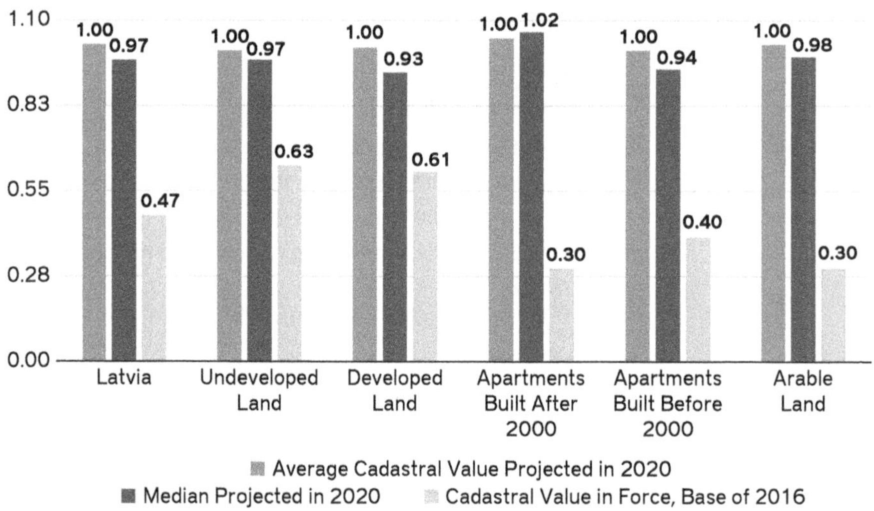

Source: State Land Service (n.d.).

The average land area of

- developed land parcels is 1,500 square meters in cities and 2,700 square meters in rural areas; and
- undeveloped land is 4,000 square meters in cities and 3,000 square meters in rural areas.

Figure 15.8 Changes in the Cadastral Value of Land and Buildings (effective 2016 versus projected 2020, € billion)

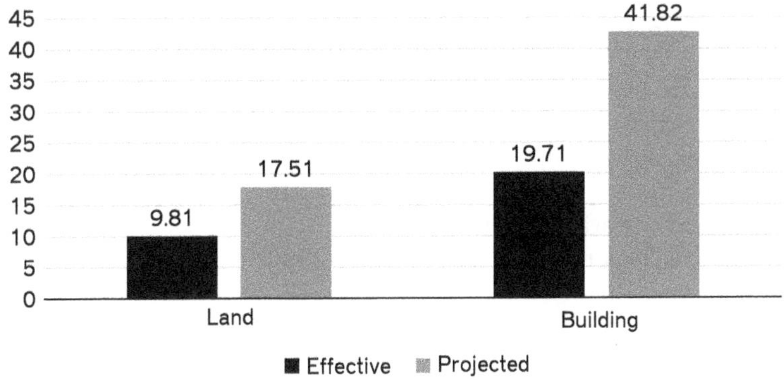

Source: State Land Service (n.d.).

Figure 15.9 Comparison of Current and Projected Land and Building Cadastral Value Totals for Main Real Estate Groups (€ million)

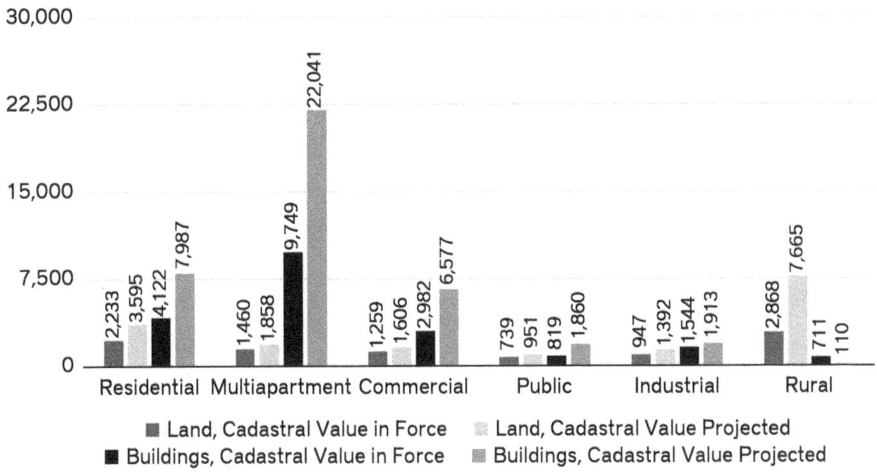

Sources: State Land Service (n.d.).

Twelve percent of the building stock was built in the 21st century, 62 percent between 1940 and 1991, and some 26 percent before 1940. Dwellings built between 1991 and 2000 account for only 4.7% of the current stock due to the extreme economic transition during that period. Newly built apartments represent 42,000 units (some 5 percent) of all building

Table 15.10 Projected Maximum and Minimum Base Values

Property Group/Parameter	Minimum Base Value (€/m²)	Maximum Base Value (€/m²)
Agricultural land, ha²	115	9,000
Residential/multiapartment land, m²	0.5	1,000
Commercial/public land, m²	0.5	1,000
Industrial land, m²	0.5	1,000
Detached houses/apartments, m²	45	1,700
Commercial buildings, m²	35	1,700
Industrial buildings, m²	12	1,000

Source: State Land Service.

Table 15.11 Projected Cadastral Value Increase by Property Group in 2020 (% of cadastral value)

Property Group/Type	Increase of Cadastral Value (%)
Rural land	167
Commercial land	28
Apartments	On average 230
Apartments in the Riga metropolitan area and national cities, built before 2000	200
Apartments built after 2000	30
New detached houses	On average 260
Industrial objects	Maximum 35
Commercial and public buildings	125

Source: State Land Service.

stock. Out of a total of 74,000 apartments, 32,000 (44 percent) are located in Riga. The cadastral value increased for 93 percent of the 15,000 commercial buildings throughout the country; in Riga and nearby municipalities, the increase was 60 percent. The cadastral value of large industrial facilities in remote rural areas corresponds to the agricultural land values. The most significant cadastral value reduction was for multiapartment land (38,500 land units, 91 percent—for low-rise buildings), observed in national cities: Rezekne (19 percent), Jekabpils (17 percent), and Jelgava (12 percent).

About 40 percent of the 325,000 detached houses (garden houses, single residential houses, and semidetached houses) have seen a cadastral value decrease due to the implementation of the assessment of construction

Table 15.12 The Most Significant Projected Increases in Total Cadastral Values in 2020 (% of cadastral values of 2016)

Property Group/Type	Estimated Increase in % of Cadastral Value
Multiapartment land	10
Multiapartment land (standard areas)	Up to 19
Detached houses built before 2000 and auxiliary buildings of residential properties	40
Unimproved apartments in urban and rural outskirts	Insignificant reduction

Source: State Land Service.

period (age group) factor. Auxiliary building stock consists of 830,000 units, whose value is less than 2 percent of the total value. The most significant increases are shown in table 15.12.

During the public review of the new cadastral value base proposal, no consensus was reached among stakeholders—namely, the Ministry of Finance, the Ministry of Justice, Saeima, the Valuation Board, real estate firms, municipalities, and property owners. The implementation of the new value base was postponed until 2025—until the Ministry of Finance decides on a new RET policy regarding tax rates and housing tax. The package of regulatory documents (the cadastral value base and the cabinet regulations draft for the value base for 2022–2025) has been submitted to the cabinet. About the cadastral value base project (2022–2025), 1,303 objections were received: 1,078 regarding cadastral values and RET, 86 regarding methodology and data, 51 regarding the forced lease, and 88 regarding the cadastral value base. Accordingly, 1,068 claims were received in the most populated and expensive region of Greater Riga, 49 in Kurzeme, 29 in Vidzeme, 24 in Zemgale, and 19 in Latgale.

The cadastral value calculation model improvements have already been implemented in the cadastral assessment. Assessed values continue to grow.

Issues Related to Ratio Statistics

The assessment ratio (i.e., cadastral value to market value) is a very sensitive topic. The cadastral valuation uses two IAAO standards as a recommendation alongside the existing regulation: the IAAO Standard on Ratio Studies and IAAO Standard on Mass Appraisal of Real Property. Ratio studies (assessed values to market values) are one of the most important steps of cadastral valuation. The ratio of the cadastral value base is determined by dividing the transaction price by the estimated cadastral value of the relevant cadastral object.

The following information regarding applied parameters is mentioned in the Mass Valuation Report of 2020 (State Land Service, n.d.):

- The limits of the central tendency measure of the ratio between the cadastral value and the price of a real estate purchase transaction are 0.9–1.1.
- Statistical "cross-checks" shall be performed for all data groups (whole state, all municipalities, all land use purposes, and groups of buildings within value zones).
- The level of statistical significance (time correction used in the market data analysis) is $\alpha = 0.05$.
- The minimum number of transactions in the group (dataset) for analysis is 20 transactions no older than 2.5 years.

According to IAAO standard recommendations, the following indicators are calculated:

- Data dispersion indicators for determining the unity of values:
  - Coefficient of dispersion (COD)—calculated based on the median.
  - Coefficient of variation—calculates the standard deviation by dividing by the ratio averages (percentage).
- Median—the lower and upper limits of the median confidence interval.
- Average values—lower and upper limits of the confidence interval of the average value.
- Weighted average value—ratio of the sum of the assessed values and the sum of the market values.
- Average absolute deviation—used to determine the dispersion coefficient.
- COD—characterizes the dispersion of the dataset.
- Regressivity index (price-related differential)—the level of evaluation of cheap and expensive properties.

The following are the evaluation quality indicators in the mass valuation report:

- The median is between 0.9 and 1.1 or the confidence interval includes the number 1.0.
- The mean is between 0.9 and 1.1, or the confidence interval includes the number 1.0.
- COD—at least 40 percent to 30 percent (the lower the COD, the lower the dispersion).
- Coefficient of variation—not less than 40 percent.
- Price-related differential—preferably precisely within the range of 0.97 to 1.3.

The main problem of the discrepancy of cadastral values and market values is the quality of property data in the Cadastre IS, which are used in the cadastral valuation. The calculated cadastral value may not coincide with the market value of the relevant property due to differently applied data, knowledge, or physical evidence about the property. This valuation problem is solved by analyzing both the level of values and the uniformity (correspondence) of values within and between property groups.

In mid-2024, the Latvian parliament Saeima, after long political debate, adopted several amendments to the cadastral legislation on mass assessment (Saeima 2005). The cadastral value base must correspond to, but not exceed, 80 percent of the average real estate transaction price level over a period of two and a half years. From January 1, 2025, until the application of the newly developed cadastral value base, the Cadastral IS will calculate and register two cadastral values for each cadastral object: the fiscal cadastral value for calculating the RET, state fees, and other budget payments (based on the cadastral value base applied for the assessment of 2024); and the universal cadastral value (calculation based on the latest valid value base). The State Land Service must publish maps of the current cadastral values (cadastral value of one square meter of each land, building, and immovable property) and real estate market data analysis applied in the value base assessment.

Issue of Undervaluation

The issue of undervalued property is a persistent problem in Latvia's cadastral valuation. This particular problem was studied in detail in a study commissioned by the State Land Service in 2013/2014. It was found very clearly that the ratio (cadastral value against market value) did not correspond to the IAAO standard requirements. The most significant ratio problems have been identified for new constructions due to outdated or insufficient cadastral data. It is also a fact that the only (most common) method used in developing the value base (base values and zoning maps) is the sales compression method. The study indicated that for some types of property (e.g., commercial properties and production facilities), the income approach would be more appropriate in determining the value base. This discrete topic did not appear publicly until 2020, when it was mentioned for the first time in the cadastral valuation report of that year.

Construction costs are used to determine the base values of engineering structures (currently only 13 percent of all engineering structures are registered in the Cadastre IS). The cadastral value of engineering structures is found by multiplying the average building costs of production facilities by a factor of 0.3. Engineering structures are essentially not a market object; however, civil engineering objects can be included in some transactions. All correction coefficients must be confirmed in the valuation rules; they may change yearly.

The main problems related to cadastral valuations are discussed in the following sections.

The Problem of Cadastral Data Sufficiency

The average "age" of cadastral data is 15 years. Planned improvements to verify and correct data have not been introduced (e.g., implementation of the owner's declaration to collect building data). Data quality is considered the main problem, and additional state financing would be required to resolve it.

A funding model is lacking for the acquisition of data needed for valuation given that data acquisition and updating are paid services. In the Cadastre IS, land data are registered from surveying cases, while building data are obtained by a cadastral survey of buildings performed by the State Land Service. Land and building surveying are mandatory processes (also relatively expensive and time consuming) without which land and buildings cannot be registered in the Cadastre IS and a building cannot be put into operation. If the owner wants to update building data (e.g., to reduce the depreciation of the building), this must be paid for. This is a real problem that has affected building mass valuation accuracy. It is a financial issue because, for example, cadastral surveying of buildings is a significant source of income of the State Land Service.

The main problems causing the mismatch of building values are related to the following omissions affecting data quality:

Depreciation of buildings

Until the introduction of methodology changes in 2020, no system had been implemented to update the building's depreciation without necessitating a data update through the expensive cadastral surveying service. With the introduction of age groups of buildings (the new methodology of 2020), this problem hopefully will be eliminated or reduced.

Year of construction

The construction year was not entered in the Cadastre IS for all buildings (especially for new constructions) because of the poor integrity of the institutional (state or municipality) operation. It has since been resolved. However, because of this improvement, the cadastral values (also RET) of the new buildings will increase sharply.

Amenities, facilities, and other value correction factors (e.g., Location of space in the building, utilities, and auxiliary spaces)

These factors are not entered in the Cadastre IS for all building objects. They are missing mostly for building objects (multifunctional or residential buildings) registered in a mass inspection project undertaken some 22 years ago, and new buildings registered by municipalities in order to capture RET income.

Land information problems

The majority of land parcels were surveyed some 25 years ago. Many of the plans of land boundaries no longer reflect the real land cover and value. In the real market, individuals sell and buy what they see in reality, which is not recorded in old documents. There is no requirement to update land parcel plans if the owner has changed. Instrumental surveying is only required for new constructions.

Funding for Updating Data

Special budgets for mass valuation data collection and updating have not been allocated in any timely way. In 2021, the state for the first time granted to the State Land Service a budget for the opening up of cadastral data; therefore, a significant amount of cadastral information has become publicly available. However, considerable raw data that have been published require detailed checking.

National Cities

About 80 percent of the Latvian population (1.53 million) live in national cities and towns. Although the urban population continues to increase, the depopulation trend that is now underway is affecting both urban and rural areas (figure 15.10).

Riga accounts for 48.7 percent of national RET revenues and 39.6 percent of total cadastral value. Most of the rest of the RET revenue is collected by national cities. In 2017–2021, the budgets of national cities grew

Figure 15.10 Population Dynamics in the Capital City Riga and in Eight National Towns (2017–2021)

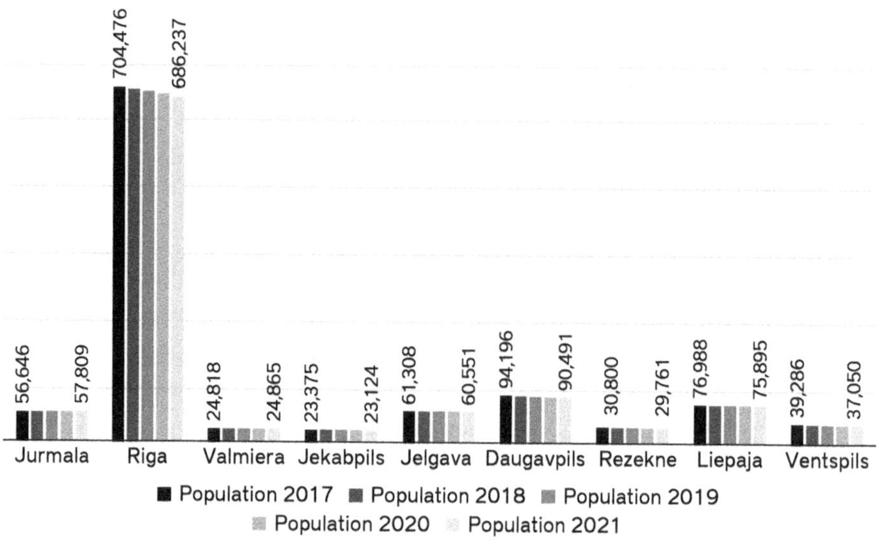

Sources: Central Statistical Bureau; State Regional Development Agency of the Republic of Latvia (2023).

faster (30 percent) than the national average RET revenues (17 percent). Expenditures of cities increased by 20 percent, maintaining a small deficit (2–3 percent of total revenues). Capital (infrastructure) expenditure grew faster than RET revenues (35 percent and 17 percent, respectively). Municipal revenue and spending statistics are shown in figure 15.11.

National cities' RET income shows an unstable trend, which can be explained by the initiatives to grant new RET reliefs for the declared residents and for vulnerable populations (the poor, disabled, families with children, etc.). RET collection trends in cities are shown in figure 15.12.

The total cadastral values of the national cities (1 percent of the territory) are 60 percent. In 2018–2021, cadastral value totals declined an average of 9 percent in Latvia and 5 percent in cities, affected mainly by a decrease in building cadastral value totals due to implementation of the new methodology.

Capital City of Riga

Riga (founded in 1201) is the national capital (population 601 million, area 303 square kilometers in 2024). It is both a cultural and a port city. Riga consists of six administrative districts and 58 "vicinities." Almost

Figure 15.11 Dynamics of Municipal Total Revenues and RET Revenues; Total and Capital Expenditures (2017–2021)

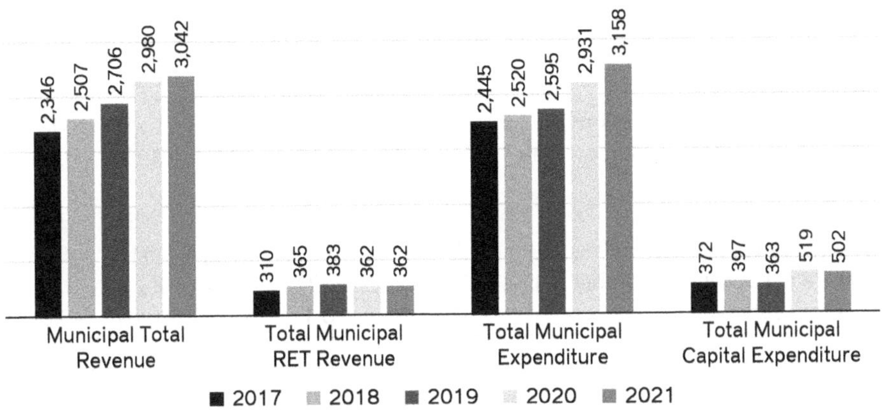

Sources: Central Statistical Bureau (n.d.-a); State Regional Development Agency of the Republic of Latvia (n.d).

Figure 15.12 RET Income Dynamics in National Cities (2017–2021, € million)

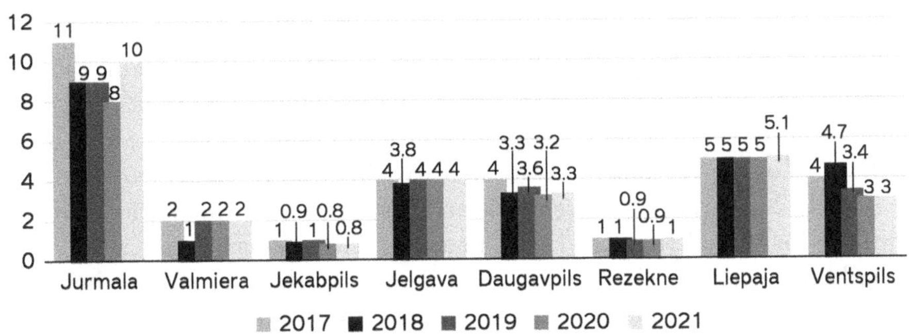

Sources: Central Statistical Bureau (n.d.-a); State Regional Development Agency of the Republic of Latvia (n.d.)

5 percent of the territory is a UNESCO heritage site—the Historical Center of Riga and its protection zone.

Almost 1.1 million (63 percent) of Latvia's population live and work in the Riga metropolitan area, and they produce 70 percent of Latvia's GDP. About 46 percent of Latvia's workforce (of 480,000) work in Riga, although only about 35 percent (about 170,000) actually reside in the

Table 15.13 General Statistics, Riga (2017–2021)

Indicator	2017	2018	2019	2020	2021
Area, capital city (km^2)	304	304	303	303	303
Population (million)	0.64	0.63	0.63	0.62	0.61
Density in Riga (people/km^2)	2,107	2,097	2,082	2,043	2,021
Population in Riga suburban area (Pieriga) (thousands)	0.36	0.37	0.37	0.37	0.38
Unemployment rate (%)	3.1	3.2	3.3	3.3	3.4
Working-age population (%)	62	62	61	61	61
Average household (number of people)	2.21	2.21	2.19	2.21	2.21
Net migration (%)	1.09	−0.17	−0.25	−0.07	−0.07

Sources: Central Statistical Bureau (n.d.-b); Reģionālā attīstības indikatoru modulis (2025).

municipality. Net migration to the region is relatively low. Riga is experiencing a significant population decline and development challenges—almost 22 percent of the national population is now concentrated in former agricultural suburbs of Riga. General statistics are shown in table 15.13.

Apartments of the modern period are a main dwelling type (0.32 million units, or 44 percent of the total number of apartments in Latvia). Dissatisfaction with the quality of urban space and housing is the main reason many leave Riga for the suburbs (Pieriga), where former residents of Riga declare residence and pay taxes, though they work in Riga. It is estimated that half of the daytime population of Riga are Pieriga residents.

Only 25 percent of households can afford to rent or qualify for a loan to purchase well-furnished new housing. The average depreciation of buildings is about 45–50 percent (26 percent of these were built before 1940). About 1,500 units have reached slum status (depreciation greater than 80 percent) (Rīgas valstspilsētas pašvaldības, n.d.). A significant amount of housing is not permanently inhabited (17 percent in Riga, 20.6 percent in the Historical Center of Riga) or is rented out (up to 15–40 percent in residential areas) (Central Statistical Bureau 2016).

Economic Indicators

Riga is the sixth-richest municipality in Latvia.[15] On average, 58 percent of the country's GDP is attributable to Riga. Unemployment has been stable and under 4 percent. Municipal revenues include tax revenues (PIT, RET, gambling tax, etc.) and state budget transfers. The economic indicators of the city of Riga are shown in table 15.14. The tax revenues

Table 15.14 Capital City of Riga, Macroeconomic Indicators (2017–2021)

Indicator	2017	2018	2019	2020	2021
GDP (€ billion)	14.5	16.1	16.84	16.0	n.a.
Total budget revenues (€ million)	684	691	972	931	940
Total budget tax revenues (€ million)	667	691	707	598	671
State budget transfers (€ million)	266	178	205	170	149
State budget transfers (% of total budget revenues)	39	26	21	18	16
Total revenue per capita (€ thousands)	1,286	1,319	1,154	1,150	1,049
Tax revenue per capita (€/year)	970	985	952	950	950
PIT payers (individuals)	0.33	0.34	0.34	0.33	0.32
PIT revenues (€ million)	562	575	582	598	559
PIT revenues per capita (€/year)	797	820	840	842	839
RET revenues (€ million)	116	110	98	110	112
RET per capita (€)	165	157	175	177	179
RET per 1 km^2 (€ million)	0.38	0.36	0.43	0.36	0.36
RET of all tax revenues (%)	17	16	14	18	17
RET (% of cadastral value)	7.45	6.98	6.09	7.26	6.92
MFEF (€ million)	53	57	59	42	97

Sources: Central Statistical Bureau (n.d.-a); Ministry of Finance; Valsts reģionālās attīstības aģentūra (2025); Riga City Portal.

Note: n.a. = not available.

(PIT, RET totals, RET per capita) have not changed significantly in recent years. There has been a significant reduction in state transfers (EU and state investments). In 2021, despite a reduction in the PIT share of 5 percent, municipal payments to the MFEF increased by 111 percent.

Over five years, RET revenues have fluctuated around 14–18 percent of total tax collections (see table 15.14). Riga accounts for 45 percent of the total cadastral value of cities, which is less than its population or income share. The share of collected RET in the total cadastral value (a rough measure of the effective rate) is about 7 percent and showing a downward trend. The number of cadastral objects remains stable, with a slight upward trend (table 15.15).

RET Administration in Riga

The Riga Municipality Revenue Department oversees RET administration (tax calculation, reliefs, debt management, handling of complaints, etc.). The state Cadastre IS, Land Register, Population Register, and

Table 15.15 Statistics of Cadastral Objects and Assessed Cadastral Value Totals for Riga (2017–2021)

	Land		Buildings		Engineering Structures	
Year	Number	Cadastral Value (€ million)	Number	Cadastral Value (€ million)	Number	Cadastral Value (€ million)
2021	51,807	3.91	104,863	11.02	2,908	1.36
2020	51,481	3.84	105,335	10.96	2,880	1.35
2019	50,987	3.83	106,042	10.91	2,908	1.36
2018	50,725	3.82	103,722	10.57	2,908	1.36
2017	50,725	3.82	104,349	10.46	2,769	1.29

Sources: Valsts reģionālās attīstības aģentūra (2025).

municipal IS (taxpayer register, building board, housing, land use administration, etc.) data are used for RET administration. The assessed current cadastral value is the only base used for calculating the amount of RET.

RET Rates and Relief

The RET rates, relief, and taxable objects are specified in the Law on Immovable Property Tax and in the binding regulations of the Riga municipality (Rīgas Dome 2015). The municipality applies standard tax rates for land (1.5 percent) and buildings (0.2–3.0 percent), as prescribed by the Law on Immovable Property Tax. As noted earlier, however, municipalities have some authority to provide additional relief to property taxpayers.

In Riga, the tax rates are adjusted for certain types of property as follows:

- Owner-occupied housing is assessed at 50 percent of the cadastral value of the building or apartment.
- Unoccupied dwellings are taxed at rates up to 1.5 percent of the cadastral value of the land.
- Auxiliary buildings associated with residential property are taxed at a rate depending on whether the dwelling is occupied or unoccupied.
- Slums (depreciation greater than 80 percent) are taxed at a rate of 3 percent of the cadastral value of the land.

More specific relief measures may be granted by the municipality, either automatically, if the system provides the justification for applying the relief, or by application. The reliefs granted are significant and include many that cover low-income people or specific types of properties.

Conclusion

In Latvia, the tax revenue share in GDP (31 percent) is low compared with the EU average (39 percent). Latvia's tax system relies more heavily on indirect taxation than on direct and local taxes. The RET is one of the strategically important instruments to support the fiscal capacity of municipalities. RET revenues have grown throughout the country in the last 10 years. However, the proportion of RET in state and municipal revenues has not changed significantly. All municipalities (except the Riga region) have suffered a long-term decline in their PIT income. Due to continuing population decline, many regional municipalities have little chance of increasing fiscal revenues in the medium term.

Within the framework of the Law on Immovable Property Tax and local regulations, municipalities have successfully implemented a socially responsible policy of RET. The RET burden on households remains low. The RET policy can be considered fair to owner-occupied housing and to the most vulnerable social groups. However, there is a risk that the RET burden is not fairly assessed, as many statutory reliefs are granted automatically.

In Latvia, about 80 percent of the population owns real estate (one of the largest percentages in Europe), and housing occupancy is relatively small (on average, two people live in a house). About 20 percent of the population owns several residential properties. Society has gradually come to realize that higher RET rates should be applied to abandoned or second homes.

Since 2016, some real estate owners and their social partners have been actively promoting a reduction in the weight placed on cadastral value in the RET calculation. Their argument is based on an evaluation of European practice in taxing primary residences, which they use to defend the opinion that the cadastral value's role in determining RET liability must be minimized. Therefore, RET should be considered a fixed (long-term expected) tax. Basically, the argument is against the value base of RET. On the other hand, improving the cadastral valuation models (methodology) would allow the tax base to be improved and made more fair with a cadastral value base that corresponded to market values. The freezing of the cadastral valuation base until 2025 has had the greatest impact on the total collections of RET because the cadastral value base of 2016 is still applicable. The weakest point of the cadastral assessment is the inconsistency between the assessed values and the actual condition of the real estate (e.g., age and amenities). On average, the data of buildings and rural lands used in the evaluation are 15–20 years old.

Inadequate data on building and land cover, along with weak updating procedures and costs, discourage owners' compliance in cadastral updating. However, new mass assessment and building data acquisition strategies have not been fully implemented. It is necessary to develop systematic and comprehensive building (external and internal) and land cover data acquisition practices to ensure the resilience of the cadastral valuation system. The immediate problem is the physical condition of multiapartment buildings, which, if taken into account, would lead to a significant decline in cadastral value and RET.

The country has a large number of private dwellings compared with the population. However, many of them are in poor physical condition, which has caused the housing shortage throughout the country. Construction of new housing occurs mainly in attractive low-density parishes and on the outskirts of Riga, contributing to sprawl, leapfrog development, commuting, marginalization, municipal capital expenditure, and an unbalanced population.

The real estate market in Latvia started to cool down in the housing sector, however, with a slight positive trend, following the European Central Bank's Euribor rate cut in 2024. The population viewed negatively the decision by municipalities to set various RET rates for an owner's occupied and unoccupied residential properties (e.g., second homes and gardening societies). Arguably the most negatively viewed was the RET policy of Riga (since 2016), where the land tax rate of 1.5 percent (building tax volume in certain cases up to seven times higher than before) was applied to unoccupied dwellings. This decision had only a short-term positive effect (the number of Riga's residents showed steady growth for only a few years), because all municipalities gradually implemented similar RET regulations.

It has been recognized that it is precisely the lack of integrity on the part of national and municipal databases (e.g., local fiscal, taxation, and income data) that slows down the planning of socially responsible policy in the field of taxation (e.g., the relation of RET and PIT to the total tax burden of a household). Implementing a fairer tax policy is recommended, in which all annual taxable income of individuals (households) would be evaluated in connection with the granting of statutory benefits for residence. The main challenges of operating the taxation system are the integrity, timeliness, and interoperability of national registry data.

The central government's tax and municipal tax administration processes are not mutually integrated. Municipal systems are still highly decentralized (fragmented) and are not properly analyzed in order to resolve the most critical local social-economic problems. RET calculations and amounts are not integrated into the Cadastre IS or other registers of national importance. Lists of taxable objects, taxpayers, and RET amounts are not publicly available.

The recent amendments to the cadastral legislation establishing two cadastral values (for taxes and fees and the value determined according to the new value base) rather indicate a political unwillingness to review the current RET policy.

The establishment of a single tax account for each taxpayer would help to achieve better tax administration and assess the common tax burden on individuals and households.

The main reason why taxpayers often oppose taxes is the public's low trust in government institutions and those institutions' inability to provide detailed review of the use of the tax revenue, including revenue from RET.

Notes

1. According to unofficial information at ManaBalss.lv, the website of a Latvian civic organization where citizens propose initiatives to submit to the Saeima. See Liana Hirschson, "Par nekustamā īpašuma nodokļa atcelšanu vienīgajam īpašumam" [in Latvian], March 16, 2016, https://manabalss.lv/par-nekustama-ipasuma-nodokla-atcelsanu-vienigajam-ipasumam/show?locale=lv.

2. Latvia has a progressive income tax system for earned annual income: a rate of 20 percent on income up to €20,004; a rate of 23 percent on income between €20,004 and €78,100; and a rate of 31 percent on income over €78,100.

3. People with dual citizenship are subject to international double taxation agreements.

4. PIT is imposed on income acquired by a natural person, including salary, economic activities, license fees, the parts of the micro-enterprise tax, seasonal work, and capital gain.

5. Article 52, Part 1, Clause 24 of the Value-Added Tax Law.

6. The legal possessor of immovable property shall be considered a person whose property rights to buildings or engineering structures have been restored in accordance with the procedures laid down in law and who has assumed them; or a person who has come into possession of immovable property on the basis of inheritance rights or on another basis.

7. The taxes are not the subject of referendums in accordance with Satversme.

8. Carnikava had a population of 8,738 in 2019.

9. The term used in Latvia is *mass valuation*.

10. The State Land Service performs an assessment forecast and publishes forecasted values in its data distribution portal (www.kadastrs.lv). Since 2016, valuations have been frozen and new information has not been published.

11. Value calculation models are approved by regulation of the Cabinet of Ministers and are incorporated into the Cadastre IS for automated cadastral valuation.

12. The rural land valuation model is applied to rural land units with the intended purpose of valuing "agricultural land"; "forest land and specially protected natural

areas, where economic activity is prohibited by laws and regulations"; and "land under water bodies." In other cases, building land valuation models are applied.

13. This means that zoning maps will be subject to changes annually.

14. The Law on Immovable Property Tax amendment proposal prepared by populist parties before the municipal elections of 2018 proposed to exempt from taxation one of the owner's properties in which they reside and have declared the address and the land under particular building up to 1,500 square meters (urban), and in farmsteads of up to two hectares.

15. Per capita incomes are 20 percent lower than in the richest city (Marupe municipality).

References

Barvika, S. 2020. "The Role of the Property Tax in Sustainable Land Management and Planning: The Latvian Experience." Lincoln Institute of Land Policy. (July 8). https://www.lincolninst.edu/app/uploads/2024/04/barvika_role_of_the_property_tax_in_sustainable_land_management_and_planning.pdf.

Barvika, S., and S. Treija. 2014. "The Requirements of European Union for the Development of Contemporary Spatial Planning System in Europe." In *Riga Technical University 55th International Scientific Conference*, Riga, Latvia, October 14, 2014, 100–101. Riga: Rīgas Tehniskā Universitāte.

Berzīte, I., and I. Grumolte-Lerhe. 2022. *Nekustamā īpašuma nodokļu sistēmas Baltijas valstīs un Ziemeļvalstīs*. Riga: Latvijas Republikas Saeima. https://www.saeima.lv/petijumi/Nekustama_ipasuma_nodoklu_sistemas_Baltijas_valstis_Ziemelvalstis.pdf.

Cabinet of Ministers. 2020. "Regulations Regarding Mass Appraisal, Regulation No. 103." Likumi: Legal Acts of the Republic of Latvia, February 18. https://likumi.lv/ta/en/en/id/312662-regulations-regarding-mass-appraisal.

CEIC. 2022. "European Union Tax Revenue: % of GDP." https://www.ceicdata.com/en/indicator/european-union/tax-revenue--of-gdp.

Central Statistical Bureau. 2016. "Results of the Population and Housing Census 2011 in Latvia." https://stat.gov.lv/en/statistics-themes/population/population/publications-and-infographics/1299-results-population-and.

———. 2021. "Population and Housing Census 2021." https://www.csp.gov.lv/en/population-and-housing-census-2021.

———. n.d.-a. "Gross Domestic Product and Value Added—Annual Data." Official Statistics Portal. Accessed May 15, 2024. https://stat.gov.lv/en/statistics-themes/economy/national-accounts.

———. n.d.-b. "Private Households and Families, Size of Family Nucleus in Regions, Cities and Municipalities at the Beginning of Year 2020–2025." Official Statistics Portal.

Cenu Banka. n.d. Home page. Accessed November 25, 2024. https://cenubanka.lv/.

Elkins, A. 2016. "Management of Real Property Valuation System in Latvia." State Land Service, Riga.

EU (European Union). 2007. "Directive 2007/2/EC of the European Parliament and of the Council of 14 March 2007 Establishing an Infrastructure for Spatial Information in the European Community (INSPIRE)." EUR-Lex. http://data.europa.eu/eli/dir/2007/2/oj.

IAAO (International Association of Assessing Officers). 2017. *Standard on Mass Appraisal of Real Property: A Criterion for Measuring Fairness, Quality, Equity and Accuracy.* Kansas City, MO: IAAO.

Latio. 2022. *Housing Market Report.* Riga: Latio, Riga. https://latio.lv/uploads/marketanalysis/Housing-market_2022_1.pdf.

LVS (Latvian Valuation Standards). 2013. "LVS 401:2013, The Latvian National Standardization Body." https://www.lvs.lv/lv/products/33614.

Ministry of Finance. 2021. Presentation to Latvijas Pašvaldību savienības finanšu komiteja Ziņojums [The Latvian Association of Local and Regional Governments] (virtual). Riga.

OECD (Organisation for Economic Co-operation and Development). 2020. *Policy Actions for Housing Affordability in Latvia.* https://issuu.com/oecd.publishing/docs/latvia_housing_report_web-1.

Rīgas Dome. 2015. "Par nekustamā īpašuma nodokli Rīgā, Rīgas domes saistošie noteikumi Nr. 148." Likumi: Legal Acts of the Republic of Latvia, June 15. https://likumi.lv/ta/id/275681-par-nekustama-ipasuma-nodokli-riga.

Rīgas valstspilsētas pašvaldības, Īpašuma departaments. n.d. "Vidi degradējošo objektu saraksts." Accessed November 24, 2025. https://grausti.riga.lv/objekti/.

Saeima. 2005. "Nekustamā īpašuma valsts kadastra likums." Likumi: Legal Acts of the Republic of Latvia, December 1. https://likumi.lv/ta/id/124247-nekustama-ipasuma-valsts-kadastra-likums.

———. 2020. "Law on Administrative Territories and Populated Areas." Likumi: Legal Acts of the Republic of Latvia, June 10. https://likumi.lv/ta/en/en/id/315654.

Sauka, A., and T. J. Putnins. 2022. "Shadow Economy Index for the Baltic Countries." Stockholm School of Economics Riga. https://www.sseriga.edu/shadow-economy-index-baltic-countries.

State Construction Control Bureau. 2023. "Administration of Building Information System." https://www.bvkb.gov.lv/en/administration-building-information-system.

State Land Service. 2020. "Kadastrālo vērtību bāzes izstrāde." Valsts zemes dienests. https://www.vzd.gov.lv/lv/KVB.

———. n.d. "Kopsavilkums par projektēto kadastrālo vērtību izmaiņām." Accessed May 15, 2024. https://www.vzd.gov.lv/lv/media/2557/download?attachment.

State Regional Development Agency of the Republic of Latvia. n.d. "Regional Development Indicator Module, Municipal Profile." Accessed June 12, 2023. https://raim.gov.lv/.

State Revenue Service. 2024. "Income Tax on Capital Gains." February 13, 2025. https://www.vid.gov.lv/en/income-tax-capital-gains?utm_source=https%3A%2F%2Fwww.google.com%2F.

Tiesu administrācija. "Mani dati Zemesgrāmatā." 2021. https://www.ta.gov.lv/lv/pakalpojumi/mani-dati-zemesgramata.

Valsts reģionālās attīstības aģentūra. 2025. *Reģionālās attīstības indikatoru modulis.* Riga: VRAA. raim.gov.lv.

Vides aizsardzības un reģionālās attīstības ministrija. 2023. "Teritorijas attīstības plānošanas informācijas sistēma." https://tapis.gov.lv/.

Vides un reģionālās attīstības ministrija. 2022. "Pieņemts jauns Pašvaldību likums, kas paredz lielāku sabiedrības iesaisti pašvaldību darbā." Balance plz. https://www.plz.lv/br-pienemts-jauns-pasvaldibu-likums-kas-paredz-lielaku-sabiedribas-iesaisti-pasvaldibu-darba/.

World Population Review. n.d. "Total Population by Country." Accessed 2022. https://worldpopulationreview.com/countries.

Legislation

Law on Administrative Territories and Populated Areas of 2020.

Law on Construction.

Law on Immigration of 2002.

Law on Immovable Property Tax of 1997.

Law on Land Management of 2015.

Law on Land Privatization in Rural Areas of 1992.

Law on Land Registration of 1993.

Law on Personal Income Tax of 1993.

Law on Spatial Planning Development of 2011.

National Real Estate Cadastre Law of 2006.

Value-Added Tax Law of 2011.

16

The Netherlands: A Mature Property Tax

RUUD KATHMANN, LUC HERMANS, AND MARCO KUIJPER

The Netherlands, located in the northwest of Europe, has an area of almost 42,000 square kilometers and 17.7 million (2024 estimate) inhabitants. With around 50 percent of the area being agricultural land, it is a densely populated country. The gross domestic product per capita was €49,100 in 2021.

Most tax is collected at the central level by means of income tax, profit tax, and value-added tax. The total revenue of taxes is €223 billion (excluding social funds for unemployment and benefits for elderly and sick people). A further breakdown of the total tax revenue can be found in table 16.1. Of these revenues, around €11 billion can be seen as property tax on the level of municipality, polder board (also known as "water board"), or central government.

The Netherlands is a kingdom, but more significant is that it is a parliamentary democracy. There are three levels of government (figure 16.1). Besides the central government, there are provinces at the intermediate level of government and local governments. The most important local governments are the municipalities. The 344 municipalities cover the entire area of the Netherlands and regulated in terms of the Municipalities Act of 1851. Furthermore, there are 21 polder boards (water boards) covering the total area as a functional local government responsible for water management (groundwater level, water level in rivers and other water bodies, quality of groundwater as well as open water, and cleaning of

Table 16.1 Total Tax Revenues in the Netherlands (€ billion; % of GDP)

	2018	2019	2020	2021	2022
Central government	€178 23.1%	€196 24.0%	€194 24.4%	€212 24.8%	€223 24.9%
Of which property tax (based on value, recurrent)	€5.4 0.69%	€5.5 0.68%	€5.3 0.66%	€5.3 0.62%	€4.7 0.52%
Of which transfer tax	€3.0 0.39%	€3.0 0.37%	€3.6 0.45%	€3.8 0.45%	€4.3 0.48%
Provinces	€1.7 0.21%	€1.7 0.21%	€1.7 0.22%	€1.7 0.20%	€1.8 0.20%
Of which property tax (based on value)	€0 0.0%	€0 0.0%	€0 0.0%	€0 0.0%	€0 0.0%
Municipalities	€6.0 0.78%	€6.3 0.77%	€6.4 0.81%	€6.8 0.79%	€6.4 0.71%
Of which property tax (based on value)	€4.0 0.51%	€4.1 0.50%	€4.3 0.54%	€4.6 0.53%	€4.8 0.53%
Other rates on property by municipalities	€3.3 0.43%	€3.5 0.42%	€3.7 0.42%	€3.9 0.46%	€4.0 0.44%
Polder boards	€2.8 0.36%	€2.9 0.36%	€3.0 0.38%	€3.1 0.37%	€3.2 0.36%
Of which property tax (based on value)	€0.73 0.09%	€0.73 0.09%	€0.77 0.10%	€0.80 0.09%	€0.85 0.09%
Of which property tax (based on land area)	€0.18 0.02%	€0.19 0.02%	€0.20 0.03%	€0.20 0.02%	€0.20 0.02%
Total revenues of recurrent property tax based on value	€10.0 1.3%	€10.3 1.3%	€10.4 1.3%	€10.7 1.3%	€10.4 1.2%

Source: Centraal Bureau voor de Statistiek (2023b).

wastewater from households and smaller businesses). The main reason the Netherlands has a special functional government for water management on a local level is that large parts of the country are below sea level. The polder boards date back to the Middle Ages but are becoming even more important because of sea level rise and extreme weather events. The members of the polder boards are (partly) elected by the inhabitants of the polder board's region through a direct voting system. These elections take place every four years. Polder boards are regulated by the Water Boards Act of 1991.

Figure 16.1 Three Governmental Levels Below the Central Government

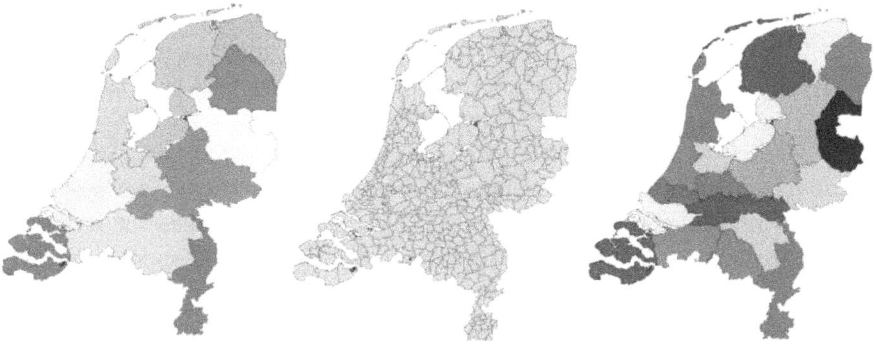

Provinces: 12 Municipalities: 344 Polder boards: 21

Source: Publieke Dienstverlening op de Kaart (n.d.).

Note: Shading denotes area of the government tier.

On the central level, the Netherlands has a parliament with 150 seats, called Tweede Kamer (second chamber), for which there are general elections at least every four years, but sooner when a cabinet dissolves. There are only minor requirements for a party to gain seats in Parliament. For instance, there is no threshold for entering other than getting enough votes. The number of votes needed is the total number of votes divided by 150 (number of seats in Parliament). Furthermore, the seats are assigned to the person instead of the party; therefore, over the course of time, breakaway parties and single-person factions can arise. The Senate in the Netherlands is called Eerste Kamer (first chamber) and has 75 seats. For the Senate, there are indirect elections every four years just after the elections for the provinces, because members of the boards of the provinces (Provinciale Staten) elect the members of the Senate.

Because there has never been a party in Parliament with an absolute majority, the Netherlands is used to having a coalition of parties within the cabinet, usually with a combined majority in Parliament, although this is not a necessity. The prime minister is head of government and head of the cabinet. The king has nearly no formal role in government anymore, though formally he is head of state. Legislation on the (property) tax system is decided on the central level.

For provinces, municipalities, and polder boards, there are general elections every four years.

Every level of government is free to set the rates of the taxes they levy, but the tax must fit within the legal framework set in central legislation. Municipalities are free to set the rates for the municipal property tax, but the tax must be based on the annually assessed value of the property, and the only difference in rate can be between residential and nonresidential property. Provinces, municipalities, and polder boards can also decide not to levy a certain tax. For instance, some municipalities choose not to levy property tax for the users of nonresidential property, and they only levy the tax for the owners of nonresidential property.

All levels of government are free in setting their budget and are therefore free in spending the revenues of the taxes. Only the revenues of the specific rates of the municipalities must be spent on the relevant activity. That is, the revenues of the rate for waste collection must be spent on waste collection and waste handling; the revenues from the rates on sewage systems must be spent on maintaining the system of sewage pipes, and so on.

Moreover, there is a system of leveling the potential revenues of property tax between municipalities. This leveling is done by granting a lower amount from central-government funds to a municipality that has a high total value of real estate and therefore a larger base for the property tax. These grants from the central government are particularly important for municipalities, because the grants form nearly 90 percent of their budget.

Land and Property Markets

The Netherlands has an open market for real estate for both ownership transactions and rental transactions. Any person or company can own property in the Netherlands, with no restrictions for people living abroad or companies without an agency within the country. However, rules apply for rental transactions for residential property to protect the renters of residential property—for instance, against instantaneous one-sided ending of the rental contract or against large increases in rental price.

A result of this open real estate market is that transaction prices (sales) can be seen as a good indicator of market value. The market value of the property is determined mostly by location and the allowed use of the property according to physical planning (Bervoets et al. 2024). The board of the municipality decides on the physical plans (*omgevingsplan* or *bestemmingsplan*).

Real estate in the Netherlands is considered the combination of land and buildings. In general, the owner of the land is also the owner of the buildings on the land. Even the owner of an apartment is not considered solely the owner of the part of the building that he uses but also the co-owner of the parts of the building that are for general use (for instance, the elevators) and the co-owner of the land on which the complex is built.

Residential property in the Netherlands is around 60 percent owner occupied; the other 40 percent is renter occupied. Most of the rental houses (nearly 30 percent of all residential property) can be seen as social housing and are owned by social housing institutions. Special rules are in place for social housing—for instance, to determine the maximum rent price. These social housing institutions are private organizations but subsidized by government. The other 10 percent of residential property is rented out on the free market and can be seen as the upper part (in price) of the rental market. A property is considered to be social housing if the base rent is below €808.06 (as of 2023).

The owner-occupied residential property market consists of both single-family and multifamily properties. The market for residential apartments is a sizable proportion of the residential real estate market. Investing in the ownership of apartments is considered a stable investment because of the formal registration of real estate in the cadastral registry of the Netherlands. All land in the Netherlands and all apartment rights are registered in the central cadastral registry. For each part of the Netherlands, an owner can be found in this registry.

The cadastral registry in the Netherlands is based on the registration of deeds. The ownership of a parcel of land or an apartment right must be derived from the last deed (for instance, sale) of that parcel of land or apartment right. The legal transfer of real estate takes place the moment the notary deed is registered by the cadastral registry. Therefore, there is always a complete registry of all formal transfers of real estate.

The cadastral registry is open to everyone, though a small service fee must be paid in order to receive information. This means that anybody can get up-to-date information on the ownership of land parcels and apartment rights. The cadastral registry is owned and maintained by a central-government organization (the Netherlands' Cadastre, Land Registry and Mapping Agency, known as Kadaster). This organization has no role in updating tax rolls but makes the information on land parcels, apartment rights, and transactions available for the tax-collecting authorities by means of the Base Register Cadastre (Bervoets et al. 2024).

However, the cadastral registry is important for the property tax in multiple ways. It is the primary source of information on sales prices to be used for mass appraisal and assessment of real estate for property tax.

In this way, the information on sales prices is made complete (in nearly all notary deeds, the price sold is stated) and available for tax-collecting governments as well as for the taxpayer. However, both must pay the cadastral organization to obtain the data.

The sales prices in the cadastral registry in the Netherlands are considered reliable in the sense that there is (nearly) no underdeclaration of the price paid, even though these prices are used to levy the transfer tax as well. The actual price paid is registered in the notary deed and in the

Figure 16.2 Residential Price Index for Existing Residential Real Estate in the Netherlands

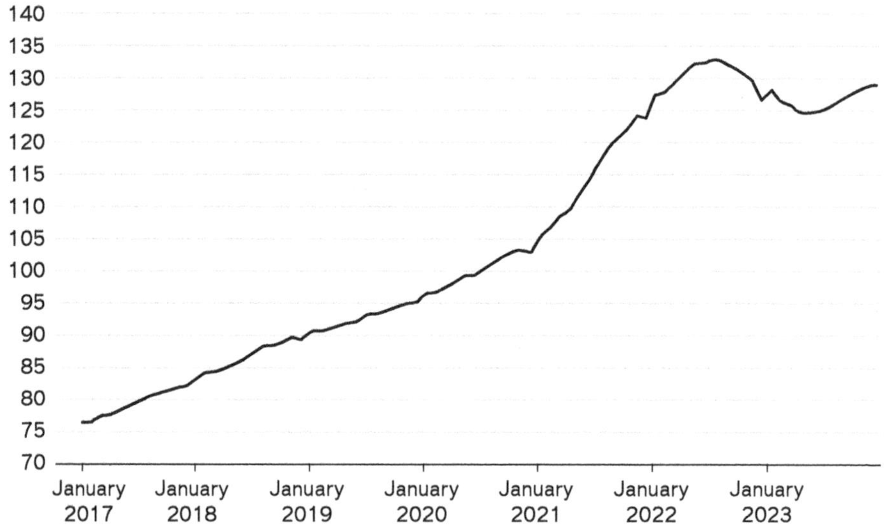

Source: Centraal Bureau voor de Statistiek (2023a; 2023b).

Note: Prices compared to 2020 (2020 = 100).

cadastral registry because, in the Netherlands, in most cases the buyer of the property takes a full 100 percent mortgage for paying the price. The reason people buy property with a mortgage and a low amount of own capital is that the mortgage interest paid can be deducted from income tax under the Income Tax Act of 2001.

The sales prices registered in the Base Register Cadastre are used by the national statistics bureau to publish a monthly price index for previously existing residential real estate (Prijsindex bestaande koopwoningen). This index is publicly available and free of charge, and it gives figures for the Netherlands as a whole. Next to the price index for the whole country, which is visualized in figure 16.2, the national statistics bureau publishes specific figures for the main regions within the country. For other types of real estate, such as commercial properties or agricultural land, the number of transactions is too small to make a reliable price index. The national statistics bureau is investigating whether it is possible to make a price index for commercial real estate using the market data that are collected by municipalities for the appraisal and assessment for taxation.

The cadastral registry is fully digitized. The notary office submits the deed using digital services, and the register (the Base Register Cadastre) can be used by the tax-levying governments through different types of web services. Furthermore, there is an option available to buy a subscription to access all new transfers registered and all other changes in the registry. Only a notary office within the Netherlands is allowed to submit a deed on a real estate transaction. Therefore, people or companies that want to buy or sell real property need the services of a notary office located in the Netherlands.

Sales prices registered in the cadastral registry are the primary source of market data on sales transactions for the mass appraisal and assessment of real estate. However, the real estate listings of brokers and real estate agents are used as well. This possibility exists because most brokers and potential buyers use an online central (private) marketplace for real estate listings.

For mass appraisal and assessment, sales prices cannot be the only source of market data. For instance, for commercial real estate like shops and offices, most market data must be found in rental transactions. For specific properties like schools, hospitals, and large industrial plants, investments (building costs) are the most important source of market data. Unlike ownership transactions, there is no official registry of rental transactions or of rent prices. Because rent prices for commercial real estate are a vital source of market data, they must be collected for the appraisal and assessment from either the owner or the renter of the property. The same limitations apply for collecting information on building costs and investments in specific properties.

Real Estate Taxes

National Level

An overview of the importance of property tax on the national level is given in table 16.2.

Table 16.2 Share of Real Property Tax in Relation to the Total Levied Tax (€ billion; % of GDP)

	2018	2019	2020	2021	2022
Central government	€178	€196	€194	€212	€223
	23.1%	24.0%	24.4%	24.8%	24.9%
Of which property tax	€5.4	€5.5	€5.3	€5.3	€4.7
(based on value, recurrent)	0.69%	0.68%	0.66%	0.62%	0.52%
Of which transfer tax	€3.0	€3.0	€3.6	€3.8	€4.3
	0.39%	0.37%	0.45%	0.45%	0.48%

Source: Centraal Bureau voor de Statistiek (2023b).

Property Transfer Tax

For all real estate transactions (sales), a transfer tax must be paid. The buyer of the property pays the tax to the national revenue office and the revenues stay on the central level.

However, the payment of this transfer tax is part of the formal transfer of the property organized by the notary office. The notary office is responsible for the formal transfer (registration in the cadastral registry) and organization of the payment to the seller. Furthermore, it is responsible for paying this tax to the national revenue office as part of handling the transaction and handling the payment of the sales price by the buyer to the seller.

The tax base is the value of the property, and for the transfer tax this value is at least equal to the price paid. The declaration for the transfer tax and payment is part of the formal procedure at the notary office. In general, there is no problem with underdeclaration. This is because arranging the mortgage (often 100 percent in the Netherlands) and handling the payment from the bank of the buyer to the bank of the seller are services offered by the notary office as well. As an extra guarantee, the notary office and the national revenue office can compare the price paid (the declared value for the transfer tax) with the formal assessed value of the property.

For a long time, there was a uniform flat rate for all transactions. But starting in 2011, the rate for buying residential property was lowered to 2 percent to stimulate the real estate market for housing. In 2021, this was changed because it was believed that new buyers on the market needed an extra support, while private investors in residential properties needed to be restricted, because they often were able to offer a higher price on the market than people who tried to buy property for self-occupancy. The current and historical transfer tax rates are visualized in table 16.3.

Capital Gains Tax or Property Wealth Tax

Taxation on income from savings and investments in the Netherlands assumes that people will have a certain taxable return on their net capital. The actual level of return (e.g., interest, dividend, capital gains or losses) is not relevant. Net capital (the value of the assets minus any liability) is determined once a year, on January 1. Only capital available for savings and investment is considered. Consequently, the owner-occupied dwelling as well as the mortgage loan linked to it and capital invested in someone's own company or in a substantial interest are not taxed in what is called box 3 of the income tax (Income Tax Act of 2001). Box 1 concerns direct income and the owner-occupied dwelling. Box 2 concerns the

Table 16.3 Historical and Current Transfer Tax Rates (%)

Buyer	2010	2011–2020	2021–2022	2023
With age under 35 buying residential property for self-occupancy with price lower than €400,000; rate only applies once	6.0	2.0	0.0	0.0
Buying residential property for self-occupancy	6.0	2.0	2.0	2.0
Buying residential property for other purposes	6.0	2.0	8.0	10.4
All other properties	6.0	8.0	8.0	10.4

Source: Belastingdienst (n.d.).

income from the own company or a substantial interest in a company, and box 3 concerns all other investments.

The tax rate in box 3 was 31 percent in 2022 (before 2021, it was 30 percent). The box 3 tax rate is assessed against a hypothetical yield. People are not taxed for capital gains or actual rental income. Instead, the Dutch tax office assumes that they enjoy a yield of up to 5.53 percent (in 2022) over their total asset value, irrespective of whether actual gains are higher or lower. It is assumed, however, that when one's capital is a higher, one can obtain a higher yield. With a capital up to €50,650, the assumed yield is 1.818 percent; between €50,651 and €962,350, the assumed yield is 4.366 percent; and from €962,351, a yield of 5.53 percent (in 2022) is assumed.

However, the High Court has decided that this assumption cannot be used anymore when a taxpayer has all capital in savings, because the current market has seen times of no interest or even a negative interest. For taxpayers with only savings, the assumed yield is therefore reduced to 0.01 percent (in 2022).

Because of this High Court ruling, the minister of finance is now preparing a system change. In the new system, expected to enter into force in 2025, the actual level of return will be taxed, including the actual capital gain. This capital gain will be taxed even when the gain is not actually received. For instance, the capital gain will be calculated by comparing the value of shares at the start of the fiscal year with the value at the end of that year. However, a debate is still going on regarding how the actual capital gain on real estate property within a tax year can be calculated when there is no sale of the property. The problem is that when the tax bill for a certain year is made, the assessed value at the start of the year is known, but the official value for the end of the year will be assessed a year later. The capital gain tax is a part of the income tax in the Netherlands, so it is a tax on the central level and administered by the national revenue office.

Because this capital gains tax or property wealth tax is part of the income tax, it is not possible to determine the exact revenue from this tax. It is estimated that around €1 billion in revenues is collected with this tax based on the value and yield of real property. With the prospective change of system, the purpose is to collect at least the same level of revenues.

Income Tax

The most important property tax at the national level in terms of the number of immovable properties involved is the assumed income that taxpayers must add to their income based on the assessed value of an owner-occupied house (Income Tax Act of 2001). The amount that must be added is an annually determined percentage of the assessed value, and the assumption is that the added amount is an approximation of the financial advantage that the taxpayer has from the owner-occupied home in the sense that one does not have to pay rent. For many taxpayers, however, the owner-occupied house is not a net "addition" but rather a "net deduction," because the deduction of the mortgage interest paid is often higher than the addition of the owner-occupied home allowance.

Inheritance Tax

When real property is part of an inheritance, the inheritor must pay an inheritance tax. The rate of this tax depends on the total value of the inheritance (the total value of the assets of the deceased) and the (family) relation between the deceased and the inheritor. For instance, a child who inherits (a part of) an inheritance less than €130,425 pays a tax of 10 percent, while a sibling or an inheritor without a family relation who gets a share of an inheritance of over €130,425 pays 40 percent tax.

The value of the inheritance is assessed on the date of death. This is also done for the real property that is part of the inheritance. However, for residential property, the formal assessed value is used as an estimate of the value of the property. This assessed value is based on the valuation date January 1. For that reason, the inheritor can choose to take the assessed value of the property for the year in which the deceased died or the following year.

The inheritors are responsible for the tax declaration. It is possible for each inheritor to file a separate declaration form, but in most cases this declaration is done by all inheritors together, because the total specification of the assets must be done only once. When handling the will of the deceased is taken care of by an executor, most commonly this executor also files the declaration for the inheritance tax.

The revenues of the inheritance tax in 2021 were around €2.5 billion for all elements of the inherited assets. It is expected that around half of that amount is related to real property. The administration of the inheritance tax is done by the national revenue office, and the revenues accrue to the central government.

Value-Added Tax

The transfer of real estate is exempted from the value-added tax, because a transfer tax is paid. However, construction of a real property is not exempted. Therefore, one pays a value-added tax of 21 percent when buying a newly built residential property or other kind of newly built property, but one does not have to pay a transfer tax. Because the construction of new property is subject to the value-added tax, buying a construction site is subject to value-added tax and therefore exempted from the transfer tax.

In line with the transfer tax, the value-added tax is also entirely collected on the central level.

Landlord Tax

The owner of residential property who owns more than 50 dwellings for renting out at a rent price lower than the limit for social housing must pay a landlord tax based on the assessed value of these properties. This central-government tax has been levied since 2013 and changed often during the last 10 years. For instance, at the start, the tax had to be paid when owning more than 10 dwellings, but this number has since been increased to over 50 dwellings. So the number of taxpayers has decreased and the tax is mainly paid by organizations for social housing. Yearly, the revenues of this tax are around €1.7 billion.

However, this tax was abolished in 2023. By abolishing this tax, the government intended to give the organizations for social housing more financial means for lowering rent prices for lower-income groups and for investing in sustainability and measures to limit the energy bill for renters (insulation, solar panels, etc.).

Central Property Taxes and Influence on the Market

Property taxes of the central government are primarily intended to generate revenues. For instance, the landlord tax was introduced to generate revenues for government spendings on allowances for people with low income to pay the rent. The central government has lately started using property tax more to influence the real estate market. One of the policy themes is giving more possibilities to those striving to buy their first owner-occupied house. Because of the market, these young buyers were often outbid by people buying the property as an investment for renting out the property.

This policy goal can clearly be seen in the different rates for the transfer tax presented in table 16.3 (0.0 percent for young first-time homeowners and 10.4 percent for people buying as an investment).

The same policy goals also play a role in making the plans for the capital gains tax and property wealth tax. In the market, investing in real estate was for several years very interesting because the yields were higher than for savings and bonds. Moreover, the yields of real estate investments were taxed on a low level, because the taxable yield was a long-term average of the mean yield for savings, bonds, and real estate.

Because of the market, which had high yields on real estate and much lower yields on other investments, real estate became very interesting for investors. This made the market hard for people looking to buy a house for living and in need of a mortgage for financing this step. In the new system for the capital gains tax or net wealth tax to be implemented in 2025, the government strives to make rental income taxable as well as the capital gains because of the value increase of real estate. There is still debate about how to achieve these goals, while also considering that the value of real estate (as well as of bonds) can go down.

Whether the central-government taxes really influence the market, and whether the policy goals are met, is often hard to evaluate. Market developments, such as interest rates on mortgages or confidence in economic developments, in general often have a larger effect on the decisions of people than the tax they must pay.

Another general policy goal is a shift from tax on income to tax on assets and wealth. One way of achieving this goal is by increasing the property tax of municipalities while lowering the income tax by central government. This shift from income tax to property tax and from taxation by central government to a local tax has not started yet. This is due to the big impact it would have on financial arrangements between government levels and the need to gain acceptance by taxpayers, because the municipal property tax is much more visible than the income tax.

Subnational Level

Provinces

At the moment, provincial governments do not levy property taxes. The only taxes they levy are surcharges on the tax on motor vehicles (an annual tax on owning a motor vehicle and the right to use public roads).

Because of the developments with respect to electric vehicles, there are questions about the stability of its future revenue flow. A surcharge on the municipal property tax might be an interesting replacement.

Polder Boards

Polder boards have a system based on the distinction between unbuilt property and built-up property. All properties must pay property tax to the polder boards, because all properties benefit from the work the polder boards do to control the level of groundwater, pumping out all the water for land below sea level (the polders) and maintaining dikes along rivers and canals. All built-up property pays property tax to the polder board based on the assessed value. A parcel of land with a building on it is considered one built-up property when there is one owner. So the land that belongs to this property is considered "built-up" property. It is only "unbuilt" when there is no building on a parcel of land. The property tax for unbuilt land is based on the area of the land. Roads (including railroads) are considered by law to be unbuilt land, but the rate per square meter for roads is higher than for other types of unbuilt property like agricultural land. Also, woods, nature reserves, and other "wild land areas" must pay this property tax of the polder board, but at a lower rate per square meter.

The rates and the total revenues of the property tax of the polder boards are lower than the rates and revenues of the municipal property tax. But levying taxes and rates is more important for polder boards than for municipalities. The reason for this is that polder boards do not receive any financial transfers from the central government and must collect their complete budget from residential properties, a poll tax for inhabitants, and rates for the cleaning of sewage water.

The total revenues of the value-based property tax for built-up property are €800 million each year. The revenues of the area-based property tax are €200 million a year.

The total budget of polder boards (€3,100 million) also benefits from revenues of the poll tax (€700 million) and the charges for sewage water cleaning (€1,400 million). A breakdown of the polder board budget is presented in table 16.4.

The revenues of the value-based property tax of the polder boards have been quite stable over time. But because of the developments on the real estate market, an increasing part of this revenue is paid by the owners of residential property. This is a result of the significantly increased value of residential property. For instance, between the valuation date January 1, 2021, and January 1, 2022, the value of residential property increased by 17 percent and of nonresidential property by 2 percent. For this reason, polder boards have asked for a change in the law to enable setting

Table 16.4 Budget and Sources of Revenues for Polder Boards

	2021 (€ million)	As % of GDP
Budget of polder boards	3,136	0.37
Coming from		
Value-based property tax	801	0.09
Area-based property tax	196	0.02
Poll tax	704	0.08
Charges for cleaning sewage water	1,435	0.17

Source: Centraal Bureau voor de Statistiek (2023b).

different rates (percentage of the assessed value) for residential and for nonresidential property.

The rules for the property tax of the polder boards are set by the central government (part of the Act on Polder Boards). But each polder board sets the rates for the different taxes and charges, and all the revenues accrue to the budget of the polder boards. The budget and the tax rates are set by the general board of the polder boards, which is elected once every four years by general elections.

Municipalities

Based on the number of properties on the tax roll and the total revenues collected, the most important value-based property tax in the Netherlands is the municipal property tax. The municipalities levy three types of property tax:

- Property tax for the owners of residential property.
- Property tax for the owners of nonresidential property.
- Property tax for the users of nonresidential property.

The owner-occupier of a nonresidential property pays more tax than the owner-occupier of a residential property with the same value. This is because the tax rate for nonresidential property is considerably higher in most municipalities. The property tax for the users of residential property was abolished in 2006.

However, the valuation and tax system are still suitable for levying a property tax from the user of residential property. Furthermore, for residential properties, the demarcation of the taxable properties is based on the ownership and use of the property.

Table 16.5 Comparing Residential and Nonresidential Properties in Number, Value, and Municipal Property Tax

	2021	As % of Residential and Nonresidential Properties Combined
Number of residential properties	8,300,000	91
Number of nonresidential properties	825,000	9
Total value of residential properties	€2,295 billion	83
Total value of nonresidential properties	€465 billion	17
Total revenues of municipal property tax on residential properties	€2,375 million	52
Total revenues of municipal property tax on nonresidential properties	€2,185 million	48

Source: Waarderingskamer (n.d.).

So a multifamily complex that is owned by an organization for social housing and with 100 units that are rented out thus contains 100 taxable objects, and for each of these objects a value is assessed. For this reason, the number of taxable properties in the Netherlands is larger than the total number of cadastral parcels and cadastral apartment rights that are registered and used for the registration of ownership. More detail on the municipal property tax is given in table 16.5.

The property tax is the most important source of income that municipalities collect themselves. However, the largest part of the budget of municipalities comes from the central government. A large part of the grants from the central government is reserved for special activities. But a significant portion of the budget that municipalities can also use for their own policy goals comes from the central government. More detail on the municipal budget is specified in table 16.6.

It is considered a problem that only a limited part of the municipal budget comes from the municipalities' own sources. For instance, when the municipal board wants to increase the total budget by 5 percent to be able to reach some political goals, on average it nearly has to double the revenues from the property tax to reach that goal. This kind of large increase in the tax rate is, in most cases, not politically feasible, and that means that the board of a municipality is very limited in its options for changing the total budget to reach new political goals.

These limitations on changing the budget are a problem for the central government as well. The central government tries to divide the budget

Table 16.6 Budget and Sources of Income (including taxes) for Municipalities

	2021 (€ million)	As % of GDP
Budget of municipalities	64,475	7.53
Coming from central government		
For free spending	35,135	4.10
For specific purposes	10,900	1.27
Coming from "taxation" by municipalities		
Property tax	4,560	0.53
Other taxes (parking, tourists, dogs)	1,810	0.21
Charges for collecting sewage water	1,725	0.20
Charges for waste collection	2,170	0.25
Other charges (e.g., building permits)	1,050	0.12
Other sources of income	7,125	0.83

Source: Centraal Bureau voor de Statistiek (2023b).

for specific activities in such a way that each of the municipalities can deliver the proper level of service on that activity. However, demand for certain activities can change over time. Without a sufficiently flexible budget, it can become impossible for a municipality to maintain an acceptable service level for the taxpayer. Their only option is to increase property tax rates, which, in turn, might become unacceptable.

Next to the wish of municipalities to create more flexibility in their budget and the wish of the central government to create more flexibility in the municipal budget, there is also a third reason for an increase in the total revenues of the municipal property tax. That reason comes from the high level of income tax in the Netherlands. In light of several economic factors, it is better to lower the level of tax on income and increase the level of tax on wealth or assets. The property tax is considered a suitable tax on assets. So with a lower income tax and more possibilities for municipalities to increase the level of property tax, each of these three goals can be met.

But in spite of the fact that reducing the income tax in favor of increasing the property tax has been on the political agenda for years, there has been no significant change during the last 10 years. Municipalities are only willing to increase their property tax (or any other municipal tax) if they can explain to taxpayers that the significant increase in property tax is the result of a decrease in the income tax. But the problem is that a significant change in income tax is difficult for the central government because it also faces a budget constraint. Another problem is that, for many taxpayers, the property tax is much more visible than is the income tax.

Like the property tax for polder boards, the property tax (and all other taxes and charges) of municipalities has its formal base in rules set by the central government (in the Municipalities Act). But the boards of the municipalities set the rates for all the taxes and charges, and they can also choose not to levy one or more of the three property taxes. For instance, some municipalities only levy the property tax on the owners of nonresidential property and not the tax on users of nonresidential property.

Recurrent Land and Property Tax

The most important recurrent property taxes on the national level and the decentralized level (municipality and polder board) are based on the market value of the property (Bervoets et al. 2024; Municipalities Act of 1851; Water Boards Act of 1991). For the taxes, land and buildings together are considered a property, for which each year a market value is assessed by the municipality. The assessment of the market level is based on comparable sales (obligatory for residential property but, for instance, also used for agricultural property), on the income approach (mostly for commercial real estate) or on the cost approach (for property for which there is no or little market information, such as schools, hospitals, and large industrial estates). This assessed valued is used for taxation on different levels as well as for some other purposes. For that reason, the assessment of real estate is regulated in the Act on the Valuation of Immovable Property of 1994 that was implemented on January 1, 1995.

What is special in this act is that all immovable property is valued on the basis of the assumption that the owner has full ownership and can sell this full ownership without restrictions. This also means that the starting point is that the immovable property is not rented out when sold. This assumption is logical in the Dutch situation, because the assessed value is used for taxation not only of the owner but also of the user. For this user, it is not relevant whether the owner has full ownership or a limited right to the immovable property. In special circumstances, this can mean that the assessed value is higher than the possible sales price of the limited right that the taxpayer has on the valuation date.

This act for real estate assessment came into force in 1995 and has been used for recurrent property taxes since 1997. However, these taxes date back to an earlier period. For instance, the municipal property tax was implemented in the 1970s, while the polder boards' property tax has an even longer history. But since 1997, these taxes have all been based on the formal assessed value, and since 2007 this value has been assessed annually.

The assessment of all properties is done by municipalities. To make it possible for polder boards and the national revenue office to use this assessment, the assessed values are registered in a national base register of assessed values. This makes it possible for each level of government to administer its own property tax and use the same assessed value. However, in most cases municipalities and polder boards work together in shared service centers to administer the property tax and send out tax bills to all taxpayers for their territory.

Furthermore, municipalities are responsible for handling all objections and appeals against the assessed values. Therefore, polder boards and the national revenue office have a very low appeal rate for their property tax. Any taxpayer can make an objection against the assessed value in the municipality. When unsatisfied with the outcome of the objection, the taxpayer can go to court (tax court). At court there are three levels of appeal, of which the High Court is the final level.

A formal appeal should be made in writing, but municipalities encourage taxpayers to make informal appeals by telephone or use other informal methods of communication. The formal objections to a municipality are not published, but in general a court decision on an appeal against the assessed value is published.

The appeal rate for the assessed values is considered acceptable (2–3 percent objections for residential properties and around 6 percent for nonresidential property) but is influenced by the fact that half of these objections are made by legal fee companies (in Dutch, often referred to as no cure, no pay companies). It is regulated that these bureaus get a fee from the municipality when the assessed value is changed because of the objections made by the bureau. This fee is around €700 for each successful objection; in most cases the objection is made based on the results of an automated valuation model. The costs to make such an objection are in most cases much lower than the fee. Therefore, these bureaus advertise—for instance, on national television—to convince taxpayers to object against the assessed value of their property and let the bureau do this work for them.

The stable system of annual valuation, with an average of 2–3 percent objections for residential properties, has existed since 2007. Around the turn of the century, the system changed from requiring a revaluation once every four years to requiring an annual assessment. In the period when taxpayers only received a new assessment once every four years and could only appeal once every four years, the appeal rate for residential properties was about 8 percent. The reduction in the number of formal objections has also helped to keep the costs of the transition to annual valuation limited. Ultimately, this transition has not led to an increase in the costs of valuation and value assessment. In the period in question, a cost reduction was ultimately achieved, which is believed to have been possible mainly through the use of rapidly developing technological tools and an increase in scale because municipalities have increasingly started to cooperate in shared service centers (tax partnerships).

The current system of real estate assessment, with annual valuation by the municipalities of all properties based on the valuation date January 1 of the year before the fiscal year for which the assessment is made, is a stable system, and there are no plans for drastic changes. However, to keep it stable, small changes are continually being made—for example, in the valuation report or in the method of communication with the taxpayer to keep up with social expectations. Another change in the administration is that most of the smaller municipalities have started to cooperate with other municipalities (and polder boards) in shared service centers for the assessment and the levying of taxes.

The last major change in regulation occurred in 2016, when the assessed values of residential properties became available online so that all taxpayers could compare the value of their property with those of other properties in the neighborhood.

The main exemptions for the property tax are administered as part of the assessment. So the exemption for agricultural land results in an assessed value for an agricultural property where the agricultural land is excluded. This assessed value thus only includes the buildings and the built-up land. In the same way, the most important exemptions are administered:

- Agricultural land.
- Nature reserves.
- Public roads and railroads for public transport.
- Machinery for industrial production.
- Religious buildings like churches.

All areas of the municipality are taxed unless exempted. The same applies for the polder boards, but for polder boards a property is considered a built-up property (taxed based on the assessed value) or an unbuilt property (taxed based on the area of the land).

Each municipality can set its own tax rate. Because there is a difference in the taxes for residential and nonresidential property, the tax rates differ for these kinds of properties. Municipalities are not allowed to make other changes in tax rate. Polder boards cannot set different tax rates for built-up property, but they want the legislation to be changed so they also can set different rates for residential and nonresidential property. Each polder board can set its own tax rate for unbuilt properties, and different rates can be set for, for instance, "nature" an "agricultural land."

In the Netherlands, the rates for municipal property taxes are relatively low. This is possible because municipalities receive the largest part of their financial resources from the central government. Because all municipalities have relatively low rates, the differences between them are small, and there is no significant competition among municipalities regarding the rate for property taxes. The location choices of companies are therefore at most marginally influenced by local tax rates and much more by aspects of the physical location, such as accessibility, availability of adequate electrical connections, and the way in which the municipal government supports companies with services such as granting permits.

There is no exemption for low-value properties. But taxpayers with no ability to pay the tax can get a remission of the tax to be paid (Bervoets et al. 2024). To grant this remission, the municipality and the polder board look at the taxpayer's income as well as assets like real estate and cars.

The assessments made by the municipalities are also used on the national level. For that reason, it is important that all assessed values are on real market value. The act for real estate assessment thus also arranges for oversight to control the quality of the assessments (Bervoets et al. 2024). This oversight agency is the Netherlands Council for Real Estate Assessment (Waarderingskamer). It provides guidelines for the assessment but also performs audits in the municipalities (in shared service centers). Based on these audits and research into the quality of the valuations based on international standards, the Council for Real Estate Assessment Chamber decides whether a municipality is allowed to send out the new assessments to the taxpayers. Only when the council has given this permission, possibly only after improvement measures have been implemented, may the values be published and the property tax notices sent.

The main reason why municipalities are responsible for assessment in the Netherlands is that they have the best access to relevant data. The act for real estate assessment does not give formal guidelines for the data that should be used. Because the market for real estate is always changing, the characteristics that are relevant for the market prices are changing over time. For instance, characteristics regarding sustainability are now much more important than 10 years ago.

For the assessment of real estate, municipalities use the system of base registers in which data are registered that are used for all kinds of governmental purposes. Using this system, municipalities have access to cadastral data on ownership and the size of parcels as well as data on sales prices and the geometry of the parcels. Using the base register of addresses and buildings, municipalities have access to the size of the building and the year of construction, as well as the location of the building. But municipalities also collect and update information specifically for the assessment. For the assessment, a distinction is made between primary characteristics and secondary characteristics. This distinction does not evaluate characteristics in terms of importance but rather reflects the way the object characteristics can be changed. Primary object characteristics can only be changed by building activities. The following primary object characteristics are used in the appraisal models in the Netherlands:

- Type of property.
- Number and type of annexes (for instance, garage space).
- Size of the land plot (derived from the Base Register Cadastre).
- Size of the (main) building (derived from the base register of buildings) and of the annexes.
- Building year of the (main) building and of the annexes (derived from the base register of buildings).
- Information on building year and size for different parts of the (main) building.

Secondary object characteristics are the characteristics that can change without building activities—for instance, because of time, but also because of preferences of buyers. The secondary object characteristics registered and updated for the annual appraisal in the Netherlands are:

- maintenance condition of the property (sometimes with a distinction between maintenance condition of the structure and outside of the building, on the one hand, and the maintenance condition of the interior, on the other hand);
- quality of the property (sometimes with a distinction between the quality of materials used for the building, on the one hand, and the level to which the property meets the actual wishes for residential facilities of property owners and potential buyers, such as the quality of kitchen facilities, on the other); and
- location of the property in relation to services available in the neighborhood and potential nuisances caused by properties or infrastructure in the direct surroundings.

Both primary and secondary object characteristics are used in the computer-assisted mass appraisal in the Netherlands. A variety of approaches are used, but applications of modern approaches are limited because they are often hard to explain to the taxpayer, and it is not possible to show with a simple calculation how the valuation was done (Bervoets et al. 2024).

The taxpayer gets a tax bill each year. The tax bill combines all the municipal taxes as well as the formal assessment of the value of the property. In some regions, the tax of the polder boards is on the same tax bill. However, in most cases there is a separate tax bill for the polder board. The tax bill is sent as a digital form (PDF) when the taxpayer has a formal email address in the governmental portal (MijnOverheid.nl). Otherwise, the tax bill is sent on paper by mail.

Payment of the municipal property tax and the property tax of the polder board is mostly done through 10 monthly automatic installments by the bank. Only large companies must pay the property tax in one or two installments. When the property tax is not paid in time, there is a penalty depending on the amount that must be paid. When, even after the reminder with penalty, the property tax is still not paid, an official debt collector will start a formal procedure, which costs at least €54 extra.

Property tax administration in the Netherlands is highly digitized on all levels, and the administration for the different levels of government is connected by the use of the base register of assessed values. Not only the administration is digitized but also the communication with the taxpayer. Most taxpayers in the Netherlands receive their tax bill in their secure email account within their MyGovernment (MijnOverheid) account. Collection of the property tax for municipalities and polder boards is done for most taxpayers through automatic monthly installments.

Property Tax in Large Urban Areas

The property tax system is in force for all municipalities. Table 16.7 shows the figures for the municipality of Amsterdam (the capital of the Netherlands and the municipality with the highest number of inhabitants), giving a general view of how important the property tax is for municipalities in the Netherlands.

Reform Initiatives and Country-Specific Issues

The system of property tax has been rather stable during the last 10 years.

For the municipal (property) tax, there are plans for a substantial increase in revenues starting in 2026 (by lowering the amount of money transferred from the central government to municipalities). The details of the new system are not entirely clear just yet. Possible extra sources of revenue are

Table 16.7 Key Figures for Property Tax for Municipality of Amsterdam

Number of inhabitants	875,000
Basis of the property tax	Capital market value
Exempt properties	All properties that are exempted by law, such as public roads and parks, public waterways, and agricultural land (some within boundaries of the municipality). These properties are not registered or valued.
	Churches and all other buildings used for religious gatherings (102 properties). These building are not valued.
Valuation	Department of Municipal Taxes (staff: 69 full-time equivalent)
Revaluations	Yearly
	Valuation on January 1, 2021, for tax year 2022
	Municipality
	Number of objections: 15,600 (3.0%)
City revenue sources	Grants from central government: €3,600 million
	Property tax: €218 million
	Rates for sewage system and waste collection: €213 million
	Parking fees: €236 million
	Other taxes and rates: €290 million
	Sales of property and profit from participations: €950 million
	Leases from land lease contracts: €250 million
	Other: €670 million
Property tax as a %	7.5% of total own source revenue
	23.8% of tax revenue
	3.3% of total revenue
Role of the property tax	Used as source of revenue for the total budget of the municipality; no special regulations for spending

	2019	**2020**	**2021**
Number of taxable properties	486,000	499,000	506,000 (2021)
- Residential			468,000
- Nonresidential			38,000
Total value of the tax base	€197 billion	€225 billion	€238 billion
Collection data: Total revenue	€174 million	€178 million	€218 million

Source: Gemeentebelastingen Amsterdam (n.d.).

- the revival of the property tax for the users of residential property (for nonresidential property, both the owner and user pay a tax, but for residential property only the owner pays, because the property tax for the users of residential property was abolished in 2006);
- a fixed amount for each household or each person living in the municipality; and
- an increase in tariffs for the existing property tax.

For the national taxes, changes are expected for the property wealth tax as part of the income tax (box 3). This tax is now based on a hypothetical yield as a percentage of the assessed value of the property. But plans are being made to abolish this hypothetical yield and to tax the actual income from the property as well as the (unrealized) capital gains derived from comparing the assessed value at the end of the fiscal year with the assessed value at the start of the year.

In order to identify country-specific issues, comparative studies have been done by organizations such as the Netherlands Council for Real Estate Assessment and the Erasmus University Center for Local Taxes (Bervoets et al. 2024; Waarderingskamer, n.d.).

Impact

The rates for the property tax in the Netherlands are relatively low. As a result, the property tax appears to have little direct influence on the real estate market or the use of property. Also, the differences in rates between municipalities are limited, suggesting little tax competition among municipalities.

However, central-government taxes are used to influence the real estate market. For instance, the different rates for the transfer tax for young first-time buyers, for buyers of residential property for use, and for investors buying residential property to rent it out were intended to improve the position of young first-time homeowners on the market compared with investors. However, the effect on the market was limited.

The intended change of the capital gains tax to tax actual income derived from property as well as tax the actual increase in value also was intended to improve the positions of homeowners on the market compared with investors.

The rates for the property taxes in the Netherlands depend not on the value of the property but on the use. Also, the assessed values of property are in accordance with the differences on the real estate market (100 percent of market value). This results in a system that is neither progressive nor regressive. However, the program for (automatic) remission of taxes for people with low income (no ability to pay) has a large influence on people earning a little over the threshold for this remission. The tax is in that sense progressive.

Conclusion

The Netherlands has a stable system of property tax on different levels of government. In general, this property tax is based on the capital market value of property that is officially assessed by municipalities annually.

Despite the fact that the system is stable, the tax rates in the Netherlands for properties are low in comparison with other countries. The main reason for these low rates is that municipalities get the major part of their financial means from the central government. The system in the Netherlands is considered stable enough to generate a higher level of revenues. There are some plans to use this possibility in the near future.

Postscript

In 2024 the regulation for rent price control for residential property was broadened. These regulations were put in place for social housing with a maximum rent price of €808.06 per month. Because of a shortage of rental residential property for middle-income households, additional regulations will come into force for houses and apartments with a maximum rent price under €1,123. These regulations are quite comparable with the rent price control measures for social housing. For both categories, the assessed value of the property is one of the characteristics used to determine the maximum rent price.

Because the yield on savings increased in 2023, the assumed yield on savings for the net wealth tax increased from 0.01 percent to 0.92 percent for the 2023 tax year. For other assets, the assumed yield for the net wealth tax was increased from 5.53 percent (tax year 2022) to 6.17 percent.

Starting on January 1, 2024, the regulations for the legal fee companies were changed. The fee they get for a successful objection or appeal was decreased by 75 percent. The municipality that has to pay this fee must now pay it to the taxpayer and not to the legal fee company. This regulation is intended to make taxpayers more aware of the costs they incur by hiring these firms that work on the basis of no cure, no pay.

No final decisions have been made on the intended increase in revenues of municipal property tax combined with a decrease of central income tax or on the modernization of the net wealth tax.

References

Belastingdienst. n.d. Home page. Accessed March 10, 2023. https://www.belastingdienst.nl.

Bervoets, B. P. P., L. D. Hermans, R. M. Kathmann, and M. Kuijper. 2024. "Lessons from the Netherlands: Real Estate Assessment and Property Tax Systems." Cambridge, MA: Lincoln Institute of Land Policy. https://go.lincolninst.edu/lessons-from-the-netherlands.pdf.

Centraal Bureau voor de Statistiek. 2023a. "Bestaande koopwoningen; verkoopprijzen prijsindex 2015 = 100 1995–2023." https://www.cbs.nl/nl-nl/cijfers/detail/83906NED.

———. 2023b. "Bestaande koopwoningen; verkoopprijzen prijsindex 2020 = 100 1995–2023." https://opendata.cbs.nl/#/CBS/nl/dataset/85773NED.

———. 2023c. "Statline topic: opbrengsten belastingen." https://opendata.cbs.nl/statline/#/CBS/nl/.

Gemeentebelastingen Amsterdam. n.d. Home page. Accessed March 10, 2023. https://www.Amsterdam.nl.

Publieke Dienstverlening op de Kaart. n.d. Home page. Accessed July 2022. https://app.pdok.nl/viewer.

Waarderingskamer. n.d. Home page. Accessed June 12, 2023. https://www.waarderingskamer.nl.

Legislation

Act on the Valuation of Immovable Property of 1994 [Wet waardering onroerende zaken (Wet WOZ)].

Income Tax Act of 2001 [Wet inkomstebelasting].

Municipalities Act of 1851 [Gemeentewet].

Water Boards Act of 1991 [Waterschapswet].

17

The Need for Property Tax Reform in Poland

MAŁGORZATA RENIGIER-BIŁOZOR, SABINA ŹRÓBEK, ELŻBIETA ZYSK, MAREK WALACIK, AND RYSZARD ŹRÓBEK

Poland, according to the Central Statistical Office, had 38,179,800 inhabitants in March 2021 and an administrative area of 312,696 square kilometers (Statistics Poland 2021). The population density is 122 people per square kilometer. Poland is currently characterized by a relatively even distribution of population across regions, with a high share of population in rural regions (49 percent), much higher than the average for Organisation for Economic Co-operation and Development (OECD) countries (29 percent). Approximately 48.1 percent of the population lives in urban communes, about 28.3 percent in rural communities, and 23.5 percent in urban-rural communes. In Poland, the administrative system is divided into state (central) government and self-government. The self-government administrative system has a three-tier division into the following local-government units (LGUs): 16 provinces, 380 counties, and 2,477 communities. Of these communities, 302 are urban communities, 1,523 are rural communities, and 652 are urban-rural communities (OECD 2021). The administrative division of the state, which determines the boundaries of LGUs, is one of the basic factors shaping the ability of LGUs to perform their tasks effectively. In Poland, the heads of particular self-government units are presidents or mayors (in communities), *starosts* (in counties), and *voivodes* (in provinces).

The legal basis for the imposition of tax obligations in Poland is the Constitution of the Republic of Poland, in force since October 17, 1997.

Currently, there are two main types of taxes in Poland: direct and indirect taxes. Most are direct taxes, such as personal income tax (PIT), corporate income tax (CIT), inheritance and donation tax, tax on civil law transactions, agricultural tax, forestry tax, property tax, tax on means of transport, tonnage tax, tax on extraction of certain minerals, and lump-sum tax on the value of production sold (so-called shipbuilding tax). Indirect taxes include value-added tax (VAT), excise duty, and gaming tax. Indirect taxes are "hidden" in the prices of goods and services, so are paid when purchases are made. However, the payment of such taxes to the tax office is carried out by those who sell the goods and services.

According to Article 168 of the Constitution, LGUs have the right to determine the highest level of taxes and local fees to the extent specified by law.[1] The taxing power of communes includes the possibility of introducing exemptions from local taxes and charges. In turn, in accordance with Article 217 of the Constitution, these may only be subjective exemptions (tax exemptions, as well as those concerning rates of local taxes, made in the form of resolutions of the constituent bodies). The procedure for the adoption of tax resolutions is regulated in constitutional acts (including the Act on Municipal Self-Government [1990] and the statutes of communities). Revenues of LGUs in Poland are regulated by the Act on the Income of Local Government Units (2003), which indicates the sources of own revenues of communes, counties, and provinces.

In Poland, only communes are empowered to collect local-government taxes. These revenues constitute a significant item in their budgets. Sources of commune tax revenues include real estate tax, agricultural tax, forest tax, vehicle tax, PIT, inheritance and donation tax, and tax on civil law transactions. Communes budgets rely significantly on tax revenue, including the real estate tax, agricultural tax, forestry tax, vehicle tax, PIT, inheritance and donation tax and a tax on civil law transactions. Among these, communes have the authority to levy the real estate tax, agricultural tax, forestry tax, and tax on means of transport. The tax authority is the head of the commune, mayor, or town president. Pursuant to separate acts, the tax authority for PIT and tax on civil law transactions is the head of the tax office, who collects arrears from these titles for the commune. According to the OECD, gross domestic product (GDP) in 2021 equaled US$37,711 per capita (figure 17.1).

The per capita incomes of the LGUs of communes, counties, and provinces in US$ are shown in table 17.1.[2] The smallest communes have the smallest—not only in absolute terms but also per capita—funds for local-government tasks.

Figure 17.1 Change in Polish GDP from 2000 to 2021 and Average GDP of 27 EU Members States (per capita in US$)

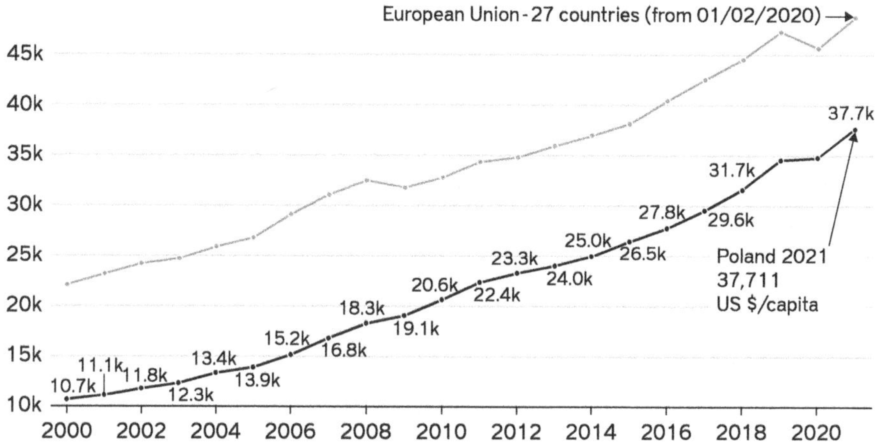

Source: OECD (2021).

Table 17.1 Per Capita Income of LGUs by Administrative Unit (US$)

	Communities					
	Cities	Cities with County Status	Urban-Rural	Rural	Counties[1]	Provinces[2]
Min.	993	1,389	953	908	1,305	1,688
Max.	2,831	3,353	2,659	9,319	2,169	2,074

Sources: Authors' calculations based on data from the Ministry of Finance (2021) and data from the Central Statistical Office from 2021 (Statistics Poland 2021).

[1] Per capita incomes of all LGUs in the counties.

[2] Per capita incomes of all LGUs from the territory of the voivodeship.

The Polish tax system is one of the most complex among OECD countries. Among the 38 OECD countries in early 2021, it ranked penultimate in terms of competitiveness (Bunn and Asen 2021).

According to the Tax Foundation (Bunn and Asen 2021), the general conclusion is that the Achilles heel of the Polish tax system is its complexity. It is also characterized by extremely high volatility, uncertainty, and often tiresome unpredictability.

It should be emphasized, however, that this opinion of significant tax institutions does not apply in particular to real estate tax, which, due to its area tax base, is not very complicated. Its administration, as discussed later, is problematic.

Land and Property Markets

The structure and function of property markets in Poland are determined by a number of factors, but the fundamental one is the Polish legal system, which describes particular kinds of properties and property rights, determines procedures for property rights transfer, and imposes certain restrictions.

The Polish legal system distinguishes three basic types of properties: land, buildings, and premises (parts of buildings, if under specific regulations, constitute an object of ownership separate from the land) (Civil Code 1964). Agricultural property is also identified as a separate category. In the context of land, the *superficies solo cedit* principle is significant, which means, "what is on the surface belongs to the ground." The law, however, indicates exceptions to this rule—they include, inter alia, buildings (as ownership objects separate from the land), which are built only when they are situated on land in perpetual usufruct. The distinction between different types of properties cannot be understood without consideration of particular types of rights established on properties. The most common and their distinctions are presented in figure 17.2.

Ownership gives the entity the broadest possible rights. The owner, within the limits set by the law, the principles of social coexistence, and the socioeconomic destination of property, may, with the exclusion of other people, use the land and dispose of it.

Figure 17.2 Property Rights in the Polish Legal System

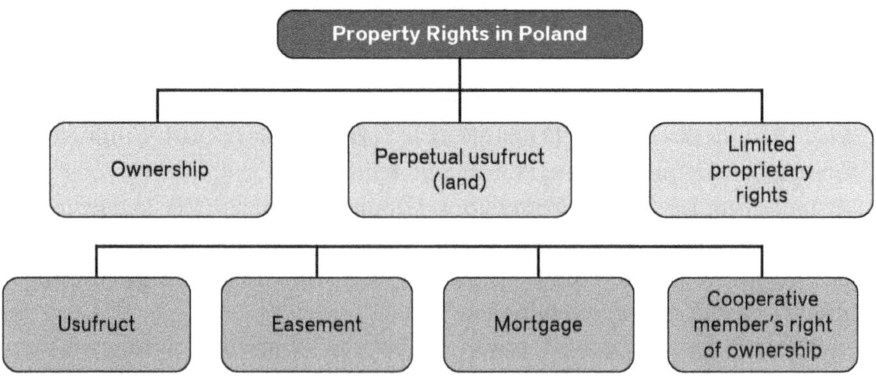

Source: Authors' study on the basis of the Act on the Civil Code (1964).

The right of *perpetual usufruct* is an intermediate right between ownership and limited rights in rem. Perpetual usufruct allows the use of the land within the limits specified by the acts, rules of social coexistence, and agreement for putting the land of the State Treasury or the commune into perpetual usufruct. As a rule, the land is put into perpetual usufruct to natural and legal persons for a period of 99 years. It is also permissible to put the land in perpetual usufruct for a shorter period, but it must be at least 40 years. During this period, the entitled person pays an annual fee. Perpetual usufruct fees are determined according to a percentage rate on the real estate price (market value).

Usufruct belongs to the catalog of limited proprietary rights. Real estate can be encumbered with the right to use it and to obtain its benefits. The user has the right to use someone else's land and to collect benefits that the land brings. Usufruct is a nontransferable right—it cannot be transferred to another person. The usufruct may be established for a definite or indefinite period, but it always expires as a result of failure to perform it for 10 years. In order to create a usufruct, an agreement between the landowner (e.g., a commune or the State Treasury) and the future user is necessary. The usufruct may be established against payment or without remuneration.

A *cooperative* right of ownership allows the owner to use and dispose of the property (e.g., apartment). However, due to the fact that it functions on the basis of limited property rights, the actual owner remains the housing cooperative. The cooperative ownership right to the premises is transferable, it may be inherited (passed to heirs), and it is subject to foreclosure, and it is possible to establish a land and mortgage register for such real estate.

The purchase or sale of real estate must always be made through a *notarial deed.* A notarial deed is a specific legal act that cannot be replaced by a regular contract. Article 158 of the Act on the Civil Code 1964 states unequivocally that the contract for the transfer of property ownership must include a notarial deed. Any other agreement will be void and cannot result in an enforceable transfer. The conclusion of the notarial deed is preceded by a clear statement of the parties to the transaction, certified by an authorized notary public. The document that parties receive is an excerpt from the notarial deed.

The structure, content, and manner of concluding a notarial deed for the sale of real estate are strictly formalized and defined by Polish regulations. This is stated in the Act on Notaries 1991. A notarial deed for the sale of an apartment or other real estate can be divided into three sections. In the first, information about the place, date, office, parties to the transaction, and, possibly, people present at the declarations of intent is stated. The second section contains the actual content of the declarations of will. This is the essential section of the notarial deed, which describes the detailed terms and conditions of what both parties agree to. The third section is information about taxes, the notary's fee, the stamp duty, and the method of their payment. At the end, there is a section in which the parties confirm that the act has been read and the signatures certify the entirety.

All necessary information, including the procedure for preparing and dealing with a notarial deed, is specified in Polish law in Articles 91–95 of the Act on Notaries 1991. It lists the most important rules that should be followed by a notary public, including information contained in a notarial deed. Most often, it is the notary who prepares the content of the notarial deed, based on the information and documents provided. However, there are also cases when one of the parties wants to prepare a preliminary draft of the real estate sale agreement in order to have a greater impact on its detailed content. Obviously, such a procedure is perfectly acceptable.

Services performed by a notary public are *confidential*. This means that a notary public may not disclose any information related to the performance of statutory notarial activities—that is, the content of notarial deeds and certificates, parties that participated in signing them, or even the fact of their preparation. In a notary's office, the details of the person requesting the extract are meticulously checked, and their entitlements are verified. Therefore, an extract of a notarial deed can only be obtained by a strictly defined group of people. An extract may be issued to the natural or legal person who was a party to the act. It will also be received by any person mentioned in the text of the act as entitled to receive it. It is the notary's obligation to transfer the notarial deeds to tax offices.

Each notarial deed is kept in the archives of the office in which it was created for a period of 10 years. During this period, it is possible to obtain an extract, which requires the payment of an appropriate fee calculated according to the applicable notarial fee. After this period, the notarial deed is transferred to the archives of the land and mortgage registers of the district court for the jurisdiction where the office is located. If more than 10 years have elapsed since the act was drawn up, it is held in the relevant archives of the district court.[3]

The purchase or sale of a property in Poland may be subject to specific *limitations*. One example is a property purchase made by foreigners. As a rule, the acquisition of real estate in Poland by a foreigner requires a permit from the minister responsible for internal affairs, if the minister of national defense does not raise an objection, and in the case of agricultural real estate, if no objection is raised by the minister responsible for rural development. The Act on the Acquisition of Real Estate by Foreigners (1920) indicates numerous exceptions to the general principle of obtaining a ministerial permit. Obtaining a permit from the minister is not required, inter alia, in the following cases (among others): purchase of an independent apartment or purchase of independent commercial premises intended for a garage or share in such premises. There are no such limitations for foreigners who are citizens or entrepreneurs of the member states of the European Economic Area or the Swiss Confederation. Since 2016, the transitional provisions introduced for these countries regarding the restrictions on the purchase of agricultural real estate in Poland have ceased to apply.

Property transactions in Poland are subject to registration. One of the core elements of the property transaction registration system is the *real estate price registry*. The concept of the register was introduced by the Act on Geodetic and Cartographic Law 1989. According to its provisions, for the entire country, databases are established and maintained in the information and communication technology system, including datasets of the spatial information infrastructure, concerning, inter alia, the real estate price register (Bydłosz, Ciechociński, and Parzych 2010; Hopfer, Cegielski, and Pietrzak 2012). The ordinance of the minister of regional development and construction on the land and building register, in turn, specifies that the obligation to keep a register of real estate prices specified in notarial deeds rests on the starost (Konowalczuk 2014). Moreover, the competent starost must, after receiving a notarial deed from a notary public, enter the provided data into the real estate price register within 30 days. This ensures that the register is always up to date. The real estate price register contains information about the location of the property, the transaction price, the registration numbers of plots, the type of property (e.g., whether it is a housing property, a building property, or an undeveloped agricultural property), the area of the property, the date of the notarial deed, and so on. The starost provides the information contained in the register in the form of extracts and lists from the register, excerpts from the cadastral map, copies of documents justifying entries in the database of the registration frame, and computer files formatted in accordance with the applicable standard of registration data exchange (Siewicz 2012). Anyone can receive these data (for a fee) because they are considered public information (R. Źróbek 2020).

The quality of the data contained in the real estate price register is a derivative of a combination of many circumstances (Kokot 2015). Some of them result directly from the specificity of the real estate market; others from the legal, organizational, and technical conditions of the principles of keeping relevant registers. The official register of real estate prices is kept, as it were, on the occasion of the census of the geodetic resource and thus does not meet the requirements of a thorough market analysis. The register is maintained on the local level (county) by the starost on the basis of notarial deeds sent by the notarial office.

The real estate price register contains prices that have been declared by both parties to the real estate sale or purchase transaction during the preparation of the notarial deed by the notary public. The notary is not obliged to check whether the price corresponds to the market value of the property being sold. The tax office to which the notarial deed is sent, in the event of a gross difference between the sale price and the average price obtained on the market for similar properties, may request that the taxpayer prove that the price has not been falsified (or has not been underestimated). This is important in order to properly determine the taxes related to the real estate transaction. There are no publications presenting the results of research concerning how often such differences occur or how big they are in practice.

The main problems affecting the low quality of data include

- poor, nonstandardized, and often untrue information contained in notarial deeds;
- data entry errors in the register of prices, usually caused by human mistakes;
- long delays in entering data into the register;
- changes in the condition of the property between the date of the transaction and the date of its description; and
- a small amount of data on market transactions (Halik 2018, 2019; Zyga 2016).

Pursuant to the Act on Real Estate Management 1997, the president of the Central Statistical Office publishes, in the form of an announcement in the Official Journal of the Republic of Poland, *Monitor Polski*, real estate price change indexes for a given type of real estate, not later than four months from the end of the quarter to which these indexes relate, broken down by voivodeships (the highest-level administrative subdivision of Poland). In addition, the Central Statistical Office collects information on the number and volume of real estate transactions, as well as the area of real estate sold, including residential and nonresidential premises and land. Data are provided by the starost directly to the Central Statistical Office. According to the mentioned act, the price index should be used for the valorization of the amounts for particular purposes given in the act (e.g., adjacent fee, compensation for expropriation). Currently, price index data are mainly used by developers and other private entities on the real estate market.

Because such price indexes currently cover only the housing market sector (despite the existence of a statutory obligation to develop price indexes for all market sectors), for official purposes, the valorization of

Figure 17.3 Revenue of the State Budget

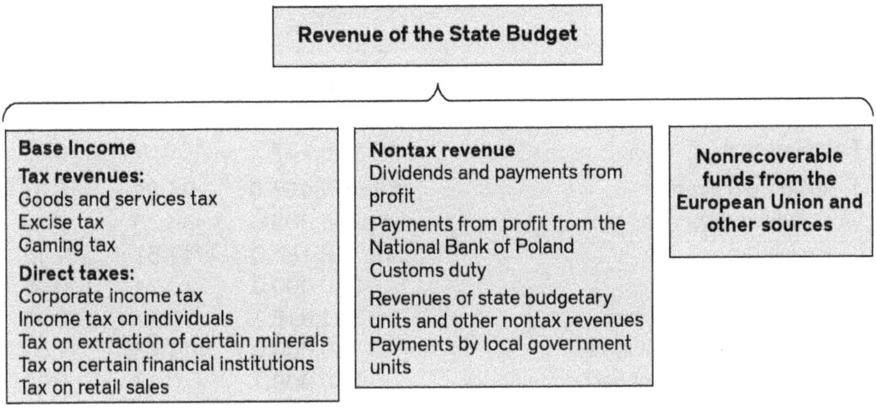

Source: Authors' compilation based on the Act on Public Finance (2009).

amounts is still carried out using indexes of growth in the prices of services and consumer goods (the so-called inflation index). Nevertheless, there are private real estate companies and portals that develop and publish indicators commercially.

Real Estate Taxes

National Level

The state budget is the primary tool used by public authorities to implement social and economic goals. In order for the goals to be realized, it is necessary to pursue this policy through an appropriate government revenue system, in which the most important place is occupied by direct and indirect taxes (figure 17.3).

In 2022, tax revenues to the state budget (table 17.2) grew by US$14.06 billion, with VAT accounting for as much as half of the growth (table 17.2). The growth in revenues was mostly influenced by the increased consumption of citizens, but also by inflation. Revenues from VAT were 16.9 percent higher than a year earlier (about US$7.09 billion), from PIT, by 15.4 percent (US$9.8 billion); from CIT, by 26.9 percent (US$2.52 billion); and from excise taxes, by 6.4 percent (US$1.06 billion). Nontax revenue for the budget in 2021 was US$13.77 billion, or about US$3 billion more (27.9 percent). This is partly the result of the National Bank of Poland profit contribution (US$2.02 billion), but mostly revenue from the auction of greenhouse gas emission allowances, which amounted to US$24.3 billion. The total tax on property as a percentage of GDP declined in 2020 (figure 17.4).

Table 17.2 Specification of Tax and Nontax Revenues in Total Revenue

	The Plan		
Specification	**US$ (billion)**	**%**	**% GDP**
Total Revenue	91,928,187.7	100.00	6.39
1. **Total tax revenue**	**83,895,457.0**	**91.26**	**5.83**
Goods and services tax	41,136,363.0	44.75	2.86
Excise tax	16,148,181.0	17.57	1.12
Gaming tax	650,000.0	0.71	0.05
Corporate income tax	8,431,818.1	9.17	0.59
Income tax on individuals	15,750,000.0	17.13	1.09
Tax on extraction of certain minerals	340,909.1	0.37	0.02
Tax on certain financial institutions	1,106,818.1	1.20	0.08
Tax on retail sales	331,366.6	0.36	0.02
2. **Nontax revenue**	**7,443,832.3**	**8.10**	**0.52**
Dividends and payments from profit	87,895.5	0.10	0.01
Payments from profit from the National Bank of Poland	302,078.5	0.33	0.02
Customs duty	1,006,363.6	1.09	0.07
Revenues of state budgetary units and other nontax revenues	5,332,605.5	5.80	0.37
Payments by local-government units	714,889.3	0.78	0.05
3. **Nonrecoverable funds from European Union and other sources**	**588,898.4**	**0.64**	**0.04**

Source: Authors' calculations based on Ministry of Finance (2021) databases and Statistics Poland (2022).

Local Taxes in Poland

In Poland, the supreme fundamental law is the Constitution, which regulates a number of legal, political, social, and economic aspects. It is in this law that the principles of financial self-reliance of LGUs and the right of municipalities to determine the amount of local taxes and fees are defined. The Act on Local Taxes and Fees (1991) systematizes the most important tax issues. As specified in Article 1 of the act, local taxes include real estate tax, transportation tax, and local fees (market, health spa, advertising, and dog ownership fees). The agricultural tax and forestry tax, regulated in separate laws, are also sources of local-government revenue (Act on Agricultural Tax 1984; Act on Forest Tax 2002). All of these taxes are included in the budgets of municipalities (Pahl 2017). Under current law, only the commune level of government has the power

Figure 17.4 Total Tax on Property as Percentage of GDP with the Average of OECD Countries (2000–2020)

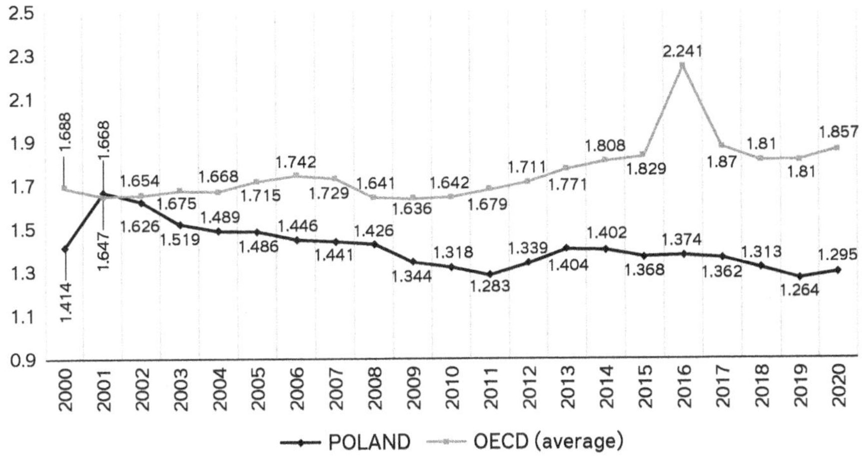

Source: OECD (2021).

to regulate the amount of these taxes and grant any exemptions. Local governments are required to prepare budget reports with selected information on property tax, agricultural tax, and forestry tax (Dworakowska-Raj 2020).

The principle of separateness and independence of LGUs from the state budget also applies to tax revenues, as shown in table 17.3. Detailed data about selected own revenues are presented in table 17.4.

The property tax in Poland accounts for about 1.28 percent of GDP when both recurrent property taxes and transfer taxes are included. This level of property taxation is low by comparison with some higher-income OECD countries and ranks Poland at about the same level as Latvia and Portugal. Available data show that recurrent property taxes account for about 19 percent of the total LGU revenues, but it should be noted that taxes on real property are also levied under the PIT and VAT regimes and neither of these are reported (OECD 2022).

Stamp Duty

Stamp duty is similar to the property transfer tax but is associated with a reciprocal, specific benefit from the state. Stamp duty is payable in individual cases in the field of public administration (e.g., performing an official action on the basis of a notification or request). The list of items of stamp duty (type of official activity) and the monetary amounts of these fees are included in the appendix to the Act on Stamp Duty (2006).

Table 17.3 Sources of Tax Revenue in the Budget of LGUs

Specification	Income Collected By: Communes	Powiats/ Counties	Provinces/ Voivodeships
Local Taxes			
Tax on real estate	Yes	No	No
Agricultural tax	Yes	No	No
Forest tax	Yes	No	No
Tax on means of transport	Yes	No	No
Tax on business of natural persons paid by tax card	Yes	No	No
Inheritance and donation tax	Yes	No	No
Tax on civil law transactions (property wealth tax)	Yes	No	No
Participation in Central Taxes			
Part of personal income tax revenues	Yes	Yes	Yes
Part of income tax revenue from legal entities	Yes	Yes	Yes

Source: Authors' compilation based on Act on Public Finance (2009); Act on the Income of Local Government Units (2003).

Table 17.4 Selected Own Revenues of LGUs and State Budget Revenue for 2021

	Total LGU Revenues (%)	Recipient Government
Tax on real estate	16.47	LGU
Stamp duty	0.37	LGU
Tax on civil law transactions	2.83	LGU
Inheritance and donation tax	0.26	LGU
CIT	9.02	LGU
PIT	39.14	LGU
National government own revenues	Percentage of total Polish government revenues	
State budget revenues	100.00	National government
VAT	43.59	National government

Source: Authors' calculations based on data from the Ministry of Finance (2021) and data from the Central Statistical Office from 2021 (Statistics Poland 2021).

The competent authority in matters of stamp duty is the president or mayor of a city or an urban-rural or rural commune. Stamp duty must be paid at the time the obligation to pay arises. The amount of stamp duty is given in the Act on Stamp Duty of November 16, 2006, and depends on the kind of the official (legal) activity—for example, issuing a decision on zoning and land development conditions at the request of the owner in 2023 was associated with a fee of US$136 (PLN 598). The amount of a stamp duty fee is not based on the value of the property.

Capital Gains Tax

In the Polish fiscal system, the sale of real estate before the expiration of five years from the time of its acquisition, which importantly applies to tax years (and not calendar years—i.e., counted from the end of the calendar year), is subject to a capital gains tax. This tax is time bound and specifically applies to the sale of real estate within the five-year period. It involves the payment of PIT at a rate of 19 percent on income—that is, earnings from the transaction. However, this is a percentage not of the value of the property but of the income it produces. Deductions are allowed for expenditures that enhance the value of the property and for the original price of acquiring the property. Sales made after a five-year holding period are not taxable.

Individuals are exempt from capital gains tax if all proceeds from the sale are used to cover their own housing needs and purposes. This can be the purchase of a new apartment or house, but also the construction of a house. The funds must be used within a maximum of three years from the end of the tax year in which the sale took place. No tax is due if the net profits from the sale are less than zero.

PIT

This legislation, in Article 30a of the Act on Personal Income Tax 1991, indicates the taxation of capital income earned by taxpayers with unlimited tax liability for incomes earned both in Poland and abroad. PIT can be paid in various forms of taxation:

- On general terms (12 percent up to approximately US$27,000 and 32 percent above approximately US$27,000).
- As a flat PIT tax (19 percent).

The tax base is income—that is, the amount earned by the taxpayer that has not been reduced by deductible expenses.

Introduced in 2002, the tax aroused much controversy and emotion among the public. Today, more than 20 years after its implementation, the public is accustomed to paying it, but nevertheless, from time to time, the ruling parties return with demands for its abolition, with the aim of gaining party electorate (Business Insider 2022; Rudke 2022).

Tax on Civil Law Transactions

The tax on wealth, formally known as the tax on civil law transactions, is among the compulsory tributes for LGUs. The tax must be paid by anyone who has made a legal action (purchase) and has not paid VAT in the process. The tax on civil legal actions is levied at a specified rate based on the market value of the real estate or right of perpetual usufruct, the market value over the value of the share in joint ownership or share in the inheritance, the amount of the secured claim, the value over the debts and burdens assumed by the recipient or the donor's obligations, or the market value of the benefits of the user or the person for whom the easement was established. The rates of tax on civil law transactions are, for a contract of sale, from 1 to 2 percent of the purchase price. For real estate sales, the tax rate is 2 percent.

Inheritance Tax

Inheritance and donation tax (Act on Inheritance and Donation Tax 1983) is a tax with respect to individuals who acquired ownership of things located in the territory of the Republic of Poland or property rights exercised in the territory of the Republic of Poland, by virtue of

- inheritance, simple bequest, further bequest, legacy bequest, or testamentary instruction;
- donation or donor's order;
- inheritance;
- gratuitous removal of co-ownership;
- a retainer, if the beneficiary did not receive it in the form of a gift made by the testator's donation or by inheritance or bequest; or
- rights acquired free of charge: annuities, usufruct, and easement.

The law indicates the tax exemption of the acquisition of property or property rights by the spouse, descendants, ascendants, stepchildren, siblings, stepfather, and stepmother if they report the acquisition of ownership of property or property rights to the competent head of the tax office within six months from the date on which the tax liability arises, in the case of acquisition by inheritance, or within six months from the date the court decision confirming the acquisition of the inheritance becomes final. In other cases, tax for inheritances and gifts must be paid when the value of the property exceeds the tax-free amount for each of the three tax groups indicated in this law.

VAT

The taxation of real estate involves the imposition of VAT. The sale of a building or land for consideration by an individual who is a businessperson can be charged VAT only if the seller acts as a taxpayer in the transaction. A VAT taxpayer on the sale of real estate can be considered such an individual who acts professionally in the transaction (Act on Tax on Goods and Services 2004). Contracts of sale are usually subject to a 2 percent tax on civil law transactions. However, if the sale of the property is subject to VAT, it is no longer subject to the tax on civil law transactions—neither on the part of the buyer nor on the part of the seller of the property.

The sale of real estate is subject to VAT at the rate of 23 percent (or at the rate of 8 percent for the sale of buildings covered by the social housing program).

CIT

The CIT is paid by legal persons (i.e., entities to which legal provisions grant legal personality). These include, among others, commercial law companies—that is, limited liability companies and joint-stock companies.

The subject of taxation is the income earned by the entrepreneur—that is, the excess of revenue over costs incurred in a given calendar year.

As of 2023, according to the act on CIT, the CIT rate is 19 percent or 9 percent of the tax base as standard, provided that certain criteria are met. The lower value applies to the taxation of income other than from capital gains in the case of start-ups (in the first tax year) and small taxpayers.

Grants

Grants are regulated by the provisions of the Act on Public Finance 2009. They constitute state public law benefits for other public entities of a nonrefundable, general, unconditional, and gratuitous nature. These form one of the revenues of LGUs. The most significant for LGUs are targeted grants (e.g., investment, for tasks realized on the basis of agreements between LGUs, from financial assistance granted between LGUs for financing own tasks).

General Remarks

There is no direct evidence that transfer taxes have affected real estate markets, such as by reducing or increasing real estate sales. Neither is there evidence about the possible underdeclaration of transfer tax liability.

If a transaction is undervalued, the tax office implements a procedure to check the declared sales price against the market value. At the contract of sale of real estate, the notary collects from the parties a tax of 2 percent of the market value (Manzhynski et al. 2018). The market value of the object of civil law transactions is determined on the basis of the average prices used in trade in things of the same type and species, accounting for their location, condition, and degree of wear and tear, and in trade in property rights of the same type, as of the date of the transaction, without deducting debts and burdens (Act on Tax on Civil Law Transactions 2000).

The notary then sends a copy of the notarial deed to the tax office, where the documents are thoroughly analyzed and verified. If the value stated in the contract does not correspond to the market value according to the assessment of the tax office, an increase in the declared value within 14 days from the date of service of the summons is called for. The tax office will provide an alternative value according to its own judgment. If the taxpayer agrees with the office's valuation, he pays the difference between the tax already paid and the tax actually due, together with interest calculated from the date of the agreement. If, on the other hand, the parties fail to agree on a value, the tax authority appoints an appraiser to make a valuation. If the value determined by the appraiser exceeds the value provided by the parties by 33 percent, the cost of the expert's opinion will be borne by the buyer. In terms of the Act on Tax on Civil Law Transactions 2000, the tax authority has up to five years to challenge the deed price.

Subnational Level

There has been an increasing trend in maximum rates of property tax set by the Ministry of Finance. In 2017, all private entrepreneurs paid a maximum of US$5.50 in tax per one square meter of building, and in 2022 it was US$5.85. A similar increase applies to the maximum tax rates for one square meter of land. In 2017, entrepreneurs paid a maximum of US$0.20 per square meter, and the limit for 2022 is US$2.10. For an entrepreneur paying the highest rates, owning 50,000 square meters of buildings and 100,000 square meters of land, this means an increase in tax liability by almost US$38,636 per year.

The increasing importance of property tax in the budget of local governments is also illustrated by data on annual revenues. Over a five-year period (2016–2020), they have increased by almost US$0.79 billion. However, this has not led to an increased surplus in local-government budgets. Instead, it is a result of changes in the structure of the central taxes in which they share, such as the introduction of a tax exemption in PIT for taxpayers up to the age of 26 (a US$0.25 billion annual loss) or the CIT—a

Table 17.5 Property Tax Revenues Relative to GDP (%)

Year	2010	2011	2012	2013	2014	2015	2016	2017	2018	2019	2020
Poland	1.32	1.28	1.34	1.40	1.40	1.37	1.37	1.36	1.31	1.26	1.29

Source: Authors' elaboration based on OECD (2022).

Table 17.6 Property Tax Revenues in Relation to Total Tax Revenues (%)

Year	2010	2011	2012	2013	2014	2015	2016	2017	2018	2019	2020
Poland	4.21	4.03	4.16	4.38	4.37	4.22	4.12	3.99	3.74	3.60	3.58

Source: Authors' elaboration based on OECD (2022).

lump sum on the income of capital companies (US$0.29 billion in 2022). The entry into force of new provisions will mean that many local governments, which have so far enacted property tax rates at less than the maximum level, may be forced to raise them.

Among European countries, France and the United Kingdom (with effective property tax revenue of about 3.9 percent of GDP each), as well as Belgium (3.45 percent), Italy, and the Netherlands (about 2.45 percent each), had the highest property taxes in recent years. Poland, with a rate of 1.3 percent, is at the bottom of the list (table 17.5), 0.55 percentage points below the average for OECD member countries, and has been declining.

With respect to property taxes as a percentage of all tax revenues, the countries cited were also well ahead of Poland. The United Kingdom in 2020 achieved a proportion of 11.8 percent; France, 8.8 percent; and Belgium, 8.0 percent. The average for all countries analyzed was 5.5 percent, whereas for Poland it was only 3.6 percent (table 17.6).

In 2020, the income of LGUs in Poland from property tax amounted to 16.5 percent of the structure of own income of LGUs. The community has other revenues such as CIT, personal tax, and revenues from property (movable and immovable property owned by the local government or community). This property consists of, for example, public real estate (squares, official buildings, nurseries, schools, etc.) owned by the local government. The structure of LGUs' own revenue is shown in figure 17.5.

The own revenue of LGUs in years 2016–2020 is presented in figure 17.6.

Based on the data presented in figure 17.6, it is apparent that there is a successive increase in the income of LGUs from property taxation. The increase is observed with the property tax, averaging about 1 percent per year over the past five years, and with revenue generated from the

Figure 17.5 Structure of LGU Revenue

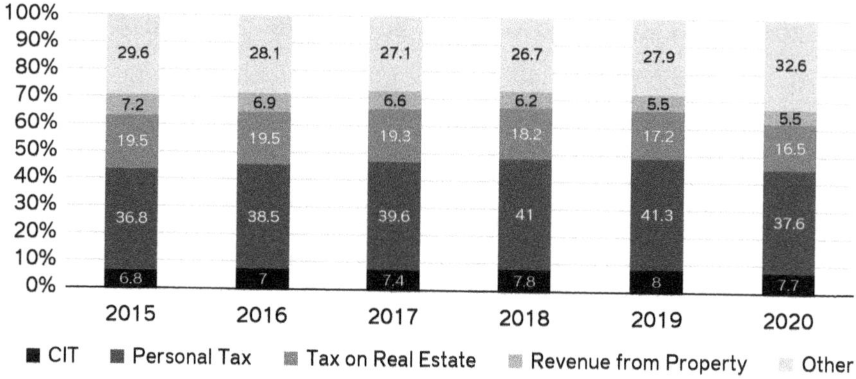

Source: Authors' calculations based on Ministry of Finance (2021).

Figure 17.6 Own Revenue of LGUs (US$ million)

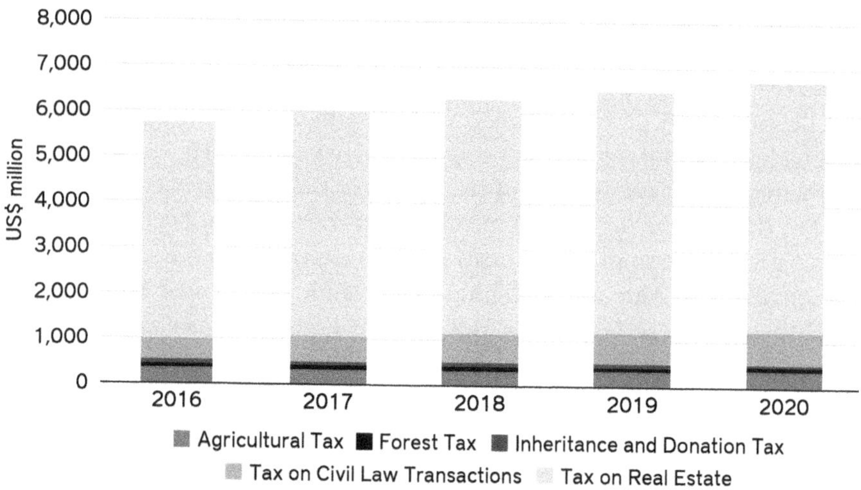

Source: Authors' calculations based on Ministry of Finance (2021).

forestry property tax, which is at 0.7 percent. The higher revenues are due to the increase in the ceiling for tax rates for the period under review. In the existing system of taxation, an increase in revenue from real estate taxes is achieved mainly by adopting the upper tax amount specified by the minister of finance for a given tax year. At the same time, there is a noticeable decline in revenue from the agricultural tax. This is related to urban sprawl, which has led to the conversion of agricultural properties located in the vicinity of large cities to areas zoned for single- and multifamily housing (Tataruch, Zysk, and Do Thi Tuyet 2019; Zysk and Wawrowska 2018). Geodetic data obtained from Head Office of Geodesy and Cartography (n.d.) also indicate an annual loss of agricultural land to developed areas.

General Remarks

It is important to emphasize that the current administrative division of the state is characterized by a fragmentation of basic LGUs and wide variation in the size of LGUs. The smallest municipalities have the fewest resources to carry out assigned local-government tasks—not only in absolute terms but also per capita.

The act of October 27, 2017, which amends the Act on Local Taxes and Fees (1991), is a continuation of the legislature's efforts to bring apparent rationalization to the local-government tax system. The main effect of the solutions proposed by the legislature is the introduction of an obligation for tax authorities to provide selected information on property tax, agricultural tax, and forestry tax. According to the Finance Ministry, the information thus obtained will increase the possibilities of analyzing and evaluating the tax policy of municipalities in terms of utilizing their income potential.

Recurrent Land and Property Tax

The real estate taxation system in Poland consists of three types of taxes: the real estate tax, which concerns nonagricultural land (i.e., built-up and intended for development); the agricultural land tax; and the forest tax. This system was developed during the period of a centrally controlled economy. Its main principles were adopted in the mid-1980s (agricultural land tax) and in the early 1990s (new forest tax). Later, small changes in the structure of taxes were made, aimed at adjusting to the changing socioeconomic situation. Every self-government commune in Poland has a certain degree of flexibility regarding the size of taxes in the form of setting tax amounts, introducing exemptions and reductions, and determining the mode of their payment. However, these may not exceed the maximum amount established by the legislator (Lesner 2021; Trojanek and Kisiała 2018).

Tax Base

The base for the recurrent property tax for land is its physical area. For buildings or parts of them (not used for business purposes), it is *usable area*. For taxation purposes, the usable area of rooms with a clear height is as follows: above 2.2 meters, 100 percent is included; from 1.4 meters to 2.2 meters, 50 percent is included; and less than 1.4 meters, the area is ignored.[4] For other structures (any construction object that is not a building) or their parts related to the running of a business, it is the *value* determined as of January 1 of the tax year. The value of the structure is determined separately from the value of the land. If the taxpayer has not specified the value of the structure or has provided a value that does not correspond to the market value, the tax authority appoints a property appraiser who determines this value. The basis for the taxation of a structure for property tax is its value, as referred to in the Act on Personal Income Tax 1991, which is the basis for determining depreciation. Thus, it is the so-called initial value of a structure as a fixed asset, or its updated value. It may correspond to either the acquisition cost or the manufacturing cost of a given structure, which are slightly different concepts:

- The acquisition cost is the price at which a given structure was purchased plus the costs of transport, loading and unloading, insurance en route, assembly, installation, notarial, stamp and other fees, interest, and commissions.
- The manufacturing cost includes the value (at the purchase price) of materials and consumption of other tangible assets, third-party services used, labor remuneration costs (including derivatives), and other costs that can be included in the value of manufactured fixed assets (structures).[5]

For urbanized land, regardless of its intended use in the local spatial development plan, the taxable amount is the area taken from the real estate cadastre. For agricultural and forest land, it is the so-called conversion area. In the case of agriculture, it depends not only on the area of land but also on the type of land use, bonitation[6] classes, and location. Table 17.7 contains conversion factors for areas of agricultural land, meadows, and pastures. The numbers of tax districts result from the division of the commune area into smaller areas characterized by similar conditions of agricultural use and result from the provisions of law (Act on Agricultural Tax 1984). For example, 1 hectare of arable land recorded in the real estate cadastre as being located in the best tax district (I district) and in the best bonitation class (I class) receives a coefficient of 1.95. This means that the agricultural tax will be calculated for a conversion area of 1.95 hectares.

In terms of the *coverage of tax base* in Poland, single plots of land are registered in the state real estate system—namely, the land and building cadastre, or in short, "cadastre"—as stated in table 17.8.

Table 17.7 Conversion Factors Used to Determine Land Area for Agricultural Tax

Type of Agricultural Land	**Arable Land**				**Meadows and Pastures**			
Tax Districts	**I**	**II**	**III**	**IV**	**I**	**II**	**III**	**IV**
Bonitation classes of agricultural land	Conversion factors							
I	1.95	1.80	1.65	1.45	1.75	1.60	1.45	1.35
II	1.80	1.65	1.50	1.35	1.45	1.35	1.25	1.10
IIIa	1.65	1.50	1.40	1.25	n.a.	n.a.	n.a.	n.a.
III	n.a.	n.a.	n.a.	n.a.	1.25	1.15	1.05	0.95
IIIb	1.35	1.25	1.15	1.00	n.a.	n.a.	n.a.	n.a.
IVa	1.10	1.00	0.90	0.80	n.a.	n.a.	n.a.	n.a.

Source: Act on Agricultural Tax (1984).

Note: n.a. = not available.

Table 17.8 Number of Plots Registered in the Land and Building Cadastre

Year	**Number of Plots in Urban Areas**	**Number of Plots in Rural Areas**	**Total**
2020	7,933,988	28,512,928	36,446,916
2021	8,176,154	29,716,614	37,892,768
2022	8,289,663	29,812,569	38,102,232

Source: Head Office of Geodesy and Cartography (2023).

Collections and Arrears

There is no collective information for the whole country on the amount of revenue lost due to exemptions and exclusions. The information obtained directly from the city of Gdańsk (one of the biggest voivodeship cities in Poland) shows that the greatest amount of arrears due to unpaid taxes concerned the agricultural tax: in the period from 2018 to 2020, it was at the level of 11–13 percent of the tax due. The arrears are the lowest in the case of forest tax; in the same period, they ranged from 0.17 percent to 0.04 percent. The level of real estate tax arrears is gradually decreasing—in 2018 it was at 5.77 percent, and in 2020 at 1.95 percent. On the other hand, in a smaller voivodeship city, Olsztyn, the analysis of analogous data indicates that the greatest arrears are in the field of real estate tax. In the same period, it was 13 percent. The lowest level of losses was related to forest tax—it was at 0.33–1.21 percent. In Olsztyn, the level of tax arrears for all types of taxes is also decreasing—in 2018 it was at 6.2 percent and in 2020 at 5.96 percent.

A *taxpayer* (responsible for payment of the tax) is a natural person, a legal person, or an organizational unit without legal personality, subject to tax liability under tax laws. Taxpayers are owners of real estate or building structures, independent owners of real estate or building structures, and perpetual usufructuaries of land. The tax from the structures is paid only by taxpayers who conduct business activity in construction. The lessee is the taxpayer for the agricultural tax, if the land of the agricultural holding has been leased on the basis of an agreement concluded in accordance with the provisions on social insurance for farmers or the provisions on obtaining structural pensions. If the property or construction work is jointly owned or owned by two or more entities, it is a separate subject of taxation. The tax obligation rests jointly and severally on all co-owners or holders of the subject of taxation.

If the owner changes over the course of the year, the property tax is apportioned in a manner that corresponds to the period of the year in which each owner managed the property. These changes should be reported to the commune office within 14 days. The obligation to notify also applies to those taxpayers who build a house and live in it. The tax will be charged to them from the next year.

Assessment

The basis for assessing real estate tax is *property data* from the land and building cadastre (real estate cadastre). The tax office is obliged to take them into account, even if they are incorrect. Correction of these data should be requested in the manner specified in the Act on Geodetic and Cartographic Law (1989). The real estate cadastre includes, among other things, information on

- land—area, types of land use, and their valuation classes;
- buildings—utility functions, built-up area, and general technical data;
- premises—utility functions and usable area; and
- information entered into the register of monuments.

The real estate cadastre is one of the main reference registers containing information on real estate. It is used during the implementation of tasks in the fields of economic planning, spatial planning, tax assessment, marking real estate in land and mortgage registers, public statistics, and real estate management. The communal tax authority obtains information as well from the following sources: land and mortgage registers, notarial deeds, registers of issued decisions on building conditions and land development, issued building permit decisions, local zoning plans, records kept by tax offices, and, above all, declarations the submission of which is the responsibility of taxpayers. In a situation where the objects of taxation are not entered in the real estate cadastre, data on the area of the building and premises are accepted on the basis of the taxpayer's declaration.

Natural persons are required to submit to the competent tax authority information on the objects of taxation within 14 days from the date of the occurrence of circumstances justifying the emergence or expiry of the tax obligation. Legal persons, organizational units, and companies without legal personality are required to submit real estate tax declarations for every tax year. The declaration includes information on land and building area, tax rate, and tax amount, among other characteristics. This information and real estate tax declarations may be submitted by electronic means of communication. In order to correctly determine the amount of the tax liability or the tax base, control activities may be carried out by authorized employees of the tax authority after obtaining the consent of the district prosecutor at its request (Article 288 of the Tax Ordinance Act 1997). The inspector has the right to enter the premises, building, or apartment under control for the purpose of doing an inspection, if they have been indicated as the place of business or the seat of the controlled entity. For the purposes of tax assessment and collection, the tax authorities keep real estate tax records in the administration system. It contains data on taxpayers and subjects of taxation. The rules of keeping real estate tax records in the information technology system and cooperation with the real estate cadastre are specified by the minister responsible for public finances (Act on Local Taxes and Fees 1991). Tax offices do not provide special incentives for taxpayers to correctly declare their property. In the declaration form (or tax statement) delivered to the tax office, taxpayers must sign a statement indicating that the data they provide is truthful. There are no lists containing estimates of revenue losses for this reason.

A tool for comparing the data from the real estate tax records with the data from the real estate cadastre, the Integrated Real Estate Information System, was supposed to be implemented in order to correctly determine the tax assessment. According to the Act on Geodetic and Cartographic Law (1989), the general surveyor of Poland is responsible for creating and maintaining the Integrated Real Estate Information System. This task is performed in cooperation with county starosts, voivodes and voivodship marshals, the minister of justice, the minister responsible for computerization, the minister responsible for internal affairs, the minister responsible for public finance, the minister responsible for the environment, the president of the Central Statistical Office, and the president of the Restructuring Agency and Modernization of Agriculture. However, this system is not as yet fully operational. The main obstacle is the incomplete supply of the central repository with data from the real estate cadastre, with which all registers communicate (including land and mortgage registers and real estate tax records) on the basis of data exchange. The land and building register (real estate cadastre) is maintained by the heads of counties, which results in 380 units being responsible for maintaining them. The cadastral data, and in particular the data on cadastral parcels, are the primary reference data for the presentation of various other objects and features collected in spatial information databases. When a parcel is found, it is also possible to access the objects located on it at the same time (Head Office of Geodesy and Cartography, n.d.). Each plot of land has a unique identifier in the real estate cadastre.[7]

A serious problem is the lack of data on the usable area of buildings in the real estate cadastre. Taxpayers must define and declare it themselves, as the usable areas indicated in construction projects may significantly differ from the usable areas that should be declared for tax purposes. Contradictory definitions of the usable area in various acts and regulations make it difficult to correctly define the area. Suggestions as to the need to enter the usable area of buildings into the cadastre are formulated by various entities (e.g., property appraisers). This problem is also being considered by the central office, the Head Office of Geodesy and Cartography. It can be hoped that this problem will be solved in near future. There are also no data on structures in the cadastre.

A further problem concerns the credibility (timeliness) of the records in the land cadastre, although there is a legal obligation to update the information contained in this system. In some situations, changes in land use (from agricultural to urbanized) are entered into the register with a delay. This may result in incorrect taxation of the land and a reduction in the revenue of communes on this account. No information is published on the amount of the lost income for that reason. Changes in the cadastral register are made by cadastral staff offices on the basis of entries in land and mortgage registers, final court decisions, final administrative decisions, notarial deeds, notifications of real estate owners regarding a change in the use of the building or its part to which the competent authority has not raised any objections, geodetic documentation adopted to the state geodetic and cartographic resource, and by way of an administrative decision (Act on Geodetic and Cartographic Law 1989).

Objections and Appeals

Property taxes in the Polish legal system can be a subject of objections and appeals. The taxpayer has the right to formulate objections against the tax decision, but also against the tax proceedings preceding its issuance. The objections may concern, for example, incorrect application or misinterpretation of tax law provisions, or omission of the evidence requested. Tax proceedings have two stages. First, the taxpayer may appeal against the decision of the tax authority to the appeal authority within 14 days. The appeal authority is the local-government appeal board. The appeal is lodged through the tax authority that issued the decision. The appeal may be submitted in writing or orally, or by electronic means of communication via the electronic inbox of the tax authority or the tax portal. Second, if the local-government appeals board does not accept the appeal, the taxpayer may go to court. In the first instance, it will be the provincial administrative court.

Tax Amounts (Rates)

The maximum amount of real estate tax for a given tax year is specified in the Act on Local Taxes and Fees (1991). It is established by the minister of finance. On this basis, the commune council, by means of a resolution, determines the amount of real estate tax rates, which may not exceed the maximum rates. The commune council may differentiate its amount for particular types of objects of taxation accounting—in particular, for the location, type of activity, type of development, and type of land use (Trojanek, Kisiala, and Trojanek 2021). In relation to buildings, it may additionally account for the type of development, technical condition, and age of the buildings; unfortunately the possibility given by law is not used in practice. A comparison between the adopted tax amount in 2022 in voivodeship cities in Poland and the maximum amount established by minister of finance is presented in figure 17.7 (see the data in the framed row).

Figure 17.7 shows that the authorities of eight large cities (municipalities with county rights: Warszawa, Gdańsk, Kraków, Wrocław, Poznań, Łódź, Bydgoszcz, and Szczecin) adopted a resolution on the determination of real estate taxes for a given tax year, assuming the maximum amounts per one square meter of taxed area allowed by law for all kinds of taxation objects.

The powers of commune councils with respect to the rates of the agricultural and forestry tax are slightly different. The amounts of those taxes depend not only on the area of land subject to taxation but also, respectively, on the price of a purchase of 100 kilos (1 quintal) of rye or a

Figure 17.7 Adopted Tax Amount (in US$ per square meter) in 2022 in Voivodeship Cities in Poland, Established by the Minister of Finance

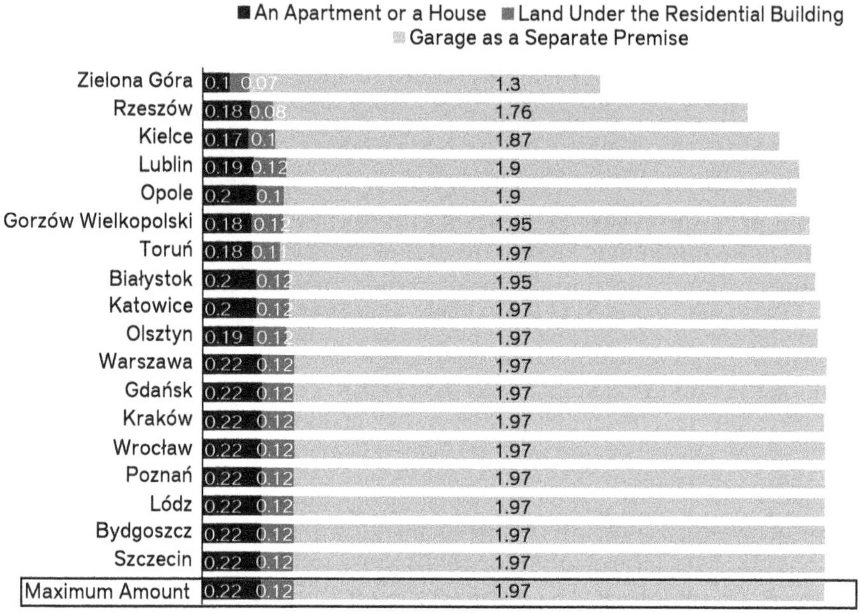

Source: Authors' study based on Podatki (2022).

sale of 1 cubic meter of wood. In the case of the agricultural tax, the statutory tax rate is the equivalent of the price of 2.5 or 5.0 quintals of rye per tax year. The forestry tax rate is the equivalent of the price of 0.220 cubic meters of wood. If the commune council does not take any action, the aforementioned values constitute the basis for calculating the tax in a given year. However, by virtue of a resolution of the commune council, it is possible to reduce both the price of rye and the price of wood for the purpose of calculating the tax for a given tax year (Dowgier 2021). Each year, the minister of finance indexes the tax rate on the basis of the index of changes (increase) in the prices of goods and services, also established annually by the president of Statistics Poland and published in the Official Journal of the Republic of Poland, *Monitor Polski*. Once established, this rate is not reduced later. If, during the tax year, there was an event affecting the amount of taxation that year—in particular a change in the use of the subject of taxation—the tax is reduced or increased, starting from the first day of the month following the month in which the event occurred.

Tax Reliefs and Exemptions

The Tax Ordinance Act 1997 also allows for the application of *exemptions* and other forms of *tax relief*. The real estate tax is not paid, for example, by farmers, because they have to pay the agricultural tax. The following are also exempt from real estate tax: port infrastructure buildings and land occupied for them; land, buildings, and structures in the area of public use airports; farm buildings for forestry or fishing activities; land and buildings entered in the register of monuments (subject to their conservation, in accordance with the provisions on the protection of monuments); and universities. The exemption from paying real estate tax does not apply to real estate on which business activity is conducted. Tax reliefs for a taxpayer running a business, as a rule, can be granted under de minimis aid (on the terms set out in applicable acts such as the Act on Municipal Self-Government [1990]).

The commune council may introduce this tax exemption in the form of a resolution constituting an aid program, while maintaining the solutions based on the European Community regulations on de minimis aid, which exempt the aid from the notification obligation; however, the draft resolution must be submitted to the president of the Office of Competition and Consumer Protection for information.

The basic legal act regulating the granting of de minimis aid is Commission Regulation (EU) No. 1407/2013 of December 18, 2013, on the application of articles 107 and 108 of the Treaty on the Functioning of the European Union for de minimis aid (European Commission 2013). The application for tax relief may be sent electronically via the electronic inbox on the tax portal, submitted to the commune office, or sent by post.

Real estate tax is also not subject to reciprocity—real estate owned by foreign countries or international organizations or transferred to them for perpetual usufruct. Agricultural land with the worst bonitation classes (V, VI, and vIz) receives exemptions. The Tax Ordinance Act (1997) also allows for the application of tax reliefs.

The tax authority, in cases justified by an important interest of the taxpayer (e.g., very difficult financial and property situation) or the public interest, may, at the taxpayer's request,

- postpone the tax payment deadline or divide its payment into installments; or
- cancel all or part of the tax arrears and late payment interest.

In 2021, property tax exemption was available to entrepreneurs facing financial difficulties due to the COVID-19 pandemic. This possibility was provided to them by the Act on Special Solutions for Preventing, Countering and Combating COVID-19 2020. Such exemptions are therefore temporary and are introduced through separate resolutions by city and municipal councils. The tax office is the part of the communal administration responsible for administration and tax billing. It delivers the tax bill in paper form to the taxpayer via a messenger of the commune office, if the taxpayer has a residence address or address for service in the commune, or by registered mail in other cases. Tax bills are received by taxpayers for all types of real estate at the same time—by March 1 in a given tax year at the latest.

As for property tax collection, owners of all kinds of private properties must wait for a decision on the amount of tax from the commune office. The taxpayer is obliged to pay the tax calculated in the declaration without being summoned. The tax is payable in installments. When the amount of property tax does not exceed PLN 100, the property owner has to pay it in a single installment by March 15. The commune council may order the collection of real estate tax from natural persons and microentrepreneurs by way of collection. Enterprises can calculate their own property tax and pay it monthly.

Legal regulations regarding the enforcement of local taxes and fees in Poland are sufficient, but they are not perfect in practice. The periodic inspections carried out by the Supreme Audit Office show that the slowness of some municipalities in issuing reminders and writs of execution, as well as the lack of preventive measures, significantly reduced the effectiveness of enforcement and strengthened the feeling of impunity among debtors.

The Supreme Audit Office recommends that municipalities enforce the submission of the required declarations and information from all taxpayers and verify them thoroughly with source documents and databases. The office also recommends increasing the scope of tax audits, conducting ongoing verification of tax arrears, and ensuring correct application and reliable documentation of the premises entitled to receive tax relief (PAP 2022).

Tax payment can be made directly to the cash desk of the commune office or by bank transfer. Agricultural tax from natural persons may be collected by the village administrator. Entrepreneurs can only pay by bank transfer. Tax regulations do not provide for discounts for early payment.

The Polish property tax system has particular rules for *enforcement* procedures. Failure to pay taxes on time may result in enforcement proceedings and the addition of late payment interest. The rate of such interest amounts to twice the National Bank of Poland Lombard rate[8] increased by 2 percentage points, but not less than 8 percent per annum. As a rule, compulsory tax enforcement is carried out in administrative enforcement proceedings and after the end of tax proceedings. In the course of tax proceedings, the tax authorities take all necessary steps to thoroughly explain the facts and settle the case. In tax proceedings, cases must be settled in one of two forms: in writing or in the form of an electronic document. The principle of two-stage proceedings applies. On January 1, 2016, the principle of resolving doubts in tax law in favor of the taxpayer was introduced. Where it is possible to choose from several enforcement measures leading directly to the performance of the obligation, the ones that are the least burdensome for the obligated should be used. It is up to the creditor and the enforcement authority to assess the severity of the individual enforcement measures. The Tax Ordinance Act (1997) provides a catalog of enforcement measures that may be applied against an unreliable debtor. Debtors are usually disciplined by the admonition itself. However, if necessary, enforcement measures may include deductions from wages and salaries, pensions, bank accounts, securities, promissory notes, movables, and real estate. The regulations introduced in 2016 regarding the information recorded by creditors brought positive results. The collection of tax arrears, even before the launch of administrative enforcement, increased significantly. However, municipalities do not fully use the enforcement measures available under the law. One example is property foreclosure, whose limited application is often explained by practical or political constraints, such as low debt amounts, the presence of other creditors, encumbered property, or the social consequences of enforcement.

Property Tax in Large Urban Areas

The previous subsections discussed in detail the scope and type of property taxes in the Polish tax system. The average GDP in 2021 was PLN 69,100 (at current prices) (figure 17.8).

The statistics in table 17.9 show the national dominance of the capital city in collections of property tax and property transfer taxes. The comparison also shows data for Olsztyn (a provincial city) and suggests the degree to which the capital city dominates. Other large cities in Poland in such comparisons with Warsaw do not reach the same level of property tax or transfer tax revenue, highlighting the capital's exceptional fiscal position.

The percentage distribution of revenues for Warsaw and Poland for the period from 2018 to 2021 is presented in table 17.10 for all major categories in local-government revenues. The share of annual property tax revenues in total collections declined during the period shown, but the share of property transfer taxes increased. This may partially reflect COVID-19 pandemic impacts. Also of note during this period is the declining importance of shared income tax revenues.

Figure 17.8 GDP per Capita in Voivodeships of Poland in Relation to National Average GDP in 2021

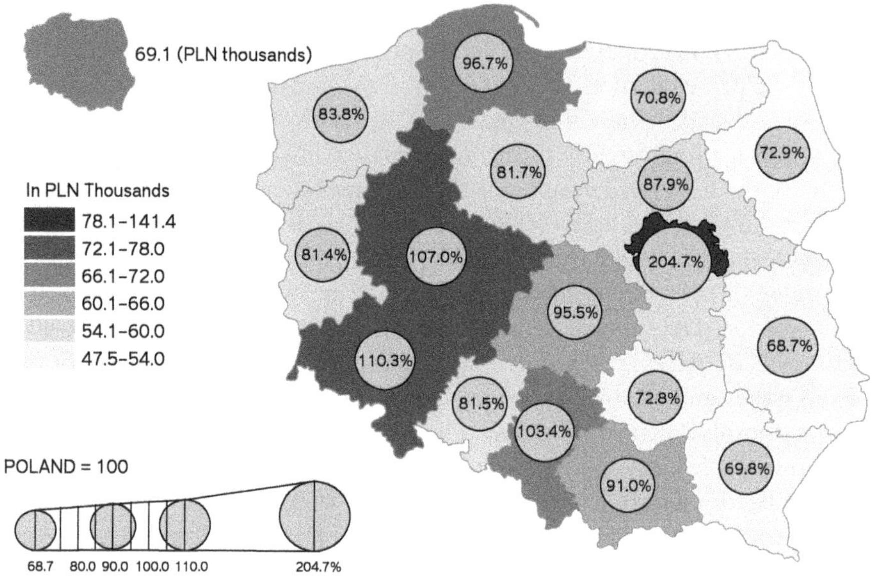

Source: Authors' elaboration based on Narodowy Bank Polski (n.d.).

Table 17.9 Property Tax Characteristics of Warsaw and Olsztyn

Characteristics Year 2021	**Warsaw**	**Olsztyn**	**Poland**
Population (million)	1.79	0.17	37.45
Per capita property tax revenues (US$)	172.75	162.41	158.50
Per capita stamp duty revenues (US$)	13.33	7.36	3.24
Per capita tax on civil law transactions revenues (US$)	134.20	32.10	27.20

Source: Authors' elaboration based on Ministry of Finance (2021); Polska w liczbach (n.d.); and interviews with officials in the Taxpayer Service Center of Warsaw and Olsztyn.

The reduction in PIT revenue shown in table 17.10 is mainly due to legislative changes, such as the reduction in the PIT rate from 18 percent to 17 percent and the PIT exemption for those under 26.

Comparing implementation with municipal budget planning gives an opportunity to look for factors relevant to diagnosing and assessing the

Table 17.10 Percentage Distribution of Revenues for Warsaw and Poland

	2018		2021	
Selected Revenues	**Warsaw**	**Poland (LGU)**	**Warsaw**	**Poland (LGU)**
Property tax	6.99	18.23	6.31	16.46
Agricultural tax	0.001	1.190	0.008	1.030
Forest tax	0.001	0.240	0.030	0.190
Inheritance tax	0.70	0.24	0.63	0.26
Stamp duty	1.06	0.38	0.93	0.36
Tax on civil law transactions	3.42	0.21	4.9	2.82
PIT	33.00	41.04	31.10	39.13
CIT	5.30	7.81	4.40	9.01

Source: Authors' elaboration based on data obtained from the Taxpayer Service Center in Warsaw City Hall.

Note: On May 29, 2019, Order No. 906/2019 was signed by the president of the city of Warsaw, amending the order on granting organizational regulations for the Office of the City of Warsaw, in which the Taxpayer Service Center was established. Until the establishment of this center, the tasks of handling the system of local taxes and fees were carried out in 18 districts of the city of Warsaw, in which unrelated, separate information technology systems were operating. Therefore, the Taxpayer Service Center does not have data for the period 2018–2019.

quality of financial management. It also identifies unexpected changes. Comparison of the planned and actual revenue from real estate taxes in Warsaw in 2018–2019 shows that actual collections exceeded the budgeted estimates by more than 3 percent in 2018 and 5 percent in 2019. Table 17.11 presents the actual revenue of selected taxes in Warsaw's budget as a percentage of the planned revenue. In subsequent years, the planned revenue of the real estate tax had been 93.5 percent (2020) and 98.8 percent (2021).

The taxes on civil law transactions in the period under review have maintained a steady trend and actual revenues have been more than 100 percent of budgeted estimates. In 2021, the execution exceeded the estimate over 111.7 percent; this may be related to turnover in the real estate market, primarily the sale of real estate and a growth of revenue from transfer real estate. The upward trend is also noticeable with the inheritance and gift tax, except for 2019, when there was a decrease; in the remaining years it remained above the estimate. In 2021, it reached an increase of more than 36 percent. Agricultural and forestry taxes have been

Table 17.11 Tax Realization Versus Plan in the Budget of the City of Warsaw, 2018–2021 (%; 100% = full plan realization)

Specification	2018	2019	2020	2021
Property tax	100.4	102.2	93.5	98.8
Agricultural tax	94.4	92.5	15.7	82.0
Forest tax	169.2	102.3	63.1	80.3
Tax on inheritances and donations	114.1	78.3	119.9	136.9
Tax on civil law transactions	132.9	126.8	124.5	211.7

Source: Authors' calculations based on compendium data (BIP Warsaw 2022).

Table 17.12 Tax Realization Versus Plan in the Budget of the City of Olsztyn, 2018–2021 (%; 100% = full plan realization)

Specification	2018	2019	2020	2021
Property tax	106.40	106.90	102.60	108.20
Agricultural tax/ forest tax	105.80	124.40	105.30	104.28
Tax on inheritances and donations	138.30	144.30	208.40	177.18
Tax on civil law transactions	90.87	88.49	99.21	150.67

Source: Authors' calculations based on compendium data (BIP Olsztyn 2020).

on a downward trend since 2020, and this may be related to the city's current spatial policy, including the de-landing of property and the allocation of land for single-family and residential development.

A comparison of the plan and execution in the areas of real estate, agricultural, and forestry taxes in the city of Olsztyn in 2018–2021 shows that the plan was executed above the estimate. An upward trend was noted in the area of tax on inheritances and donations, including a more than twofold increase in 2020. In the area of tax on civil and legal transactions in 2018–2020, it was below 100 percent, while in 2021 there was a significant increase of more than 50 percent of the estimate (table 17.12). Again, it is noteworthy that these comparisons include the COVID-19 pandemic years.

To present a detailed benchmarking analysis in terms of the implemented property tax policy in Poland, several cities were selected based on demographic and statistical data (table 17.13).

The total amounts of agricultural, forestry, and real estate taxes as percentages of own income and revenue in the selected cities are presented in table 17.14.

Table 17.13 Demographic and Statistical Data for Selected Cities in 2022

	Olsztyn	**Katowice**	**Białystok**	**Warszawa**	**Łódź**	**Gdańsk**
Province	Warmińsko-mazurskie	Śląskie	Podlaskie	Mazowieckie	Łódzkie	Pomorskie
GDP province (% per capita, 2021)	70.8	103.4	72.9	204.7	95.9	96.7
Area (km^2)	88.3	164.6	102.1	517.2	293.3	262.0
Population	170,622	289,162	296,401	1,792,718	667,923	470,633
Population density (people/km^2)	1,931.6	1,756.3	2,902.2	3,465.9	2,277.7	1,796.6
Women (%)	53.5	52.5	53.1	53.9	54.4	52.7

Source: Authors' elaboration based on Polska w liczbach (n.d.).

Table 17.14 Scope of Tax Data in Analyzed Cities

	2018	2019	2020	2021
Total Amounts of Agricultural, Forestry, and Real Estate Taxes as % of Own Income and Revenue in the City				
Białystok	6.46	6.13	6.18	6.16
Katowice	12.45	11.72	11.92	12.51
Olsztyn	12.89	13.77	15.16	13.53
Łódź	11.00	10.20	9.70	9.40
Warszawa	9.98	9.73	9.57	9.84
Gdańsk	13.90	18.63	17.80	15.00
Percentage of the Area of Land Under Real Estate Tax in the Total Area of Taxed Real Estate				
Białystok	n.a.	n.a.	n.a.	n.a.
Katowice	n.a.	n.a.	n.a.	n.a.
Olsztyn				
Land in agricultural tax	10.01	8.40	8.50	9.14
Land in forestry tax	31.37	32.61	32.43	32.64
Land in real estate tax	42.73	42.92	42.88	42.03
Łódź				
Land in agricultural tax	13.01	12.27	12.25	12.24
Land in forestry tax	36.30	36.93	36.76	36.37
Land in real estate tax	50.69	50.80	50.99	51.40
Warszawa				
Land in agricultural tax	n.a.	n.a.	17.38	17.20
Land in forestry tax	n.a.	n.a.	20.32	19.00
Land in real estate tax	n.a.	n.a.	62.30	63.80
Gdańsk	n.a.	n.a.	n.a.	n.a.
Exemption Value (%)				
Białystok	0.89	0.69	2.53	2.39
Katowice	8.23	7.58	35.99	34.69
Olsztyn	4.96	9.36	4.16	n.a.
Łódź	19.83	15.23	18.09	18.32
Warszawa	n.a.	n.a.	47.49	47.90
Gdańsk	31.89	29.33	30.03	28.76

Source: Authors' elaboration based on interviews with officials in the Taxpayer Service Center in Warsaw, Białystok, Katowice, Olsztyn, Łódź, and Gdańsk.

Note: n.a. = not available.

In 2021, the highest shares were obtained in Gdańsk and Olsztyn, and the lowest shares were recorded in Warsaw and Łódź (see table 17.14).

The percentage share of land area (buildings or parts thereof) under the property tax in the total area of taxed real estate (land and buildings or parts thereof) occurred in the period 2020–2021 in the city of Warsaw at the level of more than 60 percent. In Łódź it oscillates at over 50 percent, while the lowest level is in the city of Olsztyn at 42 percent. In terms of agricultural tax, Warsaw occupies the highest position, followed by Łódź and Olsztyn. In terms of forestry tax, Łódź occupies the highest position, followed by Olsztyn and Warsaw. The smallest property tax exemptions (value of exempted structures) were recorded in 2021 in Białystok and Łódź.

The percentage shares presented in table 17.14 are mainly a result of the structure of the land and ownership relations that are located in the area of each city.

Reform Initiatives and Country-Specific Issues

Some attempts have been made to change the real estate tax base from "area" to ad valorem. In Poland the value-based tax is commonly referred to as the cadastral tax. Such a change would bring Poland's tax regime closer to mainstream OECD practice.

Provisions on mass appraisal of real estate were introduced into the Act on Real Estate Management issued in 1997 in order to determine the cadastral value of real estate. However, ad valorem taxation has not been carried out so far (apart from the pilot studies supervised by the Head Office of Geodesy and Cartography before 2000). Many scientific articles on the methodology of mass valuation in Poland have been published (Cellmer et al. 2014; Walacik 2016; Walacik, Cellmer, and Źróbek 2013). However, no legal acts have been issued specifying the dates of commencement and completion of mass appraisal or the sources of its financing. Also, as of this writing, the comprehensive program of the Polish government does not contain any plans to introduce a cadastral tax (Źróbek, Renigier-Biłozor, and Źróbek 2024).

Government authorities are not interested in introducing this reform of the property tax system. The estimated expenditure from the State Treasury budget for its implementation is significant (especially that for designing and implementing a system for mass taxation and for periodic updating of cadastral values), and revenues from real estate taxes will become the income of local-government budgets and not the state budget. With the strained state budget, spending on the reform of taxes that stimulate local budgets is not an action that will be easily accepted by the finance minister and the Parliament. The experience gained so far with attempts to reform real estate tax justifies the claim that the majority of LGUs are also not interested in this reform. They are afraid that the costs of its implementation will be passed on by the government to municipalities, and its effects will only be visible in a longer period than the term of office of the local authorities introducing these changes.

Mass media evidence shows that taxpayers are not interested in reforming the existing tax system. They are afraid of the ad valorem tax because they do not understand it. Currently, the taxes paid are relatively low; therefore, in the opinion of taxpayers, the changes will lead to an increase. There is a view in the media that the introduction of a tax based on the value of real estate (cadastral tax, sarcastically called a catastrophic tax by some) would adversely affect the budgets of households, because the tax related to their real estate would probably increase several times. For some taxpayers, such a change could involve the need to move to a smaller or less attractive flat. The rents of real estate would also certainly increase, as the landlord would add the increased tax to the rent. A reform of real estate taxation in Poland would require a simultaneous modification of the taxation of income from agricultural and forestry activities. Currently, the lack of inclusion of this income in the income tax is explained by the nature of the agricultural and forest taxes.

At the end of 2021, the Ministry of Finance wrote on its Twitter profile, "The government has no plans to introduce a cadastral tax" (see Renigier-Biłozor, Źróbek, and Chmielewska 2025; Źróbek, Renigier-Biłozor, and Źróbek 2024). The information that appeared in the media was untrue. On the other hand, the government is analyzing the issue of the taxation of purchased apartments that remain empty, with their owners expecting to resell them at a profit. It would be referred to as a "vacancy tax." Such a tax would probably be collected by local governments. However, there was no official information on the progress of activities in this matter as of the date of the report (*Business Insider* 2021; Wara-Wąsowska 2021). In April 2024, the Ministry of Finance officially denied any intention to introduce a tax on the value of real estate. According to the deputy minister, "There are no current plans to introduce systemic changes in real estate taxation" (*Gazeta Prawna* 2024).

In recent years, the media has also discussed the concept of "improving" the definition of the term *surface* in relation to buildings and premises as the tax base. This was presented as an alternative to the ad valorem reform, costly and unpopular with taxpayers. However, so far there are no specifics on how this new surface measurement would be determined. Some would argue that one of the key conditions for changing the real estate taxation system is the need to complete the construction of and implement the Integrated Real Estate Information System, enabling efficient mass real estate appraisal. This system would also serve the needs of many other public authorities (R. Źróbek 2020; S. Źróbek et al. 2016), enabling better communication between the functioning public registers (including the Central Register and Information on Economic Activity and the National Court Register) (Act on the National Court Register 1997).

In conclusion, the attempts to reform the taxation system of land, buildings, and premises in Poland have not been successful. The system based on the area of land and buildings is still in force. The introduction of a value-based tax (cadastral tax) requires a great deal of economic, sociological, and sociopolitical research, especially in the context of the expected increase in the tax burden.

Impact

The political system in Poland is characterized by the decentralization of public authority. This involves the granting of financial autonomy to local government, which is manifested, inter alia, by income from taxes and local fees. Local taxes and fees support the implementation of local-government economic policy in many areas. Real estate tax is primarily characterized by a fiscal and redistributive function, but at the same time it contributes little to the smoothing of economic fluctuations (stabilization function) and, as a rule, does not take into account the specific situation of the taxpayer (social function). Local taxes and fees, although they have a marginal share in Poland's GDP, are an important source of local-government revenues. To a large extent, they determine the satisfaction of investment needs and may also constitute a criterion for the competitiveness of local governments.

Research has shown that the vast majority of communes in Poland applied tax reductions (reliefs) by lowering the upper rates of real estate tax. These activities were aimed at attracting new investors or retaining existing investors. In urbanized, well-developed communes, rich in natural resources or attractive for tourists, the reduction of property tax did not stimulate development. The encouragement of local tax competition is one of the attempts (apart from public intervention) to reduce the scale of disproportions and maintain the economic and territorial cohesion of the country, but the effects of these activities are not particularly spectacular. Due to the specific structure of agricultural and forestry taxes, their role in the entire tax system is average or unnoticeable (Grześkiewicz 2004).

The amount of property taxes determined according to the current system (based on area) does not show any noticeable impact on the property market or land prices. For property owners, one-off fiscal charges are often perceived as more severe, as their amount is directly linked to the increase in the market value of the property (Jackowska 2020). These charges include the planning fee for changing the designated land use in the local spatial plan and the adjacent fees applied when land is subdivided into building plots or connected to technical infrastructure funded by the commune. The intensity of land use is mainly determined by the supply of vacant land and, consequently, the market prices of land. Property taxes have a greater impact on property tenants than on landlords. This is because the landlords transfer the tax burden to the tenants by increasing the rent.

Property tax rates are set annually at a higher level by the Ministry of Finance. However, these changes do not trigger social protests as they are not too excessive. Regressive effects result from the fact that, in the current system, the amount of tax is not a derivative of the condition of the real estate market and changes in real estate prices (values), as the market value of real estate grows faster than the tax rate. The greater impact of the real estate tax system is felt in relation to the functioning of enterprises. These entities use the real estate for the purpose of running a business. For this reason, it happens that companies pay higher taxes in Poland. According to Ayming's (2021) analysis of 300 companies, the investigated companies overpaid on average PLN 200,000.00 (US$45,454.50). The report states that, annually, 65 percent of companies in Poland pay the wrong amount of tax (including 22 percent underpayment), and nearly every second company makes overpayments (about 44 percent; there are cases in which the overpayment amounts to PLN 30 million [US$6.81 million]), which illustrates the complexity and ambiguity of tax regulations (Ayming 2021). Taxpayers can recover overpaid amounts up to five years back.

There are many reasons for this type of irregularity, the main ones being

- frequent changes in the legal acts and tax regulations;
- the fact that there are 2,478 municipalities in Poland, with the same number of local tax offices;
- incorrect classification of taxable objects to the appropriate taxation category; and
- lack of annual verification by the state of fixed assets of enterprises and ambiguity of regulations as to the proper determination of their usable area constituting the tax base.

The type of industry is also important. The largest numbers of overpayments are in the following industries: transport, chemical, thermal energy companies, water supply, and sewage systems. The analyses show that these companies had the greatest problem with identifying the appropriate building or structure category for the object and determining the appropriate category (type of land use) for the land. This is due to, inter alia, the fact that the term *real estate* as defined in the civil code is not the same as the subject of real estate tax.

Conclusion

In Poland, the legal basis for imposing taxes (including property taxes) is Article 217 of the Constitution of the Republic of Poland of April 2, 1997, while the rules for imposing them are regulated by acts—for example, the Tax Ordinance Act (1997). The Polish system of property taxation has many unique features. The tax system in Poland under discussion has undergone countless changes. These changes were supposed to lead to the construction of a rational model of real estate taxation, except that it was not clear what the assumptions of the target system were. Thus, through more than 20 years of amending regulations, a taxation model was created that was difficult to apply, contradictory, and in need of constant adjustments.

Reform of the Real Estate Taxation System in Poland

At the start, it should be explained why this reform has not been implemented. The delay is due to the country's historical background and the widespread conservatism and conformism of Polish society. At the beginning of the 1990s, the property tax system, which is still in force today, was shaped quickly and without detailed analysis or research. The real estate tax was regulated in the Act on Local Taxes and Fees of March 14, 1985, which remains in force. It reiterated the content of the act, which in turn was largely based on the solutions contained in the Act on Certain Area Taxes and Fees of December 19, 1975. In addition, the complexity of the Polish tax system is increased by the fact that agricultural and forestry taxes, which are not covered by the Act on Local Taxes and Fees, are covered in other legal provisions (Act on Agricultural Tax 1984; Act on Forest Tax 2002). Apparent reforms of the Polish tax system have created a situation in which solutions that were developed in the 1950s are still in force today, though they have nothing in common with today's legal or economic reality.

Disadvantages of the Current System of Property Taxation

The surface area of land and buildings, as opposed to their value, is the main factor in determining the amount of tax on land and buildings. This creates inequity, as the owner of an expensive property would pay the same tax as the owner of an equal-size but low-value property. The same is true with land. A square meter of land in the center of a capital city is taxed at very similar rates to a square meter of nonagricultural land in the countryside.

The continued use of the current real estate taxation model results in the following issues:

- The majority of communes do not receive adequate revenue for local budgets.
- A relatively large amount of real estate is either not taxed at all or unjustifiably subject to preferential taxation—for example, if land of a poor class is predominant in a commune and at the same time it is completely exempted from agricultural taxation (classes V, VI, and VIz), the commune is deprived of tax revenue.
- The differences in the level of taxation of specific landholdings encourage the search for ways to escape taxation. Taxpayers create artificial landholdings only to reduce the amount of taxation and to benefit from various financial preferences (e.g., subsidies or excise refunds).
- A poorly constructed statutory definition of what counts as a structure (e.g., telecommunications networks, mine workings, and wind power stations) causes numerous problems of interpretation and results in lower tax revenue.
- The lack of a uniform and reliable register of taxable objects is a major problem. The taxable area of property is intended to be taken from the land and building register. In reality, however, only the land register functions reasonably well. For buildings and premises, not all the data are included in the register, and even if they are (as in the case of premises), the usable floor area can be quite different from the registered area.
- A lack of vision for the taxation of agriculture is a problem. At present, taxes are charged only to owners of agricultural holdings—in essence, it is an area property tax with remaining elements of income taxation (reflected by conversion factors) from previous periods. In addition, the definition of an agricultural holding, which determines the preferential taxation of agricultural land, is problematic—for

example, a farmer is someone who has more than one hectare of physical or conversion area of agricultural land, though the individual may not actually carry out agricultural activities.

Why Is Real Estate Tax Reform Not Being Implemented?

One of the key prerequisites for changing the real estate taxation system in Poland is to complete the construction of the Integrated Real Estate Information System. This system would also serve the needs of many other public authorities, enabling communication between functioning public registers (including the Central Register of Land and Buildings and the National Court Register). The introduction of a cadastral tax based on cyclically updated, reliable real estate values would require research into the economic, sociological, and sociopolitical effects of this tax. A positive advantage of this land information system would be to support real estate mass valuation.

There are major barriers to moving forward with such a reform:

- Political authorities are reluctant to introduce a cadastral tax on values due to the adverse impact on voters and influential taxpayers.
- There is a high financial cost of mass valuation, and the source of funding for this expenditure is undetermined. Local government is not in a position to finance this reform, and the central government is not interested in doing so.
- Property owners—potential taxpayers—are hesitant to accept any changes to the current taxation system. This reluctance is mainly due to the fact that taxpayers fear an increase in the taxation of their real estate assets. This fear, in the case of property tax reform, is so strong that most taxpayers, not even knowing what a cadastre and a property value tax are, are opposed to their introduction.
- Changing attitudes require an extensive campaign to make the public aware of the need for a value-based tax and to show that this does not necessarily involve an increase in the tax burden, especially for residential and agricultural real estate. The communes themselves are not in a position to advance any reforms. At the same time, there is little interest in central government carrying out these reforms. It should be noted that their implementation—which is costly and would generate social conflicts—will not bring direct revenue to the state budget. Hence, there is no such determination on the part of the

government to initiate and implement reforms concerning property taxes, especially on agricultural land.

The presented characteristics of property taxation in Poland can be summarized as follows:

- Property taxes are the main source of own income for communes.
- Local governments are entitled to change the taxation amounts within the limits imposed by the Ministry of Finance.
- Property tax, with reference to the register of land and buildings, is determined on the basis of area expressed in square meters or hectares; for the agricultural tax, it is converted hectares or physical hectares; and for the forestry tax, it is physical hectares.
- Among the tax reliefs and exemptions applied, the legal status of the entity and its specifics are of paramount importance. According to tax law, exemptions are applied to state and communal real estate, and they are also granted for specific activities.

It is worth mentioning that new taxes are planned in Poland—for example, a vacancy tax for owners of uninhabited real estate. The main idea behind its introduction is to increase the supply of flats, which are lacking on the market (Spurgiasz 2022). It is not yet known whether and when such taxes will be introduced, and who would be liable for paying them.

Poland seems prepared for property tax reform in terms of having a sufficient number of specialists to carry out mass property valuations. There are about 20,000 state-authorized surveyors and about 9,000 certified property valuers to value all types of property. But there is a lack of full integration of property data held by many entities operating under different ministries. Due to the complexity of the present Integrated Real Estate Information System, the large number of entities involved in its creation, and the varied state of the data maintained by the starosts (some data are still stored in analog form), the process of achieving full functionality of the system will take time.

Notes

This research was funded in part by the National Science Center (grant number 2023/49/B/HS4/00701).

1. The maximum tax rates are established every year in the announcement of the minister of finance on the upper limits of specific rates of local taxes and fees.
2. Converted to US dollars at the exchange rate on June 13, 2022: US$1.00 = PLN 4.40.

3. From April 9, 2018, Polish legislation provides for and regulates the possibility of making electronic excerpts and notarial extracts prepared in the territory of the Republic of Poland. In accordance with the amendments to the Act on the National Court Register 1997 and some other acts of that day, the operation was started by the Central Repository of Electronic Extracts of Notarial Deeds established by the National Council of Notaries.

4. This means that if the height of the room is in the range of 1.4 meters to 2.2 meters and its usable area is 52 square meters, the tax will be calculated on the area of 26 square meters, because 50 percent of 52 square meters is 26 square meters.

5. In addition, in the case of a fully depreciated structure, the tax is calculated on the depreciation base in the last year of its depreciation. Thus, if the last year of depreciation was 2022, and depreciation was then calculated on a value of US$200,000, the tax base in subsequent years after 2022 will be US$200,000; in the case of construction or acquisition of a structure during a tax year, the tax base is its value on which the depreciation of the structure is calculated in that year. Thus, if the construction of a structure is completed in May and it is entered in the fixed asset register with an initial value of US$150,000, then the basis for calculating the tax on the structure will be precisely US$150,000. If a given structure is not depreciated, the taxable base is the market value—more on this later. If the structure in question was leased and the lessee is making depreciation write-offs, then after its takeover by the owner of the property, the tax will be calculated according to the initial value from before the conclusion of the first lease agreement for that structure, taking into account updates and improvements. Repayments of the initial value are not taken into account. In the case of updates or improvements, the tax base is the market value of the structure in force on January 1 of the tax year following the date of the update.

6. *Bonitation* (from Latin *bonus*, meaning "good"), in soil science, is an assessment of the usable quality and the impact on its fertility: relief, degree of culture, and difficulty of cultivation in relation to the climate, terrain, and economic elements.

7. The identifier takes the following form: WWPPGG_R.XXXX.NR, where WW=voivodeship code; PP=county code in the voivodship; GG=commune code in the county; R=type of commune, e.g., urban or rural; XXXX=registration precinct number in the commune; and NR=plot number within the cadastral area in a given commune.

8. The Lombard rate determines the maximum interest rate on loans granted by the central bank to commercial banks against securities (so-called Lombard loans).

References

Ayming. 2021. "Webinarium: Podatek od nieruchomości: Oszczędności w obliczu rosnących kosztów." https://www.ayming.pl/analizy-i-aktualnosci/wydarzenia/podatek-od-nieruchomosci-oszczednosci-w-obliczu-rosnacych-kosztow/.

BIP (Biuletyn Informacji Publicznej) Olsztyn. 2020. "Biuletyn informacji publicznej Urząd Miasta Olsztyna—Zarządzenia prezydenta 2020." Accessed June 15, 2022. http://bip.olsztyn.eu/bip/dokument/364239/zarzadzenia_prezydenta_2020/.

BIP (Biuletyn Informacji Publicznej) Warsaw. 2022. Home page. Accessed June 15, 2022. https://bip.warszawa.pl.

Bunn, D., and E. Asen. 2021. *International Tax Competitiveness Index 2021.* Washington, DC: Tax Foundation.

Business Insider. 2021. "Podatek katastralny w Polsce? Rząd zaprzecza. nie wyklucza jednak innych." December 22. https://businessinsider.com.pl/twoje-pieniadze/podatek-katastralny-w-polsce-rzad-zaprzecza-nie-wyklucza-jednak-innych/95gmwrb.

———. 2022. "Chcą zlikwidować podatek Belki. To ma pomóc Polakom." May 10. https://businessinsider.com.pl/gospodarka/chca-zlikwidowac-podatek-belki-to-ma-pomoc-polakom/121wtrl.

Bydłosz, J., P. Ciechociński, and P. Parzych. 2010. "Możliwości wykorzystania danych rejestru cen i wartości nieruchomości na potrzeby gospodarki przestrzennej." *Acta Scientiarum Polonorum—Administratio Locorum* 9(1): 5–16.

Cellmer, R., M. Bełej, S. Źróbek, and M. Subic-Kovac. 2014. "Urban Land Value Maps—a Methodological Approach." *Geodetski Vestnik* 58(3): 535–551. https://doi.org/10.15292/geodetski-vestnik.2014.03.535-551.

Dowgier, R. 2021. "The Polish System of Property Taxation." *Prawo Budżetowe Państwa i Samorządu* 9(3): 33–52. https://doi.org/10.12775/PBPS.2021.014.

Dworakowska-Raj, M. 2020. "Które podatki zasilają budżet samorządu terytorialnego?" *Gazeta SGH.* April 27. https://gazeta.sgh.waw.pl/po-prostu-ekonomia/ktore-podatki-zasilaja-budzet-samorzadu-terytorialnego.

European Commission. 2013. Commission Regulation (EU) No. 1407/2013 of 18 December 2013 on the application of Articles 107 and 108 of the Treaty on the Functioning of the European Union to de minimis aid. *Official Journal of the European Union* L 352: 1.

Gazeta Prawna. 2024. "Zmiany w podatku od nieruchomości: Czy wróci podatek katastralny?" April 3. https://podatki.gazetaprawna.pl/artykuly/9475618,podatek-od-nieruchomosci-czy-wroci-podatek-katastralny-szykuja-sie-zmiany.html.

Grześkiewicz, W. 2004. "Znaczenie podatków w finansowaniu rozwoju lokalnego." *Samorząd Terytorialny* 3: 24–41.

Halik, Ł. 2018. "Information and Communication Systems Used for Keeping the Register of Real Estate Prices and Values (RREPV) in Poland." *Real Estate Management and Valuation* 26(4): 43–51. https://doi.org/10.2478/remav-2018-0035.

———. 2019. "Analysis of County Geoportals in Terms of Opportunities to Purchase Data of the Register of Real Estate Prices and Values Online." *Real Estate Management and Valuation* 27(1): 69–78. https://doi.org/10.2478/remav-2019-0007.

Head Office of Geodesy and Cartography. 2023. Ewidencja gruntów i budynków—liczba działek według stanu na 31.12.2022 r. https://www.gov.pl/web/gugik/liczba-dzialek-ewidencyjnych.

Head Office of Geodesy and Cartography. n.d. Home page. Accessed June 15, 2022. https://www.gov.pl/web/gugik-en.

Hopfer, A., S. Cegielski, and L. Pietrzak. 2012. "Rejestr cen i wartości nieruchomości w świetle projektu rozporządzenia Rady Ministrów w sprawie Zintegrowanego Systemu Informacji o Nieruchomościach—Wpływ Rozporządzenia na Jakość i Wiarygodność RCiWN." *Rzeczoznawca Majątkowy* 74: 4–11.

Jackowska, I. 2020. "Podatek od nieruchomości pod lupą gmin." *Puls Biznesu*, January 20. https://www.pb.pl/podatek-od-nieruchomosci-pod-lupa-gmin-980305.

Kokot, S. 2015. "Jakość danych o cenach transakcyjnych na rynku nieruchomości." *Acta Scientiarum Polonorum—Administratio Locorum* 14(1): 43–49.

Konowalczuk, J. 2014. "The Corporate Real Estate Market in Public Statistics in Poland." *Real Estate Management and Valuation* 22(2): 41–51.

Lesner, D. 2021. "Gmina ma wpływ na wysokość podatku od Nieruchomości." https://www.prawo.pl/samorzad/podatki-od-nieruchomosci-w-gminie,506307.html.

Manzhynski, S., S. Źróbek, O. Batura, and E. Zysk. 2018. "Why the Market Value of Residential Premises and the Costs of Its Purchase Differ: The Examples of Belarus and Poland." *Land Use Policy* 71: 530–539. https://doi.org/10.1016/j.landusepol.2017.11.012.

Ministry of Finance. 2021. "Data Bases of Ministry of Finance from 2021." https://www.gov.pl/web/finanse/bazy-danych4.

Narodowy Bank Polski. n.d. Home page. Accessed June 15, 2022. https://www.nbp.pl.

OECD (Organisation for Economic Co-operation and Development). 2021. *Lepsze zarządzanie, planowanie i dostarczanie usług w jednostkach samorządu lokalnego w Polsce.* https://web-archive.oecd.org/2021-10-20/593713-OECD-Poland-Report-Highlights-PL-REV.pdf.

———. 2022. "Tax on Property (Indicator)." https://doi.org/10.1787/213673fa-en.

Pahl, B. 2017. *Podatki i opłaty lokalne: Teoria i praktyka.* Warsaw: Wolters Kluwer Polska.

PAP (Polska Agencja Prasowa). 2022. "Supreme Audit Office Recommends Expanding Tax Audit Scope and Enhanced Verification in Municipalities." Polska Agencja Prasowa.

Podatki. 2022. "Podatki od nieruchomości 2022—stawki w największych miastach." Accessed January 2023. https://ksiegowosc.infor.pl/podatki/podatki-i-oplaty-lokalne/46%2C4145%2CPodatek-od-nieruchomosci.html.

Polish Committee for Standardization. 2015. *PN-ISO 9836:2015-12: Performance of Buildings—Definition and Calculation of Area and Volume Indicators.* Warsaw: Polish Committee for Standardization.

Polska w liczbach. n.d. Home page. Accessed June 15, 2022. https://www.polskawliczbach.pl.

Renigier-Biłozor, M., Źróbek S., and Chmielewska. A. 2025. "Mass Appraisal and Fair Taxation: Why Property Valuers Matter?" *Real Estate Management and Valuation* 33. https://doi.org/10.2478/remav-2025-0033.

Rudke, M. 2022. "Nowy podatek od nieruchomości. Co powinieneś wiedzieć o pomyśle rządu i jakie standardy panują w innych krajach." *Business Insider*, May 17. https://businessinsider.com.pl/finanse/nowy-podatek-od-nieruchomosci-co-powinienes-wiedziec-o-pomysle-rzadu-i-jakie/2x3gmce.

Siewicz, K. 2012. "Prawne aspekty korzystania z Rejestru Cen i Wartości Nieruchomości." *Roczniki Geomatyki* 10(3): 126–135.

Statistics Poland. 2021. *Area and Population in the Territorial Profile in 2021.* Warsaw. https://stat.gov.pl/download/gfx/portalinformacyjny/pl/defaultaktualnosci/5468/7/18/1/powierzchnia_i_ludnosc_w_przekroju_terytorialnym_w_2021_roku.pdf.

———. 2022. "Local Data Bank Territorial Cross-Sections." https://www.bdl.stat.gov.pl/en/.

Spurgiasz, K. 2022. "Podatek od Pustostanów—na czym ma polegać i kiedy będzie wprowadzony w Polsce?" Direct.money.pl, November 9. https://direct.money.pl/artykuly/porady/podatek-od-pustostanow-najwazniejsze-informacje.

Tataruch, A., E. Zysk, and M. Do Thi Tuyet. 2019. "Changes in the Landscape of Rural Areas Located Close to City—Case Study of Olsztyn." *Acta Scientiarum Polonorum—Administratio Locorum* 18(4): 397–410. https://doi.org/10.31648/aspal.4653.

Trojanek, M., and W. Kisiała. 2018. "Recurrent Property Taxes in Communal Budgets—Identification of Types of Communes and Their Spatial Differentiation." *Real Estate Management and Valuation* 26(1): 39–50. https://doi.org/10.2478/remav-2018-0004.

Trojanek, M., W. Kisiała, and R. Trojanek. 2021. *Do Local Governments Follow Their Neighbours' Tax Strategies? Tax Mimicking amongst Polish Municipalities.* Land Use Policy 108: 105545. https://doi.org/10.1016/j.landusepol.2021.105545.

Walacik, M. 2016. "Property Taxation in Poland: Legislation Without Implementation." *Land Tenure Journal* 15(2): 101–116.

Walacik, M., R. Cellmer, and S. Źróbek. 2013. "Mass Appraisal—International Background, Polish Solutions and Proposal of New Methods Application." *Geodetski List* 67(90/4): 255–269.

Wara-Wąsowska, E. 2021. "Podatek od zysku ze spekulacji—Nowe rozwiązania rządu." Bezprawnik, November 4. https://bezprawnik.pl/podatek-od-zysku-ze-spekulacji/.

Źróbek, R., ed. 2020. *Podstawy i procedury gospodarowania publicznymi zasobami nieruchomości: Teoria i Praktyka.* Olsztyn, Poland: Wydawnictwo Uniwersytetu Warmińsko-Mazurskiego w Olsztynie.

Źróbek, S., S. Manzhynski, E. Zysk, and Y. Rassokha. 2016. "Some Aspects of Local Real Estate Taxes as an Instrument of Land Use Management." *Real Estate Management and Valuation* 24(3): 93–105. https://doi.org/10.1515/remav-2016-0024.

Źróbek, S., M. Renigier-Biłozor, and R. Źróbek. 2024. Analysis of Legal Regulations Relating to Comprehensive Property Taxation in Poland: Proposals for Amending Selected Legal Provisions. *Studia Iuridica* 104: 111–132. https://doi.org/10.31338/2544-3135.si.2025-104.7.

Zyga, J. 2016. "The Usefulness of Real Estate Prices and Values Register in Appraisal by Comparative Methods, on the Basis of Lublin Voivodeship Registers." *Infrastructure and Ecology of Rural Areas* 4(3): 1673–1688.

Zysk, E., and P. Wawrowska. 2018. "Instrumenty planistyczne—Kreowanie polityki przestrzennej w odniesieniu do zabudowy jednorodzinnej i wielorodzinnej w wybranych gminach podmiejskich Olsztyna." *Acta Scientiarum Polonorum—Administratio Locorum* 17(1): 87–100.

Legislation

Act on Agricultural Tax 1984.

Act on Certain Area Taxes and Fees 1975.

Act on Forest Tax 2002.

Act on Geodetic and Cartographic Law 1989.

Act on Inheritance and Donation Tax 1983.

Act on Local Taxes and Fees 1991.

Act on Municipal Self-Government 1990.

Act on Notaries 1991.

Act on Personal Income Tax 1991.

Act on Public Finance 2009.

Act on Real Estate Management 1997.

Act on Special Solutions for Preventing, Countering and Combating COVID-19 2020.

Act on Stamp Duty 2006.

Act on Tax on Civil Law Transactions 2000.

Act on Tax on Goods and Services 2004.

Act on the Acquisition of Real Estate by Foreigners 1920.

Act on the Civil Code 1964.

Act on the Income of Local Government Units 2003.

Act on the National Court Register 1997.

Constitution of the Republic of Poland 1997.

Tax Ordinance Act 1997.

18

Russia's Transition to Using Market Values for Real Estate Taxation

ANDREY TIMOFEEV

As of December 31, 2021, the Russian Federation had a population of 145.6 million, out of which 74.8 percent resided in urban areas.[1] After the annexation of the Republic of Crimea and the city of Sevastopol in 2014, the federation comprised 85 units: ethnic republics, krais, and oblasts, as well as autonomous okrugs and autonomous oblasts—hereafter referred to as regions. Below the regional level, there are 19,675 jurisdictions at the two tiers of local government, with a distinction made between urban and rural types at each tier.[2] Separate packages of functions are assigned to each type of jurisdiction at each tier of subnational government uniformly throughout the country (see the appendix for more details).

The federal legislation does not allow any level of government to introduce taxes beyond those enumerated in the Tax Code of 1998 (as amended).[3] The list of permitted taxes and charges is broken into three categories: federal, regional, and local. Classification of a tax into a particular category does not always determine the level of government that receives the proceeds from that tax. For instance, revenues from the tax on the assets of organizations, which is classified as a regional tax, are shared between regional and local governments in some regions.

More importantly, the designation of taxes as "local" or "regional" says little about the degree of tax autonomy associated with the taxes assigned to each level of government (Martinez-Vazquez, Timofeev, Boex 2006). As discussed later, the fact that a tax is classified as local or regional does not generally mean that either local or regional governments have the discretion to change the structure of the tax. Even for the taxes designated as regional or local, subnational discretion is limited to

- setting tax rates (within limits set by the Tax Code);
- granting tax reliefs; and
- determining procedures and deadlines for the payment of these taxes.

Likewise, the fact that a tax is classified by law as federal does not mean that regional or local governments have no control over the base or rate of the tax (e.g., the exemption of capital gains from the personal income tax). Finally, similar to other Eastern European and central Asian countries, all taxes in Russia are administered by the national tax authorities, and the accounts of all government entities at all levels of government are kept in the national treasury. Therefore, when discussing specific taxes, national or subnational, this chapter does not repeat details about the collection process, modes of payment, or enforcement, since these arrangements are the same for all taxes in Russia.

As an alternative to receiving hard copies of tax bills, since 2016 taxpayers have been able to access them electronically after creating an account in the internet portal of the Federal Tax Service. Reportedly, for the tax on natural persons' property, out of 68 million tax bills issued for the tax year 2017, 14.3 million were delivered through the portal (Kholyavko and Terchenko 2018).

Overdue taxes incur interest at the rate of one three-hundredth of the current refinancing rate of the Central Bank of the Russian Federation for each day of delay. The Tax Code (articles 46–58) provides two very different sets of enforcement powers: one for businesses and the other for natural persons not involved in entrepreneurial activities. For the latter group of taxpayers, only courts can order collection. By contrast, for taxes owed by legal entities and sole proprietors, the federal tax authorities can issue a collection order and send it to the bank where the taxpayer's account has been located. If the available funds are not sufficient to recover back taxes, the tax authorities have powers to recover unpaid taxes from other assets of the taxpayer by sending a writ of enforcement to the Federal Bailiffs Service.

After the sales tax was eliminated in January 2004, the current list of "regional" taxes included the tax on the assets of organizations, the transport tax (levied based on engine horsepower, gross tonnage, etc.), and the gambling tax (table 18.1). In addition, regional legislatures are empowered to introduce an individual entrepreneur's patent as a special tax

Table 18.1 Delineation of Taxing Powers

Tax	Tax Is Imposed By	Tax Base Is Set By	Tax Rate Is Set By	Payments Go To	2021 Revenue as % of GDP
Value-added tax	Federal government	Federal government	Federal government	Federal government	4.19
Enterprise profit tax (including capital gains and rental income)	Federal government	Federal government	3% federal rate +regional rates within federal limits 13.5%–17%	Federal budget from federal rate Shared between regional and local budgets for regional rates	4.65
Personal income tax (including capital gains and rental income)	Federal government	Federal government Regional authorities: shorten possession period for exemption of capital gains	Federal government	Shared among regional and local levels	3.73
Gambling tax	Federal government simultaneously for the entire country	Federal government: per slot machine, bookmaking office, etc.	Regional authorities within federal limits	Shared among regional and local levels	<0.01

Transport tax	Federal government simultaneously for the entire country	Federal government: engine horsepower, jet thrust, gross tonnage, etc.	Regional authorities within federal limits	Regional budget	0.15
Enterprise assets tax	Federal government simultaneously for the entire country	Federal government: book value Regional authorities: apply cadastral values for select types of nonindustrial objects	Regional authorities within federal limits	Shared among regional and local levels	0.74
Natural persons' property tax	Federal government simultaneously for the entire country	Federal government: cadastral values (regions were to phase in by 2022)	Local authorities within federal limits	Local budget	0.06
Land tax	Federal government simultaneously for the entire country	Federal government: cadastral values	Local authorities within federal limits	Local budget	0.15
Trade levy	Federal government simultaneously for the entire country	Federal government	Local authorities within federal limits	Local budget	0.01

Source: Prepared by the author based on the Tax Code and Federal Tax Service data.

regime that would replace liabilities for natural persons' income and property taxes arising from selected (hard-to-tax) business activities. Proceeds from all regional taxes can serve as "regulated" sources of revenue for subregional budgets so that regional governments can share those revenues with their localities on a derivation (point-of-collection) basis.

Since 2005, the list of "local" taxes has included the land tax, the natural persons' property tax, and the trade levy (essentially a business permit fee). As of January 2025, municipalities are also allowed to introduce the tourism tax, up to 1 percent of the accommodation rate.

Land and Property Markets

The Civil Code of the Russian Federation (Article 130) defines real estate as land parcels and everything affixed to the land that cannot be moved without significant damage to the use of buildings, structures, and construction in progress. In addition, the legal definition of real estate also includes residential and nonresidential premises, registered parking spaces, aircraft, seagoing vessels, and inland navigation ships.

In Russia, structures are separate real estate objects and are registered in the same real estate register discussed in this chapter (Konevsky and Konstantinov 2020). Land and structures can therefore be owned by different persons under separate titles. However, Russian law generally requires that the same person have some rights both to the underlying land parcel and to the structure located on it.

Currently, Russian legislation allows for six types of interest in property:

- **Ownership (freehold):**
    - public (federal-regional or municipal);
    - private (by natural persons and legal entities); and
    - co-ownership, which can be either shared ownership (shares are determined) or joint ownership (shares are not determined).
- **Easement** (can be contractual or established by a court). This is a right of the owner of one land parcel to a limited use of a neighboring land parcel that is owned by somebody else.
- **Public easement** (can be mandated by law or established by a public authority). This is a right for every person or entity to a limited use of a land parcel for specific purposes of public importance (e.g., access to a public beach).

- **Mortgage** (can be contractual or prescribed in law). This is regulated by a dedicated federal law. Only land parcels that are already within the stream of commerce can be pledged. A mortgage can be set for the term of a loan agreement only.

- **Leasehold** (can only be contractual). Long-term lease agreements (for more than one year) require state registration. There are no restrictions on the time term of a lease between private parties. For a lease of publicly owned real estate, a maximum lease term is set in the law (up to 49 years). It varies depending on the type of land parcel and the purposes of the lease. Furthermore, for public leases with a term of over five years, lease rights can be reassigned without consent of the public authority that owns it (Land Code, Article 22[9]).

- **Permanent (perpetual) use.** This applies to publicly owned land used by public entities (Land Code, Article 39.9).

In addition, inheritable lifelong possession, while no longer granted, is still recognized for formerly granted titles of this type. The Russian Civil Code (Article 266) contains a provision under which such titles used to be granted to natural persons in respect of public land. Since the enactment of the Land Code of 2001, this form of interest only applies to such titles for land parcels that had been previously granted, but it would have to be converted to ownership in order to make any kind of transfer other than inheritance.

Generally, foreign persons and legal entities can freely hold real estate titles in Russia. There are, however, a few restrictions (Konevsky and Konstantinov 2020). Thus, neither natural nor legal foreign persons can hold ownership title to agricultural land as well as land plots located in the border areas, seaports, and other areas specified in federal laws. With respect to the restriction on agricultural land, which also applies to Russian companies with over 50 percent of foreign ownership, only leasehold is allowed.

An interest in any kind of real estate (including land parcels) generally requires state registration in the Unified State Register of Real Estate (referred to as the Unified Register throughout this chapter).[4] Until recently, the Unified Register was operated by the Federal Service of State Registration, Cadastre, and Cartography (known by its Russian abbreviation Rosreestr). In turn, Rosreestr, initially established in 2004 as the Federal Registration Service (Rosregistratsiya), transformed into its current form in 2009 by taking over functions of the abolished Federal Real Estate Cadastre Agency (Rosnedvizhimost) and the Federal Agency for Geodesy and Cartography (Roskartografiya). As part of this reorganization,

Rosreestr had to merge legacy databases originating from different predecessors, which required resolving various issues, such as duplicate and incomplete records. Though in 2009 it inherited 1,800 databases covering different types of objects in different regions, by 2015 it was able to consolidate them into 85 databases, 1 per region, and has been working on consolidating all records into a single database accessible throughout the country.

Rosreestr also inherited two separate networks of territorial offices (i.e., in each region, city, and district), with each network having about 30,000 employees throughout the federation. One network of offices (Federal Cadastral Chamber) deals with land surveying and property records, while the other network (Regional Divisions) deals with ownership titles, land use permitting, and monitoring. These territorial offices are in addition to the federal headquarters employing about 600 staff and the directly subordinated Center for Geodesy, Cartography and Spatial Data Infrastructure, with a staff of about 500.

As the procedure of state registration was introduced only on January 31, 1998 (per the Law on the State Registration of Property Rights and Transactions, Law 122-FZ of 1997), titles acquired before that date are also recognized in Russian law and still exist despite not being recorded in the Unified Register. In order to enter into transactions in respect of such real estate, the titleholder has to register the title (with a few minor exceptions—e.g., an unregistered lease is binding between the contracting parties but not against third parties). There are other exceptions when a right (or a title) can be obtained without state registration. These include cases of inheritance and corporate reorganization. All land that is not in the ownership of a natural or legal person or municipalities is presumed state-owned (i.e., federal-regional) property (Konevsky and Konstantinov 2020). In practice, most of commercially valuable land remains in state ownership and can be leased, in most cases, only through a public tender.

Except for pre-1998 titles, a record in the Unified Register (at Rosreestr) is the only proof of ownership. The Unified Register contains key information about each real estate object (e.g., year of construction, size, location, and permitted use), cadastral number, titleholders (i.e., current and past owners), and encumbrances and limitations. State registration is required for most transactions with real estate (title transfers, leases and subleases over one year, easements, etc.), but not for leases and free-of-charge land use under one year.

In the case of purchasing an existing property, in order to transfer the title in the Unified Register, the buyer would need to attach the purchase contract, which would be considered null and void without a price explicitly stated (Civil Code, Article 432). Thus, Rosreestr possesses data on transaction prices.

Basic information recorded in the Unified Register is available to the general public by request for a fee. Requests can be made only with respect to specific objects rather than a specific titleholder. Furthermore, confidential data, such as copies of sale and purchase agreements, can be obtained only in specific cases required by law.

Extracts from the Unified Register with a description of the title, the titleholder, and any encumbrances and limitations are available for a fee (from approximately US$3 to US$80, depending on the type of extract). Some information (e.g., the contents of documents related to previous transactions) is available only to the current owner, tax authorities, courts, and law enforcement bodies. An extract can be obtained in an electronic form (on the official website of Rosreestr) or as a hard copy. In order to request an extract, it is sufficient to know the address of the real estate object. By presenting an ID (or a digital signature if done online) and submitting an application form, anyone can request information from the Unified Register concerning a particular property object.

Within 10 days of the registration of property or recording of transactions with registered properties, a territorial branch of Rosreestr is required to pass this information to the corresponding territorial branch of the Federal Tax Service. By February 15 of each year, a territorial branch of Rosreestr is required to provide to the corresponding territorial branch of the Federal Tax Service information on all property objects registered in that territory as of January 1.

In December 2021, Federal Law on the Public Law Company 'Roscadaster' (Law No. 448-FZ) was passed establishing a public legal company (Roscadaster) as an operator of the property database previously maintained in-house by Rosreestr. Roscadaster was created by combining assets and staff of a number of public entities, including the aforementioned Federal Cadastral Chamber and Center for Geodesy, Cartography and Spatial Data Infrastructure. With the creation of Roscadaster, the roles of regulation, supervision, and operation of the Unified Register have been delineated among three separate entities. The Ministry of Economic Development is responsible for the normative and regulatory framework, as well as methodological guidance, including methodologies for the valuation of different types of property. Rosreestr, a federal cadastre and cartography agency with branches in every region, is responsible for the Unified Register, as well as the spatial data infrastructure in Russia. In January 2023, Roscadaster took over from Rosreestr the tasks of operating and maintaining databases containing records of property objects and ownership titles, as well as facilitating interagency and public access to this information. In my later discussion of specific land and property taxes, I describe the roles of Roscadaster, but one should note that before 2023, these tasks were performed in-house by Rosreestr.

Real Estate Taxes

National Level

There is no formal "property transfer tax" in Russia. However, other taxes levied by the federal government (e.g., value-added tax [VAT] and income taxes) do cover sales or income involving real properties and landlord rents received.

Property Transfer Tax or Stamp Duty

The buyer of real property or a property right must pay stamp duty for the state registration of ownership title. Until January 2025, it was a fixed amount of RUB 2,000 (about US$30) for natural persons and RUB 22,000 (about US$330) for legal entities, regardless of the property value. The nominal amounts of this stamp duty did not change between 2014 and 2025. However, since January 2025 the stamp duty amount has increased with the cadastral value of the property object. For objects acquired by natural persons, the amount is RUB 4,000 (about US$40 as of 2025) for cadastral value under RUB 20 million (about US$200,000) or no cadastral value; for higher-value objects, it is 0.02 percent of the cadastral value or sales price (whichever is higher) but capped at RUB 500,000 (about US$5,000). For objects acquired by legal entities, the amount is RUB 44,000 (about US$440) for cadastral value under RUB 22 million (about US$220,000) or no cadastral value; for higher-value objects, it is 0.02 percent of the cadastral value or sales price (whichever is higher) but capped at RUB 1 million (about US$10,000). Furthermore, in January 2025, an option to expedite processing for double the standard rate of the stamp duty was introduced.

Mortgage rights must also be registered with Rosreestr. The registration fee is a fixed amount of RUB 1,000 (about US$15) for natural persons and RUB 4,000 (about US$60) for legal entities.

Property Wealth Tax

There is no wealth tax in Russia. However, higher rates of property taxes can be set by subnational governments for pricier categories of vehicles and real estate.

Inheritance Tax

Currently, there are no death, estate, or inheritance taxes in Russia. However, if there are any outstanding property taxes that the deceased has not paid, these taxes must be paid by the heirs after they have registered their rights to the estate.

The inheritance and gift tax was abolished effective January 1, 2006. While this tax was classified as a federal tax, traditionally, its entire revenue yield was allocated to the subnational budgets at the point of collection (i.e., fully shared on a derivation basis).

Since 2006, the inheritance of property has not been taxable, except for royalties from intellectual property (remunerations payable to heirs of authors of works of science, literature, and art and patent holders of discoveries, inventions, and industrial samples). Payments to heirs from trusts and other foreign structures are not generally treated as inheritance and therefore are taxed as ordinary income at the applicable progressive rate ranging from 13 to 22 percent.[5]

Gifts between individuals are also generally exempt from taxation in Russia. However, gifts of real estate, vehicles, and shares are only exempt from income taxation when made between family members or close relatives. In all other cases, gifts of real estate are taxed as ordinary income at the applicable progressive rate (13–22 percent).

VAT

Sales of nonresidential real estate (except vacant land parcels) are subject to VAT at 20 percent (18 percent before January 1, 2019). VAT is only applicable when the seller of real estate is a legal entity or a registered individual entrepreneur. The buyer pays the VAT-inclusive purchase price to the seller, and then the seller remits VAT to the national treasury. Further, in certain cases, the seller can be exempted from VAT. For example, the seller may qualify for a VAT exemption if its average receipts in the previous three months did not exceed RUB 2 million (about US$30,000). Unless the tenant has tax privileges or benefits, VAT applies to rent at 20 percent (again assuming that the landlord has a sufficiently large turnover to require VAT registration). Foreign representative offices and branches are generally exempt from VAT in respect of office premises leased in Russia.

If the ownership of a real estate holding company (i.e., a special purpose vehicle) is transferred solely or primarily in order to transfer ownership of nonresidential real estate, there is a risk that VAT may be assessed. Nevertheless, acquisitions of complex real estate assets are usually structured as purchases of the company that owns the respective assets (a share deal), usually a Russian limited liability company or an offshore company, rather than the purchase of the property itself (an asset deal). Offshore companies (typically in Cyprus or the Netherlands) used to be commonly established to hold real estate before recent tax changes concerning controlled foreign companies made it less attractive. Asset deals are mainly used for purchasing land parcels (as they are exempt from VAT) or nonoperating real estate objects. If the seller is a foreign legal entity without a tax presence in Russia and the buyer is a Russian taxpayer, the buyer will be required to withhold and pay the enterprise profits tax and VAT (if applicable) on the payment to the seller.

Capital Gains Tax

Receipts under a sale and purchase agreement may be subject to the enterprise profit tax or personal income tax, according to the legal status of the seller.

For tax-resident natural persons, the income from the sale of property (other than shares) that was owned for less than the minimum period of possession is taxed at a flat 13 percent rate rather than the rate of 15 percent applied to total taxable income exceeding 5 million RUB (about US$75,000) between 2021 and 2025 or even a steeper schedule of rates in force thereafter. The income from a property sale by nonresident natural persons is subject to a flat 30 percent rate.

Income received from the sale of real estate or other property may be exempt from the personal income tax if the property has been owned by a natural person for the minimum period of possession, except where the property has been used for business or entrepreneurial activities. Generally, the minimum period of possession of real estate is five years. However, if the real estate has been acquired as the result of an inheritance or gift from a family member or a close relative, was under a life care contract, or served as the primary residence of its owner at the time of its sale, the minimum period is three years. The minimum period of possession for property other than real estate is three years. Starting from 2019, non–tax residents are also entitled to a tax exemption of income from sales of movable and immovable property if the aforementioned minimum period of possession is met.

The Tax Code (Article 217.1) allows regional legislatures to broaden the exemption of capital gains from the personal income tax by shortening the minimum period of possession or further lowering the 70 percent share of the cadastral value used as a floor for the declared sales price.

If the property has been owned by the seller for less than the minimum period of possession, Russian tax-resident natural persons may be able to reduce their taxable income either by a standard deduction—which is RUB 1 million (about US$15,000) per taxpayer for residential property sales and RUB 250,000 (about US$3,750) per taxpayer for the sales of garages and other noncommercial nonresidential property—or by the amount of their documented actual expenses incurred in connection with the acquisition of that property. If the sale price is below 70 percent of the cadastral value, the latter is used to assess the personal income tax liability for the seller (Tax Code, Article 24.10). In turn, the buyer might be unwilling to underreport the purchase price, as it will result in a higher capital gain liability when this property is sold in the future.

When the seller is a legal entity, capital gains from real estate are subject to the enterprise profit tax at the standard rate (20 percent before 2025, 25 percent thereafter). In addition to the sale of real estate (an asset deal), capital gains are generally included in taxable income; they are also taxed at a standard rate of 20 percent for share deals (or share purchases) where assets derive more than 50 percent of their value directly or indirectly from Russian immovable property (EY Russia 2021). In such a share deal, when the seller is a foreign company without a tax presence in the Russian Federation, then the buyer that is a Russian taxpayer will be required to withhold the enterprise profit tax from the payment to the seller.

Since capital gains are taxed as part of the comprehensive income taxes, the delineation of the tax authority and revenue collections can only be analyzed for these two broader taxes (individual income tax and enterprise profit tax) rather than capital gains alone. While tax returns lump together proceeds from selling real estate and other proceeds (e.g., a retail chain would lump proceeds from selling one of its shops together with the sales of merchandise in all of its shops in a given tax period), something can be gleaned by looking at subtotals of tax payments for industries related to real estate (table 18.2).

Furthermore, since the yield of the national taxes on the income of legal and natural persons is partially shared with subnational budgets at the point of collection, table 18.3 reports the contribution of these taxes

Table 18.2 Revenues from Federal Taxes Paid by Industries Related to Real Estate, 2020 (% of GDP)

Revenue Source	Construction	Warehousing and Auxiliary Transport Activities	Hotels and Other Places for Temporary Residence	Real Estate
VAT	0.3907	0.0196	0.0067	0.1493
Enterprise profit tax	0.1130	0.0023	0.0004	0.1350

Source: Calculated from Federal Tax Service data.

Table 18.3 Share of General Government Tax Revenues Accounted for by National Taxes Whose Bases Are Related to Property Transactions (%)

Revenue Source	2016	2017	2018	2019	2020	2021
VAT	18.47	17.85	16.91	18.92	20.58	19.48
Enterprise profit tax	19.26	19.13	19.39	20.19	19.38	21.62
Personal income tax	20.97	18.91	17.28	17.58	20.50	17.04
Total of three taxes	**58.70**	**55.89**	**53.58**	**56.69**	**60.46**	**58.14**

Source: Calculated from Federal Tax Service data.

as a share of total tax revenues of the general government, including national and subnational budgets.

The trends shown in table 18.3 reveal an increase in the relative contribution of the enterprise profit tax vis-à-vis the personal income tax when measured as a share of the total tax revenues of the general government. Since both are taxes on the comprehensive income, these collection figures do not allow one to parse out the contributions related to capital gains. The relative contribution of VAT had been declining until the rate was increased from 18 percent to 20 percent in 2019.

Table 18.4 reveals that, as a share of gross domestic product (GDP), the yield of all three national taxes increased over the 2016–2021 period. However, the enterprise profit tax and the VAT appear to be much more buoyant than the personal income tax. There was a noticeable jump in the VAT yield after the standard rate was raised from 18 to 20 percent in 2019. Given that the fixed nominal amount of the stamp duty was set in 2014 and had not changed until 2025, it is not surprising that its revenues had declined when measured as a percentage of GDP.

Table 18.5 summarizes the relative contributions of revenues from federal taxes and duties related to property transactions in 2020.

Subnational Level

The bulk of revenues from the national taxes on the income of legal and natural persons, covering capital gains among other types of income, is allocated to subnational budgets at the collection point.

All property taxes on the list of regional or local taxes are recurrent taxes on land and structures, which are described in more detail in the next section.

To provide some context, table 18.6 reports the contributions of these three recurrent property taxes to the total tax revenues of all subnational

Table 18.4 Revenues from Federal Taxes and Duties Related to Property Transactions (% of GDP)

Revenue Source	2016	2017	2018	2019	2020	2021	2016–2021 Buoyancy
VAT	3.09	3.43	3.44	3.90	3.99	4.19	2.04
Enterprise profit tax (including capital gains)	3.22	3.68	3.95	4.16	3.76	4.65	2.30
Personal income tax	3.51	3.64	3.52	3.62	3.97	3.73	1.19
Total of three taxes	**9.82**	**10.75**	**10.91**	**11.68**	**11.72**	**12.57**	**1.82**
Total tax revenues of all levels of government	**16.73**	**19.24**	**20.36**	**20.60**	**19.39**	**21.50**	**1.83**
Stamp duty for property title registration	0.0619	0.0525	0.0406	0.0408	0.0426	n.a.	n.a.

Source: Calculated from Federal Tax Service and Ministry of Finance data.

Note: n.a. = not available.

Table 18.5 Relative Contributions of Revenues from Federal Taxes and Duties Related to Property Transactions, 2020

Tax	Amount (RUB billion)	Percentage of GDP	Comments
Stamp duty for title registration	45.515	0.0400	2020
VAT	740.639	0.5663	Total VAT remitted by the four industries in 2020
Construction	511.001	0.3907	Total VAT remitted by this industry in 2020
Warehousing and auxiliary transport activities	25.591	0.0196	Total VAT remitted by this industry in 2020
Hotels and other places for temporary residence	8.802	0.0067	Total VAT remitted by this industry in 2020
Real estate	195.244	0.1493	Total VAT remitted by this industry in 2020
CIT (including capital gains, rents)	327.809	0.2506	Total CIT remitted by the four industries in 2020
Construction	147.826	0.1130	Total CIT remitted by this industry in 2020
Warehousing and auxiliary transport activities	2.960	0.0023	Total CIT remitted by this industry in 2020
Hotels and other places for temporary residence	0.494	0.0004	Total CIT remitted by this industry in 2020
Real estate	176.528	0.1350	Total CIT remitted by this industry in 2020

Source: Calculated from Federal Tax Service and Ministry of Finance data.

Note: CIT = corporate income tax.

budgets combined, including regional and local levels. Over the 2016–2021 period, there was a steady decline in the contribution of the land tax to the total subnational tax revenues. Furthermore, the contribution from the enterprise assets tax also started to decline in 2019, when movable assets were excluded from taxation. At the same time, the contribution from the tax on the property of natural persons increased every year except in 2020, when tax relief was granted in response to the COVID-19 pandemic. By 2021, the three recurrent property taxes accounted for

Table 18.6 Share of Total Subnational Tax Revenues Accounted for by Recurrent Property Taxes (%)

Revenue Source	2016	2017	2018	2019	2020	2021
Enterprise assets tax	10.12	10.47	10.48	9.07	8.37	7.63
Natural persons' property tax	0.48	0.64	0.65	0.70	0.57	0.67
Land tax	2.34	2.27	1.99	1.82	1.59	1.55
Total of three taxes	**12.94**	**13.38**	**13.12**	**11.59**	**11.65**	**9.86**

Source: Calculated from Federal Tax Service data.

about 10 percent of all tax revenues in subnational budgets, inclusive of derivation-based sharing of national taxes.

The data in table 18.7 reveal similar trends in the relative performance of the three recurrent land property taxes when measured as a share of GDP. With a share at less than 1 percent of GDP, Russia ranks well below most European countries. This might be partially explained by the fact that little land is privately owned in Russia compared with other countries. Over 92 percent of the land was publicly owned as of 2014 (Paul 2021). And the bulk of the private land is owned by natural persons, such as subsidiary farming plots. Legal entities own less than 1 percent of land in Russia and therefore have to lease public land. Thus, revenue from leasing publicly owned land accounted for 0.24 percent of GDP in 2020, which exceeded the revenue from the land tax.

Moreover, over the last five years, the land tax and the enterprise assets tax exhibited a low revenue buoyancy with respect to GDP. Thus, there was a dramatic drop in revenue from the enterprise assets tax as a percentage of GDP in 2019, the year when movable assets were excluded from the enterprise assets tax. This just eliminated the double taxation of vehicles, which continued being taxed under the regional transport tax. By contrast, the tax on the property of natural persons appears to have had a very high buoyancy of 2.58. The latter could be partially explained by the phasing in of cadastral values coinciding with the period of tepid GDP growth in 2016–2019.

Recurrent Land and Property Tax

Tax on the Assets of Organizations

Historical Context

Historically, the regional tax on corporate assets has been levied on the annual average balance sheet value of assets of legal entities. Since the

Table 18.7 Subnational Budget Revenues (% of GDP)

Revenue Source	2016	2017	2018	2019	2020	2021	2016–2021 Buoyancy
Enterprise assets tax	0.89	0.96	0.95	0.84	0.85	0.74	0.51
Natural persons' property tax	0.04	0.06	0.06	0.06	0.07	0.06	2.58
Land tax	0.21	0.21	0.18	0.17	0.17	0.15	0.22
Total of three taxes	**1.14**	**1.22**	**1.19**	**1.07**	**1.11**	**0.95**	**0.53**
Total tax revenues of subnational budgets (including tax sharing)	**8.78**	**9.15**	**9.05**	**9.27**	**9.38**	**9.67**	**1.30**
Total nontax revenues of subnational budgets	**0.86**	**0.90**	**0.79**	**0.80**	**0.71**	**0.77**	**0.69**
Total intergovernmental revenues of subnational budgets (excluding tax sharing)	**1.90**	**1.98**	**2.09**	**2.36**	**3.84**	**2.98**	**2.66**
Total revenues of subnational budgets	**11.54**	**12.03**	**11.93**	**12.42**	**13.93**	**13.42**	**1.48**

Source: Calculated using data from the Federal Tax Service and Federal Statistics Service (Rosstat).

1990s, Russia has planned to adopt a modern real estate (immovable property) tax. Thus, the General Part of the Tax Code, adopted in July 1998, envisioned that, as soon as the regional legislatures introduced the real estate tax in their jurisdictions, the three legacy taxes on land and property (land tax, natural persons' property tax, tax on assets of organizations) would cease to be levied in those regions.

Two pilot cities (Novgorod and Tver) started working on the introduction of the real estate tax in 1997 (Martinez-Vazquez, Timofeev, and Boex 2006).[6] The city of Novgorod created a municipal register of property specifically for taxation purposes. For every property object, the register contained data on its physical characteristics, its legal status, and holders of property rights. These data were used for a mass appraisal of the registered property objects. In the city of Novgorod, the introduction of the real estate tax was supposed to be implemented in stages. In the first stage, the existing property taxes were supposed to be replaced with the real estate tax only for those legal entities that owned both land parcels and improvements. Initially, this was done only for a dozen large enterprises that owned the land under their facilities. Although the city property tax roll did cover all property objects in Novgorod, the system of intergovernmental revenue sharing reportedly discouraged city officials from tapping this tax base. The idea was that at a later stage, the experiment would cover legal entities that leased land parcels. The experiment in the city of Tver fell behind that in Novgorod.

Both experiments were to be completed by 2003 but were subsequently extended through 2005. While these experiments made some headway in terms of valuation methodology, the results were hampered by the lack of reliable data on market transactions. At that time, housing was the only segment of real estate with a substantial number of sales transactions, but even that was concentrated in a few major urban centers (Overchuk 2004). The results of the pilots were supposed to inform the development of federal legislation on the real estate tax. However, in the summer of 2003, the federal government proposed amendments to the Tax Code that would essentially modernize the three legacy land and property taxes. While this indicated a lack of readiness to introduce the real estate tax, it was expected to improve revenues from the existing property taxes by tweaking the tax structure and administration procedures.

In May 2004, a group of prominent members of the federal parliament, including vice-speaker Georgy Boos, initiated a bill (No. 51763-4) amending the Tax Code with a new chapter dedicated to the real estate tax designated as a local-government revenue source. The bill passed the first reading in the lower house of the federal parliament on June 10,

2004, and was scheduled for deliberations in the second reading on July 10, 2004. However, the second reading did not take place until 2013. The cabinet's review of the bill stated that the arrangements required for implementation—namely, the property cadastre, mass valuation methodology, training of assessors, and actual valuation—would not be ready before January 2007.

Furthermore, in August 2004, an amendment to the Tax Code eliminated the clause (Paragraph 2 of Article 14) envisioning the replacement of the three legacy land and property taxes (land tax, natural persons' property tax, and enterprise assets tax) with one (regional) real estate tax. Nevertheless, the planned replacement of the three property taxes with one real estate tax was repeatedly mentioned in the president's budget address to the federal parliament every year between 2006 and 2011. Incremental implementation steps were made along the way. The Law on the State Register of Real Estate (No. 221-FZ of July 24, 2007) was enacted in March 2008. In May 2010, the cabinet's fiscal policy guidance for 2011–2013 stated that the cadastral valuation methodology had been tested for nonresidential properties in four regions (the Tatarstan Republic and the Kemerovo, Tver, and Novgorod oblasts). Cadastral valuation was supposed to be rolled out to other regions in 2011–2012, and the cadastral values were to be ready in early 2012.

In November 2011, in a letter to the prime minister, the Ministry of Finance reported that it was working with the Ministry of Economic Development on drafting amendments to Bill 51763-4 and expected the introduction of the real estate tax in January 2013. In a July 2012 letter, the Ministry of Finance again reported ongoing work with the Ministry of Economic Development on drafting amendments to Bill 51763-4. However, the letter stated it would not be feasible to implement the real estate tax before January 2014.

The cabinet's fiscal policy guidance for 2012–2014 mentioned the possibility of introducing the real estate tax in selected regions that have completed a cadastral valuation. The guidance for 2014–2016 again stated that the introduction of the real estate tax was contingent on the completion of cadastral valuation. However, now it mentioned the possibility of introducing the real estate tax for natural persons only but still expected it to cover both land parcels and buildings and structures.

In November 2013, Article 378.2 was added to the Tax Code, allowing regional governments to use cadastral values instead of book values for the nonindustrial real estate objects owned by legal entities.

The 2014 sanctions and subsequent collapse of energy prices created more fiscal pressure and prompted proposals for the partial introduction of the real estate tax as a way to boost local-government revenues. In September 2014, Bill 51763-4, amended to apply only to structures owned by natural persons, was passed in the second and third, final readings and enacted in January 2015. This appears to have closed the chapter on the two decades of trying to introduce a single real estate tax in Russia.

Reportedly, for legal entities, cadastral values were intended to be applied only to assets generating rental income, while other assets, used as means of production, would still be taxed according to their book value, which is only a fraction of the cadastral value (Yastrebova, Chervonnaya, and Bazanova 2019). This is reflected in the range of corporate assets that regions were allowed to tax by cadastral values starting from 2014 per Article 378.2 of the Tax Code. In 2019, this list was revised in order to align it with the taxation of property of natural persons and thus to remove any incentives for households to move the title of their assets into shell companies.

Basis of the Tax on the Assets of Organizations

Currently, the tax base is defined in the Tax Code (Chapter 30, enacted in January 2004) as the annual book value of fixed assets (including movable assets until 2019), recorded on the balance sheet of legal entities except for specific types of real estate objects that a given region has chosen to tax according to the cadastral value as allowed by Article 378.2 of the Tax Code (i.e., nonindustrial objects). As of 2022, there was a significant amount of variation among regions in terms of the range of property objects taxed on the cadastral value. A handful of regions used cadastral values for taxing all types of objects allowed in Article 378.2. Other regions used cadastral values only for objects exceeding a certain size. For example, for shopping centers, this threshold can be as large as 10,000 square meters in Yamal-Nenetsk Autonomous Okrug. Overall, foreign-owned assets are more commonly taxed on the cadastral values (since they have no book values kept in Russia and thus would be untaxed otherwise). By contrast, for residential premises, it is less common to tax legal entities based on the cadastral values.

Coverage of the Tax Base

After the adoption of Chapter 30 of the new Tax Code in 2003, regional governments reintroduced this tax to conform to the new federal framework. Thus, inventories, intangibles, and capital outlays had to be excluded from the tax base. Since 2014, the Tax Code (Article 378.2) has allowed regional governments to use the cadastral value for the following real estate objects owned by legal entities: office and retail space, real

Figure 18.1 Evolution of the Taxable Base (% of GDP)

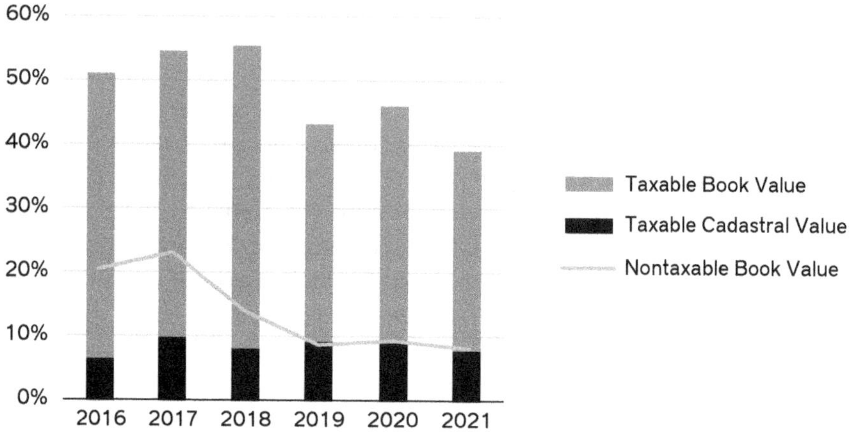

Source: Calculated from Federal Tax Service data.

estate owned by a foreign entity without a permanent establishment, and residential property and garages. In particular, until a region adopted cadastral values for the purpose of taxation of assets of legal entities, unsold residential property was treated as the developer's inventory and thus subtracted from the balance sheet value subject to this tax. Furthermore, other than the aforementioned types of property taxed according to the cadastral value, all other corporate fixed assets were taxed according to their book value, regardless of the ownership status. By contrast, for property objects to be taxed per cadastral value, there is no tax liability until the ownership is recorded in the Unified Register.

As shown in figure 18.1, objects taxable on cadastral values account for about one-fifth of the taxable base of this regional tax. This taxable cadastral value jumped from 6.5 percent of GDP in 2016 to 9.9 percent of GDP in 2017, in part driven by the 2016 revaluation in Moscow City and many other regions. However, by 2021 it declined to 7.8 percent of GDP. There was a dramatic drop in the book value of taxable assets after movable assets were excluded from taxation in 2019.

Taxpayers

Taxpayers of the tax on the assets of organizations are Russian legal entities (RLEs) and foreign legal entities (FLEs) carrying out activities in Russia through permanent establishments (PEs) or owning real estate in Russia.

Responsibility for Valuations

Quarterly, RLEs and FLEs that carry out activities in Russia through PEs self-assess the tax base as the average annual value of fixed assets on the basis of their net book value in each tax reporting period cumulative from the start of the year.

For certain types of property objects, rather than the book value, taxpayers can be required by the respective regional government to use the cadastral value of

- office and retail space;
- immovable property of FLEs that do not have PEs (or which is not related to the PEs' activities);
- construction in progress;
- residential premises;
- car parking spaces and garages; and
- noncommercial residential buildings and outbuildings built on land parcels designated for subsidiary farming or single-family houses.

For these property objects, the cadastral value is included in the tax base even if they are not recorded as fixed assets in the accounts of a corporate titleholder. However, if such property objects were not in the official cadastral valuation report for that tax year, then the old rules based on net book value apply to determine the tax base for that property in that year.

Since January 2017, cadastral valuation has had to follow the sequence of steps set in the Law on the State Cadastre Valuation, Law 237-FZ of July 3, 2016 (hereinafter Law No. 237 of 2016) as described later for the local land and property taxes.

Valuation Cycle

For fixed assets taxed based on the book value, every quarter, taxpayers are required to calculate the taxable base as the average monthly book value year to date.

Cadastral values are revalued every two years in Moscow and Saint Petersburg, while in other regions, it has to be done every four years. Since 2022, cadastral revaluation has had to cover all registered structures or all registered land parcels, but in any given region, these two categories of real estate can follow two separate valuation cycles (Federal Law on Amendments to certain Legislative Acts of the Russian

Federation, Law No. 269-FZ, of July 31, 2020). Before 2022, each of the different types of land and structures could have its own valuation cycles in the same region.

For newly registered property objects or modifications of the previously registered objects, within 3 days of recording this information in the Unified Register, Rosreestr has to notify the designated regional valuation agency, which in turn has to assign or update the corresponding cadastral value within 10 business days.

Valuation Methodology

Unless regional legislation requires the use of cadastral values for the taxation of a particular category of property owned by legal entities, the Russian accounting standards are applied to determine the net book value of fixed assets.

For railways, pipelines, and similar objects spanning several regions, the taxpayer is required to determine the share of the net book value pertaining to each region and report it in the tax return filed in that region.

For cadastral values, the methodology is prescribed in the federal guidelines for state cadastral valuation (Order of the Ministry of Economic Development of Russia No. 358 of June 6, 2016, "On Approval of the Guidelines for State Cadastral Valuation," same as described later for the local land and property taxes).

Valuation Quality Control Measures

For those categories of property taxed on cadastral values, the same quality controls apply as described later for the local land and property taxes.

For other categories of property, the Russian accounting standards are applied to determine the net book value of fixed assets and scrutinized by tax authorities in connection with the corporate income tax and VAT. For publicly traded companies, the net book value of fixed assets is also scrutinized by external auditors.

Property Valuation Data

A territorial branch of Rosreestr is required to provide to the corresponding territorial branch of the Federal Tax Service the information, including cadastral values, on all property objects registered in that territory as of January 1.

Objection and Appeal

For those categories of property taxed on cadastral values, the same appeal procedures apply as described later for the local land and property taxes.

Tax Rates

The tax rate is set by regional legislatures but cannot exceed the following ceilings:

- 2 percent for property taxed based on the cadastral value.
- 2.2 percent for property taxed based on the book value.
- 1.6 percent for public railways and similar complex property objects (specified in the list approved by the cabinet).[7]
- 0 percent for certain types of property specified in the list approved by the cabinet (e.g., trunk pipeline facilities, gas extraction facilities, helium production and storage facilities, and facilities provided for in technical plans for the development of mineral deposits) if certain conditions are met (EY Russia 2021).

For the taxation of fixed assets based on the book value, the maximum allowed standard tax rate of 2.2 percent was found in all regions (excluding the Republic of Crimea and the city of Sevastopol) as of 2022. However, in many regions, reduced rates apply to specific industries, such as telecommunications (e.g., 1 percent in the Adygeya Republic), distribution of natural gas (e.g., 0.7 percent in the Altai Republic), health care (e.g., 0.4 percent in Voronezh Oblast), regional and municipal roads (e.g., 1.5 percent in Kemerovo Oblast), and agro-processing (e.g., 1.8 percent in the Karachayevo-Cherkessk Republic).

For the taxation of fixed assets based on the cadastral value, a dozen regions set the standard rate below the maximum allowed 2 percent: the Republic of Kalmykia (1.5 percent), the Republic of North Osetia (1.6 percent), the Chuvash Republic (1.3 percent), Amur Oblast (1.3 percent), Vladimir Oblast (1.5 percent), Irkutsk Oblast (1.25 percent), Kursk Oblast (1.8 percent), Moscow Oblast (1.9 percent), Omsk Oblast (1.5 percent), Perm Oblast (1.7 percent), Smolensk Oblast (0.8 percent), Tambov (1.5 percent), Yaroslavl Oblast (1.6 percent), and Moscow City (1.9 percent). In addition, many regions set reduced rates applicable to the cadastral value of property objects of specific types and sizes.

Exemptions

Regional authorities can set tax rates of 0 percent for specific categories of legal entities.

With the enactment of the dedicated chapter of the Tax Code in 2004, the federally imposed list of tax exemptions had been significantly shortened to include only correction facilities, pharmaceutical manufacturing, entities dealing with oil and gas exploration in the territorial waters, federal highways, and buildings dedicated to religious services, services for disabled individuals, prosthetic care, legal defense, and science (Article 381).[8]

Certain assets are excluded from the tax base, such as land parcels (subject to a separate local tax) and other natural resource sites (e.g., bodies of water), nuclear installations, spacecraft, ships registered in the Russian International Register of Vessels, and assets recognized as cultural heritage assets. Some regions provide full exemptions from the enterprise assets tax for entities involved in specific investment projects.

Tax Relief Measures

Tax rates are to be set by the regional legislatures and can vary by type of property and category of taxpayer (previously they could vary by type of production utilizing these assets). However, it is prohibited to set individual rates for specific entities.

Foreign taxes paid by an RLE for property located outside Russia can be offset against the enterprise assets tax due in Russia on the same property objects. Figure 18.2 reports the magnitude of forgone revenues, through exemptions and reduced rates, either mandated in federal legislation or introduced by specific regions. As shown in this figure, there was a dramatic drop in federal tax expenditures in 2018, which was only partially offset by an increase in subnational tax expenditures. This was primarily driven by the elimination of the federally mandated exemption of movable assets (vehicles, medical furniture, etc.) and provision of the ability for regions to either exempt these assets at the regional level or tax them at a reduced rate of 1.1 percent or some combination of the two approaches. Furthermore, in 2019, movable assets were removed from the definition of taxable objects altogether.

Billing

Quarterly, taxpayers are required to make advance estimated payments for the tax reporting period cumulative from the start of the year. After the end of the tax year, taxpayers are required to self-assess the amount of tax for the entire year and pay the balance remaining after subtracting advance payments made throughout the tax year. A tax return must be submitted no later than March 30 of the year following the tax year.

Deadlines for advance and final payments are set by the respective regional legislatures. In particular, regional legislatures can choose not to require advance payments so that this tax would be paid annually.

In every year from 2016 to 2021, collection rates exceeded 99 percent of the assessed amounts.

Figure 18.2 Tax Expenditures Related to the Assets of Legal Entities (% of GDP)

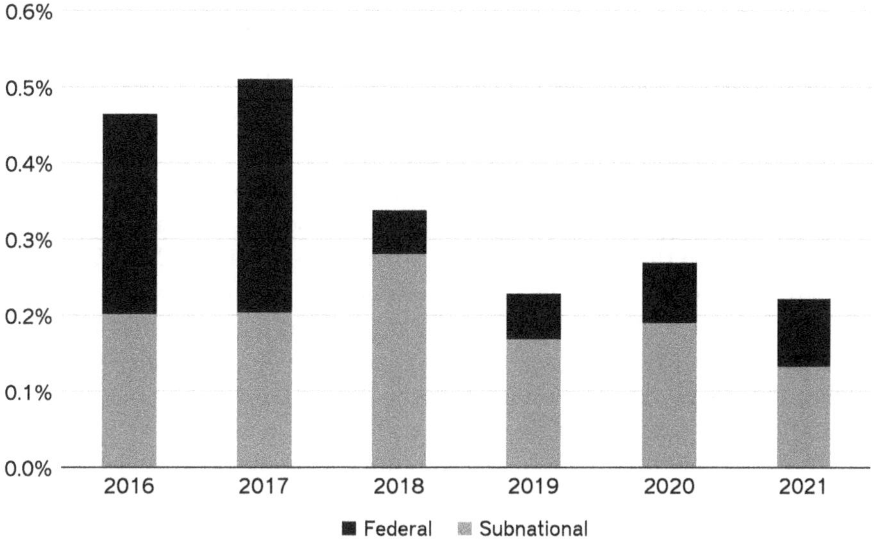

Source: Calculated using data from the Federal Tax Service and the Federal Statistics Service (Rosstat).

Land Tax and Land Lease Fee

Historical Context

In Russia, land use requires payment to the government. According to the Land Code of 2001 (Article 65[1]), there are two mutually exclusive forms of payment: the land tax and the land lease fee. Furthermore, the Land Code envisioned levying the land tax only until the introduction of the real estate tax (Article 65[1]).

Land parcels and shares of land parcels in ownership, possession, or use of legal entities and natural persons have been subject to the legacy land tax. Since it is classified as a local tax, the land tax revenues have been allocated to local budgets.

The land lease fee is paid by lessees of state—that is, federal and regional—and municipal land. The amount and terms of payments are set separately in each lease, which can but is not required to be informed by the cadastral value (Land Code, Article 65[5]). For federal land parcels leased without a public auction, federal regulation (issued with Cabinet Resolution No. 582 of July 16, 2009) prescribes the amount of the lease fee as a certain percentage of the cadastral value, ranging from 0.01 to 2 percent depending on the land type and permitted use. For regional and municipal land, the respective subnational authorities prescribe the formula for determining and revising land lease fees, which cannot increment any variables, except inflation and cadastral value, more often than once in three years (Cabinet Resolution No. 582). Between 2007 and 2015, the Land Code had a clause (Article 65[3]) setting the floor for the land lease fee at double the land tax rate in cases of leasing public land for the purpose of construction if the structure has not been commissioned within three years.

The Land Code (Article 66) clearly distinguishes between the market value assessed by independent appraisers (governed by the Law on Valuation Activity in the Russian Federation, Law 135-FZ of July 28, 1998) and cadastral values produced by designated regional valuation agencies (governed by Law 237-FZ of 2016). Among other things, an assessment of the market value is required for any transaction involving publicly owned land. While, by law, the cadastral value has to be equal to the market value at the revaluation date, they are allowed to diverge in the periods between revaluations. However, if the entire segment of the regional real estate market (e.g., agricultural land) experiences a substantial downturn in any given year, then cadastral values have to be indexed down for all property objects in that segment.

Before Law 237-FZ took effect on January 1, 2017, cadastral valuation had been governed by Law 135-FZ (Chapter III) of 1998, as further elaborated in the regulation issued with Cabinet Resolution No. 316 of April 8, 2000. This regulation required cadastral revaluation at least every five years but not sooner than three years after the previous one. Different valuation approaches were prescribed for different types of land. For urban land, the assessment of the cadastral value was supposed to be based on mass appraisal methodologies, while for agricultural land and forests, it was supposed to be based on the capitalization of rental income. The Ministry of Economic Development has issued numerous methodologies dealing with the valuation of specific types of land. Reportedly, regional entities tasked with cadastral valuation have been facing difficulties in selecting the correct methodology as, for many land parcels, the Unified Register lacks information on the permitted land use.

The Land Code envisioned that the taxation of land should be based on cadastral value (Article 65[5]). In November 2004, the federal parliament adopted a new chapter of the Tax Code, changing the taxable base of the land tax from the acreage to the cadastral value, effective January 1, 2005.

Before 2005, the tax rates were set by local governments per unit of land area within a narrow range prescribed by the federal and regional governments (Martinez-Vazquez, Timofeev, Boex 2006). Separate rates for agricultural and nonagricultural land were applied to the area of land parcels. Tax rates were doubled for land parcels not in use or used for purposes different from the intended use. Regional governments could provide tax preferences to different categories of taxpayers and specific taxpayers on the portion of the tax liability due to the regional budget. At the same time, local governments were allowed to provide tax preferences on the portion of the tax liability due to their budgets but only with respect to specific taxpayers.

Basis of the Land Tax

Since 2005, the tax base has been the cadastral value of the land parcel. If the land parcel crosses municipal boundaries, the cadastral value is apportioned according to the land area located in each respective municipality, and then each portion is multiplied by the tax rate set in the respective municipality.

Coverage of Tax Base

By 2007, case law and subsequently issued tax instructions established that there is no tax liability until the registration of property rights in what has eventually become the Unified Register (at Rosreestr). Until the registration of the property rights by the new owner, the previous owner remains liable for the land tax. Thus, technically the land tax has 100 percent coverage. However, failure to register property rights can be interpreted by tax authorities as a form of tax evasion and result in penalties set for tax registration violations. Furthermore, the Unified Register might not have records of the titles acquired before the procedure of state registration was introduced on January 31, 1998 (per Law 122-FZ of 1997). Those titles represent a minor fraction of the land because, at that time, most of the land was state owned, as it remains today for the bulk of commercially valuable land.

As shown in figure 18.3, between 2016 and 2017, the share of untaxed land parcels doubled from 7.3 percent (2.5 million out of 34.9 million parcels) in 2016 to 14.6 percent (5.3 million out of 36.4 million parcels) in 2017. This was entirely driven by parcels owned by natural persons, through both a reduction of taxed parcels and an increase in the total number of tax-registered parcels. The latter could be partially explained by the amnesty for back taxes on unregistered land parcels if self-declared by January 1, 2017. It should be noted that the total number of tax-registered land parcels, 39.9 million as of 2021, is significantly lower than the 61 million land parcels covered by the 2022 cadastral valuation nationwide. Therefore, the 6 million land parcels reported as untaxed by the tax authorities in 2021 appear not to capture exclusions but only

Figure 18.3 Evolution of Land Parcels in the Tax Net (million objects)

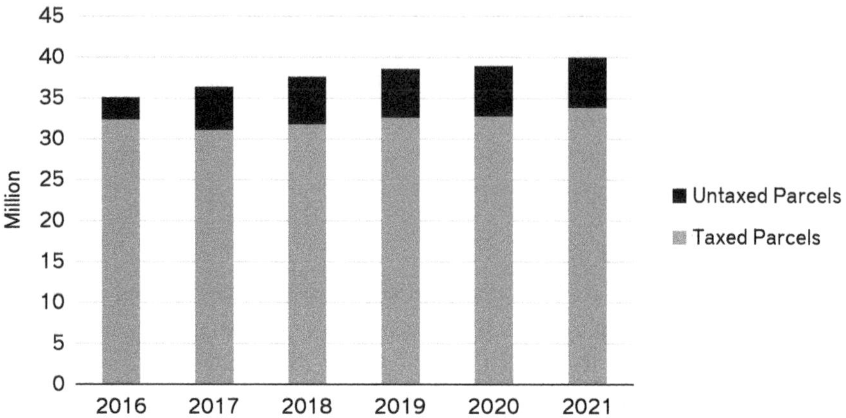

Source: Calculated using data from the Federal Tax Service.

include those parcels that generally fell under the definition of tax objects but that did not incur any tax either due to a tax-exempt status of the owner or allowed deductions (see the later discussion on exemptions and tax relief).

Taxpayers

Taxpayers of the land tax are legal entities and natural persons who own land or enjoy the right of inheritable lifelong possession or the right of permanent (perpetual) use. The Tax Code (Article 388[2]) explicitly rules out tax liability for lessees or users of land parcels other than under permanent (perpetual) use.

Responsibility for Valuations

Since January 2017, cadastral valuation has been required to follow the sequence of steps set in Law No. 237-FZ of 2016 (figure 18.4). These steps are further elaborated in the federal guidelines for state cadastral valuation (Order of the Ministry of Economic Development of Russia No. 358 of June 6, 2016, "On Approval of the Guidelines for State Cadastral Valuation").

Under this new law, rather than contracting private appraisers, each regional government had to designate a public entity (thereafter referred to as the regional valuation agency) to carry out a cadastral valuation of all properties in that region. Law 237-FZ (Article 7[2]) explicitly prohibits these regional valuation agencies from outsourcing property valuation or engaging any assessors other than their permanent staff. Furthermore,

Figure 18.4 Cadastral Valuation Steps

1. Regional line department issues a revaluation decision.
2. Regional line department publishes revaluation decision and solicits property declarations to the valuation agency.
3. Roscadaster provides regional line department with a list of objects to be forwarded to the valuation agency.
4. Valuation agency carries out revaluation, produces a draft valuation report, publishes it on its website, and submits it to Rosreestr.
5. Rosreestr reviews the draft valuation report and requests the valuation agency to rectify deficiencies, if any.
6. Affected parties submit objections to the valuation agency.
7. Valuation agency accepts or rejects objections, finalizes the valuation report, and submits the final report to Rosreestr and regional line department.
8. Regional line department approves valuation report, publishes the approval act, and submits it to Rosreestr.
9. Rosreestr updates cadastral values.

Source: Prepared by the author based on Federal Law No. 237-FZ of 2016.

these entities are required to deny appeals citing independent market valuations if the latter involved any staff of these entities. While the establishment of these regional valuation agencies was completed in all 85 regions by 2020, reportedly there were some initial problems. According to a survey of regions conducted by a parliamentary working group, only 50 regions established their designated valuation agencies by 2018 (Kholyavko 2018b). In just over half of these 50 regions, the valuation agencies were created from scratch rather than through the reorganization of existing agencies, such as the Bureaus of Technical Inventory (BTIs) described later in this chapter.

I am not aware of any studies tracking revaluation dates, which were set independently in each region for each category of real estate within the mandated three-to-five-year window before 2020. After Law 237-FZ required the establishment of regional valuation agencies in 2017, revaluations were reported in 34 regions in 2018 and 65 regions in 2019, and 45 regions were still planning to conduct it in 2020 before the pandemic outbreak. However, it is not clear which categories of real estate (land, structures, etc.) were covered in which year by which region.

With the 2020 federal law amendment mandating a four-year revaluation cycle in all regions (except for Moscow and Saint Petersburg, where the cycle was two years), all regions completed their revaluation of land parcels (totaling 61 million parcels nationwide) in 2022 (Kozlov and Molotkova 2023).

I am aware of instances in which the regional valuation agency produced new cadastral values but they were not approved by the regional executives on time. Thus, the 2022 revaluation of tax parcels in Tatarstan was endorsed by the regional executives on December 2, 2022, just one day short of the required lead time for these cadastral values to be applied in the 2023 tax year, so these new values only became effective in 2024. Furthermore, in March 2022, an amendment to the Tax Code (Article 391) introduced a moratorium on increases in the taxable value of land compared with the levels before the 2022 revaluation.

Based on information reported in one study narrowly focused on agricultural land (Komarov et al. 2021), table 18.8 reports the share of regions completing the revaluation of that category of real estate in each five-year period. It should be noted that during the last five-year period, the mandated periodicity changed from five to four years per Law 237-FZ, which took effect on January 1, 2017. Furthermore, the same law required regional authorities to establish designated valuation agencies by 2020 rather than relying on contracted assessors. These legal changes,

Table 18.8 Share of Regions Completing the Revaluation of Agricultural Land (%)

	Round 1	Round 2	Round 3	Round 4
Federal District	**2001–2005**	**2006–2010**	**2011–2015**	**2016–2020**
Central	94	94	94	72
Northwestern	91	91	73	64
Southern	100	100	100	63
North Caucasian	n.a.	86	86	57
Volga	100	100	93	43
Ural	100	100	100	50
Siberian	100	90	90	30
Far Eastern	100	100	100	45
Nationwide	**98**	**95**	**92**	**54**

Source: Prepared using data from Komarov et al. (2021) and the Federal Statistics Service (Rosstat).

Note: n.a. = not available.

combined with the pandemic, might explain why only half of the regions were able to complete a revaluation of agricultural land in the 2016–2020 period. With the 2022 revaluation of all types of land parcels completed in all regions, the cadastral values have finally caught up with the market.

Valuation Cycle

In Moscow and Saint Petersburg, revaluations must take place every two years, while in other regions it is every four years. No later than six months before January 1 of the revaluation year, the relevant line department of the regional government (e.g., the Moscow City Department of Public Assets) issues its decision to carry out revaluation, specifying the revaluation year and the categories of properties to be covered. Within 30 days of issuing its revaluation decision, the regional line department has to disseminate it through multiple channels (internet, press, information boards, letters to municipalities, submission to the Rosreestr database) and prompt owners to declare property characteristics to the respective valuation agency. By January 20 of the revaluation year, Roscadaster provides the regional line department with a list of property objects and populates the cadastral valuation database. Within three days of receiving the property list, the regional line department has to forward it to the valuation agency. After a valuation report is drafted by the valuation agency, it has to be reviewed by Rosreestr and then undergo a public consultation period allowing affected parties to submit objections. After the conclusion of the public consultation period, the draft valuation report becomes the final valuation report. Once the final valuation report is approved by the regional line department, Rosreestr will update cadastral values in the Unified Register.

In 2020, an amendment to Law 237-FZ (Article 19.1) introduced the concept of real estate indexes and required Roscadaster to annually produce such indexes for each type of property (land parcels, apartments, parking spaces, etc.) in each region. Furthermore, this amendment requires that, within three months of the issuance of annual indexes, Rosreestr has to index cadastral values for property categories where these indexes fell by more than 30 percent compared with the year following the last cadastral revaluation, except for objects that had their cadastral value replaced with the market value after the last cadastral revaluation.

Valuation Methodology

Regional valuation agencies have to follow the methodological approaches prescribed in the federal guidelines for state cadastral valuation (Order of the Ministry of Economic Development of Russia No. 358 of June 6, 2016, "On Approval of the Guidelines for State Cadastral Valuation"). When determining the cadastral value, mass valuation methods are to be used. If it is impossible to apply mass valuation methods, the determination of the cadastral value is to be carried out individually for respective real estate objects. In practice, mass valuation appears to be the only feasible option given the limited staff of regional valuation agencies; Kholyavko (2018b) reports 500,000 objects per specialist in a regional valuation agency.

The use of mass valuation methods involves determining the cadastral value by grouping real estate objects with similar characteristics. When conducting a mass valuation, a comparative sales, cost, or income approach to valuation is to be used.

For modeling the cadastral value, any of the three methodological approaches can be used. The choice of a particular approach—or a justified decision not to use it—is to be based on the object characteristics and the type of permitted use, as well as the sufficiency and reliability of available market information. In each region, the designated regional valuation agency must justify its choice of approaches and methods used either for mass valuation or for determining the value of an individual object. Where more than one valuation approach is used, the results obtained using different approaches should be reconciled in order to determine the final value. The reconciliation method, as well as all judgments and assumptions made in the course of reconciling the results, must also be justified. In the case of reconciliation by weighing, the choice of weights must be justified.

If there is sufficient and reliable market information on prices (the amounts requested, offered, or paid as the result of a completed or proposed transaction), the determination of the cadastral value should be carried out mainly on the basis of the comparative sales approach. For each type of property, the federal methodological guidelines also rank the appropriateness of alternative valuation methods. Thus, the income approach is ranked higher than the comparative sales approach for land parcels used for agriculture, business, water objects, and common or special use.

Valuation Quality Control Measures

Article 14(4) of Law No. 237-FZ of 2016 requires the regional valuation agency to carry out quality control of its evaluation results based on prevailing market conditions in its region as specified in the federal methodological guidelines, among other things by cross-checking with the information on property transactions recorded by Rosreestr. Within 3 business days of drafting a valuation report listing all property objects, the regional valuation agency must post the report on the internet and provide it in an electronic form to Rosreestr (Article 14[9]). Rosreestr has 10 business days after receiving the draft valuation report to verify its conformity with the normative and quality requirements and then 3 business days to communicate the verification outcome to the valuation agency and the regional line department (Article 14[10]). Then the designated regional valuation agency has 7 business days to rectify any deficiencies found by Rosreestr and post the rectified draft evaluation report on the internet, as well as to resubmit it to Rosreestr (Article 14[12]).

After acceptance of the draft valuation report by Rosreestr, the latter has 3 days to commence a 30-day period of public consultation by providing the link to the draft report posted on the internet by the designated regional valuation agency as well as arranging for the submission of public comments. Any natural or legal person can submit a comment on the draft valuation report (Article 14[17]). In cases where public comments lead to the correction of the cadastral values of some property, the designated regional valuation agency has to verify whether a similar correction is required for adjacent properties or property objects of the same type (Article 14[22]). If public consultations result in changes in cadastral values for some properties, the designated regional valuation agency has to post on the internet an updated version of the draft valuation report along with a summary of accepted and declined comments and extend the public consultation period by at least five days beyond that announced for the previously posted version. At the same time, Rosreestr will again have 10 business days after the updated draft valuation is posted to verify its conformity with the normative and quality requirements (Article 14[28]). If no more updates or corrections are required after the conclusion of the (possibly extended) public consultation period, the draft valuation report becomes the final valuation report. In that case, the designated regional valuation agency has five days to notify Rosreestr and provide it with a summary of accepted and declined comments. Since 2022, Rosreestr has been allowed to delegate some of its tasks just listed to Roscadaster (Article 14[22]).

In addition to the quality control of revaluations, Rosreestr is also responsible for ongoing monitoring of the performance of the relevant regional line department (typically the department for public assets) and the entity designated by this regional department to conduct cadastral valuation (often successors of the former BTIs). If such monitoring identifies noncompliance with the law on cadastral valuation (Law No. 237-FZ),

Rosreestr can issue a motivated opinion requiring the relevant regional line department or its valuation agency to rectify noncompliance within 30 days or submit a rebuttal. Within 10 business days of receiving a rebuttal, Rosreestr has to rescind, amend, or sustain its request, which becomes mandatory for rectification within 30 days.

Property Valuation Data

Article 13 of Law 237-FZ of 2016 requires Roscadaster to populate the cadastral valuation database with information from all relevant records in the Unified Register and other sources by January 20 of the valuation year.

According to survey responses from 50 regions that had established their valuation agencies by 2018, there were numerous issues with the valuation data (Kholyavko 2018b). For example, 42 percent of responding regions reported missing geolocational information on land parcels. Missing information on permitted land use was reported by 34 percent of responding regions, while 32 percent of respondents reported conflicting information on permitted land use. About 24 percent of responding regions reported missing information on administrative borders (e.g., municipal boundaries). A few years earlier, the chamber of commerce also reported widespread instances of erroneous, missing, or duplicate records in the valuation data (Korytin and Patel 2016).

Objection and Appeal

In addition to submitting comments on the draft valuation report during the public consultation period, anybody can request the correction of an error made by the regional valuation agency designated for cadastral valuation in a region. There are four types of errors that can be reported:

- Noncompliance of the determination of the cadastral value with the provisions of the methodological guidelines on state cadastral valuation.
- A typographical error, misprint, arithmetic error, or other error that affected the assessment of the cadastral value of one or more real estate objects.
- Incorrect determination of the circumstances affecting the value of the property (location of the property, its intended purpose, permitted use of the land parcel, emergency or dilapidated state of the property, the degree of wear and tear, or the location of the property

within the boundaries of a zone with special conditions for the use of the territory).

- The use of inaccurate information about the characteristics of the property in determining the cadastral value.

Law 237-FZ (Article 21) requires that the designated regional valuation agencies review such error correction requests within 30 days and either correct the cadastral value or deny the request. Refusal to correct a reported error can be appealed in an administrative court.

Per the Land Code (Article 66), when the market value of a land parcel is determined, its cadastral value has to be set to the market value. In practice, this requires filing an appeal by the taxpayer, and even then, it applies only until the next cadastral revaluation cycle.

The results of cadastral valuation can be appealed either in court or through an appeal commission if established by the regional government (Article 22).[9] The commission has to include at least five members, including representatives of the regional government and Rosreestr, as well as the business ombudsperson. State and municipal officials cannot account for more than half of the commission membership.

Appeals can be filed by legal or natural persons affected by the valuation or by the state or municipal governments that own the affected property objects. The appeal has to be substantiated with an independent assessment of the market value of the property object in question. The commission forwards the market value assessment to the regional valuation agency designated for cadastral valuation. The commission can request information and testimony from those involved in cadastral and market valuations of the property object in question. It has to rule by a simple majority within 30 days of receiving the appeal.

Naydenova (2021) reports that, in 2019, courts ruled to reduce the cadastral value in 96 percent of cases. Domnina and Savoskina (2021) report that, on average, court-mandated reductions were about half of the cadastral value every year from 2014 to 2020. By contrast, they report that the reductions granted by the appeal commissions were only about one-third of the cadastral values in the same years. Similarly, Mereminskaya and Yastrebova (2019) report a 30.3 percent reduction of cadastral values resulting from appeals submitted to regional commissions nationwide, totaling over 20,000 appeals concerning over 40,000 property objects (both land and structures) between January and August 2019. For comparison, a year earlier, between January and August 2018, regional commissions received 19,594 appeals concerning 32,260 objects, and in 61 percent of cases they ruled in favor of the owners (Kholyavko and Terchenko 2018). Between

January and October 2020, regional commissions received 14,276 appeals, out of which about one-third (4,824) were denied, two-thirds (8,311) led to cadastral values reset in line with market value appraisals, 104 led to cadastral value corrections addressing inaccurate data, and 1,037 appeals were still pending.

Paul (2021) also reports that the cadastral value often exceeded the market value of property objects. However, all these reports are based on the evidence arising from appeals and litigation, which can be expected to involve cases where the cadastral value exceeded the market value. Furthermore, given the costs of private appraisals and litigation,[10] such cases are more likely to be filed when the discrepancy between the cadastral and market values is substantial. In addition, notwithstanding the 2018 Supreme Court ruling, there is still confusion about whether the legal definition of the market price is inclusive of the 20 percent VAT, which for the same object might be invoiced to the buyer and claimed on the buyer's VAT return in one buyer-seller pairing but not in another depending on their VAT-registration status. Some private appraisers and regional valuation agencies make adjustments for VAT, some do not, and others prefer not to mention it at all rather than having to justify their approach (Mavrina 2021).

All these reports seem to suggest that the existing quality control arrangements still allow cases of significant, sometimes multifold differences between cadastral and market values (Solntsev 2020). However, there are reasons to believe that overestimation is more likely to be reported and corrected than underestimation. For Moscow City, Popova (2019) reports one expert opining that the cadastral value was higher than the market value for about 50 percent of objects, close to the market value for 30 percent of objects, and lower than the market value for about 20 percent of objects.

Tax Rates

For each kind of land and type of land use, municipal authorities can set any rate within the federally prescribed limits.

The rate ceiling is set in the Tax Code (Article 394) at 1.5 percent except for the following types of land subject to the 0.3 percent rate ceiling:

- Land reserved for agriculture and farming.
- Land under housing stock and communal infrastructure.
- Land granted for private subsidiary farming, horticulture, gardening, or livestock breeding.

- Land that cannot be freely traded because it is subject to restricted use for military, security, and customs needs.

Land parcels acquired by legal and natural persons for the construction of residential structures other than owner-occupied ones are subject to a double rate of taxation in the first three years of design and construction and a quadruple rate thereafter (Article 396[15]). The land tax rate on parcels acquired by natural persons for the construction of owner-occupied residential structures doubles after 10 years of design and construction (Article 396[16]).

Exemptions

Certain types of land are exempt from the tax, such as

- land under objects of cultural and historical heritage;
- land parcels included in the common area of an apartment building;
- land officially recognized as forest;
- land under state-owned water basins (with some exceptions); and
- land under public roads.

In many cases, a building is owned by a private entity but the land is leased from a public authority. In that case, only property tax (on the structure) is due.

Tax Relief Measures

The Tax Code allows the deduction of the cadastral value of 600 square meters of land to some socially vulnerable categories of people, such as disabled people, retirees, and families with three or more children (Article 391[5]). Some organizations are entirely exempt from the land tax (Article 395), such as religious organizations, organizations of people with disabilities, and those domiciled in special economic zones (for a limited period). Some additional exemptions for specific categories of taxpayers may be set in local normative acts (Article 387[2]). However, it is prohibited to grant exemptions to specific entities or individuals (Article 56).

While upper limits on annual increases in the tax liability were initially introduced as part of the phasing in of cadastral values for the taxation of structures owned by natural persons, since 2019 a 10 percent ceiling has also been applied to increases in land tax liability, again for natural persons only.

Figure 18.5 reports the magnitude of forgone revenues, through exemptions and deductions, either mandated in federal legislation or introduced

Figure 18.5 Tax Expenditures Related to Land Parcels (% of GDP)

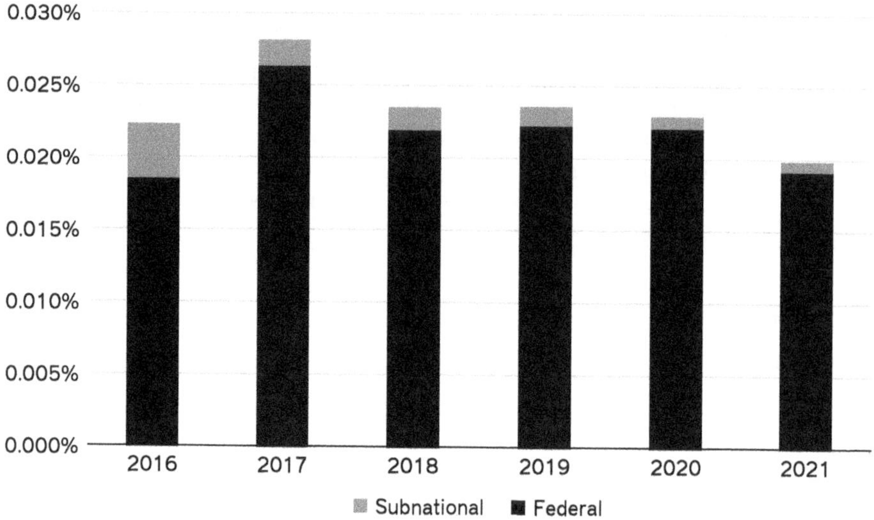

Source: Calculated using data from the Federal Tax Service and the Federal Statistics Service (Rosstat).

by specific regions and municipalities. As shown in this figure, tax expenditures are dominated by those mandated at the federal level, which experienced a dramatic spike in 2017, entirely driven by parcels owned by natural persons. The likely explanation for the spike is the amnesty on back taxes offered to entice self-declaration of parcels not registered by tax authorities. Tax expenditures have been steadily declining since 2017.

Billing and Collection

Legal entities are required to assess their tax liabilities, submit tax returns, and pay the tax on their own. Each local government can set its own schedule of payments for legal entities. In particular, they can require quarterly filings and advance payments at one-quarter of the tax rate (articles 393 and 396–397 of the Tax Code).

For land parcels owned by natural persons, the local branch of the national tax authorities must issue a tax assessment note and demand payment. Natural persons (i.e., individuals) pay the land tax annually.

From 2016 to 2021, collection rates ranged from 91 percent of assessment in 2016 to 107 percent in 2021 (table 18.9). Repayment of back taxes pushed the collection rates over 100 percent in some years. As expected, collection rates are generally higher for parcels owned by legal persons.

Table 18.9 Land Tax Collections as a Percentage of Assessed Amounts

Ownership	2016	2017	2018	2019	2020	2021
Legal persons	94.18	95.31	96.64	101.44	97.22	111.05
Natural persons	79.71	88.44	87.30	101.41	98.68	96.28
All owners	**90.87**	**93.54**	**94.21**	**101.43**	**97.57**	**107.44**

Source: Calculated using data from the Federal Tax Service.

Natural Persons' Property Tax

Historical Context

The natural persons' property tax, designated in the Tax Code as a local-government revenue source, applies to structures (houses, apartments, cottages, garages, etc.) owned by natural persons (as opposed to legal entities liable for the regional tax described earlier). Before January 1, 2013, the tax rate applied to the sum of the inventory values of all structures located in the local jurisdiction and owned by one individual. The inventory value of structures used to be determined by a local BTI as the cost of reconstruction depreciated for the deterioration of the structure.[11] In November 2011, in its letter to the prime minister, the Ministry of Finance acknowledged that the inventory values bore little resemblance to market values, as the former were based on reconstruction cost tables issued in 1970–1971 with some subsequent price adjustments. However, at that time, the Ministry of Finance opposed updating the methodology for assessing the reconstruction value of structures, arguing that the introduction of cadastral valuation was imminent. Reportedly, most objects had an inventory value under RUB 500,000 (US$7,500), which is significantly less than the market value of an apartment in most localities (Korytin and Patel 2016; Petrova and Tretyak 2019). However, for recently built structures, the inventory value could reportedly exceed the market value (Kornya and Kholyavko 2018).

BTIs stopped estimating or updating inventory values in 2013. But during the transition period—initially envisioned as ending in 2020 but extended through 2022 in some regions—the inventory values assigned before 2013 could still be used for taxation after being adjusted for inflation. With the enactment in January 2015 of Chapter 32 of the Tax Code, dedicated to the taxation of natural persons' property, local governments were given the discretion to set tax rates subject to either of the two separate sets of rate limits, depending on which value is used for taxation—that is, inventory or cadastral. Furthermore, the Tax Code (Article 408[8]) required a gradual phasing in of cadastral values by defining the tax base as a weighted average of inventory and cadastral values, with the weight on the latter progressively increasing from 0.2 to 0.6 during the first three years of transition and jumping to 1.0 starting from the fourth year. In addition, even after the three years of transition, annual increases in the tax liability are capped at 10 percent. Reportedly, in 2015, cadastral values were set to be applied for the taxation of natural persons' property in less than one-third of regions (Zykova 2014). According to one source, by 2018, 28 regions had completed all three years of phasing in cadastral values, 21 regions were in the second year of phasing in, 15 regions were in the first year of phasing in, and the remaining regions were not yet applying cadastral values for the taxation of properties of natural persons (Kholyavko and Terchenko 2018). Another source states that only 13 regions had not started using cadastral values by 2018 (Kornya and Kholyavko 2018). The latter source also suggests that regions were not in a hurry to transition to cadastral values because they would not be able to apply a progressive schedule of rates that were allowed for the inventory values (see table 18.10).

Rather than exempting all structures valued under RUB 500,000 (US$7,500), as had been done before 2015, the new law gives each taxpayer a deduction equal to the value of a fixed area of the property object (e.g., 50 square meters of a house). While the initial draft of Bill 51763-4 envisioned significant shortening of the federally mandated list of exempt individuals, the final text of Tax Code Chapter 32, enacted in January 2015, contained much the same list as the previous federal law, "On the Property Tax for Natural Persons" (No. 2003-1; December 9, 1991). However, since 2015, these exemptions have been limited to one property object of each type per taxpayer: one apartment, a part of an apartment, or a room; and one residential building or part of a residential building. Furthermore, these exemptions cannot be claimed for property objects used for any kind of business.

Basis of the Natural Persons' Property Tax

Cadastral values (or inventory values during the transition period until 2022) exceeding the amount of the standard deduction are used as the basis for this tax.

Coverage of Tax Base

According to the Tax Code (Article 401), the tax base should include the following types of property objects owned by natural persons:

- A residential building.
- An apartment or a room.

- A garage or parking space.
- A single real estate complex.
- Construction in progress.
- Other buildings, structures, and premises.

Common areas of multiunit residential buildings are explicitly excluded (Tax Code, Article 401[3]). This has implications in a situation when an owner of a unit in a multiunit residential building is denied ownership registration for an underground or outdoor parking space assigned to that unit. There is no tax liability when property rights are not granted, but the de facto owner can still pursue legal recourse to have the property rights registered because ownership security can outweigh tax implications.

Case law has established that illegally built structures are not taxable, as no property rights can be granted or recognized according to the Civil Code.

Similar to the tax on assets of legal entities, land parcels are excluded from the tax base, as they are subject to a separate local tax.

Before January 1, 2015, natural persons were not legally required to pay land or property taxes unless furnished with a tax bill by the Federal Tax Service. Since January 1, 2015, natural persons have been required to declare property ownership if they have not received tax bills in the past. Until January 2017, voluntary submission of property declarations did not require paying any back taxes. After January 2017, whether ownership is self-declared or identified by tax authorities through other means, three years of back taxes can be assessed, which is the maximum look-back period allowed in the Tax Code for any tax. The total number of tax-registered property objects (other than land) owned by natural persons increased from 55.6 million in 2014 to 68 million in 2017, and then to 75.7 million in 2021.

As shown in figure 18.6, the share of untaxed property of natural persons slowly but steadily decreased from 41.1 percent (27.2 million out of 66.1 million objects) in 2016 to 39.4 percent (29.8 million out of 75.7 million objects) in 2021.

Taxpayers

The taxpayers of the natural persons' property tax are natural persons who own property recognized as taxable objects under this tax.

Responsibility for Valuations

One designated regional valuation agency is to be established by each regional government to carry out a cadastral valuation of all property objects (land and structures) located in that region and registered by Rosreestr.

Figure 18.6 Evolution of the Natural Persons' Property Objects in the Tax Net (million objects)

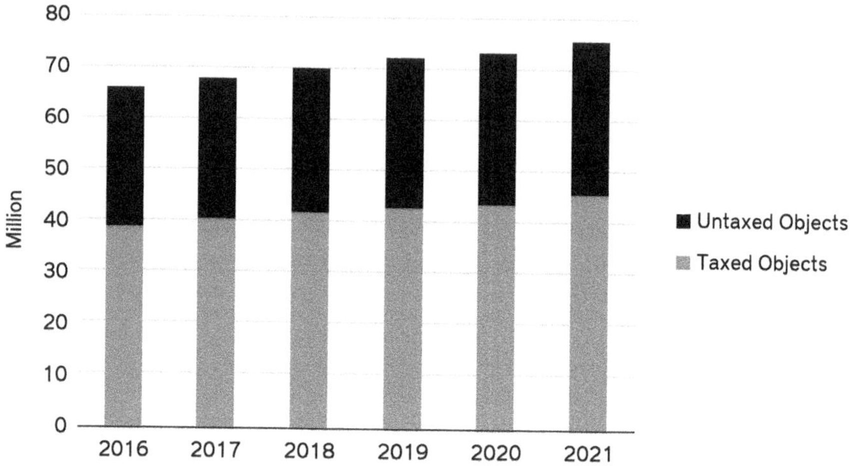

Source: Calculated using data from the Federal Tax Service.

Valuation Cycle

The cadastral value is reassessed every two years in Moscow and Saint Petersburg, while in other regions it has to be done every four years. Since 2022, cadastral revaluation has had to cover all registered structures or all registered land parcels, but these two categories of real estate can follow two separate valuation cycles. Furthermore, with the newly mandated four-year revaluation cycle, all regions were scheduled to undertake the revaluation of structures in 2023–2024.

For newly registered property objects or modifications of the previously registered objects, within 3 days of recording this information in the Unified Register, Rosreestr has to notify the regional entity responsible for valuation, which in turn has to assign or update the corresponding cadastral value within 10 business days.

Valuation Methodology

If there is sufficient and reliable market information on prices (the amounts requested, offered, or paid as the result of a completed or proposed transaction), the federal methodological guidelines recommend that the determination of the cadastral value should be carried out mainly on the basis of the comparative sales approach. For each type of property, the federal guidelines (Order of the Ministry of Economic Development of Russia No. 358

of June 6, 2016, last revised August 9, 2018) also rank the appropriateness of alternative valuation methods. Thus, the income approach is ranked higher than the comparative sales approach for retail, hospitality, and office space.

Valuation Quality Control Measures

The quality control measures for valuation of the natural persons' property tax are the same as for the land tax described earlier.

Property Valuation Data

The data on property valuation for this tax are the same as for the land tax described earlier. According to survey responses by 50 regions that had established their valuation agencies by 2018, there were numerous issues with the valuation data (Kholyavko 2018b). For example, 22 percent of responding regions reported missing or conflicting information on construction in progress.

Objection and Appeal

Just as for the land tax described earlier, payers of the natural persons' property tax can commission a private appraisal and then have the cadastral value updated through an appeal commission or court (starting from January 2023, also by submitting the market valuation directly to the designated regional valuation agency). However, this updated value will be valid only until the next cadastral revaluation cycle. Just as for the land parcels, there are numerous reports of cadastral values substantially exceeding market values (Mavrina 2021). A three-year period of phasing in the cadastral values helped to dampen the financial impact of these discrepancies on taxpayers. Yet it seems that the extra time allowed by this transition period was not enough to improve the quality of mass valuation, and such incidents were still reported in 2021 after another revaluation cycle conducted by the regional valuation agencies.

Tax Rates

Rates for the natural persons' property tax are set in the normative acts of representative bodies of municipal governments. Tax rates can vary with the amount of combined cadastral values (or inflation-adjusted inventory values if still used in some regions, at least until 2022) of all property objects owned by one taxpayer. Representative bodies of municipal governments set tax rates within federal limits according to cadastral (or inventory) value and type of usage of a taxable object.

In cases where cadastral values are used to determine the tax base, tax rates set by municipal councils cannot exceed

- 0.1 percent for the following objects:
  - Residential buildings, parts of residential buildings, apartments, parts of apartments, and rooms.
  - Construction in progress if the intended use of such objects is residential.
  - Single real estate complexes that include at least one residential building.
  - Garages and parking spaces.
  - Outbuildings, the area of each of which does not exceed 50 square meters, and which are located on land parcels designated for personal subsidiary farming, gardening, or single-family houses.
- 2 percent for the following objects:
  - Office and retail space.
  - Property objects with cadastral values exceeding RUB 300 million (about US$4.5 million).
- 0.5 percent for all other objects.

In cases where inventory values are used to determine the base, municipal governments have to stay within the federal limits listed in table 18.10 when setting tax rates.

Exemptions

The cadastral value is reduced by the amount of a standard deduction equal to the value of a fixed area of the property object:

Table 18.10 Federal Limits for Tax Rates on Natural Persons' Property

Total Inventory Value of Properties	Tax Rates
Below RUB 300,000 (US$4,500)	Up to 0.1%
From RUB 300,000 (US$4,500) to RUB 500,000 (US$7,500)	0.1%–0.3%
Over RUB 500,000 (US$7,500)	0.3%–2.0%

Source: Tax Code (Chapter 32).

- 10 square meters for a room + 5 square meters per child in households with three or more children.
- 20 square meters for an apartment + 5 square meters per child in households with three or more children.
- 50 square meters for a residential building + 7 square meters per child in households with three or more children.
- RUB 1 million for a single real estate complex that includes a residential building or residential premises.

Tax Relief Measures

Tax Code (Article 407) mandates exemptions for some socially vulnerable categories of people, such as disabled people and retirees, for one property object of each type: a room or an apartment, a residential building, and a garage or a parking spot.

In addition to these federally mandated exemptions, other specific categories of taxpayers may be granted exemptions in local normative acts (Article 399). However, it is prohibited to grant exemptions to specific individuals (Article 56).

In addition to mandating exemptions for specific categories of natural persons, the Tax Code (Article 407) also mandates exempting one object per taxpayer from the following specific types of properties:

- Apartment or room; house; garage or parking spot; premises or structures used by individuals engaged in professional creative activities such as creative workshops, ateliers, and studios; and residential premises used as private museums, galleries, or libraries open to the public.
- Outbuildings or structures with an area under 50 square meters located on land parcels provided for personal subsidiary farming, gardening, or individual housing construction.

As part of the phasing in of cadastral values for the taxation of structures owned by natural persons, since 2018, annual increases in the tax liability have been capped at 10 percent.

Figure 18.7 demonstrates the magnitude of forgone revenues, through exemptions and deductions, either mandated in federal legislation or introduced by specific regions and municipalities. As shown in this figure, tax expenditures are dominated by those mandated at the federal level. Both kinds of tax expenditures were declining before 2018 but started to rise again thereafter.

Figure 18.7 Tax Expenditures Related to Natural Persons' Structures (% of GDP)

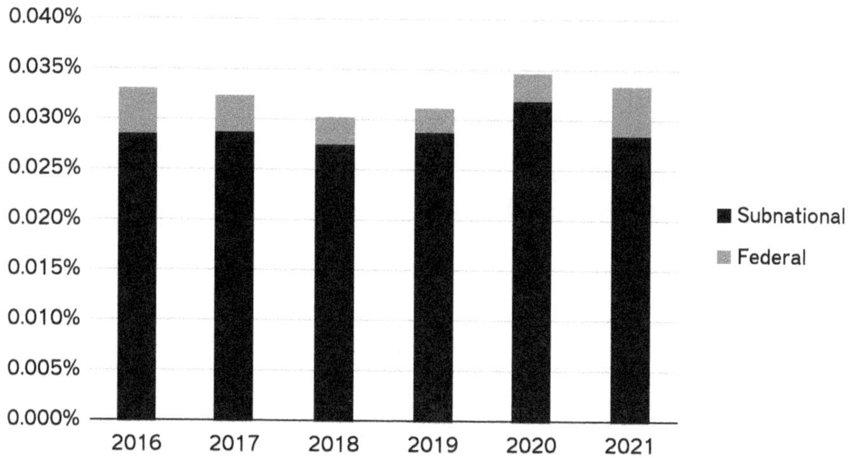

Source: Calculated using data from the Federal Tax Service and the Federal Statistics Service (Rosstat).

Billing

The tax year for the natural persons' property tax is the calendar year from January 1 to December 31. Private individuals are not required to submit any tax returns concerning property tax. The tax authorities calculate the tax amount based on their records obtained through the interagency exchange from Rosreestr as well as by surveying companies that maintain technical records of buildings (BTIs). However, if the tax authorities have incorrect information about the taxable assets or some assets of the taxpayer are not registered with the tax inspectorate, the taxpayer must provide the relevant information to the tax authorities.

Payment

Each municipality can set its own due date for tax payment, but it has to be before November 1.

From 2016 to 2021, collection rates ranged from 75 percent of assessment in 2016 to 103 percent in 2019.

Property Tax in Large Urban Areas

The cities of Moscow and Saint Petersburg enjoy a special administrative status that gives them the same powers as regions.[12] In 2021, the city of

Moscow accounted for 8.68 percent of the national population and 20.1 percent of GDP (table 18.11). In 2021, the city of Saint Petersburg accounted for 3.69 percent of the national population and 7.7 percent of GDP. At the same time, out of all land and property tax collections in the country, the city of Moscow accounted for about 16 percent, while the city of Saint Petersburg accounted for 4 percent.

As shown in figure 18.8, as a share of the total tax revenues of Moscow City, the contribution from the three land and property taxes peaked at 9.18 percent in 2017 and has been declining since. The decline has been mostly driven by the tax on enterprise assets and land tax. By contrast, the share of the natural persons' property tax continued to grow until 2020.

Table 18.12 reveals that, as a share of the gross regional product (GRP), the enterprise assets tax was declining while all three property taxes underperformed when compared with the personal income tax, the main tax source for the city of Moscow. This is despite the fact that, since the introduction of the cadastral values for the taxation of corporate assets, Moscow City has been gradually increasing the applicable tax rate, from 0.9 percent in 2014 to 1.5 percent in 2018, to 1.6 percent in 2019, to 1.7 percent in 2020, and finally to 1.9 percent in 2020, the rate that remains in place today. The decline in revenues from the tax on enterprise assets could be partially explained by a decline in cadastral values of most objects, on average by 16 percent, after the 2018 revaluation applicable to the 2019–2021 tax years (Kholyavko 2018a). Reportedly, the decline in cadastral values was a product of overestimation in the previous revaluation cycle (carried out in 2016 and applied to the 2017–2018 tax years). The results of the 2016 valuation had been appealed by a majority of large taxpayers in court, often successfully.

For almost all types of land, Moscow City set maximally allowed tax rates: the standard rate of 1.5 percent and a reduced rate of 0.3 percent. The only exception is for land under housing stock, parking spaces, garages, and communal infrastructure (0.1 percent) and land granted for private subsidiary farming, horticulture, gardening, or livestock breeding (0.025 percent). As these rates are generally lower than those set on structures, in particular those owned by legal entities, it is not surprising that in Moscow City the land tax generates significantly less revenue than the two taxes levied on structures owned by legal and natural persons, respectively. Further, for retail and office space with cadastral values under RUB 300 million (about US$4.5 million), the tax rate is lower for natural persons (1.5 percent) compared with that on similar objects owned by legal entities (1.9 percent).

As shown in figure 18.9, as a share of total tax revenues, the contribution from the three land and property taxes to Saint Petersburg's budget

Table 18.11 Land and Property Taxes in Moscow and Saint Petersburg

	Moscow City (12,635.5 million residents in 2021)	**Saint Petersburg City (5,377.5 million residents in 2021)**
Number of taxable properties	In 2021, the cadastral valuation roll included 7 million objects, including 342,000 land parcels. In 2022, the cadastral valuation roll included 348,000 land parcels. In 2021, the total cadastral value of tax-registered property was equivalent to about 140% of GRP. In addition, book value of other taxable corporate assets was equivalent to about 22% of GRP.	In 2020, the cadastral valuation roll included 3.2 million objects, including 145,000 land parcels. In 2022, the cadastral valuation roll included 150,000 land parcels. In 2021, the total cadastral value of tax-registered property was equivalent to about 129% of local GRP. In addition, book value of other taxable corporate assets was equivalent to about 21% of GRP.
Basis of the property tax	Cadastral value of land Cadastral value of structures owned by natural persons Book value of corporate assets except land and select categories of structures taxed per cadastral value: • Office and retail centers • Commercial structures over 1,000 m^2 or specifically designated commercial space over 3,000 m^2 in one residential building or specifically designated immovable property of FLEs that do not have PEs (or which is not related to the PEs' activities) • Construction in progress	Cadastral value of land Cadastral value of structures owned by natural persons Book value of corporate assets except land and select categories of structures taxed per cadastral value: • Office and retail space over 3,000 m^2 • Immovable property of FLEs that do not have PEs (or which is not related to the PEs' activities) • Construction in progress • Residential premises • Car parking spaces and garages

	• Residential premises • Car parking spaces and garages • Residential buildings and outbuildings built on land parcels designated for subsidiary farming or single-family houses	
Total value of the tax base	Between the 2018 and 2021 revaluations, cadastral values increased by 40% for apartments and 4%–8% for commercial property. During the same period, Moscow City's GRP increased by 22.51% in nominal terms and 3.29% in real terms.	Compared with 2018, cadastral values increased by 32% for land parcels in 2022. During the same period, Saint Petersburg City's GRP increased by 120% in nominal terms and 23.16% in real terms.
Exempt properties	As long as tax-exempt properties have cadastral registration (even if they have no ownership titles), they are included in the cadastral valuation roll. For natural persons, there are only federally mandated exemptions.	As long as tax-exempt properties have cadastral registration (even if they have no ownership titles), they are included in the cadastral valuation roll. For natural persons, in addition to federally mandated exemptions, the city also exempts citizens enrolled in educational organizations, as well as orphans over 18 in military service and children left without parental care.
Revaluations	Revaluations occur every two years (disrupted by the pandemic in 2020). The last revaluation was in 2022 for land parcels and in 2021 for other properties.	Revaluations occur every two years (disrupted by the pandemic in 2020). The last approved revaluation was in 2022 for land parcels and 2018 for other objects. In 2020, revaluation of all types of property was carried out but not approved by the city government.

Source: Prepared using data from the Federal Tax Service and Federal Statistics Service (Rosstat).

Note: GRP = gross regional product.

Figure 18.8 Land and Property Taxes in Moscow City (% of total tax revenues)

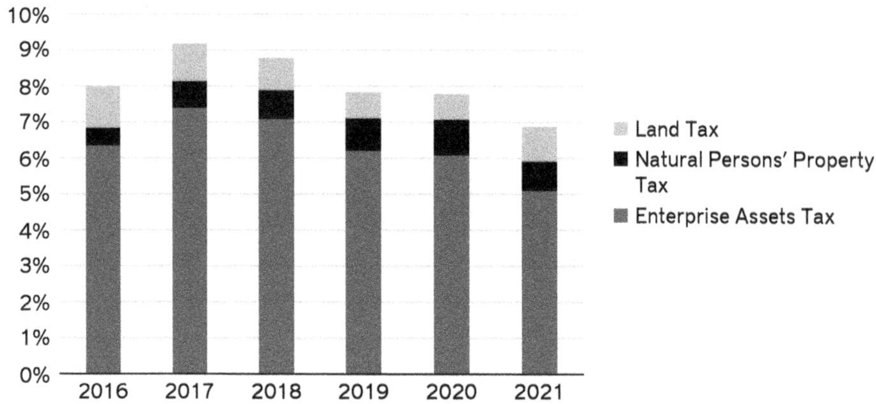

Source: Calculated using data from the Federal Tax Service.

Table 18.12 Composition of Moscow City Revenues (% of GRP)

	2018	2019	2020
Total revenues	12.71	13.34	14.51
Tax revenues	10.92	11.62	11.75
Enterprise profit tax	4.07	4.38	3.99
Personal income tax	5.02	5.27	5.85
Enterprise assets tax	0.77	0.71	0.71
Natural persons' property tax	0.09	0.10	0.09
Land tax	0.10	0.09	0.11
Trade levy	0.04	0.04	0.04
Excises	0.15	0.22	0.21
Other tax revenues	0.68	0.81	0.74
Nontax revenues	1.39	1.36	1.30
Grants	0.41	0.37	1.45

Source: Calculated using data from the Federal Tax Service and Federal Statistics Service (Rosstat).

peaked at 9.6 percent of the city tax revenues in 2016 and has been declining since. As in Moscow City, this decline was driven by the taxes on land and enterprise assets.

Table 18.13 reveals that, as a share of GRP, the enterprise assets tax was declining while all three property taxes underperformed when compared

Figure 18.9 Land and Property Taxes in the City of Saint Petersburg (% of total tax revenues)

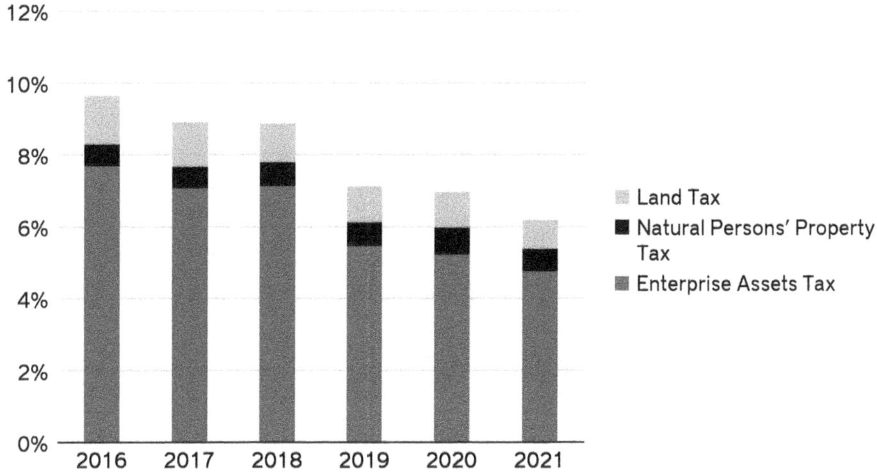

Source: Calculated using data from the Federal Tax Service.

Table 18.13 Composition of Saint Petersburg Revenues (% of GRP)

	2018	2019	2020
Total revenues	12.32	12.51	12.98
Tax revenues	11.03	11.24	11.33
Enterprise profit tax	3.35	3.64	3.36
Personal income tax	5.37	5.33	5.74
Enterprise assets tax	0.78	0.60	0.58
Natural persons' property tax	0.07	0.07	0.08
Land tax	0.12	0.11	0.11
Trade levy	0.00	0.00	0.00
Excises	0.42	0.48	0.47
Other tax revenues	0.93	1.01	1.00
Nontax revenues	0.76	0.71	0.61
Grants	0.52	0.57	1.01

Source: Calculated using data from the Federal Tax Service, Ministry of Finance, and Federal Statistics Service (Rosstat).

with the personal and corporate income taxes, the main tax sources for the city of Saint Petersburg.

For almost all types of land, the city of Saint Petersburg set maximally allowed tax rates: the standard rate of 1.5 percent and the reduced rate of 0.3 percent. The only exception is for land under housing stock and communal infrastructure (0.05 percent) and land granted for private subsidiary farming, horticulture, gardening, or livestock breeding (0.01 percent).

Similarly, for almost all types of natural persons' structures, the city of Saint Petersburg set maximally allowed tax rates except for structures with cadastral values under RUB 300 million (about US$4.5 million), other than those intended for residential, parking, retail, or office use, where a 0.3 percent rate applies rather than the maximum allowed 0.5 percent. Also, for retail and office space with cadastral values under RUB 300 million (about US$4.5 million), the rate is aligned with the one set on similar objects owned by legal entities (1.5 percent) rather than being set at the maximum allowed 2 percent.

Even by focusing on these two entirely urban jurisdictions of regional status, one can see that the uniform federal framework allows considerable discretion for subnational authorities in both setting rates and defining the taxable bases. These two urban jurisdictions appear to make quite different choices along all these dimensions: statutory rates, the extent to which cadastral values are to be used instead of book values of corporate assets, and acceptance of cadastral revaluation results (see table 18.11). Saint Petersburg appears to have been more cautious in making all those choices, and this seems to be reflected in its fiscal outcomes.

Conclusion

In the last five years, Russia has largely completed its transition to the scaled-back vision for property taxation that it settled on after abandoning in 2014 its earlier attempts to introduce a single real estate tax. In terms of tax policy, it has entrenched the fragmented system with three separate land and property taxes (land tax, natural persons' property tax, and tax on assets of organizations) split between two subnational tiers of government. The only integration on the tax policy side was allowing regions to substitute cadastral values for (much lower) book values of corporate assets, but only with respect to the type of assets that are not used in production and might otherwise be shifted by natural persons into shell companies to avoid the local tax on natural persons' property.

Even more integration and harmonization between the three property taxes have been achieved on the tax administration side. All spatial cadastres (land, water, forests, etc.), previously scattered across various federal agencies, were brought under one roof (Rosreestr). The same agency is now responsible for maintaining the Unified Register, which covers both land and structures and includes the cadastral value among the property characteristics. Thus, when property ownership is transferred from a natural to a legal person, the taxation is switched from the local tax on natural persons' property to the regional tax on the assets of organizations. However, at least for nonindustrial objects, there is continuity in terms of recording the ownership, physical characteristics, and cadastral values of property objects. Even though the valuation of land and structures is carried out by the same regional entity, in each region it can follow two separate revaluation cycles and use different valuation methods. Since 2017, these regional valuation entities have been required to carry out valuation in-house by their permanent staff rather than outsourcing it to private appraisers.

On the one hand, this chapter chronicles the failure of Russian authorities to implement an ambitious vision for a unified tax on real estate. After almost two decades of stalled efforts, Russia had to settle on a much less ambitious version of this reform by narrowing its focus on the property of natural persons. In terms of fiscal outcomes, this narrow version of reforms appears to be quite successful, with the revenue buoyancy for this tax on natural persons' property above 2.5 over the 2016–2021 period. On the other hand, this might represent a one-off gain associated with the gradual phasing in of market values in place of inventory values for taxing the property of natural persons. Indeed, the land tax, which underwent a similar transition to cadastral values in 2004, shows a meager 0.22 revenue buoyancy just a decade later.

Even within this scaled-back policy framework, the revenue potential of the property taxes has not been exhausted. Many regions are still using book values for taxing many categories of corporate assets, in particular residential structures and small commercial premises. This might reflect the pushback from businesses in response to the inadequate quality of mass valuation of property conducted by the recently established regional valuation agencies.

Existing land and property taxes in Russia were conceived in the early 1990s when virtually all land was owned by the state. This explains why structures were and still are taxed separately from the land. While the taxation of land and nonindustrial structures had transitioned to market values by 2022, with these values determined for both land and structures by the same valuation agency in each region, there is still a disparity in tax rates applied to land compared with structures. While the actual rates are set locally in each municipality, they are capped by the federally imposed ceilings, which are lower for land (1.5 percent) than for rent-generating structures (2 percent).

By 2000, subnational governments were still receiving 2.5 times more revenues from taxing structures than from taxing private land and leasing public land (Timofeev 2004, 236–245). Even that disparity constituted a dramatic drop from the 4.3 ratio recorded in 1997, and this drop could be explained by the 1998 currency devaluation that eroded the book value of enterprise assets. By 2020, this ratio had increased again to 3.2.

Furthermore, the relative contributions of revenues from land taxes vis-à-vis public land leases dropped from five to one in 1997 to two to one in 2000, and then to one to one in 2020. This conforms to the fact that the bulk of commercially valuable land parcels are publicly owned and can generally only be leased, rather than owned privately. It appears that over time, subnational governments became better at capturing the commercial value of publicly owned land, among other things by using public tenders and cadastral values to set the amount of lease payments.

In September 2023, the Ministry of Finance declared that it was still considering the possibility of applying cadastral values for the taxation of all corporate assets, with the possible exception of railways and similar complex property objects. However, in its Main Directions of Budget, Tax and Customs Tariff Policies for 2024 and the outyears 2025–2026, the ministry used a more tentative wording compared with the same document issued a year earlier. In both cases, the ministry clarified to reporters that it had no specific or immediate plans for this reform (Grinkevich, Boyko, and Kozlov 2023).

Appendix

Table A18.1 Expenditure Responsibilities of Regional and Local Government

Expenditure Functions	Settlements	Urban Districts	Municipal Districts	Regions
General public services				
Archives	Formation of the settlement archive	Formation and depository of the municipal archive	Formation of the district archive, depository for district and settlement archives	Formation and depository of the regional archive
Public order and safety				
Street patrolling	None	By local police	By local police	None
Education				
Preschool	None	Maintenance of buildings, financing of utilities, and organization of the rest with regional financing	Maintenance of buildings, financing of utilities, and organization of the rest with regional financing	Financing of wages, textbooks, equipment, and supplies
Primary	None			
Secondary	None			
Tertiary	None			
Vocational/technical	None	None	None	Provision
Health				
Ambulance	None	Organization of ambulance service, primary health care, and obstetrical services	Organization of ambulance service, primary health care, and obstetrical services	Airlift

(continued)

Table A18.1 Expenditure Responsibilities of Regional and Local Government (*continued*)

Expenditure Functions	Settlements	Urban Districts	Municipal Districts	Regions
Outpatient clinics and hospitals	None			Provision of special treatment (dermatology, sexually transmitted diseases, tuberculosis, narcology, oncology, etc.)
Public health	None	None	None	
Insurance for the unemployed	None	None	None	Financing
Social security and welfare				
Social protection	None	None	None	Child benefits, support to labor veterans, orphans, homeless/destitute children, single mothers, and mothers with many children
Guardianship	Facilitation	Provision	Provision	None
Labor market policy	None	None	None	Retraining, public works
Housing and community amenities				
Social housing	Provision	None	None	Financing of subsidies to households
Garbage/waste	Collection	Collection and utilization	Utilization	None

Water	Organization	Organization	None	None
Sewerage	Organization	Organization	None	None
Planting of greenery, forest protection	Provision	Provision	None	None
Street sweeping, lighting, and signs	Provision	Provision	None	None
Funeral services and maintenance of cemeteries	Organization	Organization	Organization	None
Firefighting/fire protection	Basic fire protection	Basic fire protection	None	Organization of firefighting
Recreational and cultural affairs				
Physical culture development	Facilitation	Facilitation	None	Organization of regional programs
Libraries	Municipal libraries	Municipal libraries	Library collectors	Regional libraries
Museums	None	None	None	Organization and support of regional museums, folk crafts, and other cultural activities
Arts	None	None	None	
Entertainment	Facilitation of service provision	Facilitation of service provision	None	None
Places of recreation	Arrangement	Arrangement	None	None

(continued)

Table A18.1 Expenditure Responsibilities of Regional and Local Government (*continued*)

Expenditure Functions	Settlements	Urban Districts	Municipal Districts	Regions
Protection of historical sites	Within the settlement	Within the settlement	None	Sites of regional importance
Fuel and energy				
Central heating	Organization	Organization	None	None
Heating fuel (natural gas, firewood, coal)	Organization	Organization	Organization (natural gas)	None
Electric power supply and lighting	Organization	Organization	Organization	None
Agriculture, forestry, fishing, and hunting	None	None	None	Support to agricultural producers
Transportation and communication				
Telecommunications	Facilitation of service provision	Facilitation of service provision	Facilitation of service provision	None
Road network	Organization within the settlement	Organization within the settlement	Organization between settlements	Organization between districts
Public transport	Organization within the settlement	Organization within the settlement	Organization between settlements	Organization between districts and suburban

Railroads	None	None	None	Organization between districts and suburban
Airlines	None	None	None	Organization between districts and suburban
Other economic affairs and services				
Urban planning and land management	Development of plans and zoning of settlement land	Development plans and zoning, maintenance of land records	Maintenance of land records, zoning of intersettlement lands	Planning the use of agricultural land
Other expenditures				
Environmental protection	Organization within the settlement	Organization within the settlement	Organization between settlements	Organization between districts
Prevention and handling of emergency situations	Participation in responding to local incidents	Participation in local incidents	Participation in district incidents	Regional and intersettle-ment incidents
Ecological control	None	Provision	Provision	None
Equalization of constituent jurisdictions	None	None	Equalization of settle-ments with district funds according to regional methodology	Equalization of districts and settlements accord-ing to federal guidelines

Source: Martinez-Vazquez, Timofeev, and Boex (2006), updated with subsequent amendments of the law.

Notes

1. This chapter uses official data ranging between 2016 and 2021, which include the (Autonomous) Republic of Crimea and the city of Sevastopol in the national aggregates. However, I do not intend to make any judgment as to the legal or other status of any disputed territories or prejudice the final determination of the parties' claims.

2. A 2019 amendment to the law on local self-government introduced a third, mixed urban-rural type of top-tier municipality, which was expected to be used to guide the formation of new municipalities by 2025 through mergers of some cities with surrounding rural districts. These changes are not reflected in the data used for this chapter, which only extend to 2021.

3. In the course of 2000–2005, gradual enactment of the Tax Code chapters replaced respective provisions of the previous Law on the Basic Principles of Taxation (Law 2118-1 of 1991) and other federal laws dedicated to specific taxes.

4. All property rights acquired after the enactment of the Law on the State Registration of Property Rights and Transactions (Law 122-FZ of 1997) are subject to state registration. Before 2008, state registration of property rights was carried out by justice offices established by regional governments in accordance with federal legislation and under the supervision of the federal government. According to Malme and Kalinina (2001, 68), this registration process had been "burdensome for new owners and costly for governments. . . . As a result, much property remain[ed] unregistered, including valuable new construction."

5. Russia had a flat 13 percent rate for the personal income tax until 2021, when an increased rate of 15 percent was introduced for taxable income exceeding RUB 5 million (US$62,700). Since January 2025, Russia has had five income tax brackets ranging from 13 percent for taxable income under RUB 2.4 million (US$30,000) and progressively increasing to 22 percent applicable to taxable income exceeding RUB 50 million (US$627,000).

6. Federal Law on Real Estate Tax Experiment in the Cities of Novgorod and Tver (110-FZ; July 20, 1997). For a more detailed account of this experiment, see Malme and Kalinina (2001, 76–80) and Martinez-Vazquez, Timofeev, and Boex (2006).

7. Lower rate ceilings were set at 1.6 percent for 2020–2021, 1.3 percent in 2019–2018, and 1 percent in 2017 (EY Russia 2021).

8. Previously, municipal housing stock and communal amenities, as well as assets used for agricultural production, education, culture, health care, and sports, were exempted from taxation.

9. Since 2017, it has been up to each region whether to have such a commission. Thus, since Moscow City opted not to have one after 2019, the only way to challenge the value has been in a court. But next door in the Moscow Oblast, such a commission is still functioning and provides an alternative route for property owners to dispute cadastral value (Solntsev 2020).

10. The court route reportedly requires one to spend RUB 80,000–270,000 (US$1,200–US$4,050) on an appraisal and might additionally include RUB 300,000 (US$4,500) in attorney's fees and, if ordered by the court, RUB 200,000–500,000 (US$3,000–US$7,500) for an independent expert evaluation of the market appraisal. Reportedly, the latter is more likely when the cadastral value exceeds the submitted appraisal by more than 20 percent (Popova 2019).

11. BTIs were authorized agents of the Ministry of Construction Industry, Housing and Utilities Sector of the Russian Federation (Minstroi).

12. The same status was also granted to the city of Sevastopol after it was annexed along with Crimea in 2014.

References

Domnina, S. V., and E. V. Savoskina. 2021. "State Cadastral Valuation of Real Estate in the Conditions of Market Development." [In Russian.] *Fundamental Research* 2021(11): 66–72. https://doi.org/10.17513/fr.43124.

EY Russia. 2021. "Doing Business in Russia." March. Ernst & Young Valuation and Advisory Services.

Grinkevich, D., A. Boyko, and A. Kozlov. 2023. "The Ministry of Finance Has Returned to the Idea of Levying the Business Property Tax Based on the Cadastre." [In Russian.] *Vedomosti*, October 10. https://www.vedomosti.ru/economics/articles/2023/10/10/999687-minfin-vernulsya-k-idee-nachisleniya-naloga-na-imuschestvo-biznesa-po-kadastru.

Kholyavko, A. 2018a. "Moscow Agreed to Reduce Business Property Tax Rate." [In Russian.] *Vedomosti*, December 11. https://www.vedomosti.ru/economics/articles/2018/12/11/789019-pravitelstvo-soglasilos.

———. 2018b. "Regions Cannot Solve the Problem with the Quality of Information Required for Cadastral Valuation." [In Russian.] *Vedomosti*, September 2. https://www.vedomosti.ru/economics/articles/2018/09/02/779667-regioni-ne-mogut-reshit-problemu.

Kholyavko, A., and E. Terchenko. 2018. "Why the Property Tax of Many Citizens Has Increased Again." [In Russian.] *Vedomosti*, November 16. https://www.vedomosti.ru/economics/articles/2018/11/16/786604-nalog.

Komarov, S. I., S. A. Gal'chenko, R. V. Zhdanova, and A. A. Rasskazova. 2021. "State Cadastral Valuation of Agricultural Land in Russia." In *Land Economy and Rural Studies Essentials*, vol. 113, European Proceedings of Social and Behavioral Sciences, ed. D. S. Nardin, O. V. Stepanova, and V. V. Kuznetsova, 240–249. European Publisher. https://doi.org/10.15405/epsbs.2021.07.30.

Konevsky, A., and P. Konstantinov. 2020. "Russia." In *Real Estate 2021*, ed. D. Wagerfield. London: Global Legal Group.

Kornya, A., and A. Kholyavko. 2018. "The Constitutional Court Will Check the Property Tax." [In Russian.] *Vedomosti*, October 29. https://www.vedomosti.ru/economics/articles/2018/10/29/785047-nalog-na-imuschestvo.

Korytin, A., and S. Patel. 2016. "Improving the Mechanism of Taxation of Natural Persons Property." SSRN, March 23. http://dx.doi.org/10.2139/ssrn.2760350.

Kozlov, A., and D. Molotkova. 2023. "Business Complained About the Sharp Increase in the Cadastral Value of the Land." [In Russian.] *Vedomosti*, January 31. https://www.vedomosti.ru/business/articles/2023/01/31/961023-rezkii-rost-kadastrovoi-stoimosti-zemli.

Malme, J. H., and N. Kalinina. 2001. "Property Tax Developments in the Russian Federation." In *The Development of Property Taxation in Economies in Transition*, ed. J. H. Malme and J. M. Youngman, 67–83. Washington, DC: World Bank Institute.

Martinez-Vazquez, J., A. Timofeev, and J. Boex. 2006. *Reforming Regional-Local Finances in Russia*. World Bank Institute Learning Resources Series, Washington, DC.

Mavrina, L. 2021. "The Pandemic Did Not Prevent the Growth of Revenue from Property Taxes on Citizens." [In Russian.] *Vedomosti*, March 8. https://www.vedomosti.ru/economics/articles/2021/03/08/860606-pandemiya-nalogov.

Mereminskaya, E., and S. Yastrebova. 2019. "The Government Wants to Tighten the Mechanism for Contesting the Cadastral Value." [In Russian.] *Vedomosti*, October 11. https://www.vedomosti.ru/economics/articles/2019/10/11/813436-pravitelstvo-uzhestochit.

Naydenova, M. N. 2021. "Consideration of Disputes About the Results of Determining the Cadastral and Market Value of Land Parcels." [In Russian.] *International Journal of Humanities and Natural Sciences* 5–4(56): 119–124. https://doi.org/10.24412/2500-1000-2021-5-4-119-124.

Overchuk, A. 2004. "Mass Valuation of Land in the Russian Federation." *Land Lines*, April.

Paul, A. 2021. "Problems with Cadastral Value in the Russian Federation." In *Real Property Taxes and Property Markets in CEE Countries and Central Asia*, ed. M. Radvan, R. Franzsen, W. J. McCluskey, and F. Plimmer. Maribor, Slovenia: Lex Localis.

Petrova, Y., and A. Tretyak. 2019. "The Population Pays More and More in Property Taxes." [In Russian.] *Vedomosti*, November 22. https://www.vedomosti.ru/personal_finance/articles/2019/11/21/816898-naselenie-imuschestvennih.

Popova, A. 2019. "How a Business Can Reduce the Cadastral Value." [In Russian.] *Vedomosti*, May 29. https://www.vedomosti.ru/management/blogs/2019/05/29/802680-biznesu-umenshit.

Solntsev, M. 2020. "How to Appeal the Cadastral Value of a Warehouse and Workshop." [In Russian.] *Vedomosti*, March 20. https://www.vedomosti.ru/management/blogs/2020/03/19/825708-osporit-kadastrovuyu.

Timofeev, A. 2004. "Land and Property Taxes in Russia." In *International Handbook of Land and Property Taxation*, ed. R. M. Bird and E. Slack. Cheltenham, UK: Edward Elgar.

Yastrebova, S., A. Chervonnaya, and E. Bazanova. 2019. "Business Spooked by the Prospect of Increased Tax Burden on Real Estate." [In Russian.] *Vedomosti*, September 27. https://www.vedomosti.ru/economics/articles/2019/09/27/812206-biznes-ispugalsya-riska.

Zykova, T. 2014. "The Federal Tax Service Named 28 Regions Introducing a New Tax on the Property of Natural Persons." [In Russian.] *Rossiyskaya Gazeta*, December 16. https://rg.ru/2014/12/17/nalog.html.

Legislation

Civil Code of the Russian Federation, Law 51-FZ of 1994 (Part 1), Law 14-FZ of 1996 (Part 2), Law 146-FZ of 2001 (Part 3), and Law 230-FZ of 2006 (Part 4) (as amended).

Land Code of the Russian Federation, Law 136-FZ of 2001.

Law on the Basic Principles of Taxation, Law 2118-1 of 1991.

Law on the Property Tax of Natural Persons (now chapter 32 of the Tax Code).

Law on the Public Law Company "Roscadaster," Law No. 448-FZ of 2021.

Law on the Real Estate Tax Experiment in the Cities of Novgorod and Tver, Law 110-FZ of 1997.

Law on the State Cadastral Valuation, Law 237-FZ of 2016.

Law on the State Registration of Property Rights and Transactions, Law 122-FZ of 1997.

Law on the State Register of Real Estate, Law 221-FZ of 2007.

Law on Valuation Activity in the Russian Federation, Law 135-FZ of 1998.

Order of the Ministry of Economic Development of Russia on Approval of the Guidelines for State Cadastral Valuation, No. 358 of June 6, 2016.

Tax Code of the Russian Federation of 1998 (as amended).

19

Property Tax Reform in Slovenia: A Missed Opportunity

NEVA ŽIBRIK AND TINA HUMAR

Slovenia is an independent European country in the south of Europe. It shares borders with Italy to the west, Austria to the north, Hungary to the northeast, and Croatia to the east and south.

With an area of 20,271 square kilometers, Slovenia is one of Europe's smaller to medium-sized countries. Throughout a turbulent history, the territories of today's Slovenia were usually part of different empires (from the Roman Empire, to the Austro-Hungarian Monarchy, to the Kingdom of Yugoslavia). From 1944 until independence, it was one of the republics of the Socialist Federal Republic of Yugoslavia; Slovenia gained its independence through a referendum decision on December 23, 1990, and secession from Yugoslavia on June 25, 1991. It was admitted as a member of the United Nations on May 22, 1992. It is also a member of the Council of Europe, the World Trade Organization, the Organization for Security and Co-operation in Europe, the Organisation for Economic Co-operation and Development (OECD), the North Atlantic Treaty Organization, and other world organizations. In 2004, Slovenia joined the European Union. In 2007, it became a member of the Economic and Monetary Union and adopted the single European currency, the euro.

According to official statistics, Slovenia's population on October 1, 2022, was 2,110,547 (Statistični urad 2022). The majority of the population is Slovene, but the country's constitution also recognizes three national minorities—Italian, Hungarian, and Roma—which together make up around 0.6 percent of the population. Politically, Slovenia is a constitutional parliamentary democracy. Ordinary parliamentary elections are held every four years.[1] Ljubljana is the capital city of Slovenia. It is an administrative, educational, cultural, and political center. It has around 295,000 inhabitants, which is nearly 15 percent of the total Slovene population. Additionally, more than 130,000 people commute to Ljubljana daily to work or study (Wikipedia 2025a).

Slovenia's economy is based on the free market, private property, and free economic initiatives. With a gross domestic product (GDP) per capita of US$34,089 (World Bank, n.d.-a), Slovenia ranks among the advanced economies in terms of economic indicators. The main part of value added is contributed by industry, primarily processing activities (around 25 percent of value added) and trade and logistic services (around 22 percent of value added). Financial services and research each contribute around 4 percent of value added, and agriculture adds around 2 percent. Slovenia also ranks very high on the equality scale, as indicated by a Gini coefficient of around 24 (World Bank, n.d.-b; World Population Review, n.d.).

According to the Constitution of the Republic of Slovenia, the country is governed by the rule of law and the rule of social law. These principles are also applied through a modern tax system that pursues fairness, equal treatment, and social redistribution.

Taxes are the main source of funding for government functions, accounting for around 90 percent of total government revenue (table 19.1). Apart from social contributions (for pensions, health insurance, and the provision of social rights), the most important tax source is taxes on the turnover of goods and services—that is, value-added tax (VAT) and excise duties, which account for one-third of tax revenue. This is followed by revenue from income taxation—that is, taxes on corporate and personal income, which contribute around 20 percent of tax revenue. Property taxes are a modest source of tax revenue, contributing less than 2 percent of tax revenue, or only around 1.5 percent of total revenue. The share of these taxes in the GDP is consequently very low, at only around 0.6 percent.

The Constitution of the Republic of Slovenia allows for several levels of local self-government (regional and local), but in practice the only local self-governing units are municipalities. Slovenia is therefore governed at two levels, the central state level and 212 municipalities, of which 12 have the status of city municipalities.[2] Most municipalities are small, with more than half having fewer than 5,000 inhabitants.

The tasks of the state and the municipalities are separate and regulated by legislation. General competence allows a municipality to define its

Table 19.1 Total National Public Finance Revenue (consolidated budget) (€)

	2017	2018	2019	2020	2021
Tax Revenue					
Taxes on income and profits	2,966,958,551	3,296,364,661	3,613,981,088	3,261,830,308	3,981,337,802
Taxes on property	274,233,567	277,932,827	296,378,312	316,865,460	316,865,460
Taxes on goods and services	5,722,785,817	5,989,285,287	6,126,746,074	5,493,269,705	6,359,191,677
Other taxes	105,931,893	111,938,245	120,734,180	98,610,998	200,134,225
Social contributions	6,092,096,588	6,549,768,474	7,021,304,741	7,289,869,198	7,928,127,746
Total tax revenue	**15,162,006,416**	**16,225,289,494**	**17,179,144,395**	**16,460,445,669**	**18,785,656,910**
Nontax Revenue					
Entrepreneurial and property income	616,446,047	835,915,383	601,572,008	450,085,989	630,229,929
Fees, sales, fines	162,353,529	157,504,032	174,934,561	156,508,954	171,621,224
Other nontax revenue	310,560,652	357,224,017	337,676,166	511,653,334	536,501,596
Total nontax revenue	**1,089,360,228**	**1,350,643,432**	**1,114,182,735**	**1,118,248,277**	**1,338,352,749**
Capital revenue	**91,166,433**	**152,815,618**	**136,361,873**	**146,936,767**	**228,305,222**
Grants	**9,498,619**	**12,430,536**	**13,758,239**	**17,506,830**	**21,856,534**

(continued)

Table 19.1 Total National Public Finance Revenue (consolidated budget) (€) (*continued*)

	2017	2018	2019	2020	2021
Transfers	**52,284,243**	**55,552,200**	**58,327,715**	**54,770,321**	**57,298,267**
European Union funds	**398,977,361**	**796,879,940**	**730,510,055**	**730,675,747**	**951,162,190**
Total revenue	**16,803,293,300**	**18,593,611,219**	**19,232,285,012**	**18,528,583,611**	**21,382,631,871**
Tax revenue as % of total revenue	90.2	87.3	89.3	88.8	87.9
Property tax revenue as % of total revenue	1.6	1.5	1.5	1.7	1.5
Property tax revenue as % of GDP	0.64	0.60	0.61	0.61	0.61

Source: Ministrstvo za finance (n.d.-a).

powers by its own rules. It exercises them independently, and they concern only its own inhabitants, without interfering with the powers of the state and other municipalities. For services, municipalities have their own funding, infrastructure, and staff. However, the state may delegate to a municipality a range of specific tasks falling within the competence of the state, provided that the municipality has the capacity to undertake these services. This is called a system of delegated powers, which allows municipalities to regulate the delegated tasks by means of their own bylaws and to exercise them through their own organs and administration (Republika Slovenija 2021).

Despite the small size of some municipalities, they have a relatively wide range of competences (Brezovnik 2022). The state has delegated to the municipalities tasks that mainly concern the local area, such as spatial planning, pre-primary and primary education, primary health care, local public services (e.g., utilities, local transport, funeral services, and provision of essential infrastructure such as local roads, water supply, and protection against natural disasters). In total, between 11 and 12 percent of total government expenditures in Slovenia is provided by municipalities.

The law governing the financing of municipalities (Financing of Municipalities Act) provides what is deemed to be adequate financial resources to carry out these tasks. The most important of these is the share of the income tax that the state cedes to municipalities. By law, 54 percent of the personal income tax is transferred to municipalities. The state sets an amount of eligible expenditure each year that represents the recognized costs of carrying out the compulsory tasks.[3] For these purposes, the state transfers directly to the municipalities 70 percent of the 54 percent of the personal income tax recognized, which is allocated to the municipality in whose territory the taxable persons reside. The excess of this amount over the eligible expenditure and the remaining 30 percent of the personal income tax attributable to the municipalities is used to create a solidarity compensation fund. From this fund, municipalities that do not reach the amount of eligible consumption with 70 percent of their personal income tax shall be reimbursed for the shortfall. The solidarity-based transfer equalizes the distribution of the shared personal income tax revenue between more and less developed municipalities.

In addition to the personal income tax, municipalities are also entitled by law to revenues from property taxes and from a tax on winnings from traditional gambling. These revenue entitlements of local governments are not considered in calculating the income tax revenue share.

The total revenue budget of municipalities (table 19.2) represents around 12 percent of the consolidated state budget. Taxes are the most important source of revenue for municipalities, contributing around

Table 19.2 Total Revenue of Municipalities (€)

	2017	2018	2019	2020	2021
Tax Revenue					
Personal income tax	1,096,669,339	1,167,111,336	1,200,496,935	1,323,466,228	1,331,312,687
Taxes on property	273,935,730	277,440,785	295,979,498	286,944,099	316,065,190
Taxes on goods and services	47,909,702	54,144,325	60,444,430	51,185,466	50,760,681
Other taxes	0	1,185,944	317,889	255,263	0
Total tax revenue	**1,418,514,771**	**1,499,882,390**	**1,557,238,752**	**1,661,851,057**	**1,698,138,558**
Nontax Revenue					
Entrepreneurial and property income	225,474,125	226,983,505	234,758,121	220,271,197	221,713,639
Fees, sales, fines	13,842,158	14,930,725	18,534,351	16,971,733	19,776,582
Other nontax revenue	99,768,786	155,489,188	129,034,716	124,086,792	148,156,173
Total nontax revenue	**339,085,069**	**397,403,418**	**382,327,188**	**361,329,722**	**389,646,394**
Capital revenue	**50,991,187**	**68,848,463**	**53,910,307**	**67,503,093**	**84,146,685**
Grants	**1,445,508**	**5,025,209**	**863,834**	**1,783,552**	**3,043,294**
Transfers	**163,171,966**	**180,598,916**	**234,526,513**	**229,364,112**	**319,086,118**
European Union budget funds	**3,450,650**	**2,680,633**	**3,415,465**	**5,288,659**	**4,064,249**
Total revenue	**1,976,659,150**	**2,154,439,030**	**2,232,282,059**	**2,327,120,194**	**2,498,125,298**
Tax revenue as % of total revenue	71.8	69.6	69.8	71.4	68.0
Property taxes as % of total tax revenue	19.3	18.5	19.0	17.3	18.6

Source: Ministrstvo za finance (n.d.-b).

70 percent of local budgets, with income taxes contributing the largest share of tax revenue, around 80 percent. The next-largest tax source is property taxes, which contribute around 19 percent of municipal tax revenue. The most important of these are the charge for the use of building land and the property transfer tax, which together account for about 90 percent of these revenues (table 19.3). Moreover, the property tax is an important fiscal instrument for municipalities in the field of spatial planning.

Land and Property Markets

Throughout history, the territory of Slovenia has been part of various empires and has rarely been politically independent. In the 18th and 19th centuries, it was part of the Austro-Hungarian Empire. This period was the time of the Enlightenment, which, despite the territory's political subordination, brought progress to the system of land registration and compulsory primary education in the Slovene language. The territory also saw the establishment of a land cadastre with an inventory of status and characteristics of each parcel of land, especially its fertility and type of use. The primary purpose of the original land register was to levy a tax on farming, which was the main source of income for the population at that time. The so-called land tax has been maintained to the present day as a form of flat-rate taxation of agricultural activities under the income tax (flat-rate taxation based on cadastral income). It is important to note that this was the first time that a comprehensive inventory of all parcels of land was established, with measurements and collated attributes of land data. At the same time, the land book, a land register with the ownership status of all parcels, was also established.

Parcel data were also kept during the period of the Socialist Federal Republic of Yugoslavia, within which Slovenia had the status of one of the republics, and those data have been retained to the present day. After Slovenia's independence, at the same time as ownership relations were being regulated (through the abolition of public ownership and establishment of transparent ownership, privatization, and denationalization), the land cadastre underwent an overhaul during the two-decades-long reform. It was gradually unified throughout the country, updated, and digitized, while at the same time a register of buildings and parts of buildings was also established.[4] Slovenia now has a land registry that keeps data on all plots of land, buildings, and parts of buildings. For each unit, there is a unique identifier, information on size (usually based on a geodetic survey), and a description of basic characteristics, such as the actual and intended use for the land, the productive capacity of agricultural and forest

Table 19.3 Revenue from Taxes on Property of Local Governments (€)

	2017	2018	2019	2020	2021
Property tax	5,927,961	3,859,126	9,925,280	8,188,549	8,156,950
Charge for the use of building land	215,914,236	223,394,001	225,307,115	228,012,881	243,023,522
Tax on water vessels	322,625	409,183	392,082	403,850	426,342
Inheritance and gift tax	10,555,397	9,689,271	15,973,551	10,117,227	10,639,459
Tax on the transfer of real estate	41,215,511	40,089,204	44,381,469	40,221,593	53,818,916
Total tax revenue of taxes on property	**273,935,730**	**277,440,785**	**295,979,498**	**286,944,099**	**316,065,190**
Property taxes as % of GDP	**0.64**	**0.60**	**0.61**	**0.61**	**0.61**

Source: Ministrstvo za finance (n.d.-b).

land, the year of construction, the building type, maintenance, and equipment. For all parcels, buildings, and parts of buildings, information on ownership is also obtained from the land register. The register is the most complete record of immovable property and its components, and it is intended to reflect the actual status of each parcel, both for the administrative purposes of the state, including taxation, and for the regulation of the area, including the protection of real estate rights.

New parcels are registered through surveys, the registration of which in the cadastre is compulsory, as this legally creates a new immovable property. Any newly constructed building may be registered in the cadastre as soon as its area is measured, but it must be entered no later than three months after the completion of the construction. The existence of unregistered buildings is verified on the basis of aerial photographs, which are taken for several purposes over the whole surface of the country at least once every two years. These data can also be used to verify the accuracy of the information on buildings and parts of buildings. Verification may also be carried out by means of field visits or notifications. In the event that an irregularity is detected, the owner can be called upon to rectify the data.

The law establishes the obligation to enter immovable property into the register and, through controls and various measures, ensure its integrity and quality. The Surveying and Mapping Authority of the Republic of Slovenia (SMA), which is responsible for real estate registration, is organized at the national level with three special offices (for geodesy, real estate, and mass appraisal of real estate). They cover the area of the whole country through 12 regional geodetic offices (Republika Slovenija 2025). The SMA (Geodetska uprava Republike Slovenije 2025) reported that, as of year-end 2024, 5,810,112 plots of land, 1,172,070, buildings, and 1,909,815 parts of buildings were registered in the land cadastre.

With its independence, Slovenia adopted all the principles of a democratic free society based on human rights, free economic initiative, free market, and private property. It inherited a land register from the socialist period. Žibrik and Humar (2021a) state that though the land register contained data on property rights and the owners of the property rights for all real estate, parcels, and buildings, the record of ownership of real estate was not maintained or updated systematically, so the quality of data was poor. A large share of real estate was publicly owned (especially building land, industrial properties, etc.), and priority was not placed on registering and updating data; in other cases, registration of ownership was even discouraged due to the philosophy of the socialist system.

After Slovenian independence, private property became more important. As a part of the transition from a socialist to a democratic system, a process of denationalization and privatization was initiated. As a result, the owners of real property were deemed to be those owners or their legal successors who were owners before the nationalization that followed World War II, and at the same time, all building land was redistributed to the holders of land use rights in the previous system.

One of the first laws in this area was the Law of Property Code, which, following the example of the central European legal order, regulated property relations, making it possible to put into practice the newly created property statutes. Generally, the legal order is based on the principle of *superficies solo cedit* with regard to ownership of immovable property, which establishes a connection between the land and the building constructed above or below it. The owner of the land is therefore also the owner of the building that stands on that land. However, the law also allows for a special right to be created—the building right; that is, the possibility of owning a building separately from land ownership. Such a right constitutes an exception to this general principle, since it allows the holder of the right to own an object that is built on someone else's land. According to the law, the building right is time limited and cannot exceed 99 years of duration.

In principle, ownership of immovable property is not limited, but there is a constitutional provision regarding the ownership of real estate for foreigners (Article 68 of the Constitution of the Republic of Slovenia). They can acquire property in Slovenia under the conditions of reciprocity.[5]

Availability of Real Estate Data

Transparent regulation of property ownership enhances activity on the property market. However, the availability of subinformation on the property market is also essential for the normal functioning of the market. The first systematic collection of sales and rent data was initiated with the enactment of the Real Property Mass Valuation Act in 2006. This act established a special database (the Real Estate Market Register) in which all transactions involving real estate have been recorded since 2007 (see figure 19.2). The recorded data include information on the location, price or rent paid, and most important characteristics of the real estate (except personal data of the owner) that is the subject of agreement (Žibrik and Humar 2021a). The register is maintained by the authority for mass valuation of real estate, which is part of the SMA. The data are made public and available on the internet; however, to protect the privacy of the owners, no personal data or unique identification numbers of real property are revealed.

Data on transactions are obtained from different sources. The main source for price data is the assessment of the real estate transfer tax, reported monthly by the tax authority of the Republic of Slovenia, the

Financial Administration of the Republic of Slovenia (FARS). The prices of real estate transactions for which VAT has been paid are reported by the sellers. The data on rents received by natural persons are collected once a year from the assessment of tax on rental income. Information on other rental contracts is reported by lessors. Data on the characteristics of real estate, reported through the price and rent collecting systems, are systematically compared with data on the same property held in the real estate cadastre. If differences are detected, the mass real estate valuation office informs the real estate office, which performs control procedures, including sending a query to the owner.

Before they are included in the register, all collected data are subject to a review that focuses on reliability and credibility, comparing the data with those for other transactions and the actual characteristics of real estate that was the subject of transactions. In the process of mass valuation, nonmarketable transactions are filtered out by means of various statistical tools and genuine marketable transactions are specifically identified in the registry. During periods of high prices, taxpayers tend to be inclined to lower the declared price for transfer tax purposes. However, these deviations are relatively rare for property sales, as the tax authority exercises control when assessing the property tax. According to the financial authority, the detected underestimations of contract prices reach up to 3.5 percent of all contracts, but on average it is around 2 percent.

The data on rents are particularly problematic, and such income is often underestimated, as the tax authorities have limited power to verify the accuracy of this income when it is declared for tax purposes. In principle, when the authorities assess the quality of data, they pay more attention to the data that are used for the valuation of commercial real estate. However, data on residential rents are less reliable and more attention should be paid to their collection in the future.

To allow a transparent overview of the real estate market, the SMA publishes annual reports on the real estate market in Slovenia that contain collected sales and rental data (Ministrstvo za naravne vire in prostor, n.d.-b). Data from the Real Estate Register are another basic source of information for the general public and for professional users such as banks, courts, and valuers. The register's data are also used for economic analyses, research, and statistical analyses. All collected data are in the public domain and freely available. In the Real Estate Register portal, it is possible to sort data according to the type of property and market period (figure 19.1). Transaction data are georeferenced on maps showing the locations of properties. Clicking on a dot will open a window containing information on the transaction (price, characteristics of the real estate, and characteristics of the transaction).

Figure 19.1 Public View into the Real Estate Market Register

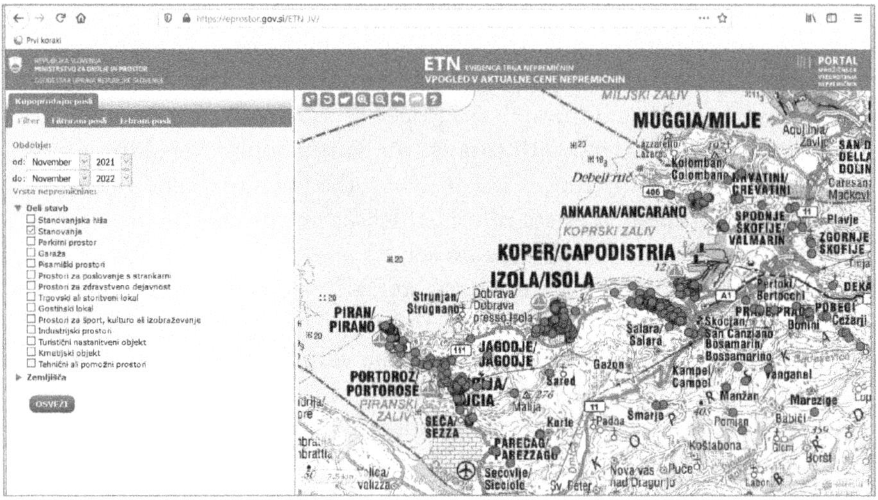

Source: Surveying and Mapping Agency of Republic of Slovenia (Ministrstvo za naravne vire in prostor, n.d.-a.).

Note: Dots represent transactions concerning apartments in the coastal area of Slovenia in the period from November 2021 to November 2022.

Real Estate Market Register data allow for the monitoring of real estate market activity, which has changed dramatically over the years. Having experienced a dynamic market in 2006 and 2007, Slovenia, like many other countries, faced a financial recession with a significant drop in the number of transactions between 2008 and 2013, especially in the housing and commercial real estate sectors (Žibrik and Humar 2021a). The recovery was slow until 2016 (figure 19.2). The real estate market has recovered significantly and in last two years, 2021 and 2022, exceeding pre-crisis levels. However, because of the experience of real estate bubble in 2007, the dynamics in rising prices, especially on the housing market, is a concern (figure 19.3).

An important indicator is the housing index (calculated based on data in the Real Estate Market Register by the Statistical Office of the Republic of Slovenia), which shows that average housing prices in 2020 and especially in 2021 increased above the average for the previous 15 years by more than 50 percent (figure 19.4).

The cost of purchasing an apartment is currently high, although it is lower than it was during the period from 2007 to 2008. Measuring the cost of housing in terms of the number of monthly salaries required to

Figure 19.2 Number of Recorded Sales by Type of Real Property, Slovenia, 2007–2021

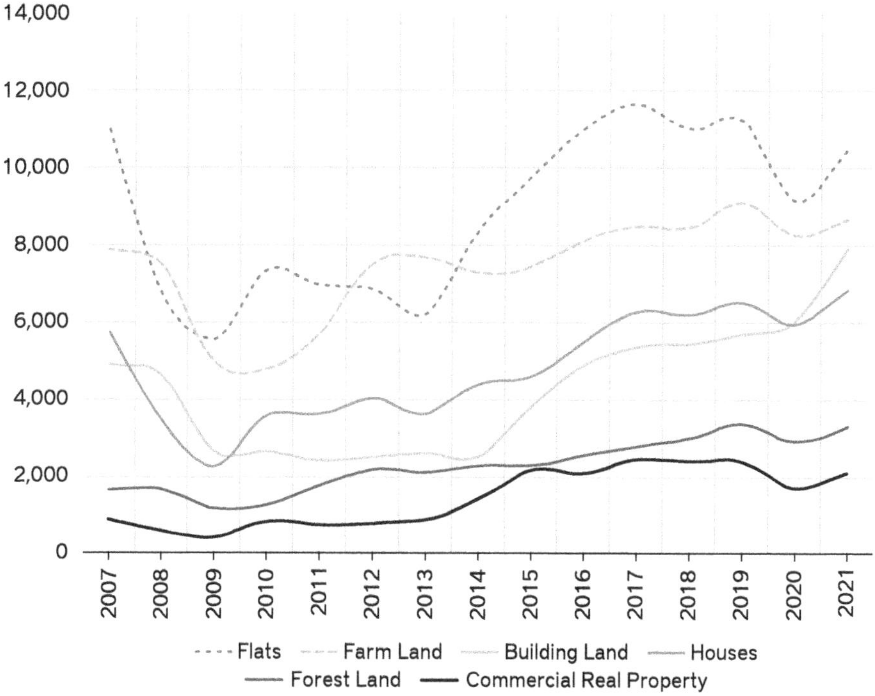

Source: Compiled based on data on prices from annual reports on the real estate market in Slovenia (Ministrstvo za naravne vire in prostor, n.d.-b).

pay for one square meter of a used (not new) apartment shows that, at the beginning of the economic crisis (2007–2008), on average 2 monthly salaries were required per square meter of an apartment. At the lowest point of the crisis curve, between 2014 and 2020, less than 1.5 monthly salaries were needed, and after 2020 the curve began to rise toward 2 monthly salaries (figure 19.5). Rising apartment prices are a consequence of many factors, including limited supply, increases in employment and income, an increase in demand, and relatively favorable credit conditions. These trends are the current reasons for concern and are being closely monitored by responsible authorities.

According to the Statistical Office of the Republic of Slovenia, as of January 1, 2021, Slovenia had around 864,300 residential properties, of which 38 percent were apartments and 62 percent residential houses. Sixty-six percent of all inhabitants lived in family houses. Some 92 percent of residential properties were in private ownership, 5 percent were owned by

Figure 19.3 Average Prices for Used Flats in Select Market Analysis Areas, Slovenia, 2007–2021

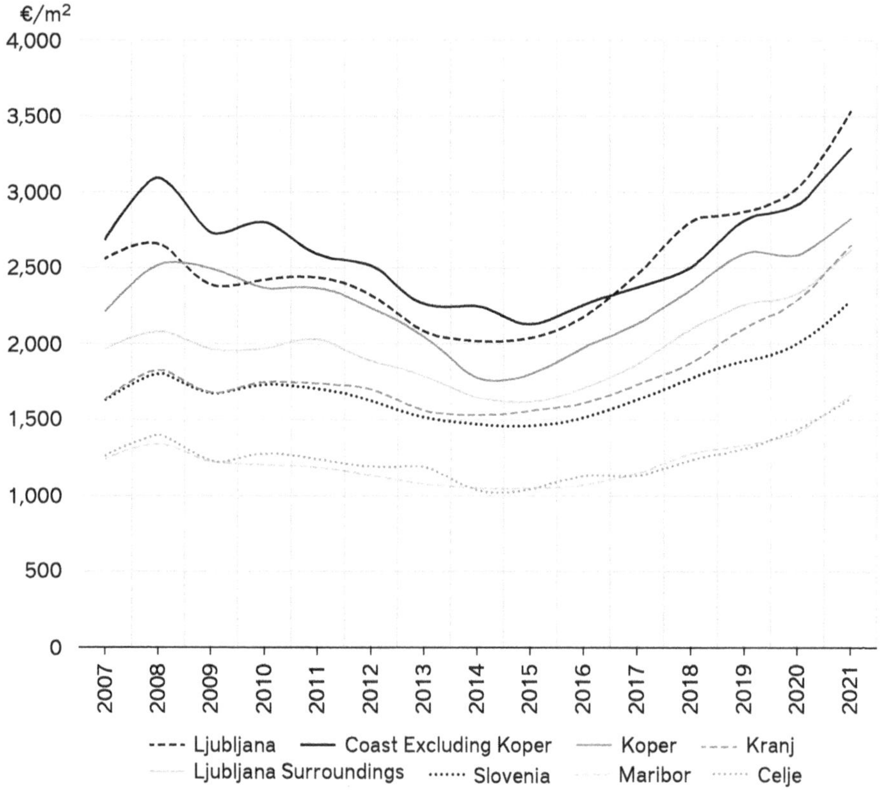

Source: Compiled based on data of the Surveying and Mapping Authority on prices from annual reports on the real estate market (Ministrstvo za naravne vire in prostor, n.d.-b).

public legal persons, and the rest were owned by private business. Eighty percent of populated housing real estate was occupied by the owners and their family members; only about 9 percent was rental apartments. Housing real estate ownership dominates, and rental housing is very limited. The government has undertaken major interventions in the housing market, especially to increase the construction of public rental housing.

The main aim of collecting market data is to build models for the mass valuation of real estate. According to the Real Property Mass Valuation Act, the valuation cycle is carried out at least every two years, resulting in a regular reassessment of real estate market values. Those revised values are used to determine the generalized value for each registered real estate property.

Figure 19.4 House Price Index in Slovenia (2015 = 100)

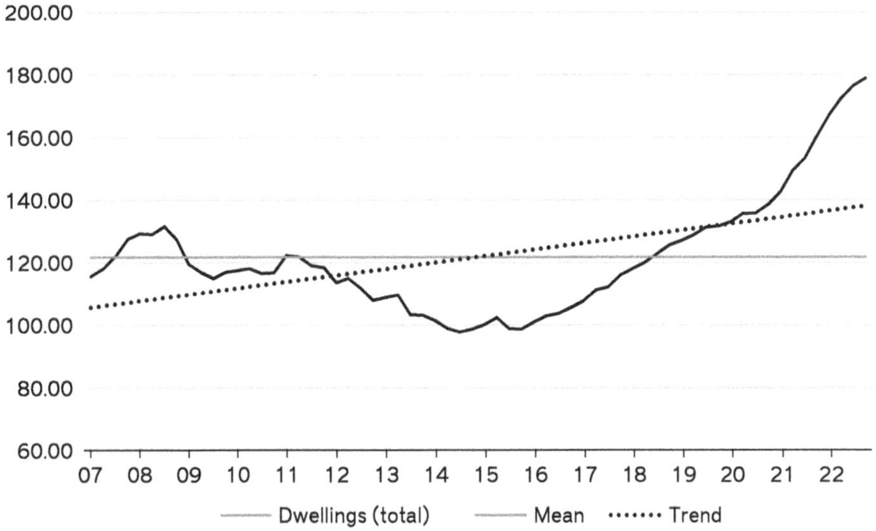

Source: Compiled based on data of the Statistical Office of the Republic of Slovenia (Statistični urad, n.d.-a).

Mass Valuation of Real Estate in Slovenia

Žibrik and Humar (2021b) describe the mass valuation of real estate as a process of estimating the value of a large number of properties on the same valuation date using uniform property data and standardized procedures. As the system requires large databases and relies on computerized procedures, it is often referred to as a computer-assisted mass appraisal system.

Slovenia developed a mass valuation system for real estate with a World Bank project that also supported development of the real estate database and other legal and technical activities. The legal framework for the mass appraisal system was designed to focus on several aspects: international experience, objectivity in value appraisal, the organization responsible for mass appraisal, the cost effectiveness of a system, and supporting legislation.[6]

The first Real Property Mass Valuation Act was adopted in 2006, and the first mass valuation was carried out in 2012, followed by several revaluations. The mass valuation system in Slovenia was intended for multifunctional use (i.e., not only taxation), so the main goal was to follow the market (Mitrović 2010). When the market changes to the extent that the modeled values do not correspond to the quality criterion, a

Figure 19.5 Number of Monthly Salaries Required to Buy a Square Meter of a Used Apartment in Slovenia (average net salary/average price)

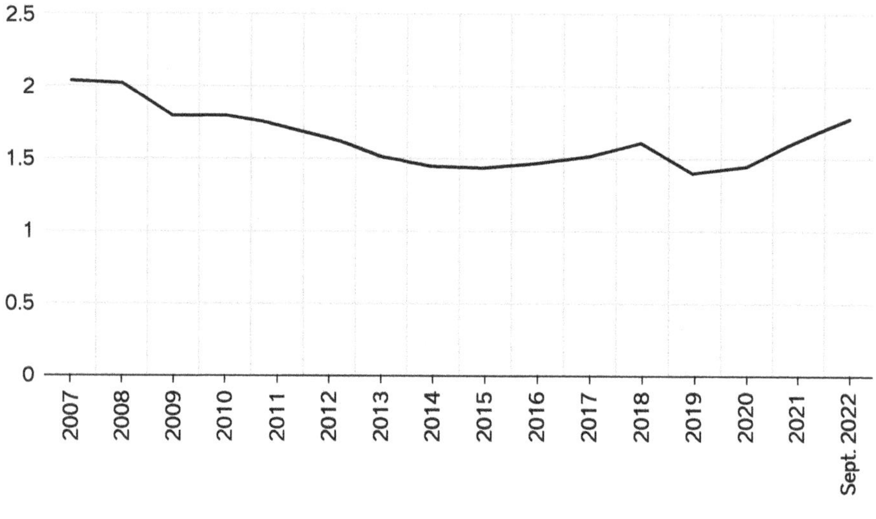

Source: Compiled based on data of the Statistical Office of the Republic of Slovenia on salaries and prices of apartments.

revaluation takes place. The system also relies on up-to-date real estate data records. Whenever there is a change in the real estate data (despite the unchanged valuation models), the system carries out the appropriate recalculation and determines a new value for the real estate.

The law defines the valuation models as mathematical equations using value zones with associated value levels, the characteristics of the property, and the magnitude of their effect on the value of the property. The mass valuation system presents models in formulas, tables, scorecards, factors, and graphs. All model elements are officially published and allow the public to check the accuracy of the valuation of any registered real property.

The legal basis of the mass valuation of real property was subject to a Constitutional Court revision in 2013, together with the Real Property Tax Act. Based on the Constitutional Court's decision, all issues were addressed and a new legal basis was adopted (Real Property Mass Valuation Act). The main issue was upgrading the law to include the procedures on appeal to value.[7] The basic principle for the valuation of real estate is according to the best economic use of the property, with the result of the valuation being a generalized (market) value. The law determines the development of 17 valuation models, which are divided into three groups: models for the valuation of buildings and parts of buildings, models for the valuation of land, and models for the valuation of specific valuation units. Within these three groups, models are defined for specific types of property for which the behavior of buyers and sellers in the market is similar, as they have similar market characteristics.

Because the determined values of real property can also be used for taxation and assessment related to other public obligations and rights of the owners, it is possible to further individualize the value of each property by undertaking a specific revaluation in light of special circumstances (e.g., micro-location, quality, and disrepair or damage to the building that cannot be reflected in the model).

The results of mass appraisal are constantly being compared with current market data. According to the law, the accuracy should be in a range of plus or minus 20 percent, but the actual values are much more accurate, especially those calculated with the use of models based on market prices (specifically apartments, houses, and land). In these cases, based on the statistics for the models from 2020, the average ratio between the generalized values and actual market prices is between 0.9 and 1.10. For houses, this ratio is between 0.84 and 1.14; for offices, between 0.81 and 1.20; for agricultural land, between 0.81 and 1.24; and for building land, between 0.75 and 1.20. These data are part of the public information on every model (Ministrstvo za naravne vire in prostor n.d.-c).

According to the law, if the SMA, on the basis of regular analysis, detects that the quality ratio has moved out of the legally prescribed boundaries of accuracy, a new valuation cycle must be carried out. In any case, the new valuation cycle has to be carried out at least every two years.

The first mass valuation was carried out in Slovenia in 2012, followed by several revaluations (table 19.4). The next valuation cycles took place in 2017 and 2020. The valuations followed developments in the property market. Thus, in 2017, the values reflected the downturn in the real estate market, with the total value of all properties decreasing by almost 15 percent. The 2022 valuation increased the total value of all properties by 30 percent. Due to the COVID-19 pandemic, the then-current government decided not to publish the newly assessed values in 2020. Consequently, while the current data can be consulted as public information, it cannot be used for official or public purposes (e.g., to determine rights or obligations like taxes or social support), and the new values are not considered data from the official register.

Slovenia is in the process of completing the next cycle of mass valuation, which will estimate generalized values for all properties according

Table 19.4 Results of Mass Valuation (€)

Type of Property	Model Name	Value (value date April 25, 2012)	Value (value date January 25, 2017)	Model Name	Value (value date April 1, 2020)
House	HIS	51,808,076,089	44,872,625,879	HIS	52,161,119,375
Apartment	STA	31,510,335,555	26,821,640,518	STA	31,336,496,637
Office	PPP	11,379,874,191	9,474,598,702	PPP	6,997,881,901
Shop	PPL	6,639,848,689	5,395,325,615	PPL	6,696,231,275
Tourism	n.a.	n.a.	n.a.	TUR	1,505,349,612
Industry	IND	4,696,491,601	4,468,553,789	IND	6,571,920,759
Power plant	PNE	3,973,387,938	3,585,339,541	PNE	3,746,473,161
Public building	PNJ	1,960,429,395	1,535,192,594	PNJ	4,027,788,414
Garage	GAR	1,678,025,806	1,826,969,719	GAR	1,910,262,017
Petrol station	PNB	1,090,561,684	550,999,569	PNB	598,968,830
Heavy industry	INP	807,478,644	749,760,590	INP	868,466,891
Port	PNP	516,401,616	682,953,316	PNP	687,349,855
Wine cellar	PKZ	467,428,254	474,296,175	n.a.	n.a.
Other buildings	PND	259,891,690	310,222,075	n.a.	n.a.
Farm building	PKO	234,899,980	279,483,318	KDS	3,126,798,478
Mine	PNM	140,275,241	52,915,428	n.a.	n.a.
Special real estate	PPN	134,521,055	110,229,504	n.a.	n.a.
Farmland	KME	7,098,383,180	7,115,765,879	KME	8,329,673,147
Building land	ZGS	6,121,086,124	1,806,834,934	n.a.	n.a.
Forestland	GOZ	4,580,969,300	4,509,518,383	GOZ	5,250,268,980
Urban land	n.a.	n.a.	n.a.	STZ	20,845,204,618
Other land	ZDR	3,289,219,633	3,395,228,386	DRZ	147,292,285
Built land	PSZ	1,304,328,479	999,930,761	n.a.	n.a.
Total		**139,691,914,144**	**119,018,384,675**		**154,807,546,235**

Source: Data obtained upon request from the SMA.

Note: n.a. = not available.

to the state of the market at the end of 2024. The new values were published and open for public inspection and formal use in May 2025. Preliminary estimates from the mass valuation office predict that the total value of all real estate will increase by more than half compared with 2020. The increase in prices and consequently values is mostly the result of the weak construction cycle (especially for housing) during the economic crisis and COVID-19 pandemic, the postpandemic economic boost, and favorable credit terms, which strongly increased the demand. Part of the increase of total value is attributed to the new approach in the valuation of urban land, as well as land that is already developed, which is going to be valued based on the prices of land intended for construction, whereas in previous valuation cycles all building land was valued according to the average prices of land intended for building.

Mass valuation of real estate in Slovenia is provided as a public service, implemented by a valuation department at the SMA. The department employs between 25 and 30 experts in various disciplines, as well as around five professionals with real estate valuation skills. The central office is in Ljubljana, where the system is supported by performing market analyses and developing models, and there are seven regional units, which are placed in the regional geodetic offices that cover areas important in terms of real estate market activities (i.e., Maribor, Murska Sobota, Celje, Koper, Nova Gorica, Kranj, and Novo Mesto). The main task of the regional units is to analyze the local market characteristics and to check the reliability of collected transaction data.

Generalized (market) values are calculated primarily for different public services, but they can also be used for private purposes, because data on generalized values are considered public information about the property. Data can be seen in the separate register, and they can be acquired for free by any interested party.

Information on generalized values is used for public purposes only in procedures for determining rights and obligations in the context of public entitlements, as a benchmark for the valuation of available immovable property. Data are also used in the process of managing state- and municipality-owned real estate. They provide important information for statistical analyses, such as the calculation of residential price indices. They are used also for tax purposes, but only as information on the real estate market used for checking the accuracy and reliability of reported real estate prices in order to assess the real estate transfer tax, income tax on capital gains, or tax on inheritance and gifts. The data are not yet used to set the tax base for any tax, as the Constitutional Court, when repealing the Real Estate Tax Act, held that the mass valuation system should be upgraded to provide legal certainty for owners, including the possibility to appeal the value. The Law on Mass Valuation of Real Estate has since been revised accordingly (2017), meeting all required constitutional principles as described earlier in this chapter, but the reform of property taxation has not been implemented. Within the private and business spheres, the data can be used in court disputes, in the banking system for mortgage purposes, and in private contracts (e.g., to provide general information on price levels).

Taxes on Real Estate

In the Slovenian tax system, real estate is a taxable object for the purposes of income tax, VAT, and property transfer tax, and it is a subject of taxation as a source of income, as a transfer of property, and under the general local-government property tax (see also the section on recurrent land and property tax).

Real Estate as a Source of Income

As a source of income, real estate can be taxed under the personal income tax (Personal Income Tax Act) or the inheritance and gift tax (Inheritance and Gift Tax Act).

Personal Income Tax

After its accession to the European Union, Slovenia largely reformed its structure of income taxes. The new system was introduced in 2005 with the adoption of the Personal Income Tax Act and was upgraded in 2007, with the main changes including the taxation of worldwide income of residents and the exclusion of so-called passive revenues, which are taxed independently. The law was amended more than 30 times. Personal income tax is fully administered by a central government body, FARS, which is a subdivision of the Ministry of Finance, responsible for implementing tax law provisions.

The Personal Income Tax Act distinguishes between active and passive income The former includes income from employment, business income, income from basic agriculture and forestry, and other income; and passive income, which includes income from rents and royalties, as well as income from capital (interest, dividends, and capital gains). All taxable income from all sources forms the annual tax base, after compulsory social security contributions and certain allowances are deducted. The annual tax base is then taxed according to a progressive tax rate. Passive income is taxed at a flat rate separately for every passive income source. The tax is treated as a final tax for residents and nonresidents alike.

Income from Renting Real Estate

The income earned from short-term rentals used for tourist purposes (such as Airbnb) is treated as ordinary business income. Income from long-term rentals is treated as passive income. Personal income tax on this type of rental income is levied on the amount of actual rent reduced by 10 percent (norm costs) or by actual cost. The tax rate was lowered in 2022 (with a law amendment) from 25 percent to 15 percent, but in 2023 the rate was increased again to 25 percent. Long-term rental income is reported to the central government's income tax authorities once a year, no later than February 28 of the year, for all income from that source in the previous year. The tax is levied by means of a decision, which is normally issued by the tax authority within 30 days of receipt of the return.

The law does not state that the rent must reflect the real market rent, and therefore the tax authority has limited powers to verify the real value of the reported rent. Notwithstanding the regulation, the Tax Procedure Act gives the tax authority the right to issue a decision based on its assessment of the true value of the rent in case of suspicion of a misrepresentation. In carrying out this procedure, the tax authority relies on a variety of information, including advertised rents and data on comparable rents from other reported contracts, but the assessment captures only extremely underdeclared reporting, which is rare. If taxpayers disagree with the tax authority's assessment, they may object by submitting evidence proving the actual amount of rent received. The appeal is to be decided by the second-instance authority, which, if it agrees with the evidence submitted, will either rule in favor of the taxable person or refer the case back to the first-instance authority for reconsideration; or, if it disagrees with the taxable person, will issue a dismissal order. Irrespective of the procedure, the taxable person must pay the tax on the basis of the decision issued. An appeal shall not suspend the obligation to pay the tax. Any reduction of the liability resulting from the appeal shall be credited to the taxable person by way of a refund of the tax overpaid.

It is estimated that a small part of the rental property market in Slovenia is outside the scope of taxation (the estimates vary but extend to more than 15 percent), and a significant proportion of underreported rents is also recognized. The lack of relevant subdata on the rental market (though registration of rental contracts is required) and a failure to monitor the number of "empty" apartments make the collection of these data difficult. FARS conducts independent analyses every few years, but it relies on official data and does not try to resolve the issue through the usual control practices. A more systematic approach will be necessary to address the problem. Nevertheless, the data currently available indicate that revenues from long-term rental income represent around a quarter of total tax revenues from passive income and amounted to around €57 million in 2020.

Income from Capital Gains

Capital gains are taxed based on the difference between the selling price (contract price or estimated market value) and the acquisition price (contract price or estimated market value). The selling price and acquisition price are increased for acknowledged costs. The value at the time of acquisition and disposal is based on the price in the sale and purchase agreement but may also be supported by other evidence. If the tax authority is in doubt as to whether these values correspond to market values during the relevant period, it may correct the values, and the taxable person has the right, as in the case of a tax on rents, to challenge this decision by submitting an appraisal. Determining the selling price in this procedure is not so problematic because the price is already checked during the real estate transfer tax assessment.

FARS corrects between 2 and 3 percent of reported transactions. A dilemma can arise in determining the acquisition price, particularly where the real estate is acquired by inheritance or gift and the tax was not assessed, but a problem may be also be encountered in other cases. Of around 40,000 transactions reported yearly for the capital gains assessment, approximately 1 percent are corrected by FARS.

The tax rate decreases according to the length of ownership: it is 25 percent if the real estate property has been possessed for less than 5 years, 20 percent if it has been possessed for 5 to 10 years, and 15 percent if it has been possessed for more than 10 years. No tax is payable after 15 years of ownership. These provisions were amended in 2022 by abolishing the rate for holding periods of more than 15 years (which was 10 percent) and reducing the period of taxation from 20 to 15 years of holding.

Capital gains tax is levied on the basis of a return of the taxpayer who is the vendor of the property. The taxable person must file the return within 15 days after the conclusion (signing) of the contract of sale of the immovable property.

Capital gains are not assessed in the case of inheritance, disposal of immovable property under a lifetime maintenance contract, disposal under a gift contract in the event of death, or in the case of the transfer of immovable property under expropriation. Homeowners of apartments or houses with no more than two apartments, upon proof that they have lived at the address for at least the last three years, are exempt from income tax on capital gains. In the case of a gift of real estate between spouses or between parents and children, the tax obligation can be postponed until the

Table 19.5 Tax Revenue from the Income of Natural Persons in Connection to Renting or Disposing of Real Estate

	2017	2018	2019	2020
Long-term rental income tax (€) (% of GDP)	50,613,987 (0.118)	53,204,649 (0.116)	58,372,778 (0.121)	57,147,479 (0.121)
Capital gain tax on real property (€) (% of GDP)	7,423,119 (0.017)	9,001,358 (0.020)	11,122,817 (0.022)	12,241,970 (0.026)

Source: Tax assessment data obtained upon request from the Ministry of Finance.

next disposal. In such a case, the acquisition time is considered to be the time when the donor acquired the real estate, and the acquisition value is the value at the time when the donor acquired the real estate.

The assessment of this tax is administratively costly for the tax authority, and the revenue from this source is modest. In 2020, it amounted to around €12 million (table 19.5).

Inheritance and Gift Tax

Tax on inheritance and gifts is administered by the central government (FARS). The assessment of gift tax is conducted on the basis of the taxpayer's declaration, which must be made to the local tax authority within 15 days upon receiving a gift. The assessment of inheritance tax, in contrast, is conducted without the taxpayer's declaration according to the inheritance decision sent by the court to the tax authority. The tax object is property received by a natural or legal person in the form of inheritance or a gift. Taxable persons are legal persons and natural persons. The tax for natural persons is determined based on categories that take into account their relationship to the deceased or donor: Class I is all direct descendants and spouses; Class II is parents, siblings, and their descendants; Class III is grandfathers and grandmothers; and Class IV is all others.

The tax base is the value set in the gift contract or in the inheritance decision for the inherited or donated property, reduced for debts, costs, and other burdens in connection to the property. If the value does not reflect the market value, the tax administration can set the tax base on market value. The taxpayer, if not satisfied with the changed tax base, can justify another value based on a valuation undertaken at the individual's expense.

Tax rates are determined progressively according to the class of taxable person and the value of the tax base: Class II at 5–14 percent, Class III at 8–17 percent, and Class IV at 12–39 percent. Class I is fully exempt from taxation, which means that more than 90 percent of all inheritance and gifts are tax-free.

There are additional exemptions, such as movable property up to a value of €5,000 received from the same person in a year; gifts or inheritance to a legal person of private law if intended for religious, humanitarian, educational, cultural, charitable, and certain other activities; and agricultural land or an entire farm inherited by a farmer. The revenue belongs to the municipalities. Due to comprehensive exemptions, the revenue is low. In 2021, it amounted to only €10.6 million, which was 3.3 percent of the total revenue from property taxes.

Taxes on Real Estate Transactions

Real estate transactions are subject to VAT or real estate transfer tax. VAT is, in general, paid only on transactions involving newly built buildings and building land if the seller is conducting business activity and is a registered VAT vendor. For all other transactions involving real estate, even if performed by a VAT taxpayer, real estate transfer tax is assessed.

VAT

VAT is a general consumption tax on a net basis included in the price consumers pay for goods and services, based on Value Added Tax Act. It is an indirect tax, which means that consumers pay this tax while paying for goods or services, and a taxable company or person engaging in commercial activity must remit the tax to the tax administration office. In principle, all companies pay VAT, but there are some exemptions. These include companies carrying out certain defined activities, small businesses, and farmers with a turnover and income below defined thresholds, as well as in cases concerning products intended for export and international transport.

In general, transactions with real estate are exempt from VAT, except those involving new buildings or building land. But the law allows optional taxation for real estate when the transaction is carried out between two VAT taxpayers who conclude an arrangement and inform the tax authority before the transaction. If the option is chosen, the real estate transaction becomes liable to VAT. There are three VAT rates: a standard rate of 22 percent, a reduced rate of 9.5 percent, and a special, lower rate of 5 percent. The reduced rate of 9.5 percent applies to the provision of newly constructed housing real estate and also to renovation and alteration of housing and the repair of private dwellings, excluding materials that account for a significant part of the value of the service supplied.

VAT is revenue of the central government and represents the most important state budget revenue at around 20 percent of all revenue and 22 percent of all tax revenue. Real estate activities contribute between 2 and 3 percent of total VAT turnover, which was around €4.231 million in 2021.

Tax on the Transfer of Real Estate

All transactions involving real estate that are not subject to VAT are taxed under the Real Property Transfer Tax, which was introduced in Slovenia in 1990. The legal base is the Real Property Transaction Tax Act, which was modernized in 2006. Initially the tax rate was set at 5 percent. The tax originally belonged to the state budget. However, since 1995, the tax has belonged to the municipalities and the tax rate has been reduced. All features of the tax (tax object, taxpayer, tax base, tax rate, exemptions or reliefs) are set in the law and local communities have no power to influence them. Tax is assessed by FARS and allocated to the municipality where the real estate is located. The present tax rate is 2 percent.

The tax object is the payable transfer of the ownership of real estate or building right if not subject to VAT. The taxable persons are legal persons and individuals who are sellers. The taxpayer is the seller, legal person, or individual. The tax base is the selling price[8] set in the contract. If the contract price does not reflect the market value, the tax authority can set the tax base on market value. The taxpayer, if not satisfied with the changed tax base, proves the value with individual valuation at the taxpayer's expense.

In 2022, FARS assessed the real estate transfer tax for 38,052 real estate transfer documents. In some 843 cases (about 2.22 percent), the tax base was the corrected price determined in the assessment procedure. In all the remaining cases, the tax base was set as the contract price. During periods of high prices, the detected underestimations of contract prices can reach up to 3.5 percent of all contracts.

As an aid in determining whether the contract price corresponds to the comparable market value of the real estate, the data on the mass appraised values of the real estate are still used as a guideline, but in the final determination of the tax base, the financial office must not refer to this value and must instead find comparable market values.

There are several exemptions:

- Transfers to diplomatic and consular missions, if reciprocity is valid, and other international organizations according to international contracts and conventions.

- Transfers of agricultural land within the agrarian bond operations.
- Transfers connected with enforcement of tax collection.
- Transfers of real estate that contains a cultural monument.
- Transfers back to the previous owner if the contract is canceled.
- Transfers at division of property between spouses upon divorce and between shareholders in company liquidation proceedings.
- Transfers at division of property upon liquidation of a company.

FARS assesses the tax based on a tax return filed by the taxpayer within 15 days after the conclusion (signing) of the contract. It sends the decision with the date of payment. The tax is due to be paid within 30 days after receipt. If the tax is not paid, the signatures on the contract cannot be authenticated and the ownership in the land book cannot be changed.

The revenue from the real property transfer tax belongs to municipalities. In general, it is the second most important tax revenue of municipalities, but it depends on the market activity; thus, with the real estate market reduction during the recent economic crisis, the revenue diminished significantly. In 2021, the revenue was again at the same level as during 2007–2008 at €53.8 million, which represented 3.2 percent of the total tax revenue of municipalities.

Recurrent Land and Property Tax

Slovenia imposes two taxes on the possession (and use) of real property: the tax on property and a duty called "charge for the use of building land." Both originated in the mid-1980s and are obsolete and problematic in many ways. The base of both taxes is some measure of area (in square meters). The Constitutional Court in the 1990s determined that these taxes were unconstitutional. Consequently, nearly every Slovenian government since has included property tax reform in its program, but rarely has it been a political priority. Only one government actually attempted reform, but it failed at the Constitutional Court level in 2014 when the court annulled the Real Property Tax Law even before the first assessment was made. It mandated returning to the previous system. More detail on the subject is presented later, but it is safe to say that the real estate tax in Slovenia is still based on an outmoded system.

Tax on Property

The smaller of the two property taxes is the tax on property (Civil Tax Act). It is an annual duty levied on premises such as buildings and parts of buildings, including apartments, garages, and second homes. The tax on property is not levied on land. By design, this tax is a kind of luxury tax, since it is levied mostly on real estate that is not primarily used by its owners (for living or carrying out a business). The tax objects are premises registered by FARS. The taxpayer is the individual who is the owner or usufructuary of the premises (legal persons are not taxpayers for this tax) on a certain date.

Tax obligation starts with the conclusion of the purchase contract. New owners must report the acquisition to FARS. When reporting, the taxpayer must provide data about the real estate (e.g., year of construction; area of all parts of the real estate; building quality, including quality of windows, floor, tiles, and other parts; and type of heating). Based on this information, the property is assigned "data points" according to a points system prescribed by law. The data on buildings and their characteristics, together with attributed points, are maintained by FARS. These data points are used to differentiate between newer and older houses, renovated and nonrenovated, and between good and poor construction quality. Higher-quality, larger, and updated real estate is allocated more points. The regulations on the points system, which sets the number of points for each characteristic, have not changed in decades (the system was adopted in 1981 and upgraded in 2004). Points are only a technical aid, derived from the building regulations (connected to building costs), with no connection to market conditions. Location is not considered in the points system.

The taxable base is the value ascertained as a multiplier of points and the value of a point, or the area in square meters and the value of a square meter. The value of the point, or square meter, is set by local communities mainly based on their fiscal needs. In most cases, points are allocated only once (when the property is first reported to FARS). The law binds taxpayers to report all changes in the real estate characteristics affecting the amount of tax liability, but the FARS database cannot be directly connected to the state real estate cadastre, and most real estate characteristics, which are considered for valuing real estate for tax on property, are not systematically collected. Reporting on changes is the owners' responsibility and is not performed systematically. Local communities can also change the value of the area unit or point every year before the tax assessment. The tax base can, in theory, be changed every year.

The tax rates depend on the type of property and are progressively assessed according to the use of the property. The tax rate for dwellings varies from 0.10 percent to 1 percent, the tax rate on premises used for recreation is in the range of 0.20 percent to 1.50 percent, and the tax rate for business premises varies from 0.15 percent to 1.25 percent. For business premises that are not used for attendant business activities and are not rented (unused premises), the tax rate is increased by 50 percent.

The exemptions to the property tax are quite extensive and include incentives and reliefs linked to other policies of the state:

- Residential buildings of less than 160 square meters, if used by the owner or his close family member (spouse or child). If an owner-occupied apartment exceeds the area limit, only the surplus area is taxed. Because of this exemption, this tax is considered a wealth property tax, since only very large or luxury apartments and second homes are taxed.
- Buildings used for agricultural purposes. The exemption is linked to the principle that a real property that is used for making taxable income is not considered wealth since it is taxed through income taxation.
- Business premises used by the owner or user for business activity.
- Cultural or historical monuments. The exemption serves as an indirect aid to the owners of such real property, in light of the public interest in preserving historical monuments and the high costs that are linked to their maintenance.
- A newly constructed building or repaired or renovated building, if the value of the building has increased because of renovation by more than 50 percent. The exemption is temporary (10 years) and serves as an incentive for owners to invest money in renovations or new building, but it also reflects the fact that when a building permit is required, the local community receives additional communal fees, which are much higher than tax on property.
- Taxpayers with more than three family members who live in the owner's premises. The tax decreases by 10 percent for the fourth and every additional family member. This exemption serves as a tool of the social and family policy of the state, which is an encouragement for families with more than two children.

Tax assessment is performed by FARS as a part of the central government's duties. The tax authority assesses tax on the property and sends the written order with the date of payment. The tax is due to be paid in three months or in half-yearly installments (if less than €200). Monthly installments are payable the first day of every month and must be paid within 15 days. Three-month and half-yearly installments must be paid within 45 days. The tax authority first sends the notice of unpaid tax and instructions to pay the tax within eight days from the time of delivery of the notice; in the final stage of collection, the tax authority can enforce the tax obligation by selling the property.

The tax on property is revenue of municipalities. Due to the incompleteness of the registers at the tax authority, which is the result of a lack of controls in the past (data are self-declared by the owners, there are no field inspections, and the only control is comparing the tax authority register with the central real estate cadastre, which is difficult, since real estate properties in the tax authority register are not marked by a unique real estate identifier), and due to broad exemptions, this tax is a less important revenue source with only €8.2 million in 2021, which represents less than 0.5 percent of the total tax revenue of municipalities. But the situation is improving, since new owners are now asked to submit a return in connection to the real estate transfer tax assessment. Also, more regular checks are being performed based on the comparison of data in the tax register with data in the real estate cadastre, and owners who did not submit a return at the time of acquisition are invited by FARS do it subsequently.

Charge for the Use of Building Land

With respect to the charge for the use of building land, every municipality has its own real estate register. There are no common rules on the collection of data, quality control, or comparability with other municipalities. Data are mostly collected from municipal sources (e.g., planning, register of communal infrastructure, administrative sources) and the land book (for ownership). The only obligation is that data on buildings and parts of buildings be collected from the central real estate cadastre. Owners (or users) of real estate are obliged to report any changes in their property or in its ownership to the municipality.

The charge for the use of building ground (Construction Land Act)[9] is levied on undeveloped and constructed building land, registered as such in the registers of municipalities. The law defines undeveloped building land as land where the zoning act provides that the construction of buildings or civil engineering structures not intended for public use is permissible, having access to a public road and connected to water, sewerage, and electricity. Constructed building land is land on which buildings and civil engineering works have been constructed. In principle, the charge should be assessed for every real estate within the municipality that meets the conditions of the law. But in practice, municipalities independently set the locations in which the charge is assessed.

The taxpayer is the individual or legal person who is the immediate user (owner, tenant, or actual user). If not reported differently to the municipality, the charge is assessed on the owner. If the owner wants to transfer the obligation to the tenant, the owner must register the tenant as the actual user in the municipality's register.

The charge is determined for vacant building land based on the area of the land; for planned buildings and for constructed buildings, the charge is based on the land area of residential houses or business premises. The tax base is assessed on the value of the charge (rate), set by municipalities. The amount of the charge (rate) is set by local communities based on different criteria (type of property, location, etc.). For every type of property (according to the location), the municipality sets the number of points in the municipal decree and every year sets the value of a point. The criteria for the points system are not fixed in any regulation but can be set independently by every municipality. The points system and the values of points differ among municipalities. As a rule, the rates significantly differ among municipalities, but generally they are higher for business properties than for residential. The amount (rate) of the charge can be changed every year.

Calculation of the tax burden on a real property is rather complex. It requires the multiplication of the number of months, number of points per square meter (or number of points per property), area (if the charge is set by number of points per square meter), and value of the point (or square meter).

By law, exemptions are set only for building land planned for public structures. Municipalities can also grant a temporary five-year exemption for new residential buildings or apartments and partial or full exemption for taxpayers with low incomes. Municipalities also do not assess the charge for properties owned by them.

The charge is levied by FARS up to March 31 (or when the local community provides data) for the present year. The tax authority sends the written order with the date of payment. The tax is due to be paid in three-month or in half-yearly installments (if less than €200). For legal persons, monthly installments are payable the first day of every month and must be paid within 15 days. Three-month and half-yearly installments must be paid within 45 days.

If the tax is not paid in a timely way, the tax authority first sends the notice of unpaid tax with instructions to pay the tax within eight days from the time of delivery of the notice; in the final stage of collection, the tax authority can enforce the tax obligation by selling the property.

This charge is the most important own tax revenue of municipalities (in 2021, €243 million). It represents around 14–16 percent of all revenues of municipalities. The revenue is intended as a support for municipal development and is mostly used for investment in public infrastructure (communal infrastructure, roads, schools, medical facilities, social apartments, etc.) and development projects.

The charge is also one of the most common grounds for appeal, as almost half of all tax appeals are made on these grounds.

Property Tax in Large Urban Areas

Slovenia has a policy of supporting decentralized development.[10] Out of a total of just over 6,000 settlements, only 2 (Ljubljana and Maribor) have more than 50,000 inhabitants. Around 30 percent of Slovenia's total population lives in urban areas, with the remaining 70 percent living in suburban and rural areas.

In Slovenia, the real estate tax is seen as the charge for the use of building land. And since the tax objects are only building land and buildings, it is primarily an urban tax. The tax revenues are earmarked for the development of public infrastructure, which is particularly demanding and wasteful in urban areas. It is therefore not surprising that the bulk of tax revenues are generated by properties in urban municipalities, and that the amount of tax per property is comparatively high in these environments. Of the total annual revenue of around €250 million, urban municipalities account for roughly 55 percent. The highest share, with more than a quarter of all tax revenue from this source, annually belongs to Ljubljana.

According to mass valuation data, Ljubljana has around 23 percent of the total market value of real estate in the country. However, for the time being, property tax is based not on these data but on data on real estate properties from the municipalities' records, which are valued for taxation purposes through a scoring system and assigned a point value that can be adjusted annually (the method is described in more detail the previous section).

While the law obliges municipalities to account for the data on immovable property from the central real estate cadastre for the purposes of levying the charge for the use of building land, it leaves them free to determine the amount of the tax base.

According to the data from the cadastre of real estate, Ljubljana has more than 164,000 residential properties, around 16,600 business premises, some 4,800 industrial buildings, 3,300 buildings in public use, and 85,000 other types of buildings. It also has approximately 181,000 plots that are considered building land.

Comparing these data with the data on the properties included in the municipal assessment, it is estimated that Ljubljana's assessment covers practically all residential properties in the cadastre, while only around three-quarters of the other types of property are assessed for the purpose of the charge. It excludes from taxation a large part of undeveloped building land and completely excludes from taxation properties owned by the municipality, although the law does not explicitly allow for this. As a result, Ljubljana uses for tax purposes a smaller part of its real estate than it could potentially use.

In assessment of the charge for the use of building land, the tax base is also the amount of the tax liability. As already explained, municipalities are free to determine the tax base independently. For these purposes, the Ljubljana City Municipality, in its ordinance on the charge for the use of building land, divides the city into seven zones: Zone I (building land in the narrow city center), Zone II (building land in the greater city center), Zone III (building land with dense construction at city entry roads and areas of the city that are important for the development of the town), Zone IV (mainly developed building land outside the built-up city area, in city districts important for the economy with highly developed transport and business infrastructure), Zone V (mainly developed building land at the outskirts of the city and important local centers near communication and infrastructure corridors), Zone VI (sparsely developed building land at the outskirts of the city and smaller local centers near communication and infrastructure corridors), and Zone VII (remaining building land on the territory of Ljubljana City Municipality connected to the water distribution system, electricity grid, and road network). Every zone has points assigned for the provision of urban installations and other facilities and devices to the building land, such as roads, parking spaces, green areas and areas for recreation, sewage systems, water distribution systems, pipelines, heating installation systems, electricity, telecommunication infrastructure, and public transportation. Many of the facilities include detailed division. It is possible to deduct points for exposure to noise, odor, dust, shade, or other adverse effects that exceed the usual limits.

The ordinance also determines exemptions from the payment of the charge for a limited period for all exemptions that are determined by the law, for a taxable person who receives a permanent social relief, due to natural and other disasters, and when the payment would jeopardize the subsistence of a taxable person and the person's family members. There are also permanent exemptions (although the law does not allow such exemptions) for Ljubljana City Municipality's public institution dealing with social activities and welfare, for the city fire brigade, for businesses that are situated in the technological park, and for some parcels used for retail shops located at specific addresses in Ljubljana (Žibrik and Humar 2021a).

The ordinance was last changed in 2009, but the municipality ensures adequate revenue by periodically revaluing the value of a point. For 2020 (Decision on Determining the Revalued Value of the Point for Calculating Compensation for the Use of Building Land in the Municipality of Ljubljana for the Year 2020), the value of the point was set at €0.000513 per square meter per month for built building ground and at €0.000768 per square meter per month for unbuilt building ground; for 2021 (Decision on Determining the Revalued Value of the Point for Calculating Compensation for the Use of Building Land in the Municipality of Ljubljana for the Year 2021), the value of the point was set at €0.000507 per square meter per month for built building ground and at €0.000760 per square meter per month for unbuilt building ground; and for 2022 (Decision on Determining the Revalued Value of the Point for Calculating Compensation for the Use of Building Land in the Municipality of Ljubljana for the Year 2022), the value of the point was set at €0.000532 per square meter per month for built building ground and at €0.000797 per square meter per month for unbuilt building ground.

For 2023 (Decision on Determining the Revalued Value of the Point for Calculating Compensation for the Use of Building Land in the Municipality of Ljubljana for the Year 2023), the Ljubljana municipality announced new values: €0.000587 per square meter per month for built building ground and €0.000879 per square meter per month for unbuilt building ground, which is 10.3 percent higher than the previous year.

On the basis of the adjustment of the point value, the revenue of the municipality of Ljubljana from the charge for the use of building land (or from taxes on property) has been increasing from year to year, with the exception of the most crisis-ridden pandemic year of 2020, in which, as a rule, all municipalities had established certain reliefs for the real estate in their territory, bypassing the legal bases.

As already mentioned, the municipality is granted a considerable degree of autonomy in the system of charges for the use of building land. The municipalities have services in place to implement the levy, but they are not involved in valuation and mainly keep property records and plan the levy policy through the adjustment of the point value. As a rule, these decisions are influenced not by property market or inflation trends but rather by the fiscal needs of the municipality. The level of taxation is therefore adapted to the budgetary needs of the municipality in light of planned investments and other optional tasks. The value of a point may vary annually.

Table 19.6 shows that property taxation in the municipality of Ljubljana represents an above-average tax source, as its share in total tax revenue in Ljubljana (20.6 percent in 2021) is much higher than the national

Table 19.6 Total Revenue of Ljubljana City Municipality (€)

	2019	2020	2021
Tax Revenue			
Personal income tax	155,926,711	168,890,165	170,449,004
Taxes on property	76,618,272	70,891,801	79,387,175
Property tax	1,820,519	1,116,995	1,321,617
Charge for the use of building land	58,843,684	55,966,461	62,032,951
Tax on water vessels	90,018	99,273	98,225
Inheritance and gift tax	3,275,368	2,848,633	2,229,247
Tax on transfer of real property	12,588,683	10,860,439	13,705,135
Taxes on goods and services	10,628,635	6,460,127	6,207,139
Other taxes	0	0	0
Total tax revenue	**243,173,618**	**246,242,093**	**256,043,318**
Nontax Revenue			
Entrepreneurial and property income	26,477,925	22,859,677	23,696,275
Fees, sales, fines	5,276,822	4,849,705	4,891,185
Other nontax revenue	28,815,342	20,217,007	21,228,993
Total nontax revenue	**60,570,089**	**47,926,389**	**49,816,453**
Capital revenue	**10,143,195**	**16,699,903**	**14,495,547**
Grants	**7,255**	**2,450**	**6,840**
Transfers	**25,315,140**	**23,822,570**	**27,855,649**
European Union funds	**184,471**	**280,874**	**243,444**
Total revenue	**339,393,768**	**334,974,279**	**384,461,251**
Tax revenue as % of total revenue	71.6	73.5	66.6
Property taxes as % of total tax revenue	22.6	21.2	20.6

Source: Ministrstvo za finance, n.d.-b

average (18.6 percent in 2021). The largest share of this revenue, almost 80 percent, is from the charge for the use of building land, which accounts for more than a quarter of all municipal revenue in Slovenia from this source. This revenue is also the second most important single budgetary resource of the municipality of Ljubljana, after the personal income tax, which is the most important resource for all municipalities in Slovenia for the implementation of their statutory tasks.

The largest share of the municipality's expenditure, almost 55 percent, is accounted for by various transfers, including the subsidization of kindergarten prices (around 30 percent of this amount), the financing of public institutions (primary schools, health centers, libraries, etc.), and various public services. These are generally tasks that are conferred on municipalities by various laws and which they are therefore obliged to carry out. Around 30 percent of the municipality's revenue is allocated to various investments (building schools, kindergartens, public housing, roads, etc.), the costs of which it covers from its own tax resources (property taxes) and from the revenues from the management of its assets. To provide for investments, municipalities also may request an investment transfer from the state. In 2021, the municipality of Ljubljana obtained around €11 million from this source. Around 15 percent of its revenues are earmarked for the operation of the municipal administration.

Reform Initiatives and Country-Specific Issues

Žibrik and Humar (2021a) state that the need to change the system of property taxation was first discussed over 20 years ago; however, a reformed system still has not been put in place. The current system of property taxation remains as it was established in times of socialism and limited private property ownership. Both taxes related to real property (the tax on property and the charge for the use of building land) have many legal, operational, and constitutional issues and are kept in use only to ensure the source of local finance until a reformed property tax system is put in place.

In 2002, Slovenia reformed its legal basis regarding property rights, and in 2006 it introduced rules for registration of property and rules for a mass valuation system. Based on this, it established a complete real estate register (cadastre) and implemented a mass valuation system, which has provided the generalized value for every real property in Slovenia since 2012. Since then, properties are revalued every two to three years.

Since the introduction of mass valuation, different Slovenian governments have been planning to replace the old system by introducing a modern real estate tax based on market value. The new Real Property Tax Act, which established generalized market value as the tax base, was adopted in December 2013 and enforced as of January 1, 2014. The law stipulated that the new property tax should replace all existing forms of taxation of real property (i.e., the tax on property and the charge for the use of building land), so the law abolished all previous legislation. The goal of the new Real Property Tax Act was to raise the revenue from property taxation from 0.6 percent to 1.2 percent of GDP and divide the revenue evenly among the state and the local communities.

The new property taxation system was designed to replace the existing property tax system with a unified, transparent, fair, and effective real estate tax with a broad definition of tax objects. The goal was to include all types of real estate and to determine a market value for each property.

However, the Real Property Tax Act was subject to constitutional review, which was initiated by opposition members of Parliament, the National Council, the City Municipality of Koper, two associations of municipalities, and the small municipality of Rogašovci (the only municipality that did not levy property tax at that time). The Constitutional Court, with Rule No. U-I-313/13 (dated March 20, 2014), decided that the Real Property Tax Act was to be repealed, the Real Property Mass Valuation Act was not in accordance with the Constitution when used for taxation purposes, and until the proper legislative arrangement of the taxation of real estate could be introduced, previous legislation should remain in use.

The Real Property Tax Act was found to be unconstitutional in several respects, but mainly because the different tax rates did not correspond to the actual situations of taxpayers (unconstitutional lower rates for so-called "residential" apartments in comparison to normal rates for empty apartments; higher rates for buildings without building permissions); there was an inappropriate division of revenue between state and municipality, since, in the opinion of the court, more than half of revenue should belong to municipalities; and there was an unconstitutional limitation of appeal, which was only allowed concerning data of the real property and not concerning estimation of market value by the mass valuation system. The Constitutional Court repealed the Real Property Tax Act as a whole, and because the tax base was set on generalized market value, the provisions of the Real Property Mass Valuation Act were deemed to be unconstitutional if used for tax purposes.

The Constitutional Court decided that the generalized market value used as a tax base did not meet the principle of determination in the law, which is a constitutional requirement for taxation. According to the Constitutional Court, the Real Property Mass Valuation Act did not provide enough legal certainty and safety for the taxpayer because it allowed essential elements of the mass valuation system to be determined by executive regulation instead of the law and explicitly did not allow the generalized market value to be argued against. The court also ruled that the provisions that defined the valuation models were not clear to the extent that taxpayers could already, within the law, check whether their tax bases were set properly. The court said that it was not in accordance with the principle of legal certainty if some definitions and criteria of mass valuation and detailed definitions of the data were determined in the sublaw (Žibrik and Humar 2021a).

In the decision that repealed the Real Property Tax Act, the Constitutional Court also reinstated the previous system and banned the mass valuation system for tax purposes. Since 2014, the "old" system of tax on property and charge for the use of building land has been used again.

After the annulment of the Real Property Tax Act, the Constitutional Court also, based on the initiative of the Administrative Court, banned the use of the mass valuation system for the purpose of the tax on capital gains from the selling of building land (Rule No. U-I-139/14, dated March 26, 2015), for the purpose of the real estate transfer tax (Rule No. U-I-168/15, dated March 23, 2016), and for the purpose of the tax on inheritance and gifts (Rule No. U-I-190/15, dated May 5, 2016).

As Žibrik and Humar (2021a) indicate, the decision of the Constitutional Court had a huge impact on ongoing reform of property taxation, but the court did not identify the possible constitutional issues with using the system of mass valuation as a tool for setting the tax base.[11]

Based on the decision of the Constitutional Court, the new Real Property Mass Valuation Act was adopted at the end of 2017 and implemented on January 10, 2018. The new law upgrades the mass valuation system with more detailed regulations and criteria for model building (previously set in executive acts), regulates the procedures for ensuring the quality and correctness of real estate data in registers, enables wider cooperation with independent professions, and increases the ability of owners to argue the value (proving special circumstances).

Since the adoption of the new Real Property Mass Valuation Act, almost every government in power has announced a reform of real estate taxes, but none have been implemented.

New valuation models with a valuation date of January 1, 2020, were prepared and adopted by the government at the beginning of March 2020. By the end of that month, Slovenia had a new government and had faced an pandemic of COVID-19. As previously mentioned, the government decided that the public announcement of the new general values should be postponed until after the pandemic, or at least the next valuation cycle.[12] Official data with generalized values still are not shown in the real estate registers, so they cannot be used for any official purpose.[13]

Slovenia currently has a fully operational, high-quality, and comprehensive mass valuation system that is consistent with constitutional principles but is not officially available to users and is not yet built into the Slovenian tax system. Many real estate experts highlight that the reform must be resumed in real time since the current situation from both a formal and a material point of view presents huge risks for the financing of local government. Experts also advocate a change in the system of real property taxation because of other positive side effects of a modern taxation system: support for housing policy, improvement of spatial planning policy, and transparency in maintaining public real property.

In June 2022, a new government took office in Slovenia and started its mandate in a challenging context, having to deal first with the fiscal consequences of the COVID-19 crisis and, almost simultaneously, with the energy shock (electricity, gas, fuels), inflation, and rapidly rising interest rates. In its coalition agreement, the government encouraged an analysis of the state of the existing tax system and expressed support for the real estate tax reform, with a view to ensuring new revenue resources for addressing structural reform challenges that Slovenia is facing (long-term care, pension system reform, and health system reform). Immediately after the first public announcement of real estate tax reform activities was made, with the intent to start broad public debate, opposition was announced, especially by minority groups (such as churches and farmers). In order to lessen the public opposition, the prime minister declared that the current system of the charge for the use of building land was fully functional and that the new system of real estate tax would not be implemented before 2025 at the earliest.

Since real property tax reform is not imminent, Slovenia faces yet another dilemma linked directly to the mass valuation system. Because it is hoped that the system will be used as the tax base for a new real estate tax, the law requires that an extensive expert and public debate be conducted about the mass valuation models before they are declared, in order for the system to gain transparency and support. Also, a special appeal process was put in place so that owners would have an opportunity to appeal the values of their properties. This process is time and resource consuming, and it hinders regular updating of the values.

One wonders whether this process is necessary if the values are not used for the purpose that prompted the establishment of these requirements in the first place.

However, considerable political support has been declared for the introduction of net property taxation in Slovenia. Because of inflation and the deteriorating economic position of its citizens, it is widely argued that people with more assets should contribute more to the state budget. Many issues remain unsolved at the moment regarding the taxation of property, however, and a final political decision has not been made yet.

Impact

The existing system of property taxation in Slovenia, which essentially consists of two levies (property tax and charge for the use of building land), has not only legal and organizational problems but also negative economic, fiscal, housing, spatial planning, agricultural, and social effects.

For the past 10 years, the legal bases for property taxation have been invalid, and, in line with the Constitutional Court's decision, they will only remain applicable until the new system of property taxation is introduced. This raises significant legal complications. The existing legal bases are also believed to be subnormative and to encourage municipalities to act arbitrarily. Many municipal ordinances are contrary to the law or even contrary to the Constitution. Due to the separation of powers between the state and the municipalities, the state has no effective instrument to enforce legality except constitutional litigation. Since existing regulations are no longer in force, they do not have the full function of law, as they cannot be interfered with, amended, corrected, or supplemented. This problem can be resolved only by adopting new legislation, which requires political determination and a sufficient parliamentary majority, as described earlier.

As regards organizational constraints, it should be highlighted that the two current levies are completely independent and unrelated to each other. Each has a different tax base, taxable person, and subject matter. Each has different deadlines and procedures, and each uses a different real estate database.

The administration and assessment of both levies is complex and irrational from a database maintenance point of view. The property tax uses a database created for this purpose at the tax authority and is not linked in content to the already established official state records of property data at the SMA. It is therefore very deficient. For assessment of the charge for the use of building land, because municipalities use different criteria for this purpose, each municipality creates its own independent database. As a result, there are 212 real estate databases in Slovenia, which are also not directly linked to the records of the state in terms of content and type of data. Each municipality has its own rules and valuation methods for the assessment of the charge of the use of building land. This arrangement requires that each municipality (even the smallest, with a population of just over 350 inhabitants) have its own department for keeping records, calculating the value of points or units of area, conducting procedures with taxpayers, and preparing the data for assessment. It has been estimated that the establishment of a single property tax system and the transition to the use of a single central state register of real estate and its values would reduce administrative costs to 1/10 of the present level.

Regarding the charge for the use of building land, the practice of keeping the records on the municipal level and the resultant lack of supervision over the quality and the completeness of the data used for tax assessment create possibilities for corruption. If the data for an individual real property are not sent from the municipality to FARS, the charge for the use of building land is not levied. As mentioned earlier, Slovenia is locally very fragmented, so there is a lot of opportunity for special arrangements to be made.

Some inefficiencies are due to the lack of databases at the tax authority and municipal levels; additionally, the loose legal rules and extensive exemptions cause the assessment of the charge for the use of building land and property tax to be flawed. It is estimated that there is a shortfall of up to 30 percent of the revenue from the charge for the use of building land at the national level, and that the charge for the use of building land and especially the property tax are negligible and completely ineffective tax measures in some municipalities.

In terms of fiscal efficiency, revenues from both levies have been steadily increasing (see table 19.3), due to the increase in the charge for the use of building land, but also in recent years due to the increased attempts of the tax authority to improve the database for the assessment of the property tax. The upward trend in the revenue from the charge for the use of building land is visible in all municipalities, partly because of the improved coverage of the subjects of taxation and the inclusion of undeveloped building land in taxation, and partly because of the steady increase in the value of points. However, the share of revenue from this source remains modest and is even slightly decreasing in relative terms.

There are significant differences among municipalities. The most recent detailed analysis was carried out for 2019 and showed that in 51 municipalities, the share of real estate taxes in tax revenue is less than 5 percent (these are municipalities that together realize only around 3 percent of total property tax revenue); in 183 municipalities, it is below 15 percent of tax revenue. In 13 municipalities, the share of the charge for the use of building land is between 20 and 30 percent (over 50 percent of total property tax), while in the 2 municipalities with the highest shares (i.e., municipalities with large industrial complexes or with a port), it can reach 40 percent or more. From property taxation, the City Municipality of Ljubljana realizes around 25 percent of total tax revenue and 18 percent of total revenue.

Property taxation is therefore of varying importance for different municipalities. Each of them regulates it by setting the level of the tax liability independently and often quite arbitrarily. Consequently, there is also wide variation in the level of taxation between municipalities, between different types of property, and between types of taxable persons.

Legal persons (i.e., commercial and industrial real estate) have, on average, for many years contributed the bulk of the taxation, around 70 percent. In particular, the burden on commercial and industrial real estate is found to be disproportionately higher than that on private real estate. This is evidenced by the data from 2017 on the average charge for the use of building land levied per surface area of each type of property by municipality

Table 19.7 Spreads in Average Burden per Surface Area by Property Type Between Municipalities (€/m²)

	Property Type					
	Residential	Industry and Business	Other Buildings	Public Buildings	Farm Buildings	Building Land
Min. average value	0.02	0.08	0.07	0.14	0.003	0.01
Max. average value	1.85	40.19	5.51	7.02	2.490	6.21
Average value	0.51	4.03	1.07	0.89	0.500	0.46

Source: Tax assessment data for 2017 obtained upon request from the Ministry of Finance.

(table 19.7). Commercial and industrial buildings are the most heavily burdened, on average eight times more than residential properties.

But the data also show large differences between municipalities. For example, for industrial and commercial real estate, the average charge for the use of building land per surface area is just over €4 per square meter, but the differences between municipalities are extremely large, with the highest average value per municipality for this type of real estate exceeding €40 per square meter. There are also large differences in the level of the charge on residential property, ranging from as little as €0.02 to €1.85 per square meter, a difference of almost 10 times.

However, a more detailed analysis shows that even properties of the same type are burdened very differently within each municipality. As an example, in one municipality, for commercial and industrial properties, the charge for the use of building land can be assessed at €18 per square meter up to €106 per square meter.

When comparing the current system of taxation (charge for the use of building land) with the mass valuation system, it can be concluded that the current taxation of real estate places a proportionately higher burden on less valuable properties, which is contrary to the principles of the welfare state. However, since the registers in the current system are not public, socially uneven distribution of the burden is not detected and perceived as a problem that needs to be fixed.

By shifting the taxation toward market value, one could expect to lower the tax burden for less valuable properties and to raise it for more valuable ones. Another impact of such a reform would be to connect the tax burden more directly to the costs of local communities and to the values of local spaces. Properties in more developed areas would more transparently pay more. Analyses of the first attempt to introduce a real estate tax based on market value in 2014 also showed that business properties would be taxed less arbitrarily and in most cases would pay lower real estate taxes than in the present system. The tax revenue would rise in general, but this shift would likely differ between municipalities. A group of municipalities, mainly those with important business and industry objects taxation, would lose revenue. When the new tax was introduced in 2014, it did not affect the system of financing municipalities through the income tax.

International comparisons show that the current level of property (real estate) taxation is relatively low (OECD, n.d.). In Slovenia, property taxation contributes only around 0.6 percent of GDP, compared with an OECD average of around 1.9 percent. Available data show wide variation between countries (OECD, n.d.). This is partly due to the extent of fiscal decentralization, but it is also due to preferences regarding the financing of services. Property taxes play a more important role in the Anglo-Saxon countries (Australia, New Zealand, Canada, the United States, England), where they are generally the most important, if not the only, source of local tax revenue. This is not the case in most European countries, where local authorities are generally financed from a variety of sources, of which property taxes are a minor part. This is the situation in Slovenia, and Austria, the Czech Republic, Slovakia, and the Baltic states have similar local-government financing structures. It can be said that the share of property taxes in Slovenia is internationally comparable.

However, it is estimated that this tax could represent an additional source of tax revenue. The OECD has already recommended that Slovenia improve the structure of its tax sources, precisely by introducing a property tax, which would ensure higher tax revenues for municipalities and create the possibility of a different financing regime for municipalities. The OECD has also reminded Slovenia that reforming the burden on immovable property is an essential condition for balancing the tax burden in general. The current level of taxation is quite low and does not fully support even the main purpose of taxation: to provide part of the revenue for municipalities' development projects. For more ambitious objectives, an appropriate increase in taxation should be considered in the future.

Taxes on real property are, in principle, a fiscal instrument to raise revenue for the state and municipalities to provide public goods. They are also expected to play a role in supporting the implementation of other policies such as property management, spatial and environmental policy, housing, and social policy (Režek 2004). However, the current system, with its many disadvantages, cannot be used effectively as an incentive measure.

In Slovenia, because of its history, property ownership is considered one of the most important values. Thus, around 42 percent of Slovenian citizens own at least a part of one residential real property. They strive to buy residential property because of high rental prices, which can be compared to the average repayment costs for a housing loan. A properly designed tax policy could be an effective supportive measure for this segment, but the current system of property taxation does not play this role at all. It does not encourage the owners of vacant dwellings to rent them out, which could reduce rents in the rental market. Lower rental prices would act as an attraction for younger people and change the mentality about the necessity of home ownership. Another problem is that, due to the low levels of property tax and charge for the use of building land, the wealthy are putting resources into real property rather than other investments, which is pushing up property prices and, due to the lower supply, making it unaffordable for young people to address their basic housing needs. Although an additional tax is levied on real property in the present system, this has had no significant impact on the housing market because of the low tax burden. That is why Slovenia should consider introducing a more efficient real estate tax based on market values and also introduce a kind of wealth tax, which would, besides taxing Slovenian citizens with higher wealth, also address the housing problems. However, based on the ruling of the Constitutional Court, measures in support of a housing policy that would treat investment or empty apartments differently from residential properties within the property tax are not in accordance with the Constitution and the principle of equal treatment.

The existing system also does not efficiently fulfill its role of contributing to agricultural policy and spatial planning (Rakar, Černe, and Šubic Kovač 2008). In Slovenia, municipalities are in charge of land use and spatial development planning, but their plans are subject to the approval of the state authorities. Settlement planning thus necessarily clashes with the state's interest in maintaining, among other things, a sufficient amount of good-quality and suitable land for agriculture. A municipality will not obtain permission to convert agricultural land into developable land if the municipality has sufficient developable land that has not yet been developed. In many cases, individuals who want to solve their housing problem by building are denied a chance to get suitable land. In the past, at the municipal level, significant areas of land have been converted into developable land on the basis of the owners' wishes, even though the owners had no intention of building on the land and only requested the conversion because of its potential for future generations or to increase the value of the land. In some cases, developable land is not equipped with public utilities (i.e., roads, electricity, water) and is therefore not subject to taxation, either through the charge for the use of building land or through the property tax.

In essence, tax policy does not play its role in preventing undesirable actions by individuals and municipalities. All of the aforementioned issues will be essential considerations in the preparation of any new property tax regime. Without reform of this part of the tax system, it will be difficult to increase the effective role of local authorities in providing public goods, developing the property market, and, finally, balancing the system of financing public goods.

Conclusion

Real property taxation is a highly political topic in Slovenia. The taxation of residential property is a particularly sensitive issue, particularly because these levies are the responsibility of local authorities. Local governments are more susceptible to pressures from their environment and are therefore very conservative when it comes to reforms. They often defend their autonomy, even though, as in the case of Slovenia, this can be linked to highly arbitrary and nontransparent tax practices.

It is therefore not surprising that, in Europe, mass valuation is mostly not accepted and real estate taxes in most countries, including Slovenia, are still based on area. Only a few countries in Europe have managed to modernize property taxation based on the market value of real estate. These systems can sometimes be exposed to extreme political pragmatism, and most of the countries employing them face obstacles to the regular implementation of valuation, pressures for extensive tax exemptions, and requirements to limit the influence of market elements.

Area-based approach is in contrast to the constant proclamation of the need to relieve labor income, which is relatively highly taxed in Europe, and to increase the taxation of wealth. Of course, taxation of property alone cannot resolve this disparity. Some analyses show that there is indeed a disproportionate increase in the volume of wealth in the higher income brackets, but this is not only in the form of real property and instead mainly in other forms of financial assets. A real estate tax cannot, therefore, resolve all wealth disparities. Moreover, as a rule, this tax has a clear objective of financing the activities of local authorities. It is thus necessary to increase the fairness and efficiency of real property taxation but to relieve it of ambitions to progressively tax wealthier taxpayers.

The current system of real estate tax, apart from not being linked to the market value of real property, provides some incentives that run counter to the general principle of taxing according to ability to pay. This chapter argues that the right way forward is to modernize Slovenia's property tax system, but in a way that strives for fairness in the distribution of tax burdens. This might be best accomplished by linking the tax base of real estate tax more directly to the (market) value of the property. This solution could move the property tax in the direction of wealth taxation. Properties that are worth more would be more heavily taxed. The first steps toward such a market-based solution are the establishment of appropriate property and real estate market records and the development of methods and models for the mass valuation of real estate. Slovenia managed to fulfill these preconditions back in 2012. But since then, there has been no political will to reform real estate tax.

The professional community in Slovenia has been supporting the implementation of mass valuation of real estate for many years and has also been promoting the diversified use of its results. It is increasingly being used by various public administrative bodies.[14] Unfortunately, in the public eye, this system is directly linked to real property taxation reform and therefore does not enjoy political support. Its use for tax purposes is continuously hindered by various arguments against it, including questioning the quality of the property data used for this purpose, questioning the methods of mass valuation by raising suspicions about the constitutionality of the system, and questioning the assessment outcomes.

While there is a broad awareness in Slovenia of the inadequacy of the current real estate tax system, it is proving very difficult to reach a consensus on the most appropriate direction for its modernization. The timing of the next reform is therefore hard to predict. Today, the most vocal advocates are those for retaining the area-based approach, with only a modernization of scoring. This approach is supported by municipalities that want to maintain decision-making autonomy, but also by those in the legal profession who see legal shortcomings in the mass valuation of real estate due to the use of models and automated calculations and express concerns about ensuring the possibility of objections at all stages of the process. The mass valuation system also faces objections that it would be wasteful in terms of staff and finances. Its effective implementation at the level of all the real estate in the country would require around €2.5 to €3 million per year, which is equivalent to about 1 percent of the revenue generated by the current property taxation.

Notes

1. In June 2022, the 15th Government of the Republic of Slovenia took office with Robert Golob as the prime minister. For more information, see Wikipedia (2024, 2025b).

2. Since Slovenia is a small country, one in three municipalities shares a national border with one of the four neighboring countries (Republika Slovenija 2024).

3. The calculation of costs for state-delegated expenditures and the data about eligible expenditure amounts, the amount of personal income tax to be shared, and other items are made publicly available on the government website (Republika Slovenija 2023).

4. From 2000 to 2006, the Law on the Registration of Immovable Property and State Boundaries and Spatial Units was the legal basis that determined rules for the land cadastre and register of buildings; from 2006 to 2021, it was the Law on the Registration of Immovable Property; and since 2021, it has been the Law on the Cadastre of Immovable Property.

5. The rules for establishing reciprocity as a condition for the acquisition of ownership rights of foreigners and foreign states to immovable property in the Republic of Slovenia are prescribed in the Reciprocity Act (*Official Gazette of the Republic of Slovenia*, No. 27/17).

6. In October 2015, the International Monetary Fund carried out an international audit of the mass valuation system and the property taxation system as part of its technical assistance. Its report states that the mass valuation system in Slovenia—which had been found unconstitutional by the Constitutional Court when used for property taxation—is modern, of high quality, and in most respects internationally comparable, offering highly innovative and sophisticated quality assurance solutions despite the relatively low activity of the heterogeneous real estate market (see International Monetary Fund 2015).

7. Due to the system's multifunctional use, there was significant debate on how to ensure a constitutional right to an appeal in the process of mass valuation of real property, taking into consideration when a real estate owner obtains the legal interest to challenge the value of the property (Krševan 2014).

8. Since the mass valuation system was introduced in 2011, the selling price could be corrected if it was lower than 80 percent of generalized market value, but the taxpayer could prove the tax base with individual valuation. However, due to the decision of the Constitutional Court No. U-I-313/13-86, dated March 21, 2014, according to which the generalized market value is not in accordance with the Constitution if it is used for taxation of real estate, this provision was annulled with the decision of the Constitutional Court No. U-I-168/15, dated March 23, 2016.

9. With the introduction of the Real Property Tax Act in 2013, all previous legislation and municipal ordinances regarding the charge for the use of building land and the property tax were annulled. After the Constitutional Court decided to repeal the Real Property Tax Act, the old legislation on the charge for the use of building land and the property tax was reinstated. For the past decade, both the charge for the use of building land and the property tax have been assessed based on legislation that is no longer valid but is still in use. Such a situation raises many legal issues (Gerbec 2014).

10. In 2021, Ljubljana was the most densely populated municipality, with an average of 1,068 inhabitants per square kilometer. The municipality of Ljubljana belongs to the Central Slovenia Statistical Region, which is also the most densely populated—at the regional level—with an average of 238 inhabitants per square kilometer. The second most densely populated municipality was Maribor, with an average of 765 inhabitants, and the third most densely populated municipality was Izola, with an average of 587 inhabitants. The most sparsely populated municipality was Solčava, with five

inhabitants per square kilometer, followed by Bovec and Osilnica (both with nine inhabitants per square kilometer) (Statistični urad, n.d.-b).

11. Just recently, the Constitutional Court issued another decision regarding the Mass Valuation of Real Property Act, based on the proposal of an opposition party. In this decision, the court had to analyze quite a few articles of the law to assess whether they are in line with the Constitution. It was decided that the provisions are indeed in accordance with the Constitution, but one provision, related to criteria the valuation office must follow when establishing the database for the building of valuation models, was found not to be clear enough (Ustavno sodišče 2023).

12. The 14th Government of the Republic of Slovenia started its mandate on March 13, 2020, just a day after the pandemic of COVID-19 was declared in Slovenia. The coalition parties of the new government, when in opposition in previous mandates, publicly expressed a lack of support for real estate tax reform. Furthermore, the government, using the excuse that it did not wish to burden property owners with new values during the pandemic, hid them from the public records.

13. After public access to the new generalized values was denied, there were many requests for the new data from the general public and also from large system users (real estate value assessors, banks, public entities, etc.). Their application to get the data as information of a public nature was denied at first, but the appeal to the Data Protection Board of Slovenia was successful. The access to the data was at first granted only to the applicants, but after three successful appeals, the Data Protection Board ordered that the database be made public. The new values can be accessed as public information.

14. The results from the mass valuation are widely used by other government authorities as a financial measure—for example, to determine the validity of declared transaction prices for transfer tax purposes, to assist in determining social security payments, and to provide evidence for the banking industry in supporting loan requests.

References

Brezovnik, B. 2022. "Pristojnosti in naloge slovenskih občin (s pregledom splošnih in posamičnih aktov ter aktov poslovanja občine): šestnajsta spremenjena in dopolnjena izdaja." Maribor: Inštitut za lokalno samoupravo Maribor.

Geodetska uprava Republike Slovenije. 2025. "Slovenija v številkah." https://www facebook.com/GeodetskaupravaRS/posts/-slovenija-v-%C5%A1tevilkah-%EF%B8%8F-koliko-je-hi%C5%A1nih-%C5%A1tevilk-ulic-parcel-stavb-naselij-v-na/673349872210421/.

Gerbec, F. 2014. "Odprta pravna vprašanja sedanje ureditve nadomestila za uporabo stavbnega zemljišča." *Podjetje in delo* 40(6–7): 1158–1170. https://www.dlib.si/details/URN:NBN:SI:doc-VQZQZAY7.

International Monetary Fund. 2015. *Republic of Slovenia: Technical Assistance Report—the 2013 Property Tax Act: Evaluation of Its Design and the Employed Mass Valuation System.* IMF Country Report No. 16/53. Washington, DC: International Monetary Fund. https://web.archive.org/web/20260114081827/https://www.imf.org/en/Publications/CR/Issues/2016/12/31/Republic-of-Slovenia-Technical-Assistance-Report-The-2013-Property-Tax-Act-Evaluation-of-its-43716.

Krševan, E. 2014. "Postopek za odmero davka in pravna sredstva." *Podjetje in delo* 40(6–7): 1145–1157. https://www.dlib.si/details/URN:NBN:SI:DOC-PWHYDKT0.

Ministrstvo za finance. n.d.-a. "Javnofinančna statistika." Republika Slovenija. Accessed February 16, 2026. https://www.gov.si/teme/javnofinancna-statistika/.

———. n.d.-b. "Financiranje občin." Republika Slovenija. Accessed February 16, 2026. https://www.gov.si/teme/financiranje-obcin/.

Ministrstvo za naravne vire in prostor. n.d.-a. "Evidenca Trga Nepremičnin." Republika Slovenija. Accessed February 16, 2026. http://eprostor.gov.si/ETN-JV/.

———. n.d.-b. "Trg nepremičnin." Republika Slovenija. Accessed February 16, 2026. https://www.e-prostor.gov.si/podrocja/trg-in-vrednosti-nepremicnin/trg-nepre micnin/.

———. n.d.-c. "Evidenca modelov vrednotenja." Republika Slovenija. Accessed February 16, 2026. https://www.e-prostor.gov.si/podrocja/trg-in-vrednosti-nepremicnin /modeli-vrednotenja/.

Mitrović, D. 2010. "Uporaba sistema množičnega vrednotenja nepremičnin." *Geodetski vestnik* 54(2): 228–241. https://www.dlib.si/details/URN:NBN:SI:DOC-1R G2LYOI/?language=eng.

OECD (Organisation for Economic Co-operation and Development). n.d. "Tax on Property (Indicator)." Accessed February 16, 2026. https://doi.org/10.1787/213 673fa-en.

Rakar, A., T. Černe, and M. Šubic Kovač. 2008. "Fiskalna in usmerjevalna vloga javnih dajatev pri izvajanju aktivne zemljiške politike." *Geodetski vestnik* 52(4): 743–757. https://www.dlib.si/details/URN:NBN:SI:DOC-FV9A0DR2.

Republika Slovenija. 2021. "Naloge občin." Last revised October 27. https://www.gov .si/teme/naloge-obcin/.

———. 2023. "Financiranje občin." Last revised October 30. https://www.gov.si /teme/financiranje-obcin/.

———. 2024. "Občine v številkah." Last revised September 23. https://www.gov.si /teme/obcine-v-stevilkah/.

———. 2025. "O Geodetski upravi." Last revised June 11. https://www.gov.si/drzavni -organi/organi-v-sestavi/geodetska-uprava/o-upravi/.

Režek, J. 2004. "Značilnosti davka na nepremičnine in ocena njegove družbene sprejetost." *Geodetski vestnik* 48(1): 18–31. https://www.dlib.si/details/URN:NBN:SI :DOC-4E2SQ5IW.

Statistični urad. 2022. "V 3. četrtletju 2022 število prebivalcev naraslo." Republika Slovenija, October 1. https://www.stat.si/StatWeb/News/Index/10848.

———. n.d.-a. "Indeksi cen stanovanjskih nepremičnin po vrstah stanovanjskih nepremičnin." Slovenija, četrtletno." Republika Slovenija. Accessed February 16, 2026. https://pxweb.stat.si/SiStatData/pxweb/en/Data/Data/0419001S.px/.

———. n.d.-b. "Slovenske statistične regije in občine v številkah." Republika Slovenija. Accessed February 16, 2026. https://www.stat.si/obcine/sl/Theme/Index /PrebivalstvoGostota.

Ustavno sodišče. 2023. "Odločba Ustavnega sodišča št. U-I-262/19 z dne 6. 4. 2023." Republika Slovenija, May 10. https://www.us-rs.si/odlocba-ustavnega-sodisca-st-u -i-262-19-z-dne-6-4-2023/.

Wikipedia. 2024. "Vlada Republike Slovenije." Last revised December 30. https://sl .wikipedia.org/wiki/Vlada_Republike_Slovenije.

———. 2025a. "Ljubljana." Last revised June 16. https://en.wikipedia.org/wiki/Ljubljana.

———. 2025b. "Predsednik Vlade Republike Slovenije." Last revised May 26. https://sl.wikipedia.org/wiki/Predsednik_Vlade_Republike_Slovenije.

World Bank. n.d-a. "GDP per Capita (current US$)." Accessed February 16, 2026. https://data.worldbank.org/indicator/NY.GDP.PCAP.CD.

———. n.d-b. "Gini Index." https://data.worldbank.org/indicator/SI.POV.GINI.

World Population Review. n.d. "Gini Coefficient by Country 2025." Accessed February 16, 2026. https://worldpopulationreview.com/country-rankings/gini-coefficient-by-country.

Žibrik, N., and T. Humar. 2021a. "Real Property Taxation in the Emerging Economy of the Republic of Slovenia." In *Real Property Taxes and Property Markets in CEE Countries and Central Asia*, ed. M. Radvan, R. Franzsen, W. J. McCluskey, and F. Plimmer, 327–374. Maribor, Slovenia: Lex Localis.

———. 2021b. *Zakon o množičnem vrednotenju nepremičnin (ZMVN-1): Z uvodnimi pojasnili in komentarjem.* Ljubljana: Uradni list Republike Slovenije.

Legislation

Civil Tax Act, *Official Gazette of the Socialist Republic of Slovenia*, Nos. 36/88 and 8/89, and *Official Gazette of the Republic of Slovenia*, Nos. 48/90, 8/91, 14/92—ZOMZO, 7/93, 18/96—ZDavP, 91/98—ZDavP-C, 1/99—ZNIDC, 117/06—ZDVP, 117/06—ZDDD, 24/08—ZDDKIS, 101/13—ZDavNepr—Real Property Tax Act and 22/14—dec. of CC.

Constitution of the Republic of Slovenia, *Official Gazette of the Republic of Slovenia*, No. 33/91-I, 42/97—UZS68, 66/00—UZ80, 24/03—UZ3a, 47, 68, 69/04—UZ14, 69/04—UZ43, 69/04—UZ50, 68/06—UZ121,140,143, 47/13—UZ148, 47/13—UZ90,97,99, 75/16—UZ70a.

Construction Act, *Official Gazette of the Republic of Slovenia*, No. 102/04, 14/05—corr., 92/05—ZJC-B, 93/05; 111/05 126/07, 108/09, 61/10—ZRud-1, 57/12, 101/13—ZDavNepr—Real Property Tax Act, 110/13, 19/15 and 22/14—dec. of CC.

Construction Land Act, *Official Gazette of the Socialist Republic of Slovenia*, No. 18/84, 32/85—corr., 33/89, *Official Gazette of the Republic of Slovenia*, No. 24/92—dec. of CC, 44/97—ZSZ, 101/13—ZDavNepr-Real Property Tax Act, and 22/14—dec. of CC.

Decision of Constitutional Court, No. U-I-313/13-86, *Official Gazette of the Republic of Slovenia*, No. 22/14.

Decision on Determining the Revalued Value of the Point for Calculating Compensation for the Use of Building Land in the Municipality of Ljubljana for the Year 2020, *Official Gazette of the Republic of Slovenia*, No. 82/19.

Decision on Determining the Revalued Value of the Point for Calculating Compensation for the Use of Building Land in the Municipality of Ljubljana for the Year 2021, *Official Gazette of the Republic of Slovenia*, No. 204/20.

Decision on Determining the Revalued Value of the Point for Calculating Compensation for the Use of Building Land in the Municipality of Ljubljana for the Year 2022, *Official Gazette of the Republic of Slovenia*, No. 209/21.

Decision on Determining the Revalued Value of the Point for Calculating Compensation for the Use of Building Land in the Municipality of Ljubljana for the Year 2023, *Official Gazette of the Republic of Slovenia*, No. 166/22.

Financing of Municipalities Act, *Official Gazette of the Republic of Slovenia*, No. 123/06, 57/08, 36/11, 14/15—ZUUJFO, 71/17 in 21/18—popr.

Inheritance and Gift Taxation Act, *Official Gazette of the Republic of Slovenia*, No. 117/06.

Law on Property Code, *Official Gazette of the Republic of Slovenia*, No. 87/02, 91/13.

Ljubljana City Municipality ordinance on the charge for the use of building land, *Official Gazette of the Republic of Slovenia*, No. 103/03, 120/05, 4/06, 57/06, 122/07, 107/09.

Personal Income Tax Act, *Official Gazette of the Republic of Slovenia*, No. 54/04, 56/04—popr., 62/04—popr., 63/04—popr., 80/04, 139/04, 17/05—UPB1, 53/05, 70/05—UPB2, 115/05, 21/06—UPB3, 47/06, 59/06—UPB4 in 117/06—ZDoh-2.

Real Estate Recording Act, *Official Gazette of the Republic of Slovenia*, No. 47/06, 65/07—odl. US, 79/12—odl. US.

Real Property Mass Valuation Act, *Official Gazette of the Republic of Slovenia*, No. 50/06, 87/11, 40/12—ZUJF, 22/14—odl. US in 77/17—ZMVN-1.

Real Property Mass Valuation Act, *Official Gazette of the Republic of Slovenia*, No. 77/17.

Real Property Tax Act, *Official Gazette of the Republic of Slovenia*, No. 101/13 in 22/14—odl. US.

Real Property Transaction Tax Act, *Official Gazette of the Republic of Slovenia*, No. 117/06.

Reciprocity Act, *Official Gazette of the Republic of Slovenia*, No. 27/17.

Tax Procedure Act, *Official Gazette of the Republic of Slovenia*, št. 13/11—uradno prečiščeno besedilo, 32/12, 94/12, 101/13—ZDavNepr, 111/13, 25/14—ZFU, 40/14—ZIN-B, 90/14, 91/15, 63/16, 69/17 in 13/18—ZJF-H.

Value Added Tax Act, *Official Gazette of the Republic of Slovenia*, No. 117/06, 33/09, 85/09, 85/10, 18/11, 78/11, 38/12, 83/12, 86/14, 90/15, 77/18, 59/19, 72/19, 196/21—ZDOsk, 3/22, 29/22—ZUOPDCE.

20

Spain's Comprehensive Taxation of Property

PALOMA TALTAVULL DE LA PAZ

Spain is one of the largest economies in the European Union (EU). Located in southern Europe between the Mediterranean and Atlantic Seas, it is Europe's second-largest country, covering 505,370 square kilometers, and with an estimated population of 47.43 million in 2022. The Spanish economy is the fourth largest in the EU, with a gross domestic product (GDP) of €1,206,842 million in 2021, which is equivalent to 9.8 percent of the euro area's GDP (19 countries) and 8.3 percent of the EU's GDP (table 20.1).

The Spanish institutional organization is region based, with the so-called autonomous communities (regions), provinces, and autonomous cities having a large degree of independence in policy decisions and regulations, especially in some areas with exclusive competencies, such as education, health, planning, construction, and housing. However, the central government retains responsibility for decisions concerning energy, roads, national security, and transport, among others. It coordinates activities across the regions to guarantee that the main rules and actions are homogeneous across the Spanish territory. This power separation means that many taxes are directly managed by the regions and cities (most of these are property taxes and inheritance taxes, as explained later). In addition, direct taxes (income and societal taxes) are shared between the central government and the regions, with the latter defining part of the tax structure.

Table 20.1 General Indicators of the Spanish Economy

	Population	Population Density (% of total Spanish population living in)				GDP						GDP per Capita		
	Thousands of People	Three Largest Spanish (greater) Cities[1]	Cities	Towns and Suburbs	Rural Areas	€ Million	% of EU	% of Euro Area	H. Consumpt.[2]	INV[3]	Growth Rate[4] (%)	In Real Euros, 2015	% of EU	% of Euro Area
2015	46,449.6	21.20	51.2	22.3	26.5	1,087,112	8.83	10.25	57.2	18.3	4.06	23,440	84.4	74.7
2016	46,440.1	21.30	51.4	22.8	25.7	1,122,967	8.88	10.30	57.0	18.2	2.91	24,190	85.0	75.3
2017	46,527.0	21.36	51.5	22.4	26.1	1,170,024	8.89	10.34	57.3	18.9	2.89	25,160	85.0	75.6
2018	46,658.4	21.46	50.7	23.4	25.9	1,212,276	8.90	10.37	57.1	19.7	2.39	25,950	84.9	75.7
2019	46,937.1	21.55	49.6	24.3	26.1	1,253,710	8.88	10.80	56.3	20.3	1.96	26,620	84.2	75.4
2020	47,332.6	21.70	50.6	23.4	26.0	1,129,214	8.32	9.76	55.0	20.6	−10.94	23,850	78.4	70.7
2021	47,398.7	21.48	55.6	31.3	13.1	1,235,474	8.35	9.84	55.0	20.2	6.68	26,090	78.6	71.3
2022	47,781.35	21.27	54.5	32.1	13.4	1,373,629	8.51	10.06	55.3	20.4	6.18	28,750	79.9	72.5
2023	48,320.52	21.36	54.4	32.3	13.3	1,498,324	8.71	10.32	54.3	19.7	2.67	30,970	81.2	74.0

Sources: Eurostat; Spanish Institute of Statistics (INE).

Note: €1 million is 1×10^6 euros.

[1] The three main cities computed are Madrid, Barcelona, and Valencia; the metropolitan areas are included.

[2] H. Consumpt. = final household consumption, in % of GDP.

[3] INV = gross fixed capital formation–total investment, in % of GDP.

[4] Real yearly growth rate of GDP.

There are 17 regions in Spain, containing 50 provinces plus 2 autonomous cities (Ceuta and Melilla). The largest in terms of population is Andalucía (7.47 million inhabitants), followed by Cataluña (7.76 million inhabitants), the Madrid region (with 6.75 million), and the Valencia community (5.1 million).[1] As in other developed economies, the population is concentrated in urban areas. In Spain, this concentration is the third largest in the EU, after Malta and Cyprus, following the classification of Eurostat (see European Commission, n.d.). Around 51 percent of residents live in cities (more than 50,000 inhabitants), almost 23 percent live in towns and cities' suburbs, and around 26 percent of the population lives in rural areas (see table 20.1). Since the COVID-19 pandemic, residents have tended to move toward suburbs and cities, abandoning rural areas, which remain almost empty in some central Spanish regions.

Three main cities stand out for their size: Madrid, the Spanish capital, with 5.09 million inhabitants and a total of 6.8 million in the metropolitan region;[2] Barcelona, with 1.6 million and 3.75 million, respectively; and Valencia, with 1.42 million and 1.77 million, respectively. In addition, there is a long list of medium-sized cities, with between 300,000 and 680,000 inhabitants, across Spain, most of which are provincial capitals (Seville, Málaga, Zaragoza, Murcia, Las Palmas, Alicante, etc.). In total, 280 cities, out of 8,130 Spanish municipalities, have over 25,000 inhabitants.

Wealth Generation

The Spanish economy has a similar GDP generation structure to that of other EU countries, with a larger role played by services (which contribute 68.1 percent to total GDP) and the industry sector (contributing 14.6 percent to total GDP), while the construction sector, which has shrunk, plays a much smaller role (around 5.5 percent of total GDP in 2021, with the historical contribution being 9–10 percent on average until 2008). The primary sector accounts for 2.7 percent of total GDP, which is a little more than in other EU countries, due to the relevance of food production and exports. The total indirect tax was 9.1 percent on average between 2015 and 2023 (the total value-added tax [VAT] on domestic products plus import taxes; figure 20.1).

The GDP per capita reached €30,970 during 2023, which is equivalent to 81.2 percent of the average in the EU and 74.0 percent in the euro area. This figure has decreased from the level reached during the expansion period after the Great Recession (85.0 percent and 75.6 percent, respectively) of 2016–2018, a sign of the divergence of the Spanish economy in relation to its peers.

Figure 20.1 Spanish GDP by Main Sectors: Average, 2015–2023 (% of total GDP)

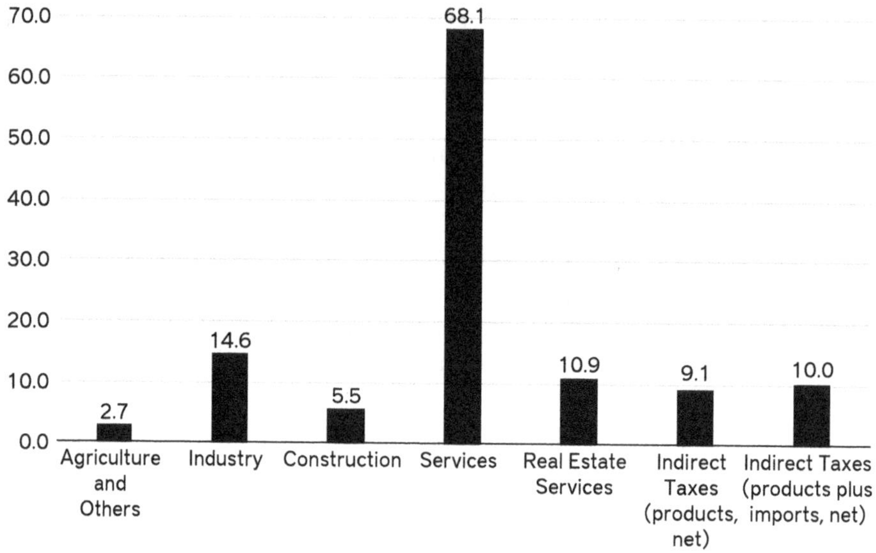

Source: INE National Accounts.

The pandemic was the starting point of a rapid concentration of population in cities, suburbs, and midsize towns. This phenomenon is due to two reasons: the increase in the number of people who work from home, together with the need for more space after the general lockdowns, which led households to move to medium-sized cities or suburbs; and the concentration of jobs in the main cities (following the trend started after the global financial crisis, which drove migrant workers' permanently toward the main cities). Both have strong implications for tax revenues at the local level.

The tax system, as harmonized in the EU, is based on the main direct and indirect taxes, plus other general taxes, including property taxes. A summary of the total income from the tax system can be seen in table 20.2. The property tax is considered a revenue source of the local authorities.

Table 20.2 contains information about tax revenues. Revenues (from income tax, VAT, and other taxes) reached 17–18 percent of GDP from 2015 to 2022, while the tax on production and imports was around 10.5 percent. All this income is collected by the central government and equates to, together with social security payments and other small sources, around 40 percent of GDP. Direct and indirect taxes are collected by the government, but revenues are shared with the regions

Table 20.2 Tax Revenues, Economic Relevance, and the Regional Share in the Spanish Economy

	Tax Revenues by Type of Tax					Tax Revenues Shared Between Central Government's and Regional/ Local Government's Budgets (% of total tax revenues)				Taxes on Production and Imports		
	Total		Direct Taxes	Indirect and Special Taxes	Other Tax Income		Regional and Local Administrations			Net, National Accounts	Property Tax	
Year	€ million	% of GDP	% of GDP	% of GDP	% of GDP	Central Government	Total	Regions	Local and municipalities	% of GDP	€ million	% of GDP
2015	182,008,642	16.74	8.90	7.61	0.23	59.80	40.20	39.31	0.89	10.40	12,992.968	1.21
2016	186,248,520	16.59	8.71	7.67	0.20	57.01	42.99	42.07	0.92	10.26	13,159.836	1.18
2017	193,950,549	16.58	8.93	7.48	0.17	54.43	45.57	44.63	0.94	10.30	13,661.553	1.18
2018	208,684,965	17.21	9.27	7.78	0.16	55.74	44.26	43.34	0.91	10.48	13,985.883	1.16
2019	212,807,546	16.97	9.10	7.70	0.17	54.93	45.07	44.15	0.92	10.24	13,708.386	1.10
2020	194,050,638	17.18	9.47	7.57	0.15	47.10	52.90	51.84	1.05	9.57	13,875.808	1.24
2021	223,384,806	18.08	10.08	7.84	0.16	55.08	44.92	44.00	0.92	10.44	14,026.950	1.14
2022	239,789,387	17.46	10.56	7.90	0.14	63.56	36.44	35.68	0.76	10.58	14,188.120	1.03
2023	271,935,075	18.15	10.66	7.36	0.12	63.90	49.51	48.47	1.04	10.00	14,237.890	0.95

Sources: Agencia Tributaria; Informe Mensual de Recaudación Tributaria; INE National Accounts; Spanish Cadastre.

because of a guarantee that part of the income tax generated at the national level will be returned to the regional and local authorities. The share varies every year and depends on annual agreements.

The last columns of table 20.2 indicate the proportion of the total tax revenues that is retained by each government level, with a share of around 55–60 percent to the central government, around 44 percent to the regional governments, and around 0.9 percent to the local authorities. Annual property taxes are collected by the municipalities and represent an independent source of income for them. The amount of annual property tax collected is equivalent to approximately 1.1 percent of GDP.

Tax revenues are used to cover the costs of providing essential services that have been transferred from the state to regional and local authorities. This transfer is part of the decentralized decision-making structure in Spain that was established at the beginning of the 1980s, with the creation of regions with different degrees of autonomy in decision-making. The responsibility for key areas, such as education, housing, the health system, and regional transport, lies with the autonomous communities (regions), and their costs should be covered by the income from general taxation.

Property tax has been a main source of income for municipal budgets since before the change to a federal system, together with some taxes on construction and other local activities. However, as table 20.2 shows, the total amount of annual property tax collected is just over 1 percent of GDP,[3] which suggests a relatively small income for covering most of the municipal budget. Although the responsibility and the right to collect the money lie with the municipalities, property regulation is determined and monitored at the central-government level. The Spanish general tax regulation is defined as the fundamental set of rules established by the central government to be applied throughout the entire territory, excluding Basque Country and Navarra. Property taxes, such as the Impuesto sobre Bienes Inmuebles (IBI) and the Impuesto sobre el Incremento del Valor de los Terrenos de Naturaleza Urbana (Increase Value of Urban Land Tax, known as the Plusvalía tax), are sometimes considered individual taxes, while at other times they are included in broader tax categories, such as income or corporate taxes. The regional and local authorities have the authority to determine the percentage of reduction, but these reductions must be in accordance with the general regulations.

Land and Property Markets

The tenure structure of the property stock in Spain is similar to that in other developed countries, with a slightly larger ownership rate. The information available is not complete, as real estate in the total housing stock can be used as the main residence for a household or for other purposes (such as second homes, holiday homes, or other nonresidential uses). The 2011 census only recorded in depth those units used as a main residence, and there is limited information about how the remaining stock is being used. The EU Building Stock Observatory was created in January 2023 to publish estimated data about the use of residential and nonresidential buildings. These data for Spain are presented in table 20.3. The Spanish ownership rate is consistent in both the census and the EU Building Stock Observatory, with 78.9 percent of main residences being owned by the household living in them. The rental share is around 13.5 percent (2011 census) or 12.1 percent (European Commission, n.d.), with 7.6 percent of units being provided free.

These data refer to main homes. Secondary dwellings and those with other uses represent 30 percent of the total residential unit stock, and there is no official information in any source regarding either tenure in that group or nonresidential building use.

The estimation of the number of nonresidential buildings reveals that almost three million buildings are being used for nonresidential purposes. The majority are owned (55.7 percent) rather than rented (44.3 percent). The office market has the highest ownership rate in the real estate market (70 percent of the total). In contrast, those buildings used as hotels or for health purposes have the highest rental rate (more than 50 percent), while buildings for education purposes have the lowest.

This higher residential ownership rate comes from a long period in which ownership became the most popular way to have a house, rising to account for almost 90 percent of the market. This trend was partially propelled by strong public housing construction, enabling homes to be sold to eligible households, alongside a flexible mortgage system. Public housing construction strongly diminished after the global financial crisis, alongside changes made to the mortgage system.

Spanish Land and Property Registration

The Spanish regulations regarding property ownership establish that any right associated with buildings or land must be registered in order to be legally effective. In this way, property rights are only considered valid if they are recorded in the Property Registry, as well as those rights associated with real estate (use, usufruct)[4] and any other limitation that may exist regarding the property. The property itself and its characteristics must also be detailed in the registration to be recognized, including property boundaries or common properties, which are especially important in the case of landownership.

Table 20.3 Tenure Structure in Spanish Building Stock

		Tenure/Ownership Status and Distribution			
		Total Units	Owner-Occupied Dwellings/Units	Private Rented Dwellings/Units	Social Housing Dwellings/ Units
		Million of Units	Million of Units	Million of Units	Million of Units
Residential	Total residential buildings	34.840	27.280	3.702	3.858
Nonresidential	Total services	2.972	1.656	1.317	0.000
	Offices	1.208	0.845	0.362	0.000
	Trade	1.291	0.574	0.716	0.000
	Education	0.044	0.044	0.000	0.000
	Health	0.196	0.094	0.102	0.000
	Hotels and restaurants	0.196	0.094	0.102	0.000
	Other nonresidentials	0.197	0.079	0.118	0.000

Percentage Structure		%	%	%
Residential	Total residential buildings	78.30	10.63	11.07
Nonresidential	Total services	55.70	44.30	0.00
	Offices	70.00	30.00	0.00
	Trade	44.50	55.50	0.00
	Education	100.00	0.00	0.00
	Health	47.83	52.17	0.00
	Hotels and restaurants	47.83	52.17	0.00
	Other nonresidentials	40.00	60.00	0.00

		Units, Thousands	Owner-Occupied, Thousands	Rent at Market Price, Thousands	Provided Free, Thousands	Other, Thousands
Residential	Total dwellings	25,849.338				
	Total main homes	18,083.692 (69.96%)	14,274.990 (78.94%)	2,438.574 (13.48%)	430.516 (2.38%)	939.614 (5.20%)
	Total second or other use homes	7,765.646 (30.04%)				

Sources: European Commission (n.d.); Census (2011).

The Spanish Civil Code of 1889 establishes sole and shared property rights, the right to ownership of the asset without the right to use it (bare ownership), and usufruct, while allowing both the ownership and the transfer of the asset to be subject to conditions (usually temporary) decided by the initial owner. For example, it is common to find transaction limitations derived from a purchase under nonmarket conditions or from an inheritance. For these limits to be legally valid, they must be registered. Another aspect affecting properties is encumbrances and liens, especially financial ones, such as mortgages or any other charges that are associated with the property.

The registration system is a traditional institution in Spain. The Property Registry (n.d.-a) is the administrative public body in charge of officially declaring the ownership of real estate, as well as the rights and charges.[5] It is a mechanism that seeks to increase the guarantees of all interested parties in relation to real estate (see ES Registro, n.d.). The Property Registry is a public registry of an official nature in which private property rights over real estate are registered for general knowledge, as well as all other property rights affecting the property. It falls under the remit of the Ministry of Justice and is managed by the property registrars, who are public officials for all legal purposes. As a public institution, the Property Registry has jurisdiction throughout Spain; its aim is to provide reliable information to citizens—who can trust what is registered when making contracts that imply the disposition of registered assets—through the creation of ownership by virtue of public power and publicization of the legal status of real estate, in order to protect legal traffic. Its main task is thus to provide (legal) certainty for acts related to real estate and property, which, by the provision of the law, must produce effects against third parties; this activity is essential to strengthening the legal regime.

The purpose of the Property Registry is the registration of all constitutions, modifications, transfers, and extinctions of real rights over assets, as well as those judicial decisions that affect the property, in order to provide legal certainty and provide proof of property ownership.

The operation of the Property Registry is governed based on six principles:[6]

- Voluntary: All registration is a voluntary act (albeit recommended), although mortgage registration is compulsory.
- Principle of rogation: Whoever wants to register a title must request it in the corresponding Property Registry.
- Priority: The older right registered is applied before any later rights.

- Legality: The property registrars will qualify, under their responsibility, the legality of the extrinsic forms of documents of all kinds by virtue of which the registration is requested, as well as the capacity of the grantors and the validity of the dispositive acts contained in the public deeds.
- Specialty: For titles to be recorded in the Property Registry, they must meet the requirements of form and content in the terms established by law.
- Successive contracts: To register titles, the right of the person granting it must be previously registered.

The Property Registry is highly mechanized and advanced, fully integrated at the national level, and coordinated among all regions (organized in provinces) (see Registradores de España, n.d.-b). It is linked with the cadastre for the confirmation of property details and has implemented an agile, cheap, online information system through which it is possible to know immediately the situation of any property in Spain. However, although this process is fully online and the registration management is highly mechanized, it relies on robust verification for each registration, which is carried out by an expert civil servant (the property registrar) who verifies each of its characteristics, since the responsibility for any potential error lies with the property registrar.

These information technology innovations have allowed the Property Registry to implement digital procedures secured by blockchain systems, creating (anonymized) interoperable datasets for public administration, judicial authorities, and individuals with legitimate interest and allowing access to the information at an extremely low cost. The use of specific geographic software (Cyperurban) has also been promoted to improve data analytics (see Registradores de España, n.d.-a), as well as the adoption of technical tools to facilitate agile license provision and urban environmental checks.

The Property Registry issues a *nota simple* (literally "simple note"), which is a certification serving as the proof of ownership and the property description. These notes can be obtained online according to client requirements.

Land Registration Coverage and Potential Future Reforms

The land registry covers the whole Spanish territory, except for the Basque Country and Navarra.[7] The registration system is a centralized government service with a presence in each province via a network of centralized registries. The registry does not control the stock of the properties, as they are all included in the cadastre. In cases in which a property arrives without cadastre details, the differences are resolved by the two institutions. The registry records all components of a property by describing their characteristics.

The Property Registry has been implementing technology and making the management system more flexible in order to improve communication and transparency regarding property information. This encompasses both exchanging information with other institutions and streamlining the process to facilitate the sending of information from notaries, public information offices, and individuals. Thus, the whole Spanish territory has digitized information for 100 percent of existing properties.

The system is already fully integrated, allowing the interaction of private and public institutions to exchange information and perform procedures. That is, the electronic system encompasses the Property Registry, cadastre, and public institution records. Periodically, the Property Registry provides users free access to various institutions through which they can receive more detailed information. Currently, basic documents can be obtained through the website, but certain procedures that involve more detailed data still require the submission of physical documents. This is because these documents may contain sensitive data, and it would be a violation of privacy protection regulations if the information were accessed by unauthorized individuals.

The Process for Recorded Sales and Rental Transactions

The systems for recording property market transactions differ for the sale of property assets and rent transactions. Both are based on the private contract system (regulated by the Civil Code) but, in the former case, due to property rights transfer laws, it is compulsory to record the transaction. After the property transaction is agreed to at a private level, the parties should complete two steps to secure legal recognition of the property right: obtain authorization of the formal transaction by a notary, and perform the registration. Therefore, the reflection of a private transaction in a contract is not sufficient for definitively transferring rights. As a consequence, the transaction is normally made within the notarial system, whereby the notary certifies the aims of two parties in a transaction,[8] their eligibility to act in the transaction procedure, and that the data included are true and advises the parties regarding their rights and encumbrances. The document signed by the notary is then sent to the Property Registry, which checks the details and, once it is accepted, proceeds to the registration.

The process is as follows: First, as a preliminary phase, the client normally reviews the property information (checking details such as location, size, and quality), ensuring that the property has the listed features, that it is a debt-free property, and that the seller has the right to sell it, normally by asking the Property Registry for a document called a *nota simple* (as mentioned earlier), which contains the basic property information and is free. Subsequently, the two parties sign a compromise transaction contract, which is called a *contrato de arras* (earnest money contract), through which the seller agrees not to sell the property to anybody else and the purchaser signals the intent to purchase via a deposit (around 10 percent of the price), which is valid for an agreed period of time. This deposit will be discounted when the transaction is finally made, while the period allows the purchaser to arrange for a mortgage or any other required procedure for the transaction. Formally, the transaction is supported (and formal rights are created) when it is made in presence of the notary. The notary creates a public deed including all details of the transaction and a full description of the property. The deed is sent to the Property Registry, and the property's and the transaction's features are double-checked before registration.

There is no assessment of the value declared for the transaction at this stage. The declared price is agreed by both parties of the transaction, and neither the notary nor the Property Registry should control, declare any opinion concerning, or change it. The tax authorities, once the transaction is recorded and registered, will perform a valuation to estimate the transaction tax accordingly. This happens once the buyer has paid the transfer taxes based on the declared value. The tax authorities confirm the property value by comparing it with *reference values* they have for the location, adapted to the specific characteristics of the property. If the declared value is lower than these reference values, the tax authorities issue a parallel liquidation (compulsory to be paid) of the remaining taxes and notify the Property Registry. Thus, the reevaluation has the purpose of calculating the transaction tax based on a value closer to the real value. The lists are updated at least every two years. The buyer has the ability to complain and demonstrate that the declared value is the right one.

There are no statistics concerning the underdeclaration of values. The tax authorities verify every declared transaction value in depth; when it is lower than the so-called reference value estimated by the cadastre (which is the minimum price considered for a property in a particular location), the authority corrects the values and issues a complementary tax declaration that should be paid (sometimes with additional charges as a fine and interest). The price verification rule is contained in Article 57.1 of the General Tax Law (Ley General Tributaria 58/2003), and the more recent law (11/2021) provides the definition of the cadastral reference value as the objectively determined value for each real estate property based on the data available in the cadastre. This value corresponds to the most likely price at which a property could be sold between independent and unencumbered parties and has a limit, which is the market value that it cannot exceed. To ascertain this, a reduction factor will be applied in its determination. The list of reference values is published on the cadastre website or by the tax authorities, and it is applied in the verification process for all taxes related to properties. Such a system encourages both parties in the transaction to give the fair value in the notarial act.

Data are held electronically for all processes of the notary and registration, although access to the notarial deed is reserved for interested parties only, while the registration data are public.

All these processes create transaction costs that can reach around 13 percent of the transaction value. This amount accounts for the VAT or transfer tax with the notary and the Property Registry (all at the rates detailed later) and also includes the estate agent rate (which varies substantially from 3 percent to 6 percent of the total transaction price). The expenses are shared between seller and buyer as determined by law, although the parties are free to agree to a different distribution. Spanish law[9] assigns the notary costs of the transaction to the seller (a fixed amount of around €800 for a basic housing transaction), but the cost for authorized copies (subsequent to the transaction) and the rest of the expenses are the responsibility of the buyer. The latter include all Property Registry costs (which vary depending on the property value declared, from €24 to a maximum of €2,182 [see Property Registry of Spain, n.d.-a], depending on the property features and the amount transacted), the transaction taxes, and other costs levied on the property that are not considered in the contract or in the deed. The estate agent fee is not regulated, and it would be charged to buyer and seller.

There are three taxes applied in property transactions: the Impuesto de Transmisiones Patrimoniales (ITP), or the transfer tax, which is applied to existing property transactions and has different rate levels (7 percent for all properties but 4 percent if it is a house and 2.5 percent in the case of main households); the Impuesto sobre el Valor Añadido, or VAT, which is applied to the transfer of a new property; and the Actos Jurídicos Documentados, or stamp duty, which is 0.5 percent of the declared value. There is another transfer tax called the Plusvalía, which is charged based on the increase in the land value since the last transfer and is collected by the municipality and paid, according to the law, by the seller (as it is based on the capital gains tax generated during the time the seller was the property owner). Proposals were made in 2021 (see Agencia Estatal Boletín Oficial del Estado 2021) to change this tax calculation method, with two possible tax base values. The first would be calculated using cadastral values (the difference in land values between the last and current transaction) by applying fixed coefficients (0.14 to 0.45 of the value difference), depending on the period the house has been owned by the seller. The second possibility is a calculation based on evidence about the difference in the transaction price (of the land). The seller would choose the lower one.

In the case of rental transactions, the entire process is in the private domain. Until 1997, there was a public institution controlling (at the national level) rental contracts and keeping the "deposit of guarantee" in a public account. This institution no longer exists, and the rental market has become fully private. The notarial and registration steps for rental transactions are voluntary, and most contracts are never formally registered; the rental market has thus been free since the late 20th century. This means that the deposit is kept by the landlord for the time the contract is active, and most management is conducted by brokers and property managers, a professional body traditional in Spain. In the case of commercial properties, the regulation to be applied is the Urban Rent Law (Law 29/1994), which established that a deposit is to be created equivalent to two months' rent when the contract is signed and which is quite flexible in the terms of the agreement.

The process for rental transactions is much simpler than that for purchases: The usual situation is that tenants find information about the available units in property managers' listings. After visiting and checking the property, including the legal situation of the property (by asking the Property Registry), they may sign a private contract. Rental contracts do not have to be intermediated by a lawyer or a notary system, which reduces the transaction costs. There is no responsibility for the real estate manager in case the contract includes mistakes, and most of the responsibility lies with the landlord (regarding maintaining the property in a state ready to be used, guaranteeing the facilities, etc.), while the tenant is responsible for maintaining the property and making rental payments on time. Depending on the use of the house, tenants have benefits in terms of minimum stay time and limited rent increase.

The lack of regulation in the rental market has relevant impacts on the quality of transactions, and it contrasts with the clear and specific duties of the landlord and tenant after the contract has been signed, which are fully regulated. All rules are contained in the Urban Rent Law, which specifies the rights, time of duration, rent evolution, unpaid claims, property restitution, and other aspects of the rental agreement. Related to the costs, there is a second relevant law, the Horizontal Property Law (Law 49/1960), which establishes the duties related to the property and the distribution of costs. Both are reference laws for the Spanish rental market.

Consistent with its private nature, transaction costs are the sum of two values: the security fund (normally one monthly rent deposit) to be paid to the landlord, and the broker intervention amount, which is normally another full monthly rent amount (sometimes two). No public taxes are applied.

Since the early 2010s, some municipalities have used rent controls (on residential property) to avoid rental increases, and the regulations have the potential to be extended following the implementation of the Law on the Right to Housing (Law 12/2023). However, at the time of writing this chapter, such intervention is not widespread.

Data

Data concerning transactions in these two markets are quite different, in terms of both volume and quality. In the property transaction sector, the available statistics cover almost 100 percent of formal transactions. Data are collected from the notary system, checked against data from the Property Registry, and managed and published by statistical experts in the Spanish Ministry of Transport and Urban Agenda (MITMA). These data are released quarterly and cover the whole of Spain, although data at a monthly level can also be retrieved from the notary system (see Consejo General del Notariado, n.d.). This dataset contains information from 1987 and later, although Taltavull de La Paz and Juárez Tárraga (2015) developed a back-estimation from the 1960s. These data show the price per square meter in euros, calculated based on a spatial weighted median price, which makes it extremely convenient for tax estimations and business analysis.

A second source of housing prices is a hedonic index, built by the INE, based on the Eurostat methodology. The index uses the notary dataset, and it has been published since 2005 on a quarterly basis.

In contrast, there are no continuous sets of official data on rental contracts and rental prices. The INE recently published a new "experimental statistic" with a yearly housing rental price index from 2011 to 2020, detailing the micro-municipal level and the type of housing (two categories) (INE 2025). The data come from rental payment information obtained from fiscal sources (direct tax declarations), but there is no market information from rent contracts. The data for the rental market come from a massive platform (see Idealista 2023), which prepares averages at the national, regional, provincial, and municipal levels for the whole of Spain but only includes "asking rents." The absence of data to illuminate the market and the number of real transactions is a barrier to understanding the rental market in depth.

Real Estate Taxes

The taxation of real estate in Spain is complicated because several different bases are taxed and because there are linkages with the intergovernmental system. First, real estate taxes are levied on the possession, transfer, or refurbishing of properties. Most of these taxes exist at the local level. Second, some central-government taxes have been transferred to the regions (autonomous communities), which have a certain margin of freedom to introduce exemptions, set tax rates, and establish deductions and rebates. Moreover, both the regions and the local governments can establish real estate taxes at different rates. This means that the impact of the fiscal structure on the Spanish real estate market varies with respect both to the type of tax and to where it is levied.

A classification of real estate taxes according to the institutional level of responsibility is shown in table 20.4.

National Level

The two main taxes the state collects are income tax and VAT. Income tax is a direct tax applied to those workers with wages or any other source of income. In Spain, income tax can be declared by the family unit or individually, with the latter being popular in households with more than one active worker. In relation to real estate, income tax is levied on real property in two ways. The first is by adding to the taxable income base 1.1 percent or 2 percent of the cadastral value of those properties (not land) reserved for the owner's use (not rented) and that are not the principal home.[10] The amount is considered the yearly yield (imputed rent), which is added to the personal income (for both resident and nonresident owners). When the property is used for commercial purposes, the declaration is made and taxation is applied following the rules for taxing an economic activity—that is, taking into account the total income received less expenses. Second, when the property is sold, the owner should include in her taxable income tax the equity gains. The amount taxed is the amount by which the owner's income has increased since she purchased the property, weighted by coefficients depending on the length of time the property has been held.

VAT is also applied to real estate activity in two areas. The first is when the initial sale of the property takes place, and the second is on the income generated by the rental of real estate. VAT is only taxed on the first sale after completion of the construction, and it is exempt in successive transactions, which are taxable under the ITP. The calculation base on which VAT is charged is the transaction value declared in the deed by the builder.

Table 20.4 Real Estate Tax Typology

Tax Name	Level	Base of Value	Tax Reductions or Discounts	Overcharges
Wealth tax (Impuesto sobre el Patrimonio)	Regional (transferred)	Larger of the three values: transaction, cadastral value, or tax value if it exists	Yes if it is a primary home Limits on property value	
Property tax	Municipal	Cadastral value of land plus construction Cannot exceed the market value	Public houses up to 50% for first three first years, 90% for households with more than three children, and 50% for solar energy installation buildings	Unused or empty houses 50%, and metropolitan areas 0.2%
Income tax	State/tax income shared with regions; two charges:			
		1. Over yields derived from property ownership (concept of real estate capital): 2% of cadastral value	Principal home is exempt	
		2. Over benefits or losses at time of transfer (equity gains or losses): applied to the difference between selling price and acquisition price actualized	Properties bought before 1986 are exempt	
Capital gains tax (Plusvalía)	Municipal	Percentage of cadastral land value at transfer date times years of tenancy[1]	All transactions less than one year old are exempt	

Construction tax (Impuesto sobre Construcciones, Instalaciones y Obras)	Municipal	Total cost of construction or works	Public houses are reduced by 50%, 90% for work to favor accessibility, and 90% for installations of solar energy or isolation	
Inheritance and donation tax (Impuesto sobre Sucesiones y Donaciones)	Regional (transferred)	A percentage of the cadastral value[1]	Several deductions by kinship, age, or disability; 95% for direct relatives	
Transfer tax (ITP) and stamp duty	Regional (transferred)	The property value according to the valuation table determined by the authority	Levy second property transfers, housing rents, and other real estate rights transfer Public houses, mortgage cancellation or subrogation, and other public acts are exempt	The authority can calculate the fair value when there are doubts about the declared value
VAT	State although shared with regions	The declared value in the deed in the first housing transfer	Second and posterior transfers are exempt Rental housing contracts are exempt	
Private or special use of public domain tax (*tasas por utilización privativa o aprovechamiento del dominio público*)	Municipal	Land rent		

Note: In the case of the coincidence of fiscal subjects, only one tax is applied, avoiding double taxation.

[1] The percentage is determined by the municipality.

In the case of nonresidential real estate rent, rental income is taxed with VAT (21 percent); when a dwelling is rented to serve as a home, the rent is exempt from VAT if the owner uses it as the main residence, and it is subject to ITP otherwise.[11]

In both cases, the tax income collected is shared with the regions. The shared weight is recalculated every year, although the central government's intent is to transfer 50 percent of the total income tax and VAT to the regions.[12]

Some details regarding the income tax are presented in table 20.5. The table provides information about the number of taxpayers and the details of the real estate components in the income tax structure, as well as the amounts for each. The second part of the table contains relative measures to identify the revenue potential. The total tax filers for income tax represent around 40 percent of the total population on average,[13] a proportion that increased during the analyzed period from 2015 to 2019 (from 38.6 percent to 42.4 percent), while the amount declared (payable base to be levied) is equivalent to around 36 percent (from 32.2 percent to 40.2 percent during the studied period) of the Spanish GDP. The amount of income tax collected is equivalent to 6.6 percent of GDP on average, with an increasing weight throughout the period, reaching 7.7 percent in 2020.[14]

The three main categories for which income taxation is related to real estate are nonprincipal homes, properties rented, and properties transacted.

About 42.5 percent of income tax filers had imputed rents or income from real estate, mostly coming from second or extra homes and real estate assets (around 38 percent), with a small number declaring income from renting their second properties (13.3 percent on average of all tax filers). The increase in taxable income added due to real estate is, on average, 3.3 percent (diminishing from 3.4 percent in 2015 to 3.1 percent in 2020). The extra income for those tax filers not renting the properties[15] is 1.2 percent on average, while for those who are renting their properties it is 2.1 percent, which suggests that real estate is mainly devoted to own use and that rental activity adds more than the basic imputed rent estimated by income tax.[16]

The efficiency of this tax measure can be evaluated by calculating the number of tax filers who own nonprincipal homes. This can be done using the official data on the stock of nonmain units, which allows us to determine the extent of the income tax coverage on real estate investors.[17] The weight of tax filers over the total nonmain residential units suggests that the tax is quite efficient by taxing more than 100 percent of owners with a secondary or extra home. The fact that the percentage is larger than 100 suggests that declarations include cases in which the household rents its extra dwellings and nonresidential real estate.[18] The exchange of information between the tax authorities and the cadastre allows the authorities to know all the details of real estate ownership for each Spanish tax filer, as both tax systems are linked in real time. On average, each household's imputed income for nonmain housing units increases the payable base (in the income tax) by around €759.

Regarding transactions, around 2.8 percent of income tax filers declare yields from properties transacted at a quite stable rate, with a small increase for transactions in 2020. The amount of equivalent yields included in the tax declaration is around 0.3 percent of the taxable base.

Finally, the income tax allowed owners to deduct the capital and interest of primary home purchases until 2013. Around 19.5 percent of income tax filers are still deducing the amounts of these purchases due to the rights created to do so, though this number has declined, reaching almost 15.9 percent in 2020; the amount deducted represents 3.2 percent of the total tax payments on average, with a decline to 2.3 percent in 2020.

The Real Estate Rental Market in the National Tax System

The regulations governing the taxation of real estate rental appear in the legislation on the two main direct taxes (income and corporation) and reflect how the rental market in Spain is managed through two sources (individuals and companies), accounting for almost 50 percent each. Regarding the relevance of housing rent in the income tax, it can be assumed that most rent taxes in corporate tax refer to nonresidential activity, but there is no information publicly available that can fully support analysis of the real estate subsectors that are the origin of these taxes. The final collection of income from real estate is not known, since it forms part of the consolidated tax base in both taxes, but the details of the withholdings made for specific categories allow an approximation of the collection capacity of real estate, the data for which are shown in table 20.6.

The Spanish rental market produces tax payments equivalent to 0.21 percent of GDP, with an average of €2,500 million (nominal terms) a year. The relative weight over GDP is quite stable and suggests a consistent tax-collection capacity according to the business cycle, as well as the association between the tax results of rental activity and the evolution of the general economy.

VAT

VAT is levied on properties in two ways: through rent for the economic use of building space and through real estate transactions, including those concerning land.[19] Building transactions in general are taxable at a reduced rate of VAT (10 percent; 4 percent for public houses), covering

Table 20.5 Real Estate and Housing Components in Income Tax for Spain, 2015–2020

Selected items of income tax	Number of Taxpayers (declarants)				
	2015	2016	2017	2018	2019
Yield derived from real estate assets not affected by economic activities	7,690,298	7,892,410	8,071,333	8,345,477	8,474,803
Total Real Estate Imputed Income (principal home is not included)	**6,984,242**	**7,117,181**	**7,226,908**	**7,455,754**	**7,563,689**
Total Returns on Real Estate Housing on Rent	**2,231,383**	**2,372,449**	**2,524,274**	**2,669,669**	**2,776,246**
Other income under special regimes	867,333	77,753	766,281	786,398	791,076
Of them, Net Imputed Returns on Real Estate Capital (from property transactions)	**483,465**	**500,823**	**5,306,120**	**551,892**	**564,477**
General payable base and savings subject to income tax	17,946,121	18,793,509	19,107,856	19,614,231	19,809,781
General deductions	6,763,374	6,809,128	6,854,530	6,690,988	6,535,873
Of Them, Principal Houses	**4,073,071**	**4,080,876**	**3,962,584**	**3,682,630**	**3,445,320**
Resulting income tax	13,813,683	12,672,823	13,331,405	13,693,242	13,745,529
Total population (residents)	46,440,099	46,527,039	46,658,447	46,937,060	47,332,614
GDP nominal (€ million)	1,078,092	1,114,420	1,162,492	1,203,859	1,245,513
Total Nonprimary Homes (thousand units, MITMA estimates)	**6,565.9**	**6,529.8**	**6,524.7**	**6,477.1**	**6,439.9**

Sources: Agencia Tributaria; INE; MITMA; and own calculations.

	Amount (€ million)						
2020	**2015**	**2016**	**2017**	**2018**	**2019**	**2020**	**Average**
8,431,576	11,808.0	12,492.9	13,276.3	14,133.5	14,822.9	14,001.6	
7,525,176	**4,468.8**	**4,682.5**	**4,872.2**	**4,994.3**	**5,204.7**	**5,371.4**	
2,818,043	**7,339.1**	**7,810.4**	**8,404.1**	**9,139.2**	**9,618.3**	8,630.2	
809,205	4,787.9	4,032.0	4,093.1	4,196.4	4,261.4	3,663.8	
588,661	**1,225.4**	**1,264.9**	**1,325.2**	**1,388.5**	**1,463.8**	**1,278.3**	
20,094,178	347,369.4	389,888.9	409,140.9	433,605.2	450,934.5	448,972.3	
6,403,772	3,590.5	3,596.5	3,440.6	3,298.8	3,108.0	2,953.4	
3,194,958	**2,787.5**	**2,707.8**	**2,546.5**	**2,336.4**	**2,170.6**	**1,964.3**	
13,813,683	58,585.1	70,495.2	74,828.0	81,371.8	86,601.3	86,580.8	
47,398,695							
1,117,989							
6,473.3							

(continued)

Table 20.5 Real Estate and Housing Components in Income Tax for Spain, 2015–2020 (*continued*)

Selected items of income tax	Number of Taxpayers (declarants)				
	2015	2016	2017	2018	2019
	Weight accounted in number of tax declarants (%)				
Tax filers per capita (%)	38.6	40.4	41.0	41.8	41.9
Income tax payable based on GDP (%)					
Tax income by GDP (%)					
Real Estate in Income Tax Components					
% of tax filers with nonmain home or nonresidential real estate over the total declarants	42.9	42.0	42.2	42.5	42.8
From those, nonrented real estate income filers over total declarants (%)	38.9	37.9	37.8	38.0	38.2
From those, rental real estate income filers over total declarants	12.4	12.6	13.2	13.6	14.0
% of tax imputed income from nonmain homes or nonresidential real estate over the total payable base					3.4
% of imputed rent of nonrented homes or real estate over income tax payable base					
% of net rental income of real estate (residential and nonresidential) over payable base					

	Amount (€ million)						
2020	2015	2016	2017	2018	2019	2020	Average
	In total income (€ in imputed rent, and % otherwise)						
42.4							
	32.2	35.0	35.2	36.0	36.2	40.2	35.80
	5.4	6.3	6.4	6.8	7.0	7.7	6.61
42.0							
37.4							
14.0							
3.2	3.2	3.3	3.3	3.1	3.25		
	1.3	1.2	1.2	1.2	1.2	1.2	1.20
	2.1	2.0	2.1	2.1	2.1	1.9	2.06

(continued)

Table 20.5 Real Estate and Housing Components in Income Tax for Spain, 2015–2020 (*continued*)

Selected items of income tax	Number of Taxpayers (declarants)				
	2015	**2016**	**2017**	**2018**	**2019**
Real Estate Imputed Income Over Non-principal Homes					
% of tax filers with imputed income in real estate over total nonprincipal homes and real estate	106.4	109.0	110.8	115.1	117.5
Average real estate imputed income (€)					
Real Estate Transactions in Income Tax					
% of filers of housing transactions over total declarants	2.7	2.7	2.8	2.8	2.8
% of real estate transaction yields over payable base					
Income tax real estate deductions					
% primary home tax deductions filers over total declarants	22.7	21.7	20.7	18.8	17.4
% primary home tax deductions over total payable base					

only the first transfer for any completed property from a developer to its first owner (VAT Law, articles 20, 22A). The second and all following transactions are VAT exempted but are covered by the transfer tax in Spain. Agricultural land transactions are also exempted when they are not considered urban land with the possibility to be developed.

If a rented dwelling is used as a main home, the landlord is exempted from VAT. When the dwelling is also used as a professional office or the

	Amount (€ million)						
2020	2015	2016	2017	2018	2019	2020	Average
116.2							
	680.62	717.09	746.74	771.07	808.19	829.78	758.91
2.9							
	0.4	0.3	0.3	0.3	0.3	0.3	0.32
15.9							
	0.8	0.7	0.6	0.5	0.5	0.4	49.59

landlord is a real estate agent, the exemption is not applied, and the rate is 21 percent. If the use is short term, seemingly providing hotel services, the VAT is 10 percent.[20]

Therefore, real estate appears on VAT tax declarations when the building is first transmitted or associated with any real estate services other than main-housing rent. The VAT statistics for total tax income collected do not distinguish by source of income. The only indication of the VAT

Table 20.6 Tax Withholdings of Rental Properties

	Income Tax	Corporate Tax	Total Rental Withholdings	% of GDP
		€ Million		
2010	1,450.140	1,421.024	2,871.164	0.27
2011	1,404.178	1,371.614	2,775.792	0.26
2012	1,450.421	1,421.869	2,872.290	0.28
2013	1,337.078	1,335.034	2,672.112	0.26
2014	1,300.362	1,296.709	2,597.071	0.25
2015	1,226.093	1,251.773	2,477.866	0.23
2016	1,205.653	1,245.800	2,451.453	0.22
2017	1,242.942	1,294.133	2,537.075	0.22
2018	1,280.668	1,348.616	2,629.284	0.22
2019	1,306.039	1,408.858	2,714.897	0.22
2020	1,117.597	1,278.574	2,396.171	0.21
2021	1,172.619	1,347.753	2,520.372	0.21

Sources: Agencia Tributaria (n.d.); INE (2025).

share coming from housing transactions is the value of the base on which the tax is applied (figure 20.2).

In the top panel of figure 20.2, the amount of the VAT base of expenses is shown to have grown rapidly until the global financial crisis, then recovered in 2013, reaching around €500,000 million. This created a net VAT income of €72.5 million, which exceeded the historical maximum (2006). The payable base of housing is counted as the "household housing purchase expenses." The strong fall in Spanish construction after the global financial crisis explains why the base of housing transactions in VAT shows a dramatic decrease and a very weak recovery after 2013, as most transactions made are for existing homes not covered by this tax. The size relative to GDP of the VAT income reached its maximum in 2021 (6 percent of total GDP). The VAT collection capacity of new housing transactions shows a dramatic fall after the financial crisis,[21] due to the decrease in construction activity, from 0.85 percent to 0.21 percent of VAT during the analyzed period (bottom panel in figure 20.2).

An estimation of VAT from housing transactions is shown in table 20.7. The calculations were made by taking the number of transactions of new homes, distinguishing between private and public units, and computing 10 percent over the private units' declared value and 4 percent of the public units' value. Results indicate that VAT would be around 0.1 percent of GDP on average, varying from 0.06 to 0.29 percent.

Figure 20.2 Total VAT Base During the Available Period (1995–2021) in Millions of Euros (top panel) and the Tax Income Relative to GDP (bottom panel)

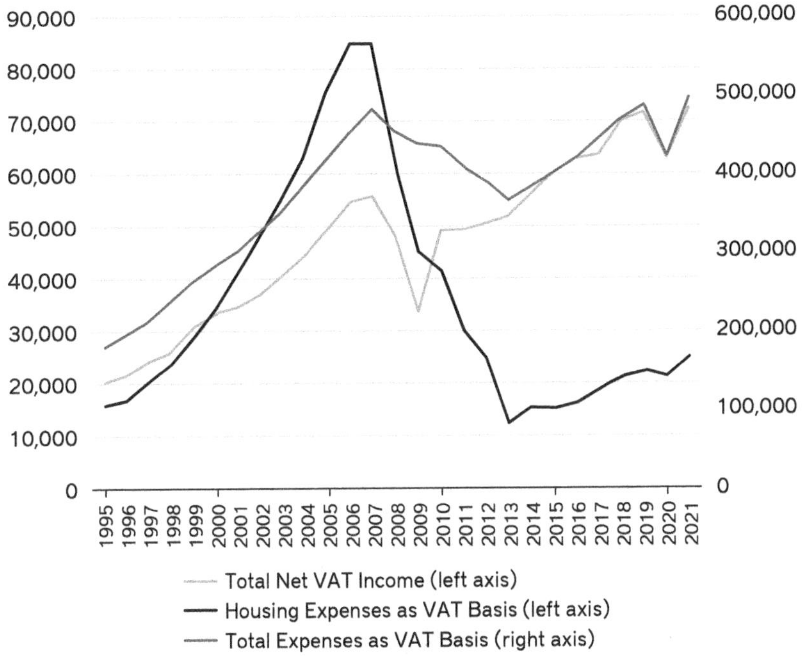

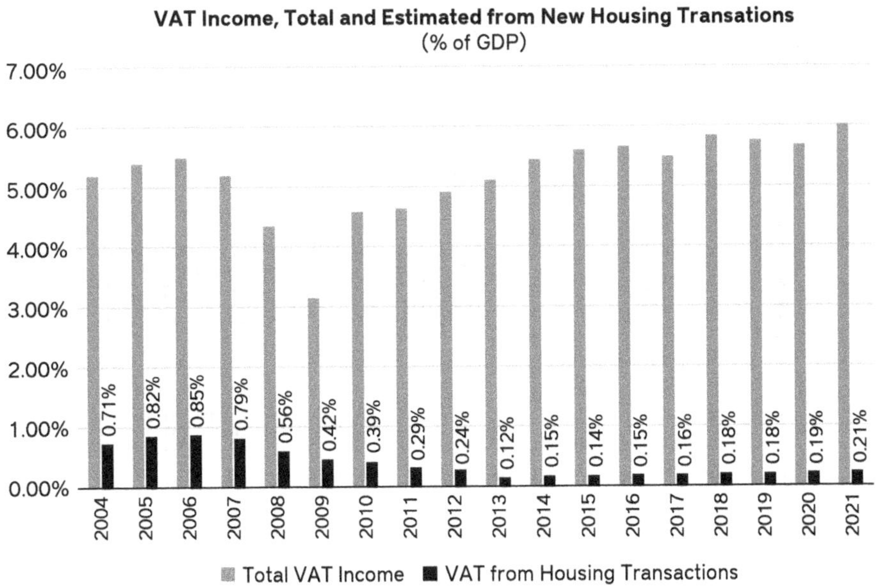

Sources: Agencia Tributaria (n.d.); INE (2025).

Table 20.7 Estimated VAT from Transactions of Dwellings in Spain

	Total Dwelling	New Units				Estimation of VAT			
		Number of units		Value (€ thousand)		€ Thousand		Total VAT	
	Transactions (number)	Private	Public Housing	Private	Public Housing	Private Unit (10%)	Public Housing (4%)	Income	% of GDP
2010	444,388	165,215	34,516	31,490,471.2	34,516	3,149,047.12	1,380.64	3,150,428.0	0.29
2011	309,138	98,094	29,786	17,714,734.8	29,786	1,771,473.00	1,191.44	1,772,665.0	0.17
2012	327,172	89,838	26,511	14,734,103.7	26,511	1,473,410.00	1,060.44	1,474,471.0	0.14
2013	285,304	49,487	7,031	7,705,352.1	7,031	770,535.00	281.24	770,816.0	0.08
2014	347,170	46,915	7,948	7,289,237.0	7,948	728,924.00	317.92	729,242.0	0.07
2015	383,107	42,072	7,038	7,048,489.3	7,038	704,849.00	281.52	705,130.0	0.07
2016	436,574	40,564	6,550	7,214,157.8	6,550	721,416.00	262.00	721,678.0	0.06
2017	509,847	44,915	5,482	8,522,462.6	5,482	852,246.00	219.28	852,466.0	0.07
2018	558,990	50,937	5,541	10,638,337.0	5,541	1,063,834.00	221.64	1,064,055.0	0.09
2019	546,592	50,723	5,563	11,939,966.2	5,563	1,193,997.00	222.52	1,194,219.0	0.10
2020	467,839	54,731	5,661	13,657,275.0	5,661	1,365,727.50	226.44	1,365,954.0	0.12
2021	650,913	66,129	5,698	16,880,325.9	5,698	1,688,033.00	227.92	1,688,260.5	0.14
2022	360,531	31,880	2,684	12,242,106.0	2,684	1,224,211.00	107.36	1,224,318.0	0.09

Sources: INE; MITMA.

Subnational Level

Most taxes related to property in Spain are decentralized and are a main source of income for the municipalities and regions (see table 20.4). The main regional taxes are the wealth tax, inheritance tax, transfer tax, and stamp duty, while the main municipal taxes are capital gains tax (Plusvalía), property tax (IBI), and construction tax.

Wealth Tax (Impuesto sobre el Patrimonio)

The wealth tax is currently regulated by Wealth Tax Law (Law 19/1991 of June 6) and is managed by the Spanish regions (autonomous communities) (Agencia Estatal Bolétin Oficial del Estado 1991). The wealth tax is a direct, general, and single personal tax that is levied on the net value of the property or other types of personal wealth on a periodic basis. It falls on individuals and is complementary to (natural or legal) personal income tax. The tax application was interrupted in 2008 but was reestablished in 2010. It affects both Spanish residents and nonresidents when they have taxable properties or rights within the Spanish territory (in the case of nonresidents or foreigners) and on their entire wealth (in the case of residents). The tax exempts individuals with a wealth less than €2 million and a family business or professional wealth, although this limit varies by region from €1 million to €3 million.

Wealth tax is considered together with income tax in order to avoid double taxation. Thus, both tax quotas cannot exceed 60 percent of the taxable base; when this happens, the wealth tax will be reduced accordingly to reach this rate. Wealth tax is regulated by the Spanish state, although the regions (autonomous communities) are empowered to change some of the regulations to adapt them to the local reality, specifically the tax base brackets, the minimums to be exempted, and tax reductions. Real property is one of the assets covered by this tax.

The base of the property in the wealth tax is applied to the difference between the value of all properties, goods, and real estate rights less the debts. The tax exempts from payment the main home (until €300,000) and a minimum (which varies by region from €500,000 to €700,000) in order to obtain the net patrimony. The tax bracket ranges from 0.2 percent to 3.5 percent and, after calculation of the tax reduction, can be applied to obtain the final tax payment.[22] Properties are valued as the maximum amount among three values: the cadastral value (the value estimated by the cadastre based on location and construction costs), the transaction price, and the administrative value (from a list of values estimated by the authorities to verify the declared value in transactions). Pension plans are

Table 20.8 Wealth Tax Revenue Distribution Between Central Government and Regions

	State (€ million)	Regions (autonomous communities) (€ million)	Total (€ million)	% Growth	% GDP	Transferred to Local Authorities[1] (€ million)
2015	32.38	1,143.61	1,175.99	1.2	0.109	150.84
2016	38.09	1,213.79	1,251.88	6.5	0.112	161.19
2017	54.52	1,267.53	1,322.06	5.6	0.114	162.37
2018	56.75	1,348.14	1,404.89	6.3	0.117	183.83
2019	61.42	1,355.61	1,417.03	0.9	0.114	164.51
2020	59.42	1,441.17	1,500.59	5.9	0.134	176.80
2021	64.92	1,451.24	1,516.16	1.0	0.126	
Average	52.50	1,317.30	1,369.80			

Sources: INE; Ministry of Finance and Civil Service (2021), Table III.7.

[1] The amount includes the autonomous cities of Ceuta and Melilla; it is transferred from the regional and national amounts.

specifically exempted. There has been much discussion in Spain concerning elimination of this tax (Ministry of Finance and Civil Service 2014).

The statistics concerning wealth tax revenues can be seen in table 20.8, which shows the distribution of tax revenues among the regions, the state, and local authorities. The wealth tax raises little revenue, an average of 0.11–0.13 percent of the Spanish GDP.

Almost 96 percent of the total tax is retained by the regional governments, with a residual average of 4 percent of tax revenues going to the state. The regions transfer around 12.8 percent to local regions, and the state does this for Ceuta and Melilla.[23]

As might be expected, regional variations in wealth tax revenues are unequally distributed. For instance, the region with the largest tax collection capacity is Cataluña, which collects more than 38 percent of the total wealth tax payments, followed by the Basque Country and the Valencia community, with around 12 percent and 10.3 percent, respectively. Andalusia and the Balearic Islands have around 6.4 percent and 5 percent, and Madrid, one of the two largest economies in Spain, collects 0.1 percent of the total tax, showing that wealth is mainly exempted for Madrid residents.

The differences among exemptions from this tax and a desire to avoid double taxation have led to the wealth tax being reviewed. Although there are currently no changes to these regulations under consideration, the regions are empowered to modify their exemptions at any time.

Property Transfer Tax and Stamp Duty (Impuesto sobre Transmisiones Patrimoniales y Actos Jurídicos Documentados)

The property transfer tax (PTT) and stamp duty are two mandatory indirect taxes that are imposed whenever a transfer of goods, including real estate, between individuals is carried out. In Spain, it is defined as one tax (the Impuesto sobre Transmisiones Patrimoniales y Actos Jurídicos Documentados)[24] with three modalities: transfer tax, corporate tax, and stamp duty.

The first and second modalities, PTT for individuals and corporations, are mandatory taxes whenever a transfer of goods between individuals or corporations is carried out within the Spanish territory. It is normally applied to transactions of properties and cars, but it also applies to the constitution of rights, bonds, leases, bails, contract options, pensions, and administrative concessions, as well as corporate operations (second modality). It is never applied to any operation subject to VAT to avoid double taxation. The tax-passive subject is the individual (or corporation) whose wealth increases with the operation, which has to cover the amount of the tax. There are some exemptions as, in the case of mortgage generation, PTT is levied to the financial institution (Royal Decree Law 17/2018).

The taxable base of PTT is the real value of the property, good, or right transmitted. In property transfers, as well as in the cases of wealth and inheritance taxes, the base declared is verified when the authorities determine that the value declared is too low. The process is as follows.

Each region decides the taxable base to apply the tax between the cadastral value or the transaction (declared) value. Then the tax authority applies a coefficient to correct the value by adjusting it to be closer to the actual market value. The correction coefficient varies depending on the duration of property ownership by the taxpayer. As the ownership period increases, the coefficient also increases, reaching its maximum value after 20 years (the coefficient correction varies by region). Coefficients are normally published—for example, the regional Valencia community's are in Generalitat Valenciana [n.d.], and the national level is published according to Order HAC/37/2011 of December 26.

The final taxable value varies among regions due to the choice of the tax base and the different coefficients applied. Traditionally, the cadastral value has been the most popular tax base applied in all regions except for Castille-Leon, Madrid, La Rioja, and Murcia until 2021 with the launch of the Law for the Prevention and Fight Against Tax Fraud (Law 11/2021).

When the declared value is lower than the estimated value (base times the coefficient), the tax authorities may verify the price according to a list of administrative values and assign an arbitrary value that would be the base for estimating the tax.[25]

As in the PTT declaration, the transfer must be made within 30 days, and the buyer should self-declare the transaction according to the price agreed to and included in the deed, thus paying PTT immediately after the transfer. The payment for the tax can be made at a bank. However, it is common for the payment to be handled by the notarial office, which oversees the entire process of tax payments and registration.

The revision of the values is carried out once the tax payment is made, and this can generate an additional tax payment for the difference between the declared value and the one assigned by the tax authority. The difference in values is subject to a fine, adding late payment interest and penalties. The declarant has the right to object to the value set by the authorities by presenting evidence for the one declared, and they can reach agreement on the final value. Since the 1990s, there have been many court decisions overturning the public values defined by the authorities.

In 2021, the system to calculate the taxable base for verification changed,[26] with the introduction of a reference value known as the *reference market* value (*valor de referencia del mercado* [VRM]) as the minimum taxable base in PTT and inheritance tax. The new value is calculated by the cadastral authorities and will be greater than the cadastral value, in some cases up to 90 percent of the market value.[27] In cases in which the VRM is not yet calculated, the taxable base will be calculated as in the previous system. The VRM is public, is calculated every year, and can be found on the cadastre's website with precise location details.[28]

The PTT rate is defined by the region where the operation is levied, although the national regulation establishes 6 percent as a reference rate (in case the region has not yet determined any other figure), with rates ranging from 4 percent to 10 percent across regions. The corporate rate is 1 percent for rights (such as guarantees, pensions, bails, or loans, and any corporate operations). The property rental contracts tax rate is determined by the regional authorities.

Stamp duty is the third modality. It taxes notarial, commercial, and administrative documents containing the proof of transactions made in Spain or that have effect in Spanish territory. The tax is applied through a fixed or variable amount depending on the type of document and also differs by region, ranging from 0.5 percent to 1.5 percent, while it is always a fixed amount paid for registration in the Property Registry or the Intellectual Property Registry, or any other juridical act that should be registered in a public deed.

The tax is managed by the regional authorities, which can change the rates and include tax exemptions or benefits that will depend on their regulatory laws as well as the specific circumstances of the buyer. For instance, the acquisition of primary homes by young people or large families has discounted rates, as does public housing. In housing transactions, PTT is applicable only to the second and subsequent transfers. In the case of renting a house as a main home, the regional tax is applied to the amount of rent and the time agreed, and it should be paid by the lessee, who must settle and pay the tax after signing the contract (Agencia Estatal Bolétin Oficial del Estado 1987).[29]

There are several exemptions for PTT to be applied in the property arena. Some of the most common exemptions established by the regions are

- the transfer of goods and rights in the creation or dissolution of a conjugal partnership;
- the rent contract of the main house for permanent living (Article 2 of the Urban Rent Law 29/1994);
- the transfer of land and the assignment of surface rights for the construction of buildings under the subsidized housing regime Viviendas de Protección Oficial, as well as the public deeds granted to formalize acts and contracts related to the housing regime;
- the first copies of notarial deeds that document the cancellation of mortgages of any kind; and
- notarial document costs for mortgage debtors in mortgage novations and credits during the pandemic period (Royal Decree-Law 6/2012 on urgent measures for the protection of mortgage debtors without resources).

The amount of tax income collected is shown in table 20.9. The table distinguishes between transfer tax and stamp duty tax. Following a similar pattern for ceded taxes, the amount of PTT is collected by the regions and partially shared with the state and the local administrations. In the case of PTT, almost 99.8 percent of total tax collection is kept in the regions.

Inheritance and Donations Tax

Inheritance and donations tax is levied at the national level in terms of the Inheritance and Donations Tax Law 29/1987, with compulsory application to the whole Spanish territory, although its management is ceded to the regions and its regulation varies between regions, as in the case of other taxes also ceded. Inheritance and donations tax is an indirect tax levied on increases in natural persons' wealth due to assets obtained free of charge (by inheritance, donation, or legacy, among other methods). Thus it does not apply to legal persons, which are liable for corporate tax in such cases.

Table 20.9 Transfer Tax Revenue Distribution Between Central Government and Regions

	State (€ million)	Region (€ million)	Total (€ million)	% Growth	% of GDP	Local Authorities % of Total Tax Revenues
A. Transfer Tax (modalities I and II)						
2015	5.7	5,138.7	5,144.4	15.5	0.48	2.81
2016	5.5	5,473.1	5,478.6	6.5	0.49	2.92
2017	6.5	6,351.1	6,357.5	16.0	0.55	2.87
2018	6.1	6,944.6	6,950.7	9.3	0.58	2.97
2019	6.4	6,891.7	6,898.1	–0.8	0.55	3.03
2020	5.6	5,464.2	5,469.8	–20.7	0.49	3.21
2021	8.4	8,203.3	8,211.7	50.1	0.68	3.04
Average				9.1	0.50	3.00
B. Stamp Duty (modality III)						
2015	0.21	2,174.59	2,174.80	14.4	0.17	0
2016	0.12	1,752.55	1,752.67	1.6	0.17	0
2017	0.17	1,533.85	1,534.02	12.3	0.18	0
2018	0.20	1,606.42	1,606.63	12.5	0.20	0
2019	0.21	1,838.23	1,838.44	3.0	0.20	0
2020	0.20	1,867.46	1,867.66	–15.3	0.18	0
2021	0.18	2,096.78	2,096.96	26.5	0.22	0
Average				2.8	0.20	0

Sources: INE; Ministry of Finance and Civil Service (2021), Table III.7.

The natural person should present a declaration of this tax when receiving assets and rights by any succession title (mortis causa acquisitions—inheritance tax) or by donation (inter vivos acquisitions—donation tax), or when the beneficiary of life insurance. The period for presenting the tax declaration is short in the case of donations (30 days) and longer in the case of inheritances (six months plus six months' extension).

The law specifies that, when property assets are donated or inherited, the declaration should be made in the region where the property with the largest value is located.

The payable base is determined by adding the real value of all goods included in the donation or inheritance (at the time of acquisition) and subtracting debt and deductible expenses. The real value is considered to be the greater of the market value (Article 9.2) or the declared value. In the case of real estate, the taxable value will be the cadastre's "reference value" of the property on the accrual date of the tax or the declared value if it is larger. In the case that the cadastre has not calculated the reference value, the taxable base will be the greater between the value declared and the market value. The tax base will be determined by the tax authorities under the "direct estimation" regime.

In the case of the inheritance tax, there is a list of deductible amounts determined at the national level depending on the kinship degree (up to second-degree relatives—siblings), as well as the type of inherited asset, to calculate the taxable base. Once it is estimated, the tax rate (ranging from 7.65 percent to 34 percent, depending on the amount inherited) determines the amount to pay, which is computed as the base times the rate and adjusted by a multiplier coefficient that can range from 1 to 2.4. There are reductions established by law that can be applied to the tax rate and the final payments. The regions normally modify the deductions determined in the national law, as well as the reductions applied, in the final quota.

In the case of the donation tax, there is no reduction at all in the taxable base (following national regulations), although the regions can apply them. For instance, donations from parents to children are subsidized at 99 percent in Andalusia, Madrid, Murcia, and Rioja. The lack of a declaration, however, would be heavily fined.

The tax revenues are reported in table 20.10.

The total amount of revenues corresponds to the tax income generated by the two main taxes: inheritance tax and donation tax. The two

Table 20.10 Inheritance and Donation Tax: Distribution of Revenues Across Spanish Regions

	State %	**Region %**	**Total (€ million)**	**%**	**% of GDP**
2015	8.0	92.0	2,787.983	4.02	0.26
2016	5.8	94.2	2,691.713	–3.45	0.24
2017	5.0	95.0	2,709.089	0.65	0.23
2018	5.3	94.7	2,682.143	–0.99	0.22
2019	–0.8	100.8	2,512.657	–6.32	0.20
2020	2.3	97.7	2,460.236	–2.09	0.22
2021	3.3	96.7	3,565.272	44.92	0.30
Weighted average	4.6	95.4	2,639,430	5.70	0.23

Source: Ministry of Finance and Civil Service (2021), Table I.7.

combined are equivalent to around 0.23 percent of the total Spanish GDP. The regions keep around 95 percent of total revenues from this tax, with a marginal 4.6 percent on average being collected by the central government. The amount collected annually fell substantially from 2015 to 2021, with the pandemic effect being the reason for the increase of 44 percent in revenues from inheritance tax. However, there are no details about the relevance of either the inheritance or donation tax.

The distribution among regions reveals a large concentration of revenues in Cataluña, Madrid, Andalusia, and the Valencian community, which together account for more than 50 percent of the total revenues from this tax.

Municipal Level

The Spanish public decentralization of service provision has driven the need to share most public tax resources at the subnational level. This decentralization took place in the early 1980s after recognition of the regional organization in the Constitution (1978), which involved ceding sovereignty over the management and control of different economic and social activities to the regions. This also implied the transfer (progressive over time) of taxes in three ways. First, by recognizing the regional generation of tax benefits and compensating for this by sharing the income with the regions; second, through tax cession (decentralization) but with some degree of centralized regulation; and third, by completely assigning some taxes to the regions or the municipalities. Municipalities kept the main taxes they had traditionally used because of their direct responsibilities for land policy and management. This included the capital gains tax for land and the annual property tax. In addition, municipalities created other taxes associated with real estate, including the building and construction tax, the tax for private use of public space, and a new tax on unoccupied housing that has not yet been implemented.

Capital Gains Tax

There are two levies on capital gains from real property in Spain. One is an income tax (described earlier) where the increase in the value of the property (when it is transferred) is taxed according to the seller's income tax rate. The second is the property tax on the increase in the value of the property. In Spain, the local-government capital gain tax is called the Impuesto sobre el Incremento del Valor de los Terrenos de Naturaleza Urbana (Increase Value of Urban Land Tax), or the Plusvalía tax. It is levied against the increase in the land value in urban areas during the period in which the ownership was held (whether by transaction, donation, inheritance, or legacy). The base of the tax is land value (buildings are not included).[30] The Plusvalía tax is defined, structured, and managed by each municipality and constitutes a main source of income for local authorities. It is regulated by Royal Decree-Law 2/2004 of March 5, which approves the revised text of the Law Regulating Local Treasuries. Specifically, Article 104 defines it as a direct tax on the increase in value of urban land revealed at the time of transfer. The taxpayer is the person who has obtained the economic benefit in the transaction—that is, the seller, the donee, or the heir—who is obliged to pay the municipal capital gains. The conditions to settle the tax are that the property be located in the urban area (rural is not taxable); that the property be sold, donated, or inherited; and that the value has increased during the time owned.[31] The tax should be paid within 30 days after the transaction date (or six months if an inheritance).

The calculation of municipal capital gains tax liability has been a legally controversial issue. Its estimation procedure was declared unconstitutional in 2021 after several rulings against the formula used by municipal authorities during periods when the value did not increase. Royal Decree-Law 26/2021 established a new regulation in the system,[32] with the aim of adapting the tax to fluctuations in the price of the property in order to identify the real capital gain. It defines two systems for estimating the Plusvalía tax: objective and direct or real.

To obtain the "objective" estimate, the municipality calculates the property value based on the cadastral value multiplied by specific administrative coefficients. Such coefficients quantify the period elapsed from the land acquisition to the current transfer and take into account the time period, ranging from less than 1 year to 20 or more years. The greater the elapsed time, the more the coefficients increase, up to a maximum coefficient of 0.45 (20 years or more).

The "direct" estimate of municipal capital gains is determined by comparing the original purchase value with the current transaction value of the entire property. The comparison is made by calculating the difference between the sales price and the acquisition price of the land, which is obtained by applying the proportion that represents the cadastral value of the land over the total cadastral value. If this value is lower than the previous one, it is set as a taxable base. The law allows municipalities to apply a reduction coefficient of up to 15 percent on the estimated taxable base. For instance, for a dwelling bought in 2014 for €250,000 and sold in 2021 for €260,000, in the objective system, the property's cadastral value is €100,000 of which €20,000 is the land value (published values in the cadastre). The coefficient rate to apply, for 7 years, is 0.12, thus the taxable base value is $20{,}000 \times 0.12 = €2{,}400$. In the direct (or real) system, the ratio of land over the cadastral value is 20 percent (20,000 / 100,000); the capital gains are $260{,}000 - 250{,}000 = €10{,}000$; thus, the land capital gains are $10{,}000 \times 20\% = €2{,}000$ as a taxable base.[33] The taxpayer can choose the lower taxable base—that is, that determined through the objective system (2,000 versus 2,400).

The subject of the tax can freely decide the type of calculation to apply that provides the greatest benefit. Such a possibility has meant a change in the fiscal philosophy that normally allows the authorities to choose the most beneficial payment base. As the new calculation has been recently implemented, its effectiveness is still under analysis.

The tax rate to be applied is determined by the municipality, with a limit of 30 percent, and reductions can also be applied to lower the resulting amount, up to 95 percent of the final quota.

Regarding exemptions, there are also cases in which there is no obligation to present the tax declaration of the municipal capital gains:

- When the property transfer is made within a married couple—for example, when the matrimonial economic regime is liquidated.
- When the transaction subject is a historical, cultural, or artistic heritage site or has been declared of cultural interest.
- When the transfer of real estate is made between certain entities (the state, autonomous communities, municipalities, local entities, charities, or educational institutions).

Capital gains tax is regulated by the Law regulating Local Treasuries mentioned earlier, which also determines the rules for other taxes managed by the municipalities (such as property tax).

The resources raised from this tax are mainly collected by the municipalities. Table 20.11 shows the relevance and distribution of these tax revenues.

The tax revenues from capital gains tax are equivalent to about 0.20 percent of the Spanish GDP. The amount grew during the observed period until 2017, with a large negative impact in the first pandemic year, 2020, which is the last year for which data are available. The municipality's accounting function establishes a budget estimate for this tax. By 2020, the level of collections was 25 percent below expectations. This shortfall is partly due to measures enacted in 2020 to mitigate the pandemic's effect, which delayed various payments until the following year, including rents, mortgage payments, and tax payments. It is assumed that the accounting in 2021 will include some of these late payments.

Building and Construction Tax

The building and construction tax (Impuesto sobre Construcciones, Instalaciones y Obras [ICIO]) is a municipal and indirect tax that is levied

Table 20.11 Capital Gains Tax for Spanish Municipalities: Revenues Collected and Differences from the Expected

	Final Tax Revenues (consolidated, € million)	Difference from Budget and Effective Tax Collection (€ million)	% of Spanish GDP
2015	2,152.042	369.488	0.20
2016	2,301.410	277.139	0.21
2017	2,268.502	–41.445	0.20
2018	2,148.680	–170.140	0.18
2019	2,202.927	–76.117	0.18
2020	1,869.135	–467.054	0.17

Source: Ministry of Finance and Civil Service (2021), Table III.7.

Table 20.12 Building and Construction Tax

	€ Million	% Annual Growth Rate	% of Spanish GDP
2015	462.01		0.043
2016	598.10	29.5	0.054
2017	674.89	12.8	0.058
2018	884.36	31.0	0.073
2019	970.84	9.8	0.078
2020	788.37	–18.8	0.071

Source: Ministry of Finance and Civil Service (2021), Table III.7.

for any construction project in the municipality and regulated by Royal Decree-Law 2/2004 of March 5 and by the local treasury (table 20.12). The taxable event is a construction or installation project having obtained the corresponding building or planning permission issued by the municipality. The tax subject is the developer or the person who holds the status of construction owner. Thus the subject can be either a natural person or a legal person acting as a developer.

The taxable base of the ICIO is the effective cost of the construction or installation and includes the cost of materials (Article 103.2 of the Law regulating Local Treasuries) but not taxes, professional honorariums, or business benefits. The tax rate is determined in the tax ordinance approved by the town hall with a maximum rate of 4 percent. The special-interest construction projects recognized by the law, such as roads, railways, ports, airports, hydraulic works, and sanitation projects, are exempt from the ICIO tax.

Municipalities define different level of tax reductions to grant specific constructions declared of special interest for the municipality due to social, cultural, historical, artistic, or employment promotion circumstances. Some examples are solar energy system installations (95 percent of reductions), private investments in infrastructure (50 percent), public housing construction (50 percent), and electric vehicle charging point construction (90 percent).

Revenues from this tax are equivalent to about 0.06 percent of the Spanish GDP, and it is an increasing stream of income as developments start again in Spanish municipalities.

Recurrent Land and Property Tax

Property is taxed with different time frames, either when it is transferred or annually. When property is transferred or inherited, the tax is levied according to the increase in value or the value at sale (the Plusvalía tax and transaction tax, explained earlier), by VAT (charged on the total amount of the transaction value), and by income tax (charged on the difference in property values between transactions). Property ownership is taxed yearly through income tax if the property is not used as a main home or if it is rented, through the wealth tax declaration (charged based on the full value), and through a recurrent property tax, the IBI.

The IBI is a mandatory direct tax levied by municipalities on the ownership of any of the three categories of property recognized in Spain (urban, rural, or with special characteristics) and within the municipality's limits. It is the only annual tax applied to real estate, and it is defined and managed by the municipalities, although the general regulation comes from the central-government administration. It is levied on the value of the property rights and usufruct (right of use of the property), the administrative concession on the real estate, and those public services affected, thus taxing both the rights and services associated with a property.

The type of property is determined by the category of the land registered in the cadastre. The different types of properties are categorized by their use, such as single-family homes, apartments, offices, and warehouses. These properties can be built on either urban or rural land. Properties classified as infrastructure, such as energy suppliers, ports, or bridges, are categorized based on their technical conditions. Consequently, the cadastre includes three categories of property: urban, rural, and goods of special use (known as *bienes de características especiales* [BICE]).

The tax collection is the responsibility of the city council, which also determines the tax rate and the discounts applicable according to the limits set in the law. The IBI is one of the most important sources of income for the municipalities in terms of tax revenues.

Historical Views of Property Tax and the Cadastre System

The real estate tax (IBI) was established on January 1, 1990. It replaced three different property taxes levied on property, thus avoiding potential double taxation: the rustic and livestock land tax, the urban land tax, and the municipal tax on lots (Ortega-Piga 1990). The IBI is regulated by articles 60–77 of the Law regulating Local Treasuries (Gencat 2004). Cadastral management issues were subsequently addressed by the tax reform that came into force on January 1, 2007, and by Law 36/2006 on measures for the prevention of tax fraud. The IBI gives city councils more powerful tools to issue construction and first occupancy permissions, and it defines the taxable base and reductions for certain properties. The cadastre plays a key role in the IBI, as it determines the bases on which the tax will be levied.

The cadastre is a national institution established by the central government per the Real Estate Cadastre Law 48/2002, as amended and consolidated by Royal Legislative Decree 1/2004.[34] It is defined as an administrative registry in which rural, urban, and "special characteristics" real estate is described, as set out by the Spanish Ministry of Finance and Civil Service. The main role of the cadastre is to be the source of property information to serve the needs of general public administration, the Court of Justice and tribunals, and the Property Registry, as well as to provide the official database with precise information about the territory for public institutions and citizens. The cadastre's information does not compete with the information from the Property Registry, which prevails over it.

The cadastre in Spain dates back to the 18th century,[35] created by Felipe V with the general objective of providing the calculation base to apply wealth taxes. The first cadastre was created in the former Aragon Crown (today's regions of Catalonia, Valencia, and Aragón) to ascertain the existing wealth and formulate the tax system to which those territories must submit after losing the War of Succession (Llombart Bosch 1996). The first one to cover the full Spanish territory and to be based on topographic and cartographic materials was the Catastro Topográfico Parcelario (1906–1913),[36] and the first to create legal effects on property rights documents issued by the cadastre was the one established in 1925. In 1987, the Center for Cadastral Management and Tax Cooperation was created to unify the information for the entire national territory. The former Local Treasury Law of 1988 gave it cadastral competence and gave the local authorities the mandate to manage and collect property tax. In 2004, the amended Real Estate Cadastre Law came into force, consolidating the cadastre as a section in the Spanish Treasury that covered the whole territory and establishing the current structure and tasks, which include making property data available using geographical technologies, enforcing legal procedures to obtain compulsory documents, and engaging in administrative collaborations and international agreements (see Dirección General del Catastro, n.d.-a).

The IBI

Generally, the IBI is levied on any type of property registered in the cadastre. Both the natural and legal persons owning the property rights have an obligation to pay the tax (Article 63 of the Law regulating Local Treasuries), which is billed and collected yearly. The municipality is responsible for determining the tax rate, maintaining the property tax base, and updating and managing the tax collection.

The list of existing and new properties in the municipality is managed by the cadastre. It has the mandatory task of continuously checking the properties, exchanging information with other institutions, and providing clear descriptions to enable changes to be registered. For this purpose, the cadastre is in close collaboration with the notaries and the Property Registry, which send information about the creation of, changes to, or inscription of properties (new constructions, demolitions, or boundary changes), and the cadastre then incorporates the information and estimates values and other features.

The property tax is exclusively determined and managed by the municipalities, although the base and property listing are the exclusive responsibility of the state through the cadastre system.

Land and Property Tax Base

The taxable base of the property tax is the cadastral value, which is calculated based on the regulations determined by Royal Decree 1020/1993. The cadastral valuation has the aim of defining a stable value for properties, lower than in the market, which will serve as a base for taxation.

The cadastral authorities have the mandate to maintain information and keep property values updated, and they thus revise the values periodically. They use mass valuation techniques yearly to update the values and conduct partial or individual valuations for new land developed or special properties. They use three procedures: the "general" valuation, the "partial" valuation, and the simplified procedure. The first two require what is called *ponencia de valores* (appraisal report), which is a list of unitary values (values by square meter) calculated by the territorial services of the cadastre based on valuation modules, urban planning, and other tools. The modules are prices by square meter estimated yearly, both for land and for the total construction, published in the official bulletin (by province) for the calculation of the cadastre value, which should also be agreed on with the municipality.[37]

A simplified cadastral review model is a streamlined process that enables property owners to update the cadastral value of their property more quickly and at lower cost than a full appraisal, focusing only on aspects that have changed, such as planning regulations or market conditions. Owners must provide evidence of discrepancies or changes, submit the necessary documentation, and maintain active collaboration with the cadastral administration; while offering efficiency and transparency, the model is not suitable for major modifications or significant valuation gaps.

Valuation Methodology

The cadastral value is calculated by summing the land value and the construction (buildings') value. To calculate the land value, the residual method is applied (RD 1020/1993, Norma 9.2) based on the market value less the construction value, as explained in the appraisal valuation methodology regulated in Spain by Order ECO/805/2003 of March 27, on the rules for the valuation of real estate and certain rights for certain financial purposes.[38] To value the construction, the "reposition" method is used, which is a variant of the residual method that takes into account the use, quality, historical values, and other market features in order to find a final value that captures the whole costs and values.

The cadastral method describes in detail the correction coefficients to be applied and how to measure land and construction components of the final value (RD 1020/1993, Norma 16.1).

The definition of the value is formulated as follows:

$$V_c = [V_L + V_C] * C_L * C_c * M_m \tag{1}$$

where:

$$V_L = V_R * S_{CONS} * Coef_s \tag{2}$$

$$V_C = MBC * Coef_i x CoefH_i \tag{3}$$

where V_c is the cadastral value; V_L is the land value (estimated); V_C is the value of construction (also estimated); C_L is the land correction coefficient; C_c is the coefficient of construction expenses; M_m is a coefficient correcting for the market moment; V_R is the unitary value of land taken from the *ponencia de valores* (a list of unitary values); S_{CONS} is the building size in square meters; $Coef_s$ is the correction coefficient of land; *MBC* is the basic construction module assigned to the municipality (related to the planning); $Coef_i$ is the coefficient applied to the construction typology (*i*) among residential, industrial, office, commercial, and tourism properties by land use and density (RD 1020/1993, Normas 9, 18); and $CoefH_i$ is the correction coefficient of the construction value (Silvan Mon 2015). All components calculated refer to homogeneous economic areas—that is, regions or areas that share similar economic characteristics. This classification allows for the grouping of areas with common economic influences. The concept is comparable to that of housing submarkets or industrial areas. The classification of these areas is determined jointly by the cadastre and the ministry at the subregional level.

As can be seen, the valuation methodology is based on the principles of appraisal in the primary estimation of the different modules of values (the *ponencia de valores*) that also refer to the market value. After estimating the basic values, the calculation uses several correction coefficients to ascertain the individual cadastral value. The method is complex and requires large databases with real data (existing in the cadastral database). The mass appraisal made for the whole portfolio employs an automated version of the method approved in the law, as well as spatial georeferenced statistics and artificial intelligence methodologies.

The cadastre updates the value via a process of mass valuation when directed to by the General State Budget Law 47 of 2003. Regulations updating the methodology are not frequently passed. The last changes to the regulations were introduced by Royal Decree 1464/2007 and covered the modification of certain modules' estimation and the methodology for specific types of properties. This decree introduced a specific method for cadastral value estimation in the case of properties with special characteristics" (such as airports, ports, and central rail terminals), the methodology for which is regulated via modules for depreciation, subsector, and quality, among others.[39]

In terms of Law 11/2021, a reduced factor applicable to the determination of the reference values of the properties was approved to avoid cadastral values exceeding the market value.[40]

In 2013, the cadastre initiated a review and mass process to update the information on existing properties to reflect the actual situation. This affects those properties that have changed due to an extension of the available land, the coverage of open areas, or any other constructions that changed the property value and that the owner has not declared. Accordingly, the whole property dataset is being reviewed and updated. The information about the municipalities under review is published on the cadastre's website.[41]

In 2021, the High Court rejected the method to estimate taxes (other than property tax) based on cadastral values. As a result, the cadastres began calculating an alternative value, the so-called *valor de referencia* (reference value, defined in Law 11/2021), which is based on the prices from property transactions carried out by a public notary and registered by the Cadastre. It will never exceed the market value and will serve as the basis to calculate transfer tax, inheritance tax, and stamp duty but not the IBI, which has as a base the cadastral value. The reference value is determined yearly and simultaneously in all municipalities.

Valuation Quality Control Measures

Owners can reject the values applied by the Cadastre and litigate for a fair value. The system is transparent, and there are several mechanisms for complaints. There is a Taxpayer Defense Council, and the system contains the possibility to elaborate single valuations when there are doubts about the value.

The reestimation of values serves also as a control for valuation quality from an internal perspective. The regulation establishes that the values assigned by the cadastral method should be discussed with the municipality, and the final values should be agreed on by both the Cadastre and the municipality. This system serves as an external control process in property valuation.

In addition to exchanging information with the Property Registry, the cadastre uses different methods to check the accuracy of information on built properties, such as periodic aerial photographs and satellite images.

Coverage of the Tax Base

The coverage of the tax base is almost 100 percent. Through the modernization process—with an updated regulation establishing clear steps to register new constructions and renovations—as well as interaction with the tax authorities and the Property Registration System, the cadastres have registered almost all Spanish properties, as shown in table 20.13. In addition, the administrative system itself requires registration to generate the effects of legal property rights, and private facility providers (services, financial) also require registration documents to provide services.

As table 20.13 shows, there are 39.1 million properties in urban areas and a similar number of rural plots. The coverage rate is 98.35 percent, with an average amount of €331.68 per property. In the case of BICE (infrastructure and equipment), the coverage is also close to 99 percent and shows a tax amount of almost €14,000 a year, consistent with these properties'

Table 20.13 Coverage of Property Tax, 2021

	IBI-Issued Bills	Number of Properties	Total Tax Collection		Coverage Rate (bills/properties)	Tax Collection/ Property (mean)
Typology	**Number**	**Number**	**€**	**% of GDP 2021**	**%**	**€**
Urban properties	38,509,952	39,155,277	12,987,018,429	1.08	98.35	331.68
Rural lots	5,719,183	39,138,283	461,313,028	0.04	14.61	11.79
BICE (infrastructure and equipment)	39,250	39,762	553,269,908	0.05	98.71	1,3914.54

Sources: Dirección General del Catastro (n.d.-c) and own calculations.

features. In the case of rural property tax, the coverage seems to be low due to the bills issued containing multiple plots associated with one owner.

The total amount represents 1.17 percent of the Spanish GDP, which is in line with other countries' collection (Slack 2010). Agricultural land and buildings are subject to the IBI for rural property tax. This tax typically encompasses both the buildings on the rural property and the land itself when it is effectively used for agricultural production, including cooperatives. In some cases, there may be a reduction of up to 95 percent of the tax rate for agricultural properties.

Exemptions

IBI exemptions are contained in the Law regulating Local Treasuries (Article 62). Those properties exempt from IBI payments are public properties owned by public institutions, communal properties, properties owned by recognized religious groups or associations, Red Cross properties, diplomatic buildings, railway buildings and installations, properties used in education, historical monuments, health centers, and some buildings owned by nonprofit entities. Properties with low value are also exempt (Law 49/2002 on the tax regime of non-profit entities and tax incentives for patronage, Article 15).

Table 20.14 contains the number of urban and rural properties registered in the cadastre by use in 2022, and it can be seen (italicized rows) that 0.32 percent of the total buildings are exempt. The amount of revenue excluded due to the exemptions is not estimated in public data.

The cadastre takes into account when the property is not used only in the residential sector, allowing municipalities to increase the tax by 50 percent (Article 72.4). The number of exempt buildings shown in table 20.14 is not complete, as public buildings and other exemptions are not precisely identified.

Taxpayers

Article 35.4 of the General Tax Law determines that any natural or legal entity that holds property rights is the taxpayer. Others subject to the IBI include those holders of administrative concessions, of surface rights, and of real rights of usufruct. In the case of transfer, the new holder must pay the IBI from the year following the date of acquisition. Therefore, the tenants have no obligation to pay property tax.

There are no special rules when the owner is a nonresident. The tax should be paid at the time it is issued. In the case of nonpayment, the final tax amount will be incremented by 20 percent or more, and the property can be auctioned by the municipal authorities.

Table 20.14 Total Properties Registered in the Spanish Cadastre, 2022

	Thousands of Properties	%
Total urban properties	**39,392.008**	**50.25**
Residential	23,898.695	30.49
Warehouse	8,704.780	11.11
Retail	1,367.567	1.74
Cultural	*52.801*	*0.07*
Hospitality	211.098	0.27
Industrial	1,688.284	2.15
Sport	*94.159*	*0.12*
Urban lots	2,960.964	3.78
Offices	302.693	0.39
Single buildings	*21.538*	*0.03*
Religious	*43.085*	*0.05*
Leisure	5.461	0.01
Health	*40.883*	*0.05*
Total rural plots	**38,993.848**	**49.75**
Total urban + rural	78,385.856	**100.00**
% of properties tax-exempted by use		*0.32*

Source: Spanish Cadastre.

Taxpayers declare their ownership in the cadastre, and this should be done at the time of acquiring the property rights. In the transaction, a demonstration that the property tax has been paid should be shown to the notary. Thus, the new owner is provided with all information to self-declare ownership to the cadastre. Outstanding property tax debt is secured by the property, so the debt amount would be settled by auctioning off the property.

Responsibility for Valuations

Valuations are made by the cadastre at the national level. As the valuation methodology is uniquely prescribed for the cadastre, no external experts or valuers take part in it. The cadastre has a provincial section that is assigned to perform the valuation and agree with the municipality on the final values to be applied. The valuation is public and can be consulted on the cadastre's website.

The system to update the cadastre allows registration of variations on a continual basis, and the procedure for requesting changes in the property definition can be initiated by the owner.[42] Any alteration to properties will have an effect on the property tax in the following natural year.

Valuation Cycle

The cadastral values of properties undergo annual updates through two methods. First, a specific number of properties are valued each year as mandated by the General State Budget Laws; thus, the valuation system is not automatic, but starts at the request of municipalities or through annual updating coefficients approved in the State Budget. The valuation update can be done via valuation reports (a full revision, or *ponencia de valores*) or through coefficients (a partial adjustment). The first method involves a direct requirement for the cadastre to review property values using the complete methodology in a certain number of municipalities, typically accounting for a maximum of 50,000 properties a year. The valuation reports normally cover all properties in a municipality and are carried out when there is a significant gap between market and cadastral values. The second method uses coefficients, which are established each year in the Spanish State Budget Law, approved by the government, and applied across cadastral values (thus, without a full valuation). The coefficients align cadastral values with market trends by comparing the date of a municipality's last revision to the market price changes that have occurred since.

Property Valuation Data

Property data are collected by the cadastre in three ways: from the Property Registry or the notarial system after the transaction is made, through self-reported information provided by the new owners to be accounted for property tax purposes, and through the cadastre's own collection, following a mandate by the national authorities for testing and quality control, or due to planning. There is no requirement to physically inspect the properties, as the technical details in the official documents should be complementary to the declaration. However, the cadastre is able to perform inspections if required.

The information exchange between the Property Registry and the Treasury (both public institutions) is achieved by sharing the database electronically.

Objections and Appeals

The owners can use an official procedure to challenge any decision made by public institutions that is against their interests. The cadastre implements the procedure via its website through the Taxpayer Defense Council, which is an institution within the Treasury Ministry that analyzes complaints and objections. The system for appealing value decisions is also regulated. The complaints should be made in writing, and they are not published. There are no data available regarding the number of objections.

Tax Rates

Municipalities are solely responsible for setting the tax rates once a year, and the cadastre determines the value. The exemptions are contained in the Law regulating Local Treasuries (Article 62), and several reductions regarding the taxable base are considered (Article 67) when the property's cadastral value has increased according to the last mass valuation (not when the increase is due to updating the value with multiplier coefficients). The rates are approved by the municipality annually within a range regulated in Article 72 of the Law regulating Local Treasuries. This is generally between 0.4 percent and 1.3 percent of the cadastral value, but the law allows an increase of the rates currently applied depending on the municipality type and size, from 0.05 percent to 0.15 percent (Article 72.3).

A reduced rate (minimum 0.1 percent in urban areas and 0.075 percent for rural properties) can be applied during the first six years after the cadastral value has undergone mass updating.

Tax Relief Measures

Other than exemptions, the IBI accounts for reductions to specific properties, which should be granted on request. For example, the IBI can be reduced by 50–90 percent for construction activity and the refurbishing of properties after completion, public housing receives a reduction of 50 percent during the first three years after completion, and rural properties devoted to agricultural production have a 95 percent tax reduction (Article 73). Other than these reductions, municipalities also have the right to reduce the tax by up to 90 percent for buildings devoted to agricultural activity under certain conditions (and not covered by the general bonus) and by 50 percent for those with energy efficiency installations.

IBI Tax Management

The billing process is fully electronic. Bills are sent at the start of the tax period defined for the whole municipal property list, and owners are provided the opportunity to arrange automatic charges to their accounts; advice is sent to the property address in the case that the owner is not registered for electronic billing.

Public administration can establish collaboration with financial institutions to collect the tax revenues according to the law.[43] Any tax can usually be paid directly by bank using the tax declaration document, adding the revenues to the public account. The system is quick and fully controlled electronically.

There are no data concerning tax payments other than those coming from final budgets shown in table 20.15. Property tax arrears are not published either, because the information system adopted does not enable such publication and because any debt is guaranteed by the property, so the amount of unpaid tax assessment bills will be low. Direct debit from the owner's account is possible, in the case that the relevant information is provided and direct payment from a financial institution has been authorized using the tax liquidation document that the municipality issues to owners. There is no possibility to pay by cash.

Spanish regulations establish a system to recover the amounts of taxes or public services fees that have not been paid. When the tax bill is issued, it has a payment term that varies between one month and two months before payment is due; this is the "voluntary" period for payment. A direct debit is normally issued in the middle of the period. If the payment is not made, the public administration can use progressive sanctions, including surcharges and seizure of the house. The day after the deadline, the tax bill enters the "executive" period, with a 5 percent surcharge that can be paid by the owner via city hall. If this period elapses and no payment is made, the surcharge is increased to 10 percent and recovery is transferred to the courts, which send a payment order to the owner. If the tax is still not paid, the surcharge increases to 20 percent plus default interest and the city council, based on what is established by the tax law, can start an embargo process for the property.

As this procedure applies to all public taxes, the system normally has a strong collection capacity. Each step is published publicly, and the owner is also notified, so it is rare that the debt collection reaches the last step with embargoes. However, the law establishes that tax debt can be collected up to four years from the end of the regulatory term in the voluntary period, so the municipalities should start the third step in the process promptly to avoid being unable to recover the tax debt.

Technology

Both the cadastre and the tax administration are well supported through technology and high levels of automation. The cadastre uses information and communications technology systems to maintain the data, evaluate the market reality, and discover new properties by checking the territory with geographical measures (geographic information systems are widely implemented), together with information obtained from drones and satellite imagery. The valuation system in the cadastre uses artificial intelligence to manage and store data, as well as econometric methods to perform the value estimations. The system for billing, collection, and accounting is fully electronic and controlled by the public administration system.

Fiscal decentralization

The discussions regarding the distribution of income from the state to the regions have motivated reviews of the tax collection sharing (white papers on Spanish taxation). Contributing to this policy discussion are court decisions forcing changes to the calculation of the taxable base of real estate (Plusvalía tax) and a strong debate regarding the system adopted by the central government for resource and investment distribution across the regions. The latter is known as the Sistema de Financiación Autonómica,[44] which is a model of resource distribution established at the start of the administrative decentralization process in the 1980s. It is based on the so-called principle of fiscal coresponsibility, by which the tax and income resources are shared across the state according to basic needs, irrespective of where the tax revenue is generated.[45]

Two decentralization models are applied: those of the Provincial Treasury (Hacienda Foral), applied to the Navarra and Basque Country regions; and the Common Treasury, applied to the rest of the regions. In the latter, an initial sharing model did not substantially modify the percentage distribution of resources. As expenses in most of the areas were transferred to the regions, those worst treated (the Valencian community and Murcia) complained that the unequal distribution of income had led to increased debt in the regional accounts.[46] Several reports supported the finding that an unequal financial distribution in some regions over many years had created a disequilibrium in the public accounts (Espasa 2015; Perez 2002). But this did not result in a substantial modification of the distribution system.

The model of resource distribution among the regions and the difficulties in increasing the efficiency of the tax drove an initiative to transfer more of the management of the main taxes to the regions. The present financing system is designed to cover the expenses of all transferred services and to channel financing through two funds: the Transfer of Guaranteed Funds for Fundamental Public Services and the Global Sufficiency Fund. Both are defined at the national level to cover the provision of basic services in the whole territory.[47] Two additional funds are used to promote convergence: the Competitiveness Fund and the Cooperation Fund.

Analyses of the fiscal system have highlighted a weaker revenue mobilization than in other European countries, suggesting the need for tax system reform. This would focus on both broadening the tax base and curbing fiscal fraud (Zabalza 2014). Discussion of such reforms has established the idea that the federal system needs to be updated, mostly to address ceded taxes (Laborda and Zabalza 2015), taking into account the fact that regional finances are extremely sensitive to the business cycle and that the decisions of the central government compromise certain essential services such as the health system (Cuenca and Gonzalez 2015).

The analysis of potential models to modify the tax system has evolved, culminating in the last expert report, the *White Book of Fiscal Reform* (Ministry of Finance and Civil Service 2022).

Regarding real estate taxes, most were ceded to local authorities at the beginning of the process, and evidence suggests a high degree of efficiency in tax collection. For example, a study by Laborda and Zabalza (2015) showed that the elasticity of "traditional" ceded tax revenues, such as the tax on net wealth, inheritance tax, capital transfer tax, and gaming taxes, was approximately 1.0 and exceeded that of income tax, VAT, and excises from 2002 to 2011. This implies that the newly collected tax revenues can be beneficially integrated into the existing framework for managing real estate taxation.

Until recently, there were few analyses estimating whether property tax would affect housing or real estate markets, mainly due to the lack of statistics. In a theoretical analysis, López-García (2004), by analyzing the tax structure for housing in Spain, demonstrated that the elimination of housing subsidies in personal income tax and the inclusion of investment incentives for housing would reduce the price increase by increasing supply.

Property Tax in Large Urban Areas

Table 20.13 showed that while the number of properties in urban and rural areas is quite similar, the tax contributions differ significantly. Urban areas generate 98.5% of total property tax revenue, whereas rural areas contribute only 14.6%. In table 20.14, consistent data also showed that about one-third of urban properties are used for residential purposes. In this section, in-depth property tax information is shown for the two main Spanish cities, Madrid (the capital city) and Barcelona, as well as three other large Spanish municipalities that are representative of the second- and third-tier groups by size—namely, Valencia and Seville (representative of cities larger than 500,000 inhabitants) and Alicante (representative of cities larger than 200,000 inhabitants). Details about the amount of property tax, its collection, and its relevance are presented using data obtained from the official registers of the Spanish Treasury and the cadastre. A summary is contained in table 20.15.

Table 20.15 Property Tax and Municipalities: Five Main Spanish Cities, 2021

	Variable	**Madrid**	**Barcelona**	**Valencia**	**Seville**	**Alicante**	**Source**
Main cities by size	Population (January 1, 2022), thousand residents in the city	3,280.782	1,636.193	792.490	682.000	338.580	INE
Number of taxable properties in 2021	Data by property use, category, etc., 2021, urban (see table 20.16)	2,223,638	1,155,183	683,388	484,122	296,695	Cadastre
	Growth rate (2019–2021)	1.39	0.87	0.50	1.21	1.24	Cadastre
Base of the property tax	Tax base value, 2021 (thousand)	291,361,486.06	120,112,011.96	32,183,773.52	23,960,217.31	14,456,875.59	Cadastre
Total value of the tax base	Growth in the value of the tax base (2019–2021)	0.90	0.03	3.29	4.13	1.06	Cadastre
Exempt properties	Number of exempt properties (by type),[1] 2021 (see table 20.16)	6,028	4,986	2,307	1,696	1,284	Cadastre
	Are these properties valued?	Yes	Yes	Yes	Yes	Yes	Cadastre
Valuation	Does the city have a valuation department?	No[2]	No	No	No	No	Cadastre

Revaluations	Average frequency of revaluations (years)	10	10	20	20	20	Cadastre
	Date of last revaluation	2012	2018	1998	2001	1996	Cadastre
	Responsibility for revaluation	Cadastre	Cadastre	Cadastre	Cadastre	Cadastre	Cadastre
Collection data	Revenue collected (2019–2021), urban + rural + BICE (infrastructure and equipment) (€)	4,536,537,767	2,044,881,530	706,768,000	528,983,489	254,839,942	Treasury
	Arrears (2019–2021) (% of total income)[3]	12.77	13.52	13.24	6.37	2.45	Treasury
Property tax as a %	Of tax revenue	59.43	58.11	60.52	52.46	60.54	Treasury
	Of total revenue	28.96	24.52	25.63	20.99	30.87	Treasury
Role of the property tax	How is the revenue spent?	There are no precise expenses assigned to property income (see table 20.17)					Treasury
	Use as security for borrowing (% of total municipal income)	12.77	13.52	13.24	6.37	2.45	Treasury

[1] The number of exempt properties is unknown. Here it is calculated by adding the properties with some uses clearly exempted, although public houses and government offices cannot be identified here.

[2] For property valuation purposes.

[3] Only for 2021; it is calculated based on the overcharges collected for taxes not paid on time and other rates and taxes.

The number of properties in each city is consistent with the size of the population—that is, larger in Madrid (2.2 million) than in Alicante (around 300,000)—but it shows a different dynamism, with more growth in Madrid, Seville, and Alicante than in Barcelona and Valencia. The tax base value (set by the cadastre) has grown more in Seville (4.13 percent) and Valencia (3.29 percent) than in Madrid (0.9 percent). Barcelona has maintained almost stable property values for tax purposes. These differences are due to the systems used for revaluating properties, depending on the cadastre, which recalculates the values every decade, even though there is a system in place to update values according to property value changes. As can be seen in table 20.15, values were last reestimated long ago in Valencia, Seville, and Alicante (more than 20 years ago) but more recently in Barcelona and Madrid (around 10 years ago), although the updated coefficients are applied yearly for value actualization.

Revenues from property taxation come mainly from urban properties, as most rural properties are exempt from taxation. This same pattern holds in the select cities where space for rural land generates low property tax payment, with more than 95 percent coming from urban properties. The BICE (infrastructure and equipment) generates around 3 percent of property tax income in the main cities, but it is almost 0 percent elsewhere.

The typology of properties is large, and all properties are valued (even if exempt from taxation). As shown in detail in table 20.16, residential, warehouse, and retail are the three main groups of properties in all cities, although in terms of value, office buildings are also relevant for total property tax.

Settled financial accounts enable identification of the amount of property tax as a proportion of the total municipal budget. The total tax revenues coming from direct taxation are more than 90 percent, with one of the sources being the property tax (table 20.17). Revenues coming from the property tax represent more than half of the tax collected, mostly around 60 percent (Madrid, Valencia, and Alicante) but a little less in Barcelona (58.1 percent) and Seville (52.46 percent). Regarding the total income of the municipalities, property taxes represent around 29 percent of the total in Madrid, 24.5 percent in Barcelona, 25.6 in Valencia, 21 percent in Seville, and 30.8 percent in Alicante. These figures indicate the reliance on property taxation for the successful provision of public services.

Finally, the municipality budgets forecast a surplus of 13 percent on average in the largest cities, but less in Seville and Alicante, to serve as a security fund.

Reform Initiatives and Country-Specific Issues

Since 2018, legal reforms affecting property taxes have been enacted to reduce the effects of rising rental prices for homes and the associated severe lack of affordable housing since the global financial crisis. One of the most recent measures, Royal Decree-Law 7/2019, is designed to improve housing affordability and promote affordable rent by reducing taxes. This legislation includes amendments to the Law regulating Local Treasuries and the Law on the Tax on Property Transfers and Documented Legal Acts (Royal Decree-Law 1/1993).

The most recent tax reforms have affected the transfer tax, stamp duty, and inheritance tax rather than the property tax. The first was set out in Law 11/2021 regarding prevention measures and the fight against tax fraud, which determined, among other changes to the inheritance tax and donation tax, a new property valuation method to find the reference value (closer to the market value) to serve as a new base, which is prepared by the cadastre (Parón Garcia 2022).

Second, a decision by the High Court on October 26, 2021, declared as unconstitutional the tax base of the tax due to calculations made in recessionary periods when property prices diminish. This decision forced the authorities to fully revise the base of this tax by creating a new reference value (calculated by the cadastre) to tax wealth and transactions.

There is also a major ongoing debate about the low level of tax revenues in relation to expenditures, which is a common problem in the EU (European Commission 2020, 6, 35). The Recovery, Transformation and Resilience Plan published in 2021 included two chapters devoted to addressing the need to adapt the tax system to the twenty-first century. The secretary of state for finance initiated the Resolution of April 12, 2021, and a committee of experts was commissioned to draft the White Paper on the Comprehensive Reform of the Tax System, which focused on harmonizing taxes related to the environment, corporations, the digital economy, and wealth. Basically, the expert group discussed the country's low tax collection capacity, especially for VAT and corporate tax, as well as the inadequate income tax base and the existence of tax benefits or exemptions. The opinion of the group of experts is that some taxes, such as wealth and transfer tax, are unfair, especially because they tax property assets that have been previously taxed. Individuals pay taxes on earned income, do it again when they collect the benefits of their investment, and also do so when they die. At the same time, there is taxation for things that have already been taxed, through property tax (IBI) and other taxes. The experts' proposal for property tax is that the cadastral value accommodate the current real estate reality in a dynamic way through a

Table 20.16 Property Tax by Use: Main Variables, 2021

	Madrid		Barcelona	
	Number of Properties	**Total Tax Base Value (€ thousand)**	**Number of Properties**	**Total Tax Base Value (€ thousand**
Total urban	**2,223,638**	**291,361,486**	**1,155,183**	**120,112,01**
% structure by type of use	**%**	**%**	**%**	**%**
Warehouse	25.12	3.92	31.74	4.21
Retail	4.46	8.12	5.03	8.59
Cultural	0.10	3.05	0.18	3.16
Hospitality and leisure	0.35	2.40	0.22	4.69
Industrial	0.54	2.29	0.33	1.03
Sport	0.06	1.26	0.05	0.89
Urban lots	0.62	3.01	0.66	1.80
Offices	1.42	10.27	1.58	7.47
Single buildings	0.02	2.06	0.04	0.86
Religious	0.03	0.49	0.03	0.52
Private buildings for public shows (cinema, theaters, etc.)	0.01	0.27	0.02	0.35
Residential	67.21	61.07	59.99	64.43
Health buildings	0.06	1.80	0.13	2.01
Property Tax Bills Issued				
	Number	**Total Tax Base Value (€ thousand)**	**Number**	**Total Tax Base Valu (€ thousan**
Total urban bills	2,225,550	291,687,217	1,155,950	105,150,23
Total rural bills	3,826	221,129	486	22,114
BICE (infrastructure and equipment) bills	261	4,497,733	130	1,820,558
Tax Collection Amounts Accounted in Local Public Budgets				
Property tax (€)		1,505,120,414		712,976,81
Urban tax (%)		96.54		98.20
Rural tax (%)		0.05		0.00
BICE tax (%)		3.41		1.80

Source: Dirección General del Catastro (n.d.-b).

Note: Italics indicate those use types exempt from property tax.

Valencia		Seville		Alicante	
Number of Properties	Total Tax Base Value (€ thousand)	Number of Properties	Total Tax Base Value (€ thousand)	Number of Properties	Total Tax Base Value (€ thousand)
683,386	**32,183,576**	**484,121**	**23,948,773**	**296,695**	**14,456,876**
%	%	%	%	%	%
31.59	6.87	24.69	4.22	27.49	5.02
5.09	11.50	5.17	9.82	5.78	10.89
0.16	3.25	0.12	3.69	0.06	2.36
0.07	1.79	0.31	3.13	0.10	1.29
0.75	1.78	1.12	4.48	0.81	6.01
0.05	1.04	0.05	1.68	0.24	0.79
0.85	1.98	0.39	2.22	1.82	2.09
1.10	4.96	2.07	6.65	1.21	4.28
0.03	1.79	0.04	2.45	0.02	0.64
0.04	0.41	0.05	0.61	0.03	0.32
0.01	0.64	0.01	0.46	0.00	0.18
60.18	61.64	65.89	58.39	62.36	64.53
0.06	2.34	0.09	2.19	0.07	1.60
Number	**Total Tax Base Value (€ thousand)**	**Number**	**Total Tax Base Value (€ thousand)**	**Number**	**Total Tax Base Value (€ thousand)**
681,084	30,025,326	567,975	23,960,217	33,1684	14,456,876
7,092	28,599	1,243	48,906	3,756	21,991
119	552,948	12	1,856	1,930	189,026
	238,223,000		175,043,561		85,610,152
	96.67		100.00		99.81
	0.05		0.00		0.19
	3.27		0.00		0.00

Table 20.17 City Revenue Sources from the Public Budget, 2022

	Madrid	**Barcelona**	**Valencia**	**Seville**	**Alicante**
Resources: Income					
Total municipal income (€)	5,414,736,464	2,924,909,545	949,586,556	834,036,093	281,834,158
Total tax revenue (€)	2,638,316,747	1,234,396,436	402,240,620	333,641,367	143,716,184
Direct tax (%)	91.78	90.02	90.62	91.20	89.26
Indirect tax (%)	8.22	9.98	9.38	8.80	10.74
Total property tax (urban, rural, and BICE) (€)	1,568,058,859	717,319,690	243,423,000	175,043,561	87,007,000
Property tax in % of total municipal income	28.96	24.52	25.63	20.99	30.87
Property tax in % of total taxes	59.43	58.11	60.52	52.46	60.54
Expenses					
Total (€)	4,723,111,719	2,529,550,568	823,893,498	780,933,891	274,933,427
Chapter I, Personnel (%)	33.31	18.42	39.39	40.66	41.75
Chapter II, Goods and services (%)	45.86	26.69	34.88	17.71	43.43
Chapter III, Financial expenses (%)	2.34	0.62	1.15	1.45	0.10
Chapter IV, Current transfers (%)	16.97	52.31	22.36	40.01	14.15
Chapter V, Contingency funds (%)	1.52	1.96	2.23	0.18	0.57
Income less expenses as a security fund	691,624,745	395,358,976	125,693,058	53,102,202	6,900,731
% of total budget income	12.77	13.52	13.24	6.37	2.45

Sources: Local authorities' budgets; Spanish Treasury.

change in the valuation of the tax base or by allowing lower territorial authorities to perform the valuations. They also propose the possibility of extending the limits of the municipalities to determine the tax rate.

Changes based on these experts' proposal are on the way but, taking into account the large degree of decentralization in Spain, any new measure entering the regional or local arena would come up against constitutional provisions, because the autonomy of local authorities is guaranteed in articles 137 and 140. A wide-ranging debate is expected regarding tax system reform.

Impact

The keys to a modern and adjusted financial system are precise allocation to the taxpayer with the obligation to pay, equity so that the same tax is not levied twice, and efficiency in the collection of tax revenues. Efficiency depends both on allocation and on tax management.

As explained earlier, the mechanisms implemented to manage the property tax, including regulation and technological procedures, are held to quite high standards in Spain, making the system largely efficient in a technical sense. Allocation is less discussed with reference to the property tax, as the land asset is immobile and it is easy to find for tax purposes.[48] On the other hand, capital is mobile, and an increase in property tax rates or the tax on buildings might cause some investors to look for a lower-cost location (OECD [Organisation for Economic Co-operation and Development] 2022).

The structure of property taxes in Spain has a long tradition, but there seems to be a general opinion that it has become outdated.[49] Some argue that it is inequitable in a modern economy, since it generates numerous double taxations that increase the fiscal pressure on the owners of real estate. Revising the system is not an easy task due to the number of regulations and the decentralized system in Spain. The regulatory changes proposed by experts would take some years to be implemented. Moreover, it would require altering the tax system shared across the regions that was established 50 years ago. The aim should be increasing the tax management capacity at the regional and municipal levels, improving the allocation impact, and enabling local authorities to set the tax rate, as well as increasing equity in the property tax system. However, this necessitates significant changes to tax management, which would be difficult to implement.

More equitable property taxation would affect the demand side positively if the reforms could avoid multiple taxes on the same base. There are no estimations of the potential effect that changes to the property tax would have on different uses or development. For instance, the overcharging of property tax (already approved and starting to be implemented by the municipalities) for owners of unoccupied homes would convince landlords to rent the units, mobilizing the real estate sector in the market. However, it is hard to see how the impact would be strong on nonresidential properties. The difficulty of demonstrating when a unit is unoccupied or being used for different purposes by the owner is another key issue hotly debated in the courts, and this is crucial to assessing the success of tax measures.

An OECD report by Slack and Bird (2014) recognized the higher relevance of the property tax when it is managed at a local level. After analyzing several developed countries, the authors concluded that "the future of local property taxation in any country seems highly dependent on the role that local governments are expected (and able) to play" and that "a local property tax reform accompanied by changes in the transfer system[,] . . . as well as perhaps some realignment of functions and finances between levels of government, may be a more promising path to reform than a 'stand-alone' reform effort" (Slack and Bird 2014, 25).

As that report recognizes, Spain is one of the few countries with this tax so fully decentralized, but the recent changes to allow regional and municipal valuation systems would represent a step toward bringing the tax system closer to the realities in the real estate market. The reestimation of the tax base is the central change in the tax, starting with the creation of the new value (not yet for property tax) in 2022.

Progressive taxation is a much-studied issue in the context of Spanish income tax but is largely disregarded in the context of Spanish property taxation. An exception is the study by Figari, Verbist, and Zantomio (2022), who suggest a regressive effect on the bottom decile of taxpayers on income distribution related to housing, meaning that the poorest homeowners bear a property tax burden that is disproportionate to their share of income. While higher-income taxpayers pay more in absolute terms, it is disproportionate to their share of income. Figari and coauthors conclude that property taxes are regressive in the case of Spain (and the least progressive in comparison with other countries), in contrast to the high progressivity of income tax. They argue that the sources of regressivity are the exemptions and the property tax base definition in the cadastral value (Figari, Verbist, and Zantomio 2022, 72).

Using property tax to increase the overall progressivity of the tax system could have poor results in Spain. Due to the ownership structure, in which a large percentage of poor households are homeowners, changes in exemption policies could lead to unwanted impacts on low-income families (Gómez Bengoechea and Quan 2020).

Conclusions

The consideration of changes to taxation in Spain is driven by two issues: the need to adapt the taxation system to the new requirements of the EU economy for modern coordination purposes; and the challenges created by the global financial crisis and the COVID-19 pandemic, which required the government to increase the debt to cover basic needs. As both challenges have affected most EU countries, the regulatory analysis in this context follows general rules to be adapted for the main taxes, although property tax is more difficult to design and manage, primarily owing to local traditions and local characteristics deriving from social idiosyncrasies and heterogeneity.

The way to make property tax both more reflective of the reality and more efficient is by increasing the amount of information and applying new technology for its management. The Spanish cadastres and the property tax management system have been adopting modern technology for the past two decades, increasing the capacity for the identification and collection of tax. However, the tax base estimation is still an aspect whose reform could lead to improvements in the tax system's quality in order to achieve a neutral impact.

Notes

I would like to acknowledge the support of my former student and now an expert on regulation, Daniel Llorens Hernandez, for his explanations of the tax structure, its logic, and management issues.

1. Spanish Institute of Statistics (INE), data for 2021.
2. Data for metropolitan areas come from Eurostat for functional urban areas for 2020. In the case of Madrid, the metropolitan influences exceed the regional limits.
3. There is no information published regarding the proportion of property tax bills that are unpaid.
4. Lifetime right to use a real estate asset.
5. Civil Code, Article 605: "The purpose of the Property Registry is the registration or annotation of the acts and contracts related to the domain and other real rights over real estate"; and Article 607: "[It] will be public for those who have a known interest in ascertaining the status of real estate or property rights recorded or registered."
6. Detailed rules can be found in Ministry of the Presidency, Justice and Relations with the Courts (n.d.).
7. These two regions have had a tax system in line with the state's unified system since the creation of the regional system in the late 1970s.
8. The notary is a semipublic civil servant who must pass exams organized and recognized by the state and who is assigned within a city according to the available notary positions in the geographic network of notarial offices. Notaries have the duty to guide transactions and changes in civil or economic status to make them eligible for the creation of rights.
9. Civil Code, Article 1455, which assigns the notarial deed costs to the seller, while the first and later authorized copies will be paid for by the seller.
10. The 1.1 percent rate is applied to those dwellings with a recently revised cadastral value, while the 2 percent rate is applied to the rest.

11. The deposit is exempt from VAT, as well as parking and other space annexed to the dwelling, if the house is rented as a main home. When the rental is short-term and the landlord is an individual with no activity in the hotel sector, it is also exempt. See Bolétin Oficial del Estado (1992).

12. The VAT shared by regions in Spain is explained in INE (n.d.).

13. As it is possible to declare income tax separately in a household, we do not use the number of households to estimate the scope of the tax.

14. Note that the amount of direct taxes shown in table 20.2 is the sum of income tax, corporate tax, and other direct taxes.

15. The imputed rent is 2 percent of the cadastral value of the property.

16. The figure of 2.1 percent is calculated in this section as the difference between gross rental flows and property expenses per year.

17. Data derived from MITMA statistics.

18. As nonresidents are subject to VAT with few exemptions, the amount collected in income tax refers mainly to the residential sector. The few exemptions (and the estimation of nonmain home dwellings) would affect the larger than 100 percent weights estimated here.

19. Nonbuildable land is exempt. See the Value-Added Tax Law 37/1992 of December 28.

20. The list of activities outside the exemptions can be found in articles 20 and 23b of the Value-Added Tax Law 37/1992.

21. The estimated VAT is based on the number of housing transactions from 2004, the first year when transaction data were available, onward. The calculation estimates 10 percent of the private housing value published in the statistics, although it does not publish the transaction value for public housing, only the number of transactions. The latter has been calculated considering the public value as 20 percent less than the average of the private value and applying 4 percent VAT. The values obtained are lower than the VAT source reports, so the total amount of tax income is adjusted to the difference.

22. For instance, the Madrid region provides a 100 percent tax reduction for the tax payment to residents, thus reducing to zero any result of this tax, although it is compulsory to present the tax liquidation when the taxpayer's wealth is greater than €2 million. See the Royal Decree 1/2010 of October 21.

23. Through a mechanism known as the Inter-Territorial Compensation Fund (Fondos de Compensación Interterritorial).

24. Royal Decree-Law 17/2018 of November 8, which modifies the Ley del Impuesto sobre Transmisiones Patrimoniales y Actos Jurídicos Documentados approved by Royal Decree 1/1993 of September 24.

25. There is no specific methodology outlined for determining administrative values. Assessments seem to be not hedonic based but a combination of cadastral values and the market price evolution.

26. See the Ley de Prevención y Lucha contra el Fraude Fiscal (Law for the Prevention and Fight Against Tax Fraud), Law 11/2021 of July 9, replacing the EU Directive 2016/1164 of July 12, 2016

27. Orden HFP/1104/2021 of October 7 determines a correction factor of 0.9 for the market value in transactions, for both urban and rural real estate. The calculation is based on the analysis of prices declared in the notary documents.

28. See, for example, https://www1.sedecatastro.gob.es/Accesos/SECAccvr.aspx.

29. A landlord who receives the first rent without demanding proof of payment of the PTT becomes the subsidiary responsible for the payment of the tax.

30. In the two-tax approach, income tax is levied on the increase in personal income occurring in one year due to a transaction, while property tax taxes the transaction as a property sale when the ownership change generates a money transfer. Neither property donation nor inheritance involves monetary movement as a countervalue.

31. Per the High Constitutional Court judgment of May 11, 2017.

32. Royal Decree-Law 26/2021 (of November 8) amends the consolidated text of the Law Regulating Local Treasuries, approved by Royal Legislative Decree 2/2004 (of March 5), to comply with Constitutional Court jurisprudence regarding the tax on the increase in value of urban land.

33. That is, tax base = the proportion that represents the cadastral value of the land over the total cadastral value × capital gain obtained in the transaction.

34. The term *cadastre* comes from the Latin word *capitastrum*, or "units registered per capita." Detailed information regarding the cadastre's history can be found in a two-volume work edited by Segura i Mas and Canet Rives (1988).

35. Though historians have uncovered information about the cadastres of the Roman period and those created up to the eighth century in Spain, they are not considered precedents of the modern system. "The land of the Spanish Cadastre will have as its object the determination and representation of territorial property in its various aspects, in order to make it serve effectively for all economic, social, and legal applications, with specialty for the equitable distribution of the land tax, and, as far as possible, for the mobilization of the value of the property" (Article 1). For further details, see Llombart Bosch (1996).

36. The model of *catastro parcelario* was finally chosen for the creation of the cadastres, as opposed to an alternative methodology based on a statistical list of crops, production, and taxpayers known as *amillaramientos*, which was used as a model for the previous cadastres in Spain. The debate on these models was intense during second half of the 19th century (Moreno-Bueno 2008, 34–35).

37. The regulation in which the application is explained is Royal Decree 1020/1993 of June 25, concerning the technical valuation rules for determining the cadastral value.

38. See McGreal and Taltavull de La Paz (2012) for more details about property valuation in Spain.

39. Properties with special characteristics are real estate such as airports, ports, and central rail terminals. See Royal Decree 1464/2007 of November 2 (Agencia Estatal Bolétin Oficial del Estado 2007).

40. See Order HFP/1104/2021, of October 7, https://www.boe.es/diario_boe/txt.php?id=BOE-A-2021-16584.

41. See Ministerio de Hacienda, Dirección General del Catastro, "Procedimiento de regularización catastral," accessed March 3, 2026, www.catastro.hacienda.gob.es.

42. The online procedure for requesting changes can be found at https://www.sedecatastro.gob.es/Accesos/SECAccTramites.aspx.

43. Law 30/1992 of November 26 regarding the legal regime of the public administration and the common administrative procedure

44. Regulated by the Law 22/2009 of December 18th of the common regime to finance the autonomous communities (regions), which was slightly modified by the Law 21/2001 of December 27.

45. See *Papeles de Economia* (2000). This is a full issue devoted to fiscal topics in the Spanish regions.

46. A full explanation of the process is contained in several articles in prominent Spanish journals; see, for instance, "La nueva reforma de la financiación autonómica: Análisis y propuestas," *Papeles de Economía*, no. 143 (2015): v–xv.

47. For more information, see Local Treasury Law at https://www.base.cat/web/_recursos/PDF/Lleis/Llei_hisendes_locals.pdf.

48. This is one of the real estate features commonly covered in most handbooks. See, for instance, chapter 5 of Dasso, Shilling, and Ring (1995).

49. See López-García (2001, 2004) for a discussion of the impact of tax measures on housing prices and debate of the fiscal efficiency of real estate markets.

References

Agencia Estatal Boletín Oficial del Estado. 1987. "Ley del impuesto sobre transmisiones patrimoniales y actos jurídicos documentados." Madrid: AEBOE.

———. 1991. "Ley 19/1991, de 6 de junio, del Impuesto sobre el Patrimonio." BOE no. 136, 7 de junio de 1991. www.boe.es.

———. 1992. "Ley 37/1992, de 28 de diciembre, del Impuesto sobre el Valor Añadido." BOE no. 312, 29 de diciembre de 1992. www.boe.es.

———. 2007. "Real Decreto 1464/2007, de 2 de noviembre, por el que se aprueban las normas técnicas de valoración catastral de los bienes inmuebles de características especiales." BOE no. 278, 20 de noviembre de 2007. www.boe.es.

———. 2021. *Real Decreto-ley 26/2021, de 8 de noviembre, por el que se adapta el texto refundido de la Ley Reguladora de las Haciendas Locales.* BOE no. 268, 9 de noviembre de 2021. www.boe.es.

Agencia Tributaria. n.d. "Informes mensuales de Recaudación Tributaria." Gobierno de España. https://sede.agenciatributaria.gob.es/Sede/datosabiertos/catalogo/hacienda/Informe_mensual_de_Recaudacion_Tributaria.shtml.

Consejo General del Notariado. n.d. Home page. https://www.notariado.org/portal/.

Cuenca, A., and R. Gonzalez. 2015. "Sistema de financiación autonómica y gasto sanitario en España." *Papeles de Economía Española* 143: 65–93. https://web.archive.org/web/20240524132245/https://www.funcas.es/wp-content/uploads/Migracion/Articulos/FUNCAS_PEE/143art06.pdf.

Dasso, J., J. D. Shilling, and A. A. Ring. 1995. *Real Estate.* 12th ed. Englewood Cliffs, NJ: Prentice-Hall.

Dirección General del Catastro. n.d.-a "Catastro topográfico parcelario (Escala 1:5.000) (cartografía catastral rústica 1930–1970)." https://web.archive.org/web/20241105024523/ https://www.catastro.hacienda.gob.es/esp/productos_ficha15.asp.

Dirección General del Catastro. n.d.-b. "Estadísticas catastrales." https://www.catastro.hacienda.gob.es/esp/estadisticas.asp.

Dirección General del Catastro. n.d.-c. "Sede Electrónica del Catastro." https://www.sedecatastro.gob.es/.

Espasa, M. 2015. "La financiación autonómica: Una historia interminable." MQITE Working Paper No. 15-02. Universidad de Alicante. https://web.ua.es/es/dmcte/documentos/qmetwp1502.pdf.

ES Registro. n.d. "¿Qué es el Registro de la Propiedad?" https://www.esregistro.es/registro-de-la-propiedad.

European Commission. 2020. "Commission Staff Working Document: Country Report Spain 2020." Brussels: European Commission. https://eur-lex.europa.eu/legal-content/EN/TXT/?uri=CELEX%3A52020SC0508.

———. n.d. "EU Building Stock Observatory." https://energy.ec.europa.eu/topics/energy-efficiency/energy-efficient-buildings/eu-building-stock-observatory_en.

Figari, F., G. Verbist, and F. Zantomio. 2022. "Homeownership Investment and Tax Neutrality: A Joint Assessment of Income and Property Taxes in Europe." *International Journal of Microsimulation* 15(2): 62–76. https://repository.uantwerpen.be/docman/irua/89f615/ijm_00263.pdf.

Gencat. 2004. "Reial decret legislatiu 2/2004, de 5 de març, pel qual s'aprova el text refós de la Llei reguladora de les hisendes locals." https://portaljuridic.gencat.cat/ca/document-del-pjur/?documentId=898578.

Generalitat Valenciana. n.d. "Cálculo del valor de inmuebles de naturaleza urbana (para devengos entre 01/01/2013 y 31/12/2021)." https://atv.gva.es/es/simulador-bienes-inmuebles-naturaleza-urbana.

Gómez Bengoechea, G., and S. Quan. 2020. "Fiscal Incidence in Spain in 2016." Working Paper 95, CEQ Institute, Tulane University. https://repositorio.comillas.edu/xmlui/bitstream/handle/11531/51272/ceq95.pdf?sequence=1.

Idealista. 2023. "Evolución del precio de la vivienda en venta en España." https://www.idealista.com/sala-de-prensa/informes-precio-vivienda/.

INE (Spanish Institute of Statistics). 2025. "Índice de Precios de la Vivienda en Alquiler (IPVA): Base 2015." https://www.ine.es/dynt3/inebase/es/index.htm?padre=8306&dh=1.

———. n.d. "Nota sobre el indicador de consumo para la distribución territorial del Impuesto sobre el Valor Añadido (IVA) correspondiente al año 2017." https://www.ine.es/daco/daco42/cre00/iciva/nota_calculo_indicador.pdf.

Laborda, J. L., and A. Zabalza. 2015. "A vueltas con la autonomía tributaria." *Papeles de Economía Española* 143: 94–109. https://www.funcas.es/articulos/a-vueltas-con-la-autonomia-tributaria/.

Llombart Bosch, M. J. 1996. "El catastro en España." Monograph. Ministry of Economy and Treasury. https://www.catastro.hacienda.gob.es/documentos/publicaciones/ct/ct28/art1.pdf.

López-García, M. A. 2001. "Tratamiento fiscal de la vivienda y exceso de gravamen." Universidad de La Laguna. https://dialnet.unirioja.es/descarga/articulo/3125541.pdf.

———. 2004. "Housing, Prices and Tax Policy in Spain." *Spanish Economic Review* 6(1): 29–52.

McGreal, S., and P. Taltavull de La Paz. 2012. "An Analysis of Factors Influencing Accuracy in the Valuation of Residential Properties in Spain." *Journal of Property Research* 29(1): 1–24.

Ministry of Finance and Civil Service. 2014. "Informe: Comisión de Expertos para la Reforma del Sistema Tributario Eespañol." Madrid: Ministry of Finance and Civil Service. https://web.archive.org/web/20240810130024/https://www.hacienda.gob.es/es-es/prensa/en%20portada/2014/documents/informe%20expertos.pdf.

———. 2021. *Informe anual de recaudación tributaria 2021.* https://sede.agenciatributaria.gob.es.

———. 2022. *Libro blanco sobre la reforma tributaria.* Madrid: Institute of Fiscal Studies. https://www.ief.es/docs/investigacion/comiteexpertos/LibroBlancoReformaTributaria_2022.pdf.

Ministry of Finance, First Vice-Presidency of the Government. n.d. "Informes sobre la financiación definitiva de las comunidades autónomas a través del sistema de financiación." Madrid: Ministry of Finance. https://web.archive.org/web/20251207133935/https://www.hacienda.gob.es/es-ES/CDI/Paginas/SistemasFinanciacionDeuda/InformacionCCAAs/Informes%20financiacion%20comunidades%20autonomas2.aspx.

Ministry of the Presidency, Justice and Relations with the Courts. n.d. "Registro de la Propiedad." https://www.mjusticia.gob.es/es/ciudadania/registros/propiedad-mercantiles/registro-propiedad.

Moreno-Bueno, T. 2008. "Breve crónica de un siglo de catastro en España (1906–2002)." *CT: Catastro*, no. 63: 31–60. https://oposicionarquitectoshacienda.wordpress.com/wp-content/uploads/2011/02/historia-del-catastro.pdf.

OECD (Organisation for Economic Co-operation and Development). 2022. *Tax Challenges Arising from the Digitalisation of the Economy—Commentary to the Global Anti-Base Erosion Model Rules (Pillar Two): Inclusive Framework on BEPS, OECD/G20 Base Erosion and Profit Shifting Project*. Paris: OECD. https://www.oecd-ilibrary.org/taxation/tax-challenges-arising-from-the-digitalisation-of-the-economy-commentary-to-the-global-anti-base-erosion-model-rules-pillar-two-first-edition_1e0e9cd8-en.

Ortega-Piga, E. 1990. "El impuesto sobre bienes inmuebles: Antecedentes e incidencia en los de naturaleza urbana." Monograph. Spanish Cadastre. https://www.catastro.hacienda.gob.es/documentos/publicaciones/ct/ct1/EL%20IMPUESTO%20SOBRE%20BIENES%20INMUEBLES,%20ANTECEDENTES%20E%20INCIDENCIA%20EN%20LOS%20DE%20NATURALEZA%20URBANA%20Emilio%20Ortega%20Piga.pdf.

Papeles de Economia. 2000. "Corresponsabilidad fiscal." Special issue. Vol. 83. https://www.funcas.es/revista/corresponsabilidad-fiscal-enero-2000/.

———. 2015. "La nueva reforma de la financiación autonómica: Análisis y propuestas." Special issue. Vol. 143. https://www.funcas.es/revista/la-nueva-reforma-de-la-financiacion-autonomica-analisis-y-propuestas-febrero-2015/.

Parón Garcia, G. 2022. "Algunas novedades en la Ley de prevención y lucha contra el fraude fiscal: El valor de referencia y la acumulación de donaciones, contratos y pactos sucesorios." *Revista CESCO de Derecho de Consumo* 41: 33–43. https://doi.org/10.18239/RCDC_2022.41.2957.

Perez, F. 2002. "La financiación del estado autonómico: Una lectura de veinte años de descentralización." https://www.uv.es/~perezgar/publicaciones/organizacionterritorial.pdf.

Property Registry of Spain. n.d.-a. Home page. https://e-registradores.com.

———. n.d.-b. "Registro de la Propiedad." https://www.registradores.org/el-colegio/registro-de-la-propiedad.

Registradores de España. n.d.-a. "Geoportal." https://geoportal.registradores.org/.

———. n.d.-b. Home page. https://sede.registradores.org/site/home.

Segura i Mas, A., and I. Canet Rives, eds. 1988. *El catastro en España*. 2 vols. Madrid: Ministerio de Economia y Hacienda, Centro de Gestión Catastral y Cooperación Tributaria. https://dialnet.unirioja.es/servlet/libro?codigo=377623.

Silvan Mon, N. 2015. "El procedimiento de valoración catastral y su regularización." Universidad Politécnica de Valencia. https://riunet.upv.es/bitstream/handle/10251/54636/Silv%C3%A1n%20Mon%20Noelia_EL%20Procedimiento%20de%20%20valoraci%C3%B3n%20catastral%20y%20su%20regularizaci%C3%B3n_Memoria.pdf?sequence=4.

Slack, E. 2010. "The Property Tax—in Theory and Practice." IMFG Working Paper No. 02. Institute on Municipal Finance and Governance, Munk School of Global Affairs, University of Toronto. https://imfg.munkschool.utoronto.ca/uploads/2/property_tax_paperwithlogos.pdf.

Slack, E., and R. M. Bird. 2014. "The Political Economy of Property Tax Reform." OECD Working Papers on Fiscal Federalism No. 18. Paris: OECD. https://www

.oecd-ilibrary.org/taxation/the-political-economy-of-property-tax-reform_5jz5pzvzv6r7-en.

Taltavull de La Paz, P., and F. Juárez Tárraga. 2015. "Una serie histórica de precios residenciales para España." *Ciudad y Territorio, Estudios Territoriales* 186: 639–656. https://recyt.fecyt.es/index.php/CyTET/article/view/76437.

Vicepresidencia Primera del Gobierno. n.d. "Informes sobre la Financiación Definitiva de las Comunidades Autónomas a través del Sistema de Financiación." https://web.archive.org/web/20260115134650/https://www.hacienda.gob.es/es-ES/CDI/Paginas/SistemasFinanciacionDeuda/InformacionCCAAs/Informes financiacion comunidades autonomas2.aspx.

Zabalza, A. 2014. "Retos actuales de la Hacienda Pública Española." *Papeles de Economía Española* 139: 2–20. https://www.funcas.es/articulos/retos-actuales-de-la-hacienda-publica-espanola/.

Legislation

Civil Code of 1889.

General State Budget Law 47/2003.

General Tax Law 58/2003.

Horizontal Property Law 49/1960.

Inheritance and Donations Tax Law 29/1987.

Law for the Prevention and Fight Against Tax Fraud 11/2021.

Law on the Right to Housing 12/2023.

Law on the Tax Regime of Non-profit Entities and Tax Incentives for Patronage 49/2002.

Local Treasury Law of 1988.

Real Estate Cadastre Law 48/2002.

Royal Decree-Law 1/1993 which approves the Consolidated Text of the Law on the Tax on Property Transfers and Documented Legal Acts.

Royal Decree-Law 1464/2007 approving technical standards of cadastral valuation of real estate with special characteristics.

Royal Decree-Law 6/2012 on urgent measures for the protection of mortgage debtors without resources.

Royal Decree-Law 7/2019 which approves amendments to the Consolidated Text of the Law on the Tax on Property Transfers and Documented Legal Acts 1/1993.

Royal Decree-Law 26/2021 amending the consolidated text of the Law Regulating Local Treasuries 2/2004.

Royal Legislative Decree 1/2004, approving the revised text of the Real Estate Cadastre Law.

Royal Legislative Decree 2/2004 approving the revised text of the Law Regulating Local Treasuries.

Urban Rent Law 29/1994.

Value-Added Tax Law 37/1992.

Wealth Tax Law 19/1991.

21

The United Kingdom: Shouldering a Heavy (Property Tax) Burden?

PEADAR DAVIS, THOMAS MURPHY, MICHAEL MCCORD, AND JOHN MCCORD

The United Kingdom (UK) is a unitary state taking the form of a parliamentary democracy. Parliament is sovereign, under an elected cabinet government led by the prime minister, with a constitutional monarch as head of state. It is made up of four main constituent elements, with England, Wales, and Scotland on the mainland forming Great Britain (GB), along with Northern Ireland (NI) on the island of Ireland. Traditionally, the UK has been a highly centralized nation politically, but this has been less true in recent decades with the devolution of powers, initially to the constituent "countries" of Wales, Scotland, and NI, and more recently to city regions within England. The UK faces ongoing centripetal pressures from active independence movements, most prominently within NI and Scotland. Notably, there is far less pressure for further devolution and no appreciable pressure for any significant fiscal devolution within England, which contains most of the UK population.

Devolved and local government is a complex combination of structures; England's most notable are the Greater London Authority, 10 regional authorities, and 333 local authorities of various forms. Wales has a devolved Welsh Parliament (Senedd Cymru) with 22 single-tier local authorities referred to as counties, Scotland has a devolved Scottish Parliament with 32 local authorities referred to as councils, and NI has a devolved assembly and 11 local authorities referred to as district councils. In terms of fiscal decentralization, local-government expenditures on

Figure 21.1 Public Spending in the UK by Region and Level of Government

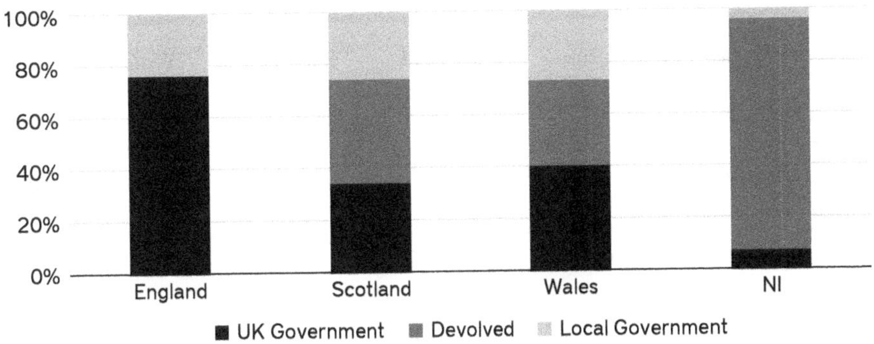

Source: Authors' compilations from Office for National Statistics (ONS 2023).

services account for approximately 21 percent of total government spending in the UK (GOV.UK 2022). Figure 21.1 depicts the regional breakdown of public spending by government level in the UK. As it shows, in Scotland and Wales, the breakdown is similar, with devolved spending largely replacing UK government spending, and the proportion allocated to local government is about the same across England, Scotland, and Wales. The picture is quite different in NI, where there is a much larger role for regional devolved government and a much smaller role for local government, a legacy of reduced local-government responsibilities during the period of political instability known as the Troubles.

In terms of the contribution of recurrent property taxes to local-government finances, table 21.1 depicts the percentage contribution of residential and business property taxes to local-government revenue and expenditure in each UK jurisdiction. As shown, under the devolved NI scenario, property taxes are more significant to local revenues. This is mostly because local authorities have fewer responsibilities than do the GB jurisdictions. Notably, NI property taxes also contribute significantly to the devolved regional budget, with regional domestic and nondomestic rates (levied from the same tax base, in a shared tax demand) providing at least as much revenue, and currently exceeding district rates revenue by approximately 15 percent.

According to the 2021 census, the population of the devolved regions across the UK was 56,490,048 in England, 3,107,494 in Wales, 5,479,900 in Scotland, and 1,903,175 in NI—adding up to the 21st most populated country worldwide. About 83 percent of the UK is urbanized and has a relatively high population density, particularly in South East England and in London, with its population of approximately 9 million.

Table 21.1 The Role of Property Taxes in Local-Government Revenue and Expenditure in UK Jurisdictions

Property Tax Contribution	England	Scotland	Wales	NI
Residential % revenue	21	14	24	36
Commercial % revenue	12	11	12	32
Total % revenue	33	25	36	68
Total % expenditure	47	22	35	65

Source: Authors' compilations from ONS (2023).

The UK is considered a wealthy nation, ranking approximately fifth by gross domestic product (GDP) (International Monetary Fund, n.d.). It has a service-based, postindustrial economy with an annual GDP of US$3.64 trillion and a GDP per capita of US$56,327 (World Bank, n.d.). The economy is anchored by the city of London, which is one of the world's foremost financial centers and a globally integrated economy. Despite friction associated with the UK's decision to leave the European Union in 2016, and postpandemic economic uncertainty, its environment for business is very stable, ranking 11th out of 180 countries in terms of transparency (Transparency International 2022) and 1st out of 89 countries (most transparent) in the Jones Lang LaSalle Global Real Estate Transparency Index Rankings (Jones Lang LaSalle 2024).

The UK's relative durability and stability are well suited to the accumulation of wealth in fixed assets such as real estate and to taxation of that wealth. The UK has an established history of property taxation—on ownership, income, occupation, and transfer. While many aspects of these property-based taxes are similar, England and Wales (which share a legal system) and Scotland and NI (which have distinct legal systems) have certain differences that have been accentuated by devolution's fiscal decentralization and divergence between England and Wales under the devolution of powers to the Welsh Parliament.

In the financial year (FY) 2021–2022, the UK's national tax revenue was £714 billion, representing approximately 30 percent of GDP (ONS 2023). This is the highest percentage of GDP in over 20 years, during which time the revenue has fluctuated narrowly between 25 percent and 30 percent and has fallen midway between revenues of the United States and levels typical of national taxes in continental Europe.

The UK's national taxation figure includes property-based taxes on income, capital gains, transactions, and transfers, either under taxes for individuals or taxes for corporate entities. Overall, the UK raises about

£65 billion in recurrent property taxes levied or administered locally. Of that, approximately 54 percent is levied on residential or domestic property, via devolved forms of council tax (GB) and domestic rates (NI), with the rest levied on nondomestic properties via devolved forms of business rates.

Land and Property Markets

The principles and laws applicable to land and property taxation are broadly similar throughout the UK, but some regional variations arise due to the constitutional framework. The UK has three distinct legal jurisdictions: England and Wales, Scotland, and NI. Each has its own system of courts, with the UK Supreme Court the ultimate appellate court for each. The UK (Westminster) Parliament passes legislation applicable throughout the UK. However, it also passes some laws applicable only in England, because Wales, Scotland, and NI each have their own specific legislatures governing devolved matters. The following discussion will focus on the law in England, which has by far the largest population, noting regional variations if they are relevant.

Tenure, Estates, and Ownership

The concepts of tenure and estates, still utilized to varying degrees in many jurisdictions around the common law world, originate from the feudal system introduced to England by William the Conqueror after 1066 and, in modern times, from a system of taxation based on land ownership. In the original feudal system, the king had absolute sovereignty over all land in the realm and distributed estates in land on tenure to his followers and those who swore allegiance to him. Tenure included an onerous set of obligations—for example, to supply the Crown armed horsemen or agricultural produce—and an estate was the duration for which tenure was granted. Those who had received land directly from the Crown then distributed land to their followers on a similar basis and those people did likewise, thus creating a complex revenue-raising pyramid of land interests with the Crown at its apex.

While the feudal pyramid and its system of taxation have long since disappeared, in England, Wales, and NI, the Crown remains (at least in theory) the ultimate owner of all land, and the concepts of tenure and estates still provide the conceptual framework for ownership rights to land by any other entity (allodial or outright ownership is not possible).[1] This system's practical relevance is limited, so it is generally appreciated only by lawyers and can cause confusion. In common parlance and in practical terms, it is customary to distinguish "owned" property from "rented" property. For example, the Office of National Statistics (ONS) estimated that, in 2020, England contained over 24 million dwellings, of which

- 8.8 million (36 percent) were owned outright;
- 6.8 million (28 percent) were owned with a mortgage or a loan;
- 4.8 million (19 percent) were privately rented; and
- 4.2 million (17 percent) were socially rented, mainly from housing associations and local authorities.

Asserting that someone is the "owner" of land is often shorthand for saying that they are the holder of a fee-simple estate (potentially lasting forever)[2] held on freehold tenure from the Crown. However, the description "owner" may well also encompass the holder of a long lease (for example, of 999 years) held on leasehold tenure directly or (much more likely) indirectly from the Crown and who may well be paying rent. In this context, in a recent House of Commons Library Research Briefing (Wilson 2023, 6) describes trends in the leasehold market as follows:

> There are around 4.98 million leasehold homes in England, of which 70% are flats and 30% are houses. Most flats in the private sector are leasehold (an estimated 94% of owner-occupied flats and 71% of privately rented flats). Around 8% of houses in England are leasehold. Land Registry data tells us more about leasehold sales in England and Wales. 24% of residential property transactions in 2022 were leasehold—around 207,000 transactions in total. Almost all flats are sold on a leasehold basis compared to 7% of houses. The proportion of new-build houses sold as leasehold rose from 7% in 1995 to a peak of 15% in 2016. The proportion has subsequently fallen and was less than 1% in December 2022.

In many respects, drawing a distinction between a freehold and a long leasehold will be irrelevant, as both will last for a very long time. Nevertheless, key differences exist. The vendor of a freehold estate will generally be unable to exercise any control over that land after conveyance, unless the parties have agreed to a restrictive freehold covenant limiting what the purchaser can do with the land or the vendor has reserved an easement such as, typically, a right of way over the land. Enforcement of, in particular, restrictive covenants purporting to bind freehold land has long been difficult, and thus freehold estates are highly problematic in the context of individual units of multioccupancy buildings, in which complex relationships between the occupants must be managed.[3] While a new form of interest, the commonhold, similar to the concept of condominiums in the United States and strata title in Australia, was introduced in 2002 in an attempt to address such issues, its uptake has been very limited (Law Commission 2020). Consequently, in such circumstances, leasehold is the predominant form of tenure.

Leasehold tenure is contractual in nature (rather than feudal in origin). While one party (the landlord) grants the other (the tenant) exclusive possession of land or premises for a term (duration), they can agree to a potentially complex set of agreements about how the lands or premises are to be used; these agreements are generally enforceable not only between the original parties to the lease but also between any successors in title. A lease also best facilitates the short-term use of property, with the tenant paying a rent (sometimes known as a rack or market rent) reflecting the property's capital value, hence the common distinction between renting and owning discussed earlier. However, as already indicated, tenants of property on long-term leases will also often pay rent. Generally, in a long lease, the value of the property will reflect (in whatever proportion the parties agree to) both an up-front (in essence, purchase) premium and a "ground" rent typically payable annually throughout the duration of the lease. In recent years, concerns have arisen over growing exploitation of unwary purchasers who pay apparently modest ground rents on long residential leases. Those rents then, because of a rent review clause, quickly rise onerously and unsustainably and could prevent future sale or (re)mortgaging of the property (Department for Communities and Local Government 2017).

The result has been the Leasehold Reform (Ground Rent) Act 2022, which, subject to some exceptions, will prohibit the charging of ground rent on new residential leases of more than 21 years.[4] But this solution may create a two-tier market in which potential purchasers are unwilling to consider leasehold property to which the new law does not apply. Consequently, the Competition and Markets Authority has been investigating potential misselling and unfair contract terms. Some freeholders and developers have voluntarily agreed to amend rent review clauses, and the Competition and Markets Authority is taking action against others. While this may benefit tenants, investors who lawfully acquired freehold on the basis of projected ground rent returns—at least in part—are liable to feel aggrieved, and further legislation may be required (Thompson-Copsey 2022; Wilson 2023).

Registration of Title to Land and Buildings

Each of the three legal UK jurisdictions has a land register administered by its own land registry. While the three differ in practice, they share the broad approach and principles of registration.

In England and Wales, registration is the responsibility of HM Land Registry,[5] a nonministerial government department. In 2021–2022, HM Land Registry had, according to its annual report and accounts (HM Land Registry 2022a, 7), a total revenue of £318.9 million, which helps underpin the state guarantee that the register is an accurate and complete reflection of the property rights in question (the mirror principle) and that anyone who does suffer loss will be compensated (the insurance principle). In March 2016 the government launched a public consultation on potential privatization of HM Land Registry; however, concerns were raised about potential breaches of data privacy, conflicts of interest, and lack of transparency. Consequently, in 2018, it was ultimately decided that the registry should remain in the public sector (Department for Business, Energy and Industrial Strategy 2018).

In England and Wales, approximately 26 million titles are registered, covering 88 percent of land (HM Land Registry 2022a, 4).[6] Since 1990, a system of compulsory first registration of title has been in operation, requiring (in respect of unregistered land) an application for first registration to be made when a freehold estate or a leasehold estate with more than seven years left to run is transferred, when a lease of more than seven years is granted, or when a mortgage is taken out. Under the Land Registration Act 2002, failure to register in the context of such transactions will render the transfer, grant, or creation void (sections 4, 6, and 7) and, for land that has been registered, subsequent transfers of a registered estate or charge, or the grant of a lease of more than seven years, must be registered for legal title to pass (Section 27). The government's objective is to completely eliminate unregistered titles by 2030 (Ministry of Housing, Communities and Local Government 2017), though no plans currently exist to require compulsory first registration without a relevant transaction. Because an owner's death will trigger registration, unregistered land is increasingly focused on land owned by institutions, if the land has not been bought in recent times and is unmortgaged. The proprietor of a registrable title may, of course, voluntarily apply for registration, and some incentives do encourage voluntary first registration.

In England and Wales, the key legislation is the Land Registration Act 2002.[7] The overarching objectives of that act have been noted by Lord Justice Rimmer in the (English) Court of Appeal case of *Chief Land Registrar v. Franks* [2011] EWCA Civ. 772 at [25] as follows: "The essential purpose . . . is to provide a system of state guaranteed registered title. Subject to exceptions, the register is intended to provide a comprehensive and accurate reflection of the title to registered land at any given time, so that it is possible to investigate title on line with the 'minimum of additional enquiries and inspections.'"

The Land Registration Act 2002 requires the chief registrar to keep a register of title for all freehold estates and all leasehold estates of more than seven years[8] (thus a property may have more than one registered title). The title has its own unique number and file, as well as three constituent elements: the Property Register, which describes the nature of the property, refers to a title plan, and notes any appurtenant beneficial rights such as rights of way to enable access; the Proprietorship Register, which notes the name and address of the proprietor, the nature of their title, and any restrictions on their ability to deal with the land; and the Charges Register, which records notices of the rights of others (such as mortgagees and the owners of neighboring properties) that burden the land.

The system is largely computerized, and anyone can search (or at least initiate a search) online. A basic free search, Title Summary, immediately reveals whether a registered freehold or leasehold title exists, whether there are any easements or restrictive covenants, and (if sold since April 2000) when it was last sold and for how much. If further details are needed, such as the owner's name and address, whether there is a mortgage, and the specific nature of any restrictive covenants or easements, a Title Register or a Title Plan must be purchased for a small fee and will generally be delivered online. Official copies of the register for the purposes of proving title will generally be provided online (if available in electronic format) within seven working days. Subject to some specific exceptions, any person may, as of right, apply to inspect or obtain the following:

- The register of an individual title.
- Any title plan of an individual title.
- Any document referred to in the register.
- Any document not referred to in the register that relates to an application.

For the registration process, automation and digitization are being promoted (HM Land Registry 2017 and 2021),[9] and since November 30, 2022, applications submitted using the HM Land Registry customer portal have been digital by default (HM Land Registry 2022b). Instead of submitting a scan or PDF, customers now directly input application details, capturing the data digitally. A basic goal of the Land Registration Act 2002 was to enable a mandatory electronic system that would remove the "gap" between the conveyance from registered proprietor to transferee and subsequent registration (by HM Land Registry) of the transferee as the new proprietor (Hopkins and Griffin 2018; Owen 2017), by fusing both stages in one simultaneous transaction. Despite the obvious attractions, mandatory electronic conveyancing has yet to be introduced. The issue was reconsidered by a Law Commission report in 2018, which advocated a more gradual approach toward simultaneous completion and registration, but the government has not (yet) acted upon these recommendations.

Issues of contention and consequent litigation are inevitable in a system on the scale of the Land Register, and where errors occur, disputes may arise as to how best to minimize the impact, and also any knock-on consequences that may arise from alteration or rectification of the register. In many such instances, the register is incorrect due to fraud or forgery, and it can be questioned why the state should, in essence, take the blame and bear the burden. The need to provide certainty in the property market continues to be the dominant consideration in that debate.

From the early days of land registration, the goal of a fully comprehensive (mirror) register has been pursued, to minimize the impact on purchasers of interests that are not deemed capable of registration. Thus, for example, the Land Registration Act 1925 introduced the "curtain principle," whereby a purchaser could, by following procedures, avoid worrying about (look "behind the curtain" at) any beneficial entitlements under a trust. Similarly, the law of adverse possession, whereby a squatter can gain title to land by virtue of mere possession, while not abolished, was significantly curtailed by the Land Registration Act 2002. In this context, an enduring criticism of the legal framework, and a significant source of litigation, has been the continued recognition of a group of overriding interests—unregistered interests that override registered dispositions. Key examples are leases of seven years or less and, most significantly, minor interests (such as the right of a spouse or family member) that existed at the time of the registered disposition, the holder of which was in actual occupation of the land or premises and whose occupation would have been obvious upon a reasonably careful inspection of the land. The need for a potential purchaser to make such inspection can be regarded as a significant "crack" in the mirror of title principle (Qingmei 2022; Zilou 2021). The Land Registration Act 2002 reduced the number of overriding interests, and the Law Commission (2018) has subsequently recommended some further streamlining; however, as the interests in question are considered socially and economically significant and registration is considered unreasonable and impractical, no significant change is likely.

Overseas Ownership

Since January 1999, HM Land Registry has required overseas companies acquiring property in England and Wales to identify where they are set up.[10] Since 2016, companies registered in the UK have been required to disclose beneficial ownership in the People with Significant Control Register. Schedule 1A of the Companies Act 2006 provides that this will include anyone who directly or indirectly controls more than 25 percent of shares (or 25 percent of the voting rights) or who has the right, directly or indirectly, to appoint or remove a majority of the board of directors; or has the right to exercise, or actually exercises,[11] significant influence or control over the company. It will also include the trustees of a trust (or members of any unincorporated body) to which the aforementioned conditions apply (GOV.UK 2024a).

Following the Russian invasion of Ukraine, the UK Parliament fast-tracked passage of the Economic Crime (Transparency and Enforcement) Act 2022. This legislation introduced the Register of Overseas Entities, which became operational in August 2022. Any overseas entity acquiring property[12] in the UK has to be registered, has to update the registered details annually, and in the case of companies, has to declare any beneficial owners on the same basis as UK registered companies. Both registers are publicly searchable and are administered by Companies House.[13] The provision of false information to Companies House and failure to comply with these registration requirements are both criminal offenses. Failure to register will also mean that an entity will be unable to register acquisitions with HM Land Registry, and therefore will be unable to legally acquire, dispose of, or enforce a charge over any such property.

The 2022 act also amends the law on unexplained wealth orders introduced by the Criminal Finances Act 2017 and on civil recovery orders introduced under the Proceeds of Crime Act 2002. An unexplained wealth order can be issued by the High Court to anyone who is a politically exposed person or who is reasonably suspected of being involved in, or being connected to someone involved in, serious crime and when the known legitimate sources of income for that person do not explain how they were able to obtain the property (if of a value in excess of £50,000) that they currently hold.[14] Politically exposed persons are, in essence, politicians or public officials from outside the UK and the European Economic Area, members of their families, or those associated with or connected to them.[15] In the event of failure to comply, or failure to provide evidence to explain a legitimate source of funding, the normal burden of proof in civil cases is reversed and a rebuttable presumption arises that the property will be recoverable via civil recovery order without the need for any criminal proceedings. Additionally, the Sanctions and Anti-Money Laundering Act 2018 gives the government wide powers to impose sanctions, such as in compliance with UN obligations, and to accordingly freeze the assets of designated individuals.

Data Sources

In terms of the capture of data from market transactions and its usefulness to the property taxation process, the situation is broadly similar across UK jurisdictions. Property sales, transfers, and leases subject to stamp duty land tax (SDLT) (England, NI); land and buildings transaction tax (LBTT) (Scotland); and land transaction tax (LTT) (Wales) are recorded by HM Land Registry in England and Wales, Registers of Scotland, and the Land Registry section of Land and Property Services in NI. HMRC (2023) reports 76,920 residential transactions in the year to February 2023, which was 18 percent lower than in February 2022. Nonresidential transactions also decreased in the same period, down 7 percent to 8,710 transactions. Details of the transactions are made available to both government and the public via the Price Paid Registry in England and Wales and via a web search tool in Scotland. The information is available but currently less accessible in NI due to the lack of a curated data source or web tool.

In all areas of the UK, the property market is monitored via a variety of private sector and official house price indexes. Within the UK, official property indexes are produced to capture the entire market of transacted properties for each devolved administration. The UK House Price Index (HPI), launched in June 2016 and designated as an official ONS statistic in 2018, applies sales data for all transacted residential properties for full market value, whether for cash or with a mortgage, from HM Land Registry for England and Wales, Registers of Scotland, and Land and Property Services for NI. The construction of the UK HPI amalgamates a range of comprehensive administrative data sources:[16]

- Price data from HM Land Registry for England and Wales, Registers of Scotland, and HMRC; SDLT sales for NI processed by Land and Property Services of NI.
- Information on attributes of data sold from the Valuation Office Agency (VOA), Land and Property Services of NI Valuation List, and Energy Performance Certificates Scotland.
- Demographic characteristics of the area in which the property is located through the Acorn dataset, produced and licensed by CACI (HM Land Registry 2023).

The index is calculated by the ONS using a hedonic regression methodology to provide estimates of the change in house prices for a standardized property with weights used to combine low-level estimates with higher-level aggregates. For the mainland UK (England, Wales, and Scotland), the index is published on a monthly basis, with the data available in England and

Wales since 1995 and in Scotland since 2004. For NI, price change statistics are produced on a quarterly basis (see HM Land Registry 2023) and available since 2005. Overall, for the UK, historical data are available under the historical path of the ONS, which dates back to 1968. The UK HPI dataset contains information (approximately four million triples) on more than 441 areas in England, Scotland, NI, and Wales. The dataset is available in various forms from HM Land Registry, with a version also available that is linked to datasets published by the Ordnance Survey and the ONS. The data collection process follows the Quality Assurance of Administrative Data toolkit, as described by the Office for Statistics Regulation.

While no official indexes exist for the nondomestic market, private sector organizations such as Morgan Stanley Capital International (the leading provider of investment property performance indexes) do monitor the market and publish indexes aggregating individual transaction data in most of the UK's major office, industrial, and retail market areas. The combined effect is that the UK market is well analyzed and is a relatively data-rich environment for the type of property market analysis involved in the operation of property taxes. This helps to mitigate against any significant market manipulation with the aim of reducing tax liability. Reported transaction values are generally considered accurate. While aggressive tax planning does occur, this tends to be in the nature of special purpose vehicles or other liability-mitigation measures, rather than any significant underdeclaration of transaction value.

Real Estate Taxes

National Level

Property Transfer Tax and Stamp Duty

Stamp duty was one of the oldest taxes in the UK. Via the Finance Act 2003, it was replaced by SDLT, which is charged on the purchase of property or land. Under the auspices of fiscal devolution, Scotland now has a separate property transaction tax (the LBTT, from 2015), as does Wales (the LTT, from 2018). All of the versions are charged on the consideration (if a sale), ostensibly on the basis of market value. Leases are also subject to the tax, on the basis of the net present value of the lease payments. Tax returns for all forms are typically made by the solicitor acting on behalf of the buyer, via an online portal. While there are penalties for underdeclaration, including prosecution, there is no widespread experience of underdeclaration, and it is not perceived to be a notable issue in the UK context. Gifts and transfers without consideration generally do not attract these taxes, unless there is outstanding debt transferred also.

In all of the UK jurisdictions, the revenue is retained at the higher level and is not shared with local government. The taxes are similar in that there are different tax rates for residential property and for commercial property. Unlike the preceding stamp duty, which had a "slab" tax rate structure, all of the replacement versions have progressive graduated tax rates, with more expensive properties facing higher tax rates that apply to the part of a property's selling price that falls within a designated value band "slice." The main differences among the three taxes are the value bands adopted, the tax rates applied, and the specifics of the exemptions available.

SDLT in England and NI

SDLT is administered by HMRC. In FY 2021/2022, SDLT raised £14.3 billion (Office for Budget Responsibility 2022). Of this, £10.1 billion was raised from residential property and £4.2 billion was raised from non-residential property. OBR states that this makes up 1.7 percent of all tax receipts and 0.7 percent of national income. For context, it estimates this as £600 per household (Office for Budget Responsibility 2022). In terms of data transparency, HMRC publishes regular SDLT revenue statistics.

SDLT for residential property largely depends upon how many properties are owned and the residency status of the buyer. Commercial SDLT is largely dependent upon the sale price or lease payments. There are a number of reliefs available for identified groups, such as first-time buyers, social landlords, and others for whom full application of the tax would be punitive, such as for compulsory purchases.

Temporary reductions in SDLT in response to economic challenges arising from COVID-19 have been strongly associated with the robust housing market performance witnessed after market restrictions were lifted. These reductions were removed in September 2022, coinciding with the recessionary and inflationary pressures that have since emerged and combined to end strong housing market growth.

The main details of the SDLT tax thresholds and tax rates under the different circumstances are detailed in table 21.2.

LBTT in Scotland

LBTT replaced the UK SDLT in Scotland on April 1, 2015. LBTT is similar to SDLT in that it is administered by Revenue Scotland, with support from Registers of Scotland. Recent changes include an increase in the additional dwelling surcharge rate (charged when a buyer owns another residential property *anywhere in the world*), which was increased to 6 percent in December 2022.

The main details of the LBTT tax thresholds and tax rates under the different circumstances are detailed in table 21.3.

Table 21.2 SDLT Value Bands and Tax Rates, England and NI

Residential Purchase Price (£)	Rate from September 2022 (%)	Rate from 2025 (%)	Commercial Purchase Price (£)	Rate (%)	Lease Rent Payable Net Present Value (£)	Rate (%)
0–125,000	0	0	0–150,000	0	0–150,000	0
125,001–250,000	0	2	150,001–250,000	2	150,001–5 million	1
250,001–925,000	5	5	Over 250,000	5	Over 5 million	2
925,001–1.5 million	10	10				
Above 1.5 million	12	12				
First-time buyers: 0% up to £425,000; 5% for £425,000–£625,000						
3% surcharge for additional homes						
2% surcharge for non-UK residents						

Source: Authors' compilations from HMRC (2024).

Table 21.3 LBTT Value Bands and Tax Rates, Scotland

Residential Purchase Price (£)	Rate (%)	Commercial Purchase Price (£)	Rate (%)	Lease Rent Payable Net Present Value (£)	Rate (%)
Up to 145,000	0	0–150,000	0	Up to 150,00	0
145,001–250,000	2	150,001–250,000	1	150,001–2 million	1
250,001–325,000	5	Over 250,000	5	Over 2 million	2
325,001–750,000	10				
Over 750,000	12				
First-time buyers: 0% up to £175,000					
6% surcharge for additional residential purchases greater than £40,000					

Source: Authors' compilations from Revenue Scotland (2022).

LTT in Wales

LTT replaced SDLT in Wales on April 1, 2018. LTT operates in a way broadly similar to SDLT. The Welsh Revenue Authority collects and manages the tax on behalf of the Welsh Government. Unlike the provisions for SDLT and LBTT, the LTT has a separate value band scale for buyers who have a qualifying interest in another residential property (criteria include that the interest is worth greater than £40,000 and is for a period longer than seven years). Also, unlike in the other jurisdictions, there is no first-time buyer rate in Wales.

One of the peculiarities of Wales is its complex property market interaction with that in England. Scotland's border with England is largely rural, relatively sparsely populated, and clearly delineated. The Welsh border is quite different, with many local property markets straddling it, resulting in the potential for notable market effects from the differential tax rates and value bands employed.

The main details of the LTT tax thresholds and tax rates under the different circumstances are detailed in table 21.4.

The various transfer tax bands and the fundamentals of the property markets in which they operate create a complex pattern of taxation. Table 21.5 depicts the revenue implications according to value band between the regions (reporting bandwidths differ in official sources).

The first item of note is the implications of England and NI sharing a tax band structure. NI's property value profile is generally lower: 46 percent

Table 21.4 LTT Value Bands and Tax Rates, Wales

Residential Purchase Price (£)	Rate (%)	Additional Residential Property (£)	Higher Rate (%)	Commercial Purchase Price (£)	Rate (%)	Net Present Value Lease Rent Payable (£)	Rate (%)
0–225,000	0.0	0–180,000	4.0	0–225,000	0	0–225,000	0
225,001–400,000	6.0	180,001–250,000	8.0	225,001–250,000	1	225,001–2 million	1
400,001–750,000	7.5	250,001–400,000	9.0	250,001–1 million	5	Over 2 million	2
750,001–1.5 million	10.0	400,001–750,000	11.5	Over 1 million	6		
Over 1.5 million	12.0	750,001–1.5 million	14.0				
		Over 1.5 million	16.0				

Source: Authors' compilations from Welsh Revenue Authority (2022).

Table 21.5 Transfer Taxes by Property Value and Region

England and NI Reporting Bands	**£250,000 or Less**	**£250,001–£500,000**	**£500,001–£1 Million**	**£1 Million–£1.5 Million**	**£1.5 Million–£2 Million**	**Over £2 Million**	
England revenue (%)	8	22	29	12	7	22	
NI revenue (%)	46	31	15	8	0	0	
Scotland Reporting Bands	**£0–£145,000**	**£145,001–£250,000**	**£250,001–£325,000**	**£325,001–£750,000**	**£750,001 and Above**		
Scotland revenue (%)	0	7	12	58	23		
Wales Reporting Bands	**Up to £180,000**	**£180,001–£225,000**	**£225,001–£250,000**	**£250,001–£400,000**	**£400,001–£750,000**	**£750,001–£1.5 Million**	**Over £1.5 Million**
Wales revenue (%)	14	6	4	29	33	10	3

Source: Authors' compilation from HMRC (2024).

Table 21.6 Transfer Tax Amounts and Percentage of GDP by Region

Country	Revenue	FY 2019 Revenue (£ million)	2019 % GDP	FY 2022 Revenue (£ million)	2022 % GDP
England	SDLT residential	8,370	0.43	10,105	0.52
Scotland	LBTT residential	354	0.21	573	0.34
Wales	LTT residential	146	0.19	278	0.36
NI	SDLT residential	50	0.10	65	0.13
England	SDLT commercial	3,570	0.18	3,895	0.20
Scotland	LBTT commercial	169	0.10	228	0.13
Wales	LTT commercial	73	0.09	131	0.17
NI	SDLT commercial	30	0.06	35	0.07

Source: Authors' compilations from ONS (2023).

of revenue is derived from the lowest reporting band, as opposed to 8 percent for England, with 77 percent derived from the lowest two bands, in comparison with 30 percent in England. The top three value bands for England represent 41 percent of revenue, as compared with 8 percent for NI. This makes practical sense in a market value context, but it makes less sense when transfer taxes are viewed as wealth taxes, particularly in terms of intra-UK tax equity. The comparison of Wales and Scotland with England is similar but perhaps less stark, partly due to the differing reporting bands. This does highlight limitations to devolution and also the limited or stalled devolution in NI.

It is also possible to examine the outflowing implications in terms of revenue significance of the separate systems. Table 21.6 depicts the revenue significance of the three transfer taxes across the four regions, overall and as a percentage of regional GDP. Clearly, the same system (SDLT) has quite different revenue implications for England (0.61 percent of England's GDP in 2019, 0.72 percent in 2022) and NI (0.16 percent of NI's GDP in 2019, 0.2 percent in 2022). SDLT in NI is a clear low outlier, even between the systems, but England raised roughly double the revenue of the others in terms of the percentage of GDP in 2019, with the gap narrowing, but still significant, in 2022. These differences in incidence are largely opaque, obscured as they are by differences in market value profile and the band structures in place to reflect those differences.

In addition to the various forms of transfer tax and stamp duty, the UK has another tax due on residential property held by nonnatural persons. This is meant to limit the ability to hold high-value residential property in companies, thereby allowing transfer of the beneficial (but not legal) ownership via sale of shares, which are taxed at a much-reduced rate. The need for such measures is evident when considering the practice of transferring high-value commercial property and development land, which invariably occurs via the sale of controlling interest in a special purpose vehicle.

Capital Gains Tax

Unlike in the various versions of stamp duty–based transfer tax, the rules for capital gains tax (CGT) are consistent across all UK jurisdictions, under the Taxation of Chargeable Gains Act 1992. The tax is charged as a separate tax on individuals and as part of the corporation tax mechanisms for corporate entities. In terms of revenue performance, the OBR (2022) estimates CGT revenue to be £15 billion, or 1.5 percent of receipts and 0.6 percent of national income, characterized as approximately £530 per household. The tax is levied on "unearned" capital gains made by the seller on disposal of assets, from the point of purchase or from the base date of April 1, 1982, if the property was acquired before then. The tax is administered by HMRC, with the revenue accruing to the National Treasury. The CGT base is effectively self-declared, via a requirement to report any chargeable disposal within 60 days of the sale. Most reporting now takes place via the online Government Gateway.

The main exemption from CGT is for gains made on the sale of residential property that is the principal private residence of the seller. Failure to report on time incurs interest and penalty charges. Payment can be made via online banking or via more traditional methods.

Tax is paid on gains above a threshold, referred to as the annual exempt amount, which in FY 2021–2022 was £12,300 for individuals and £6,150 for trusts. Once a chargeable gain is established, differential tax rates are applied depending upon the income tax status of the taxpayer. The income tax thresholds used are the thresholds common for England, Wales, and NI. These thresholds are also applied to taxpayers in Scotland, although it has different income tax thresholds, because the income tax is devolved to the Scottish Government. If the income amount is within the basic income tax band, the tax is charged at 10 percent, rising to 18 percent on residential property. Higher rate taxpayers are charged 20 percent, rising to 28 percent on residential property.

This tax calculation effectively assumes market value has been achieved at purchase and disposal. Therefore, if property is disposed of at a lower amount without qualifying as an exempt gift (e.g., to a spouse or to a charity), or where a property was acquired as a gift or inheritance, market value is used to determine the amount of tax due.

There are several relevant reliefs for the disposal of business assets. For periods up to 2017, Retail Price Index–based indexation is available, to

Table 21.7 CGT by Region

Country	FY 2019 Revenue (£ million)	2019 % GDP	FY 2022 Revenue (£ million)	2022 % GDP
England	8,995	0.46	13,427	0.69
Scotland	447	0.26	504	0.30
Wales	163	0.21	223	0.29
NI	125	0.25	160	0.32

Source: Authors' compilations from ONS (2023).

properly reflect the purchase price. Various reliefs that can reduce or delay liability are available to businesses, including business asset disposal relief (for sole traders and partners when they dispose of part or all of their business), at a reduced rate of 10 percent; rollover relief, where business assets are replaced; incorporation or disincorporation relief, when companies are created or wound up; and gift holdover relief, when an asset is gifted.

The CGT revenue breakdown by region in absolute terms and as a percentage of GDP is depicted in table 21.7. As shown, CGT performance is heavily weighted toward England, where it makes up over double the revenue in terms of the percentage of GDP in comparison with the other regions, where it is relatively similar in terms of the percentage of GDP.

According to official sources, 45 percent of UK CGT is incurred on transactions with gains exceeding £5 million, representing less than 1 percent of the reported transactions. Receipts are heavily dominated by London and the South East of England, with over 45 percent of receipts from these areas. CGT from residential property gains in FY 2021 is depicted in table 21.8, which shows that CGT from residential capital gains accounts for approximately 12 percent of total revenue raised.

Inheritance Tax

Like CGT, inheritance tax (IHT) is charged in the same way throughout the UK. It is administered by HMRC, and the income accrues to the National Treasury.

IHT is a significant tax affecting property raising £6.1 billion in FY 2021/2022, a 14 percent increase on the previous year. IHT is levied on the estates of deceased persons above the threshold in place at the time; for FY 2022–2023 this threshold amount was £325,000. Amounts above this threshold are not taxable if left to a spouse, a civil partner, a charity, or certain clubs or societies. Amounts left to children or grandchildren enjoy a threshold of £500,000.

Table 21.8 CGT from Residential Property Gains, FY 2021

Taxpayer Type	Number of Taxpayers (thousand)	Number of Disposals (thousand)	Amount of Gains (£ million)	Amount of Tax (£ million)	% UK GDP
Individuals	127	139	8,041	1,594	0.074
Trusts	2	2	385	105	0.005
All	129	141	8,426	1,699	0.079

Source: HMRC (2022).

Gifts made within seven years of death can be retrospectively included in the deceased person's estate for tax purposes. This can potentially be reduced by taper relief, depending upon how much time has elapsed since the gift was made.[17] Property transferred before death, if the deceased remains in possession, is fully included in the estate (deemed gifts with reservation of benefits), unless a full market rent was charged for the continued occupation.

Any tax due is ordinarily paid by the person dealing with the estate (the executor if there is a will), under probate (if required). Those receiving gifts in the final seven years of life may be required to pay tax, depending on the size and timing of the gift. All amounts subject to the tax are charged at 40 percent on the entire eligible estate.

IHT has garnered focus due to the UK's relatively large rise in house prices relative to small increases in the threshold, gaining it a reputation as a "stealth tax."

The IHT revenue and percentage of GDP for each of the jurisdictions are depicted in table 21.9, which shows that England dominates revenue, both overall and as a GDP percentage.

Value-Added Tax

Value-added tax (VAT) was introduced as part of the accession to the European Union and again, like CGT and IHT, is administered in the same way across the UK, by HMRC. Although the regulations are common, the nature of the transaction and its VAT implications are subject to variation, primarily due to different legal definitions within the legal systems of England, Wales, Scotland, and NI. In all jurisdictions, the revenue accrues to the National Treasury.

The VAT rules for the many forms of property transactions are complex. Sales of residential land and buildings, both newly constructed and at subsequent transfers, and commercial buildings under the same

Table 21.9 IHT Revenue by Percentage of GDP and Region, FY 2022

Country	Revenue (£ million)	% GDP
England	4,230	0.22
Scotland	231	0.14
Wales	97	0.12
NI	42	0.08

Source: ONS (2023).

circumstances are the main aspects that are handled differently. VAT status can be separated into three main categories, exempt, zero rated, and standard rated. With exempt supplies, no VAT is charged on any transactions, so any VAT incurred (e.g., on services rendered) cannot be reclaimed. Zero-rated supplies charge VAT at 0 percent but thereby allow VAT incurred to be reclaimed. Standard-rated supplies incur 20 percent VAT on all transactions.

Existing residential property is exempt from VAT for both property sales and lettings, and VAT costs incurred during refurbishment cannot be reclaimed. A special rule allows vacant property in a poor state of repair for at least two years to be refurbished at a reduced rate of 5 percent. When a newly constructed residential building is sold, the supply is considered to be zero rated, enabling recovery of VAT expended on the construction works. If a newly constructed residential building is let, the exempt status continues, precluding reclamation of input VAT.

Sales and other VATable supplies of newly constructed commercial property for the first three years after completion are considered standard rated. After this period, commercial property is considered exempt, meaning no VAT is charged on supplies (e.g., rent or sale proceeds) or can be recovered (e.g., on professional services rendered). However, an option to tax can be enacted at any time, by charging VAT or informing HMRC of the option to tax. From this point, all supplies, including rent and sales, are subject to VAT at the standard rate of 20 percent, which can have important effects, particularly if significant elements of the occupier and ownership market are VAT-exempt organizations. This includes financial services industries, which sometimes dominate occupation and ownership markets, but for which VAT is a real cost as they do not make use of VATable supplies and thus cannot recover the VAT they pay on rent and purchases. Owners who make the supply can also be dramatically affected, if rental agreements do not allow the recovery of VAT in addition to rent if charged, making the rent received gross of VAT and effectively lowering the net rent by 20 percent.

The main issue with VAT and property in the UK is the complexity of the regulations and the risk for operational missteps, which can have unintended tax consequences.

In terms of revenue from property, HMRC (2023) reports VAT returns for "real estate activities" for FY 2022 as £4.22 billion, an increase from £3.8 billion in FY 2019.

Property Income Tax

Property income in the form of rent is taxed under the income tax regulations for individuals and under corporation tax for incorporated entities. Transaction profits deemed to accrue from "trading" are also subject to income tax under these regulations. Under both regimes, tax is due to be paid on net income after allowable expenses. In the case of corporation tax, income is treated in the same way as other business income.

Individuals receive a £1,000 initial tax-free allowance for property income and are then treated differently if they are determined to be running a property business, in which case they are subject to additional National Insurance contributions. Income exceeding £2,500 after allowable expenses (or £10,000 before allowable expenses) must be reported to HMRC via a Self-Assessment Tax Return. Allowable expenses are slightly different for properties subject to long-term lets and for short-term holiday lets. Short-term let property has increasingly been registered for business rates, as opposed to for council tax, often then avoiding any property tax as the property's ratable value often falls within the ambit of the various small business relief schemes. Consequently, regulations have been updated to extend the minimum period of short-term lettings per annum. This level of reporting allows statistics to be compiled regionally on unincorporated property income tax revenue. Figure 21.2 depicts the regional revenue, clearly showing that income tax from property is heavily concentrated in London and South East England. The latest figures available are from FY 2023, with a reported total of approximately £50.17 billion, a slight increase from the previous year's approximately £49.1 billion.

Recurrent Land and Property Tax

Property taxation at the subnational level in the UK is relatively complex. Recurrent property tax falls into two broad categories, residential and commercial. It can also be distinguished by jurisdiction, with commercial taxation largely consistent across the UK, while residential property

Figure 21.2 Total Property Income Declared by Unincorporated Landlords by Region of Taxpayer Address, 2022–2023

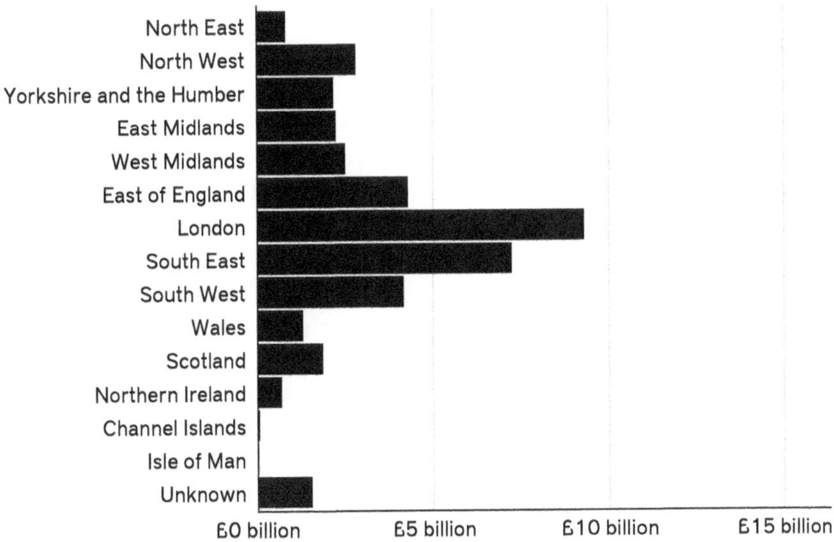

Source: GOV.UK (2024b).

falls into three GB jurisdictions (which are similar), and one in NI, which is quite distinct. In terms of tax rate setting, GB jurisdictions have a certain amount of power to establish their domestic property tax (council tax) revenue potential base via striking the "Band D" reference tax bill against which all other bands are established (see the later section on the council tax in England; increases of more than 5 percent are only possible after a local referendum).

With regard to the nondomestic property tax in GB, the local authorities have no practical role. However, in certain locations, police and crime commissioners and metro mayors can place an additional surcharge on council tax bills and a supplementary charge to business rates, in agreement with the local business community, mainly for infrastructure improvements (Institute for Government 2018). Local authorities can influence their recurrent tax revenues mainly via their collection role, application of discretionary reliefs, and involvement in development and urban regeneration activity to grow the tax base. District councils in NI do have the power to set their own rates for the district rates elements of both domestic and nondomestic rates, though they have considerably reduced mandates compared with those of GB authorities. The more significant responsibilities and thus fiscal role are retained at the regional level, with one overall regional rate established.

Responsibility for Valuation

In England and Wales, the VOA, under HMRC, values property for both council tax and business rates, alongside a range of other valuation services on behalf of the public. The VOA is an executive agency of HMRC, employing over 3,800 staff in 35 offices across England, Wales, and Scotland. It is the largest single employer of qualified valuers in the UK. The VOA produces a wide range of property market statistics, alongside the ONS.

In Scotland, most properties are valued by Scottish assessors. Scottish assessors are independent public officials, but they must join the Scottish Assessors' Association (SAA), an umbrella body, and must be members of the Royal Institution of Chartered Surveyors. Some property continues to be valued by the VOA. The SAA produces a range of statistical analysis and customer services regarding valuation and taxation in Scotland, accessible via its website (SAA, n.d.).

In NI, valuation and management of both domestic and nondomestic rates is carried out by Land and Property Services, part of the Department of Finance of NI, which was created to include progenitor entities the Valuation and Lands Agency, the Land Registry, the Ordnance Survey, and the Rates Collection Agency. This "one-stop shop" for land- and property-related services is in itself innovative and has helped modernize each element to its current status as a data-driven center of excellence for land and property government services. Land and Property Services operates Spatial NI, a geographic information system–based information service focused on rating valuations that puts out publications explaining how the rating values are assessed.

In general, the UK property taxation system is very transparent, with valuation rolls and supplementary information available electronically via official sources.

Residential Property Tax

Residential property taxation is generally a decentralized local-government tax in terms of billing, collection, and revenue allocation, except in NI, where it is shared between local and regional government.

In GB jurisdiction, the recurrent property tax is the council tax. The tax was introduced in 1993 to replace the ill-fated community charge, popularly known as the poll tax, which itself had several years earlier

Table 21.10 Total Dwellings by Region

Region	Total Domestic Dwellings	% of UK Total
England	25,114,150	83.8
Wales	1,462,660	4.9
Scotland	2,562,357	8.6
NI	822,083	2.7
Total	**29,961,250**	**100**

Source: ONS (2023).

replaced domestic rates, an annual rental value–based system (Butler, Adonis, and Travers 1994; Gibson 1994; Smith 1991). The council tax is value based, with a broad capital value band structure that differs in each GB jurisdiction. It is levied on the occupier of the property, under a broad definition that includes the owner if the property is owner occupied or if a separate occupier cannot be determined.

In NI the residential property tax is domestic rating, which is also a capital value-based tax. Unlike the council tax, it is a discrete (individual values) value-based system, resembling other international property taxes, notably those in the United States and Canada. As in those jurisdictions, it is a tax levied on the property owner, not the occupier as is the case elsewhere in the UK. This has historically been true, with the previous domestic rating system (otherwise largely consistent across the UK) also levied on the owner. The domestic rate was subject to reform in 2007, after extensive analysis of the potential implications of moving to a banded system like in GB, as opposed to a discrete value system (as finally adopted).

From a UK-wide perspective, England dominates in residential property tax, given its relative market size. The total number of chargeable residential properties by region and percentage of the UK total are depicted in table 21.10. Despite England's dominance, the devolved nature of residential property tax and its inherently local nature keeps it high profile in all four jurisdictions.

The Council Tax in England, Scotland, and Wales

A banded property tax system (council tax) for domestic property was introduced in GB in 1993 (Department of the Environment 1991). The Department of Environment green paper (1991) laid out the basic underpinnings of the banded system:

- Eight valuation bands (A through H).
- A three-to-one ratio between the bill paid by the highest band (H) and by the lowest (A).
- Band D to represent the reference band to which the tax paid for the other bands is related.
- A system of "ninths" to determine the relevant tax multipliers per band, with Band D representing "nine-ninths," or one.
- A starting point for Band A of "six-ninths," or 0.67.

A key attraction for the government of the council tax was the establishment of a series of value bands developed by reference to the average value of dwellings in the different regions, rendering distinct bands for England, Scotland, and Wales. The council tax system was established in April 1993 and was loosely based on property values as of April 1, 1991. The council tax has another key feature: a single-occupancy discount of 25 percent. Because the bands are relatively broad, large tracts of urban areas can typically fall within the same, or adjoining, bands. When added to the flat nature of the charging mechanism, which does not differentiate liability between bands much, and the fact that in the UK the average number of adult occupants in a household is about two, the discount for one adult occupant makes the council tax very similar to a poll tax. The design is by no means accidental, as this political and technical sleight of hand defused the poll tax tensions by removing its most egregious aspects, with a policy that performed in a similar fashion on a global level.

The banding system finally adopted in GB is depicted in table 21.11. Tax is payable in the proportions on the eight bands A–H. The banding system means that the amount of council tax payable will vary according to the value of the property but within limits. People in the lowest band of property pay about two-thirds what people in the middle bands in that area pay; those in the highest band will pay three times more than those in the lowest band.

A white paper by the Department of the Environment, Transport and the Regions (1998b) stated that the council tax was working well as a local tax, as it had been widely accepted and was generally well understood. Despite considerable criticism of the tax more recently during election campaigns and amid calls for reform or replacement (with some form of local income tax, for example), it still performs well in terms of compliance, with collection percentages in the high 90s for the three GB jurisdictions. For example, in England in FY 2020–2021, 96 percent of council taxes were collected, while the previous five years all reported over

Table 21.11 Original Council Tax Valuation Bands and Multipliers in GB

	Range of Values			
Valuation Band	**Scotland (£)**	**England (£)**	**Wales (original bands) (£)**	**Proportion of Band D Bill Payable**
A	Up to 27,000	Up to 40,000	Up to 30,000	6/9
B	27,001-35,000	40,001-52,000	30,001-39,000	7/9
C	35,001-45,000	52,001-68,000	39,001-51,000	8/9
D	45,001-58,000	68,001-88,000	51,001-66,000	9/9
E	58,001-80,000	88,001-120,000	66,001-90,000	11/9
F	80,001-106,000	120,001-160,000	90,001-120,000	13/9
G	106,001-212,000	160,001-320,000	120,001-240,000	15/9
H	Over 212,000	Over 320,000	Over 240,000	18/9

Source: Authors' compilations from VOA (2016).

97 percent (DLUHC [Department for Levelling Up, Housing and Communities] 2022). In Wales in FY 2021–2022, 99.6 percent of budgeted council tax was collected (Welsh Government 2023). The fairness and equity of the council tax have been increasingly undermined by the lack of an effective revaluation in England and Scotland, as well as by the length of time since the revaluation in Wales.

The creeping reduction in equity was noted by Lyons (2007), who estimated that over 17 percent of taxpayers were paying substantially more than they would in a revalued and reformed system, with most of those affected being in the lower-valued, lower-value bands. The situation has only worsened since 2007.

Table 21.12 depicts the tax bill–setting methodology for a hypothetical jurisdiction of 11,874 properties and a £10 million revenue requirement.

Current Status of the Council Tax

The council tax in England and Scotland has remained relatively unchanged since its inception, without any revaluation or changes to the number or the width of the bands or adjustment of the multiplier system between the bands. This is despite several policy reviews in each jurisdiction (Beecham 2006; Burt Review 2006; Lyons 2007) and considerable academic and press criticism of the tax, particularly due to the vintage of the valuation exercise and the perceived lack of fairness (Jones, Leishman, and Orr 2006; Kenway and Palmer 1999; Longley, Higgs, and Martin 1996). To illustrate the lack of currency of the values, table 21.13

Table 21.12 The Council Tax Bill–Setting Methodology

Identify number of Band D equivalent properties in the jurisdiction
Multiply total number of properties in each band by the band "ninths" ratio

Band	Band Total Property Count	Ninths Ratio	or	Band D Equivalents	Resulting Tax Bills (£)
Band A	800	6/9	0.66	528	479
Band B	1,650	7/9	0.77	1,271	558
Band C	1,702	8/9	0.88	1,498	638
Band D	2,002	9/9	1.00	2,002	725
Band E	1,750	11/9	1.22	2,135	885
Band F	1,602	13/9	1.44	2,307	1,044
Band G	1,503	15/9	1.66	2,495	1,204
Band H	865	18/9	1.80	1,557	1,305
Total properties	11,874	Total Band D equivalents		13,792	
Municipal revenue requirement budget				£10,000,000	
Band D bill calculation		Budget / Band D equivalents		£725	
Each band bill calculation		Band D bill × ninths ratio = Resulting tax bills			

Source: Authors' compilations.

Table 21.13 Value Change and Assessment-to-Sale Ratio, 1991–2023

	UK Average Value	London Average Value
April 1991	£56,853	£75,199
January 2023	£289,818	£533,986
% growth	410	610
Assessment-to-sale ratio (%)	20	14

Source: Authors' compilations from UK House Price Index (n.d.).

Table 21.14 Current Welsh Council Tax Bands and Multipliers

Band	Lower Threshold (£)	Upper Threshold (£)	Ratios 1:3.5
A	0	44,000	0.667
B	44,001	65,000	0.778
C	65,001	91,000	0.889
D	91,001	123,000	1.000
E	123,001	162,000	1.222
F	162,001	223,000	1.444
G	223,001	324,000	1.667
H	324,001	424,000	2.000
I	424,001	Above 424,001	2.333

Source: Authors' compilations from VOA (2016).

depicts the average property value in the UK and in London, at the date of valuation (April 1991) and January 2023. Not only has the value changed considerably, but there has been differential change between areas.

In Scotland, the Council Tax Reform Policy of the Scottish Government (2016) advocated amending the banding ratio in the upper bands to reduce regressivity, but this policy has not been adopted to date.

In Wales, more reform activity has occurred since the system began. The Welsh council tax was reformed and revalued in 2005, with a valuation date in 2003 as opposed to 1991. It was altered with full knowledge of a decade of analysis and criticism. The current Welsh system has nine bands and adopts a 3.5:1 ratio. The bands and multiplier ratios are detailed in table 21.14.

The council tax continues to be reviewed in Wales, with ongoing research into the possibility of rebanding using computer-assisted mass appraisal (CAMA). The goal would be to use CAMA to make individual assessments, with properties then allocated to a band in a banding structure devised to fit the range of values determined. Right now, no live policy exists to deploy such a method, or to move toward a discrete valuation basis like that currently used in NI.

Council tax valuation in England and Wales is undertaken by the VOA for new or modified properties. The VOA carried out approximately 50 percent of the original exercise and the rest was undertaken by private sector firms, which conducted a very limited external inspection amounting to a "drive-by" exercise in a very short time and with a very limited budget. In Scotland, banding was originally and is still carried out by the Scottish assessors.

Performance

The council tax, in all its forms, can be viewed as extremely regressive, particularly in regard to the maximum ratio of tax liability between the lowest tax bill and the highest in any local authority (1:3; 1:3.5 in Wales), in comparison with the market's general range of values, which exceeds 1:8 in capital value terms. It is even more regressive against income, with very poor performance against any metric based on ability to pay. Set against this is the excellent, efficient performance of the tax over many years and its relatively good performance against a benefits principle–based metric. On average, households with similar numbers of adults pay relatively similar taxes on a per capita basis. That said, the passage of time has made the tax, with the same values, increasingly untenable from a fairness and equity perspective.

Given the differential property market changes since 1991, the issue of horizontal equity is significant, as is the built-in vertical equity issue (Jones, Leishman, and Orr 2006; Kenway and Palmer 1996). The technical investigation into the use of cost-effective CAMA approaches to revalue and reband in Wales likely forms a test case for the broader application of CAMA to revalue elsewhere in the UK, as either a new banding exercise or wholesale reform of the tax. The highly political nature of such reform may, however, further delay this type of activity. The council tax has been a political football, with successive governments restricting local governments' capacity to freely set their revenue targets, either with freezes or with limitations to inflation-linked increases. This is against a backdrop of reduced government transfers, resulting in a significant fiscal gap for local governments.

Domestic Rating in NI

NI was not included in the short-lived "poll tax experiment," or its council tax replacement, retaining the domestic rating system based on annual rental values until 2007. By that time, rental values, last reviewed in 1976, had become extremely inaccurate, in absolute and in relative terms. Market areas had performed differentially through several decades marked by economic stagnation and the political and societal upheaval associated with both the Troubles and the transition from an industrial economy. This resulted in considerable disparities in the tax treatment of properties. A further reform challenge related to the basis of the tax. Since the mid-1960s, tenure throughout the UK transitioned from mainly rented to mainly owner occupied, and NI followed this trend. When the dated annual rental values were compared with contemporary capital values, the lack of fairness and equity was stark (DFP 2002; McCluskey, Plimmer, and Connella 1998). The requirement to raise more revenue from the tax base to fund services absolutely required rates reform; eventually the case was made to both revalue and rebase the tax on capital value, better reflecting the pattern of occupation (DFP 2002; McCluskey, Lim, and Davis 2007).

Unlike the council tax, domestic rates are levied on the property owner. A subsequent amendment to the law introduced full rating of vacant properties. This difference in local taxation liability is important to note in any comparative analysis of residential property markets among the UK jurisdictions, particularly in terms of investment rental and yield performance.

Reform brought revaluation of residential properties to capital value using contemporary—and in some ways innovative—CAMA techniques (Gloudemans and Montgomery 2008). The valuation utilized multiple regression analysis and expert valuer–determined market areas. The valuation assumptions include actual external repair (assuming normal repairs and maintenance, and average internal condition), limiting the need for internal inspection of the unsold population of properties. The revaluation became effective in April 2005 and the new system in April 2007.

One controversial new element was a value cap above which additional value would not be taxed. This was initially pegged to the highest council tax liability in GB, above which the tax liability does not increase. This is currently £400,000. While the value cap does not preserve equity and fairness, it is perhaps pragmatic in that it can defuse opposition from the wealthiest property owners—the people best placed to mount the sustained, well-organized protests that have proved so successful in the United States. (In California, such protests have resulted in far more distorted tax systems through Proposition 13 [McGuire 1999], and in Florida through the Save Our Homes Amendment [Allen and Dare 2009].)

The history of direct rule in NI has left a legacy of local authorities' diminished responsibilities for expenditures, with regional bodies responsible for housing, health, education, infrastructure, and other areas,

Table 21.15 NI Domestic Rating Tax Rates (%)

District Council	District Rate	Regional Rate	Total Rate
Antrim and Newtownabbey	0.37	0.46	0.83
Ards and North Down	0.36	0.46	0.82
Armagh City, Banbridge, and Craigavon	0.46	0.46	0.92
Belfast	0.36	0.46	0.81
Causeway Coast and Glens	0.41	0.46	0.87
Derry City and Strabane	0.53	0.46	0.99
Fermanagh and Omagh	0.38	0.46	0.84
Lisburn and Castlereagh	0.33	0.46	0.78
Mid and East Antrim	0.46	0.46	0.91
Mid Ulster	0.35	0.46	0.81
Newry, Mourne, and Down	0.41	0.46	0.87

Source: Authors' compilations

such as regeneration and economic development. The NI Assembly has inherited these functions, which continue to be delivered by centrally administered departments. This structure has required the establishment of a split rate, with one rate set for the centrally delivered functions, which is the same across NI (the regional rate), and one set independently by each of the 11 district councils (the district rate). Table 21.15 details the tax rate structure for FY 2022–2023 for each of the 11 district councils.

The overall revenue performance of the UK's various domestic property tax systems, and their relative performance against GDP, is depicted in table 21.16. In all areas, both the revenue and the performance against GDP increased between 2019 and 2022.

Nonresidential Business Rates or Commercial Property Tax

In all UK jurisdictions, the nonresidential or commercial property tax is known colloquially as business rates and is devolved to the different jurisdictions. Rates in the jurisdictions share many common features, differing mainly in how the tax is administered, the revaluation cycle, the tax rate applied, and the exemptions and reliefs available. In all jurisdictions, the valuation basis is net annual value (NAV), which closely approximates annual rental value under a full repairing and insuring lease (a net rent to the landlord with the tenant paying for all repairs, maintenance, and insurance premiums) for the combined value of the land and buildings.

Table 21.16 Domestic Property Tax Revenue and GDP Percentage by Region

Country	Revenue	FY 2019 Revenue (£ million)	2019 % GDP	FY 2022 Revenue (£ million)	2022 % GDP
England	Council tax	29,293	1.51	33,875	1.75
Scotland	Council tax	2,336	1.37	2,607	1.54
Wales	Council tax	1,573	2.01	1,880	2.41
NI	Domestic rates	730	1.45	791	1.58

Source: ONS (2023).

While the UK legislation does not specify valuation methodology, valuation practice and case law indicate three valuation approaches to arrive at NAV: rental comparison, which should always be used if the rental market is active; profits method, for when no clear rental market exists but the property is operated for profit; and the contractors or cost approach, in which neither situation pertains. For the cost base approach, statutory decapitalization rates are established to generate a NAV from the capital value established.[18] Detailed coverage of the legal and technical basis and operation of the business rates in the UK is provided by Bond and Brown (2017).

The tax is fundamentally a tax on occupation, levied upon the occupier of a "ratable hereditament." Hereditament is defined as "a property that would have a separate entry in the rating list" and is largely delineated via a series of legal cases. The property is valued *rebus sic stantibus*, or "as it stands," which means in its actual condition, assuming normal repairs and maintenance have been conducted. While rating is fundamentally a tax on occupation, there are now rates applied to vacant property after a statutory qualifying period of three months, with the owner deemed the occupier. The tax base includes land occupied with buildings and some qualifying plant and machinery—wind turbines, for example, because their base and mast would be considered ratable, while the turbines themselves would be considered exempt.

The business rates are not applied to properties statutorily defined as nonhereditaments, including agricultural land and buildings and crematoria. A relatively broad array of exemptions and reliefs are deployed on the business rates, differing from jurisdiction to jurisdiction, and some are statutory (particularly in NI), while others are discretionary at the local-government level.

In each jurisdiction, reduction or removal of rate liability is generally similar but with some differences. The basis for exemption and relief in each is as follows.

Reliefs in England:

- Small business rate relief.
- Rural rate relief.
- Charitable rate relief.
- Enterprise zone relief.
- Hardship relief.
- Retail, hospitality, and leisure relief.
- Local newspaper relief.
- COVID-19 additional relief fund.
- Exempted buildings and empty buildings relief.
- Transitional relief if the taxpayer's rates change by more than a certain amount at revaluation.
- Supporting small business relief.

Recent reforms have abolished downward transitional relief. Upward transitional relief remains in place and is actioned depending on the ratable value of the property. The framework for relief is indicated in table 21.17.

Reliefs in Wales (Welsh Government 2025):

- Retail, Leisure, and Hospitality Rates Relief Scheme.
- Small Business Rates Relief Scheme (approximately 70 percent of properties benefit from this scheme, with approximately 50 percent paying no rates).
- Charitable and nonprofit organizations rates relief.
- Relief on empty properties.
- Hardship relief (if the local authority believes that it is in the interests of the local community to do so).
- Upward Transition Scheme.

Recent reforms have abolished downward transitional relief. Upward transitional relief remains in place and is actioned depending on the amount

Table 21.17 Transitional Relief for Tax Bills Increasing After April 1, 2023

Ratable Value	2023–2024	2024–2025	2025–2026
Up to £20,000 (£28,000 in London)	5%	10% plus inflation	25% plus inflation
£20,001 (£28,001 in London) to £100,000	15%	25% plus inflation	40% plus inflation
Over £100,000	30%	40% plus inflation	55% plus inflation

Source: GOV.UK (2023).

Table 21.18 Transitional Relief in Wales

Welsh Upward Transition Scheme
Where Increased Liability Exceeds £300

Year	% of Uplift Paid
Year 1	33
Year 2	66
Year 3	100

Source: Business Wales (2017).

of increase experienced at the revaluation. The framework for relief is indicated in table 21.18.

Reliefs in Scotland (mygov.scot 2025):

- Small Business Bonus Scheme.
- Reliefs for empty or newly reoccupied properties.
- Charitable rate relief.
- Business growth accelerator relief.
- Hardship relief.
- Rural rate relief.
- Disabled persons relief.
- Enterprise areas relief.

- Transitional relief.
- District heating relief.
- Renewable energy generation relief.
- Day nursery relief.
- Telecommunications relief.
- Reverse vending machine relief.

Reliefs in NI (nibusinessinfo.co.uk, n.d.):
Exemptions and reliefs in NI are not discretionary but rather are established under statutory instruments.

- Back in business rate support.
- Small business rate relief.
- Small business rate relief for small post offices.
- Charitable exemption for rates.
- Sports and recreation rate relief.
- Residential homes rate relief.
- Industrial derating.
- Nondomestic vacant rating.
- Hardship rate relief.
- Rural ATM relief.
- Any hereditament that is considered to be altogether of a public nature and is occupied and used for the purposes of the public service.

Various other levies and reliefs have been introduced to limit the rates burden on certain sectors affected by issues such as the pandemic and other economic factors. There is a move toward increased support for traditional retail stores to ameliorate the tax discrepancy between traditional and online retailers, but the major approaches used to assess general economic circumstances are efforts to regularly revalue the tax base and to determine the impact on value of changing economic practices.

There is no rating liability applied to bare development land or derelict property that is deemed to be incapable of beneficial occupation. This is a significant fiscal gap, which has been the subject of numerous policy initiatives over several decades (Wightman 2013) and has been considered most recently in Wales (Welsh Government 2018), Scotland in the Beveridge review (Beveridge, Biberbach, and Hamilton 2016), England in the Barker review (Barker 2006) and Mirrlees review (Adam et al. 2011), and NI (DoF 2016). It has never been successfully addressed, in light of significant pushback from the property industry and landowner interests.

One notable variation pertains to NI, where certain types of industrial property are entitled to industrial derating, which reduces the liability to 30 percent of the full NAV. This was a national scheme originally established at 100 percent exemption intended to aid post–World War II recovery of the industrial base. The relief has been repealed in the GB jurisdictions but has been retained in NI, initially due to the detrimental economic effects of political violence and in recognition that such specific state aid would be impossible to reintroduce under World Trade Organization rules if it were abolished. Eligibility rules are in place, and an extensive case law surrounds the issue.

This system of determining nonhereditaments, exemptions, and reliefs does have an effect on the revenue raised, with a concomitant effect of increasing the liability on those properties within the rating ambit. For example, in NI, reliefs total £226.6 million and are applied to approximately 75% of nondomestic properties. This support represents a value equivalent to 26% of the region's total non domestic rates revenue (Ulster University 2021). In England the combined cost of all reliefs was approximately £4.4 billion in 2019 and rose to approximately £10.5 billion in 2022 (DLUHC 2022). In Scotland, rates relief increased from £684 million in 2017–2018 to approximately £1.4 billion in 2021–2022 (Scottish Government 2023). In Wales in FY 2022, mandatory and discretional reliefs amounted to approximately £387.4 million.

Rate Setting

In the GB jurisdictions, the commercial rates are not truly "local" taxes, being partially administered at a national or regional level.

In England and Wales, business rates multipliers are set annually as a percentage of the ratable value by the central government (for England) and the Welsh and Scottish Governments, respectively. This is effectively the tax rate against the NAV tax base. The multipliers for each region from 2016 to the present are depicted in table 21.19. The policy has been to increase the multipliers in line with inflation, but this has been on hold since the onset of the COVID-19 pandemic and the "cost-of-living crisis" that followed, as the UK witnessed extremely high rates of inflation for the first time in a generation.

Table 21.19 History of the Tax Rate by Region (%)

FY	Wales	Scotland Higher	Scotland Medium	Scotland Lower	England Higher	England Lower
2023/2024	53.5	52.4	51.1	49.8	51.2	49.9
2022/2023	53.5	52.4	51.1	49.8	51.2	49.9
2021/2022	53.5	51.6	50.3	49.0	51.2	49.9
2020/2021	53.5	52.4	51.1	49.8	51.2	49.9
2019/2020	52.6	51.6		49.0	50.4	49.1
2018/2019	51.4	50.6		48.0	49.3	48.0
2017/2018	49.9	49.2		46.6	47.9	46.6
2016/2017	48.6	51.0		48.4	49.7	48.4

Source: Authors' compilations from various official sources.

Local authorities administer the tax, undertaking billing, collection, and enforcement. In Scotland and Wales, the proceeds are remitted to the respective governments. The revenue is then redistributed to the local authorities on a formula based on population and several other needs- and capacity-based metrics.

In England, the situation was the same as for Scotland and Wales until 2013, after which additional revenue identified or created by local authorities' actions, such as regeneration schemes, could be retained under the Business Rates Retention Scheme (BRRS), incentivizing the local authorities in this fashion. By 2017, this had risen to almost 50 percent of rates revenue in some local authorities. Since 2017, the BRRS has been altered to experiment with 100 percent rates retention. The revenue implications of this approach have been investigated by Amin-Smith, Phillips, and Simpson (2018), who identify a number of opportunities and risks, with upside opportunities for wealthier areas and revenue shortfall risks for more deprived areas. The BRRS was intended to be rolled out to 100 percent for all areas in 2018, but this has not occurred, partly due to the end of some pilot schemes and the onset of the COVID-19 pandemic, which perhaps encouraged a risk-averse attitude toward revenue based on business property occupation. In 2021, most councils reverted to 50 percent retention, with the exception of the City Deal devolution locations, which were central to the 100 percent BRRS project and which have retained 100 percent BRRS (DLUHC 2022).

In Scotland, the Scottish Government sets the business rates multipliers for the whole of Scotland, striking three rates based on ratable value level. Scottish local authorities are incentivized to maximize rates revenue, albeit to a lesser extent than in England, under the Business

Table 21.20 NI Nondomestic Rating Tax Rates (%)

District Council	District Rate	Regional Rate	Total Rate
Antrim and Newtownabbey	24.50	27.90	**52.40**
Ards and North Down	24.33	27.90	**52.23**
Armagh City, Banbridge, and Craigavon	26.46	27.90	**54.36**
Belfast	27.20	27.90	**55.10**
Causeway Coast and Glens	26.37	27.90	**54.27**
Derry City and Strabane	32.02	27.90	**59.92**
Fermanagh and Omagh	22.72	27.90	**50.62**
Lisburn and Castlereagh	23.49	27.90	**51.39**
Mid and East Antrim	32.27	27.90	**60.17**
Mid Ulster	24.39	27.90	**52.29**
Newry, Mourne, and Down	24.46	27.90	**52.36**

Source: Authors' compilations.

Rates Incentivisation Scheme. Each local authority has a "buoyancy target" for rates income. If this is exceeded, 50 percent of the excess can be reflected by additional funding through the rates grant (Scottish Government 2023).

In NI, the nondomestic rates follow a similar structure in terms of the tax base and valuation methodologies. The tax rate (rate poundage) follows the pattern of the domestic rates, striking two rates, one regional common rate and 11 distinct district rates. The rates in use in FY 2022–2023 are detailed in table 21.20. The regional rate is struck each year by the Department of Finance to raise the budgeted revenue. The district rates are struck each year by each district council. This is a somewhat complicated process that requires estimation of the collection rate, bad debt write-offs and the revenue loss attributable to the operation of the statutory exemptions, reliefs, and the results of appeals from the current and previous years. All of these factors are dynamic, requiring a certain amount of informed "crystal ball gazing" in setting what is known as the "Penny Product." While it is frowned upon and politically risky, most councils will attempt to incorporate a slight surplus. Nevertheless, the impact of events such as the COVID-19 pandemic are difficult to model within the regular budget and rate-setting framework. The pandemic witnessed considerable regional reliefs for affected sectors, such as hospitality and certain retail, resulting in the requirement for considerable external support from the Department of Finance to maintain revenue levels for the delivery of essential services.

Table 21.21 Nondomestic Property Tax Revenue and Percentage of GDP by Region

Country	FY 2019 Revenue (£ million)	2019 % GDP	FY 2022 Revenue (£ million)	2022 % GDP
England	25,748	1.33	21,752	1.12
Scotland	2,847	1.67	2,108	1.24
Wales	1,001	1.28	1,036	1.33
NI	682	1.35	666	1.33

Source: ONS (2023).

Table 21.21 depicts the overall regional revenue from nondomestic property taxes and performance measured against regional GDP. While the revenue from England dwarfs those from Wales, Scotland, and NI, the revenues from the regions are more significant locally in GDP terms, a situation that has become more pronounced in recent years.

Revaluation

Revaluation in the UK has traditionally been established by legislation within a five-year revaluation cycle (e.g., in England and Wales, the Local Government Finance Act 1988), with efforts made to achieve coterminosity between the different constituent jurisdictions as part of a "harmonization" effort. This has frequently been delayed by events, typically recessions or other sociopolitical disruption. There has been a concerted effort to move toward revaluations once every three years, with all parts of the UK converging with a 2023 revaluation to come into force effective April 2023, using values established around an antecedent valuation date of April 2021 in England, Wales, and NI, and April 2022 in Scotland.

Table 21.22 depicts the pattern of nondomestic revaluations in GB and NI. It can be seen that despite good intentions, revaluing at a common date has proved unachievable until recently. This has been the result of oft-cited "circumstances" such as the financial crisis in 2008, and the policy decisions flowing from that. Failure to revalue at a common date does carry its own complications, particularly with the valuation of large-scale linear infrastructure, such as the telecoms network, which has a value base that covers the entire UK and which must all be valued in order to extract any geography-based proportion.

Table 21.22 Pattern of Nondomestic Revaluations

NI	1957	n.a.	1976	n.a.	1997	n.a.	2003	2010	2015	2020	2023
GB	1956	1963	1973	1990	1995	2000	2005	n.a.	2017	n.a.	2023

Source: Authors.

Note: n.a. = not applicable.

Valuation Approach

Business rates valuation can be described as a process of computer-aided valuation. Taxpayers are required by law to complete and return very detailed questionnaires, which seek to identify all valuation-significant features and all relevant transactional evidence. "Bulk" property types, such as shops and offices, are valued against "standard" property types in valuation zones, with differences from the standard property accounted for via a series of adjustments. More specialist property types, such as infrastructure, petrol filling stations and oil refineries, and leisure properties, are valued using valuation schemes that are frequently developed with input from industry, to maximize acceptance and minimize objections, while retaining accuracy, fairness, and impartiality in respect of the entire property roll.

In all parts of the UK, valuation is carried out by highly technically skilled professional valuers, almost exclusively qualified members of the Royal Institution of Chartered Surveyors, drawing upon extensive market evidence. The evidence is a combination of details of property characteristics and lease agreements reported via legally required self-declarations by owners and occupiers of let premises, as well as close monitoring of market transactions as they occur and later, to fully understand the state of the market at the valuation date. The ability to require occupiers to furnish comprehensive data on value-significant physical, legal, and economic property characteristics, and the established practice of compliance with this, is a major advantage of the UK property tax system. Government valuers liaise closely with market participants and carry out revaluation exercises with a high degree of skill and accuracy, with NAVs being as close to the market rental value as practicable. Of course, certain issues will always remain up for debate, and these are generally dealt with via the objection and appeals system, with a view to achieving accuracy and fairness in the rating list.

Once a revaluation has become established and the bulk of initial objections have been settled, future additions or objections are valued against the "tone of the list," with regard to properties on the list in the same state and circumstances as the property in question, rather than against primary market evidence. This works to maintain fairness and equity between properties existing at the time of the revaluation and later additions. Wholesale rebasing to, for example, properly reflect the changing value relationship between sectors, such as retail, industrial, and leisure, and also between different locations, is dealt with by revaluation. In this context, the delays, cancellations, and other causes of long periods without revaluation can be seen as a major friction in the operation of the tax system. This is particularly true in times of market dynamism and given the high tax burden carried by the rating system in the UK. This can result in some sectors and some locations carrying an excessive burden, and it can also result in significant burden redistribution at the eventual revaluation. While this restores fairness and equity, it may not be bearable by the businesses in the location seeing sharp increases. The rental base of the system also has a significant effect on incidence, when compared against the capital value of the property. Different sectors and different locations have varying capitalization rates applied in the market, and these rates are dynamic. Therefore, the flat rate on rent can result in a varying and dynamic effective rate of tax when measured against capital value.

In terms of the technological support for valuations, the VOA has conducted a deep reform of its technical processes and technology through its Business Systems Transformation initiative, transitioning from a number of outdated systems to a new digital one in an effort to transform into "a more flexible, efficient and agile organization" (InRule 2023, 1). The process has addressed people, customers, compliance, policy, processes, and data. The VOA also launched a digital transformation initiative "to replace outdated and end-of-life core IT systems to improve resilience" (InRule 2023, 1). This mirrors technology improvements in the Land and Property Services in NI and in the operations of the Scottish assessors. In technology terms, public valuation in the UK can be viewed as appropriately supported.

Valuation Objections and Appeals

Valuation objections and appeals are handled differently between the jurisdictions. In England (and Wales from April 1, 2023), there is a system of check and challenge, accessed via an online Business Rates Valuation Account and a Government Gateway user ID. The initial process is a check with the VOA, largely aimed at discovering factual inaccuracies in the subject property. If the matter is not satisfactorily resolved, the next stage is a formal challenge to the VOA. Further challenge is via an appeal to the Independent Valuation Tribunal Service. A subsequent appeal can be made to the Lands Tribunal, which is the final arbiter on points of fact and value. Further recourse to the courts can be made on points of law only.

Before 2023, the process in Scotland was broadly similar, with an initial review by the local assessor and a right to appeal to a local valuation committee. Further recourse was available on points of law to the Lands Valuation Appeals Court, and onward potentially to the UK Supreme Court. Coinciding with the 2023 revaluation, a new process was introduced. Appeals are now referred to as proposals and must be submitted within four months of the valuation date. Proposals must include a statement of the perceived issue and must be accompanied by comparable evidence and detailed reasons why the assessed value is incorrect. Furthermore, the Scottish assessors may reject the proposal if they believe that it does not meet the statutory standard. This is perceived to be a more onerous process for the appellant. It seems likely that aspects of the new system will be subject to challenge as the implications of the change are manifested in response to the new valuation list.

In NI, there is an opportunity for an informal objection, again largely to confirm details, followed by an initial appeal to the commissioner of valuation. Further appeals are made to the Northern Ireland Valuation Tribunal (for properties with a NAV less than £12,500) or to the Lands Tribunal, which are the final arbiters on matters of fact and value. Further recourse to the courts can be made on points of law only.

Major Issues

The predominant issue of concern with business rates in the UK is the high rates applied, which are among the highest, if not the highest, effective property tax rates in the world, at approximately 50 percent of rent, equating to between 2 and 5 percent annually in capital value terms (Lyons 2007). This fact drives the majority of the controversy in terms of business rating, resulting in frequent calls for reform, most recently in Scotland under the auspices of the Barclay review (Scottish Government 2017) and in England under the "Business Rates Review" (HM Treasury 2021). Fundamentally, these reviews indicate a desire to reduce the burden of business rates over time and to introduce more regular revaluations. There is a general acceptance that there is no significant alternative to the continued use of business rates that provides a comparable revenue potential and that does not present equivalent economic challenges. The latest manifestation of business rates reform is included in a nondomestic rates bill currently being considered by Parliament that seeks to

- support more frequent revaluations;

- deliver administrative reform to facilitate efficiency, support more frequent revaluations, and provide more transparency to ratepayers, including support for the Digitalizing Business Rates Program, which seeks to improve targeting of reliefs and increase compliance;
- support decarbonization by introducing a relief for low-carbon heat networks and a 12-month rates holiday on qualifying improvements;
- remove downward transition and removal of the requirement for revenue neutrality to support this; and
- replace the Retail Price Index with the Consumer Price Index as the measure of inflation for annual increases in the multiplier.

While these reforms are widely supported, they do not address the fundamental concerns of industry commentators, who continue to identify the overall tax burden as the most significant issue with the current system, an opinion that prevails across all four jurisdictions.

The reform proposals in England also appear to place additional legal and financial reporting obligations on ratepayers, including those in receipt of 100 percent exemption, which could be viewed as onerous, without necessarily supporting additional revenue (Webber and Allen 2023).

While the high tax burden is generally cited as a disincentive to business, it is most notably seen as a significant cost burden on retail, hampering the ability of brick-and-mortar retailers to compete with online retailers (Greenhalgh, Johnson, and Huntley 2019). This is an issue everywhere, but the high property tax burden in the UK is seen as a significant factor. Online retailers are subject to the tax on their occupation of warehouses and distribution centers, but they do not incur an equivalent tax burden at the point of sale. This has resulted in a range of actions to support retail but no overall reduction delivered via the rating system itself. A number of short-term, piecemeal reliefs have been introduced to ameliorate the pressure on retail, but the main approach to dealing with this remains revaluation, with the 2023 rating list in England showing an average reduction in retail valuations of approximately 10 percent and warehouses and distribution centers increasing by 27 percent on average. While this does rebalance the tax burden toward online activity, traditional retailers also use these facilities.

Calls for a significant reduction in liability, potentially funded by the introduction of a considerable online sales tax, are not currently deemed viable, although this remains a policy aspiration in many quarters, along with considerable political opposition support for the abolition of business rates entirely. Set against these calls is the argument that such a move would lead to a considerable capture of the forgone tax revenue by landlords, who would seek higher rents, and the absence of any viable, proven, efficient alternative. This point was made by Lyons (2007), who noted that enterprise zones (business incentive areas) with reduced business rates had witnessed increased rents, capturing most, if not all, of the benefit for the landlord.

The 2023 revaluation addressed one particularly unpopular aspect in the removal of downward transition, where properties due a reduction would have this phased in, to offset the revenue loss of upward transition for those with liability increases, which were similarly phased in.

Despite the criticism, business rates perform extremely well in terms of revenue generation, with high levels of collection. In FY 2021 the collection rate in England, for example, was 93 percent, but it had exceeded 98 percent in each of the previous five years (DLUHC 2022).

Property Tax in the Capital City, London

Table 21.23 depicts the key statistics for the capital city of the UK, London. The city in many ways dominates the economic life of the UK. Given the high level of urbanization in the UK, it is clear that property taxes are a heavily urban phenomenon.

Conclusion

Property taxation has a long history in the UK across all of the constituent jurisdictions. The various property taxes place a considerable burden on both household and business budgets. Indeed, the UK is at the very top end in revenue from its taxes on property.

In terms of residential property, recurrent property taxes have performed extremely well, raising considerable revenues despite extended periods of policy inaction, a situation that has led to tax bases that are universally agreed to be out of date, to greater or lesser extents, and also perhaps, in the case of council tax, outmoded. There is no doubt that the UK has the professional expertise, technology, and market maturity to modernize the recurrent property taxes, in line with international best practice.

Indeed, the system of domestic rates in NI is very close to best practice, lacking only a revaluation (and consideration regarding the valuation cap). The vital ingredient that is perhaps missing in each of the jurisdictions of the UK is the political will to begin such a monumental task as reform, in the face of considerable taxpayer (and voter) antipathy toward property taxes. The very bluntness of the council tax in GB lends it a degree of legitimacy, retaining as it does a considerable element of a service charge for local services. The extreme length of time elapsed since the last revaluation in all of the GB jurisdictions promises, or perhaps threatens,

Table 21.23 Property Tax in the UK's Capital City

City (name and population)	London Population: 9,648,000			
Number of taxable properties		**2020**	**2021**	**2022**
	Retail stock	91,590	92,260	91,980
	Office stock	108,930	110,120	109,770
	Industrial stock	50,050	50,680	50,780
	Other commercial	74,100	72,180	71,790
	Residential stock	3,679,910	3,713,460	3,749,970
	Total stock	**4,004,580**	**4,038,700**	**4,074,290**
	Council tax stock by type			
	Bungalow	57,500		
	Flat/maisonette	2,113,160		
	Terraced house	939,420		
	Semidetached house	466,910		
	Detached house	132,290		
	Annex	3,070		
	Caravan / houseboat / mobile home	2,630		
	Unknown	35,000		
Basis of the property tax	• Residential–banded capital value (council tax) • Commercial–annual ratable (Rental) value (ARV) (business rates)			
Total value of the tax base		**2020**	**2021**	**2022**
	Retail ratable value	£4,644,594,000	£4,611,893,000	£4,542,546,000
	Office ratable value	£9,062,197,000	£8,980,515,000	£8,822,352,000
	Industrial ratable value	£1,745,937,000	£1,735,003,000	£1,725,327,000
	Other ratable value	£4,843,522,000	£4,831,081,000	£4,835,453,000
	Total ratable value	**£20,296,251,000**	**£20,158,492,000**	**£19,925,678,000**

	Council tax stock by band			
	A	144,580		
	B	491,480		
	C	1,013,180		
	D	954,210		
	E	569,930		
	F	288,660		
	G	220,130		
	H	66,340		
Exempt properties	• Are these properties valued?–Yes			
Valuation	• Valuation undertaken by the VOA • High percentage of Royal Institution of Chartered Surveyors–qualified valuers			
Revaluations	• Most recent revaluation: commercial, April 1, 2023 (previous April 1, 2017); residential, April 1, 1993 • VOA undertakes valuations and revaluations			
Collection data		**2020**	**2021**	**2022**
	Rates revenue	£25,565,978,000	£14,299,520,000	£21,209,356,000
	Rates collection rate	98%	92%	94%
	Council tax revenue	£31,577,732,000	£32,176,246,000	£34,583,678,000
	Council tax collection rate	96%	94%	94%
City revenue sources	• Complex structure of London boroughs and Greater London Authority			
Property tax as a %	• Of total own source revenue: 72% • Of tax revenue: 29%			
Role of the property tax	• How the revenue is spent: general expenditure–not hypothecated[1] • Can be used as security for borrowing			

Source: Authors' compilation from various official sources.

[1] Hypothecated indicates earmarked revenue to be spent on specific activities.

considerable redistribution of the tax burden. While this is likely to create more "winners" than "losers," it raises the specter of public dissatisfaction and organized opposition (from the more vocal losers). As a result, council tax reform and revaluation seem likely to remain on the "too difficult" list, at least until the UK weathers the aftereffects of BREXIT, the COVID-19 pandemic, the cost-of-living crisis that has followed, and the concomitant political uncertainty that has seen regime change at a rate unprecedented in recent decades.

Commercial property taxation is under the spotlight like never before. Despite performing extremely well in fiscal terms and despite a currently successful revaluation across the UK jurisdictions, the business rates have drawn constant criticism from the business community regarding the level of the rates charged. It is a peculiarity of the structure of the rates that the effective burden rises as values fall (in between revaluations), accentuating the perceived burden. Calls for significant reform have crystallized into a Labour Party Manifesto pledge to abolish business rates, should they be elected. This pledge is not backed up by firm suggestions of alternatives, and indeed there is no consensus on how the revenue from business rates could be adequately replaced, and no official investigation into the subject has recommended replacement. It thus seems likely that the business rates will continue in largely their current form for some time to come.

Postscript Updates, January 2025

The Economic Crime and Corporate Transparency Bill was given royal assent on October 26, 2023, and is now law.

The Non-Domestic Rating Act 2023 received royal assent on October 26, 2023. The act implemented various changes to the system known as business rates in England and Wales. One key change was to reduce the revaluation cycle for business rates in England from five years to three years. The act introduced a limited relief on certain qualifying works of improvement to occupied (but not vacant) buildings, conferring 12 months' relief from completion. The act also made a number of procedural changes designed to clarify the reliefs system (particularly for long-term vacant properties) and to improve information provision and exchange between the rating authority and the taxpayer. Most, if not all, of these changes were well anticipated due to extensive preimplementation consultation.

In November 2024 the incoming Labour Government published the Non-Domestic Rating (Multipliers and Private Schools) Bill. This contains draft legislation to bring in higher nondomestic rating multipliers in England for large businesses and lower multipliers for retail, hospitality, and leisure businesses. It also proposes the removal of charitable relief for private schools (mirroring the introduction of VAT on private school fees). The actual size of these changes is not yet finalized. The autumn 2024 budget also included a discussion paper titled "Transforming Business Rates," which is now open for consultation and responses, with a relatively wide remit in terms of business process modernization and stakeholder engagement.

Notes

1. In Scotland, as part of a program of law reform, feudal tenure has been abolished and interests in (formerly) feudal estates are now simply known as ownership. A similar approach has been advocated (but not implemented) in NI.

2. A fee-simple freehold estate can continue forever, unless the current holder dies intestate and no one can be identified to inherit for the purposes of the law of intestacy. In that event, the right to possession of the land will revert to the Crown and tenure will end.

3. Lenders will typically refuse to offer loans secured on a freehold estate relating to an individual unit within a multistory building. For a discussion of the issues, see the case of *Hickland v. McKeone* [2018] NIQB 81.

4. Not yet fully in force at the time of writing (December 2022).

5. In Scotland, the equivalent is Registers of Scotland, a nonministerial department of the Scottish Government, and in NI the Land Registry is administered by Land and Property Services within the Department of Finance of the Northern Ireland Executive.

6. In Scotland, Registers of Scotland aimed for 88 percent of a functionally complete Land Register by March 2023 with 85 percent land mass coverage by March 2023 and over 90 percent by December 2024 (Registers of Scotland 2022, 4).

7. In Scotland, the key legislation is the Land Registration (Scotland) Act 2012, and in NI it is the Land Registration Act (Northern Ireland) 1970.

8. And also, less commonly, any rent charge, franchise, or profit à prendre in gross: Section 2 of the Land Registration Act 2002.

9. In NI, the Department of Finance is currently considering tenders to create a new digital registration system (Northern Ireland Department of Finance 2022).

10. Since 2014 in Scotland.

11. Such as where shares are held by a nominee. This situation is also specifically addressed by paragraph 19 of Schedule 1A to the Companies Act 2006 and by paragraph 19 of Schedule 2 to the Economic Crime (Transparency and Enforcement) Act 2022. A share held by a nominee for another will be treated as though the shares were held by the true owner.

12. The act has retrospective effect in this context and applies to any acquisition after January 1, 1999 (December 8, 2014, in Scotland).

13. In December 2022, additional legislation, the Economic Crime and Corporate Transparency Bill, was being considered by Parliament. This legislation would inter alia seek, through the provision of new powers and responsibilities, to give Companies House a more active gatekeeper role in regulating company creation.

14. Under Section 362 of the Proceeds of Crime Act 2002, this will encompass cases in which the property is held through a trust or some corporate structure, including a company registered outside the UK.

15. Section 362B of the Proceeds of Crime Act 2002. For a discussion, see *National Crime Agency v. A* [2018] EWHC 2534 (Admin).

16. For a full discussion, see HM Land Registry (2023).

17. "Taper relief" reduces tax liability based on the duration of asset ownership.

18. Decapitalization rates are used to convert a capital sum into an annual sum. For example the capital cost of a building can be converted into an annual rental cost by applying the decapitalization rate.

References

Adam, S., T. Besley, R. Blundell, S. Bond, R. Chote, M. Gammie, P. Johnson, J. Mirrlees, G. Myles, and J. M. Poterba. 2011. *Tax by Design*. Oxford: Oxford University Press. https://ifs.org.uk/books/tax-design.

Allen, M. T., and W. H. Dare. 2009. "Changes in Property Tax Progressivity for Florida Homeowners After the 'Save Our Homes Amendment.'" *Journal of Real Estate Research* 31(1): 81–92.

Amin-Smith, N., D. Phillips, and P. Simpson. 2018. "100% Business Rate Retention Pilots: What Can Be Learnt and at What Cost?" IFS Briefing Note BN233. London: Institute for Fiscal Studies. https://ifs.org.uk/sites/default/files/output_url_files/BN233.pdf.

Barker, K. 2006. "Barker Review of Land Use Planning: Final Report Recommendations." https://assets.publishing.service.gov.uk/media/5a7c35b6ed915d76e2ebbd10/0118404857.pdf.

Beecham, J. 2006. "Beyond Boundaries: Citizen-Centred Local Services for Wales." Review of Local Service Delivery: Report to the Welsh Assembly Government. Welsh Assembly Government Cardiff.

Beveridge, C., P. Biberbach, and J. Hamilton. 2016. *Empowering Planning to Deliver Great Places*. Edinburgh: Scottish Government. https://tinyurl.com/54y9wyzz.

Bond, P. H., and P. K. Brown. 2017. *Rating Valuation: Principles and Practice*. Abingdon: Routledge.

Burt Review. 2006. "A Fairer Way." Report by the Local Government Finance Review Committee." LGRFC Edinburgh.

Business Wales. 2017. "Business Rates in Wales." https://businesswales.gov.wales/topics-and-guidance/business-tax-rates-and-premises/business-rates-wales.

Butler, D., A. Adonis, and T. Travers. 1994. *Failure in British Government: The Politics of the Poll Tax*. Oxford: Oxford University Press.

Department for Business, Energy and Industrial Strategy. 2018. *HM Land Registry: Moving Operations to the Private Sector—Consultation Response*. https://www.gov.uk/government/consultations/land-registry-moving-operations-to-the-private-sector.

Department for Communities and Local Government. 2017. *Tackling Unfair Practices in the Leasehold Market—a Consultation*. https://assets.publishing.service.gov.uk/media/5a82d4c1e5274a2e8ab5991f/Tackling_unfair_practices_in_the_leasehold_market.pdf.

DFP (Department of Finance and Personnel). 2002. *Review of Rating Policy: A Consultation Paper*. Northern Ireland: Department of Finance and Personnel.

DoF (Department of Finance). 2016. "A Rates Rethink—Consultation." https://www.finance-ni.gov.uk/sites/default/files/consultations/dfp/Rates%20Rethink%20Consultation%20paper%20%28full%20document%2C%2055%20pages%29.pdf.

———. 2022. "Land and Property Services: Data Available Online." https://www.finance-ni.gov.uk/articles/land-property-services-lps-data-available-online.

Department of the Environment. 1991. *The New Tax for Local Government: A Consultation Paper*. London: Department of the Environment.

Department of the Environment, Transport and the Regions. 1998a. *Modern Local Government: In Touch with the People.* London: DETR.

———. "1998b. Modernising Local Government: Improving Local Financial Accountability." London: DETR.

DLUHC (Department for Levelling Up, Housing and Communities). 2022. *Main Non-Domestic Rating Account 2021–22.* https://assets.publishing.service.gov.uk/government/uploads/system/uploads/attachment_data/file/1091970/MNDRA_21-22.pdf.

Gibson, J. G. 1994. "Voter Reaction to Tax Change: The Case of the Poll Tax 1." *Applied Economics* 26(9): 877–884.

Gloudemans, R. J., and E. Montgomery 2008. "Domestic Revaluation in Northern Ireland." *Journal of Property Tax Assessment and Administration* 5(4): 17–31.

GOV.UK. 2022. "Public Spending Statistics: July 2022." July 21, 2022. https://www.gov.uk/government/statistics/public-spending-statistics-release-july-2022/public-spending-statistics-july-2022.

———. 2023. "Business Rates Relief: Transitional Relief." https://www.gov.uk/apply-for-business-rate-relief/transitional-relief.

———. 2024a. "Economic Crime and Corporate Transparency Act: Beneficial Ownership." Updated March 1. https://www.gov.uk/government/publications/economic-crime-and-corporate-transparency-act-2023-factsheets.

———. 2024b. "Official Statistics: Property Rental Income Statistics." https://www.gov.uk/government/statistics/property-rental-income-statistics/property-rental-income-statistics-2024.

Greenhalgh, P. M., L. Johnson, and V. Huntley. 2019. "An Investigation of the Impact of 2017 Business Rates Revaluation on Independent High Street Retailers in the North of England." *Journal of Property Investment and Finance* 37(3): 241–254.

HM Land Registry. 2017. *Business Strategy 2017 to 2022.* https://assets.publishing.service.gov.uk/media/5a82c94040f0b6230269cb16/HM_Land_Registry_Business_strategy_2017_to_2022.pdf.

———. 2021. *Business Plan 2021–24.* https://assets.publishing.service.gov.uk/media/6113d14f8fa8f506cbee533b/HM-Land-Registry-Business-Plan-2021-2024.pdf.

———. 2022a. "Annual Reports and Accounts 2021–22." https://assets.publishing.service.gov.uk/media/62f1084de90e071435aa478e/Annual-Report-and-Accounts-HM-Land-Registry-2021-22-web_2___1_.pdf.

———. 2022b. "HM Land Registry Marks the First Major Milestone in Fulfilling Automation Ambitions." Press Release. November 30. https://www.gov.uk/government/news/hm-land-registry-marks-the-first-major-milestone-in-fulfilling-automation-ambitions.

———. 2023. "About the UK House Price Index." https://www.gov.uk/government/publications/about-the-uk-house-price-index/about-the-uk-house-price-index.

HMRC (HM Revenue and Customs). 2022. "Capital Gains Tax Statistics." https://www.gov.uk/government/statistics/capital-gains-tax-statistics.

———. 2023. "Value Added Tax (VAT) Annual Statistics." https://www.gov.uk/government/statistics/value-added-tax-vat-annual-statistics.

———. 2024. "UK Stamp Tax Statistics." https://www.gov.uk/government/statistics/uk-stamp-tax-statistics.

HM Treasury. 2021. "Business Rates Review." https://assets.publishing.service.gov.uk/media/6177dda98fa8f52982a861ea/BRR_final.pdf.

Hopkins, N., and J. Griffin. 2018. "Updating the Land Registration Act 2002." *Conveyancer and Property Lawyer* 3: 207–212.

InRule. 2023. "Using New Technology for Valuation: How InRule Is Putting the VOA in Control of Valuation Logic." HMRC Case Study. https://inrule.com/wp-media/resources/casestudies/CaseStudy_Gov_VOA-HMRC.pdf.

Institute for Government. 2018. "Tax and Devolution." https://www.instituteforgovernment.org.uk/explainer/tax-and-devolution.

International Monetary Fund. n.d. "GDP, Current Prices." Accessed March 4, 2026. https://www.imf.org/external/datamapper/NGDPD@WEO/OEMDC/ADVEC/WEOWORLD.

Jones Lang LaSalle. 2024. "The Global Real Estate Transparency Index 2024." https://www.jll.co.uk/en/trends-and-insights/research/global-real-estate-transparency-index/greti-global-rankings-and-methodology.

Jones, C., C. Leishman, and M. Orr. 2006. "The Potential Impact of Reforms to the Essential Parameters of the Council Tax." *Fiscal Studies* 27: 205–229.

Kenway, P., and G. Palmer. 1999. "Council Tax: The Case For Reform." London: New Policy Institute.

Law Commission. 2018. *Updating the Land Registration Act 2002*. Report No. 380. London: Law Commission. https://webarchive.nationalarchives.gov.uk/ukgwa/20250109142155mp_/https://cloud-platform-e218f50a4812967ba1215eaecede923f.s3.amazonaws.com/uploads/sites/30/2018/07/Updating-Land-Registration-final_WEB_230718.pdf.

———. 2020. *Reinvigorating Commonhold: The Alternative to Leasehold Ownership*. Report No. 394. London: Law Commission. https://assets.publishing.service.gov.uk/media/61b9f00dd3bf7f05522e302d/Commonhold-Report-final-N14.pdf.

Longley, P., G. Higgs, and D. Martin. 1996. "The Rates Revisited? A Geographical Reassignment of Property Valuations and Local Tax Burdens Under the Council Tax." *Environment and Planning C: Government and Policy* 14: 101–129.

Lyons, M. 2007. *Lyons Inquiry into Local Government: Place-Shaping, a Shared Ambition for the Future of Local Government*. London: Stationery Office. https://assets.publishing.service.gov.uk/media/5a7c093540f0b645ba3c64cb/9780119898545.pdf.

McCluskey, W. J., F. Plimmer, and O. Connella. 1998. "Ad Valorem Property Tax: Issues of Fairness and Equity." *Assessors Journal* 5(3): 47–55.

McCluskey, W., L.-C. Lim, and P. Davis. 2007. "Brownfield Development Land Tax Assessment of Revenue Potential: An Initial Investigative Scoping Study." University of Ulster: School of the Built Environment.

McGuire, T. J. 1999. "Proposition 13 and Its Offspring: For Good or Evil." *National Tax Journal* 52(1): 129–138.

Ministry of Housing, Communities and Local Government. 2017. *Fixing Our Broken Housing Market*. Cm 9352. London: Her Majesty's Stationery Office. https://assets.publishing.service.gov.uk/media/5a7f355f40f0b6230268e1a5/Fixing_our_broken_housing_market_-_print_ready_version.pdf.

mygov.scot. 2025. "Non-Domestic Rates Relief: Overview." Last updated April 1. https://www.mygov.scot/non-domestic-rates-relief.

nibusinessinfo.co.uk. n.d. "Help Available for Business Rates." Accessed June 25, 2025. https://www.nibusinessinfo.co.uk/content/help-available-business-rates.

Northern Ireland Department of Finance. 2022. "Improving Land Registers NI." https://www.finance-ni.gov.uk/topics/improving-land-registers-ni.

Office for Budget Responsibility. 2022. "Public Finance Databank 2022." https://obr.uk/publications/?_keywords=public%20finance%20databank%202022.

ONS (Office for National Statistics). 2022. "Subnational Estimates of Dwellings and Households by Tenure, England: 2020." January 31. https://www.ons.gov.uk/peoplepopulationandcommunity/housing/articles/researchoutputssubnationaldwellingstockbytenureestimatesengland2012to2015/2020.

———. 2023. "Country and Regional Public Sector Finances Revenue Tables." https://www.ons.gov.uk/economy/governmentpublicsectorandtaxes/publicsectorfinance/datasets/countryandregionalpublicsectorfinancesrevenuetables.

Owen, G. 2017. "Priorities and Registered Land During the Registration Gap: Baker v Craggs [2016] EWHC 3250 (Ch)." *Conveyancer and Property Lawyer* 3: 230–241.

Qingmei, D. 2022. "Can Overriding Interests and the Crack on the Mirror Principle Be Reconciled?" *Coventry Law Journal* 27: 157–160.

Registers of Scotland. 2022. "Corporate Plan 2022–2027." https://www.ros.gov.uk/__data/assets/pdf_file/0007/209437/Corporate-plan-2022.pdf.

Revenue Scotland. 2022. *Annual Report and Accounts 2021–22—Devolved Taxes Accounts.* https://revenue.scot/news-publications/publications/corporate-documents/annual-report-accounts-2021-22-devolved-taxes.

SAA (Scottish Assessors' Association). n.d. Home page. Accessed June 25, 2025. https://www.saa.gov.uk/.

Scottish Government. 2016. *Council Tax Reform.* Edinburgh: Scottish Government. https://web.archive.org/web/20160811200944/http://news.scotland.gov.uk/News/Council-tax-reform-2347.aspx.

Scottish Government. 2017. *Report of the Barclay Review of Non-Domestic Rates.* https://www.gov.scot/binaries/content/documents/govscot/publications/independent-report/2017/08/report-barclay-review-non-domestic-rates/documents/00523643-pdf/00523643-pdf/govscot%3Adocument/00523643.pdf.

———. 2023. *Scottish Local Government Finance Statistics 2021–22*. Edinburgh: APS Group Scotland. https://tinyurl.com/c6ayer97.

Smith, P. 1991. "Lessons from the British Poll Tax Disaster." *National Tax Journal* 44(4): 421–436.

Thompson-Copsey, S. 2022. "The Leasehold Reform (Ground Rent) Act 2022." *Landlord and Tenant Review* 26: 50–53.

Transparency International. 2022. "Corruption Perceptions Index." https://www.transparency.org/en/cpi/2022.

UK House Price Index. n.d. "Compare UKHPI Statistics Across Locations." Accessed June 25, 2025. https://landregistry.data.gov.uk/app/ukhpi/compare?from=1991-01-01&in=avg&location[]=K02000001&location[]=E12000007&st=all&to=2023-01-01&lang=en.

Ulster University. 2021. "Non-Domestic Rates: UUEPC Evidence Paper for Committee of Finance." Accessed June 25, 2025. https://www.ulster.ac.uk/epc/pdf/2021/review-of-non-domestic-rates-and-covid-19-recovery/UUEPC-Evidence-paper-Review-of-Non-Domestic-Rates-June-2021-Final.pdf.

VOA (Valuation Office Agency). 2016. "How Domestic Properties Are Assessed for Council Tax Bands." https://www.gov.uk/guidance/understand-how-council-tax-bands-are-assessed.

Webber, J., and R. Allen. 2023. "Why the New Non-Domestic Rates Bill Won't Solve the Business Rates Question." Colliers, April 3. https://www.colliers.com/en-gb/news/05-04-23-why-the-new-non-domestic-rates-bill-wont-solve-the-business-rates-question.

Welsh Government. 2018. "Welsh Tax Policy Report 2018." https://www.gov.wales/sites/default/files/publications/2018-10/welsh-tax-policy-report-2018.pdf.

———. 2023. "In Year Council Tax, by Billing Authority." StatsWales. https://statswales.gov.wales/Catalogue/Local-Government/Finance/Council-Tax/Collection/inyearcounciltax-by-billingauthority.

———. 2025. "Business Rates in Wales." Business Wales. https://businesswales.gov.wales/business-rates-wales.

Welsh Revenue Authority. 2022. "Changes to Main Residential Rates and Bands for Land Transaction Tax." https://www.gov.wales/changes-rates-and-bands-land-transaction-tax-october-2022.

Wightman, A. 2013. "A Land Value Tax for England: Fair, Efficient, Sustainable." Report commissioned by Caroline Lucas. https://commongroundorwa.org/LVT_england_final.pdf.

Wilson, W. 2023. "Leasehold and Commonhold Reform." House of Commons Library Research Briefing CBP08047, December 22.

World Bank. n.d. World Bank Open Data Databank United Kingdom. Accessed June 25, 2025. https://data.worldbank.org/indicator/NY.GDP.MKTP.CD?locations=GB.

Zilou, F. 2021. "An Analysis of Land Registration and Overriding Interests." *Coventry Law Journal* 26: 130–135.

Legislation

Companies Act 2006.

Criminal Finances Act 2017.

Economic Crime (Transparency and Enforcement) Act 2022.

Finance Act 2003.

Land Registration Act 1929.

Land Registration Act 2002.

Land Registration (Scotland) Act 2012.

Land Registration Act (Northern Ireland) 1970.

Leasehold Reform (Ground Rent) Act 2022.

Local Government Finance Act 1988.

Non-Domestic Rating Act 2023.

Proceeds of Crime Act 2002.

Sanctions and Anti-Money Laundering Act 2018.

Taxation of Chargeable Gains Act 1992.

22

Technology and Methodologies for Valuation

LUC HERMANS, RUUD KATHMANN, AND MARCO KUIJPER

The property tax assessment industry is, and has always been, subject to change. The primary goal of this chapter is to provide insight into these developments. While a broad spectrum of changes will be addressed, it is not possible to cover all. The chapter elaborates on five major developments: advances in real property data, the transparency of market data, automated valuation modeling techniques, quality control for automated valuation models, and communication.

Real Property Data

Automated Change Detection

Automated change detection is a developing technique in real property data collection. The principle is to compare an input dataset at a given time with a similar input dataset at another time. Using machine learning algorithms, changes within the dataset will be identified and filtered. Typically, these input datasets are aerial photographs. However, the technique can also be used on (digital) large-scale maps, digital surface models, digital elevation models, and point cloud data (Charalabos, Psaltis, and Potsiou 2009; Heywood, Cornelius, and Carter 2005).

Automated change detection has proved to be especially useful in identifying (small) buildings or alterations that are placed without the necessity of a building permit, such as solar panels, swimming pools, and small standalone garages. The technique can also be used to identify small improvements or alterations in real estate. For instance, it has been successful in identifying roofs that have been replaced due to asbestos contamination. Similarly, recently placed roof dormers can easily be identified using automated change detection.

The use of machine learning algorithms has made this technique much more effective. Changes in vegetation, for instance, are filtered out automatically, and changes in parked vehicles will not result in a detected change relevant for the updating of property data.

Automated Data Interpretation

Automated data interpretation is used to collect data from written documents or photographs—for instance, real estate listings on the internet. Automated data interpretation scrapes the information of interest from the listing and collects it in a useful format to be used in the real estate assessment practice. This approach is highly effective if a market has one or a few central platforms that are used for real estate listings. If the information is too scattered, this technique will be harder to implement due to the inconsistency of listing setups from platform to platform. Another possible downside is that real estate listings are less necessary to make a sale in a highly pressurized real estate market. This can result in real estate listings that lack detailed or verified information, or even in the absence of a listing for a given property if the sale was completed before the realtor could create an online listing. It should be noted that the legality of scraping is dependent on the context and the legal framework of the country it is exploited in. Therefore, the technique should be used prudently and only after conducting a test of legality.

Like the technique of automated change detection, the extraction of information from text in a listing also takes advantage of the developments in artificial intelligence (AI) and machine learning. Using these developments, it also becomes possible to extract information that is not to the letter in the text. For instance, a poor maintenance condition is usually not mentioned directly in the text of a listing. But using the text, and sometimes also the presented photographs, it is often possible for these algorithms to give a rating of the maintenance condition of the property.

Automated data interpretation can also be used for extracting object characteristics from photographs—for instance, collecting information on the facilities of a residential property from the pictures that are part of the real estate listing. Extracting characteristics from aerial photography is also possible—for example, to pinpoint all properties with solar panels on the roof, including sorting by the size and type of these panels.

Additionally, automated data interpretation can be combined with other techniques such as georeferencing and 3D city modeling. Tools have been developed that create low-quality 3D city models for given properties based on their location, building permits, and building layouts.

The developments in collecting 3D information using laser scanning and extracting information from 3D models are growing rapidly. In research settings, it is already possible to automatically generate a 3D model of a property's interior with the use of scanners. This model can then be used to automatically measure floor area and other characteristics within the property. We expect that, within a few years, these techniques will also be available for use in assessment practice.

Open-Source Data Availability

The first two techniques presented in this section aid in the collection of data specifically for assessment purposes. In recent years, governments and other organizations have been creating a growing number of data platforms designed to distribute open-source datasets. The central premise is that data, once collected, can be a driver for companies and governmental organizations to better their practices (Welle Donker, van Loenen, and Bregt 2016). When organizations share data that are not affected by the General Data Protection Regulation (GDPR), the costs of collecting data drop significantly. This data availability can lead to lower initial costs for start-up companies and the implementation of new techniques such as automated change detection by already-existing organizations.

Currently, open-source data platforms are widely available. These are typically run by organizations with broad data infrastructures such as national cadastral offices and national statistics bureaus. The main challenges in providing data concern interoperability and findability. For use in valuation models, geographic information system techniques help to convert data into useful information—for instance, on the distance or traveling time from a certain property to schools or shopping districts.

The quality and completeness of the data must be given special consideration. When data used for assessment do not align with the actual situation of the property assessed, extra costs and loss of trust in the system may result. Thus, when using an open-source dataset, it is essential to evaluate the metadata with regard to quality and the date of collection.

Transparency of Market Data

Transparency of Real Estate Listings

Real estate listings should be considered an important information source for the valuer in addition to the sales price. Advertisements include characteristics and photos of the objects for sale in combination with the list prices. These data are a crucial addition to the market data sourced from the official sales registers.

In all European countries, advertisements for the supply of real estate properties are presented on websites that are intended to be used easily by potential buyers. These listings also benefit valuers, allowing them to look inside the property and collect up-to-date data on maintenance of the property without necessitating onsite visits or questionnaires. Online listings offer several other benefits to the valuer:

- The list price gives the valuer insight into the market. Of course, the asking prices that are shown in real estate listings do not necessarily reflect the market value of real estate properties, but they can play a role in the valuation process, especially when compared with the sales price. In addition, changes in the market will be evident earlier in the asking prices than in the sales prices, because sales prices are typically only available from the moment the property is transferred to the buyer.
- The length of the period between the first advertisement on the internet and the actual date of sale is important market information.
- The listed property characteristics can help the valuer keep the property registration up to date.

Valuers should thus use the data from real estate listings in a systematic way. However, as soon as a property is sold, the information on these websites usually becomes unavailable online. For that reason, the valuation industry should develop tools to systematically collect, register, and store the information that is presented in real estate listings. For privacy reasons (per GDPR), these systems may only be used by organizations responsible for the formal assessment of real estate.

Transparency of Sales Price Data

The availability of sales price data is crucial for the valuation process. That is why we argue that, for a well-functioning property tax system, selling prices should be

- actual;
- easily accessible (for the appraiser as well as for the taxpayer);
- reliable; and
- complete.

If one of these conditions is not met, actions must be taken. For instance, if a transfer tax with relatively high rates is applicable, this can indicate that certain amounts of money are being paid "privately" by the buyer to the seller. In that case, the officially registered amount of money does not reflect the price paid and thus the market value, and it is therefore less useful for the appraiser. An example of a well-functioning system of sales price data transparency is outlined in box 22.1.

For a transparent real estate market, which has many benefits, sales price data must be freely available not only to the valuer but also to the public. For property tax purposes, this will give taxpayers an instrument to verify the assessed value.

Transparency of Rent Price Data for Commercial Real Estate

For commercial real estate like office space and shops, we cannot only use sales transactions for valuation because of the limited availability of

Box 22.1 The Netherlands' Cadastre, Land Registry and Mapping Agency

The Netherlands' Cadastre, Land Registry and Mapping Agency collects and registers administrative and spatial data on property and the rights involved. Cadastral information is available predominantly through online web services.

It is the responsibility of the Netherlands' cadastre to maintain a central database containing all real estate properties, including all transactions that have taken place regarding those properties. So, when the ownership right of a certain property is transferred from one person to another, this transaction, including the sales price, is registered, in a central database. This database is a part of the system of key registers, which contains the most important governmental information in the Netherlands. All key registers are connected. Through this system of key registers, municipalities are connected to the cadastral database, which means that they receive records of all real estate transactions that have taken place on a daily basis.

This information is publicly available in the Netherlands; however, one has to pay for these data, so the goal of ensuring transparency of the market as part of a transparent tax system is not met entirely.

information on these transactions. Therefore, rental transactions must be considered as well. In most countries, the data on rental transactions are much less transparent than those on sales transactions, as there is no official registry of rental transactions and thus no organized source of data on them.

Consequently, private valuers, as well as the government agencies responsible for the assessment and taxation of real estate, have to collect market data on rental transactions themselves. For instance, these data can be collected by asking owners and users of such properties for their rental contracts. The obtained rental prices and other information in the contracts can be used for the formal assessment. But in most countries, the valuer or government agency is not allowed to share these collected data with other organizations because of privacy regulations. This also limits the possibility to show such market data on a valuation report and therefore limits the transparency of the tax system.

Transparency of Building Cost Data

For the valuation of nonmarketable, nonresidential real estate, the replacement cost method is often used for assessment and taxation. Important factors in this approach are the estimation of building costs and the land value. Location is a primary factor in the land's valuation. Building costs are less affected by location. This means that the building cost data can, in most cases, be collected systematically on a national level.

For rental transactions, we have seen that private valuers, as well as government agencies, have to collect market data. The same is true for building cost data. In general, these are less interesting for private valuers, but they are particularly of interest for building companies and companies specialized in making building cost estimates.

Creating a building cost database for the most common categories of nonmarketable, nonresidential real estate, such as schools, hospitals, and sports facilities, can be important to establish a base for key figures, such as the building cost per square meter for a small modern school building with 10 classrooms.

The actual building costs of newly built properties cannot be shared between organizations. However, the key figures on building costs used by government agencies and used by building companies for calculating building costs can be compared in order to improve the quality of the key figures, but also to improve transparency (key figures may be published) and trust in the assessment.

Developments in Automated Valuation Modeling Techniques

Machine Learning Models

The wider availability of computers, improved computing power, and open-source software have led to the creation and increased accessibility of statistical approaches to make automated valuation models for real estate assessment. Traditionally, such models have been based on general linear model (GLM) regression or multiple regression analysis approaches. Since the early 1990s, AI-based approaches have been studied with various levels of success. Early studies on the use of these approaches find that their traditional counterparts produce better results (Beimer and Francke 2019; Lenk, Worzala, and Silva 1997). However, later studies have found that the AI-based approaches do outperform their traditional counterparts (Beimer and Francke 2019; Kok, Koponen, and Martinez-Barbosa 2017).

One of the main shortcomings of AI-based approaches is that they are affected by the black-box problem, a phenomenon in which the influence of an independent input variable is hard or impossible to explain in a meaningful way, which thereby limits the explainability of real estate assessments made with these methods.

Gloudemans and Sanderson (2021) identify four AI-based approaches that are adaptive learning methods. These methods—classification and regression trees, random forests, neural networks, and gradient boosting methods—have been demonstrated to be superior to traditional approaches. However, they are all affected by the black-box problem, which limits their use for property tax purposes (Gloudemans and Sanderson 2021).

Spatially Aware Models

Comparative studies of AI-based approaches and traditional GLM-based approaches tend to overlook spatially aware models. Various spatially aware models exist, most notably the spatial error model, the spatial lag model, and geographically weighted regression. These spatially aware models allow for the adjustment of independent variable coefficients over space. Spatially aware models can thus incorporate what is arguably the most important factor in real estate, location, at their very core. Often these spatially aware models require significant computing power even compared with their AI-based alternatives.

Depending on the underlying urban form of the modeling study area, a spatially aware model can outperform both its GLM and its AI counterparts (Hermans 2020; McMillen 1996). In terms of explainability, spatially aware models perform very well. They maintain the explainability of the GLM approach and are not affected by the black-box problem that occurs in their AI-based counterparts (McCluskey et al. 2013).

Spatially aware models also have drawbacks. Given the spatial dependence of housing prices, they tend to overfit (McCord et al. 2022).

Spatially Aware Models

In addition to the three main statistical spatially aware modeling approaches just outlined, cross-category approaches have been researched and developed. Recent studies have tried to mitigate the shortcomings of both the AI-based approaches and the spatially aware models. This is done by placing constraints and integrating spatial techniques into advanced regression approaches. The aim of this field of research is to build new statistical approaches for real estate assessment that contain the improvements of both spatially aware models and AI-based approaches but do not encounter the black-box problem or the overfitting tendency. Early results from these studies tend to be promising (Helbich and Griffith 2016; McCord et al. 2022).

To ensure that an automated valuation produces trustworthy results, quality controls must be established in order to examine which of the approaches works best in a given study area. Quality control is an integral step in any valuation practice. Reflection on the quality of assessments aids in the acceptance of the assessed values by the public and also provides a way for assessors to reflect on their own capabilities. The following section provides an outline of quality-control checks as used in the assessment practice for property tax. It also offers insight into alternative quality checks used in the broader valuation and assessment industry.

Quality Control

Automated valuation models must be tested for their performance. Academic debate on which indicators should be used has been ongoing since the early 1970s. All the proposed model performance indicators, both in the property valuation industry and in property tax assessment, are based on observed and predicted values. However, market value, which is the phenomenon that automated valuation models aim to predict, is unobservable (Clapp 1990; Kochin and Parks 1982; Paglin and Fogarty 1972).

Traditionally, there have been three approaches to this problem of error in the variable. The first approach was proposed by Paglin and Fogarty (1972), who suggested that the sale price of a property be used as the indicator for market value. In the second approach, which was introduced by Kochin and Parks (1982) a decade later, the assessed value is used as the preferred indicator for market value. While this debate was taking place, research determined that approaches using the sale price as the indicator for market value are biased to find regressivity in vertical equity tests, and the approaches using assessed value as the indicator for market value tend to be biased toward finding progressivity in vertical equity tests. To mitigate the biases of these approaches, Clapp (1990) suggested a third approach, the use of both the sale price and the assessed value in a two-stage model performance indicator.

Central to all quality-control indicators is the use of the assessment-to-sale price ratio (ASR). This ratio is calculated by dividing the assessed value by the sale price, as visualized in equation 1.

$$ASR = \frac{Assessed\ Value}{Sale\ Price} \tag{1}$$

Market Level and Horizontal and Vertical Equity

In real estate assessment, model performance is often operationalized by analyzing three aspects. The first is whether the model output is in line with the market level. This measure for assessment level is based on a central tendency statistic. The International Association of Assessing Officers (IAAO) *Standard on Ratio Studies* (IAAO 2013), the leading international standard for ratio studies, suggests the use of the median ASR. Alternatively, a weighted or arithmetic mean can be used to obtain the assessment level indicator. The level of assessment, or market level, gives an indication of the accuracy of the assessments made by the automated valuation model (IAAO 2013).

The second aspect for determining automated valuation model performance is horizontal equity, which indicates whether assessments are similar in precision between different categories. These categories can be neighborhoods or property types, among other things. The IAAO Standard on Ratio Studies suggests the calculation of the coefficient of dispersion (CoD) for each of the categories. The CoD gives the percentage deviation from the median ratio as a result. Therefore, comparing the CoDs between categories gives a meaningful indicator of the precision of the assessments made by the automated valuation model.

The third aspect for determining automated valuation model performance is vertical equity, which indicates whether assessments are consistent between different strata of housing values. Indicators for vertical equity can indicate regressivity, where lower-value properties are assessed at a greater percentage of their market value than higher-value properties. In contrast, indicators for vertical equity can indicate progressivity when lower-value properties are assessed at a lower percentage of their market value than higher-value properties. The IAAO *Standard on Ratio Studies* suggests the use of the price-related differential (PRD) as an indicator for vertical equity. The PRD is centered just above 1. Therefore, a PRD score lower than 0.98 indicates progressivity. A PRD score higher than 1.03 indicates regressivity in the assessments (IAAO 2013).

The IAAO *Standard on Ratio Studies* suggests, in addition, the use of the price-related bias (PRB), another measure for vertical equity. Compared with the PRD, the PRB is less prone to the influence of outliers. The PRB is centered at 0. A significant PRB score of lower than −0.05 indicates progressivity in the assessments made by the automated valuation model, and a significant PRB score of higher than 0.05 indicates regressivity (IAAO 2013).

The current academic consensus is that a variety of vertical equity measures should be used to mitigate between the advantages and disadvantages of certain configurations. A discussion of all possible vertical equity measures, as well as their advantages and disadvantages, is beyond the scope of this chapter. A more in-depth overview can be found in Carter (2016); McMillen and Singh (2023); Quintos et al. (2023); and Sirmans, Gatzlaff, and Macpherson (2008).

Industry Measures of Quality Control

The IAAO *Standard on Ratio Studies* is used by assessment offices throughout the world. However, next to the model performance indicators proposed by the standards, some other measures have been used in the valuation and assessment industry to check for model performance (Rossini and Kershaw 2008). These measures focus on accuracy and can therefore be used to give insight into the horizontal equity of the valuations or assessments made by a given automated valuation model if the measures are calculated for different subsets, such as property types or neighborhoods. One of the most common indicators used in the assessment industry is the mean absolute percentage error (MAPE). The MAPE is a common indicator discussed in the academic debate concerning forecasting. It can be used with the sale price or the assessed value as the indicator for observed market value. One of its advantages is that the calculation is often incorporated as a function in free open-source statistical software. A reasonable MAPE for an automated valuation model is around 10 percent and not above 13 percent (Rossini and Kershaw 2008).

Another model performance indicator that has its roots in the academic field of forecasting is the root mean squared error (RMSE). Like the MAPE, the RMSE is often incorporated as a function in free open-source statistical software. The RMSE can also be used with sale prices or assessed values as the indicator for market value. Both the RMSE and the MAPE are measures for accuracy. Calculating these model performance indicators for different subsets of the assessments made by an automated valuation model can give insight into horizontal equity.

Next to the RMSE and the MAPE, academic literature concerning forecasting recommends accuracy indicator percentages, more commonly referred to as hit rates, as an indicator for accuracy. They can be seen as an inverse version of the MAPE. However, instead of indicating the percentage error, the hit rates indicate what percentage of the assessments made fall within a certain percentage error margin. Commonly, hit rates are calculated for at least percentage margins like 5 percent, 10 percent, and 15 percent (Rossini and Kershaw 2008). Calculating hit rates for different subsets of the assessments made by a given automated valuation model gives an indication of horizontal equity. Hit rates are not often incorporated as a function in free open-source statistical software. However, due to their simplicity, the calculations can easily be defined within such software.

Use of Parallel Valuation Models

As stated earlier, automated valuation models have become readily available in a wide range of statistical approaches. Academic debate has been ongoing about which approach yields the preferred model performance in a chosen study area. While this debate is extremely productive for the comparison of statistical approaches, the underlying urban form has a heavy influence on the performance of any of them. Given this knowledge, a new debate is emerging on how to make use of parallel valuation models—that is, using two separate automated valuation models instead of one. Early examples of this approach are the work of Allen and Dare (2009), who investigated the effects of the Florida Save Our Homes Amendment, and that of Davis et al. (2012), who investigated the performance of simplified valuation approaches in a more specified automated valuation model.

A more recent example is the work of Hermans et al. (2022), who constructed a nine-scenario framework based on the notion that both sale price and assessed value can be used as indicators for market value. The main argument they make is that the outcome of an automated valuation model can be used as an indicator for market value if it passes the model performance tests proposed by the IAAO *Standard on Ratio Studies*. With this new indicator, a new ratio is constructed: the assessment-to-model value ratio (AMR), given in equation 2. With the availability of three indicators for market value, the sale prices and the outcomes of two separate automated valuation models, a comparison framework can be

Table 22.1 Nine-Scenario Framework

Scenario	Description	Initial Model Value	Validation Model Value	Observed Sale Price	AMR	ASR
1	Unsold undervaluation	300,000	360,000	n.a.	0.83	n.a.
2	Unsold overvaluation	300,000	260,000	n.a.	1.25	n.a.
3	Unsold consensus	300,000	300,000	n.a.	1.00	n.a.
4	Unsold compromise	300,000	295,000	n.a.	1.02	n.a.
5	Sales price chasing	300,000	360,000	300,000	0.83	1.00
6	Sold undervaluation	300,000	360,000	370,000	0.83	0.81
7	Sold overvaluation	300,000	250,000	260,000	1.20	1.15
8	Sold compromise	300,000	295,000	305,000	1.02	0.98
9	Absolute agreement	300,000	300,000	300,000	1.00	1.00

Note: n.a. = not available.

created. The nine-scenario framework Hermans et al. (2022) propose is visualized in table 22.1.

$$AMR = \frac{Initial\ Model\ Value}{Validation\ Model\ Value} \tag{2}$$

In the proposed framework, the first four scenarios are used for properties that lack an observed sale price. The first scenario occurs when the AMR violates a predefined lower bandwidth value, indicating that the initial model value is significantly lower than the parallel automated valuation model. The second scenario occurs when the AMR violates a predefined upper bandwidth value, indicating that the initial model value is significantly higher than the parallel automated valuation model. The third scenario occurs when the values from the initial and parallel automated valuation models are exactly equal. The fourth scenario occurs when the values from the initial and parallel automated valuation models differ but the AMR does not violate the upper or lower bandwidth boundary.

The subsequent five scenarios deal with properties that do have an observed sale price and therefore have the advantage that an ASR can be calculated. The fifth scenario occurs when the initial model value is exactly equal to the observed sale price but the validation model violates the upper or lower bandwidth boundary. This scenario can indicate sales price chasing.[1] The sixth scenario occurs when both the ASR and the AMR violate the predefined lower bandwidth boundary, indicating sold undervaluation. The seventh scenario occurs when both the ASR and the AMR violate the predefined upper bandwidth boundary, indicating sold overvaluation. The eighth scenario occurs when the observed sale price and the values from both automated valuation models differ but do not violate the upper or lower bandwidth boundary. The ninth scenario occurs when all three of the market value indicators are exactly equal. It is important to note that the scenarios can be altered to fit the goal at hand. For instance, one might not be interested in the occurrence of possible sale price chasing; in that case, the fifth scenario can be left out of the framework. In line with this reasoning, subsequent work by Hermans et al. (2023) proposes a 12-situation framework.

Communication

Digital Personalized and Protected Interaction

People and organizations have predominantly shifted from using paper to using digital technologies for communication. In most countries, this also applies to government communication. In this section, we provide examples of digital communication methods in the Netherlands. Comparable practices can be found in several other countries.

In the Netherlands, most communication between inhabitants and different levels of government is done via a digital platform called Mijn Overheid (My Government), a personal inbox for all governmental affairs. By logging in with a personal digital identification number, citizens and firms can see all the information that is sent to them and also the information that is registered about them. This central digital personalized and protected interaction platform facilitates clear and to-the-point communication with the government.

It is possible to see the assessed value of one's properties on this platform. Mijn Overheid also acts as a gateway to the digital facilities that municipalities offer for users to ask questions about the assessment process or the assessed value, as well as to file an objection. These digital platforms can also help the government to communicate with the taxpayer before the property assessment is available and before the tax bill is issued. For instance, during the valuation process, the taxpayer can be asked to check the object characteristics of the property that will be used for the assessment.

Valuation and the GDPR

The GDPR is a regulation in European Union (EU) law on data protection and privacy in the EU and the European Economic Area (EEA). It is an important component of EU privacy law and of human rights law. It also addresses the transfer of personal data outside the EU and EEA. The GDPR's primary aim is to enhance individuals' control and rights over their personal data and to simplify the regulatory environment for international business. The regulation contains provisions and requirements related to the processing of personal data of individuals (formally called data subjects in the GDPR) who are located in the EEA and applies to any enterprise—regardless of its location and the data subjects' citizenship or residence—that is processing the personal information of individuals inside the EEA.

The GDPR was adopted on April 14, 2016, and became enforceable beginning May 25, 2018. As the GDPR is a regulation, not a directive, it is directly binding and applicable for all member states, and it provides flexibility for certain aspects of the regulation to be adjusted by individual member states.

For property tax and mass appraisal, a significant amount of data is needed that is controlled by the GDPR. The reason for this is that all data that are connected to an address can also be connected to the people living at that address. Therefore, caution is needed when handling all data on property, but especially market data, assessed values, tax bills, and information on tax payments. Within an organization, the handling of the GDPR can be improved by periodically conducting risk analysis and maintaining an up-to-date registry of privacy violations. It is advised that organizations keep close contact with the national data protection authority.

Self-Declaration and Quality Control of Data

The involvement of taxpayers in the valuation process has a positive effect on the trust they have in the outcome. That is why, for valuation and taxation purposes, government organizations should try to interact with their taxpayers. This interaction should take place before the tax notices with the assessed values are sent out. In this phase, the interaction can take different forms. For instance,

- governments ask taxpayers to declare property characteristics for valuation;
- governments ask taxpayers to declare a value estimate for their property;
- governments allow taxpayers to check registered property characteristics; or
- governments allow taxpayers to check the estimated value before the assessment is made formal.

The involvement of taxpayers to check or self-declare property characteristics is not only an important data source for valuation purposes ("Owners know their properties best"), it can also give the taxpayer a positive view of the valuation process. People are more likely to appreciate the process if they have contributed to it themselves. There are a few conditions that must be met, however.

First, if a jurisdiction asks the taxpayer to check the object characteristics, the information that is presented to the taxpayer must be of good quality, otherwise the taxpayer will lose trust in the assessment immediately. Second, it is important that the taxpayer is able to provide the information in a straightforward way—for instance, in a protected digital environment. Third, the information that is provided by the taxpayer must always be checked by the government before it is used for the assessment.

Self-Declaration and Quality Control of Value

As mentioned above, the involvement of taxpayers can positively affect the trust they have in the assessed value. This will also be the case when the assessed value is presented to the taxpayer before it is formally set. At this point, the taxpayer may be asked to indicate whether the determined value matches the taxpayer's view of the market value. In that instance, the communication between the government (assessor) and the taxpayer can be of a more informal nature. After the assessment is made formal, all communication should be seen as pertaining to an objection, and more formal communication procedures should be instated.

Figure 22.1 Dutch Key Register on Assessed Values

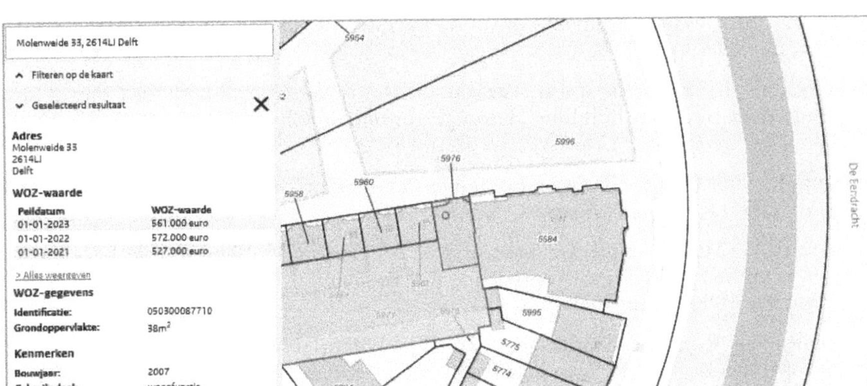

Source: Wozwaardeloket (n.d.).

Transparency of Assessed Values

To achieve more transparency, the Dutch government has developed a system for the public disclosure of assessed values of residential property. This enables homeowners to check and compare the assessed values of their own properties with the assessed values of other properties. Through a national website, municipalities automatically disclose the assessed value of residential properties, which are displayed on a map (figure 22.1). Other countries use public websites with assessed values to give taxpayers the opportunity to compare the assessed values of properties. This not only allows taxpayers to verify the assessed values of their own properties, it also instills trust in the fairness of the system.

In general, transparency in assessed values fosters the trust of the taxpayer. The direct relation between a higher level of trust and a lower number of objections and appeals is obvious, though differences in legal systems must be considered.

Note

1. Sales price chasing refers to the unprofessional practice of selectively revaluing properties close to their sale price while leaving the values of unsold properties unchanged. This creates significant disparities between similar properties, resulting in inequitable tax liabilities.

References

Allen, M., and W. Dare. 2009. "Changes in Property Tax Progressivity for Florida Homeowners After the 'Save Our Homes Amendement.'" *Journal of Real Estate Research* 31(1): 81–92.

Beimer, J., and M. Francke. 2019. "Out-of-Sample House Price Prediction by Hedonic Price Models and Machine Learning Algorithms." *Real Estate Research Quarterly* 18(2): 13–20.

Carter, J. 2016. "Methods for Determining Vertical Inequity in Mass Appraisal." *Fair and Equitable* 14(6): 3–8.

Charalabos, I., C. Psaltis, and C. Potsiou. 2009. "Towards a Strategy for Control of Suburban Informal Buildings Through Automatic Change Detection." *Computers, Environment and Urban Systems* 33(1): 64–74.

Clapp, J. 1990. "A New Test for Equitable Real Estate Tax Assessment." *Journal of Real Estate Finance and Economics* 3(3): 233–249.

Davis, P., W. McCluskey, T. Grissom, and M. McCord. 2012. "An Empirical Analysis of Symplified Valuation Approaches for Residential Property Tax Purposes." *Property Management* 30(3): 232–254.

Gloudemans, R., and P. Sanderson. 2021. "The Potential of Artificial Intelligence in Property Assessment." *Journal of Property Tax Assessment and Administration*, 18(2). https://doi.org/10.63642/1357-1419.1241.

Helbich, M., and D. Griffith. 2016. "Spatially Varying Coefficient Models in Real Estate: Eigenvector Spatial Filtering and Alternative Approaches." *Computers, Environment and Urban Systems* 57: 1–11.

Hermans, L. 2020. "Implementation of Geographically Weighted Regression in Automated Valuation Models in the Netherlands." *Journal of Property Tax Assessment and Administration* 17(1): 23–48.

Hermans, L., P. Bidanset, P. Davis, and M. McCord. 2022. "Using Property-Level Ratio Studies for the Incorporation of Validation Models in Single-Family Residential Real Estate Assessment." *Journal of Property Tax Assessment and Administration* 19(1): 83–102.

Hermans, L., M. McCord, P. Davis, and P. Bidanset. 2023. "An Exploratory Approach to Composite Modeling for Real Estate Assessment and Accuracy." *Journal of Property Tax Assessment and Administration* 20(1): 43–61.

Heywood, I., S. Cornelius, and S. Carter. 2005. *An Introduction to Geographical Information Systems.* Upper Saddle River, NJ: Prentice Hall.

IAAO (International Association of Assessing Officers). 2013. *Standard on Ratio Studies.* Kansas City, MO: IAAO.

Kochin, L., and R. Parks. 1982. "Vertical Equity in Real Estate Assessment: A Fair Appraisal." *Economic Inquiry* 20(4): 511–532.

Kok, N., E. Koponen, and C. Martinez-Barbosa. 2017. "Big Data in Real Estate? From Manual Appraisal to Automated Valuation." In "Special Real Estate Issue," *Journal of Portfolio Management* 43(6): 202–211.

Lenk, M., E. Worzala, and A. Silva. 1997. "High-Tech Valuation: Should Artificial Neural Networks Bypass the Human Valuer?" *Journal of Property Valuation and Investment* 15(1): 8–26.

McCluskey, W., M. McCord, P. Davis, M. Haran, and D. McIlhatton. 2013. "Prediction Accuracy in Mass Appraisal: A Comparison of Modern Approaches." *Journal of Property Research* 30(4): 239–265.

McCord, M., D. Lo, P. Davis, J. McCord, L. Hermans, and P. Bidanset. 2022. "Applying the Geostatistical Eigenvector Spatial Filter Approach." *Applied Sciences* 12(20): 10660.

McMillen, D. 1996. "One Hundred Fifty Years of Land Values in Chicago: A Nonparametric Approach." *Journal of Urban Economics* 40(1): 100–124.

McMillen, D., and R. Singh. 2023. "Measures of Vertical Inequality in Assessments." *Journal of Housing Economics* 61: 101950.

Paglin, M., and M. Fogarty. 1972. "Equity and the Property Tax: A New Conceptual Focus." *National Tax Journal* 25(4): 557–565.

Quintos, C., K. Foster, M. Hayes, L. Hermans, M. McCord, J. Myers, V. Vielma, C. Yemen, and S. York. 2023. "A Review of Vertical Equity Measures in Property Assessments." *Journal of Property Tax Assessment and Administration* 20(2): 101–132.

Rossini, P., and P. Kershaw. 2008. "Automated Valuation Model Accuracy: Some Empirical Testing." Paper presented at the 14th Pacific Rim Real Estate Society Conference (January).

Sirmans, S., D. Gatzlaff, and D. Macpherson. 2008. "Horizontal and Vertical Inequity in Real Property Taxation." *Journal of Real Estate Literature* 16(2): 167–180.

Welle Donker, F., B. van Loenen, and K. Bregt. 2016. "Open Data and Beyond." *ISPRS International Journal of Geo-Information* 5(4): 48.

Wozwaardeloket.nl. n.d. Accessed January 30, 2025.

Contributors

Editors

ROY BAHL
Professor Emeritus
Georgia State University, United States

WILLIAM MCCLUSKEY
Extraordinary Professor
African Tax Institute
University of Pretoria, South Africa

RIËL FRANZSEN
Professor and Research Chair in Tax Policy and Governance
University of Pretoria, South Africa
Fellow, Stellenbosch Institute for Advanced Study, South Africa

Chapter Authors

SARMITE BARVIKA
Riga Technical University, Latvia

GUILLAUME CHAPELLE
Professor, CY Cergy Paris University, France

PEADAR DAVIS
Ulster University, N. Ireland, United Kingdom

NIALL DEEGAN
TU Dublin: Technological University, Ireland

THOMAS DIMOPOULOS
Neapolis University, Pafos, Cyprus

HEIDI FALKENBACH
Associate Professor, Aalto University, Finland

GUY GILBERT
Professor, ENS Paris-Saclay, France

FRANK HARRINGTON
TU Dublin: Technological University, Ireland

LUC HERMANS
Netherlands Council for Real Estate Assessment, The Netherlands

TINA HUMAR
Director General, Ministry of Finance, Slovenia

VERONIKA ILSJAN
National Land Board, Estonia

RUUD KATHMANN
Netherlands Council for Real Estate Assessment, The Netherlands

ANTHONY KENNEALLY
Tailte Éireann, Ireland

PAULIINA KRIGSHOLM
Finnish Geospatial Research Institute, National Land Survey, Finland

MARCO KUIJPER
Netherlands Council for Real Estate Assessment, The Netherlands

WENJING LI
Peking University–Lincoln Institute Center for Urban Development
and Land Policy, China

JOHN MCCORD
Ulster University, N. Ireland, United Kingdom

MICHAEL MCCORD
Ulster University, N. Ireland, United Kingdom

THOMAS MURPHY
Ulster University, N. Ireland, United Kingdom

JOHANNES NÕUPUU
National Land Board, Estonia

MAŁGORZATA RENIGIER-BIŁOZOR
Professor, University of Warmia and Mazury, Poland

POUL SCHOU
Chief Economist, Danish Economic Council, Denmark

PALOMA TALTAVULL DE LA PAZ
Professor, University of Alicante, Spain

ANDREY TIMOFEEV
Research Associate Professor, Georgia State University, United States

AIVAR TOMSON
Kinnisvaraekspert, Estonia

ALAIN TRANNOY
Professor, Aix-Marseille University, France

MAREK WALACIK
Assistant Professor, University of Warmia and Mazury, Poland

ETIENNE WASMER
Professor, New York University of Abu Dhabi, Abu Dhabi

JAN WERNER
Professor, Cologne Business School, Germany

NEVA ŽIBRIK
Head of the Department of Property Taxation (retired),
Ministry of Finance, Slovenia

RYSZARD ŹRÓBEK
Professor, University of Warmia and Mazury, Poland

SABINA ŹRÓBEK
Professor, University of Warmia and Mazury, Poland

ELŻBIETA ZYSK
Assistant Professor, University of Warmia and Mazury, Poland

Index

Page numbers in italic indicate tables or figures.

About the Lincoln Institute of Land Policy

The Lincoln Institute of Land Policy seeks to improve quality of life through the effective use, taxation, and stewardship of land. A nonprofit private operating foundation whose origins date to 1946, the Lincoln Institute researches and recommends creative, nonpartisan approaches to land as a solution to economic, social, and environmental challenges. Through education, training, publications, and events, we integrate theory and practice to inform public policy decisions worldwide. We organize our work around three impact areas: land and water, land and fiscal systems, and land and communities. We envision a world where cities and regions prosper and benefit from coordinated land use planning and public finance, where communities thrive from efficient and equitable allocation of limited land resources, and where stewardship of land and water resources ensures a livable future. We work globally, with locations in Cambridge, Massachusetts; Washington, DC; Phoenix, Arizona; and Beijing, China.

LINCOLN INSTITUTE
OF LAND POLICY

113 Brattle Street
Cambridge, MA 02138-3400 USA
P 1.617.661.3016 1.800.526.3873
F 1.617.661.7235 1.800.526.3944
help@lincolnist.edu
lincolninst.edu